A Grand Delusion

Also by Robert Mann

The Walls of Jericho: Lyndon Johnson, Hubert Humphrey, Richard Russell, and the Struggle for Civil Rights

Legacy to Power: Senator Russell Long of Louisiana

A GRAND DELUSION

America's Descent into Vietnam

ROBERT MANN

BALSAM LAKE PUBLIC LIBRARY
404 Main St. • P.O. Box 340
Balsam Lake, WI 54810

BASIC
BOOKS

A Member of the Perseus Book Group

Copyright © 2001 by Robert Mann

Published by Basic Books
A Member of the Perseus Books Group

All rights reserved. Printed in the United States of America. No part
of this book may be reproduced in any manner whatsoever without
written permission except in the case of brief quotations embodied
in critical articles and reviews. For information, address Basic Books,
10 East 53rd Street, New York, NY 10022-5299.

Library of Congress Cataloging-in-Publication Data

Mann, Robert
    A grand delusion : America's descent into Vietnam / Robert Mann.
        p.   cm.
    Includes bibliographical references and index.
    ISBN 0-465-04369-0 (alk. paper)
    1. Vietnamese Conflict, 1961–1975—United States.   2. Asia—Politics and
government—1945–   3. Vietnam—Politics and government—1945–1975.   4. United
States—Politics and government—20th century.   I. Title.

DS558.M34 2000
959.704'3—dc21   00-049824

Designed by Jim Buchanan of Nighthawk Design

FIRST EDITION

00 01 02 03 / 10 9 8 7 6 5 4 3 2 1

959.70
Man

donated '12003

For Robert and Avery,
With my love

Contents

Introduction

MORE THAN A QUARTER CENTURY AFTER THE LAST AMERICAN combat troops left Southeast Asia, the social and political fires of the Vietnam War continue to burn throughout the United States and Vietnam. Millions of citizens in both countries bear the deep, painful scars of a twenty-five-year conflict that wreaked havoc on the political and social landscapes of the United States and Vietnam. Even today, legions of war veterans endure the physical and emotional wounds inflicted during their tours of duty, while the 3 million people who perished on all sides are only memories to millions of husbands, wives, children, grandchildren, parents, siblings, and friends.

In the United States, the nation's ill-advised military foray into Vietnam continues to impact our political institutions. The war has emerged as an issue in virtually every presidential election, and many congressional elections, since it ended. Lately, those candidates who avoided service must, decades after the fact, defend impetuous—and sometimes calculating—decisions made in their teens.

More significant for Americans, however, may be the war's lasting impact on the country's government and its foreign and defense policies. The ghosts of Vietnam, former combat journalist Ward Just has observed, will not leave us, "rising whenever Washington contemplates a military adventure." In the years since the war's end, every American military action has been influenced by the experience of Vietnam. "For American statecraft," Just argues, "the legacy is as profound as that of World War II." Journalist Myra MacPherson's astute observations about the war, from her 1984 book, *Long Time Passing: Vietnam & the Haunted Generation*, remain timely: Vietnam's "consequences are still being felt in our foreign policy . . . in a haunted generation, in the new generation faced with possible new Vietnams, and in our hearts and minds."

The Vietnam War also profoundly altered Americans' view of their public institutions. While polls suggest that public confidence in the federal government has not declined significantly in more than thirty years, Vietnam did awaken millions of Americans to the fact that their presidents had routinely lied to them—about the American military role in Southeast Asia, about Watergate, and about a host of other issues.

Vietnam was, indeed, a turning point in American political history. The war destroyed the New Deal political coalition that dominated American politics for nearly four decades, opening the door to new and equally potent political forces that lasted into the twenty-first century. Vietnam unleashed a level and variety of public dissent never before seen in American politics, but one that profoundly altered the ways that the American people communicate with their elected leaders.

Before the war, and the Watergate scandal it helped to spawn, news reporters, the public, and even members of Congress generally accepted information supplied from presidents and their advisors. In the wake of the war and the Watergate scandal, the press and the American people grew, if not less trustful, more apathetic about government and doubtful of its ability to positively impact their lives. Congress, in turn, grew more adversarial in its relationship with the executive branch and—beginning with the War Powers Act in 1973—more zealous of its own constitutional prerogatives. Without a war in Vietnam and the political turmoil it sparked, it is unlikely that Richard Nixon, and perhaps even Ronald Reagan, would have been elected president.

The Vietnam War, a renowned sociologist has observed, actually divided America's historical view of itself: "On one side of that history," Todd Gitlin wrote, "America, whatever its rights and its wrongs, stands triumphant, its glorious destiny manifest. On the other, America knows defeat, even shame."

The tragedy of Vietnam, however, cannot be measured only by the conflict's dead-and-wounded statistics or by its impact on American society, politics, or diplomacy. Compounding the calamity is the simple fact that millions of deaths might have been averted had the American people and their leaders opened their eyes to the delusions leading them progressively deeper into the morass of Southeast Asia in the 1950s and 1960s— a national crusade undertaken to defeat an enemy that had once been our ally and that had originally wanted nothing more than independence from brutal colonial rule.

From beginning to end, America's political, military, and diplomatic leaders deluded themselves, accepting a series of myths and illusions about Vietnam that exacerbated and deepened the ultimate catastrophe.

- Most Americans and their leaders were deluded about the nature of the threat to freedom in Indochina, concluding that it was only "international" communism and not French colonialism. They also believed that the communist-supported nationalistic movement in Indochina was not indigenous, but directed from Moscow and Peking.

- President Eisenhower and his advisors were deluded about the success of their policies in Indochina and wrongly concluded that the
armed struggle against the Vietminh guerrillas in the mid- and late-
1950s was being won.
- American leaders in the 1950s were deluded about South Vietnamese Prime Minister Ngo Dinh Diem, wrongly concluding that
he was a reformer dedicated to democratic ideals.
- President John F. Kennedy was deluded about the course of the conflict during his administration. With disastrous results, he disregarded the young reporters in South Vietnam who alerted him and
their readers to the serious deficiencies of the American-backed
South Vietnamese government and its military forces. Relying on
advisors like Vice President Lyndon Johnson, Defense Secretary
Robert McNamara, Secretary of State Dean Rusk, and National
Security Advisor McGeorge Bundy, Kennedy rejected a fundamental reappraisal of U.S. policy in Vietnam that might have halted or
slowed the nation's descent into the quagmire of Southeast Asia.
- Throughout the 1960s, Kennedy, Johnson, and other American
political leaders were deluded about the true nature of the conflict.
They wrongly assumed that the war was primarily a military, not a
political struggle and that the application of military might was a
legitimate substitute for an educated program to help the South
Vietnamese regime win the "hearts and minds" of its people.
- American voters in 1964 were innocently deluded about Johnson's
intentions in Vietnam, believing his promises of "no wider war."
- Leaders in Congress were deluded and misled about the nature of
the incidents in the Gulf of Tonkin in August 1964, which resulted
in a breathtaking grant of war-making power to Johnson from Congress in days following the incidents.
- Like Kennedy, President Johnson and his advisors were deluded
by the prospects of military might—particularly bombing—and
believed that a military solution, short of destroying North Vietnam,
was possible.
- Both Johnson and his successor, Richard Nixon, successfully deluded American voters about the steps they were willing to take to
achieve peace. In the 1968 election, American voters were again
deluded by a winning presidential candidate when Nixon suggested
that he possessed a plan to end the war with "honor." During the
early months of Nixon's presidency, opponents of the war in Congress were also deluded into believing that Nixon planned to move
quickly to end the fighting.

For the United States, Vietnam itself was a grand and very tragic delusion—a country that the American people and their leaders believed could be "saved" from what they believed was a Soviet-controlled communist regime that threatened to consume all of Southeast Asia. Indeed, for almost two decades, American leaders mistakenly concluded that the United States had the power, the will, and the means to win the war—if a definition of victory could ever be universally accepted.

This book is a political history of the Vietnam War, the story of the well-meaning, but misguided American leaders whose virulent, one-dimensional anticommunism led the nation into its tragic misadventure in Vietnam in the 1950s and 1960s. A primary feature of this story is its focus on the political tension over U.S. foreign and military policy during the early 1950s and how the political decisions about these issues paved the way for the country's eventual full-scale military involvement in Vietnam. Indeed, I believe the strength of this book is its examination of the events of the late 1940s and early 1950s that helped shape the foreign and military policies of Presidents Eisenhower, Kennedy, Johnson, and Nixon.

Because this was America's most politically charged war in the twentieth century, I have focused primarily on the roles of U.S. political leaders in the partisan turmoil that embroiled the nation during the early years of the Cold War. I show how the political repercussions of the communist takeover in China in 1949, the outbreak of war in Korea in 1950, and the rise of anticommunism (particularly McCarthyism) in the early 1950s taught each president from Eisenhower to Ford important lessons that they later applied to their foreign policies in general and to Vietnam in particular.

This book is also the first comprehensive single-volume account of the Vietnam War that places the roles of leading members of Congress in their proper perspective. Ultimately, I believe, it helps to answer a compelling question that historians, journalists, and tens of thousands of veterans have posed for more than twenty-five years: Why did the supposedly brilliant men of five successive presidential administrations involve the nation in and build public support for a tragic, ill-conceived war that ultimately claimed as many as 3 million lives and ended in a humiliating defeat for the United States? It is not an easy question to answer. Scores of historians have analyzed this war to a degree that would rival studies of the American Civil War or World War II.

I am the first to admit that no simple answers to the question are readily available or easily agreed upon. I do believe that a large part of the answer, however, lies in the delusions about Vietnam and how they blinded American leaders and the American people to the dangers of the nation's deepening involvement in Southeast Asia. If this book does nothing else,

I am hopeful that it will point to the need for a Congress and an electorate better informed about foreign policy, as well as a political leadership resolved to thoroughly educate its citizens about their country's military and foreign policies. I do not wish this book to be used in support of the argument that the United States should never again deploy its armed forces abroad. I do hope, instead, that it will point forcefully to the importance of rational, informed public debate about the means, objectives, and possible consequences of such decisions.

In order to make informed, wise decisions about military and foreign policy, Congress and the American people need more, not less information from their presidents about why American troops should be deployed abroad. No matter what presidents and their advisors have almost always believed and practiced regarding the deployment of U.S. troops, the Constitution still invests Congress with the solemn responsibility and power to declare war. Therefore, I am hopeful that this book will serve as a chilling reminder of what can happen when Congress and the public take an ancillary role in the making of military and foreign policy.

During the Vietnam era, had our presidents been honest with Congress and the American people, had members of Congress more closely guarded their constitutional war-making prerogatives, and had the American people and their leaders been better informed about Vietnam and the American policy there, millions of lives might have been spared and untold misery avoided.

History at its best helps us to understand our past while providing some guidance for the future. My hope is that this book will shine a beacon of light on the nation's future path that might help prevent another tragedy like Vietnam.

ROBERT MANN
BATON ROUGE, LOUISIANA
JULY 2000

That Little Pipsqueak

February 1965

F RANK CHURCH HAD CHOSEN HIS WORDS CAREFULLY. BUT HE KNEW that his criticism of President Lyndon B. Johnson's Vietnam policies would undoubtedly damage his standing at the White House. In early February 1965, as he composed a Senate speech and a companion column for the *New York Times Magazine*, the 40-year-old Idaho Democrat was prepared to take that risk. After months of private and public deliberation, Church was about to challenge Johnson over the most important military and foreign policy question of the day—whether to increase the nation's military presence in South Vietnam. Church was uneasy about the article and the subsequent speech he would deliver in the Senate. He was not altogether certain his public dissent was wise. "I'm reluctant to repudiate the President on Vietnam," he later confessed to a friend. His reluctance was justified. Church knew the tempestuous president well and understood that his forceful speech would enrage Johnson and would, in Church's words, erase "any chance that may be left to me to exert some moderating influence upon the future course of events."[1]

Yet Church also knew that his words would break through the wall of silence that surrounded the burgeoning American military role in Vietnam. Despite the fact that Johnson was planning a massive, protracted air assault on North Vietnam, neither the country nor Congress had been consulted or informed. While some members of the Senate, particularly the taciturn majority leader, Mike Mansfield, knew of plans to widen the U.S. role in the conflict, most members were ignorant of the nation's dangerous and steady drift toward war. Church's bold speech would mark the cautious beginnings of a fierce and contentious nine-year congressional debate over U.S. military policy in Southeast Asia. For the first time, the Senate would debate the new direction of the nation's Vietnam policy, as Church and Democratic Senator Gale McGee of Wyoming, a loyal Johnson supporter, challenged each other over the growing U.S. role in that region. Within days, however, the civilized discourse that Church initiated would dissolve into a far wider and more belligerent debate over Vietnam policy.

Church would not, however, be the first senator to air his concerns about Johnson's Vietnam policy. The president already had outspoken critics in the Senate—two, to be exact. Wayne Morse of Oregon and Ernest Gruening of Alaska, both liberal Democrats, had dissented the previous summer as Johnson made his first moves toward escalating American involvement in Vietnam. In August 1964, after North Vietnamese torpedo boats had reportedly attacked two American destroyers in the Gulf of Tonkin, members of Congress had rushed to express their righteous indignation and gave Johnson a free hand to expand the war. Indeed, Church had joined that bipartisan stampede. Through it all, Gruening and Morse had stood alone and virtually ignored—opposed to Johnson and fully aware that their puny dissent would do nothing to slow the president's steady march toward war. Mavericks, well known for their willingness to champion unpopular causes, the two men had caused barely a ripple on Washington's political waters.

Yet Church was no maverick. Unlike Gruening and Morse, he did not rise routinely on the Senate floor to challenge the president of his party over important foreign policy issues. In fact, in 1957 as a 32-year old freshman senator, Church had quickly established himself as one of majority leader Johnson's favorite newcomers. After Church helped him pass the Civil Rights Act of 1957, Johnson had rewarded his promising young friend with a seat on the prestigious Senate Foreign Relations Committee. Church was progressive, smart, and one of the Senate's better orators. On most political issues, he and Johnson had shared the same outlook. Like Johnson, Church was pragmatic—an astute political leader willing to compromise in pursuit of his legislative and political goals. This stand, against a president who had once predicted that Church himself had the stuff to one day be president, would create quite a stir.

Days earlier, as Church knew from news accounts, the nature of the Vietnam conflict had begun to change dramatically. During the early morning hours of February 7, communist Viet Cong guerrillas had staged a daring raid on a remote U.S. airstrip in the central highlands of South Vietnam, near the village of Pleiku. When the sky finally stopped raining mortar shells, eight American soldiers lay dead and a hundred more were wounded. The guerrillas had destroyed ten U.S. aircraft. From Vietnam, Johnson's national security advisor, McGeorge Bundy, urged "graduated and continuing" reprisals against North Vietnam. It was, Bundy advised, "the most promising course available."[2] After consulting his advisors, Johnson agreed. Within hours, U.S. bombs destroyed a North Vietnamese military site near the

Demilitarized Zone. Johnson's decision was the humble beginning of a bombing campaign that would mushroom into a long and deadly offensive. Bombs would fall on North Vietnam for the next three-and-a-half-years.

Although most Americans did not know it yet, their country was drifting toward an all-out war with North Vietnam. At the beginning of 1965, only twenty-three thousand American troops were stationed in South Vietnam. By year's end, that number would swell to more than one hundred eighty thousand. As a leading member of the Foreign Relations Committee, Church sensed the inherent dangers of Johnson's retaliatory actions, and he was worried. "Nothing would be more futile," he had told an interviewer several months earlier, "than to permit ourselves to be sucked into a war which would pit Western forces against Asian forces." Even if we succeeded in taking control of the country, Church said, "we could not stay there long." The result, he predicted, would be "implacable hostility on all sides and the tides of history would, in the end, wash over us." A lasting victory was impossible, he insisted.[3]

In February, persuaded more than ever that Johnson was propelling the nation headlong into a disastrous conflict, Church prepared to formally announce his dissent to the Senate and to the nation. He knew what his critics, particularly Johnson, would say in reply. They would charge that he did not comprehend the serious threat communism posed to Southeast Asia and the whole of the Pacific. "To ignore aggression now," Johnson had warned in his January 4 State of the Union speech, "would only increase the danger of a much larger war."[4] Church knew that the supporters of Johnson's policies would undoubtedly call him an appeaser, evoking the memory of Britain's capitulation to Adolf Hilter at Munich in 1938. They would also accuse him of harboring the political isolationism of the political hero of his youth, Senator William E. Borah of Idaho. With that in mind, he would begin his speech with praise for the lofty motives behind Johnson's intervention in Vietnam. He would assure his colleagues, geographical and ideological similarities notwithstanding, that he was no isolationist.

On February 17, three days after Church had emerged as an outspoken critic of Johnson's Vietnam policies by publishing his controversial views in the *New York Times Magazine*,[5] he formally presented his treatise to his colleagues. "All Americans," he told the Senate, "agree with the President. Head-in-the-sand isolationism died a generation ago. It isn't likely to be resurrected." He insisted that he was "a confirmed internationalist." But over the previous thirty years, he said, the ideological pendulum of American policy had swung too far in the opposite direction— toward interventionism. "Once, we thought that anything which happened abroad was none of our business; now we evidently think that everything which happens abroad has become our business."

He wondered why had America spread itself so thin. "What compulsion draws us, ever deeper, into the internal affairs of so many countries in Africa and Asia, having so remote a connection with the vital interests of the United States?" The answer, he concluded, "stems from our intensely ideological view of the cold war." Americans were no longer able to distinguish between the different forms of communism and, therefore, regarded every communist regime as "the enemy." The result, he said, was that "we fancy ourselves as guardian of the 'free' world, though most of it is not free, and never has been. We seek to immunize this world against further Communist infection through massive injections of American aid, and, wherever necessary, through direct American intervention." That policy, he insisted, would be "self-defeating" because "in many, if not most of these emergent lands, it is capitalism, not Communism, which is the ugly word."

Turning to South Vietnam, Church urged recognition of the "limits" of U.S. military power to stop a communist uprising. Alluding to the lagging public support in South Vietnam for the regime of Prime Minister Nguyen Khanh, he declared that "if the people themselves will not support the government in power, we cannot save it. We can give arms, money, food and supplies, but the outcome will depend, in the final analysis, upon the character of the government helped, and the extent to which the people are willing to rally behind it." In Church's view, the Viet Cong were winning the war "not because they are better supplied than Saigon, but because they are united in their will to fight." Such unity could not be imported, Church insisted. "It must come from within," he said. "A family feud is never settled by outsiders."

Expressing hope that Johnson's retaliatory air strikes against North Vietnam would demonstrate "the strength of our will and purpose" to honor U.S. commitments to Saigon, Church doubted that military might alone would prove successful. He urged negotiation, he said, aware that "cries of 'appeasement' are being directed at anyone who speaks up for a negotiated settlement of this escalating war." But he cautioned that "the systematic and sustained bombing of North Vietnam, unattended by any proffered recourse to the bargaining table, can only lead us into war." The next step, he sagely predicted, "will be to send American land forces into battle, thus converting the struggle into an American war on the Asian mainland." It would be, he predicted, "a war we cannot finish. In the end, after a tragic trail of casualties out of all proportion to our real national interest, we will have to negotiate a settlement with the Communists, even as such a truce was finally negotiated in Korea." To Church, the real question was "not whether we should negotiate, but when."[6]

Minutes after Church sat down, Johnson gained another public Senate critic when South Dakota's George McGovern endorsed Church's call for negotiations. Like Church, McGovern was a liberal Democrat who had enthusiastically backed many of Johnson's foreign and domestic policies. While he had supported the Gulf of Tonkin Resolution, McGovern also

nursed concerns about Johnson's refusal to negotiate with the North Vietnamese and the Viet Cong. Like Church, McGovern supported Johnson's
"selective air strikes" and opposed an abrupt withdrawal of U.S. troops.
However, he said that he also feared that "bombing attacks in the north
will not solve the guerrilla struggle in the south." He expressed hope "that
such tactics are aimed at increasing pressure on the North Vietnam government and perhaps on the Chinese for negotiation rather than following the false hope that military victory is possible for either side." Johnson's "military embrace of the South Vietnam rulers," McGovern said,
"may actually have opened the way for Communist gains in Southeast Asia
and delayed the development of responsible government."[7]

McGovern, like Church, had not attacked his president over Vietnam.
His disagreement with Johnson, like Church's, was mostly over tactics and
was designed not to embarrass or harm Johnson, but to influence him. "Perhaps naively," McGovern later explained, "we still hoped that by avoiding
direct attacks on the administration and pressing instead for a negotiated
settlement, we might persuade the president to modify his course."[8]

At the White House, an irritated Johnson was in no mood to heed advice
from Church and McGovern—even if that advice was couched in faint praise
for the overall wisdom of his policies. After all, as Johnson knew, the vast
majority of senators and congressmen still publicly supported his policies.
Criticism from two additional Democrats would not deter him. Yet, Johnson
and his aides had begun to worry about the growing congressional dissent and
how demands for negotiation might undermine the strong, unified message
the administration hoped its retaliatory strikes would send.[9] Johnson believed
that Church and McGovern were not only intemperate, but uninformed about
the seriousness of the conflict and the stakes involved. "They ought to be told
the other side [of the story]," an irritated president told his national security
advisor, McGeorge Bundy, after Senate Minority Leader Everett Dirksen
phoned Johnson to report that McGovern and Church were "teeing off on
your Vietnam policy" in Senate speeches. Johnson told Bundy that both senators needed to know "that the thing that hurts us the most is not hitting our
compound or blowing up our hotels." Rather, it was "these goddam [Senate]
speeches that the communists blow up and that show we're about to pull out."

The next afternoon, hoping to prevent the spread of this minor uprising within the Democratic party, Bundy arrived on Capitol Hill to meet
with the small band of senators who had publicly questioned his Vietnam
policy.* Vice President Hubert Humphrey, who privately nursed his own
nascent doubts about the course of U.S. policy in Vietnam, hosted the

---

*The group included Gaylord Nelson of Wisconsin, Eugene McCarthy of Min-
nesota, and Stephen Young of Ohio. Administration supporter Gale McGee of
Wyoming also attended.

meeting in his spacious Capitol office. As the senators settled into their chairs for the meeting, McGovern and the others waited for the normally didactic, unyielding national security advisor to offer a lecture on the "logic and wisdom" of the administration's actions—the kind of presentations they had heard so often during White House briefings. But Bundy had no lecture this time. Instead, Humphrey simply handed the national security advisor copies of the speeches Church and McGovern had delivered in the Senate the previous day. For an uncomfortable ten minutes, Bundy devoured the speeches as McGovern and the others studied his face for any sign of disapproval or anger.[10]

Finally, Bundy looked up. Although he was undoubtedly familiar with Church's well-publicized views, he acknowledged that the press had greatly exaggerated the differences between Johnson and his critics in the Senate. In fact, he said, the speeches were rather constructive. Still, Bundy hoped the second-guessing from the Senate would end. Johnson, it was clear, wanted no public debate in the Senate on Vietnam. "I wonder if you could hold off on these speeches until we can have some further discussions with you," Bundy said. Church, not inclined to stifle his public criticism, spoke up. A public debate over Vietnam, he said, might actually be helpful to Johnson and increase his options. McGovern and the others agreed. Politely, but firmly, they told Bundy they would continue pressing their case for a negotiated settlement, painfully aware that this would surely provoke a president notorious for the creative ways he often punished his political opponents. After Bundy left the room, Humphrey was clearly pleased by the resolve of his former Senate colleagues. "You boys don't scare easily, do you?" he said.[11]

The meeting was over, but the pressure from Johnson had only begun. That afternoon, when they returned to the Senate floor, Church and McGovern discovered a full-fledged discourse over Vietnam. They found themselves under fire from several of Johnson's Senate allies, including Everett Dirksen. "To negotiate in South Vietnam while Communist aggression is spreading throughout the entire Southeast Asian peninsula," Dirksen said, "is like a man trying to paint his front porch while his house is on fire." Dirksen ridiculed Church and McGovern for leading "a chorus of despair sung to the tune of a dirge of defeat." [12]

That evening, Johnson turned up the pressure on Church in an effort to stifle his public dissent. At a White House briefing for a small group of senators, the president brought all of his immense persuasive powers to bear on the Senate's skeptics. As he commenced the briefing, Johnson fixed his steely eyes on Church, who sat, uncomfortably, only a few feet away. "There was once a senator who thought he knew more about war and peace than the president," Johnson began. "And he predicted, a few months before the outbreak of the Second World War, that there would be no war in Europe." Those who knew anything of history understood the thrust of Johnson's message. The "senator," Church knew, was his boyhood idol—the eminent senator of the 1920s and early 1930s, William E. Borah of Idaho.

It was Borah's enormous personal magnetism and his legendary rhetorical skills that had first inspired Church and drawn him toward politics at age 15. When Borah died in 1940, the immense crowds that descended on Boise to pay homage to the fallen senator had electrified the 16-year-old Church. He had been among the solemn, worshipful throng that filed past Borah's coffin in the rotunda of the state capitol. To Church, Borah was Idaho's greatest statesman and he hoped to follow in his footsteps. "Because he was a senator," he later acknowledged, "I wanted to become one."[13]

In an impassioned tribute to Borah the previous year at the University of Idaho, Church had defended his hero, noting that "Borah did not regard himself as an isolationist, in the general sense of that term." Borah, he correctly noted, favored cooperation with other countries, supported the codification of international law, and backed international trade. In fact, Church insisted, "the only way in which he was an isolationist was that he sought to isolate America from war." Borah's role in U.S. foreign affairs, Church explained, "was neither so negative, nor so naïve, as it is depicted nowadays." He argued that his own study of Borah's life had drawn him "not to those views of his which are now irrelevant, but to those premises he held so strongly which still remain applicable to our life and times. I think of his reluctance to use force, his anti-imperialism, and his toleration for diversity in the world at large."[14] In so many ways, any comparison to Borah clearly flattered Church. But there was no flattery intended in Johnson's words—only scorn. (Had Church been aware of Johnson's past, he might have noted that the president himself had once been among those, like Borah, who were wary of American involvement in the European war. In 1940, while pandering to his substantial German-American constituency, Johnson had insisted that "the ability of the American people to think calmly and act wisely during a crisis is going to keep us out of a war.")[15]* Church, however, remained silent throughout the briefing. He resisted the urge to question or challenge the president or his two principal advisors on Vietnam, Secretary of State Dean Rusk and Defense Secretary Robert McNamara.[16]

Later, at a reception in the State Dining Room, Mike Mansfield, the Senate majority leader and a quiet critic of U.S. policy in Vietnam, approached Church. "Frank, I was expecting you to speak up." "Well,"

---

*By the following year, Johnson was running for the U.S. Senate and enthusiastically supported Roosevelt's efforts to mobilize the country for war.

Church replied, "the president is so excited. He looks to me like a light bulb about ready to go out. I didn't want to aggravate him any further. I though it best just to remain silent."

Suddenly, Church caught sight of Johnson plowing through the crowd toward him—"like a dreadnought parting the destroyers left and right," he later recalled. Johnson slowly backed Church into a corner. Johnson, of course, wanted to talk about Vietnam. Best as he could, Church tried to explain his position. He had not advocated withdrawal or abandonment of U.S. commitments in Vietnam. He had even supported Johnson's firm response to the Pleiku attack. While Johnson appeared surprised to learn of Church's support, he pressed his case even harder. Finally, several guests, including Church's wife, Bethine, and Lady Bird Johnson, tried unsuccessfully to pry Church from Johnson's clutches. Johnson, showing the effects of several scotches, waved Bethine and Lady Bird away. "Frank and I are old friends," he insisted. "We want to talk this thing out." Finally, after even more intense discussion, Johnson relaxed his grip on Church. The gathering broke up. As the group left the White House, Eugene McCarthy of Minnesota joked, "If Frank Church had just surrendered, we all could have gone home thirty minutes ago."[17]

Church seemed to be unfazed by the confrontation,[18] but his wife was deeply concerned. Johnson had carried Idaho in 1964—although barely—and she worried about the political consequences of Church's appearing to oppose the nation's commander in chief in his struggle to defeat communism in Southeast Asia. She thought not of the towering Borah—who had died before America entered the war—but rather of her cousin, former Senator D. Worth Clark of Idaho, who had suffered politically after opposing American intervention in World War II. As Bethine knew, to be labeled an isolationist in 1965 was, at its worst, to stand accused of pacifism or, at best, to be indifferent to the threat of communism in Latin America, Asia, Africa, and Eastern Europe.[19]

The next week, just as Bethine feared, the isolationist charge emerged in a sharply worded speech delivered in the Senate by Thomas Dodd of Connecticut, one of Johnson's most reliable allies. While Dodd did not name Church or anyone else, his intended targets were known to all present. Dodd decried "the new isolationism" that he said grew out of a "national weariness" with the Cold War. "The basic premise of the new isolationism," Dodd said, "is that the United States is overextended in its attempt to resist Communist aggression around the world, over-committed to the defense of distant outposts, and over-involved in the murky and unintelligible affairs of remote areas." Dodd asserted that calls to withdraw from Vietnam—something that Church, McGovern, and other Johnson critics had not yet proposed—"add up to a policy which I can describe by no other name than 'appeasement,' subtle appeasement, unintentional appeasement, to be sure, but appeasement nonetheless."[20]

As Dodd and Church well understood, pure American isolationism was a relic of a more innocent period. In fact, Americans had never been isolationist in the broadest sense of the term. Commercially and culturally, Americans had long been actively engaged with other nations in virtually every corner of the globe. Politically, however, the United States had almost always conducted its affairs in isolation. Beginning with George Washington, who left public life with the exhortation for future presidents "to steer clear of permanent allies with any portion of the foreign world," American leaders had generally declined to involve the nation in what Thomas Jefferson called "entangling alliances." To most American leaders, nothing short of a direct threat to the United States or its vital interests would ever justify involvement in a foreign war.

Prior to World War II, many Americans—parochial and largely ambivalent about foreign affairs—had ignored the pleas of Great Britain and France for help in resisting Hitler's aggression. Throughout the 1930s, many American leaders discounted the actual threat posed to the United States by the turmoil in Europe and Asia. Few believed that their nation had any duty to provide leadership among the community of nations. In the words of historians William L. Langer and S. Everett Gleason,

> most Americans felt secure enough and beguiled themselves with arguments supplied them in quantity by some of their most respected public figures: war is inherently evil and settles nothing in any case; being not immediately menaced, the first duty of Americans is to maintain their unique civilization and protect it from foreign contamination; the best way, therefore, to deal with Fascism and Nazism is to stay away from them and concentrate all efforts on the solution of national social and economic problems, so as to preserve intact the great stronghold of democracy.[21]

Throughout the 1930s, a determined group of influential senators— many of them Republicans from the South, Midwest, and West—had managed to make political isolationism the policy of the U.S. government. Among their leaders were Borah, the former chairman of the Senate Foreign Relations Committee, Arthur Vandenberg of Michigan, Hiram Johnson of California, Burton Wheeler of Montana, and Gerald Nye of North Dakota. A principled and dogmatic man, Borah was a liberal Republican who counted among his greatest achievements the Senate's 1920 rejection of the League of Nations. In 1924, his commitment to pacifism led him to introduce a resolution outlawing war under the law of nations. Borah, however, was slightly ahead of his time. By 1928, the notion of rejecting war as an instrument of national policy had gained currency, when the

United States and fifteen other nations ratified the Kellogg-Briand Pact. The pact would ultimately prove meaningless, but Borah's isolationism grew more determined as another war brewed in Europe. A fiery orator, whose influence extended far beyond the Senate chamber, Borah believed that President Franklin Roosevelt—in cahoots with Britain and the French—had greatly exaggerated the danger of war. Twenty-six years later, even Lyndon Johnson recalled Borah's famous, but tragically wrong prediction: "My feeling and belief," Borah told Roosevelt in 1939, "is that we are not going to have a war. Germany isn't ready for it."[22]

Borah died in 1940, almost two years before Congress declared war on Japan, Germany, and Italy. In his absence, however, the congressional isolationists continued the fight. Added to their number was Ohio's Robert Taft, an energetic and intelligent leader of the conservative, Midwestern wing of the Republican Party. A dour, partisan man, Taft argued that "even the collapse of England is to be preferred to participation for the rest of our lives in European wars."[23] In 1943, even after the nation was completely committed to the war, Taft continued to argue that the world should not look to the United States to solve its problems. He opposed calls for postwar military alliances to keep the peace and he ridiculed *Time* magazine publisher Henry Luce's concept of an "American Century" in which the United States would become the world's "Good Samaritan." Whether Frank Church realized it or not, twenty-two years later, portions of his February 1965 speech to the Senate would bear an uncanny likeness to Taft's wartime calls for American neutrality. Taft had argued that Luce's vision was "based on the theory that we know better what is good for the world than the world itself. It assumes that we are always right and that everyone who disagrees with us is wrong." In Taft's view, military alliances meant imperialism. "Our fingers will be in every pie," he sternly predicted. Later that year, when Taft was forced to support the resolution that committed the United States to participation in the United Nations, he grumbled that "we do not wish to be a meddlesome Mattie, interfering in every trouble throughout the world."[24]

World War II had driven political isolationism to the fringes of American political thought. There it stayed until 1965, when men like Church, McGovern, and Senate Foreign Relations Committee Chairman J. William Fulbright revived a more pragmatic, sophisticated version of the discarded ideology. While these men rightly and forcefully eschewed the strict isolationist label and enthusiastically supported foreign and economic alliances, they also rejected the perceived interventionism or militarism of Lyndon Johnson, his Democratic supporters, and the modern-day leaders of the Republican Party. While they considered themselves neither isolationist nor interventionist, there were definite strains of the old political isolationism in their rhetoric and reasoning. Like Borah, Taft, and other pre–World War II isolationists, they argued that the nation's ever-expanding foreign commitments had diverted the nation's attention from important domestic concerns. Fulbright, for example, believed that the nation's obsession with fighting the Cold War had become "an excuse, as well as a genuine cause, for the diversion of our energies from domestic well-being to external security." He and others believed that the Cold War mentality had "encroached upon our sovereignty; it has given the Communists the major voice in determining what proportion of our budget must be allocated to the military and what proportion therefore cannot be made available for domestic social and economic projects."[25]

Long before his dissent over U.S. involvement in Vietnam, Church had argued in his 1964 paean to Borah that "we have permitted ourselves to become so massively involved that we regard every little country's frontier, no matter how remote, as our responsibility." He questioned: "Do we not wonder whether we haven't extended our commitments beyond our capacity to fulfill? Was there not some wisdom in Borah's attempt to limit the American sphere of responsibility?" He insisted that Borah's instinct against "the folly of war was true. War was bad enough in Borah's time; it has become incalculably worse since the advent of nuclear weapons. Borah was groping for a way to eliminate war. In this, he was not behind his times, but ahead of them."[26]

The emerging voices of Church, Fulbright, and McGovern notwithstanding, in 1965 most Americans supported the activist role their country had played in world affairs since World War II. Perhaps this is why in April 1965, Johnson could boldly assert that the United States was in Vietnam not merely to help South Vietnam "defend its independence," but also to "strengthen world order."[27] Like it or not, most Americans believed their nation could no longer afford the outdated isolationism of Borah and Taft. In the dangerous postwar era, America needed military allies. Most believed that the country, indeed, had a proper and leading role in world affairs. But how much of a role, what kind of role, and at what expense to important domestic concerns? These were questions that plagued Johnson's small, emerging band of critics in the Senate. Yet even these critics agreed that the United States had a role in the maintenance of world peace. Virtually no one—certainly not Church or McGovern—wanted a precipitous American withdrawal from Vietnam or any other part of the world. But, as some influential senators began asking: Should the nation become embroiled to this degree in every regional dispute involving a communist threat? "We're trying to police the world," complained Republican Senator George Aiken of Vermont, "and we can't do it."[28]

However, the threat of Soviet communism was real—and quite

menacing in almost every region of the world, particularly in Latin America, Asia, Eastern Europe, and Africa. In the years following World War II, America had aggressively met that threat in Europe with a massive expansion of the nation's military might. For more than a generation, U.S. foreign and defense policy was predicated on one, primary aim: containing communism by attempting to stop its spread at every turn. By 1965, most Americans considered the nation's European containment policy a brilliant success. Yet Asia, as they knew, was another story altogether.

PART ONE

THE ROOTS OF WAR

The Democratic label is now the property of men and women who have . . . bent to the whispered pleas from the lips of traitors . . . men and women who wear the political label stitched to the idiocy of a Truman, rotted by the deceit of an Acheson.

—SENATOR JOSEPH McCARTHY, 1950

We cannot win the next election unless we point out the utter failure and capacity of the present Administration to conduct foreign policy and cite the loss of China and the Korean war as typical examples of their very dangerous control.

—SENATOR ROBERT TAFT, 1951

CHAPTER I

The "Loss" of China

1949–1950

THE CONGRESSIONAL ELECTION RETURNS WERE HARDLY SURPRIS-
ing, considering the momentous events of the previous year. President
Harry Truman and his Democratic Party had endured an especially turbulent political season—and the voting on November 7, 1950, reflected
the political misfortunes that had befallen the White House. While the
president confidently predicted an electoral endorsement of his foreign
and domestic policies, a restless and disgruntled nation expressed precisely
the opposite. Voters were worried about the course of the Korean conflict
and disturbed that Truman and his State Department had allowed China
to fall into communist hands in late 1949. They were largely indifferent to
the president's liberal Fair Deal proposals. Perhaps most significant, many
voters were not as eager as Truman to reject the charges of communist
infiltration that Senator Joseph McCarthy had leveled against the State
Department. Where there was smoke, there might be fire—and the reckless Wisconsin Republican had generated plenty of smoke.

Earlier in the day, after voting in his hometown of Independence, Missouri, a beleaguered Truman returned to Washington to await the election
results. That evening, as he and his military and White House aides cruised
the Potomac River on the presidential yacht *Williamsburg*, the depressing
election news arrived over radio telephone: in the Senate, Republicans had
come within two votes of seizing control. The Democrats' 54-to-42 margin had all but disappeared and, with it, most chances that Truman would
have his way with the new 82nd Congress. In the House, the Democratic
losses were just as distressing—twenty-seven Democratic seats now
belonged to the Republicans.

It was a severe blow. Truman appeared to blame himself for the losses.
At first, he tried to lessen his shock by consuming generous quantities of
bourbon. One aide later remarked it was the only time he had ever seen

Truman drunk. Finally, at 9:00 P.M., weary and depressed, he turned in
for the evening.[1] The next morning, the *Chicago Daily News* summed up
the election's import in a front-page story. "President Truman's policies
were stingingly repudiated," the paper reported—and its characterization
was beyond dispute.[2] Truman had not only lost five crucial votes in the
Senate; voters had rejected the Senate's two Democratic leaders, leaving
Truman and his troubled legislative agenda adrift in uncertain and treacherous waters. A coalition of Republicans and southern Democrats—
hostile to most of Truman's Fair Deal agenda—would now have a working
majority on a host of issues. Some even speculated that the decidedly
more conservative majority might elect a southerner—Richard Russell
of Georgia or Harry Byrd of Virginia—as majority leader. Regardless of
who ran the Senate, Truman knew that his ambitious domestic agenda
was dead.[3]

The defeats of Majority Leader Scott Lucas of Illinois and the Democratic whip, Francis Myers of Pennsylvania, were the sharpest rebukes and
left the Senate Democrats in disarray. While the two men had not always
been strong or innovative legislative strategists, the president could usually rely on them to champion his programs and defend him against the
verbal assaults of conservative Republicans. Now the fates of his foreign
and domestic policies would depend on the questionable loyalty of a
narrow, more conservative Senate majority.

Other losses were also disheartening. The election claimed Armed
Services Committee Chairman Millard Tydings of Maryland and Labor
Committee Chairman Elbert Thomas of Utah. The Maryland veteran had
fiercely disputed McCarthy's charges of communism in the State Department and, thus, had drawn the withering enmity of McCarthy's right-
wing loyalists. At least two new members had gained entrance to the
Senate with charges that their opponents were communist sympathizers.
In Florida, conservative Democrat George Smathers had knocked off
incumbent Democrat Claude Pepper with a barrage of innuendo and
invective. With help from Smathers and his supporters, the Florida incumbent became, among other things, known as "Red" Pepper. In California,
an ambitious House member named Richard Nixon scored a decisive
victory over his liberal Democratic opponent, Congresswoman Helen
Gahagan Douglas, by questioning her patriotism and her adherence to
Truman's China policies.[4] Nixon dubbed her "the Pink Lady." She, in turn,
named him "Tricky Dick."

In every region but the South lay the dead political bodies of Truman's
House and Senate supporters. It was not as devastating as the absolute
repudiation Truman had suffered in 1946, when Republicans seized both
houses of Congress, but it was an electoral disaster by almost any defini-

tion. "Senate Democrats," *Newsweek* observed in the aftermath, "were a battered army whose command post had been blown up."[5]

THE CARNAGE OF November 1950 was, in large measure, the first electoral reaction to a series of unfortunate political and foreign policy developments that had begun in the late summer of 1949. In September, Truman had stunned the American public when he announced that the Soviet Union had recently detonated an atomic bomb. Since the end of World War II, America's sole possession of the bomb had been regarded as the most effective deterrent to another World War and had firmly secured the nation's status as the world's most powerful military force. It was a distinction that comforted an American public still weary from the turmoil and sacrifice of nearly four years of World War. Truman's staggering announcement, however, changed the essence of the Cold War and reordered America's worldview. No longer a war of words waged with strong rhetoric and competing economic assistance, a new militaristic Cold War had dawned. Some believed that a military showdown between the United States and the Soviets was now inevitable. Those fears appeared more justified than ever in January 1950, when Truman announced that the nation would respond to the Soviet bomb test by developing a hydrogen bomb—a device vastly more destructive than any existing atomic weapon.

U.S. relations with the Soviets had turned sour in the aftermath of World War II and had only grown more adversarial in subsequent years. With increasing alarm, Truman's foreign policy and defense advisors had come to see a Soviet Union bent on imposing communism on the rest of the world—a chilling declaration that former British Prime Minister Winston Churchill eloquently expressed in his famous "Iron Curtain" speech in early 1946. "From what I have seen of our Russian friends and allies during the war," Churchill said, "I am convinced that there is nothing they admire so much as strength, and there is nothing for which they have less respect than weakness, especially military weakness." While Truman, having accompanied Churchill to Missouri for the speech, did not immediately endorse the former British leader's thesis, U.S. foreign policy soon reflected the president's deep distrust of Stalin and his communist regime. In particular, the visionary thinking of George F. Kennan, a Russian scholar and Foreign Service officer stationed in Moscow, greatly influenced official attitudes toward the Soviets. It was Kennan who turned official heads when he asserted that the nation's approach to the Soviet Union "must be that of a long-term, patient but firm and vigilant containment of Russian expansive tendencies." Thus was born the nation's "containment" policy in Europe, aimed at Soviet expansionism and later widened, to Kennan's dismay, to include military opposition to communism around the globe.*

Events in early 1947 had placed the United States in direct conflict with the Soviets' perceived hegemonic aims. In February, Great Britain informed the Truman administration that it could no longer afford to keep the peace in Greece and Turkey in the wake of a budget crisis that forced the country to withdraw half of its military force from the region. From Athens, U.S. diplomats sent word that the British withdrawal would almost certainly mean the collapse of the Greek government. The message was clear: if the government fell, it would fall in the lap of a totalitarian government with close ties to the Soviet Union. In a foreshadowing of the later rationale for U.S. involvement in Vietnam, one of Truman's advisors warned that the outcome might be that "the whole Near East and part of North Africa" were "certain to pass under Soviet influence."[6]

Without consulting its leaders, Truman quickly demanded that Congress appropriate $400 million in aid to prop up the governments of Greece and Turkey. Dominated by members of their isolationist Midwestern wing, congressional Republicans were initially cool to the idea. But Truman had one important Republican ally: Senate Foreign Relations Committee Chairman Arthur Vandenberg of Michigan, a former political isolationist himself, who urged the president to present the threat of Soviet expansionism to Congress and the nation in the starkest of terms. The only way to get the aid, Vandenberg advised, was to "make a personal appearance before Congress and scare the hell out of the American people." On March 12, 1947, Truman, before a joint session of the House and Senate, did just that, painting the picture of a world teetering toward communist domination. In articulating a set of principles—later known as the Truman Doctrine—the president declared: "I believe that it must be the policy of the United States to support free peoples who are resisting attempted subjugation by armed minorities or by outside pressures."

In May, both houses of Congress overwhelmingly approved Truman's plan and, thus, set the nation on a determined and idealistic forty-five-year crusade against communism—from Europe to Africa to Latin America to

---

*In later years, Kennan was disappointed that his containment philosophy, which he meant only as a response to Soviet expansion, had been used as the pretext for a general, worldwide military response to communist hegemony. In his memoirs, he lamented that two decades of U.S. foreign policy were "bedeviled" by those wedded to the belief "that all another country had to do, in order to qualify for American aid, was to demonstrate the existence of a Communist threat" (Kennan, 322).

Southeast Asia. The Truman doctrine was a major turning point in U.S. foreign policy, not simply because Truman identified the Soviet empire as a totalitarian threat to the rest of the world (this had already been articulated), but because the United States had, for the first time, intervened on behalf of nations threatened by communism.[7]

Still reeling from the news about the Soviets' atomic test, Americans were far more aroused in October 1949, when Mao Tse-tung's communist forces in China finally drove General Chiang Kai-shek's Nationalist army from the mainland onto the island of Formosa. For years, China had held a special place in the hearts of many churchgoing Americans who regarded the nation as the world's most fertile field for Christian evangelism and Chiang as a devout Christian. American churches and Christian organizations had supported missionaries in China for generations and had developed a deep and lasting affection for the country and its people. Thus, many Americans were shocked and heartbroken by the communist victory, largely unaware that Chiang actually ruled a corrupt and undemocratic regime destined to fall of its own weight—although its collapse was greatly hastened by an effective, intense, and ideologically driven communist opposition.

Truman and his State Department knew the truth and understood that the president could have turned the tide in China's civil war only by massive military intervention. That would have meant making the country a U.S. protectorate—something that even Chiang's most ardent supporters opposed. In truth, U.S. efforts to save China had been far from paltry. Since the end of World War II the United States had given $3 billion in economic and military assistance to the Nationalist government—with little to show for it. The communists routed Chiang's poorly trained and unmotivated troops over and over. As Secretary of State Dean Acheson aptly observed, the Nationalists failed because "the almost inexhaustible patience of the Chinese people in their misery [had] ended. They did not bother to overthrow this government. There was really nothing to overthrow. They simply ignored it throughout the country."[8] Additional U.S. aid to China would have been wasted. "There is no evidence," Acheson accurately told Senate Foreign Relations Committee Chairman Tom Connally in March 1949, "that the furnishing of additional military materiel would alter the pattern of current developments in China."[9]

That Chiang was a corrupt leader in charge of an inept army was obvious to anyone with even a passing knowledge of China. Truman's political enemies, however, saw China's woes in a far different light. Foremost among those critics was *Time* publisher Henry Luce, born in China to missionary parents, who argued that the communist victory was a result of American irresolution, not Chiang's perfidy. "At no time in the long chron-

BALSAM LAKE PUBLIC LIBRARY
404 Main St. • P.O. Box 340
Balsam Lake, WI 54810

icle of its failure [in China] had [Truman's administration] displayed a
modest fraction of the stamina and decisiveness which had checked communism in Europe," *Time* said in a vitriolic broadside against the Truman
administration in August 1949.[10]

Congressional Republicans exploited the developments in China with
a relentless assault on the Truman–Acheson foreign policy. Leading
Republicans echoed Luce's charge that while Truman and Acheson were
preventing communist expansion into Western Europe, they had, in the
words of New Jersey Republican H. Alexander Smith, "left the back door
wide open in Asia."[11] In the Senate, California Republican William Knowland—whose intense devotion to Chiang earned him the mocking title
"Senator from Formosa"[12]—led a vigorous Republican attack on Truman
and Acheson. Truman's policies, he charged, had "accelerated the spread
of communism in Asia" so much that "gains for communism there have far
more than offset the losses suffered by communism in Europe." Chiang's
corruption and inept leadership notwithstanding, Knowland charged that
the "debacle solely and exclusively rests upon the administration which initiated and tolerated it." Truman and Acheson, he suggested, were guilty of
"appeasement," as well as "aiding, abetting and giving support to the
spread of communism in Asia."[13]

Further compounding the political damage were allegations—partly
true—that some U.S. Foreign Service officers had systematically dispar-
aged and undermined Chiang while expressing their admiration and support for the Communists, thereby abetting the Nationalists' defeat. Senate Republican leader Robert Taft, in arguing that the United States could
have prevented the communist victory, charged that Truman's State
Department was "guided by a left-wing group who obviously have wanted
to get rid of Chiang, and were willing at least to turn China over to the
communists for that purpose."[14]

U.S. disillusionment with Chiang, however, was nothing new, nor was
it indigenous to a small coterie of Foreign Service officers. It dated back
to early 1942, when General Joseph Stilwell arrived to oversee military
operations in the China-Burma-India Theater. Given the task of repelling
Japanese aggression in China and Southeast Asia, Stilwell quickly concluded that Chiang, was far more interested in preserving his crumbling
regime—that is, fighting the Chinese Communists—than in stopping
Imperialist Japanese aggression. Unable to persuade Chiang to provide the
troops needed to oppose Japan, a frustrated Stilwell finally suggested that
communist forces should be enlisted for the fight. Supporting Stilwell were
a handful of respected State Department China experts—men like John
Patton Davies, John Stewart Service, and John Carter Vincent—who
shared an intensive disdain for Chiang and urged U.S. pressure to force

him to reform. Taft, Knowland, and other conservatives thought it even more appalling that the "China hands," as they became known, had expressed respect for Mao's communist disciples, particularly their personal asceticism, espousal of self-government, and the easy way they moved among the peasants. In October 1944, at Chiang's insistence, Roosevelt finally recalled Stilwell.

In late 1945—more than a year after President Franklin Roosevelt had dispatched Major General Patrick Hurley to China to persuade Chiang to unify the Nationalist and communist forces against Japan—this newest general resigned and blamed his failure on the China hands. In a letter to President Truman, Hurley charged that "the professional Foreign Service men sided with the Chinese Communist armed party and the imperialist bloc of nations whose policy was to keep China divided against herself." The China hands, Hurley said, "continuously advised the Communists that my efforts in preventing the collapse of the National Government did not represent the policy of the United States."[15]

The fall of China was a call to arms for the conservative Republicans. Frustrated by their inability to regain the White House after seventeen years in political exile, they sensed the makings of a potent campaign issue. Chiang's Nationalist government, they alleged, did not fall because of economic and political forces beyond the control of U.S. policymakers; liberal Democratic foreign policy experts, sympathetic to communism, had "lost" China and thereby jeopardized U.S. national security.[16]

In light of world developments, the allegation seemed plausible. Less than five years after the end of World War II, Russia had, indeed, made substantial gains throughout the world. As *U.S. News & World Report* observed in early 1950, "Communist governments—many of them led by men trained in Moscow—are in command of nations ruling almost 800 million people." The result, the magazine reported, "is that the West finds it has lost more than 1 billion people from its sphere in less than 60 months."[17] A "Red Tide," it seemed, was consuming the nations of the world. And Truman's stubborn refusal to dispatch a military mission to bolster Chiang's exiled regime only served as further proof to the Republicans that Democrats could no longer be trusted to stop the march of communism across the world stage. "This is the year," the liberal *New Republic* observed,

> when the feverish fear of Communism is fanned higher by elections; when the men who legislate our futures think less of a hundred million votes in Asia than of a thousand votes in the Fourth Ward; when any gesture of conciliation to end the cold war is smeared as a surrender by an opposition whose dearest ambition is to pin the communist label on our chief of state.[18]

But the demagoguery was not confined to the Republican Party. Some conservative Democrats, aware of their constituents' alarm over the communist victories, also fanned the flames of fear. Speaking to a veterans group in January 1950, U.S. Representative John F. Kennedy of Massachusetts said Truman should send troops to Formosa and blamed him for Chiang's failure in China. "What our young men had saved, our diplomats and our president frittered away." The nation must now "prepare ourselves vigorously," he said, "to hold the line in the rest of Asia."[19]

If the "loss" of China was a call to arms for Republicans, the conviction in January 1950 of Alger Hiss, a former State Department official charged with perjury for lying about his Communist Party activities, gave them even more ammunition against Truman. Although not among the country's top diplomats, Hiss was well regarded by his colleagues and was among the advisors President Roosevelt had consulted at the Yalta Conference in early 1945. It was at Yalta, conservatives alleged, that Roosevelt had sentenced millions of Eastern Europeans to communist slavery by acceding control over their nations to the Soviet Union. Hiss's perjury conviction (the three-year statute of limitations on his alleged espionage activities had expired) vindicated Republican Congressman Richard Nixon and other members of the House Committee on Un-American Activities (HUAC) who exposed Hiss's communism during the committee's wide-ranging investigation.

The Hiss conviction gave Truman's foes yet another opportunity to buttress their argument that a decade of treachery and treason by liberal Democrats had reaped a whirlwind of communist gains throughout the world. Hiss, they alleged, was the thread that connected the "fall" of China to the "giving away" of Eastern Europe. South Dakota Republican Karl Mundt, a former HUAC member, wondered aloud about "what influence Alger Hiss might have had in writing a pro-Soviet foreign policy toward China" and suggested that Hiss had engineered "that most calamitous of all decisions at Yalta by which we agreed to give to the Russians control of the Communists in China." To Mundt and other conservatives, the Hiss case suggested a State Department crawling with Communists.[20]

To be sure, Acheson's subsequent public defense of Hiss—the brother of a close family friend—only made matters worse for Truman and increased the Republicans' antipathy toward the secretary of state. It did not help that only six days after Hiss's conviction, authorities in England arrested German-born Klaus Fuchs—a noted physicist who had worked on the Manhattan Project—for passing atomic secrets to the Soviets. Arrested in connection with Fuchs were two New Yorkers, Ethel and Julius Rosenberg. "How much more are we going to have to take?" Republican Homer Capehart of Indiana asked the Senate on February 9. "Fuchs and

Acheson and Hiss and hydrogen bombs threatening outside and New Dealism eating away at the vitals of the nation! In the name of Heaven, is this the best America can do?"[21]

To regain the White House and Congress, the Republicans would have to do much more than smear a few mid-level diplomats. Maximum political gain would result only if the "plot" to support Soviet communism could be traced to the higher echelons of Truman's administration. For this purpose, Acheson made the perfect villain. The son of a English-born Episcopal bishop, Acheson exuded an air of East Coast intellectual elitism that masked his lifelong devotion to liberal democratic cares. A committed New Dealer, he served briefly in Franklin Roosevelt's Tasury Department and later as FDR's assistant secretary of state for economic affairs. In Truman's administration, he had distinguished himself as effective and brilliant under secretary of state. To his friends, he was a firm and witty man with an impressive intellect and a high degree of personal rectitude. To his enemies in Congress, however, Acheson was an arrogant, intellectual snob who communicated an infuriating air of superiority.[22] As Truman biographer Alonzo L. Hamby observed,

> Angry Republicans, most of them embittered isolationists, s[Acheson] as representing all the trends that had disturbed them for that twenty years: the rise of the welfare state and big government, the finance of an Ivy League-northeastern establishment, the embrace of rope they considered distant and corrupt, the "loss" of China, the spe of international Communism. He would become the focal point politics of revenge bent on deposing Democrats and restoring "true Aicanism" in Washington.[23]

Although Republicans saw political gold in their attton Truman, Acheson, and the State Department, they never anticipahat the primary standard-bearer in their unseemly election-year entse would be a dishonest, second-rate senator from Wisconsin—Josepl Carthy.

CHAPTER 2

Paralyzed with Fear

1950

O N FEBRRY 9, 1950, SENATOR JOSEPH R. MCCARTHY TOOK THE Republican artisan attacks on Truman and Acheson to a new level when he addresse Republican women's club in Wheeling, West Virginia. The Wisconsin ator told them that he had a list of 205 names "known to the Secretary cate as being members of the Communist Party who nevertheless are l working and shaping policy in the State Department." Of course, Mcthy—who later reduced the number of Communists to 57— had no suıst. What he had was a three-year-old document prepared for the theepublican-controlled House Appropriations Committee in 1947. WItthe report contained 108 case studies, the subcommittee had ident no Communists in the State Department. In a gross distortion of t!port that actually absolved these employees of disloyalty, McCarther claimed to have a list of 57 "card-carrying Communists" who wercking in the State Department in February 1950.[1]

With reckless but politically explosive charges, the Wisconsin Republicas at once a blessing and a curse to the Republicans and their anticomst crusade: a curse, because in the hands of a more responsible anutable advocate, the movement might have been more respectaud effective; a blessing, because no other member of Congress was so rs, audacious, and effective in wreaking havoc among a bewildered Lratic Party thrown off balance by his sensational charges. McCartd no evidence to substantiate his allegations. His story changetantly, and many Washington insiders knew him as nothing more twomanizing drunkard who had faked a war record and won his Sent in 1946 by unfairly suggesting that his Democratic opponent wmmunist sympathizer. None of that, however, mattered to the prallible and receptive public, and a Republican Party hungry for a pssue to usher them back into power.

McCarthy was, by no means, the first Republican member of Congress to exploit public fears of Communists in government in the postwar years. The issue had been a favorite of Republican candidates for years and was practiced by the likes of Robert Taft, who had once said that Democratic programs "bordered on Communism"; House Minority Leader Joseph Martin, who advocated the election of Republicans to rid the government of communists and fellow travelers; New York Governor Thomas Dewey, who charged that Democrats were "adventurers" loyal to foreign ideologies; and Richard Nixon, who won a House seat in 1946 by smearing incumbent Democrat Jerry Voohis as a communist sympathizer.[2] Virtually every member of the House Committee on Un-American Activities, Democrat and Republican, had made a career out of the Communists-in-government issue. In fact, many Democrats were also not averse to using the smear on their opponents. In 1948, a Texas congressman, Lyndon Johnson, had suggested that Communists supported his Senate opponent, Coke Stevenson.[3] Truman himself had engaged in anticommunist demagoguery during his 1948 election when he encouraged supporters to label third-party candidate Henry Wallace a communist sympathizer.[4]

While he was no pioneer in Red-baiting, in 1950 McCarthy perfected the practice with an utter shamelessness and reckless audacity that has not since been matched in American politics. In the wake of his earthshaking charges, he tore viciously into the party of Truman and Roosevelt. "The Democratic label is now the property of men and women who have . . . bent to the whispered pleas from the lips of traitors . . . men and women who wear the political label stitched with the idiocy of a Truman, rotted by the deceit of a[n] Acheson." The Roosevelt and Truman years, he said, represented "twenty years of treason."[5] Initially, Truman and some of his Senate allies underestimated McCarthy, unable to imagine an American public so gullible and eager to accept his fantastic and baseless allegations. "I think we have these 'animals' on the run," an overconfident Truman wrote to Acheson in late March.[6]

Hoping to examine McCarthy's evidence, the Senate directed its Foreign Relations Committee to appoint a special investigative subcommittee and named Maryland Democrat Millard Tydings, chairman of the Armed Services Committee, to lead the inquiry.* A wealthy, conservative Democrat, Tydings was widely respected as a tough, intelligent, no-nonsense legislator who would lead a thorough and fair investigation. In the beginning, at least, his mind was skeptically open. After examining McCarthy's

---

*Also appointed to the subcommittee were Democrats James McMahon of Connecticut and Theodore Francis Green of Rhode Island and Republicans Bourke Hickenlooper of Iowa and Henry Cabot Lodge of Massachusetts.

"evidence," however, the utter bankruptcy of the charges became apparent.
In open session, a combative Tydings demanded that McCarthy supply the
subcommittee with any information that supported his allegations. Lacking
hard evidence, McCarthy demurred and simply suggested that everything the
subcommittee wanted would be found in the State Department's loyalty files.

Unfortunately for Tydings and the Senate's Democrats, Truman
intended to stand by a 1948 executive order that prohibited release of personnel files to Congress. For three months, McCarthy and the Republicans waged a campaign of relentless attacks on Truman and suggested that
his refusal to release the files was proof that they contained incriminating
evidence. To many Americans, that charge seemed plausible. What was
Truman hiding? they wondered. By the time Tydings devised a plan allowing release of the information without breaching executive privilege, the
damage was done. McCarthy now suggested that the State Department
had "completely rifled" the files.[7]

Moving to bolster his credibility, McCarthy finally named names.
Those standing accused of communism included Philip C. Jessup, the
State Department's ambassador at large; Owen Lattimore, a noted Asian
scholar at Johns Hopkins University and occasional State Department and
United Nations consultant; and, John Stewart Service, one of the China
hands who had been so critical of Chiang Kai-shek. But under the weight
of tough questioning by the subcommittee, McCarthy's flimsy evidence
collapsed. Although he succeeded in smearing Jessup, Lattimore, Service,
and others, he had proved nothing but that his capacity for prevarication
knew no limits. By July, the subcommittee—split down partisan lines—
declared McCarthy's charges "perhaps the most nefarious campaign of
untruths in the history of our Republic." The majority further concluded
that "with nothing, Senator McCarthy plunged headlong forward, desperately seeking to develop some information which, colored with distortion and fanned by a blaze of bias, would forestall a day of reckoning. . . .
Were this a campaign founded in truth it would be questionable enough;
where it is fraught with falsehood from beginning to end, its reprehensible and contemptible character defies adequate condemnation."[8]

Despite overwhelming evidence that McCarthy had, indeed, perpetrated a hoax on the Senate, the American public failed to see the issue as
clearly as Tydings and the White House. During the lengthy investigation,
Truman and Tydings committed several tactical errors that allowed a wily
McCarthy to escape the wrath of the public and the press. But Truman's
refusal to release the loyalty files had been, perhaps, the most damaging
error. The delay gave McCarthy several months to trumpet his baseless
charges with little fear of contradiction. "The President is hiding behind
those files," Senate Minority Leader Kenneth Wherry eagerly charged.
Republican William Jenner of Indiana, who labeled the Tydings commit-

tee "Whitewash, Inc.," supported him.[9] By the time of the subcommittee's scathing report, McCarthy's charges of a partisan Democratic cover-up had gained credence with the public.

The cowardly silence of most Senate Democrats as well as the public support of Senate Republicans, who perceived a political windfall for their party in the fall elections, also enhanced McCarthy's credibility. Conservatives like Homer Capehart and William Jenner of Indiana, Bourke Hickenlooper of Iowa and Karl Mundt of South Dakota, and Chiang Kai-shek disciples William Knowland of California and Styles Bridges of New Hampshire, all rushed to McCarthy's defense on and off the Senate floor. More helpful was the support he received from influential Republican leaders like Wherry and the party's ideological leader, Robert Taft. A sometimes-isolationist, who nursed a five-year political grudge against Acheson, Wherry lent McCarthy his considerable support in a number of savage attacks on the administration. Like other conservative Republicans, Wherry skillfully associated the spread of communism in Asia and elsewhere with the Communists McCarthy claimed to have discovered in the State Department. "Is it any wonder that an administration which harbors so many radicals at home is tolerant of the spread of socialism and its twin brother Communism abroad?" Wherry asked a Los Angeles Republican audience in February.[10]

Wherry's well-known antipathy toward Acheson made him a predictable, if disappointing, McCarthy ally. To many, however, Taft's vocal support for McCarthy's recklessness was a larger disappointment and one more piece of evidence that a destructive partisanship had afflicted the nation's foreign policy. For years, the wise and steady Arthur Vandenberg of Michigan had been the Senate Republicans' chief spokesman and leader in matters of foreign policy. Once an isolationist, Vandenberg—like many Republicans—had evolved during World War II. To Truman's delight he became a confirmed internationalist, a leading proponent of a bipartisan foreign policy, and one of Truman's most valued allies in Congress. In 1949, it was Vandenberg who had reluctantly helped Acheson—his nomination as secretary of state endangered by his defense of Alger Hiss—win a unanimous recommendation from the Senate Foreign Relations Committee and eventual confirmation by the Senate.

By 1950, however, Vandenberg's influence had waned. A serious illness hobbled him for much of the year and left the administration's foreign policy exposed to the attacks of more partisan foes. "While [Vandenberg] was out of action, and partly because of his absence," *Time* observed in April 1950, "the nation's bipartisan foreign policy had gone to pot."[11]

Into this vacuum stepped Taft, a committed foe of Truman's foreign and domestic policies. Facing a tough reelection in the fall and nursing ambitions for his party's presidential nomination in 1952, Taft fully appreciated McCarthy's usefulness to the task of destroying Truman's presidency and, with it, any prospects for the continuation of his liberal domestic policies. With his unbridled attacks on the "treason" of the Democrats, McCarthy just might pave the way for a Taft presidency. Although McCarthy had not yet identified one Communist in government, Taft said he told him to "keep talking and if one case doesn't work out, he should proceed with another one."[12]

Angry at the Republican attempts "to sabotage bipartisan foreign policy," Truman had condemned McCarthy and his supporters as the Kremlin's "greatest asset."[13] An indignant Taft rushed to McCarthy's defense, praising him as "a fighting Marine who risked his life to preserve the liberties of the United States."[14]*

While Taft's open support of McCarthy emboldened many Senate Republicans to ally themselves with their controversial colleague, a few Republicans were less than smitten by his poisonous tactics. In June, led by Margaret Chase Smith of Maine, seven liberal Republicans issued a "Declaration of Conscience" that deplored the right wing's enthusiastic embrace of McCarthyism.* "Certain elements of the Republican party," the senators said, "have materially added to this confusion in the hopes of riding the Republican party to victory through the selfish political exploitation of fear, bigotry, ignorance, and intolerance." Strong as it was, the declaration was signed by an insignificant minority of Republicans. It did not mention McCarthy by name and it took an obligatory swipe at Truman's "complacency to the threat of Communism here at home." More significant was the multitude of Republican senators who, out of fear of retribution, refused to sign. On June 1, after Smith finished reading the statement to the Senate, few of her colleagues rose to offer support. "Joe had the Senate paralyzed with fear," Smith later said. "The political risk of taking issue with him was too great a hazard to the political security of senators." Over time, even Smith found herself lending qualified support to McCarthy, as did every other senator who signed the declaration—except Wayne Morse, the maverick Republican from Oregon who would eventually abandon his party in disgust.[15]

By the summer of 1950, Republican exploitation of the communist threat—real and perceived, foreign and domestic—had deeply wounded Truman and his party in Congress. In May, only 16 percent of voters who were questioned in a national poll believed that the United States was winning the Cold War. In July, another survey indicated that almost half of the

---

*Other signers included George Aiken of Vermont, Wayne Morse of Oregon, Edward Thye of Minnesota, Irving Ives of New York, Charles Tobey of New Hampshire, and Robert Hendrickson of New Jersey. H. Alexander Smith of New Jersey later expressed his support for the statement.

electorate invested at least some belief in McCarthy and his charges.[16] Further compounding the president's woes were the bitter partisan debates that had stymied much of his domestic legislative agenda, including his controversial civil rights, farm, and health care proposals. Allegations of corruption also dogged the administration. A Senate investigation headed by freshman Arkansas Democrat J. William Fulbright had shed unfavorable light on alleged influence peddling and other unethical practices involving several of the president's aides and associates.[17]

In some respects, McCarthy was not the worst of Truman's troubles in the spring of 1950. In April, at Acheson's direction, National Security Council staff members had produced a sobering assessment of the nation's military strength. The paper, known as NSC Memorandum 68 (NSC-68), concluded that the Soviets posed a very real threat to world peace and would become only more menacing by 1955, when they could amass a nuclear arsenal of up to two hundred bombs. "We must realize that we are now in a mortal conflict," a Defense Department official somberly informed Truman. "Just because there is not much shooting as yet does not mean that we are in a cold war. It is not a cold war; it is a hot war. The only difference between this and previous wars is that death comes more slowly and in a different fashion."[18] Truman's aides believed that to keep pace with Soviet military expansion the United States would have to spend as much as $50 billion a year for nuclear and conventional weapons—an amount about 4 times the current military budget. As alarming and significant as it was, NSC-68 was a flawed document. It exaggerated the Soviets' current and potential military might and assumed the worst about their plans for world conquest. In 1950, however, the peril of Soviet expansionism was hardly a matter for debate. The only question was how Truman would react to the explosive report. Reluctant to call for a dramatic military buildup, he hesitated. As one biographer noted, "He would make no drastic moves until he knew more."[19] Without a looming international crisis to influence public opinion and spur Congress to action, Truman seemed to understand the sheer folly of proposing such a drastic increase in military spending. But Korea, as Acheson would later remark, changed everything.

JUST WHEN IT APPEARED the political challenges for Truman and his party had reached their zenith, an even larger one appeared on the Korean peninsula in late June, setting the stage for an even greater escalation of Republican assaults on Truman and Acheson. In the early morning hours of

June 25, 1950, communist North Korea staged a surprise invasion of the Republic of Korea. Encountering little resistance from the poorly trained, ill-equipped South Korean military, Soviet-backed communist forces surged south across the 38th Parallel—the arbitrary border created by the United States and the Soviet Union at the end of World War II—and headed for Seoul. Within days, the capital fell and a devastated South Korean army fled in full retreat. In the United States, administration officials viewed the situation with alarm and concluded the invasion was a Soviet-backed operation designed to test Truman's mettle.

The communist attack suddenly turned Korea into the first major battleground of a newer, more dangerous Cold War. Only eleven months earlier, when Truman had ordered U.S. troops removed from Korea, the Joint Chiefs of Staff and the State Department had not viewed the region as an area of strategic importance. By the time of the invasion, however, the political turmoil of the previous year had raised the stakes in Asia considerably. Despite the fact that Korea was, indeed, of no real strategic value to the United States, Truman and Acheson knew that the entire world would be watching their response. Failing to respond decisively to communist aggression in Asia would undoubtedly expose Truman to charges from Republicans that he had allowed two Asian nations to fall into communist hands within the span of nine months. Had Truman wavered or refused to assist South Korea in the critical days following the invasion, it would have effectively ended his presidency and spelled an end to Democratic control of Congress.

It is not known if Truman and his advisors, in the early days of the crisis, discussed the Korean situation's long-term political implications. Yet the political consequences of inaction—or of providing inadequate assistance to South Korea—could not have been far from their minds. Responding decisively, Truman ordered a significant expansion of the U.S. military presence in Asia. First, he directed General Douglas MacArthur, commander of the U.S. occupation forces in Japan, to supply South Korea with weapons and ammunition. He sent the Seventh Fleet steaming toward Taiwan to protect Chiang Kai-shek's forces from a possible Chinese attack. He also increased and accelerated shipments of aid to the Philippines and the French forces in Indochina.

On June 30, after an urgent request from MacArthur, Truman made one of the most fateful decisions of his second term. After a series of intense discussions with his advisors, the president informed congressional leaders that he would commit ground, air, and naval forces to the United Nations effort to defend South Korea. At a press conference announcing the decision, Truman agreed with a reporter who asked if the effort was a "police action." Unlike his successors, Truman would make no effort to conceal the extent of U.S. military involvement in Asia. But his unilateral decision to inform congressional leaders, not to consult them, would have broad implications for the nation's future involvement in the political and military affairs of Southeast Asia. Relying on varying interpretations of Truman's precedent, rarely would another president feel compelled to consult members of Congress before committing the United States to the armed struggle against communism in Asia.

CHAPTER 3

Korea

1950

T HE VITRIOLIC DEBATES OVER THE KOREAN WAR, AND WHO WAS responsible for it, would have long-lasting implications for the way American politicians approached communism in Asia. For more than twenty years, American presidents and other political leaders would be guided by the political fallout over Truman's military decisions in the summer and fall of 1950. Dwight D. Eisenhower would view Truman's troubles over Korea as evidence that Americans had no stomach for fighting another war in Asia—an interpretation that may have kept the nation out of the Indochina war in 1954. Lyndon Johnson, however, would learn different lessons from Korea. Truman's distasteful experiences would be part of the reason this Democratic president would eventually conceal the extent of the Vietnam War from the American people and their representatives in Congress. Ironically, however, the Korean experience would also teach Johnson the necessity for formal congressional assent for his military actions—even if he would obtain it with deception and the most negligible degree of formal consultation.

The first signs of domestic trouble over Korea first appeared on June 30, 1950, when Truman met with congressional leaders, not to consult, but to inform them of his decision to send U.S. troops to South Korea. Senator Kenneth Wherry aggressively challenged the president and wanted to know, recalled one Truman aide, "if the President was going to advise the Congress before he sent ground troops into Korea." Truman matter-of-factly responded that "I just had to act as Commander-in-Chief, and I did." Should the need arise for full-scale military action, Truman assured the congressional leaders, he would consult Congress.[1]

Earlier, when Truman spoke with Senate Foreign Relations Committee Chairman Tom Connally, the plainspoken Texas Democrat had advised him that "if a burglar breaks into your house, you can shoot him without

38

going down to the police station and getting permission. You might run into a long debate by Congress, which would tie your hands completely. You have the right to do so as Commander-in-Chief and under the UN Charter."[2] Truman may have had the constitutional right to dispatch U.S. troops unilaterally to Korea. But because he declined to make congressional leaders partners in his decision, the Republicans would feel no obligation to share the blame if the conflict went badly. In fact, they would attack him mercilessly at the first opportunity.*

As it turned out, that opportunity came early. Republican leaders were seething, not only over the way Truman had excluded them from his decision, but because of administration policies that they believed had encouraged the North Koreans to think that the United States would not challenge an attack on South Korea. Acheson had seemed to say as much in a widely heralded speech to the National Press Club in January. While he forcefully articulated a North Pacific perimeter that the United States would defend against communist aggression (a line running along the Aleutian Islands southward to Japan to Okinawa to the Philippines), the secretary of state had curiously omitted South Korea.[3] That glaring omission, Republicans later charged, was an open invitation to aggression, especially considering other signs that Truman did not regard Korea as a region of strategic importance to the United States. Ironically, the position of some prominent Republicans toward Korea seemed uncomfortably similar to Acheson's position. Heavily influenced by the military isolationists who had once strongly opposed direct U.S. involvement in Europe during World War II and who had only managed a good rhetorical game when it came to fighting communism in Asia, many Republican leaders were instinctively opposed to sending troops into Asia. Thus, in the early days of the conflict, while much of the nation rallied to Truman's support, most Republicans remained on the sidelines.

At a Republican caucus to discuss the Mutual Defense Assistance Act—legislation containing military assistance for South Korea—William Jenner complained that it was "just downright idiotic" for the State Department to place so much emphasis on Korea. Taft advised his colleagues not to be "stampeded into war" over Korea. While he supported sending military equipment, he said the communist invasion "should not be considered provocation for

---

*Fourteen years later, as President Lyndon Johnson considered retaliatory strikes against North Vietnam for its aggression in the Gulf of Tonkin, Truman's political woes over Korea were instructive. Unlike Truman, Johnson insisted that members of Congress share responsibility for any escalation of hostilities between the two countries. The result was the Gulf of Tonkin Resolution, approved in August 1964.

war." Senator Styles Bridges of New Hampshire speculated that South Korea might be "written off" in less than ten days, and there "isn't a thing we can do about it." Senator Arthur Watkins of Utah doubted the whole idea of sending military supplies to countries threatened by communism, believing that Truman's policy relied too much on military force. Following the caucus, Senator Eugene Milliken of Colorado met with reporters to summarize the Republican view of the Korean situation. Republican lawmakers, he said, were "unanimous" in believing the communist invasion "should not be used as a provocation for war." The nation had no obligation to fight with South Korean soldiers, although he said there was "perhaps a moral commitment to help the Koreans help themselves, to wit, with supplies."[4]

Within days, however, the winds of public opinion swept through Capitol Hill like a tornado. After months of attacking the president for having abandoned the fight against communism, Republicans realized they could only offer Truman their grudging support. "The general principle of the policy is right," Taft admitted, "and I see no choice except to back up wholeheartedly and with every available resource the American men in our armed forces who have been moved into Korea."[5] Congress promptly ended its debate over whether to allow Truman to reinstate the draft. A unified House and Senate not only gave the president that authority, but handed him power to call up the National Guard and reservists. Both houses also gave speedy assent to a $1.2 billion military aid program with provisions allowing Truman to spend up to $460 million to assist South Korea. In the Senate, the vote demonstrated that Republicans had heard public opinion. Both measures were approved unanimously.[6]

Immediately following the invasion, however, Taft—as the ideological leader of his party's military isolationist wing—gave his Republican colleagues the rhetorical framework for their political opposition to Truman's Korean policies: Truman's show of force was late in coming, he told a party caucus. Had such a policy been in place before the invasion, Taft said, "there never would have been such an attack by the North Koreans. In short, this entirely unfortunate crisis has been produced, first, by the outrageous, aggressive attitude of Soviet Russia, and second, by the bungling and inconsistent foreign policy of the administration" that had, among other things, acquiesced to communism in China. Furthermore, Taft argued, the postwar decision to divide Korea at the 38th Parallel was evidence of the Roosevelt–Truman policy of cooperation with the Soviet Union.[7]

Throughout the summer of 1950, as U.S. troops fought communist forces in the mountains and hills of South Korea, a political war broke out in Washington and across the country. With the fall congressional elections just months away, the Republican attacks on Truman intensified. In Iowa, a group of Republican Party chairmen from twelve states demanded the resignations of Acheson and Secretary of Defense Louis Johnson for "demonstrated ineptitude."[8] Speaking to 1,800 cheering American Legionnaires in Green Bay, Wisconsin, Joseph McCarthy also called for Acheson's head. "The Korea death-trap," he said, "we can lay to the doors of the Kremlin and those who sabotaged rearming, including Acheson and the President, if you please."[9] In Illinois, where Majority Leader Scott Lucas battled for his political life, Republican opponent Everett Dirksen turned from attacking Lucas over the economy and began focusing, instead, on the Korean conflict. Reminding a state fair audience that only eight months earlier Truman had bragged about the robust state of the nation, Dirksen said, "It is not good now, Mr. President, because of your neglect of our defenses. . . . The blunderers and stupid policy makers sowed the seeds of war in Washington. That's why young people die today."[10]

But these and other strong words belied a high degree of dissension over Korea among various Republican factions. Moderates and liberals within the party (men like Vandenberg, Henry Cabot Lodge of Massachusetts, and H. Alexander Smith of New Jersey) shied away from the more virulent personal attacks on Truman and Acheson, while the most conservative Republicans urged open warfare on the president and his controversial secretary of state. In mid-August, four prominent Republican members of the Senate Foreign Relations Committee tried their hand at propounding what they considered a moderate party doctrine for Asia.* In their sharply worded manifesto, the senators blamed the Truman–Roosevelt foreign policy, in general, and the Yalta and Potsdam agreements, in particular, for most of the world problems. Truman and Acheson, the senators said, gave the Soviet Union a "green light to grab whatever it could in China, Korea and Formosa."[11] Despite its sharply partisan tone, the manifesto was indeed a relatively moderate document and the product of several compromises. For example, to gain the signatures of Lodge and Smith, the statement stopped short of demanding Acheson's resignation and did not call for direct U.S. support of Chiang Kai-shek's forces in Formosa.

To Wherry, however, even this sharp rebuke of Truman's foreign policy was far too weak. In a separate Senate speech, he not only questioned Acheson's judgment, but his patriotism, and declared him "100 percent responsible for what has happened" in Korea. "The way to win the minds of men to the principles for which the United States stands," Wherry told the Senate on August 14, "is to get rid of Secretary Acheson and to put in charge of the State Department someone who has not blundered the

*The senators were H. Alexander Smith, Alexander Wiley of Wisconsin, Bourke Hickenlooper of Iowa, and Henry Cabot Lodge. Arthur Vandenberg let it be known that he was in "general agreement" with the statement.

United States into another war." He congratulated his Republican colleagues who, he said, were "trying to get rid of the alien-minded radicals
and moral perverts in the Truman administration."[12]

In the Senate, Truman's Democratic supporters reacted to the Republican attacks with a furious counterassault. One of McCarthy's detractors
on the Tydings committee, Brien McMahon of Connecticut, attacked
Wherry and other Republicans as "masters of hindsight" who sought to
"cut themselves in on the victories of our foreign policy and to divorce
themselves from our defeats." McMahon bitterly noted that more than half
of the Senate's Republicans had opposed U.S. assistance to fight communism in Turkey and Greece, had tried to block enactment of the Marshall
Plan for economic recovery in Europe, and had opposed the North
Atlantic Treaty. Tydings angrily challenged a Republican assertion that
only two hundred dollars' worth of military assistance had actually made
its way to South Korea before the invasion. Actually, Tydings told the Senate, U.S. occupation forces had left behind $301 million in military sup-
plies and U.S. aid to South Korea had totaled almost $500 million. When
Wherry rose to challenge Tydings' figures, the Maryland Democrat issued
a stern lecture: "It does not lie well in the mouths of any of us, particularly
those who have opposed the arms-assistance program by their speeches
and their votes, to find fault." Turning red with anger, Wherry responded
that he had, indeed, voted for aid to China and Korea. Sharpening his
attack and ignoring the evidence of his own previous ambivalence to assistance for the South Koreans, Wherry brazenly declared that it mattered
not whether he voted for the aid, "the blood of our boys in Korea is on
[Acheson's] shoulders, and not on the shoulders of anyone else."[13]

The truth was that the minority leader, like many isolationist Republicans, had supported economic assistance for Korea, while opposing the
entire military assistance program that included military aid. He had also
opposed authorizing foreign economic aid, including assistance to China,
had called the Greek-Turkish aid bill "a military adventure," and had
insisted that "tremendous savings" could be found in the military budget.[14]
But as *Newsweek* presciently noted, while the Democrats were correct in
highlighting the Republican hypocrisy, "Republican strategists were sure
that the average voter did not concern himself with voting records. The
mistakes, if such they were, had been made by a Democratic President and
a Democratic Congress."[15]

FOR ALMOST THREE MONTHS, U.S. troops struggled to prevent the powerful, well-supplied communist forces from driving them off the Korean

peninsula. Throughout the early days of the conflict an embarrassing series of setbacks and retreats served only to intensify Republican attacks on Truman. With the November election less than seven weeks away, MacArthur launched a military counterstrike that changed the course of the war and finally put communist forces on the defensive. On September 15, American forces staged a daring amphibious landing at the Yellow Sea port of Inchon, 30 miles from the South Korean capital of Seoul. The invasion was a remarkable success. By September 26, Seoul was liberated. By month's end, the North Korean army had retreated to the 38th Parallel and MacArthur began lobbying the administration for permission to cross into North Korea and rout the communist forces.

With the conflict finally in hand—many wrongly concluded that the war had actually been won—Republicans faced the irony of having been denied a potent campaign issue by the heroic actions of their favorite general, a man well known as a conservative with Republican leanings. But the reversal of fortune in Korea did not quell the fury of Truman's most ardent critics. With partisan gusto, they continued to look for ways to exploit the administration's perceived foreign policy "blunders." Within days, some of Truman's foes had found their new issue: the "treason" of former Secretary of State George C. Marshall.

ONLY DAYS BEFORE THE successful invasion at Inchon, Truman reluctantly forced the resignation of Secretary of Defense Louis Johnson. It was not the partisan Republican attacks on the president's military policies that irreparably damaged Johnson, but his arrogance and an inability to cooperate with other members of Truman's cabinet, particularly Acheson. Truman quickly nominated General George C. Marshall as Johnson's successor. A legendary soldier with forty years in uniform, Marshall was Army chief of staff during World War II and later Truman's secretary of state. It was no secret that Truman virtually worshiped the highly decorated soldier and believed him to be the greatest living American.[16] At age 69 and retired from active duty for five years, Marshall remained a national hero. Truman hoped that a man of such enormous stature and unquestioned integrity might help to keep the partisan hounds at bay and rally the country around his foreign policy. But some Republicans did not share Truman's high opinion of the esteemed general, and they thought even less of his nomination to head the Defense Department. The reason, as expressed in the words of *Time*, was that Marshall's appointment meant that "a political issue was being snatched right from under their noses."[17]

There were other reasons for their antipathy. Conservatives, most of whom admired MacArthur, had always viewed Marshall with suspicion because of his liberal, New Deal political leanings. As the president's emissary to China and later as secretary of state, they believed Marshall had turned his back on Chiang Kai-shek and allowed China to fall to the Communists. Some military isolationists actually believed that Marshall and Roosevelt knew about the Japanese attack on Pearl Harbor, but withheld the information to force direct American intervention in World War II. Marshall's detractors also blamed him for the "outrageous lies" used to "cover up the Yalta sell-out of the Orient."[18]

In mid-September, as Congress considered waiving legislation that prohibited the former general from heading the Defense Department, Marshall's critics roared to life. House Republicans stood and cheered when their colleague, Dewey Short of Missouri, shouted that Marshall was "a catspaw and a pawn" whom Truman had called back into service "to bail out desperate men who are in a hole." In the Senate, Republican William Jenner of Indiana—a fierce isolationist—shocked the Senate with a withering personal attack on Marshall. Jenner called him a "front man for traitors," a "living lie," and "either an unsuspecting, well-intentioned stooge or an actual co-conspirator with the most treasonable array of political cutthroats ever turned loose in the executive branch of our government." Jenner alleged that Marshall had supported the communist victory in China and would now join "the Communist-appeasing, Communist-protecting betrayer of America, Secretary of State Dean Acheson." In remarks not delivered, but supplied to the press, Jenner went even further and suggested that "only a Republican victory and the impeachment of the President can save our form of government."[19]

To Senate Majority Leader Scott Lucas, Jenner's attack on Marshall comprised "the most venomous, the most diabolical, the most reprehensible, the most unfortunate and irresponsible speech I have ever heard made on the floor of the Senate or of the House of Representatives." (Truman later called Jenner "one of those dirty sonsabitches.") Jenner's diatribe made Republican Leverett Saltonstall of Massachusetts so angry that he visibly shook as he rose to address the Senate immediately after the Indiana senator had finished. The dignified and courtly Saltonstall said he lacked "the words and the voice to express how strongly I disagree with what has been said here. If any man in public life is more above censure than General George Marshall, I do not know of him." While disassociating himself from Jenner's particular vitriol, Taft made it clear he had nothing but disdain for Marshall. If he supported Marshall, Taft said he would be "confirming and approving the sympathetic attitude toward Communism in the Far East which has dominated the Far Eastern division of the State Department." In the House, one hundred Republicans and five

Democrats opposed legislation permitting Marshall's nomination, while twenty Republicans and one Democrat opposed him in the Senate.[20]

Marshall won, but with the partisan fires raging in Congress, it was now apparent that even a man of his immense stature and legendary skills could not unify the country around a bipartisan foreign policy—especially in an election year. The bruising battle demonstrated the futility of bipartisan rapprochement over Asia. That Truman's critics had not hesitated to attack an American hero like Marshall suggested the lengths to which they would go in their quest to recapture the White House.

As the November election drew near, Truman handed his opponents yet another enticing political opportunity. In September, after several years of inaction, the Senate had finally approved the Internal Security Act, a sweeping measure that tightened federal laws against espionage and sedition, and required registration of all communist-front organizations and the detention of anyone considered likely to commit espionage or sabotage. Originally sponsored in the House in 1948 by Republicans Karl Mundt and Richard Nixon, the bill had been bottled up in the Senate Judiciary Committee. By 1950, however, events in China and Korea and McCarthy's dramatic allegations of communism in government provided ample leverage to force the bill onto the Senate floor. In short order, the measure became a prime vehicle in the conservative effort to link the turmoil in Asia to the alleged communist subversion of the State Department. Truman despised the bill and argued that it "adopted police-state tactics and unduly encroached on individual rights." He would veto the legislation, he told a friend, "regardless of how politically unpopular it was—election year or no election year."[21] Although he hoped to persuade Congress to amend the legislation to his satisfaction, the issue had become far too emotional and politicized. Conservatives were in no mood to compromise.

The bill, in fact, was nothing short of veto bait. The last thing Truman's opponents wanted was the president's support. The outcry over Truman's opposition to the bill would be a wonderfully potent political issue for Republicans as they entered the campaign's final weeks. What better way to prove that Truman and the Democrats were weak on communism? True to his word, Truman rejected the bill, tartly claiming it would "put the government in the thought control business." As Congress considered overriding his veto, courage was a scarce commodity among Democrats, especially those who would face the voters in November. Frightened by the potential repercussions of appearing soft on communism, senators followed the House in overriding Truman's veto. Only ten Democrats voted to uphold their president.[22]

As the fall campaign went into full swing, so did the war in Korea. U.S. forces fared so well that MacArthur gained permission to attempt a total rout of communist forces. In October, he finally took the battle into North Korea in hopes of reunifying the two countries under the South Korean government. But there were disturbing signs that MacArthur's foray into North Korea was about to draw Chinese forces into the war.

Despite evidence of Chinese intervention—a potentially disastrous result—the Republicans were stymied when it came to Korea. No longer able to attack Truman for military setbacks in the conflict, they instead focused their attacks on the patriotism and judgment of Truman and his foreign and military advisors. As usual, McCarthy's attacks were the most vicious—and the most effective. Although the Korean conflict had bumped him and his hunt for Communists from the front pages, McCarthy was still a potent and influential political force. As he stumped the country on behalf of Republican candidates, the Wisconsin senator painted a vivid picture of an administration-controlled Democratic Party infested with Communists and communist sympathizers. In late September, campaigning in Maryland against nemesis Millard Tydings, McCarthy unveiled a new smear that cleverly distinguished between the larger Democratic Party and the national "administration" party. While "millions of loyal Americans" had long voted for Democrats, McCarthy informed his Republican audience that the "administration Democratic Party . . . is no longer an American Party."

> Unfortunately, the men of little minds who control the administration Democrats, and who do not represent the millions of loyal American Democrats, have placed themselves on the side of the Communists, traitors, and dupes in order to gain a short-term political advantage. Apparently the Tydings, the [Brien] McMahons and the Lucases do not realize that they cannot save the face of the Democratic Party if the face of America is lost. I do not ask the Democrats in this country to desert their party. I do ask them in the name of America to realize that at long last the administration Democratic Party has deserted them and has made it a party which protects Communists and hides corruption.[23]

Across the country, Republicans borrowed McCarthy's tactics with varying degrees of sophistication. In Illinois, Republican Everett Dirksen challenged Majority Leader Lucas for reelection with the charge that Democrats had "shielded and defended and coddled" Communists since the early days of the New Deal.[24] Facing a tough reelection campaign of his own, Taft joined Dirksen on the stump and insisted the election was a referendum on whether "we are going to establish a socialistic state. If you elect a Democratic Congress and if you move them just a little to the left of the present Congress, you will get the whole [socialist] program."[25]

In California, one of Richard Nixon's campaign advisors, Murray Chotiner, adopted a more sophisticated strategy. He cautioned his candidate and campaign workers against painting all Democrats as communist sympathizers. "We must appeal to Democrats to help win the election," Chotiner wrote in a campaign manual. "Therefore, we do not make a blanket attack on Democrats. Refer to the opposition as a supporter of the socialistic program running on the Democratic ticket."[26] By following this strategy, Nixon seized the upper hand against Democratic Congresswoman Helen Gahagan Douglas when he charged that she was "pink right down to her underwear" and linked her to New York's leftist congressman, Vito Marcantonio.[27] In the words of one Douglas supporter, Alvin Meyers, Nixon's strategy "was a *masterful* hatchet job."[28] If Douglas had her way, Nixon said on one radio broadcast,

> the Communist conspiracy in the United States would never have been exposed and Alger Hiss, instead of being a convicted perjurer, would still be influencing the foreign policy of the United States. . . . If she had her way, our troops in Korea would have been even less prepared than they are. . . . It just so happens that my opponent is a member of a small clique which joins the notorious Communist party-liner Vito Marcantonio of New York in voting time after time against measures that are for the security of this country.[29]

Nixon made much of Douglas's House speech in 1946 in which she asserted that "communism is no real threat to the democratic institutions of this country." What voters could not appreciate was that Douglas's words had represented one of the more courageous and principled early stands against the excesses and demagoguery of the House Un-American Affairs Committee, a panel whose controversial tactics far overshadowed whatever legitimate evidence it uncovered. She had, indeed, risen on the House floor to deliver her "Democratic Credo" that dismissed the so-called communist threat. The real danger, she asserted, was "the irresponsible way the term 'communism' is used to falsely label the things the majority of us believe in." In her speech, Douglas had celebrated free enterprise and democracy and attacked the communist Soviet regime as "the cruelest, most barbaric autocracy in world history." But her passionate plea for a rational fight against domestic communism also hinted at the deplorable methods a generation of politicians, including Nixon, would employ in their rise to political power.

"The fear of communism in this country is not rational," Douglas observed, referring to the near panic created by HUAC's deplorable tactics. "And that irrational fear of communism is being deliberately used in many quarters to blind us to our real problems. . . . I am nauseated and sick to death of the vicious and deliberate way the word communist has been forged as a weapon and used against those who organize and raise their voices in defense of democratic ideals."[30]

But Nixon's blistering attacks on Douglas's patriotism were effective, as were his demands for American support of Chiang Kai-shek's struggle against the Chinese Communists. Truman was guilty of neglecting Asia at the expense of Europe, he charged. "While engaging in a cold war against the spread of Communism in some parts of the world, we have adopted a policy of virtual isolationism elsewhere," Nixon said. "Communism requires a worldwide resistance."[31]

In scores of Senate and House races, the message was clear to anyone listening: the Communists who had infiltrated the State Department had undermined the cause of democracy in China and Eastern Europe. These traitors would not have been discovered without the courage and diligence of patriotic Republican leaders. Furthermore, American troops would not be fighting in Korea and Chiang's Nationalist government would still be in power in China had Republicans been in charge of U.S. foreign policy.

Truman, meanwhile, resisted the urge to directly challenge his critics and refused to hit the campaign trail. Yet, had he chosen to campaign, it is unlikely that his help would have been welcomed. With his public approval ratings sagging, few Democrats were eager to associate themselves with this unpopular president and his equally unpopular foreign and domestic policies.

Throughout the fall, the president's strongest reply to his critics was issued through his special assistant, W. Averell Harriman, the former U.S. ambassador to the Soviet Union. In a speech to the AFL-CIO—a group that despised Robert Taft for his sponsorship of the antilabor, Taft–Hartley legislation—Harriman blasted the Ohio Republican for his military isolationist voting record that had included opposition to the North Atlantic Treaty, support for cutting the Marshall Plan, and efforts to stop the arming of America's allies in the early days of World War II. "When you look at his record," Harriman observed, "you cannot escape the conclusion that if Congress had adopted his positions, Communist objectives would thereby have been furthered." Harriman also charged that "actions which further the designs of the Kremlin cannot be forgiven on the ground that they were taken unwittingly. The most charitable thing one can say about Taft it that he knows not what he does."[32] Harriman's speech might have warmed the hearts of Truman and his allies, but it did nothing but spark renewed assaults on the president in Congress. As an isolated attack, the broadside had no long-term impact. More significant, it was a cheap and ham-handed imitation of the tactics the Republicans had used repeatedly against Truman for much of 1950.

When Truman finally entered the race himself—he delivered a radio speech from St. Louis the Saturday before the election—it was too late.[33] The damage had already been done. At every turn throughout the previous eighteen months, Republicans had masterfully exploited each foreign policy mishap. By election day, the perception was clear in enough minds: adverse developments in Asia had not only been caused by Truman's ineptitude; they were the direct result of the treachery and disloyalty of those who had managed U.S. foreign policy during the Roosevelt and Truman years. When "patriots" like McCarthy, Wherry, and Taft exposed the Communists, the Senate Democrats—led by Tydings—had tried to protect Truman by perpetrating a massive whitewash. Perhaps just as effective was the Republican tactic of giving Truman's Fair Deal proposals the "socialist" label. In doing so, Republicans succeeded in making a damaging connection between Truman's liberal Fair Deal agenda and his "pro-Communist" foreign policy.

To almost any aspiring politician, the lessons of 1949 and 1950 seemed clear enough: woe to the leader who tolerated the slightest hint of disloyalty in his ranks and who allowed one square inch of Asian soil to fall into communist hands. Truman and Acheson were almost crucified for their misfortunes in Asia. And a new generation of political leaders—John F. Kennedy, Lyndon Johnson, and Richard Nixon included—were watching and learning.

CHAPTER 4

The Part-Time Isolationists

1951

THEIR IMPRESSIVE SHOWING IN THE 1950 ELECTION EMBOLDENED the congressional Republicans. By exploiting the "failures" of Truman's Far East policies, they had discovered a potent political weapon. Therefore, it was only natural that some would conclude that if a vigorous assault on Truman's foreign policy had put them in reach of a congressional majority, an even more audacious assault on the president and his party might just push them over the top in 1952. Not only Congress, but the White House and the reins of the domestic and foreign policies of the United States now seemed within their reach. Two more years of unbridled opposition to the Democrats, and it could all be theirs.

No one seemed more devoted to this strategy than Robert Taft, whose hard-fought reelection campaign in Ohio—as well as his presidential aspirations for 1952—persuaded him of the need to intensify the Republican attacks on Truman. Taft not only survived a strong reelection challenge; he defeated his Democratic opponent by the widest margin of his political career. Some attributed the win to a variety of factors—a new ballot that favored incumbents, a highly effective Republican campaign organization, Taft's own immense stature and seniority in Washington, and the excesses of his union-backed opposition. Taft, however, chose to believe that it was primarily his prominence as the leading congressional opponent of Harry Truman.

As one who took seriously his role as de facto leader of the opposition party, Taft believed Truman had survived in 1948 because the Republicans had nominated, in Thomas Dewey, what he called "a me-too-man." Already plotting his 1952 presidential campaign, Taft believed that his party would not prevail unless it rejected the philosophies of the Dewey loyalists and Eastern internationalists. Strong, vigorous, dogged opposition to Democrats and their programs was the route to victory, he now believed. The 1950 elections only confirmed Taft's decision to strike an even more partisan, hard-line position against Truman in the new 82nd Congress. In the words of one sympathetic biographer, *New York Times* reporter William S. White, Taft believed that "Ohio had very greatly preferred him, and all that he represented." To win in 1952, Taft thought that his Republican colleagues "needed only his type of campaign in Ohio, the smashing, rock-breaking sort of campaign full of nothing but attack."[1]

For Taft, however, the matter was more than political expediency. He seemed to fear for the future of his country under Democratic leadership. As he told one constituent, "Their policies have led America into a dangerous situation, and they are utterly incapable of getting us out."[2]

Taft wasted no time. In January, he launched his renewed campaign against Truman by embracing the nationalistic "Fortress America" sentiments of former President Herbert Hoover, who had only recently advocated a drastic reduction of America's military commitments around the world, especially in Europe and Asia. "We Americans alone," Hoover said, "with sea and air power, can so control the Atlantic and Pacific Oceans that there can be no possible invasion of the Western Hemisphere by Communist armies." Hoover, who consulted often with Taft and other Senate Republicans on foreign policy, wanted the United States to withdraw from Korea and Japan, but increase its role in the protection of Formosa and the Philippines. Western European allies, Hoover maintained, should be denied U.S. military aid until they had organized defenses of their own "of such large numbers as would erect a sure dam against the Red flood." In other words, Hoover seemed to believe America should defend Europe only when it no longer needed America's help. Hoover's isolationist speech struck a chord with leading Senate Republicans. "He exactly expressed my opinion," said Senate Minority Leader Kenneth Wherry. Taft offered that he, too, agreed "with many of the principles he states."[3]

Taft, of course, had long held that the Far East was "more important to our future peace than is Europe."[4] He demonstrated just how much he agreed with Hoover when he formally opposed Truman's plans to implement the North Atlantic Treaty Organization (NATO) in 1949. Taft had voted against NATO and now he stood adamantly opposed to Truman's plan to send four divisions to protect Western Europe from the Soviet Union. In early January 1951, Taft told the Senate that the U.S. should "commit no American troops to the European continent at this time." When Illinois Democrat Paul Douglas reminded Taft that the fall of Western Europe would leave the Continent's industrial potential in Soviet hands, Taft replied that, in that event, the United States could destroy those industrial facilities with bombs. Taft's extraordinary logic was too much for J. William Fulbright of Arkansas, who interrupted to say that it was "a very shocking thing for Europeans to realize that we are willing to contemplate their destruction."[5]

While Taft and his allies forcefully rejected the isolationist label, their curious indifference to Europe's defense needs raised several interesting questions. What else could one call an ideology that sought to make the United States a virtual fortress, with little or no regard for the security of its European allies? What else to call a philosophy that denied the inextricable ties between the military and economic futures of Europe and the United States? How could Taft and his colleagues, on one hand, castigate Truman for failing to challenge communism in China, when they were unwilling to defend Europe, a Continent with close economic and cultural ties to the United States and the ancestral home of most Americans?

The answer was that Taft and many of his colleagues were, indeed, isolationists—especially where Europe was concerned. Their aversion to U.S. military intervention in Europe, in particular, was fed by strong historical animosities and racial prejudices toward the varied, feuding ethnic and religious factions throughout the European Continent. Said Herbert Hoover of Europe:

> Here are four hundred million people on the Continent divided into twenty-six races. They are crowded cheek by jowl in an area less than two-thirds of the United States. Suppose each of twenty-six of our states had its own language, its own racial inheritance, its own economic and political problems. And suppose through all these races for centuries have surged the forces of nationalism, of imperialism, of religious conflict, memories of deep wrongs, of age-old hates, and bitter fears. Suppose each had its own army and around each of these states was a periphery of mixed populations that made exact boundaries on racial lines hopeless. The outcries of separated minorities would be implacable and unceasing cause of war. Suppose they all had different forms of government and even where it was a democratic form of government it was class government. That would be Europe. . . . And periodically there boils up among these people some Pied Piper with silver tongue, calling some new Utopia. . . . With a victorious rhythm these malign forces seem to drive nations like the Gadarene swine over the precipice of war.[6]

While antipathy toward Europeans might explain an unwillingness to defend Europe, it could not explain the Taft Republicans' eagerness to challenge communism in Asia. Given their historic isolationist and nationalistic tendencies, how could they argue that America should intervene in Asia, but not in Europe? One explanation is that many conservative Republicans believed, in the words of Douglas MacArthur, that Europe was "a dying system." Asia, with its hundreds of millions of people and its emerging economies, seemed a much more promising market for American goods—as well as economic and military alliances. European leaders, they believed, were hopelessly allied with the liberal East Coast establishment that dominated American foreign policy and had spurned the Asian ally near and dear to the hearts of most conservatives—the former Chinese leader Chiang Kai-shek.

Another explanation was America's more paternalistic relationship with Asian nations. "Whereas America's intervention in Europe necessarily implied entangling relationships with nations that would be roughly our equals (Great Britain and France)," wrote historian Robert W. Tucker, "intervention in Asia was based on the assumption that such relationships could be avoided, since our putative adversary (Japan) was the only major power in the region. Accordingly, it was in Asia that some isolationists were willing to engage the nation's interests and power, while refusing to do so in Europe."[7]

Over time, the conservative Republicans' great antipathy toward Europe only served to make them more sympathetic toward Asia, notwithstanding the apparent contradiction of their policies. For years, these Republicans had been sympathetic to complaints by MacArthur and other conservatives that Franklin Roosevelt had undermined Asian security during World War II with his "Asia-last" policy that gave greater priority to the defense of Europe. Furthermore, they believed that Roosevelt had "sold out" Asia at the Yalta Conference and that Truman finished the job in the late 1940s when he refused to aid Chiang and his Nationalist forces. By the early 1950s, this attraction to the notion of a liberal conspiracy against Asian democracy had become Republican Party orthodoxy and emerged as a tremendous force motivating the party's rank-and-file opposition to Truman and the Democratic Party. Thus, it was only natural that Taft and other conservative Republican's were tempted to cast aside their military isolationism—in this one case—and employ Asia as a political issue with which to challenge Truman and his foreign policy.

Despite having spent most of their political lives arguing against foreign military entanglements, particularly in Europe, Taft and his disciples blithely and audaciously became Asian interventionists without sufficient explanation of the contradictions in their positions: they deplored military intervention in Europe while excoriating Truman for failing to adequately intervene in Asia. The best Taft could do was to explain that he wanted Truman to pursue the same policy in Asia as he did in Europe.

Fortunately for Taft, events in Korea in the winter and spring of 1951 riveted the nation's attention on Korea and allowed him and his colleagues to avoid questions about these troubling and politically inspired contradictions. Truman and his Far East policy, meanwhile, were about to endure the most withering and partisan attacks yet.

FOLLOWING GENERAL Douglas MacArthur's foray into North Korea in October 1950, China had begun secretly funneling troops into North Korea. Oblivious to the threat, Truman and the United Nations authorized MacArthur to press northward in an effort to liberate the whole

Korean peninsula, an expedition with tragic consequences. In late November, some three hundred thousand Chinese troops had struck back with a vengeance and forced a humiliating and hasty retreat. By January, Communist troops had pushed MacArthur's beleaguered forces back below the 38th Parallel and once more controlled Seoul. Months earlier, MacArthur had boldly predicted the war would end by Christmas. Now, it was clear that the conflict was far from over. Only weeks before, an eventual UN victory seemed assured. Even that was now in doubt.

The Chinese attack caught Truman and his advisors by surprise. Responding quickly, the administration declared a national emergency, increased draft calls, imposed wage and price controls, and asked Congress to quadruple defense spending. Yet the last thing Truman had wanted was a direct conflict with Communist China. Truman hoped to end the war—quickly—and was willing, therefore, to abandon the forcible reunification of the two Koreas. Reluctantly, the United States prepared to accept the prewar status quo of a divided Korean peninsula that was one-half communist. MacArthur, however, saw the Chinese intervention as a perfect opportunity to take the battle directly to China and end the conflict, not by negotiation—as Truman seemed to want—but with a decisive military victory. The general urged Truman to bomb and blockade Mainland China, offering a proposal to bring Chiang Kai-shek's Nationalist army into the fight by equipping them to lead a ground offensive against the Chinese.

Just as troubling were MacArthur's dire reports from the field concerning the condition of his troops. To the Joint Chiefs of Staff came official reports that MacArthur's army suffered from fatigue and low morale—an assessment that later proved erroneous. The fact was that MacArthur's troops were down, but far from out. Under the able leadership of Lieutenant General Matthew Ridgway, the new commander of the 8th Army, they reversed their retreat and regained the initiative. By late January, retreat turned into offensive and U.S. forces were again on the march.

MacArthur, however, continued urging his own aggressive strategy on Truman, with embarrassing and harmful results. As Acheson later observed: "While General MacArthur was fighting the Pentagon, General Ridgway was fighting the enemy." [8] Embarrassed that his promise to have U.S. troops home by Christmas had collapsed under the weight of the strong and unexpected Chinese offensive, MacArthur—still the darling of the conservative Republicans in Congress—publicly tried to shift the blame to Washington and Truman. In early December, he had argued that his inability to resist the Chinese was the result, not of his own military missteps, but of limitations—"without precedent"—imposed on him by Washington. U.S. officials, he complained, had refused permission to bomb Chinese bases in Manchuria and to pursue enemy planes across the Chinese border.

Fearing that a direct confrontation with China might bring the Soviet Union into the conflict and precipitate another World War, Truman refused to allow his trigger-happy commander to take the country into war against Communist China. "I should have relieved General MacArthur then and there," Truman later said. "The reason I did not was that I did not wish to have it appear as if he were being relieved because the offensive failed." Instead, on December 6, Truman ordered that no military official publicly discuss anything but the most routine foreign policy matters without first consulting his superior.[9]

MacArthur ignored the order. On March 15, he escalated his dispute with the president by informing the president of the United Press that he opposed the administration's decision to stop the 8th Army's advance at the 38th Parallel. The general ventured further into forbidden territory when he erroneously stated that his mission was "the unification of Korea"—a matter of policy and one that Truman had expressly rejected. Nine days later, MacArthur did it again. In the words of Acheson, the general "perpetrated a major act of sabotage."[10] While U.S. officials labored on the wording of a cease-fire proposal, MacArthur unilaterally issued an inflammatory ultimatum to the Chinese in which he threatened to widen the war. Communist China, he said, "must by now be painfully aware that a decision of the United States to depart from its tolerant effort to contain the war to the areas of Korea, through an expansion of our military operations to his coastal areas and interior bases, would doom Red China to the risk of imminent military collapse."[11] Back home, Republicans enthusiastically took up their favorite general's call for the war's expansion. "Broadly speaking," Taft said, "my quarrel is with those who wish to go all-out in Europe, even beyond our capacity, and who at the same time refuse to apply our general program and strategy to the Far East." In Korea, Taft complained, Truman had "refused to fight that war with all the means" at his command.[12]*

MacArthur's hostile and threatening declaration torpedoed Truman's carefully crafted cease-fire initiative. Furious at the flagrant disregard for his December 6 order, Truman again resisted the urge to fire the general

---

*Taft failed to explain another one of the fundamental contradictions in his Asian policy versus his European policy. At the very time he backed MacArthur's intemperate plan to bomb Mainland China—dismissing concerns that such an aggressive action might draw the Soviets into the war—he was warning that the presence of several divisions of U.S. forces in Western Europe would provoke a Russian attack.

and, instead, issued a stern warning. The final straw came in early April, when House Republican Leader Joseph Martin released a March 20 letter from MacArthur in which the general agreed with Martin's view that the Nationalist Chinese forces should be brought into the war.

> It seems strangely difficult [MacArthur wrote] for some to realize that here in Asia is where the Communist conspirators have elected to make their play for global conquest, and that we have joined the issue thus raised on the battlefield; that here we fight Europe's war with arms while the diplomats there still fight it with words; that if we lose the war to Communism in Asia the fall of Europe is inevitable, win it and Europe most probably would avoid war and yet preserve freedom. As you point out, we must win. There is no substitute for victory.[13]

Acheson saw the letter as "an open declaration of war on the administration's policy."[14] And so it was. So rebellious were MacArthur's words that they could have easily been delivered in the Senate by Taft or Wherry. In fact, conservative Republicans had repeatedly expressed the same sentiment in the House and Senate. "The time had come to draw the line," Truman later said. "MacArthur's letter to Congressman Martin showed that the general was not only in disagreement with the policy of the government but was challenging this policy in open insubordination to his Commander in Chief."[15] Truman had no choice but to relieve MacArthur of his command, which he did on April 11.

MacArthur's firing sparked an unprecedented display of popular furor. Angry citizens inundated the White House with more than 250,000 telegrams of protest. [16] A Gallup poll revealed that almost 70 percent of voters supported MacArthur. Across the country, flags were flown upside down or at half-mast. In some places, Truman and Acheson were burned in effigy. Although most Americans did not favor MacArthur's belligerent strategy to widen the war, they liked and admired him and wanted the war to end. As explained by MacArthur biographer William Manchester,

> MacArthur's contempt for half measures and a brokered truce, his determination to punish the evil men who had disturbed the peace—peace, in American eyes, being the normal relationship between nations—struck a chord deep within [the American people]. His moral challenge, his vow to crush wickedness, appealed to what they regarded as their best instincts. The fact that they could not respond to it saddened, even grieved, them, and they felt untrue to themselves.[17]

On Capitol Hill, Republicans were privately gleeful and publicly outraged. They were gleeful because Truman, they believed, had once again fumbled the ball in Asia. Publicly, they were more than ready to milk the public's wrath for everything it was worth. "Impeach him," rolled off the tongues of many Republicans, despite the fact that Democrats still controlled Congress and could block any move to oust the president. That fact did not stop Truman's more irresponsible critics from demanding his removal from office. In a Senate speech the morning of MacArthur's dismissal, William Jenner of Indiana even suggested that Truman was a Soviet agent.

> I charge that this country today is in the hands of a secret inner coterie, which is directed by agents of the Soviet Union. They have formed a popular front government like that in France in the thirties and we know how France was taken from within. . . . We must cut this whole cancerous conspiracy out of our Government at once. Our only choice is to impeach President Truman and find out who is the secret invisible government, which has so cleverly led our country down the road to destruction.

As Jenner finished, spectators in the Senate gallery applauded.[18] Also piling on Truman that day was California's William Knowland, who observed that "Mao Tse-tung in Peking and Josef Stalin in Moscow must have received great satisfaction" from Truman's decision. Knowland said he believed that the U.S. position in Japan and the Far East "is placed in jeopardy by an action, which most observers will interpret as a preliminary step to a far-eastern Munich."[19]* Joseph McCarthy used the occasion to launch an attack, not just on Truman, but also on the Democratic Party. "Unless Democrats in the Senate and House—after all, they are in control—stand up and let themselves be counted as being against treason they will forever, and rightly, have labeled their party as the party of betrayal."[20]

In most cases, however, Republicans assailed Truman, not so much for firing MacArthur, but for his unwillingness to follow MacArthur's advice to take the United States into direct military conflict with Communist China. Typical was Richard Nixon's critique of the episode, which the Senate gallery greeted with applause:

> I believe that rather than follow the advice of those who would appease the Communists, who would gain a cessation of hostilities by letting the Communists have what they wanted when they started the war—and that is what we are going to do if we follow the critics of MacArthur—rather than do that, what we should do is to do what we intended to do when we went into Korea, and that is to bring the war to a successful military con-

---

*It was at Munich in 1938 that British Prime Minister Neville Chamberlain, in pursuit of peace, had allowed Hitler to seize the Sudetenland part of Czechoslovakia. Winston Churchill called the Munich agreement a "disaster." Churchill's damning assessment proved correct and Munich thereafter became synonymous with appeasement, serving as proof to an entire generation of American foreign policy leaders that aggression should always be met with force, not conciliation.

clusion by taking the necessary steps in implementation of the resolution
passed by the United Nations, to the effect that Communist China was
an aggressor.[21]

Nixon and others were, in effect, urging the United States to launch a
full-scale assault on China in the calculated belief that the Soviet Union
would not enter the fight. It was precisely this point that so outraged Senator Robert Kerr, a freshman Democrat from Oklahoma. A fiery, fearless
debater, Kerr had planned to attack MacArthur in a Senate speech on April
11, not knowing that Truman would fire the general on the same day. More
than any other Democratic senator, Kerr was prepared to engage Republicans over U.S. policy in Korea and he wasted no time going after what
he saw as the party's hypocrisy in Asia. "MacArthur said over and over again
that he should be furnished with the men and material to carry the war into
China," Kerr said. "If the Republicans want that, let them say so. If they
do not, their support of MacArthur is a mockery."[22]

Of course, no Republican senator dared take up Kerr's challenge. Very
few of them were actually interested in war with Communist China. They
were, instead, engaged in a far more productive war with Harry Truman
and the Democratic Party. Judging by public opinion, they were winning
in a big way.

As the nationwide vilification of Truman continued, MacArthur
returned to a hero's welcome in the United States. On April 19, eight days
after his dismissal, the defrocked general stood at the podium in the chamber of the House of Representatives. In perhaps one of the most bizarre
public events in U.S. political history, the elected representatives of the
American people stood and cheered an arrogant, insubordinate general
who had single-handedly threatened the constitutional principle of civilian control of the foreign and military policy of the United States. This
frenzied MacArthur worship—William S. White called it "a *politico-
military* cult"[23]—was not confined to the halls of Congress. All across the
country, millions of Americans seemed perfectly willing to choose the
risky, ill-advised foreign policy of an unelected general over that of the
president of the United States.

Standing before a joint meeting of Congress, MacArthur defiantly
articulated his own foreign policy. In the ensuing orgy of public adulation,
few members bothered to ask the fundamental question of whether any
military man should even be permitted to *have* a foreign policy, much less
the right to present it to Congress. Decrying the Truman administration's
refusal to fight the Chinese, MacArthur indirectly accused his critics of
appeasement. "Like blackmail," said MacArthur, such an attitude "lays the
basis for new and successively greater demands until, as in blackmail, vio-

lence becomes the only other alternative. Why, my soldiers asked of me, surrender military advantages to an enemy in the field? I could not answer." While neither MacArthur nor any other political leader invoked the concurrent Chinese threat to French Indochina, the implications were clear enough in the tenor and tone of MacArthur's words to Congress: any ambivalence toward or accommodation of the communist threat in Asia amounted to appeasement. "Like a cobra," MacArthur said, "any new enemy will more likely strike whenever it feels that the relativity in military or other potential is in its favor on a worldwide basis."

As MacArthur staged his triumphant return to the United States, Republicans fell all over themselves in praise of the general and his policies. "I have long approved of General MacArthur's program," Taft said. Said William Jenner, "MacArthur has bought us another, perhaps final chance, to destroy the Administration's pro-Communist, pro-Socialist foreign policy." But this praise for MacArthur was more predicated on an appreciation of the general as a political club with which to pound Harry Truman than as a valuable foreign policy advisor. Despite the Republicans' professed agreement with MacArthur's desire to take the battle to the Chinese, no one had answered Kerr's challenge to introduce a formal congressional resolution that embodied that policy. As *Time*, generally favorable in its assessment of MacArthur, astutely observed: "Though Republicans in Congress considered MacArthur a godsend to the party, there were few who publicly endorsed all his proposals."[24]

Writing privately to a friend in July, even Taft acknowledged that MacArthur was more valuable as a political tool. Taft knew that the Republicans would not succeed politically in 1952 if the issues were purely domestic. "We cannot win the next election," he wrote, "unless we point out the utter failure and capacity of the present Administration to conduct foreign policy and cite the loss of China and the Korean war as typical examples of their very dangerous control. We certainly can't win on domestic policy, because every domestic policy depends entirely on foreign policy."[25]

Throughout the entire episode, Truman was strangely silent. Only occasionally did he emerge to offer a vigorous defense of his foreign policy and the decision to fire the popular general. For weeks, his Republican critics dominated the debate and inflicted serious and lasting political wounds on the president and his party. Truman did recover somewhat during a seven-week Senate inquiry into MacArthur's dismissal. During joint hearings of the Senate's Armed Services and Foreign Relations Committee— chaired by Georgia's Richard Russell—a different image of MacArthur began to emerge. He was strangely uninformed and disinterested in world affairs and expressed confused and contradictory opinions about the nature and objective of Soviet communism. Worst of all, the Joint Chiefs of Staff, Joint Chiefs Chairman Omar Bradley, and Defense Secretary George C. Marshall each contradicted MacArthur's claims that they supported his military strategy for Korea.[26]

But MacArthur's fading fortunes provided no political boost for Truman. The crisis had arrived on the heels of the Democrats' embarrassing showing in the 1950 congressional elections and an election year that had seriously and deeply weakened Truman's standing with the American public. Piled on top of other perceived mistakes in China and the damaging attacks on the loyalty and competence of his State Department, the MacArthur episode made the weight of negative public opinion almost unbearable. By now, Americans were weary of the war (a conflict, in stalemate, that would continue for two more years). They also harbored serious and lasting doubts about the Democratic foreign policies—doubts that were only confirmed by MacArthur's dismissal.

Americans could be forgiven if they were confused about Truman's foreign policy goals. After years of insisting that the real threat to peace was the Soviet Union's designs on Western Europe, Truman now presided over a military that had much of its manpower tied down, inexplicably, in an excruciating and maddening conflict in Asia. Even as the Soviet Union continued to loom as a greater threat in Europe, the United States was moving toward an even deeper and more consequential commitment to the defense of Asia. Not only had Truman committed troops to Korea, he had increased shipments of military and economic assistance to colonial French forces for their armed struggle against communist guerrillas in Indochina. While it was MacArthur who wanted to defend all of Asia and had declared that "I believe we should defend every place from Communism,"[27] it was Truman and Acheson who were busy implementing that very strategy in Korea and, now, in Indochina. Indeed, fifty years later, one might be forgiven for pondering the question of just who—in the spring and summer of 1951—actually won the debate over America's Asian policy.

PART TWO

THE INITIAL DESCENT

We have now allied ourselves with the French in this struggle, allied ourselves against the Communists but also against the rising tide of nationalism. We have become the West, the proponents of empire—carriers of what we had traditionally disdained—the white man's burden.

—SENATOR JOHN F. KENNEDY, 1951

Step by step, we are moving into this war in Indochina, and I am afraid we will move to a point from which there will be no return.

—SENATOR JOHN STENNIS, 1954

CHAPTER 5

Nothing But a Grim Joke

1945–1950

In October 1949, the same month Mao Tse-tung declared victory in China, Democratic Congressman Charles Deane of North Carolina returned to the United States from a fact-finding mission to the Far East. His extraordinary and prescient report to President Truman contained a sober warning about the dangers of any potential U.S. military involvement in Indochina. "Southern and Southeast Asia are aflame with militant nationalism," he told the president in an October 19 memo. France, he observed, was coming to grips with the demise of its colonial empire in Indochina, but had "yet to learn to live with its replacement." In the midst of the social and economic upheaval of the postwar years, Deane observed that "the shadow of Communism overhangs the entire political situation in the Far East." Communism, he said, had "waxed fat on human misery and economic despair and on the aspirations of colonial peoples for political independence."

Deane's may have been the first warning ever issued from Congress about the dangers of a U.S. military role in Indochina. Military might alone, he insisted, was not the answer. To defeat communism in Asia would require the United States to treat the Far East holistically. The United States must work to alleviate poverty and identify with—not suppress—the nationalistic urges of the people. "A negative U.S. policy which ignores these factors and is designed merely to 'check Communism' by military means is not likely to accomplish its purpose," Deane wrote. "If we remain true to our heritage of freedom, however, and with missionary zeal dedicate our policies in the Far East to the principles of the advancement of human freedom and the uplift of the level of material well-being and human dignity, we shall not only check Communism but place it decisively on the defensive."[1]

There is no evidence that Deane, not known for any foreign policy expertise, ever shared his astute observations with his House colleagues; nor did his analysis attract the attention of the Washington reporters who covered foreign and military affairs. All that is known is that the North Carolina congressman put his views in a memorandum and sent it to the White House. One can only imagine what might have happened had Truman and his aides heeded his advice or if Deane had pressed his case more vigorously with the White House or the Washington press corps.

How seriously Truman took Deane's warning—indeed, if he even read the report—is not known. In practice, however, the Truman administration, battered as it was after the "fall" of China, rejected it out of hand, as would subsequent administrations. Like his next four successors, Truman would see nothing but communist shadows cast by the light of the militant nationalistic flames that Deane identified. From its earliest days, the struggle in Indochina was a military conflict that progressively drowned out the meager efforts to challenge communism with economic and humanitarian assistance. Few American policymakers bothered to examine the marked differences between nationalism and communism in Asia. When they did engage in attempts to channel nationalistic passions into programs that would provide realistic and popular alternatives to communism, their efforts were often clumsy or misinformed and revealed a woeful misunderstanding of Asian culture.

The states of the former French Indochina—Vietnam, Laos, and Cambodia—had been a worrisome part of the world for the United States since the end of World War II. But it was more the conduct of France, and not the Indochinese governments, which most concerned U.S. policymakers. Since the nineteenth century, France had dominated the region, after setting up shop in Cochinchina (the southern tip of Vietnam) in 1859. In later years, it added to its colonial possessions the protectorates of Annam and Tonkin (the other two regions of Vietnam), as well as the nations of Laos and Cambodia. Arrogant and harsh rulers, the French maintained uninterrupted control of the region—overcoming an outbreak of armed resistance in the 1930s—until the outbreak of World War II. Japan finally broke the back of French rule in 1940 when it took advantage of France's capitulation to Nazi Germany. As they swept into the region, the Japanese left the French administrators only nominally in charge of government operations.

Almost immediately after the war ended in September 1945, the French prepared to reassert their claim to the former colonies. But moving back into Indochina would be no easy task. The war had unleashed powerful passions for independence in the region, especially in Vietnam, where nationalist forces led by the League for the Independence of Vietnam—popularly known as the Vietminh—were determined to assert their country's independence from colonial rule. To these fervent Vietnamese nationalists, the French were not only former colonial rulers seeking to restore the faded glory of their war-ravaged empire; they had conspired with the brutal Japanese occupation during World War II. Determined to prevent another era of French rule, the Vietminh vowed to fight the restoration of French dominion at every turn.

The Vietminh were not the only ones who recognized the severe toll French rule had exacted in Indochina. The suffering of the Vietnamese people was evident to Americans who visited the country shortly after the war's end. In October 1945, a young American Navy lieutenant, Mark Hatfield, sailed into Vietnam for the first time and witnessed the disastrous impact of the war and the detrimental impact of French reign. Ordered to the northern city of Haiphong to transport Chiang Kai-shek's Nationalist army (which had helped to free Vietnam from Japanese rule) to northern China for the fight against Mao's communist troops, Hatfield's ship docked in the muddy waters of Haiphong harbor. Almost immediately, small boats surrounded the vessel and their pitiful Vietnamese occupants began begging for food and clothing. In an emotional letter to his parents, Hatfield—who, twenty years later, would become a Republican U.S. senator from Oregon and a vigorous opponent of America's military involvement in Vietnam—wrote:

> It was sickening to see the absolute poverty and the rags these people are in. We thought the Philippines were in a bad way, but they are wealthy compared to these exploited people. The Philippines were in better shape before the war, but the people here have never known anything but squalor since the French heel has been on them. . . .
>
> I tell you, it is a crime the way we occidentals have enslaved these people in our mad desire for money. The French seem to be the worst and are followed pretty closely by the Dutch and the English. I can certainly see why these people don't want us to return and continue to spit upon them.[2]

In mid-1945, as a new president facing hundreds of momentous postwar decisions, Harry Truman regarded Indochina as among the least pressing of a bewildering assortment of problems and challenges. With Truman absent from the early deliberations, State Department officers waged a vigorous, but short-lived debate over U.S. policy in Indochina. In the Office of Far Eastern Affairs, officials stressed the importance of recognizing the "independence sentiment" in Indochina. "If really liberal policies toward Indochina are not adopted by the French," a prescient State Department analyst wrote, "there will be substantial bloodshed and unrest for many years, threatening the economic and social progress and the peace and stability of Southeast Asia." But the administration's postwar emphasis was on containing communism in Europe, not nurturing a nascent Asian independence movement that threatened U.S. relations with France and Great Britain. This Europeanist sentiment was prevalent in the department's Division of Western European Affairs, where officials argued persuasively that forcing France to relinquish Indochina would "run counter to the established American policy" of helping that country "regain her strength in order that she may be better fitted to share responsibility in maintaining the peace of Europe and the world."[3]

This was a debate that advocates of Indochinese independence were bound to lose. In the postwar, Cold War era, concerns about France's ability to fight off internal communism far outweighed American desires for the immediate independence of Indochina. A distracted Truman eventually sided with the French, although he approved mild language encouraging eventual independence for the region. "The United States recognizes French sovereignty over Indochina," the State Department declared in a policy paper in June 1945. "It is, however, the general policy of the United States to favor a policy which would allow colonial peoples an opportunity to prepare themselves for increased participation in their own government with eventual self-government as the goal."[4]

In Vietnam, meanwhile, a charismatic 55-year-old nationalist Vietnamese leader, Ho Chi Minh, had formed his own views about Indochina's independence from a more celebrated American document. In one way or another, from Paris to Peking to Hanoi, Ho had been a leader in the struggle for Vietnamese independence since the First World War. On September 2, 1945, in Hanoi, he declared Vietnam a free and independent nation. Addressing a massive crowd that had gathered in the center of town, Ho sounded like an American revolutionary recounting King George's crimes against the American colonies when he detailed the excesses and brutality of French rule. In the reviewing stand sat a group of friendly U.S. army officers.[5] Reading aloud from the "Declaration of Independence of the Democratic Republic of Vietnam," Ho said:

> All men are created equal; they are endowed by their Creator with certain unalienable Rights; among these are Life, Liberty and the pursuit of Happiness.
>   This immortal statement was made in the Declaration of Independence of the United States of America in 1776. In a broader sense, this means: All peoples on the earth are equal from birth, all the peoples have a right to live, to be happy and free.[6]

"It would be wrong to make too much of those opening lines of the proclamation of independence," biographer Jean Lacourture observed as he considered Ho's shrewd reliance on the most sacred document in American history. "Yet a revolutionary patriot like Ho Chi Minh would scarcely have quoted the words of the Philadelphia Convention at that most solemn moment unless he felt a strong historical affinity with the rebels of 1776."[7] Although Ho had been a Communist since the end of World War I, when he first began working for Vietnamese independence, a State Department appraisal of him in 1948 acknowledged the absence of evidence establishing a "direct link between Ho and Moscow." Yet the department assumed, nonetheless, that such a link existed. Another State Department study of communist influence in Southeast Asia found that Moscow was directing communist activities in virtually every country—except Vietnam. "If there is a Moscow-directed conspiracy in Southeast Asia," the report concluded, "Indochina is an anomaly so far."[8] In any event, as historian Robert D. Schulzinger later observed, "Americans thought that Ho did not need to consult Moscow regularly because he knew what the Kremlin wanted."[9]

But Ho's communism did not prompt any overt hostility to the United States—at least in the mid-1940s. Sensing that World War II had fundamentally changed the equation in Indochina with the occupation of his region by the Japanese and the Nazi invasion of France, he had aggressively sought the assistance of the United States in his struggle to free his country from French rule. At first, he had invested great hope in the words of the Atlantic Charter, a wartime statement of the "common principles" of the United States and Great Britain. To Ho's delight, the Charter affirmed "respect" for the "right of all peoples to choose the form of government under which they will live" and declared that the two countries "wish to see sovereign rights and self-government restored to those who have been forcibly deprived of them."

Indeed, Ho's wartime objectives—defeating Japan and ridding his country of the French colonialists—were virtually identical to Washington's early wartime policy toward Indochina. After the war, Ho believed, the United States would oppose the reintroduction of French colonialism. Thus, he worked closely with American intelligence agents during the war and hoped that the alliance would earn his cause special consideration, especially in light of the Atlantic Charter's lofty proclamations about "sovereignty" and "self-government." In one of his several messages to Washington, Ho wrote that "the carrying out of the Atlantic Charter and the San Francisco Charter implies the eradication of imperialism and all forms of colonial oppression."[10] Yet he was also pragmatic. He told one American intelligence officer that "if we want to get a sufficient share [of freedom and democracy] we have still to fight."[11]

To Ho's regret, American officials greeted each of his friendly contacts with stony silence. Finally, in desperation, he turned to Communist China and the Soviet Union for assistance. Within a matter of years, Ho would angrily denounce the United States, his former ally, as "American imperialists."[12]

Caught in the grip of Cold War hysteria, the Truman administration believed the communism of Ho's guerrilla forces tainted them irrevocably. Truman was not alone. Few American leaders cared to examine the nuances and subtle differences in the various ideologies that thrived under the label of communism. To most U.S. leaders, every Communist was a tool of a vast, monolithic Soviet conspiracy to rule the world. Most American foreign policy leaders believed that "nationalism" was simply the fraudulent label that Asian Communists used to conceal Soviet designs on the region. They concluded that Ho's repugnant political ideology far outweighed his professed desire for Vietnamese independence. Besides, the U.S. commitment to France had been irrevocably made. American leaders, considering their nation's historic and ethnic ties to Western Europe, simply believed they had far more to gain by helping France resist communism in Europe—and that meant not undermining its economic and military interests in Indochina.

The frightening specter of Soviet communism in Europe trumped the budding aspirations for freedom and independence in Southeast Asia. By 1945, after U.S. State Department officials had repeatedly ignored Ho's pleas for American assistance, he ruefully asked a friendly American intelligence agent if the Atlantic Charter was "applicable only to white European nations."[13] Maybe not, but U.S. policymakers did believe it more important to keep France strong and vibrant in Europe as a bulwark against Soviet hegemony. Grudging acquiescence to the recolonization of the Indochina was the price to pay. Almost twenty years later, the authors of the *Pentagon Papers*—the Defense Department study of early U.S. involvement in Vietnam—pointed to the "basic incompatibility" of the early naïve U.S. position toward France and Vietnamese nationalism: "Washington wanted France to fight the anti-Communist war and win, preferably with U.S. guidance and advice; and Washington expected the French, when battlefield victory was assured, to magnanimously withdraw from Indochina."[14]

But no matter how much American leaders wanted to believe otherwise, France was not fighting to defeat communism in Indochina. Its goal was simple: the reconquest of its former colony and, thereby, the partial restoration of its world position and prewar glory. For the duration of their struggle against the Vietminh, the French would howl about the dangers of Vietnamese communism only to the extent that it generated U.S. support.

Although American officials repeatedly pressed France to make concessions to the nationalist forces in Indochina, they made no attempt to prevent the reoccupation. Officially, the Truman administration was neutral in the struggle. In France, meanwhile, negotiations with the Vietminh collapsed. As far as France was concerned, Indochina was again a French colony. But it was not the same colony France had ruled before World War II. The war had reordered not only the balance of power in Europe, but in Asia and the Pacific as well. Colonialism was fading on every continent. The forces of militant nationalism, unleashed with a fury throughout Southeast Asia after the war, now gave France two basic options: relinquish its hold on Indochina or have it torn away in a violent, bloody struggle.

Not afraid to fight for independence, Ho and his wily Vietminh guerrillas took the battle directly to the French. War finally broke out in 1946 after the French summarily established Cochinchina as a "free republic." In November, the French shelled the northern city of Haiphong—then under Vietminh control—and killed several hundred Vietnamese citizens. Throughout the struggle, the United States remained on the sidelines, regarding Indochina as little more than a French concern. Despite French pleas for military assistance, the State Department informed Paris in early 1947 that the United States would not offer military hardware and armaments for sale "in cases which appear to relate to Indochina."[15]*

But Southeast Asian experts at the State Department correctly perceived American neutrality as tacit support for the French position. As the fighting escalated, Abbot Low Moffat, chief of the State Department's Division of Southeast Asian Affairs, cabled Washington from Thailand to express his concern that the department's hands-off policy regarding Vietnam "appears as US approval [for] French military reconquest."[16] Moffat was undoubtedly correct. He later said that by the end of 1946 "a concern about Communist expansion began to be evident in the [State] Department," leading to a "fixation on the theory of monolithic, aggressive communism" that began "to affect our objective analyses of certain problems."[17]

U.S. vice consul in Hanoi, James O'Sullivan, obliquely suggested to Washington in July 1947 that the French amply perceived Washington's fear of communism and seemed to be manipulating the United States by stressing the communist ideology of Ho Chi Minh's nationalist forces. It was "curious," he wrote, that the French "discovered no Communist menace in Ho Chi Minh until after September 1946, when it became apparent that [the Vietnamese government] would not bow to French wishes." O'Sullivan later reported that it was "apparent that Ho's support . . . derives from [the] fact that he represents [a] symbol of [the] fight for independence.

---

*The substantial economic aid that the United States poured into France as part of the Marshall Plan gave France the ability to spend considerably more in its war against the Vietminh.

He is supported because he is acting like [a] nationalist, not because he was or is a Communist." The intellectuals backing Ho, O'Sullivan later reported, had been "driven to Communism" not by the belief in the ideology, but by "French colonial policy" in Indochina. "Hate for [the] French blinds them to many things and makes them accept others they do not like."[18]

Tacit U.S. support for the French in Southeast Asia deeply concerned several American officials who feared the consequences should their nation become too intimately identified with the reintroduction of Western colonialism. Indeed, the substantial U.S. prestige in the region was on the line and it appeared that the United States was prepared to squander it in order to mollify France. In a separate message to Washington, O'Sullivan later reminded Washington that the United States still exerted tremendous influence in Vietnam and that Vietnamese leaders "would be more than willing" to allow U.S. intervention to resolve "their political and economic needs."[19]

Secretary of State George C. Marshall, whose earlier mission to China had exposed him to the nationalistic passions sweeping Asia, also grew concerned that a protracted war between the French and the Vietminh might damage American credibility in the region. Marshall hoped to keep the U.S. strictly neutral in the conflict. In May 1947, he warned the U.S. ambassador in France that Vietnam was becoming a "rallying-cry for all anti-Western forces" and was "playing into" the hands of Communists. "We fear," Marshall wrote in his cable, that "continuation [of the] conflict may jeopardize [the] position [of] all Western democratic powers in southern Asia and lead to [the] very eventualities of which we [are] most apprehensive."[20] As a State Department policy statement on Vietnam aptly explained the following year, "hatred of the Vietnamese people toward the French is keeping alive anti-western feeling among oriental peoples, to the advantage of the USSR and to the detriment of the US."[21]

By 1948, despite France's efforts to strengthen its hold on Vietnam, including increasing armed forces in the colony to 150,000, its grip on the country had slipped. Led by a brilliant military strategist, General Vo Nguyen Giap, the outnumbered, but well-trained and highly dedicated Vietminh army had gradually seized the vast rural areas of northern and central Vietnam (and would control roughly two-thirds of Vietnam's territory by late 1949).[22] Hoping to ease the political turmoil while luring nationalist followers away from Ho Chi Minh, French leaders had tried to manufacture the image of self-rule by negotiating the return of Bao Dai, the former emperor of the central Vietnam state of Annam who had abdicated in 1945. Most Vietnamese, however, regarded him as a weak, ineffectual leader, and many, particularly the most militant nationalists, bitterly recalled his complicity with Japanese occupation forces during World War II. But France enticed the former emperor with the prospect of returning to his prewar glory. Bao Dai gradually dropped his original demand for greater Vietnamese autonomy and agreed to do France's bidding in exchange for the comfortable and lucrative position as head of state.

On March 8, 1949, Bao Dai and the French government finally agreed on the political, economic, and military future of Vietnam. An "independent" Vietnam—comprised of the unified states of Tonkin, Annam, and Chochinchina—would join the French Union as an "Associated State," along with the newly "independent" associated states of Cambodia and Laos. The three states would comprise an Indochinese Federation and would be governed by a French governor-general. The Elysee Agreement, as it became known, hardly amounted to a real grant of independence. Under its terms, France would direct Vietnam's economy, diplomacy, and military forces, while French citizens would enjoy special legal rights. "There did not seem to be a single right accorded Vietnam," George Abbott, the U.S. consul-general in Saigon, informed Acheson in July 1949, "which was not limited [in] some way to requirement for approval or consultation with [the] French."[23] As the *New Republic* observed, "this independence is nothing but a grim joke."[24]

Although the United States formally recognized the new Associated State of Vietnam in February 1950, France's good faith remained the subject of much doubt not only among American leaders, but also in the Southeast Asian countries that withheld formal recognition of the new government. As Acheson explained to French Ambassador Henri Bonnet, French officials had not yet allowed Bao Dai to occupy the royal palace in Saigon. The fact that the palace remained the residence of the French high commissioner, Acheson noted, "was the sort of thing which in Oriental minds meant a great deal."[25] As Bao Dai himself remarked shortly after his return to "power," "What they call a Bao Dai solution turns out to be just a French solution."[26]

Unwilling to press the French to grant Vietnam full independence, and frightened of the consequences if they did so, the United States unenthusiastically cast its lot with Bao Dai. Acheson pledged an unspecified amount of American economic and military assistance for France and the Associated States. Realistically, there appeared to be no other reasonable stance—other than strict neutrality, which the American desire for closer relations with France precluded. "It was a case," explained a State Department working paper, "of backing Bao Dai or accepting the Communist government of Ho Chi Minh."[27] From Hanoi, Ho summed up the feelings of many skeptical Vietnamese—and other observers—when he derided the French for having created "a puppet government under Bao

Dai." The purpose, he concluded, "was to back up their war of reconquest and to hoodwink the world."[28] While the French may not have completely hoodwinked Truman, they had at least forced Washington's hand—the Bao Dai "solution" resulted in grudging U.S. support for France's "reconquest" of Vietnam.

Despite the growing tension in Southeast Asia, Indochina's turmoil attracted little public attention in the United States. News reports about the region were rare in the popular press and were almost always footnotes to larger, more significant stories about the political upheaval in China. Most Americans knew little about Indochina, had never heard of Ho Chi Minh or Bao Dai, and certainly did not understand the historical background of the war between the French and the Vietminh. The ambivalence or ignorance about Indochina extended to Congress as well, where House and Senate members had virtually nothing to say about France's military struggle in Indochina.

But the collapse of the Nationalist forces in China in the fall of 1949 suddenly raised the stakes in Indochina. "All of a sudden," as *U.S. News & World Report* observed in February 1950, "Indo-China is out front in the power struggle between Russia on the one hand and the Western world on the other."[29] Right or wrong, there it would stay for most of the next twenty-five years.

IN 1950, DESPITE THEIR persuasive arguments that China had been a hopeless cause and the belief that much of Southeast Asia was of no strategic importance to the United States, Acheson and Truman knew they could afford no more communist victories in Asia. With its budding communist movement, Indochina seemed as good a place as any for the West to finally challenge the Soviet Union and China and persuade Americans that Democrats, like Republicans, were serious about stopping communism in Asia. Administration officials were not blind to the domestic and international political implications of Southeast Asia's future. A National Security Council study completed in June 1949 had ominously warned that "if southeast Asia also is swept by communism we shall have suffered a major political rout the repercussions of which will be felt throughout the rest of the world."[30]

By early 1950, with China firmly in communist hands, the debate over whether to assist France in Indochina was brief and perfunctory. Mao's forces now occupied the region of China bordering Indochina. That and the other alarming events in China had moved Indochina toward the top of Washington's foreign policy agenda. The focus of U.S. concern, however, was no longer the conduct of the former French colonizers, but rather the alarming threats posed by Soviet and Chinese communism. Those concerns increased all the more in January 1950, when the Soviet Union and China extended diplomatic recognition to Ho's government.[31] To Acheson, the Kremlin's action proved that Ho was more communist than nationalist and, he declared, "reveals Ho in his true colors as the mortal enemy of native independence in Indochina."[32] The country was now, in the alarmist words of Saigon consul George Abbott, the "advance bastion against [the] 'Bolshevist' tide" in Southeast Asia.[33]

In February 1950, as expected, France urgently requested U.S. aid for the war in Vietnam. "There is no other alternative," a State Department staff analysis concluded.

> The choice confronting the United States is to support the French in Indochina or face the extension of Communism over the remainder of the continental area of Southeast Asia and, possibly, farther westward. We then would be obligated to make staggering investments in those areas and in that part of Southeast Asia remaining outside Communist domination or withdraw to a much-contracted Pacific line. It would seem a case of 'Penny wise, Pound foolish' to deny support to the French in Indochina.[34]

Almost three months later, on April 24, Truman endorsed NSC 64, with its requirement that "all practicable measures be taken to prevent further communist expansion in Southeast Asia." In the first official argument for what would become the "domino theory," NSC 64 argued that "the neighboring countries of Thailand and Burma could be expected to fall under Communist domination if Indochina were controlled by a Communist-dominated government. The balance of Southeast Asia would then be in grave hazard."[35]

On May 1, Truman committed the United States to the struggle against communism in Indochina. After considering Acheson's recommendation that he direct $15 million in military supplies to the French, the president agreed to a paltry $10 million in assistance.[36] But in making his decision, Truman established a presidential precedent regarding Vietnam that would last into the 1970s: he did not consult the House or Senate. While he might have talked privately to individual members about his decision, he did not inform Congress as a whole, nor did he formally consult the foreign or military affairs committees of the House and Senate. Notoriously remote in his approach to congressional relations, Acheson may well have argued that Truman had no need to seek congressional approval for his actions. If so, he would have been on firm ground. After all, Congress had appropriated the money, specifying only that it be used to defend nations that might fall under the influence of Chinese communism. Furthermore, language tucked away in the Mutual Defense Assistance Act of 1949 had authorized the president to go a step beyond merely sending military supplies. An obscure provision gave the president permission to dispatch noncombat U.S. military advisors to any "agency or nation" that the president deemed worthy of assistance.[37]*

But not every member of Congress went along quietly with Truman's plan. During closed-door hearings on the bill in 1949, former Foreign Relations Committee Chairman Arthur Vandenberg worried aloud that the bill "extends to the President of the United States the greatest peacetime power that was ever concentrated in an Executive. He is entitled to sell, lend, give away, anything he wishes to any nation on earth on any terms that he defines at any time he feels like it." To bolster his argument, Vandenberg inserted into the hearing record a column by Walter Lippmann, an influential foreign policy journalist, who complained that the bill was "a general license to intervene and to commit the United States all over the globe, as, when and how the President and his appointees decide secretly that they deem it desirable to intervene." As if he were looking into the future by fifteen years, Lippmann contended that the legislation "would invest the President with unlimited power to make new commitments which Congress would have to support but could not control."[38]

Vandenberg aside, few members of Congress complained about the way the president had committed the nation to support France's military effort in Indochina. For starters, Congress had already appropriated and authorized the meager expenditure. By virtue of the Mutual Defense Act, Truman now had unfettered authority to spend the money as he wished. If challenged, he could simply argue that Congress was adequately consulted in 1949, during hearings in both houses of Congress. Consulted or not, most Republicans could hardly fault Truman for coming to France's aid in the fight against communism. Most Democrats meanwhile—weary of defending their president on charges of having "lost" China—were delighted to join the battle against communism in Asia. Most of all, few members of Congress knew enough about the remote, murky region of Indochina to mount anything resembling an effective challenge to the U.S. assistance.

---

*Yet another provision of the same measure set the stage for creation of the Southeast Asia Treaty Organization (SEATO) in 1954. In the bill, Congress advocated a "joint organization" to, among other things, "protect" the "security and independence" of threatened nations in Southeast Asia. In the 1960s, President Lyndon Johnson would argue that membership in SEATO gave the United States permission for direct intervention in Vietnam (Gravel Edition, *PP*, vol. 1, 36–37).

Ironically, those members of Congress who did object were far more troubled by Truman's proposal to fight communism in Indochina with economic assistance than by his decision to supply the French with military material. After Truman first advanced his idea for foreign aid to poor nations in his 1949 inaugural address, the idea became known as "Point Four" (because it was the fourth point in the speech). As Truman later explained it, the goal was to export "not the ideal of democracy alone, but the tangible benefits of better living through intelligent co-operation."[39]

Providing economic assistance to Indochina through the Point Four program gained momentum in May 1950 after a special State Department survey mission recommended at least $60 million in economic and technical assistance for the region. Endorsing the proposal, Acheson explained that the United States believed that economic and military assistance was required to assist the states of Indochina "in restoring stability" and permitting them to "pursue their peaceful and democratic development."[40] Congress included Truman's first Point Four program request in the Foreign Economic Assistance Act of 1950, a bill that extended the Marshall Plan for European recovery to the noncommunist forces in China and Formosa and provided economic assistance for "the general area of China."[41]

In early 1950, no part of Asia seemed more in need of economic and political stability than Indochina, where the Vietminh had masterfully exploited the French colony's economic and political inequities. Some Republicans and conservative Democrats, however, were skeptical, doubtful of Point Four's potential impact and concerned about the ultimate budgetary implications of establishing what one member of Congress called a "world-wide WPA." Robert Taft predicted that Point Four would only open "a new field for spreading government money around the world." Kenneth McKellar, a senior Democrat and chairman of the Appropriations Committee, was even more outspoken. "We're going mad," he protested, "we're going wild."[42]

Although the Truman administration clearly intended to make Indochina its first foreign aid laboratory, the subject was rarely raised during debate over the bill. Yet a haunting exchange between Acheson and Theodore Francis Green, a senior member of the Senate Foreign Relations Committee, served as an early warning about U.S. military involvement in Indochina. During a closed-door committee session in late March, Green pointedly questioned Acheson about the U.S. mission in Indochina. Was the nation, he wondered, "getting into a position where we are rather defending in part what is left of French colonial policy there, and also supporting against the revolutionaries an unpopular king whom they are trying to put out, and a corrupt government there?" Acheson did not disagree with Green's characterization, but noted that the United States was "pressing the

French to go forward as far and as fast as they can." But, as he cautioned, prudence was appropriate, because pressing the French too much might provoke them to say, "All right, take over the damned country. We don't want it."

Acheson's answer clearly left Green unsatisfied. "We have jockeyed ourselves into a position where we had to take the position of one or the other parties in the country against the rising masses," he said. "Everywhere the masses in these countries . . . are rising, and they are conducting what will ultimately be—it is a question of time—successful revolutions, but we are identified to those masses as being the defenders of the status quo."[43]

History would prove Green correct. Without knowing it, Truman and Acheson had started the nation down the road toward an active, ever-expanding involvement in Indochina that would last for twenty-five years. Yet even as Truman made the initial U.S. commitment in Vietnam, members of Congress, as would so often be the case, were ignored or left in the dark. In making these momentous decisions, Truman and Acheson appeared only to consider the views of their critics—the vociferous, partisan opponents of their beleaguered China policy. Truman's political opponents had forced his hand—first, in Indochina, and months later, in Korea—pushing him to commit the nation to defend a region barely understood by policymakers and possessing little or no strategic importance for the United States. As *Time* caustically noted in a May 29, 1950, cover story devoted to Indochina, Truman's decision "to go into such a doubtful project as the defense of Indo-China was the result of an idea that it ought to do something, somehow, to stop the Communists in Southeast Asia." Frightened by the political consequences of another Asian country succumbing to communism, Truman and Acheson had made Indochina, in the words of *Time*, "a new frontier" in the Cold War.[44]

In June 1950, the United States Military Assistance Advisory Group set up shop in Saigon.[45] The first of many dominoes began to fall.

CHAPTER 6

The Keystone in Southeast Asia

1951

IT HAD BEEN, IN HIS WORDS, "A RATHER EXHAUSTING JOURNEY." IN September 1951, a young Democratic congressman, John F. Kennedy, set out from Boston for the Middle and the Far East. Later, he would explain that he had hoped to gather "facts that I could really bite on, for I wanted to know how those peoples regarded us and our policies."[1] To another audience, he would confess that he had been "confused, as most of us are, about the many problems there and what, if anything, we were doing about them."[2] Kennedy also knew, of course, that upon his return the press would dutifully report his observations about the political and economic upheavals afflicting almost every nation on his itinerary.

It was also no coincidence that most of the nations he would visit were of particular interest to the American foreign policy community. In Iran, the government had recently nationalized British oil interests. In Egypt, trouble brewed over disputed control of the Suez Canal. In India, a vast population had begun adjusting to its long-sought independence from British rule. Seven hundred thousand Arab refugees crowded the area near Israel's new borders. War raged in Korea. In Japan, the U.S. postwar occupation had just ended in April.

For seven long weeks, Kennedy would hopscotch the globe with his brother Bobby and sister Patricia. First, a stop in Paris for a visit with General Dwight Eisenhower, commander of NATO forces in Europe. From there, to Israel for a meeting with Prime Minister Ben Gurion, and then to the Arab states for meetings with various leaders. In Pakistan he would talk with Prime Minster Liaquat Ali Khan—only hours before his assassination. Kennedy would discuss world politics with Indian Prime Minister Nehru. Next, to Singapore and Thailand. While in Indochina, he planned meetings with Bao Dai, the Vietnamese head of state, and the famous gen-

eral Jean de Lattre de Tassigny, who commanded the French forces in their
struggle against the Vietminh. Finally, his marathon journey would end
with visits to Korea and Japan.

Besides widening his geopolitical horizons, Kennedy knew the trip
would provide him with foreign policy experience and an air of seriousness
that would help him in his upcoming Senate campaign against the incumbent Republican, Henry Cabot Lodge. Only the previous spring, he had
spent four weeks in Europe, investigating the status of its postwar recon-
struction efforts, as well as the Continent's success in resisting the powerful influence of Soviet communism. This trip would bolster his foreign policy credentials and disarm any attacks on his youth or lack of experience.

Kennedy's five-year House career had to that point been decidedly
unremarkable. Like many junior members of Congress, he had avoided
controversial issues while diligently tending to the parochial interests of
his conservative, working-class Boston constituency. On domestic issues
he was a moderate who generally supported Truman's Fair Deal programs,
although he championed economy in government. His foreign policy outlook, however, was decidedly conservative. Like many conservative Republicans, he had assailed the Truman administration over China and
blamed much of the political troubles in Asia on the mistakes of Roosevelt
and Marshall at Yalta. "Whatever share of the responsibility was Roosevelt's and whatever share was Marshall's," he had declared in 1948, "the
vital interest of the United States in the independent integrity of China
was sacrificed, and the foundation was laid for the present tragic situation
in the Far East."[3]

Kennedy had also trafficked with Senator Joseph McCarthy. Shortly
after McCarthy burst into the national consciousness in 1950, Kennedy
bragged to a group of Harvard students about his friendship with the Wisconsin demagogue and suggested that "he may have something."[4]

FOR PRESIDENT TRUMAN, the outbreak of war on the Korean peninsula
finally settled the question of whether the United States would employ its
military and economic might against further communist gains in Southeast Asia. The president acted decisively. Widely supported by members
of both parties in Congress, he increased the paltry $10 million in military
assistance he had promised to the French in 1950 to a pledge of $107 mil-
lion in 1951.

To those who might question whether nationalism, not communism,
was the true sentiment motivating the Vietminh, Truman administration
officials warned of the potential danger of taking lightly the communist

threat in Indochina. Testifying before a joint meeting of the Senate's Foreign Relations and Armed Services committees in the summer of 1951, Dean Rusk, the assistant secretary of state for Far Eastern affairs, assured committee members that the Communists were busy exploiting nationalist sentiment in the Far East. To Rusk, the dynamic looked all too familiar.

Like many leaders of his generation, Rusk intensely dreaded communist totalitarianism—a sentiment that had been profoundly shaped by the experience of World War II and the years leading up to that cataclysmic conflict. As a graduate student, Rusk had been in Berlin in March 1933 when Hitler's nationalist forces seized power. Later, back in the United States, he watched ruefully as European leaders appeased Hitler at Munich in 1938. Recalling how he had once been fined for "tempting thieves" by the German authorities who returned his stolen canoe, Rusk said he concluded that "the United States and Western democracies, with our pacifism, isolationism, and indifference to aggression, were guilty of 'tempting thieves' " in Europe. "It was the failure of the governments of the world to prevent aggression," he later said, "that made the catastrophe of World War II inevitable."[5] Like others in the Truman State Department, Rusk was determined that the United States not repeat the mistakes of 1938 in Asia. Rusk, like most others in Truman's administration, had embraced the "lesson" that Hitler taught an entire generation of American leaders: aggression unchecked is aggression unleashed.[6] He concluded that "Communist absorption of additional countries in Asia would create vast new problems for the United States and, in fact, for the rest of the free world." Walking away from such a challenge, Rusk maintained, would amount to another Munich.[7]

The future secretary of state's persuasive presentation went mostly unchallenged by the committee, not because of apathy, but ignorance. Those members of Congress who had never traveled to Indochina knew little about this mysterious region, its people, and its politics. Lacking the staff resources enjoyed by the White House and State Department, they were not usually privy to independent information, other than scattered news reports. Many had no choice but to accept the administration's dire warnings about potential communist domination of the entire Far East, a threat now heightened considerably by the war in Korea, and a fact that would give several administrations a decided advantage when promoting policies toward Indochina.

A typical congressional supporter of U.S. military assistance to the French was Democratic Senator Hubert Humphrey, a liberal, anticommunist freshman from Minnesota who strongly backed Truman in Korea and who wanted to protect Indochina from "the Communist onslaught." Humphrey told the Senate in August that the loss of Indochina would be "as severe a blow as if we were to lose Korea." Like many members of Congress, Humphrey believed that a communist victory in Vietnam would only lead to "the loss of Malaya, the loss of Burma and Thailand, and ultimately the conquest of all the south and southeast Asiatic area."[8]

Another Truman supporter, Senate Foreign Affairs Committee Chairman Tom Connally, demonstrated how some leading members of Congress believed that the Vietminh were inspired and actually controlled by the Soviet Union. Connally argued that "Communist conquest" of the region would enable the Soviet Union to capture Indochina's oil, rubber, tin, and quinine resources. But Connally, like other U.S. leaders, was of two minds on Indochina. Another reason to assist France, he said in an echo of official U.S. policy, was "to release French manpower and resources now committed in Indochina to the defense of Western Europe."[9]

The news from Vietnam only worsened in the fall of 1951. By October, as the Vietminh continued to seize rural areas in the northern region of Vietnam, some American officials began to fear a Chinese invasion. As a consequence, support for the French grew even stronger among American officials. At least one member of the Joint Chiefs of Staff, General Lawton Collins, went so far as to suggest that under certain conditions the United States should consider dispatching ground troops to Indochina to prevent a communist victory.[10]

These developments in Indochina were disheartening to the U.S. government primarily because they had been so encouraging only months earlier. The appointment of the dynamic Marshal de Lattre de Tassigny in December 1950 had coincided with the infusion of additional military assistance from the United States. The general was aggressive, predicted he would win the war quickly, and pleased American and Vietnamese officials with his talk of full independence for Vietnam. Indeed, the convergence of charismatic leadership and increased shipments of military hardware and armaments had briefly helped France to turn the tide in the spring and summer of 1951. But by the fall, worried that their advantage was slipping again, the French pressed wary American officials for even more military aid.

In September, French Foreign Minister Robert Schuman arrived in Washington to plead for additional help, arguing that France could no longer fulfill its defense obligations in Europe without more American help in Indochina.[11] On the heels of Schuman's visit came a disgruntled de Lattre, who urged American officials to speed up the delivery of much-needed military equipment. In a contentious meeting at the State Department on September 17, the general sternly warned his American hosts that a settlement of the Korean conflict might have disastrous consequences. In that event, de Lattre predicted that "Mao, in order to save face, would immediately release his troops in an effort to gain a quick victory in the South, and at that moment all Chinese troops would fall on his shoulders." If U.S. officials really believed that Indochina "was the keystone in Southeast Asia," de Lattre argued, then "the U.S. must provide the weapons to make continued resistance possible."[12] Speaking to the National Press Club on September 20, de Lattre artfully spoke directly to American fears about the threat of international communism.

> The loss of Southeast Asia would mean that Communism would have at its disposal essential strategic raw materials, that the Japanese economy would forever be unbalanced, and that the whole of Asia would be threatened. Once Tonkin is lost there is really no barrier before Suez, and I will leave to your imagination how defeatism and defeat would swell up as time passes, how Communist fifth columns would get into the game in every country as strong external Communist forces apply pressure on their frontiers.[13]

As much as Truman's military and diplomatic advisors wanted to help—and as much as they admired the general for having turned the tide, if only briefly, in Indochina —they were not yet prepared to support a massive increase in aid to Indochina, especially if that meant diverting vital military support from Europe or Korea. The American hesitancy to commit even greater resources to Indochina was further complicated by the nagging concerns that the French were still not sincerely committed to true independence for their former colonies. De Lattre insisted the struggle was "the war of Vietnam for Vietnam" and claimed "we have no more interest here. . . . We have abandoned all our colonial positions completely." Privately, however, some State Department officials wondered if the war was still not primarily a French affair. For one thing, de Lattre and the French stubbornly opposed any direct U.S. aid to the Vietnamese military and had permitted only minimal latitude for the Vietnamese fighting forces which made up only one-third of the army that fought under de Lattre's command.[14]

If France continued resisting complete independence for the Vietnamese—in other words, if the war was seen only as a colonial battle between the French and the Vietminh and not one of independence fought by the Vietnamese—some U.S. officials doubted its forces would ever prevail. Observed Robert Shaplen, a *Newsweek* reporter with extensive experience in Vietnam in the early 1950s: "It should have been apparent to anyone with any knowledge of the situation that only a strong nationalist counterforce would have any chance of achieving victory or even containment of the Vietminh."[15]

Despite these concerns about France's real intentions in the war, the

Truman administration never went so far as to threaten an end to U.S. military support. As Rusk argued many years later, while the United States could not have forced France to grant greater independence, "we could have seduced it more forcefully." At best, he admitted, attempts to influence France were "half-hearted." At the time, however, differences of opinion between the State Department Far Eastern and European bureaus complicated and muddled U.S. policy toward Indochina, although the Europeanists usually prevailed. Acheson, Rusk explained, was a "North Atlantic man," who "really didn't give a damn about the brown, yellow, black and red peoples of the world." What Acheson ultimately wanted, Rusk believed, was "full cooperation with the French." [16]

Another reason for the high degree of American forbearance was the always implicit threat by French officials that they might simply withdraw from the war. To be sure, France's military struggle was highly unpopular back home and a severe drain on the nation's budget. Without more military assistance, France made it clear that dumping the entire problem in the lap of the United States was not out of the question. "In effect, then," the writers of the *Pentagon Papers* later observed, "because of the overriding importance given to holding the Communist line in Indochina, the French in being able to threaten to withdraw possessed an important instrument of blackmail."[17]

Although some American officials doubted that France was really in the fight as a bulwark against encroaching Asian communism, Truman and Acheson chose to believe otherwise, persuading themselves that the struggle was essentially one of communism versus anticommunism—not nationalism versus colonialism. In his testimony before the Foreign Relations and Armed Services committees that summer, Rusk had touted the State Department line and expressed absolute confidence in France's willingness to grant full independence to Indochina. "We believe the French have passed the point of no return in solving this colonial issue," he assured committee members. Rusk also insisted that Indochina's "armed struggle" was not, "on any realistic basis, about whether or not it will remain a colonial power. The issue is whether the Associated States [Vietnam, Cambodia, and Laos] will be allowed to develop their independence along constitutional lines or whether the country will be taken over by Communist conspiracy."[18]

It was in the midst of this confusion over France's ultimate goals in Indochina that John F. Kennedy arrived in southern Vietnam on October 19, gaunt, pale, and exhausted from a life-threatening illness that had struck him in Okinawa, sending him to a hospital for several days with a 106 degree temperature.[19] Kennedy was resilient, however, and insisted on continuing the trip. But his party had no sooner arrived in Saigon than it found itself in the midst of the war. Throughout the visit, as brother Robert later noted, fighting between the French and the Vietminh guerrillas was so heavy that it confined the group to the city. Kennedy could not explore the countryside. "[We] could hear shooting as evening wore on," Robert wrote in his diary during the trip. Although restricted to Saigon, Kennedy did not sit still. He and Robert met with Bao Dai, the Vietnamese leader who, a bemused John Kennedy later noted, appeared "in [S. J.] Perelman's words" to be "fried in Crisco."* Assessing the political situation more astutely than many U.S. observers, Robert Kennedy concluded that in a national election Ho Chi Minh would get 70 percent of the vote. [20]

It was in Saigon that John Kennedy renewed his friendship with Edmund Gullion, the chargé d'affaires of the American legation. They had first met four years earlier in Washington when Gullion, then a young State Department assistant to Acheson, helped Kennedy prepare a foreign policy speech. While the U.S. legation was officially supportive of the French and their puppet, Bao Dai, Gullion was among a faction of Foreign Service officers becoming sharply critical of the French military effort. Gullion and others worried that without more direct intervention by the United States, the French might never gain the upper hand.[21] Furthermore, Gullion—like many officials in Washington—believed the United States should pressure the French to grant greater freedom to the Vietnamese. He also favored sending some military assistance directly to Bao Dai's government, instead of channeling all aid through the French.[22]

Influenced by Gullion's thinking, Kennedy boldly challenged the legation's official policy and questioned staff members sharply during a briefing in Saigon. Why should the Vietnamese people, he asked, be expected to join the struggle to keep their country a part of the French empire? Pointed questions like this irritated not only Donald Heath, the new American minister in Indochina, but also de Lattre, who fired off a formal complaint to Heath after his own contentious meeting with Kennedy.[23] Nonetheless, de Lattre confidently assured Kennedy that the French would win the war.[24]

Robert Kennedy later recalled that the trip made a "very, very major impression" on his older brother. "These countries from the Mediterranean to the South China Sea, all [were] searching for a future," he wrote. Among the questions Congressman Kennedy pondered after this trip, Robert said, was: "What [these countries'] relationship was going to be to the United States; what we were going to do in our relationship to them; the importance of the right kind of representation; the importance of associating ourselves with the people rather than just the governments, which

---

*Actually, Perelman, a journalist, had described Bao Dai as a "short, slippery-looking customer rather on the pudgy side and freshly dipped in Crisco" (Karnow, 187).

might be transitional, transitory; the mistake of the war in Indochina; the mistake of the French policy; the failure of the United States to back the people."[25]

Kennedy returned to Boston on November 11 and quickly went to work touting the trip and eagerly sharing the foreign policy insights he had gained. Three days after his return, he spoke to a national radio audience on the Mutual Broadcasting Network and described his "long journey" of "some 25,000 miles." To the young congressman, the struggle in Indochina was no longer an abstract conflict between communism and democracy in Southeast Asia. For the first time, he had witnessed the deleterious impact of French colonialism on the region. His understanding of the power of nationalism in the Far East was now more sophisticated. He now knew more about the region than 95 percent of Congress. "Here," he told his radio audience,

> Colonialism is not a topic for tea-talk discussion. It is the daily fare of millions of men. This is also an area of revolution, which manifests itself at times in bloody riots and assassinations. . . . In Indo-China and in Korea, this spirit of revolution has now reached the stage of pitched battles and full-scale modern war. Basically, this is an area of human conflict between civilizations striving to be born and those struggling desperately to retain what they have held so long. As such, it is obviously open to the inroads of Communism, but it also holds an enormous challenge to the penetration of American faiths and beliefs.[26]

Several days later, speaking to attendees of a Boston Chamber of Commerce luncheon, Kennedy again revealed a growing antipathy toward the French in Indochina. France, he said, was "trying desperately to hang on to a rich portion of its former empire against a Communist-dominated nationalistic uprising." To Kennedy, Bao Dai's government was "a puppet government, manned frequently by puppeteers once subservient to the Japanese, now subservient to the French." All the neutral observers he questioned had told him that "a free election . . . would go in favor of Ho and his Communists." Although Kennedy acknowledged General de Lattre's brilliance, he told his audience that the war was exacting "a fearful toll on the young officers of the French Army." De Lattre, according to Kennedy, "will probably win tactical victories, but security in that area will never be finally achieved until France clearly makes up her mind to work for the ultimate independence of those areas." His indictment of American support of the French was severe. "We have now allied ourselves with the French in this struggle," he said, "allied ourselves against the Communists but also against the rising tide of nationalism. We have become the West, the proponents of empire—carriers of what we had traditionally disdained—the white man's burden."

In retrospect, the principles Kennedy said he learned from his trip were striking and instructive—and more so, because under his presidential leadership he seemed to abandon them in favor of more, not less, U.S. involvement in the affairs of Vietnam. "We cannot reform the world," he insisted in 1951. "We cannot and should not impose upon this Eastern world our values, our institutions or our customs. True, there is a basic sameness in all men, the desire to be free from want, from illness, from tyranny. But, however much we may value our conceptions of suffrage, our mechanical well-being, even our bathtubs, the East may think little or nothing of them." Furthermore, Kennedy asserted, "there is just not enough money in the world to relieve the poverty of all the millions of this world who may be threatened by Communism. We cannot and should not attempt to buy their freedom from this threat; all we can do is help them achieve that freedom if they really wish to do so." Although he supported President Truman's Point Four program of economic aid to the region, he cautioned against "broad, unlimited" grants to any government. "More grants of money are debilitating and wasteful," he said. "More than this, they favor the 'ins' as contrasted from the 'outs.' " While he praised the American diplomats that he encountered during this journey abroad, the politician in Kennedy noticed that many of "our representatives abroad seem to be a breed of their own, moving mainly in their own limited circles not knowing too much of the people to whom they are accredited, unconscious of the fact that their role is not tennis and cocktails, but the interpretation to a foreign country of the meaning of American life and the interpretations to us of that country's aspirations and aims."

Perhaps what most troubled Kennedy, however, was the way the United States had so clearly identified itself with French colonialism. "We cannot ally ourselves with the dreams of empire," he said. "We are allies with our Western European friends and we will aid and befriend them in the defense of their own countries. But to support and defend their colonial aspirations is another thing. That is their problem, not ours."[27] And a worsening problem it was.

The French failed to build upon the military successes for which de Lattre and his intrepid leadership had largely been responsible in early 1951. Despite those victories, the French struggle had lagged considerably by year's end. Kennedy's wise and prescient warning notwithstanding, de Lattre's untimely death in January 1952 would mean that Indochina would become, increasingly, an American problem.

JOHN KENNEDY WAS NOT alone in believing the United States suffered from its substantial support of France in Indochina. Although most members of Congress would eventually come to regard the conflict in Vietnam as a struggle against Communist China's hegemony in the region, in 1951, at least, a surprising cross-section of knowledgeable Republicans and Democrats viewed the clash primarily in terms of France's desire to reestablish its fading colonial empire. This may have had more to do with the fact that France's oppressive colonial rule was still in force throughout Indochina. By the late 1950s and early 1960s, however, the issues would become muddier, as many members of Congress forgot the excesses of the French colonial era.

Senator George Malone, a freshman Republican from Nevada, informed the Senate in April 1951 that he believed the French continued to hold Indochina "in colonial slavery." As one of the few members of Congress to have visited Indochina, Malone observed that the United States was "now making enemies faster than any nation can make friends in the Far East . . . through the system of fostering colonial slavery under the guise of keeping down Communism."[28]

During a lame-duck December Senate session, outgoing Florida Democrat Claude Pepper described a recent visit to Asia during which he was asked, "Why are you identifying yourselves with the most hated form of exploitation so far as the Asiatic peoples are concerned, namely western colonialism?" Like Kennedy and Malone, Pepper believed the United States was not doing enough to disassociate itself from colonialism in Asia, and he proposed United Nations intervention to mediate an end to French rule. "Then the United States as well as the United Nations would properly support the democratic forces that might be recognized," he explained, "and then we would be free of the charge that we were aligning ourselves with the hated imperialism of the past." Oregon's Wayne Morse agreed with Pepper and supported "an honorable negotiation" on Indochina's independence arrived at by "international arbitration."[29]

Even Tom Connally, chairman of the Senate Foreign Relations Committee and a strong supporter of Truman's assistance to the French in Indochina, had begun to question the degree to which the United States injected itself into the political strife sweeping Asia. "I do not subscribe to the doctrine that we are obligated in any sense whatever to intervene in these quarrels between these countries in Asia, unless they affect directly the interests of the United States," Connally told Rusk during the joint committee hearing in 1951. "You folks do not realize that our back is going to break after a while."[30] In a February 1952 Foreign Relations Committee executive session, Connally again pressed his case when he told Acheson that, "Ultimately, I think France is going to have to get out or acknowledge this anti-colonialism, because they are not going to put up with this colonialism any longer."

Asked by Connally if, as Pepper and Morse had earlier suggested, Indochina's problems could be settled by the United Nations, Acheson dutifully trumpeted the French line and replied that he doubted it. Indochina's problem, he explained, "is no longer any conflict between the French and the Vietnamese. The Vietnamese have got all the liberty and opportunity that they can possibly handle or want. In fact, they have got a lot more than they can either handle or want." Acheson pragmatically insisted that the aim of the United States was "to keep [the French] doing what they are doing, which is taking the primary responsibility for this fight [against communism] in Indochina and not letting them in any way transfer it to us."[31]

At another executive session of the committee in March, Acheson hedged when asked what the United States would do if the French withdrew from Indochina. "Well," he replied, "I just can't answer that. I don't know." On this occasion, the interrogator was a newer Democratic member of the committee, J. William Fulbright from Arkansas. In response to Acheson's nonanswer, Fulbright ventured his own answer and, in the process, seemed to capture the sentiment of other committee members and some Truman administration officials who struggled to understand the complicated and confusing situation in Indochina and America's response to it. Said Fulbright: "We have to do *something*."[32]

CHAPTER 7

A Great Crusade

1951–1952

From General Dwight D. Eisenhower's vantage point in Paris on March 17, 1951, the prospects for a French victory in Vietnam were bleak. As the new supreme commander of NATO forces in Europe waited for France's General de Lattre to arrive, he mused about France's prospects against Ho's Vietminh guerrillas. "The French have a knotty problem on that one," he wrote in his diary. Indeed, the American general could appreciate the enormous burden French people shouldered as they recovered from the devastation of war in the menacing shadow of Soviet communism and struggled against another communist army in the jungles of Southeast Asia. "The campaign out there," Eisenhower noted, "is a draining sore in their side."

But Eisenhower was also a firm believer in what would come to be known as the "domino theory," the notion that a communist victory in Vietnam would eventually draw all of Southeast Asia, including India, into the communist orbit. "That prospect," he wrote, "makes the whole problem one of interest to us all." To "get the thing over at once," Eisenhower favored "heavy reinforcement" of the French army. Yet he worried that "no military victory is possible in that kind of theater." For "even if Indochina were completely cleared of Communists, right across the border is China with inexhaustible manpower."[1] In other words, as of 1949—when Mao's communist forces first occupied the Chinese provinces along Vietnam's northern border—Eisenhower believed that war in Indochina may have already been a futile exercise for the French. The truth of that astute observation—although not shared with the American public—would be increasingly apparent by year's end, although American and French officials would continue to ignore the abundant evidence.

In deeming the cause futile, Eisenhower may have considered the military setbacks France had suffered in the fall of 1950, particularly the calamity that befell them in October near the Chinese border. When Vietminh forces threatened to overwhelm the garrison they had established in the Cao Bang province, the French beat a hasty but ill-conceived retreat through uncharted jungle. In the ensuing confrontations with Vietminh forces, the French lost six thousand troops and more than ten thousand weapons—enough firepower to equip an entire Vietminh division. The renowned Vietnam historian Bernard Fall later observed:

> For the French, the Indochina War was lost then and there. That it was allowed to drag on inconclusively for another four years is a testimony to the shortsightedness of the civilian authorities who were charged with drawing the political conclusions from the hopeless military situation. American military aid—the first trickle of which had made its appearance in the form of seven transport planes in June, 1950, after the Korean War had broken out—was to make no difference whatever in the eventual outcome of the war.[2]

Futile or not, the French were not prepared to quit. They pressed Washington for more money, arguing that their government could not continue its costly military operations in Europe and Asia without greater U.S. assistance. A National Intelligence Estimate prepared for the State Department in March 1952 concluded that if forced to choose between Europe and Asia, the French "would view their Indochina commitment as of lesser importance." France estimated that even with current levels of U.S. aid, it would come up "several hundred million dollars short" of honoring its military obligations in Europe and Indochina.[3] With U.S. defenses stretched to the limit in Europe and Korea, the last thing Truman wanted was France's ugly war in Indochina.

In the short run, therefore, prudence called for continued financial support of the French in hopes that, at the very least, it might help preserve the status quo. In early 1952, Truman asked Congress to appropriate $293 million in military aid for Indochina in 1953. The United States had already poured more than $600 million into the "defense" of Indochina, but Truman was prepared to send more.[4]

Dissatisfied with the level of U.S. support for a war that drained their own military budget by more than $1.2 billion a year, French officials pressed for even more than Truman proposed. In what British Foreign Minister Anthony Eden later described as a "long and difficult" conference with American, French and British officials in May 1952, French Defense Minister René Pleven complained that—hundreds of millions in U.S. aid notwithstanding—"France cannot continue to bear *alone* such a considerable share of this burden." Acheson assured Pleven that the United States believed the French effort in Indochina "is essential for our security, not just in the Far East but also in the Middle East and Europe."

Pressing their case even further, French officials exploited the Americans' desire to see France play a greater role in the collective security of Europe by joining the European Defense Community, but not without linking it to U.S. support for the French military effort in Indochina. Without such assistance, Pleven said, France could not afford to field troops for the defense of Europe. It was a cynical strategy that Acheson later described as "blackmail."[5] Leaving the conference, Eden later recalled that Acheson ruefully told him that if Congress approved additional aid to France, the United States would be paying for almost half the cost of the war. "Yet," As Eden wrote, "to hear the French talk, one would think that [the U.S.] Government were only supplying them with the odd revolver or two." Eden said that he "reflected that if the French really wanted American aid, they were going about it in the worst possible way."[6]

Yet to Eden's surprise, Truman—in spite of the distasteful French approach—demonstrated the extent of his desire to keep France, and not the United States, fighting in Indochina when he offered an additional $150 million in June. This meant that the United States would now be assuming almost one-third of the entire cost of France's ill-fated Asian crusade while U.S. officials exerted almost no influence over French military operations and were often uninformed about France's military strategy, or lack thereof.[7]

Ultimately, Truman decided he had no option but to support the French in Indochina wholeheartedly. As long as the ill political winds over China and Korea continued to blow, a Democratic administration—and for that matter, any Republican administration—could not ill afford to bear the blame for losing another Asian nation to communism. Truman believed he had little choice but to subsidize the French. (France, of course, well understood the Americans' inordinate fear of communism and continued to masterfully exploit those fears.)

Viewing the issue only in its foreign and military policy contexts, U.S. support for Indochina had its decided advantages. As long as the French and the Vietminh fought, China's military energies remained divided between Indochina and Korea—a distinct advantage for U.S. forces in Korea. An early end to either war, as everyone understood, would only unleash the Chinese to pour even greater resources into the remaining conflict. For Truman, a holding action in Indochina, even if it cost the United States as much as $440 million a year, seemed well worth the price because of its positive impact in Korea. It is, therefore, not surprising that Truman agreed with the conclusions of his National Security Council staff in February 1952 that

Communist domination of Southeast Asia, whether by means of overt invasion, subversion, or accommodation on the part of the indigenous governments, would be critical to United States security interests. Communist success in this area would spread doubt and fear among other threatened non-communist countries as to the ability of the United States and the United Nations to halt communist aggression elsewhere. It would strengthen the claim that the advance of communism is inexorable and encourage countries vulnerable to Soviet pressure to adopt policies of neutralism or accommodation.[8]

Despite their belief in the anticommunist nature of the Indochina war, Truman and his advisors remained concerned about France's overtly colonial aims. Despite its rhetoric about seeking true independence for Indochina, France continued to exercise considerable control over Indochina's internal political matters. In January, when U.S Ambassador Donald Heath urged Bao Dai to exert greater supervision over his country's government and military, the Vietnamese leader complained that he could not "actively take over" his government unless France gave him more authority.[9]

Not that the United States accorded Bao Dai or his government any significant degree of deference either. In the early 1950s, State Department officials routinely held bilateral and trilateral talks with French and British officials to discuss Indochina, as if the region were still a French colony. France routinely touted Indochina's independence, while the United States continuously professed its support of true independence for the Associated States. Yet, Vietnamese officials were not invited to these discussions and were rarely consulted in a substantive manner.

France could not, however, completely ignore the Vietnamese—at least to the extent they would be urged to fight for the "independence" of their country. For years, however, the only way a Vietnamese citizen could participate in the military struggle against the Vietminh was to enlist in the French Expeditionary Corps. Once enlisted, however, the French made certain that no Vietnamese soldier rose above the rank of small unit commander. So, in November 1950, when France reluctantly took steps to form a Vietnamese National Army, it found—thanks to years of French discrimination—that few Vietnamese possessed the military training and experience to lead men in battle.[10]

Initially, French officials had hoped to train and equip an indigenous fighting force of one hundred fifteen thousand men, but their effort fell far short of expectations. Less than forty thousand Vietnamese had enlisted by early 1951, an indication that many Vietnamese distrusted French motives, regarded the war as a French operation, or believed they had no personal stake in the war's outcome.[11] As Acheson told the Senate Foreign Relations Committee in January 1952, a majority of Vietnam's citizens "are sitting on the fence waiting to see who wins. . . . It is a dangerous thing for an Indochinese to commit himself. He is likely to have his throat cut."[12]

As the military stalemate dragged on in Indochina, an ideological battle of another sort unfolded in the United States. Shut out of the White House since 1933, and painfully denied its best opportunity for victory by Harry Truman in 1948, the Republican Party of 1952 featured an irate, power-starved collection of political partisans who were deeply divided on foreign policy between the dominant ideological strains—isolationism and internationalism. But when Truman announced his retirement and suddenly withdrew from the race in early 1952, he revived the Republicans' hopes for victory—but only if they could find someone to span the deep ideological chasms that separated both sides of their fractious party.

Into this breach stepped Eisenhower, the World War II commander who vacated his NATO post in the summer of 1952. Few doubted that a heroic figure like Eisenhower represented the party's best opportunity to regain the White House after twenty years in the political wilderness. Yet the isolationist, fiscally conservative Midwestern and Western wing of the party was decidedly cool to Eisenhower and favored Senator Robert Taft of Ohio.

The personal and political differences between Taft and Eisenhower were stark. Taft was a pedigreed Republican, the son of President and Chief Justice William Howard Taft and the ideological leader of the Senate Republicans. Although Eisenhower was a wily politician, he was also a lifelong solider who had only recently declared his political affiliation. Taft had voted against NATO. Eisenhower not only supported the organization, but had commanded its multinational military force in Europe. Taft railed against the Democrats' "sellout" at Yalta and their "loss" of China. Eisenhower had worked to implement Franklin Roosevelt's foreign policy during World War II and had served as Truman's Army chief of staff in 1949, when China's Nationalist government fell to the Communists.

Eisenhower and his advisors knew they had to win over the isolationists and Taft loyalists if they were to win the nomination. In June, shortly after returning from Europe, the general launched a campaign to distance himself from the foreign and defense policies that he had once advocated and implemented. During a speech in Denver, he launched into a surprisingly partisan attack on the party of the Democratic presidents he had served in several capacities. Without naming Truman or the Democratic Party, Eisenhower decried the "trust" that had been placed "for too long" in "a godless dictatorship."

> Think of the places that stand as black monuments to this misplaced trust.
> Our loss of China, a divided and almost naked Germany, the enslaved

countries of the Baltic and the Balkans, the long and bloody struggle in Greece. They, the consequences of that misplaced trust, come home to every one of us in the war in Korea. If we had been less trustful, if we had been less soft and weak, there might easily have been no war in Korea.[13]

Eisenhower's transition from the role of aloof, apolitical military leader to pandering, partisan politician was gradual and reluctant. Accompanying him as he tentatively made his peace with the compromise and ideological obfuscation necessary for victory was the Republicans' chief foreign policy spokesman, John Foster Dulles, who would eventually help Eisenhower implement U.S. policy in Indochina. A deeply religious and extremely conservative Presbyterian with a strong sense of moral rectitude, Dulles was born in 1888 into the rarified world of international diplomacy, the grandson and nephew of former secretaries of state. Now a successful Wall Street lawyer, Dulles had years of foreign policy experience to his credit, earned during service in the state departments of presidents Wilson, Roosevelt, and Truman. He had negotiated virtually all of the postwar international treaties, including the United Nations charter. Although he had served as the token Republican in Truman's State Department, he was the undisputed choice for the job of secretary of state in the next Republican administration.

Some believed that Dulles viewed the world in black and white. To Dulles, two forces—good and evil—vied for world domination. America, of course, had only noble aims and stood for that which was just. Conversely, the communist Soviet regime, aided by its clients in China, personified evil.* Despite having served three Democratic presidents, including Truman, Dulles came to believe that the incumbent Democrat's containment policies smacked of appeasement. Like many who applied the lessons of Munich to their foreign and military policy views, he believed the United States should never compromise in the name of peace with the Soviets or their puppet states. Dulles believed that General MacArthur had said it best when he maintained that there was "no substitute" for victory. Containment, Dulles maintained, meant that "we are not working, sacrificing and spending in order to be able to live *without* this peril—but to be able to live *with* it, presumably forever."[14]

In a celebrated article for *Life* magazine in May 1952, Dulles argued that the only proper response to Soviet communism "is for the free world to develop the will and organize the means to retaliate instantly against open aggression by Red armies, so that [if an attack] occurred anywhere,

---

*Dulles, of course, was not alone in his views. Most Americans of that era ascribed only good and noble purposes to their country and believed that the Soviet Union was the source of virtually every evil.

we could and would strike back where it hurts, by means of our choosing."
What Dulles meant, of course, was that the United States should consider
using its nuclear arsenal in the fight against communism. But it was not
enough, Dulles maintained, to simply secure the good behavior of the
Soviets by means of a nuclear threat. Dulles wanted the free world, led by
the United States, to undertake "the political offense" against communism
by exchanging a containment policy for "liberation" of the "captive peoples" in the Soviet orbit. Although Dulles made it clear he did not expect
the United States to enforce his liberation policy with military might, he
left many wondering what other means the country might use to liberate
the "captive" nations.[15]

Despite all his bellicose rhetoric and a moralistic view of the world,
Dulles was also pragmatic and politically astute. Believing that only Eisenhower could make peace between the isolationist and internationalist
wings of his party, Dulles patiently helped his candidate understand the
need to honor—and in many cases, embrace—certain aspects of the isolationists' foreign policy agenda. He knew, too, that after years of turmoil in
the United States over communism—foreign and domestic—great political gains were possible in 1952 if foreign policy issues were properly
exploited. In that enterprise, Taft, despite his considerable political skills
and aggressive partisanship, was no match for a war hero like Eisenhower.
While Dulles' assistance was only one aspect of Eisenhower's successful
strategy to deny Taft the Republican nomination, it was significant and
would pay handsome dividends in the fall election when voters began
focusing on the Democrats' purported foreign policy failures.

At the Republican National Convention in mid-July, Eisenhower
invited Dulles to draft the party's foreign policy platform plank. Mirroring
the prevailing mood of party members, Dulles' rhetorical product was
audacious and vitriolic, laying the blame for virtually every significant
international problem at Harry Truman's doorstep, and serving up red
meat to internationalists and isolationists alike. It began:

> The present Administration, in seven years, has squandered the unprece-
> dented power and prestige, which were ours at the close of World War II.
> In that time, more than 500 million non-Russian people of fifteen differ-
> ent countries have been absorbed into the power sphere of Communist
> Russia, which proceeds confidently with its plan for world conquest.[16]

More than spelling out the *perceived* stark differences in the Democratic and Republican approaches to the international communist threat,
Dulles' product included a pledge that, when fulfilled, would have long-
lasting implications for the country. Eisenhower's party promised to "end
neglect of the Far East, which Stalin has long identified as the road to vic-

tory over the West. We shall make it clear that we have no intention to sacrifice the East to gain time for the West." It was an old conservative Republican saw meant to comfort and energize those former Taft supporters who doubted Eisenhower's commitment to Asia. Therefore, it was music to the conservatives' ears to learn that Eisenhower believed that the people of the region "not under Communist control find it difficult to sustain their morale as they contrast Russia's 'Asia First' policy with the 'Asia Last' policy of those in control of the Administration now in power."* Further pandering to the far right of their party, Eisenhower and Dulles paid homage to the McCarthyites, pledging to "repudiate all commitments in secret understandings such as those of Yalta, which aid Communist enslavements." This, of course, was also a tribute to the liberation policy that Dulles hoped would supplant containment. Here, however, Dulles' language was so ambiguous as to have no meaning: "It will be made clear, on the highest authority of the President and the Congress, that United States policy, as one of its peaceful purposes, looks happily forward to the genuine independence of those captive peoples."[17]

The choice of Richard Nixon as Eisenhower's running mate was another way the nominee narrowed the ideological chasm between the party's disparate wings. While men like Taft and McCarthy were wary of the internationalist Eisenhower, they liked and trusted Nixon. Even more than Dulles, the Californian instinctively understood the political gold mines that were Truman's woes in the Far East and U.S. State Department. A fierce and effective anti-Communist during his House years, Nixon became famous for his expertise in the art of the smear, which he had used to win seats in the House and Senate by reviling his opponents as communist sympathizers. Only the year before, it was Nixon who had proved a skillful practitioner in the art of exploiting the fallout over Truman's dismissal of General MacArthur. Avoiding the wild and extreme rhetoric of Republicans like McCarthy and Jenner, Nixon carefully played to his strength as an expert on domestic communism. "The happiest group in the country," Nixon had said, "will be the Communists and their stooges. . . . The president has given them what they always wanted—MacArthur's scalp." Nixon then introduced a Senate resolution deploring the dismissal and, instead of demanding the president's impeachment, called on Truman

*In their platform, Republicans arrogantly declared that "there are no Communists in the Republican Party." The document also condemned the Truman administration's "appeasement of Communism at home and abroad" and charged it with covering up evidence of Communists in government while prosecuting only "the most notorious Communists after public opinion forced action" (*CQA*, 1952, 491).

to reinstate the general.[18] Compared to many of his intemperate colleagues, he appeared judicious and statesmanlike.

Now that he had the nomination, Nixon was more than willing to campaign like a street fighter. For the next four months, he would not only play the role traditionally reserved for vice presidential candidates—that of a fierce partisan who employed the most negative, hard-hitting, cutthroat invective—he would forever define the role. While Eisenhower largely took the high road and promised to clean up "the mess in Washington,"[19] Nixon traveled low. In an August newspaper interview, he issued veiled accusations about Truman's patriotism. "The most devastating thing that can be said about the Truman record is that he has lost 600 million people to the communists."[20]

Later in the campaign, Nixon struck at Truman even harder. Stevenson, Truman, and Acheson, he told a Texarkana audience on October 27, were "traitors to the high principles in which many of the nation's Democrats believe." Days later in Los Angeles, he ridiculed Stevenson's patriotism when he said that the Democratic candidate "holds a Ph.D. degree from Acheson's College of Cowardly Communist Containment." Unbowed by criticism of his tactics, Nixon declared that "if the record itself smears, let it smear. If the dry rot of corruption and Communism, which has eaten into our body politic during the past seven years, can only be chopped out with a hatchet, then let's call for a hatchet."[21]

Not that Nixon was alone in his assaults on Truman. He and Eisenhower employed rhetoric that would limit their options in Indochina and might ultimately expose them to attacks from Democrats if they failed to produce the results they appeared to be promising in Indochina and elsewhere. Eisenhower, although less personal, was not above attacking Stevenson and Truman over communism and Far East policy. He and his advisors understood the widespread public discontent over the stalemated Korean War and made it their most prominent issue in the campaign's homestretch. In fact, Eisenhower assailed the Truman administration so often that a casual observer might not have known that Stevenson, and not Truman, was the Democratic nominee. In Philadelphia in early September, he delivered a hard-hitting speech in which he charged that "seven years after victory in World War II this Administration has bungled us perilously close to World War III." Blaming Truman for having "grossly underestimated" the communist threat, Eisenhower claimed that "we are in that war because this administration abandoned China to the Communists . . . [and] announced to all the world that it had written off most of the Far East as beyond our direct concern."[22]

In Korea, Eisenhower had found a defining issue. As the nation's most respected military leader, he could speak about war with unquestioned authority. Despite his inexperience in Asia, Eisenhower enjoyed a degree of credibility regarding Korea that far eclipsed Stevenson's.

The former general's enormous stature—a war hero of unquestioned integrity and patriotism, Eisenhower was widely regarded as a man "above politics"[23]—was such that his nomination virtually ended the division among Republicans over Truman's Korean policies. Prior to Eisenhower's candidacy, the East Coast internationalist wing of the party—Eisenhower's Republican base—had generally supported Truman's Korean policies, particularly his dismissal of General Douglas MacArthur in April 1952. Members of the more conservative, Taft-isolationist wing, however, fiercely opposed Truman's war in Korea, although they occasionally found it difficult to explain why. (Sometimes, they attacked American involvement in the conflict and called for complete withdrawal from Korea. On other occasions, however, they criticized Truman for failing to wage an all-out war with the Chinese.) Despite their differences and largely because of the respect he commanded on military issues, Eisenhower now gave both sides a home with his, and Nixon's, pungent criticisms of Truman's "no-win" policy in Korea.[24]

Less than two weeks before the election, Eisenhower dropped a bombshell that ensured his victory. In Detroit, he vowed to focus his energies on ending the war and declared that, if elected, "I shall go to Korea." That electrifying speech not only sealed the election, it provided a telling view into the philosophy that would guide Eisenhower's policies toward the rest of Asia, including Indochina. "There is a Korean War," Eisenhower said, "and we are fighting it for the simplest of reasons: because free leadership failed to check and to turn back Communist ambition before it savagely attacked us."

At the heart of Eisenhower's criticisms of Truman's Korean policies was the lesson he and other leaders had learned from Munich—and which Truman's advisors were now applying to Indochina. "World War II should have taught us all one lesson," Eisenhower declared. "The lesson is this: To vacillate, to hesitate—to appease even by merely betraying unsteady purpose—is to feed a dictator's appetite for conquest and to invite war itself. That lesson—which should have firmly guided every great decision of our leadership through these later years—was ignored in the development of the Administration's policies for Asia."[25]

On Election Day 1952, the voters finished the repudiation of Harry Truman and the Democratic Party that had begun in 1950. Not only did voters elect Eisenhower as the first Republican president in twenty years; they did so in a landslide while handing his party control of the House and Senate, if only by slim margins. While voters did not speak with one voice— Democratic congressional candidates actually out-polled Republicans by more than three hundred fifty thousand votes [26]—they demonstrated that the turmoil and upheaval in Asia and in the State Department was a potent political weapon for Eisenhower's party. While Truman had also suffered from mounting concerns about the nation's economy and charges of corruption in his administration, nothing hurt him and his party more than two years of relentless, vituperative attacks on the wisdom of their foreign policy as well as their personal patriotism. While those attacks were instrumental in the Republican strategy to regain the White House, their political consequences and the impact they had on leaders of both parties would have great and lasting implications for the nation's military and foreign policies in Indochina. Fearing a repeat of the attacks that had played such a role in Truman's downfall, future presidents like Kennedy, Johnson, and Nixon would be careful never to expose themselves to charges that they lacked sufficient resolve to defeat Asian communism.

Almost from beginning to end, Eisenhower and Nixon had run not against Stevenson, but Truman. By election day, the polls revealed the extent of the damage to Truman's popularity: only 32 percent of Americans approved of his job performance and only 43 percent believed the United States should have gone to war in Korea.[27] For Stevenson, those numbers were devastating. He had failed to persuade a majority of voters to view him independently of the politically crippled incumbent.

In the polling that fall, no one asked the American people for their opinion about the United States' support of the French in Indochina. Had they, it is doubtful that the small percentage familiar with the day-to-day struggle in Southeast Asia would have objected. As Harry Truman prepared to leave office, support for the French effort in Indochina was an article of faith among most leaders in Washington, as were other accepted "truths" about the conflict: communism, not nationalism, was the enemy. The French were merely fighting to prevent Indochina from falling into the Soviet orbit, not to preserve the frayed remnants of their formal colonial empire. Furthermore, the Vietminh were not nationalists, but pawns of Communist China who were, in turn, soldiers in the worldwide communist conspiracy directed by the Soviet Union. While there were a few senators who did not share these views, including John F. Kennedy and George Malone, most members in both houses knew too little about Indochina to challenge the information disseminated by the White House and the State Department. Nonetheless, this was Washington's conventional wisdom concerning the Indochina war—an understanding profoundly molded by the domestic political events of the previous two years. It would serve as the wellspring for the nation's military policies in Vietnam for the next generation.

In Indochina, in 1952, were applied all the accumulated "lessons" of

Munich, China, and Korea: aggression must never again be appeased in the tragic manner of the European leaders of 1930s and the Truman administration of 1940–50. Negotiation, conciliation, or ambivalence— all synonyms for appeasement—would only lead to a wider, more destructive war.

Tragically, however, most American leaders did not arrive at these conclusions after a considered examination of the powerful forces of nationalism and communism that were sweeping Asia in the early 1950s. More than anything, it was the "lessons" of China and Korea—manipulated and distorted by Truman's opponents for political purposes—that set in stone the belief that communism in Southeast Asia posed a direct threat to the national security of the United States and, furthermore, that this threat should be challenged with nothing less than the collective might and determination of the entire Western world. This was the lesson that a generation of U.S. leaders, including presidents Eisenhower, Kennedy, Johnson, and Nixon, learned and would apply all too well.

As Dean Rusk later observed, the lessons of Munich were liberally applied in Indochina, and few questioned them. "We belonged to that generation," Rusk said, "who had been led down the path into the catastrophe of World War II, which could have been prevented." At different times, "decisive action could have been taken" that would have prevented the outbreak of war, Rusk believed. "Many of us were fed to the teeth about that story."[28] Echoing Rusk, historian James R. Arnold observed that Truman, Acheson, and other leaders of the day

> saw a straight chain of events from German reoccupation of the Rhineland, to the Austrian Anschluss to the dismemberment of Czechoslvakia at Munich, to general war in Europe. Almost everyone was less familiar with events in the Pacific, yet here too there had been a similar chain of events beginning with Japan's seizure of Manchuria, subsequent invasion of the rest of China, occupation of Indochina, and [the] strike on Pearl Harbor. Viewed differently, after the toppling of the first domino, the remainder of the chain had inevitably collapsed leading to world war.[29]

Out of that story about Munich—a powerful, prevailing mind-set about how best to challenge totalitarianism in the modern world—sprang America's involvement in Vietnam. Although propelled by several other motivations, including his desire to see France participate fully in the defense of Western Europe, Truman came to France's aid in Indochina primarily because his understanding of history, his view of communism, and the audacity of his political opposition gave him no choice. If Truman had allowed the Communists to snatch another Asian nation, it would have spelled political disaster. In the end, the Vietnam War would become one legacy of a politically weakened president who sought political refuge in Southeast Asia from a highly partisan and unscrupulous political opposition determined to hound his party from power in Washington. Seeking to maintain Democratic Party predominance, preserve world peace, and prove their determination to fight communism in Asia, Truman and Acheson had ushered the nation into the first stage of a tragic crusade in Indochina.

CHAPTER 8

Pouring Money Down a Rat Hole

1953

Among the nine members of the U.S. Supreme Court in 1953, none was more outspoken than the fiercely liberal associate justice William O. Douglas. A former law professor and once the chairman of Franklin Roosevelt's Securities and Exchange Commission, Douglas was a most unusual man—a noted jurist and champion of civil liberties whose interests were not limited to the law and the Constitution. Although his position on the nation's highest court prohibited his playing an active role in U.S. diplomatic policy, Douglas was deeply interested in the world beyond the United States. Breaking with court tradition, the 54-year-old justice often commented on foreign relations and urged American policymakers to pursue an activist, internationalist approach to foreign policy—particularly when it came to fighting communism.

As an avid outdoorsman and prolific writer, Douglas had begun melding these two interests in the early 1950s when he published the first in a series of travelogues based on his adventures in several exotic lands. His fourth book, *North from Malaya: Adventure on Five Fronts*, scheduled for release in the summer of 1953, documented his 1952 journey to the nations of Southeast Asia, including the then-obscure French colony of Vietnam.[1]

Despite his sophistication about the world—he recognized and appreciated the powerful nationalistic forces that were sweeping Southeast Asia—Douglas embraced the conventional American view of the role of communism in the region. His recent trip to Indochina had persuaded him all the more that the Soviet Union's quest for world domination was the driving force behind the communist insurgencies on the "five fighting fronts" of Southeast Asia—Indochina, Malaya, Korea and Formosa, the Philippines, and Burma. "Each front is, indeed, an overt act of a Communist conspiracy to expand the Russian Empire," he asserted in the foreword of *North from Malaya*.[2]

Douglas' experiences in Indochina in August 1952 troubled him deeply. He found the U.S.-backed Bao Dai government woefully out of touch with the people and maddeningly ambivalent toward democracy. "Their political philosophy was similar to that of George III when he dealt with the American colonies," Douglas observed. "The people were an unstable, unreliable force not to be trusted." But the French, he found, were no better. "The French are afraid of the democratic counterrevolution—the only force that can turn back the tide of Communism," he wrote. "For the counterrevolution would make as its foremost slogan ridding the country of the power of the foreigner."[3]* Douglas, however, had discovered just the man to supplant Bao Dai, someone he believed could lead Vietnam to democracy and victory over the Vietminh. At lunch in early May 1953, he would introduce his new friend, a reserved, 52-year-old Vietnamese nationalist residing at a Catholic seminary in New Jersey, to two freshman U.S. senators—John F. Kennedy and Mike Mansfield—known for their interest in Southeast Asia.

Kennedy and Mansfield had arrived in the Senate in January 1953, after having defeated their state's incumbent senators in close races. Of the two, Kennedy in Massachusetts had attracted more national attention because he had vanquished the powerful Henry Cabot Lodge. Among the nation's most prominent political families, the Lodges had been synonymous with political leadership in New England for almost fifty years, since the days when the first Henry Cabot Lodge, his grandfather, had served in the U.S. Senate. Widely acknowledged as the front-runner, Lodge was so confident that he had volunteered to manage Eisenhower's presidential campaign—to his own political detriment, as it turned out. Although Eisenhower carried the state by more than two hundred thousand votes, the general's coattails were not long enough to help the Republican incumbent. Kennedy had made too many inroads with disgruntled voters of Lodge's own party, shoring up the support of traditional Democrats and winning the election by a margin of seventy thousand votes out of more than 2.4 million votes cast.

---

*So discouraged was Douglas by the failure of the French and their Bao Dai government, that he spoke openly to a wire service reporter in Saigon. "There is no place in Southeast Asia I have so far visited," he said, "where I have seen so many forces of disintegration pulling asunder as in Indochina." Douglas said he believed that if "all the popular forces" supported the fight against the Vietminh, "the war should end in a matter of a few weeks." Douglas' statement prompted a French complaint to the U.S. ambassador in Saigon, Donald Heath, who informed them that the justice's views were "highly personal and highly independent" (*FRUS*, 1952–54, 13:249).

Mansfield, meanwhile, won by an even smaller margin. Like Kennedy, the lanky, plainspoken former college professor from the University of Montana had defied the Eisenhower electoral tide to carry his state by a mere 5,700 votes, in what would be the narrowest victory of a long congressional career.

In almost every way, Mansfield's path to the Senate was different from that of his privileged Massachusetts colleague. Born in New York City to Irish Catholic immigrants in 1903, Mansfield went to live with relatives in Montana following his mother's death in 1910. In later life, those who knew him only as a staid and assiduous professor-turned-politician would have been surprised by the rebellion and defiance of Mansfield's checkered youth. He ran away from home three times and was jailed twice for minor offenses. In 1918, only 15 years old, he dropped out of the eighth grade, lied about his age, and joined the Navy. In four years' time, during service in the Navy, Army, and Marine Corps, Mansfield traveled the world and acquired a deep affection for the Far East. He loved, he later said, "the sights, sounds, smells and people of China."

His brief military career over by 1922, Mansfield returned to Montana, where he labored in the Butte copper mines for six years. In 1928, his girlfriend and future wife, Maureen Hayes, persuaded him that that he was wasting his life in manual labor. Impulsively, Mansfield quit the mines and enrolled at Montana State University. By 1933, with a master's degree in political science, he was teaching courses in Asian and Latin American history. Eventually, politics beckoned. After one unsuccessful campaign for Congress in 1940, Mansfield won his first election in 1942 when he defeated the well-known pacifist House member, Jeanette Rankin.* In the House, the freshman Mansfield quickly won a seat on the Foreign Affairs Committee, where he aggressively cultivated a reputation as an authority on what were then viewed as the mysterious and enigmatic ways of the Orient.[4]

In late 1944, after returning from the first of several congressional trips to China, Mansfield reported to the House on his mission with a knowledgeable and evenhanded analysis of Chinese politics. While this trip established his Asia credentials, his frank assessment of Mao's Communists would later haunt him. Although he made it clear that he favored Chiang Kai-shek's Nationalist government, he had nonetheless characterized the Communists as "more reformers than revolutionaries" who "have attacked the problems most deep-seated in agricultural China." While the Communists were

---

*Rankin was the first woman ever elected to the House and the only member of Congress to have voted against America's war declaration against Germany in 1917 and against Japan in 1941.

"totalitarian and dictatorial in their own way," Mansfield asserted that "there is more democracy in their territory than in the rest of China." He complained that Chiang's government "speaks democratically but acts dictatorially." Echoing the assessment of many State Department officials—the China hands who would later be attacked on charges they favored the Communists—he maintained that Chiang's government "is afraid of the will of the people [and] has lost much of its popular support."[5]

His unorthodox assessment of the communists did Mansfield no good during his unsuccessful Senate race in 1950. His well-publicized interest in Asia earned him the derogatory label "China Mike" and the charge that he cared more about China than Montana. Worse, his opponent dug up his unfortunate 1945 characterization of the Chinese Communists as agrarian reformers. Two years later, they aired the remark again, accusing him of contributing to the "loss" of China and suggesting that he was a Communist. In a passionate statewide radio address, only days before the election, Mansfield forcefully defended himself and disingenuously protested that he had not praised the Communists, but had only quoted an American general's description. In spite of the attacks over China, his Catholicism, and a campaign visit on behalf of his opponent by Senator Joseph McCarthy (who declared that Mansfield was "either stupid or a dupe") Mansfield possessed one distinct advantage that resulted in his narrow victory: his opponent, incumbent Zales Ecton, was widely regarded as one of the more ineffective members of the Senate.[6]

While Mansfield and Kennedy were not close friends, they did share common ground. Both were Irish Catholic, considered themselves moderate Democrats, and were keenly interested in world affairs. Each also knew something, although not much, about Indochina. It was for those reasons that Douglas had invited them to meet the promising Vietnamese nationalist Ngo Dinh Diem over lunch.

An enigmatic and deeply religious Catholic Mandarin, Diem had earned the respect of Bao Dai, whom he served as interior minister in 1933, *and* Ho Chi Minh, who had offered him a position in the communist government in 1945. Yet his intense animosity toward the French colonialists as well as the Communists eventually precluded Diem's service in either government and led him into a self-imposed exile, first in France and finally in the United States. When he arrived in the United States in 1951, Catholic leaders, particularly Francis Cardinal Spellman of New York, welcomed Diem warmly and offered him refuge at the church's Maryknoll seminary in New Jersey.

Douglas had first learned of Diem during his travels in Indochina the previous year. When they finally met, Douglas was impressed with what he saw. In *North from Malaya*, Douglas exalted his new friend as "a hero" with a "considerable following" in several regions of the country. Adding to that exaggeration of Diem's popularity, Douglas asserted that he was "revered by the Vietnamese because he is honest and independent and stood firm against the French influence."[7]

At the luncheon, Diem told Kennedy and Mansfield that the Vietnamese people would not fight against the Communists until France granted them greater independence. Acknowledging that the French had recently made some concessions, Diem feared that they were "too little and too late." They could not beat the Communists, he said. To Diem, the Communists were worse than the French. "He thought there could be no liberty under the Communists," wrote Kennedy's old friend, Edmund Gullion, who was back from Saigon and in attendance as a State Department representative. "The trouble in Vietnam was, he said, that there was no rallying point in between the Communists and the French." Diem expressed his desire to return to Vietnam, but doubted the French would issue him an exit visa and, furthermore, he feared that the Communists would assassinate him if he returned. "What he lacked," wrote Gullion in paraphrasing Diem, "was a platform of any political context in which he could do useful work for his country."[8]

Diem impressed Kennedy and Mansfield enormously. For Mansfield, not yet an expert on Indochina, the meeting marked the beginning of an intense interest in the region. He later recalled that he was taken with Diem's "independence, integrity" and concluded that his new Vietnamese acquaintance was "a man who had one goal in mind, and that was the full independence of his country."[9] While impressed with Diem's "deep conviction and almost buoyant confidence that he would some day steer his country between colonialism and communism toward freedom," Mansfield doubted that Vietnam's leader-in-waiting would ever get the chance. At the time, he said, "there seemed no likelihood that this man—outlawed by both sides in the Indochina conflict—would ever have an opportunity to put his nationalist idealism into practice."[10]

The meeting with Diem had a profound impact on Kennedy as well. That afternoon, when he returned to his office, the freshman senator dictated a letter to Secretary of State John Foster Dulles that included forty-seven questions about the war in Indochina. Diem's misgivings about the French seem to have influenced Kennedy's questions: "Have the French a plan for the next two years for success in French Indochina—military, economic and political? . . . Is it possible for the French to give assurances to the Associated States of increasing autonomy within the French Union? . . . If the French had offered to the Vietnamese in 1946 the same extent of economic liberty they now profess, is it not possible that the Vietnamese would not now be tempted by the Communist camp?"[11]

Kennedy had expressed private concerns about Vietnam ever since his Far East journey in 1951 had opened his eyes to the deplorable conduct of the French. Only three weeks before his meeting with Diem, Kennedy had asked his staff to investigate whether France was spending less on the economic welfare of Indochina than it had publicly claimed. In a memorandum requesting the report, an aide also noted that Kennedy "suspects the French are still too much in control of the Government and that is one reason for the trouble. And therefore the US should insist on reforms being made there *before* aid is given." Responding to Kennedy's questions, special assistant Priscilla Johnson wrote that it was impossible to determine exactly how much the French were spending on economic aid except to say that the assistance was "small in proportion to its military aid." Regarding French intransigence on reforms, Johnson quoted a State Department official who told her that the United States "certainly should press harder for reform" but had not done so because they feared that it might drive the French to make peace with the Vietminh.[12]

Coincidentally, Mansfield had also found fault with the French in Indochina. In 1949, as a House member, he had offered an amendment to the Marshall Plan aimed directly at France. Mansfield had wanted to deny Marshall Plan assistance to any participating country if it denied "to its citizens or citizens in any dependent area under its jurisdiction, the principles of individual liberty, free institutions and genuine independence." Asked if his amendment was aimed at the French, Mansfield pleaded ignorance about the situation in Southeast Asia, but ventured that "there is a lot the French must answer for in Indochina." He later withdrew the amendment.[13]

The meeting with Diem proved pivotal for Kennedy and Mansfield. For these two men with doubts about France's ability to hold the line against the Vietminh, Diem seemed to be the leader with just the right amount of vision and determination to turn the war around—that is, if he ever got the chance. When Diem finally did get his chance to lead Vietnam the following year, he would have no stronger advocates in Washington than Kennedy and Mansfield.

AT THE SAME HOUR that Mansfield and Kennedy dined with Diem at the Supreme Court, Canadian Prime Minister Louis St. Laurent arrived at the White House for a meeting with President Dwight Eisenhower and Secretary of State John Foster Dulles. When the wide-ranging discussion turned to Indochina, Eisenhower made clear his belief that the French had not adequately demonstrated their desire to grant Indochina's full independence. (It was, in fact, the same argument Diem was simultaneously making to Mansfield and Kennedy.) Absent such a declaration, U.S. officials knew it was unlikely that the Vietnamese people would ever join the French in their war against the Vietminh. The new president maintained "that the only chance of preserving South East Asia lay in making sure of the support of the native peoples." According to official minutes of the meeting, both sides seemed to agree "that time was lacking for gradualism in Indochina and that the French should not take counsel of their fears over the effects elsewhere in their empire of a forthright political declaration with regard to Indochina."[14]

Eisenhower was disturbed by France's stubbornness and the way it affected the country's ability to fight the war. As he knew, the conflict had been a costly and deadly enterprise. Despite a substantial U.S. contribution, France had diverted $3.5 billion of its own funds to the war in Indochina—precious francs that could have been used for the defense of Europe or to rebuild the nation's war-torn economy. France had now deployed over half a million men in Southeast Asia. Of that number, 48,000 had died and another 132,000 had been wounded. In 1952 alone, the French army lost more officers in battle than had graduated that year from St. Cyr, the nation's military academy. Yet despite all of the death and sacrifice and expense, France was no better off than when the war began. In fact, a report on the Indochina war for Dulles in late January had grimly concluded that "no region in the entire French-held territory can be considered secure against Viet Minh raids and large-scale sabotage."[15]

France was handicapped in several ways. After years of waging a frustrating war, its resolve was waning. Only the day before he left office, on January 19, 1953, Acheson testified before the Senate Foreign Relations Committee and painted a dismal picture of sagging French morale. "The French are periodically in great depression about their position in Indochina," Acheson said, adding that "the French like to be encouraged by having everybody say that this is not merely a little French venture all by itself; it is part of a whole struggle against Communist aggression."[16]

Eisenhower had done his best to exhort the French without suggesting that U.S. support was unconditional. In late March, when French officials, including Prime Minister Rene Mayer and Foreign Minister Georges Bidault, arrived in Washington for consultations with American officials, Eisenhower hosted them aboard the presidential yacht, *Williamsburg*. As they cruised leisurely down the Potomac River toward Mount Vernon, the president expressed his interest in "hearing of any French program for the solution of the Indochina question." He emphasized that "we recognize that [the war] is part of the general struggle against Communism and that it is not merely a French colonial effort." Having said that, Eisenhower

tactfully impressed upon Mayer the importance of elucidating his country's intentions in Indochina if they desired greater U.S. financial support.
"Many Americans," Eisenhower told Mayer, "continue to think of the war
in Indo-China as a French colonial operation rather than as part of the
struggle of the free world against the forces of Soviet Communism." In
exchange for additional financial aid, Eisenhower made it clear that he
expected France to keep the United States fully informed about its plans
for the war. Not only did Mayer dodge that request, but Eisenhower
recalled that he failed to offer reassurances about "an out-and-out renun-
ciation of any French colonial purpose."[17]

France's tepid response—and its lack of any plausible military or political plan to resolve the conflict—only caused Washington more anxiety. At
a National Security Council meeting on April 28, General Hoyt Vandenberg, the Air Force chief of staff, informed the president that the Joint
Chiefs believed that absent a "realistic plan" in Indochina, "further U.S.
assistance amounted to pouring money down a rat hole." Vandenberg
wanted Eisenhower to "make clear to the French that unless they formed
larger units of native forces and took the offensive against the enemy, further U.S. aid could not be forthcoming."[18]

Of course, it was not military considerations alone that factored into
Eisenhower's exhortations for a more imaginative military strategy and
greater emphasis on independence for the Vietnamese people. He had
another reason for pushing the French: congressional pressure. In late
March, some leading members of Congress had informed Dulles that they
could not support additional military aid for Indochina unless "the American people could be given reason to believe that the difficulties in Indo-
China will end by the French according Indo-China a real autonomy," as
well as "giving real promise of military and political success."[19]

Despite his anxiety over France's intransigence and the timidity of its
military strategy, Eisenhower believed the French were engaged in a noble
cause—the struggle against international communism as sponsored and
exported by the Soviet Union. He and Dulles had entered office in January firmly persuaded that the conflicts in Korea and Indochina were simply two facets of the same communist offensive in Asia. Indochina was now
the next potential battleground between democracy and communism.
"You have the broader considerations that might follow what you would
call the 'falling domino' principle," he asserted at an April 7 press conference. "You have a row of dominoes set up, you knock over the first one,
and what will happen to the last one is the certainty that it will go over very
quickly." The resulting "disintegration," Eisenhower feared, "would have
the most profound influences."[20]

Although Eisenhower thought the French "were slow to awaken to the
seriousness of the problem of making their intentions plain," he ultimately

concluded that additional aid "should not be delayed."[21] On May 5, he finally swallowed his doubts about French resolve and sent Congress a request for the 1954 Mutual Security Program that, in his words, proposed to provide France and Indochina's Associated States with "substantial additional resources." Later that day, defending the administration's request for $400 million, Dulles painted a disturbing picture of the stakes in Indochina. Testifying before House and Senate committees, the secretary of state claimed that "Communist aggression in Indochina represents one of the most serious present threats to the free world."[22]

Determined as he was to provide additional aid to France, Eisenhower was far from persuaded the money would do any good. Discussing the issue with his National Security Council the following day, Eisenhower insisted that "two, and only two, developments would really save the situation in French Indochina." The first, Eisenhower said, was a definitive statement from the French about independence for Indochina. The second was the need for a strong leader. Unless something could be done to persuade the French to give up their lingering colonial designs on Indochina, Eisenhower insisted that "nothing" could save Indochina. Continued financial assistance, he feared, quoting General Vandenberg, "would amount to pouring our money down a rat hole."[23]

The next day—the same day that Mansfield and Kennedy met Diem for the first time—Eisenhower wrote to the U.S. ambassador in Paris, Douglas Dillon: "An outstanding [French military] leader is needed, empowered with the means and authority to win victory—a man who is at once eminently qualified in training and organization of military forces, and who is at the same time *a forceful and inspirational leader.*"[24] Dillon dutifully communicated Eisenhower's views to French officials, who responded to his prodding by appointing General Henri-Eugene Navarre to lead the French forces in Indochina. Although he was not quite the inspiring personality that Eisenhower had wanted, Navarre did, in the words of Admiral Arthur Radford, exude "a spirit of vigor and determination reminiscent of Marshall de Lattre."[25] Backed by a new French government led by new prime minister Joseph Laniel and France's first promise of real independence for Indochina, Navarre developed an aggressive military strategy that won Washington's grudging approval. Under the Navarre Plan, as it became know, France resolved to take the offensive, especially in northern Vietnam. It promised greater emphasis on guerrilla warfare and the fortification of its military units with increased manpower—two hundred fifty thousand additional French troops. Navarre's strategy also involved greater efforts to organize and train native forces who would be given greater autonomy in military operations.

Eisenhower, Dulles, and the Joint Chiefs supported Navarre's plan because they had no other viable options. They knew that if this latest offensive failed to defeat Ho Chi Minh's forces, public opinion in France would turn strongly against a continuation of the war. France would likely withdraw and leave the United States as the only nation capable of any meaningful intervention to prevent the fall of Indochina to communism. Having just concluded a presidential campaign that had severely faulted Truman and the Democrats for "losing" China and almost losing South Korea, Eisenhower knew that he could ill afford the political consequences if Indochina fell to the Communists on his watch.

The potential for the Navarre Plan's failure raised the question of whether the United States would consider military intervention—sending U.S. troops to Indochina—if France ultimately withdrew from the war. Although a report commissioned by the Joint Chiefs of Staff contended in June that the region was so important to U.S. security that Eisenhower should consider sending American forces to protect it, the chiefs generally opposed the notion. The man most determined to prevent direct U.S. intervention was General Lawton Collins, the Army Chief of Staff who presciently predicted to a gathering of military and State Department officials on July 10 that "if we go into Indochina with American forces, we will be there for the long pull. Militarily and politically we would be in up to our necks . . . we would be in for a major and protracted war."[26]

For now, at least, the best way of closing the door on direct U.S. involvement was to support the Navarre Plan—and pray that it worked. The French, however, could not proceed with the plan without the support of American resources. The resources they requested were substantial. In addition to the $400 million Eisenhower had already requested for the 1954 fiscal year, the president was also considering a recommendation, made by his National Security Council in August, to approve an *additional* $385 million in aid. Appreciating the advantage of continuing to finance France's stand against communism in Southeast Asia, versus the infinitely greater cost to the United States if France withdrew completely, few members of Congress opposed the massive increase. The sentiment Dulles expressed to the National Security Council in September was embraced by most members of Congress: "If we don't spend the money, the French will certainly get out of Indochina promptly, and the whole area will be immediately overrun by the Communists, and neighboring areas as well." In that event, Dulles argued, the United States would be forced into spending far more than $400 million.[27]

Although House approval for the Indochina appropriation came quickly, the Senate's debate over the bill turned on an amendment by freshman Republican Barry Goldwater of Arizona. Offered on July 1, Goldwater's amendment to the Mutual Security Assistance bill would have prohibited expenditures for Indochina unless France gave "satisfactory assurance" of its plans to establish the "complete independence" for the Indochinese states. Despite repeated assurances that it wanted real independence for Indochina, France's statement did not impress Goldwater. "Here today, on the floor of the United States Senate," he said, "we are proposing to support a country, France, that has colonial intentions." To Goldwater, that meant Congress would be spending money to support the continued subjugation of the people of Southeast Asia. Approval of the $400 million expenditure would, in Goldwater's eyes, amount to telling the world "that perhaps we have a right to support countries who wish to enslave other peoples." What worried Goldwater more, however, were the military consequences for the United States if France failed in Indochina. "As surely as day follows night," he said, "our boys will follow this $400 million."

Although Goldwater's amendment failed by a hefty margin in the face of substantial Republican and Democratic opposition, the debate over his amendment was significant for several reasons. It was the first meaningful, full-scale debate in the Senate over Indochina since the fighting had erupted in 1945. In a single afternoon, Republican senators William Knowland of California (the new Senate majority leader), Everett Dirksen of Illinois, and John Sherman Cooper of Kentucky, and Democrats Walter George of Georgia, John F. Kennedy, and Warren Magnuson of Washington all flocked to the Senate floor for a spirited, nonpartisan debate.* In fact, the debate marked one of the few times in recent years that Asian policy had been discussed in the Senate without rancor or partisanship. More important, however, was that senators on both sides of the amendment made clear their desire to keep U.S. forces out of the fighting in Indochina. Like Goldwater, Knowland wished to see France, not the United States, bear the burden for the fighting in Vietnam. He opposed the amendment because he believed that conditions like those spelled out by Goldwater might precipitate France's abrupt departure from Indochina. Knowland, while far more willing than Goldwater to see the United States intervene directly in Asia, undoubtedly gave voice to the anxieties of many colleagues who were torn between their concerns over French conduct in

---

*The debate was full of ironies. Future proponents of American involvement in Vietnam like Goldwater and Dirksen based their arguments on a desire to keep U.S. forces out of the conflict. Kennedy supported Goldwater—perhaps remembering his reaction to France's treatment of the Vietnamese during his 1951 visit— by offering substitute language designed to make Goldwater's amendment more palatable. Minority Leader Lyndon Johnson, who did not speak on the amendment, sided with the Republican leadership in opposing Goldwater, Kennedy, and Dirksen.

Indochina and their desire to do whatever necessary to keep France in the fight.

> It would not be in the best interest of the people we want to help [Know-land said] to have France lay down her burden, and for us, at that point, to take it up. . . . I submit to the distinguished Senator [Goldwater] that if France lays down the burden and we do not pick it up, the people in those states will not be in a position to defend themselves. We might lose all of Southeast Asia, including Malaya, Thailand, and Burma, and per-haps then have the Communist forces under Mao Tse-tung on the very borders of India and Pakistan.

As the senior Democrat on the Foreign Relations Committee, Walter George may have been the most persuasive Democratic voice in the debate. He, too, feared the impact Goldwater's amendment would have on France's willingness to continue the fight. "France may be compelled to withdraw from Indochina," he warned. "Believe me . . . the total with-drawal of France from Indochina at this moment might present us with graver problems than the continuation of the unhappy state and condition that exist in that quarter of the globe at this time."[28]

Attempting to help Goldwater attract more votes by mitigating his tough proposal to "prohibit" U.S. funds in the absence of a firm French plan for Indochina's independence, Kennedy offered a substitute amend-ment. His language merely required that U.S. aid to Indochina—"to the extent that it is feasible"—would be administered to "encourage the free-dom and independence desired" by the Associated States of Vietnam, Cambodia, and Laos. Only the day before, Kennedy had delivered a lengthy speech in the Senate full of strong criticism for France's continued economic and political control over Indochina. "The degree of military, civil, political and economic control maintained by the French," he insisted, "goes well beyond what is necessary to fight a war." A case in point, Kennedy noted, was France's near-complete dominance over the economic affairs of the Associated States:

> The French control over the economic life of the country is extensive, and the possession of property belonging to the French cannot be changed without permission of the French. The French still control the country's basic resources, transportation, and trade. In Viet-Nam, the French con-trol 66 percent of the rice import trade; 100 percent of the rubber prod-ucts for export; practically all export and import businesses; all interna-tional shipping and the principal coastal shipping. In the field of foreign commerce, it is estimated that the French control is nearly 100 percent.

Like Eisenhower and others, Kennedy believed France's greatest mistake was its unwillingness to address the "large numbers of the people of Vietnam" whose "sullen neutrality and open hostility" to French control kept them from joining the fight against the Communists. "This can never be done," he said, "unless they are assured beyond doubt that complete independence will be theirs at the conclusion of the war."[29] The next day, in offering his amendment to the Goldwater proposal, Kennedy again focused on France's failure to rally the indigenous population. "In fact," he said, "the majority of the population appears to be in sympathy with the Communist movement of Ho Chi Minh." Like Knowland, George, and others, Kennedy was gravely concerned that Goldwater's "ultimatum" might be "regarded by the French as an adequate excuse for withdrawing their effort." Despite the moderate nature of Kennedy's amendment, which Goldwater accepted as a substitute for his own, the Republican and Democratic leadership lined up against him—and brought most of the Senate with them. The Senate killed the amendment, 64–17.[30] While the debate revealed strong sentiment in the Senate against the conduct of France in Indochina, few members were willing to risk taking action that might precipitate a sudden French withdrawal. As the fighting continued on the Korean peninsula few, if any, public officials were eager to see the United States engaged in yet another war in Asia.

To most in Congress and many officials in Eisenhower's administration, there appeared little else to do. As the State Department reported in August to the National Security Council, the new government of Prime Minister Joseph Laniel "is almost certainly the *last* French government which would undertake to continue the war in Indo-China." Failure meant that a successor government would "almost certainly . . . seek a settlement on terms dangerous to the security of the U.S. and the Free World." Any negotiated settlement between France and Ho Chi Minh "would mean the eventual loss to Communism not only of Indo-China but of the whole of Southeast Asia." Ominously, the State Department report concluded that "if the French actually decided to withdraw, the U.S. would have to consider most seriously whether to take over in this area."[31]

In September, with the fate of the Navarre Plan hanging in the balance, Eisenhower approved the National Security Council's recommendation for an additional commitment of $385 million. Added to the $400 million Congress had approved earlier, this meant that the United States would be spending $785 million in Indochina in just one year. With Congress out of session for the remainder of the year, a congressional vote on spending the additional amount would be out the question until early 1954—possibly too late to help the French. The money would, instead, come out of the budgets of existing foreign aid programs. Sensing, however, that Congress might balk if the additional funding commitment were presented as a *fait accompli*, Eisenhower directed the State Department to consult leading members of Congress prior to an announcement of the decision.

In mid-September, Thruston Morton, the assistant secretary of state for congressional relations, consulted two leading members of the Senate—Democrats Walter George and Richard Russell of Georgia.* When Morton arrived at George's farm in Vienna, Georgia, where the elderly senator was busy harvesting his peanut crop, he found a compliant and willing supporter of the administration's decision. Morton recalled that as the two men sat on George's front porch and chatted, "George just accepted it and never asked a question." As the ranking Democrat on the Foreign Relations Committee, George was widely respected for his bipartisanship in foreign affairs and was known to be a loyal supporter of U.S. aid to Indochina. His strong support was expected.

In Atlanta, however, where Morton caught up with Russell, the questioning was far tougher. As the former chairman and now senior Democrat on the Armed Services Committee, Russell was far more skeptical of the administration's escalating support for the French. He told Morton that he believed "the French had out-traded us and that they could probably carry more of the burden if forced to." He would support Eisenhower, but with serious reservations. "You are pouring it [the money] down a rat hole, the worst mess we ever got into, this Vietnam," he complained to Morton, echoing the phrase first employed by General Vandenberg and later by Eisenhower. "The president has decided it. I'm not going to say a word of criticism. I'll keep my mouth shut, but I'll tell you right now we are in for something that is going to be one of the worst things this country ever got into."[32] (More than ten years later, Russell would repeat essentially the same advice to his close friend and former Senate colleague, President Lyndon Johnson. Then, as in 1953, Russell would suppress his deep misgivings about American involvement in Vietnam out of loyalty to the president.) On September 29, with Russell's tacit support, the United States announced that it would make available an additional $385 million "for the intensified prosecution of the war against the Viet Minh."[33]

Like Russell, few in Washington wanted to see the United State's become bogged down in another Asian war. Yet the end of the Korean War (an armistice agreement was signed in July 1953) raised the risk of this for the United States by freeing up China to devote to Indochina the military supplies and ammunition it had once used exclusively in the Korean conflict. While Eisenhower was generally opposed to the idea of putting

---

*Morton, a former Republican House member from Kentucky, would later serve in the Senate and emerge as a vocal opponent of U.S. policy in Vietnam.

American troops in Indochina, he and Dulles did not want to encourage direct Chinese intervention in the conflict by demonstrating a lack of American resolve.

Dulles, in a speech to an American Legion convention in St. Louis on September 2, drew a threatening line in the sand over Indochina: "There is the risk that, as in Korea, Red China might send its own army into Indochina. The Chinese Communist regime should realize that such a second aggression could not occur without grave consequences which might not be confined to Indochina."[34] While it would soon be apparent that Dulles' bellicose speech was part of his strategy of speaking loudly while carrying a small stick, the speech also opened a window into the administration's attitudes toward the conflict. Dulles demonstrated that he and Eisenhower, like Truman and Acheson before them, were still burdened with a narrow, ideological view of the Indochina war that left little room for acknowledgment of the intense nationalistic passions that had sparked and continued to fuel Ho Chi Minh's struggle—and that continued to foster an intense hatred of the French that hindered the war against the Communists. To Eisenhower, the Korean and Indochina conflicts were only two fronts in the same war of Soviet-Chinese communist aggression. China, not Ho Chi Minh, was the real enemy. But, as the French journalist and historian Bernard Fall observed, Dulles' thinly veiled threats of U.S. intervention were of little consequence:

> The Eisenhower Administration was about to reap, in Indochina, the bitter fruits of its foreign-policy promises during the 1952 electoral campaign. Having branded the Democrats a "war party" and made the slogan "Peace in Korea" its major foreign-policy drawing card (along with such other phrases as "rolling back the Iron Curtain," and "unleashing Chiang Kai-shek"), it had virtually ruled out even the threat of force—much less the use of force itself. Thus, the President and the Secretary of State were compelled to walk a diplomatic tightrope; Dulles continued to sell a "hard" policy to America's allies abroad, while the President at the very same moment faced the delicate task of explaining those statements to Congress and to an anxious American public without openly contradicting Dulles.[35]

Indeed, for all their campaign talk about reordering America's approach to communism in Europe and Asia, in their first year in office Eisenhower and Dulles had not substantially changed the face of U.S. foreign policy. Despite the Republican Party's 1952 campaign pledge to discard the "negative, futile and immoral policy of containment" in favor of a more active "liberation" strategy for the "captive peoples," Eisenhower was actually quite content to pursue Truman's successful policies.[36] In

Korea, for example, he settled for a truce agreement that restored the pre-war status quo. Unlike many of the conservatives he had wooed during the election, the new president did not insist on a reunification of the two nations under democratic rule. In fact, the Korean armistice as approved by Eisenhower and Dulles was an acceptance of the policy that Truman and Acheson had pursued and for which they had been so thoroughly vilified by the members of the Republican Party, including Eisenhower himself.

Instead of the promised end to Truman's containment policy, Eisenhower actually sought to make it even more effective. This he would accomplish through significant changes at the Defense Department, including a wholesale change in the membership of the Joint Chiefs of Staff. In the summer of 1953, at the urging of congressional Republicans who viewed Joint Chiefs chairman General Omar Bradley as having been overly sympathetic to the Truman–Acheson policies, Eisenhower appointed a new chairman, as well as new chiefs for the Army, Navy, and Air Force. The most significant appointment was that of Admiral Arthur Radford, who replaced Bradley as chairman. A highly respected naval officer who had served as commander in chief in the Pacific since 1949, Radford was regarded as something of an Asian expert who shared conservative Republican views about China and believed that Indochina was vital to America's security interests.

With his new chiefs in place, Eisenhower set about redefining the nation's military objectives. When adopted in late October, the administration's "New Look" policy—spelled out in a top-secret report by the National Security Council—sought to bolster the effectiveness of the U.S. military's response to communism while simultaneously reducing its cost. In a dramatic speech to the Council on Foreign Policy in January 1954, Dulles would explain that the administration now envisioned a more effective and economical system of mutual security that placed "more reliance on deterrent power, and less dependence on local defensive power." That meant that the United States would no longer base its expensive containment policy on military forces spread throughout the globe, but would, instead, withdraw much of its foreign ground forces in favor of "massive retaliatory power." In other words, the nation would now rely on the threat of nuclear retaliation to prevent communist aggression. Dulles, in fact, broadly hinted that even in localized military situations the United States would consider the use of nuclear weapons.

The massive retaliation policy articulated by Dulles was only one part of a policy that also relied on increased dependence on collective security—that is, mutual defense agreements with other nations, more training and equipping of indigenous troops, and a greater dependence on the Air Force and Navy to support the armies of those nations. Dulles explained that his announcement that the United States now considered nuclear weapons a legitimate part of its anticommunist arsenal was issued so that a "potential aggressor" would have a "crystal clear" understanding of the response it could expect from the United States. The speech, however, was far too ambiguous to have any great effect. Dulles failed to clearly state when and where the United States would regard its interests so threatened as to justify a nuclear response.

The public reacted to the new policy—or, more accurately, Dulles' bellicose explanation of it—with fear and confusion. As Dulles' biographer Townsend Hoopes observed, "the press and the public read it either as the serious intent of the U.S. government to transform every border incident into a nuclear showdown, or else as a glaringly transparent bluff that would (by proving wholly inapplicable to the task of guiding revolutionary change in the fringe areas) serve to weaken the credibility of American policy everywhere."[37]

Dulles' ham-handed presentation notwithstanding, the "New Look" was Eisenhower's first radical departure from the Truman–Acheson defense policy. Driven by a desire for economy as much as by strategic military concerns, it ushered the United States into a new era of greater dependence on its nuclear arsenal. With expenditures for conventional forces reduced (in one year, the overall defense budget declined from $42 billion to $34.5 billion), the Eisenhower administration forced the country to rely almost exclusively on the threat of nuclear attack to deter communist aggression.

Indochina would be the first place Eisenhower and Dulles would put their "New Look" policy to the test. In time, however—in only a few months, in fact—the strict and debilitating limitations it placed on the use of military force would become painfully apparent.

CHAPTER 9

You Shall Not Fight Unaided

1953

"THE WORLD'S ONE REMAINING WAR," U.S. NEWS & WORLD
Report told its war-weary readers in September 1953, just two months after
the Korean armistice, "is flaring into action again in the jungles and rice
plains of Indochina." Framing the conflict as a clash between American-
style democracy and Chinese-backed communism, the magazine noted
that "anyone in Saigon can see proof that the U.S. is deeply involved in
Indochina's war."[1] The increased American role was, by all appearances,
having the desired effect. That same month, *Time* described a "new spirit
and optimism" among the soldiers "who must fight the ugly war" in
Indochina and attributed it partly to the American decision to "plunge
fresh resources into the war"—$785 million in 1953 alone.[2]

Despite all this heightened activity, most Americans still viewed the
region as an isolated and murky outpost in the lush valleys and dense
mountain jungles of Southeast Asia. While many knew that American-
backed French troops were engaged in an armed struggle somewhere in
Southeast Asia—newspapers and periodicals routinely reported news
of the war—most Americans paid only scant attention to Indochina.
Nonetheless, Eisenhower and Dulles regularly warned the public that the
war's outcome would profoundly impact U.S. security, although most
Americans, including many members of Congress, could not have articulated exactly how the downfall of a remote region like Indochina would
directly and adversely affect the United States. Even though they had
voted over the years for more than $1 billion to aid the French in the mil-
itary struggle against Ho Chi Minh, most House and Senate members
remained blissfully ignorant about Indochina and its war. Europe was far
more familiar territory and was viewed by most members of Congress as
more significant. That accounted for the $2.1 billion in defense aid Con-
gress appropriated for Europe in 1953 alone, compared to half that amount

for all of Asia and the Pacific. Dulles had signaled the beginning of a "shift in emphasis" toward Southeast Asia and Formosa, and yet Indochina remained only one of the fifty-six nations the United States had supported with foreign aid funds since 1945.[3]

For years, congressional trips to that part of the world had usually skipped Vietnam, Cambodia, and Laos in favor of more alluring places like India, Thailand, and Japan. Prior to 1953, members of Congress had ignored the region. The war, after all, was France's to fight. America was simply footing most of the bill. Few American lives were at risk in Indochina. Furthermore, with the Korean War essentially over, the nation's attention had turned again to the more serious threat posed in Europe by the Soviet Union. To most, Indochina was a secondary and far less significant battleground.

But as the costs of the conflict rose, congressional leaders began to pay more attention. By 1953, congressional trips to Indochina by U.S. government officials were on the rise. In fact, the fall of that year saw visits from nine members of Congress, as well as Vice President Nixon. In early September, Senate majority leader William Knowland of California stopped in Indochina during a lengthy Far East trip that included Japan, Korea, Formosa, Thailand, Burma, India, and Pakistan. It was Knowland's first visit to Indochina and the briefings he received from American and French officials only reinforced his narrow view of the conflict as a classic struggle between democracy and communism. Judging from his simplistic public comments to reporters afterwards, if Knowland had gained anything more than superficial insight into the conflict, he did not admit it. Careful not to offend his French hosts, the Republican leader declared that "the age of colonialism . . . is dead" and, despite substantial evidence to the contrary, he spoke about a "free" and "independent" Vietnam.[4]

On the heels of Knowland's largely uneventful visit arrived a visitor who, in time, would prove far more thoughtful and influential on U.S. policy toward Indochina. Mike Mansfield's first trip to Indochina in late September would be the first of many visits he would make to the region in the decades to come. In a short time, in fact, he would be the most influential voice in Congress on Southeast Asia and Eisenhower's most important ally in the administration's effort to deepen U.S. involvement in the region.

Although he had taught college courses in Asian history in Montana, Mansfield was not an expert on Indochina. Earlier that summer, when he phoned Francis Valeo, an Asian expert with the Legislative Reference Service of the Library of Congress, Mansfield had confessed his ignorance about the region and invited Valeo to accompany him on his trip, which he was making under the auspices of the Senate Foreign Relations Committee.

Even Valeo knew little of the region, having concentrated primarily on Korea and China.

Mansfield and Valeo flew first to Paris for talks with French officials and then to Saigon. They arrived the afternoon of September 21 and spent the rest of the day in meetings with the Vietnamese prime minister, the French high commissioner, and U.S. Ambassador Donald Heath. The next day, Mansfield met first with U.S. military officials and then with Navarre. It was Navarre, the small, shy soldier whose optimism and steely determination ("We will not let go of one inch of terrain"), who had reinvigorated the French forces and raised Washington's hopes that France was finally on the verge of gaining the upper hand in the struggle.[5]

Mansfield and Valeo did not know it at the time, but they were soon to be among the first American officials to learn of a military plan that would prove to be a tragic turning point in the war. Speaking in English, the French general briefed them on plans to break the back of the communist forces by setting a trap. It was at their outpost at Dien Bien Phu, located in a remote river valley in northwestern Vietnam near the Laotian border, that the French would make their stand, hoping to lure the Vietminh out of the surrounding hills. Once they emerged from hiding, the Communists would be destroyed, Navarre said. The poorly equipped Vietminh, he explained, could never install artillery pieces in the steep hills surrounding the French garrison. Navarre assured Mansfield that he was "quite confident this strategy is going to work" and added that his superior fighting force would finally defeat the Vietminh at Dien Bien Phu. Asked by Mansfield what more he needed from the United States, Navarre—who expressed his gratitude for the generous American aid already bestowed upon France—asked only for additional helicopters.

The trip, in Valeo's words, "was an eye-opener for Mansfield."[6] Unlike Kennedy in 1951, Mansfield learned about the conflict in Indochina almost entirely from official briefings. Like Knowland, he returned home even more persuaded of Indochina's importance to world peace. "The security of the United States and of other free nations is no less involved in Indochina than in Korea," he wrote in his report to the Foreign Relations Committee. Among the first members of Congress to spell out the nature of the U.S. stake in Indochina specifically, Mansfield observed that "Indochina is the key to control of southeast Asia, rich in the raw materials of war. . . . To deny these sinews of power to the Communists is to limit their capacity to engage in further aggressive adventures."

Like many U.S. officials, Mansfield was now enamored of Navarre and his bold military strategy. A decorated World War II intelligence officer who had fought in the French underground, Navarre had predicted the exact strategy of the German army against France in 1939. Still widely respected as an astute warrior with extensive experience in underground military tactics, Navarre and the audacious plan he had for Dien Bien Phu captured Mansfield's imagination. "There are indications," he wrote in his report to Congress, "that the stalemate in Indochina may be coming to an end. The months ahead could witness the beginning of a series of significant military engagements." Navarre, he said, was bringing an end to the "defensive mentality" that had crippled the French since the death of General de Lattre in early 1952. Based partly on Navarre's confident portrayal of what would prove to be a deeply flawed military plan, Mansfield argued for more American aid to Indochina, which he believed "has provided the margin of material assistance necessary for continuing resistance to the Communist advance." His only concern appeared to be that some U.S. aid was being poorly administered, resulting in "unduly wasteful" spending. As much as Mansfield supported Navarre and his push for a decisive showdown in the war, he was certain that his support for continued American assistance would not include the commitment of U.S. combat forces in Indochina. "Sacrifices for the defense of freedom must be equitably shared," he wrote, "and we have borne our full burden in blood in Korea."

Mansfield appeared to accept France's characterization of the war, writing in his report that the French were "trying to halt Communism in an area where nationalism is giving a new birth of freedom to peoples who have not known it for a long time." Yet he was perceptive enough to recognize Ho Chi Minh's popular appeal. Mansfield took note of the "current of nationalism [that] runs strong throughout Indochina" and acknowledged that much of Ho's appeal was derived from "a desire for independence from foreign control that is deep-seated and widespread." Ho, he astutely observed, "has been publicized not as an exponent of Communism but as the figurehead of anti-colonial, anti-western nationalism." Perhaps remembering the political headaches he had endured in 1950 for once describing the Chinese Communists as "more reformers than revolutionaries," Mansfield carefully avoided characterizing Ho as a true nationalist. His strategy, Mansfield charged, was merely "a form of misdirected nationalism" aimed at winning the support of non-Communists.

Mansfield's report would give Eisenhower and Dulles plenty of bipartisan ammunition for their effort to sustain and increase a program of military assistance to the French. To support the French was to support a winning cause, Mansfield concluded. "The military prospects of the non-Communist forces in Indochina are improving," he declared.[7] Mansfield's enlistment in the effort to assist the French in Vietnam had a considerable impact in Congress and at the White House. As a Democrat, his support for Eisenhower's policies in Southeast Asia would guarantee them bipartisan support. Because of the respect he was gaining among his Senate colleagues for his understanding of the political climate throughout Asia, Mansfield's views on Indochina could not be easily ignored. If someone as steady, studious, and thoughtful as Mike Mansfield supported American assistance to the French in Vietnam—a murky and confusing issue for most—then few senators would be inclined to refute him. Most important of all was the image that he was successfully cultivating as the senator most knowledgeable about Asia.

As important as Mansfield's trip was, the visit of yet another U.S. official to the region in October 1953 played an even greater role in cementing the nation's long-term commitment to the region. Dispatched by Eisenhower on a ten-week, nineteen-nation tour of Asia and the Far East, Vice President Nixon and his wife, Pat, departed Washington on October 5. The tour, Nixon's first official foreign excursion as vice president, would give the young politician—at age 40—an opportunity to demonstrate his diplomatic skills. Admittedly, the maiden voyage of a new vice president was no monumental world event. With a small staff, two Secret Service agents, and only three reporters in the traveling party, Nixon's trip would not be a major news story in the United States.

Years later, Nixon would say that his mission had three major goals: to "explain American policies" to those countries with a neutral posture in the Cold War, to "assess Asian attitudes" toward Communist China, and to gain "a firsthand look at the rapidly developing situation in Indochina."[8] At the time, however, Nixon's enthusiasm for orchestrating press coverage and arranging media events during the trip suggested that the domestic impact of the trip—that is, how his foreign travels would influence his public image—was foremost in his mind. Like John F. Kennedy before him, Nixon understood that a successful foreign trip could burnish one's domestic standing. Nixon also knew that favorable press coverage and positive reports from U.S. embassy officials would help transform his image from that of an aggressive partisan into a statesman capable of comporting himself with poise on the world stage.[9]

For six "fascinating and frustrating" days, as he would write in 1978, Nixon toured the three nations of Indochina. After two days of meetings with Cambodian officials, he and Pat arrived in Saigon on October 31, hoping to meet with Bao Dai, the reclusive leader who rarely emerged from the refuge of his luxurious mountaintop villa in Dalat. The former emperor received Nixon and Ambassador Heath for an hour on November 1.

Eager to achieve what others had failed to gain, Nixon prodded the Vietnamese leader to work harder to generate more public participation in the struggle against the Vietminh. But the discussion proved unfruitful. As Heath later reported in a cable to the State Department, "Bao Dai steadfastly refused to meet the Vice President's questions as to the possibility of greater personal activity on his part in assuming the functions of Commander-in-Chief of the Vietnamese Armed Forces." Instead, he insisted that he was already commander in chief, "but wound deviously around the point of whether or not he should get into a uniform and stand in front of his soldiers."[10]

Although he was, in part, France's puppet, Bao Dai was growing increasingly impatient with the French. To Nixon, he revealed that this was at least part of the reason why he had not done more to motivate his army or his people. Like most Vietnamese, the former emperor seemed to view the war as a struggle between the French and the Vietminh. Only two weeks earlier, Bao Dai's National Congress—voicing its frustration with France's refusal to grant independence to Vietnam—had voted against membership in the French Union, an association of France and its overseas territories and states. The union, the Vietnamese Congress had declared, was "quite contrary to sovereignty of an independent nation." Vietnam's decision caused great consternation among officials in Washington and Paris. But Bao Dai seemed not to care. Speaking with Nixon, he forcefully declared his belief that the French had failed to fulfill their promises about independence.

Although he was concerned about Bao Dai's increasing alienation from the French, Nixon was encouraged by his determination to resist negotiations with the Communists. "There is no point in trying to negotiate with them," he told Nixon. "At the least we would end up with a conference which would divide my country between us and them. And if Vietnam is divided, we will eventually lose it all."* That evening, at a dinner hosted by Bao Dai, Nixon papered over his differences with the former emperor. "The verdict of history," Nixon said in a toast, "will be that Your Majesty and your government are following the right course for all those who desire complete independence and a free Vietnam."[11]

After a brief visit to Laos for discussions with Prince Souvanna Phouma, Nixon arrived in the northern, cosmopolitan city of Hanoi on November 3.[12] At a dinner given in his honor by the governor of North Vietnam, Nguyen Huu Tri, Nixon pledged America's continued support for those Vietnamese fighting communism and praised the anticommunist nature of the struggle. "The hopes and vital interests of all the nations of the free world are focused here, as they are focused in Korea and in those European nations lying just outside the zone of Communist darkness," Nixon said. "We know that you are determined to resist aggression, even

---

*Bao Dai's were prescient words. Less than a year later, after negotiations with the Vietminh were completed, his country was divided at an international conference in Geneva.

as we are determined to resist it. And we are resolved, as our past actions have proved, that you shall not fight unaided."[13]

The next night, after a visit with French and Vietnamese troops, Nixon attended a dinner hosted by the ranking French official in Vietnam, Commissioner General Maurice Dejean. The vice president spoke optimistically—if not sincerely—about the struggle in Vietnam. "I believe that the turning point has been reached in the fight of the forces of freedom against the forces of totalitarianism which is centered in Vietnam," he said. "The tide of aggression has reached its peak and has finally begun to recede. The foundation for decisive victory has been laid." Although he had observed the apathy of the Vietnamese and the French contempt for them, Nixon hewed faithfully to administration policy. He insisted that "the people have learned that the true friends of Vietnam are not the Communists, but they are their own leaders and the leaders of the French Union forces, both of whom strive for freedom."[14]

Yet Nixon's words certainly did not reflect his personal views on Indochina. Years later in his memoirs, he acknowledged that he was convinced that the French were failing "primarily because they had not sufficiently trained, much less inspired, the Indochinese people to be able to defend themselves. They had failed to build a cause—or a cadre—that could resist the nationalist and anti-colonialist appeals of the Communists." Nixon recognized the "deplorable conditions" that existed for the Vietnamese under French rule. They lacked leadership and inspiration, he observed. "Most important," he said, "they did not have a battle cry, a *merdeka*, to make the difference between having to fight and wanting to fight."

Despite his deep misgivings about the progress of the war, Nixon reached the same conclusion as Mansfield, Kennedy, Knowland, and virtually every other policymaker who contemplated Indochina's problems: if the French evacuated Indochina, the whole region "would fall like husks before the fury of the communist hurricane." He concluded that the United States "would have to do everything possible to find a way to keep the French in Vietnam until the Communists had been defeated."[15]

On December 23, after his return to the United States, Nixon sat down with members of the National Security Council—including Eisenhower and Dulles—to share his observations about Indochina. While he encouraged NSC members to talk "optimistically" about Indochina because "we have put good money in, and we must stick by it," he acknowledged the "pessimistic side" of the situation. First of all, he recognized that the Communists possessed a "sense of history" and that meant that "time is on their side." Without China's support, Nixon believed that Ho Chi Minh's army would collapse in three months. But he cautioned that "a present military defeat of the Communists does not mean that the problem cannot again be stirred up by the Chinese." Besides the inadequate training of Vietnamese natives, Nixon deplored Bao Dai's anemic leadership. "We have no real leaders in Vietnam," he said. On balance, however, Nixon advised continued U.S. support for the French. "I am convinced in my own mind," he said, "that what happens in Indochina is more important, from the standpoint of strategic interests of Europe, than what happens in Korea."

For the immediate future, Nixon was most concerned about the impact of growing domestic opposition to the war in France. In late October, Prime Minister Joseph Laniel had announced his willingness to negotiate with Ho Chi Minh for an end to the conflict. Like Eisenhower, and Truman before him, Nixon knew that if France bowed out of the war, the United States would be forced to assume even greater responsibility for fighting communism in the region. With the nation barely out of the mire of the Korean War, no one was eager to see the nation bogged down in another Asian conflict. "If there is negotiation now, the only thing that will result," Nixon predicted to NSC members, "is Communist domination. If the French get out, the only capable leadership at the present time in Vietnam is Communist leadership."[16]

That evening Nixon delivered a far more optimistic report to the American people. In a nationwide radio and television address Nixon explained that the war was not an isolated outcropping of communist aggression. At its root, he said, was "the problem of China." Completely ignoring the misery and unrest wrought by decades of corrupt French rule, Nixon parroted the Republican Party line when he asserted that "China is the basic cause of all of our troubles in Asia. If China had not gone Communist, we would not have had a war in Korea. If China were not Communist, there would be no war in Indochina, there would be no war in Malaya." Without mentioning the Truman administration's "failures" in Asia, Nixon made it clear that he believed Eisenhower had ushered in a new approach to communism. "We should recognize that the time is past when we should try to reach agreement with the Communists at the conference table by surrendering to them," he said. "We are paying the price in Asia for that kind of diplomacy right now."[17]

While Nixon hoped to present an image of a new and forceful Republican approach to communism, the truth was that the nation's policy had changed little. His strong words rang hollow in the face of the historical record. Despite Nixon and Dulles' bold rhetoric, almost no one in the administration or Congress supported an American combat role in Vietnam. With or without France, the nation would continue to pay someone else to wage a struggle against communism in Vietnam—a struggle that Nixon and others claimed was so important that it might determine the future of Southeast Asia and, by extension, that of the United States.

Meanwhile, Dulles' bellicose New Look policy, which emphasized American nuclear deterrence to communist aggression, effectively limited the nation's military options in places like Indochina. Henceforth, in cases of aggression, the United States would either bring the world to the brink of nuclear war or risk being known as a paper tiger. While he obliquely blamed the Truman administration for the current situation with an unspecified charge of "surrendering" to communism through negotiation, Nixon conveniently ignored Eisenhower's role in ratifying the recently concluded Korean armistice—a clear case of negotiation with the communist leaders of North Korea.

Beneath its tougher exterior, America's approach to the world had barely changed under Eisenhower. Truman's containment policy lived on, although cloaked in more strident rhetoric and more budget-conscious clothing. Mansfield and Nixon, their firsthand experience in Indochina notwithstanding, had also changed little. Their simple, black-and-white outlook on the world was not unlike that of most American leaders in the early years of the Cold War. On one side was the West, led by the United States, standing gallantly for liberty and freedom and everything good, decent, and humane. On the other side was the Soviet Union, an evil empire that sought, through clients like Communist China, to control the world. "If there was a certain arrogance discernible in American leaders," Cold War historian Thomas J. McCormick observed, "it was an arrogance of righteousness as well as of power."[18] After leading the world out of a World War and now the Korean War, American leaders rarely, if ever, considered that their actions, not to mention their motives, might be subject to question.

Despite an intellectual acknowledgment of the nationalistic passions that burned in Indochina, the bright light of communism blinded Nixon, Mansfield, and other American leaders and prevented the kind of nuanced view of the conflict that might have fostered a more rational and humane approach to U.S. policy in the region. When they examined Indochina, these leaders saw not a legitimate nationalistic, anticolonialist crusade led by people who had found outside support from no one but the Communists; rather, they saw an evil international communist conspiracy directed from Moscow and Peking that cleverly camouflaged its communist ideology with nationalism and anticolonialism. In order to buttress the French in this fight—that they also believed would determine the fate of Southeast Asia—men like Mansfield and Nixon would reluctantly indulge France's colonialist intentions.

American leaders were also tolerant of French excesses in Indochina because they were eager to see that country's beleaguered army prevail, and then return to the task of restoring the balance of power in Western Europe. No less important to some was the impact that war might have on Japan's emerging industrial economy if Vietnam—rich in raw materials like coal, tin, gold, iron ore, and rubber—fell into the communist orbit. Yet, determined as they were to support France for these and other reasons, leaders like Mansfield and Nixon were also at a loss about what to do if and when the French lost or defected. Neither Eisenhower, Nixon, nor Mansfield bothered to explain why, if this region was so vital to world security, the United States would not send troops there to restore peace and establish democracy if France proved unequal to the task. The answer, of course, was domestic American politics. With the Korean War barely over, no one wanted U.S. troops embroiled in another Asian conflict—especially at a time when Eisenhower was looking to cut the nation's defense budget. While it footed much of France's bill for the war, the simple fact was the U.S. government was unprepared to fight for what it officially considered the future of Southeast Asia. This suggests that, to some extent, American leaders, particularly Eisenhower and Nixon, may not have believed everything they said about Indochina's transcendent importance.

Nonetheless, visiting the region in 1953 had afforded Mansfield and Nixon their first experiences with the conflict that would come to dominate the later parts of their political careers. Despite evidence to the contrary, each man returned from the region publicly confident that France could prevail. Each was more determined than ever to support continued U.S. assistance to the French. Privately, however, both doubted the French would ever enact the fundamental reforms necessary to entice more Vietnamese to join the fight. While neither Nixon nor Mansfield was blind to the anticolonialist passions sweeping the region, they did seem blissfully unaware that their nation was increasingly viewed as a defender, not of democracy and freedom, but of the French colonial empire. Worse, neither man seemed to appreciate fully the nature of France's desperate situation in Indochina—and just how soon the entire problem would fall into America's lap.

CHAPTER 10

La Guerre Sale

1954

P RESIDENT EISENHOWER MIGHT HAVE BEEN UNCERTAIN ABOUT how the United States would respond to a French withdrawal from Indochina, but one thing was sure: American troops would not replace them. "No one could be more bitterly opposed to ever getting the United States involved in a hot war in that region than I am," the president told reporters at a press conference on February 10.[1] That was not exactly what Under Secretary of State Walter Bedell Smith had wanted to hear. Although he did not favor sending United States troops to Indochina, Smith worried that Eisenhower's unequivocal statement had denied the administration a potent psychological weapon in the war against the Vietminh. "I wish to God we could leave that suspicion or fear in their minds," Smith sheepishly confessed to members of the Senate Foreign Relations Committee on February 16, in a closed-door session, explaining that Eisenhower had removed American troops from the equation to calm public fears.

But the question of American troops was not the only issue over which Smith differed with his administration. Contradicting Vice President Nixon's recent argument on behalf of the domino theory in Southeast Asia, Smith told the committee that Indochina's partial loss would be "dangerous," but not necessarily catastrophic. "I think that, even at the worst, part of Indochina might be lost without losing the rest of Southeast Asia."

As for what the United States would do if Indochina were "lost" to the Communists, Smith stopped short of an unequivocal statement that Eisenhower would not send American troops to Indochina. "Nothing would be done without bringing the problem to the Congress and getting its decision," he said. "We would not go into any all-out war anywhere." Perhaps more reassuring than Smith's noncommittal statements about troops was

Joint Chiefs Chairman Arthur Radford's disingenuous argument that the French would never request American reinforcements because "they feel perfectly competent in handling the situation with their own troops."[2]*

Despite any discomfort over the absence of a clearly articulated policy toward Indochina, most committee members would refrain from public criticism of Eisenhower, although several expressed concerns behind closed doors. Democrat Guy Gillette of Iowa pressed Smith to explain "under what concept are we in Indochina." He was not satisfied when Smith answered that, essentially, the United States was helping France liberate Vietnam. Likewise, Hubert Humphrey complained to Dulles at a hearing the following week that "it is patently obvious that we just do not have any plan." When Humphrey asked what the United States would do if the French abandoned Indochina, Dulles said only that the administration still had faith in the Navarre Plan. "I feel," Dulles said, "that the program upon which we are now embarked will probably hold the situation in Indochina."[3]

Despite the smattering of discord at the February 16 hearing, no one suggested an alternative course. "I want to say," Mansfield told Radford, "that I am very glad that this Government is spending $1,200 million this year in Indochina, and as far as I am concerned, I will vote for another billion or more next year." That said, Mansfield spoke for many on the committee when he urged administration officials to be more forthcoming about Indochina. "I hope that you folks will see to it," he told Smith and Radford, "that the proper committees of Congress are informed before any large developments are undertaken, because if you do not, then I think you are just asking for a lot of trouble."[4]

The "situation in Indochina," as Dulles described it to the Foreign Relations Committee on February 24, was a very precarious one. After more than six years of fighting, at a cost of about $10 billion and thousands of lost lives, domestic French support for the nation's foreign adventure had all but collapsed. As Bernard Fall later noted, France's military leaders seemed to have forgotten why they were fighting—if indeed they ever really knew. For some, the struggle was to hold a marginally independent Indochina within the French Union. Others fought because they had finally come to believe what their leaders had told Washington for years: they were standing up to an international communist threat that menaced all of Southeast Asia.[5]

Whatever the purpose of the war, the French people were fed up. The

---

*While Radford's statement may have comforted some who feared that U.S. troops might be drawn into the conflict, Radford himself would attempt to persuade the French to request the involvement of U.S. troops a mere six weeks later.

endless struggle had become their *la guerre sale* (the dirty war). By 1954, what forces Navarre had were getting weaker and smaller. Since 1950, a succession of French governments had placed increasingly stricter limitations on the number of French troops dispatched to Indochina. Draftees were barred from the region. Reinforcements for the dead and wounded were pitifully inadequate. All the while, the Vietminh grew stronger and more determined as supplies and equipment from Communist China began pouring across the border following the Korean armistice in July 1953.

Even before its inauguration, the much-touted Navarre Plan was in shambles. Escalating Vietminh activity in the southern Mekong Delta, as well as successful invasions of southern and central Laos, had foiled French plans for a decisive offensive against the Vietminh in the fall of 1953. Now, with Vietminh forces pressing toward northern Laos, Navarre put into action his plan to staunch the enemy supply lines into northern Laos at Dien Bien Phu. Success at Dien Bien Phu, the French believed, would invigorate their war on both military and diplomatic fronts. Navarre not only hoped to inflict heavy casualties on the Vietminh army, his superiors hoped that by slowing the enemy they could increase France's bargaining position at the expected international conference at Geneva.*

There was no question about Dien Bien Phu's importance. *Time* described it as "one of the most important places in the world" and suggested the outcome of the impending battle there "could decide the fate of all Southeast Asia."[6] From the beginning, however, the French effort was doomed. Situated in a wide river valley, Navarre's garrison would be a sitting duck for the heavily armed Vietminh who occupied the surrounding high hills. With no decent roads to supply the outpost, the French built an airstrip and began flying in supplies and men. Within a matter of weeks, they had completed a strong fortification of barbed wire and bunkers, manned with ten French battalions. Thus began their wait for the emergence of tens of thousands of Vietminh guerrillas perched in the nearby hills.

The entire enterprise spoke to the hubris of Navarre and his commanders. Almost any first-year military school student would have questioned the wisdom of occupying the low ground in a valley with no overland escape route. Compounding the strategic error was Navarre's miscalculation about the ability and determination of the Vietminh, led by General Vo Nguyen Giap, to move men and heavy artillery into the well-

---

*Representatives of the People's Republic of China, France, Great Britain, the Soviet Union, and the United States were scheduled to meet in Geneva to discuss the postwar issues relating to Berlin and Korea. They were also expected to discuss the status of Indochina in a separate conference that included representatives of Cambodia, Laos, Vietnam, and the Vietminh.

protected, densely overgrown hills surrounding the garrison. Concealed by heavy jungle cover, Giap's troops nestled into the hills and waited patiently for weeks.

Although Navarre was concerned by France's unwillingness to reinforce his garrison with additional troops, he revealed nothing to American officials.[7] In early January, after speaking to the general, Ambassador Donald Heath reported to the State Department that Navarre had "expressed entire confidence in [the] ultimate success of his military plan." In what would become a monumental understatement, Navarre acknowledged the "possibility of reverses." Nonetheless, he boldly predicted, even the "loss of Dien Bien Phu or even as many as 10 battalions of his battle corps would not prevent his moving on to eventual victory."[8] However, Navarre did ask Heath if the United States would consider supplying aircraft and pilots to fly logistical, noncombat missions. That, he said, would give French pilots more time to concentrate on missions against Vietminh artillery.[9]

At the White House, administration officials had first viewed that request with a mixture of concern and dread. They expected that the coming spring rainy season would temporarily quell the fighting and give them until at least the summer to decide on military intervention. But now, before the battle had even begun, time appeared to be running out. Despite Navarre's public confidence about victory at Dien Bien Phu, French air power had failed to sever the Vietminh supply lines and the French had been forced to suspend ground patrols around the garrison as Vietminh troops inched closer. At the January 8 meeting of Eisenhower's National Security Council, CIA Director Allen Dulles, the brother of Secretary of State Dulles, had delivered a sobering assessment of the French position. While the garrison was not imminently threatened, Dulles observed that the French were growing anxious. While Dien Bien Phu was a "strong position," he noted that "the French were actually locked up in it, and fresh Vietminh battalions were en route." Eisenhower made clear his determination to resist sending American ground forces to Indochina. The prospect was "simply beyond his contemplation." He insisted that the "key to winning this war was to get the Vietnamese to fight." It was futile, he said, to talk about United States forces replacing the French troops in Indochina. In that event, the Vietnamese would only "transfer their hatred of the French to us." Forcefully, the president declared that "I cannot tell you . . . how bitterly opposed I am to such a course of action. This war in Indochina would absorb our troops by divisions."

While Eisenhower may have strongly opposed replacing American troops in Indochina with French troops, he was amenable to an Air Force mission to relieve the French at Dien Bien Phu, who would soon come

under withering attacks. Although his position would shift several times in
the coming months as he grappled with a worsening Dien Bien Phu situation, Eisenhower would consider virtually every contingency but a long-
term American military commitment. Other administration officials, particularly Chairman Radford, were more open to the idea. The former
commander of two aircraft carrier divisions during World War II, Radford
was respected for his intelligence and vision. Until his appointment as
chairman in 1953, the admiral had served as commander in chief, Pacific,
where he cultivated an understanding of Indochina and had arrived at the
belief, shared by Eisenhower and Dulles, that the region's protection
against communism was vital to U.S. security. The importance he placed
on Indochina was apparent at the January 8 NSC meeting, when Radford
urged Eisenhower to "do everything possible to forestall a French defeat
at Dien Bien Phu." He suggested that the United States could send an aircraft carrier to assist the French if they appeared in danger of losing the
battle.

Eisenhower did not respond to Radford's advice, but Treasury Secretary George Humphrey did. More devoted to reducing military spending
than to a costly military intervention in Indochina, Humphrey asked:
"When we start putting our men in Indochina, how long will it be before
we get into the war? And can we afford to get into such a war?" Radford
replied that the United States already had a significant contingent in
Indochina, although not in combat positions.

Sympathetic to a French request for additional U.S. airplanes and
pilots to fly logistical missions to relieve French pilots for combat, Eisenhower informed his advisors that, at the very least, he favored providing
the requested aircraft. He seemed prepared to go even further only
moments later when Radford argued that only American pilots could
destroy Vietminh antiaircraft guns in the hills overlooking the French garrison. "The president commented," the minutes recorded, "that if any of
our people were to get into this jungle fighting, they should certainly be
given the proximity fuse or VT fuse bombs, not just ordinary bombs. Let's
hurry up and give them some."

But there was nothing in any NSC directives, National Security Advisor Robert Cutler noted, that specifically authorized the introduction
of combat forces into Indochina. Eisenhower, however, made clear his own
distinction between "general policy" and a "specific action" to assist
the French. It would be necessary "to work out some way," Eisenhower
said, "by which our planes could be used. Obviously we couldn't just fly
them into combat off the carrier." Although he insisted that "no one
was more anxious" to keep U.S. troops out of "these jungles," Eisenhower
was reluctant to "forget our vital interests in Indochina." As the meeting

drew to a close, Radford had revisited the issue of using air power to relieve the French garrison. "If we could put one squadron of U.S. planes over Dien Bien Phu for as little as one afternoon," he said, "it might save the situation."[10]

One week later, with the distressing situation in Vietnam virtually unchanged, the talk at the weekly National Security Council meeting again turned to the possibility, this time raised by Dulles, that "the French position in Indochina would collapse." Dulles argued against giving up, saying, "Too bad. We're licked and that's the end of it," if France left Indochina. He argued, instead, for a more aggressive approach involving an "effective guerrilla operation against this new Vietminh government." The costs would be low, Dulles said, and would present the United States with "an opportunity" in Southeast Asia. "We can raise hell and the Communists will find it just as expensive to resist as we are now finding it."

Eisenhower embraced Dulles' suggestion and observed that something similar should have been done after the communist victory in China. It was left to Vice President Nixon, drawing on knowledge from his recent trip to Indochina, to inject a dose of reality into the meeting by noting that not only would a U.S.-backed guerrilla force be difficult to assemble, "the Vietnamese would not like this role." Nixon added that the departure of the French "might provide just what was lacking to the Vietnamese by way of the will to fight." In that case, Nixon believed that the Vietnamese might "allow us to come in and build up their native forces and in general do for them what the French had thus far failed to do." That, he hastened to add, did not mean United States combat troops.[11]

Throughout January and February, as the French dug in deeper and the Vietminh reinforced their positions in the hills surrounding Dien Bien Phu, Eisenhower and his advisors continued to struggle over how to respond if the expected battle went badly for the French. For weeks, the president and his advisors toyed with, but never committed themselves to, direct intervention. Their indecision partially grew out of uncertainty about whether the French—zealously guarding their predominant role in Indochina—would welcome direct U.S. military assistance. Mostly, however, they worried that direct action might draw the United States into a much wider and more costly adventure on Asian soil.

What Eisenhower and most of his advisors *could* agree on was France's request for more airplanes and additional personnel to keep them flying. After a vigorous debate among his advisors, Eisenhower agreed in late January to send the French twenty-two B-26 bombers and two hundred uniformed U.S. Air Force mechanics.[12] When news of the decision leaked to the press, some senators worried aloud about further involvement in Asia only six months after the Korean armistice and expressed concern that it was the kind of escalation that might eventually lead to full-scale U.S. involvement in Indochina. As *Time* reported on February 15, Republican leaders in Congress "believe the Korean peace is one of their greatest political assets in this election year [and] shudder at the thought of involvement in a fresh war in Indo-China."[13] On the other hand, Eisenhower and his advisors knew they could not afford the political damage that would result if Indochina fell to the Communists on a Republican administration's watch. For years, Republicans had occupied the high ground when it came to fighting communism in Asia. A French defeat in Indochina would leave Eisenhower and the Republicans—in an election year—open to the same partisan attacks leveled against Truman after the "loss" of China in 1949.

The Senate's Republican leaders aired those fears in a February 8 meeting with Eisenhower during which Senate Armed Services Committee Chairman Leverett Saltonstall told Eisenhower that his committee had been "very loath to agree to this involvement of U.S. personnel." While they were not opposed to sending civilian mechanics, Saltonstall said most members of the Armed Services Committee objected to the involvement of uniformed personnel. Furthermore, he said, the decision might also cause problems with members of both parties on the Senate Appropriations Committee, the panel that approved funding for the administration's massive aid program for Indochina. Eisenhower listened to Saltonstall's complaints, but protested that he had no other choice but to grant the request. He appealed to the Republican leadership to help him build congressional support for his decision.[14]

Elsewhere in the Senate, another small revolt brewed among three prominent Democrats—Mansfield, Richard Russell of Georgia, and John Stennis of Mississippi. Russell, the senior Democrat on the Armed Services Committee and its former chairman, labeled Eisenhower's decision to send the mechanics a "mistake" that would likely draw U.S. ground troops into the war.[15] While Mansfield generally supported Eisenhower's decision as "a logical extension of a practice already underway," he complained that the White House was not keeping the Senate and the American public informed about evolving U.S. policy in the region. Alluding to the administration's New Look policy and its reliance on the nuclear threat to fight communist aggression, Mansfield wondered:

> If we are about to be drawn more deeply into the military situation on the Asia mainland, as some persons seem to fear and as some press reports hint at, has the administration undertaken at this point to replace our conventional forces and place reliance on atomic weapons? One need not be a military strategist to know that the kinds of wars being fought in Asia are largely rifle wars, not atomic wars. . . . We cannot afford to permit the situation in Indochina to drift any longer.[16]

Like Mansfield, Stennis—a senior Democrat on the Armed Services Committee—did not strenuously object to Eisenhower's decision, but expressed grave concerns about the eventual consequences of the expansion of United States assistance to France. "Step by step," he told the Senate, "we are moving into this war in Indochina, and I am afraid we will move to a point from which there will be no return."[17]

Asked at a February 10 press conference about his decision to send the air force mechanics, Eisenhower assured reporters that he saw "no opportunity" for them to be "touched by combat." Responding to Stennis's and Mansfield's concerns, the president insisted that "no one could be more bitterly opposed to ever getting the United States involved in a hot war in that region; consequently, every move that I authorize is calculated, as far as humans can do it, to make certain that that does not happen." Later, answering another question about deeper American involvement in Indochina, Eisenhower insisted that he could not "conceive of a greater tragedy for America than to get heavily involved now in an all-out war in any of those regions, particularly with large units."[18]

Hoping to mollify members of Congress, Eisenhower later promised that the mechanics would leave Indochina by the end of June.[19] Eisenhower's strong statement eased congressional anxiety. Stennis told the *New York Times* he was pleased the president "is now firmed up against possible direct involvement." Foreign Relations Committee member Walter George of Georgia, one of the Senate's most influential Democrats, said he, too, was comforted by Eisenhower's words. "Only one thing would bring China in, in force," George said. "That is if we sent any sizeable number of men over there. That would bring on real trouble."[20]

As Eisenhower pondered how to honor his promise to keep U.S. ground troops out of Indochina while preventing a French defeat, the Vietminh finally attacked Dien Bien Phu. On the afternoon of March 13, deadly fire from enemy artillery, bunkered in the well-protected hills, began raining terror on the embattled garrison. Within hours, it was apparent that Navarre had drastically overestimated the French position and tragically underestimated the strength of the Vietminh as well as their ability to place artillery pieces on the hillsides. The French response proved so ineffectual in the early hours of the battle that the embarrassed French artillery commander committed suicide with a grenade.[21]

A week into the battle, on March 20, General Paul Ely, the chief of staff of France's military, arrived in Washington at Radford's invitation for consultations with American officials. With the Geneva Conference on the future of the Far East set to begin on April 26, Ely was under orders to solicit American support for negotiations to end the war. Tired and frustrated by years of costly fighting, France finally wanted out. Officials in Washington, however, were largely unaware of Dien Bien Phu's desperate condition. Eisenhower, Radford, and Dulles desperately hoped that they could persuade the French to continue fighting.

Throughout Ely's weeklong visit, the necessity of a French victory at Dien Bien Phu was *the* major area of mutual agreement between the two nations—although for entirely different reasons. In preparing for the Geneva talks, France hoped to strengthen its bargaining position for eventual withdrawal from Indochina by enlisting American firepower to critically wound the Vietminh at Dien Bien Phu. This they hoped to achieve, on their own terms, without additional concessions to the Americans. While they wanted American assistance, the French were as determined as ever to resist American efforts to exert more influence over their military strategy. American officials, meanwhile, also wanted the French to prevail at Dien Bien Phu, but primarily because they believed a victory might persuade the French to continue fighting and, thereby, eliminate any pressure to commit United States troops to the fighting.

Radford, however, was not among those officials opposed to direct military intervention in Indochina. Although he had previously assured the Senate Foreign Relations Committee that France could win the battle unaided, the Joint Chiefs chairman began lobbying his French counterpart to request U.S. military intervention at Dien Bien Phu from almost the moment he arrived in Washington. As the dismal reports about the embattled French garrison finally began pouring into Washington, Ely gradually relented. Although he had not been authorized to request American intervention, the changing circumstances of the battle dictated a new strategy. With Radford's help, he was now more inclined to explore the possibilities of more direct U.S. assistance. Eisenhower's ambiguous directive to Radford to provide the French with whatever assistance they needed to save Dien Bien Phu led Ely to believe that the president and the more hawkish admiral were in complete agreement over U.S. policy toward Indochina. Actually, while Eisenhower was willing to entertain sending U.S. bombers to attack the Vietminh camped in the hills overlooking Dien Bien Phu, he was not nearly as eager as Radford. But Ely, encouraged by Radford, apparently heard only what he wanted.[22]

By the time Radford brought the French general to meet Dulles on March 23, three days into his visit, Ely was eager to extract a promise of U.S. intervention in the event that China sent jet fighters into Indochina. Dulles, however, was still aligned with those opposing intervention. Frustrated by France's intransigence, Dulles was reluctant to intervene if the result would be nothing more than a better bargaining position in Geneva. To Ely's disappointment, Dulles hedged when asked about direct U.S. intervention. Instead, he reminded the general "that if the United States sent its flag and its own military establishment—land, sea or air—into the Indochina war, then the prestige of the United States would be engaged to a point where we would want to have a success." That, of course, meant the United States would demand a greater role in determining military strategy—something the French were loath to consider.[23]

Ely did not leave Washington empty-handed. Unknown to Eisenhower and Dulles, Radford had presented to him a detailed plan for air strikes of Vietminh positions around Dien Bien Phu and other strategic sites. Ely left town believing that Radford would persuade Eisenhower to approve the plan—as long as the French government requested it.[24] Whether Radford promised more than he could deliver is not certain. What is certain is that as the French position at Dien Bien Phu worsened, Radford—alone among the members of the Joint Chiefs of Staff—urged Eisenhower to intervene.

By March 25, when Eisenhower met again with his National Security Council, the Vietminh assault on the French garrison had abated. According to Allen Dulles, the guerrillas appeared to be low on ammunition and supplies. But the French were unable to stop their reinforcement. Eisenhower reacted with disgust. His caustic reaction shed light on the basic reason for his reluctance to aid the French: while he hoped to prevent a communist victory in Indochina, he believed that French ineptitude, and not the absence of U.S. intervention, would prove the decisive factor. Eisenhower observed "that if the point had been reached when the French forces could be moved only by air, it seemed sufficient indication that the population of Vietnam did not wish to be free from Communist domination."

Despite his frustration with the French and his public assurances that he would not send ground troops into Indochina, Eisenhower continued to entertain the notion that a single day of air strikes on Vietminh positions around Dien Bien Phu might be enough to turn the battle around. Only the day before, the president told Dulles of his unwillingness to "get involved in the fighting in Indochina unless there were the political preconditions necessary for a successful outcome." That meant, of course, a more prominent strategic role for the U.S. military. According to Dulles' minutes of the conversation, Eisenhower also did not "wholly exclude the possibility of a single strike [at Dien Bien Phu], if it were almost certain this would produce decisive results."

Dulles' previous public bravado about "massive retaliation" to fight communist aggression had no meaning for the battle at Dien Bien Phu. Eisenhower understood that he was not free to act unilaterally—even if he ultimately determined that a single bombing attack on the Vietminh at Dien Bien Phu might be effective. He knew that the American public, and thus many in Congress, would be skeptical of anything that threatened to involve the nation in another war in Asia. Moreover, taking unilateral action without consulting Congress was dangerous. He knew that the small but boisterous furor in the Senate over his decision to send the air-craft mechanics was but a taste of the outrage that would surely erupt should he send the U.S. Air Force into the battle.

Even if Eisenhower took his case to Congress and requested a resolu-tion authorizing military action, a successful outcome was far from certain. With slim majorities in both houses of Congress (48–47–1 in the Senate and 221–213–1 in the House), Eisenhower knew he could not depend on his Republican allies. In the Senate, in particular, the debate over Joseph McCarthy's sensational allegations that the Army had covered up alleged foreign espionage activities had deeply fractured the Senate's Republicans. Beyond that, Republicans lacked a fundamental consensus on foreign pol-icy. Thus, they would be ill suited to mount an effective defense of his actions. Meanwhile, Democrats who vividly recalled the Republican attacks on Truman for his unilateral decision to send American troops to defend South Korea in 1950 could not be expected to rush to the aid of a Republican president who committed a similar "offense."

In any event, Eisenhower was not willing for the United States to go it alone without help from its allies, particularly Great Britain. Not only was it a matter of principle, he knew that a majority of Congress was unlikely to support unilateral military action in Indochina. Any full-scale military involvement in the war beyond Dien Bien Phu, Eisenhower argued, should involve a coalition of governments acting under the aus-pices of the United Nations—or at least a loose alliance of Pacific and Western European powers. At the March 25 NSC meeting, Eisenhower had raised the issue of UN action, saying that he did not "see how the United States or other free world nations could go in full-out in support of the Associated States without UN approval and assistance." In any event, the president insisted, he would not involve American troops in Indochina without first consulting Congress. "It [is] simply academic," Eisenhower said, "to imagine otherwise." That in mind, he suggested that "this might be the moment to begin to explore with Congress what sup-port could be anticipated in the event that it seemed desirable to intervene in Indochina."[25]

While Radford mounted a campaign among Eisenhower's advisors to build support for air strikes, Dulles began looking beyond Dien Bien Phu. While he had once hoped U.S. military intervention might save the day, the unfolding military debacle had changed his mind. By early April, he had decided to begin exploring the formation of an international coalition for the continuing defense of Indochina—not to help the French hold on, but to take their place. Moreover, Dulles believed the United States risked undermining its position in Southeast Asia unless it made a strong state-ment supporting independence for Indochina. On March 24, he told Eisenhower that he believed the time had come to declare "that the freedom of the Southeast Asia area was important from the standpoint of our peace, security and happiness, and that we could not look upon the loss to Communism of that area with indifference." Eisenhower agreed, and authorized Dulles to deliver a speech that would explain clearly the U.S. position on Indochina.[26]

Despite a CIA report to Eisenhower in late March that suggested reason for optimism, the French position at Dien Bien Phu was deteriorating as the Vietminh rearmed and staged their attacks with renewed vigor.[27] The pause in fighting had been but the calm before another storm of brutal Vietminh artillery and antiaircraft fire. The antiaircraft guns were highly effective and laid waste to so many French transport planes that the aerial resupply of the garrison was finally halted. By March 28, Dien Bien Phu was virtually isolated from the outside world. Henceforth, supplies would be dropped by parachute—and much of that would fall into enemy hands. Worse, wounded soldiers could no longer be evacuated.

Faced with reports that the garrison might fall within days, Eisenhower, Dulles, and other administration officials abruptly reassessed their earlier reservations about U.S. intervention. Although they had once expected that the rainy season would postpone the day of reckoning, the French position had deteriorated so quickly that they no longer had the luxury of ample time to debate intervention at Dien Bien Phu. During the next several days, Eisenhower's strategy would change several times— sometimes daily—as he and Dulles struggled with their conflicting military and political objectives.

Eisenhower met with Republican congressional leaders, including Knowland and House Speaker Joseph Martin, on the morning of March 29 to brief them about the worsening situation. Judging from Vice President Nixon's recollection of the meeting, recorded in his diary, it appeared that many of Eisenhower's reservations about unilateral intervention at Dien Bien Phu had suddenly evaporated. Nixon remembered that "Eisenhower said that if the military situation at Dien Bien Phu became desperate he would consider the use of diversionary tactics, possibly a landing by Chiang Kai-shek's Nationalist forces on China's Hainan Island or a naval blockade of the Chinese mainland."

Eisenhower may have been simply thinking aloud, or gauging the reaction that such a drastic move might elicit from Congress. In any event, he made it clear to Knowland, Martin, and the others that the situation at Dien Bien Phu was growing desperate. "I am bringing this up at this time," he said, "because at any time within the space of forty-eight hours, it might be necessary to move into the battle of Dien Bien Phu in order to keep it from going against us, and in that case I will be calling in the Democrats as well as the Republican leaders to inform them of the actions we're taking." Eisenhower's use of the word "inform," instead of "consult," suggests the distinction he made between the kind of congressional approval needed for a sustained U.S. intervention involving ground troops versus that needed for a strong, but limited air strike requiring only congressional notification. Days earlier, he had seemed unwilling to take any action without congressional approval. Now, however, he appeared to limit congressional consultation to situations involving a larger infusion of military power. Within days, after a dramatic meeting between Dulles and congressional leaders, his view of presidential prerogatives would change again—dramatically.[28]

But for now, at least, Eisenhower seemed to be thinking and acting on two tracks. On one hand, he continued to consider the possibility of a surgical attack by American bombers on Vietminh artillery positions in the hills surrounding Dien Bien Phu. He knew, however, that such an action would not itself decisively alter the course of the war, even if it resulted in a French victory at Dien Bien Phu. For this reason, he and Dulles had agreed that the efforts of a coalition of nations—"united action," as Dulles called it—might be the only way to achieve a definitive victory in Indochina.

On the evening of March 29, Dulles went to New York to deliver the Indochina policy speech that Eisenhower had authorized the previous week. In a nationally broadcast speech to the Overseas Press Club, Dulles stressed the importance that the United States attached to the region and raised the specter of military action to "save" it. "The area has great strategic value," Dulles declared, reminding his audience of Eisenhower's statement the previous week that Indochina was of "transcendent importance." Should the Communists win in Indochina, Dulles said, they would control "the so-called 'rice bowl'" that fed millions of people, from India to Japan. Furthermore, he said, the free world risked losing "the many raw materials" of Indochina, such as tin, oil, rubber, and iron ore. Dulles warned that the war in Indochina was the direct result of communist Soviet expansionism, carried out by "its Chinese Communist ally." Attempting to lay the groundwork for some unspecified course of action, he insisted that a communist victory "should not be passively accepted, but should be met by united action. This might involve serious risks. But these risks are far less than those that will face us a few years from now, if we dare not be resolute today."[29]

Whether Dulles meant the united action of a coalition of nations to augment or replace the French, or whether he was signaling the possible beginning of a new militant phase of U.S. involvement in Indochina was not immediately clear to those who heard the speech. With the partisan backlash over Truman's sudden commitment of troops to Korea in 1950 still fresh in his mind, Dulles hoped the speech would prepare the American public for possible U.S. intervention in Indochina. It is also likely that he and Eisenhower simply hoped that a certain amount of ambiguity would throw the Chinese off balance and persuade them to forestall greater assistance to the Vietminh.

The practical effect of the speech, however, was to muddy the already murky diplomatic waters between the United States and France. Dulles' rhetoric persuaded French leaders that Ely had not misinterpreted Radford's offers of military assistance. The United States might be serious, after all, about air strikes to relieve Dien Bien Phu. The speech also created confusion in the Senate, where some members were unsure about exactly what policy the Eisenhower administration had in mind. This, of course, was understandable; Eisenhower and Dulles were themselves less than certain about how to proceed.[30] Although leading members of Congress were briefed on Dulles' call for "united action," the speech caught others—mostly Democrats—by surprise and added to the confusion over whether Eisenhower and Dulles were trying to lead the nation into war in Indochina. "It is not clear," Mansfield told the Senate, "that the policies of the administration have yet established the minimum conditions to prevent Communist seizure of Indochina without full-scale war. It is not clear that these conditions are even understood by the administration."[31] Despite their confusion about administration policy, Democrats were clearly conscious of the political risks that Eisenhower faced in Indochina. After interviewing several prominent Democrats in early April, *New York Times* reporter William S. White observed that "the Senate atmosphere in this developing crisis is serene on the surface, even though to nearly all its members the Truman Administration's intervention in Korea is still remembered as a frightening political experience."[32]

What Dulles and Eisenhower did not anticipate was how the secretary of state's speech would elevate the importance of Dien Bien Phu to almost epic proportions in the public consciousness. Of course, Dulles had addressed his remarks to saving Indochina, not Dien Bien Phu. But with much of the world focused on the battle, and not the war, such a misperception was inevitable, especially considering the speech's ominous tone. Creating an atmosphere of crisis and then indirectly linking the fate of the entire region to a battle in which the French were destined for defeat was hardly what Dulles could have intended. After all, he had previously attached relatively little importance to the outcome at Dien Bien Phu, especially now that the situation appeared so hopeless.

In the Senate on March 31, Democrat Paul Douglas of Illinois sparked a small debate in the Senate over Indochina with a speech strongly supportive of Eisenhower. "In this critical moment," he said, "we must support the president." Yet, like other members of Congress, Douglas admitted he was unsure about U.S. policy toward Indochina. "I do not know what measures this administration plans." But conservative Republican Arthur Watkins of Utah, not so eager to give Eisenhower a blank check, better represented the views of many senators from both parties who were reluctant to relinquish their constitutional role of advising the president on military and foreign policy.

A gaunt, gray-haired figure of rectitude, the 68-year-old Watkins was serving in his second Senate term. Once described by an admirer as "an almost painfully ethical Mormon," Watkins was among the Senate's most admired Republicans—a quiet, shy man known for his political courage.[33] He would soon chair the select Senate committee on the censure of Wisconsin's Joseph McCarthy. While he was usually loyal to Eisenhower, he was also concerned about the Senate's constitutional prerogatives. "It is the duty of the President," he said, "to advise the Congress, so that the Congress can grant him, under its constitutional power, authority to go ahead." Then, in a slap at Democrats that evidenced the lingering animosity over Korea, Watkins added that he hoped "the President will not follow the example of President Truman and take action without consulting the Congress." While Watkins believed Congress would give Eisenhower authority for whatever emergency military action he might take, he did not believe Eisenhower "has any right to send American armed forces to intervene in that war without an authorization from the Congress."[34] Judging from this Senate debate, Eisenhower must have known that he risked a congressional revolt even if he ordered a single air strike at Dien Bien Phu without congressional assent.

The emotion in Watkins speech was no isolated or spontaneous outburst related only to fears of U.S. military involvement in Indochina. It came in the wake of a fierce Senate debate in February over amending the Constitution to restrict considerably the president's power to negotiate treaties and other agreements. The "Bricker amendment" had been the brainchild of Republican Senator John Bricker of Ohio and was the culmination of years of frustration and anger over treaties that its supporters believed undermined the nation's security. Foremost in Bricker's mind had been the Yalta agreements and his fear, expressed in an October 1953 speech, that "American sovereignty and the American Constitution . . . are threatened by treaty law." Behind such treaties and executive agreements, Bricker saw "reactionary one-worlders" who were "trying to vest legislative powers in non-elected officials of the UN and its satellite bodies," controlled, he claimed, by "a socialist-communist majority." While not all supporters of Bricker's amendment were worried that a president would sell out the country to the Communists, most were worried that the executive branch had too often usurped the power constitutionally vested in Congress to ratify treaties and declare war. It is likely that a majority of the sixty-one senators who voted for the amendment on February 26—one vote shy of the necessary two-thirds majority—had in mind Harry Truman's 1950 decision to involve the nation in the Korean War without first consulting Congress.[35]

Despite the narrow failure of the Bricker amendment, the Senate had made clear that a majority of its members held a strict constructionist view of the Constitution's language regarding congressional prerogatives in foreign and military affairs. Although Eisenhower had fiercely opposed the amendment, the import of the vote did not elude him. While not constitutionally constrained from taking unilateral action in Indochina, Eisenhower was now well aware of the political constraints imposed on him by the Senate. Watkins, therefore, undoubtedly gave voice to the frustration of most Bricker amendment supporters regarding unilateral presidential decisions involving the United States military.

Eisenhower got the message. At a White House press conference on March 31, he reiterated his opposition to injecting American troops into Indochina, saying that he could conceive "of no greater disadvantage to America than to be employing its own ground forces, and any other kind of forces, in great numbers around the world, meeting each little situation as it arises."[36] While Eisenhower did not say whether he considered Indochina a "little situation," his statement calls into question whether he believed, as he previously argued, that the region was of "transcendent importance."

This public opposition to sending ground troops to Indochina notwithstanding, Eisenhower had not actually given up on military intervention at Dien Bien Phu. At the April 1 NSC meeting, the president again raised the issue with his advisors. Aware that the Joint Chiefs of Staff—except for Radford—opposed air strikes to relieve the French, Eisenhower admitted that he was unsure about his response to the steadily deteriorating situation. It was a question, he said, for "statesmen." But although he said he saw "a thousand variants in the equation and very terrible risks," the president said "there was no reason for the Council to avoid considering the intervention issue."[37]

After the NSC meeting, Eisenhower met privately with a smaller group of advisors to discuss his options for Dien Bien Phu. While no record exists of that meeting, it seems clear that one decision emerging from the discussion was a newfound determination by Eisenhower to formally consult the Republican and Democratic leaders of Congress. That afternoon, Dulles, whose opposition to U.S. intervention had also given way to his fears about an imminent collapse of the French position in Indochina, phoned Attorney General Herbert Brownell to tell him that he would be meeting soon with congressional leaders and wanted "something" to show them. That "something" became the draft of a congressional resolution authorizing Eisenhower to use the Navy and Air Force, until June 30, 1955, "to assist the forces which are resisting aggression in Southeast Asia, to prevent the extension and expansion of that aggression, and to protect and defend the safety and security of the United States."[38]

How serious was Eisenhower about seeking congressional authorization for military action? According to presidential Press Secretary James Hagerty, as late as the afternoon of April 1, the president may have been weighing the option of bypassing Congress and ordering a covert air strike on the Vietminh at Dien Bien Phu. Hagerty recalled that during lunch with two newspaper publishers, who were also close friends, Eisenhower said the "US might have to make decisions to send in squadrons from 2 aircraft carriers off coast to bomb Reds at Dien Bien Phu." Hagerty said Eisenhower added that, "Of course, if we did we'd have to deny it forever."[39]

Whatever thoughts Eisenhower had about covert action must have been discarded by the next day. That Friday morning, April 2, at 9:30, Eisenhower met with Dulles, Radford, and Defense Secretary Charles Wilson to discuss Saturday's meeting with congressional leaders. Shown the congressional resolution, Eisenhower told Dulles that he agreed with the language, but advised him not to share it with the members of Congress. Instead, he said, the first objective of the meeting would be to "develop the thinking of congressional leaders."

This meeting, held ostensibly for the purpose of developing a strategy for persuading members of Congress to approve air strikes to save Dien Bien Phu, shifted abruptly to discussion of a long-term United States military strategy for Indochina. Dulles' minutes of the meeting show that Radford had again changed his mind about air strikes—he now believed that an American attack would be fruitless. "He felt the outcome there would be determined within a matter of hours," Dulles recalled, "and the situation was not one which called for any US participation." Radford maintained that "he had nothing presently in mind," although he did not exclude "the prospect of future U.S. military involvement in Indochina." Eisenhower, who sat silently through most of the meeting, did not challenge Radford's view. With Radford's opposition to air strikes, Eisenhower's senior advisors were now unified in their opposition to U.S. intervention at Dien Bien Phu. The government of the U.S. would allow the garrison to fall. But more than the fate of Dien Bien Phu was hanging in the balance. Whether they knew it or not, Eisenhower and his men had just sealed the fate of the French in Indochina. Although the beleaguered garrison would not succumb for several more weeks and the last French troops would not officially leave Indochina for another two years, the first Indochina war effectively ended, unceremoniously, with Eisenhower's April 2 decision against intervention.[40]

CHAPTER 11

We Cannot Engage in Active War

1954

Saturday, April 3, dawned breezy and cold in Washington, D.C. It was cherry blossom season in the capital. By mid-morning, thousands of tourists and area residents would be flocking to the area near the Jefferson Memorial to see the explosion of snow-white blooms ringing the Tidal Basin. Just a few blocks north, in an area of town called Foggy Bottom, a smaller and far more serious gathering was about to take place. Shortly after 9:00 A.M., a group of Democratic and Republican members of Congress—five senators and three representatives—arrived at the State Department for a meeting with Secretary of State Dulles, Admiral Radford, Under Secretary of Defense Roger Kyes, and Navy Secretary Robert Anderson. The congressional group was small, but influential: Republican senators William Knowland, the majority leader, and Eugene Millikin of Colorado; Democratic senators Lyndon Johnson, the minority leader, Richard Russell of Georgia, and Earle Clements of Kentucky; House Speaker Joseph Martin, a Republican from Massachusetts; the Demo cratic House minority whip, John McCormack of Massachusetts; and Democrat J. Percy Priest of Tennessee.

Eisenhower, the leaders knew, was at Camp David. The task of briefing the congressmen would be left to Dulles, Radford, and the other officials. At 9:30, after the congressmen and senators had settled into their chairs, Dulles—seated before a huge map of the world—called the meeting to order. In an instant, the friendly, informal atmosphere in the room turned deadly serious. "The president has asked me to call this meeting," Dulles said. His purpose quickly became clear. He and Eisenhower wanted congressional approval for a resolution approving deployment of naval and air forces—but not ground troops—in Indochina through June 1955.[1]

On one level, Eisenhower and Dulles hoped that by approving an Indochina resolution, Congress might simply give the United States a stronger bargaining position with its European allies. The day before, Dulles had agreed with Defense Secretary Charles Wilson, who argued that a congressional resolution was not so much a pretext to actual military intervention, but would " 'fill our hands' so that we would be stronger to negotiate with France, the UK and others."[2] Yet it is also possible that Eisenhower suspected Congress would never give him such a resolution. He may have concluded that involving Congress in the decision—indeed, inviting legislators to tie his hands—might inoculate him against charges that his administration had single-handedly allowed the fall of Indochina to the Communists.

Perhaps revealing the president's desire to share the blame with Congress for any disastrous outcome in Southeast Asia, Dulles informed the leaders of Eisenhower's wish that he and Congress would be of one mind on Indochina. He then abruptly turned the meeting over to Radford. In a detailed discussion of Indochina's military situation, the Joint Chiefs chairman devoted special attention to Dien Bien Phu—so much so that the congressmen were to be forgiven if they mistakenly concluded that a U.S. mission to relieve the garrison was still under consideration. The administration was very concerned about the situation in Indochina, Radford said, especially Dien Bien Phu. Some form of American intervention, he argued, was urgently necessary to save the situation, although he was doubtful the French at Dien Bien Phu could hold out for more than a few days.*

Dulles agreed with Radford and explained that Indochina was of great strategic importance to the United States. "If the Communists gained Indochina and nothing was done about it," Dulles told the group, it would be "only a question of time until all of Southeast Asia falls along with Indonesia, thus imperiling our western island of defense." Therefore, Dulles argued, the president deserved the backing of Congress "so that he could use air and sea power in the area if he felt it necessary in the interest of national security."[3]

Knowland—always eager for a greater U.S. role in Asia—initially supported Radford and Dulles. But he quickly fell silent as skeptical questions poured forth from Johnson and Russell. It was Johnson who noted Knowland's earlier complaints that in Korea as much as 90 percent of the personnel and funding had been supplied by the United States. If this was an unacceptable situation, as the Republican majority leader had once suggested, then Johnson argued that "we want no more Koreas with the United States furnishing 90 percent of the manpower." The group agreed. But Radford countered that the administration did not "now contemplate

---

*Radford was referring to the overall war. But some of the congressional leaders undoubtedly thought that he was talking about Dien Bien Phu.

the commitment of land forces." French and Vietnamese troops would do the fighting on the ground.

But these congressional leaders, especially Russell, had little confidence that France would bear its share of the burden in a joint military enterprise. Furthermore, Russell worried that Indochina would prove a quagmire. "Once you commit the flag," Russell argued, "you've committed the country. There's no turning back. If you involve the American air force, why, you've involved the nation."[4] If the nation were committed, he argued, land forces would soon follow. Russell was "weary," he told the group, "of seeing American soldiers being used as gladiators to be thrown into every arena around the word."[5] At this, the eight leaders agreed that a congressional resolution should not be considered "until the Secretary had obtained commitments of a political and material nature from our allies."[6]

Dulles assured them he was already talking with British and Philippine leaders and would be discussing the matter with the French ambassador later that morning. But his problem, he explained, was that he could go only so far in building support for united action in Indochina without the support of his own government. Russell and the other leaders expressed little confidence that Dulles could persuade the British to participate in a coalition effort in Indochina.[7]

While the meeting did not expose any deep rift between congressional leaders and Eisenhower, it did reveal that the congressional group was decidedly against any form of *unilateral*, long-term U.S. intervention. Before the meeting ended, Russell, Johnson, and the others made it clear they would support U.S. intervention only after three conditions were met: (1) allies were a found to participate in joint military action; (2) any U.S. military intervention would be predicated on French assurances to remain in the war until the end; (3) France would agree to grant a greater level of independence to Indochina. While these were not unreasonable conditions, they did severely limit Eisenhower's flexibility in responding to the unfolding events.* Forcing Dulles to first secure French concessions and allied support for united action effectively gave Britain and France veto

---

*Indeed, the president may actually have wanted his options limited and, in fact, welcomed the conditions set by Russell, Johnson, and the others. Eisenhower almost certainly understood that the congressional leadership would never embrace unilateral U.S. military intervention in Indochina. If the Senate vote on the Bricker amendment was not enough, the dissent that erupted in Congress over the American aircraft technicians, as well as the controversy over Dulles' "united action" speech, would have made clear the congressional reluctance to allow Eisenhower a free hand in Indochina.

power over U.S. intervention. Furthermore, the congressmen had greatly weakened Dulles' bargaining position. How could the secretary of state plead with Britain to join an international coalition in Indochina when his own Congress was withholding support for the same action?[8]

The meeting ended with one brief moment of partisanship. McCormack mischievously expressed surprise that Dulles would expect the "party of treason," as Joseph McCarthy had once described the Democrats, to support a policy that might lead to general war.[9] Dulles wisely let the jab pass without comment, and the meeting ended with the congressmen unanimous behind the conditions imposed on U.S. intervention.

Dulles could not have been pleased by the uncertain outcome of the meeting. He had wanted a virtual blank check from the congressional leaders, not a list of conditions that further complicated his job. Characterizing the encounter in general terms, Dulles told an impassive Eisenhower later that afternoon that "on the whole it went pretty well—although it raised some serious problems." He said that he believed Congress would be "quite prepared to go along on some vigorous action if we were not doing it alone. They want to be sure the people in the area are involved, too." Neither criticized the congressional leaders for the conditions they imposed—which supports the notion that Eisenhower, at least, was pleased to have the leading members of Congress join him in resisting military intervention in Indochina. In the meantime, if united action was what the congressmen demanded, then Dulles would try to deliver it, despite the overwhelming odds against persuading reluctant British leaders to go along.[10]

Eisenhower returned to Washington on Sunday, April 4. That evening, at 8:20, he convened his military and foreign policy advisors in his upstairs study at the White House. For the first time, his advisors presented him with the three conditions the congressional leaders had established. Eisenhower's top White House assistant, Sherman Adams, recalled that the president "agreed with Dulles and Radford on a plan to send American [naval and air] forces to Indo-China under certain strict conditions [imposed by Congress.]"[11] Yet each man surely knew that the British and the French would almost certainly balk at the conditions. But so fearful was Eisenhower of the political criticism almost certain to come his way if he passively allowed a French military collapse in Indochina, he was willing to watch Dulles go through the futile public charade of attempting to build an international coalition around "united action."

A desperate French government, meanwhile, had finally decided to redeem Radford's offer to work for U.S. intervention, although on terms vastly different from those envisioned by the congressional leaders. By early April, Dien Bien Phu was on the verge of collapse. Because of the garrison's psychological impact on the French people and their army in

Indochina, the impending disaster threatened to undermine the entire French position in Indochina. For the first time since the war began, the French government was prepared to ask the United States for something more than money and military equipment. During his March 22 meeting with Ely, Radford had laid out the framework of a proposed aerial bombardment of the hills surrounding Dien Bien Phu, which the French called Operation *Vautour* (Vulture). On April 4, Prime Minister Joseph Laniel summoned U.S. Ambassador Douglas Dillon and requested "immediate armed intervention of US carrier aircraft" to save the situation at Dien Bien Phu.

In his cable to the State Department early on the morning of April 5, Dillon informed Washington that Ely had reported to his government "that Radford gave him his personal assurance that if [the] situation at Dien Bien Phu required US naval air support he would do his best to obtain such help from US Government." Dillon reported that General Navarre believed that "a relatively minor US effort could turn the tide but naturally hoped for as much help as possible." Dillon said that Foreign Minister Georges Bidault made it clear that the French now believed "that for good or evil the fate of Southeast Asia now rested on Dien Bien Phu." Furthermore, Bidault said that the outcome of the upcoming Geneva Conference—the international gathering to discuss the dispositions of Berlin, Korea, and Indochina—also depended on the fate of the crumbling French garrison.[12]

But the French request had arrived too late. Eisenhower had already decreed that he would initiate no U.S. military intervention in Indochina unless the congressional leaders' three conditions were met. As for Radford's indiscretion, Eisenhower was not pleased and partly blamed the admiral for the ill-timed entreaty. Eisenhower and Dulles agreed that, for now, intervention was implausible. Dulles recalled that Eisenhower remarked that "in the absence of some kind of arrangement getting support of Congress" any decision to intervene "would be completely unconstitutional and indefensible." While Eisenhower suggested the United States should take "a look to see if anything else can be done," he was firm in his belief that "we cannot engage in active war." After discussing the situation with Eisenhower, Dulles dispatched a cable to Paris, informing Dillon that the United States would not intervene "except on [a] coalition basis with active British Commonwealth participation."[13]

Dulles, it appears, genuinely hoped that he could arrange the kind of united action the congressional leaders wanted. Fearful that the French position in Indochina would dissolve in total defeat at Dien Bien Phu—with disastrous consequences for the Geneva talks and the future of Southeast Asia—he worked furiously to cobble together his international military coalition. In a letter telegraphed to British Prime Minster Winston Churchill that he prepared for Eisenhower's signature, Dulles argued that "Geneva is less than four weeks away. There the possibility of the Communists driving a wedge between us will, given the state of mind in France, be infinitely greater than at Berlin."* He reminded the prime minister of the stakes in Indochina and asserted that communism posed "a grave threat to the whole free community." Such threats, he said, "should now be met by united action and not passively accepted."

> The important thing is that the coalition must be strong and it must be willing to join the fight if necessary. I do not envisage the need of any *appreciable* [emphasis added] ground forces on your or our part. If the members of the alliance are sufficiently resolute it should be able to make clear to the Chinese Communists that the continuation of their material support to the Viet Minh will inevitably lead to the growing power of the forces arrayed against them.[14]

In a terse telegram on April 5, Churchill acknowledged Eisenhower's message and said only that "we are giving it earnest Cabinet consideration."[15] The following day, the National Security Council met to discuss the Indochina situation and, in the words of national security advisor Robert Cutler, "whether or not the United States should intervene with armed forces in Indochina in the event that there was no other means of saving the area from Communist control." Judging from Eisenhower's comments, the president was resigned to the reality that Dulles was unlikely to assemble the kind of international coalition that would permit direct military intervention by the United States. Engaging in a bit of prospective revisionist history, Eisenhower told the group that if Dien Bien Phu "were lost to the French, it could hardly be described as a military defeat, since the French would have inflicted such great losses on the enemy." The French, the president observed, appeared to have "a fifty percent superiority in manpower nearly everywhere in Indochina." He did not understand why they were unwilling or unable to capitalize on that advantage. The minutes of the meeting record that, "with great emphasis," Eisenhower declared "there was no possibility whatever of U.S. unilateral intervention in Indochina, and we had best face that fact. Even if we tried such a course, we would have to take it to the Congress and fight for it like dogs, with very little hope of success."

Later, the president again attempted to downplay the consequences of nonintervention in Indochina by contradicting his own earlier statement—and years of conventional American wisdom—about Indochina's "tran-

---

*A reference to the post–war conference at Potsdam, July, 1945.

scendent importance" to the future of Southeast Asia. After months of publicly promoting the domino theory, Eisenhower now privately objected to "the notion that because we might lose Indochina we would necessarily have to lose all the rest of Southeast Asia." As he noted, the NSC had not always held that view. In fact, he said, an NSC special committee had been asked to "recommend measures for saving the rest of Southeast Asia in the event that Indochina were lost."[16] That evening, Nixon wrote in his diary that he believed Eisenhower "had backed down considerably from the strong position he had taken on Indochina the latter part of the previous week. He seemed resigned to doing nothing at all unless we could get the allies and the country to go along with whatever was suggested and he did not seem inclined to put much pressure on to get them to come along."[17]

Eisenhower was not the only administration official looking beyond the prospects for armed intervention in Indochina. While briefing NSC members on his efforts to build a coalition that included the British, Dulles said that he regarded the NSC's task, not as "a decision to intervene with military forces in Indochina, but as an effort to build up strength in the Southeast Asia area to such a point that military intervention might prove to be unnecessary." In other words, short of an effective program of "united action," the best Dulles could hope for was to increase U.S. assistance to the French in order to keep them from abandoning the war. "The French will to resist," he said, "may be sustained if the French believe that they will get real help in the reasonably near future."

When Eisenhower raised the possibility of a regional organization of nations dedicated to the defense of Southeast Asia* in the event that Indochina "should be lost," Nixon placed his finger on the fundamental problems preventing a French victory in Indochina. The war, he pointed out, was not one primarily of outside aggression, but a "civil war." It was this understanding, Nixon predicted, that would ultimately prompt Congress to oppose U.S. intervention. A regional defense organization might "prove very useful as a means of resisting overt Communist aggression," he said, but could it effectively combat the increase in "internal Communist subversion, especially if Indochina fell?" Dulles, who had previously blamed the Soviets and the Chinese for the war, associated himself with Nixon's comments and provided an interpretation that Nixon, perhaps, did not intend. The real problem, Dulles said, "was indirect, rather than direct aggression," suggesting that the support for the Vietminh by Peking and

---

*It was one of the first mentions of what eventually became the Southeast Asia Treaty Organization, or SEATO, formed later in the year.

Moscow may not have been as consequential as the administration had argued.

From the muddled tone of the April 6 NSC meeting, it was clear that neither Eisenhower nor his advisors had a clear vision of how to reverse a steadily declining situation. Torn between the desire to prevent a certain French defeat and the knowledge that nothing short of direct military intervention could make a difference, the NSC members, including Eisenhower, were at a loss. With American intervention increasingly unlikely, the president obviously hoped to downplay the consequences of what he feared would be the inevitable outcome if the French abandoned the fight—thus, his stated uncertainty about the future of Southeast Asia in the event of a French defeat.

Despite occasional statements to the contrary, Eisenhower seemed to believe in Indochina's "transcendent importance." When Treasury Secretary George Humphrey doubted the wisdom of a regional defense alliance—because it might eventually lead to "a policy of policing all the governments of the world"—Eisenhower responded passionately. Waving aside his earlier ambivalence about the risks if the Vietminh gained control of Indochina, the president argued that "Indochina was the first in a row of dominoes. If it fell, its neighbors would shortly thereafter fall with it, and where did the process end?" Eisenhower objected to Humphrey's concern that the United States might eventually adopt a policy "of intervening every time that local Communist forces became strong enough to attempt to subvert free governments." "George," he said, "you exaggerate the case. Nevertheless, in certain areas at least we cannot afford to let Moscow gain another bit of territory. Dien Bien Phu itself may be just such a critical point." While Eisenhower noted that he was not prepared to save the garrison, he argued that the regional alliance was important enough to begin pursuing "as a matter of the greatest urgency."[18]

IF NSC MEMBERS WERE confused about how to handle the deteriorating situation in Indochina, Congress was even more in the dark. While the bleak reports out of Dien Bien Phu were widely reported in the press in early April, Eisenhower showed no desire to brief members of Congress again about the course of events in Indochina or the military options under consideration, saying that he believed the decision was one only for "statesmen." The substantial Senate support for the Bricker amendment was just the latest evidence to the president that statesmen were sometimes a rare commodity on Capitol Hill. However, the decision to leave all but a handful of members out of the debate was risky. Democrats, especially, were mindful of how Harry Truman had suffered at the hands of Republicans for his refusal to consult members of Congress in the hours following the outbreak of war in Korea. They would repay Eisenhower in kind if given the opportunity.

The frustration and confusion voiced in the Senate the previous week by senators Watkins, Stennis, and others grew even more pronounced in the early days of April. On the afternoon of April 6, Kennedy addressed the Senate and excoriated Eisenhower and Dulles for withholding the facts about Indochina. He said "the time has come for the American people to be told the blunt truth about Indochina." While he favored Dulles' policy of "united action," he worried about where such a policy would lead the nation. "To pour money, materiel, and men into the jungles of Indochina without at least a remote prospect of victory," he said, "would be danger-ously futile and self-destructive." For his part, Kennedy said he doubted the United States could make much difference in Indochina. "No amount of American military assistance in Indochina can conquer an enemy which is everywhere and at the same time nowhere, 'an enemy of the people' which has the sympathy and covert support of the people."

When Mansfield entered the debate, the discussion turned to the prac-tical implications behind Dulles' call for united action. "I wonder," Mans-field asked Kennedy, "if the senator can tell the Senate what he thinks Sec-retary Dulles had in mind when he was making his speech before the Overseas Press Club in New York recently."

"There is every indication," Kennedy replied, "that what he meant was that the United States will take the ultimate step."

"And that is what?" Mansfield asked.

"It is war."[19]

That same day, as the Senate Democratic Policy Committee—a group of about a dozen leading Democrats—gathered for their weekly meeting, the discussion turned Indochina. When Walter George assumed the role of devil's advocate and argued for U.S. intervention, the group erupted. Oklahoma's Robert Kerr became especially incensed. When George said that "If we don't go to war we'll lose face," Kerr slammed his fist on the table. "I'm not worried about losing my face," he said. "I'm wor-ried about losing my ass." As the meeting ended, one observer later recalled, "there was no doubt whatsoever where the Democratic Policy Committee stood. They were against it. And [Minority Leader Lyndon] Johnson so reported back to Eisenhower."[20] Perhaps as important as the April 3 meeting between congressional leaders and Dulles, the April 6 dis-cussion among these senators was more evidence for Eisenhower that direct U.S. intervention in the Indochina war would not attract broad bipartisan support in Congress.

At a press conference the following day, Eisenhower made it clear where he stood—in public, at least—on the strategic importance of Indochina, his vacillations in the NSC meeting notwithstanding. Asked what importance he would assign to Indochina, the president defined the "broader considerations that might follow what you would call the 'falling domino' principle." With the possible loss of Burma, Thailand, Indonesia, and other nations in the region, Eisenhower said that "you are really talking about millions and millions and millions of people. . . . So the possible consequences of the loss are just incalculable to the free world." Asked if the United States was prepared to "go it alone" in the event that attempts at united action failed, Eisenhower refused to answer. [21]

Dulles, meanwhile, addressed a group of Republican women on April 7 and issued a veiled threat to China and the Vietminh. He seemed to confirm Kennedy's assumption that "united action" was the equivalent of war. The united will of free nations', he said, would "diminish the need for united action." Most of the nations, "great problems," Dulles observed, "come from not making sufficiently clear in advance what the dangers are to a potential aggressor." Ironically, Dulles himself failed to articulate the consequences of the aggression he and Eisenhower opposed in Indochina. [22]

By sending conflicting and confusing signals, Eisenhower and Dulles risked painting themselves into a political corner. In speeches and statements over the previous months, both men had raised the stakes in Indochina by declaring that the region was of vital importance to the security of all democratic nations in Southeast Asia. The "loss" of Indochina, they argued, would not only threaten Southeast Asia, but ultimately the forward Pacific defenses of the United States. Yet Eisenhower had also made clear that he opposed involving U.S. ground troops in the region, despite his argument that Indochina's "loss" would jeopardize U.S. security interests. He rejected air strikes to help the French win the crucial battle at Dien Bien Phu. After years of deriding Harry Truman for allowing China to "fall" to the Communists, Eisenhower and his men seemed prepared to do the same in Indochina—only with a much more determined effort to demonstrate a sincere *desire* to do *something*.

Eisenhower's remarks did nothing but heighten public and congressional anxiety about U.S. plans for Indochina. Among those most anxious was Mansfield. A strong supporter of U.S. assistance to France in Indochina, Mansfield worried that the United States was drifting toward war because of the administration's muddled and incoherent policy.

On April 14, Mansfield justifiably complained to the Senate that Eisenhower, while taking several members of Congress into his "confidence," had not yet consulted the chairmen and ranking minority members of the Senate Foreign Relations Committee and the House Foreign Affairs Committee. "While the Senate may discuss this problem, and the press may write about it, the President and the Secretary of State must bear the responsibility for dealing with the situation," Mansfield said. "They, and they alone, must lay down our official policy with respect to Indochina, in clear and unmistakable language." While Mansfield understood that the administration "believes our strategic stake in Indochina is very great," he worried that Eisenhower had not yet "established the minimum conditions to prevent Communist seizure of Indochina without full-scale war. It is not clear that these conditions are even understood by the administration."

Although he was not ready to break with Eisenhower over Indochina, Mansfield was not happy with the general drift of events. With the rapid deterioration of France's position, Mansfield worried that it would soon be "too late . . . to keep Indochina from falling or slipping into the net of Communist totalitarianism." While Dulles would soon be carrying the nation's "hopes" for a solution to Geneva, Mansfield questioned if those hopes were "a substitute for the actions which are necessary, which must be taken to prevent either a settlement of appeasement or our full military commitment in Indochina?"

Attending the Geneva Conference, "without a change in the present state of affiars," Mansfield said, would only postpone an inevitable crisis. "At worst, we can expect an unmitigated disaster. Out of this conference may come a truce, which will insure ultimate Communist control of Indochina with all that implies for our own security and the security of other free nations." The foremost fear in Mansfield's mind was that the conference might throw France's political system into a tailspin, resulting in the "collapse of all plans for the united defense of Western Europe. Out of this conference may come, in the last analysis, world war III."

At the heart of Mansfield's argument was his fear that Eisenhower had already made a decision to send U.S. troops to Indochina, an action he believed wholly unnecessary. There were more peaceful, prudent means to avert a dangerous escalation of the conflict, he argued. Like Kennedy, Mansfield believed that Indochina's problems were primarily political, not military. He proposed a seven-part plan of action designed to "clarify the objectives of the struggle in Indochina" and to "prevent the Geneva Conference from ending in disaster." His prescription included complete independence for Indochina's Associated States, the unequivocal endorsement of that independence by the United States "and other free nations," the reorganization of the governments of Indochina "on the basis of more popular representation," and the abdication of French citizenship by all nationalist leaders. Knowland agreed with Mansfield's point about granting complete freedom to the Associated States. "No matter how powerful their friends abroad may be," he said, "unless people desire freedom and have the will to resist, their resistance will not be effective."

When challenged by Democrat Albert Gore of Tennessee to elaborate on his suspicions that Eisenhower had already decided to intervene in Indochina, Mansfield responded that "the only information I get is what I read in the newspapers or what I happen to hear." He explained that he had simply been reading newspaper accounts of the April 3 congressional leaders' meeting with Dulles and Radford. He understood, he said, that the men had raised "two possibilities" at the meeting: limited air strikes to relieve Dien Bien Phu and a congressional resolution giving Eisenhower a free hand in Indochina.* Neither option pleased him. "People can talk all they wish about our air support and air strikes," Mansfield said, "but any time such action is taken, it will not be long before the foot soldier will have to move in." Furthermore, a congressional resolution, Mansfield believed, "would mean the abdication of responsibility by Congress, and I should be very much opposed to it. I think Congress ought to be informed, and informed minutely, of events as they are developing."†

Later in the debate, when John Stennis asked Mansfield if he believed that "we are approaching a state of facts that could involve us in a full-scale military involvement in this conflict," Mansfield answered, simply, "I think we are approaching a conference pregnant with possibilities."[23]

LESS THAN TWO WEEKS before the opening of the Geneva Conference, Dulles was having only limited success in forming a regional or international coalition around his concept of "united action." Britain and France wanted no part of a military or diplomatic endeavor that would threaten negotiations at Geneva. As French Foreign Minister Georges Bidault told Dulles on April 14, France was weary of the "heavy burden" of war. The government, he said, "must have an opportunity to negotiate an honorable peace." Should the conference fail to produce an acceptable agreement regarding the future of Indochina, Bidault held out hope for some form of "collective security," but refused to even discuss details of that arrangement until after the conference.[24]

Undeterred, Dulles doggedly lobbied British officials to join an international coalition. After a series of meetings with British Foreign Minis-

---

*While Dulles had, indeed, prepared the draft of a congressional resolution, at Eisenhower's direction he had not discussed it with the congressional leaders.

†Mansfield would repeat, in similar language, his warnings against aerial bombing eleven years later as he tried to dissuade President Lyndon Johnson from initiating a sustained bombing campaign against North Vietnam. However, in supporting the 1964 Gulf of Tonkin Resolution, he would abandon his 1954 opposition to giving the president a free hand to intervene militarily in Vietnam.

ter Anthony Eden that began on April 11, the secretary of state extracted Eden's approval of a communiqué affirming the U.S.-British desire for "an examination of the *possibility* of establishing a collective defense" for Southeast Asia (emphasis added). Overly optimistic about Eden's intentions, Dulles read into those words Britain's willingness to finally consider "united action," a sentiment that Eden promptly tempered with a disclaimer that his first priority was the success of the Geneva Conference. Dulles also persuaded the French to sign a similar communiqué, pledging only their willingness to "examine the possibility" of collective action in Indochina. These tentative, lukewarm endorsements for Dulles' program of united action represented small steps, but the secretary of state believed that they represented a good starting point for building an international coalition. Returning home, he invited nine nations to send representatives to Washington on April 20 to begin staff-level talks on a collective security agreement for Southeast Asia.[25]

But just as quickly as hope appeared, it vanished. On April 16, Vice President Nixon spoke to a luncheon meeting of the American Society of Newspaper Editors and single-handedly revived fears that Eisenhower might send U.S. troops to Indochina. The weeklong convention had been a less-than-exciting affair to this point, partly because the editors had refused to allow their guest speakers to talk off the record. The result was that government officials who briefed the group understood that they might be quoted in the next day's newspaper and, not surprisingly, were largely unwilling to disclose information that was not already public knowledge. On Friday, by the time Nixon spoke, the editors were eager for something more than the bland, uninformative briefings they had endured all week. They urged Nixon to speak openly with the understanding that he would be identified only as a "high administration official."[26] Seemingly freed by the assurance of anonymity, Nixon delivered an impressive, wide-ranging discussion of the issues surrounding the Indochinese conflict.

Speaking to the newspaper editors, Nixon was clear about his views on intervention. He doubted the French had the "will to win," and cited the battle at Dien Bien Phu—which by then had been raging for four weeks—where he said a loss "would be almost catastrophic." Should the garrison fall, Nixon feared—and justifiably so—that France "would apply more pressure in the forthcoming Geneva conference to settle in Indochina at any cost." One answer, he suggested, was greater support for France's effort. That, he said, meant that "more men are needed and the question is where to get them." Should the Geneva Conference result in the withdrawal of French forces from Indochina, Nixon predicted that "Indochina would become Communist-dominated with a month." Asked by an editor

if U.S. troops should be sent to Indochina in the event that France withdrew, Nixon startled the group with his frank response:

> The United States as a leader of the free world cannot afford further
> retreat in Asia. It is hoped the United States will not have to send troops
> there, but if this government cannot avoid it, the administration must face
> up to the situation and dispatch forces.
>
>   Therefore, the United States must go to Geneva and take a positive
> stand for united action by the free world. Otherwise it will have to take
> on the problem and try to sell it to the others. . . . This country is the only
> nation politically strong enough at home to take a position that will save
> Asia.[27]

The next day's newspapers did not identify the "high administration
official" who called for dispatching U.S. troops to Indochina in the
event of a French withdrawal. But reaction in the Senate was immediate.
"What these speeches amount to is telling, not consulting," complained
Humphrey, who along with Republican Bourke Hickenlooper, told
reporters that the policy, as explained by the unnamed official, went
beyond U.S. policy as they understood it. Mansfield demanded disclosure
of the anonymous official's name "so that Congress can question him to
find out who and what he is speaking for."[28] Two days after the speech, on
April 18, several newspapers disclosed that Nixon had made the controversial remarks.[29]

That disclosure set off another round of attacks on the administration
in the Senate—this one led by Humphrey, who complained that administration officials would discuss Indochina with reporters, but not with senators. "I feel that if all we have to do is get information as to the security
of this country from reading the newspapers," Humphrey said, "then we
can easily conserve our time by doing away with some of the committee
meetings." Democrat Herbert Lehman of New York complained that
Nixon's speech "confused and frightened" the nation's allies. "We still do
not know who is speaking for this nation in matters of foreign policy. Is it
the president? Is it the secretary of state? Is it the vice president? Is it some
assistant secretary in the State Department? We do not know." The Senate's lone independent, Wayne Morse of Oregon, observed that the administration "is still not of one mind." Like Humphrey, Morse lamented the
failure of Eisenhower to brief the Senate properly on Indochina.

Democrat Edwin Johnson of Colorado told the Senate he was not surprised in the least by Nixon's remarks. He had recently overheard Nixon
discussing Indochina at a private party. "I heard the vice president, Mr.
Nixon," Johnson said, " 'whooping it up for war' in Indochina." In some
of the strongest senatorial language yet in opposition to American military

intervention, Johnson said that he opposed "sending American GI's into the mud and the muck of Indochina on a blood-letting spree to perpetuate colonialism and white man's exploitation in Asia."[30]

The commentary on Nixon's remarks was not confined to the Democratic side of the aisle. Majority Leader Knowland said the president should seek Senate approval before any commitment of armed forces in Indochina. The American people "would not be satisfied with having this country assume 90 percent of the burden, as it did in Korea," Knowland said, repeating the familiar argument that Lyndon Johnson had used with such deadly effect during the April 3 congressional conclave with Dulles.[31]

Eisenhower's allies worked quickly to clear up the confusion Nixon's statement had created. On April 19, Senate Armed Service Committee Chairman Leverett Saltonstall told the Senate that Defense Secretary Charles Wilson and Assistant Secretary of State Thruston Morton had both assured him the nation's policy toward Indochina had not changed. Saltonstall said that senators would be "fully advised of any broad changes in policy."[32]

Those assurances did not satisfy Morse, among others. The Oregon senator insisted "the time has come when the administration must give the American people the facts," and added that "the administration should not be talking in terms of trial balloons sent up by vice presidents."[33] Humphrey also challenged Saltonstall and insisted that he could only conclude that Nixon had announced a change in administration policy "because apparently plenty of people in the administration knew of the speech. What is more, the vice president is a member of the National Security Council."[34] In a lengthy April 20 editorial, the *Washington Post* was as skeptical of the true intent of Nixon's remarks as Humphrey and Morse. Arguing that Nixon had almost certainly anticipated the question about sending U.S. troops to Indochina, the paper said "the answer, then, bears the earmarks of a calculated attempt to prepare the American people for the possibility of direct involvement of their own ground forces."[35]*

Trying to put the best face on Nixon's comments, a State Department spokesman insisted that Nixon had not broken ranks with Eisenhower— and, in one sense, he had not. As the spokesman noted, in his "united action" speech of March 29 Dulles had warned that "united action" might involve "serious risks."[36] Dulles' artful and ambiguous remarks, however, were open to wide interpretation. Nixon's speech had been anything but

---

*In a 1965 interview, Nixon emphatically denied that his speech had been "an administration trial balloon." The speech was entirely his, he said. But, he added, "I do know this. I do know that Dulles shared that view, at the time I made that statement" (DOHP).

ambiguous. For the first time, a member of Eisenhower's administration had openly discussed what the National Security Council had been debating for weeks. Nixon disclosed nothing of Eisenhower's determination to avoid sending U.S. troops to Indochina. Yet by asserting that a French loss at Dien Bien Phu would be a "catastrophe" and that concessions to the Vietminh at Geneva would be a "retreat" from communist aggression, Nixon had publicly parted ways with his president.

Nixon's remarks elicited strong reaction from a public unaware that Eisenhower and his advisors were debating whether to send U.S. forces to Indochina. In a Gallup poll after Nixon's speech, 68 percent of those surveyed opposed sending U.S. forces.[37] Worse was that Nixon's remarks had exposed divisions within the administration over Indochina and revealed that Eisenhower had no firm policy guiding his actions. "The more one searches Mr. Nixon's remarks," wrote columnist Walter Lippmann, one of the nation's most prominent and widely read journalists, "the more obvious it is that there is no policy behind them." Adding to Nixon's embarrassment was Lippmann's comparison of Nixon's April 16 remarks to a March 15 speech by the vice president in which he warned against allowing Moscow to determine U.S. military policy by "drawing us into little wars all over the world with their satellites." Nixon had declared that the administration had "decided that we would not fall into these traps . . . that we would not let the Communists nibble us to death all over the world in little wars." Lippmann asked: "What has happened in the past month to cause the Vice President to announce that he is prepared to eat his words?"[38]

The speech had a sobering effect on the vice president. A seemingly contrite Nixon told Dulles in an April 19 phone call that he hoped he had not "upset" what Dulles was trying to accomplish and that he had not intended to be identified with the remarks. According to Dulles, Nixon assured him that "the purpose of his answer was to say if the only way to hold Indochina was to go in, we might have to." Although Dulles did not dispute Nixon's position about U.S. troops as a last resort, later that day he assured Republican Senator H. Alexander Wiley of New Jersey that he opposed "getting American soldiers bogged down in Asia, that there were other things that could be done that were better."[39]

If Nixon's ill-timed statement irked Eisenhower, he did not show it. Press Secretary James Hagerty recalled that the president merely instructed the State Department to issue a statement clarifying U.S. policy "without cutting ground from under Nixon."[40] As historian Melanie Billings-Yun speculated, "Eisenhower may have determined, as Dulles certainly did, that Nixon's indiscretion could prove useful for frightening the communists as they headed to Geneva and that to disavow the threat under pressure would damage the West's image of strength."[41]

If Nixon's supposed gaffe served any real purpose, it was to reveal to Eisenhower and most other policymakers in Washington the extent to which the American people opposed sending U.S. forces back into Asia. Nixon, however, still hoped Eisenhower would change his mind and act to "save" Indochina. For weeks, the vice president had privately made it known around Washington that he sided with the few hard-liners in the administration who had supported Admiral Radford's call for air strikes and, perhaps, a more substantial military intervention in Indochina. The comments to the newspaper editors may have been Nixon's way of burnishing his conservative credentials with the Republican Party's far right. Or he might have simply been frustrated by the inability of administration officials to come to terms with Indochina. Nixon had indeed been briefly encouraged to believe that Eisenhower might consider sending the French something more substantial and effective than airplane mechanics. On April 6, Nixon had told National Security Council members, including Eisenhower, that "the United States must decide whether it is prepared to take action which will be effective in saving free governments from internal Communist subversion." He urged Eisenhower not to "underestimate" his ability to persuade Congress to agree to "whatever measures" he deemed necessary to save Indochina.[42] To Nixon's dismay, however, Eisenhower had been "resigned to do nothing."* But the negative public reaction to his comments, wrote *New York Times* reporter James Reston after he interviewed Nixon, persuaded the vice president that "public opinion is not yet aware of the nature of the threat to United States interests in that part of the world."[43]

Nixon was not the only one hopeful that Eisenhower might reverse course. On April 30, National Security Council chair Robert Cutler suggested, in the draft of an NSC paper, that the United States inform its allies of a willingness to use atomic weapons at Dien Bien Phu. Years later, in an interview with biographer Stephen Ambrose, Eisenhower recalled his immediate reaction: "You boys must be crazy. We can't use those awful things against Asians for the second time in less than ten years. My God."[44] Cutler was not the only advisor who had broached the issue of nuclear weapons. His suggestion was similar to one that Radford had previously presented to Dulles advocating the use of three tactical nuclear bombs in Indochina. Dulles wisely ignored the proposal.[45]

---

*In his 1985 book, *No More Vietnams* (31), Nixon wrote that not intervening at Dien Bien Phu was the "first critical mistake" the United States made in Indochina. "By standing aside as our ally went down to defeat, the United States lost its last chance to stop the expansion of communism in Southeast Asia at little cost to itself."

According to Nixon, however, Eisenhower had not been as adamantly opposed to nuclear weapons as he later led Ambrose to believe. The day after he read Cutler's paper, Nixon recalled that Eisenhower did not dismiss the idea out of hand. "Eisenhower asked me what I thought about this idea," Nixon recalled, acknowledging that while he also did not reject the proposal, he thought nuclear weapons were unnecessary. "I said that whatever was decided about using the bomb, I did not think it was necessary to have more than a few conventional air strikes by the united forces to let the Communists see that we were determined to resist." According to Nixon, Eisenhower concluded that the United States could not use nuclear weapons unilaterally. "And second," he added in a discussion with Cutler, "I agree with Dick that we do not have to mention it to anybody before we get some agreement on united action."[46]

What little chance there was that Dulles could assemble an international coalition for the defense of Indochina—and it was a very remote chance—had all but vanished with Nixon's remarks to the newspaper editors. Judging by Nixon's comments about their lacking "the will to win," the French government concluded that Eisenhower was already preparing to push them aside in Indochina. Eden, who had assured his skeptical colleagues that any collective security pact would be oriented toward the defense of Southeast Asia—and not just Indochina—was furious. He refused to send a representative to the April 30 meeting Dulles had convened to discuss the first steps toward building an international coalition.[47]

His campaign for united action in shambles, Dulles was left to focus on the Geneva Conference, where the prospects for a successful outcome were even less hopeful. Dulles knew that France would undoubtedly compromise with the Vietminh and leave the Communists in control of at least some portion of Indochina. If that happened, Eisenhower would be exposed to charges that his policy toward Indochina had failed. The Republican high ground on Asia would be forfeited. It could, therefore, be said that Eisenhower had "lost" Indochina as Truman "lost" China.

As he left for Geneva, Dulles knew the conference would be littered with political pitfalls—especially for a Republican president who had campaigned to end the "futile and immoral policy of containment."[48] At best, it appeared that Eisenhower could claim that he had contained the spread of communism in Indochina—although even *that* claim could be easily disputed by any evidence of Vietminh victories. As historian David Anderson noted, "Either way, compromise was not consistent with the New Look strategy of regaining the initiative against world communism."[49]

Indochina was one of several issues the Geneva conferees planned to address. Before that, representatives of the United States, Great Britain, China, France, and the Soviet Union would discuss the postwar dispositions of Berlin and Korea. This schedule gave Dulles some room to maneuver. He would go to Geneva, but only as an observer. He would not participate directly in the talks, and he planned to leave the conference before it took up Indochina.

On his way to Geneva, however, Dulles stopped to confer with Eden and Bidault in Paris, where the French—desperate for anything to strengthen their hand at the conference table—again proposed U.S. air strikes to save Dien Bien Phu. After talking with Eisenhower, Dulles told Bidault that the U.S. position on unilateral intervention had not changed. "Under the circumstances," he told Bidault, "we should first need congressional authorization for any such war action." That authorization would not be possible in "a matter of hours," Dulles said, "nor do I think it can be obtained unless it is within the framework of a political understanding which would include other nations directly and vitally interested in Southeast Asia."[50] Arriving in Geneva on April 24, Dulles glumly told reporters that "we hope to find that the aggressors come here in a mood to purge themselves of their aggression."[51]

The Vietminh, on the other hand, exuded the confidence they had earned on the field of battle. Observed Chester Cooper, a member of the American delegation: "The French were in Geneva to admit defeat, to surrender what was once a rich empire." The Americans, he recalled, "were there, sulking, wriggling, agonizing—and all the other delegations knew that too."[52]

While Dulles contended with the problems of Geneva, Eisenhower met with Republican congressional leaders on April 26 to persuade them of his resolve to stay out of Indochina. Eisenhower told them that "if we were to put one combat soldier into Indo China, then our entire prestige would be at stake, not only in that area but throughout the world." While emphatic about keeping American ground troops out of the region, Eisenhower continued to play a cat-and-mouse game on intervention with naval and air forces. Leaving the door ajar, he said the United States might "eventually . . . use some of our planes or aircraft carriers off the coast and some of our fighting craft we have in that area for support."[53] Why he remained coy about his willingness to inject the U.S. military into Indochina became clear when Republican Congressman Charles Halleck, the House majority leader, told Eisenhower that suggestions that he might send American troops to Indochina "really hurt" politically. Nixon recalled that Eisenhower "immediately stepped in and said he felt it was important that we not show a weakness at this critical time and that we not let the Russians think that we might not resist in the event that the Communists attempted to step up their present tactics in Indochina and elsewhere."[54]

Recalling the pounding Truman took over China, Eisenhower reiterated his "determination to lead the free world into a voluntary association, which would make further Communist encroachment impossible."[55] Of course, it probably did not occur to a single Republican leader—all of them so thoroughly disdainful of Harry Truman's foreign policy—to observe that Eisenhower had just embraced the very containment policy that he and other Republicans had so vilified during the 1952 election. With another Asian country about to become dominated by a communist government, Dulles' lofty rhetoric about achieving the "genuine independence" of the "captive peoples" had quietly gone the way of Dien Bien Phu.

CHAPTER 12

Diplomacy of Bluster and Retreat

1954

In Washington, inconsistency reigned on Indochina. For all of the impassioned rhetoric about the region's importance to U.S. security, the actions of those trumpeting the rhetoric did not, in the spring of 1954, match their words. Despite the fact that almost everyone in power claimed to agree with Eisenhower's characterization of the domino theory, no one—except perhaps Radford and Nixon—believed in it strongly enough to call for the commitment of U.S. troops. When faced with the prospect of losing all or part of Vietnam to the Vietminh, Eisenhower demurred and offered rationalizations that would have sparked howls of Republican protest and condemnation had they been put forth by a Democratic president.

Congressional supporters of Indochina's independence were no less inconsistent. Typical of this intellectual inconsistency was Mike Mansfield's interview on CBS's "Man of the Week" radio and television program on April 25. When reporter Carleton Kent of the *Chicago Sun Times* reminded Mansfield of Eisenhower's argument that losing Indochina might lead to the "collapse" of Southeast Asia and "a grave and irreparable loss to the free world," he responded with a quick "That is correct." But what was Mansfield prepared to do to prevent this significant blow to freedom in Southeast Asia? Having asserted the previous October that "world peace hangs in balance" in Indochina, Mansfield now said, simply, that "I do not see why we should be called upon at this time to pull the chestnuts out of the fire in that area." The struggle, he maintained, was up to the people of Indochina. "They are the ones who have to get in and show the determination and fight for their own independence and their own liberty."[1]

As Mansfield's contradictory remarks demonstrated, the cumulative impact of the political turmoil over China, Korea, and McCarthyism was a powerful political force that contorted the rhetoric of more than one political leader in Washington. The inordinate fear of Chinese communism was at the root of it all. Most American political leaders believed, with some justification, that the communist victory in China was part of a Soviet plan for world domination. The Soviet-influenced communist leaders in China, most American officials believed, would not be satisfied until they ruled all of Southeast Asia.

However, this did not necessarily mean that the Vietminh and their political supporters were motivated only by communist ideology. The situation was far more complicated than that. But Eisenhower, Mansfield, and other political leaders—their eyes riveted on a menacing shadow of Chinese communism creeping southward across Southeast Asia—failed to see the extent to which nationalism, not communism, motivated the fight for independence in Indochina. Even if they had, it is unlikely that they would have been free to express that view. After years of McCarthyite bullying by Republicans and some conservative Democrats, the fear of being branded a communist dupe or sympathizer ensured a heightened level of rhetoric about the need to aggressively challenge communism, whether foreign or domestic. Yet because of America's painful experience in Korea, hardly any leader could be found who actually advocated the return of U.S. troops to Asia to fight the communist menace—regardless of the supposed threat to America's security. The product of these related, yet conflicting, political forces were leaders like Eisenhower, Dulles, Mansfield, Kennedy, Knowland, and others who—for various reasons—shouted "fire!" and then proposed only to provide a limited supply of water so that someone else could extinguish it.

It was just this type of political tightrope that Dulles walked in late April as he arrived for the opening session of the Geneva Conference. Inside the conference, the dour secretary of state could do little. To participate in negotiations resulting in a French compromise that ceded territory to the Communists would open up the administration to blistering attacks from Democrats and conservative Republicans. Outside the conference, Dulles could do even less. With the stringent conditions on intervention imposed by Eisenhower and Congress, the secretary of state knew the United States could have almost no impact on the conference's outcome—especially considering the refusal of the British and the French to endorse Dulles' program of united action.

After several days at Geneva, where he sat only as an observer, Dulles watched his worst fears about France's determination to compromise being confirmed. He sent word to the National Security Council that he feared the government of Joseph Laniel might soon be replaced by "a government further to the left, which would be committed to liquidate the French position in Indochina." Furthermore, Dulles reported, the French were amenable to "a settlement" that gave them parts of Cochinchina and some enclaves in the center of Vietnam. After Under Secretary of State Smith presented this depressing news at an April 29 meeting of the NSC, Nixon and Harold Stassen, director of the State Department's Foreign Operations Administration, urged Eisenhower once again to consider military intervention. Stassen wanted U.S. ground troops to replace French troops in southern Vietnam, while Nixon said he favored air strikes at Dien Bien Phu and, perhaps, other places.

Eisenhower aggressively blunted Stassen's forceful presentation. It was all "well and good," he said, to suggest that American troops should replace French troops. "But if the French indeed collapsed and the United States moved in," the president argued, "we would in the eyes of many Asiatic peoples merely replace French colonialism with American colonialism." To Nixon's suggestion, Eisenhower replied that he would only consider air strikes if he were certain such action would strengthen the French resolve to remain in the war. Considering Dulles somber report from Geneva, that appeared to be a remote possibility, indeed.[2]

At Dien Bien Phu, the French garrison was crumbling fast. Radford told the NSC at its April 29 meeting that, after seven weeks of fighting, the French now controlled an area only 1,500 yards in diameter, making it almost impossible for relief planes to drop supplies. French casualties were estimated at 5,500. Even worse, the Vietminh now vastly outnumbered the French by 40,000 to 9,700 (including French casualties).[3] Dulles' report to Eisenhower upon his return to Washington on May 5 decisively foreclosed any possibility of U.S. action to save the garrison. While France had asked for air strikes, Dulles asserted that the French government had never made a formal request. "What the French fear," Dulles told the president, "is if the U.S. is brought into the struggle, France will not have a free hand to 'sell out and get out.' " Both men agreed the United States could do nothing to change the situation.[4]

On May 1, the Vietminh launched their final assault with a brutal artillery barrage that eventually brought the garrison to its knees on May 7. At Geneva, French Foreign Minister Bidault received the news in a note delivered to him during the conference proceedings, only two days before diplomats were scheduled to begin the discussions over Indochina. The note said, simply, "DBP Fini."[5]

Sensing the beginning of the end for France in Indochina, Democrats in Congress were quick to assail Eisenhower for his failed policy. Senators Herbert Lehman of New York and Theodore Francis Green of Rhode Island said the president's policy had resulted in a "diplomatic disaster" that was "insulting toward our allies and friends."[6] Only the night before Dien

Bien Phu's fall, Lyndon Johnson addressed a Democratic Party fund-raising dinner and in a sharply worded speech blamed the approaching debacle on the administration's public vacillations over Indochina. Encouraged by several informal advisors to take a tougher stance on Indochina, Johnson—who normally supported Eisenhower on foreign policy—made a very public declaration of independence from the president. "What is American policy on Indochina?" Johnson asked.

> All of us have listened to the dismal series of reversals and confusions and alarms and excursions which have emerged from Washington over the past few weeks. We have been caught bluffing by our enemies, our friends and Allies are frightened and wondering, as we do, where we are headed. We stand in clear danger of being left naked and alone in a hostile world.[7]

Making France's position in Indochina appear even more desperate, the defeat of France at Dien Bien Phu raised fears that the United States might now succumb to even greater pressure to intervene militarily to prevent a total French collapse. That prospect was foremost in the minds of Senate Foreign Relations Committee members on the morning of May 12 when Dulles went before them to discuss the latest developments in Indochina and Geneva. In an artfully worded statement, Dulles assured senators that "it is the *present* decision of the president not to send any American forces into the area under *present* conditions and not to recommend it to Congress" (emphasis added). Dulles, however, assured the committee that "I personally feel very strongly against the commitment of American land forces on the continent of Asia." Dulles, of course, meant that he and Eisenhower opposed *unilateral* U.S. intervention, a point made clear later in answer to a question from J. William Fulbright. "It is the firm decision that under *existing conditions*," Dulles said, "that we will not fight for Indochina. We are trying to make the conditions into conditions which might make it seem that a fight for Indochina was justifiably worthwhile and would succeed"[8] (emphasis added).

What he heard at the hearing concerned Mansfield enough that he invited Paul Sturm, an official with the State Department's Office of Philippine and Southeast Asian Affairs, to lunch that day. Sturm recalled afterwards that Mansfield told him "it is now evident that our most serious mistake thus far . . . has been to assume that a military victory was possible in the absence of suitable political settlements between France on the one hand and the Associated States [Vietnam, Laos, and Cambodia] on the other." Sturm also recalled that the Montanan asked him "what it might be possible for us to do militarily" in Indochina. When Sturm mentioned the possibility of introducing limited numbers of ground forces into northern Vietnam, he thought it significant that Mansfield "did not react adversely."[9]

However, several days later, in a lengthy interview with the *New York Times*, Mansfield reiterated his opposition to sending U.S. troops to Indochina. "I don't see how it can be applied there with any effect," he said, meaning that his opposition to ground troops was primarily based on his concerns about the practical implications of force, rather than any moral or philosophical compunctions about sending the U.S. military into another Asian country. The meaning of his statement became clear when he added, "Of course, that doesn't take into consideration the dropping of the atomic bomb, but where would you drop them in Indo-China?" If the United States used nuclear weapons, Mansfield was certain the Chinese and other Asian nations "are going to say, 'Why, these white folks are taking it out on us. They don't drop atom bombs on white people but they drop them on the Japanese, the Chinese.' And I think the revulsion against us would be great." Underlying all of Mansfield's concerns about Indochina was his strong conviction that the region's problems would never be solved militarily. "It is essentially a political problem," he insisted, "and that is one thing we have lost sight of all the way through this Indo-Chinese operation."[10]

HAVING THREATENED A military solution in vain and now desperately hoping for a political resolution, Dulles—disillusioned by France's desire to leave Indochina and reluctant to be seen negotiating with a communist country—abandoned the Geneva talks as they turned to Indochina. Back home in Washington, he tried to comfort a nervous American public in a nationally broadcast speech on May 7—the day the French garrison at Dien Bien Phu collapsed—when he assured them that "*present conditions . . . do not provide a suitable basis for the United States to participate with armed forces*" (emphasis added). Dulles quickly added, however, that any settlement in Geneva that led to "a Communist takeover" would be cause for serious concerns.[11]

Dulles' remarks on May 7 were not his last words on the matter. While he hoped to assure Americans that their country was not on the verge of another Asian war, he also hoped to strengthen France's hand at Geneva by suggesting just such a possibility. Therefore, in a June 4 speech in Los Angeles, he declared that the United States would not intervene *unilaterally*, but was still considering military action as part of a united effort involving France, Vietnam, and other Southeast Asian nations. But Eisenhower's conditions for taking action had changed considerably in the weeks since Dulles' meeting with congressional leaders. He no longer insisted that Great Britain join the coalition. At the same time, however, he imposed even more stringent conditions on France and Vietnam: the "local

authorities" must request U.S. intervention; France must give "clear assurance of complete independence" to Vietnam, Laos, and Cambodia; the
United Nations must show "evidence of concern"; other nations in the
region must become involved; and France must promise that it would not
"withdraw from the battle until it is won." Dulles told his audience that
"only if these conditions were realized could the President and the Congress be justified in asking the American people to make the sacrifices incident to committing our nation, with others, to using force to help restore
peace in the area."[12]

Despite his rhetoric, it is unlikely that Dulles was actually trying to find
a way for the United States to intervene in Indochina. It is more likely
that he was engaging in a two-tiered public relations campaign: one was
designed to calm public and congressional anxieties about American intervention; the other was to increase French leverage at Geneva by leading
the Communists to believe that the United States was refining a process
under which it might eventually intervene. As one Dulles biographer
observed, the conditions were "a set of interlocking booby traps" that actually foreclosed any chance of U.S. military intervention. Even had the
French been able to "render [the booby traps] harmless and acceptable,"
biographer Townsend Hoopes wrote, "it is likely that a now thoroughly
disenchanted Eisenhower would have developed further obstacles."[13] On
June 11 Dulles spoke out again, but this time with a message aimed more
directly at the Chinese. He said that if China were to invade Indochina,
"that would be a deliberate threat to the United States itself."[14]*

Dulles' perplexing gamesmanship and his conflicting public statements clearly frustrated some members of Congress. One senator particularly irked by the administration's policy was Fulbright. A former president of the University of Arkansas, Fulbright was an intellectual given to
independent, critical analysis of U.S. foreign policy issues, especially where
Dulles and Eisenhower were concerned. But he was no opponent of U.S.
military intervention in Indochina. While his conventional views about
the monolithic nature of communism were evolving, the second-term

---

*In a 1966 interview, a former aide to Dulles, John Hanes, acknowledged the
"schizophrenic" nature of the administration's public statements on intervention.
"I think we did too much of too many things," he said. "We did intervene enough
to get ourselves tagged with intervention, which I think was done largely to placate the military, and yet, we certainly didn't do enough to be decisive. Nor did we
think it could be decisive because we didn't think the French had a winning battle
on their hands. Some of our policies, therefore, were schizophrenic, which merely
reflected the fact that we had differing forces that were pushing us" (Hanes OH,
1/29 and 8/12/66, DOHP).

Arkansas senator was, at least for now, in the mainstream of American thought about the communist threat and the military means required to prevent its encroachment.

At a June 15 hearing on the authorization of the Mutual Security Act of 1954—the foreign aid bill—Fulbright subjected Everett Drumright, deputy assistant secretary of state for Far Eastern affairs, to a rigorous line of questioning about U.S. policy toward Indochina. Saying that he was weary of sending hundreds of millions in economic and military assistance to Indochina with little positive results, Fulbright asked Drumright, "What is the long-term solution, assuming we are not going to war?" Drumright had no comprehensive answer, other than to assure Fulbright that "we have been studying these things over in our department."[15]

What Drumright did not say, and may not have known, was that the Eisenhower administration was already hard at work preparing for a post-Geneva Indochina without the French army. Since January, Dulles and his brother Allen, the CIA director, had been developing plans to begin working directly with Vietnam's "native leadership." The first step in this operation was the appointment, in late May, of Colonel Edward Lansdale to head the CIA's Saigon Military Mission, the arm of the American government that would direct covert operations in Vietnam. An ebullient and colorful character, Lansdale enjoyed a reputation as the wily and resourceful operative who had most recently helped Philippine leader Ramón Magsaysay defeat the communist-led Hukbalahap rebels. In Vietnam, Lansdale—a former advertising executive who had served with the Office of Strategic Services during World War II—would eventually become famous for his war of dirty tricks and sabotage against the Vietminh.[16]*

As Lansdale was slipping quietly into Vietnam in early June, the Geneva talks ground to a virtual standstill, and Dulles became even more concerned about the outcome. Although conferees were nowhere near an agreement on Indochina's future, France's leverage was dwindling fast. All the while, the Vietminh forces grew stronger in the northern Tonkin region of Vietnam as the moribund Vietnamese government of Bao Dai languished—largely because of the perpetual absence of its nominal leader. Ensconced in the French Riviera, the former monarch refused to return home to provide the leadership his government desperately needed. The French, meanwhile, having lost the will to fight, were no more aggressive at the conference table. Still clinging to their fading colonial prerogatives,

---

*By the late 1950s, his many exploits would be chronicled in two novels loosely based on his activities in Vietnam—Graham Greene's *The Quiet American* in 1956 and *The Ugly American* by William J. Lederer and Eugene Burdick in 1958.

they stubbornly resisted all efforts to persuade them to internationalize the conflict by taking the issue to the United Nations.[17]

Dulles had not wanted to go to Geneva in the first place and once there had behaved, according to Townsend Hoopes, "with the pinched distaste of a puritan in a house of ill repute."[18] By early July, however, the pressure on Dulles to return to Switzerland increased just as the likelihood for a successful conference diminished. Among others, French Prime Minister Mendès-France urged Dulles to return to Geneva when the conferees reassembled July 14 after a three-week recess. U.S. Ambassador Douglas Dillon, believing the secretary of state's presence might lead to a favorable settlement, told Dulles that the French interpreted the U.S. absence as evidence that Eisenhower would oppose whatever settlement was reached. That, he argued, "greatly weakens our influence with [the] French." Dulles, however, remained reluctant to associate himself in advance with any agreement that might well give Vietnamese territory to the Communists.[19]

But Dulles knew that going back to Geneva, while it might stiffen French resolve against a deal with the Communists, would only more closely associate Eisenhower with a situation that now seemed destined for failure. When and if the talks in Geneva failed to produce a favorable result, Dulles also knew that congressional Democrats were ready to pounce, as evidenced by the strident Senate debate on July 8. Supported by Fulbright, Humphrey, Kennedy, and Henry Jackson of Washington, Mansfield attacked the administration's policy toward Indochina, especially as Dulles articulated it. Opposed to American participation in the Indochina portion of the Geneva Conference, Mansfield argued that the talks had "served to increase vastly the stature of the Chinese Communists in Asia and throughout the world."

Blaming Dulles and Eisenhower for their conflicting statements about U.S. intervention—"the air around [Eisenhower] was full of military sound and fury"—Mansfield urged the administration to be more discreet in public. "We ought to be spared the ludicrous spectacle," he said, "of this great nation being led to the brink of war in public statements and actions on one day and backed away from the next. If this diplomacy of bluster and retreat is designed to confuse the enemy, it succeeds only in confusing the American people."

In his most prescient of moments, Mansfield warned that sending the American military to Indochina would involve the nation "in every sense" in a "nibbling war." "The terrain of the Indochinese conflict—the flooded deltas, the thousands of scattered villages, the jungles—is made to order for the nibbling of mechanized forces," he said. "The French have been nibbled and chewed for eight years."

The heart of the problem, Mansfield believed, was that Eisenhower continued to apply military solutions to a political problem. Although Dulles had hoped to build support for united action by inviting various nations to participate in an international coalition—"an ill-conceived alliance"—Mansfield faulted the administration for having placed too much emphasis on the military power of Western nations. "Asian freedom," he insisted, "must be defended primarily by Asians. A people, whether in Asia or in the Americas, can preserve their independence only if they have it in the first place and if they are willing to fight to keep it."[20]

The following day, July 9, Dulles was still leaning against returning to Geneva. His consultations with several leading senators, including Knowland and Lyndon Johnson, solidified his decision, as did a discussion with Nixon. Having taken note of Mansfield's speech the day before, Nixon advised Dulles to stay home. After Mansfield's speech, he said, "the line will be that Geneva is a sell-out—a failure of diplomacy. We would be put on the spot where we have to go along or repudiate what we have said."[21]

In Geneva, the talks inched along without progress until mid-June, when the French parliament replaced Prime Minister Laniel with the liberal Pierre Mendès-France, who promptly promised to reach an agreement on the future of Indochina in four weeks or resign. The new French leader quickly opened secret negotiations with Chinese Prime Minister Zhou Enlai and agreed to Zhou's proposal for partitioning Vietnam into two regions. Forced to bargain with France and China for the future of his nation, Pham Van Dong—Ho Chi Minh's foreign minister—fought to keep the partition line as far south as possible. (Exhibiting their typical disregard for the Vietnamese, France excluded representatives of Bao Dai's government from the private talks.)

On July 20, with Mendès-France's self-imposed resignation deadline fast approaching, the parties to the negotiations—now joined by Soviet Foreign Minister Vyacheslav Molotov and British Foreign Minister Eden, but still absent a representative of Bao Dai—carved up Vietnam in an act of blatant disregard for the wishes of the Vietnamese people. The agreement established a cease-fire throughout the country and divided the nation at the 17th Parallel. France would still maintain its influence in the south, while Ho Chi Minh's government would operate from the north. Within three hundred days, French troops would withdraw from the north and Vietminh troops would vacate the south. No new military equipment or forces could be introduced into either part of the country and neither side was permitted to enter into a military alliance or allow a foreign nation to establish a military base on its soil. The Geneva accords, however, never envisioned a permanent partition of Vietnam. National elections were to be held in 1956 to determine the future of the reunified nation.[22]

To *New York Times* reporter Thomas J. Hamilton, the agreement "brought to a close the eight-year struggle for Indochina."[23] The bitter reality was, however, that Geneva merely signaled a brief, uncertain truce in a war that would last for another twenty years. In the end, Geneva was more the product of a search for political, economic, and military advantages than a quest for peace. Exhausted by the war, France was desperate to cut its losses. Hoping to solidify his shaky coalition government, Mendès-France had jumped at the opportunity to secure at the conference table what his country could not win in battle. Chinese leaders, although supportive of the Vietminh, may have viewed a united Vietnam, even under communist rule, as a challenge to their preeminence in Asia. Prolonging the war, the chief legacy of the Geneva accords, kept Vietnam weak, divided, and less of a threat. For the Soviets and the Chinese, a continuing conflict in Vietnam offered an added advantage—it might force the United States to maintain the commitment of significant resources that would not be available in other regions, particularly in Europe and elsewhere in Asia.

The agreement placed Eisenhower and Dulles in the uncomfortable position of promising not to undermine an agreement which they opposed. While the president said the United States would not be bound by the agreement, he added that the country would "not use force to disturb" it. Dulles echoed Eisenhower, but was more defensive. "The important thing from now on is not to mourn the past," he said at a news conference on July 23, "but to seize the future opportunity to prevent the loss in northern Vietnam from leading to the extension of Communism throughout Southeast Asia and the Southwest Pacific."[24] Perhaps unknowingly, Dulles had articulated a containment policy for Southeast Asia.

Try as he might to forget the aggressive liberation rhetoric of Eisenhower's 1952 campaign, Dulles could not escape the critics who claimed that the president's Indochina policy had failed to stop the march of communism. For a few days, his critics treated Dulles to a taste of the bitter medicine forced on Harry Truman and Dean Acheson beginning in 1950. *Time* declared that "the balance of world power lurched, and tilted in favor of Communist power." The agreement's specifics were detailed on an entire page in the magazine's August 2 edition under the headline: "Terms of Surrender."[25] Knowland, who had opposed any American involvement in the talks, called the agreement "one of the great Communist victories of this decade."[26] The harshest rhetoric, however, came from the House. "The Geneva Conference resulted in a complete sellout of all that is dear to all liberty-loving people in the free world," said Democratic Representative Michael Feighan of Ohio. "The United States cannot escape responsibility for the sellout at Geneva." Said Republican Representative Patrick Hillings of California: "At the dawn this morning, twelve million human beings were sold into Communist slavery by the action of leaders of the free world with the exception of the United States. . . . Today is indeed a black day for freedom." Democratic Representative Ray Madden of Indiana charged that the agreement placed the people of northern Vietnam "under the yoke of Communist slavery."[27]

Despite the criticism, the political fallout over Geneva could have been worse. By refusing to participate in the talks, Dulles had insulated Eisenhower from even more widespread and vehement attack. Refusing to sign the agreement, Under Secretary of State Bedell Smith, who went to Geneva as an observer, merely "took note" of its provisions. Although they refused to embrace the talks' outcome, Dulles and Eisenhower had not been entirely displeased. As Dulles noted, the agreement "advances the truly independent status of Cambodia, Laos and southern Vietnam." Under Mendès-France's leadership, France had finally agreed to complete the independence promised so long to the nations of Indochina. Dulles viewed this as a hopeful sign and believed the native populations might be more willing to fight for their own freedom now that French colonialism would be removed from the equation.

Dulles and Eisenhower believed the agreements also bought the United States valuable time to build up the noncommunist forces in the south in preparation for the 1956 national elections. They also hoped the accords would provide additional time to formulate a longer-term arrangement for Southeast Asia's defense. Dulles, therefore, promised "prompt steps" toward "arrangements for the collective defense" of the region.[28]

While the conferees were busy dividing Vietnam, Dulles had worked to prepare the United States for the defense of Indochina after the French departure. Although he remained officially aloof from the negotiations, he and Smith quietly did their best to influence the settlement so that it would not inhibit future U.S. involvement in Vietnam. Nothing in the Geneva accords prohibited the United States from assisting the noncommunist government of Vietnam to defend itself against the Vietminh. In fact, to many members of Congress, the impending withdrawal of French forces sparked renewed optimism about Vietnam's future. With France out of the picture—and, therefore, the impediment of colonialism gone—most congressional leaders believed the fight would now become an unadulterated struggle to contain the spread of communism.

Fulbright seemed to reflect the feeling of many in Congress when he told the Senate in early July that he might have supported unilateral American intervention in Vietnam under different circumstances. "I was reluctant," he said, "to recommend intervention so long as Indochina was still a colony and there was no real commitment that it would someday cease to be a colony."[29] After Geneva, the United States would no longer be forced to deal with the Vietnamese government via the French. Assistance and advice would be dispensed directly to the Vietnamese leadership. Dulles told the National Security Council on July 22 that he would "almost rather see the French get completely out of the rest of Indochina and thus permit the United States to work directly with the native leadership in these states."[30]

With the pending French withdrawal, Eisenhower's National Security Council turned to establishing U.S. policy toward Indochina in the post-Geneva environment. The NSC concluded that the United States should move quickly to "protect its position and restore its prestige" in the Far East with a "new initiative" in Southeast Asia. One objective of this new strategy was the negotiation of a Southeast Asia security pact binding member nations to act against communist aggression in the region. In its final report, the NSC also agreed that the United States should "make every possible effort . . . to defeat Communist subversion and influence" in Southeast Asia, work to maintain and support friendly noncommunist governments in Vietnam, Cambodia, and Laos, and "prevent a Communist victory through all-Vietnam elections" set for 1956. Eisenhower also agreed that the United States should work through the French "only insofar as necessary" to support and strengthen South Vietnam's military forces and its economy. In an effort to stymie Vietminh inroads into South Vietnam, and to "prevent North Vietnam from becoming permanently incorporated in the Soviet bloc," he also approved covert operations "on a large and effective scale."[31]

But any tentative optimism about Vietnam's future was more than overshadowed by the dark clouds of doubt, deceit, and mistrust that blanketed the country in the summer and fall of 1954. Dulles, for one, worried that the Vietminh had been willing to negotiate at Geneva only because they believed "they will secure what they really want gradually in the course of time."[32] What worried Dulles most in the short term was not "overt Communist military aggression," but "subversion" and the "disintegration" of the noncommunist South Vietnamese government. Given its instability and disorganization, it was not altogether clear how long the shaky government of Ngo Dinh Diem, the fledgling country's new premier, could hold on—especially if the French beat a quick retreat before the United States had the chance to determine what level of support it could provide.

The only certainty was that Ho Chi Minh and his North Vietnamese government were determined to "liberate" South Vietnam. Claiming that Geneva was a "great victory," on July 22 Ho pledged his government's "utmost efforts" to "win the unification, independence and democracy of the whole nation." He vowed that the "struggle" would be "long and difficult."[33]

CHAPTER 13

The Best Available Prime Minister

1954–1955

In a stinging critique of Eisenhower's Indochina policy, John F. Kennedy told a Chicago business group on May 28, 1954, that he believed "the very foundation" of American assistance to Indochina rested on "a miscalculation of the military program of the French Union forces in Indo-China." Even before the Geneva Conference, Kennedy had concluded that Eisenhower's policy in Indochina had been plagued by nothing so much as "glaring errors of conception and judgment." In April, in his first public criticism of Eisenhower over Indochina, Kennedy had demanded that the president tell the American people "the blunt truth about Indochina." He had also warned of the futility of sending American resources to Southeast Asia with little prospect for victory. Now, after the debacle at Dien Bien Phu and the partition of Vietnam at Geneva, Kennedy was certain that the United States had invested too much in the Navarre Plan. The administration, he charged, had underestimated the potency of the Vietminh, as well as the impact of the assistance they received from Communist China. Kennedy believed that Eisenhower had not "recognize[d] the nature and significance of the independence movement" throughout Indochina. Like their predecessors in the Truman administration, Eisenhower and his advisors, Kennedy said, "chose to support the myth—and it was no more than a myth—that the Associated States of Cambodia, Laos and Vietnam were genuinely independent."

Worse, Kennedy charged, the administration simply did not understand Asia. Eisenhower's men failed to comprehend that "young and struggling governments, with a traditional hatred for the white man who had exploited them for several centuries, held no strong hostility for the Communist movement which was and still is to some extent identified in many sections with independence. In Indochina, the cause of the West was blurred by the visual impact of colonial powers fighting native people."

Kennedy concluded that the Eisenhower administration had based its military strength "upon mistaken analysis by the National Security Council of the future course of events in the world in general, and in Indo-China in particular." In implementing his New Look policy, Eisenhower had imposed deep cuts on the nation's military budget. Therefore, by drawing down U.S. conventional forces around the world, including the Far East, Kennedy argued that the Eisenhower–Dulles policy of threatening nuclear retaliation—"massive retaliatory power"—was based upon the dubious assumption that the nation could have "security at bargain prices."

> If the United States can meet aggression only by risking hydrogen warfare, we hand an advantage to the aggressor nation willing to achieve its conquest by methods short of those inducing us to take that risk. In short, we must reverse our air cuts and our "new look" military cuts, and place national security ahead of balancing the budget.

As for future involvement in Indochina, Kennedy maintained that the United States needed the support of "more than our traditional European allies." Specifically, he argued, that "the battle against Communism in Asia—with its long history of Western exploitation—cannot be won without the full support of the nations of that continent." Neither could the fight be won until the United States learned that "it cannot ignore the moral and ideological principles at the root of today's struggles." From the beginning, he said, the United States should have insisted that the French grant "complete" independence to the people of Indochina.

Still, Kennedy believed that the United States had a legitimate role in Southeast Asia—indeed, a responsibility to protect and promote democracy in the region. "The mantle of leadership has been placed upon our shoulders, not by any nation nor by our own government or citizens," he said, "but by destiny and circumstance, by the sheer fact of our physical and economic strength, and by our role as the only real counter to the forces of Communism in the world today." [1]

Despite his misgivings about U.S. misjudgments and missteps in Indochina, including the risks of deeper involvement in the region, Kennedy's view of Indochina was not unlike that of any other American political leader in the early years of the Cold War. Like so many others, Kennedy believed that international communism was the predominant evil in the world and that the United States was the only nation capable of providing the leadership for the free world's challenge to its threat. Although they harbored serious doubts about the ability of the United States—even in concert with other nations in the region—to effectively stem the tide of communism allied with nationalism in Asia, Kennedy, Mansfield, and others were politically and philosophically unable or unwilling to turn their backs on Vietnam. They were heavily invested in the Cold War orthodoxy that had helped elect them to the Senate, but also constrained by the political realities of their time: to reveal any lack of resolve in the struggle against communism—foreign or domestic—invited political ruin. Despite their personal concerns about the administration's Indochina policy, Kennedy, Mansfield, and most other congressional critics of Eisenhower were never anything more than *reserved* in their basic enthusiasm for the continued struggle against communism in Indochina.

In 1954—in the wake of the Geneva Conference—their "enthusiasm" for U.S. involvement in Indochina centered on the short, stocky Mandarin, Ngo Dinh Diem, whom Bao Dai persuaded in June to serve as prime minister of the newly formed government of South Vietnam. The exact circumstances surrounding his selection are still a mystery. Many, however, suspect the appointment was the result of U.S. pressure. In any event, Diem was certainly a most unlikely choice to head the new nation in the days after France's capitulation. He was neither a skilled politician, nor particularly popular with or well known to the country's population. A CIA report in late August charitably described him as a man of "great courage and implacable stubbornness . . . an uncompromising moralist, nationalist and rebel."[2]

Most of all, Diem was a man under fire, leading a new nation badly divided by eight years of war with the French and—because of France's reluctance to grant Indochina its complete independence—pitifully short of competent, visionary leadership. With more than eight hundred thousand refugees—most of them Catholic—streaming from the north into South Vietnam, the many social and political challenges facing Diem would have confounded the ablest politician. Few observers, especially the French, believed that the introverted and self-righteous Diem possessed the political skills necessary to unify and lead his new country into peace and prosperity in the dangerous and daunting months following Geneva.

Making his job even more difficult was Diem's fundamental distrust of democracy. "I know what is best for my people," would become his mantra whenever his policies were challenged. In describing Diem's governing style, the French journalist Bernard Fall once observed that, to Diem, "compromise has no place and opposition of any kind must of necessity be subversive and must be suppressed with all the vigor the system is capable of."[3] This was the man upon whom the fragile hopes for independence in South Vietnam now rested.

Diem's immediate troubles emanated from the opposition of three sects—the Hoa Hoa, the Cao Dai, and the Binh Xuyen—that had sprung up since the end of World War II in the south and had extended control over virtually every aspect of life in the country's rural areas and, to a great extent, even the capital city of Saigon. Organized around ethnic or religious ties, the sects had established alliances with the French, who armed them and found them convenient associates in their struggle for power against the Vietminh in the country's southern region. Combined, the three sects boasted armies of more than forty thousand men and posed a significant threat to Diem's power, especially considering his own tenuous control over the country's armed forces. Deepening Diem's troubles was the open rebellion of his army's chief of staff, General Nguyen Van Hinh, a citizen of France known to be plotting with leaders of the sects—with some French encouragement—to overthrow Diem's fledgling government.[4]

The new leader of South Vietnam was also no favorite of U.S. diplomats in Indochina. As he struggled to gain control of his government, fending off these factions and sects vying to share his power or seek his overthrow, cables poured in from Saigon almost uniformly critical of Diem and doubtful of his ability to hold onto power. "Diem is a messiah without a message," complained U.S. Chargé Robert McClintock from Saigon in early July. "His only formulated policy is to ask [for] immediate American assistance in every form including refugee relief, training of troops and armed military intervention. His only present emotion, other than a lively appreciation of himself, is a blind hatred for the French."[5] Reported U.S. Ambassador Donald Heath in an August 27 cable from Saigon: "Diem still has [a] reputation for honesty and patriotism. However, he seems scarcely capable of influencing people, making friends, or undertaking determined action." The problem was, however, that U.S. officials, even those most critical of Diem, could identify no other Vietnamese figure able to provide better leadership. "No successor government that we can envisage at this time," Heath admitted, "would have any real appeal to nationalist or anti-Communist sentiment." Still, Heath advised, "we must keep our eyes open for another leader."[6]

After years at the Maryknoll seminaries in New York and New Jersey, Diem did have his American admirers, especially among Catholics like Francis Cardinal Spellman, Justice William O. Douglas, Kennedy, and Mansfield. Fortunately for him, one of his most prominent supporters— Mansfield—was on his way to Vietnam. As Dulles prepared to convene an international conference in Manila to create a defensive alliance for Southeast Asia, he had devised a clever strategy to ensure the treaty's quick approval in the Senate. He would invite two influential senators—preferably Foreign Relations Committee members—to accompany him as members of the American delegation. As signatories to the treaty, these senators would be expected to fight for the treaty's ratification and serve as influential lobbyists among their committee colleagues. When Dulles consulted Foreign Relations Committee Chairman Alexander Wiley, the Wisconsin Republican recommended Mansfield and Republican H. Alexander Smith of New Jersey. Dulles readily agreed and invited both men to serve on the delegation.

Mansfield, although only a junior senator, was a shrewd choice because he had been openly skeptical of America's role in Geneva. In a CBS television appearance in May, he had specifically warned against any Southeast Asia defense agreement made up of only majority-white nations. "This must be an Asiatic pact, primarily," he insisted.[7] With a respected sometime-administration-critic like Mansfield supporting the treaty, it would be virtually assured of Senate ratification.

Mansfield, predictably, jumped at the chance. Before going to Manila, however, he stopped in France and then Vietnam, for his second visit to the region. In Paris, U.S. Ambassador Douglas Dillon gave him bad news about the new South Vietnamese leader. He told Mansfield that Diem "lacks what it takes" and might soon be overthrown. French officials, Mansfield found, had little confidence in or affection for Diem. They believed that "some coalition of religious sects" and "assorted military figures offers the only hope of holding the area." The French, Dillion assured Mansfield, "are anxious to get out of South Vietnam as quickly as possible." On the plane to Southeast Asia, reporter Jim Lucas of the Scripps-Howard newspapers reiterated this, telling Mansfield he doubted that Diem had "the drive or capacity to rally the Viet Namese Nationalists" and that he believed a coup was imminent.[8]

When he arrived in Saigon, Mansfield saw what he later described as a city in the midst of "an orgy of conspiracy and subversion. Teacup speculation centered on predicting the day or hour when the Diem government would be ousted."[9] In a September 2 meeting, he found U.S. Ambassador Heath extremely pessimistic about Diem's chances. For weeks, Heath had tried to persuade Diem to behave more like a politician and, as Mansfield observed, "play ball with the sects." Heath told Mansfield of his own forceful intercession with the sect leaders and how his stern warnings had so far prevented a coup. Diem, he said, spent most of his time worrying about the resettlement of Catholic refugees pouring into South Vietnam from the north. Heath's message to Mansfield was the same he had given to the State Department: if Diem fell, there was no one to replace him. Therefore, Heath argued, it was imperative that Diem negotiate with the sects to save his government.[10]

Later that day, when Heath escorted Mansfield to a meeting with Diem, the ambassador reported to Washington his surprise at Diem's sanguinity. Diem told Mansfield he was confident that General Hinh would return to the fold. "It is my opinion," Heath told Washington, "that Diem glossed over his difficulties in order that [Mansfield] should not have too dark a picture of [the] situation here." Other Vietnamese officials who briefed Mansfield were more realistic about Diem's precarious situation.[11] "I don't think anyone expected Diem to be able to rally anyone," recalled Francis Valeo, the Library of Congress expert who accompanied Mansfield on this and his earlier visit to Indochina. "At most, he was seen as an interim figure."[12]

In Manila, Mansfield and Wiley enthusiastically supported and signed the Southeast Asia Collective Defense Treaty (it became known as SEATO, the Southeast Asia Treaty Organization, although delegates created no formal governing organization).* Representatives of the United States, Great Britain, France, Australia, New Zealand, the Philippines, Thailand, and Pakistan signed the document and bound themselves to "act to meet common danger" according to each nation's "constitutional processes." Unlike the North Atlantic Treaty Organization (NATO), however, signatories did not stipulate that an attack on one member nation was an attack on all. Instead, in the event of "aggression by means of armed attack," the parties to the treaty would "consult immediately in order to agree on the measures which should be taken for the common defense." The United States supported the treaty only after the addition of an "understanding" that stipulated its willingness to "act" primarily in cases of "Communist aggression."

From the beginning, the treaty's deficiencies were obvious. At best, it was an anemic framework for the "united action" that Dulles had wanted before Geneva. In the words of one State Department official, the treaty was a "paper tiger," binding the countries to do nothing more than "consult" in the event of communist aggression.[13] Because of the Geneva accords, Vietnam, Laos, and Cambodia were prohibited from signing the treaty, although their protection was the primary motivation for the agreement. Burma, India, and Indonesia declined to participate.

Leaving Manila at the end of the conference, Mansfield returned to Vietnam persuaded that, whatever his shortcomings, Diem was—by default—the best person to lead South Vietnam. During the conference, Mansfield had expressed his pragmatic support for Diem to Dulles, who later relayed the information to skeptical French officials. Mansfield believed, he told Dulles, that "Diem might possibly be the last chance of a Prime Minister who could be effective." While not so enthusiastic about Diem as Mansfield, Dulles was as determined to give him a chance. Dulles told France's Minister of State Guy La Chambre on September 6 that "while we had no particular fondness for Diem, he nonetheless appeared to be a man of integrity and honesty, and we did not know of anyone who

---

*Other than the United Nations treaty, it was the only time members of Congress had served as treaty signatories.

might be any better."[14] On the evening of September 8, before leaving Manila, Mansfield and Randolph Kidder, the counselor in the Saigon embassy, met with La Chambre. After politely listening to the French official's discussion of various options for replacing Diem, Mansfield reacted strongly. A change in governments "every few weeks" would be "extremely unhealthy," he insisted. Absent a viable alternative, Mansfield said that Diem deserved support and should be encouraged to broaden his government.[15]

Upon his return to Saigon to discuss the SEATO conference developments with U.S. and South Vietnamese officials, Mansfield found that Diem's woes had only deepened. "The rumors of a *coup d'etat* persist and seem to grow more insistent," he wrote on September 10, after meeting with Heath and General John "Iron Mike" O'Daniel, the chief of the U.S. military mission in Vietnam. "Diem has still been unable to obtain control of his government."[16]

On his way back from Indochina, during a stopover in Berlin, Mansfield received a cable from Dulles requesting his views about the situation in Vietnam, especially concerning Diem's "ability to form a government worthy of our support."[17] Mansfield's September 24 reply was a strong endorsement of Diem. The political crisis, he said, was the result of Diem's attempts to form a government "free of corruption and dedicated to achieving genuine national independence." While he acknowledged that Diem was "inexperienced" and reluctant to compromise, he did not believe those "personal shortcomings" were the "root" of Diem's problems. "If Diem falls, the alternative is a government composed of his present opponents, no combination of which is likely to base itself strongly in the populace."[18]

Mansfield's backing of Diem strengthened Dulles' hand in discussions with the French by giving the U.S. policy a strong bipartisan flavor. Under Secretary of State Smith read Mansfield's message to French officials the day after it arrived, describing the Montanan as "a powerful Democratic Senator in opposition who believes that Diem is the best hope there is."[19] In a September 25 meeting among officials of the State and Defense departments, Dulles cited Mansfield's appraisal and observed that "the Senator's views would carry a lot of weight in the Foreign Relations Committee, especially with the Democrats."[20] For now, at least, Mansfield's strong endorsement of Diem had silenced the French complaints.[21]

On October 15, Mansfield reported on his study mission—a forty-eight-page document that, in the words of the authors of the *Pentagon Papers*, "elated Diem, subdued the French and annoyed Paris."[22] With its strong endorsement of Diem, the paper solidified the administration's support for the South Vietnamese leader and persuaded the president to proceed with direct military and economic aid to the South Vietnamese government. Prefacing his observations with a lengthy review of the history of Indochina, Mansfield criticized the failures of the French and the noncommunist Vietnamese government. But he was particularly critical of the administration for "overpromoting to itself and to the American people the capacity for material military aid alone" to win the struggle in Vietnam. "It is difficult to see what more could have been added, short of some foolhardy commitment of American troops on the Asian mainland against an outpost of international communism—literally its third line of defense in Asia," Mansfield wrote. "What was lacking in the situation was not military power but a sound political substructure for this power."

Concerning the immediate crisis, Mansfield observed that "the situation in Vietnam, and in a larger sense in Indochina, is grim and discouraging." And, he added, "it would be misleading and futile to report it to the Senate and to the people of the Nation in any other fashion." Mansfield warned that unless the nation's political problems were quickly resolved, South Vietnam might fall to the Communists in the 1956 elections. "Even before 1956, south Vietnam could give way to complete internal chaos."

As for Diem, his assessment was pragmatic. "The political issue in south Vietnam is not Diem as an individual, but rather the program for which he stands," Mansfield argued. "It is unlikely that any independent non-Communist government can survive in Vietnam, let alone recover the Vietminh-held area unless it represents genuine nationalism, unless it is prepared to deal effectively with corruption, and unless it demonstrates a concern in advancing the welfare of the Vietnamese people."

Concluding that the "the visible alternatives to the Diem government are not promising," Mansfield warned that any replacement for Diem "would probably take place in the form of a military dictatorship." U.S. officials must have found Mansfield's conclusions sobering and encouraging all at once: "In the event that the Diem government falls, I believe that the United States should consider an immediate suspension of all aid to Vietnam and the French Union forces there, except that of a humanitarian nature. . . . Unless there is a reasonable expectation of fulfilling our objectives the continued expenditure of the resources of the citizens of the United States is unwarranted and inexcusable."[23]

His two visits to Vietnam in 1954 had deeply influenced Mansfield. Inspired by the flood of Catholic refugees that poured into South Vietnam—"with nothing but the rags on their backs rather than to live under Communism"—the Catholic Mansfield had disregarded evidence that, to more dispassionate observers, provided ample proof of Diem's shortcomings. To be sure, Mansfield recognized many of those shortcomings. But he also appeared to have abundant faith that Diem was a work in progress and that he could be molded into the kind of leader who would inspire and lead the South Vietnamese to victory. As Gregory Olson observed in *Mansfield and Vietnam*, despite all his sophistication and his keen insights into

Asia, Mansfield could not see that communism and nationalism were not necessarily mutually exclusive philosophies. Like most other Americans, Mansfield was blind to the realities of Vietnamese politics. His Cold War philosophy, Olson wrote, "prevented him from seeing what his report made obvious, that Diem lacked the support to succeed."[24]

Mansfield's report was nonetheless greeted with consternation by U.S. embassy officials in France who worried that the senator's all-or-nothing ultimatum about U.S. aid to Vietnam might backfire if Diem, as expected, lost control of his government. "Senator Mansfield's report," Ambassador Dillon cabled Washington on October 16, "does not appear to allow for any substitute formula in such an eventuality." While Dillon believed the report might help persuade Diem and other South Vietnamese officials of the "urgency" of their situation, he expressed concern that it might also "increase the conviction" in Vietnam that Diem was "finished." Mansfield's absolute support of Diem did not appeal to Dillon or the French. "We cannot help but feel that we must continue to try [to] save South Vietnam regardless [of] individual personalities involved including Diem."[25]

From Saigon, however, Ambassador Heath saw more promise in the wide publication of Mansfield's views. "It has evidently made [an] impact on French and Vietnamese official circles," he wrote in a cable to the State Department. Diem's delight with Mansfield's considerable support was evidenced by his decision to print and distribute one hundred thousand copies of the report throughout South Vietnam. In Washington, Everett Drumright, deputy assistant secretary of state for Far Eastern affairs, agreed with Heath. He told Dulles that the Mansfield report "should greatly strengthen the Diem Government and give its opponents pause to consider." In light of Mansfield's much-welcomed support for Diem, Drumright was also willing to overlook pointed criticism aimed at the administration as "not unbearable." Mansfield's reproach, he believed, was "put forward in an effort to help and is not partisan in nature."[26]

Mansfield's report—despite its criticism of administration policy—not only endeared him to Dulles and Eisenhower; it encouraged the administration to bypass the French and finally offer financial assistance directly to Diem's government. After a month of intense debate among State and Defense department officials, Eisenhower made a firm commitment to Diem in an October 22 letter delivered by Heath. American aid would be given to South Vietnam, but only if Diem promised that "needed reforms" would be accomplished.[27]* Of course, Diem—who would always be reluctant to heed

---

*As Chester Cooper later noted, "It was that letter that was cited by members of the Kennedy Administration and even more often by officials of the Johnson Administration to relate the origin and continuity of U.S. policy in support of Diem in the earliest years of the Eisenhower Administration" (Cooper, 134).

the advice of U.S. officials—encouraged the eager Americans to believe
that he would, indeed, institute the desired reforms. But the long-term
changes in South Vietnam's system of government were actually the least
of Washington's worries. Keeping Diem in power through year's end was
a far more urgent concern.

IN THE WAKE of his impressive and influential report, Mansfield enjoyed
administration officials' utmost favor. Not only had he supplied Eisenhower and Dulles with powerful ammunition to bolster their support for
Diem, he was also among the most enthusiastic advocates for the Southeast Asia Collective Defense Treaty. Mansfield's support was now more
significant than ever after the 1954 elections in which the Democrats
regained control of both houses of Congress. By a 48–47 margin (with one
independent), Lyndon Johnson was now the Senate's majority leader. Walter George of Georgia was chairman of the Senate Foreign Relations
Committee. Mansfield, no longer the committee's most junior member,
now chaired the subcommittee with jurisdiction over State Department
operations.

   In January 1955, Mansfield flexed his new muscle by helping deflect a
reservation to the SEATO treaty proposed by former Republican congressman Hamilton Fish of New York, an isolationist in the tradition of
Robert Taft. Fish wanted a congressional declaration of war before the
president could commit U.S. troops to the defense of Indochina. In a
forceful presentation before the Foreign Relations Committee on January
10, Fish argued presciently that a president might someday use the treaty
to send American troops to Vietnam without specific congressional
approval.* "The danger is," he said, "that the United States government
may now be able to make war without a declaration of war, and may feel it
is duty-bound to react in a retaliatory or military way to any form of Chinese interference, aggression, direct or indirect."[28]

---

*Later, in defense of the massive American involvement in Vietnam in the 1960s,
Johnson administration officials like Secretary of State Dean Rusk would often cite
American commitments to the defense of Southeast Asia made in the treaty. As
historian George McT. Kahin later observed: SEATO "provided what the executive branch came to assert was congressional authority for direct military intervention" in Vietnam. "Indeed, SEATO's significance ultimately lay more in what
came to be construed as a congressional licensing of unilateral U.S. anti-communist military intervention in Southeast Asia than in its role as a collective defense
organization" (qtd. in McMahon, 154).

In a closed-door hearing three days later, Republican Homer Capehart of Indiana asked Mansfield to respond to Fish's concerns. Capehart
wanted to know if "there is no possibility then for the President under this
treaty to go to war on the scale, let us say, of the Korean war, without getting a declaration of war by Congress. Is that your thought?" Mansfield
replied, "That is my understanding."[29] After perfunctory debate with little dissent, the Senate ratified the treaty, 82–1, on February 1. The only
opposing vote was that of Republican William Langer of North Dakota,
who argued that the United States "ought to mind its own business."[30]

Meanwhile, the administration pursued its goal of placing South Vietnam and its leader on the right footing. The goal was to build a strong,
new nation to serve as a bastion of democracy from which to fight communism throughout Southeast Asia. To build this new government—one
that could persuade its people that it embodied the true nationalist spirit
of Vietnam—would have been a Herculean task under the best of circumstances because of the nation's inexperience with democratic institutions.
State Department officials believed it would require hundreds of millions
of dollars in American assistance, as well as the enthusiastic cooperation of
a unified South Vietnamese government and armed forces—a dubious
prospect given Diem's reluctance to accept advice from anyone outside his
own tight circle of advisors.

Despite the overwhelming odds against success, the process of creating a new nation in a most inhospitable political environment did not deter
Eisenhower and Dulles. With the kind of hubris that would characterize
the U.S. attitude toward Vietnam for the next twenty years, the president
expressed supreme confidence in the ability of U.S. policymakers to give
South Vietnam the kind of government and army it needed to fight the
North Vietnamese Communists. "In the lands of the blind, one-eyed men
are kings," the president had told the National Security Council on October 22. In other words, even a meager dose of American might and know-
how could win the battle against the Communists. What he wanted,
Eisenhower insisted, was a Vietnamese army that would support Diem.
"Let's get busy and get one," he commanded. He was certain, he said, "that
something could be done and done quickly."[31]

It would never be as simple as Eisenhower imagined. Not only was
Diem's weak leadership a severe impediment to progress; the Americans
suspected that the French—with one hundred sixty thousand troops still
stationed in the south—were quietly attempting to reassert their influence
in Indochina by undermining Diem's authority and, at the same time,
exploring accommodations with the communist government in Hanoi. It
was not a propitious time for conflicts between the United States and
France. They were, however, inevitable after the United States signaled its

determination in September to assist Diem's government with direct aid. At this, French officials concluded—and correctly so—that the United States was trying to supplant their country's role in Indochina. France's decision to reject membership in the European Defense Community—it did not want German troops to serve in the military alliance arrayed against the Soviet Union—did nothing to create warmer relations between the two countries and, in the words of one historian, "left the Western alliance in disarray."[32]

The new American effort to save Vietnam required someone who could work well with the French and who was capable of directing all aspects of the military and political solution that the United States hoped to implement. For this task, Eisenhower personally selected General J. Lawton Collins, who had served as Army chief of staff during the Korean War and who was then the U.S. commander in chief assigned to NATO's European Command. To associates, Eisenhower expressed tremendous respect for the man known as "Lightning Joe," one of the more successful World War II corps commanders. By early November 1954, Collins was on his way to Saigon with the title of "special representative," the rank of ambassador, and the short-term assignment of helping stabilize and strengthen Diem's government. Eisenhower instructed Collins to coordinate and direct a program that promoted internal security and political and economic stability throughout South Vietnam, while counteracting Vietminh infiltration into the country.[33]

Collins arrived in Saigon on a typically chaotic day. What he heard on the radio utterly amazed him: the chief of staff of the Vietnamese army was attacking Diem from a radio studio financed by the U.S. government. "I put a stop to that right off the bat," Collins recalled, not bothering to explain how the suppression of dissent would encourage the fuller development of democracy in South Vietnam.[34] While he was able to prevent the occasional renegade radio broadcast, Collins found himself much less effective when it came to persuading Diem to exhibit the kind of strong leadership that U.S. officials desired. After only one month at his post, Collins reported to the State Department on December 6 that "Diem still presents our chief problem." His initial unfavorable impression of Diem, he said, had "worsened rather than improved." Collins was blunt. Soon, he suggested, "some thought should be given" to a possible replacement, a prospect that he speculated might be necessary within as little as two weeks. Collins, however, had no one in mind as a replacement. "But time is running out," he said, "and it will take a lot of doing to make him into an effective leader."[35]

Diem did occasionally show signs of developing into an effective leader. His impressive skill in managing the influx of hundreds of thousands of refugees from the north was one such sign. Yet this feat was more than negated by a troublesome refusal to exert his leadership at crucial moments and a maddening penchant for adhering to uncompromising stances at the very moment that compromise was most needed. For example, during the crucial early months after Geneva, Diem had delayed selecting a leader for the nation's army while he vacillated and pondered the decision; meanwhile, he stubbornly refused to consider any accommodation with the sects that posed the greatest immediate threat to his government.

Collins, however, found that he could not instigate a program to remove Diem without Mansfield's acquiescence. After three visits to Vietnam, a prominent role in the ratification of the SEATO treaty, and an influential report on Indochina, Mansfield was now considered the senator most knowledgeable about Indochina. Such was his newfound stature that Dulles refused to consider Collins' criticisms of Diem without first consulting Mansfield. On December 7, 1954, Dulles personally sent three State Department officials—including assistant secretaries Walter Robinson and Thruston Morton—to solicit Mansfield's views on Collins' assessment. After reading the cable, Mansfield acknowledged that Collins had not overstated the degree of Diem's difficulties. Nonetheless, he believed the United States should continue backing Diem "even if it will cost a lot." To Mansfield, Diem represented "what small hope there may be in building something in Vietnam."[36]

In mid-December, after another of Collins' gloomy dispatches had arrived in Washington—"Diem does not have the capacity to unify [the] divided factions in Vietnam"—Mansfield was invited to review it and comment on whether the United States should consider seeking another leader, possibly the return of Bao Dai to a preeminent leadership position.[37] This time, Mansfield equivocated. "I cannot advise on the making of these judgments from an office in Washington," he wrote of possible disengagement from Vietnam. If the United States did withdraw, he predicted Diem would fall and that France would select a leader "with an eye to carrying out whatever policies they have in mind in connection with Viet Minh Communists under Ho Chi Minh." He urged the administration to subject all policy options to one question: "Will actions contribute to [the] development of [a] stable, independent non-Communist government in Viet-Nam and are they within our prudent capacity to discharge? If they are not, then in my judgment they should be avoided."[38]

To Collins, however, Diem's prospects grew progressively weaker. By mid-December, the general was voicing the unthinkable: a gradual American withdrawal from Vietnam. While he stopped short of recommending such a policy, Collins did make it clear that Diem had little time left to

solidify control over the government. Abandoning Diem would be embarrassing. Yet such an embarrassment, he cautioned, "would prove insignificant" compared to the damage the United States would suffer if Vietnam
fell to the Communists. "I believe it would be better to take [a] slight loss
of prestige in [the] near future," he said, "while time to attempt other solutions remains, rather than continue support [for] Diem should failure
appear relatively certain."[39]

Just as Collins was prepared to give up on him, Diem finally began to
exert more leadership. In a hopeful sign of flexibility, the prime minister
had finally agreed to bring leaders of the Cao Dai and Hoa Hoa sects into
his cabinet. That success, however, was not entirely due to Diem's new
spirit of cooperation. Edward Lansdale, the CIA operative who had
become an intimate advisor of Diem, bought the cooperation of some Cao
Dai leaders with bribes. As stubborn as he was arrogant, Diem refused to
be overthrown. By January 1955, even Collins began to see glimmers of
promise in Diem's leadership. Reporting some "successes" in Diem's deal-
ings with the sects and his "increased self-confidence" with officials in his
government, Collins reluctantly concluded that Diem might become the
kind of leader the United States wanted. Although the general cautioned
that Diem "has much yet to learn about practical politics and public relations," in a stunning turnabout Collins concluded in a cable to Washington that his "integrity, strong nationalism, tenacity, and spiritual qualities
render him the best available Prime Minister" for Vietnam.[40]

At the White House for a June 27 National Security Council meeting,
Collins told Eisenhower, Dulles, and others that his assessment of the situation in Saigon had improved considerably. There was now, he said, at
least a 50–50 chance of saving South Vietnam from the Communists.[41]
Diem's authority and stature in Vietnam was further bolstered by public
and private expressions of support from U.S. officials, including Dulles,
who met with the South Vietnamese leader in Saigon on March 1. While,
like Collins, Dulles urged Diem to neutralize potential opponents by
bringing them into his government, he assured the South Vietnamese
leader that his survival was strongly supported by the U.S. government.[42]

By late March 1955, however, Collins' evaluation of Diem's chances of
survival again turned—this time for the worse. The tranquillity between
Diem and the sects dissolved when Diem rejected their demands to control and administer the governments within their territories. The sects
now joined forces with the Binh Xuyen, a Mafia-style organization that
exerted a virtual stranglehold on Saigon, and signaled that they were prepared to wage open war against the embattled prime minister. Diem's militant and unyielding approach and his steadfast refusal to reorganize and
diversify his cabinet troubled Collins and the French high commissioner

for Vietnam, General Paul Ely. Both men worried that Diem might spark a civil war if he mishandled the delicate situation. Diem's threats of a military response to the sects particularly concerned Collins and Ely. In a tense meeting on March 30, Collins bluntly informed Diem that unless he changed tactics, he risked losing U.S. support. Diem promised only to consider Collins' advice.[43]

By late March, Collins had again given up all hope for Diem's survival. "I seriously doubt he can last long," he cabled on March 31, urging the State Department to begin consideration of "possible alternatives" to Diem.[44] Dulles was hesitant to take Collins' advice, but did not rule it out. However, when he took the matter to Eisenhower, the president cautioned against giving up too soon on the Vietnamese leader. Eisenhower, Dulles recorded in a memorandum, "does not see that we can do much except tell [Collins] not to give up on Diem until it is quite certain, because we bet on him heavily."[45]

Immediately after his meeting with Eisenhower, Dulles invited Mansfield to the State Department to discuss the situation in Vietnam. His report to Mansfield was grim. As Dulles saw it, the United States had several options: it could engineer Diem's replacement, persuade Bao Dai to influence Diem to broaden his government, or seek Bao Dai's return to Vietnam to assume the role of president, with Diem as premier. If Dulles was leaning toward replacing Diem, Mansfield's reaction did not offer any hope of congressional support. Still firmly in Diem's corner, Mansfield replied that all of his alternatives were worse than keeping Diem in office. If Diem quit or was overthrown, he said, a civil war would almost certainly erupt. At that, Ho Chi Minh "could walk in and take the country without any difficulty."[46]

Although Dulles dutifully reaffirmed Washington's support for Diem, Collins persisted in his efforts to prompt a change in governments. He complained that Diem's "inability to compromise, his inherent incapacity to get along with other able men, and his tendency to be suspicious of the motives of anyone who disagrees with him, make him practically incapable of holding this government together."[47] Shown Collins' latest cable by a State Department official, Mansfield was unfazed. Diem was the only true nationalist leader in South Vietnam, he said. Eliminating him would only "leave the field to Ho." Furthermore, he argued that dropping Diem would only increase the power of the sects and, in the process, diminish American prestige in Asia.[48]

Mansfield's strong support for Diem apparently had its desired effect—at least temporarily. In an April 9 telegram to Saigon, Dulles stopped short of rejecting Collins' conclusions, but cautioned against abandoning Diem too soon. "We have always known the qualities which

Diem possesses and those which he lacks," Dulles said. "Nevertheless, our
two countries agreed to support him in default of anyone possessing better qualifications." Since no one better was available, Dulles saw no reason
to move precipitously on a replacement. Two factors influenced Dulles'
decision to remain in Diem's corner. First, to dump Diem, the United
States would be caving in to French pressure and, thereby, weakening
American influence over the next leader, who "will clearly know where the
real authority lies." Second, Dulles told Collins that congressional support
for continued U.S. involvement in Vietnam might collapse if Diem were
replaced. While such opposition might eventually be overcome, Dulles
warned that "Mansfield, who is looked on with great respect by his colleagues with reference to this matter, is adamantly opposed to abandonment of Diem under present conditions."[49] Collins replied by saying, in
effect, that Mansfield did not know enough about the current situation to
offer an informed judgment. The conditions in Vietnam were "rather different" from those during Mansfield's last visit in September 1954, when
the senator said he feared the only alternative to Diem was a military dictatorship. "As practical politicians," Collins wrote, "I would think that
Mansfield and his colleagues on Senate committees would give considerable weight to the arguments I have advanced." Those arguments included
the recommendation of two South Vietnamese leaders as possible replace-
ments for Diem. According to Collins, Pham Huy Quat, a former Vietnamese defense minister, and Tran Van Do, the current minister of foreign
affairs, both possessed "far more flexibility than Diem and [have] an infinitely more practical approach" to the country's problems.[50]

In the face of Collins' relentless assaults on Diem, Dulles began to
waver. In an April 11 telegram, the secretary of state finally appeared
resigned to replacing Diem, although he cautioned Collins against moving too quickly. He also urged him to find a way to keep Diem in the government while making the "mechanics of the change-over seem Vietnamese inspired."[51] By late April, it appeared that Collins had finally
prevailed. Eisenhower, the State Department, and the French government
all agreed: Diem must go. Now, the only major impediment to ridding
South Vietnam of Prime Minister Ngo Dinh Diem was the dogged opposition of one junior senator—Mike Mansfield.

CHAPTER 14

This Is Our Offspring

1955–1956

Pierre Millet, minister of the French embassy in Washington, came to Mansfield's Senate office on April 21, 1955, to talk about Diem. Mansfield, however, quickly realized the meeting was far more significant than he had expected. He was being lobbied to change not only his mind, but that of Dulles and, therefore, the U.S. government's posture on the South Vietnamese leader. Mansfield stood his ground. "I still feel he [Diem] is the only man who stands a chance, and it is a long chance, of keeping South Vietnam free," he wrote afterwards in a memo, grumbling that "the administration in discussing the Indo-China situation with the French ambassador here is, in effect, putting the major responsibility on me." Mansfield refused to assume that responsibility. He made it clear to Millet that any decision on Diem rested with Eisenhower and Dulles. "All I could do was to make my views known."[1]

Of course, Mansfield, whose influence on Vietnam far outweighed his lack of seniority on the Foreign Relations Committee, could do far more than make his views known. He had the stature to influence the Senate's attitude toward future military and foreign aid to South Vietnam. In his widely heralded report the previous October, he made clear what he believed should occur if Diem's government fell. In that event, he had suggested, "the United States should consider an immediate suspension of all aid to Vietnam and the French Union forces there."[2]

Despite Mansfield's adamant support for the current South Vietnamese government, Collins' visit to Washington seemed to seal Diem's fate. Although Eisenhower emphasized the problems he would face in Congress if Diem were replaced, Collins pressed his case relentlessly. At the State Department, he told officials from the departments of State and Defense that in light of Diem's well-known inability to comprehend the political, economic, and military problems of his country it would be a "major error in judgment" to continue supporting him.[3] By the end of Collins' visit, he had finally persuaded Eisenhower and Dulles that Diem should be supplanted. "What the exact terms of our future policy will be" toward South Vietnam, "I can't say," Eisenhower said publicly on April 27, signaling a shift from the administration's previous strong support for Diem.[4] That same day, Dulles cabled the U.S. embassy in Paris to advise that "it appears that some change in political arrangements in Viet-Nam may be inevitable."[5]

Despite public professions of support for a free and independent Vietnam, U.S. State Department officials were now actually involved to a remarkable and ironic degree in the planning and implementation of a new government to replace Diem. In another cable to U.S. diplomats in France on April 27, Dulles cautioned that while the Vietnamese in Saigon should be permitted to form a new government, "Collins and Ely will probably have to be in practice the catalysts." Yet Dulles feared such involvement by outsiders might result in stories about a Collins–Ely "formula." To avoid that impression, the secretary explained that the United States would "make every attempt to keep the Vietnamese label."

American policy toward Diem was about to change—and dramatically so. Collins, backed by Eisenhower and Dulles, was about to engineer a bloodless coup of a foreign nation for the sake of saving it. Dulles' second cable on April 27 left little doubt about U.S. intentions: in pushing Diem out, Collins and Ely would urge him to serve in the new government. "If Diem refuses," Dulles wrote, "the program should nevertheless be carried out anyway."[6]

Before the new American policy could be implemented, however, Diem made a dramatic move. Undoubtedly aware that Collins was in Washington to engineer his ouster, Diem gambled on an all-or-nothing strategy to seize the upper hand. Encouraged by Mansfield and other American supporters, Diem made his move against the sects.[7] Without notifying U.S. officials, he ordered his Vietnamese National Army (VNA) to engage Binh Xuyen forces. In the ensuing struggle, the VNA emerged victorious. Diem's last-minute gamble had paid off. In the Senate, Mansfield and Humphrey immediately pressured Eisenhower to reaffirm the government's support of Diem. In a veiled threat to push for suspension of U.S. aid to Vietnam if a change in government occurred, Mansfield expressed confidence that "this [U.S] government will not align itself with the kind of forces which are now in military and conspiratorial opposition to Diem." Supporting any other regime with "hundreds of millions of dollars," he said, would be "entirely unwarranted." American support for Diem, Mansfield insisted, "should be unwavering and to the hilt."

Humphrey agreed and asserted that Diem "is the best hope that we have in South Vietnam. . . . For America to default in backing him at this hour would be a display of weakness and irresponsibility that cannot be explained or condoned."[8] Other members of Congress, including Knowland and several members of the House Foreign Affairs Committee, also expressed strong support for Diem.[9]

Privately, Mansfield vigorously lobbied the administration to continue supporting Diem. On May 2, he wrote to the newly appointed ambassador to South Vietnam, Donald Heath—still at his post in Beirut—to caution him against falling prey to the anti-Diem sentiment he would soon encounter in Saigon. "I feel that if Diem goes down," Mansfield wrote, "the way will be open to civil war and chaos and the road paved for Ho Chin [sic] Minh to walk right into all of Vietnam and perhaps eventually elsewhere."[10]

Diem's uncharacteristically strong, decisive action in challenging the Binh Xuyen forced a reluctant administration back into his corner. "The present head of the legal Government of free Vietnam which we are supporting is Diem," a State Department spokesman announced on April 30.[11] Waiting on Collins when he returned to Saigon was a cable from Dulles informing him of the policy reversal. Dulles told Collins that Diem was now "a symbol of Vietnamese nationalism" in its struggle against French colonialism and "corrupt backward elements." It could not have pleased Collins that Mansfield had prevailed again.

> Since your departure, [Dulles wrote,] US public and Congressional opinion, in view of Diem's apparent success in the current military and political battle, is now even less likely than before to support or countenance a removal of Diem forced from without. There is increasing Congressional support for Senator Mansfield's views with which you are already familiar. For us at this time to participate in a scheme to remove Diem would not only be domestically impractical but highly detrimental [to] our prestige in Asia.[12]

Diem, too, understood the crucial role Mansfield's public support had played in Washington. Quoting Confucius, he told Mansfield in a letter that "only in winter do we know which trees are evergreen. Figuratively speaking, you are the evergreen, as luxuriant as always; not only have you been a stark fighter for democracy and human rights but also the true friend of the Vietnamese people." Diem was "very much moved and touched" by Mansfield's "ever-understanding gesture."[13]

While Diem's decisive actions, as well as the subsequent expression of American support, helped make him even more popular in the United States, Eisenhower's decision to terminate Collins' assault on Diem's regime—motivated by practical, not ethical considerations—had fateful, long-term consequences for U.S. policy in Indochina. As historian David L. Anderson noted, "In the long run, Collins was right and Dulles was wrong."[14] Diem may indeed have been the best person to lead South Vietnam at the time. That, however, did not mean he was the kind of leader his country needed. Autocratic, politically inept, and fundamentally disdainful of democracy, Diem was inherently unsuited to lead his nation's fight for democratic self-rule. By the late 1950s, Collins' assessment of Diem would prove all too accurate: "The man lacks the personal qualities of leadership and the executive ability successfully to head a government that must compete with the unity of purpose and efficiency of the Viet Minh under Ho Chi Minh."[15]

No matter how distasteful, Diem's government was now the client of the United States in South Vietnam. Negotiations between Dulles and French officials in May 1955 were a turning point in the new relationship. Dulles emerged from the talks with a French decision to begin a steady withdrawal of French troops from Indochina, as well as an understanding that the U.S. military would assume responsibility for the training and equipping of the ragtag military force known as the Vietnamese National Army (VNA).[16] Spending about $85 million a year for military equipment alone, the U.S. military poured itself into the Herculean task of transforming the poorly trained and equipped VNA into a first-rate fighting force. Directed by General Samuel Williams, the U.S. Military Assistance and Advisory Group (MAAG)* in Saigon first worked to pare down the VNA from an unwieldy force of two hundred and fifty thousand to a more manageable and trainable one hundred and fifty thousand. The idea was to replicate the genius of the U.S. military system in South Vietnam by reorganizing and streamlining the indigenous forces, as well as training officers and officer candidates at special military schools.

From the perspective of 1955, a crash program to create a model fighting force to repel communism in South Vietnam seemed sound policy. Time, however, would prove otherwise. Supporting the axiom that each generation's military leaders fight the last war, General Williams and his men—almost all of them Korean War veterans—began applying the training and strategic techniques to Vietnam that had worked so well in Korea. As in South Korea, the American military primarily focused on protecting its ally from invading forces from the north. But Korea had largely been a

---

*The U.S. MAAG was limited by the Geneva agreements to a force of no more than 342 men. Through various accounting sleights of hand and outright subterfuge, the number would be gradually increased over the years until it would reach more than 1,500 in 1961.

conventional conflict fought over a defined territory with clearly drawn battle lines. The struggle in Vietnam would prove anything but conventional and its battle lines anything but defined. By the early 1960s, it would be apparent that the VNA was engaged in a war not only with a hostile power to the north, but with a potent indigenous guerrilla force in the south that fought effectively on both military and political fronts.[17] The South Vietnamese army was, by comparison, an inferior fighting force—made even more so by Diem's summary dismissal of more than six thousand experienced noncommissioned officers whom he suspected of loyalty to the French. In Diem's new army, politics and personal loyalty to the prime minister, not military skill or dedication to the new country's sovereignty, would be paramount.

Along with support and training for the VNA came more American money for strengthening South Vietnam's economy. Through 1959, the U.S. aid program would generate almost $1 billion for South Vietnam's government, in addition to $143 million in direct economic assistance and technical aid provided by Washington.[18] The commitment to nation building in South Vietnam was enormous. From 1955 through 1961, the United States would spend more than $1.5 billion in military and economic assistance to fight communism in Vietnam. Added to funds already appropriated to support France's efforts, the 1950s saw Washington pour more than $3.5 billion into "defending" South Vietnam.[19]

Washington's interest in South Vietnam's future was not merely confined to how it could train and finance the country's military force. The State Department also worried about how South Vietnam might be threatened by elections to unify the country as provided in the Geneva agreements and scheduled for July 1956. While they formally advised Diem to honor the agreement as long as North Vietnam agreed to support "genuinely free elections," U.S. officials shared Diem's reluctance to expose his country's future to the uncertain outcome of an election that he, as a nonparticipant in the Geneva talks, had never endorsed.[20]

In this, Diem enjoyed strong support from Mansfield and Kennedy. In March, Mansfield matter-of-factly told Democratic Senator Clinton Anderson of New Mexico that "it is my belief that there is a strong possibility that these elections will not be held on the grounds that south Viet Nam was not a signatory to the Geneva Convention."[21] Kennedy, too, supported Diem's decision to avoid elections. "We can hardly blame him," Kennedy later said, meaning that Diem was being urged to abide by an agreement to which he had not been a party.[22] Dulles also shared these views. "We did not sign [the Geneva accords] and the government of Vietnam did not sign them," he said on June 28, signaling to the world that elections would not take place in 1956. While he was fearful of any election that pitted him against the vastly more popular Ho Chi Minh, Diem later insisted that although he supported "essentially free elections," the North Vietnamese could not be trusted.[23]

By the time Mansfield left for his third visit to Vietnam in as many years, Diem was a much more confident, self-assured leader.[24] When the two men met on August 18, the prime minister told Mansfield that "for all practical purposes" the dissident sects had been defeated. (This was not a view shared by U.S. embassy officials, who told Mansfield that "the problem of the opposition was still a considerable way from being solved.") Nonetheless, Diem exuded confidence. Communist strength in the countryside, he told Mansfield, was down by half. Mansfield later recorded that Diem had "stressed that for the past year he has had to deal essentially in negatives. The problem was one of consolidating his authority in rooting out the dissidents and of making the government a going concern. He now felt Viet Nam was entering a new and a constructive phase."[25]

Mansfield's subsequent report to the Foreign Relations Committee was an optimistic tribute to Diem's "dedication and courage." Other than a "general review" of the U.S. aid program in Vietnam, however, he believed no major policy changes were necessary. The most important goal, he insisted, was keeping Diem in power. More than anything, Mansfield's report demonstrated that despite his many visits to Vietnam, his attitudes were still greatly influenced by an anticommunist Cold War mentality. Communism, not nationalism, was the driving force in Southeast Asia, he still believed. "The tide of totalitarian communism in Viet Nam has slackened," Mansfield wrote. "A year ago it was on the verge of overrunning the entire country and much of the rest of southeast Asia." Now, he said, that threat had been reduced. "There is today a reasonable chance of the survival and development of a free Viet Nam." But should war break out again in Indochina, Mansfield warned that it would endanger the world. "A resumption of hostilities by the Communists in that part of the world," he asserted, "is bound to be a serious threat to world peace and would produce the gravest international repercussions."[26]

By the time Mansfield left Vietnam in late August, Diem had begun moving decisively to shore up his power. With France's influence in Vietnam steadily eroding, Diem knew that Bao Dai's authority as head of state had also diminished. Although the monarch had elevated him to power in 1954, he now viewed the French-backed former emperor as a threat to his independence. When Diem called a national referendum in the south on October 23, it was his way of ridding the country of its titular leader. In a one-sided, rigged election in which voters were inundated with virulent anti-Bao Dai propaganda,* Diem "won" an astounding 98 percent of the vote. "It should not be assumed, however," warned the new U.S. ambassador in Saigon, Frederick Reinhardt, "that Diem's overwhelming victory over Bao Dai is a true measure of his popularity in Vietnam." Another embassy official in Saigon, Daniel V. Anderson said that in a sense, the election was "a travesty on democratic procedures, since the Diem forces maintained absolute control over all avenues of propaganda and did not permit the opposition to make its case."[27]

Diem, of course, embraced the "mandate" as an excuse to exert absolute control over the fledgling nation. Although Diem's methods in achieving his victory were not widely reported in the American press, the election was a vivid demonstration of the extent to which Diem and his regime now dominated the country's political, economic, and social landscape. While that regime had an American seal of approval for its ostensible adherence to democratic principles, in practice its nature perfectly matched Diem's authoritarian philosophy. As one British diplomat in Saigon remarked: "The campaign preceding this referendum was conducted with such a cynical disregard for decency and democratic principles that even the Viet-Minh professed to be shocked."[28] The referendum was quickly followed by creation of a constituent assembly made up exclusively of Diem supporters. Subsequent ratification of a national constitution gave Diem, as president, extraordinary executive powers that he employed in a form more reminiscent of a dictator than a democratically elected president. In January 1956, Diem issued a decree that effectively banned all political opposition. Within months, as many as twenty thousand peasants suspected of harboring Vietminh sympathies were herded into "reeducation camps." Diem abolished elected local governments in favor of administrators appointed by the Saigon government.[29]

Of Diem's government and its origins, Bernard Fall observed in 1963 that "not one out of ten governments in the United Nations today holds power from a popular source any less tainted than that of the Saigon regime."[30] Diem's government was so lacking in basic democratic practices that Ambassador Reinhardt warned the State Department of its "increasingly totalitarian character." At the very least, Reinhardt hoped that the

---

*According to Saigon embassy counselor Daniel V. Anderson, "In the heart of Saigon an enormous twenty foot high dummy of Bao Dai was put up depicting him in his yellow royal robes, carrying money bags and playing cards in one hand, a broken dragon scepter in the other, a woman on his knees. Behind him was a Vietnamese, representing the common people, breaking Bao Dai's throne with a long pole" (*FRUS*, 1955–57, 1:590).

administration could influence Diem to make his government more democratic by insisting that American financial and military aid should not be
taken for granted.[31] Washington, however, was more concerned with
short-term security in South Vietnam. In their haste and determination to
prop up Diem and his government as a shield against communism in
Southeast Asia, Eisenhower's advisors failed to heed Reinhardt's prescient
warnings about the perils of unconditional support for Diem.

While the president continued to support Diem's government with
increasing amounts of military and economic assistance, news reports from
Saigon and Hanoi were now relegated to the back pages of American newspapers and newsmagazines. The popular assumption, trumpeted by the
administration, was that a new nation was blossoming and the struggle against
the Vietminh was being won. This did not mean, however, that domestic
American supporters of Diem and the South Vietnamese government were
complacent. In fact—with some administration prodding—Diem's backers
were encouraged to become even more energetic and vocal by forming, in
the spring of 1955, the American Friends of Vietnam (AFV). Led by retired
General John W. "Iron Mike" O'Daniel, the former U.S. military mission
chief in Vietnam, the AFV quickly attracted a high-profile membership that
included dozens of prominent religious leaders, business executives, and a
politically diverse collection of senators and representatives. Billed as a "non-
partisan group supporting a free and democratic Republic of Vietnam," its
two most prominent Senate members were Mansfield and Kennedy. While
the organization was dedicated to influencing American policy in favor of
South Vietnam, it spent most of its time supporting Diem and little, if any,
promoting a "free and democratic" government.[32]

The myth of a "free Vietnam" persisted, aided by Diem's American
supporters like Kennedy, who addressed a June 1956 conference of AFV
members in Washington. Ignoring mounting evidence to the contrary,
Kennedy claimed that Vietnam "represents a proving ground of democracy in Asia." The country's "political liberty is an inspiration to those seeking to obtain or maintain their liberty in all parts of Asia—and indeed the
world." Hailing the "amazing success of President Diem," Kennedy also
chided the administration and the news media for its "neglect of Vietnam."
Policymakers, he argued, should not "conclude that the cessation of hostilities in Indo-China removed that area from the list of important areas of
United States foreign policy." Adding his own metaphors to Eisenhower's
"domino theory," Kennedy described Vietnam as "the cornerstone of the
Free World in Southeast Asia, the keystone to the arch, the finger in the
dike." Burma, Thailand, India, Japan, the Philippines, Laos, and Cambodia were all threatened "if the Red Tide of Communism overflowed into
Vietnam," he said.

Articulating a philosophy regarding Vietnam that would guide four presidential administrations—including his own—Kennedy insisted that the country "represents a test of American responsibility and determination in Asia."

> This is our offspring—we cannot abandon it, we cannot ignore its needs. And if it falls victim to any of the perils that threaten its existence—Communism, political anarchy, poverty and the rest—then the United States, with some justification, will be held responsible; and our prestige in Asia will sink to a new low.[33]

Although South Vietnam gradually receded toward the administration's foreign policy backburner after 1955—largely because of a belief in some quarters that the situation was well in hand—some administration officials privately worried about increased levels of communist subversion and infiltration. According to a CIA analysis presented to the National Security Council in January 1956, Diem's regime "was having serious troubles." CIA Director Allen Dulles reported that infiltration from the north was on the rise and that Diem's government was "not sufficiently broadbased." On the whole, Dulles said, "Diem had made a good record." However, he added, "the military situation in South Vietnam was not as good as might be hoped."[34] Part of the problem rested with Diem and his paranoiac personality. A State Department intelligence report in February described Diem in less-than-glowing terms: "He remains almost pathologically sensitive to criticism and potential opposition, with the result that the regime is becoming increasingly autocratic despite his democratic principles."[35]

Despite these concerns, the administration refused to demonstrate anything but unflinching support for Diem in its public pronouncements. In a state visit to Vietnam in July 1956, on the second anniversary of Diem's rise to power, Nixon reiterated the strong U.S. backing of Diem and his government. Speaking to the country's Vietnamese national constituent assembly, Nixon claimed that despite the geographical division of their country, "the militant march of Communism has been halted. I do not exaggerate when I say that your friends everywhere have derived great inspiration from the successes which have marked the first two years of President Ngo Dinh Diem's administration."[36]

Four years of economic prosperity and world peace—threats of war in Indochina notwithstanding—stood Eisenhower in good stead with the American people. For most, the Korean War was a faint memory. Any miscalculations over Indochina were long forgotten and never fully exploited by the Democrats, most of whom supported Eisenhower's policy in Southeast Asia. A flare-up of violence in the Middle East in early November came too late to have an appreciable impact on the election. Combined with a lackluster repeat matchup in 1956 between Eisenhower and his 1952 Democratic challenger, Adlai Stevenson, Election Day produced a resounding reelection victory for the Republican president. Without mentioning Vietnam in his inaugural address, Eisenhower sounded, biographer Herbert S. Parmet observed, "as though Taft and the isolationists had never existed." The speech was a eulogy for the isolationist philosophy of his party's right wing. America's responsibility, he declared, was "to help others rise from misery, however far the scene of suffering may be from our shores." Isolationism was dead, he said. "No people can live to itself alone. The economic need of all nations—in mutual dependence—makes isolation an impossibility; not even America's prosperity could long survive if other nations did not also prosper. No nation," he told the audience, "can be a fortress, lone and strong and safe."[37]

CHAPTER 15

A Blank Grant of Power

1957–1958

By approving the Gulf of Tonkin Resolution in 1964, Congress would give President Lyndon Johnson every bit of legal authority he needed to wage all-out war against North Vietnam. All but two members of Congress—both of them Democratic senators—would endorse a blank check for war that required only Johnson's decision to cash it. In fact, the resolution would stand for decades as a stunning and breathtaking abdication of congressional responsibility and prerogative that led directly to the subsequent, sustained escalation of the war in 1965.

But as we have already seen, the events of 1964 and 1965 would be only additional links in a chain of political events that began much earlier—in 1950, with Harry Truman's unilateral decision to dispatch American troops to defend South Korea. The adverse political fallout over that decision would spawn a series of resolutions in the 1950s and early 1960s—starting in 1955 with the Formosa Resolution—that ushered Congress and the president into a unique sharing of responsibility and power for certain foreign military operations.

Almost always reluctant to assume responsibility in the area of foreign affairs, Congress had traditionally deferred to the president during foreign emergencies. This was especially true when the country faced possible military intervention abroad. In a foreign crisis, Congress was loath to challenge the president's power to defend America's interests, especially when the enemy was the Soviet Union or its perceived client. Even when members of Congress did openly object to a president's decision to deploy military forces, such as Truman's 1950 decision regarding Korea, their protests were better characterized as grudging approval, not outright opposition.

For more than 165 years, Congress had never rebuffed a commander in chief's request to declare war. The events of 1955, however, presented a new situation. For the first time, a president would ask Congress for advance authorization to deploy U.S. armed forces abroad. In late January, facing a crisis in the Formosa Straits, where Communist China had attacked several islands controlled by Chiang Kai-shek's Nationalist troops, Eisenhower requested congressional authority to "employ the Armed Forces of the United States as he deem[ed] necessary" to defend the islands "against armed attack."

To members of Congress, this was something entirely new. No president had ever asked Congress, in advance, for permission to exercise his constitutional powers in the military field. Nonetheless, House approval was easy and overwhelming—410–3—reflecting Eisenhower's enormous stature in the field of foreign and military affairs. Like the House, the Senate was persuaded to give the former World War II commander the military authority he wanted, but not before a vigorous debate during which Mansfield and others questioned why Eisenhower wanted to share with Congress constitutional authority they argued was already his. The situation, a joint Armed Services–Foreign Affairs committee report concluded, "call[s] for the two branches of the Government to stand together in the face of a common danger," and that spirit prevailed when senators voted, 83–3, to approve the resolution.*

In late 1956—after Israel, Britain, and France had attacked Egypt in a bitter dispute over possession of the Suez Canal—Eisenhower and Dulles worried that the Soviets might enter the conflict on Egypt's behalf. On January 5, 1957, Eisenhower went before Congress to request— in language similar to that of the Formosa Resolution—the authority to send American troops "to secure and protect" the region from "overt armed aggression from any nation controlled by international Communism."[2] Addressing Congress, Eisenhower did not explain why he wanted authority that most members of Congress believed he already possessed. In assuring members that he would not make unilateral decisions without consulting them, he seemed to be saying that he only wanted to present a united front to the Soviet Union and the world. Indeed, this was the practical impact of the resolution.

Yet Eisenhower may also have had sound political reasons for making Congress his partner in Middle East policy. In fact, he was following a pattern that began in 1954 when he consulted congressional leaders about Dien Bien Phu and, later, the Formosan crisis: when faced with U.S. intervention in a foreign conflict, Eisenhower involved Congress to the degree that he immunized himself from political attack should his policy fail.

---

*Voting against the measure were Democrats Wayne Morse of Oregon and Herbert Lehman of New York and Republican William Langer of North Dakota.

Eisenhower and Dulles undoubtedly knew that if Truman had sought and obtained a "Korean Resolution" prior to sending in American troops, the war might never have become a political albatross. With a congressional resolution in the mold of Eisenhower's Formosa and Middle East authorizations, the U.S. role in Korea would have been authorized by a bipartisan act of Congress.

Congress greeted Eisenhower's Middle East Resolution in 1957 (it became known as the "Eisenhower Doctrine") with only slightly more skepticism than his 1955 Formosa Resolution. The House Foreign Affairs Committee approved it in a 24–2 vote after amending it to require semi-annual administration reports on military activity and to ensure that Congress could unilaterally repeal its provisions. Passed by the full House, 355–61, the resolution went to the Senate, where senators were somewhat more hesitant. During joint hearings of the Armed Services and Foreign Relations committees, Fulbright complained that Congress was being asked to give an "unprecedented delegation of authority to make wars and to spend money without restriction." More concerned about Congress's abdication of its responsibility to declare war, Fulbright asked:

> Shall we strike down the Senate's rights and duties in the conduct of foreign affairs, as defined by 168 years of constitutional practice? . . . Shall we say yes to a radical proposal whose adoption would mean that we are abandoning our constitutional systems of checks and balances; that from now on, naked Executive power will rule the highest and most fateful interests of the nation?

Fulbright worried that the resolution "asks for a blank grant of power over our funds and armed forces, to be used in a blank way, for a blank length of time, under blank conditions, with respect to blank nations, in a blank area . . . in filling the blanks, the President need not consult, much less be accountable to any other constitutional organ of government." In words that would one day seem ironic given his role as floor manager of the Senate debate over the 1964 Gulf of Tonkin Resolution, Fulbright declared:

> I do not believe that even for a short time the Congress should abdicate its constitutional powers. History will demonstrate that the periods of greatest danger of the rights of the people, in a democracy, are those periods when adulation for a popular idol diverts their attention momentarily from the implications of their actions.[3]

Fulbright was not alone in his opposition. During a floor debate with Kennedy on March 1, Morse made it clear that he would refuse to "vote to give the President any power to make war in the Middle East by a predated declaration of war."[4] In joint committee, Morse fought unsuccessfully to amend the resolution to require the president to request congressional approval for military action "prior to the employment of armed forces," unless "such notice is not possible." Said Morse:

> If a president in the exercise of the so-called emergency powers believes that the lives and the property and vital interests of the United States are so at stake in an emergency situation that troops have got to be sent in immediately to protect our interests, there goes along with that the responsibility of the President to submit his action to the checking power of the Congress, and the Congress has the residual power to repeal or reject the action of the president and order the troops home.[5]

Fulbright and Democrat Sam Ervin of North Carolina agreed with Morse and argued that Congress should at least reserve the right to approve or disapprove of the president's actions after the fact. Morse, however, was opposed not only by the committee's Republicans, but also by four influential Democrats—Theodore Francis Green (chairman of the Foreign Relations Committee), Richard Russell (chairman of the Armed Services Committee), John Stennis (a respected member of the Armed Services Committee), and Stuart Symington (the former secretary of the Air Force). While displeased with the secretive ways that Eisenhower and Dulles presented information to their committee, Russell almost always gave wide berth to presidents in these situations. "In my opinion," he said in a closed-door committee session, "the Congress of the United States is being treated as a group of children, and very small children, and children with a low IQ at that, in the manner that this resolution has been presented to us." However, Russell grudgingly supported the president.[6]

No two men had more impact on the resolution's eventual outcome than Humphrey and Mansfield, the latter whom Johnson chose in 1956 to serve as the Senate's assistant majority leader.* Both men proposed compromise language to strengthen the president's hand while refusing to give him a blank military check. Instead of "authorizing" military action, Mansfield and Humphrey proposed that Congress simply declare that if the president "determines the necessity" for military action, "the United States is prepared to use armed forces" in defense of the Middle East.

---

*Mansfield maintained that he was Johnson's unwilling compromise choice for the position. "Lyndon insisted I had to take it because I was the least objectionable to most of the Democratic senators. It was not a flattering argument, but after several meetings I finally lost my resolve against becoming whip." Later he argued that the job was far from glamorous. "[I] just sort of held the title and Johnson kept in control—even when he was absent—so [it] didn't amount to much" (Olson, 87; Evans and Novak, 98; Mansfield interview, by Mann).

When asked by Kennedy if Congress was "granting the President the right to use Armed Forces without coming again to Congress," Mansfield replied that "we are not granting him the right. We are, in effect, reasserting or reaffirming his right." On a straight party-line vote, the committee adopted the amendment.[7]

When the amended resolution came before the joint committee, it passed overwhelmingly—20–8. All the opposing votes were cast by Democrats: Russell (who now opposed the resolution's economic assistance language), Fulbright, Mansfield, Morse, Sam Ervin of North Carolina, Harry Byrd of Virginia, Russell Long of Louisiana, and Estes Kefauver of Tennessee. On March 5, after twelve days of listless debate, the Senate approved the amended resolution, 72–19.* Accepting the Senate's version, the House overwhelming approved it, 350–60.[8]

The Middle East Resolution would prove significant in at least two respects: it established and strengthened the precedent for congressional approval in advance of military excursions, it also made it less likely that any president would unilaterally employ the nation's armed forces in a substantial, long-term way without some kind of prior congressional affirmation.

Yet it might also be argued that because the Senate watered down the resolution by dropping the "authorizing" language, the Johnson administration—in the 1964 debate over the Gulf of Tonkin Resolution—would feel an even greater need to assert the president's prerogatives as commander in chief. As the historian William C. Gibbons later observed, the resolution may have established "a very important precedent for avoiding such authorization in the future." This, he argued, "resulted in language in the Gulf of Tonkin Resolution . . . that affirmed the President's right to use the armed forces without requiring specific approval or authorization by Congress."

Indeed, as Gibbons later noted, the Gulf of Tonkin Resolution would not authorize Johnson to wage war in Vietnam; it would merely approve and support the president's "determination . . . to take all necessary measures to repel any armed attack" against the U.S. military. Furthermore, it stated that the nation was prepared, "as the President determines, to take all necessary steps" to assist any nation requesting assistance under the provisions of the SEATO treaty.[9]

Viewed by itself, the Gulf of Tonkin Resolution would appear to be nothing more than a quasi-war declaration that Johnson coerced out of a

---

*Voting for the transfer of constitutional war-making power to the president were future Vietnam War opponents Mansfield, Frank Church of Idaho, Joseph Clark of Pennsylvania, John Sherman Cooper of Kentucky, and Albert Gore of Tennessee. Fulbright was among five senators who did not cast a vote.

pliant Congress. Viewed in its historical context, however, it would prove to be a continuation of a series of political and foreign policy calculations given birth by the political turmoil over foreign policy in the early 1950s. In effect, the Gulf of Tonkin Resolution would be little more than a pragmatic refinement of Eisenhower's Middle East Resolution. While it authorized Eisenhower's July 1958 decision to send the Marines into Lebanon, the resolution's long-term implications would not be fully appreciated until after Johnson, with congressional approval, sent half a million American troops to Vietnam in the mid-1960s.

CHAPTER 16

Nothing More Than a Mirage

1957–1960

O<small>N AN UNUSUALLY WARM AFTERNOON IN</small> M<small>AY</small> 1957, D<small>WIGHT</small> Eisenhower stood on the tarmac at Washington's National Airport awaiting the arrival of Ngo Dinh Diem, the South Vietnamese leader upon whom that country's tenuous hopes for democracy now rested. Eisenhower had invited the 58-year-old president for a four-day state visit—Diem's first trip to the United States since he had taken office in 1954—primarily to reaffirm America's support for South Vietnam and its president. The invitation from the American president was a precious gift to Diem. As *Time* unabashedly observed that week, it was "a triumph almost as great as Viet Nam's freedom is a shining vindication of U.S. foreign-aid policies."[1] Although *Time* certainly overstated the extent to which South Vietnam's citizens enjoyed freedom, Eisenhower and his advisors were most eager to claim success for the administration's policies. During an elaborate, red-carpet airport welcoming ceremony, Eisenhower praised the South Vietnamese people for having "exemplified, in your part of the world, patriotism of the highest order."[2] To all the world, Diem and his government were touted as democracy's proud champions and beacons of hope for liberty in Southeast Asia.

The story out of the American embassy in Saigon, however, did not match this stirring rhetoric. According to the new American ambassador, Elbridge Durbrow, a statesmanlike devotion to democratic ideals was not among Diem's qualities. Diem had his own autocratic ideas about running his government and they did not involve anything that remotely resembled government by, for, and of the people—no matter what Pentagon and State Department propagandists said. While the enigmatic leader did not hesitate to accept American dollars and military equipment, he was far more reluctant to receive American advice about how to spawn and nurture a real

democracy. Only a week before Diem's arrival in the United States, Durbrow had reported to Washington that Diem had "become more intoler-
ant of dissenting opinions" and continued to "rely heavily on [a] small circle of advisors including members of his family." Durbrow worried that
"Diem's rigidity in pursuing goals and brooking no opposition has alienated many able persons."[3]

Diem also had mismanaged several basic reforms designed to placate
his opposition, most notably land redistribution. Although he had heeded
American advice to institute the first phase of a badly needed land reform
program in 1955—rent reduction and the assurance of the continued use of
rented farmland—he failed to implement the second, more important phase
of his reform program. While he had announced plans to break up the own-
ership of large tracts of farmland—40 percent of the nation's rice land was
owned by one-quarter of one percent of the rural population—the program
was enacted so slowly that it never won popular support. Diem's plodding
reforms did not compare well with those of the Communists, who captured
and controlled large tracts of rural farmland and quickly redistributed them
to the peasants and thereby guaranteed the sympathy and devotion of thousands of new rural converts. As journalist Bernard Fall later observed, "a
large floating population of landless peasants was (as it always is) an ideal
breeding ground for Communist agitation." But Diem had little political
incentive to institute real agrarian reforms. Breaking up large estates would
have deprived members of his own family.[4]

But Eisenhower and other administration officials did not press Diem
on the land reform issue or about other ways to democratize his country.
Instead, they primarily discussed ways to strengthen the South Vietnamese
military. Fearing a North Korean-style attack from the north, Diem
pressed for a continuance of the annual $250 million in U.S. economic and
military aid ($170 million of which was allocated for defense needs). He
also wanted enough additional assistance from the United States to
increase his army by twenty thousand troops. Eisenhower's response to
Diem's pleas was noncommittal. The U.S. had many commitments around
the world, he reminded Diem, and this meant that he could only use his
best judgment when determining how to allocate the nation's limited
resources in the fight against international communism.[5]

Concerned about American resolve to defend his nation, South Vietnamese Ambassador Tan Van Chuong later told Ambassador Durbrow that
he doubted the United States would ever make good on the veiled threats
Dulles had once issued about massive nuclear retaliation in the event of a
communist invasion. Durbrow disagreed.[6] By the time Diem, Chuong,
and Durbrow arrived in Honolulu on May 20 for a conference with American military officials, Admiral Felix Stump, commander of the Pacific
Fleet, assured Diem in the strongest terms of the nation's unqualified sup-

port for South Vietnam. Stump added that the United States would use "all means at its disposal" to repel a communist invasion of "any free-world country." He went on to explain that this included the use of tactical and other nuclear weapons.[7]

Heartened by the strong assurances of U.S. support for his regime, Diem returned home to a South Vietnamese capital that was becoming less democratic and more oppressive by the month. In practice, Diem now presided over a police state—one that routinely quashed its political opposition by arresting and imprisoning those it "suspected" of being Communists or "enemies of the state." Diem's government manipulated the judicial system and completely controlled the news media. Meanwhile, his brother Ngo Dinh Nhu—a ruthless and corrupt politician who served as South Vietnam's interior minister—commanded a corrupt, murky political operation known as the Can Lao Party, an organization that more closely resembled the Mafia than a political party. Its members were mostly civil servants and military officials; anyone who hoped to achieve a leadership position in South Vietnam's government understood that party membership was mandatory. In reality, the party largely served as a secret police force that employed intimidation and even terror tactics to suppress political opposition.

As in early periods, while U.S. State Department officials and many in the American news media continued to publicly hail South Vietnam publicly as "the bastion of the free world against Communism in Southeast Asia," some journalists and American embassy officials knew better. One of the first public voices to point out the appalling lack of democratic values in the Diem government was a correspondent for the *London Times* and *The Economist*, David Hotham, whose essay "South Vietnam—Shaky Bastion" appeared in the November 25, 1957, edition of *The New Republic*. After three years in Vietnam, Hotham concluded that Diem's much-hailed "success" was nothing more than a mirage. "We should not suppose that the Communists have done nothing because Diem has been in power," he wrote. "It is rather that Diem has remained in power because the Communists have done nothing." The so-called democratic Diem government, Hatham argued, was nothing of the sort. "There is in South Vietnam no freedom of the press," he said. "There are ordered verdicts in the courts, and the clauses of the liberal constitution are a dead letter. The whole regime is a façade, propped up by money from across the seas." Hatham had equally harsh criticism for the way the United States devoted most of its effort to establishing and training South Vietnam's army.

> The upshot is that more than four-fifths of the whole gigantic aid program has failed to contribute in any direct way to the well-being of the Southern population, which should of course have been the primary

objective since the beginning. None of it has been used to cure the growing unemployment. Almost none has been used to build houses for the
people. Not a single industry has been created in the South since the end
of the Indo-China War. The Southern population, which knows well
enough what large sums have been spent in its country, knows equally
well that almost none of this money has come its way. This not only
breeds hatred of the West, it contradicts the whole principle of Western
aid to "backward" countries—the principle of preventing Communism
by improving the lot of most of the people.[8]

In a year-end report on the status of South Vietnam, Ambassador Durbrow was only slightly less critical when assessing Diem's regime. Expressing "considerable concern" about the progress of U.S.-recommended governmental and economic reforms, Durbrow complained that Diem was far
more interested in internal "security matters." Diem's "suspiciousness and
authoritarianism" had not benefited him politically, Durbrow concluded,
adding that the "base of the regime's popular support remains narrow."
"Jails and camps," he wrote, "are reportedly still filled with hundreds of
Diem's opponents." While he did credit the South Vietnamese leader for
having given his country "a much needed stability," Durbrow found him a
less-than-exemplary leader. His complaints were echoes of those relayed
to Washington by each of his predecessors:

> He overrides most of his ministers, reduces their authority, and assumes
> personal responsibility for the smallest details of government. He is
> inclined to be suspicious of others; he lacks an understanding of basic eco-
> nomic principles; and seems absorbed in pet ideas and schemes which
> detract from work on other urgent questions. . . . He remains a mandarin
> with the autocratic attitude of "I know best," a good trait at the present
> state of development of a new country, provided it does not lead to a ster-
> ilizing inflexibility.[9]

While Diem's authoritarian methods were repugnant, internal secu-
rity in South Vietnam was a legitimate concern. Two separate bombings in
Saigon on October 22 injured a busload of Americans and a group of U.S.
Army officers. A third bomb that day caused extensive damage to a U.S.
Information Service library. While the Vietminh were never directly
linked to the bombings, the attacks did coincide with a marked increase in
Vietminh activity in the south in 1957.[10] By year's end, even after Diem's
army had arrested as many as sixty-five thousand people suspected of communist activities, Vietminh activity had expanded substantially.[11] In early
December, Durbrow reported to Washington "a concerted, stepped-up
communist campaign to try to throw the regime off balance by terrorism
and intimidation." He also noted that the MAAG chief, General Samuel

Williams, believed "the present military posture of Vietnam is not too strong." [12]

Activity by the communist guerrillas that U.S. officials in Saigon now derisively called the "Viet Cong" became even more worrisome when Washington informed Diem that, as part of an across-the-board reduction in foreign aid, financial assistance to South Vietnam would be cut by 20 percent. Durbrow and other officials in Saigon were astounded. They thought it foolhardy to cut aid just as Viet Cong pressure on Diem's government was escalating. And, they argued, the reduction in funds would make it more difficult to persuade Diem to pursue economic reforms.[13] Dulles simply said that he found Diem's arguments against the reductions "not convincing," and called the 1958 funding level of $175 million an "equitable allocation" of resources.[14]

The funding cut notwithstanding, Washington devoted its efforts almost entirely to building and reinforcing South Vietnam's military forces. Significant economic reforms would wait until internal security was assured. What little economic aid the United States actually provided to South Vietnam appeared to have little effect. Few strings were attached to the assistance and, as Durbrow had noted, Diem and his government were unlikely to change their approach as long as they believed U.S. aid was unlimited and unconditional.

As early as 1956, Mansfield had warned against allowing the U.S. aid program for Vietnam to grow without focus or limit. Following his third visit to Vietnam in 1955, he told the Senate that "aid-other-than-military"—a "cumbersome term" that he claimed best described nonmilitary assistance to South Vietnam—was "bogged down in bureaucracy." Then, as in 1958, he believed that financial assistance to Diem's government should be carefully disbursed to achieve the greatest positive effect while not creating a destructive overdependence on U.S. largesse. "Such aid programs," he argued, "must be clearly designed to achieve a given purpose over a set period of time. They should not carry an implication of a continuing, general commitment by this country." In place of grants, Mansfield favored long-term loans because he believed they would carry "no implication of dependency."[15]

By 1958, congressional criticism of U.S. foreign aid programs was no longer limited to the two dozen conservative Democrats and Republicans who had traditionally opposed the increasing expenditure of American funds abroad. Since 1953, Congress had consistently appropriated far less than Eisenhower requested—a cut of $1.1 billion from his 1957 request, followed by a $652 million reduction the following year.[16] Conservative critics of foreign aid were now joined by a group of Senate Democratic moderates and liberals who began to question the disproportionate emphasis that U.S. policymakers placed on military programs in South Vietnam and elsewhere at the expense of economic development.

Some of their skepticism was reinforced by a disturbing report of the Senate Foreign Relations Committee's "Special Committee to Study the Foreign Aid Program," chaired by U.S. Chamber of Commerce chairman Clement Johnston. Although Johnston's March 1957 report praised the U.S. military's aid program for a "superb job," he was deeply concerned about the declining efficacy of U.S. military assistance. Written before the eruption of Viet Cong violence in late 1958, Johnston's report questioned whether the military had not yet "reached a period of relative balance against Communist aggression" and, therefore, if "our best weapon is not more arms, but more happy people?" Like Mansfield before him, Johnston feared that the inevitable result of the current aid program was to make the South Vietnamese government only more dependent on the United States. "The greatest disservice that we can do to these new countries," he maintained, "is to fail promptly and sharply to disabuse them of their current apparent assumption that there are no limits to American generosity and that any and all budgetary deficits will be supplied promptly and cheerfully by the American taxpayer." The time had come, he concluded, "to start a prompt and rapid tapering off of United States aid, both military and economic, if the countries [of Southeast Asia] are ever to learn to stand on their own feet."[17]

Johnston's report and other supporting information out of South Vietnam concerned Wayne Morse enough that in September 1958 he enlisted Mansfield, Fulbright, Kennedy, and four other senators to urge Eisenhower to place greater emphasis on economic assistance in Vietnam and elsewhere.[18] Eisenhower, however, was no longer intimately involved in the formation of Vietnam policy. Following the 1954 Geneva accords, the president had largely ceded day-to-day policy matters to Dulles and General Lawton Collins and, later, to Dulles, Dubrow, and General Williams. After his heart attack in 1955, the ailing Eisenhower showed even less interest in Indochina; his trusted military advisors assured him, after all, that the conflict was well in hand. Thus, instead of a personal inquiry into the alleged foreign aid abuses, Eisenhower appointed a committee to study the issue. He named former under secretary of the army William H. Draper, Jr.—then chairman of Mexican Light & Power Company—to head the inquiry. In the end, Draper's committee split the difference and recommended a substantial increase in funds for military *and* economic development programs.[19] Heartened by the committee's conditional support of U.S. aid, the administration remained steadfast. It would not increase economic aid at the expense of military assistance. Assistant Secretary of State Robertson maintained that "while economic development is effective for combating subversion, it is no defense against actual aggression. Prosperity does not, therefore, mean security."[20]

By the time the Senate considered the Mutual Security Program for the 1960 fiscal year, frustrations over Eisenhower's refusal to reform the program had boiled over. In April 1959, Humphrey and Kennedy joined Fulbright—the new chairman of the Senate Foreign Relations Committee—in proposing several amendments to force Eisenhower to put more emphasis on economic development.

As a loyal supporter of foreign aid, Fulbright had nonetheless worried about the emphasis that each successive foreign aid measure placed on military expenditures, almost always at the expense of nonmilitary programs. In 1957, he had fought for significant reforms in U.S. foreign aid and pushed most of them through the Senate, only to watch as the House virtually gutted most of the important provisions.[21] In 1958, Fulbright was even more determined to reform foreign aid. "My colleagues and I," Fulbright told the Senate, "have been concerned that military considerations have played too great a part in the formulation of the program." Disputing the notion that communism was best challenged by military might, Fulbright insisted that "we are also of the opinion that there are serious problems for the United States arising from the economic and social revolutions in Asia and Africa which arise irrespective of communism." In suggesting his own reforms to the bill, Mansfield warned that "time is running out on foreign aid." Noting that military aid, defense support, and special assistance programs accounted for 70 percent of the funds proposed by the administration, Mansfield charged that "these are the areas of decay in foreign aid."

> These are the areas in which, over the years, a one-sided dependency has developed for which an end is not yet in sight. These are the areas in which the fissures of corruption have begun to appear. These are the areas of great waste and inefficiency. These are the areas of burgeoning hostility between the American people who must foot the bill and the peoples of the recipient nations who, sometimes, as distinct from their governments, see very little benefit from the hundreds of millions, the billions that have been poured into their lands.

In the end, the Senate accepted only one of the ten amendments Fulbright and Mansfield had proposed—a Fulbright measure directing American ambassadors to consider the "political and economic" impact of the military aid programs administered from their embassies. For Fulbright, the military assistance bill debate was a turning point, an experience that solidified his resolve to reform the nation's foreign aid program and rein in its abuses.[22]

It was not Fulbright's actions, but a series of sensational newspaper articles in July 1959 by investigative reporter Albert Colegrove of the Scripps-Howard newspaper chain that prompted the first critical, in-depth study of Washington's aid to the Diem government. Colegrove spent three weeks in South Vietnam and produced a series of six articles alleging a scandal in the administration of foreign aid funds in South Vietnam. His first story on July 20 set the damning tone of the series: "The American aid program in little free Vietnam is an outrageous scandal. The true story of this fiasco has been hidden from the American public, which is paying for it."

In his series, Colegrove described a level of American decadence, graft, corruption, mismanagement, and incompetence that alarmed the public, shocked members of Congress, and put an angry Eisenhower administration on the defensive. "We have wasted many millions of dollars," Colegrove alleged, "and still are." In another article, Colegrove described the American practice of giving "Jeeps, trucks, guns, tractors, factories, even whole radio networks" to an undeveloped nation "that quite admittedly lacks the know-how to use them."[23]

In the wake of the sensational reports, the House and Senate foreign affairs committees launched investigations into Colegrove's charges. As chairman of the Foreign Relations Committee's Subcommittee on State Department Organization, Mansfield inherited responsibility for the Senate's inquiry.[24] Almost immediately, however, he butted heads with Fulbright over the investigation's scope. Although he supported foreign aid reform, Fulbright feared the sensational nature of Colegrove's stories might undermine crucial support for South Vietnam, a country that he, like most, regarded as important to U.S. national security.[25] Ironically, Fulbright urged Mansfield to submit a mildly critical "interim" report of his findings. Mansfield refused and, instead, directed a wide-ranging investigation, during which he summoned various State and Defense department officials, including Ambassador Durbrow and General Williams, to testify about the aid program.[26]

Colegrove's damning reports from Saigon suddenly raised the debate over the U.S. role in Vietnam to a fever pitch. Colegrove had hoped his reports would help improve the operation of various aid programs administered by the State and Defense departments. He did not urge ending foreign aid to Vietnam. Diem's supporters in Congress, however, perceived the stories as a full-scale attack on U.S. support of the South Vietnamese government. The ensuing political pressure to rebut Colegrove, and thus preserve U.S. aid to South Vietnam, was substantial. The chairman of the American Friends of Vietnam, retired General John O'Daniel—the former MAAG chief in Vietnam—wrote the managing editor of the Scripps-Howard papers to accuse Colegrove of "disgraceful" journalism. In what would soon become a standard criticism of anyone who questioned U.S. policy in Vietnam, O'Daniel charged that the series had generated "much joy in Moscow, Hanoi and Peiping . . . because what the Communists failed to achieve in five years—to cast doubt on the Free Vietnamese and the American aid program there—was accomplished in one week of head-lines." Other prominent AFV members accused Colegrove of "unfactual muckraking" and of having written articles "filled with falsehoods, half-truths and distortions."

Before the investigation even began, Fulbright was inclined to agree with O'Daniel. He told the retired general that "I'm afraid that these arti-cles have done a great deal of damage—how much I cannot even guess—to our efforts in Viet-Nam." In the House, where Democratic Representative Clement Zablocki of Wisconsin chaired a similar inquiry, members were even more disposed to disregard Colegrove's evidence. Admitting that he had read only one of the six articles, Zablocki revealed his biased approach in a question he posed to a witness: "Shouldn't we let the public know how [the] Scripps-Howard organization has aided the Communists?"[27]

During several long days of testimony before the more impartial Mansfield subcommittee, administration officials subjected Colegrove's allegations to a barrage of attacks. Durbrow told the subcommittee that Colegrove had presented "a distorted picture" of foreign aid to the Amer-ican people and then offered a detailed rebuttal of the reporter's charges. Despite the apparent convincing nature of the administration's argument, Mansfield and other committee members were still skeptical enough to press Durbrow, Williams, and others on the exact nature of U.S. aid to South Vietnam.[28]

Mansfield did not end his inquiry after the hearings. He sent an inves-tigative staff mission to South Vietnam for a firsthand look at the aid pro-gram. It returned with an inconclusive report that did, nonetheless, cor-roborate some of Colegrove's accusations. Ultimately, the Mansfield report, submitted to the Senate in early 1960, did not deliver the results that his vigorous investigation had originally suggested. Instead of prompting calls for sweeping reforms, Mansfield bowed to political realities, no doubt aware that the kind of foreign aid reforms that he and Fulbright had once advo-cated would never be implemented as long as Eisenhower opposed them. Despite the persuasive evidence Colegrove had uncovered, Mansfield stopped far short of accusing American officials of willful negligence or wrongdoing. He proposed only modest changes in the way the United States distributed foreign aid in Indochina. The subcommittee recom-mended only a minor "reshaping" of the program "to make it more efficient and, eventually to bring about a termination of the need for it as Vietnam achieves a reasonable means of economic self-sufficiency."[29]

But the Colegrove hearings were important, if only for the profound impact they had on Mansfield's evolving opinion of Diem. It was during the hearings that Mansfield finally began to see the full extent of the South Vietnamese leader's shortcomings. Ambassador Durbrow, who returned to Washington to testify before Mansfield's subcommittee, found Mansfield to be "cold" when discussing Diem. "He talked to me personally about Diem's lack of democracy and alleged corruption and all of that," Dubrow recalled. "As far as I was concerned, he was turned off to Diem by that time."[30]

But Mansfield's frustrations over the administration's unwillingness to force Diem to address his country's economic and political problems were soon overshadowed by deepening concerns over South Vietnam's deteriorating internal security. For many, including Mansfield and Fulbright, it did not seem a propitious time to talk about reducing military aid to Diem's government. In 1959, as many as ninety thousand cadres (unit leaders) had infiltrated South Vietnam as part of a concerted communist effort to wage revolutionary war against Diem and his government.[31] Assassinations, kidnappings, bombings, and various acts of terrorism were becoming a common tool of the Viet Cong in their ever-escalating guerrilla war against the South Vietnamese government.

At the same time, Diem's political troubles deepened, as his regime became increasingly more detached from the public and even more repressive and authoritarian. Although he believed that Diem, despite his many faults, was the "best available Vietnamese leader," Ambassador Durbrow reminded Washington in September 1960 that the ultimate objective in Vietnam was to preserve an anticommunist government in general, not Diem in particular. Should Diem's political position continue to weaken because of his refusal to enact political, military, and economic reforms, Durbrow argued that "it may become necessary for [the] US Government to begin consideration [of] alternative courses of action and leaders in order to achieve our objectives."[32]

Diem's support was particularly weak in rural areas, as the Viet Cong exploited the animosity of villagers whose local leaders had been summarily replaced with officials appointed from Saigon. In his struggle to rid the countryside of the influence of the Viet Cong, Diem played right into their hands. To insulate the rural villagers (the idea was to "protect" them from terrorist activity), the government forced thousands of families out of their ancestral homes and villages and herded them into sterile, well-protected encampments known as *agrovilles*. Designed to improve the lot of most rural Vietnamese—providing them with improved housing, heath, sanitation, and educational services—the *agrovilles* were also built to protect villagers from the contaminating influence of Viet Cong propaganda.

Unfortunately for Diem, the villagers, who had not been consulted by the government, simply wanted to be left alone. As a Saigon embassy analysis in June 1960 observed, the *agroville* program "is a complete reversal of tradition and the social and economic pattern of the people affected." By August 1960, Diem reluctantly abandoned the project, but only after it had done irreparable damage to his political standing in rural South Vietnam—areas that would soon become the Viet Cong's major stronghold.[33]

The *agroville* program was only one example of Diem's increasingly remote and authoritarian nature. To the vexation of American officials, he micro-managed the daily operations of his government and the military to a maddening degree, refused to delegate authority to his military leaders or cabinet ministers, and reserved for himself decisions on the most mundane of matters. Obsessed with loyalty to his regime, Diem irreparably damaged the country's military by promoting military officers for personal and political reasons, rather than basing his decisions on ability. He constantly bypassed and ignored his military leaders and ordered troop movements throughout the country. He also clamped down ever more tightly on the press.

Frustration with Diem's regime had begun to boil over in April 1960, when a group of noncommunist political leaders, including some former Diem cabinet ministers, met in Saigon to issue a manifesto excoriating the president for his repressive tactics. By October of that year, with rumors of coup attempts sweeping Saigon, Durbrow requested and was granted Washington's permission to talk frankly with Diem about reform. Durbrow spelled out in detail the changes Washington believed necessary for Diem to remain in power: delegation of military day-to-day operations to a minister of national defense and the strict observance of a chain of command; the end of favoritism in the promotion and assignment of military officers; decentralization of responsibility for government operations; reformation or dissolution of brother Nhu's Can Loa Party; greater news media autonomy; and freedom for local populations to elect their own officials.[34] While Diem was noncommittal, he did not reject Durbrow's recommendations out of hand.

By mid-November, the exasperation of some military officers came to a head, as a group of junior officers stormed the presidential palace in Saigon. Forced to meet their demands to save his life, Diem promised political reforms and free elections. But his empty pledges bought him just enough time for the intervention of troops loyal to his government. The coup was forcibly rebutted and Diem reneged on the agreement.

After the coup attempt, Diem became even more determined to crush his enemies, arresting even more political opponents and further tightening his grip on the government. Because the leaders of the aborted coup were known to be closely associated with U.S. military commanders, Diem

developed a basic distrust of his American military advisors and their relationships with Vietnamese army commanders. His suspicions about his
own military officers also grew, as did his determination to serve as his own
commanding general.

Alarmed by the deteriorating situation, Durbrow urged Washington
to put on hold the twenty thousand additional troops Diem wanted until
he demonstrated a willingness to ease "his heavy-handed methods of operation." Like each of his predecessors, Durbrow had grown weary of Diem.
If the South Vietnamese leader refused to reform, Durbrow said in a
December 4 cable, "we may well be forced, in the not too distant future,
to undertake [the] difficult task of identifying and supporting alternate
leadership."[35]

Indeed, it did seem a good time to give up on Diem. As 1960 ended,
the South Vietnamese leader was under siege, surrounded by political and
military opponents—communist and noncommunist, from North Vietnam and South Vietnam—all seeking a violent end to his government.
Encouraged by the North Vietnamese government, Diem's opposition had
coalesced into three affiliated organizations, all dedicated to his overthrow:
the Central Office for South Vietnam, the southern arm of North Vietnam's official Workers Party; the People's Liberation Armed Forces (the
PLAF or Viet Cong, as Westerners dubbed it) that unified southern Communists with the vestiges of the vanquished sects that had opposed Diem
in 1954; and the National Front for the Liberation of South Vietnam
(NLF), the political successor to the Vietminh, an organization that included a broad spectrum of Diem's political opponents, including militant
Communists, religious organizations, and members of various political
parties. Drawing its strength from the rural areas of South Vietnam, the
NLF masked its dominant communist ideology with broad appeals for
national independence, social justice, and governmental reforms.[36]

This renewed communist effort to depose Diem signaled the formal
beginning of Indochina's second war and the beginning of the end of
Diem's troubled government. Since 1954, an idealist and fiercely anti-
communist Eisenhower administration—desperate to avoid the political
fate that befell Harry Truman over China—had supported the autocratic
and recalcitrant Diem through hard times and two attempted coups. In
that time, three frustrated American ambassadors had vainly tried to persuade Diem to broaden his government, reform the country's political and
economic structure, and reorganize the armed forces. In the end, however,
Eisenhower stood by Diem, assured by his advisors that the South Vietnamese leader, despite his faults, was still the leader best capable of leading his country to victory over the Communists.

Having entered office by dismissing Harry Truman's containment policy as a failed experiment bordering on appeasement, Eisenhower—in Vietnam and elsewhere—had eventually made that very policy the center-piece of his foreign policy. Even when he no longer had a personal inter-est in Indochina, Eisenhower remained steadfastly committed to propping up South Vietnam as a shield against Chinese hegemony in Southeast Asia.

As his second term ended, however, it was Eisenhower's own ability to contain communism that was now in doubt. In support of Diem's fragile government and his army, the U.S. government—that is, the Eisenhower administration supported by an often-enthusiastic Congress—had poured hundreds of millions of dollars into South Vietnam in pursuit of an ambi-tious and audacious goal: to build a new, democratic nation from the ground up. Yet, by 1960, what did the United States have to show for all its mighty effort and staggering expense? Nothing more than a teetering, despotic regime masquerading as a democracy upon which the United States had eagerly staked its international reputation. With the election of a new American president just as committed to fighting communism in Asia as Eisenhower, there was little chance of a major shift in American policy toward Vietnam. Despite the widening cracks in the dike in Viet-nam, few members of Congress demanded a change in U.S. policy.

By virtue of the administration's unequivocal rhetoric, the language of the SEATO treaty, and Washington's sometimes-mindless infusion of mil-itary and economic assistance into Southeast Asia, America was already waist deep in the quagmire that would become its Vietnam War. Once committed to fighting communism in Asia, the politics of the day—still decidedly anticommunist—would continue to influence the course of events. Tragically, there would be no turning back.

PART THREE

INTO THE MORASS

The basic decision in Southeast Asia is here. We must decide whether to help these countries to the best of our ability or throw in the towel in the area and pull back our defenses to San Francisco and a "Fortress America" concept.

— VICE PRESIDENT LYNDON JOHNSON, 1961

On the basis of the present policies that prevail there, South Vietnam is not worth the life of a single American boy.

— SENATOR WAYNE MORSE, 1963

CHAPTER 17

Vietnam Is the Place

1961

"LET EVERY NATION KNOW, WHETHER IT WISHES US WELL OR ILL,"
the newly inaugurated president announced to the assembled crowd from
the U.S. Capitol's East Front, "that we shall pay any price, bear any burden, meet any hardship, support any friend, oppose any foe, in order to
assure the survival and the success of liberty." As he took office on the sub-
freezing afternoon of January 20, 1961, President John F. Kennedy signaled to the world that, like Eisenhower and Truman before him, he would
stand firm against communism. Without naming Indochina, Kennedy
promised that the United States would support those nations recently
freed from colonial domination. To those in "huts and villages" around the
world, "struggling to break the bonds of mass misery," Kennedy promised
the nation's "best efforts to help them help themselves, for whatever period
is required—not because the Communists may be doing it, not because we
seek their votes, but because it is right."[1]

After an eight-year hiatus, the Democrats were back in the White
House, having weathered the storm of the anticommunist crusades of the
1950s. Dean Rusk, the unassuming diplomat who had headed the State
Department's Far East Division during the bleak years of Truman's presidency, was now secretary of state. In the Senate, Mansfield was the majority leader, assisted by majority whip Hubert Humphrey. Fulbright chaired
the Foreign Relations Committee; Russell, the Armed Services Committee. In virtually every office, the government was now led by a group of
determined but pragmatic Cold Warriors, whose attitudes toward communism in Asia had been shaped, in large part, by the painful political turmoil of the early 1950s. That their party had survived and reemerged to
control the government was a testament to their political acumen, as well
as their steely determination never again to allow the Democratic Party to
be on the losing end of a debate over communism.

The Democratic revival of 1960 was in no small part attributable to liberal internationalist senators like Kennedy, Mansfield, and Humphrey, who had sometimes gone overboard in trumpeting their strong opposition to communism. (The liberal Humphrey, for example, had sponsored legislation in 1954 to outlaw the Communist Party.) Few Democrats, however, had been more resolute in that fight than Kennedy, a World War II veteran thoroughly persuaded by the perceived lessons of Munich. William Colby, a CIA official assigned to Saigon in 1961, recalled in 1993 that Kennedy believed "there was a communist tide running in the world that had to be stopped, in Latin America, Southeast Asia, and Europe."[2] As Kennedy's defense secretary, Robert McNamara, explained it more than thirty-five years later: "We believed our interests were being attacked all over the world by a highly organized, unified communist movement, led by Moscow and Beijing, of which we believed, and I now think incorrectly, that the government of Ho Chi Minh was a pawn."[3]

Of course, in light of the political events of 1949–50, a strong stand against communism in Asia was also good politics. Kennedy was nothing if not a good politician. In 1950, he had gone so far as to criticize Harry Truman publicly over the "fall" of China, observing that "what our young men had saved, our diplomats and our President frittered away."[4] Throughout the McCarthy era, the young senator had refused to condemn the Wisconsin senator's demagoguery and was absent—due to illness—when the Senate censured him in 1954.

Entering the White House in 1961, Kennedy would prove to be a different sort of Cold Warrior from Eisenhower and Dulles—as distrustful of the Soviet Union, but far more willing to expend military resources in the struggle. Kennedy's aides would later write of the new president's pragmatism, his willingness to probe for accommodation with the Soviet Union, and his rejection of military solutions to most foreign policy challenges. Yet, Kennedy's actions and rhetoric (beyond his pursuit of détente that culminated in a U.S.-Soviet limited nuclear test ban treaty in 1963) would often suggest a different approach. Instead of merely bolstering his tough anticommunist policies with bellicose rhetoric—like Dulles had— Kennedy was prepared to pour additional money and conventional military forces into the nation's effort to defeat communism around the world. In his first year alone, he increased the defense budget by 14 percent. While he may not have seemed as rigid and reflexive as Dulles, Kennedy was no less a believer in a menacing, monolithic communist world threat. "Our greatest challenge," he told Congress in his first State of the Union Address in early 1961,

is still the world that lies beyond the Cold War—but the first great obstacle is still our relations with the Soviet Union and Communist China. We must never be lulled into believing that either power has yielded its ambitions for world domination—ambitions which they forcefully restated only a short time ago. On the contrary, our task is to convince them that aggression and subversion will not be profitable routes to pursue these ends.[5]

When it came to Vietnam, Kennedy proved that his foreign policy would never be as daring and unconventional as his aides and admirers would later contend. In Vietnam, Kennedy, like Eisenhower and Dulles before him, saw the looming communist monsters of China and the Soviet Union, but not the passionate, militant nationalism that had pragmatically embraced communism in its pursuit of independence. While Kennedy saw no reason to reassess basic assumptions underlying the nation's Vietnam policies, he distinguished himself by an eagerness to find innovative ways of implementing America's *existing* policy. Indeed, Kennedy's earliest presidential action regarding Vietnam was to expand U.S. involvement in Vietnam significantly and send the nation down the road of military escalation that would culminate, almost seven years later, with more than half a million American troops.

Although he and Eisenhower had discussed the escalating communist threat in Laos in January 1961, Kennedy had assumed upon entering office that the basic U.S. military policy in South Vietnam was a success. In early January 1961, however, a report on Vietnam entitled, "Basic Counterinsurgency Plan for Viet-Nam"—prepared by the Country Team Staff Committee, a group of leading U.S. military and civilian officials in Saigon—caught the new president's eye. Warning of a "mounting increase" of Viet Cong "terrorist activities and guerilla warfare" in South Vietnam, the report predicted that "the gravity of this threat" would remain "until a maximum offensive and coordinated retaliatory effort is made by civil and military authorities." To meet the threat, the committee recommended granting Diem's request to increase his army by 20,000 to a total force of 170,000 men and increase his civil guard by 32,000 to 68,000 men. Beefing up South Vietnam's forces would hike the U.S. government's annual defense payments to Vietnam by $42 million to a total of $267 million.[6] It would also require a new American program to develop innovative ways to fight an unconventional guerrilla war. "This is the worst one we've got, isn't it?" a surprised Kennedy asked Walt Rostow, his deputy national security advisor, after he read the report. "You know," he added, recalling the two preinauguration briefings by his predecessor, "Eisenhower never uttered the word Vietnam."[7] From that afternoon forward, Rostow later said, "my job was not merely to follow Laos and Vietnam. It was to help the president get the Pentagon and the whole town to take guerrilla warfare seriously."[8]

Although Kennedy was somewhat skeptical that increasing the South

Vietnamese army by twenty thousand men was necessary to meet a threat posed by ten thousand Viet Cong guerrillas, his staff urged him to act decisively. On January 30, in his first official action regarding Vietnam, Kennedy ordered the increases, setting in motion his administration's escalating role in Vietnam.[9] Just as significant as the action itself was the hubris and arrogance of Kennedy and some of his advisors. Kennedy and his men—many of them bright, young, and energetic professionals recruited from some of the nation's best universities and corporations—were thoroughly persuaded that additional money, newer military techniques, and a more activist management style would solve Vietnam's problems. They approached the country persuaded that by force of intellect and will they could produce the desired results. Like Eisenhower and his advisors before them, Kennedy and his new team saw no reason that the South Vietnamese could not win the war if they learned to fight like Americans. "The Kennedy people," observed historian Thomas G. Paterson, "considered themselves 'can-do' types, who with rationality and careful calculation could revive an ailing nation and world. They believed that they could *manage* affairs."[10]

Even Diem himself could be managed, they thought. In a February 1 memorandum to Kennedy, National Security Council Aide Robert Komer revealed that he saw the conflict in Vietnam as an American operation: "While the first priority must be to meet the impending crisis—*using Diem as our chosen instrument*—we cannot neglect the longer term viability of South Vietnam" (emphasis added). In arguing for "prompt action" to meet Diem's requests for funding to increase his army, Komer also noted that the additional U.S. aid would "probably require circumvention of the Geneva Accords."[11]

Despite Vietnam's attraction as a proving ground for the administration's new approach to the struggle against international communism, the worsening situation in neighboring Laos assumed center stage in the administration's early days. Although supposedly neutral under the terms of the 1954 Geneva accords, the government of Prince Souvanna Phouma had for years received covert military assistance from the United States—about $300 million funneled mostly through the CIA. An outbreak of civil war in 1959 attracted the attention of U.S. and Soviet officials, who saw the conflict as an opportunity to achieve dominance in the region. By the time Kennedy took office, both countries had taken sides and were supplying the opposing factions with military assistance, although the Viet Cong-backed Pathet Lao were gaining ground. The issue had concerned Kennedy enough before he took office that he requested a preinauguration meeting with Eisenhower on January 19 in hopes, he later said, of getting "some idea as to how prepared they were for military intervention."[12]

It was a difficult issue that Kennedy dreaded facing. Before the meeting, he confided to advisor Ted Sorenson: "Whatever's going to happen in Laos, an American invasion, a Communist victory or whatever, I wish it would happen before we take over and get blamed for it."[13] Kennedy recalled that during his meeting with Eisenhower, outgoing Secretary of State Christian Herter argued that the United States was duty-bound to intervene if Laos requested assistance under terms of SEATO. "He said very directly," Kennedy recorded later that day, "that he felt we should [intervene if requested]. It was the cork in the bottle. If Laos fell, then Thailand, the Philippines, or of course Chiang Kai Shek would go." When Kennedy turned to Eisenhower for his views, he remembered that the retiring president "felt we should intervene." Kennedy concluded "that the Eisenhower administration would support intervention—they felt it was preferable to a communist success in Laos." Kennedy's friend and personal lawyer, Clark Clifford, also attended the meeting and recalled the conversation similarly. "President Eisenhower stated that he considered Laos of such importance that if it reached the stage where we could not persuade others to act with us, then he would be willing, *as a last desperate hope, to intervene unilaterally*'" (emphasis Clifford's).[14]

In late March, after Pathet Lao troops appeared to be sweeping the country, Kennedy ordered the Seventh Fleet on alert for possible deployment to the waters off Thailand. On March 23, he went before a national television audience to threaten American military action in pursuit of a "neutral"—as opposed to a "free"—Laos. "The security of all Southeast Asia will be endangered if Laos loses its neutral independence," Kennedy said, pointing to several large maps of the region. To his reiteration of the domino theory, Kennedy added two days later, "No one should doubt our resolution on this point."[15]

If Kennedy's rhetoric was resolute, his true intentions were less so. While it was not entirely clear exactly what he intended in defense of Laotian neutrality—and Kennedy wanted it that way—his message was designed to intimidate the Kremlin and the Viet Cong, while also sending a strong political message to Congress and the American people. To the Communists, he threatened unilateral military intervention. To his domestic audience, he made it clear that his administration, like Eisenhower's, understood the political perils facing any president who allowed the Soviets to draw another Asian nation into their orbit. There would be no "Who lost Laos" debate during his administration. Kennedy may have kept military action in the back of his mind for several weeks during the spring—until a foreign policy debacle arose that would define the early part of his administration.

The Bay of Pigs incursion in mid-April 1961—enthusiastically advo-

cated and its success virtually guaranteed by Kennedy's military advisors—
was a military blunder of historic proportions that badly shook Kennedy's
faith in the Joint Chiefs of Staff.[16] Recalled Deputy Defense Secretary
Roswell Gilpatric: "It had such a traumatic effect on everybody at the top
of the government—in State, Defense, the Agency [CIA], and the White
House—that it was bound to shake up any assurance we had in just carrying forward with existing programs or concepts. It led us to reexamine all
our premises."[17]

Speechwriter and advisor Ted Sorenson and Attorney General Robert
Kennedy believed that events early in his administration might have drawn
Kennedy toward military intervention in Laos—that is, until the Bay of
Pigs disaster made him far more skeptical of the military advice he received
from the Pentagon. "Based on the Bay of Pigs," Robert Kennedy recalled,
the president "started asking questions that were not asked at the Bay of
Pigs." He was not happy with the answers he received. The president's
tough questioning of Joint Chiefs Chairman Lyman Lemnitzer led him to
the painful conclusion that the Pentagon had not done its homework.
Sending American troops to the primitive, landlocked country of Laos
would have almost certainly resulted in another debacle like the Cuban
disaster.

When Lemnitzer presented his plan for military intervention in Laos
during a White House meeting in late April—an operation requiring the
deployment of a thousand troops a day into the Laotian airfields at
Savanaket and Peske—a skeptical Kennedy peppered the Joint Chiefs
chairman with a series of tough, probing questions.

Kennedy asked: "How many can land at the airports?"

"Well, if you have perfect conditions," Lemnitzer replied, "you can
land a thousand men a day."

"How many troops of the Communists are in the surrounding area?"

"I guess, three thousand."

By now, Kennedy believed he was dealing with a fool. "Well now,
what's going to happen if on the third day you've landed three thousand
and then they bomb the airport. And then they bring up five or six thousand more? What's going to happen? Or, if they land two thousand and
then they bomb the airport?"

Lemnitzer replied that he had not given such a contingency much, if
any, thought.[18]

If Kennedy had any lingering doubts about the inadvisability of intervention in Laos, an April 27 meeting with more than a dozen House and
Senate leaders settled the matter. Because the United States did not yet
have any significant military presence in Laos, congressional leaders
undoubtedly found it easier—and without political risk—to advise caution.

Joined by Vice President Johnson, Kennedy learned that only New Hampshire Senator Styles Bridges, a conservative Republican, supported sending in U.S. forces. Majority Leader Mansfield told Kennedy that a Laotian operation would be "fruitless." Said the Senate's Republican leader, Everett Dirksen: "When we got through we would have nothing to show for it." Democrat Richard Russell urged Kennedy to "get our people out and write the country off."[19]*

It became clear to Kennedy that a foray into Laos would be ill-advised at best, and a calamity at worst. Unlike Truman, he had the support of congressional leaders of both parties, which would provide political cover if Laos fell to the Communists. However, the principal motivation for Kennedy's decision against intervention was his strong doubts about the military's ability to carry out the mission. "The President," Arthur Schlesinger observed in his chronicle of Kennedy's presidency, "was appalled at the sketchy nature of American military planning for Laos—the lack of detail and the unanswered questions." Kennedy later told Ted Sorenson: "Thank God the Bay of Pigs happened when it did. Otherwise, we'd be in Laos by now—and that would be a hundred times worse." While Kennedy believed that France's military ineptitude had protected Eisenhower from attacks over the "loss" of northern Vietnam to the Communists after the fall of Dien Bien Phu, he knew that he, alone, would inherit the blame if a mission in Laos failed. "I can't take a 1954 defeat today," he told Rostow.[20]

The painful lessons of the Bay of Pigs allowed Kennedy to avoid disaster in Laos and taught him to be more skeptical of military advice from the Joint Chiefs of Staff. Sorenson noted that after the experience in Cuba, the new president tended to rely more on his White House staff and "his own common sense."[21] By May 1961, U.S. and Soviet representatives agreed to support a cease-fire in Laos and began work in Geneva on a negotiated settlement. By the fall, the negotiations produced a neutrality agreement for Laos. (By early 1962, the agreement would still not be implemented and the fighting would continue. In May 1962, after the Pathet Lao appeared ready to thrust across the Thai border, Kennedy raised the stakes in an attempt to force compliance with the neutrality accord. Prodded by U.S. officials, Thailand requested assistance under terms of SEATO. Kennedy then moved naval and air forces into the area and dispatched more than five thousand Marines and Army personnel—

---

*Alexis Johnson, Kennedy's under secretary of state, recalled that while all but Bridges opposed a U.S. military action in Laos, "some of the senators favored putting American troops in Vietnam and Thailand" (Johnson, *The Right Hand of Power*, 324).

joined by troops from Britain, Australia, and New Zealand—toward the Thai-Laotian border. The bold move would have its desired effect. The Pathet Lao backed down and by June, an uneasy truce—guaranteeing a coalition government dedicated to the country's neutrality—emerged from the Geneva talks.)[22]

The adverse political fallout from Kennedy's failure in Cuba and his decision to seek compromise in Laos made it all the more essential to take a strong stand elsewhere against communist hegemony. "Vietnam is the place," advisor Walt Rostow told the president on April 21, 1961, "where . . . we must prove that we are not a paper tiger."[23] Rostow believed that, other than Cuba, no country provided a better example of the Soviets' appetite for supporting "wars of national liberation." Here, Kennedy's men believed, the resolve of the United States was being tested. "The administration was impregnated with the belief," observed William Bundy, the deputy assistant secretary of defense for international security affairs, "that Communism worldwide . . . was on the offensive, that this offensive had been allowed to gain dangerous momentum in the last two years of the Eisenhower Administration, and that it must now be met solidly."[24] Vietnam would be the place where Kennedy would take his stand.

On April 20, the president had appointed Deputy Defense Secretary Roswell Gilpatric to lead a Presidential Task Force on Vietnam (comprised of representatives from the White House, the CIA, and the Defense and State departments). Defense Secretary McNamara directed the group to develop a "program of action to prevent Communist domination of South Viet-Nam."[25] Less than two weeks later, Gilpatric's group returned with its report, declaring in urgent, ominous tones the dire threat posed by the Viet Cong. "South Viet-Nam is nearing the decisive phase in its battle for survival," the group had concluded. "If the situation continues to deteriorate, the Communists will be able to press on to their strategic goal of establishing a rival 'National Liberation Front' government" in one of the country's regions and "thereby plunge the nation into open civil war."

The situation, they said, was "critical, but not hopeless." With help from the United States, the group asserted, the Viet Cong could be defeated. The task force urged Kennedy to promptly initiate "a series of mutually supporting actions of a military, political, economic, psychological and covert character designed to achieve this objective," including increasing U.S. funds to provide for a South Vietnamese army of two hundred thousand men. In addition, the group called on Kennedy to accelerate the direct intervention of U.S. troops into South Vietnam—as many as three thousand two hundred military "instructors" to assist and train Diem's army, an increase in U.S. military strength of one hundred men, and a new four hundred-man group of specially trained Army "Green

Berets" to instruct the country's special forces.[26] If carried out, the implications of the task force's recommendations were sobering. The United
States would openly violate the 1954 Geneva accords (which Dulles had
not signed, but had pledged not to violate) that placed strict limits on
American troop strength in Vietnam.*

The task force report, however, worried several of Kennedy's top advisors. Secretary of State Rusk reacted cautiously, telling Kennedy that sending U.S. troops to Vietnam might complicate the upcoming talks on
Laos.[27] Other advisors were concerned that the United States would be
taking a gradual first step away from simply assisting South Vietnam and
moving toward assuming responsibility for the country's defense. That
possibility particularly troubled Ted Sorenson, National Security Advisor
McGeorge Bundy, and Budget Director David Bell. In an April 28 memorandum, they advised Kennedy to approve only "the basic concept" of the
task force report. Any steps to help Diem, they maintained, should be part
of a "joint plan to be implemented by both countries."

> There is no clearer example [they wrote] of a country that cannot be saved
> unless it saves itself—through increased popular support; governmental,
> economic and military reforms and reorganizations; and the encourage-
> ment of new political leaders. We do not want Vietnam to fall—we do not
> want to add to Diem's burdens—and the chief purpose of insisting on
> such conditions should not be saving of American dollars but the saving
> of Vietnam.[28]

On May 11, Kennedy approved a large part of the task force report
and set in motion the first escalation of direct American military involvement in Vietnam during his administration. He authorized deployment of
the special forces training team, increased the U.S. MAAG contingent, and
ordered the military to study increasing South Vietnam's army to two hundred thousand. While these actions might seem limited, Kennedy was
moving the U.S. military gradually, but steadily, into South Vietnam. Perhaps his most momentous decision that day was to order his military advisors to explore the "size and composition of forces" that might be needed
"in the case," he said, "of a possible commitment" of U.S. troops.[29]

---

*The violations would not be new, just in the open. The United States had been
flouting the Geneva agreements for years.

CHAPTER 18

You're Just Crazier Than Hell

1961

"LYNDON," KENNEDY SAID TO HIS VICE PRESIDENT ON THE AFTER-
noon of May 5, 1961, "I still want you to go to Vietnam. You've just got to
go out there."

"Mr. President," Johnson said, "I don't want to embarrass you by getting my head blown off in Saigon."

It was the third or fourth time Kennedy had broached the subject that
week, and the president was beginning to wonder if Johnson was more concerned about his hide than the administration's foreign policy. "Don't
worry, Lyndon," Kennedy jibed. "If anything happens to you, Sam Rayburn and I will give you the biggest funeral Austin, Texas, ever saw."[1]

This apparently did not ease Johnson's resistance. In frustration,
Kennedy finally leaked word to the *New York Times* that the vice president
would be leading an administration delegation to Vietnam. When Johnson heard the news on the radio, he exploded. This time, however,
Kennedy was adamant. "You're going tonight," Kennedy barked when
Johnson vehemently protested at an NSC meeting, "and the Foreign Service and [McGeorge] Bundy will brief you." Johnson responded by leaving the meeting and getting drunk. "He came back and went to sleep on
his couch and finally let the Foreign Service guys in," recalled Johnson's
military representative, Air Force Colonel Howard Burris. One of those
officials was Carl Rowan, the deputy assistant secretary of state for public
affairs and the first black man ever appointed to a senior State Department
post. Rowan and the other officials found Johnson in an exceedingly foul
mood. "I want you State Department folks to know that I think you're a
bunch of little puppy dogs, leaking on every hydrant," Johnson said,
explaining that he expected soon to uncover the official who had leaked the
news of his upcoming trip. "I tell you," Johnson said, "you just write down
the name of the reporter who wrote that goddam story, and you wait a few

weeks and you're gonna see that reporter write something nice about the leaker because the reporter's got to pay that guy off, and I can tell you I'm waiting to see if there's a nice profile about old Chester Bowles, 'cause I think he's the one who leaked the story about my trip." Rowan was astonished that Johnson suspected Bowles because he was "absolutely certain that the leak came not from Chester Bowles but from the president of the United States."[2]

Regardless of who leaked the story, Kennedy had many good reasons for sending Johnson to Vietnam. To begin with, he understood the dimensions of his vice president's enormous ego and the personal and professional sacrifices Johnson had made when joining his administration. One day, Johnson had been among the most powerful Democrats in the nation; the next, was vice president to a former Senate colleague—and a junior one, at that. Even on the night of the election, Johnson was downcast and fully aware of the vast power and influence that had slipped through his hands. "I don't think I ever saw a more unhappy man," recalled journalist Margaret Mayer, who encountered Johnson on election night. "Lyndon looked as if he'd lost his last friend on earth."[3] After only four months in office, Johnson was having problems—his heavy drinking and his obvious depression was common knowledge around the White House. Kennedy knew that the former Senate majority leader was a very miserable man who despised the political emasculation inherent in the vice presidency.

Kennedy also knew about the ridicule and scorn that his staff sometimes heaped upon the vice president in his absence. "I don't know what to do with Lyndon," the president confided to his friend and journalist Arthur Krock. "I've got to keep him happy somehow. My big job is to keep Lyndon happy."[4] One way to keep Johnson happy was to keep him busy traveling abroad. On his first foreign trip, in April, he had traveled to Senegal and Geneva. He was barely back in Washington before Kennedy had begun urging him to go to Vietnam.

But the trip to Vietnam was more than Kennedy's way of easing Johnson's misery. As part of its comprehensive report in late April, Kennedy's Task Force on Vietnam had suggested sending Johnson—whose powers of persuasion were substantial—to Saigon with the hope that he could prod Diem into greater cooperation with U.S. officials in a coordinated effort to defeat the Viet Cong. The group believed that Johnson's visit would also bolster Diem's authority and strengthen his resolve by affirming U.S. confidence in his leadership. In addition, Kennedy's missteps in Cuba and his unwillingness to send troops to Laos suggested to some Southeast Asian leaders a lack of American resolve in the fight against communism. Kennedy wanted Johnson to reassure Diem that the United States was determined to help his country win its fight.

To Kennedy, sending his vice president also had the added political benefit, in the words of historian William Conrad Gibbons, of making it appear that "Johnson's conclusions and recommendations were his own, and represented his point of view rather than Kennedy's." In fact, the White House would choreograph much of Johnson's trip and State Department personnel would largely compose his recommendations for greater U.S. support for South Vietnam. To the public and particularly Congress—where Johnson enjoyed enormous respect—Kennedy would simply be responding to Johnson's endorsement of an increased U.S. role in South Vietnam. Because the recommendations would come from Johnson, Kennedy—by implementing them—could insulate himself from criticism from the more conservative House and Senate Democrats.[5]

"Briefed to the gills on Vietnam,"[6] in the words of Secretary of State Rusk, Johnson left Washington on May 9, with his wife, Lady Bird, Kennedy's sister, Jean, and her husband, Stephen Smith. The two-week trip would take them throughout the Far East—to Vietnam, Thailand, the Philippines, Taiwan, Hong Kong, India, and Pakistan. Johnson and his party arrived in Saigon on the evening of May 11 and were greeted by thousands of enthusiastic South Vietnamese citizens. Like any good politician, Johnson warmed to the large, receptive audience. "He played it to the hilt," recalled Mansfield's aide, Francis Valeo, who also accompanied Johnson on the trip. "He didn't know what else to do except play it as a politician." Valeo remembered that Johnson treated the gathering to an energetic "stump speech, as though he were running for office in Vietnam," and then plunged into the crowd to shake hands. With Jean Smith at his side, Johnson bragged that "we think so much of this country, I've even brought the president's little sister with me."[7]

The next morning, still exhausted from the long trip halfway around the globe, Johnson met Diem for the first time. His first order of business was to secure the South Vietnamese leader's agreement to accept the program of additional assistance that Kennedy had authorized in May— including the special forces training for Diem's troops and an expansion of the U.S. Military Assistance Advisory Group (MAAG). Diem, it was feared, might be hesitant to allow an expansion of U.S. military involvement in his country for fear of losing control of his government. Johnson presented Diem with a four-page letter outlining the additional support the United States was prepared to extend. In the letter, Kennedy told Diem that "we are ready to join with you in an intensified endeavor to win the struggle against Communism and to further the social and economic advancement of Viet-Nam."[8]

Diem ignored the letter and launched into a lengthy, meandering monologue about Vietnamese history and politics. Impatient, Johnson broke in and turned the conversation back to Kennedy's letter. Did Diem support what Kennedy had proposed? he asked. Diem reviewed the letter point by point. He agreed to an increase in the U.S. MAAG and readily accepted additional assistance for beefing up his army and the nation's civil guard. Diem was far less enthusiastic about the economic and political reforms that Kennedy suggested. The United States should understand, he said elliptically, that any reforms he pursued would be "appropriate" for a country, like Vietnam, that was "under attack and underdeveloped."[9]

Diem would accept what help he could get but when Johnson raised the possibility of a U.S.-Vietnamese mutual defense pact that might eventually lead to the introduction of U.S. troops, the South Vietnamese leader was reticent. He would support a plan to send U.S. troops to train his army, but not any greater role for U.S. troops in his country. "Diem showed no appetite for American combat troops mixing among the Vietnamese people," wrote Kenneth Young, the U.S. ambassador to Thailand who accompanied Johnson on his trip to Saigon, in a cable to Washington. "He told me privately that we should be extremely careful about such a proposal, and pleaded with me that American military personnel—and all Americans— exercise tact and restraint in Vietnam in this critical and delicate period."[10]

Despite the talk about economic and political reforms, it was the military situation that dominated the discussion, as well as Johnson's subsequent talks with U.S. embassy and military officials in Saigon. At a late-night meeting with a group of about twenty officials—including members of Johnson's traveling party, his personal staff, and U.S. embassy and military personnel assigned to Saigon—Johnson demanded a coherent plan of action to end the fighting in Vietnam. Valeo recalled that after being briefed for about twenty minutes on the U.S. aid program in South Vietnam, Johnson interrupted. "That's all very fine," he said, "but what I really want to know is: what can we do to end this situation? The American people are getting very tired of what is going on over here. We're spending something like $350 million a year on this country, and they're tired of spending that kind of money. They want to wind it up. Now, what's it going to take to end it, to get rid of the Communists?"

Responding to Johnson's aggressive prodding, the U.S. MAAG commander, Lieutenant General Lionel McGarr, reluctantly agreed that a drastic increase in U.S. military funding and personnel might help defeat the Viet Cong within a year. Johnson "loved to put words in people's mouths and then say, 'Well, he agreed with me,'" Valeo observed when recalling the discussion. "The fellow [McGarr] didn't say it, in so many words, that it would end in a year. But he permitted Lyndon to think that." Valeo concluded that the result of the meeting was that Johnson "came away with an optimistic view that a solution could be found. All we had to do was increase the amount of aid."[11]

Johnson met once more with Diem, for about twenty minutes, on the morning of May 13. Afterwards, the two men issued a joint communiqué agreeing that their governments would "extend and build upon existing programs of military and economic aid" and would "infuse into their joint actions a high sense of urgency and dedication." In negotiating the language of the document, however, Diem had insisted on watering down the draft wording that endorsed social, political, and economic reforms. The new American ambassador to Saigon, Frederick Nolting, observed in a telegram to Washington that while Johnson had stressed "economic and social measures to accompany military action, we think Diem will be inclined to put main stress on [the] military side."[12]

As he left Saigon for Manila that morning, Johnson gave every indication that he trusted Diem's leadership and believed that more money and men would solve the country's problems. An interim report sent to Washington by Nolting hailed Johnson's visit and declared that "Diem's confidence in [the] US has been greatly increased by [Johnson's] visit."[13] Kenneth Young was even more ebullient. Speaking of Johnson and the Smiths, he cabled Washington: "They came, saw, and won over."[14]

In his official report to Kennedy—approved beforehand by State Department and White House officials—Johnson offered Kennedy what would prove to be an unrealistically narrow set of options. "The basic decision in Southeast Asia is here," he said. "We must decide whether to help these countries to the best of our ability or throw in the towel in the area and pull back our defenses to San Francisco and a 'Fortress America' concept." It was as if the Viet Cong were waging war on the United States, not South Vietnam. To blunt the Viet Cong, Johnson recommended a "three-year plan of increased aid—military and economic" that he characterized as a "major effort to help these countries defend themselves." Although in Saigon he had referred to Diem as the "Churchill of today,"* Johnson was more realistic about the South Vietnamese leader in his report. "He has admirable qualities, but he is remote from the people, is surrounded by persons less admirable and capable than he." All the same, Johnson believed the United States had no choice but to back Diem—and to the hilt. "We must decide whether to support Diem—or let Vietnam fall."[15]

---

*In a 1969 interview, Johnson defended his seemingly hyperbolic remark and explained that he had not meant to suggest that Diem possessed the same leadership qualities as Winston Churchill, only that South Vietnam was threatened by communist aggression in the same way that Britain had been threatened by Nazi Germany in the 1930s. Reminding Diem that Churchill had inspired the British people by vowing to "meet them [the Nazis] on the beaches," Johnson said he told Diem that "you're going to have to be like Churchill—you're going to have to use your beer bottles on them" (LBJ OH, LBJL).

In an attachment to his report, Johnson tried to identify South Vietnam's "basic problem." The economic conditions he found in Vietnam were not unlike the problems he would address in the United States four years later with the Great Society programs of his own administration: "The ordinary people need decent houses. They need schools. They need better conditions of health. They need productive industries, the thriving agriculture and the safe and adequate transportation and communications which will make all of these things possible. They need an understanding government which is close to them and in which they feel a stake."

Johnson also believed that South Vietnam could be secured from an "invasion" from the north. "An increase in military aid will be necessary for this purpose," he said. "It will not be cheap. Yet, if this effort will in fact produce the security necessary for progress in freedom in Viet-Nam . . . then it is in our interests as well as the interests of the Vietnamese people and all free nations that the effort be made." But Johnson also warned Kennedy against sending U.S. troops to Vietnam to fight alongside the South Vietnamese army. "If we use our own forces to help put down Communist rebellion in South Viet Nam," he wrote, "we will also bear the onus of helping to put down the Vietnamese people." Johnson believed that "we should make clear, in private, that barring an unmistakable and massive invasion of South Viet Nam from without, we have no intention of employing combat U.S. forces in Viet Nam or using even naval or air-support which is but the first step in that direction. If the Vietnamese government backed by a three-year liberal aid program cannot do this job, then we had better remember the experience of the French who wound up with several hundred thousand men in Vietnam and were still unable to do it."[16]

Testifying before an executive session of the Senate Foreign Relations Committee on May 25, Johnson reiterated his support for a substantial increase in American assistance to South Vietnam. "If a bully can come in and run you out of the yard today," he told the committee, "tomorrow he will come back and run you off the porch." But Johnson also repeated his warnings about American troops in Vietnam. While he maintained "there is no alternative to U.S. leadership in Southeast Asia," he made it clear that "Asian leaders at this time do not want American troops involved in Southeast Asia, *other than on training missions*" (emphasis added). Not only were they not required, American troops were "not desirable." Johnson explained that "possibly Americans fail to appreciate fully the subtlety that recent colonial peoples do not look with favor upon governments which invite or accept the return this soon of Western troops." The nations of Southeast Asia, he insisted, "cannot be saved by the U.S. help alone."[17]

While the vice presidential trip had begun as a public relations effort to fortify Diem's leadership—with the added benefit of soothing Johnson's ego—it ended up as something far more important. Johnson recast the United States's position on Vietnam. Before his visit, the U.S. government's role was simply to provide military, financial, and technical assistance to the South Vietnamese government. But following the script written by Kennedy's State Department, Johnson had redefined his country's role. By agreeing that the two governments would take "joint actions" to fight the communist threat, the vice president—despite his insistence that U.S. troops should be used only for training purposes—had moved the United States closer to assuming the role of partner in the enterprise to save the country from communism.

WHILE JOHNSON'S REPORT HAD conveyed a restrained sense of urgency in Vietnam, Walt Rostow believed that the situation was much worse than Johnson or officials in Saigon had perceived. On May 26, he informed Kennedy that "the Viet-Nam situation is extremely dangerous to the peace," and argued that "we must push on all fronts to force a deflation of that crisis before it builds to a situation like that in Laos."[18] In the months to come, Rostow's sense of panic about Vietnam would be increasingly shared among Kennedy's aides and would prompt the president to move more rapidly toward even greater U.S. involvement.

In June, Kennedy would leave a turbulent summit meeting in Vienna with Nikita Khrushchev persuaded that the Soviet leader would continue testing the American leader's mettle around the world—particularly in Vietnam. Kennedy's handling of the Bay of Pigs invasion had apparently convinced Khrushchev that Kennedy was a weak leader who was easily intimidated, and this impression was deepened by Kennedy's lackluster performance at Vienna. Kennedy, who knew he had been bested, emerged from his meeting with Khrushchev shaken and all the more resolved to challenge the Soviets. "Now we have a problem making our power credible," Kennedy had confided to James Reston of the New York Times immediately after his meeting with Khrushchev, "and Vietnam looks like the place."[19]

The increasing U.S. presence in South Vietnam, meanwhile, concerned Senate Foreign Relations Chairman Fulbright, who worried that Kennedy's actions in Vietnam might be related to the public's anxiety over "a series of dramatic events," each challenging the supremacy of the United States. The first was the Soviet Union's successful mission to put a man in space in April. Then, there was "the misadventure in Cuba," followed by escalating tensions in Laos. Now, it was Vietnam. Fulbright believed that Americans might be drawing the wrong conclusions from the events of the spring of 1961 and that Kennedy might believe the answer was to find a place—perhaps Vietnam—to take a strong, determined stand against Soviet hegemony. That, he feared, could prove to be a tragic mistake.

As one of the Senate's leading internationalists, Fulbright believed strongly in an activist American foreign policy designed to challenge Soviet communist expansionism. Yet, for years he had questioned the Eisenhower administration's tactics in that enterprise. In the late 1950s, in fact, he had emerged as one of the administration's most vocal Senate critics, arguing that the president and Dulles lacked the vision, flexibility, and creativity to respond to Soviet hegemony with anything other than the threat of nuclear retaliation and a mindless increase in military assistance to America's allies around the world. The foreign aid program, weighted so heavily with military aid, concerned him greatly. "The shipment of arms to any nation not practiced in the art of democratic self-government," Fulbright told the Senate in June 1958, "promotes maintenance of the *status quo*. Military aid to nonrepresentative governments means the use of that equipment to maintain nonrepresentative government. That aid has a tendency to pit the United States against the rising tide of self-determination and fertilizes foreign soil for the Communists to till."[20]

Fulbright had rarely hesitated to question conventional wisdom. Since his arrival in Congress in 1943—and especially since coming to the Senate in 1945—the handsome, athletic Democrat had enjoyed a well-earned reputation as a thoughtful, yet fiercely independent man unafraid to challenge the status quo. In 1946, he had called on Harry Truman to resign after that year's Democratic electoral debacle handed control of both houses of Congress to the Republicans. An angry Truman called Fulbright, a former Rhodes scholar, "that over-educated s.o.b." Fulbright's courageous challenge to Senator Joseph McCarthy in the early 1950s had earned him another title; McCarthy derisively referred to his Arkansas colleague as "Senator Halfbright."

Despite McCarthy's name-calling, no one thought Fulbright an intellectual lightweight; quite to the contrary, he was regarded as one of the Senate's most powerful intellectuals. A graduate of the George Washington University Law School, Fulbright had taught law school and had served briefly—at age 34—as president of the University of Arkansas before launching his political career. Early in his legislative career, Fulbright had secured his place in history. As a freshman House member, he had the vision to offer a simple measure, approved by Congress, that became the framework for America's participation in the creation of the United Nations. In 1945, as a freshman senator, he sponsored legislation to create an international student exchange program—later known as the Fulbright Fellowships—which became law.

An intimate of Lyndon Johnson, Fulbright was the most influential Senate voice on foreign policy, even before he became chairman of the Foreign Relations Committee. "Bill's *my* secretary of state," the Senate majority leader had bragged to associates.[21] Johnson proved his loyalty to Fulbright in 1959 when he engineered the resignation of the committee's elderly chairman, Theodore Francis Green. Fulbright took over the committee's reins and appeared destined to become the next secretary of state in a Democratic administration. After Kennedy's election, some concluded that Fulbright was the odds-on favorite to lead the State Department. As a result of Johnson's vigorous lobbying and his own relationship with Fulbright, Kennedy appeared ready to appoint his former Senate colleague.[22] But just as quickly as he settled on Fulbright, Kennedy decided that the Arkansas senator's opposition to civil rights legislation was a disqualifying factor.[23]

Fulbright remained in the Senate and served as a valued advisor to the new president, all the while maintaining his freedom to offer constructive criticism of Kennedy's foreign policy. His speech to the Senate on June 29, while not specifically critical of Kennedy, served as a stern warning to the new president about the need to review the foreign policy he had inherited from Eisenhower and Dulles. Concerned that the Soviets' success in space and America's lack of success in Cuba and Laos would propel an embarrassed nation toward a showdown in Vietnam, Fulbright urged Kennedy to reexamine the nation's reflexive response to the communist threat. The president, he said, should ignore the "voices" that argued that "the United States is the strongest country in the world and should not hesitate to commit its strength to the active defense of its policies anywhere outside the Communist empire." That, Fulbright said, "is dangerous doctrine; nothing would please Communist leaders more than to draw the United States into costly commitments of its resources to peripheral struggles in which the principal Communist powers are not themselves directly involved. . . . Cuba, Laos, the Soviet cosmonaut—none of these by itself is a threat to our national security or to the long-term success of our policies. But by exaggerating their significance and reacting to them injudiciously we disfigure our national style and undermine our policies."

When he looked at Vietnam—and he admittedly knew little about Southeast Asia in 1961—Fulbright saw a country hampered by Diem's autocratic leadership. He wondered aloud: "How is it that the Communist Viet Cong guerillas in South Vietnam have managed to gain a foothold in much of the countryside?" The answer, he said, "appears to rest" with Diem's regime. While Diem had been "courageous and diligent in bringing order and economic progress out of the chaos that attended the country's birth," Fulbright worried that Diem's rule had been overbearing. "It is a regime that of necessity has been authoritarian," he said, "but one that also has been perhaps unnecessarily severe." In the end, Fulbright believed

South Vietnam's success would not depend on the amount of military assistance the United States provided, but on "the economic and social progress that flow from the programs and policies of its government." The proper course for the United States, he said, "is to continue sustaining and supporting efforts of the Vietnamese army to cope effectively with the foe in being—tough bands of hit-and-run Communist guerillas—while devoting at least as much effort to assisting and guiding the Vietnamese people in their struggle for dignity and economic independence."

Were he the leader of South Vietnam, Fulbright said he would work to keep his country neutral in the power struggle between the United States and the Soviets. He would ask for economic and technical assistance from the United States, but would also be open to "limited aid" from the Communist bloc. "But I would discreetly point out that the United States cannot with guns, tanks, jeeps—or even with dollars—keep communism out of my country. The United States can help me keep communism out of my country by imaginatively and dispassionately supporting my efforts to promote the welfare of my people."[24]

Of course, in the White House, Kennedy's advisors did not see the Cold War through Fulbright's more dispassionate eyes. In South Vietnam, they did not see a country whose primary need was economic and social reform. They saw, instead, a government under increasingly fierce attack from armed communist subversives who were dutiful agents of the Soviet Union. In August, Ambassador Nolting predicted from Saigon that Viet Cong activity would increase significantly in the coming months. "Indiscriminate terror campaign or one directed at Americans in Saigon," he warned, "[is] a continuing grim prospect."[25] MAAG officials also noted a "significant increase in Viet Cong capabilities."[26]

Added to these warnings, and to Rostow's in-house alarms, was advice from NSC staff member Robert Komer, who addressed the domestic political ramifications of Vietnam in a July 20 memorandum to Kennedy. Komer argued that "there are some strong political reasons for stepping up momentum in South Vietnam." Among them was his belief that "this government [should] have a major anti-communist victory to its credit in the six months before the Berlin crisis is likely to get hot.* Few things would be better calculated to show Moscow and Peiping that we mean business than an obvious (if not yet definitive) turnaround in Vietnam."[27]

In their effort to force Kennedy to make what Rostow called "a bold

---

*In August, the U.S.-Soviet dispute over the status of Berlin culminated in an effort by East Germany, a Soviet client, to stop the exodus of German citizens from East Berlin. To prevent refugees from fleeing into West Germany, Khrushchev allowed the East Germans to build a wall that split the city in two and ended the East Germans' flights to freedom.

decision,"[28] he and Komer found an ally in General Maxwell Taylor, the former Army chief of staff who had assumed the role of Kennedy's military representative. "Taylor's ideas of flexible response, employing a whole array of military options," historian Robert D. Schulzinger observed, "seemed the perfect complement to Rostow's belief that the developing world represented the new arena of the Cold War."[29] While Taylor—a once-strong critic of the Eisenhower administration's military cost-cutting efforts—did not urge Kennedy to intervene, he made it clear that events in South Vietnam were reaching the point where such a decision might become necessary.

As Taylor saw the situation, Kennedy had three options: (1) withdraw from Vietnam "as gracefully as possible"; (2) "find as soon as possible a convenient political pretext and attack with American military force the regional source of aggression in Hanoi"; or (3) empower South Vietnam to resist the Viet Cong "while preparing to intervene with U.S. military force if the Chinese Communists come in or the situation otherwise gets out of hand."[30]

Kennedy listened, but moved cautiously. While he would not rule out direct U.S. intervention, he was clearly reluctant to take this course. Perhaps still smarting from the Bay of Pigs disaster, he wanted more time and better information. In October, he named Taylor to head a special mission to South Vietnam to assess the situation and, as Kennedy said, "to evaluate what could be accomplished by the introduction of SEATO or United States forces into South Vietnam."[31] Publicly, the administration billed the mission as an "economic survey." But Taylor and his traveling companions—including Rostow and General Edward Lansdale—knew their charge was, in the words of Deputy Defense Secretary Roswell Gilpatric, to report to Kennedy on the "feasibility" of a plan for "military intervention."[32]

Taylor presented the mission's recommendations to Kennedy on November 3. Like the leaders of the two previous administrations, his and the other participants' views were guided by an unquestioning acceptance of the domino theory. Taylor, Rostow, and the others did not see the war in Vietnam as an internal struggle between nationalism and colonialism, but concluded that "the Communists are pursuing a clear and systematic strategy in Southeast Asia." The Kennedy administration, they said, "must decide how it will cope with Khrushchev's 'wars of liberation' which are really para-wars of guerilla aggression." At stake was the future, not just of Vietnam, but the entire region: "It is evident that morale in Vietnam will rapidly crumble—and in Southeast Asia only slightly less quickly—if the sequence of expectations set in motion by Vice President Johnson's visit and climaxed by General Taylor's mission are not soon followed by a hard U.S. commitment to the ground in Vietnam."

It is clear to me [Taylor wrote in his introduction] that the time may come in our relations to Southeast Asia when we must declare our intention to attack the source of guerilla aggression in North Vietnam and impose on the Hanoi Government a price for participating in the current war which is commensurate with the damage being inflicted on its neighbors to the south.

What Taylor and Rostow wanted was "a shift from U.S. advice to limited partnership and working collaboration with the Vietnamese." While they cautioned Kennedy that the war would not be won "by direct U.S. action," the chances of a South Vietnamese victory would be "substantially improved if Americans are prepared to work side by side with the Vietnamese on the key problems."[33] According to the Taylor report, a new partnership between the United States and South Vietnam meant a drastic increase in the level of American involvement: joint planning of offensive military operations, better coordination with South Vietnamese intelligence, increased covert operations throughout Vietnam and in Laos, three new helicopter squadrons and additional light aircraft, and "a radical increase" of U.S. trainers at every level, as well as additional special forces. Most significant, however, this new partnership would mean a force of eight thousand to ten thousand American soldiers sent to South Vietnam and thinly disguised as a flood relief force. Even at ten thousand, it was a relatively small number that, as Secretary McNamara observed in a November 4 meeting with Defense and State department personnel, "does not convince anyone of our resolve."[34]

While those numbers were not substantial and, as McNamara noted, were unlikely to intimidate the Viet Cong, an imminent decision to send thousands of American troops to Vietnam alarmed Mansfield. On November 2, several days after Kennedy told him that Taylor would likely recommend sending American troops to Vietnam,[35] the Senate majority leader sent Kennedy a four-page memorandum. Setting aside his earlier, politically inspired rhetoric about South Vietnam's significance to U.S. national security, Mansfield urged the president to approach his decision with "the greatest caution." The memorandum was a dispassionate appeal to Kennedy's pragmatic, analytical side—an attempt to force him to consider the long-term ramifications of a decision to commit U.S. forces to Vietnam. It was, by any standard, an intelligent, well-reasoned argument against the most significant recommendations of the Taylor report. Moreover, it was a stunning example of Mansfield's prescience and his understanding of the risks involved:

The sending of American armed forces to Viet Nam may be the wrong way and probably would be, in present circumstances. In the first place,

we would be engaged without the support of significant allies. Our troops
would be engaged by third-string communist forces (North Vietnamese).
South Vietnam . . . could become a quicksand for us. Where does an
involvement of this kind end even if we can bring it to a successful conclusion? In the environs of Saigon? At the 17th parallel? At Hanoi? At
Canton? At Peking? Any involvement on the mainland of Asia would
seem to me to weaken our military capability in Berlin and Germany and,
again, leave the Russians uncommitted.

Although he acknowledged Vietnam's importance to the United
States, Mansfield argued that "we cannot hope to substitute armed power
for the kind of political and economic social changes that offer the best
resistance to communism." If the "necessary reforms" had not occurred in
the past seven years, he said, "I do not see how American combat troops
can do it today." While he told Kennedy that he would enthusiastically
support "a substantial increase" in military and economic assistance to
South Vietnam, he maintained that the "burden of meeting communist
infiltration, subversion and attack" should be left to the South Vietnamese,
"whose country it is and whose future is their chief responsibility." Admitting that U.S. combat forces "might provide that bare margin of effectiveness which would permit a solution of the guerilla problem in South Viet
Nam or prevent further encroachments southward," Mansfield nonetheless believed the ultimate costs would far outweigh the benefits. "Even
then, we will have achieved a 'victory' whose fruits, if we would conserve
them, will cost us billions of dollars in military and aid expenditures over
the years into the future."[36]

While there is no record of Kennedy's response to Mansfield's advice,
the Senate majority leader was not the only advisor to warn Kennedy that
accepting Taylor's recommendations might well lead the nation into a
quagmire of unimaginable proportions. Under Secretary of State Chester
Bowles and Averell Harriman, America's chief negotiator at the Geneva
talks on Laos, both urged Kennedy to defer any commitment to Diem until
the Laotian situation was resolved and Americans could be confident that
the conflict would not spread beyond Vietnam.[37] At the White House,
National Security Council staff member Robert Johnson warned National
Security Advisor McGeorge Bundy that the troops that Taylor envisioned
were not likely to stay in a flood-relief mode for long. "Many in Washington are convinced that the longer the forces remained in Viet Nam, the
more they would come under attack and the more they would become
involved in combat." Furthermore, Johnson reasoned, by sending a force
of that size, the United States would be placing its reputation on the line.
"We need to face and to decide in principle the question of whether we are
prepared, if necessary, to step up very considerably our military commit-

President Harry Truman with foreign policy advisors Secretary of State Dean Acheson and Defense Secretary George C. Marshall during a conference with French Prime Minister René Pleven (*seated on right*) in 1951. Following World War II, Truman sided with France in its quest to reassert dominance over Indochina. A bloody, eight-year war with the Vietminh ensued. (National Park Service photograph, courtesy Harry S. Truman Library)

Republican Senator Joseph McCarthy of Wisconsin created havoc with his reckless charges of communism in the U.S. government in the early 1950s. "The Democratic label," he said in 1950, "is now the property of men and women who have . . . bent to the whispered pleas from the lips of traitors." (CORBIS)

As the philosophical leader of Senate Republicans, Robert Taft of Ohio often led his party's opposition to Harry Truman's foreign and domestic policies. That included encouraging Joseph McCarthy to trumpet his charges of communism in Truman's State Department in 1950. Taft described him as "a fighting Marine who risked his life to preserve the liberties of the United States." (Library of Congress)

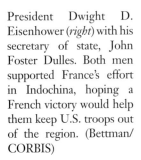

President Dwight D. Eisenhower (*right*) with his secretary of state, John Foster Dulles. Both men supported France's effort in Indochina, hoping a French victory would help them keep U.S. troops out of the region. (Bettman/CORBIS)

In 1953, Vice President Richard Nixon became the most senior American official to visit Indochina. Upon his return, he strongly urged Eisenhower to continue U.S. support for the French in their fight against the Vietminh. (Richard Nixon Library)

President John F. Kennedy and Vice President Lyndon Johnson. After Kennedy sent Johnson to South Vietnam in 1961, the new vice president urged Kennedy to increase military aid to the government of Premier Ngo Dinh Diem. (John F. Kennedy Library)

In leading America deeper into Vietnam in the early 1960s, Kennedy relied on the advice of two trusted advisors, (*left to right*) Secretary of State Dean Rusk and Defense Secretary Robert McNamara. (John F. Kennedy Library)

President Kennedy discusses the situation in Laos during a State Department press conference in March 1961. While increasing the U.S. military role in Vietnam, Kennedy searched vigorously for a peaceful solution to the conflict in neighboring Laos. (AP/Wide World Photos)

President Johnson with former President Eisenhower in August 1965. Eisenhower publicly backed Johnson's escalation of the war and helped give his Vietnam policies a bipartisan flavor. (Yoichi R. Okamoto, LBJ Library)

Oregon Senator Wayne Morse, an early opponent of American military involvement in Vietnam, was one of only two members of Congress to vote against the Gulf of Tonkin Resolution in 1964. "South Vietnam," he told the Senate in 1963, "is not worth the life of a single American boy." (Yoichi R. Okamoto, LBJ Library)

Senator Ernest Gruening with Johnson in the Oval Office. The Alaska senator also opposed the Gulf of Tonkin Resolution. Along with Morse, he was defeated for reelection in 1968. (Yoichi R. Okamoto, LBJ Library)

Defense Secretary Robert S. McNamara. The architect of the military policies of presidents Kennedy and Johnson, McNamara later confessed that he had viewed the Vietnam War not as a nationalistic movement but as "a unified Communist drive for hegemony in Asia." He later acknowledged his error. (Yoichi R. Okamoto, LBJ Library)

Senate Foreign Relations Committee Chairman J. William Fulbright (majority leader Mike Mansfield in background) led the 1964 Senate debate in support of the Gulf of Tonkin Resolution. Within eighteen months, he would become one of the Senate's most vociferous critics of Lyndon Johnson's Vietnam policies. (Yoichi R. Okamoto, LBJ Library)

Mississippi Senator John Stennis—a leading member of the Armed Services Committee and a supporter of Johnson's war policies—had initially been skeptical about U.S. involvement in Indochina. By 1967, in the midst of questions about the efficacy of the bombing campaign, Stennis urged Johnson and McNamara to persevere. (Yoichi R. Okamoto, LBJ Library)

Secretary of State Dean Rusk. Although he was the nation's chief diplomat, Rusk initially argued against seeking a peaceful end to the war. "Any 'truce' which might be 'won now in Vietnam,'" Rusk told Johnson in early 1964, "would be bought at a price . . . far more costly to us than the peace which we hope to see established there by the action of the new South Vietnamese government." (Frank Wolfe, LBJ Library)

Republican Senate Leader Everett Dirksen. Angered by opposition to his Vietnam policies from members of his own party, Lyndon Johnson welcomed the support of many Republicans. "I'm irked as hell," Johnson complained to Dirksen in 1965. "I'm getting kicked around by my own party in the Senate and getting my support from your side of the aisle." (Yoichi R. Okamoto, LBJ Library)

Johnson tried to preserve congressional support for his Vietnam policies with a series of White House briefings for House and Senate members in 1965. At this one, in February, he declared his dedication to preserving the government of South Vietnam. "We are there to stay," he said. "We don't plan to pull out and tuck our tail and come home." (LBJ Library)

ment in Viet Nam," Johnson wrote on October 31. "If we commit 6–8,000 troops and then pull them out when the going got rough we will be finished in Viet Nam and probably all of Southeast Asia."[38]

At the State Department, the under secretary for economic affairs, George Ball, had read the Taylor report and was "appalled" by its recommendations. A respected New Deal-era lawyer and political strategist with close ties to Adlai Stevenson, Ball also knew something about military operations, having helped direct the United States Strategic Bombing Survey in Europe during and after World War II. Among his many attributes, and the reason his colleagues respected him, was a willingness to speak his mind during private meetings—even when his views differed from official U.S. policy. At a November 4 meeting with Taylor, McNamara, and Gilpatric, Ball was blunt. He warned against committing American forces to South Vietnam, "or we would find ourselves in a protracted conflict far more serious than Korea." Ball explained that the Viet Cong were "mean and tough," a fact the French had learned "to their sorrow." Worst of all, Ball argued, "the Vietnam problem was not one of repelling overt invasion but of mixing ourselves up in a revolutionary situation with strong anti-colonialist overtones." But Ball was butting against a brick wall. "To my dismay," he recalled years later, "I found no sympathy for these views." He observed that McNamara and Gilpatric seemed "preoccupied" with only one issue: "How can the United States stop South Vietnam from a Viet Cong takeover? How did I propose to avoid it?" To Ball, "the 'falling domino' theory was a brooding omnipresence."[39]

Three days later, Ball had his chance with the president. Visiting the White House on an unrelated topic, Ball waited until the meeting's conclusion before he raised the subject of Vietnam. He told Kennedy that he strongly opposed the Taylor report's conclusions and believed ratifying them would be a tragic error. "Within five years," he told the president, "we'll have three hundred thousand men in the paddies and jungles and never find them again. That was the French experience." Ball, who had once practiced law in France, knew something about France's misadventure in Indochina. "Vietnam," he warned Kennedy, "is the worst possible terrain both from a physical and political point of view." To Ball's surprise, Kennedy did not wish to discuss the matter. "Well, George," he said, "I always thought you were one of the brighter guys in town, but I think you're just crazier than hell. It isn't going to happen." Whether Kennedy meant that he would never accede to committing that many troops or that such escalation would never be necessary, Ball did not know. Returning to his office "in a mood of dark futility," Ball confided to an aide: "We're heading hell-bent into a mess, and there's not a Goddamn thing I can do about it. Either everybody else is crazy or I am."[40]

DEFENSE SECRETARY ROBERT McNAMARA was among the most prominent and influential members of Kennedy's cabinet. Harvard-educated, the
former president of Ford Motor Company, and renowned for a razor-
sharp intellect and a passion for quantifying every problem and solution,
McNamara had undertaken an ambitious reorganization of the Defense
Department. Virtually every problem could be resolved, he believed, as
long as the right statistical information, properly analyzed, was brought to
bear. His renowned ability to identify problems and inefficiencies with a
cold, hard examination of an organization's books had served McNamara
well during his World War II service under Robert Lovett, the assistant
secretary of war for air. He had transferred his legendary analytical skills
to Ford Motor Company with outstanding results. Arizona Senator Barry
Goldwater called him "an IBM machine with legs."[41]

Now McNamara, a liberal Republican and an avowed Cold Warrior,
meant to apply those same principles to winning the struggle in Vietnam—
a cause he believed was just and necessary. "Like most Americans," Mc-
Namara later wrote, "I saw Communism as monolithic. I believed the
Soviets and the Chinese were cooperating in trying to extend their hegemony." To McNamara—and to Kennedy and most of his advisors, for that
matter—it was "obvious that the Communist movement in Vietnam was
closely related to guerrilla insurgencies in Burma, Indonesia, Malaya, and
the Philippines during the 1950s. We viewed these conflicts not as nationalistic movements—as they largely appear in hindsight—but as signs of a
unified Communist drive for hegemony in Asia."[42]

Although McNamara largely discounted Ball's dire warnings about the
numbers of U.S. troops that might eventually be needed to win in Vietnam, the statistician in him had to acknowledge that the upper limits of
American military manpower required to defeat the Viet Cong might,
indeed, reach as high as two hundred twenty thousand. He understood that
an initial force of less than ten thousand "will not convince the other side
. . . that we mean business." McNamara suspected—accurately, it turned
out—that "the response would be an intensified effort that would probably outrun the successive increments of our own efforts as it developed."
In other words, as he told Kennedy in a November 5 memorandum, as the
United States gradually increased its forces, the Viet Cong would respond
in kind. "We would thus be almost certain to get increasingly mired down
in an inconclusive struggle." Yet to prevent the fall of South Vietnam to
the Communists would require "the introduction of U.S. forces on a substantial scale." Despite his tragically accurate prediction of the war's long-
term flow, McNamara's unquestioning belief in the "domino theory" pro-

pelled him toward supporting the Taylor–Rostow recommendations. "The fall of South Vietnam to Communism," he told Kennedy, "would lead to the fairly rapid extension of Communist control, or complete accommodation to Communism, in the rest of mainland Southeast Asia right down to Indonesia. The strategic implications worldwide would be extremely serious."[43]

In urging Kennedy to approve the Taylor report's recommendations, Rostow—like McNamara—framed the issue in terms of his own Cold War philosophy. "The lesson of the post war, it seems to me, is that we must be prepared on our side of the line to do whatever we believe necessary to protect our own and the Free World's interest," Rostow advised. "No one is proposing that we liberate North Vietnam. . . . General Taylor's proposals are, in my view, conservative proposals for action on our side of the Cold War truce lines, to buy time and permit negotiation to take over for an interval, under reasonably favorable circumstances."[44]

Despite the near unanimity among his top administration advisors, Kennedy was still uncertain about Vietnam. "He is instinctively against introduction of U.S. forces," Taylor had told McNamara, Rostow, Ball, and the others at their November 4 meeting.[45] As if the decision about troops were not difficult enough, the president also weighed advice from some aides that, for the good of South Vietnam, he should force Diem from office. Indeed, the Taylor report had included a devastating assessment of Diem's government written by William J. Jorden, a former *New York Times* reporter now serving on Taylor's staff. Jorden warned Kennedy that the pressure for political change in South Vietnam had "reached the explosion point." As for how the United States should respond, Jorden offered a broad range of options—"from giving full and unquestioning support to the present Government in Saigon, to engineering a coup against the Diem regime." According to Jorden's bleak assessment:

> Vietnamese officials, military men and ordinary citizens . . . have lost confidence in President Diem and in his leadership. . . .
>
> There is near paralysis in some areas of administration. . . . Many men of intelligence and ability have been kept out of government or been forced to resign if their complete loyalty to the President came into doubt. The National Assembly has become a rubber stamp for the President's measures. Elections are a meaningless exercise that can only produce contempt for the democratic process.
>
> A chance remark in a café can produce a jail sentence. Those who express political opposition are harassed. Men are held indefinitely without indictment or even the placing of charges. One member of the National Assembly has been in jail for almost a year without his legislative immunity from arrest having been lifted.[46]

Kennedy was buffeted on all sides. Among those urging war were the Joint Chiefs of Staff, who offered belligerent advice that was none too comforting in light of Kennedy's experience with the military's mishandling of the Bay of Pigs invasion. Former President Eisenhower, who had publicly criticized Kennedy's "indecision and uncertainty" regarding Cuba and Vietnam, also advocated strong action,[47] as did Democratic Senator Stuart Symington of Missouri—Harry Truman's former Air Force secretary—who told Kennedy in a personal note that "we ought to hold this place . . . otherwise this part of the world is sure to go down the drain."[48]

But Kennedy knew that it was not as simple as Symington, Eisenhower, and the Joint Chiefs imagined. Many of the leading members of Congress simply would not support sending U.S. troops into Vietnam. "We have a congressional problem," Kennedy informed his advisors during a November 11 meeting to discuss the Taylor report. "[Richard] Russell and others are opposed." At the meeting, however, Kennedy had finally begun to reveal his hand. Seeking to dampen the in-house enthusiasm for sending U.S. combat forces to Vietnam, Kennedy said that "troops are a last resort." Robert Kennedy backed him up. "We are not sending combat troops," the attorney general insisted. "[We are] not committing ourselves to combat troops."[49] To Arthur Schlesinger the president said: "They want a force of American troops. They say it's necessary in order to restore confidence and maintain morale. But it will be just like Berlin. The troops will march in; the bands will play; the crowds will cheer; and in four days everyone will have forgotten. Then we will be told we have to send in more troops. It's like taking a drink. The effect wears off, and you have to take another."[50]

At a November 15 meeting of his National Security Council, Kennedy finally revealed the full extent of his opposition to sending U.S. troops. With the United States still engaged in a tense confrontation with the Soviets in Berlin, he was wary of "becoming involved simultaneously on two fronts on opposite sides of the world." Furthermore, he doubted the basic wisdom of getting the country so deeply involved in Vietnam because—despite the vociferous arguments of his many advisors—the fundamental basis for intervention was far from clear. Korea, he noted, had been "a clear case of aggression," which drew opposition from a broad range of United Nations members. "The conflict in Vietnam is more obscure and less flagrant," he believed, especially when compared to "the clarity" of the U.S. position in Berlin. Such a contrast, he feared, might make leading Democrats in Congress wary of deeper U.S. involvement in Southeast Asia.

Turning to McNamara, Kennedy asked whether he would be urging action "if SEATO did not exist." McNamara said that he would. Why?

Kennedy asked. Because, Joint Chiefs Chairman Lemnitzer interjected, "the world would be divided in the area of Southeast Asia on the sea, in the air and in communications." The resulting "Communist conquest," he said, "would deal a severe blow to freedom and extend Communism to a great portion of the world." How, then, Kennedy asked, could he justify going into Vietnam while ignoring Cuba? Lemnitzer's reply probably only strengthened Kennedy's determination to reject the strongest portions of the Taylor report. Lemnitzer replied that the Joint Chiefs believed that "at this point the United States should go into Cuba." Kennedy was clearly not persuaded. Other nations were not likely to offer their public support of U.S. intervention—and Congress was another problem entirely. Probably recalling the advice he had received from Mansfield, Fulbright, and Russell, Kennedy observed that even the Democrats in Congress were not "fully convinced."[51]

A week after that meeting, Kennedy approved National Security Action Memorandum No. 111 (NSAM-111), authorizing the United States to provide additional helicopters and aircraft, manned by U.S. uniformed personnel; equipment and uniformed personnel for air reconnaissance and "instruction in and execution of air-ground support techniques, and for special intelligence"; training and equipping of the civil guard and the self-defense corps to free up the South Vietnamese army for mobile offensive operations; additional personnel and equipment to improve the country's military and political intelligence system; and additional economic assistance. While he did not authorize the large infusion of troops recommended by Taylor, Rostow, and McNamara, Kennedy did declare that "the United States is prepared to join the Viet-Nam Government in a sharply increased joint effort to avoid a further deterioration in the situation in South Viet-Nam." In return, Diem's government was expected to "put the nation on a wartime footing to mobilize its entire resources" and to "overhaul" its "military establishment and command structure" into a more effective organization.[52]*

Diem, however, balked at the strict reforms the United States urged in the memorandum. "Vietnam, he said, did not want to be a protectorate,"

---

*Kennedy that day also approved the use of herbicide defoliants—later known as Agent Orange—to clear underbrush from along roadsides and to destroy food crops in territory controlled by the Viet Cong. In 1962, 6,000 acres would be subjected to aerial application of Agent Orange. By 1967, the Air Force program would cover 1.7 million acres. In the nine years that the United States would actively destroy crops and underbrush with the chemical agent, it would spray 20 percent of Vietnam's jungles and 36 percent of its mangrove forests (Reeves, *Profile of Power,* 259; Kolko, 144–45).

Ambassador Nolting informed the State Department on November 18 after a long conversation with Diem.[53] Although some administration officials briefly explored the possibilities of finding a replacement for Diem, the effort fizzled when it became apparent that, in Kennedy's words to journalist Ben Bradlee, "Diem is Diem and the best we've got."[54]

Kennedy's approval of NSAM-111 marked a compromise. While he did not heed the advice of his eager advisors—Cold Warriors like Rostow, Taylor, McNamara and Gilpatric—on the numbers of American troops that should be sent to South Vietnam, he did agree with their basic argument: to help South Vietnam was to place a finger in the dike of Southeast Asia. While he questioned the need for America's full-scale involvement, his doubts were primarily political and practical military concerns, and not reflective of any distrust of his advisors' assessment of Vietnam's status as the first, most crucial domino in Southeast Asia.

While some may have regarded it as something less than a full commitment to South Vietnam's future, Kennedy's decision to volunteer the United States as an active partner in the struggle against the Viet Cong was a major step in the country's steady progression toward total intervention. Although he stopped short of committing a specific number of combat personnel to the fight, NSAM-111 actually made the commitment open-ended and almost guaranteed that the number of U.S. uniformed personnel in South Vietnam would rise steadily as the military situation deteriorated. In effect, Kennedy had unlocked the door to eventual full-scale U.S. involvement.

Besides Mansfield and Ball (whom Kennedy promoted to under secretary of state in late November), no one seemed to understand the potential consequences of Kennedy's actions better than his old friend and mentor John Kenneth Galbraith, a former Harvard economist whom Kennedy had named ambassador to India. Visiting Saigon at Kennedy's request, Galbraith cabled the White House on November 20 to warn the president against expecting Diem to reform his government to any significant degree. Instead of reforming Diem, Galbraith preached replacing him. Only then did he believe a military solution was possible. The next day, back in New Delhi, Galbraith put his concerns into a more lengthy cable to Kennedy:

> We must not forever be guided by those who misunderstand the dynamics of revolution and imagine that because the communists do not appeal to us they are abhorrent to everyone. In our enthusiasm to prove outside intervention before world opinion we have unquestionably exaggerated the role of material assistance especially in the main area of insurrection in the far South. . . . It is my completely considered view, as stated yesterday, that Diem will not reform either administratively or politically in

any effective way. That is because he cannot. It is politically naïve to expect it. . . . A time of crisis in our policy on South Vietnam will come when it becomes evident that the reforms we have asked for have not come off and that our presently proffered aid is not accomplishing anything. Troops will be urged to back up Diem. It will be sufficiently clear that I think this must be resisted.[55]

Despite Galbraith's astute warnings, Kennedy's decision had been made. All the while, most members of Congress were completely unaware of the decision. By virtue of the 1961 renewal of a 1949 law—the Act for International Development—Congress had handed Kennedy broad, unfettered authority to dispatch U.S. personnel overseas as long as they remained noncombatants. In addition, the Mutual Defense Assistance Agreement with Vietnam, approved by Congress in 1960, authorized the United States to send equipment, service, and military personnel to Vietnam. Thus Kennedy felt little need to consult Congress, much less ask for its permission as he began taking the country all the more deeper into Vietnam.[56]

On December 12, the *New York Times* reported that the first contingent of American helicopters had arrived in Saigon—"the first fruits" of the Taylor mission, as the *Times* described it. The next day, the newspaper reported further that the International Control Commission—the governing body for the 1954 Geneva accords—was now considering ceasing operations in Vietnam, "in the face of an increase in United States assistance to South Vietnam's struggle against Communist guerrillas."

A few paragraphs later, the story noted: "With the arrival yesterday of the *Core*, a former escort carrier, bearing the helicopters, four single-engine training planes and about 400 men, the United States military personnel here are believed to total about 1,500." As the paper noted, presciently, "Many more are expected."[57]

CHAPTER 19

A World of Illusion

1962

Back in Washington to consult with the president and
State Department officials, Ambassador Frederick "Fritz" Nolting went to
Capitol Hill on the afternoon of Friday, January 12, 1962, to see the Senate Foreign Relations Committee. Behind closed doors, Nolting—a solid
and respected career Foreign Service man serving his first Asian assignment—made a brief, extemporaneous opening statement. "I think we have
a reasonable chance, a good chance of sustaining the independence of
South Vietnam," Nolting offered, admitting that despite the country's
"determination" to fight the Viet Cong, "there is some disorganization."

Indeed, as Nolting suggested, the tide did appear to be turning in
South Vietnam. The Americans had gradually increased their presence in
Vietnam—up to as many as three thousand five hundred uniformed personnel by early February—sending the Viet Cong scurrying for refuge. A
reorganized military command structure accompanied the additional military assistance. Kennedy replaced the Military Assistance and Advisory
Group (MAAG) with the larger Military Assistance Command, Vietnam
(MACV)—a move that reordered the American military mission. Instead
of merely advising the South Vietnamese, American officers would now be
training and assisting the country's rapidly expanding army. To head up the
new military effort, Kennedy would soon appoint General Paul Harkins,
a protégé of General George Patton and a thoroughly optimistic man,
absolutely confident that the U.S. military would vanquish the Viet Cong.
For now, Nolting told the committee, he was "sufficiently encouraged to
think that the move of the United States toward greater support and
greater commitment is a wise move in our own national interest."

Committee members were mostly in the dark. Their questions were
respectful and basic, revealing only a rudimentary understanding of the

nation their government had determined to defend. "Are we at war now in Vietnam?" asked Republican Homer Capehart of Indiana. "In other words, are U.S. troops killing other people or are they killing our people?"

"No, sir," Nolting replied. "I think the answer to that is no."

Later, Capehart approached Nolting from another angle. "So, we have a situation, then, where we are technically at war. We are on the sidelines furnishing men, ammunition and training, and they are doing the same thing in North Vietnam. Other people are doing the fighting for both the Chinese and the Russians, and the other people are doing the fighting for us?"

"This is about the situation," Nolting answered.

Asked about U.S. manpower in Vietnam, Nolting said that the number would soon escalate to as many as five thousand. "These are not combat forces," he hastened to assure the committee. "They are service forces." He warned them that the struggle to defeat the Viet Cong would likely be a long one. "In my judgment," Nolting said, "this is going to be a long, drawn-out, hard campaign without prospects of dramatic victory in the military sense."

"You said it would be a long pull," Capehart said. "What are you thinking of one, two, five, ten, fifteen, twenty years?"

"I hate to put a date on it, senator," Nolting replied, "but I am thinking in terms of five years or more."

Doing his best to dispel "speculation" that the United States was considering a plan to force Diem from office, Nolting told the committee: "The best way to win, the best way to maintain the independence of South Vietnam is to give his government full backing."[1]

Oregon Democrat Wayne Morse, the crusty Republican-turned-independent-turned-Democrat, was unimpressed. A former law school professor noted for his brilliant and incisive intellect, Morse was one of the Senate's leading mavericks—a man who had once brazenly instructed a Foreign Relations Committee staff member to draft articles of impeachment against John Foster Dulles. When the aide reminded Morse, a noted constitutional scholar, that such proceedings must originate in the House of Representatives, Morse replied, "I know that. Draft them anyway!"[2] Lyndon Johnson's aide Harry McPherson described Morse as a man who "could easily be the most irritating man in the Senate. Yet he was also indispensable: he would fight a bad bill when others wanted to but were afraid."[3]

More than most members of the Foreign Relations Committee, Morse was skeptical about America's role in Vietnam. That skepticism opened his eyes to the dangers and pitfalls that others—blinded by the bright light of anticommunism—could not, or would not, see in Kennedy's decision to send thousands of military "advisors" to South Vietnam. "Mr. Ambassador," Morse asked, "how many Americans have been killed or wounded thus far in the guerilla warfare in Vietnam?" Nolting was not sure, but he informed Morse that a sergeant had recently been killed. Another soldier was recently kidnapped, another had been shot in the leg, and a U.S. Operations Mission engineer had been killed. Before that, he said, "no military man on our side, no American, had been killed for about a year and a half."

To be effective in fighting the Viet Cong, Morse continued, U.S. troops "are bound to come in increasingly close proximity to the line of action, aren't they?"

"Yes, sir."

"And we have to be prepared for and expect an increasing number of casualties, don't we?"

"I think that is true."

Noting that the French people had finally reached the point that they "would no longer support a policy that cost that much French blood," Morse asked: "Do you think, as a matter of American policy, with an increasing number of flag-draped coffins coming back to our shores, that the American people are going to continue to be willing to make that sacrifice of American blood with no corresponding sacrifice on the part of the British and the French and the other countries that claim to be our allies?"

Nolting replied that Morse would be a better judge of public opinion. But, he added, "my own judgment would be that the number of American casualties to be expected would be sustained by public opinion at home under the circumstances that you describe." Morse responded: "I just want to be one voice of dissent in this discussion. I just want to go on record as saying that, in my judgment, if you make this a unilateral American military action, you will be surprised how quickly American public opinion will leave you in regard to the sacrifice of American boys in Southeast Asia, because you will find a very strong feeling developing that we don't intend to take on the French burden or make the same mistake that the French made."[4]

If the American people were to learn about the extent of American involvement and the likely consequences, they would not soon learn it from their president. Asked in January if U.S. troops in Vietnam were engaged in combat, Kennedy answered, "No."[5] "We are out there," the president told a reporter in early February, "on training and on transportation, and we are assisting in every way we properly can the people of South Vietnam." But Kennedy refused to provide much more information about the U.S. mission because "we don't want to have information which is of assistance to the enemy."[6]

Just how much the American people, or Congress, knew about the new American commitment in Vietnam would soon become a subject of some debate in Washington. The first inkling came in the form of a February 14 *New York Times* article by the paper's Washington bureau chief, James Reston:

The United States is now involved in an undeclared war in South Vietnam. This is well known to the Russians, the Chinese Communists, and everybody else concerned except the American people. . . . This raises some fundamental questions. Has the President made clear to the Congress and the nation the extent of the U.S. commitment to the South Vietnam Government and the dangers involved? Is he acting within the spirit of the Geneva accord that limited the number of military advisors and set up the South Vietnam Government?[7]

Reston was not the only one to raise such questions. *Newsweek*—which examined the burgeoning war in a cover story in its February 12 edition and concluded that it was "the biggest in the world"—would soon raise serious questions about attempts by the American military to conceal the extent of U.S. involvement in Vietnam. "With this new U.S. commitment has come a controversial blackout on the details of American military operations in the combat areas," the magazine observed on February 26, raising some "fundamental" questions: "Will the sending of U.S. troops lead to escalation, more guerillas, more Americans, and an eventual confrontation of the U.S. and Red China? Above all, can the U.S. strategy win the war?"[8]

With this kind of debate germinating in the news media, it was only a matter of time before the issue became embroiled in partisan politics. Ironically, it was the Republican Party, the ideological home of those who had historically urged a more forceful American challenge to Asian communism, that fired the first shot. Indeed, only the day before Reston's *Times* story, the Republican National Committee's weekly publication, *Battle Line*, suggested that Kennedy had been "less than candid" about "the pretense that the U.S. is merely acting as military advisor to South Vietnam." "Is the country moving toward another Korea which might embroil the entire East?" the Republican statement asked. Echoing Morse's private concern of a month earlier, the Republicans added that "the people should not have to wait until American casualty lists are posted before being informed about the real nature of the nation's commitment to South Vietnam." Asked about the Republican charge, Kennedy explained to reporters at a February 14 press conference that his policy was simply the continuation of a long process of support for South Vietnam that had been thoroughly explained to leaders of both houses. He insisted, "we have not sent combat troops there."[9]

Perturbed by Reston's story and the Republican volley, and perhaps goaded by the White House, Mansfield went to the Senate floor the next afternoon to rebut Reston's suggestion that Kennedy was hiding an undeclared war from Congress and the public. He maintained that "it borders on the irresponsible to suggest that Congress has not been well informed" about Vietnam. Not only had "countless" members of Congress visited Vietnam, Mansfield said, but "the [Kennedy] administration has made a special point of keeping Congress informed—as did its predecessor—on developments in Vietnam." Mansfield, of course, could not know exactly how much information the administration had withheld from Congress. Yet he insisted that "we have had, if anything, a surfeit of information on the situation in Vietnam and on our policies with respect thereto."

Mansfield, however, took note of the way the Republicans seemed to be experimenting with Vietnam as a political issue. The Republicans' invocation of Korea no doubt reminded him and other Democrats of the political damage their party had suffered over their Asian policy barely ten years earlier. With these memories undoubtedly in mind, the majority leader addressed the political implications and issued this stern warning:

> I hope that this effective collaboration and mutual accommodation will continue, because it is essential for the welfare of the Nation that they continue. But they are not likely to continue if the party headquarters become involved. They will not continue if partisans on one side insist that Congress has no concern in this matter or if partisans on the other insist that Congress should look over the President's shoulder 24 hours a day and should tell him how to conduct the foreign policy of the United States. That is the President's responsibility.[10]

While Mansfield may have been personally satisfied with the degree to which he and his colleagues were being informed about Vietnam, some in the administration were, indeed, proceeding with a clear intent to conceal as much information as possible from the American public and their elected representatives. Kennedy's assistant secretary of state for Far Eastern affairs, Averell Harriman, made this clear when objecting to a proposal to permit greater press coverage of military operations. Clearly mindful of the political ramifications of increased media scrutiny in Vietnam, Harriman forwarded his copy of the proposal to Carl Rowan, the department's assistant secretary for public affairs, and scribbled in the margin: "I believe our press will [bill] this assistance to Vietnam as our participation in this war—a new war under President Kennedy—the Democratic War Party, so skillfully avoided by the Republican President Eisenhower." Harriman was emphatic. "The press do not belong on these aircraft, but can be kept fully informed by briefings in Saigon by our military or Embassy."[11]

While Harriman worried about the reporting, Rowan fretted over the reporters. Concerned about the possible fallout if disgruntled reporters were kept away from the action, Rowan cautioned his counterpart at the Pentagon on February 15: "We seem headed for a major domestic furor over the 'undeclared' war in South Viet-Nam and of US imposed 'secrecy regulations' that prevent American newsmen from telling our people the truth about US involvement in that war." Based on the recent critical press coverage, Rowan said he believed that "we run the risk of serious domestic political consequences if we fail to give proper attention to our information policies." Ultimately, Kennedy grudgingly sided with Rowan and authorized Nolting to allow reporters to accompany U.S. troops on certain missions. But, as Rusk cautioned, the reporters were not to be taken on missions "whose nature [is] such that undesirable dispatches would be highly probable." As Rusk put it, bluntly, "It is not in our interest . . . to have stories indicating that Americans are leading and directing combat missions against the Viet Cong."[12]

Which is, of course, exactly what they were doing. Although officially described as "advisors," American soldiers were, in many cases, actively engaged in planning and executing joint operations with the South Vietnamese military. U.S. Navy warships worked closely with South Vietnam's fledgling Navy to protect the country against communist seaborne infiltration from North Vietnam, while American helicopters, flown by U.S. pilots, ferried South Vietnamese infantrymen to and from battle. Heavily armed UH 1-B helicopters, commonly called "Hueys," often reached the battlefield ahead of the infantry and initiated the attack. U.S. Air Force pilots, meanwhile, regularly accompanied South Vietnamese pilots on bombing missions.[13]

Behind closed doors, on February 20, Harriman assured the Foreign Relations Committee that "there are no [American] combat forces, as such" in South Vietnam. Challenged by Tennessee Democrat Albert Gore to explain that assertion in light of Robert Kennedy's recent statement, in Saigon, that "we are here to win and we are going to stay here until we do win," Harriman meekly explained that the statement was not "authorized." Morse, meanwhile, was more combative than ever, demanding written answers to a series of tough questions about the American mission in South Vietnam and revealing that he questioned the legality of Kennedy's actions. "From what provision of the Constitution or treaty or statute does President Kennedy receive the right for the U.S. military personnel to transport South Vietnamese troops into combat, to return the fire of North Vietnamese, to patrol the sea approaches to South Vietnam, and to drop propaganda leaflets over areas held by guerillas opposing the Government of South Vietnam?" Morse left Harriman with no doubt where he stood:

> I said earlier in this committee that when those ships start coming back to the west coast with the flag-[draped] coffins of American boys, look out, because the American people, in my judgment, are going to be very much divided. We have to avoid division in American public opinion on foreign policy—the American people are going to be very much divided if we follow a foreign policy in Southeast Asia that starts to slaughter thousands of American boys. . . . I think we have to take the American

people into our confidence, out in the open right now, and get these legal
questions cleared up, because I have grave doubts as to the constitution-
ality of the President's course of action in South Vietnam.[14]

But Kennedy's advisors assured him that his actions were constitutional. In any event, despite Morse's warnings that a failed, unconstitutional U.S. military enterprise would soon incur the public's wrath, the
public face of the American role in Vietnam was nothing but upbeat. With
the sudden application of new manpower and firepower, the South Vietnamese and their American allies finally appeared to have seized the initiative. Despite another attempted coup on Diem in late February—an
attack on the presidential palace by two dissident air force pilots—American officials in Washington received word from military and civilian officials in Saigon that the situation was steadily improving. No one epito-
mized the confident outlook more than General Harkins, a man whose
byword was optimism. "I am optimistic," the sanguine general bragged,
"and I am not going to allow my staff to be pessimistic."[15]

Nor would he permit them to acknowledge the bitter truth about the
course of the war. Armed with MACV's rosy portrayals of the struggle
against the Viet Cong, the official word on the joint South Vietnam-Amer-
ican effort was always sugarcoated. Officials claimed that because of the
Herculean American effort, a renewed will to fight had emerged among
Diem's army. Diem himself, Washington learned, was gradually, but surely,
winning the confidence and loyalty of the South Vietnamese people. The
Viet Cong were on the run. Judged by the cold statistics that Defense Secretary McNamara used to judge the war's progress—"kill ratios," the percentage of the population "pacified," and the declining number of enemy-
initiated attacks—Diem's American-backed army appeared to be winning.

But this "progress" was largely an illusion. MACV officials processed
and fed only positive information to administration officials, who eagerly
accepted it as accurate and objective. Typical was a November 1962 briefing given to John Newhouse, a member of the Senate Foreign Relations
Committee staff. After talking with Chalmers Wood, the State Department officer in charge of Vietnam affairs, Newhouse prepared a memorandum for Fulbright that offered reasons for "limited encouragement"
about a military situation that had "brightened somewhat." Based on his
conversation with Wood, Newhouse reported that the South Vietnamese
army "is gaining in confidence and morale as a result of its growing ability to catch the elusive enemy. . . . The GVN forces have been strengthened. They are being better equipped, better supplied and, as noted, better trained."[16]

A similar tone influenced reports on the apparent success of the
"strategic hamlet" project, promoted by Diem and his brother Nhu and

enthusiastically supported and funded by American officials. In truth, the program was little more than a reprise of the disastrous *agroville* program of the late 1950s. Like that effort, the hamlet initiative herded thousands of Vietnamese peasants into "secure" compounds to protect them from the influence and terror of the Viet Cong and, thereby, deprive the Communists of their primary source of political support and new recruits. In many cases, however, the project had the opposite effect. Driven from ancestral homes, often at gunpoint, and forced to work for little or no pay as they constructed their new villages, thousands of disgruntled peasants began defecting to the Viet Cong. One U.S. embassy official in Saigon, however, coolly dismissed concerns about the project by noting that "the Vietnamese are wonderful gripers."[17]

The official reports to Washington on the success of the program were, of course, always optimistic. "The strategic hamlet program promises solid benefits," an early report in May 1962 concluded.[18] A Joint Chiefs of Staff report perhaps best reflected the degree to which U.S. officials would delude themselves about the program. Because the Viet Cong had overrun less than one percent of the hamlets, the chiefs concluded that "the Vietnamese people must surely be finding in them a measure of the tranquility which they seek." Actually, the absence of attacks should have set off alarms. As the British expert who advised Diem on the project later observed, tranquillity was evidence that the Viet Cong had no need to attack; they had quietly infiltrated most of the hamlets.[19]

While optimistic reports about the progress of the U.S. military effort dominated the official news from Vietnam, the truth occasionally found its way to administration officials. Vice President Johnson, who played no significant role in the administration's policy toward Vietnam after his trip there in 1961, heard from his military aide, Colonel Howard Burris, that "the U.S. program in South Viet Nam still has not reversed the level nor intensity of Viet Cong operations."[20] Two weeks later, Burris reported more bad news to the vice president: "Viet Cong activity is being intensified on an increasingly broader spectrum." The news on the South Vietnamese side, according to Burris, was "somewhat alarming. Desertions from the regular forces have increased to 1,000 a month." He predicted that "an overall increase in the effectiveness of the South Viet Nam armed forces is doubtful."[21] Such news should have not been a surprise. Burris' reports comported with predictions in a February 21 Special National Intelligence Estimate:

> In South Vietnam, we believe that there will be no significant change over the short run in the current pattern of Viet Cong activity, although the scope and tempo of the Communist military and political campaigns will probably be increased. The Viet Cong will probably resort to large-scale

attacks, seeking to dramatize the weakness of the Diem forces and to reduce both civilian and military morale.[22]

Just as troublesome was a growing awareness that in their haste to prop up Diem's shaky regime, the Americans were no longer insisting on the political and economic reforms that had loomed so large when Kennedy had first increased military assistance to South Vietnam. "The US has 'capitulated' to Diem," a *New Republic* editorial complained on March 12, "and has bound itself to the defense of a client regime without exacting on its part sacrifices necessary for success." Indeed, the magazine's editors had correctly identified the problem that began to plague the American effort in Vietnam.

It was all a vicious cycle. In order to "save" South Vietnam from collapse, the United States could not afford to wait for Diem to move toward reform. Yet precisely because the Americans did not wait for or demand those reforms, Diem believed he could casually ignore advice and criticism from Nolting and other U.S. officials. The result was that with each passing month the leverage of the United States diminished all the more. Reforms did not occur and, therefore, were delayed. Diem and his repressive, distant government became all the more isolated and unpopular, while the Viet Cong increased in popularity throughout the countryside. As the *New Republic* assessed the situation: "American lives are to be risked in a holding action based on the inexplicable hope that with sharpened-up counter-guerilla operations and marginal reforms the regime will last."[23]

As one of the few members of Congress following the daily events in Vietnam, Mansfield was concerned. The previous November, he had warned Kennedy about the risks inherent in sending troops to Vietnam. For the next eight months, he had remained mostly silent on Vietnam, believing it his duty as majority leader to support Kennedy, especially in the tough and difficult area of foreign affairs. But when Michigan State University—the home of Professor Wesley Fishel, an acquaintance of Mansfield and a former advisor to Diem—invited him to deliver its spring commencement address on June 10, Mansfield readily accepted.* He had

---

*From 1955 to June 1962, Fishel's Michigan State University Group (MSUG) worked for the governments of the United States and South Vietnam to provide police training and public administration consultation to Diem's government. Of the more than fifty advisors under Fishel's direction, at least five had been CIA agents who, among other duties, were assigned to train Vietnamese mountain tribes in paramilitary operations. MSUG would later be criticized for its role in training the South Vietnamese police and civil guards, both noted for their brutality and disregard for basic human rights (Schulzinger, 89–90; Gibbons, 1:264, 313–14).

also began composing a speech that would reveal his growing doubts about the U.S. role in Vietnam, as well as his emerging belief that the Cold War orthodoxy of the 1950s was no longer suitable for the 1960s, at least in Southeast Asia. In delivering the speech, Mansfield would become the first prominent Democrat in Congress to publicly voice his concerns about the direction of U.S. policy in Vietnam. Because he was no ordinary observer, but the member of Congress who spoke with the most authority about Southeast Asia, Mansfield's speech signaled the first real dissent against a more activist U.S. policy in Vietnam. By later standards, Mansfield's critique was mild indeed. But in 1962, his criticisms—especially his relatively harsh words about Diem's regime—generated tremors that were felt as far away as Saigon.

Mansfield told the graduates that he was speaking about Vietnam not only because of the "close association" between the university and South Vietnam, but "because events appear to be moving in Southeast Asia toward a point of critical decision." The United States, he said, was undergoing "a deepening of an already very deep involvement on the Southeast Asian mainland."

Mansfield's first complaint about U.S. Vietnam policy was the virtual abdication of responsibility by America's SEATO allies. "We have allies under SEATO to be sure," said Mansfield, who had signed the SEATO treaty in 1954, "but allies either unwilling or unable to assume but the smallest fraction of the burdens of the alliance." Other nations, he knew, had their problems. "But this nation, too, has its problems," he said. "And one of them is to avoid miscalculations in policies which may derive from the gap between the presumed promise and the actual fulfillment in any military alliance."

As one of Diem's closest friends in the United States, Mansfield turned to the more delicate subject of the South Vietnamese government. Diem was a man, he said, "for whom I have the highest respect and deepest admiration, a man whose integrity and honesty are unquestioned, and without whom there would be no free Vietnam." Even so, he said, Diem's government had to come to grips with several challenges before its struggle against the Viet Cong could succeed. Mansfield said that much of the military assistance during the first Indochina war "went to build the wrong kinds of forces." Furthermore, he said—using extremely diplomatic language— Diem must consider undertaking substantial political and economic reforms: "It is also discovered that a great deal more emphasis on political and economic development is now required in Vietnam, although the need for the latter course has been pointed out time and time again in the Congress for many years." Mansfield still had faith in Diem. But he could not avoid the obvious fact that the South Vietnamese government was beset with enormous challenges. Despite "years of enormous expenditures of aid in

South Vietnam," Mansfield told the students it was an inescapable fact that the country "is more, rather than less, dependent on aid from the United States." In fact, he added, "Vietnam's independent survival is less rather than more secure than it was five or six years ago."

Mansfield also challenged the Cold War orthodoxy that America's security was directly tied to Asia's future—a point of view Mansfield himself had espoused in the 1950s. The majority leader suggested "that our enduring interests in southeast Asia are limited," and that those "limited interests" had always been best protected, "by a policy of minimum involvement." That policy, however, had shifted by "about 180 degrees to the point of very deep involvement and enormous cost." What worried Mansfield was that the shift might become permanent. "If it is [permanent]," he said, "then we must be prepared, at best, to carry an annual burden of several hundred millions of dollars of military and economic subsidies to anti-Communist governments in the region for many years. . . . At worst, we must be prepared for a possible conflict of indefinite depth and duration, dependent largely on our forces for its prosecution."

Mansfield concluded his remarks by recommending a six-point "new approach" to U.S. policy in Southeast Asia that included greater use of diplomacy and less emphasis on military aid, while exploring ways to minimize the "unilateral activity" of the United States in Vietnam. He also advocated a reassessment of SEATO's role, greater emphasis on "the need for collective allied and friendly activity in every sphere," and use of the United Nations to "diffuse" the burden of assisting the nations of Southeast Asia to "bring their economies and social structures up to date." But Mansfield's prescription for Southeast Asia—like those of most congressional critics—was little more than a collection of broad generalities. While he advocated more emphasis on collective action and a reexamination of SEATO, he failed to suggest specific, concrete ways that the United States could elicit more cooperation from other countries in the region. Moreover, his call for greater diplomacy and less emphasis on military aid did not include details about what he regarded as an acceptable political settlement to the civil war raging in Indochina.

The bottom line, Mansfield maintained, was his simple belief that the Kennedy administration must pursue a diplomatic end to the conflict. "This nation owes apology to no nation," he said, "if it seeks to lighten its commitments in Southeast Asia through a vigorous diplomacy—as we have been doing with respect to Laos—and a much more discriminating and prudent use of its resources." While the United States would continue to meet its treaty obligations to the nations of Southeast Asia, Mansfield insisted, without offering specifics, that "the time is long past due when we must explore every avenue which may lead to a situation in Southeast Asia, less dependent on the resources of this nation."[24]

While Mansfield's temperate dissent made little news in the United States outside of Washington, it sent minor shock waves through official Saigon. That a friend so loyal and unquestioning as Mansfield would go public with even the mildest of criticisms persuaded Diem that his American friend had fallen prey to a news media hopelessly biased against the South Vietnamese government. For months, the government had been tormenting several American reporters for their critical reporting; now it would turn up the heat even more, convinced that their news stories were to blame for the new critical tone evident in Mansfield's speech—and therefore, the apparent shift in Kennedy's policy toward Diem's government.[25] "Mansfield had been an early, invaluable supporter of the regime in the mid-fifties," recalled John Mecklin, a public affairs officer at the U.S. embassy in Saigon, "and now [he] seemed to have turned against Diem." Because of Mansfield's leadership position in the Senate, Mecklin believed that Diem and his brother Nhu "assumed (erroneously) that the speech had been cleared with President Kennedy and thus reflected high-level American opinion."[26]

Four days after the speech, South Vietnam's ambassador to Washington, Tran Van Chuong (Madam Nhu's father), asked to meet with Francis Valeo, Mansfield's legislative assistant. In a scene reminiscent of the way Dulles and French officials had courted Mansfield in the early 1950s, the South Vietnamese government hoped to affect American policy by influencing Mansfield's position. The next day, in a memorandum to Mansfield, Valeo described his three-and-half-hour meeting as "confused and disjointed" and supposed that the ambassador had wanted to communicate with Mansfield, but only indirectly. Tran told Valeo that "the Diem government is in very deep trouble and has little prospects for survival." A coup, he intimated, was imminent. Valeo believed that Tran was attempting "to find out through me what Senator Mansfield's position would be in the event of such a coup." The last time Diem's future had been discussed (in 1954), Tran recalled, Mansfield had made it clear that without Diem, he would no longer support U.S. aid to South Vietnam. "Would it mean," Tran inquired, "that Senator Mansfield again would say, in effect, Diem or no foreign aid?" Valeo said he did not know how Mansfield would respond, but speculated that "he would very likely support President Kennedy who had to make the critical decisions." Regarding the Michigan State speech, Valeo tried to calm Tran's fears about a sudden reversal of Mansfield's support for Diem. His words were probably not comforting at all. Valeo assured Tran that "Senator Mansfield had given and would undoubtedly continue to give full support to whatever the President decided."[27]

Mansfield's speech also caused ripples within the Kennedy administration. After reading the speech, Chester Bowles—now U.S. ambassador at large—advised Kennedy to articulate U.S. policy in Vietnam more clearly. Perhaps overestimating the speech's domestic impact, Bowles cautioned that because Mansfield had "focused public and congressional attention on our ultimate aims for Southeast Asia," it was time to "spell out our objectives for Southeast Asia as a whole." The objective, articulated by Bowles, was: "Here, as elsewhere in the world, what we want for the people of the region is almost precisely what the people want for themselves: *guaranteed national independence, more rapid economic development, and maximum freedom of choice within their own cultures and religions*"[28] (emphasis Bowles'). Asked to comment on Mansfield's speech at a June 14 press conference, Kennedy replied that he had carefully read Mansfield's remarks and agreed with him that "we should constantly review" U.S. policy for the region. "I know Senator Mansfield would not think we should withdraw," he added, "because withdrawal in the case of Vietnam and in the case of Thailand might mean a collapse of the entire area."[29] Asked if a review of U.S. policy might be appropriate, Kennedy agreed and observed that the country might be "on a collision course."[30] No broader official statement on the long-term U.S. objectives in Vietnam would be forthcoming.

Concerned as he was about the direction of U.S. policy in Vietnam, Mansfield would, for now, confine his public dissent to the Michigan State speech, which he inserted into the *Congressional Record* on June 11. As he made clear to the graduating students, he "wholeheartedly" supported Kennedy, although he also reserved the right to engage in "public discussion" about his policies. "In his view of the Senate," Francis Valeo later explained, "Mansfield drew a distinction between the formation of foreign policy and its execution. In the latter case, he readily conceded that the president's role, if not absolute, was certainly paramount."[31] Mansfield was hardly alone in the belief that it was unwise for a member of Congress to directly challenge a president's foreign policy. No less than the chairman of the Senate Foreign Relations Committee, William Fulbright, had written in a late-1961 law journal article that "the existing requirements of American foreign policy have hobbled the President by too niggardly a grant of power." Although subsequent events in Vietnam would prompt him to abandon that sentiment, Fulbright argued in the *Cornell Law Quarterly* that presidential power was being unduly constrained by the constitutional system of checks and balances. He doubted that "the harsh necessities of the 1960s" would permit "the luxury of 18th century procedures of measured deliberation" by Congress on foreign policy questions. "I submit that the price of democratic survival in a world of aggressive totalitarianism is to give up some of the democratic luxuries of the past," he wrote, adding that while "it is distasteful and dangerous to vest the executive with powers unchecked and unbalanced . . . my question is whether we have any choice but to do so."[32]

For most members of Congress, even those on the Senate Foreign Relations Committee, Vietnam was still a minor world problem in 1962—and one better left to the president and his State Department. Evidenced by the questions put to Nolting in January, few members understood or cared about the complex cultural, economic, and political issues at stake in Southeast Asia. "The war was being waged by the executive branch," explained Carl Marcy, the committee's chief of staff. "Committee members didn't feel that they were in a good position to criticize the professional [policymakers]."[33]

In fact, in 1962, only Morse was willing to say publicly that he believed America's military adventure in Vietnam was an outright mistake. Prior to June, he had kept his concerns off the Senate floor and confined to the closed-door sessions of the Foreign Relations Committee. But on June 8 he went public, telling the Senate that "I have heard no evidence which convinces me that it would be militarily wise for us to get bogged down anywhere in Asia in a conventional war. We make a great mistake in letting Russia pick the spot to which we will send American boys to fight for freedom. If we get an American army over there, I fear that it might suffer heavy casualties. Then we would find a demand that we resort to nuclear weapons."[34]

But Morse's concerns fell largely on deaf ears. Many administration officials were instead persuaded that, skeptical press reports notwithstanding, the tide was indeed turning in Vietnam. In a bullish report to the president on September 11, National Security Council staff member Michael Forrestal wrote that "it does appear that we have finally developed a series of techniques which, if properly applied, do seem to produce results."[35] The following week, William Trueheart, the Saigon embassy's deputy chief of mission, told a meeting of Kennedy's Southeast Asia Task Force that he was "tremendously encouraged" by developments in South Vietnam and described the military "progress" as "little short of sensational."

There was one bit of gloomy news in Trueheart's report. The news media, he complained, "believes that the situation in Viet Nam is going to pieces and . . . we have been unable to convince them otherwise."[36] Topping the list of the obstinate, troublemaking reporters was New York Times' David Halberstam, a brash 28-year-old Harvard graduate who had cut his journalistic teeth covering the emerging American civil rights movement for newspapers in Mississippi and Tennessee. He had arrived in Vietnam in the fall of 1962, after the Diem government had expelled Times correspondent Homer Bigart. Halberstam was one of several correspondents for American publications—a group that included Newsweek's Francois Sully, UPI's Neil Sheehan, the Associated Press' Malcolm Browne, and NBC's Jim Robinson and who were highly skeptical of the optimistic briefings routinely dispensed by MACV headquarters and the U.S. embassy.

Even the U.S. mission's public affairs officer, John Mecklin, later acknowledged the problem and explained that American officials had failed to distinguish between the unreliable field reports of Vietnamese sources and
those from the American military "advisors." "The root of the problem was
the fact that much of what the newsmen took to be lies was exactly what
the Mission genuinely believed, and was reporting to Washington," Mecklin said. "Events were to prove that the Mission itself was unaware of how
badly the war was going, operating in a world of illusion. Our feud with
the newsmen was an angry symptom of bureaucratic sickness."[37]

Instead of accepting the official U.S. propaganda, Halberstam and his
colleagues relied on junior military officers, many of them disappointed by
the poor performance of the South Vietnamese military and not privy to
the political strategy behind Washington's official line on the war. "It
should be reported that there is considerably less optimism in the field than
in Washington," Halberstam wrote in a November 21 story, adding that
"the closer one gets to the actual contact level of this war, the farther one
gets from official optimism." Halberstam was well aware of the official
American attempts at press manipulation. "In the continual attempt to
judge how well the war is going and how the increased American aid has
affected it," he told his readers, "there sometimes seems a tendency to
describe results before they have been attained and a parallel tendency to
discredit pessimistic reporting."[38]

In Washington, Kennedy continued receiving conflicting reports
about the "progress" in Vietnam. From McNamara on down, the official
news was blithely optimistic—so much so that in July the Defense secretary, believing "tremendous progress" had been achieved, ordered a long-
range program for the gradual phasing out of the 10,700 U.S. troops in
South Vietnam.[39] Yet the unofficial reports in the press were still far less
than encouraging, a circumstance that Kennedy's advisors assured him had
more to do with the quality of the reporting than with the facts. "Part of
this," Forrestal assured Kennedy on September 18, "is due to the fact that
the newspapers and news magazines have not sent top drawer people to
the area."[40] In fact, U.S. officials at virtually every level were now engaged
in a desperate attempt to preserve public support for Kennedy's Vietnam
policies by discouraging all negative reporting. It was a strategy that Mecklin deplored. Furthermore, he argued, it simply would not work. "I think
we should all accept the reality that the newsmen here will continue to find
access to very much of the truth of what's going on, regardless of what we
may do," he told Nolting. "I think it is futile to try to 'control' them, or
cut off their sources."[41]

Later, Mecklin observed that the real problem in Saigon was the
Americans' "all or nothing policy," marked by "a state of mind in both

Washington and Saigon" that "tended to close our reason." The real problem was not a critical news media. "The policy of support for Diem became an article of faith," he said, "and dissent became reprehensible."[42] Kennedy, meanwhile, did not know what to make of the conflicting reports out of Vietnam. One day, after reading one of Halberstam's damning reports from Saigon, a frustrated and confused Kennedy tossed the *New York Times* on his desk and growled: "Why can I get this stuff from Halberstam when I can't get it from my own people?"[43]

CHAPTER 20

The Beginning of the Beginning

1962

K ENNEDY WAS NOT THE ONLY ONE PERPLEXED BY THE CONFLICT-
ing reports out of Saigon. The dreary news from Vietnam also worried
Mansfield. By the fall of 1962, he suggested that the president ask him to
lead a congressional fact-finding trip to Europe and Southeast Asia. Eager
for some objective information about Vietnam, Kennedy sanctioned the
trip—a forty-five day trek that would take Mansfield throughout Europe
and Southeast Asia, including Germany, Greece, Egypt, India, Burma,
Cambodia, Laos, and Vietnam.

On November 7, Mansfield and a party that included Democratic senators Claiborne Pell of Rhode Island, J. Caleb Boggs of Delaware, and
Benjamin Smith of Massachusetts departed from Washington, arriving in
Saigon on November 30. At the American embassy, Ambassador Nolting
and General Harkins exuded their usual optimism about the war's
progress, telling Mansfield and his colleagues of the "greatly increased
effectiveness" of the South Vietnamese forces. They were now, Nolting
said, more willing than ever to engage the Viet Cong in battle and were
fighting with better skill and increased morale. "We are moving ahead at
a good pace," Nolting concluded. "We can see the light at the end of the
tunnel, but we are not yet at the point of emerging into the sunlight."
Harkins was just as encouraging, telling Mansfield that the U.S. efforts in
Vietnam were "now beginning to pay off." The months to come, he predicted, would bring a "rapid improvement on the military side." He
insisted that he was "definitely encouraged" with the progress made and
with "prospects for the future."

The briefing's only discordant note came from Nolting's deputy,
William Trueheart. Diem's government, he reported, "could be considered as essentially a dictatorship."[1] When Pell asked Nolting, "If there

were an election in Vietnam today, how would Diem come out?" Nolting turned to Trueheart for the answer. "I'm not sure that's a meaningful question," Trueheart answered, "because I honestly think that if you really went out in the boondocks of this country, I'm not sure that half the people know who Diem is, if you really mean the peasants." Clearly annoyed by Trueheart's answer, Mansfield said, "Well, I don't take that. Diem has been head of this country for a long time."[2]

As he arrived in Saigon, Mansfield still firmly believed in Diem. He believed in the basic integrity and leadership of his old friend—a man in whom he had invested much hope and trust over the years. Following Diem's leadership, he thought, remained South Vietnam's only route to victory. Mansfield may have questioned Diem's tactics, but never his honesty. Sometimes he doubted his wisdom, but never his patriotism. Yet, what he would see on this visit to Vietnam would completely change his opinion of Diem—and almost completely shatter his confidence in the South Vietnamese government.

During their first meeting, Diem staged a two-and-a-half-hour filibuster about the strategic hamlet program. Frustrated, Mansfield merely sat and listened. "There was primarily no opportunity to ask questions on other matters," he later complained.[3] But what most bothered Mansfield was the physical change he saw in Diem. "He seemed to be faltering in speech and not at all certain about what he was saying," recalled Francis Valeo, who observed the discussion.[4] Mansfield recalled that the Diem he once knew as outgoing and energetic now "seemed to have turned into a recluse. . . . He was very withdrawn, very secluded. He wasn't the Diem I knew, so the only conclusion I could come to—and it was at best a guess, an estimate—was that he had fallen under the influence of his brother and his wife, and they were taking over control. . . . I think he was gradually being cut off from reality."[5]

Mansfield's next conversation with Diem came during an official dinner hosted by the South Vietnamese leader. On this occasion, however, Mansfield found himself talking more with an agitated and "quite aggressive" Madame Nhu, who upbraided him for his Michigan State speech as well as comments that she mistakenly believed he had made about official treatment of American reporters in South Vietnam. Although Mansfield told her that she was misinformed about his alleged remarks, he did insist that "Congress was quite concerned about these stories coming out of Vietnam."[6]

A more productive official discussion occurred with Diem's brother, Ngo Dinh Nhu, who delivered a comprehensive report on his pet project, the strategic hamlet program. Mansfield expressed great interest in the enterprise, prompting Nhu to brag that two-thirds of South Vietnam's population would be living in strategic hamlets by year's end. Nhu's vision for the program, however, seemed to center on an unusual philosophy of government that, as he explained to Mansfield, involved using the forces of "authoritarianism and democracy to combat underdevelopment." The strategic hamlets, he claimed, would be the testing ground for his theory. Mansfield and Nolting pressed Nhu to give American reporters more latitude and freedom.[7]

By the time Mansfield arrived at a Saigon restaurant for a lengthy, off-the-record discussion over lunch with the American press corps, he was thoroughly persuaded that U.S. policy in Vietnam was on the wrong track. His discussion with the reporters only solidified that conclusion. "If you wanted to get a non-official, non-embassy briefing in Saigon in those days," recalled David Halberstam of the *New York Times*, "there was only one place—American reporters." For several hours, Mansfield, who skipped an official briefing provided by American officials, discussed the war with a group that included Halberstam, Neil Sheehan of United Press International, Malcolm Browne of the *New York Times*, and Peter Arnett of the Associated Press. "What was clear," Halberstam recalled, "was that Mike Mansfield was really listening. He wanted to know."[8] The reporters—none of whom opposed U.S. military intervention in Vietnam—told a receptive majority leader what they had told their readers for months: the South Vietnamese army was moribund and unwilling to fight. Diem was an impediment to a successful struggle. The blind optimism of Harkins and Nolting had led them to deceive Washington about the war's bitter realities.[9]

Mansfield had seen many of the dispatches these men had filed from Saigon in recent months. Even before he had arrived in South Vietnam, he had reluctantly concluded that their reporting was probably more reliable than the official reports he and Kennedy had received through official channels. Now, however, he was certain.

At the airport, as the majority leader and his party gathered to depart from Saigon, Nolting handed Mansfield a prepared statement—a courtesy the embassy customarily provided visiting dignitaries. In thanking the Diem government for its hospitality, the embassy suggested that Mansfield and his colleagues tell reporters that "we are convinced" that Diem had "found the key to victory and peace" and that the discussions in Saigon had strengthened "our belief that the United States is on the right course in its determination to support your many-sided efforts to secure your freedom." While it did urge "a more tolerant attitude" toward American journalists, the statement also applauded Diem for his efforts to "restore justice and respect for human liberties."[10] As he reviewed Nolting's prepared statement, Mansfield must have known that the American journalists would find its sanguine language absurd and surreal—especially in light of their extensive briefing on Diem's shortcomings and the failings of the U.S. policy in Vietnam. To Nolting's amazement, Mansfield refused to read the prepared remarks. Instead, he gave reporters only a brief statement of personal praise for Diem.[11]

Before he boarded his airplane, Mansfield walked through the assembled crowd and sought out Trueheart, the U.S. official who had earlier drawn Mansfield's ire by speculating that few peasants even knew their president's name. Shaking the diplomat's hand, Mansfield acknowledged that "I think you're right." Although Trueheart did not affirm Mansfield's decision to accept the reporters' bleak assessment of the U.S. effort in Vietnam, he believed that Mansfield's reliance on their stories was wise. "These guys' reporting over the time," Trueheart later acknowledged, "had been a lot more accurate than ours had been."[12]

In Washington, William Jorden, the special assistant to the under secretary of state for political affairs, saw the press stories in the same light as Trueheart. In March 1963, Jorden would inform Averell Harriman, the new assistant secretary of state for Far Eastern affairs, that the press coverage coming out of Saigon was "exceedingly good" and the reporters had been unfairly maligned by U.S. officials. He would identify the major problem bedeviling Kennedy as he tried to guide the nation's evolving policy in Vietnam: "To ignore the many negative features of the situation in Vietnam," Jorden wrote, "is to dangerously delude ourselves. There is a vast multitude of problems and only by recognizing them can we hope to do something about them. A reporter who exposes such a problem may well be opening the door to its solution."[13] At the White House, meanwhile, Kennedy's aides continued to assure the president that, troubling news reports from Saigon notwithstanding, the situation in Vietnam was well in hand.

BY THE TIME OF HIS return to Washington on December 17, Mansfield—with Valeo's help—had prepared a confidential, sixteen-page report to the president, detailing the grim news about developments in Vietnam. The next day, he sent the document to Kennedy at the president's vacation home in Palm Beach. Kennedy called the following week and invited Mansfield to Florida to discuss the report. When he arrived at the Kennedy compound on December 26, Mansfield found a lively party underway around the swimming pool. "Let's talk alone," Kennedy said, as the two men left for a two-hour cruise on nearby Lake Worth.[14]

The report contained a bombshell. Mansfield had finally reached the painful realization that he had been wrong about his friend Diem. Diem's government had failed to live up to his promise as a champion of democracy. Mansfield's reluctant conclusion was that Kennedy should reconsider the level of American military support to South Vietnam. The Diem government, he informed Kennedy, had done "little with the time which was bought at Geneva in the sense of stimulating the growth of indigenous roots for the political structure in Saigon. That structure is, today, far more dependent on us for its existence than it was five years ago. If Vietnam is the cork in the Southeast Asian bottle then American aid is more than ever the cork in the Vietnamese bottle."

Despite the "new concepts and a new American approach in Vietnam," Mansfield wrote that it had been "distressing on this visit to hear the situation described in much the same terms as on my last visit, although it is seven years and billions of dollars later. Vietnam, outside the cities, is still an insecure place which is run at least at night largely by the Viet Cong." Diem's government had made little progress with the "ordinary people" in the countryside. "In short, it would be well to face the fact that we are once again at the beginning of the beginning." Although he praised the tentative success of the strategic hamlet program, he noted that it was too early to determine whether any real progress had been made against the Viet Cong.

"It is true that Vietminh casualty counts have been rising," he acknowledged, "but the accuracy of these counts is open to question. Moreover, it should be noted that the estimates of Viet Cong core strength have also been rising." Currently, he said, the "optimistic predictions" came only from the promise of the strategic hamlet program and "the injection of new energy" from the American military. "The real tests are yet to come," he wrote. "If experience should prove that there is less rather than more truth in the assumption that fear or indifference are the keystones of the Viet Cong hold over the countryside, the target date for success will be delayed indefinitely beyond the year or two of the present predictions." Still, he argued that the strategic hamlet project might achieve results "if we were prepared to increase the commitment of men and military aid."

Turning to Diem, he noted that while he remained "dedicated, sincere, hardworking, incorruptible and patriotic," the South Vietnamese leader had grown "older and the problems which confront him are more complex" than when he faced, first, the French and Bao Dai and, then, the sects. He observed that Diem's brother Nhu was increasingly asserting himself and had assumed the primary "energizing role" in government. While he acknowledged that Nhu was talented, Mansfield also noted that "it is Ngo Dinh Diem, not Ngo Dinh Nhu, who has such popular mandate to exercise power as there is in south Vietnam. In a situation of this kind there is a great danger of the corruption of unbridled power." The real problem, he said, was not the "reports and rumors" of corruption, but the "effect on the organization of the machinery for carrying out the new concepts. The difficulties in Vietnam are not likely to be overcome by a handful of paid retainers and sycophants."

While Mansfield held out some hope "that success will be achieved quickly," he added a large caveat. "My own view," he said, "is that the problems can be made to yield to present remedies, *provided* the problems and their magnitude do not change significantly and *provided* that the remedies are pursued by both Vietnamese and Americans (and particularly the former) with great vigor and self-dedication" (emphasis Mansfield's).

> Certainly, if these remedies do not work, it is difficult to conceive of alternatives, with the possible exception of a truly massive commitment of American military personnel and other resources—in short going to war fully ourselves against the guerillas—and the establishment of some form of neocolonial rule in south Vietnam. That is an alternative which I most emphatically do not recommend. . . .
>
> To ignore that reality will not only be immensely costly in terms of American lives and resources but it may also draw us inexorably into some variation of the unenviable position in Vietnam which was formerly occupied by the French. We are not, of course, at that point at this time. But the great increase in American military commitment this year has tended to point us in that general direction and we may well begin to slide rapidly toward it if any of the present remedies begin to falter in practice. . . .

The bottom line of Mansfield's report was a fundamental questioning of the notion that the United States had overriding national security interests in Southeast Asia.

> The real question which confronts us, therefore, is how much are we ourselves prepared to put into Southeast Asia and for how long in order to serve such interests as we may have in that region? Before we can answer this question, we must reassess our interests, using the words "vital" or "essential" with the greatest realism and restraint in the reassessment. When that has been done, we will be in a better position to estimate what we must, in fact, expend in the way of scarce resources, energy and lives in order to preserve those interests. We may well discover that it is in our interests to do less rather than more than we are now doing. If that is the case, we will do well to concentrate on a vigorous diplomacy which would be designed to lighten our commitments without bringing about sudden and catastrophic upheavals in Southeast Asia.[15]

As he watched Kennedy read the report, Mansfield recalled that he could "see his neck getting red." The president had undoubtedly seen the report before Mansfield's arrival, but a second reading did not make the news any more palatable. "You expect me to believe this?" Kennedy asked when he finished reading the report. "This isn't what my people are telling me." Mansfield was resolute. "You've got my opinion, as I see things," he told the president.[16] For two hours, Kennedy and Mansfield discussed the report. "His reaction was not a very happy one," Mansfield recalled in 1969. "He was perturbed by what I had to say and he queried me closely and, at times, it seemed aggressively on a number of comments and conclusions which the report contained."

While he did not mention it in his formal report, in 1969 Mansfield remembered that he told Kennedy "that military intervention was not his answer" to the situation in Vietnam and that "I strongly advised a curb and then a withdrawal of U.S. troops."[17] (In his report, Mansfield reached a slightly different conclusion: "If we were to withdraw abruptly . . . there would be a major collapse in many places and what would follow is by no means certain.") Still, such a strong recommendation is not entirely implausible. It is possible that Mansfield might have regarded advice about withdrawal too explosive and controversial to put in writing—even in a secret communication to the president. To suggest that the United States should end its military assistance to South Vietnam would have been an audacious recommendation in the fall of 1962. One could understand why Mansfield—if, indeed, his memory was correct—might have hesitated to commit such counsel to paper. At the time, Mansfield did not know how his advice might have influenced Kennedy. "He did start to raise a few points," Mansfield said, "which were in disagreement with what I had to say. But at least he got the truth as I saw it and it wasn't a pleasant picture that I had depicted for him."[18]

Nolting, however, had definite opinions about the impact of Mansfield's report. It was, he later observed, "the first nail in Diem's coffin." The American ambassador, for one, faulted Mansfield for the time he had spent with the American journalists. "He had gotten most of his information, I think, on this point from the American press corps in Saigon."[19]

In January 1963, information from another objective source further suggested that Mansfield's assessment had been correct. A CIA report observed that the Viet Cong "continue to expand the size and effectiveness of their forces" and had become "increasingly bold in their attacks." The war was, the report concluded, "a slowly escalating stalemate."[20] General Harkins saw things differently. He and Nolting, fed optimistic reports by obsequious underlings, believed the Viet Cong had finally been forced into a corner. Like the French general Navarre at Dien Bien Phu, Harkins longed for the chance to lure the enemy into the open where his army could finish them off. In January 1963, at the remote village of Ap Bac, Harkins would finally get his wish—with disastrous consequences for the U.S. military mission in Vietnam.

CHAPTER 21

You Did Visit the Same Country, Didn't You?

1963

Ten American H-21 helicopters—they were commonly called Flying Bananas—thundered through the Mekong Delta mist southeast of Saigon early on the morning of January 2, 1963. Their mission was to assist the Army of the Republic of Vietnam (ARVN) as it engaged three Viet Cong companies thought to be hiding in the vicinity of Ap Bac, a small farming village 40 miles southwest of Saigon. The chief American military advisor for the Seventh Division, Colonel John Paul Vann, had urged his Vietnamese counterpart, Colonel Bui Dinh Dam, to launch the offensive the previous morning. But Bui, a favorite of President Diem, had hesitated, saying that he wanted to give the American helicopter pilots time to recuperate from their New Year's Eve revelry.

The delay would be costly. Warned of the attack, the Viet Cong guerrillas fortified their position and waited patiently among the trees and brush along a canal between Ap Bac and a neighboring village. As the South Vietnamese soldiers disgorged from the American helicopters in a nearby rice paddy, the Viet Cong held their fire until the fourth wave of soldiers hit the ground. In an instant, the guerrillas opened fire and turned the paddy into a killing field. Within hours, five helicopters were downed and dozens of soldiers were trapped by intense enemy fire.

Watching in horror from an observation plane high above the battlefield, Vann took to the radio and frantically relayed news of the situation to the Vietnamese armored commander, pleading with him to dispatch armored personnel carriers to rescue the downed soldiers. Back came the terse reply: "I don't take orders from Americans." Three hours later, after the commander finally deployed his carriers, they crept onto the battle area so slowly that Viet Cong machine gunners picked them off one by one. Later, on the ground, Vann would count the cost of the South Vietnamese reluctance to engage the outnumbered Viet Cong: fourteen South Vietnamese and three American soldiers dead.

To the east of the village, mayhem also reigned. As darkness fell across the delta, the Viet Cong escaped through an area of open farmland. When Vann urged the South Vietnamese commander to deploy troops to block their retreat, General Cao balked. He argued that his men had suffered enough for one day. A political appointee under the direct supervision of Diem, Cao knew that his leader would not look kindly on the day's losses. His logic proved simple, if not perverted: if no more men were committed to battle, no more would die. To risk additional men, even to save those trapped on the battlefield, meant jeopardizing his job. For hours, Cao opted to save his job and not the lives of his men. Only after an intense barrage of cursing and badgering from Vann did the reluctant general finally send troops to intercept the fleeing Viet Cong, and then only after he was certain the guerrillas had escaped and were no longer a threat. In the darkness, however, ARVN paratroopers mistook other South Vietnamese soldiers for the Viet Cong and opened fire. When the barrage ended, the day's casualty list totaled sixty-one ARVN soldiers dead and another hundred wounded. The Viet Cong, meanwhile, had escaped virtually unscathed. The bodies of only three guerrillas were left behind.

To a disgusted Vann, the battle was "a miserable fucking performance, just like it always is." He shared that scathing assessment with the American reporters who rushed to Ap Bac as news of the botched battle found its way to Saigon. Of the guerrillas who had routed the South Vietnamese army, Vann paid a grudging tribute. "They were brave men," he said. "They gave a good account of themselves today."[1]

News of the debacle reached Washington on January 3 and dominated the reports from Vietnam for the next week. One press report described it as "a major defeat."[2] Another quoted Vann, described only as an "officer," characterizing the battle—in language more suitable for a family newspaper—as a "miserable performance." Wrote reporter Hanson Baldwin in the *New York Times*: "More proof was provided this week—if any more was needed—that the war in South Vietnam is likely to be long and hard with the ultimate outcome in doubt." Baldwin observed that "the setback was perhaps a grim but needed correction to the aura of optimism about South Vietnam generated by over-optimistic Washington statements."[3] The American public had been given its most painful insight into the "progress" of the war—and the news was disquieting, to say the least.

Disturbed that the reports in the *Washington Post* and the *New York Times* were at odds with the dispatches coming to him from official sources in Saigon, President Kennedy demanded answers. From South Vietnam came the soothing assurance that all—or almost all—was well. "It appears," Deputy Secretary of Defense Roswell Gilpatric wrote Kennedy on January 3, "that the initial press reports have distorted both the importance of the action and the damage suffered by the US/GVN [Government of Vietnam] forces." General Harkins completely ignored warning signs that South Vietnamese military commanders were more concerned with their personal and political relationships with Diem than with aggressively challenging the spreading Viet Cong influence throughout the country's rural areas. "It took a lot of guts on the part of those [South Vietnamese] pilots and crews," Harkins wrote in a report that landed on Kennedy's desk, "to go back into the area to rescue their pals." Harkins even suggested that the battle resulted in a partial South Vietnamese victory. "This day they got a bear by the tail and they didn't let go of it," he wrote. "At least they got most of it." In another distorted report of the battle, Admiral Harry Felt, the U.S. commander in chief in the Pacific, tried to shift blame for the debacle to the journalists. Felt insisted that the most serious problem was "bad news about American casualties filed immediately by young reporters" who had not checked their facts. "There is good news which you may not read about in *The Washington Post*," he asserted.[4]

Kennedy was still concerned, but accepted the assurances with few, if any, probing questions. He never seriously considered talking about Vietnam with the correspondents covering the story. "Kennedy gave me hell when I suggested that you get more by talking to the correspondents coming back," George Ball recalled. "The idea that you talk to the press about anything was anathema." Kennedy hated Halberstam, in particular, Ball said. "He worried about a fellow who had ideas that were so contrary to his own."[5] But Halberstam—and indeed most of the reporters in Saigon— had never questioned the wisdom of U.S. involvement in Vietnam. What they criticized was the dismal performance of the U.S.-backed South Vietnamese military and the competence and integrity of Diem's government.

Harkins, Nolting, and Felt, meanwhile, refused to see what had become so clear to the reporters and mid-level American commanders like Vann: the American effort in South Vietnam was doomed unless the United States persuaded Diem to clean up his government and reorganize his military. Nolting was especially intransigent on this point. Although he may have been justified in believing there was no attractive alternative to Diem's leadership, he was resolutely unwilling to demand reforms in return for continued U.S. military assistance. Most of his superiors in Washington were reluctant to order him to do so, believing the war could be won despite the corruption and mismanagement in Diem's regime. "I would not find it possible," Nolting confessed to Averell Harriman in a February 27

letter, "to be the agent in a change of US policy away from forthright support of the legitimate government."[6]

Other than the newspapers and Mansfield's blunt assessment of
December 1962, the only remotely reliable information that Kennedy
received on Vietnam came from the CIA report in January that warned of
a "slowly escalating stalemate" and a more optimistic report in January by
NSC staff member Michael Forrestal. In late 1962, Forrestal and State
Department official Roger Hilsman had traveled to Vietnam at Kennedy's
behest. While their subsequent report was upbeat, it was also laced with
clear warnings about the obstacles facing the U.S. military. "The war in
South Vietnam is clearly going better than it was a year ago," began Forrestal, drawing much of his optimism from official South Vietnamese government reports about the strategic hamlet program that boasted of four
thousand protected villages around the country. Yet Forrestal also warned
that "the negative side of the ledger is still awesome."

> The Viet Cong continue to be aggressive and are extremely effective. In
> the last few weeks, for example, they fought stubbornly and with telling
> results at Ap Bac. . . . My overall judgment, in sum, is that we are proba-
> bly winning, but certainly more slowly than we had hoped. At the rate it
> is going now the war will last longer than we would like, cost more in
> terms of both lives and money than we anticipated, and prolong the
> period in which a sudden and dramatic event could upset the gains already
> made.[7]

Most official news from Vietnam, including the Forrestal–Hilsman
report, was unrealistically positive. Typical was the report of the Army
chief of staff, General Earle Wheeler, who arrived in Saigon in late January to size up the situation for the Joint Chiefs of Staff. In his report to
Kennedy—which Forrestal later characterized as "rosy euphoria" and
described as "a complete waste" of Kennedy's time—the general claimed
that the situation had been "reoriented . . . from a circumstance of near
desperation to a condition where victory is now a hopeful prospect."
Wheeler, too, adopted the by-now-familiar practice of dismissing much of
the discordant information coming out of Vietnam as a consequence of
inaccurate press coverage.[8]

If Kennedy had an unrealistic view of the situation, the American people and Congress were being completely hoodwinked by American officials in Saigon and Washington. Returning from a conference in Honolulu
with top U.S. military and civilian officials in Vietnam, McNamara's
spokesman, Arthur Sylvester, told reporters in Washington that "the corner definitely has been turned."[9] In fact, McNamara let it be known that
he hoped to begin reducing the thirteen thousand-plus U.S. military con-

tingent in Vietnam. In Honolulu he had requested from Harkins a plan to shrink the American military contingent in South Vietnam to about one thousand five hundred by the fall of 1967 and had complained that the current plans for force reductions were "too slow."[10]

Like Kennedy's, McNamara's optimism grew from a belief shared widely in Washington that Harkins, if given the right kind of weapons and men—and enough of them—could subdue the Viet Cong within five years. The alternative, pulling out completely before the job was completed, was unthinkable. But this is exactly what Mansfield may have suggested when discussing his December 1962 report with Kennedy. In March 1963, after Mansfield released a revised version of the report that suggested a reduction in U.S. aid to South Vietnam, reporters asked Kennedy if he agreed. Annoyed, Kennedy answered: "I don't see how we are going to be able, unless we are going to pull out of Southeast Asia and turn it over to the Communists, how we are going to be able to reduce very much our economic programs and military programs in Viet-Nam, in Cambodia, in Thailand."[11]

Mansfield's blunt assessment of the situation in Vietnam gave White House officials headaches. Contrary to the official administration line, Mansfield now had declared publicly that no grounds for "optimistic conclusions" about the conflict existed. After seven years and more than $2 billion in U.S. aid, "the same difficulties remain if, indeed, they have not been compounded." The only way for Diem to rally the people around him, Mansfield insisted, was to institute economic and political reforms while broadening his government. The U.S. military, he believed, could not and should not fight a war for the South Vietnamese. "It is not an American war," he said. "It is their country and responsibility. We don't want to take the place of the French."[12]

Mansfield's report created a stir in Saigon. Diem's tempestuous sister-in-law, Madam Ngo Dinh Nhu, complained that Diem's critics—meaning Mansfield and the American reporters—"dream of reducing us to the passive state of Helots, judging us worthy only to be mercenaries or abandoned halfway like so many other patriots who have courageously fought against the Communists."[13] Her husband, Ngo Dinh Nhu, called the report "treachery" and told the U.S. embassy's public affairs officer, John Mecklin, that Mansfield's comment "changes everything," although he declined to elaborate on the exact nature of the changes. Like his wife, Nhu seemed to believe that the harsh criticism of a former ally like Mansfield would not have been released without Kennedy's approval. Mecklin tried to explain to a skeptical Nhu that the president had nothing to do with the report's dissemination and that official U.S. policy toward his brother's regime had not changed.

In Washington, Mansfield's report caused a minor tumult, prompting Kennedy to confess privately—his anger of the previous December notwithstanding—that the majority leader had been correct in his assessment of the situation. During a White House meeting with the congressional leadership, Mansfield reiterated his strong opposition to the current course of U.S. policy. Kennedy fumed, but later called Mansfield back for a more intimate discussion. What he had to say was astonishing. Face to face with the unrepentant majority leader, Kennedy acknowledged that Mansfield's criticism was probably valid. "He indicated that he was having second thoughts on our position in Southeast Asia," Mansfield recalled in 1969, "and, specifically, in Viet Nam." But what Kennedy told Mansfield next was even more surprising. Kennedy, he said, went so far as to say "that he was seriously considering the withdrawal of all U.S. troops from Viet Nam if he were reelected to a second term."[14] Presidential aide Kenneth O'Donnell later claimed that Kennedy had stated himself even more strongly. O'Donnell, who was present for the meeting, recalled in 1970 that Kennedy informed Mansfield that he believed all U.S. troops should be withdrawn from Vietnam. "But I can't do it until 1965—after I'm reelected." As if Mansfield needed a lesson in politics, Kennedy explained that the political consequences of a sudden withdrawal from Vietnam would spark a conservative outcry against him and probably result in his defeat in 1964. After Mansfield left, according to O'Donnell, Kennedy said: "In 1965, I'll become one of the most unpopular Presidents in history. I'll be damned everywhere as a Communist appeaser. But I don't care. If I tried to pull out completely now from Vietnam, we would have another Joe McCarthy red scare on our hands, but I can do it after I'm reelected. So we had better make damned sure that I *am* reelected."[15] In an interview in 1969, *Chicago Sun-Times* columnist Charles Bartlett, a close friend of Kennedy, recalled that the president was perplexed—"completely at sea"— by Vietnam. But Bartlett did believe Kennedy was committed to keeping U.S. troops in South Vietnam—at least until the 1964 elections. But, he said, Kennedy also told him in 1963 that "we've got to face the fact that the odds are about a hundred to one that we're going to get our asses thrown out of Vietnam."[16]

According to Mansfield and O'Donnell, Kennedy had grown weary of the conflict and wanted out. In a sense, they were correct. Pentagon officials were under orders to begin planning a gradual reduction of U.S. forces with the goal of removing most or all U.S. military "advisors" by 1966. But Kennedy may have wanted out for far different reasons than Mansfield and O'Donnell supposed. While the president may have led Mansfield and other friendly critics to believe that he agreed with their dismal assessments of the prospects for a successful outcome in Vietnam, he was actually far more frustrated with Diem than with Nolting and Harkins.

Secretary of State Dean Rusk, for one, derided the notion that Kennedy would have ever decided on a withdrawal of American troops, but delayed the decision for domestic political reasons. "That would have meant that he was committing men to combat for what would amount to domestic political purposes," Rusk said in 1970, as if all wars did not have their political components. "I just don't myself believe that President Kennedy, or indeed any president, would be cynical enough to commit men to combat for electoral purposes."[17] Furthermore, as Rusk wrote in his memoirs, "Kennedy liked to bat the breeze and toss ideas around." While it was possible that he might have left Mansfield with the impression that he planned to withdraw from Vietnam in 1965, Rusk insisted that "had he done so, I think that I would have known about it."[18]

Judging his policy by his actions and not his private rhetoric, Kennedy appeared as strongly committed as ever to an American presence in Vietnam. As then-Assistant Defense Secretary William Bundy argued, Kennedy *was* preparing for a "progressive reduction and eventual withdrawal" of the American "advisors." But Bundy believed that he was doing so with the understanding "that the effort was working and that the South Vietnamese were growing in strength, so that they could handle the job. . . . It wasn't the case of abandoning the cause or commitment at all."[19]

Despite Mansfield's warnings and the troubling newspaper reports that he chose to discount, Kennedy had made a firm public commitment to Vietnam that he had enthusiastically reiterated on several occasions. Were he nursing a plan to order a precipitate withdrawal of all American troops from Vietnam in 1965, it is doubtful that he would have discussed the idea with the Senate majority leader but not his own secretaries of state and defense or any other national security advisor. In fact, whether he planned to withdraw after the 1964 elections was an irrelevant proposition in early 1963, almost two years before the election. There was, in the meantime, a war to be won or lost. Two years was a lifetime—in politics and war.

It is most likely that Kennedy, Mansfield's advice notwithstanding, had reluctantly decided that he could maintain an American presence in Vietnam for another two years—with slight, but steady reductions in troop strength. By then, perhaps, the South Vietnamese government—by virtue of political and military reforms or new leadership—would turn the tide so that the American people would view an eventual withdrawal as a victorious exit, not a cowardly retreat. Yet it is impossible to determine conclusively exactly what it was that Kennedy planned in Vietnam. He was undoubtedly, like the presidents before and after him, uncertain and fearful of the potential consequences of a massive American military commitment, but also afraid of the political consequences if South Vietnam fell to the Communists. "I think Kennedy's view," George Ball later said, "was that he very much wanted to avoid getting in deeply in the war. At the same time he didn't want to be regarded as a coward."[20]

Diem and Nhu, meanwhile, appeared far more uncomfortable than Kennedy about the presence of U.S. troops in their country. Fed up with efforts to force governmental reforms, Nhu told the *Washington Post*, in a front-page story on May 12, that "South Vietnam would like to see half of the 12,000 to 13,000 American military stationed here leave the country."[21] Some particularly gruesome events of that May, however, would persuade American officials that it was Diem, not U.S. troops, that had to go.

An eruption of government-sponsored violence on May 8 in Hue, a coastal city south of the North Vietnamese border, only intensified that sentiment. That day, Diem's troops opened fire and brutally attacked a group of Buddhists gathered to protest a government decree banning the display of flags to commemorate the 2,527th birthday of the Buddha. The clash had been long in coming. Although 70 percent of the country's population considered itself Buddhist, aloof Catholics like Diem and Nhu ruled the nation's government. Believing they were being persecuted for their faith, Buddhist leaders launched a sustained period of vocal protest, hoping to gain greater religious freedoms.[22]

The protest finally reached a dramatic and appalling climax on June 11 in Saigon, when an elderly Buddhist monk, doused with gasoline, squatted in the middle of a busy downtown intersection and waited as another monk set him on fire. As the man burned to death before a horrified crowd, Associated Press reporter Malcolm Browne snapped photographs. The next day, Browne's disturbing picture—he described the grisly scene as a "horror show"—appeared on the front page of virtually every newspaper in the world.[23] To John Mecklin, the photograph "had a shock effect of incalculable value to the Buddhist cause, becoming a symbol of the state of things in Vietnam."[24] Observed William Colby, the top CIA official in Saigon: "The party was almost over in terms of the imagery that was affecting American opinion."[25] Madame Nhu only reinforced the negative image of her brother-in-law's cruel, repressive regime when she reacted to the suicide with glee. She later called it a "barbecue," and told a reporter: "Let them burn, and we shall clap our hands."[26]

With Nolting away from Saigon on leave, his deputy, William Trueheart, took temporary command of the embassy and—in contrast to Nolting's sanguine strategy of conciliation—immediately adopted a harder line toward Diem. "If Diem does not take prompt and effective steps to reestablish Buddhist confidence in him we will have to reexamine our entire relationship with his regime," Rusk told Trueheart in a June 11 cable.[27] Trueheart enthusiastically delivered the message, but Diem was unmoved. The Buddhist problem had been blown out of proportion, he said, disregarding ample evidence to the contrary.[28] Throughout the country, citizens were on the verge of revolt. It was not just the Buddhists who were exorcised. College and high school students, including some Catholics, gathered for massive protests of Diem's repressive policies. Meanwhile, the self-immolation continued. As Diem approved only token reforms, seven more monks burned themselves to death.

Relations between Diem and the U.S. government reached an all-time low when the *New York Times* reported on June 14 that the Kennedy administration would "publicly condemn [Diem's] treatment of the Buddhists unless he takes prompt action to meet their grievances."[29] Despite official South Vietnamese protests that the U.S. approach was threatening Diem's negotiations with Buddhist leaders, Kennedy, Rusk, and other administration officials had clearly reached the limits of their patience with the intransigent Diem. Just as distressing were the rumors, later proven true, that Diem and Nhu were seeking a negotiated settlement with Hanoi and were engaging in secret negotiations with the Communists.[30] Rusk, meanwhile, urged Trueheart to press Diem even harder to reform his government, advising a "very hard-hitting approach."[31]

About the same time, Mansfield again weighed in and strongly urged Kennedy to reconsider continued U.S. military support to Vietnam. In an August 19 memorandum, he bluntly framed the issue. Whether to continue supporting Diem's government, Mansfield argued, was a "secondary" question. "It is the question, to state it simply and frankly, of which way is likely to be least costly in American lives and money." The debate over the future of Diem's government was not paramount, Mansfield argued, because "with the present government or with a replacement—we are in for a very long haul to develop even a modicum of stability in Viet Nam." Mansfield continued: "The die is not yet finally cast but we are very close to the point when it will have to be. Therefore, we may well ask ourselves, once more, not the tactical question, but the fundamental question: Is South Viet Nam as important to us as the premise on which we are now apparently operating indicates?"

Mansfield answered his own question by observing that the United States had overstated South Vietnam's importance and that "we have talked ourselves and 'agencied' ourselves into this premise." Vietnam, he wrote, "is not central to our defense interest or any other American interest but is, rather, peripheral to these interests." The way out of "the bind," he advised, "is certainly not by the route of ever-deeper involvement. To be sure it is desirable that we do not spend countless American lives and billions of dollars to maintain an illusion of freedom in a devastated South Viet Nam."[32]

Kennedy's nascent doubts about Diem's viability were finally confirmed on August 21 when, fearing a coup, Diem declared martial law and sent troops from his brother's special forces to raid Buddhist pagodas all across the country. Armed with rifles, machine guns, and teargas, the troops stormed the Buddhist sanctuaries and arrested more than a thousand monks, nuns, and students. Public reaction throughout South Vietnam was swift, as massive demonstrations erupted.

From Honolulu, Henry Cabot Lodge rushed to Saigon to succeed Ambassador Nolting, whose two-year term had expired and whose loyalty to Diem now made him ill-suited for the job. Kennedy chose Lodge—a wealthy, 61-year-old former Republican senator from Massachusetts—partially out of respect for his stature and toughness, but also because of his need to bolster Republican congressional support for his Vietnam policies. Lodge—Kennedy's opponent in his first Senate race and later vanquished again by Kennedy when he campaigned as Nixon's 1960 running mate—proved an able choice. "The real problem," Chester Cooper observed, "was that one needed in Vietnam an ambassador of sufficient stature so that the military commander would not outrank him either in terms of rank or in sheer terms of prestige and power."[33] Lodge seemed to fit the bill in every way. In his first meeting with Diem, on August 26, the new ambassador was firm and direct when he told Diem that judging from Madame Nhu's outrageous and incendiary statements, many Americans erroneously believed that she, not Diem, was South Vietnam's chief of state. Furthermore, he said, government persecution of the Buddhists was "shocking American opinion which favors religious toleration." All these factors, Lodge said, were "threatening American support of Viet-Nam."[34]

Lodge's exhortations, however, were largely pro forma. Only two days before he had received a crucial telegram from Under Secretary of State George Ball. Over the weekend, while most of the administration's leading military and foreign policy leaders were away from Washington, three of Diem's strongest detractors, Harriman, Forrestal, and Hilsman, had drafted a message instructing Lodge to offer U.S. support to military leaders plotting the overthrow of Diem's government. Ball, the official who would sign the telegram in Rusk's absence, recalled that Harriman and Hilsman "appeared in a great sweat" at a public golf course where he was finishing a round with Deputy Under Secretary of State Alexis Johnson.[35] "My position was that something had to give," Hilsman later explained. "We could not go on like this."[36] Harriman and Hilsman informed Ball that Lodge had notified them that "certain generals" in the South Vietnamese army were considering a coup.[37] They urged Ball to approve the telegram, which advised Lodge that Diem "cannot be preserved" and instructed him to "tell key military leaders that [the] US would find it impossible to continue support [of] GVN militarily and economically" unless reforms were undertaken "which we recognize requires [the] removal of the Nhus from the scene."[38]

From his home, Ball reviewed the telegram and recognized its "considerable importance." He later acknowledged that "I personally was not unsympathetic with what it said because I had felt that we had really run our course with the Diem regime."[39] Ball phoned Kennedy at his home in Hyannis Port. Asked for his opinion about the proposed cable, Ball replied that Harriman and Hilsman were pressing hard for its approval. "I thought to send this telegram to Lodge," Ball recalled, "was probably all right." Kennedy cautiously agreed, but inquired about McNamara's whereabouts. Told that his defense secretary was mountain climbing in Wyoming, the president instructed Ball to consult Deputy Defense Secretary Ross Gilpatric. Then, he concluded, "If Rusk and Gilpatric agree, George, then go ahead." Ball then phoned Rusk, who was in New York on United Nations business, and advised him of the telegram. But because they were not on a secure telephone line, Ball could only describe its language in the vaguest of terms. Assured that Kennedy understood the telegram's implications, Rusk finally said, "Well, go ahead."

That afternoon, Forrestal phoned Gilpatric, who was spending the weekend at his Maryland farm. Based on Forrestal's description of events, Gilpatric quickly concluded that the telegram was "basically a State Department matter, a political matter." Informed that Rusk and the president had approved the telegram, Gilpatric concurred. "I regarded it as something between the White House and the State Department," he later said, "and, therefore, I didn't object to it. . . . I went along with it just like you countersign a voucher."[40]

Later that evening, at 9:36 P.M., Washington time, the State Department dispatched Ball's telegram. "You may also tell appropriate military commanders," Ball said, "that we will give them direct support in any interim period of breakdown [in] central government mechanism." While Ball would not give "detailed instructions as to how this operation should succeed," he assured Lodge that "we will back you to the hilt on actions you take to achieve our objectives."[41]

On Monday, with all the principals back in Washington, the import of the weekend telegram became clear. What had been characterized to Kennedy as the unified counsel of his foreign policy advisors began to look more like an end run by Harriman, Hilsman, and Forrestal. Some advisors were having second thoughts. Vice President Johnson, McNamara, CIA Director John McCone, and Joint Chiefs Chairman Maxwell Taylor all opposed a U.S.-backed coup.[42] "It was the only time, really, in three years," Robert Kennedy said, "that the government was broken in two in a very disturbing way."[43]

The president was annoyed by the deep divisions among his advisors about Diem's future, but hesitated to countermand the instructions in the August 24 telegram. "I think the president felt uneasy about this telegram

to Lodge," recalled Nolting, who met with Kennedy in the days following, "but he couldn't find any way to retrieve it."[44] Instead, he wavered and
told his men that he saw no reason to support a coup without a good chance
of success. He instructed the State Department to ask Lodge and Harkins
for "their estimate of the prospects of a coup by the generals."[45] Back came
the reply from Lodge: "On [the] basis of what we now know both General
Harkins and I favor [the] operation."[46] Several days later came a more
definitive response:

> We are launched on a course from which there is no respectable turning
> back: the overthrow of the Diem government. There is no turning back
> in part because U.S. prestige is already publicly committed to this end in
> large measure and will become more so as the facts leak out. In a more
> fundamental sense, there is no turning back because there is no possibil-
> ity, in my view, that the war can be won under a Diem administration, still
> less that Diem or any member of the family can govern the country in a
> way to gain the support of the people who count, i.e., the educated class
> in and out of government service, civil and military—not to mention the
> American people. . . . I am personally in full agreement with the policy
> which I was instructed to carry out by last Sunday's telegram.[47]

Yet Kennedy remained cautious and worried about the consequences
of a U.S.-backed coup. "Until the very moment of the go signal for the
operation by the Generals," he told Lodge, "I must reserve a contingent
right to change course and reverse previous instructions. . . . When we go,
we must go to win, but it will be better to change our minds than fail." But
Kennedy's approval of the August 24 telegram had released the genie from
the bottle. In truth, there was little the United States could do to stop
Diem's overthrow—short of warning Diem and confessing U.S. complicity in the plot. Lodge's reply reflected this reality: "To be successful," he
said, "this operation must be essentially a Vietnamese affair with a momentum of its own. Should this happen you may not be able to control it, i.e.
the 'go signal' may be given by the Generals."[48] In other words, as the CIA's
Richard Helms observed, the telegram and the subsequent push for a coup
"was a truck that was rolling down the road."[49]

Publicly, Kennedy turned up the heat on Diem by sending him a
strong message: reform or lose the war. In a nationally televised interview
from Hyannis Port on September 2 with CBS newsman Walter Cronkite,
Kennedy said:

> I don't think that unless a greater effort is made by the Government to
> win popular support that the war can be won out there. In the final analy-
> sis, it is their war. They are the ones who have to win it or lose it. We can
> help them, we can give them equipment, we can send our men out there

as advisers, but they have to win it, the people of Viet-Nam, against the Communists.

As for withdrawing American troops from Vietnam, Kennedy was emphatic. "I don't agree with those who say we should withdraw," he said. "That would be a great mistake."[50]

In the effort to pressure Diem to reform his government, Kennedy and his men opened another front in early September—pointing to a congressional resolution to end U.S. aid to South Vietnam. On September 5, after a closed-door session of the Far East subcommittee of the Senate Foreign Relations Committee, Democratic Senator Frank Church of Idaho had threatened to introduce just such a resolution unless Diem's government changed its ways. Also that day, Church's subcommittee colleague Democrat Frank Lausche of Ohio seemed to signal a similar displeasure with the course of events when he delivered a Senate speech advocating "a change of policy" and "a change of personnel" in South Vietnam.[51] In a telegram that evening to Lodge, Hilsman reported news of the possible resolution and observed that the subcommittee's mood "augurs heavy sledding" in the upcoming debate over U.S. aid to South Vietnam. A delighted Lodge responded that he had immediately put Hilsman's telegram to use, apparently sharing it with the plotting generals who, he said, planned to tell Nhu that "he and his wife have no choice but to leave the country for six months." Lodge also believed the telegram would "open the way for my showdown conference with Diem."[52]

On September 9, Lodge had his meeting with Diem. Nhu had to leave the country, Lodge insisted, and not return until at least late December—after Congress approved the appropriations bill for Vietnam. But Diem would not hear of it, insisting that his brother had been unjustly accused. He put the onus on Lodge to persuade Congress to maintain U.S. assistance to his country. "If American opinion is in the state that you describe," Diem said, "then it is up to you, Ambassador Lodge, to disintoxicate American opinion." Lodge left feeling that his discussion had accomplished little.[53]

McGeorge Bundy and Hilsman, meanwhile, encouraged Church to pursue his resolution in hopes that Diem might respond to concrete evidence that Congress planned to cut off assistance to his government. "Good idea," Bundy told him. "Keep going."[54] Bolstered by the White House's support, Church circulated the text of his resolution—drafted with help from the State Department—to every member of the Senate: "*Resolved*, That is it the sense of the Senate that unless the Government of South Vietnam abandons policies of repression against its own people and makes a determined and effective effort to regain their support, military and economic assistance to that Government should not be continued."[55]

Kennedy, however, worried that the effort might backfire—especially if the resolution was offered and defeated.[56] Later, he expressed concerns that Church's resolution might take on a life of its own, becoming not just an expression of congressional disapproval of Diem's regime, but a binding amendment to the foreign aid appropriations bill. Rusk also fretted that the resolution "might get out of control." He wanted to give senators the opportunity to "sound off," but hoped the resolution would not come to a vote.[57] On balance, however, Kennedy's men believed a nonbinding resolution was worth the risk. Hilsman told the president he believed it could become "useful ammunition" for Lodge in his discussions with Diem, especially if it passed the Senate by a wide margin.[58] On September 12, Church and Republican Senator Frank Carlson of Kansas—supported by twenty-one senators, most of them liberal Democrats—offered the resolution in the Senate. "To persist in the support of such a regime," Church told the Senate, "can only serve to identify the United States with the cause of religious persecution, undermining our moral position throughout the world."[59]

At the White House, the debate over Church's resolution merely reflected the widening internal divisions over Diem that had developed in September. Kennedy was torn. On one hand, he knew he had given momentum to a conspiracy that might eventually topple the leader of South Vietnam. By September, however, he and his advisors had drawn back from their active support of a coup and focused more on ways to persuade Diem to save his regime, including banishing his brother and sister-in-law. In a September 9 interview, broadcast on the NBC television network, Kennedy told interviewers David Brinkley and Chet Huntley that "we are using our influence to persuade" Diem to take steps necessary "to win back support. That takes some time and we must be patient, we must persist." Despite his private support for Church's resolution, the president gave no public indication that he favored a reassessment of U.S. aid to Vietnam or a withdrawal of U.S. troops. "If you reduce your aid, it is possible you could have some effect upon the government structure there," he said. "On the other hand, you might have a situation which could bring about a collapse." Kennedy, however, made one thing clear. He still believed strongly in the "domino theory."

> I believe it. I think that the struggle is close enough. China is so large, looms so high just beyond the frontiers, that if South Vietnam went, it would not only give them an improved geographic position for a guerilla assault of Malaya, but would also give the impression that the wave of the future in Southeast Asia was China and the communists. So I believe it.

As for removing American troops, Kennedy acknowledged domestic complaints about the general course of the struggle as well as about the

Diem government. Withdrawing, however, "only makes it easier for the Communists," he said. "I think we should stay. We should use our influence in as effective a way as we can, but we should not withdraw."[60]

Much of Kennedy's indecision about where to go next in Vietnam was the result of the deep divisions among his advisors. Taylor and McNamara, for instance, believed that forcing Diem from office was unwise because there was no attractive alternative to his leadership. "McNamara and Taylor just don't buy the assessment this is going to get worse and something serious must be done," McGeorge Bundy told Rusk in a September 11 telephone conversation.[61] That same day, Lodge cabled Rusk and presented the other side of the argument. "The ship of state here is slowly sinking," Lodge wrote. "This brings me to the conclusion, that if there are effective sanctions which we can apply, we should apply them in order to force a drastic change in government."[62]

Nothing, however, characterized the uncertainty about Diem and his government more than the diverse conclusions reached after a joint, four-day visit to Vietnam by Major General Victor Krulak and a State Department official, Joseph Mendenhall. "The shooting war is going ahead at an impressive pace," Krulak reported when the two men briefed Kennedy on September 10. Furthermore, he said, the relationship between U.S. and South Vietnamese military forces had not been damaged by the political crisis. Krulak boldly predicted that the war would be won "if the current U.S. military and sociological programs are pursued, irrespective of the grave defects in the ruling regime."

Mendenhall's report, by contrast, was bleak. The civil government in Saigon had virtually broken down in the "pervasive atmosphere of fear and hate arising from the police reign of terror and the arrests of students." The war against the Viet Cong was now "secondary" to the "war" against Diem's regime. Contrary to Krulak's assessment, Mendenhall concluded that the war could not be won as long as Nhu remained part of the government. When Mendenhall finished, an exasperated Kennedy said, "The two of you did visit the same country, didn't you?"[63]

CHAPTER 22

A Stone Rolling Downhill

1963

"As long as Diem is the head of the government of South Vietnam," Wayne Morse indignantly told the Senate on September 9, "we continue to support a tyrant; we continue to support a police-state dictator." Morse, who had first spoken out against American involvement in Vietnam more than a year earlier, was now even more certain that the United States should leave Vietnam "and save the American people the hundreds upon hundreds of millions of dollars that our government is pouring down that rat hole." Morse knew that his protest was not widely popular, in the Senate, in his home state of Oregon, or in most parts of the country. "But I shall continue to speak it," he vowed. "On the basis of the present policies that prevail there," he concluded, "South Vietnam is not worth the life of a single American boy."[1]

Morse was not alone in his belief that the United States should leave Vietnam. Another senator, freshman Democrat George McGovern of South Dakota, also nursed growing concerns about Kennedy's policies. An amiable, soft-spoken man of 41 years, McGovern had arrived in the Senate in January 1963, having been Kennedy's Food for Peace director and, before that, a member of the House of Representatives. From his positions on the Agriculture and Interior committees, McGovern—like most freshmen—had worked to protect his state's interests. Far more, though, than a parochial member of Congress who cared only about securing pork barrel appropriations for his state, McGovern was a thoughtful and passionate man, a former college history professor who combined a love of politics with an equally intense enthusiasm for liberal causes. That liberalism had come naturally. As the son of a Methodist minister, he was inculcated early with John Wesley's teachings about "practical divinity," a theology that stressed the church's role in fighting poverty, injustice, ignorance, and disease. He was undoubtedly influenced by the pronounced strains of populism and agrarian unrest that ran through much of the Depression-era Midwest of his youth.

Nothing, however, had influenced McGovern more than his formal education. It was during his graduate studies at Northwestern University, a bastion of liberalism in the 1940s, that he learned about the history and politics of Southeast Asia. His familiarity with the views of China scholars like John King Fairbank and Owen Lattimore convinced him that the war in Vietnam was not the result of a communist-inspired, China-backed insurrection. "I felt then, as I do now," McGovern told a biographer in the early 1970s, "that U.S. foreign policy was needlessly exacerbating tensions with the Soviet Union and that we were wrong in our support of Chiang, the French in Indochina, and Bao Dai."[2] Asia was out of control, he believed, and Southeast Asia was "being convulsed by social and nationalistic upheavals that couldn't be contained by the usual sources of military power." Arriving in the Senate, the World War II bomber pilot was "struck," he recalled, "by the fact that the basic Cold War assumptions were just widely accepted in the Senate and in the executive branch and that people applied it in Vietnam without discrimination—and, therefore, we had to stand firm."

For months, McGovern had heard from various sources that the American effort in South Vietnam "wasn't working out too well." He suspected the reason for the lack of success was that "we didn't have popular support out there—the rank and file people were not all that opposed to Ho Chi Minh and not all that enamored of the regime that we were backing."[3]

On September 24, 1963, McGovern declared that the nation's foray into Southeast Asia was a "failure." He told the Senate that "the current dilemma in Vietnam is a clear demonstration of the limitations of military power. There in the jungles of Asia, our mighty nuclear arsenal—our $50 billion arms budget—even our costly new 'Special Forces'—have proved powerless to cope with a ragged band of illiterate guerrillas fighting with home-made weapons or with weapons they have captured from us." The "trap" that had lured America into Southeast Asia, McGovern insisted, "will haunt us in every corner of this revolutionary world, if we do not properly appraise its lesson."

McGovern's September 24 speech was not aimed at challenging the fundamental premise of Kennedy's Vietnam policies. His remarks on Vietnam had actually been an aside. He had, instead, come to advance his proposal to reduce funding for weapons procurement and military research and development. America, he said, echoing Fulbright and Mansfield, "will exert a far greater impact for peace and freedom in Asia and elsewhere if we rely less on armaments and more on the economic, political and moral sources of our strength."[4]

Two days later, on September 26, McGovern again took his concerns about Vietnam to the Senate floor and, after Morse, became the second member of Congress to call publicly for a withdrawal of U.S. forces. "The U.S. position has deteriorated so drastically," he told the Senate, "that it is in our national interest to withdraw from that country our forces and our aid." American guns and money, he said, "are being used, not to promote freedom, but to suppress religious freedom, harass and imprison students and teachers, and terrorize the people."[5] Press coverage of the speeches was minimal. Neither Morse nor McGovern took their concerns about Vietnam directly to Kennedy.

While some members of the Senate Foreign Relations Committee, in closed hearings, pressed McNamara, Rusk, and Taylor for more information, the leading foreign policy voices in Congress had fallen virtually silent during the months of September and October. "The Senate Foreign Relations Committee was relatively quiet," Rusk later recalled, adding that Fulbright "raised no particular problems" about Vietnam.[6] In fact, Fulbright had let it be known publicly that withdrawing U.S. forces from Vietnam would be "unacceptable."[7] As Rusk noted, "there were no doves and hawks in those days. . . . I think everybody hoped that somehow the modest steps that were taken during the Kennedy administration would be enough to pacify the situation."[8] As one of the few senators to speak out about Vietnam, McGovern was surprised that his speech did not spark some kind of reaction. "I thought it was kind of a nugget that would catch some attention," he recalled, "but it didn't."[9] McGovern concluded that "people just thought I was talking about a rather obscure and insignificant little country and that it really didn't matter all that much."[10]

But Kennedy and Rusk knew they were only one or two incidents away from a public outcry over Vietnam. The reporters in Saigon, particularly Halberstam, continued raising troubling questions about the direction of U.S. policy in Vietnam and shed new light on the divergent views about Diem among Kennedy's foreign policy advisors. The thought of a public and a Congress growing restless over a faltering U.S. policy in Vietnam and the troubling divisions among his own advisors worried Kennedy. "There is increasing concern here with strictly military aspects of the problem," Kennedy acknowledged in an "eyes only" cable to Lodge on September 17, "both in terms of actual progress of operations and of need to make [an] effective case with Congress for continued prosecution of the effort."[11]

Kennedy's response was another fact-finding mission. This time, he sent two of his top military advisors, McNamara and Taylor. Their largely optimistic conclusions, based on discussions with U.S. and South Vietnamese officials in Saigon, reinforced Kennedy's own inclination to plot a middle course between supporting Diem and promoting a coup. Claiming that "the military campaign has made great progress and continues to progress," McNamara and Taylor advised caution upon their return. While Diem's government had become increasingly unpopular, they insisted—inaccurately, as it turned out—that "there is no solid evidence of the possibility of a successful coup." Furthermore, they also led Kennedy to believe that American training of the South Vietnamese army would be completed by the end of 1965. "It should be possible," they said, "to withdraw the bulk of U.S. personnel by that time." They encouraged Kennedy to announce that he would make a down payment on that expectation by withdrawing one thousand American troops by year's end. The McNamara–Taylor report recommended that Kennedy

> follow a policy of selective pressures: "purely correct" relationship at the top official level, continuing to withhold further actions in the commodity import program, and making clear our disapproval of the regime. A further element in this policy is letting the present impression stand that the U.S. would not be averse to a change of Government—although we would not take any *immediate* actions to initiate a coup.[12] (Emphasis added)

Besides drastically underestimating the prospects for a coup and presenting an unrealistic timetable for the South Vietnamese army to withstand a U.S. troop withdrawal, the McNamara–Taylor report contained, in the words of William Bundy, the deputy assistant secretary of defense who accompanied McNamara to South Vietnam, a "clear internal inconsistency." On one hand, it claimed the war could be won if Diem made political reforms. Yet, at the same time, McNamara and Taylor said they doubted such reforms would ever be made.[13] Later, Averell Harriman and his assistant, William Sullivan, argued that the report was not only misguided—it contained a patently false characterization of the situation in South Vietnam. "The [U.S.] military are trained when they are in a battle to make the best face of what they're up against," Harriman explained in a 1965 interview. Ultimately, McNamara, Taylor, and other military leaders, Harriman believed, "were taken in by their own statements."[14] Sullivan later recalled that the State Department's opinion of the conflict—despite Rusk's aversion to advancing this point of view in meetings with Kennedy—was far different from the Pentagon's. "We felt this was going to be a long, grinding sort of thing, and we shouldn't create any illusions or delusions in the American public that it was going to be something that could be taken care of very quickly."[15]

In any event, the Taylor–McNamara report became the new guiding light for Kennedy's Vietnam policy. After the National Security Council adopted the report in early October, Kennedy approved a statement announcing a withdrawal of U.S. forces. "By the end of this year, the U.S. program for training Vietnamese should have progressed to the point where 1,000 U.S. military personnel assigned to South Viet Nam can be withdrawn."[16] In the weeks following the report, the administration began implementing the recommended "selective pressures": the CIA recalled its station chief, John Richardson, known to be one of Nhu's close friends; withheld funding for Nhu's special forces; and stopped all shipments of commodities like rice, milk, and tobacco.[17]

Although these selective pressures were not specifically designed to make Diem more vulnerable, they certainly had that effect. By the middle of October, coup plotting was again in full bloom. Lodge, believing the U.S. effort would only be successful with Diem out of the picture, was the generals' primary American cheerleader. Urging McGeorge Bundy to give him the latitude to continue his support for the generals, Lodge argued that "we should remember that this is the only way in which the people in Vietnam can possibly get a change in government."[18] Bundy did not reject that argument, but cautioned Lodge to "avoid direct engagement" with the plotters and to only support an effort that was likely to succeed. "An unsuccessful coup," he wrote, "however carefully we avoid direct engagement, will be laid at our door by public opinion almost everywhere."[19]

By October 29, according to Lodge, the coup was imminent. "We are not engineering the coup," Lodge assured Washington. "The sum total of our relationship thus far is: that we will not thwart a coup; that we will monitor and report."[20] Throughout, Kennedy—knowing that the momentum now belonged to the dissident generals—was little more than a bystander to the quickly unfolding events. Quoting Lodge, he told his national security advisors that the coup was "comparable to a stone rolling down hill which can't be stopped." His advice to Lodge, to whom he had ceded most of the responsibility for the U.S. role in the Saigon intrigue, was simple and direct: "tell the generals that they must prove they can pull off a successful coup or, in our opinion, it would be a mistake to proceed. If we miscalculated, we could lose our entire position in Southeast Asia overnight."[21]

On the afternoon of Friday, November 1, the generals launched their assault on the presidential palace. Earlier in the day, Diem had suddenly turned conciliatory, asking Lodge to inform Kennedy that "I take all his suggestions very seriously and wish to carry out them out, but it is a question of timing."[22] By then, it was too late. Nothing Diem could do would have discouraged the generals. At 4:30 P.M., Diem phoned Lodge to inform him that a "rebellion" was beginning.

"What is the attitude of the U.S.?" he inquired.

"I do not feel well informed enough to be able to tell you," Lodge lied.

"I have heard the shooting, but am not acquainted with all the facts." It was 4:30 A.M. in Washington, Lodge added, and the U.S. government "cannot possibly have a view."

"But you must have some general ideas," Diem pressed. "After all, I am a chief of state. I have tried to do my duty."

Lodge agreed, then inquired about Diem's safety. "If I can do anything for your physical safety, please call me."

"I am trying to reestablish order," Diem said.[23]

Earlier in the day, the generals had seized key military and communications installations around Saigon. That afternoon, they demanded that Diem and Nhu resign. But as soldiers under the command of the rebel generals marched toward the presidential palace, Diem and Nhu fled through an underground tunnel and sought refuge in the Chinese district of Saigon. That evening, after attending a Catholic mass, Diem and Nhu were found by soldiers loyal to the generals. Persuaded that their personal safety was guaranteed, the two men agreed to board an army personnel carrier. Within minutes, they were murdered.

At the White House, meanwhile, Kennedy was meeting with his national security advisors when Michael Forrestal brought in a telegram. Diem and Nhu, he informed the president, were dead, presumably by suicide. According to Taylor, Kennedy "leapt to his feet and rushed from the room with a look of shock and dismay on his face which I had never seen before."[24]

Kennedy was not alone in his apparent horror over Diem's death. In a November 4 letter, Richard Nixon told Eisenhower that "our complicity in Diem's murder was a national disgrace." The former president agreed. "No matter how much the administration may have differed with him," Eisenhower replied on November 11, "I cannot believe any American would have approved the cold-blooded killing of a man who had, after all, shown great courage when he undertook the task some years ago of defeating communist's [sic] attempts to take over his country."[25]

Diem's old friend and defender Mansfield was also "horrified" by Diem's death. While he was well aware of Diem's faults, he—like other American opponents of the coup—insisted that "I didn't see anyone who could replace Ngo Dinh Diem and expect to do any better." Thirty-five years after the fact, Mansfield still refused to believe—despite the overwhelming archival and anecdotal evidence—that Kennedy had supported Diem's ouster.[26] Mansfield later said his opposition to American involvement in Vietnam began with Diem's assassination. "I lost all hope," he said, "after Diem was assassinated."[27]

Addressing the Senate on November 5, the majority leader said the "tragic events" in Saigon would only have "constructive significance" if

American leaders recognized "that the effectiveness of our Asian policies cannot be measured by an overthrow of a government, by whether one government is 'easier to work with' than another, by whether one government smiles at us and another frowns." Mansfield argued that the success of U.S. policy in Southeast Asia should, instead, be weighed in light of several "basic questions," including, "Do these policies make possible a progressive reduction in the expenditures of American lives and aid in Vietnam?" and "Do these policies hold a valid promise of encouraging in Vietnam the growth of popularly responsible and responsive government?"[28]

George Ball, meanwhile, failed to see how any of that mattered in the long run. The man whose August 24 telegram to Lodge had encouraged the generals' plotting against Diem believed that the war was lost, with or without Diem and with or without a change in U.S. policy. While opposed to Diem's murder, Ball believed that Diem still had to go—not because he was inept, but because he was a corrupt tyrant. "The Nhus were poisonous connivers," Ball wrote in his memoirs, "and America could not, with any shadow of honor, have continued to support a regime that was destroying Vietnamese society by its murderous repression of the Buddhists."[29]

Yet Francis Valeo, Mansfield's aide and a noted Asian scholar, believed that the administration's support for Diem's overthrow, for whatever reason, was symptomatic of another disturbing shortcoming that would soon manifest itself: an abysmal misunderstanding of Vietnam's problems and an undeniable American hubris in the pursuit of a solution to those perceived problems. "We made the terrible mistake," Valeo observed, "of looking for a Vietnamese administrator in lieu of Diem who would do our bidding more readily. I think that was the root of the disaster." Whether Diem was competent was not the issue. What was instructive, Valeo believed, was how U.S. officials reacted when Diem proved reluctant to serve as the figure-head leader for Nolting, Lodge, and Harkins.

> This is quite apart from whether Diem was capable of dealing with the problems that existed in the country or not, but the course we took was bound to lead in the quite opposite direction from what we hoped. We would eventually have to find that the cost of what we were doing, in terms of lives and in terms of money, would be so ridiculously out of proportion with any national interest that we had in that area, that we would have to pull out. I think Diem understood that. We did not. We were still confusing the technique and the machinery with the purpose. And we were good, and we knew we had great equipment, and we knew we had brave soldiers, and we knew we had a very professional military force. But that was not the answer in that situation.[30]

A day or so after Diem's assassination, a ringing telephone awakened Assistant Secretary of State Roger Hilsman in the middle of the night. His friend, Marguerite Higgins, the hawkish foreign correspondent for the *New York Herald Tribune*, was on the line. "How does it feel to have blood on your hands?" she asked.

"God, Maggie, this is a revolution; people get hurt in revolutions. No way you can stop that."[31]

On November 22, exactly three weeks after Diem's death, Lee Harvey Oswald killed Kennedy in Dallas. In Vietnam, the slain president had left a tragic legacy. While Kennedy had wisely resisted the advice of his more hawkish advisors that he take a precipitous plunge into Vietnam, he had, nonetheless, presided over a sometimes naive and politically motivated policy that steadily ratcheted up the American role in Vietnam by degrees. All the while, he refused to examine fully the impossible challenges the United States faced in Vietnam and—like Eisenhower before him—preferred the soothing reassurances of his military and diplomatic advisors over the honest and discomforting reports from friends like Mansfield or the reporters in Saigon.

Under Kennedy's leadership—and with the unwitting support of most members of Congress—the nation was now heavily invested in South Vietnam's survival, having committed to the belief that the fate of Southeast Asia hung in the balance. Less than a year into his term, Kennedy dramatically altered the U.S. role when he approved increased military aid and economic support for an enterprise in which the United States and South Vietnam were to be partners. But the partnership was far from a success. Although his country had benefited from billions of American dollars and thousands of its fighting men, Diem proved a stubborn ally, almost always resisting military, political, and economic advice from the Americans. Advice was usually the strongest form of counsel that Diem received. For most of Kennedy's presidency, U.S. officials shrank from pressuring Diem to institute the kind of real reforms that might have attracted more popular support for his government. When the pressure was finally applied in 1963, the president's emissary in South Vietnam, Henry Cabot Lodge, inserted himself into the domestic political affairs of the country to an appalling and disastrous degree. In the name of saving the government, the United States engineered the overthrow and assassination of the nation's leader—and pushed its government into a downward spiral of repression, corruption, and ineptitude from which it would never recover.

Like Truman and Eisenhower before him, Kennedy firmly believed that he lacked the political freedom to ignore the perceived hegemonic lust that Communist China had for Southeast Asia. But his political calculations in Vietnam were also based on a genuine belief that the "fall" of South Vietnam to the Viet Cong would not only imperil his presidency but would be a stunning and disastrous defeat for Western democracy in general and

the United States in particular. While the U.S. military role in Vietnam
under Kennedy's watch was puny compared to the massive presence commanded by his successors—at the time of his death there were about sixteen thousand American soldiers in Vietnam—the slain president and his
advisors had made very public commitments to South Vietnam that would
not be easily reversed or revoked. Haunted by the same political ghosts as
Kennedy and also persuaded of Vietnam's importance to U.S. national
security, Lyndon Johnson was not about to change the nation's course in
Vietnam only a year before the 1964 presidential election. Kennedy's tragic
crusade in Vietnam now belonged to Johnson.

PART FOUR

ESCALATION AND DECEPTION

The United States intends no rashness, and seeks no wider war. . . . We are a people of peace—but not of weakness and timidity. I should like to repeat again that our purpose is peace.

— PRESIDENT LYNDON JOHNSON, 1964

All we say and all we do must be informed by our awareness that this horror is partly our responsibility; not just a nation's responsibility, but yours and mine. It is we who live in abundance and send our young men to die. It is our chemicals that scorch the children and our bombs that level the villages. We are all participants.

— SENATOR ROBERT F. KENNEDY, 1967

CHAPTER 23

Get In, Get Out, or Get Off

1963–1964

INSECURE AND UNSURE OF HIS STANDING WITH THE AMERICAN people, Lyndon Johnson moved quickly to solidify public and congressional support for his new administration. To Johnson, the surest route to legitimacy in those troubled, early days was to persuade Kennedy's aides to remain onboard—particularly his national security advisors. "I needed that White House staff," he later confessed. "Without them I would have lost my link to John Kennedy, and without that I would have had absolutely no chance of gaining the support of the media or the Easterners or the intellectuals. And without that support I would have had absolutely no chance of governing the country."[1] On the night of Kennedy's assassination—as he rode a helicopter from Andrews Air Force Base to the White House—a somber Johnson told McNamara, Ball, and McGeorge Bundy: "You're the men I trust the most. You must stay with me. I'll need you."[2]

Although Kennedy's men agreed to stay, absent demands from the new president they would not be inclined to suggest any fundamental changes in the country's Vietnam policy. "All these senior advisors to President Kennedy," Johnson's friend and informal advisor Clark Clifford later said, forgetting about Ball's dissent, "all felt that we were headed correctly in Vietnam."[3] Despite the changes at the top—in both Washington and South Vietnam—the faulty policy would continue to be guided by its inventors, who themselves would not pause to reexamine its basic, underlying assumptions. As McNamara mournfully noted years later, the government's senior leaders refused to rethink "the basic questions that had confronted first Eisenhower and then Kennedy: Would the loss of South Vietnam pose a threat to U.S. security serious enough to warrant extreme action to prevent it? If so, what kind of action should we take?"[4] Ball described the situation more vividly:

I felt as though an accelerating current were propelling us faster and faster toward a gigantic waterfall. Yet no one was questioning the navigation, only how to rev up the engines to make the ship run faster. "How?" was the obsessive question. How could we apply the vast power at our command to impose our will on the North Vietnamese and the Viet Cong?[5]

Johnson, particularly, was uninterested in questioning or reexamining the assumptions behind Kennedy's policies in Southeast Asia. A war was being fought and he believed the United States had to win it. "This nation," he told a joint session of Congress on November 27, "will keep its commitments from South Vietnam to West Berlin."[6] To a group of Foreign Service officers at the State Department on December 5, Johnson urged total commitment to winning the war in Vietnam. "We should all of us let no day go by," he said, "without asking whether we are doing everything we can to win the struggle there."[7]

Based on what Johnson was hearing from McNamara and others, the South Vietnamese needed the United States more than ever in late 1963. Despite hopes that Diem's successor, Major General Duong Van "Big" Minh, would impose the political and economic reforms necessary to unite the country against the Viet Cong, the results were proving far from spectacular. In the confusion following the November coup, the much-touted strategic hamlet program faltered as the Viet Cong made impressive gains in the rural areas. In the Mekong Delta, the guerrillas now controlled almost all territory outside the region's major cities. Months earlier, McNamara had believed the war was progressing so well that all American troops would be out of the country within two to three years. Now, the talk was about how many additional men would be required to save South Vietnam from collapse. Plans for the announced one thousand-man withdrawal were quietly scrapped.* "The situation is very disturbing," McNamara reported to Johnson after a trip to Vietnam in mid-December. "Current trends, unless reversed in the next 2–3 months, will lead to neutralization at best and more likely to a Communist-controlled state."[8]

Johnson would not stand for that. "When I took over," he said in a post-White House interview, "I believed that the president's [Kennedy's] policy was clear—namely, that we had a great interest in that area of the

---

*The Defense Department pretended, however, that the withdrawal had actually occurred. Although the one thousand men were withdrawn by year's end, the task was accomplished by concentrating scheduled rotations home in December. The troops were more than replaced in subsequent months. Johnson and McNamara, however, deceived Congress and the public by claiming American troop strength in South Vietnam had been reduced by one thousand (*PP*, GE, 2:303; Gibbons, 2:213).

world; that we had soberly concluded that although it involved a great chance, we should inform any would-be aggressors that if, in the face of common danger, when parties to the Southeast Asia Treaty asked for help, when they found themselves confronted with invasion or aggression or threats to their security, that we would come to their assistance."[9]

Although Johnson told his national security team on November 25 that he had strongly opposed the American role in Diem's overthrow and was not pleased by the Viet Cong success, he did not suggest any fundamental reassessment of administration policy. CIA Director John McCone's notes of the meeting indicated that instead of suggesting policy changes, Johnson lectured the group about supporting the existing policy. He told them "he wanted no more divisions of opinion, no more bickering and any person that did not conform to policy should be removed."[10] Far from questioning the wisdom of staying in Vietnam, Johnson was determined to press ahead. As Johnson told Ambassador Lodge in the November 25 meeting: "This is the only war we have."[11]

On November 26, Johnson approved National Security Action Memorandum No. 273, a reiteration of long-standing U.S. policy in Vietnam. NSAM-273 reflected the new president's unquestioning commitment to continue the war under the precepts and terms laid down by Kennedy and his advisors: "It remains the central object of the United States in South Vietnam to assist the people and Government of that country to win their contest against the externally directed and supported Communist conspiracy. The test of all U.S. decisions and actions in this area should be the effectiveness of their contribution to this purpose."[12]

Certain that the policy being advanced was wise, if not effective, Johnson concluded that the war was foundering because South Vietnam's leaders lacked not only resolve, but an American ambassador who could provide the necessary leadership. In demanding a suitable replacement for Lodge—whom Johnson blamed for pushing the coup against Diem—the president insisted on someone willing to enforce Washington's policies, not devise new strategies. "We need an able, tough guy to go out there as Chief of Mission," Johnson told Donald Cook, president of the American Electric Power Company, on November 30. "We've got to either get in or get out, or get off. And we need a damn tough cookie and somebody that can say, 'Now, this is it'—and that's got enough judgment to realize he can't make Vietnam into an America overnight. 'Cause if they do, the other damn government will fail."[13]

Although he was determined to win in Vietnam, Johnson was far from preoccupied with Southeast Asia. What time he spent on Vietnam in the early days of his administration was insignificant compared to the effort he poured into enacting a program of domestic initiatives—much of it a continuation

of Kennedy's unfinished agenda. "The president," said Ball, "turned immediately to the problem of how he could get the Kennedy program
through." By early 1964, Johnson was devoting most of his time trying to
persuade Congress to pass Kennedy's civil rights and tax cut proposals, as
well as his own massive government assault on poverty. "He was much
more intent on this than he was on the problems of Vietnam, which were
cranking along," Ball recalled.[14]

In the wake of Kennedy's death, Johnson heard hardly a peep about
Vietnam from Congress—and that encouraged him all the more to stay the
course. The simmering congressional dissent over Vietnam had quickly
cooled off in the face of more immediate and pressing domestic issues.
Although the armed conflict raged on, the embryonic public debate in
Congress would be shelved for months. McGovern, Morse, Church, and
a handful of other dissidents believed they could do nothing but wait for
the period of national mourning to pass. It seemed useless to critique
Kennedy's handling of the issue; their previous public complaints, no matter how valid and instructive, were now moot. The new president would
enjoy the period of national good will that naturally accrues to any new
president, especially one who assumes office in a time of crisis.

McGovern, for one, believed that pressing Johnson to make hasty
decisions about Vietnam was unwise. He reasoned that Johnson "was not
likely to make any fundamental changes in our overseas commitments" less
than a year before the 1964 presidential election. "So, in effect," he later
told an interviewer, "I just laid off the issue, although I continued to have
deep apprehension about it."[15]

Fulbright, Russell, and Mansfield were among the few exceptions to
the congressional tranquillity. "I don't think I would do anything," advised
Fulbright in a December 2 phone conversation with Johnson. While he
did not urge Johnson to reconsider the wisdom of the underlying policy,
Fulbright did express the dismal view that Vietnam was "a hell of a situation. It involves a lot more talk, but I'll be goddamned if I don't think it's
hopeless." While he acknowledged he was no expert on Vietnam, Fulbright nonetheless advised Johnson that "I think the whole general situation is against us, as far as a real victory goes." And, he cautioned, "You
don't want to send a whole lot more men in there, I don't think. . . . Some
things you can't do anything about unless you want to go all-out and I don't
believe you want to go all-out." Advised Russell in a December 7 conversation: "We should get out, but I don't know any way to get out."[16] Russell later recalled that on another occasion in late 1963 he advised Johnson, "I'd spend whatever it takes to bring to power a government that
would ask us to go home."[17]

Alone among Johnson's congressional confidants, Mansfield offered a different approach to Southeast Asia. He knew that the new president would soon be called upon to make critical decisions about the future course of American involvement there—and to him the new administration meant the opportunity to move the country in a different direction. Mansfield, therefore, moved quickly to advise Johnson not to increase America's military role. In a strongly worded memorandum on December 7, the majority leader urged Johnson to consider a negotiated settlement instead of a costly, ultimately unsuccessful effort at military victory. He cautioned the president not to repeat in Vietnam the mistakes Truman had made in Korea. He also attacked the conventional wisdom that maintained the war could be won by fighting in South Vietnam only. Mansfield took issue with those who believed "that the war can be won at a limited expenditure of American lives and resources somewhere commensurate with our national interests in south Viet Nam."

> There may be no war to be won in south Viet Nam alone. There may be only a war which will, in time, involve U.S. forces throughout Southeast Asia, and finally throughout China itself in search of victory. What national interests in Asia would steel the American people for the massive costs of an ever-deepening involvement of that kind? It may be that we are confronted with a dilemma not unlike that which faced us in Korea a decade ago. It will be recalled that Mr. Eisenhower's response was not to pursue the war to victory but to go to Korea to make peace, in reality, a truce.

What Mansfield wanted, in effect, was a truce that would leave South Vietnam neutral in the Cold War between the United States and the Soviet Union. In seeking such a truce, he told Johnson, he would enlist the help of India, Britain, France, and "perhaps even" the Soviets "in a bona fide effort" to end the conflict.[18] Johnson was not likely to follow that advice. To negotiate with the Communists would be a sign of weakness. The legacy of Truman's ignominious "loss" of China lingered. Eisenhower might have gone to Korea in search of peace, but Eisenhower was a genuine war hero, far more insulated from the attacks of Republicans who saw Korea as a mindless conflict caused by the blunders of Truman and Acheson. "I'm not going to lose Vietnam," Johnson told Lodge during their November meeting. "I am not going to be the president who saw Southeast Asia go the way China went."[19]

To Johnson, Mansfield's neutralization proposal was just "another name for a Communist take-over."[20] Francis Valeo, now Mansfield's top aide, gained some insight into the president's thinking in this regard when Johnson phoned him on the evening of December 18 to discuss routine legislative business. When the discussion turned to Vietnam, Johnson revealed that Truman's political troubles over China were still fresh in his mind. "Do you want that to be another China?" he asked Valeo. Without mentioning Mansfield's neutralization plan, Johnson invited Valeo to spell out his thoughts on Vietnam in a memo and, then, added: "I don't want these people around the world worrying about us, and they are. . . . They're worried about whether we've got a weak President or a strong President."[21]

Mansfield seized the solicitation of Valeo's views as an opportunity to bend Johnson's ear again on Vietnam. Returning to Washington after Christmas, he fired off a one-page memorandum that answered Johnson's rhetorical question about "another China."

> We do not want another China. I would respectfully add to this observation: Neither do we want another Korea. It would seem that a key (but often overlooked) factor in both situations was a tendency to bite off more than we were prepared in the end to chew. We tended to talk ourselves out on a limb with overstatements of our purpose and commitment only to discover in the end that there were not sufficient American interests to support with blood and treasure a desperate final plunge. Then, the question followed invariably: "Who got us into this mess" "Who lost China?" etc.
>
> We are close to the point of no return in Viet Nam. A way to avoid another Korea and, perhaps, another China may be found in the general policy approach suggested in the memo of December 7th. If so, there ought to be less official talk of our responsibility in Viet Nam and more emphasis on the responsibilities of the Vietnamese themselves and a great deal of thought on the possibilities for a peaceful solution through the efforts of other nations as well as our own.[22]

McGeorge Bundy provided a quick response. While he accepted Mansfield's China analogy, Bundy asserted that the historical evidence argued for a more aggressive effort in Vietnam. "The political damage to Truman and Acheson from the fall of China," explained the self-described "ex-historian" in a memorandum to Johnson, "arose because most Americans came to believe that we could and should have done more than we did to prevent it. This is exactly what would happen now if we should seem to be the first to quit in Saigon." Now was not the time for negotiation, he said. "*When* we are stronger, *then* we can face negotiation" (emphasis Bundy's).

Johnson treated Mansfield's proposal with deadly seriousness. Bundy's was only the first of three memoranda that Johnson sought from his senior advisors to help him refute the majority leader's call for a negotiated settlement; the other two came from Rusk and McNamara. On January 9, Bundy sent them to Johnson in a single document. "What the communists mean by 'neutralization' of South Viet-Nam," Rusk wrote, "is a regime which would have no support from the West and would be an easy prey to a communist takeover." He rejected the notion that "North Vietnam's terrorism can be called off by 'an astute diplomatic offensive' at this time." Neutralization, he cautioned, must wait until South Vietnam was stronger. "Any 'truce' which might be 'won now in Vietnam' would be bought at a price," Rusk wrote, "which I am convinced would eventually prove far more costly to us than the peace which we hope to see established there by the action of the new South Vietnamese Government."[23]

Any deal to neutralize South Vietnam, McNamara cautioned Johnson, "would inevitably mean a new government in Saigon that would in short order become Communist-dominated." Still, the Defense secretary was optimistic about Vietnam. *"The security situation is serious,"* he told Johnson, *"but we can still win,* even on present ground rules." McNamara further advised Johnson to stress that the war *"is essentially a Vietnamese responsibility,* and this we have repeatedly done, particularly in our announced policy on U.S. troop withdrawal" (emphasis McNamara's). But McNamara certainly knew that his rhetoric about South Vietnamese responsibility was specious; the thrust of his argument centered not on South Vietnamese responsibilities, but on the predominant U.S. role in Vietnam. "South Vietnam is both a test of U.S. firmness and specifically a test of U.S. capacity to deal with 'wars of national liberation,'" he said. "The stakes in preserving an anti-Communist South Vietnam are so high that, in our judgment, we must go on bending every effort to win."[24]

Not surprisingly, Johnson sided with his advisors and rejected Mansfield's advice. Politically and practically, he did not believe he could afford to explore even the possibility of a peaceful end to the conflict. Johnson and his advisors believed that any negotiated settlement resulting in a neutralized South Vietnam would only hasten the day when all of Vietnam was communist-controlled. Johnson, instead, pursued what he believed was his only viable option: a program to force the total capitulation of the Viet Cong and North Vietnam. In January, Johnson upped the pressure on North Vietnam when he approved a secret plan to intensify the conflict with covert offensive military operations. As approved by Johnson, Operations Plan (OPLAN) 34-A would place increasing pressure on North Vietnam to curtail its support of the Viet Cong. "As an example of what it contemplated," Lodge told General Minh on January 21, "there would be clandestine, aggressive and daring attacks, principally in the nature of sabotage, against the port of Haiphong; and destruction of petroleum reserves and of naval installations."[25]

To the Joint Chiefs of Staff, however, the plan fell far short of what was needed to regain the upper hand in Vietnam. On January 22, they informed McNamara of their plan to "put aside many of the self-imposed restrictions which now limit our efforts and to undertake bolder actions which may embody greater risks." The Joint Chiefs complained that the United States and South Vietnam were "fighting the war on the enemy's terms." To turn the conflict around, they urged McNamara to recommend ten changes in U.S. policy and tactics, including a drastic shift in policy that would take control of the fighting out of Vietnamese hands and give it over, "temporarily," to the U.S. military commander who would, in turn, replace the ambassador as the top U.S. official in South Vietnam. The other recommendations were just as breathtaking, including active U.S. participation in the aerial bombing of North Vietnam and assisting the South Vietnamese in conducting "large-scale commando raids" aimed at "critical targets" in the north. In addition, the Joint Chiefs recommended sending "additional US forces, as necessary," to support combat operations in the south and north.[26]

Much of the Joint Chiefs' dismay sprung from their deep dissatisfaction with "Big" Minh and the French-trained junta that had assumed power in South Vietnam after Diem's overthrow. The junta was politically inept and unable to put forward an aggressive program to rectify the nation's many political and economic problems. Thus, the war effort had stalled by early 1964. American officials were particularly alarmed when several government leaders endorsed a neutralization plan proposed by French President Charles de Gaulle and entertained by Mansfield.* On January 29, a cadre of junior officers headed by General Nguyen Khanh ousted Minh and his junta in a bloodless coup. "He [Kahn] is unquestionably pro-U.S.," Lodge advised Washington the day after the coup, "and may carry on the war more efficiently and energetically than the preceding government." In his first meeting with Khanh, Lodge bluntly told the new leader that "he would rise or fall, as far as American opinion was concerned, on the results which he obtained in the effort against [the] Viet Cong."[27]

The latest coup may have given some U.S. officials hope for a more efficient prosecution of the war. Johnson, however, understood that most Americans, especially congressional leaders, would be tempted to conclude that the U.S. military effort was in shambles. Three governments over the course of three months spelled trouble no matter how administration officials tried to explain it. In sending McNamara back to Vietnam, Johnson

---

*In 1963, de Gaulle had offered a plan that would have restored provisions of the 1954 Geneva accords, a proposal that included withdrawal of all U.S. troops, the neutralization of Vietnam, and a resumption of diplomatic relations between North and South Vietnam. Kennedy and his men, preoccupied with the day-to-day conduct of the war, had summarily rejected the proposal.

relayed this message to Khanh: "No more of this coup shit."[28] Indeed, in assessing U.S. policy after the latest coup, Mansfield had reached the very conclusions that Johnson feared. Writing on February 1, the majority leader told Johnson he doubted the coup would produce "any significant improvement in the situation" and said it was "likely to be only the second in a series, as military leaders, released from all civilian restraint, jockey for control of the power which resides in United States aid."

> If these are in fact the grim prospects, our present policies will be drained of any constructive significance for the political future of Viet Nam. We will find ourselves engaged merely in an indecisive, bloody and costly military involvement and the involvement will probably have to increase just to keep the situation as it is.
>
> This indecisive situation could persist for a long time, *provided* [emphasis Mansfield's] we are prepared to pour in the men and money which it takes to hold it together. Yet, if we are unprepared to do so, there is no real military alternative for us except an abject withdrawal. A deeper military plunge is not a real alternative. . . .
>
> We are already on the verge of turning a war in Vietnam which is still primarily a Vietnamese responsibility into an American war to be paid for primarily with American lives. I see no national interest at this time which would justify that plunge and I most emphatically do not recommend it.

To Johnson's consternation, Mansfield again made his pitch for de Gaulle's neutralization proposal. "We should not by word or action endorse the new junta's hostile attitude toward France," he wrote, "for if there is any hope of a satisfactory solution in Viet Nam and, indeed, throughout Indochina, it rests very heavily on France."[29] At a press conference later that day, Johnson summarily rejected Mansfield's advice about neutralization. "I think that if we could expect the Viet Cong to let their neighbors live in peace," Johnson said, "we could take a much different attitude." But as long as the Viet Cong persisted, Johnson said that the United States would not back down. In fact, he said, "I think the operations should be stepped up there."* Several days later, in remarks to a group of government officials, Johnson seemed to say that he not only rejected Mansfield's advice, but that he regarded his private dissent as something

---

*Years later, McNamara would acknowledge that he, Johnson, and other administration officials summarily dismissed all proposals for neutralization, believing "that there was no neural solution to the governance of South Vietnam because Hanoi and the NLF would not permit it." Yet, as McNamara also admitted, "we didn't properly analyze the *idea* of a neutral solution. It wasn't taken seriously. It was simply rejected" (emphasis McNamara's) (McNamara, *Argument Without End*, 101–2).

just short of treason. In a veiled reference to Mansfield, Johnson said that
when he became majority leader in 1955 he adopted the view that "we had
but one President and one Commander in Chief—that I would support his
policies and give him strength and comfort, and that I would not be aligning myself with any enemies of the United States in criticizing him."[30]

What Johnson would not say publicly was that he feared the political
fallout, especially in an election year, if he demonstrated anything less than
absolute resolve to fight communism in Southeast Asia. "We're there
now," he told John Knight, publisher of the *Miami Herald*, in a February 3
telephone conversation, "and there's one of three things you can do. One
is run and let the dominoes start falling over. And God Almighty, what they
said about us leaving China would just be warming up, compared to what
they'd say now."

Already, Johnson's political antennae had detected the first soundings
of a new "Who-lost-China" debate involving Vietnam. Only the day
before, Richard Nixon, a possible candidate for the Republican presidential nomination, had suggested that Johnson was less than resolute in his
opposition to de Gaulle's neutralization idea. Arizona Senator Barry Goldwater, another possible Republican opponent, had charged that Johnson's
foreign policy "fumblers" were "napping" as the conflict in Vietnam
drifted "toward disaster." Johnson was not about to open himself up to the
charge that he was weak on communism.[31]

Despite Johnson's strong, public feelings against neutralization, Mansfield continued pressing his case with the president. On the evening of
February 10, he went to the White House to meet with Johnson. Although
no record of their conversation has been found, McGeorge Bundy's advice
to Johnson, written in anticipation of the meeting, makes it clear the topic
was Vietnam. Reminding Johnson that Mansfield "continues to believe in
the de Gaulle approach," Bundy advised Johnson to tell the recalcitrant
majority leader that "any weakening of our support of anti-Communist
forces in South Vietnam would give the signal for a wholesale collapse of
anti-Communism all over Southeast Asia." Bundy suggested Johnson
might wish to "urge Mansfield himself not to express his own doubts in
public, at least for a while."[32]

If Johnson followed this advice and urged Mansfield to keep his dissent to himself, the president's counsel was promptly ignored. Johnson and
his advisors could not have been pleased by the strongly worded speech
Mansfield delivered in the Senate on February 19. It was time, he said, for
the United States to reassess its policy in Vietnam. "We have given extraordinary support to two successive governments in Vietnam," he said. "We
can do no more and should try to do no more for a third." The war, he said,
should not be turned into an American enterprise. "There is no national

interest at this time," he said, "which would appear to justify this conversion." While commending Johnson's commitment to helping the South Vietnamese "find a way to stability and peace," he praised de Gaulle for his "sense of history and statesmanship in seeking new ways for dealing with the continuing instability and insecurity" in Southeast Asia. Mansfield warned against dismissing de Gaulle's neutralization proposal "out of hand," as Johnson had already done.

> Indeed, we might well ask ourselves: Do we ourselves, in terms of our national interests as seen in juxtaposition to the cost in American lives and resources, prefer what exists in South Vietnam to what exists in Laos or Cambodia? Do we prefer another Vietnamese type of American involvement or perhaps a Korean-type involvement in these other countries and elsewhere in Southeast Asia? Are we eager for expenditure of the great additions of foreign aid, which they would entail? Are we to regard lightly the American casualties which would certainly be involved?[33]

Mansfield's public pronouncements on Southeast Asia almost always caused ripples that extended to Vietnam. This speech was no exception. "Mansfield's statement strengthened a growing body of opinion among Vietnamese and Americans here that the United States is sick of this war and is looking for a way out," Associated Press correspondent Malcolm Browne reported from Saigon. Judging by the reaction of at least one American official in Saigon, the Johnson administration was also sick of Mansfield's public advice. Although Browne reported no official U.S. or Vietnamese reaction to Mansfield's speech, he quoted a "top American official"—probably Lodge or Harkins—who observed: "Of course it wasn't the Senator's intention to give aid and comfort to the Communists and undermine Vietnamese and American morale. But that's exactly what he did. And he couldn't have done a better job if his speech had been written in Hanoi."[34]

As historian Lloyd C. Gardner later observed, "a pattern of dealing with dissent" was developing in the Johnson administration that "would continue throughout the Vietnam War." Despite Mansfield's impressive knowledge about Southeast Asia and his important leading role in the Senate, Johnson considered his advice "tainted," wrote Gardner, "because the Senate majority leader looked favorably upon Charles de Gaulle's proposals."[35] Over the next five years Johnson would tolerate Mansfield's opinions, and sometimes actively solicit his advice, but would rarely heed his counsel—despite that fact that experience would quickly prove the majority leader a wise and prescient advisor.

At least two of Johnson's allies in the House and Senate wasted no time challenging Mansfield. Democrat Clement Zablocki of Wisconsin, chairman of the House Far East Subcommittee, told his colleagues that "we cannot give way—or appear to give way before the expansionist policies of Communist China. Instead, we must make our stand in Vietnam as long as the freedom-loving people of that nation ask our assistance in this joint endeavor against communism."[36] The same day, Republican Senator Jacob Javits of New York—a self-described "ardent supporter of the Vietnam War"[37]—challenged Mansfield directly, although respectfully, when he insisted that "the minute we begin to talk about neutralization and neutralism, the backbone and spirit could go out of the action which is being taken in this struggle." Javits' remarks to the Senate reflected the predominant view about America's role in Vietnam among members of the House and Senate, especially those with vivid memories of the vitriolic debates over China and Korea more than a decade earlier:

> Let us remember that even a great nation must suffer casualties currently in order to avoid even greater casualties later. The present position in south and southeast Asia—representing still a rampart against the absolutely uncontrolled expansion of Communist China, which preaches to all its people that its ultimate aim is the destruction not only of the free world, but specifically the United States of America and its people—it seems to me is only insurance against a future which seems so foreboding in terms of the intentions at the moment which Communist China declared and reiterated for so very long.

Responding to Javits, Mansfield made it clear—his private counsel to Kennedy in 1962 notwithstanding—that he did not want the United States to withdraw from South Vietnam. That, he said, would be a "mistake, because then South Vietnam and the rest of southeast Asia would be placed at the mercy of elements connected with the Communist movement." Mansfield insisted that he was merely suggesting that the Johnson administration consider an "alternative" to escalation or withdrawal. Whether neutralization would work, he said, "no one can tell. But if any stability is to be brought to South Vietnam, it is not going to be done on the basis of coup after coup after coup."[38]

At the White House, a frustrated Johnson struggled with ways to bring his wayward majority leader back onto the reservation. The day after Mansfield's February 20 speech, the president told McNamara of his plan to use the just-retired Marine Corps commandant, General David Shoup, to influence Mansfield. Johnson knew that Mansfield respected Shoup and suggested that the defense secretary include Shoup on his upcoming trip to Vietnam. "I would put a stop to Mansfield's speaking up there every day on it," Johnson said, "and Shoup would put a stop to it." After his return, Johnson expected Shoup to go to Capitol Hill "and tell these boys some things."[39]

In his determination not to change the basic equation in Vietnam—to follow what Rusk called "the middle track"[40]—Johnson was not simply heeding the advice of advisors like McNamara, Bundy, and Rusk. While these men had, indeed, advised Johnson against any sudden moves—withdrawal, embarking on a drastic escalation of the American military presence, or following Mansfield's counsel about a negotiated settlement—the president had other important reasons for wanting to preserve the status quo. In the first instance, his reluctance to take drastic action in Vietnam was a result of his frustration with a situation over which he had little control and even less understanding. He simply did not know which way to turn. Every alternative offered little hope. Second, Johnson knew that to enact his legislative agenda he must keep Congress focused on domestic affairs. Foreign policy, particularly a contentious debate over Vietnam, must not intrude. Yet, more than anything, Johnson's caution on Vietnam reflected a fundamental political judgment that the safest route to election in 1964 was to defer all major decisions on Vietnam until after November. He simply would not allow Nixon, Goldwater, or other potential Republican challengers to use Vietnam against him. That meant staying the course—a prospect that looked increasingly difficult from the perspective of early 1964.

"I just can't believe that we can't take fifteen thousand advisers and two hundred thousand [South Vietnamese soldiers] and maintain the status quo for six months," Johnson complained to McGeorge Bundy on March 2, adding that "I don't know enough about it to know." That evening, Johnson expressed his frustration again, this time to Fulbright. "The only thing I know to do," Johnson said, "is more of the same and do it more efficiently." Fulbright agreed. "That's exactly what I'd arrive at under the circumstances," he replied, "at least for the foreseeable future." Johnson, however, feared he might not be able to hold the line until after the election. Referring to McNamara's upcoming trip to Vietnam, Johnson worried aloud: "Now, when he comes back, though, and we're losing what we're doing, we got to decide whether to send them in or whether to come out and let the dominoes fall. That's were the tough one's going to be."[41]

Two days later, Johnson met with the Joint Chiefs of Staff and heard their recommendations for a program of military actions aimed at North Vietnam. "The President accepted the need for punishing Hanoi without debate," Joint Chiefs Chairman Taylor wrote in a memorandum following the meeting. But Taylor also noted that Johnson "pointed to some other practical difficulties, particularly the political ones with which he was faced." He observed that it was "quite apparent" that Johnson "does not want to lose South Vietnam before next November nor does he want to get the country into war."[42]

While Johnson fretted over how to avoid losing the war without losing the presidency, Mansfield continued speaking out. This time, he urged
the president to inform the American people about the long-term risks
involved in Vietnam. "The American people had better become fully aware
of exactly what confronts us" in Vietnam, he declared in the Senate on
March 3. "The truth will hurt no one. The truth should and must be told."
As for the role of Congress in setting U.S. foreign policy, however, Mansfield expressed the minimalist view that would characterize his subdued
dissent over Vietnam for the rest of Johnson's presidency: "All we can do
here is discuss the matter."[43]

As usual, Morse was far more direct and willing to announce, unlike
Mansfield, that U.S. troops should be withdrawn from Vietnam. Furthermore, Morse also believed Congress—and indirectly, the public—had a far
more instrumental role to play in the creation of U.S. policy in Vietnam.
On March 3, in a closed-door session of the Foreign Relations Committee,
the Oregon Democrat—persuaded that public opinion would quickly turn
in favor of withdrawal—pointedly urged Rusk to "get some facts out to the
American people on South Vietnam."[44] Two days later, in a Senate speech,
Morse returned to the same theme. "Those troops should be brought
home," he said. "They never should have been sent there in the first place.
American unilateral participation in the war of South Vietnam cannot be
justified, and will not be justified in American history." Morse continued:
"As I have made clear to the State Department, this administration had bet-
ter be warned now that when the casualty lists of American boys in South
Vietnam increase until the mothers and fathers of those boys—and, yes, the
American people generally—start crying 'Murder,' no administration will
stand."[45] Morse was not alone in his strong feelings about a continued
American presence in Vietnam. When he finished, Democrat Allen Ellender of Louisiana rose to offer his support. "We should never have gone in
there," he said, adding that "we should get out."[46]

Another vocal opponent of the U.S. role in Vietnam was Democrat
Ernest Gruening of Alaska, a devout liberal and, like Morse, a maverick
who passionately opposed American involvement in Vietnam. At 77, Gruening had lived a fascinating and multifaceted life. Born in New York City,
Alaska's future senator graduated from Harvard's medical school, but never
practiced medicine. Instead, he chose the more exhilarating life of a newspaper reporter and editor for papers in New York, Massachusetts, and
Maine. A disciple of President Franklin Roosevelt, Gruening had a firm
commitment to liberalism, which finally led him into public service in the
mid-1930s, when he accepted a top position in Roosevelt's Interior
Department. In 1939, Roosevelt appointed him governor of the Alaska territory, where he soon became a leading voice for Alaskan statehood. When

the territory became the forty-ninth state in 1959, citizens sent the independent Gruening to Washington. In the Senate, he quickly earned a reputation as an intense and outspoken champion of causes like civil rights and public health.[47]

By late 1963, along with his close friend Morse, Gruening had concluded that continued American involvement in Vietnam was unwise. In October, shortly after McGovern had spoken out in the Senate, Gruening also gave voice to his concerns:

> I consider every additional life that is sacrificed in this forlorn venture a tragedy. Some day—not distant—if this sacrificing continues, it will be denounced as a crime.
>
> I would like to ask my colleagues and indeed American fathers and mothers this question: If your drafted son is sent to Vietnam and is killed there would you feel that he had died for our country?
>
> I can answer that question for myself. I would feel very definitely that he had not died for our country, but had been mistakenly sacrificed in behalf of an inherited folly.

Johnson, he noted, "inherited this mess" and, therefore, "should feel no compunction to act in such a way as to justify past actions, past decisions and past mistakes." He urged Johnson "to take steps necessary to disengage the United States immediately" from Vietnam.[48] Morse, who was present in the Senate chamber for the first part of Gruening's speech, interrupted to offer his encouragement. "It is about time the American people awakened to what is going on in South Vietnam," Morse said, "and recognize that South Vietnam is beyond the perimeter of American defense." In his strongest words of condemnation to date, Morse added: "There is no justification for murdering a single American boy in South Vietnam, for the issue has now become one of murder."[49] Afterwards, according to Gruening, Richard Russell congratulated Gruening for his remarks. In a letter to Johnson the next day, Gruening proudly touted the support he had received from Johnson's close friend, the Armed Services Committee chairman. "I was pleased," he wrote, "that Dick Russell warmly congratulated me on this speech and said he agreed with me completely."[50]

The day after Gruening's speech, Democrat Thomas Dodd of Connecticut came to Johnson's defense in a speech he entitled, "South Vietnam: Last Chance for Freedom in Asia." Dodd, who would become one of Johnson's most reliable defenders in the Senate, maintained that if South Vietnam fell to the Communists, the Pacific would become a "Red ocean." Neutralization, he said, was only a "dishonest substitute for unconditional surrender." Dodd believed the United States should fight more aggressively—and he echoed advice that Johnson was receiving from the Joint Chiefs, to initiate guerrilla operations against the North Vietnamese coast and air strikes against targets in the north.[51]

By late March, Johnson knew he must decide on a course and hope it would carry him safely through the election. McNamara and Taylor had just returned from another visit to Vietnam, and the defense secretary reported that "the situation has unquestionably been growing worse" since the previous September. The Viet Cong now dominated as much as 40 percent of the countryside. In more than half of the nation's provinces, the Viet Cong controlled more than half of the land area; in several they controlled 90 percent. "Large groups of the population," he reported to Johnson, "are now showing signs of apathy and indifference, and there are some signs of frustration within the U.S. contingent." The greatest weakness, however, was the Khanh government, which McNamara said had neither wide political appeal nor control of the country's armed forces. Morale and organization in the government was down and the constant threat of another coup persisted.

To counter the growing Viet Cong influence, while also seeking to boost morale in the Khanh regime, McNamara recommended a wide-ranging program of stepped-up measures. Among his recommendations: provide funds and training assistance necessary to increase South Vietnam's army by fifty thousand men to a total of about three hundred fifty thousand; use U.S. planes to patrol the Cambodian and Laotian borders to prevent infiltration of men and supplies from North Vietnam; and authorize "hot pursuits" into Laos to secure the country's border. McNamara also gave Johnson another option, although he stopped short of recommending its implementation. It was a proposal to send U.S. planes into North Vietnam airspace to apply what he called "graduated overt military pressure" on the North Vietnamese. "This program would go beyond reacting on a tit-for-tat basis," McNamara reported. "It would include air attacks against military and possibly industrial targets." While McNamara advised against initiating a gradually escalating bombing campaign—he knew well that Johnson would not have approved it under any circumstance—he nonetheless had, for the first time, injected the idea into the debate. He recommended that Johnson at least order U.S. forces "to be in a position" to initiate bombing of North Vietnamese targets "on 30 days notice."[52]

Johnson approved McNamara's plan on March 17, although Taylor had cautioned that the Joint Chiefs of Staff feared "it may not be sufficient to save the situation."[53] In fact, there was a strong current of dissent running through the Pentagon and the American military headquarters in Saigon. Several military leaders believed McNamara's reasoning—that the United States should consider a bombing campaign only when the Khanh government became stronger or when evidence indicated a surge in Viet Cong supplies from the north—was faulty. In a memorandum to Mc-George Bundy, Forrestal reported that the Joint Chiefs favored "strong overt action against the North." Forrestal also informed Bundy that General Rollen Anthis, the top Air Force commander in Saigon, had been quoted telling associates that if the United States could not "make the high jumps in South Vietnam, then we should pole-vault into the North." Forrestal reported a growing sentiment among some Pentagon officers that "the decision not to attack the North was made because President Johnson did not wish to face a domestic political crisis before the election."[54]

Still conflicted and unsure about Vietnam, Johnson opted for a program that simply poured more resources and energy into a strategy that had already proven to be a failure. Politically, however, he saw no other way. He determined to do his best to steer the conflict through the treacherous, uncertain middle ground between neutralization and escalation. What he did not want was criticism on the Senate floor from members of his own party—Mansfield, Morse, Gruening, and others. Their dissent only fed the fires of public discontent. Worse, it played into Republican hands by reminding people that Vietnam was slowing slipping into the grip of the Communists under Johnson's watch. "I had moments of deep discouragement," Johnson later recalled, "times when I felt the South Vietnamese were their own worst enemies. But I felt even more impatience with those who were always ready only to criticize."[55]

Johnson had never counted his friend Bill Fulbright among those annoying critics. For the longest time, in fact, Fulbright had kept his own counsel about Vietnam. When given, the Foreign Relations Committee chairman's advice to Johnson was affirming and supportive. But now he was about to alter course. Not that he planned to oppose Johnson or support Mansfield's call for neutralization. What Fulbright had in mind might, in the long run, provide even more of a challenge to Johnson's Vietnam policies by questioning the fundamental premise of American military involvement in Southeast Asia.

Fulbright was no expert on Indochina. "I didn't know anything about Vietnam at the time," he later confessed.[56] What he was, however, was one of the Senate's most daring intellectuals, that rare breed of politician given to periods of deep philosophical thought about the direction of the nation's foreign policy. Unlike many of his colleagues, and certainly many officials in the State Department, Fulbright believed the Senate floor was the nation's premier arena for debating and discussing America's relationships with the rest of the world.

On the afternoon of March 25, as the Senate debated civil rights legislation, Fulbright rose to make a bold and highly publicized address that directly challenged the Cold War assumptions on which the United States had built its foreign policy. In the speech, entitled "Old Myths and New Realities," Fulbright argued that the United States must find a new way to deal with the communist world. "We are confronted with a complex and fluid world situation," Fulbright said, "and we are not adapting to it. We are clinging to old myths in the face of new realities, and we are seeking to escape the contradictions by narrowing the permissible bounds of public discussion, by relegating an increasing number of ideas to a growing category of 'unthinkable thoughts.'" Among the thoughts Fulbright labeled "unthinkable" was the "master myth of the cold war" that held that "the Communist bloc is a monolith composed of governments which are not really governments at all, but organized conspiracies" dedicated to the destruction of "the free world." Although Fulbright acknowledged that communism was, indeed, hostile to the free world, he urged his colleagues to recognize the "great variations in its intensity and character both in time and among the individual members of the Communist bloc."

As he closed his remarks, Fulbright turned to Vietnam. The situation there, he said, "poses a far more pressing need for a reevaluation of American policy." Yet while so daring in his assessment of U.S. policy in other areas of the world, here Fulbright had little advice for Johnson. He opposed withdrawal and, therefore, saw only three options open to the administration: continuing the current effort with "renewed American efforts to increase the military effectiveness" of the South Vietnamese army; attempting to end the war through negotiation for Vietnam's neutralization; or expanding the war "either by the direct commitment of large numbers of American troops or by equipping the South Vietnamese Army to attack" the north. Ruling out negotiation, Fulbright concluded the only two alternatives open to Johnson were expansion of the U.S. effort or bolstering the capacity of the South Vietnamese. He did not say which he preferred.[57]

Fulbright's provocative speech made national and international news. "It was one of the most important foreign policy statements made by any Senator in this decade," raved columnist Drew Pearson.[58] The *New York Times* cited Fulbright's remarks as "refreshing evidence of what we hope is a new flexibility in foreign affairs and a willingness . . . to get away from blindly accepted cliches."[59] While praise for Fulbright's well-publicized thoughts came from other quarters, including as far away as the Soviet Union, his notions about an American foreign policy flexible enough to adapt to "new realities" did not sit well with some leading Republicans and the more conservative press. Ironically, the partisan attacks, far from opening Johnson's mind about a new approach in Vietnam, may actually have persuaded the president that his political judgment—that any movement toward negotiation or withdrawal would spark partisan cries of appeasement—was sound.

In the Senate, Republican senators John Tower of Texas and Strom Thurmond of South Carolina charged Fulbright with "appeasement."[60] Conservative nationally syndicated columnist David Lawrence wrote that "Senator Fulbright's speech represents a point of view of many persons inside and outside our government who believe, as Chamberlain did in 1938, that a little bit of appeasement can never be harmful or bring on a war."[61] Equally conservative, the *St. Louis Globe-Democrat* observed that Fulbright's "hypothetical 'realism' is indeed a hard realism—the realism of defeat. He had become the left-wing establishment's poobah of appeasement."[62]

At the White House, an angry Johnson seethed. Only days earlier, he and Fulbright had dined together. Fulbright had given him no inkling that he was about to make a speech of that magnitude. Now, the chairman of the Republican National Committee, William Miller, was suggesting that Fulbright's remarks were "a trial balloon which the Johnson administration is sending up to prepare public opinion for the acceptance of a foreign policy that could only lead to disaster for the United States and other free nations."[63]

From the moment news of the speech hit the wire services, Johnson knew what lay in store. "I feel mighty blue over Bill Fulbright's speech today," he told Democratic Senator Spessard Holland of Florida.

"I suppose that was done at your suggestion," Holland replied.

An angry Johnson shot back: "Oh, hell! . . . We have just gotten over Mike's [Mansfield] speech on neutralizing Vietnam and pulling out and now Bill gets up and makes a speech."

Minutes later, on the phone with McGeorge Bundy, Johnson complained that Holland believed the speech had been a trial balloon for the administration. "They all assume that Fulbright speaks for the administration," he told Bundy, adding later that "Fulbright is that way, though. He's a very unpredictable man. . . . As Truman said one time, he's 'half bright'!"[64]* Little did Johnson know just how vexing Fulbright would become—over Vietnam and other foreign policy issues. In fact, in little more than a year, the senator whom he had once considered among his closest friends in the Senate, the man that majority leader Johnson had once called "my secretary of state," would turn his back on Johnson in a very public way.

---

*That derisive moniker had actually been coined by Joseph McCarthy, not Truman.

CHAPTER 24

The Damn Worst Mess I Ever Saw

1964

CONVINCED THAT AMERICAN INVOLVEMENT IN VIETNAM WAS A ghastly mistake, Wayne Morse turned up the heat on the Johnson administration. Day after day, from March through June, the intrepid Oregon Democrat filled the Senate chamber with condemnations of what he began to call "McNamara's war." McNamara, far from objecting, proudly accepted the appellation. "I think it's a very important war," the defense secretary told a reporter, "and I am pleased to be identified with it and do whatever I can to win it." Morse, of course, had not meant to flatter the Pentagon chief. "Well, at long last we have smoked him out," Morse declared when he learned of McNamara's remark. "We now have an admission from the Secretary of Defense that this nation is engaged in war."[1]*

In all, during the spring of 1964, Morse's fiery speeches on Vietnam filled over two hundred pages of the *Congressional Record*. Seeking to preach his dissent to citizens outside Washington, Morse began barnstorming the country and delivered dire warnings about the consequences of America's military adventure.[2] It was a lonely, but brave battle. Except for Gruening and Louisiana's Allen Ellender, Morse had no allies willing to join him at the barricades. A few Democrats—McGovern, Church, and Olin Johnston of South Carolina—offered muted, private encouragement, but nothing more. McGovern's cautious attitude was typical. "I was concerned," the South Dakota Democrat explained, "about not doing anything that would unfairly put pressure on Johnson at a time when I thought he more than

---

*McGovern believed that Morse tried to make McNamara a villain in order to preserve his relationship with Johnson. "I think Morse . . . was reluctant to take Johnson head on," McGovern said, noting that Morse rarely flailed the president in his many tirades against the war. "He kind of liked Johnson" (McGovern, by Mann, 9/10/97).

had his hands full."[3] Johnson's only Republican critics, meanwhile, were senators and congressmen dissatisfied by the president's unwillingness to take the fight directly to the North Vietnamese. "We should either pull out and stop losing our men over there," said Margaret Chase Smith of Maine, "or we should go in and clean up."[4]

Most senators, the *New York Times* concluded after an informal survey in late March, "reluctantly support the present Administration policy for lack of acceptable alternatives." That, as the White House knew, was certainly no ringing endorsement of Johnson's policies. "Supporters as well as critics are deeply apprehensive and edgy over the policy's failure," reporter John D. Morris concluded, adding that Johnson's supporters "confess to a sense of frustration and a lack of optimism over prospects of satisfactory results." But on at least one matter most of Johnson's Senate "supporters" were clear: while they opposed withdrawal of the U.S. forces currently in South Vietnam, they would not back any plan to commit U.S. "advisory forces" to an active combat role.

According to Mansfield, one of the few senators willing to be quoted for the *Times* story, the "only feasible choice" for most of Johnson's Senate allies was to accept the White House plan to increase the U.S. role in South Vietnam with the understanding "that we are not escalating the war and we are not pulling out." Johnson's plan, Mansfield explained, repeating a phrase heard repeatedly over the past three years, "places emphasis on the fact that this is a Vietnamese war and it must be won by the Vietnamese." Another senator quoted was Fulbright who, Morris noted, "has some reservations about the conduct of American policy in Vietnam." But Fulbright was unwilling to share those reservations with the *Times*. "I don't think senators spouting off helps the situation," Fulbright said, explaining that he was urging his colleagues to communicate their concerns privately to Johnson. Mansfield, meanwhile, encouraged more, not less, public discussion. In a comment that undoubtedly worried a president who was interested in less, not more public debate, the majority leader predicted there would be "plenty of debating on Vietnam before the year is out."[5]

As far as Morse was concerned, the debate had already begun. On March 26, after McNamara and Taylor went behind closed doors with the Foreign Relations Committee to explain the administration's plan to increase pressure on the North Vietnamese, Morse—in his typically vituperative style—caustically dismissed the Defense secretary's testimony as "even more unsound than I thought he could concoct by way of a chain of fallacies." Disturbed by McNamara's refusal to acknowledge the true extent of U.S. involvement in Vietnam, Morse later told the Senate, that "by subterfuge and the pretense that we are not at war, we nevertheless are conducting operations that are killing American men in South Vietnam."

Morse also challenged the notion that U.S. forces were in Vietnam fighting outside communist aggression. "There are no Chinese soldiers in
South Vietnam," he said. "There are no Russian soldiers in South Vietnam. The only foreign soldiers in South Vietnam are U.S. soldiers."

Morse's vocal denunciations of the nation's role in Vietnam had begun
to attract the attention of a few informed dissenters in the Pentagon. In his
March 26 speech, Morse referred to a "Marine Corps officer of substantial
rank" who had called on him earlier in the day to express his "complete
agreement" with Morse's views on Vietnam. He claimed that he also had
the support of "some of the high-ranking officers in Vietnam who are
charged with directing local troops in their operations against the Viet
Cong" and added that he had received "some interesting correspondence
from them." Morse said the Marine officer had told him that morale among
American forces in Vietnam "is at a seriously low ebb" because of "unsound"
U.S. policy. "We are acting as though we are not at war," Morse said the
officer told him, "but we are killing men as though we were at war."[6]

Unusual among senators in 1964, Morse made clear publicly that he
did not trust McNamara, Taylor, and other Pentagon spokesmen, or the
information they supplied the Foreign Relations Committee. Frustrated
that so many of his colleagues had "abandoned" their responsibilities "for
the big things" in favor of "making the most of the small things," Morse—
speaking at Utah State College—scolded members of Congress who he
said "fear to question the Pentagon brass, the State Department, and the
Central Intelligence Agency."[7]

He put the Pentagon on notice that he would continue monitoring its
activities. On March 30, he informed the Senate that "one of the leading
correspondents" had told him of a "subtle move at the Pentagon" to
involve "American guerilla fighters" in South Vietnam. Although he noted
that the Pentagon had denied the allegation, Morse warned that "I intend
to watchdog the Pentagon day by day for a constant check on its maneuvers."[8] The next day, from the Senate floor, Morse importuned Russell, the
Armed Services Committee chairman, to obtain from the Defense Department "all information as to what its plans are, to the extent that any plans
exist, [for] sending more American Armed Forces to South Vietnam." Russell gamely said he would try and reminded Morse that he had always
opposed American military involvement in Vietnam.[9]

By early April, Morse's withering attacks had finally taxed the patience
of South Vietnam's leader, Nguyen Khanh, who told a reporter that Morse
was "a traitor of the American people" for his pointed criticism of the U.S.
effort. Morse retorted that Khanh was nothing but "a tinhorn soldier
tyrant whom the Government of the United States is supporting in an
unjustifiable war."[10]

The next day, Johnson invited Morse and other congressional leaders to attend a meeting of the National Security Council during which McNamara briefed the lawmakers about Johnson's decision, made in mid-March, to intensify the U.S. effort in South Vietnam. As he sat at the table, an incredulous Morse listened to McNamara describe the worsening situation in Vietnam. The Viet Cong, the Defense secretary said, now controlled 40 percent of South Vietnam, and the populace was becoming more apathetic toward the war, thereby increasing the military desertion rate. Many strategic hamlets had been overrun or disbanded. McNamara, Morse believed, had just made the case for withdrawal or for a negotiated settlement. But to his surprise, McNamara reviewed the available policy options, saying that only two viable alternatives remained. The United States could "broaden ... the military campaign by taking the war to other areas, such as North Vietnam," he said, adding that this option had been "seriously considered." But the course that "we have chosen to follow," McNamara reported, was that of making "the present program of assistance more effective." Although McNamara said that Khanh did not favor "broadening the military action," he noted that the Joint Chiefs believed "that to be successful in South Vietnam the war would have to be taken to North Vietnam."

Characteristically, Morse spoke up. He disagreed entirely with McNamara's program for Vietnam, he said. The only way to solve the problem, he insisted, was to work for a "peaceful settlement" involving the United Nations and the countries who were parties to the SEATO treaty. Annoyed by Morse's impertinence, Johnson replied that he had no intention of trying to undermine Morse's position or involve him in the administration's policies. But Morse was still stinging from Khanh's charge of treason. Having demanded some official response from the U.S. government the previous day, Morse seemed to imply that Johnson's unwillingness to defend him to Khanh was a tacit approval of the South Vietnamese leader's views on Morse's patriotism. Johnson's tart reply was that "no one in this room has called you a traitor."

But Morse was alone in his dissent. When Republican Senate leader Everett Dirksen wondered if seeking SEATO intervention, as Morse had suggested, was a viable option, Mansfield observed—perhaps forgetting his once enthusiastic support for SEATO—that the treaty organization was only a "paper tiger." Despite his own earlier calls for a negotiated settlement, Mansfield meekly shrunk from a direct challenge to Johnson. He offered Morse no comfort. Johnson's policy toward Vietnam, the majority leader said, was "the only one we could follow."[11]

In a speech to the Senate a week later, Morse described the NSC meeting. "I was never so depressed," he said. As he listened to McNamara's bleak assessment of the conflict, Morse said that "I kept saying to myself, 'If all these things are true, what in the world are we doing here?' [McNamara] had made the greatest statement in support of our getting out of South Vietnam, and ended by urging that we go in to a greater extent. That is the kind of mental gymnastics that I do not understand."[12]

McNamara's grim assessment of the situation in South Vietnam was no exaggeration. But the intensification of U.S. assistance that resulted from it appeared to have little effect. Despite considerable U.S. assistance, Khanh's government remained weak and ineffectual. Desperate to keep his shaky government from total collapse, the South Vietnamese leader—previously opposed to taking the war to the north—now changed course. When Rusk visited Saigon in mid-April, a now-bellicose Khanh suggested it was time to move northward. Rusk responded that a foray into North Vietnam would require a firmer base in the south. Furthermore, attacking North Vietnam might draw China into the war. Rusk said he feared a wider war might force the United States to consider using nuclear weapons. Unfazed, Khanh replied that "as far as he was concerned we could use anything we wanted against China."[13]

Ambassador Lodge seemed to share what one State Department official described as Khanh's "sense of despair and . . . panic."[14] In early May, the South Vietnamese general asked Lodge about the wisdom of placing the country on a war footing. The ambassador envisioned a Saigon similar to Washington during the Civil War. "The suspension of certain civil rights," he explained, would be necessary. Lodge told Khanh that his personal opinion was that "winning the war must come first. Afterwards, there would be plenty of time to go ahead with democratic reforms."[15] A few days later, in a cable to Johnson, Lodge warned of a steadily deteriorating situation in South Vietnam. Raising the specter of "another Dien Bien Phu," Lodge worried that "a massive Communist success . . . could end the war as a Communist victory if the US were not to react promptly." Lodge now thought it possible for North Vietnam to "seize the northern provinces" in South Vietnam. Thus, he warned the president that quick action—in other words, a massive retaliatory response—might "make all the difference between either holding or losing South Vietnam."[16]

Johnson was concerned—and very frustrated. "Let's get some more of something, my friend," he told McNamara on April 30, "because I'm going to have a heart attack if you don't get me something. I just sit here every day. And this war . . . I'm not doing much about fighting it. I'm not doing much about winning it. I just read about it." Nothing had changed much, he said, since 1954. "What I want is somebody that can lay up some plans to trap those guys and whup the hell out of them, and kill some of them."[17]

The "new plans" that Johnson had in mind, however, did not involve attacking North Vietnam. He and McNamara knew that in a volatile election year such a precipitous move would be politically risky—especially if escalating the war failed to have the desired effect. Johnson was walking a political tightrope. If he failed to escalate, he would incur the wrath of conservative Republicans and Democrats—the so-called Cold War hawks.

Yet Johnson knew that heeding the belligerent advice of his Joint Chiefs presented just as many and perhaps greater risks. He might wind up with another Korea-style conflict that involved Chinese troops. In any event, no one could guarantee that bombing North Vietnam would persuade Ho Chi Minh to withdraw his support for the Viet Cong. Moreover, there was no guarantee that turning up the heat in the north would have any effect at all in the south. Johnson knew that the current "inaction" might eventually pale compared to the inconclusive outcome of taking the war north. He understood that bombing North Vietnam might not end the war, only widen it—at considerable cost to the United States in lives and money. Just as depressing, a wider war would only spark a vigorous congressional debate and divert attention—and money—away from his civil rights and Great Society initiatives.

Worried about Khanh's sudden bellicosity, Johnson sent McNamara, Taylor, and several State Department officials back to Saigon in mid-May. They found an American ambassador just as bellicose toward North Vietnam as Khanh. Lodge told William Sullivan, Rusk's special assistant for Vietnam, that he favored a "steady escalation" of clandestine military operations against North Vietnam—the OPLAN 34-A program earlier approved by Johnson—that would eventually include "air strikes" against targets in the north. Sullivan recalled that when he skeptically asked who should fly the planes, Lodge was indifferent. It mattered not, he said, "so long as they were proficient and capable of pinpoint accuracy." If questioned, Lodge said, the United States should deny any role in the attacks.[18]*

McNamara and Taylor, meanwhile, met with Harkins, the MACV commander, and his deputy and soon-to-be successor, Lieutenant General William Westmoreland. Despite the overwhelming evidence that he was fighting a losing battle, Harkins was typically buoyant. He told his visitors that "acceptable control will have been established everywhere except in the [Mekong] Delta," which might take until the end of 1965. But Westmoreland was far more realistic. Gaining control of the countryside north

---

*A measure of Lodge's willingness to plunge the United States headlong into the war in Vietnam was his comment to McNamara that "if Khanh disappears, the U.S. should be prepared to run the country, possibly from Cam Ranh Bay" (*FRUS*, 1964–68, 1:327).

of Saigon would take at least a year, while success in the delta was two or three years away.[19] In short, nothing appeared to have changed. "The Viet Cong continue to hold the initiative," McNamara observed in his notes for a report to Johnson.[20]

Upon McNamara's return to Washington, Johnson convened another meeting of his National Security Council and invited a group of Democratic and Republican congressional leaders to attend. Johnson told them he was "extremely alarmed" by the "deteriorating" situation in South Vietnam. "Even with increased U.S. aid," he said, "the prospect in South Vietnam is not bright."[21] The extra assistance he proposed to send to Vietnam was not insubstantial. On May 15, Johnson announced that he would ask Congress to appropriate $125 million in additional economic and military aid—in addition to the $500 million already proposed for South Vietnam in the 1965 fiscal year. Publicly, though, Johnson was upbeat. "I share with Ambassador Lodge the conviction that this new Government can mount a successful campaign against the Communists."[22]

If Johnson hoped to demonstrate his determination to continue supporting the South Vietnamese, Republicans in Congress were not persuaded. To Representative William Broomfield of Michigan, such a puny appropriations request was symbolic of Johnson's unwillingness to fight aggressively enough to win in Vietnam. In late May, Broomfield offered a resolution challenging Johnson to use all means possible to gain the upper hand in Vietnam. "There should remain not the slightest doubt as to the determination of the United States Government to pursue this course of action," the resolution said, "and to fully inform the American people of what will be necessary to defend freedom in South Vietnam and Southeast Asia." In the Senate, Republican Leader Dirksen complained that the administration's "indecision" regarding Vietnam was "dribbling away both American lives and American prestige in Southeast Asia."[23]

Although Johnson complained to his press secretary, George Reedy, that "Dirksen did us awful dirty,"[24] he feared that Dirksen's criticism was sound. When he spoke to Richard Russell on May 27, he revealed the depths of his uncertainty over Vietnam. "Frankly, Mr. President," Russell said, "if you were to tell me that I was authorized to settle it as I saw fit, I would respectfully decline and not take it." Johnson chuckled, but Russell was serious. "It's the damn worst mess I ever saw, and I don't like to brag," Russell said. "I never have been right many times in my life. But I knew that we were going to get into this sort of mess when we went in there. And I don't see how we're ever going to get out of it without fighting a major war with the Chinese and all of them down there in those rice paddies and jungles . . . I just don't know what to do."

"That's the way that I've been feeling for six months," Johnson replied.

The situation would only get worse, Russell predicted, adding that he wished a new leader would come to power in South Vietnam who would say that "he wished to hell we *would* get out. That would give us a good excuse for getting out."

"How important is it to us?" Johnson asked, revealing that his pronouncements about Vietnam's strategic importance to the United States were less than heartfelt.

"It isn't important a damn bit with all those new missile systems," Russell said, adding that the time had come for Johnson to widen his circle of advisors in the search for a solution. "Now you got all the brains in the country, Mr. President. You better get ahold of them. I don't know what to do about this."[25]

Indeed, it was the current advice from McNamara and Rusk, reflected in a May 25 memorandum from McGeorge Bundy, that most worried Johnson. The trio had recommended "selected and carefully graduated military force against North Vietnam," but only after North Vietnam had been prepared with "appropriate diplomatic and political warning." While Bundy said the advisors did not believe the attacks would spark a war with China, he included a chilling cautionary note about "the risk of escalation toward [a] major land war or the use of nuclear" weapons or the risk of a Viet Cong "reply in South Vietnam" that would cause the country's collapse.[26]

Alluding to the memorandum, Johnson told Russell that his advisors wanted him to "show some power and some force." He had "avoided that for a few days," he told Russell. "I don't think the American people are for it. I don't agree with Morse and all he says, but—"

"No, neither do I, but he's voicing the sentiment of a hell of a lot of people."

"I'm afraid that's right," Johnson said. "I don't think the people of this country know much about Vietnam and I think they care a hell of a lot less."

"Yeah, I know, but you go to send a whole lot of our boys out there—"

Johnson agreed. Even a few American deaths would spark a partisan outcry. "The Republicans are going to make a political issue out of it, every one of them, even Dirksen."

"It's the only issue they've got," Russell said.

The Republicans wanted escalation, Johnson noted, while "Mansfield, he just wants to pull up and get out.* And Morse wants to get out and Gruening wants to get out. And that's about where it stops. I don't know."

---

*Not an accurate characterization of Mansfield's position on Vietnam.

But Russell knew of another potential Democratic defector. "Frank Church has told me two or three times that he didn't want to make a speech on it. He just wished to God we could get out of there."[27]*

Told by Johnson that military officials were advocating a bombing campaign in North Vietnam, Russell said he doubted that would have much effect. "We tried it in Korea," he said. "We even got a lot of old B-29s to increase the bomb load and sent 'em over there and just dropped millions and millions of bombs, day and night. . . . They would knock the road at night and in the morning, the damn people would be back traveling over it."

Here, Johnson revealed a basic instinct that prevented him from considering withdrawal. "Well, they'd impeach a President, though, that would run out, wouldn't they?" Before Russell could answer, Johnson continued. "Outside of Morse, everybody I talk to says you got to go in." That, he said, included the Republicans. "And I don't know how in the hell you're gonna get out unless they [Senate Republicans] tell you to get out."

Russell suggested installing a South Vietnamese leader who would tell the United States to "get out," but Johnson dismissed that advice, knowing that any U.S. complicity in another coup would become public knowledge. "Wouldn't that pretty well fix us in the eyes of the world though and make it look mighty bad?"

"I don't know," Russell said with a chuckle. "We don't look too good right now. You'd look pretty good, I guess, going in there with all the troops and sending them all in there, but I tell you it'll be the most expensive venture this country ever went into."

Johnson confessed that he agonized over the impending decision. "I haven't got the nerve to do it," he said, "and I don't see any other way out of it."

Minutes later, Johnson was back on the phone—this time with Mc George Bundy. His heartrending confession continued. He worried about "another Korea" during which the Chinese Communists might be provoked to enter the conflict, especially if Johnson attacked North Vietnam. "I don't think it's worth fighting for and I don't think we can get out. It's just the biggest damn mess I ever saw."

Bundy agreed. "It is. It's an awful mess."[28]

---

*Church was, indeed, growing concerned. And although he had so far resisted making a Senate speech, in April he had appeared on a Pennsylvania television show hosted by Republican Senator Hugh Scott. To Scott, Church cautioned that taking the war into North Vietnam would risk a direct confrontation with China and "a hopeless entanglement, the end of which is difficult to see." By late June, Church would take his doubts to the Senate floor (*NYT*, 4/27/64).

If Johnson was searching for a way out, Mansfield's latest memorandum on Vietnam offered little to chew on. In the missive that Johnson had read earlier in the day, Mansfield had suggested nothing in the way of radical changes in U.S. policy. What he did suggest was "an end to the reflex of pique" at de Gaulle's proposals for neutralization and "a willingness to entertain any reasonable proposals for international conferences to consider" an end to the war.[29] Johnson was less than impressed with the counsel, as he confessed to Bundy.

"Everybody I talk to that's got any sense in there says, 'Oh, my God, ple-e-e-ease give this [some] thought.' Of course, I was reading Mansfield's stuff this morning and it's just milquetoast as it can be. He's got no spine at all." But, then, neither did Johnson—as he indirectly acknowledged. "This is a terrible thing we're getting ready to do," he said. Desperate for some way out, Johnson implored Bundy to find him someone with an innovative perspective on the problem. "I think," Bundy rightly concluded in a drastic understatement of fact, "that you're constantly searching, if I understand you correctly, for some means of stiffening this thing that does not have this escalating aspect to it."[30]

Johnson was also searching for a way to avoid injecting Vietnam into the upcoming presidential campaign. "I have some idea of the pressures that you're under or going to get under with that damned Goldwater and so on," U.N. Ambassador Adlai Stevenson told Johnson later that afternoon. But the two-time Democratic presidential nominee advised that "this is the time for restraint." Stevenson characterized Johnson's political perception of the war perfectly. "This is a war-and-peace issue. The man who is the peacemonger and not the warmonger will be in the strongest political position." Even with an inconclusive peace conference, Stevenson believed that Johnson would be "better off than with a war—especially a war ten thousand miles away in a part of the world that's almost meaningless to the American people and which is a quagmire."[31]

Johnson paid for his indecision in lost sleep. During a March 31 meeting with columnist Walter Lippmann, he confessed that he had been so preoccupied with Vietnam that he had slept no more than "a few hours" the night before. As Ball later told Rusk, Johnson had pondered aloud: "How could he maintain his posture as a man of peace in the face of the Southeast Asia crisis? How could he carry a united country with him if we were to embark on a course of action that might escalate under conditions where the rest of the world would regard us as wrong-headed?" While Ball got no inkling of how Johnson might ultimately decide, he left "persuaded that the President will not act hastily."[32]

Johnson, meanwhile, continued to prod his advisors to bring him a different approach to Vietnam. But there was none—at least none that he had not already seen. And when his top advisors gathered in Honolulu on June 1 they proposed nothing new, except to agree that they would not recommend attacks on North Vietnam until the American public had been better prepared for them. "This debate will probably grow in volume," William Bundy told Rusk in preparation for his briefing of the president, "and we must get at the basic doubts of the value of Southeast Asia and the importance of our stake there that are besetting and confusing both key members of the Congress and the public."[33]

Indeed, the debate was growing in volume. While Johnson's team met in Hawaii, Republican Representative Melvin Laird of Wisconsin rose on the House floor to attack Johnson for failing to admit that his administration had devised plans to attack North Vietnam. At a press conference on June 2, Johnson responded to a reporter's question about a possible attack on North Vietnam, saying, "I know of no plans that have been made to that effect."[34] But Laird alleged otherwise. As chairman of the Republican Party's platform committee for its upcoming convention, Laird had recently spoken to Rusk, who advised him, Laird said, that the administration was involved in "the preparation of plans to go north into North Vietnam." Laird said that he regretted that Johnson "used his news conference in this way, because the American people deserve to be informed and have the right to know."[35]

At the White House, Laird's statement angered Johnson. "I've got no preparations to do it on my desk," Johnson told Rusk and Bundy, who were still in Honolulu. Technically, Johnson was correct. What he had was a broad recommendation, not a detailed plan, of how attacks on North Vietnam would be carried out. Nonetheless, the president was more than a little disingenuous to leave the impression that no one had advised him to attack North Vietnam. "I have approved no plan to carry and have made no plans at this stage to carry the war into North Vietnam," he told Rusk and Bundy. "That's what I was trying to say."[36]

Laird's unexpected assault was only the latest reminder of the treacherous road Johnson faced in Congress if he chose escalation. Recalling Harry Truman's unfortunate Korean experience in 1950, he feared that any sudden influx of American troops into Southeast Asia—without congressional assent—would provoke a partisan outcry in Congress. Just as he applied the example of Truman's experience with China to his Vietnam policy, he would also draw powerful lessons from his predecessor's painful encounter with North Korea. He was determined not to repeat Truman's mistakes. "Lyndon Johnson remembered that [episode] very clearly," Rusk later recalled.[37] As Johnson told Attorney General Robert Kennedy, he would not go deeper into Vietnam without the approval and cooperation of Congress. Without congressional approval, he said, "the resentment would be pretty widespread and it would involve a lot of people who normally would be with us."[38]

Johnson's national security team debated the need for a congressional resolution authorizing "wider action" in Vietnam for about a week. "Such a resolution is essential before we act against North Vietnam," Bundy advised Johnson, adding that Russell, who was also the leader of southern forces allied against Johnson's civil rights bill, might be persuaded to accept "a three-day truce [in the civil rights debate] on straight patriotic grounds" so the Senate could consider a Vietnam resolution.[39] A lengthy draft resolution prepared by the State Department declared that "the United States regards the preservation of the independence and integrity of the nations of South Viet Nam and Laos as vital to its national interest and to world peace." The crux of the resolution was its language authorizing military action:

> To this end, if the President determines the necessity thereof, the United States is prepared, upon the request of the Government of South Viet Nam or the Government of Laos, to *use all measures, including the commitment of armed forces* [emphasis added] to assist that government in the defense of its independence and territorial integrity against aggression or subversion supported, controlled or directed from any Communist country.[40]

While he understood the risks of escalating the war without congressional input, Johnson was hesitant to send the issue to Congress in an election year. A protracted debate with an uncertain end was more of a risk than Johnson wanted to take. "If we asked for the authority," he told Robert Kennedy, "I would shudder to think that if they debated it for a long period of time, and they're likely to do that. So I don't think the choice is very good."[41] Fulbright shared Johnson's concerns. On May 28, Ball phoned Johnson to tell him of his conversation with the Foreign Relations Committee chairman. "He is very much opposed to the idea of any resolution before November," Ball reported. "He thinks it would create a kind of war fever on the Hill that could distort the whole situation and create a lot of problems." Perhaps aware of Johnson's pique over his "Old Myths and New Realities" in March, Fulbright made it clear, Ball said, that "he is not going to do any talking and wants to do everything that keeps the maximum freedom of maneuver for the President—which distinguishes him from some colleagues."[42]

Rusk and McNamara agreed with Fulbright. "It would be disastrous," Rusk said, if Congress rejected or weakened the resolution. "We should ask for a resolution," he told Johnson's national security team on June 10, "only when the circumstances are such as to require action, and, thereby, force congressional action." Rusk believed "there will be a rallying around the President the moment it is clear to reasonable people that U.S. action is necessary." In any event, Rusk noted, persuading Congress to pass such a resolution would be difficult until Johnson had made the "basic decisions" about what to do in Southeast Asia. McNamara agreed with Rusk and told the group that a resolution before September was "unlikely unless the enemy acts suddenly in the area" which, he added, "is also unlikely."[43]

The enemy, however, *had* acted—and briefly heightened the concerns that a minor incident might become the pretext for a rapid escalation of the conflict. On June 6 and 7 the Pathet Lao—nationalist guerrillas allied with the North Vietnamese—shot down two U.S. planes flying reconnaissance missions over Laos. Johnson's military advisors recommended a proportional response—air strikes on a Pathet Lao antiaircraft installation. However, General Curtis LeMay, the trigger-happy Air Force chief of staff, wanted more. "LeMay wanted to get tougher, much tougher now," Johnson's aide Jack Valenti recalled. That worried Johnson. As they left the meeting, Johnson told Valenti that "I get anxious and look for the fire exits when a general wants to get tough. LeMay scares the hell out of me."[44]

But Johnson was finally persuaded to authorize the air strikes. "We just had to make some response," he explained to House Speaker John McCormack on June 9. "If we didn't, why, we'd just destroy ourselves."[45] Worried about the reaction in Congress—from his allies as well as his opponents— Johnson tried to keep the attacks a secret. "We sure don't want to give any indications that we're getting involved in a war," Johnson told Mansfield. Despite his many exhortations about exploring the chances for a negotiated settlement, Mansfield was supportive of Johnson's actions in Laos. "So far as I'm concerned," he assured Johnson, "I think you've done everything right."[46]

Later that day, however, Mansfield had second thoughts about Johnson's retaliatory actions—as well as the reconnaissance flights themselves. "These two steps," he wrote Johnson, "have opened up the immediate possibility of a far more direct U.S. military involvement in Laos than we now have in Viet Nam." Although Johnson had assured him that the bombing "was not to be repeated," Mansfield observed that "you cannot count on the absence of the need for repetitions of the bombings so long as the reconnaissance flights continue over Laos." While he stopped short of urging Johnson to discontinue the flights over Laos, he stressed what he believed should be the president's guiding philosophy regarding widening the war: "If it is not in the national interest to become deeply involved in a military sense on the Laotian front, we will avoid those actions which can impel us, *even against our inclination or expectation* [emphasis Mansfield's], to become more deeply involved." Once again, the majority leader urged Johnson to "take every possible initiative to bring about a peaceful settlement."

While Johnson certainly did not find Mansfield's observations on Laos comforting, he could not have been more pleased by his majority leader's remarkable, unqualified pledge of support for his ultimate course of action in Vietnam. Reflecting his very limited view of the Senate's role in formulating the nation's foreign and military policy, Mansfield wrote: "From the Senate, we can only give you, in the last analysis, our support and such independent thoughts as may occur to us from time to time in the hope that they may be constructive." Should Johnson decide to wage a bombing campaign in the north, Mansfield gave him the green light. "If our interests justify, in the last analysis, becoming involved on the Southeast Asian mainland then there is no issue. What must be done will be done." While he was clear that "I do not conclude that our national interests are served by a deep military involvement in Southeast Asia," he quickly added that "in this situation, what I or any other Senator may conclude is secondary. The responsibility rests with you and we can only give you our support in whatever decisions you may make."[47]

Mansfield's eagerness to abdicate the Senate's constitutional responsibilities for declaring war was remarkable. Although he was persuaded that greater American involvement in Vietnam was not in the nation's interests—and would, in fact, result in "an indecisive, bloody and costly military involvement"*—he was ready to support any administration decision on the grounds that a president deserved the support of his majority leader, especially on foreign affairs. Mansfield might at least have left Johnson with the impression that escalation would result in a mild public denunciation; instead he left no doubt in the president's mind. Mansfield gave the president his unconditional support for whatever course he decided to pursue. Although he would forcefully advance his position to Johnson in private, he was unable or unwilling to carry his dissent to the floor of the U.S. Senate. Like his other quiescent Democratic colleagues in the spring and summer of 1964—including Fulbright, Russell, McGovern, and others—Mansfield allowed Johnson to put political interests ahead of the national interest. Mansfield knew as well as Johnson that an ugly, protracted Senate debate over Vietnam could only harm the president politically. Such a debate would not occur on his watch.

Although Johnson appeared to dismiss most of Mansfield's reasoning—especially his calls for a negotiated end to the war—the memorandum appeared to have a sobering effect. In the days after receiving it, Johnson cited Mansfield's views in discussions with McNamara and Russell. "Now Mansfield's got a four-page memorandum that I'm getting ourselves

---

*From Mansfield's February 1 memorandum to Johnson.

involved and I'm gonna get in another war if I do any more," Johnson told Russell on June 11.

"In a way," Russell acknowledged, "I share some of his fears."

"I do, too," Johnson said, "but the fear the other way [withdrawal] is more."

"I don't know what the hell to do," Russell confessed. "I didn't ever want to get messed up down there." Like Mansfield, Russell did not believe that Vietnam was vital territory. He took issue with "those brain trusters who say that this thing has got tremendous strategic and economic value and that we'll lose everything in Southeast Asia if we lose Vietnam." But also, like Mansfield, Russell could not bring himself to advise Johnson to withdraw U.S. forces. "As a practical matter, we're in there and I don't know how the hell you can tell the American people you're coming out. . . . They'll think that you've just been whipped, you've been ruined, you're scared. It'd be disastrous."[48]

Whatever Mansfield, Morse, and others might have suspected about the administration's aggressive plans for Vietnam, Johnson *was* resisting—with all his being—the advice of his more hawkish advisors. He refused to believe that going north was the only way to change the dynamics in Vietnam. His finely tuned political antennae told him that a congressional resolution—absent any urgent crisis—was unwise. Yet, as if he were searching for a magical solution to the dilemma, Johnson refused to accept the alternatives to escalation that advisors, like Mansfield, were advancing.

No matter which way he turned, Johnson saw no acceptable alternatives. "I'm confronted," he told Russell on June 11. "I don't believe the American people ever want me to run [withdraw American forces]. If I lose it, I think that they'll say *I've* lost. I've pulled in. At the same time, I don't want to commit us to a war. And I'm in a hell of a shape."[49]

Concern about a devastating backlash from hawkish members of Congress kept Johnson from considering withdrawal, while an equally incapacitating fear of an assault from the left prevented him from turning loose the Joint Chiefs. He believed that even the slightest hint of escalation *or* "pulling back" risked an outcry that might derail his campaign and give momentum to the Republicans. Yet splitting the war down the middle was no recipe for military victory. Johnson understood that much. But he also knew it might buy him time enough to win reelection. For now, he was willing to take that chance.

In the meantime, Johnson's advisors urged him to approve the public relations campaign that they had recommended after the Honolulu conference. "If we're going to stay in there," McNamara advised Johnson, "if we're going to go strictly up the escalating chain, we're going to have to educate the people, Mr. President. We haven't done so yet." To Johnson, educating the public was simply another way of preparing the country for a wider war in Vietnam. "I think if you start doing it," he told McNamara, "they're going to be hollering, 'You're a warmonger.'"[50] But Johnson relented and agreed that, at the very least, Americans should better understand the issues at stake in Vietnam. He ordered the State Department to conduct "a broad program to bring to the American people a complete and accurate picture of the United States involvement in Southeast Asia."[51]

But Johnson thought the most useful public relations might be the selection of a strong, effective new ambassador to replace Lodge, who wanted to return to the United States. Although Johnson considered a number of nominees for the job—including Robert Kennedy, McNamara, and John J. McCloy, the former high commissioner in Germany after World War II—he settled on someone he knew as a tough, urbane, and articulate military leader: Joint Chiefs Chairman Maxwell Taylor. "Taylor can give us the cover that we need with the country and with the Republicans and with the Congress," Johnson told McNamara the day before Lodge submitted his resignation. "We need somebody to cover us with the opinion-molders."[52] On June 23, Johnson announced Taylor's appointment and said he would send Alexis Johnson, deputy under secretary of state for political affairs, to serve as his deputy. To replace Taylor, he nominated General Earle Wheeler, the Army chief of staff.[53]

Taylor was only one part of Johnson's effort to burnish his Vietnam policies. The effort to influence Congress was another. Rusk and his assistant for Vietnam affairs, William Sullivan, perceived some measure of the task before them on June 15 when they appeared before an increasingly skeptical Foreign Relations Committee. Morse was his usual acerbic self, assailing Rusk for his unwillingness to put the question of Vietnam before the United Nations. "The United States is not using the peaceful procedures available to it to try to bring peace to Southeast Asia," he said. "We apparently have decided on a military course of action."

It was Frank Church, however, who emerged as the latest agnostic regarding Johnson's Vietnam policies. Church argued, like so many others, that the military power of the United States would prove indecisive without the active support of the South Vietnamese. But Church was not prepared to give up on South Vietnam and added that he favored giving "as much aid and assistance as they can possibly use in helping them resist" the Viet Cong. But as far as a direct combat role for U.S. troops, Church was adamantly opposed.

> If the time ever comes when we permit ourselves to be sucked in and make their wars our wars and use our forces in that area, we are going to find that the Chinese will come down just as we found that out in Korea. . . .

All the Asians will regard our intrusion as an attempt on the part of the Western white world to reestablish a beachhead in Asia.

This is the thing we must avoid. Yet political forces keep sucking us further and further in this direction. That is the thing that concerns me.[54]

Church's comments gave Rusk some insight into the Idaho senator's quickly evolving opposition to a military solution in Vietnam. Church had not yet gone public; the hearing had been behind closed doors. This would not last for long. For months, he had been concerned that leaders in Washington and Saigon increasingly believed that the solution to the war in Vietnam was a direct military challenge of North Vietnam. But when he went to the Senate floor on June 23, he had not intended to air those concerns. The occasion for his remarks was the twentieth anniversary of the United Nations. However, when Fulbright challenged his assertion that the Vietnam conflict should be placed before the United Nations, Church defended himself, but agreed that "our determined support [of Saigon] at this time is indispensable to the survival of that regime." But just as Church appeared ready to yield the floor, he stopped momentarily. As Morse and Democratic Senator William Proxmire of Wisconsin sought recognition, Church suddenly decided to continue. To a silent Senate chamber, he held forth about Vietnam for ten minutes and, in the process, sparked a change in the dynamics of congressional debate over Vietnam.

He found it difficult to understand how "25,000 hard-core Viet Cong in South Vietnam" had been so far able to thwart the American-backed South Vietnamese government. The Viet Cong were being supplied "over a long and arduous jungle trail, by runners who carry what they can on their backs." Meanwhile, the United States sends "shiploads of the most modern equipment and pour[s] in hundreds of millions of dollars each year." Yet, he said, "we fear the Government of South Vietnam is about to topple."

> What concerns me is that if this war—which is essentially a political war, that can be won only by the people of South Vietnam—is being waged on terms so advantageous, with the enemy restricted to 25,000 hard-core Viet Cong, how on earth will the situation be improved by extending the war to the north? Will it help to take on the army of North Vietnam?
>
> Do we think that the bombing of North Vietnam will break the spirit of the Government, and cause it to discontinue to aid and abet the insurrection in the south? Why should we? The bombing of North Korea never broke the spirit there. And we bombed every house, bridge and road until there was nothing left but rubble. Expanding the war is not getting out. . . . It is getting further in.

As for supporting South Vietnam's effort to "put down the present insurrection," Church said, "I am for that policy." He would, he said, "vote for the added money that may be needed." He was, however "setting up some warning posts that had better be pondered if we are to avoid a tragic trail of casualties in Asia, out of all proportion" to U.S. vital interests. "Sometimes, war must be fought. I am for fighting them where the vital interests of the United States are at stake. But let us be sure. Let us be sure."[55]

After the speech, Hubert Humphrey—soon to be Johnson's vice presidential running mate—offered Church his qualified support. He agreed that the issue should be put before the United Nations. He was also opposed to escalating the war, as some believed Johnson was about to do. "What is needed in Vietnam," he said, "is a cause for which to fight, some sort of inspiration for the people of South Vietnam to live for and die for." Humphrey failed to explain why he apparently did not consider the struggle against communism in South Vietnam a cause offering sufficient inspiration for the nation's people.[56] (Privately, however, Humphrey gave Johnson a "generally pessimistic appraisal" of the Vietnam situation and reiterated his belief that the Vietnamese people needed a more stable government and "some hope" around which to rally. "No amount of additional military involvement can be successful without accomplishing this task." Military action against North Vietnam or direct participation of U.S. troops in combat, Humphrey added, "is unnecessary and undesirable.")[57]

Church's speech was significant. Until now, the only Senate skeptics of the war were the older and sometimes strident members of the body like Morse, Gruening, and Ellender. The quiet dissenters—Russell and Mansfield—were powerful senior senators. Among the younger generation, only McGovern had spoken critically of American involvement in Vietnam—but had fallen silent on the issue after his speeches of September 1963. Since then, no senator under the age of 60 had publicly questioned America's military role in Southeast Asia. At 39, Church was one of the Senate's youngest and brashest members. His aide Bryce Nelson viewed the speech as a turning point. "I think that one of the feelings of the younger and more cautious senators was that they did not want to identify too much with opposition to involvement in Vietnam because they thought that the comments of people like Morse and Gruening were so strident," Nelson said. "They did not want to be lumped in with people like Morse and Gruening, at least initially."[58] In a small way, Church's mild, but groundbreaking dissent (he did not express any significant disagreement with Johnson's basic Vietnam policy) altered the dynamics of the embryonic Vietnam debate.

If Church had hoped to avoid association with Morse and his hellfire-and-brimstone opposition to Johnson's Vietnam policies, he was successful—primarily because the Oregon senator now saw Church as a White House apologist. "Whenever I listen to a member of the Senate attempt to rationalize the U.S. outlawry in Southeast Asia," he told the Senate shortly after Church had finished his remarks, "I propose to register my dissent."

> They are not facing their responsibilities, born of the oath that they took when they came into this body. We are making war in South Vietnam, and we are making it unconstitutionally. We are killing American boys illegally. The number that we have killed thus far is a small number compared with the tens of thousands that we shall kill if we do not stop this administration's course of action in Southeast Asia.

Few of his colleagues shared Morse's dim view of U.S. policy in Vietnam. In less than six weeks—as they debated a congressional resolution giving Johnson enormous powers to prosecute the war in Vietnam— almost none would comprehend the deadly accuracy of his next statement. "The American people apparently will have choices between degrees next November," he predicted. "They will have the choice between a slower-paced Democratic war and a faster-paced Republican war."[59]

Unfortunately for Morse, more of his colleagues appeared to want a faster-paced war than no war at all. And Republican leaders were not averse to applying the necessary political pressure to force Johnson's hand. At the closed-door June 23 meeting of the Foreign Relations Committee, the committee's senior Republican, Bourke Hickenlooper, doubted that Johnson's aim in Vietnam was "to win." If Congress and the public believed that South Vietnam "is essential to the well-being of the country and to the free world," then Hickenlooper hoped that "we will support all necessary action from here on out to guarantee that victory."[60] Public statements by other leading Republicans were more provocative—aimed at Johnson, as well as North Vietnam. In a haunting reprise of their party's "Who Lost China" debate of the early 1950s, members of the House Republican Conference blamed Johnson and the Democrats on June 29 for "letting our guard down" against communism in general and North Vietnamese communism in particular. "A victory in South Vietnam over the military and subversive threats of Communism is urgently required," the conference statement said. "We must repeal today's complacent commitment to prevent a Communist victory and substitute a commitment to insure a victory for freedom." Releasing the statement was Representative Gerald Ford of Michigan, who argued that the United States should do more than simply advise and assist the South Vietnamese military. Ford said he wanted the United States to immediately "take command of the forces in Vietnam and not simply remain advisors."

Mansfield rushed to Johnson's defense and pointed to what he believed were the political motives of the administration's critics. "I am not surprised that the partisan political knives should be drawn on this issue," he said. "What amazes me is that they have come out of the sheaths so early." The majority leader could only conclude that they were "intended to be used in a preliminary rumble . . . for the political war later on." Two Republican senators, Javits and John Sherman Cooper of Kentucky, rose to defend their House counterparts. Javits insisted the issue had nothing to do with politics. He believed, he said, "regardless of party, that we must stick it out in Vietnam. I do not believe that we ought to pull out." Yet Javits also said he did not wish to "*overtly* [emphasis added] extend the war to North Vietnam, which has been recommended by some."[61]

Johnson, meanwhile, combined tough talk with promises of continued assistance to the South Vietnamese. While most Americans, and many in Congress, could be forgiven if they did not entirely understand why their nation had sent almost twenty thousand men into South Vietnam, they were not likely to misunderstand Johnson's deft characterization of the mission. "The United States intends no rashness, and seeks no wider war," Johnson said during his June 23 news conference. All the same, he said, the country would continue to "use its strength to help those who are defending themselves against terror and aggression. We are a people of peace—but not of weakness and timidity. I should like to repeat again that our purpose is peace."[62]

CHAPTER 25

Aggression Unchallenged
Is Aggression Unleashed

1964

CONGRESSIONAL REPUBLICANS AND CONSERVATIVE DEMOCRATS were not the only ones pressing Johnson to intensify the effort in Vietnam. The new ambassador, Maxwell Taylor, was getting an earful from Prime Minister Khanh about taking the war northward. After less than a month on the job, Taylor reported to Washington that Khanh appeared to have "launched [a] deliberate campaign" to associate the United States with his new policy for "increased military pressure" on North Vietnam.[1] On July 19, Khanh tried to whip up public enthusiasm for attacks against North Vietnam at a rally in Saigon where he claimed that all segments of society were demanding the attacks. "The Government cannot remain indifferent before the firm determination of all the people," Khanh declared to a desultory crowd of about one hundred thousand. Afterwards, only a group of student leaders appeared to be swayed by Khanh's new spirit of militarism. Rushing the stage, the students chanted "Bac Tien" (To the North).[2]

Taylor offered Washington several explanations for Khanh's sudden turnabout: perhaps Khanh believed a "dramatic move" would improve morale among the South Vietnamese people and help quell internal political and military dissension. More intriguing, however, was the ambassador's observation that Khanh might be influenced by American political developments. Barry Goldwater's campaign to win the Republican Party's presidential nomination, Taylor speculated, led many to believe that "now is [an] opportune time to launch [a] campaign" in the north.[3]

Compared to Johnson's relatively measured approach to Vietnam, Goldwater was a cheerleader for expanding the war. Clark Clifford later recalled that a saying in Washington at the time was: "Within the Republican Party there'd been two great figures: Lincoln was the great emancipator and Goldwater was the great defoliator."[4] Goldwater's belligerent Cold War rhetoric, like that of his congressional colleagues, was strangely reminiscent of the attacks Truman's Republican critics had employed in the early 1950s. When it came to the threat of communism in Asia, Goldwater was Robert Taft, William Knowland, and Kenneth Wherry rolled into one articulate and fiercely conservative opponent. Goldwater left no doubt where he stood on "winning" the war in Vietnam. He said that he would give the Pentagon a blank check. If he were president, military commanders would be told "that it was their problem and to get on with solving it." Goldwater suggested that Johnson did not really wish to defeat the communists in Vietnam, but "only says we will contain them." He warned that losing Vietnam to the Communists "will be a far more costly loss than the humiliating defeat we have suffered in Korea. It will mean the loss of the whole of Southeast Asia." A stalemate in Vietnam would be, he said, "placed squarely in the laps of those twin commanders of chaos, Lyndon B. Johnson and Robert S. McNamara."[5] So reckless was Goldwater in his goading of Johnson and the Pentagon that he even suggested he might consider defoliating the jungles with "low-yield atomic weapons" to expose the Viet Cong's supply lines.[6] Johnson's nightmare of another "Who lost China" debate appeared to be coming true.

In mid-July, Republican delegates in San Francisco handed Goldwater their party's presidential nomination. At a convention thoroughly disdainful of Johnson's conduct in Vietnam, the Republican platform charged that Johnson had encouraged "an increase of aggression in South Vietnam by appearing to set limits on America's willingness to act." If given control of the White House, the party vowed to "move decisively to assure victory in South Vietnam while confining the conflict as closely as possible."[7] Given Goldwater's incendiary rhetoric, it was not difficult for many Americans to imagine what steps Goldwater might take to "end" the conflict. In his acceptance speech to the convention, Goldwater drew on still-vivid memories of Korea:

> Yesterday it was Korea; tonight it is Vietnam. Make no bones of this. Don't try to sweep this under the rug. We are at war in Vietnam. And yet the president, who is commander-in-chief of our forces, refuses to say, refuses to say, mind you, whether or not the objective over there is victory. And his secretary of defense continues to mislead and misinform the American people.[8]

Although Goldwater had urged delegates not to sweep Vietnam under the rug, he was about to do just that. In private negotiations with Johnson, the Republican nominee would soon relieve Johnson of a chief political concern. When Goldwater contacted the White House shortly after the Republican convention to request a private meeting with the president, Johnson and his aides suspected he wanted to talk about civil rights. Goldwater, after all, had voted against the just-enacted Civil Rights Act of 1964. But after racial violence erupted in Harlem and elsewhere, Goldwater worried that his opposition to the civil rights legislation might be misinterpreted. He did not want to do or say anything that might incite further racial discord. Johnson and his aides never expected that Goldwater, during the July 24 Oval Office meeting, would also propose a deal to shelve Vietnam as a campaign issue. Goldwater recalled that he told Johnson "there was already too much division in the nation over the war. We should not contribute to it by making Vietnam an issue in the campaign." More than likely, however, Goldwater had begun to understand that his bellicose rhetoric about Vietnam only scared voters and was giving Johnson more ammunition with which to persuade voters of the Republican nominee's recklessness and instability.* In any event, Johnson was just as eager as Goldwater to stop talking about the war. While the deal would not give him absolute freedom to maneuver in Vietnam—Johnson's other Republican critics would not be bound by Goldwater's secret nonaggression pact—the July 24 meeting now reasonably assured Johnson that the campaign's outcome would not hinge on uncertain events in Southeast Asia.[9]

Although Johnson's election-year concerns about Vietnam had abated, he knew the issue would never go away as long as the war continued going badly. In fact, by late June, Ambassador Taylor worried that conditions had grown so dismal that Khanh might resign unless the United States showed some willingness to intensify the war. Hoping to strengthen Khanh's faltering resolve, Taylor suggested that U.S. officials express a desire to work with South Vietnam to plan "various forms of extended action" against North Vietnam. It was a cosmetic approach, as Taylor acknowledged. "We are not assuming any commitment to implement such plans," he noted. But he thought, nonetheless, it might keep Khanh at bay for a few months. "Such planning," Taylor wrote, "would not only provide an outlet for the martial head of steam now dangerously compressed but would force the Generals to look at the hard facts of life which lie behind the neon lights of the 'march north' slogans."[10] Rusk concurred "completely" and agreed that such planning would provide a "channel for [the] frustrations" of

---

*Johnson's campaign exploited fears about Goldwater's recklessness with several nationally televised advertisements—one featured a small girl plucking petals from a daisy followed by an atomic blast—suggesting that a President Goldwater might start a nuclear war (Dallek, *Flawed Giant*, 175–76).

Khanh and his generals "without committing" the U.S. government "to action."[11] Perhaps to further placate Khanh, on July 27 Johnson approved a month-old request from the new MACV commander, General William Westmoreland, for an additional five thousand military advisors, thus increasing the U.S. military advisory force to about twenty-two thousand.[12]

In another apparent attempt to pacify Khanh, while placing increasing pressure on North Vietnam, the United States and South Vietnam had also resumed in late July a series of provocative naval maneuvers in the Gulf of Tonkin along the North Vietnamese coast. One of those operations was the so-called DeSoto patrols involving a U.S. destroyer, the USS *Maddox*. The vessel supported a CIA-led South Vietnamese program of coastal commando "hit-and-run" attacks—part of the OPLAN 34-A program Johnson had approved in January—against North Vietnamese radar sites. On De-Soto patrol, ships like the *Maddox* were outfitted with sophisticated equipment designed to collect "electronic intelligence" about North Vietnamese coastal defenses. When supporting the 34-A raids, the ship approached off-shore islands and skirted the North Vietnamese coast—even crossing the country's 12-mile territorial limit—with the goal of activating enemy radar. When that occurred, the vessel's equipment locked onto the radar-emitting device, determined its location, and forwarded the information to nearby South Vietnamese commandos, who staged an attack.

Although U.S. officials would later deny that the American DeSoto patrols and the South Vietnamese 34-A raids were connected—and that the North Vietnamese were wrong to conclude that the operations were provocative—their intent was clear enough.[13] Predictably, North Vietnamese gunboats would eventually respond by attacking the *Maddox* in early August, in an incident that would provoke a furious U.S. response that would change dramatically America's approach to the war.[14]

Why were U.S. officials determined to behave so provocatively? Was Johnson or the Pentagon spoiling for a fight and actually looking for an incident to provide the impetus for a military attack on North Vietnam? Or, were they hoping to spark a conflict that would compel Congress to adopt a resolution giving Johnson unlimited authority to fight the war? Rusk's and McNamara's comments during a June 10 White House meeting are noteworthy and provide at least some evidence suggesting that U.S. officials did, indeed, hope the DeSoto patrols and the 34-A raids would eventually draw a military response from North Vietnam.

Rusk had not opposed the concept of a congressional resolution authorizing escalation, only its timing. "We should ask for a resolution *only when the circumstances are such as to require a resolution*" (emphasis added), he told the group, "and, thereby, force congressional action." At that point, the secretary of state observed, "there will be a rallying around the President," as long as it was "clear to reasonable people that U.S. action is necessary." McNamara agreed, but said he doubted a resolution could be sought until September, *"unless the enemy acts suddenly in the area"* (emphasis added)," an eventuality he deemed "unlikely." In McNamara's defense, he added later that "in the event of a dramatic event in Southeast Asia we would go promptly for a congressional resolution, but we would not plan on one."[15]

A draft memorandum prepared in September 1964 by William Bundy, assistant secretary of state for Far Eastern affairs, provides further evidence that some U.S. officials were hoping to provoke the North Vietnamese. Even after the *Maddox* was attacked, providing the pretext for a congressional resolution, Bundy contemplated ways to further provoke North Vietnam. "The main further question is the extent to which we should try to add elements . . . that would tend to provoke a DRV [Democratic Republic of (North) Vietnam] reaction, and consequent retaliation by us." Bundy saw the DeSoto patrols as the best chance for accomplishing that mission. "The main action to be considered would be running US naval patrols increasingly close to the North Vietnamese coast and/or associating them with 34A operations. Such extension might be undertaken if the initial US naval patrols had not aroused a reaction."[16]

Years later, presidential advisors like McNamara, Rusk, William Bundy, and others vehemently denied that U.S. officials had ever conspired to induce a North Vietnamese response in the Gulf of Tonkin in the summer of 1964.[17] They argued that the DeSoto patrols were legitimate, independent, intelligence-gathering operations. While this may have been the case, the *Maddox*—no matter how legitimate its primary purpose—was clearly behaving in a provocative manner when it intruded on North Vietnam's coastal territory.* At least one high-level national security official, Under Secretary of State George Ball, firmly believed that, in sending the *Maddox* so close to the North Vietnamese shore, the United States was "looking for an excuse to initiate bombing." The DeSoto patrols in August, he said, were "primarily for provocation."[18]

The real motive behind the patrols and the coordinated 34-A raids may never be fully understood. While the August patrols did have an authentic intelligence-gathering mission, they were almost certainly meant to be provocative. Yet it is impossible to prove that Johnson or his advisors, as Ball charged, were orchestrating these specific operations in order to spark an international incident. In fact, in spite of evidence to the contrary, one might argue that it was unlikely Johnson wanted a high-

---

*While North Vietnam claimed a 12-mile coastal limit, the United States recognized only a 3-mile limit.

profile incident given his desire to downplay Vietnam prior to the November presidential election.

Yet it is also exceedingly clear that Johnson well understood the political and military opportunities afforded by any incident in the Gulf of Tonkin. That his administration was prepared to exploit such an opportunity for its purposes is also certain. The most likely scenario, advanced by Edwin Moïse in his definitive study of the incidents, *Tonkin Gulf and the Escalation of the Vietnam War*, is that the provocative association of the De-Soto patrols and the OPLAN-34A raids might have been coordinated in Saigon by lower-level American officials "who were making requests and recommendations to the Navy about what the DeSoto patrols should do, and then scheduling OPLAN 34A raids" to coincide with the patrols. In doing so, the military and civilian planners in Saigon—many who wanted Johnson to fight a more vigorous war—"could have decided to maximize the chances that the North Vietnamese would think that the destroyer was somehow involved in the raids, and attack it."[19]

Given the offensive nature of the operations, it was not surprising, therefore, that the North Vietnamese military responded as it did. On the afternoon of Sunday, August 2, three North Vietnamese patrol boats attacked the *Maddox*—the only ship then conducting DeSoto patrols—and fired three torpedoes at the American vessel. None of the torpedoes hit its target, although the ship did sustain slight damage from a 14.5 mm shell fired from one of the boats. The *Maddox* returned fire and crippled one of the North Vietnamese boats.

News of the attack reached Washington shortly after 4:00 A.M.* The initial report from the White House Situation Room reached Johnson in his bedroom several hours later and erroneously stated that the attacks had taken place "30 miles off the North Vietnamese coast."[20]† That morning at 11:30, Johnson convened a meeting of his national security team.[21] The group concluded that the attack had been, in Johnson's words, the result of "an overeager North Vietnamese boat commander" or miscalculation at a shore station.[22] By all accounts, the president was calm and more interested in discussing the postal bill.[23] He was, however, disturbed that neither the *Maddox* nor the fighters from the *Ticonderoga* were able to sink the three torpedo boats. "The whole goddamn navy is out there," he said, "all those ships and planes, and you can't even sink three little PT boats?"[24] An embarrassed military official informed the president that peacetime rules

---

*A consequence of the twelve-hour time difference between Saigon and Washington.

†The *Maddox* was actually about 15 miles offshore at the time.

of engagement permitted naval forces to return fire, but not to pursue and destroy their attackers. That, Johnson resolved, would soon change.[25]

Whether the attacks were intentional or mistakes, the question remained: How to respond? Although some advisors recommended immediate retaliatory strikes, Johnson had other notions. Ball recalled that the president "wished for an even stronger record."[26] In other words, if Johnson were to hit North Vietnam over a naval incident in the Gulf of Tonkin, he hoped to be certain that the offenses were deliberate or premeditated. Therefore, he would give the North Vietnamese another chance to strike. Yet Johnson would not simply wait for another attack. Instead of instructing U.S. naval vessels to avoid what Ball described as "this now-established danger zone," Johnson ordered another destroyer, the *C. Turner Joy*, to join the *Maddox* for continued DeSoto patrols.[27] "We were determined not to be provocative," Johnson later said, failing to mention the crucial relationship between the DeSoto patrols and the 34-A raids, "nor were we going to run away. We would give Hanoi the benefit of the doubt—this time—and assume the unprovoked attack had been a mistake."[28]*

In addition to dispatching the *C. Turner Joy*, Johnson ordered a combat air patrol to protect the destroyers. He also amended the rules of engagement by instructing the pilots and destroyer commanders "to attack any force which attacks them in international waters" and "to attack with the objective not only of driving off the force but of destroying it."[29] Ball greeted Johnson's orders with quiet consternation. "The argument that we had to 'show the flag' and demonstrate that we did not 'intend to back down,'" he later observed, "seemed to me a hollow bravado."[30] It also appeared designed to provoke another attack.

Members of Congress, however, did not see the incident in the same light. When Rusk, McNamara, and Wheeler briefed the Senate Foreign Relations and Armed Services committees on August 3—informing them that the attack was "entirely unprovoked"—no one opposed Johnson's actions.[31] By now, administration officials—despite their later denials to Congress—were well aware that the *Maddox*'s DeSoto patrols and the U.S.-coordinated 34-A raids were related. In an August 3 telegram, for example, Rusk informed Ambassador Taylor that "we believe that present OPLAN 34A activities are beginning to rattle Hanoi, and [the] *Maddox* incident is directly related to their effort to resist these activities. We have no intention of yielding to pressure."[32]

Why would Johnson have gone out of his way to invite another attack

---

*Not only did Johnson assert that U.S. actions were not provocative, but he later claimed—falsely—that the 34A raids were "not connected" with the DeSoto patrols (Johnson, *The Vantage Point*, 113).

from the North Vietnamese, knowing that a second encounter would require a strong U.S. military response? American politics was at the heart of the matter. After the August 2 incident, Johnson knew that the Republicans in Congress and the news media would subject his every move to intense microscopic examination. If he had responded immediately and forcefully to the August 2 incident, Johnson would have opened himself to charges in the press that he was a trigger-happy warrior like Goldwater. However, to meekly remove the *Maddox* from harm's way would have opened Johnson up to more damaging charges that he had retreated in the face of communist aggression. While Johnson's response to the attacks on the *Maddox* seemed designed merely to provoke a stronger response from the North Vietnamese, politically, at least, Johnson saw no alternative. He believed he had no choice but to forcefully challenge the perceived North Vietnam "aggression," and hope that the enemy would back down.

The stormy night of August 3 brought another 34-A raid on the coast of North Vietnam, as the two American destroyers patrolled nearby. At 7:40 P.M., Saigon time, the *Maddox* intercepted radio broadcasts that suggested imminent attacks on both ships. At 9:12 P.M., McNamara phoned Johnson with the first reports. Later in the hour, when he and McNamara spoke again, Johnson was cautious, but expressed the desire to retaliate. "I wish we could have something [North Vietnamese targets] that we've already picked out," Johnson said, "and just hit about three of them damn quick and go right after them." McNamara assured Johnson that he and Bundy would prepare "a retaliation move against North Vietnam" if and when the attacks occurred.[33] McNamara's calls had interrupted Johnson's weekly breakfast meeting with the Democratic leaders of both houses. After apprising them of the developing events in the gulf, Johnson informed the leaders—Mansfield was absent—that he was considering retaliation in the event of another attack. The leaders agreed and also gave their assent to a resolution of congressional support for retaliation.[34]

Johnson groaned when McNamara phoned at 11:06 A.M. with reports of a second North Vietnamese attack on the destroyers.[35] By the noon hour, more details filtered in. Arriving at the White House for a series of meetings with Johnson and his advisors, McNamara relayed reports of a fierce naval engagement. "Presently," he said, "we believe nine or ten torpedoes were fired at the patrol." Two of the attacking North Vietnamese boats had been sunk, he said, and as many as six had been "fired on." He reported no U.S. casualties.[36] By now, Johnson was ready to respond—not only with retaliatory strikes on North Vietnam, but with a congressional resolution. "You know that resolution your brother's been talking about for the past few months?" Johnson said to McGeorge Bundy. "Well, now's the time to get it through the Congress." Not entirely persuaded of the wisdom of that

course of action, Bundy recalled that he advised caution. Johnson, however, was in no mood to discuss the merits of a resolution. He wanted it
done.[37] At a working lunch with Rusk, McNamara, Bundy, and others,
Johnson announced his determination to launch a "firm, swift retaliatory
strike" against the North Vietnamese. By mid-afternoon, he ordered a
series of air strikes. The targets included a North Vietnamese oil complex,
several military bases, and PT boats—the strikes were to commence at 7:00
P.M. Washington time.[38]

Simultaneously, however, a commander on the *Maddox* had suddenly
voiced doubts about whether the reported attacks had occurred at all.
Returning to the Pentagon, McNamara was confronted with a message
from naval officials in the gulf, advising that

> a review of the action makes many reported contacts and torpedoes fired
> "appear doubtful." "Freak weather effects" on radar, and "over-eager"
> sonarmen may have accounted for many reports. "No visual sightings"
> have been reported by the *Maddox*, and the Commander suggests that a
> "complete evaluation" be undertaken before any further action.[39]

From the Pacific, Admiral Ulysses S. Grant Sharp, head of the Pacific
Command, assured McNamara that the attacks had occurred. But Johnson and McNamara demanded proof. "The reports are a little confusing
on what happened," Sharp confessed in a phone conversation with Mc-
Namara. "Neither ship saw a ship or a wake." While Sharp sounded certain
that the American vessels had been attacked, he did acknowledge the
"slight possibility" of no attack at all. Speaking of the ships' "sonar men,"
Sharp observed that "these young fellows are apt to say any noise is a torpedo." Of the retaliatory strikes, McNamara told Sharp that "we obviously
don't want to do it until we are damn sure what happened." At the same
time, however, McNamara placed Sharp under tremendous pressure to
develop proof of the attacks, reminding the admiral that the retaliatory
attacks were set to begin in three hours. "If you get your definite information in two hours, we can still proceed with the execute," McNamara said,
urging Sharp to "get the pilots briefed, get the planes armed, get everything lined up to go."[40]

As Sharp and his men labored to compile enough evidence to satisfy
McNamara and Johnson, the commanders of the *Maddox* and the *C. Turner
Joy* were becoming more convinced than ever that the extent of the
engagement was greatly exaggerated—if it had ever occurred at all. Conducting tests of the sonar equipment on both ships, both commanders concluded, in the words of Captain John Herrick, commander of the Seventh
Fleet's Destroyer Division and aboard the *Maddox* in early August, that
most of the sonar reports of his ship "were probably false," the result of

"our outgoing sonar beams hitting the rudders." Although Herrick was still certain of an attack, he could not vouch for its extent. He was, however, prepared to say that some of the reported torpedoes were probably North Vietnamese boats that made "close passes at the Maddox," adding that "ship screw noises on rudders [on the *Maddox*] may have accounted for some."[41] Later, Edwin Moïse concluded that many of the supposed radar images of attacking North Vietnamese boats were probably a result of a "phenomenon sometimes called 'Tonkin Gulf Ghost' or 'Tonkin Spook,' a radar anomaly found in the Gulf of Tonkin and . . . a few other limited areas."[42]

The hard evidence of an attack was, indeed, sketchy—but it was all that McNamara needed to assure Johnson that another incident had occurred. One of the destroyers reported observing the cockpit lights of what appeared to be a North Vietnamese PT boat. Several men aboard the *C. Turner Joy* reported, as McNamara later claimed, that "the destroyer had been fired upon by automatic weapons while being illuminated by searchlights."[43] (Days later, naval officials concluded that these reports were in error. Men on one destroyer had witnessed the gunfire of another destroyer and mistook them for muzzle flashes from an attacking enemy boat.)[44]

Armed with this and other hard "evidence," McNamara finally assured Johnson that the attacks had occurred. Satisfied, Johnson ordered the retaliatory strikes to commence that evening. Later, during a meeting of his National Security Council, the president appeared perplexed about the reason for the attacks. "Do they want a war by attacking our ships in the middle of the Gulf of Tonkin?" Johnson asked, ignoring the fact that the American vessels were far closer to shore than the "middle" of the gulf.* CIA Director John McCone doubted the North Vietnamese really wanted war. Referring to the 34-A raids, he speculated that "the North Vietnamese are reacting defensively to *our* [emphasis added] attacks on their off-shore islands." McCone gave the incident an ominous interpretation. "The attack is a signal to us that the North Vietnamese have the will and determination to continue the war," he said. "They are raising the ante."[45] Johnson remained determined to respond militarily and resolved that "we

---

*But as Edwin Moïse observed: "Had the Soviet Union staged a vessel equipped with five-inch guns right off Charleston harbor, [Joint Chiefs Chairman Earle] Wheeler would have treated this as a serious provocation. Had the Soviet Union put such a vessel off Charleston during a week when the Soviet Union was also sending Cuban gunboats to shell the South Carolina coast, it is unlikely that it could have remained there even twenty-four hours without being attacked by U.S. forces" (Moïse, 68).

should do more than merely return the fire of the attacking ships." The only real question in his mind, he revealed to the group, was how many North Vietnamese targets should be attacked.

As Johnson steamed ahead, determined to answer the North Vietnamese assault with a forceful military response, McNamara revealed to the group that he had no unclassified confirmation of the attacks—although it is difficult to understand why he would have classified the reported visual sightings by the ship's crew, unless it would have exposed the Navy's support for the OPLAN 34-A raids. "Do we know for a fact that the North Vietnamese provocation took place?" inquired Carl Rowan, director of the U.S. Information Agency. The reason for his question, Rowan explained, was that "we must be prepared to be accused of fabricating the incident."* McNamara's answer seemed to suggest he had more doubt about the attacks than he had previously revealed to Johnson. Saying that definitive proof would not be available until the morning of August 5, McNamara explained the only current evidence of an attack was "highly classified" and "information we cannot use." Nothing in the official record suggests that he explained, even to the National Security Council—a group in which each member possessed the highest security clearances—the "highly classified" evidence of the attacks. Nor is there evidence that Johnson or anyone else questioned the wisdom of proceeding with attacks on North Vietnam without a thorough examination of McNamara's evidence.[46]†

The following month, after another reported confrontation between U.S. and North Vietnamese naval vessels in the gulf, Johnson revealed the extent of his doubts about the August 4 incident. "You just came in a few weeks ago," he told McNamara, "and said, 'Goddamn, they're launching an attack on us, they're firing on us.' And we got through with all the firing and we concluded maybe they hadn't fired at all." Johnson demanded more discretion from the Navy. "But I sure want more caution on the part of these admirals and these destroyer commanders, whoever they are, to whether they are being fired on or not," he told his Defense secretary. "I don't want them to be just like some change-of-life woman, running up saying, by God, that she's been raped just because a man walks in the room." Johnson clearly realized the political implications of a precipitous U.S. military response based on flimsy evidence. "That's the basic argu-

---

*Most likely, Rowan believed that charges of fabrication would come from the North Vietnamese, not from the skeptical critics of Johnson's response to the Gulf of Tonkin incidents.

†In 1995, McNamara acknowledged that the second "attack" had probably not occurred.

ment between [me] and Goldwater," he said. "Now, let's don't get sucked in on his side of it."[47]

Having determined to attack North Vietnam, Johnson was now ready to take on Congress. He had instructed the U.S. Navy to behave in a highly provocative manner following the August 2 incident. Now relying on the flimsy, inconclusive evidence of a second attack, he seized the opportunity to obtain widespread congressional support for his Vietnam policies. Although his Vietnam truce with Goldwater had been a case of great good fortune, a near-unanimous bipartisan congressional endorsement of his policies was a bonanza he never expected. As a wily politician, Johnson would take the opportunity and run with it.

McGeorge Bundy, for one, understood the political forces set in motion by the Gulf of Tonkin incidents. At a White House meeting on August 5, he jokingly urged one of Johnson's new assistants, Douglas Cater, to resist the urge to closely examine the proposed resolution. "Perhaps the matter should not be thought through too far," Bundy said, adding that "he welcomed the recent events as justification for a resolution the Administration had wanted for some time."[48]

In a meeting with congressional leaders on the evening of August 5, Johnson again presented his idea for a congressional resolution—and encountered, as Bundy no doubt anticipated, nothing but enthusiastic support. As drafted by State Department officials, the latest draft of the joint resolution in Johnson's possession declared that the United States "will not tolerate unprovoked and illegal armed attacks on its forces" and would take "such measures as may be necessary" to prevent future attacks. Congress would be asked to support the president's "determination" to "respond instantly with the use of appropriate force to repel any unprovoked attack" against U.S. armed forces. However, the resolution that Johnson and his advisors envisioned not only endorsed his response to the Gulf of Tonkin attacks, but invited Congress to give him broad authority to fight a war against the Communists in Southeast Asia. Congress would be asked to affirm Johnson's power, "upon request from any nation in Southeast Asia, to take, consistent with the Charter of the United Nations, all measures including the use of armed force to assist that nation in the defense of its political independence and territorial integrity against aggression or subversion."[49]

Yet in his presentation to the bipartisan group, Johnson implied that the resolution he sought would only give congressional assent to his retaliatory actions scheduled for later that evening. "We felt that we should move with the action recommended by the Joint Chiefs," Johnson told the group, "but I wanted to get the congressional concurrence. I think it would be very damaging to ask for it and not get it." Bourke Hickenlooper, who affirmed the right of the president "to order the armed forces into action," expressed his belief that such a resolution was not necessary. "It is my own personal feeling that it is up to the President to prepare the kind and type of resolution he believes would be proper." Congress, he said, would then debate it. In that event, he said, "I have no doubt in my mind that concrete action would be taken."

But Johnson stressed again the importance of securing formal congressional approval for his actions. He recalled Truman's difficulties in 1950 after his unilateral decision to send troops into South Korea. "I don't think any resolution is necessary," Johnson said, "but I think it is a lot better to have it in light of what we did in Korea." That statement seemed to rouse an already supportive group. "I think Congress has a responsibility," said House Speaker John McCormack, "and should show a united front to the world." House Republican Minority Leader Charles Halleck chimed in: "The president knows there is no partisanship among us." Hickenlooper called the proposed resolution "appropriate and proper."

Of the assembled congressional leaders, only Mansfield dissented. "I suppose you want us to be frank," he told Johnson, confessing that "I don't know how much good it [the reprisals] will do." Instead of reacting to the incidents by attacking North Vietnam, Mansfield urged restraint and suggested that the United States treat them as "isolated acts of terror" and then refer the whole matter to the United Nations or the governing body of the 1954 Geneva Convention. Mansfield believed that Johnson was making an international incident out of a minor naval encounter. "In this instance, Russia is remote," he said. "China is not involved directly." The United States, he feared, "may be getting all involved with a minor, third-rate state" with the prospects for an inconclusive result. "The Communists won't be faced down," he argued, adding that sending the kind of strong message that Johnson proposed would cost "a lot of lives."

As usual, Johnson was unmoved by Mansfield's overture for peace. As the meeting drew to a close, Johnson said, "I have told you what I want from you," and looked around the table, polling each member present. This time, there was no dissent—not even from Mansfield, who simply promised that the resolution would be placed before the Foreign Relations Committee. "I will support it," said Fulbright. Republican Senator George Aiken of Vermont—long skeptical about American involvement in Vietnam—may have summed up the mood of the congressional leaders when he observed, presciently, "By the time you send [the resolution] up, there won't be anything for us to do but support you."[50] Later that evening, Johnson moved to secure one more important supporter for his actions in North Vietnam. In a phone call to Goldwater, Johnson read the statement he would soon deliver to the nation. Goldwater was supportive. "I think you've taken the right steps," he said, "and I'm sure you'll find that everybody will be behind you."[51]

At 11:36 P.M., Johnson went before the television cameras to tell the nation that "a number of hostile vessels" had attacked the two destroyers in the Gulf of Tonkin. "Repeated acts of violence against the Armed Forces of the United States must be met not only with alert defense, but with positive reply." As he spoke, Johnson said, "air action is now in execution" against targets in North Vietnam. Trying to put the incidents in some perspective, Johnson argued that they reinforced the "importance of the struggle for peace and security in southeast Asia." He pledged that the American response would be "limited and fitting" and he sought "no wider war." In the first public mention of a congressional resolution, Johnson said he had discussed with congressional leaders the importance of "making it clear that our government is united in its determination to take all necessary measures in support of freedom and in defense of peace in Southeast Asia." He had, he said, been given "encouraging assurance" that his resolution "will be promptly introduced, freely and expeditiously debated, and passed with overwhelming support."[52] That evening, the United States launched sixty-four sorties against four North Vietnamese patrol boat bases and an oil storage depot. Of the twenty-five targets, the Pentagon later reported that all were "severely" damaged. In the fighting, however, the North Vietnamese downed two American planes.[53]

The next day, in a speech at Syracuse University, Johnson did his best to give his Vietnam policy a moderate, bipartisan aura and, with an eye to Congress, to elevate the incident to the level of an international crisis. As Johnson described them, the attacks on the *Maddox* were historic in proportion. Without specifically saying so, Johnson signaled his would-be political detractors that he would not succumb to the mistakes that had bedeviled Harry Truman fourteen years earlier. "Aggression — deliberate, willful and systematic aggression—has unmasked its face to the entire world," Johnson said. In a reference to Europe's appeasement of Hitler at Munich, Johnson added: "The world remembers—the world must never forget—that aggression unchallenged is aggression unleashed." Johnson closed his speech with an appeal to bipartisanship, telling his audience that "there are no parties and there is no partisanship when our peace or the peace of the world is imperiled by aggression in any part of the world."[54]

LIKE THE OTHER congressional leaders, Fulbright and Mansfield had no reason to doubt McNamara's assurances that the second incident had occurred as described. Rusk had been particularly persuasive during the briefing's early minutes when he argued that the United States "must make it quite clear that we are resolved not to overlook the threat that is posed to our forces." Furthermore, he said, Johnson's decisive response "would make it clear as we can that we are not going to run out of Southeast Asia, but that we have no national ambitions, nor either in a war to the north."[55]

In a White House meeting on August 5, Johnson and his aides gave Fulbright further assurances that reports about the second incident were accurate. What they did not tell him, however, was that days earlier the naval commander on the *Maddox* had expressed grave reservations about that incident; nor did they disclose the true relationship between the De-Soto patrols and the provocative 34-A commando raids. Although Bundy surely knew he was deceiving the chairman of the Foreign Relations Committee about a critical national security matter, he assured him that the 34-A raids had no connection with U.S. naval operations. Unlike his wide-ranging discussions with Russell over whether to expand the war into the north, Johnson never fully discussed his options in Vietnam with Fulbright. Although Fulbright had some knowledge that Johnson was considering a new military initiative in Vietnam, he did not know the extent of the discussions that had occurred behind the closed doors of the Pentagon and the White House.[56]

Satisfied that the Gulf of Tonkin incidents were nothing more than, as Johnson claimed, "open aggression on the high seas against the United States of America," Fulbright agreed to lead the debate when the resolution reached the Senate floor. "He readily agreed to the administration's wishes," recalled Seth Tillman, one of Fulbright's aides on the Foreign Relations Committee staff. "He had no reason, as he often ruefully recalled, to doubt their veracity. . . . He had no reason to doubt what he was being told by Rusk and McNamara."[57] Fulbright's chief of staff, Lee Williams, believed Fulbright "became persuaded that Johnson was sincere and this was the way to prevent a wider war" and that he merely wanted to give Johnson "the authority to react to situations such as the Tonkin Gulf" incident. "He had no reason to believe," Williams believed, "that he was used as a dupe, if you will, and that this was a ruse on behalf of Johnson to get the authority that he needed to conduct a wider war."[58] Fulbright's enthusiastic support for the resolution was crucial. For dozens of senators, the Foreign Relations Committee chairman was a bellwether on foreign policy and national security issues. His arguments for the resolution from the Senate floor would be, as Johnson and his aides knew, persuasive to any undecided senator.

Fulbright may also have been motivated by more than a simple desire to assist Johnson in Vietnam. In fact, his intense animus toward Goldwater coupled with his desire to help Johnson politically may have seriously clouded his judgment in the days following the events in the Gulf of Tonkin. "I was not in a suspicious frame of mind," Fulbright later acknowledged. "I was afraid of Goldwater."[59] According to Tillman, "Fulbright himself was quite appalled at the prospect of Barry Goldwater being elected." From his subsequent discussions with Fulbright, Tillman believed the chairman merely saw the resolution as "a resounding statement of national unity" and of support for a president "who needs to pin down his credentials as tough on Communism and deny the Republicans a weapon that they can use against him."[60] McGovern agreed. "I think that Fulbright really did just think it was for the '64 campaign," he said. "It was designed to undercut Goldwater's efforts to paint Johnson as a weakling." In fact, McGovern said, virtually every Democrat in the Senate was persuaded of that view. "That's really how everybody but [Ernest] Gruening and [Wayne] Morse were sold on it," he said.[61] As another Foreign Relations Committee staff member, Pat Holt, observed: "Compared to Goldwater, the Johnson reaction looked moderate."[62]

On the afternoon of Wednesday, August 5, Ball came to Mansfield's Capitol office for a legislative strategy session with Fulbright and the senior members of the Senate Foreign Relations and Armed Services committees, as well as members of the House Foreign Affairs Committee. Fulbright, they agreed, would introduce the resolution in the Senate later that day. Russell and Hickenlooper, as chairman and senior Republican on the Armed Services Committee, and Leverett Saltonstall, the senior Republican on the Foreign Relations Committee, would join Fulbright as co-sponsors, thereby ensuring broad bipartisan support. The senators also agreed that the Senate would refer the resolution to the two committees for joint hearings the following day.[63]

Mansfield was not an active participant in the meeting. But to a question about altering the resolution's wording, he finally spoke up. Congress, he insisted, should pass the resolution just as Johnson had submitted it. Russell, however, suggested one change—the addition of thirteen words to the last paragraph, stating that the resolution could be dissolved by presidential decree, "except that it may be terminated earlier by concurrent resolution of the Congress." With that, Russell ensured that the resolution's future would not be solely in the hands of the president. Because concurrent congressional resolutions are not subject to presidential veto, Congress could unilaterally repeal the resolution at any time.[64]

Pat Holt recalled that he and Bill Darden, chief of staff for the Armed Services Committee, watched the discussion "with growing incredulity." Recalled Holt: "I remember Darden and I whispering to each other during the meeting, 'There's no way they're going to get this thing done that fast.'" Neither man could have imagined the ease with which Congress was about to hand Johnson carte blanche in Southeast Asia on the basis of incomplete and inaccurate reports about a minor naval skirmish in the Gulf of Tonkin. "I have frequently thought since then," Holt later acknowledged, "that I should have at least raised a caution that this thing had implications that maybe ought to be considered at greater length, but the reason I didn't was that I was absolutely sure that the damn committee would do it without any prompting from me."[65]

Why did Mansfield and Fulbright want to push the resolution through the Senate so quickly? Francis Valeo thought that the two men sincerely believed they were assisting Johnson in *containing* the war. "I believe the way it was sold to Mansfield, and probably to Fulbright," Valeo said later, "was that if we do this now, we make this statement, that will put an end to this and we'll avoid getting ourselves more deeply involved. But we have to do it without debate or without discussion, because if we don't make a unified show of strength in this situation they'll pluck at our weaknesses or our divisions." When Valeo confronted Mansfield with his concerns about the Senate's haste in enacting the resolution, Mansfield hinted at his own anxiety, but showed no willingness to stand up to Johnson. "Sometimes you have to do things that you may not always agree with," Mansfield explained, "but you don't have any choice.[66]*

By now the resolution had acquired the momentum of a runaway freight train. On Thursday, August 6, the House Armed Services Committee met for forty minutes and quickly passed the resolution, 29–0.[†] As committee member Dante Fascell, a Florida Democrat, later recalled, few House members were eager to ascertain the facts behind the incident, nor did they wish to explore the important constitutional questions raised by the resolution's expansive language. Fascell believed that most members reasoned, "'Well, the president wants this power and he needs to have it.' . . . Who cared about the facts of the so-called incident that would trigger this authority? So, the resolution was just hammered right on through by everybody."[67]

Testifying before the House committee, Rusk had argued that the resolution's language giving Johnson authority to "take all necessary steps, including the use of armed forces," to defend South Vietnam was really no

---

*In a 1976 interview Mansfield, like many other embarrassed supporters of the resolution, acknowledged doubts about the Senate's actions. "I went along reluctantly, because I had my doubts about the incidents in the Gulf of Tonkin. I still have them. They're stronger now than ever before." The American destroyers, he said, "were in areas where they could expect to be attacked" (Mansfield, 12/13/76, BBC, Mansfield Papers).

†Two members, Republicans H. R. Gross of Iowa and Edward Derwinski of Illinois, voted "present." Derwinski justified his vote by saying that the White House never informed Congress on foreign policy matters "until they get in a jam" (Galloway, *The Gulf of Tonkin Resolution*, 78).

different than authority Congress had already extended to Eisenhower and Kennedy in resolutions relating to Formosa, the Middle East, and Cuba. "There can be no doubt," Rusk said, "that these previous resolutions form a solid legal precedent for the action now proposed. Such action is required to make the purposes of the United States clear and to protect our national interest."[68] The House members offered no challenge.

Meanwhile, the Senate was hardly more deliberative. The closed-door, joint session of the Armed Services and Foreign Relations committees, chaired by Fulbright, lasted all of an hour and forty minutes. But it was more than enough time for McNamara, accompanied by Rusk and Wheeler, to thoroughly deceive committee members about the incidents and the nature of the naval operations that had provoked them. In describing the events of August 4 with an air of rock-solid certainty that had eluded him two days earlier, McNamara informed rapt senators that "torpedoes were launched, automatic weapons fire was directed against the vessels." With McNamara serving up "definitive" details about the attacks, Rusk talked solemnly about the incidents in terms of their larger implications—especially in relation to China. "It is our impression that the Chinese would give at least very strong political and public support to the North Vietnamese in this situation," Rusk said, a grave statement that only emphasized the need to pass Johnson's resolution quickly.[69]

Morse, of course, was having none of it. Earlier, an informed acquaintance in the Pentagon had warned him that McNamara's version of events might not be truthful. The *Maddox*, the informant said, was actually much closer to the North Vietnamese coast than the administration acknowledged. Furthermore, the ship was not on a pure "routine patrol" when attacked on August 2. Its mission, he said, was more involved. "Get the logs," the man urged Morse.[70]

When his time to question the witnesses arrived, Morse was blunt. "I am unalterably opposed to this course of action which, in my judgment, is an aggressive course of action on the part of the United States. I think we are kidding the world," he told McNamara, "if you try to give the impression that when the South Vietnamese naval boats bombarded two islands a short distance off the coast of North Vietnam, we were not implicated." Morse believed, he said, that "those boats didn't act in a vacuum as far as the United States was concerned."

> We knew those boats were going up there, and that naval action was a clear act of aggression against the territory of North Vietnam, and our ships were in Tonkin Bay, in international waters, but nevertheless they were in Tonkin Bay to be interpreted as standing as a cover for naval operations of South Vietnam. . . . Sure, there was all the vicious infiltration of Communist technique, but the first act of open territorial aggression by

way of military operation was South Vietnam naval boats against two
North Vietnam islands with American naval vessels conveniently standing by as a backstop.

In response, McNamara, with convincing deceit, unequivocally denied
Morse's charges. "Our Navy played absolutely no part in, was not associated with, was not aware of, any South Vietnamese actions, if there were
any," he said.* "I want to make that very clear to you. The *Maddox* was
operating in international waters, was carrying out a routine patrol of the
type we carry out all over the world at all times." Despite that fact that little of what he had just said was true, McNamara insisted that "I think it is
extremely important that you understand this. If there is any misunderstanding on that we should discuss the point at some length."

"I think we should," Morse replied.

"I say this flatly," McNamara told Morse. "This is the fact."

McNamara's unequivocal denials of U.S. complicity in the 34-A raids
did not satisfy Morse. "Didn't you, as secretary of defense," Morse asked,
"have knowledge that the attack on the island was going to be made?"

Here, McNamara may have been on firmer ground. "I did not have
knowledge at the time of the attack on the island," he answered, but added,
"There is no connection between this patrol and any action by South
Vietnam."

Morse was not deterred and continued to insist that the U.S. Navy had
"backstopped this open naval attack of South Vietnam on two islands of
three to five, six miles off the coast of North Vietnam. That is where I think
we got ourselves clearly implicated and South Vietnam got herself implicated in an aggressive attack on the territorial integrity of North Vietnam."
In reply, McNamara was equally adamant that "our ships had absolutely
no knowledge of it, were not connected with it; in no sense of the word can
we be considered to have backstopped the effort."[71]

With his educated, penetrating questions, Morse was the only committee member concerned about any connection between the 34-A raids
and the DeSoto patrols. Most senators who posed questions were far more
worried about how China or the Soviet Union might react to an escalation
of the conflict. Rusk sought to relieve their anxiety with assurances that
Johnson would take no steps toward escalation without advising and con-

---

*That statement was, as McNamara knew, false. He had known about the South
Vietnamese 34-A operation. Years later, he acknowledged as much, when he wrote:
"Long before the August events in the Tonkin Gulf, many of us who knew about
the 34A operations had concluded they were essentially worthless" (McNamara,
In Retrospect, 130).

sulting Congress. He assured them that "this consultation" would "in no sense be the last contact between the executive and the legislative branches on these problems in southeast Asia." Rusk promised that "there will continue to be regular consultations not only with committees but between the president and the congressional leaders, and on a bipartisan basis." That promise—soon forgotten and broken by Rusk and Johnson—may have been comforting to Fulbright, Mansfield, and others. But not to Democrat Russell Long of Louisiana, who admonished Rusk not to waste too much time consulting Congress. "As much as I would like to be consulted with on this kind of thing," Long said, "the less time you spend on consulting and the quicker you shoot back, the better off you are."[72]

By the end of the brief hearing, committee members were satisfied with McNamara's description of events, as well as Rusk's arguments for the necessity of formal congressional approval for Johnson's Vietnam policy. In a 31–1 vote, members of both committees approved the resolution. Morse—his principled objections almost totally disregarded by colleagues who considered him little more than a contentious maverick—opposed the resolution. Throughout the hearing neither Fulbright, Mansfield, nor Russell asked a single question. In its official report to the Senate, the committee supported Johnson's actions "to meet the attack on U.S. forces in southeast Asia by the Communist regime in North Vietnam." Brushing aside the numerous constitutional concerns that had never been addressed, the joint committee gave Johnson its "full support" for his "resolute policy" of preventing "further aggression or to retaliate with suitable measures should such aggression take place." Committee members were "satisfied that the decision of the president to retaliate against the North Vietnamese gunboat attacks was both soundly conceived and skillfully executed."[73]

That afternoon, Mansfield brought the resolution to a virtually vacant Senate chamber. Opening the Senate debate, the majority leader praised Johnson for acting "in the hope of preventing an expansion of the conflict in Asia." Johnson's actions and the resolution, Mansfield told the Senate, were all designed "in the hope of restraining the dogs of war." When Mansfield finished his brief opening remarks, Fulbright picked up the theme and likewise praised Johnson for his "wise and necessary action" in responding to "the unprovoked attacks on American naval vessels." He commended to the Senate, with little elaboration, the resolution which, he explained, "expresses the approval and support of the Congress for the determination of the president to take such action as may be necessary, now and in the future, to restrain or repel Communist aggression in southeast Asia."

McGovern was the first senator to question Fulbright on the resolution. Making clear he was not "casting doubt" on its "wisdom," McGovern raised the very question Johnson had asked, but that should have given administration officials pause after the questionable events of August 2 and 4. "All of us have been puzzled, if not baffled, as to why a little state such as North Vietnam should seek a deliberate naval conflict with the United States with the overwhelming naval and air power that we have in that area." Although McGovern had not aligned himself with Morse's allegations, Fulbright took the question to mean that McGovern had concerns about collusion between the South Vietnamese and American navies. The operation of two American destroyers, Fulbright assured McGovern, "was entirely unconnected or unassociated with any coastal forays the South Vietnamese themselves may have conducted." Seemingly satisfied by Fulbright's unequivocal answer, McGovern moved on to his next concern. "Does the senator," he asked Fulbright, "think there is any danger in this resolution that we may be surrendering to General Khanh's position" about taking the war to the north? Fulbright's answer was firm and reassuring. "I do not think there is any danger of that," he replied. "The policy of our government not to expand the war still holds." Pleased with Fulbright's argument that "this is a perfectly legitimate and proper way to defend oneself from the kind of aggression South Vietnam has been subjected to for many years," McGovern responded, "I am inclined to agree with the senator."

McGovern was not the only senator with questions about the events in the gulf. Democrat Allen Ellender of Louisiana, a longtime critic of U.S. involvement in Vietnam, asked Fulbright questions about the nature of the DeSoto patrols and their relationship with the 34-A raids. "Were we there to protect them?" Ellender asked. "The ships were not assigned to protect anyone," Fulbright said accurately. But in quoting McNamara and Rusk, Fulbright unwittingly disseminated false information. "They had no connection whatever with any Vietnamese ships that might have been operating in the same general area." Ellender, however, was persistent. "I am trying to discover," he explained, "if our forces could have done anything which might have provoked these attacks." Fulbright assured Ellender "categorically" that no evidence pointed to that conclusion.

As floor manager of the resolution, Fulbright defended not only the administration's version of the attacks in the Gulf of Tonkin, but the rationale for the Southeast Asia Resolution. To a question by Republican Owen Brewster of Maine—would the resolution authorize "the landing of large American armies in Vietnam or China?"—Fulbright was candid. Nothing in the resolution "contemplates it." But, as Fulbright added, "the language of the resolution would not prevent it. It would authorize whatever the commander in chief feels is necessary." While the resolution might not prevent such escalation, Fulbright assured Brewster that "the last thing" the Foreign Relations Committee wanted "is to become involved in a land war in Asia." Later Democrat Gaylord Nelson of Wisconsin revealed similar concerns in a pointed question to Fulbright:

> Am I to understand that it is the sense of Congress that we are saying to the executive branch: "If it becomes necessary to prevent further aggression, we agree now, in advance, that you may land as many divisions as deemed necessary, and engage in a direct military assault on North Vietnam if it becomes the judgment of the executive, the commander in chief, that this is the only way to prevent further aggression?"

Fulbright's answers were honest. Although he believed that it would be "very unwise under any circumstances" to send large land forces to Asia, Fulbright could not assure Nelson that the resolution precluded such action. "I do not know what the limits are," he said. "I do not know how to answer the senator's question and give him an absolute assurance that large numbers of troops would not be put ashore. I would deplore it." Fulbright's response did not comfort Nelson. Although he said he would support the resolution, Nelson added that Congress should not "leave the impression that it consents to a radical change in our mission or objective in South Vietnam." Fulbright could offer little comfort. "In all frankness," he said, "I cannot say to the senator that I think the joint resolution would in any way be a deterrent, a prohibition, a limitation, or an expansion of the president's power to use the armed forces in a different way or more extensively than he is now using them."

Later, in answering questions from Republican Senator John Sherman Cooper of Kentucky, Fulbright went a little further in his interpretation. "We are not giving to the president any powers he has under the Constitution as commander in chief," he said. "We are in effect approving of his use of the powers that he has." Honing in further on Fulbright's understanding of the resolution, Cooper posed what would become the crucial question of the entire debate: "Are we now giving the president advance authority to take whatever action he may deem necessary respecting South Vietnam and its defense, or with respect to the defense of any other country included in the [SEATO] treaty?" Fulbright's candid response would haunt him for years. "I think that is correct," he said.

"Then, looking ahead," Cooper continued, "if the president decided that it was necessary to use such force as could lead into war, we will give that authority by this resolution?"

"That is the way I would interpret it," Fulbright said, adding that Congress could always unilaterally withdraw its approval if it disagreed with the president's actions.

Still trying to comprehend the dimension of the resolution, Cooper summarized it in the form of another question to Fulbright: "We are now providing the president, if he determines it necessary, the authority to attack cities and ports in North Vietnam, not primarily to prevent an attack upon our forces but, as he might see fit, to prevent any further aggression against South Vietnam?" Summarizing the gamble Congress was prepared to take, Fulbright explained that the provision in question "is intended to give clearance to the president to use his discretion. We all hope and believe that the president will not use this discretion arbitrarily or irresponsibly. *We know he is accustomed to consulting with the Joint Chiefs of Staff and with congressional leaders. But he does not have to do that*" (emphasis added).[74]

Fulbright's was not the only persuasive voice in favor of the resolution. As a senior member of the Senate, an intimate of Johnson, and chairman of the Armed Services Committee, Russell wielded enormous influence and power among senators of both parties. Taking the floor immediately after Fulbright's presentation, the Georgia senator sought to allay fears that the resolution might alter the balance of power between Congress and the White House. "The resolution," Russell insisted, "is intended to demonstrate that Congress approves the retaliatory action that has been taken in defense of our flag and our armed forces, and that Congress shares in the determination that this country will do everything necessary to defend our national interests, wherever they may be endangered."

To Russell, the Gulf of Tonkin incidents involved far more than congressional support for Johnson's policy in Vietnam. "Our national honor is at stake," he insisted. "We cannot and we will not shrink from defending it. No sovereign nation would be entitled to the respect of other nations, or, indeed, could maintain its self respect, if it accepted the acts that have been committed against us without undertaking to make some response."[75] With Russell's jingoistic remarks, the lines were now more clearly drawn than ever: to approve the resolution was to defend the nation's sacred honor. Observed Carl Marcy, the Foreign Relations Committee chief of staff: "You almost had to be a Wayne Morse or a fool—and I never thought Wayne Morse was a fool—to have voted against the Tonkin Resolution."[76]

To no one's surprise, Morse was still vehement in his opposition. In its basic form, his argument was simple: the Southeast Asia Resolution was an unconstitutional reaction to a contrived provocation by the United States. "All the protestations on the part of the State Department and the Pentagon cannot change a physical fact," Morse insisted.

> The presence of those ships in that proximity to the North Vietnamese coast, while an act of war was being committed against [the] North Vietnamese coast by the bombing of those islands, was bound to implicate us. We are implicated. . . .

> If we had knowledge—and we did have knowledge—that there was
> to be a South Vietnamese bombardment of the islands, we should not
> have had our ships anywhere in the area.

Challenged by Democrat Frank Lausche of Ohio, who insisted that "our government had no knowledge" about the 34-A raids, Morse responded forcefully, certain of the accuracy of his information. "I state categorically that they knew the bombardment was going to take place before the ships ever moved up there." Morse was on solid ground. In his testimony before the joint Senate committee, McNamara had acknowledged that the U.S. embassy in Saigon was "aware" of the 34-A raids.[77]

The next day, August 7, as the Senate debate wound to a close, Morse railed against the resolution for almost two hours. This time, he argued that it gave Johnson "authority to go beyond immediate self-defense of the United States and proceed with a war campaign." Morse, who had opposed the Formosa and the Middle East resolutions on similar grounds, insisted that "such resolutions" were unconstitutional because they "constitute a predated declaration of war"—a notion that, interestingly, Fulbright had not disputed in his exchange with Cooper the previous afternoon. Except for Gruening—who agreed with Morse that the resolution was "the equivalent of declaration of war"—Morse was alone.[78] His determined efforts to persuade the Senate that the resolution was ill advised had failed. As one colleague told him, "Hell, Wayne, you can't get in a fight with the President at a time when the flags are waving and we're about to go to a national convention. All Lyndon wants is a piece of paper telling him we did right out there, and we support him, and he's the kind of president who follows the rules and won't get the country into war without coming back to Congress."[79]

As the final vote neared, another skeptic was Gaylord Nelson, who remained troubled by the resolution's expansive grant of military latitude. Nelson agreed with Johnson's stated desire to send "a message" to North Vietnam. "But as I read it," he later said, "it was broad enough to authorize the president to broaden the war. And I figured that it ought to be clarified."[80] McGovern, too, was troubled. And as he walked to the Senate floor in the early afternoon, he encountered Nelson, who explained a clarifying amendment that he planned to offer. "Well, I really hope you do it," McGovern told Nelson. "I still don't feel right about voting for that thing, but I guess I'm going to do it."[81]

When he reached the floor, Nelson submitted his amendment and hoped Fulbright would accept it without a vote. The amendment was a simple statement that sought to limit Johnson's latitude. While affirming Johnson's policy of "seeking no extension of the present military conflict," Nelson's amendment stated that U.S. policy "is to limit our role to the provision of aid, training assistance, and military advice, and it is the sense of Congress that, except when provoked to a greater response, we should continue to attempt to avoid a direct military involvement in the southeast Asian conflict." Although Fulbright said he agreed with Nelson's intent, he refused to accept the amendment. "It states fairly accurately what the president has said would be our policy," Fulbright assured Nelson, explaining that he could not support the amendment because its inclusion would delay final passage by requiring a conference committee with the House. Fulbright made it clear his goal was speed, not perfecting the resolution. "I cannot accept the amendment and go to conference with it," he explained, "and thus take responsibility for delaying matters."[82]

Nelson was no different than a handful of skeptical senators. "Well, okay," Nelson later said he reasoned, "I didn't have any confidence as an expert in foreign policy. I'm talking to a person that I admired the most in this field [Fulbright]." Regretfully, Nelson said, he accepted Fulbright's "assurances that that's what the Gulf of Tonkin [Resolution] means anyway and that's the intent.[83]* McGovern explained his support for the resolution with a similar rationale. "It was a political decision on my part, influenced directly by Fulbright."[84]

Of those senators not as skeptical as Nelson and McGovern—and that meant the vast majority of senators of both parties—Republican George Aiken of Vermont best captured their sentiments. He was "still apprehensive over the outcome of his decision" to support the resolution, he said, yet believed that "since it has been made, I feel that I, as an American citizen, can do no less than support the president in his capacity as leader of our nation. I believe that our country will be in greater jeopardy if we do not now support his decision." Although he spoke of his "misgivings," Aiken said not a word about the constitutional questions Morse and Gruening had raised. "I do not believe that any of us can afford to take a position opposing the president of the United States for exercising the power which we, under our form of government, and through our legislative bodies, have delegated to his office."[85]

After less than ten hours of debate, during which the Senate chamber was less than a third full, the Senate voted in the early afternoon of August

---

*Presidential Press Secretary George Reedy later acknowledged that senators like Nelson were "misled by Fulbright's assurances and Fulbright had every reason to believe those assurances." Reedy, who was present when White House officials briefed Fulbright on the resolution, had "no doubt" that Johnson "was saying this was a one-shot thing and it was only intended for this particular operation" (Olson, *Mansfield and Vietnam*, 136).

7. Ninety of the one hundred senators were present. When the votes were tallied, only Morse and Gruening opposed the resolution. (The ten absent senators were each recorded as having supported the resolution.) Eighty-eight senators—including prominent future war opponents like McGovern, Church, Eugene McCarthy, Edward Kennedy, Albert Gore Sr., and Edmund Muskie—voted in the affirmative. Earlier that day, after a mere forty minutes of "debate," the House approved the resolution, 416–0.[86]

At the White House, Johnson welcomed the vote as "a demonstration to all the world of the unity of all Americans."[87] On this issue, at least, Americans did appear united. "In a single stroke, Mr. Johnson has, at least temporarily, turned his greatest political vulnerability in foreign policy into one of his strongest assets," pollster Louis Harris observed in the *Washington Post* on August 10. Eighty-five percent of Americans supported Johnson's military response to the Gulf of Tonkin attacks. Only the month before, 58 percent of Americans had doubts about Johnson's Vietnam policy. But in the wake of the Gulf of Tonkin incidents, 72 percent now approved the president's course. By a margin of 71 percent to 29 percent, Americans said they trusted Johnson over Goldwater in Vietnam.[88]

But the true importance of the Tonkin Gulf incidents and the resulting congressional resolution was not its impact on public opinion. Nor, as historian Marilyn B. Young later observed, was the resolution's most important aspect its authorization for Johnson to wage a wider war. Rather it was "the completeness with which [Congress] accepted administration reasoning about *why* it was doing it." Other than Morse and Gruening, Young noted that "Congress shared the world view of the administration, debating the edges of the issue but never questioning the basic premises."[89] As Johnson's soon-to-be vice presidential running mate, Hubert Humphrey, later observed in his memoirs, "Most of the criticism early in the Johnson administration had to do with the bombing, not the fact of our presence in Indochina."[90] During the Senate debate, Humphrey, like many other colleagues, supported the American presence in Vietnam and enthusiastically shared the administration's embrace of the domino theory as applied to Southeast Asia. "I do not believe," he told the Senate on August 6, "that we show any love of peace by letting the Communists take the world over piece by piece."[91]

In the hours following the vote, meanwhile, McGovern was having second thoughts. Curiously, however, his reservations did not involve any concern about how Johnson might eventually misuse the resolution, but about the determination of South Vietnam to engage the enemy in battle. McGovern told the Senate on August 8 that he did not wish his vote "to be interpreted as an endorsement of our longstanding and apparently growing military involvement in Vietnam." He simply believed that the attacks in the gulf "constituted a military challenge which had to be met with a military response."

Explaining that he had harbored "serious misgivings about our entanglement in Vietnam since we were first committed to that course ten years ago," McGovern said that "we cannot win a conflict against sustained guerrilla activity in Vietnam without enthusiastic and vigorous action on the part of the people and the Government of South Vietnam. I do not think that kind of widespread effort has been demonstrated." He deplored Khanh's renewed militancy and his calls to engage North Vietnam. "Such action on our part would be fraught with the gravest of dangers," McGovern predicted, "and could very well entangle us in a war to the death on a vast scale, claiming the lives of countless thousands of American boys." Like Mansfield, McGovern urged Johnson to heed de Gaulle's advice to convene an international conference to explore Vietnam's neutralization. "What I am saying here," McGovern explained, "is that we are involved in a terribly dangerous military conflict which can only be resolved by a political settlement."[92]*

McGovern was not alone in his anxiety about the ultimate impact of the Senate's action. In brief remarks on the Senate floor the same day, Nelson explained that he had supported the resolution because of Fulbright's "specific assurance" that "the Congress approved no change in our basic mission in Vietnam." Although "some have interpreted the resolution as a broader endorsement of any action against aggression," Nelson said that Fulbright had assured the Senate "this is not its meaning." While this was certainly what Fulbright said during their brief exchange over Nelson's proposed amendment, the Foreign Relations Committee chairman had not attempted to interpret the *Senate's* intention as much as he assured Nelson that *Johnson* had no plans to escalate the war. Earlier, in his floor discussion with Cooper, Fulbright had, indeed, acknowledged that the resolution would give Johnson a virtual blank check to wage war in Vietnam—although he doubted Johnson would ever cash it. The distinction was crucial, and Nelson—and, perhaps, other senators—apparently heard only what he wanted to hear.

Like McGovern and Mansfield, Nelson also called for negotiations to

---

*More than thirty years later, McGovern confessed that one of his deepest regrets in public life was his vote for and his support of the Gulf of Tonkin resolution. "What I regret," he confessed, "is telling audiences all over the country that Johnson would not expand the war and that he would not engage in bombing, he would not attack the northern cities, he would not escalate—all those things that proved to be wrong" (McGovern, by Mann, 1/27/97).

end the war. The United States had made its "firmness unmistakably clear," he said. "While this awareness is fresh, I believe we should attempt to make it clear that if negotiation and diplomacy can achieve the objectives of peace and freedom, this nation is more than willing to 'walk the last mile' in search of a peaceful settlement."[93]

But Johnson, profoundly influenced by the "lessons" of Munich, equated negotiation with appeasement and was, therefore, not interested in seeking a negotiated settlement. While he was not yet determined to escalate the war, he and his advisors were firmly persuaded that any peace conference would merely hasten the day when the Viet Cong, aided by North Vietnam, would overrun the south. That, administration officials believed, would have disastrous consequences for all of Southeast Asia and deal a devastating blow to U.S. national security interests. Thus, diplomacy was out—and so was any fundamental reexamination of the relative importance of Vietnam to U.S. national security. In this politically charged environment, few leaders besides Ball, Mansfield, and Morse were devoting time to the important questions: Was Vietnam really worth it? What were the ultimate risks to U.S. interests if a negotiated settlement, as expected, resulted in a communist takeover in South Vietnam? Did the domino theory still apply in Southeast Asia? Were the Viet Cong truly clients of hegemonic Chinese Communists, or simply a communist-backed nationalist movement fighting a civil war of limited scope? Might negotiations resulting in a coalition government that included NLF representatives be preferable to a massive military commitment in Vietnam by the United States? Could anything short of a massive U.S. military effort in Vietnam prevent a communist victory? What were the upper limits of the U.S. commitment to South Vietnam's "freedom"? If there was a limit, did that indicate that Vietnam's importance to the United States was also limited?

Johnson and his top advisors never formally debated these and other questions. The United States had made solemn commitments to keep South Vietnam out of communist clutches. That was the task before them. Reassessing Vietnam's strategic value or considering the possibility of a coalition government were useless notions to minds that saw communist capitulation as the conflict's only acceptable outcome.

The only diplomacy Johnson would consider was what one U.S. official called "coercive diplomacy."[94] It was just this strategy—based on a belief that the North Vietnamese would eventually end their aggression when persuaded of America's will and resolve to engage them in battle— that Johnson had embraced and that Congress, in its just-enacted resolution, had endorsed. For now, the United States would try to force a North Vietnamese surrender on the battlefield, not at the negotiating table.

Reviewing the events of the past week with his national security advisors on August 10, Johnson doubted that the engagement with North Vietnam would be the last. In his summary memorandum of the meeting,
McGeorge Bundy wrote that the president observed that "if we should do
nothing further, we could find ourselves even worse off than before" the
Gulf of Tonkin incidents. While Johnson did not wish to escalate the war
simply because the recent bombing was popular with the American public, he also did not wish to lose what initiative it had achieved for South
Vietnam. "Instead of letting the other side have the ball," Johnson said,
"we should be prepared to take it."[95]

CHAPTER 26

No Wider War

1964–1965

THE REVERBERATIONS OF THE EVENTS IN THE GULF OF TONKIN were not limited to the U.S. domestic front. Emboldened by the U.S. reprisals in North Vietnam after the gulf incidents, Khanh declared a state of emergency, dissolved the country's constitution, and fired his principal political rival, all on August 7. Assuming the role of president, Khanh then awarded himself near-dictatorial powers. In late August, after angry Buddhists and outraged students in Saigon flooded the streets in a boisterous convulsion of protest, a humiliated Khanh backed down and resigned. After two days of private machinations, however, he reemerged, but drastically weakened—this time as head of the country's Provisional Leadership Committee, which eventually reappointed him prime minister in early September.

The renewed turmoil in Saigon only stiffened Johnson's determination not to further escalate the conflict during the presidential campaign. Although Ambassador Taylor had urged him to quickly resume the DeSoto patrols and the 34-A raids—so as not to leave the "impression that we or the South Vietnamese have been deterred from our operations because of the Tonkin Gulf incidents"[1]—Johnson was hesitant. He suspended the DeSoto patrols and the 34-A raids—the very operations that McNamara had denied were directed by U.S. officials.[2]

Taylor was not the only advisor pushing for a tougher stance against North Vietnam. On August 31, Bundy informed Johnson that the national security team had been discussing "the increase of a U.S. military presence in South Vietnam, perhaps by a naval base, or perhaps by landing a limited number of Marines to guard specific installations." A far more drastic option, which no one but Bundy had mentioned, was "the use of substantial U.S. armed forces in operations against the Viet Cong." Said Bundy:

"I myself believe that before we let this country go we should have a hard look at this grim alternative," adding that he did "not at all think that it is a repetition of Korea."[3]

In a September 9 meeting, Johnson met with his military advisors—including Taylor—to consider their arguments for further reprisals against North Vietnam in the event of more attacks. They would also urge him to continue the naval patrols and 34-A raids in the Gulf of Tonkin. The meeting had barely begun, however, when McNamara reported that although the Joint Chiefs supported the recommendations, they were deeply divided over what to do next. The chiefs of the Air Force and the Marines, he said, were urging "extensive air strikes against North Vietnam." But Wheeler and his Navy and Army colleagues sided with Taylor, who believed that the "drastic action" of attacking North Vietnam might "overstrain the currently weakened" South Vietnamese government. While he did not categorically reject the bombing option, Johnson agreed with Taylor and observed that "we should not do this until our side could defend itself in the streets of Saigon." But Taylor made it clear that "sooner or later we would indeed have to act more forcefully against the north." Now, he said, was not the right time. Johnson did not disagree. He authorized Wheeler to tell the Joint Chiefs that "we would be ready to do more, when we had a base." For now, Johnson explained, he did not want to "enter the patient in a ten-round bout, when he was in no shape to hold out for more than one round. We should get him ready to face three or four rounds at least."

In one of his rare semiprivate moments of despair and confusion over Vietnam, Johnson asked his advisors if Southeast Asia "was worth all this effort." Taylor confidently assured him it was, insisting that the United States "could not afford to let Hanoi win, in terms of our overall position in the area and in the world." Just as adamantly, Wheeler argued that to give up on South Vietnam meant walking away from all of Southeast Asia. "Country after country on the periphery would give way," he said, "and look toward Communist China as the rising power of the area." McGeorge Bundy later recalled that Rusk and CIA Director John McCone registered their agreement with "considerable force."

Despite Johnson's public statements that "we seek no wider war," the president appeared persuaded—albeit reluctantly—that events would eventually force him to expand the conflict to the north. At this meeting, the question of *whether* to bomb was not paramount; rather the operative question was *how long to wait* before a bombing campaign would be effective. The reason to wait, Johnson explained, "must be simply that with a weak and wobbly situation it would be unwise to attack until we could stabilize our base."[4]

The next morning, Taylor went to Capitol Hill for a closed-door hearing of the Senate Foreign Relations Committee during which he encouraged committee members not to lose their will for continued U.S. support of South Vietnam. "We are wrapped in battle, so to speak, and the outcome is not in sight," Taylor said. "That is not the time for anyone to become fainthearted and say we cannot win." While Taylor said he could not "prove we are going to win," he said he could "think of a lot of ways we can lose and I can see the disaster of losing." The only hostile questions from an otherwise polite and deferential committee came, not unexpectedly, from Morse, who pressed him to acknowledge a deliberate U.S. provocation in the Gulf of Tonkin the previous August. Taylor was too wily to allow Morse to box him in. By now, most committee members had learned to ignore Morse's indignation and to blithely tolerate the hostile questions he fired at administration witnesses. Yet those committee members who were still paying attention were treated to an illuminating discussion when Morse engaged Taylor in a fascinating cross-examination that led the ambassador to reveal his increasingly hawkish approach to winning in Vietnam.

Asked by Morse if he knew of "any so-called American military advisors" who "engage in counter attacks . . . beyond the borders of South Vietnam into North Vietnam," Taylor replied that he knew of "no such units going across."

"If you knew of such American military participation would you raise objections to it?" Morse asked.

"No, I would not," he said. When Taylor explained that "I am not the American government" and that his reply was merely "as an individual," Morse responded tartly: "But you are not an individual. You are a symbol of the American government as our ambassador, and I am seeking to find out what our ambassadorial position is as a matter of policy."

To that, Taylor explained that he would not object to American military personnel who accompanied South Vietnamese units into the north "if I felt that contributed to approved American policy."

"Aren't you really saying that you are not objecting to American escalation of this war by indirection?" Morse asked.

Taylor's reply was simple, direct, and very illuminating. "If it is in the interest of American policy," he said.

A disgusted Morse shot back: "I think the president of the United States has the duty to tell that to the American people, and I shall do my best to challenge him to tell it to the American people." Morse finally yielded the floor with this parting shot: "I am more convinced than ever that our policy in Vietnam is against America's public interest."[5]

Of course, Morse was dreaming if he thought Johnson would ever tell the public that he was considering a massive and sustained bombing campaign in North Vietnam. Indeed, Johnson was busy telling the public just the opposite. As he traveled the country, he portrayed himself time and again as a moderate-yet-resolute advocate for peace in Southeast Asia, a leader unwilling to abandon the valiant fight against communism but determined not to escalate the war. He was, in short, the peace candidate. In one of his most celebrated speeches of the campaign, at dedication ceremonies on September 25 for Oklahoma's Eufaula Dam, Johnson ridiculed "those that say you ought to go north and drop bombs, to try to wipe out the supply lines."

> We don't want our American boys to do the fighting for Asian boys. We don't want to get involved in a nation with 700 million people [China] and get tied down in a land war in Asia.
>
> There are some that say we ought to go south and get out and come home, but we don't like to break our treaties and we don't like to walk off and leave people who are searching for freedom, and suffering to obtain it, and walk out on them. We remember when we wanted our freedom from Great Britain, and we remember the people that helped us with it, and we'll never forget them. So we don't want to run out on them. . . .
>
> But we are not about to start another war and we're not about to run away from where we are.[6]

Three days later in Manchester, before a group of New Hampshire newspaper editors, Johnson used subtler rhetoric. "Some of our people—Mr. Nixon, Mr. Rockefeller, Mr. Scranton and Mr. Goldwater—have all, at some time or other, suggested the possible wisdom of going north in Vietnam. Well, now, before you start attacking someone and you launch a big offensive, you better give some consideration to how you are going to protect what you have." On this day, Johnson was the epitome of discretion and prudence. "As far as I am concerned," he said, "I want to be very cautious and careful, and use it only as a last resort, when I start dropping bombs around that are likely to involve American boys in a war in Asia with 700 million Chinese. So *for the moment* I have not thought that we were ready for American boys to do the fighting for Asian boys." Johnson assured the editors that his efforts had gone toward persuading the South Vietnamese to "do their own fighting" with American assistance and advice. "So we are not going north and drop bombs *at this stage of the game*, and we are not going south and run out and leave it for the Communists to take over" (emphasis added).[7]

Later—after Johnson launched the very bombing offensive that led to a massive influx of American troops into South Vietnam—his defenders would point to his New Hampshire speech as proof that Johnson had never unequivocally pledged that he would not bomb North Vietnam or send in more U.S. soldiers. He was, they argued, forthright about the choices facing him and the American people. Viewed in isolation, the case for Johnson's September 28 speech is compelling. But considering the soothing promises about restraint that Johnson made, via Fulbright, during the Gulf of Tonkin resolution debate—and his promises of "no wider war" as well as his repeated pledge to let the "Asian boys" carry the fight—the New Hampshire speech was a refreshing but brief divergence from an otherwise deceitful campaign designed to give the public false choices.

Those choices were a wise, reasonable, and discerning man of peace, or an unstable, belligerent, and fanatical advocate of victory at all costs. Johnson's vice presidential running mate, Hubert Humphrey, told a Wisconsin audience in late October that a vote for Goldwater was a vote for war: "The 'solutions' he [Goldwater] offers are not solutions at all. They are instead a sure path to widening conflict—and ultimately to a terrible holocaust."[8] Even in the New Hampshire speech, Johnson did his best to leave the impression—nuances and qualifications about escalation notwithstanding—that he was the man whom voters should choose if they wanted to avoid war. "It is not any problem to start a war," he said. "That is the easiest thing in the world. I know some folks that think I could start one mighty easy. But it is a pretty difficult problem for all of us to prevent one, and that it what we are trying to do."[9] As historian Thomas Powers noted, Johnson's "lawyerly provisos" about escalation were "lost in the heat of the campaign." In any event, "they had been intended for historians, not the people, and the people had failed to hear them." As Powers concluded, "If any American president had ever promised anything to the American people, then Lyndon Johnson had promised to keep the United States out of the war in Vietnam."[10]

Johnson's choices had been false for another important reason. As he characterized it, voters could choose between Goldwater's version of all-out war or a continuation of Johnson's measured, responsible policies. Yet as Johnson well knew, these were not at all the real choices facing the voters. While most Americans did not yet know it, the administration policy that Johnson pledged to continue in Vietnam was failing. The government in Saigon was a disaster. Infiltration of men and supplies from North Vietnam was rising rapidly. With every passing day the Viet Cong controlled more of the countryside. By almost any objective measure, the U.S. military effort had fallen short of its objectives.

The *real* question, as the president knew, was how the United States should alter its faltering military policy in South Vietnam—with a more aggressive military effort, a renewed push for a peaceful settlement, or withdrawal of U.S. forces? Because Johnson had rejected the last two options, he must have known that he would inevitably be forced to decide whether to salvage the government of South Vietnam with drastic new military measures—that is, a bombing campaign, an influx of American ground troops, or both. McGeorge Bundy apparently saw the inherent danger in Johnson's false choices and urged him in early October to "give a hint of firmness" in his public utterances about Vietnam. Bundy knew that contrary to Johnson's rhetoric, the United States would likely be forced into a military escalation in the months following the election and he did "not want the record to suggest even remotely that we campaigned on peace in order to start a war in November."[11]

But Johnson, busy setting up and smashing straw men, ignored Bundy and never shared the real choices with voters, fearful that he might spark a contentious debate over Vietnam and forfeit his role as the peace candidate. In a nationally televised campaign address on October 7, Johnson invoked the memory of the men who had preceded him in the Oval Office, saying that "each of these presidents has known that guns and rockets alone do not bring peace. Only men can bring peace." His predecessors, Johnson said, "have used our great power with restraint—never once taking a reckless risk which might plunge us into large-scale war." Although he had rebuffed and ridiculed Mansfield's advice to take the Vietnam conflict to an international peace conference, Johnson associated himself with previous presidents who "have used all their efforts to settle disputes peacefully—working with the United Nations." Those men, Johnson explained, were never "afraid to sit down at the council table to work out agreements which might lessen the danger of war without increasing the danger to freedom." While he did not mention Goldwater by name, the reference to his Republican opponent was clear enough when he said that, in contrast to following the wise, restrained examples of previous presidents, "we are told we should consider using atomic weapons in Vietnam." Johnson dismissed such a strategy as contradictory to "the entire course of America in the postwar period." He would not, he insisted, "discard the tested policies of the last twenty years." Instead, he would "match firmness to strength. And I will continue, with all the skill at my command, the patient search for lasting peace."[12]

The next day, at a high school in Lake Country, Indiana, Johnson warmed to his theme and told the students that "you don't get peace by rattling your rockets. You don't get peace by threatening to drop your bombs." While he believed that the United States should remain militarily strong, Johnson argued that, in the pursuit of peace, "you must always have your hand out and be willing to go anywhere, talk to anybody, listen to anything they have to say, do anything that is honorable, in order to avoid pulling that trigger, mashing that button that will blow up the world."[13] In Louisville, Kentucky, two days later, Johnson assured his audience that "we are trying as best we can not to enlarge that war, not to get the United States tied down in a land war in Asia, and not for American boys starting to do the fighting that Asian boys ought to be doing to protect themselves."

At the same time, however, Johnson cautioned that he would not support a precipitate U.S. withdrawal. "We don't want to pull out and come home and say, 'We will turn it all over to you.'" Therefore, Johnson concluded—striking a reasonable, moderate tone—"if you don't want to enlarge it and seek no larger war, and you don't want to pull out and run home, the only thing you can do is what we are doing." That, he said, meant the restrained policy of tit for tat. "We let them know," he said, "that when they shoot at us as they did in the Tonkin Gulf, we will make prompt, adequate, and sufficient reply."[14]

After the Gulf of Tonkin incidents and the resulting congressional passage of the Southeast Asia Resolution, Vietnam had become the least of Johnson's political worries. Good to his promise—and foreclosed by the strong public and congressional support that Johnson enjoyed—Goldwater virtually dropped his criticism of Johnson's Vietnam policies. For his part, Johnson wisely accepted the political wisdom of his trusted aide Bill Moyers, who advised him in early October that "we ought to be hoping that public discussion of Vietnam could be kept to a minimum."[15] When the issue was raised, it was usually Johnson who brought it up—and, then, almost always in a context designed to contrast his determination to avoid a "wider war" with Goldwater's reckless belligerency.

But Vietnam remained on the back burner for another important reason. Despite continuing reports of growing Viet Cong strength in South Vietnam, Johnson was simply loath to take any drastic action before the election. Increasingly preoccupied with the campaign, Johnson knew that whenever events in Vietnam forced him to send men into battle, such as the Gulf of Tonkin reprisals, the confrontation would inevitably overshadow and undermine his soothing rhetoric about peace and "no wider war." As he told his advisors on August 10, from now on he wanted "maximum results and minimum danger."[16]

While Johnson preached peace, his advisors continued developing options for war. Bundy, for one, was already on record favoring discussion of the "grim alternative" of sending in "substantial U.S. armed forces" to arrest the deteriorating situation.[17] Taylor, too, continued to maintain that eventually the United States must consider "a carefully orchestrated bombing attack" on North Vietnam "directed primarily at infiltration and other military targets."[18] Like Taylor and Bundy, the Joint Chiefs were also alarmed by the rapidly deteriorating situation. The week before the general election, the military chiefs advised McNamara they believed "strong military actions" were required "*now* in order to prevent the collapse of *the U.S. position* in Southeast Asia" (emphasis added).[19]

While Johnson may not have been intimately involved in the discussions over the options in Vietnam, he knew what his advisors were discussing. He knew of Taylor's warnings about the eventuality of bombing. He had read Bundy's memorandum that suggested the need to discuss sending additional ground troops. He knew that his military advisors, as they had for a year, were still pushing for more drastic measures to turn the tide in South Vietnam. Despite these clouds of war gathering over the horizon, Johnson sought to make the election a referendum about peace versus war. "Your job Tuesday week [Election Day]," Johnson told a crowd in Columbia, South Carolina, "is how to avoid war, not to provoke war. Your job Tuesday week is to try to select a man that can unite this country instead of man that can divide this country."[20] On November 3, in overwhelming numbers, Americans voted for peace—or at least the status quo as Johnson had characterized it. When the votes were counted, Johnson had buried Goldwater in a landslide of historic proportions.

Given his many campaign speeches in which he had assured Americans—implicitly and explicitly—that a Johnson administration would not escalate the war and would, in fact, seek a peaceful solution to the Vietnam conflict, Johnson could have reasonably concluded that he had achieved a mandate for the kind of negotiated settlement supported by Mansfield and de Gaulle. Tragically, however, Johnson's statements on Vietnam had been a hollow and cynical exercise to gain votes—not by informing the voters about the legitimate military and diplomatic options available in Vietnam to American policymakers, but to so frighten them about the specter of a Goldwater presidency that they would have little choice on Election Day.

Rank-and-file American voters were not only ones to fall for Johnson's deceptive, soothing rhetoric about peace. No less than the chairman of the Senate Foreign Relations Committee had been deluded by Johnson's assurances. Fulbright later claimed that Johnson led him to believe that they shared serious concerns about escalating the war. Johnson assured him that "he was seeking a way to minimize the war and not to expand it and to find a solution and negotiate a settlement." Like most American voters, Fulbright believed Johnson. "I was taken in by the misrepresentations until it was too late."[21]

TWO DAYS BEFORE the election, a Viet Cong mortar attack on the Bien Hoa airfield in South Vietnam killed four U.S. servicemen, wounded another thirty, and destroyed or damaged twenty-seven American aircraft. The attack focused Johnson's attention on the deepening crisis in South Vietnam. Taylor described the daring assault on U.S. forces as "a deliberate act of escalation." He and the Joint Chiefs urged Johnson to respond with "an appropriate act of reprisal," fearing that if Johnson refused to respond, the Viet Cong might be encouraged to stage additional raids. This was, as Taylor described it, "a change of the ground rules" by which the Viet Cong had fought. For the first time, the guerrillas were directly targeting U.S. installations for attacks in a seeming attempt to provoke Johnson to raise the stakes.[22]

Johnson's instincts told him to reject the advice on reprisals. Rusk and McNamara agreed. Yet worried that he might look weak if he refused to respond, Johnson had instructed Bill Moyers to contact pollster Louis Harris. "The president would like to know," Moyers dutifully asked, "if a failure to respond to this attack immediately will be taken by the voters as a sign of weakness by the administration." Harris' advice: "That is the sort of thing people would expect from Barry Goldwater and probably the main reason they are voting for him."[23] Relieved, Johnson did not take the bait and refused to retaliate. But the event was, in the words of William Bundy, "another real clap of thunder in the gathering storm."[24]

Safely in office for four more years, Johnson looked toward his inauguration not with exuberance, but caution—cognizant that the strong support he enjoyed in Congress and among the American people had resulted in power that he could preserve only if he used it judiciously. With visions of ambitious, expensive domestic programs dancing in his mind, Johnson planned to proceed with circumspection and prudence. As he later would tell a group of congressional liaison officers for various government agencies, "I was just elected president by the biggest popular margin in the history of the country, fifteen million votes. Just by the natural way people think and because Barry Goldwater scared the hell out of them, I have already lost about two of these fifteen and am probably getting down to thirteen. If I get in any fight with Congress, I will lose another couple of million, and if I have to send any more of our boys into Vietnam, I may be down to eight million by the end of the summer." Because of this eventual, undeniable erosion in his popular support, Johnson had determined to wage an aggressive campaign for his Great Society domestic programs. He would use his power before he lost it. During this time, he knew that to expend any of those finite powers on Vietnam would only hinder the drive to enact his Great Society agenda. Therefore, he would weigh carefully— in fact, he would agonize over—any proposals to raise the stakes in Vietnam by launching a sustained bombing campaign.

When he finally opted to escalate the war, he would strive mightily to conceal from Congress the budgetary implications of his decisions for fear that conservatives would use the increased military commitments as a pretext for reducing funding for his domestic initiatives. As Johnson reportedly told friends after he had finally decided to escalate the conflict: "I can get the Great Society through right now—this is a golden time. We've got a good Congress and I'm the right president and I can do it. But if I talk about the cost of the war, the Great Society won't go through and the tax bill won't go through."[25]

While he hoped to defer action on Vietnam for as long as possible, Johnson knew the issue would not disappear. And so, prompted by alarm over the Bien Hoa attacks and the larger fear of an imminent total collapse of the South Vietnamese government, he authorized his aides to begin laying plans for the escalation he desperately wanted to avoid, but feared he could not. On November 2, Johnson appointed the State Department's William Bundy to lead an extensive review of U.S. policy in Vietnam by an ad hoc NSC Working Group on Southeast Asia. By November 19, the group returned with an interim report to Johnson that outlined "three broad alternatives" in Vietnam. The first was a continuation of the present policy, except for the addition of "reprisals against the Viet Cong and North Vietnam for any further 'spectaculars' of the Bien Hoa variety." Option two was the harshest—"a program of attacks of increasing intensity against North Vietnam during which negotiations would not be our immediate goal but would not be ruled out." But the third option seemed designed to catch Johnson's attention with its "slow, controlled squeeze on North Vietnam in order to bring about negotiations, increasing gradually our present level of operations against the North."[26] In a separate paper analyzing the three options, Bundy's group noted that while Johnson would probably wish to explain the new policy to the public, as well as Congress, no "new" congressional mandate was needed.[27]

Johnson listened to the discussion, but did not voice a preference, except to express the hope that "no firm decisions would be made without participation by the military." As he explained, "he could not face the congressional leadership on this kind of subject unless he had fully consulted with the relevant military people."[28] Yet the military leaders Johnson wanted to consult had marched much farther down the road toward escalation than Johnson was prepared to go. In a November 23 report to McNamara, the Joint Chiefs weighed in heavily for the second option (the rapid escalation of military pressures on North Vietnam), arguing that it "offers the best probability of achieving our objectives at the least risk, casualties, and cost, with the least probability of enemy miscalculation."[29]

Conflicted as usual, Johnson retired to his ranch in Texas for the Thanksgiving holiday. On November 22, Russell arrived for a two-day visit. During their conversations, the two men hashed over the president's dilemma in Southeast Asia. Afterwards, in an interview, Russell may have been reflecting on the choices as Johnson saw them. "We either have to get out or take some action to help the Vietnamese," Russell said, adding that the South Vietnamese people "won't help themselves." The Armed Services Committee chairman seemed clear enough about his own doubts about how Johnson should proceed. "We made a big mistake going [in] there," Russell said, "but I can't figure . . . any way to get out without scaring the rest of the world."[30]

Several days later, in a press conference at his ranch, a reporter asked Johnson about whether the "expansion" of the war into Laos or North Vietnam was "a live possibility." Johnson did not offer much insight into his thinking. "But," he said, "when you crawl out on a limb, you always have to find another one to crawl back on." As for the speculation about his intentions, Johnson cautioned that any rumors that he had decided on a course of action was "somewhat premature." Of the South Vietnamese struggle against the Viet Cong, he said, "We will do everything we can to make it more effective and more efficient. The only thing we need to do to end our real problem in that area is for some folks out there to leave their neighbors alone. We hope in due time that can be brought about."[31]

In Washington, meanwhile, Johnson's national security team had concluded that Johnson's only real option was to initiate a gradually escalating bombing campaign. At a meeting of the president's top advisors on November 27, Taylor told the group that General Westmoreland was willing to wait for six months "to have a firmer base for stronger action." His own opinion, Taylor said, was that the South Vietnamese government might not hold together that long. "We must do something sooner than this," he argued. McNamara agreed.[32] A draft position paper produced by the NSC Working Group spelled out in greater detail the tenor and objectives of the plan that Johnson's team supported. The first phase would include U.S. armed reconnaissance strikes in Laos, as well as strikes on North Vietnamese targets by American and South Vietnamese airplanes, but only "as reprisals against any major or spectacular Viet Cong action in the south." What came next was more serious. When the South Vietnamese government had recovered to "an acceptable degree," then "the US is prepared—at a time to be determined—to enter into a second phase program . . . of graduated military pressures."

> The whole sequence of military actions would be designed to give the impression of a steady, deliberate approach, and to give the US the option at any time (subject to enemy reaction) to proceed or not, to escalate or not, and to quicken the pace or not. Concurrently, the US would be alert to any sign of yielding by Hanoi, and would be prepared to explore negotiated solutions that attain US solutions in an acceptable manner.[33]

Despite the near unanimity among his staff, Johnson was not yet prepared to launch sustained, graduated air strikes against targets in North Vietnam. When the working group presented its recommendations to him on December 1, Johnson made it clear he would not be herded into a quick decision. The essential missing element, he told the group was "a stable government" in South Vietnam. There was "no point," he said, in launching strikes against the north as long as the south was not unified. Johnson vowed that he would "not send Johnson City boy[s] out to die" as long as the South Vietnamese were "acting as they are." According to notes taken by Assistant Defense Secretary John NcNaughton, Johnson added that he was "hesitant to sock [his] neighbor if [his own] fever [was] 104. [I] want to get well first. We've never been in position to attack. [It's] easy to sock. Easy to follow Morse. They'll [Congress] be back in January. We want to be prepared to answer the questions." In the meantime, Johnson wanted top congressional leaders consulted, but only in an intimate setting so as not to encourage leaks. "Give good and bad," Johnson said. "Ask for suggestions."[34]

Two days later, Taylor went before the Senate Foreign Relations Committee again. In a closed-door briefing, the ambassador gave the committee its first hint that White House officials were actively considering plans for escalation. "We are faced, then, at the proper time with going outside the country," Taylor said, explaining that this meant excursions into Laos, interdicting North Vietnamese naval traffic, retaliation for Viet Cong terrorism, "or moving into the attack on infiltration targets" in North Vietnam. "Most of us feel we will have to do some of them at some point."

"Do what?" asked the committee's senior Republican, Bourke Hickenlooper, as if he did not comprehend Taylor's statement.

Taylor's reply was forthright. "Engage in anti-, counter-infiltration military operations outside of South Vietnam," he explained, adding that the administration would not likely embark on this course without a stable government in South Vietnam.

Taylor's response disturbed Fulbright. "It seems to me futile to go on expanding it when the government itself is so shaky," he said. "If you cannot create a reasonably stable government that has the support of a good solid majority of the local people, what are we going to come back to? What are you fighting for? We don't want the country."

But Taylor argued that "there is a chicken-egg aspect" to the situation. While bombing should not occur until there was a stable government, he believed that bombing might facilitate more governmental stability. "Any action against the north that would tell the South Vietnamese, 'The old enemy is suffering just as they made us suffer for these years,' would be good for the government."

Clearly unsettled by what he was hearing, Hickenlooper worried aloud that "there is a growing impression on me that we are going down the same road the French did in Dien Bien Phu." He speculated that "an inconclusive operation" would result in "the erosion of public opinion." Frank

Church was also troubled by Taylor's testimony and remarked that "the particular question that concerns me is the growing speculation that we are about to underwrite attacks on North Vietnam of various kinds." But Taylor assured Church that while "the day is going to come when we have to do some other things," those actions would not occur "until we have a government that can speak for its own people and guarantee the effectiveness of its own armed forces."

Concluded Fulbright: "This is a hell of a problem. I don't think it is worth a war. . . . I am willing to try to work with this government [of South Vietnam]. If the government fails, if they do unseat it, I would certainly come around—I am not willing to attack North Vietnam just because this happens."[35]

Distracted by his leadership responsibilities, Mansfield could not attend the hearing. Nonetheless, he obviously learned of Taylor's disturbing testimony. A week later, he sent Johnson a six-page memorandum outlining his grave reservations about where the administration appeared headed. "We remain on a course in Viet Nam which takes us further and further out on the sagging limb," Mansfield told Johnson. Mansfield feared that "if a significant extension of the conflict beyond South Viet Nam should occur, then the prospects are appalling. Even short of nuclear war, an extension of the war may well saddle us with enormous burdens and costs in Cambodia, Laos and elsewhere in Asia, along with those in Viet Nam." Once again, Mansfield urged Johnson to seek a peaceful end to the conflict. America's "limited national interests" pointed in the direction of "an eventual negotiated settlement," he said. "Such negotiations are essential to the reduction of our present over-commitment and ultimate withdrawal."

Mansfield offered Johnson a number of policy suggestions. First among them was the admonition to "avoid United States military action beyond the borders of South Vietnam, especially if the primary purpose of such action is to demonstrate the firmness of our will or our capacity to inflict damage." Mansfield believed the United States had "amply demonstrated" its capacity to wage war and that "the greater need now is to demonstrate the astuteness to deal with the practical negotiating problems involved in a peaceful settlement in a situation in which we have few usable cards in our hands." If Johnson declined to ignore Mansfield's advice and press, instead, for escalation, the majority leader warned that "we had better begin now to face up to the likelihood of years and years of involvement and a vast increase in the commitment, and this should be spelled out in no uncertain terms to the people of the nation."[36]

Yet, as important as Mansfield believed the issue was to the nation, he was constitutionally unwilling or incapable of taking the issue to the public himself. Similar to his conduct during the Gulf of Tonkin debate, Mansfield would state his case—and then defer to Johnson. For years, under Majority Leader Johnson's leadership, the Senate's Democrats had strained under the heavy hand and overbearing personality of their energetic and powerful leader. When Johnson needed a vote, he had a dozen arguments and parliamentary devices at his disposal. He would cajole, threaten, promise, trade, and plead. In short, Lyndon Johnson would do whatever it took to get the votes he needed. In almost every way, Mansfield was Johnson's polar opposite. Where Johnson was loud and boisterous, Mansfield was subtle, quiet, and introspective. Where Johnson menaced his colleagues to win a vote, Mansfield deferred to their better judgment. "When Mansfield came in," said his Senate colleague Frank Moss of Utah, "he was totally different. Mansfield didn't *want* to be the leader. He never tried to exert leadership."[37]

"He was reasonable, accommodating and fair," Johnson aide Harry McPherson observed about Mansfield, adding that the majority leader "permitted" the Senate to be "what it was, a hundred disparate adults who ought to have been able to deal efficiently and responsibly with public affairs."[38] As the Senate majority leader for the president's party, Mansfield viewed himself as the president's spokesman and legislative strategist in the Senate. In so many ways, he did not view himself an independent legislative force like Johnson, who had never served as majority leader under a Democratic president. "I am not a political animal, really," Mansfield confessed to an interviewer in 1970. "I don't believe in going for the jugular. I believe in cooperating and accommodating and then, let the chips fall where they may."[39]

So averse to anything that smacked of a personal disagreement with Johnson, Mansfield was often unable to confront the president, in person, with his concerns over Vietnam. Although he feared that Johnson was about to lead the country into a war against North Vietnam which, he was persuaded, would have disastrous and long-lasting consequences, Mansfield often resolved to do nothing more than submit a memorandum.

Johnson merely sent Mansfield's memorandum to Bundy for a reply. "The one suggestion in your memorandum which I myself would take direct issue with is that we are 'overcommitted' there," Johnson said in a cover letter accompanying Bundy's response. "Given the size of the stake, it seems to me that we are doing only what we have to do." Although Bundy told Johnson that Mansfield's memorandum revealed "no difference in fundamental purpose," it was clear that Mansfield and Johnson were miles apart on the matter of U.S. objectives in Vietnam. For example, Bundy casually brushed aside Mansfield's admonition against "military action beyond the borders of South Vietnam." "I myself," he wrote, "do not see the grounds for the flatness of the Senator's recommendation, given the facts of infiltration and of North Vietnamese control over the Communists in the South." Bundy also rejected Mansfield's warning about a "vast increase" in the U.S. commitment toward South Vietnam. "No matter what course is taken," Bundy said, "it seems likely to us that we face years of involvement in South Vietnam, though not necessarily" the vast increase that Mansfield feared. "In general, the administration's policy seems to correspond to the view of most thoughtful Americans: We do not want a big war out there, and neither do we intend to back out on a 10-year-long commitment."[40]

As advisor after advisor came to the same conclusion about the need for escalation, the only formidable and credible dissenter in Johnson's inner circle was George Ball. While no expert on Asia, Ball was nonetheless alarmed by the haste with which Johnson's national security advisors were moving toward a full-scale assault on North Vietnam. "My colleagues in Washington and our Saigon embassy were standing logic on its head," he later wrote. "What we charitably referred to as a government in Saigon was falling apart, yet we had to bomb the North as a form of political therapy." Ball thought that "such a tortuous argument was the product of despair—the last resort of those who believed we could not withdraw from Vietnam without humiliation."

In early October, Ball had sent a sixty-seven-page memorandum spelling out his dissenting views on Vietnam to McNamara, Rusk, and Bundy. Coming down hard against a bombing assault, Ball argued that an air campaign would tempt the North Vietnamese "to retaliate by using ground forces, which they possess in overwhelming numbers." American bombs might only serve to weaken the Saigon government, he said. "Hanoi might also increase terror and sabotage in the South, including terror attacks on American personnel in Saigon and even the bombing of Saigon and other urban areas to induce demoralization." Ball's basic point was simple—and prophetic:

> It is in the nature of escalation that each move passes the option to the other side, while at the same time the party which seems to be losing will be tempted to keep raising the ante. To the extent that the response to a move can be controlled, that move is probably ineffective. If the move is effective, it may not be possible to control—or accurately anticipate—the response. Once on the tiger's back we cannot be sure of picking the place to dismount.

Instead of escalation, Ball urged his colleagues to revisit the idea of a negotiated settlement. As far as the American commitment to helping South Vietnam, Ball said it should be honored only "so long as the Vietnamese people wish us to help" and only so long as they demonstrated the

ability to fight on their own behalf. Ball believed that Johnson should simply serve notice on the government in Saigon that the United States would
continue to support its struggle "*only* if they achieve a unity of purpose in
Saigon." Such a message, Ball speculated, "might result in pulling together
the responsible elements in the country and lead to the creation of a unified government."[41]

Ball recalled that after he had distributed the paper to the three advisors, McNamara, in particular, "was absolutely horrified. He treated it like
a poisonous snake."[42] While not as visceral in their reaction, neither Rusk
nor Bundy was persuaded. "My colleagues," Ball later reflected, "seemed
somewhat more concerned with a possible leak than with the cogency of
what I had written." A meeting with the memorandum's recipients on
November 7 was all that Ball needed to conclude that "there was no point
in carrying the argument further." He decided that McNamara, Rusk, and
Bundy had regarded his arguments as little more than "an idiosyncratic
diversion from the only relevant problem: how to win the war."[43]

Winning the war. It was a spirit of purpose that prevailed within the
Johnson administration and often foreclosed a healthy examination of the
fundamental basis for America's military presence in South Vietnam. As
Johnson said in numerous speeches and public events during the 1964
campaign, America was in Vietnam to honor commitments made by three
previous presidents. Lyndon Johnson would not be the president to break
the nation's solemn promises to the people of South Vietnam.

Furthermore, Johnson made it abundantly clear that he wanted nothing other than the highly centralized foreign and military policy decision-
making apparatus that he relied upon for advice on Vietnam. While
Kennedy had favored a more relaxed, freewheeling approach—inviting a
wide variety of competing opinions and views—Johnson insisted on a more
formalized, regimented environment. "It wasn't easy to get into a reflective, back-and-forth conversation" in meetings with Johnson, William
Bundy recalled. "You didn't feel that he was sort of playing with a subject,
as President Kennedy tended to do to some extent."[44] While Johnson did
not specifically forbid his aides from lively, creative discussions about
options in Vietnam, it was understood that such internal debates had their
limits. The process that led to a formal foreign policy decision was almost
always the result of an orderly, systematic process in which Johnson relied
on advice and recommendations brought to him after his top advisors had
reached a consensus. "There was a tremendous nervousness that if you
expressed an opinion," recalled Michael Forrestal, "it might somehow leak
out, get published somewhere, and the president would be furious and
everybody's head would be cut off." Forrestal believed that this unspoken
but very real limitation on the exploration of military and diplomatic

options in Southeast Asia "inhibited, to some extent, an exchange of information and prevented the president himself eventually from getting a lot of facts that he should have had."[45]

If insiders like Ball could not persuade Johnson, the challenge was even greater for someone like Mansfield. Mansfield was among several congressional critics of Johnson's Vietnam policy whom Johnson found it easy to ignore because they were simply not part of his established decision-making process. As historian Doris Kearns noted, the "institutional forms of the decision-making process" precluded outside advisors like Mansfield from making cogent arguments about Vietnam. The insiders who advocated escalation "had daily contact with one another and access to secret information, which allowed them to prepare elaborately detailed predictions of the consequences, both immediate and far into the future, of a failure to escalate in Vietnam." Mansfield and other dissenters, Kearns wrote, "were scattered, each proceeding from his own perspective, each criticizing a different aspect of the war." Without the kind of staff resources enjoyed by officials like McNamara, Rusk, and Bundy, congressional advisors like Mansfield, Kearns said, "could do little more than express personal judgments opposed to an extensively documented and argued position shared by nearly all the top officials of government."[46] Johnson simply trusted Bundy, McNamara, and Taylor—none of them particularly knowledgeable about Vietnam—more than the Senate's foremost expert on Southeast Asia.

As an eventful year drew to a close, Johnson was no less perplexed about events in Vietnam than he had been before the election. In the weeks since the November 3 election, Saigon had endured yet another attempted coup. On December 20, Khanh—who had clung to power by appointing the former mayor of Saigon, Tran Van Huong, as premier—now enlisted his military allies to help him oust Huong after the premier suddenly declared martial law. Trying his best to help stabilize the South Vietnamese government in preparation for a bombing operation, Taylor was furious. He confronted Khanh's military cohorts in his embassy office, scolding them as if they were juvenile delinquents. "I made clear that all the military plans which I know you would like to carry out are dependent on government stability," Taylor barked. "Now, you have made a real mess." Taylor warned the group that "we cannot carry you forever if you do things like this."[47]

Taylor's gloomy "progress" from Saigon, meanwhile, gave Johnson no encouragement. "We are faced here with a seriously deteriorating situation," the ambassador said in a January 6 telegram, "characterized by continued political turmoil, irresponsibility and division within the armed forces, lethargy in the pacification program, some anti-US feeling which could grow, signs of mounting terrorism by VC directly at US personnel and deepening discouragement and loss of morale throughout SVN." As soon as the South Vietnamese government could be stabilized, Taylor believed that "we should look for an occasion to begin air operations."[48] But, as William Bundy observed, a more stable government in Saigon might involve an interminable wait. "The blunt fact," Bundy told Rusk in briefing notes for a meeting with Johnson, "is that we have appeared to the Vietnamese . . . to be insisting on a more perfect government than can be reasonably expected, before we consider any additional action." Bundy warned that might be dangerous because "the situation is now likely to come apart more rapidly than we had anticipated in November."[49]

WAITING WAS THE LAST THING that columnist Joseph Alsop wanted. An influential, nationally syndicated journalist, Alsop was among the most enthusiastic supporters of a U.S. military solution in Vietnam. Like many conservative supporters of the war, Alsop saw Vietnam through Cold War-tinted lenses, believing, like Johnson—and Kennedy, Eisenhower, and Truman before him—that the communist insurgency in Vietnam was no nationalist uprising, nor the result of civil strife. Vietnam was the latest and most dangerous front in Communist China's drive to dominate all of Southeast Asia. Alsop, however, believed when it came to fighting communism in Asia, Johnson was wavering.

When the columnist learned of Johnson's vacillation at the December 1 meeting with his Vietnam working group, he launched a private campaign to give the president the steel he needed to commit the United States to stronger military action. That included advising Taylor to "use [a] pistol on Washington to hijack the required decisions" from the Pentagon and "elsewhere." By late December, Alsop went public, telling legions of readers that Johnson had "dodged the choice" of whether to escalate the conflict because of political considerations. Alsop warned that "if sterner measures are not taken pretty soon . . . the United States is almost certainly doomed to suffer the greatest defeat in American history." Aiming his verbal arrows directly at the president and his well-known aversion to presiding over an American defeat in Vietnam, Alsop wrote that it did not seem "credible that Lyndon B. Johnson intends to accept and preside over such a defeat." In another audacious attempt to goad Johnson into a wider war, Alsop contrasted Johnson's handling of Vietnam with Kennedy's response to the Cuban missile crisis. "If Mr. Johnson ducks the challenge [in Vietnam], we shall learn by experience about what [it] would have been like if Kennedy had ducked the challenge in October, 1962."[50]

Although Johnson did not react publicly to Alsop's bullying, he was clearly concerned. Johnson's aide Jack Valenti recalled that Alsop "represented a point of view that the president took care to listen to." In 1964, at least, Johnson knew that his most severe critics were on the political right. "He was sorely afraid that Republicans and conservative Democrats would maul him unmercifully if he detached from Vietnam without leaving behind a stable enterprise," Valenti said. "He was haunted by the thought of increasing pressures from this wing of political conviction which would damage his own leadership of his domestic legislative program." In this sense, Alsop—because of his blunt outspokenness, his influence, and his enormous readership—was a potentially formidable critic. "The Alsop syndrome was the president's hairshirt," Valenti said. "Its coarse covering could be felt by the president every time he ached to be rid of Vietnam; it intruded into every presidential desire to cut losses and get out."[51]

As the pressure mounted on Johnson to act before all of South Vietnam was lost, Johnson's advisors had also begun exploring the need to send American ground troops to protect the additional personnel and vast U.S. military resources that would be involved in a sustained bombing operation. General Westmoreland's initial report, forwarded to Johnson on January 6 by Taylor, contained disconcerting news that would only make the president's decision more agonizing. Taylor characterized the results of Westmoreland's study as a "startling requirement" and reported that the commanding general thought he would need something on the order of seventy-five thousand U.S. personnel to provide "maximum security."[52]

On Capitol Hill, meanwhile, memories of Taylor's September testimony before the Senate Foreign Relations Committee—during which he had professed support for taking the war northward—troubled Fulbright. Clearly aware that administration officials were pressing Johnson to escalate the war through the air, Fulbright invited Rusk to testify before his committee on January 8. In executive session, the chairman pressed Rusk to promise that Johnson would consult the Senate before he ordered a bombing campaign. Reminded by Fulbright that Taylor had earlier promised that Johnson would not escalate the war "unless and until a stable government was established in Saigon," Rusk hedged. "Mr. Chairman, that is the present policy," he said, and then added that "I think I should say if the president should come to any other conclusion, he would do so in consultation with the leadership of the Congress." Fulbright, however, revealed a growing irritation with Johnson's style of "consultation" when he inquired of Rusk if his committee would "be told after the decision is made or before? Will we be invited to a meeting at the White House and told we have to have made up our mind tomorrow morning or in thirty minutes to launch an attack?" Rusk ignored the question and told Fulbright, in so many words, that attacks on North Vietnam could be justified because parts of the country had become "a safe haven for these depredations, which have been coming out of North Vietnam."

Fulbright, however, had made it clear where he stood on the question of escalation. "The only reason I and others have entertained the possibility, even entertained the thought, that maybe we might have to negotiate," he told Rusk in the hearing's opening minutes, "is simply that it looks hopeless." As for escalation, he was even more straightforward. "I don't think anything can justify the escalation of the war, in my opinion," he told Rusk, adding that "I just don't want another Korea." As for whether Johnson would engage the Senate in genuine consultation, Fulbright continued to press Rusk for a direct answer. "In this case it is so important that I hope the administration won't make a decision of that nature before at least feeling the pulse of this committee," Fulbright said. "Do you think that would be a reasonable thing to expect?" Again, Rusk dodged the question. "I think, Mr. Chairman, perhaps the reasonable thing on a matter of such importance is to report your remarks to the president."[53]

The following week, during another closed-door session with the committee, Rusk was more direct about Johnson's willingness to consult congressional leaders before launching any new offensive. "I myself feel that strikes against the north are a part of the problem on which the leadership and the president would be in consultation," Rusk said, "because this would be a significant development of the situation."[54]

Johnson revealed almost nothing of his inner conflicts over the war during a meeting with Democratic and Republican congressional leaders on January 21. Although he tried to flatter Senate Minority Leader Everett Dirksen and his Republican colleagues by assuring them that he wanted them "in on foreign policy take-offs rather than merely at the time of crash landings," he told them nothing about the decision his advisors were urging him to make. The briefing—as so many others would be in the coming years—was designed not so much to inform, but to inflame. Instead of inviting the assembled group to offer advice on administration policy toward Vietnam, Johnson, Rusk, and McNamara filled the senators and congressmen with statistics and anecdotal information designed to bolster the argument for greater military intervention. After a series of depressing statistics from McNamara, Johnson led the group to believe that he still strongly opposed escalation. He told them that "we have decided that more U.S. forces are not needed in South Vietnam short of a decision to go to full-scale war."[55]

The tenor and tone of the congressional briefing betrayed nothing of Johnson's mounting agony over how to proceed in Vietnam. It appeared to him that circumstances in Vietnam were forcing him to choose between achieving his Great Society programs and a very uncertain outcome in Southeast Asia. In early 1965, at least, nothing was more important to Johnson than the legacy that he hoped his Great Society would secure for him. To preserve his domestic programs Johnson knew that, for now at least, he must not give conservative members of Congress any compelling reason—such as the added expense of a wide war—to oppose his social initiatives. As he later confessed to Doris Kearns:

> I knew from the start that I was bound to be crucified either way I moved. If I left the woman I really loved—the Great Society—in order to get involved with that bitch of a war on the other side of the world, then I would lose everything at home. All my programs. All my hopes to feed the hungry and shelter the homeless. All my dreams to provide education and medical care to the browns and the blacks and the lame and the poor. But if I left that war and let the Communists take over South Vietnam, then I would be seen as a coward and my nation would be seen as an appeaser and we would both find it impossible to accomplish anything for anybody anywhere on the entire globe.[56]

When Johnson finally made his decision to start an air war in North Vietnam, he would not—despite Rusk's soothing testimony before the Foreign Relations Committee and the president's own comforting words to the congressional leadership—make Congress, nor the country, privy to the decision. Choosing the future of his Great Society over public disclosure about a dramatic expansion of American involvement in Vietnam, Johnson was about to lead the country—secretly and deceptively—into full-scale war in Vietnam.

CHAPTER 27

Harder Choices

1965

T HE MORNING OF WEDNESDAY, JANUARY 27, 1965, BROUGHT MORE
depressing news from Vietnam: yet another coup. This time General
Nguyen Khanh assumed near-dictatorial powers when he dismissed the
nation's armed forces council. Accustomed to the revolving door at the top
of their government, South Vietnamese citizens took the latest development in stride. The public's attitude, reported a State Department intelligence official, "is one of indifference."[1] Ambassador Taylor, meanwhile,
worried that the coup, which Khanh launched in cooperation with Buddhist leaders, might now result in a greater willingness by Saigon's government to negotiate with Hanoi and the National Liberation Front, the
Viet Cong's political organization.[2]

In Washington, the coup was conclusive proof to McNamara and
Bundy that the administration's status quo policy was a failure. The two
men told Johnson that the present policy would "only lead to disastrous
defeat. What we are doing now, essentially, is to wait and hope for a stable
government." The hope for a stable government had been the administration's policy since the fall of 1964 and was by now an unrealistic goal.
"The time has come for harder choices," Bundy advised Johnson in a memorandum. The choices, as the two advisors saw them, were escalation or
negotiation. As for McNamara and Bundy, they told Johnson on January
27 that they "tend[ed] to favor" escalation. Rusk, however, was far more
cautious. Bundy told Johnson that the secretary of state believed "the consequences of both escalation and withdrawal are so bad that we simply must
find a way of making our present policy work." Bundy dismissed Rusk's
concerns by noting that "this would be good if it was possible. Bob and I
do not think it is."[3]

At a White House meeting that morning with McNamara, Rusk, Bundy, and Ball, Johnson appeared ready to begin escalating the war. "Stable government or no stable government, we'll do what we ought to do," he told his advisors. Johnson made it clear that "we will move strongly."[4] Still, he wanted more information before he made the final commitment. Within days, Bundy—accompanied by a party of State Department officials—was on his way to Saigon. He arrived on February 4 and spent the next three days consulting American and South Vietnamese officials. "There was a general disposition after we were there for several days," recalled NSC staff member Chester Cooper, "to feel that the original conception was right—either we had to get out or do something more than we were doing."[5]

"The prospect in Vietnam is grim," Bundy said in a report that he began preparing before he left Saigon. "The situation in Vietnam is deteriorating, and without new U.S. action defeat appears inevitable. . . . There is still time to turn it around, but not much." Bundy's recommendation would not surprise anyone in Johnson's White House. Within days, he would urge Johnson to approve a program of "sustained reprisal." In doing so he would go right to the heart of Johnson's political insecurities about Vietnam, born of Harry Truman's political tribulations of the early 1950s. "There is one grave weakness in our posture in Vietnam which is within our power to fix," Bundy would report, "and that is a widespread belief that we do not have the will and force and patience and determination to take the necessary action and stay the course."[6] Johnson later said he was impressed and persuaded by Bundy's logic. "We were at a turning point," he wrote in his memoirs. "Though the Bundy report proposed a course of action we had considered and turned down only three months before,* I was impressed by its logic and persuaded strongly by its arguments. I knew that the situation had changed and that our actions would have to change, too."[7]

In fact, the situation was getting worse. In the early morning hours of Sunday, February 7 (Saturday afternoon in Washington), communist guerrillas staged a deadly mortar attack on the U.S. Army barracks at Pleiku, in South Vietnam's central highlands. Eight Americans died. More than 120 were wounded. The deadly attack set the wheels of escalation turning even faster. "That pulled the rug out from any sitting and waiting," said Cooper, who also observed that the Pleiku incident gave the administration "an opportunity to put in motion a policy which they had already decided upon, but needed a fairly conspicuous threshold before they could

---

*As William Conrad Gibbons observed, Johnson had never "turned down" the idea of escalation. "It had," Gibbons correctly noted, "merely been postponed" (Gibbons, 3: 59ff.).

implement."* In Saigon, Bundy, Taylor, and Westmoreland urged Johnson to order immediate retaliatory strikes on North Vietnam.[8] This time, Johnson was ready to act.

At 7:45 that evening, the president convened his National Security Council—Mansfield and Speaker McCormack included—to discuss the administration's response. Ostensibly held to assess the attack and determine the severity of the response, the meeting took on the air of a war council. Johnson went around the table and polled his advisors one by one. The gathering, however, was a charade. Johnson's eagerness to escalate was too apparent, too visceral. He had summoned his advisors not to hear their recommendations. He wanted an endorsement of his decision to launch air strikes. "I've gone far enough," he said angrily, referring to the attacks on the army barracks. "I've had enough of this."[9]

Predictably, all but Mansfield urged Johnson to retaliate. Even Ball argued forcefully that a military response was necessary "because Hanoi directs the Viet Cong, supplies arms, and infiltrates men." Mansfield was steadfast. He finally summoned the courage to challenge Johnson directly, insisting that "caution should be our watchword." The attack, Mansfield explained as he looked across the table at Johnson, "has opened many eyes. We are not now in a penny ante game." Mansfield believed the ease with which the Viet Cong had staged the attack was evidence that "the local populace is not behind us." Furthermore, he argued, there was no stable government in Saigon. He asked, rhetorically, with "what government" had the United States cleared the operation? Mansfield believed that Johnson was moving with undue haste and had not fully considered the implications of military action, especially "the possibility of engaging in a large-scale conflict with China, the position the Soviet Union would take, probably assisting the healing of the Soviet-Sino split." The results, Mansfield warned, might be "worse than Korea."[10] It was, William Bundy later said, a remarkable and tense moment—"the only time I ever saw a member of the Congress who said, 'Mr. President, I think you are wrong on basic policy,' in any direct session."[11]

To Johnson, Mansfield's words were heresy. The president's face reddened. His reply was "terse and quite biting," Bundy recalled, "but not a rational attempt to persuade" Mansfield of his position.[12] He had "kept the shotgun over the mantle and the bullets in the basement for a long time

---

*Later, Cooper, who accompanied Bundy to Vietnam at the time of the attack, hedged on this question. He suggested that Bundy's recommendation concerning escalation might have been different had the incident not occurred—or if American officials had known that the attack was carried out, not on orders from Hanoi, but from a local commander apparently unaware that American forces were stationed at Pleiku (McNamara, *Argument Without End*, 205–17).

now," Johnson said. But the enemy was killing U.S. personnel and he could no longer ask them to remain in Vietnam without giving them the authority to defend themselves. Without directly accusing the majority leader of appeasement, Johnson raised the Munich analogy and suggested that failing to respond to the attack at Pleiku was akin to the reluctance of European leaders to challenge Hilter in the 1930s. Johnson insisted that "cowardice has gotten us into more wars than response has." With that, Mansfield knew his dissent had been futile. He merely nodded.

As the meeting drew to a dramatic close, at 9:00 P.M., Johnson finally issued his orders. A contingent of 132 U.S. and twenty-two South Vietnamese airplanes would immediately retaliate by bombing North Vietnamese army barracks in the country's southern region. Johnson invited all the participants to return the next morning for another National Security Council meeting.[13]

That evening, Taylor cabled his policy recommendation from Saigon, a proposal that would become the basic blueprint for U.S. military policy in Vietnam in the ensuing months. "The concept would be that of a graduated reprisal program," the ambassador explained, echoing the advice Bundy would soon give to Johnson. Taylor advocated "a measured, controlled sequence of actions" against North Vietnam that he believed would "persuade it to stop its intervention in the South." Taylor conveniently forgot his testimony before the Senate the previous September, during which he had insisted that escalation should wait until Saigon had a secure government. This time, he advised Washington that "not much of a government is required for the GVN [South Vietnamese] to play its role."[14]

The next morning, during another meeting of congressional leaders, Mansfield returned and again urged Johnson to resist his advisors' counsel. "Why cannot we handle this matter through the United Nations?" Mansfield asked. "Can't the Geneva [accord] powers act?" Johnson scoffed at that suggestion. "This cannot be done," he said, explaining that his advisors assured him it was "hopeless" to expect anything from the United Nations (notwithstanding his 1964 campaign rhetoric that affirmed his determination to use the UN in an unending quest for peace). As for the Geneva Conference, Ball told Mansfield that negotiations "should only be entered from a position of greater strength than we now have."

This time, however, Mansfield would not be the lone congressional skeptic. House Minority Leader Gerald Ford wanted to know why Johnson had called off the previous day's air strikes after fog prevented the bombing of three of the four targets. He found it difficult to understand, Ford said, why Johnson would cancel a mission that was not completed.[15] In his memoirs, Johnson claimed that "we all felt that a second-day strike by U.S. planes might give Hanoi and Moscow the impression that we had begun a sustained air offensive."[16] But this was not what Johnson told Ford at the time. According to CIA Director John McCone's extensive notes of the meeting, Johnson merely told Ford that the response to the Viet Cong attacks was "prompt and adequate" and the target hit was "by far the biggest and had the most potential for damage."[17]

In fact, a sustained offensive had been launched, as Ball made clear in remarks early in the briefing. Johnson, Ball revealed, had embraced Taylor's strategy of "sustained reprisals." The bombing after Pleiku was not merely a proportional response to a communist attack, but the beginning of the gradually escalating bombing campaign that Taylor and Bundy had supported. As Ball explained, to continue reprisals in response only to Pleiku might suggest to the North Vietnamese that the United States was merely responding to Viet Cong attacks in piecemeal fashion. "Our officials in Saigon," Ball said, referring to Taylor's recommendation, "want a graduated response to the entire North Vietnamese military effort rather than merely retaliatory strikes to attacks by the North Vietnamese and the Viet Cong."

Mansfield remained troubled by what he had heard. If the purpose of the attacks had been to "impress" Ho Chi Minh and other North Vietnamese leaders, then that had been accomplished, he said, and it was not "necessary to go any further at this time." Johnson's reply, as McCone noted, was instructive: "He also intended to impress [Soviet Premier Alexei] Kosygin and a number of others in the world, *including our own citizens*" (emphasis added).

As the meeting ended, Mansfield relieved Johnson of any concern that he would ever go public with his grave doubts about the administration's Vietnam policy. While he had spoken "frankly" at Johnson's invitation, Mansfield observed that the decision had been made and he intended to support it.[18] Having pledged his grudging support for an escalation policy that he believed would have disastrous consequences for his country, Mansfield began to remove himself from the public debate over Vietnam.

It was a decision with enormous consequences for his country. At the time—because of his widely acknowledged expertise on Southeast Asia and his powerful role as majority leader—Mansfield was first among a handful of American political leaders capable of forcing Johnson to apply the brakes to the planned escalation of the war. Had he opposed Johnson's policy with more force—or at least in public—Mansfield might been successful. He might have taken to the Senate floor to denounce escalation in an effort to rally more senators, as well as the public, to his side. Had he done so, Congress would certainly have held more hearings. Fulbright and others might have been awakened from their postelection slumber. Johnson might have been forced to explain exactly what he hoped to achieve by taking the country into war in North Vietnam.

But Mansfield, sadly, viewed himself not as the leader of the Senate's Democrats, but as Johnson's floor leader in the Senate. He was a good soldier, committed to gently shepherding Johnson's domestic initiatives and determined to let Johnson to have his war—although he seriously doubted that Johnson, like the French and two American presidents before him, would succeed. It was Mansfield's view of his minimalist, subservient constitutional role that inhibited him from publicly expressing his grave doubts about Vietnam. It was also Mansfield's deferential and compliant approach to the majority leader's responsibilities that gave Johnson the freedom to escalate the war with no threat of public criticism from the conflict's most credible and persuasive skeptic.

To Johnson, Mansfield's pledge of public silence was an enormous relief. In the Senate, the pressure for a full-scale public debate over Vietnam was mounting. "Up until now," *Newsweek* observed in mid-January, "the relative disinterest of their constituents in a remote Southeast Asian country has allowed Washington policymakers more or less a free hand to pursue their solutions."[19] But that was changing. Within six weeks, *Newsweek* would report that more than twenty senators openly questioned, to some degree, the trim of Johnson's sails in Vietnam. Those who did so privately, *Newsweek* said, numbered "perhaps as many as 25 more."[20]

Yet the last thing Johnson wanted was a messy public discussion in the Senate focusing more attention on Vietnam as he pondered critical decisions. On January 7, the *New York Times*—noting that Johnson had virtually ignored Vietnam in his State of the Union Address—had urged just such a debate. The paper observed that while a "'great debate' undoubtedly would prove unsettling for Vietnam's factions and for American administrators" in Vietnam, "'a post-mortem' before the patient becomes a corpse might prove the best way of averting that eventuality."[21] Johnson, however, saw no use in such a public discussion. For weeks, he had worked furiously to keep Vietnam off the Senate floor by courting senators in one-on-one meetings and in the numerous private briefings he began hosting at the White House. By February, his efforts began to pay off. But nothing helped his cause more than the acquiescence of Mansfield and Fulbright—the two men who could most legitimize and elevate a Vietnam discourse. To Johnson's relief, both men, out of loyalty to Johnson and a minimalist view of the Senate's role in foreign and military affairs, agreed to keep their doubts private. For now, at least, the Senate would largely ignore the nation's most crucial foreign policy issue.[22]

BUNDY COMPLETED HIS REPORT to Johnson on his way back to Washington. "The international prestige of the United States, and a substantial part of our influence, are directly at risk in Vietnam," he wrote. Negotiation would be useless, he said, and withdrawal after a negotiated settlement would simply be "surrender on the installment plan." Like Taylor, Bundy recommended a program of "sustained reprisals" which, he explained, "will be reduced or stopped when outrages in the South are reduced or stopped." As Ball had explained to the National Security Council, the reprisals could no longer be tit-for-tat. "We are convinced," he said, speaking for Johnson's national security advisors in Washington and Saigon, "that the political values of reprisal require a *continuous* operation" (emphasis Bundy's).[23]

Johnson, however, had already accepted Bundy's recommendation when he agreed with Taylor's February 7 cable. "We face a choice of going forward or running," Johnson told his advisors on the morning of February 8. "We have chosen the first alternative." The primary question in Johnson's mind was now "how fast we should go forward?"[24] But later, when the four congressional leaders—Mansfield, Dirksen, McCormack, and Ford—joined the meeting, Johnson was far less forthcoming about the true nature of the "sustained reprisals." Attempting to describe the dramatic policy change as "a program of further pressure against North Vietnam" that he had approved in December but had not initiated, Johnson assured the leaders that "we are now ready to return to our program of pushing forward in an effort to defeat North Vietnamese aggression *without escalating the war*" (emphasis added). As for his legal authority for the reprisals, Johnson told the group that the Gulf of Tonkin Resolution, in addition to his constitutional powers as president, gave him all the authority he needed. The views of a few senators—no doubt he meant Morse and Gruening—would not deter him. He would use the congressional resolution "carefully but effectively."[25]

The meeting over, Johnson cabled Taylor. The United States would, he told the ambassador, "carry out our December plan for continuing action against North Vietnam with modifications up and down in tempo and scale."[26] As for any official notification of Congress, Johnson had engaged in little of the authentic consultation that Fulbright had sought from Rusk in January. Although they were subsequently briefed privately by Johnson, Rusk, and McNamara, Fulbright and Russell were not formally consulted prior to Johnson's decision.[27] The most comprehensive briefing for other members of Congress came on February 9, when the State Department's assistant secretary for the Far East, William Bundy, appeared before the Senate Foreign Relations Committee's subcommittee on Far Eastern affairs. But instead of disclosing to members that Johnson had approved a "sustained" bombing campaign in North Vietnam, Bundy characterized the response to the Pleiku incidents as little more than a measured, one-time military retaliation. Because Mansfield did not attend the hearing, no one was present who could have directly challenged Bundy's description of the new U.S. policy in Vietnam.

In explaining why American fighters were not allowed to complete their missions after bad weather obscured many of the targets chosen for attack, Bundy gave committee members an answer that substantially contradicted Ball's answer to the congressional leaders the previous day. While Ball had informed Mansfield, Dirksen, McCormack, and Ford that the United States wanted "a graduated response to the entire North Vietnamese military effort rather than merely retaliatory strikes," Bundy's explanation to the senators was the exact opposite. "We were anxious not to give the impression, at least at this time," Bundy said, "that we were getting into a steady or continuing course of action against the north." Bundy went out of his way to assure members that there was no continuing operation under way. "As of this moment," he said, "we do not plan any further operations related to the incident." Later Bundy added that the response to the Pleiku attacks was "the end of this episode," although he acknowledged the possibility of further attacks on North Vietnam sites. "We are looking very hard at the possibility that if the North Vietnamese continue with this whole pattern of infiltration on a stepped-up basis, whether additional actions of this sort will be necessary." Asked directly by Republican Frank Carlson of Kansas if "there has been a policy decision on expansion of this war," Bundy replied: "Sir, I cannot say at this point. We are weighing the situation very heavily, very hard."[28]

Members of Congress generally responded to the air strikes by publicly supporting the president—a reflection of the generally strong support Johnson enjoyed from the American people. An Associated Press survey of the Senate in early January revealed that of eighty-three senators questioned, thirty-one essentially agreed with Senator Alan Bible of Nevada who told a reporter that he supported Johnson's policy but also wanted more "emphasis on a stable and responsible Vietnamese Government." Ten senators favored moving directly to negotiations, while only three supported the policy change that Johnson clearly had in mind—taking the war northward. "The survey showed," the AP reporter wrote, "that many Senators shared the 'sense of frustration' voiced recently by Secretary of State Dean Rusk 'that things are now somehow moving more rapidly toward a conclusion.'"[29] Despite these concerns, few senators were courageous enough to challenge Johnson and buck public opinion by publicly voicing their doubts, especially in the wake of Johnson's decisive military response to the Pleiku attacks.[30]

FEW MEN EVER FOUND the courage or fortitude to sustain an argument with Lyndon Johnson in person, especially after he became president. Johnson was so overwhelming, his temper so searing, his personality so dominant, his office so impressive and awesome, that few men—least of all a deferential figure like Mansfield—possessed the rare combination of intellect, bravery, independence, and stamina to sustain such a confrontation for long. One exception was Wayne Morse, who seemed to savor his public and private confrontations with Johnson. Once when Johnson welcomed Morse to a White House meeting, the president remarked: "Wayne, I've never seen you looking so fit. How do you do it?" "Well, Mr. President," Morse replied, "I'll tell you. Every time I read in the papers what you're doing about Vietnam, it makes my blood boil. That purges me; it keeps me fit."[31] A circumspect man like Mansfield would never have behaved so impertinently. He would never challenge Johnson so directly. His dissent in the February 6 meeting was about as far as he was prepared to go—at least in person.

Strong, persistent doubts about Johnson's policies continued to plague Mansfield. He saw full-scale war looming over the horizon and continued privately advising Johnson against taking the fateful step toward escalation. On February 8, he sent the president yet another memorandum that spelled out his concern that a sustained bombing campaign might "force [Soviet Premier] Kosygin's hand." He worried that escalation might even bring about "a closer degree of cooperation" between the Soviet Union and China, and that China might be drawn directly into the conflict.

> What the answer to the situation is at the moment [Mansfield wrote,] I do not know nor does anyone else. But I am persuaded that the trend toward enlargement of the conflict and a continuous deepening of our military commitment on the Asian mainland, despite your desire to the contrary, is not going to provide one.[32]

Later that day, McGeorge Bundy—responding on Johnson's behalf—ignored Mansfield's fundamental concern about enlarging the conflict. The Viet Cong strikes at Pleiku had left Johnson no other choice but to respond, Bundy argued. "We think that inactivity by the United States," he wrote, "would have made it even more tempting for the Soviets to enlarge on their support for North Vietnam." As for the risk of Chinese involvement, Bundy assured Mansfield, without elaboration, that "we aim to keep the risk of that involvement as low as possible."[33]

On February 10, events again led Johnson closer toward ordering the "sustained reprisals" that he had endorsed in the hours after the attacks at Pleiku. That morning, Viet Cong guerrillas bombed a hotel in Qui Nhon, a coastal city where American soldiers were housed. Twenty-three Americans died and more than twenty were wounded—by far the most American casualties in a single incident during the war. Johnson took the incident as "a clear signal that the Communists were determined to raise the level of violence."[34]

At a National Security Council meeting that afternoon, Johnson polled his advisors on whether the United States should launch another retaliatory strike. Almost all, including McNamara and Rusk, urged Johnson to act immediately. One senior advisor, Ball, had his doubts, but remained silent. "Faced with an unanimous view," he later explained, "I saw no option but to go along."[35] Ball did, however, try what he called a "filibustering tactic," advising Johnson that the United States should proceed cautiously in light of Premier Kosygin's ongoing visit to North Vietnam. Turning to Hubert Humphrey, attending only his second National Security Council meeting as vice president, Johnson asked, "Hubert, what do you think?"[36] Only months earlier, when he had accepted the role as running mate, Humphrey had pledged Johnson his complete loyalty. Although Humphrey was free to express his views in private, Johnson made it clear he wanted nothing other than absolute fealty in the presence of others. He had been that kind of vice president to John Kennedy and he expected nothing less from Humphrey. Now, not quite a month into his term as vice president, Humphrey was about to break his promise.

For years, the liberal Humphrey had been an outspoken supporter of a strong American presence in South Vietnam. "It is my view," Humphrey had said during the Gulf of Tonkin Resolution debate, "that the minute we back away from the commitments we have made in the defense of freedom, where the Communist powers are guilty of outright subversion and aggression, on that day the strength, the freedom and the honor of the United States starts to be eroded."[37] But like many Americans, and some prominent members of Congress, Humphrey had his doubts about the effectiveness of a bombing campaign. But because he was not part of Johnson's tight circle of Vietnam advisors, he had every reason to believe the president when he campaigned on the pledge of "no wider war." As his advisor Ted Van Dyk recalled, Humphrey "had campaigned as an honest man."[38]

In January, as vice president-elect, Humphrey had accompanied retired General Edward Lansdale—an outspoken proponent of a political solution for Vietnam—to a closed-door session of the Senate Foreign Relations Committee. There, Humphrey made it clear to his Senate colleagues that he sided with Lansdale, who favored a smarter effort on the political front in South Vietnam before taking the war northward. "Everybody says we have to improve the political situation," Humphrey acknowledged to the committee. "But in the meantime they say you can't improve the political situation until you win the military situation. You know, it is just hopeless if you keep talking like that."[39]

By the time Johnson solicited Humphrey's opinion, the new vice president was thoroughly persuaded that an air campaign against North Vietnam was a terrible idea. Without weighing the consequences—and perhaps not fully comprehending that Johnson was looking not so much for advice but affirmation of a decision already made—Humphrey spoke up. "I don't think we should," Humphrey said in answer to Johnson's question about a second round of retaliatory strikes. As Johnson fumed, Humphrey explained that, like Ball, he did not necessarily oppose the strike, but believed it might be best to postpone military action until Kosygin had left North Vietnam. Furthermore, Humphrey wondered if the South Vietnamese, rather than the U.S. military, should wage the attacks. But as Humphrey soon realized, Johnson had already reached his decision. The attacks would take place "at first light."[40]

After the meeting, Bundy, McNamara, McCone, Ball, and others remained behind to begin drafting a press release concerning the American response to the Viet Cong attack. As Bundy observed, Johnson appeared to have finally "turned the corner." The country was now, he said, on track to begin conducting "sustained and continuing operations against the North." Although McCone disagreed—and said he understood that Johnson had merely approved retaliation for a particular event—the others argued that Johnson had, in fact, finally approved implementation of a bombing campaign. "A program of sustained operations," they informed McCone, "was the order of the day."[41]

Less than two hours later, Johnson met with the bipartisan congressional leaders. After the briefing—in what had become his custom—he polled the room to ensure that each advisor could not claim he had not been afforded an opportunity to object. No one spoke but Speaker McCormack, who gave Johnson his support and assured him that he was following the only available course. Mansfield sat silent. Invited by Johnson to speak, he declined. After the meeting, Mansfield handed a memorandum to White House aide Jack Valenti and asked him to deliver it to the president.[42]

In his brief memorandum, Mansfield warned Johnson that the next round of attacks would be more difficult than the first. Communist defenses in the north, he said, "have already been and will continue to be strengthened since the last attack." The latest Viet Cong assault had proven that more retaliation "will not cool off the situation—that much should now be clear." More U.S. bombing would lead to further Viet Cong attacks, he argued, and the Viet Cong would likely respond by pitting "their strength against our weakness." That, warned Mansfield, meant more attacks on vulnerable facilities like Pleiku. "Our weakness is on the ground in Viet Nam," Mansfield wrote, "where isolated pockets of Americans are surrounded by, at best, an indifferent population and, more likely, by an increasingly hostile population." To protect against the inevitable attacks, Mansfield predicted that "the outposts will have to be *vastly strengthened by American forces* [emphasis Mansfield's] or pulled into and consolidated in the Saigon area." Again, Mansfield urged Johnson to seek a peaceful way out and suggested that he seek a conference of the parties to the 1954 Geneva accords. "If it is convened," he told Johnson, "our diplomacy should strive to see to it that the first act of this Conference should be to call for a cease-fire throughout Viet Nam and Indochina."[43]

Again, it was Bundy, not Johnson, who responded to Mansfield. The national security advisor told him that the administration doubted "that any single retaliation can be expected at this stage to cool off the situation." Yet Bundy agreed with Mansfield that "Americans on the ground" did, in fact, "face the prospect of harassment by the Viet Cong." But he offered no rebuttal of Mansfield's prescient contention that the natural consequence of increased Viet Cong attacks would be an increase in American ground troops. As for Mansfield's call for peace talks leading to a cease-fire, Bundy worried that an across-the-board cessation of fighting "would seem to be an effort to apply equal standards to the cops and to the robbers."[44]

Mansfield was not the only one advising Johnson to go slow. Ball, who had hesitated to speak out during the February 10 NSC meeting, had now shifted gears and argued in a memorandum that "we cannot long continue air strikes against North Viet-Nam without facing the likelihood of engagement with the 53 Chinese MIGs sent to Hanoi to defend North Vietnam." Ball painted a terrifying scenario of a gradually escalating series of confrontations with China that might ultimately involve three hundred thousand American troops as well as nuclear weapons.[45] Ball gained support for some parts of his argument from McNamara, Bundy, and Ambassador-at-Large Llewellyn Thompson. He had hoped to "shake up the President and smoke out my colleagues," he said. But while Johnson gave Ball a hearing, the memorandum did not have the desired effect. Johnson read the document quickly and invited Ball to review it in detail. By then, however, Johnson's course was set. "He thanked me," Ball recalled, "and handed the memorandum back without further comment."[46]

Brushing aside Mansfield's objections and Ball's reservations, Johnson plowed ahead. On February 13, Ball—serving as acting secretary of state during Rusk's absence from Washington—dutifully informed U.S. officials in Saigon that the president had approved execution of "a program of measured and limited air action" on North Vietnamese sites south of the 19th Parallel, to be carried out jointly with the South Vietnamese military "until further notice." Ball added that the United States would take its case to the United Nations Security Council and argue that Hanoi was the "aggressor" and that the United States was "ready and eager" for "talks" to end the war. But that would only be for show, as Ball certainly knew. Talks would not end the conflict, Ball cautioned, because, as he explained, "we are determined to continue with military actions." Washington would not ease up, Ball said, "unless and until Hanoi has brought its aggression to an end." The attacks on North Vietnam would be limited, in the beginning, to strikes on two or three targets "about once or twice a week."[47]

By now, Johnson had done everything but issue orders to begin the bombing—a fact that troubled Bundy and McNamara and prompted Bundy to gently inform Johnson that his hesitation had caused "a deep-seated need for assurance that the decision has in fact been taken." While Bundy assured Johnson that he understood the need for secrecy, he urged him to at least make his decision "known and understood by enough people to permit its orderly execution."[48] Johnson, however, was hoping in vain for an improvement in the political situation in Saigon. That was not likely to happen. Within days, a group of insurgent generals would stage another coup. This time, they would dislodge Khanh from power and force him out of the country. He would be replaced as premier by one of the usurpers, Phan Huy Quat, a physician and longtime nationalist leader.

By February 16, Johnson finally seemed prepared to yield to McNamara and Bundy. He agreed to begin the bombing within a few days. But he was far from enthusiastic about what his new policy would accomplish. "But bombers—" he told McNamara, "I'm just hoping out of hope they'll draw people in Saigon together. But bombers won't bring 'em [the North Vietnamese] to their knees—unless we do something we wouldn't do.* We'll be called warmongers—elsewhere, and here in the U.S. that'll be more pronounced. Peacemakers'll be after us."[49]

A powerful series of arguments advanced by Humphrey in a February 15 memorandum may have added to Johnson's continuing hesitation to launch the bombing campaign. While Johnson was angered by Humphrey's impertinence at the February 10 National Security Council meeting (and refused to invite him to another NSC meeting three days later), he had apparently taken time to consider the political warnings contained in a paper the vice president had submitted the following week. But it was a hard sell—especially considering Humphrey's blunder at the meeting on the 10th. As a senator, Humphrey had always enjoyed enough independence to express his views to Johnson without fear of retribution. Once he was vice president, however, their relationship had changed dramatically. Still accustomed to the Senate's freewheeling environment, Humphrey had not yet adapted to his new role. He had neither calculated Johnson's reaction nor considered the best way to approach the president on the issue. When Johnson asked for his opinion, he simply accepted the question at face value and gave an honest, but very unwanted opinion.

---

*Johnson was probably referring to the use of nuclear weapons or the wholesale bombing of civilian targets in North Vietnam.

"When he moved," Ted Van Dyk observed, "he always went with the emotional side of himself."[50]

Although Johnson valued his vice president as a skilled legislator who could help him immensely with his domestic agenda on Capitol Hill, the president assumed Humphrey had little of substance to offer in the foreign affairs arena. He had primarily been invited to the February 10 NSC meeting because, as vice president, he was an ex offico member and could not legally be excluded. Returning to his office after the meeting, Humphrey was blithely unaware that Johnson was about to cast him into purgatory. When his former Senate aide Thomas Hughes called him at George Ball's behest, Humphrey was willing to stage one more attempt at dissuading Johnson from executing the bombing campaign.

Hughes was now director of the State Department's Bureau of Intelligence and Research. Within a week, he and Humphrey had produced an impressive and formidable paper warning of the dire domestic political consequences of the planned bombing operation.[51] This time Humphrey's approach was shrewd. Unlike Ball, he would not argue against bombing on technical, military, and diplomatic grounds. Instead, he would speak to Johnson in a language they both spoke fluently: politics. Humphrey's argument was simple: a decision to escalate and widen the war would prove a serious political and legislative blunder. To begin with, Humphrey articulated what he saw as the basic differences between the Democratic and Republican parties' approaches to Vietnam—differences that Humphrey noted had been "highlighted" during the 1964 presidential campaign. The Republicans, led by Goldwater, had advocated "a quick, total military solution in Vietnam, to be achieved through military escalation of the war," Humphrey wrote. Johnson, by contrast, had presented a much more sophisticated Democratic approach that "emphasized the complexity" of the situation, while pledging to stay in Vietnam "as long as necessary" and insisting "that the war will be won or lost chiefly in South Vietnam."

> Today the administration is being charged by some of its critics with adopting the Goldwater position on Vietnam. While this is *not* true of the Administration's position as defined by the President, it is true that many key advisors in the Government are advocating a policy markedly similar to the Republican policy as defined by Goldwater.

Humphrey warned that "a full-scale military attack on North Vietnam" would "risk gravely undermining other U.S. policies." It would prevent any warming in relations between the United States and the Soviet Union, postpone progress on arms control, encourage an end to the Sino-Soviet rift, harm relations with European allies, and weaken the U.S. position in the United Nations. It would also, Humphrey warned, "tend to

shift the Administration's emphasis from its Great Society oriented programs to further military outlays." Most important, Humphrey argued,
escalation would "damage the image of the President of the United
States—and that of the United States itself."

With that introduction, Humphrey was only warming to his argument.
He warned Johnson that a full-scale war "would not make sense to the
American people" because the administration had not adequately explained
why the freedom of South Vietnam was in the "national interest." Raising
the specter of the Korean War and the debate over the "loss" of China,
Humphrey maintained that "the American people find it hard to understand why we risk World War III by enlarging a war under terms we found
unacceptable 12 years ago in Korea, particularly since the chances of success are slimmer." Regarding China, Humphrey asked Johnson to consider
that "if a war with China was ruled out by the Truman and Eisenhower
administrations alike in 1952–3, at a time when we alone had nuclear
weapons, people find it hard to contemplate such a war with China now."

One of Johnson's concerns was the weakness of the government in
Saigon, a concern that Humphrey tried to exploit when he noted that
"politically, people can't understand why we would run grave risks to support a country which is totally unable to put its own house in order." Politically speaking, Humphrey was on solid ground—and Johnson knew it.
"Politically, in Washington and across the country," Humphrey wrote,
"the opposition is more Democratic than Republican." This point had to
concern Johnson. If his popularity among Democrats suffered because of
his Vietnam policies, it could only make it more difficult to enact his Great
Society legislation. Humphrey, therefore, saw only one politically palatable way out of Vietnam. "Politically, it is always hard to cut losses," he
wrote. "But the Johnson Administration is in a stronger position to do so
than any Administration in this century. 1965 is the year of minimum political risk for the Johnson Administration. Indeed, it is the first year when
we can face the Vietnam problem without being preoccupied with the
political repercussions from the Republican right."

> The best possible outcome a year from now would be a Vietnam settle-
> ment which turns out to be better than was in the cards because the Pres-
> ident's political talents for the first time came to grips with a fateful world
> crisis and so successfully. It goes without saying that the subsequent
> domestic political benefits of such an outcome, and such a new dimen-
> sion for the President, would be enormous.

Humphrey left Johnson with a prophetic warning about the course of
escalation that he had already approved:

If on the other hand, we find ourselves leading from frustration to escalation, and end up short of war with China but embroiled deeper in fighting with Vietnam over the next few months, political opposition will steadily mount. It will underwrite all the negativism and disillusionment which we already have about foreign involvement generally—with direct spill-over effects politically for all the Democratic internationalist programs to which we are committed—AID, UN, disarmament, and activist world policies generally.[52]

Humphrey's persuasive memorandum angered Johnson and at the same time gave him pause. Had he presented his concerns to Johnson privately on February 10, and not in front of the entire National Security Council, his arguments might have found a more receptive audience. Yet despite Humphrey's evaporating influence, his case was potent and reasoned. Johnson, as angry as he was with his vice president, could not casually ignore him, especially now that Humphrey was not alone in advising caution.[53] However, Humphrey's powerful argument may also have had an unintended and more significant consequence. Instead of dissuading Johnson from ordering the sustained bombing of North Vietnam, the vice president, by so vividly describing the potential political consequences, may have only strengthened the president's resolve not to disclose the operation. As Bundy acknowledged in a February 16 memorandum to Johnson, "you do not want to give a loud public signal of a major change in policy right now." Bundy only reinforced Johnson's penchant for secrecy, reminding him that former Ambassador Henry Cabot Lodge believed "that action speaks louder than words in this field."[54]

Thus, while among Johnson's advisors the bombing campaign was acknowledged as a "watershed decision" and a "major operational change,"[55] Johnson was careful not to give any hints in public that a major escalation of the war was imminent. To the public and most in Congress, Rolling Thunder—as the operation would be dubbed by military officials—would be nothing more than retaliation for specific acts of terrorism by the Viet Cong. "I'm not going to announce a new policy," Johnson told McNamara after some advisors suggested the need to explain Johnson's decision to the public.[56] Indeed, when he addressed a group of business leaders on February 17, Johnson relied on familiar rhetoric to describe his Vietnam policy. "We seek no wider war," he told them in a reprise of his campaign promise. To his credit, Johnson said nothing to indicate that he sought a "narrower" war. But his explanation of American policy in Vietnam was ambiguous and open to wide interpretation. "But we must all understand that we will persist in the defense of freedom, and our continuing actions will be those which are justified and those which are made necessary by the continuing aggression of others." His actions, he promised without elaboration, would be "measured and fitting and adequate."[57]

In spite of Humphrey's potent arguments, Johnson worried that he might have little choice but to escalate the conflict. The current policy had proved a dismal failure. The Viet Cong already controlled much of the countryside. Without strong intervention, the U.S. military might find itself protecting nothing more than Saigon and a few other population centers. To Johnson, withdrawal was no option—just a politically humiliating admission that he, like Harry Truman, had been unable to hold the line against communism in Asia. Negotiating for neutrality, as de Gaulle and Mansfield suggested, was no better. Johnson agreed with Bundy: entering peace talks from a position of weakness would merely be "surrender on the installment plan."

Despite the belief that bombing was his only viable option, Johnson still needed a boost of confidence. For this he reached across party lines. At 10:00 A.M. on the morning of Wednesday, February 17, former president Eisenhower joined Johnson, McNamara, Bundy, and Wheeler in the White House Cabinet Room. What Johnson heard from the former president and Allied commander was comforting. The man who had been so reluctant to send American fighters to relieve the French at Dien Bien Phu ten years earlier was now an eager warrior, enthusiastically supportive of Johnson's plan to launch a bombing operation that would, as Eisenhower acknowledged, lead the United States into "a new war." But the nation had put its prestige on the line in Vietnam, Eisenhower told Johnson. "We cannot let the Indochinese peninsula go," he insisted. While Eisenhower hoped the operation would not eventually require sending in as many as eight divisions, if that level of military commitment was necessary," he said, then "so be it."[58] That was all Johnson needed to hear.

On March 2, the bombing campaign commenced, as 104 U.S. Air Force B-57s, F-100s, and F-105s, accompanied by 19 South Vietnamese Skyraiders, thundered into the sky toward their targets in North Vietnam: the Xom Bang ammunition depot just north of the border and the Quang Khe naval base. That day, North Vietnamese antiaircraft guns downed six U.S. planes. In Washington, there was no public announcement that the United States was finally at war with North Vietnam.[59]

FOR MORE THAN five months—since his remarks following the Gulf of Tonkin Resolution—George McGovern had not spoken publicly about Vietnam. By January, however, the South Dakota Democrat had concluded that Johnson was on the verge of embarking on a disastrous policy in Vietnam. On January 15, he had joined Morse, Gruening, and Church and became the Senate's most recent public critic of the president's Vietnam policy. Unlike Morse, however, McGovern went out of his way to avoid direct criticism of Johnson. He applauded the president for his "restraint" in ordering the retaliatory air strikes against the North Vietnamese "only after careful consideration of all the factors involved in this complex crisis." Gentle as he was in his critique of the administration's policies, McGovern left no doubt where he stood on the current state of affairs in South Vietnam.

"We are not winning in South Vietnam," he told the Senate. "We are backing a government that is incapable of winning a military struggle or of governing its people." In fact, McGovern said, the United States was farther away from victory "than we were a year ago." While the United States could support the South Vietnamese government with foreign aid and military equipment, McGovern doubted that any outside force could bring stability to the country's chronically unstable, ever-changing leadership. "Personally," he said, "I am very much opposed to the policy, now gaining support in Washington, of extending the war to the North." Attacks on the north could not weaken the guerrillas in the south, McGovern argued. They were, after all, "fighters who depend for eighty percent of their weapons on captured U.S. equipment and for food from a sympathetic local peasantry."[60]

A month later, Church came to the Senate floor to expand on his criticisms in a widely publicized interview with *Ramparts*, a liberal Catholic publication. After Morse, he was now the second Foreign Relations Committee member to publicly oppose the war's escalation. In the interview, Church had insisted that "the only answer to Communist subversion" in South Vietnam "is to be found within that country itself." As for calls to directly engage the North Vietnamese, Church warned that "nothing would be more futile than to permit ourselves to be sucked into a war which would pit Western forces against Asian forces." Church worried that "even if we were able, with brute muscle power, to take a large chunk of Asian territory, we could not stay there long. Our only harvest would be implacable hostility on both sides and the tides of history would, in the end, wash over us. No lasting victory could be achieved."[61]

The interview in a publication of only limited circulation had been a mild warning shot over the White House's bow. What followed, however, was a more direct and powerful blast aimed in the administration's direction and established Church as one of the first senators to publicly doubt the domino theory in Southeast Asia. On February 14, Church published a lengthy article in the *New York Times Magazine* entitled "We Are in Too Deep in Asia and Africa." In it, he demonstrated an impressive understanding of how the complicated forces of Asian nationalism imperiled the U.S. military effort in Vietnam. "Massive American intervention is a heavy cost for Saigon to bear," Church wrote. "People who fought so long and hard to rid their country of the white man's rule," he observed, "are not likely to draw much distinction between French and American uniforms, however differently we conceive our purpose for being there." Church also challenged a basic tenet of American involvement in Southeast Asia when he maintained that the other governments of Southeast Asia "are not so many dominoes in a row. They differ from one another, in popular support, and in capacity to resist Communist subversion. We will help them by keeping our distance, extending aid at arms length."[62]

On February 17—the same day that Johnson had briefed Eisenhower on his plans for escalating the war—Church, McGovern, and Gaylord Nelson gathered on the Senate floor to discuss their mounting objections to Johnson's Vietnam policies in one of the first extended debates over the war by skeptical senators. Despite their opposition to the trend of U.S. policy in Vietnam, none of these men had abandoned Johnson completely. Church expressed hope that "our retaliatory bombing" would "persuade Hanoi and Peiping that the United States is not, and never has been, a paper tiger." While he opposed the country's creeping interventionist policies, he hoped the bombing might facilitate a negotiated settlement. "The military might we can bring to bear upon North Vietnam is formidable indeed," he said, "and so it would behoove the Communists to explore with us the way to a peaceful solution in Southeast Asia." One peaceful solution that Church envisioned was an agreement for Vietnam's "neutralization," policed by the United Nations or "a special high commission," that gave the Vietnamese people time to form "an independent and unaligned new government."

Unlike Morse, Church insisted he did not favor withdrawal from Vietnam. "I support the president in what he has done thus far," he said, unaware that Johnson was about to order the sustained bombing of North Vietnam. "When the president ordered these bombings," he said of the response to Viet Cong attacks on military personnel at Pleiku and Qui Nhon, "clearly his action was intended to demonstrate the strength of American will and purpose." But having done so, Church hoped that "our government would make clear that a peaceful settlement is our objective in Southeast Asia."[63]

In his brief remarks, Nelson congratulated Church for his "refreshing and thoughtful contribution" to the debate over the U.S. role in Vietnam, which the Wisconsin Democrat believed should be "a very limited one." Based on the nation's ten-year experience in Indochina, Nelson said, "it clearly would be folly to expand our mission" in Vietnam. "When we became engaged there in 1954, I do not think anyone expected we would still be there in 1965." Although he could not imagine how wrong he would be, Nelson added, "Certainly we do not intend to stay there until 1975."[64]

As he joined the debate near the end of Church's remarks, McGovern also made it clear that his dissent was not an attack on Johnson. "The greatest disservice senators could render to the president of the United States and to the country as a whole would be to remain silent at a time when we have an especially urgent responsibility to share our views and our convictions on important issues that might affect the future of our country and the peace of the world." McGovern's views on Vietnam, he said, were "exactly the same" as Church's. Like most Americans, he supported the retaliatory air strikes Johnson had ordered in recent days, but also strongly favored negotiations to bring the war to an end. "It is perfectly possible," he insisted, "to uphold the president's hand at a time when he is ordering *selective* air strikes . . . and at the same time urge our president to use that high office in arranging a conference in which the possibilities of negotiation can be explored" (emphasis added).

Like Church, McGovern opposed unilateral withdrawal (although he had urged removal of all U.S. forces in 1963). But he believed that continued bombing would serve a useful purpose only if it were "aimed at increasing the pressure" on the North Vietnamese to negotiate "rather than following the false hope that military victory is possible for either side." McGovern also believed the United States was on the verge of replacing the French as a colonialist occupation force. "Many of the same factors that brought the French forces into disrepute and eventual defeat in Southeast Asia," he said, "are now operating against us."[65]

Later that day, encouraged by the White House to demonstrate support for Johnson's policies, House and Senate Republican leaders issued a strong statement that deplored negotiations to end the conflict and endorsed the president's retaliatory strikes against North Vietnam. "If we have any difference with the president in this respect," the leaders declared, "it is the belief that these measures might have been used more frequently since the Bay of Tonkin decision last August and an even stronger policy formulated in the meantime."[66]

From the White House, Johnson and his aides watched the nascent Vietnam debate with growing anxiety and anger. "I'm irked as hell," Johnson told Senate Republican leader Everett Dirksen. "I'm getting kicked around by my own party in the Senate and getting my support from your side of the aisle."[67] While Johnson and the Senate could ignore the objections of mavericks like Morse and Gruening, senators like McGovern, Church, and Nelson were different. Each man, although reasonably new to the Senate, was generally respected for his thoughtful, reasoned opinions.

None would have publicly disagreed with the foreign policy of a Democratic president without considerable reflection and analysis. While only
Church served on the Foreign Relations Committee, each of these three
men had approached the issue with some degree of scholarship and a basic
understanding of the powerful revolutionary forces at play in Southeast
Asia. While Morse may have been one of the most intelligent and articulate opponents of U.S. involvement in Vietnam, his virulent, sometimes
personal attacks on the administration had rendered him ineffective and
too easy to disregard. Everyone knew that the administration no longer listened to Morse and Gruening on Vietnam. The same was not true for
Church, McGovern, and Nelson. While they were not yet powerful senators, many of their Senate colleagues regarded them as serious, honest
men. They could not be easily ignored.

Worried that the three senators might represent the beginning of a
hemorrhage of support among senators in the president's own party (support among Democrats in the House was still strong), in early 1965 the
White House embarked on a subtle, but determined campaign to shore up
congressional support. Throughout February and into March, White
House officials held ten briefings to which every member of Congress was
invited. Church, who attended the February 17 briefing with Mansfield
and Minnesota Senator Eugene McCarthy, recalled that Johnson dominated the discussion, "sometimes allowing Mr. Rusk a few minutes, sometimes Mr. McNamara, but usually jumping up and sitting them down and
answering the questions himself." He compared the president to "a carni-
val barker, using all of his persuasive powers which were always impressive
and calling upon many a folksy tale to fortify his argument."[68]

But the briefings were largely one-sided exercises. White House officials were not interested in hearing arguments for a negotiated settlement
or withdrawal. Johnson and his aides never gave Church's views, nor those
of McGovern and Nelson, anything more than a cursory nod. The hubris
of presidential advisors like Bundy, Rusk, and McNamara—as well as Johnson's fears that public disclosure about Vietnam might jeopardize his
domestic agenda—foreclosed any formal, extensive congressional consultation, not to mention simple consideration of observations or advice from
congressional sources. Even the views of an acknowledged expert like
Mansfield were largely greeted with quiet contempt out of a frame of mind
that saw members of Congress as nuisances and security risks or little more
than deferential mouthpieces for administration policies.

Yet, despite the consternation they caused at the White House, neither Church, McGovern, nor Nelson had actually articulated any fundamental opposition to Johnson's basic policies. They merely pressed the
administration to work harder in search of an unspecified negotiated settlement while pursuing the policy of retaliatory air strikes against North

Vietnam. Each man had argued, in varying ways, that a series of policy errors had brought the United States to its current state of affairs in Vietnam. Johnson, they believed, was at a crossroads. He could expand the war, with tragic results, or he could turn away from the steady course of escalation and earnestly seek a peaceful solution that limited or reduced the country's involvement in Southeast Asia. "I remember I used to react unfavorably to Morse and Gruening talking about 'McNamara's war' and personalizing it," McGovern later said. "To me, I wanted to make it easier for them to back down by calling for negotiations. Instead of saying, 'Let's get out,' my early instinct was to say, 'Let's negotiate. Let's talk to them and see what we can work out.' And that was partly designed to make it easier for the administration to embrace the course we were recommending."[69]

McGovern and Church, however, were not getting through to Johnson, a man now doggedly determined to press his views on members of Congress, not to invite theirs. The White House seminars to which Johnson invited members of Congress appeared to have their desired effect. In the House, Democratic and Republican leaders strongly supported the president's Vietnam policies, even if they were still unaware of the sustained bombing campaign Johnson had ordered. In fact, about the only dissent heard in the House came from Republicans who believed that Johnson had not prosecuted the war vigorously enough. In the Senate, Johnson also enjoyed broad bipartisan support—from conservative Minority Leader Dirksen to liberal Democrats like Connecticut's Thomas Dodd and Illinois' Paul Douglas, who answered Church's dissent in Senate speeches on February 23. In a moment of rhetorical excess, Dodd insisted that "the demand that we negotiate now over Vietnam is akin to asking [Prime Minister Winston] Churchill to negotiate with the Germans at the time of Dunkirk, or asking Truman to negotiate with the Communists when we stood with our backs to the sea in the Pusan perimeter in Korea." No doubt speaking for the White House, Dodd dismissed the notion that winning the war would require extensive bombing of the north. "Nor do I believe," he said, "that there will be any large-scale involvement of American troops on the Korean model."

Like many political leaders of both parties—conservative and liberal—Douglas applied the perceived lessons of World War II to Vietnam. "To those who say that there is no analogy between the cumulative conquests of Hitler and Mussolini in the late 1930s and the cumulative developments of the Chinese in Asia in the 1960s," he said following Dodd's remarks, "I should say that there is a grave danger that they delude themselves. It would be a terrible thing if we woke up to find all of Asia Communist."[70]

Although White House officials had prompted much of this vocal support for Johnson, the enthusiastic endorsements of his policies—by liberals and conservatives—were most welcome. While they may not have succeeded in casting Johnson's few critics as ill-informed isolationists, they did help reinforce the feeling that those who questioned the administration's course in Vietnam were far removed from the mainstream of American political and foreign policy opinion. In fact, there is no evidence that the mild dissents of senators like Church, Nelson, or McGovern had any lasting effect on the administration's position in Vietnam. "The Vietnam debate" of February and early March, William Conrad Gibbons observed, "was a substitute for other forms of action." For example, during a period when Johnson was leading the country into a full-scale war in Vietnam, neither the Senate Foreign Relations Committee nor the House Foreign Affairs Committee held hearings on the administration's Vietnam policies. Except for a handful of junior members, no one spoke out against the rapid escalation of America's military role in Vietnam.[71]

While some of this silence can be explained by Johnson's unwillingness to disclose crucial details about the sea change in Vietnam policy, another critical factor was the extreme reluctance by members of Congress, especially Democrats, to publicly challenge a president who had just been elected by the largest landslide in American history. Like Mansfield, the few who strongly opposed administration policy chose to communicate their differences in private memoranda, not public speeches. "I had supported him and we were good friends," Fulbright later said about his own glaring absence from the public debate. In private, Fulbright had advised caution, warned against a bombing campaign, and insisted that Johnson consult Congress before he embarked on any radical departure from current policy. In public, however, he was silent. "I thought," he later said, "I could persuade him to change his mind."[72] Having given Johnson—by virtue of the Gulf of Tonkin Resolution—a blank check to fight the war as he pleased, Congress had effectively abdicated responsibility for U.S. military policy in Vietnam. Johnson concluded that he needed no more congressional license in Vietnam than that which he already possessed.

In the momentous period during which Washington began its gradual descent into the quagmire of Vietnam, Mansfield, Fulbright, and Russell were quiescent, having left the debate over American policy in Southeast Asia to Johnson's enthusiastic, high-profile supporters and his marginally influential detractors. In the middle, attempting vainly to prod the administration toward a peaceful settlement of the conflict, Church, McGovern, and Nelson were humored, but largely ignored. Lyndon Johnson had his hunting license for Vietnam—and now he intended to use it.

IN LATE FEBRUARY, after Gaylord Nelson attended one of the Vietnam seminars at the White House, he caught a ride home with Humphrey in his official limousine. Nelson was astonished by the speculative talk he had just heard from other members of Congress about sending American ground troops to Vietnam. "My, God, Hubert," he said, "if we put ground troops in there, we're going to get into a hell of a big war."

Humphrey acknowledged the pressure on Johnson to increase the American commitment. "Gaylord," Humphrey said, "there are people in the Pentagon and the State Department who want to send in three hundred thousand troops." Humphrey, however, had faith in Johnson's judgment. "The president," he assured Nelson, "will never get sucked into that."[73]

CHAPTER 28

We Are Very Deep Already

1965

"Bomb, bomb, bomb," Johnson barked on March 2 as he bored his finger into the medal-laden chest of the Army chief of staff, General Harold Johnson. "That's all you know. Well, I want to know why there's nothing else. You generals have all been educated at the taxpayers' expense, and you're not giving me any ideas and any solutions for this damn little pissant country. Now, I don't need ten generals to come in here ten times and tell me to bomb. I want some solutions. I want some answers."[1] With those instructions, General Johnson left for South Vietnam in early March 1965 in search of the elusive solution that would end—or at least limit—the American presence in Vietnam and allow the president and the country to turn their attention to the administration's domestic initiatives.

It was not to be. Conditions in Vietnam only grew worse, despite a bombing campaign that had lifted the sagging spirits of the South Vietnamese but failed to dampen those of the Viet Cong. On March 6, Bundy informed Johnson that "the chances of a turn-around in South Vietnam remain less than even; the brutal fact is that we have been losing ground at an increasing rate in the countryside in January and February." There was no evidence, he reported, that the latest government leaders had the "necessary will, skill and human resources which a turn-around will require."[2] The underlying message seemed clear enough: winning the war would require a massive military commitment by the United States. After a week in South Vietnam, General Johnson found none of the easy solutions that the president had demanded. The best he could do was to recommend a more vigorous bombing campaign and more covert operations. A worried Johnson, speaking by phone to Richard Russell on March 6, confessed "the great trouble I'm under" in Vietnam: "A man can fight if he can see the daylight down the road, somewhere. But thre ain't no daylight in Vietnam."

Russell agreed. "It's the biggest damn mess I ever saw in my life," he said. "You couldn't have inherited a worse mess." To that, Johnson observed, prophetically: "Well, [if] they'd say I inherited it, I'd be lucky. But they'll all say I created it."

The Army chief of staff also returned with the distressing news that Westmoreland wanted more troops—and that meant an even deeper American role in Vietnam and the promise of a protracted, costly war. The level of U.S. ground troops in Vietnam—about twenty-eight thousand in early 1965—was already rising with the arrival of three thousand five hundred Marines at the American air base near the coastal city of Da Nang on March 8.[3]* While Ambassador Taylor recognized the need to protect the base from Viet Cong attack, he warned officials in Washington that the decision to send in the Marines would be the first step "in reversing [a] long standing policy of avoiding commitment of ground combat forces in SVN. Once this policy is breached, it will be very difficult to hold [the] line."[4] Johnson agreed, telling McNamara on March 6 that "what we've done with these B-57s [bombers] is just going to be Sunday school stuff compared to the Marines."

By mid-March, Taylor's concerns about holding the line on troop deployments proved exceedingly prophetic. This time, Westmoreland requested a Marine battalion to protect an American airfield at Hue, north of Da Nang. "Westmoreland's estimation of the war," Admiral Sharp, the commander of Pacific forces, reported to the Joint Chiefs, "has moved out of the purely guerilla phase and into a more formalized military conflict."[5] Taylor again warned Washington that another American battalion should serve as "a reminder of the strong likelihood of additional requests for increases in U.S. ground combat forces in SVN."[6] On March 20, as if on cue, the Joint Chiefs of Staff informed McNamara of "a marked deterioration in the military situation in Vietnam" and warned that if "present trends are not reversed, the counterinsurgency campaign in South Vietnam will be lost." They recommended deployment of two American divisions. Westmoreland hoped that the additional troops would serve several purposes: wresting control of the highlands region from the Viet Cong and protecting U.S. installations and coastal enclaves.[7]

At the White House, Bundy offered his tentative support for the Joint Chiefs' proposal and posed this haunting question to Johnson: "In terms of U.S. politics which is better: to 'lose' now or to 'lose' after committing 100,000 men? Tentative answer: the latter."[8] Bundy was no politician, but

---

*While he granted Westmoreland's request for the Marines, Johnson severely limited their mission. He restricted them to the airfield and allowed nothing more than defensive operations against the Viet Cong.

he did understand Johnson's political calculations. He knew that Johnson, like Kennedy and Eisenhower before him, was fearful of the prospect that he might bear the blame for the loss of all of Southeast Asia to Chinese communism. What Bundy wrote had real meaning for Johnson: better to lose Vietnam after a good fight than none at all. In a war that was increasingly associated with Johnson, Bundy knew that the president wanted it known that he was no coward; he was not afraid to stand up to the Communists.[9]

But while he was willing to authorize more bombing and an intensification of covert operations, Johnson was not yet prepared to send two divisions into Vietnam, especially for offensive purposes. The bombing was clearly not working—the Viet Cong were stronger than ever and Hanoi was unbowed—but Johnson believed it was too early to send in large numbers of troops without first trying some alternative. But where were the alternatives? Having closed the door to so many other options, Johnson knew his choices were limited. "Where are we going?" he demanded of his advisors during their now-regular Tuesday lunch meeting on March 23. Their answers were sketchy. Was the bombing having *any* effect on Hanoi? Johnson wanted to know. "Do they know we're willin' to talk?" he asked, adding later that American bombers should "revisit" targets that had already been bombed. "I don't wanna run out of targets and I don't wanna go to Hanoi. I was a hell of a long time getting into this. But I like it."[10]

MANSFIELD COULD SEE the ground troops coming. On March 6, he had received the first inkling when McNamara phoned to seek his support for sending the Marine battalions to Da Nang. Mansfield opposed the idea and told the Defense secretary that ground troops would make an "already delicate" situation even "more delicate." Instead, Mansfield recommended withdrawing some American troops from Saigon and sending them to Da Nang. Sending in the Marines, he cautioned, "would make a difficult situation more dangerous and tend to create the impression around the world that this was a preliminary to a stepped up escalation."[11] By month's end, Mansfield realized the decision to send in large numbers of U.S. troops was more imminent than he had earlier imagined. Whether Johnson revealed the Joint Chiefs' recommendation at a March 23 meeting with congressional leaders, or in a private phone conversation with Mansfield later that day, is not clear. But judging by the tone of Mansfield's memorandum to Johnson the following day, it seems evident that he knew something of the decision facing Johnson.[12]

In unusually harsh and blunt language, Mansfield characterized Johnson's "present" U.S. policy in Southeast Asia as one that involved making "whatever expenditure of American lives and resources . . . is necessary in order for us to exercise, in effect, a primacy over what transpires in South Viet Nam. If this involves going into North Viet Nam and beyond, that, too, will be done." As best he could tell, Mansfield told Johnson, the United States was insisting upon the "unconditional capitulation of the Viet Cong" and that, absent their surrender, "our military involvement must continue and be increased as necessary." Mansfield also revealed little confidence in Johnson's willingness to negotiate in good faith. The American position was, he told Johnson, that "we will not try to encourage, through sustained diplomatic efforts, the emergence of the kind of situations which exist in Burma and Cambodia, but rather, so far as I can see, that we will stress those situations which can be maintained only by continuous infusions of American aid."

While he expressed "no great hope that, at this late date, these suggestions will be useful to you," Mansfield nonetheless gave Johnson his latest observations on U.S. policy, "for what they may be worth." First, he recommended what would soon become known as the "enclave strategy"—a plan originally devised by Maxwell Taylor that would concentrate U.S. ground forces "into two or three key spots which either back up on the sea or are easily accessible from the sea." All other Americans in Viet Nam, he added, "should be drawn into these protected points as rapidly as possible." Again, Mansfield urged Johnson to seek a peaceful settlement of the conflict through a reconvening of the 1961 Geneva Conference that had secured the Laotian neutrality in 1962—but only if Hanoi and the Viet Cong agreed to a cease-fire throughout the two countries. While convening such a conference would have risks, Mansfield believed they were "risks which are far smaller than those which we now run."

"We are very deep already," Mansfield concluded, "and in most unfavorable circumstances. In my judgment we were in too deep long before you assumed office. But you know the whole situation on a day-to-day basis and I most certainly respect the decisions which you have felt compelled to make in this connection." Vowing not to "trouble you further with memorandums [sic] on this situation,"* Mansfield assured Johnson once more that despite their deep differences over the course of U.S. policy in Vietnam, he would do nothing but support him in public. "I want you to know," he wrote, "that you have my support on a personal as well as an official basis."[13]

On March 26, McGovern, worried like Mansfield that a major escalation of the war was imminent, went to the White House to discuss Vietnam with the president. "Perhaps naively," McGovern said of himself and

---

*Contrary to his assurance, the memorandum would not be Mansfield's last.

Frank Church, "we still hoped that by avoiding direct attacks on the administration and pressing instead for a negotiated settlement, we might persuade the President to modify his course."[14] In the past weeks, McGovern had become more vocal in his insistence that bombing would have little impact on the Viet Cong. "I think it's quite possible that we can bomb the people of North Vietnam into oblivion," he said on a CBS television network program on March 8, "but that won't end the fighting in the South." The only thing bombing might accomplish, McGovern warned, was to lead the nation's military forces deeper and deeper into Vietnam. "It may involve a million American soldiers in an Asiatic war before we're through," he warned.

Still walking a fine line between support for what he believed was a policy of restrained, retaliatory bombing and the inexorable tug of deeper involvement in South Vietnam, McGovern painted his own haunting picture of what escalation might bring: "I think there will be a staggering loss of human life out of all proportion to the stakes involved and I see no guarantee that once we go through that kind of a murderous and destructive kind of a military effort that the situation out there will be any better. In fact, I think it will be a lot worse."[15]

When he arrived at the White House three weeks later, McGovern quickly realized that he had little chance of getting through to Johnson who, he said, "just closed his ears to anyone who seemed to oppose him as well as the war." McGovern told Johnson that he believed the war was spinning out of control. Johnson assured him that any escalation was restrained and gradual. "I'm going up old Ho Chi Minh's leg an inch at a time," Johnson said. "Well, Mr. President," McGovern replied, "sometimes when we go up a leg we get slapped." When McGovern mentioned a memorandum he had prepared containing his arguments for ending American involvement in Vietnam, Johnson dismissed him. "Don't give me another goddamn history lesson," he snapped. "I've got a drawer full of memos from Mansfield. I don't need a lecture on where we went wrong. I've got to deal with where we are now."

Finally, near the end of an unproductive thirty minutes, McGovern asked Johnson, "What do you think is the objective of the Chinese Communists?"

"I think they want to take over the world," Johnson replied.

"You mean a Hitler-style type conquest?" McGovern asked.

"That's my view," said Johnson.

"Well, my view, Mr. President, is by tying down so many of our resources and men in South Vietnam, if in fact the Communists do have in mind an international expansionist program, we are playing into their hands because we have picked an area that is very difficult for American forces to defend. Furthermore, we are taking on a fourth-rate power involved in a complex struggle of their own, and I can't see where that serves our interest in weakening Chinese expansionism. It may be serving their purpose."

Johnson, who obviously disagreed, replied, "Well, I know there are some people who hold to that view."

As he drove out the White House gates that evening, McGovern said, "I literally trembled for the future of the nation. I was not angry at Lyndon Johnson. I was filled with sadness and foreboding that this powerful, well-meaning man who wanted so desperately to be a great president was heading down the road to disaster."[16]

McGovern and Mansfield were not the only senators very worried about the consequences of the bombing and the prospect that Johnson might commit large numbers of American troops to Vietnam. In mid-March, after hearing through an aide that the Soviets were greatly disturbed by the U.S. bombing, Fulbright had called on Soviet Ambassador Anatoly Dobrynin, who told him the air strikes were "causing deep embarrassment and concern" in the Kremlin. At the very least, the Soviets would now feel the need to increase their supplies of military equipment to the North Vietnamese. Seeing a developing deterioration in relations between the United States and the Soviet Union, Fulbright tried to sell Rusk on a deal by which the United States would halt the bombing in exchange for Russian pressure on the North Vietnamese to end the infiltration of men and supplies to the Viet Cong. At that point, as Fulbright envisioned it, the Soviets and Great Britain would reconvene a Geneva Conference in which all parties would accept the results of a national election in Vietnam—the very election scenario the United States had helped quash in 1956. Fulbright told Rusk that he was sure that a proposal to negotiate an end to the conflict would be "received with rejoicing" in Moscow. But Johnson and his aides, busy on a peace proposal that skirted the delicate subject of negotiations, rejected the idea.

Fulbright appeared to let the matter drop, but made it clear to administration officials that full-scale escalation was not the course to pursue if Johnson wanted continued congressional support for his policies. Near the end of March—after a long discussion with Richard Russell about their mutual fear that Vietnam would prove a "bottomless pit"—Fulbright went to the White House, where he informed Johnson of his fear that escalation in Vietnam would lead the nation into direct confrontation with the Soviet Union.[17] If that occurred, then one of Fulbright's greatest hopes—the restoration of normal relations with the Soviets—would be lost. For once, Fulbright believed that Johnson had given him a fair hearing. The president seemed to receive his arguments with unusual equanimity.

When he returned to his office, Fulbright summoned Seth Tillman, his speechwriter and a senior Foreign Relations Committee staff member. Immediately, the two men began work on a more detailed disquisition of his views. In a memorandum that he discussed with McNamara and handed to Johnson in early April, the Foreign Relations Committee chairman made his position abundantly clear: the threat in Southeast Asia was not communism, but Chinese imperialism. Therefore, it would be disastrous to engage in a massive ground and air war in Southeast Asia. Not only would such an endeavor be costly, Fulbright maintained, it would aggravate the Cold War. The bottom line, as Fulbright warned Johnson, was that "the commitment of a large American land army would involve us in a bloody and interminable conflict in which the advantage would lie with the enemy." On April 6, Fulbright sent the memorandum to the White House. Johnson, he later said, "was not persuaded."[18]

Several days earlier, on April 2, before a joint meeting of the Senate Foreign Relations and Armed Services committees, Fulbright had made his views unmistakably clear to Ambassador Taylor: continued escalation, especially without congressional consultation, would be a serious mistake. For almost two hours, Taylor endured tough questions from Fulbright and several other senators concerned about reports that administration officials were contemplating the deployment of as many as three hundred fifty thousand U.S. troops to South Vietnam. Taylor, who reported for the first time on the sustained U.S. bombing of North Vietnam, acknowledged that sending "anything ranging from several thousand individuals to . . . three or four divisions" had been discussed. But Johnson, he said, was considering nothing on the order of three hundred fifty thousand men.

"It seems to me that this is a major step," Republican Clifford Case of New Jersey told Taylor, adding that he doubted the Gulf of Tonkin Resolution empowered Johnson to make such a decision. "I think if the country felt that it did empower him to take it, there might be considerable pressure for recission [sic] of the resolution." Sending large numbers of American troops to Vietnam, Case insisted, "is a very grave question" that "requires more than just a determination by the [National] Security Council and the President."

"The last thing we want to do," Taylor assured Case, "is to suggest we are taking over the war and the Vietnamese can stand to one side."

Intrigued, Fulbright picked up Case's line of questioning. "Is the resolution which we passed last summer after the Tonkin affair interpreted to mean a full authorization, approval by the Congress to send either 300,000 or 500,000 or one and a half million people to Vietnam?" Did the administration believe, Fulbright elaborated, that Johnson had "no need to come and consult the Congress . . . if they are going to decide to put, well,

150,000 men? . . . If we are going into the land- war conditions, we ought to be consulted."

Taylor replied that while "careful examination of possible ground reinforcements is going on today," no one had discussed "a decision of this magnitude at this moment." Were such a decision to be considered, Taylor assured Fulbright that "this committee would be most thoroughly consulted."

Fulbright was skeptical and recalled that American force levels in Vietnam had risen from about 700 in 1960 to 28,000 in 1965 with no little or no congressional consultation. "You won't put 300,000 all at once," he explained. "You can't do that. It is only 10,000 at a time." Instead of discussing sending in ground reinforcements, Fulbright urged Taylor to "explore just a little bit more just how vital this is to the security of the United States, because it wasn't very long ago that I didn't know where Vietnam was. We had no interest. How has it become so vital to us that this particular piece of real estate must be retained at all costs?"

"It is simply the fact that Vietnam is a very important element in a very important piece of real estate," Taylor replied, "namely, Southeast Asia, a country to the defense of which we have committed ourselves publicly. For us to walk away from this one—"

Fulbright interrupted. "Maybe we made a mistake in committing ourselves publicly," he said.

"We would make a bigger mistake," Taylor said, "if we give up there, senator."

Despite Taylor's insistence that no decision had been made on ground troops, several committee members appeared persuaded that the decision was inevitable. "It looks to us as laymen," Democrat John Stennis of Mississippi said, "that we are moving rapidly in that direction."

In an antagonistic ending to an already contentious hearing, Fulbright inquired about an administration request for $1 million to rebuild the U.S. embassy in Saigon that had been severely damaged several days earlier by a bomb blast that killed 17 people and injured 183. "You asked us for one million dollars for a building," he said, "but you don't want to ask us for 300,000 men to send over there that may cost $50 billion. How about that?"

"When that day comes, senator, you are going to be consulted, I am perfectly sure."

"Are you sure?" Fulbright asked, skeptically.[19]

That afternoon, Taylor reported to Johnson and the National Security Council on his testimony and observed that "the mood of some senators was one of concern, but not disapproval." Fulbright, in particular, "was worried about reports that the U.S. might send as many as three or four divisions to Vietnam." Furthermore, he said, the Foreign Relations chairman believed that the Gulf of Tonkin Resolution "might not cover the dispatch of large ground units to Vietnam." Johnson ignored Fulbright's concerns and barely commented on the reports of senatorial skepticism. He did not believe, he said, "the sending of U.S. military forces to Vietnam would require a new congressional resolution."[20]

Later that evening, Rusk phoned Church—after trying unsuccessfully to reach Fulbright and Case—to assure him that, despite rumors of a three hundred thousand-man deployment to Vietnam, "no such operation was at all in contemplation." That undoubtedly left the distinct misimpression that administration officials were considering nothing more than small troop deployments. Furthermore, Rusk assured Church that if and when such a decision were made "there would be the fullest consultation with Congress."[21] Rusk, however, had neglected to give Church some important news. The day before, with no consultation or notice to Congress, Johnson had reached two momentous decisions: he had approved sending as many as twenty-four thousand new troops to South Vietnam—nearly doubling the number of American troops in Indochina—and had drastically altered the mission of U.S. ground forces. Hereafter, U.S. forces that were previously permitted to conduct only advisory, defensive operations would be authorized for offensive "counterinsurgency operations."[22] The American "advisors" were now combatants.

Fulbright and his committee would not learn of the decision until April 7, when McNamara informed them of Johnson's order to send the additional troops. During his testimony, however, the Defense secretary held back the other important piece of information—the change in mission of U.S. forces from defensive to offensive. "It looks now as if the administration is assuming," a perturbed Fulbright said, "that . . . further consultation or approval from the Congress is necessary in view of the resolution last summer." Ball, who accompanied McNamara, disagreed. "No, Mr. Chairman," he said. "I would say that the president has every intention of keeping in the closest consultation with Congress on all moves of this kind." Echoing Ball, McNamara assured Fulbright that Johnson would consult the Congress "before undertaking any combat moves of personnel that would potentially enlarge the war."[23]

"It wasn't that he was double-crossing people," Ray Cline, deputy director of the CIA, later said in defense of Johnson's obsession with secrecy. "He kept deluding himself that it would all be easier than it was. He never wanted to bite the bullet of going downtown and telling his congressional cronies, 'I'm sorry, you guys, I got you into a situation here where you've got to do some unpopular things, we've got to do them.'"

Johnson, meanwhile, had Bundy and other aides busy preparing a major speech that he would deliver on April 7 at Johns Hopkins University in Baltimore, during which he would unveil a dramatic bid for peace while simultaneously characterizing U.S. involvement in Vietnam as an effort to "strengthen world order." "We will not be defeated," he would declare. "We will not grow tired. We will not withdraw, either openly or under the cloak of a meaningless agreement." While Johnson would acknowledge that "air attacks alone" would not win the war, he would also insist that they "are a necessary part of the surest road to peace." Yet he would insist that the United States was prepared to enter into "uncondi- tional discussions" that would lead to an "independent South Vietnam." The hallmark of Johnson's speech, however, would be his sensational offer to spend $1 billion on a vast program of economic development in the Mekong Delta, providing food, water, and power "on a scale to dwarf even our own TVA [Tennessee Valley Authority]." In effect, Johnson planned to deal with Ho Chi Minh as if he were a congressman from Louisiana in need of a flood-control project. In this case, surrender would bring Ho $1 billion for economic development.[24]

Johnson loved the idea and was eager to share it with his detractors. In a White House meeting with Walter Lippmann, Johnson informed the columnist that he planned to "hold out that carrot you keep talking to me about." In the end, however, Johnson could not resist hectoring his critic while also revealing the insincerity of his expressed determination to pur- sue a negotiated settlement. "I'm not just going to pull up my pants and run out on Vietnam," he told Lippmann. "Don't you know the church is on fire over there, and we've got to find a way [to put it] out?" Dismissing Lippmann's calls for negotiation, Johnson insisted that "there's nobody over there to negotiate with. So the only thing there is to do is to hang on. And that's what I'm going to do."[25]

On the day of the speech, in a meeting with Fulbright and Mansfield, Johnson declined to discuss the arguments for negotiations that Fulbright had included in his memorandum delivered to the White House the day before. Instead, he handed the two men a text of the Johns Hopkins speech and drew their attention to his statement of support for unconditional negotiations. Fulbright was pleased by the "affirmative tone" of Johnson's remarks.[26] Later that day, Johnson reached out to two more critics when he invited Church and McGovern, along with pro-war senator Gale McGee, to the White House to read the speech. Knowing that McGovern and McGee would appear on the CBS television network afterwards to critique his remarks, Johnson hoped to neutralize McGovern by giving him the impression that he was eagerly seeking negotiations to end the war. John- son read aloud his entire speech to the three men. "In effect, he was say- ing," McGovern later speculated, "'Now I'm giving you what you've been asking for, an offer to negotiate. Now I hope you bastards will shut up.'"[27]

Despite Johnson's seeming eagerness to negotiate, McGovern and

Church also noted that the speech contained the disheartening passage that the United States "will not withdraw, either openly or under the cloak of a meaningless agreement." Although McGovern and Church were initially pleased with Johnson's rhetoric about negotiations, McGovern recalled that "we both made it quite clear that simply making the offer and then accelerating the military effort would not accomplish what we had in mind."[28] McGovern later said he believed that Johnson's Johns Hopkins speech "was primarily calculated to disarm the dissenters at home and abroad without changing policy."[29]

With no real intention of entering into negotiations to end the war, Johnson knew that the success of his much-heralded peace "plan" hinged on North Vietnam's acceptance of his billion-dollar economic program. "Old Ho can't turn me down," Johnson told aide Bill Moyers after the speech.[30] But Ho could turn him down—and did. Johnson's miscalculation was his failure to see the Viet Cong and their North Vietnamese supporters as committed nationalists. Having fought against foreign domination for more than twenty years, they were unlikely to drop their struggle the minute that Johnson promised a billion dollars in *additional* American involvement in Southeast Asia. "I think he wrongly thought that the same assumptions prevailed there that prevailed here," Moyers observed. "He'd say, 'My God, I've offered Ho Chi Minh [$1 billion] to build a Mekong Valley. If that'd been [labor leader] George Meany, he'd have snapped at it!'" Yet because "LBJ had no particular grasp of foreign cultures," explained NSC staff member Robert Komer, he could not have foreseen North Vietnam's adamant refusal of his offer. "He felt no particular need to delve into what made Vietnamese Vietnamese—as opposed to Americans or Greeks or Chinese," said Komer. "He was a people man, and he thought people everywhere were the same." Johnson saw no difference, Komer said, between a Vietnamese rice farmer and a farmer from Oklahoma or Texas.[31]

Johnson had also tailored his economic development proposal to the desires of his domestic critics, hoping to prove that he was serious about a peaceful resolution to the conflict and that the United States genuinely wanted to improve the lives of the average South Vietnamese citizen. "These countries of Southeast Asia are homes for millions of impoverished people," Johnson said, revealing a firmly held American misperception of Vietnam as a nation uniformly and widely racked by misery and poverty. "Each day these people rise at dawn and struggle through until the night to wrestle existence from the soil," he said at Johns Hopkins. "They are often wracked by diseases, plagued by hunger, and death comes at the early age of 40." Johnson promised to change all of that with massive amounts of American money and Yankee know-how. It was a massive social welfare and public works plan Johnson hoped would capture the hearts and imaginations of the traditional liberals, while charming fiscal conservatives with a $1 billion insurance policy that promised to prevent a far more costly war.

The speech that Johnson hoped would soothe nascent critics like Church, McGovern, and Fulbright had the unintended consequence of antagonizing at least one of Johnson's important conservative supporters— Senate Republican leader Everett Dirksen, who suggested that the president wanted to pay for peace in Southeast Asia. "Do you buy freedom for a humble people with a billion-dollar package?" Dirksen wondered. "I doubt it, and I also doubt that we can preserve face and prestige with such an approach."[32] From the other end of the political spectrum, Morse derided Johnson's bid for negotiations as "a lot of lip service paid to the theory of peace." While Morse observed that while "grandiose utopian verbiage was plentiful and the dollar sign was liberally displayed," he heard nothing more from Johnson than "the United States is going to continue shooting fish in the barrel until they are all dead."[33]

In the days following the speech, Johnson was particularly determined to secure Fulbright's support—or at least "neutralize" him, as Bundy put it. Knowing that Fulbright was a close friend of World Bank President Eugene Black, Johnson importuned Black to become administrator of the Mekong Delta project.[34] For his part, Fulbright welcomed Johnson's willingness to engage in negotiations, but told reporters in mid-April that he doubted peace talks would be possible as long as the United States continued to bomb North Vietnam. Before things spun out of control in Vietnam, Fulbright said, Johnson should consider a temporary halt to the bombing "just to give opportunity for reflection and possibly to go to discussions as proposed by the President."[35]

The day after the speech, North Vietnamese Premier Phan Van Dong responded with a four-point program that in some respects comported with the fundamental U.S. objectives in Vietnam: "recognition of the basic national rights of the Vietnamese people: peace, independence, sovereignty, unity and territorial integrity." But Phan also insisted that the United States withdraw all of its troops, end the bombing, and "cancel its military alliance with South Vietnam." But the real sticking point was the North Vietnamese demand that the affairs of South Vietnam should be settled by the people, "in accordance with the program of the South Vietnam National Front for Liberation, without any foreign interference."[36] U.S. officials regarded that point as nothing more than a demand for U.S. capitulation to the Viet Cong and flatly refused to consider the North Vietnamese proposal.[37]

By now, Fulbright had clearly awakened from his slumber over Vietnam. Having served as the legislative midwife for the pivotal Gulf of

Tonkin Resolution, he and his committee had been a virtual nonentity in the early months of 1965 as Johnson prepared to exercise the vast authority and latitude given to him by Congress in 1964. After its February 9 hearing, the committee did not meet again to discuss Vietnam until early April. "Your staff . . . are much worried at the role of the Committee on U.S. policy in Vietnam," committee staff director Carl Marcy had told Fulbright in a March 30 memorandum. "The United States is on the verge of decisions there that can be the most important of the decade, if not of this half century." Instead, Marcy noted, the committee was deeply enmeshed in debate over the president's foreign aid request. No doubt Marcy captured Fulbright's attention when he asserted that "if the president wanted a free hand he couldn't have planned a better way to keep the committee occupied." Marcy's own survey of committee members led him to conclude that a majority would oppose sending substantial numbers of ground troops to Vietnam. "Yet everyone is silent," he wrote. "They are silent despite the fact that you (with tacit committee approval) asked Secretary Rusk that the Committee be informed of any plans to escalate in Vietnam."[38]

One thing was for sure. Fulbright would be silent no longer. While not ready to publicly break with the president—like Mansfield, Church, and McGovern, he believed that he still might dissuade Johnson from sending in ground troops—he was now more prepared than ever to employ the influence of his committee to assert the Senate's constitutional prerogatives regarding Vietnam.

THE SMALL BAND OF Democratic senators was not alone in its concern over the direction of the conflict in Vietnam. Dissent began to bubble on college campuses with the first "teach-in"—an informal lecture or debate on the war between students and faculty members that began on March 24 at the University of Michigan and quickly spread to colleges across the country. By May 15, the idea was so popular that students and teachers on 122 college campuses debated the war in a massive teach-in that was broadcast to a nationwide radio audience. On April 17, a small but passionate crowd of more than fifteen thousand demonstrators organized by the liberal organization, Students for a Democratic Society (SDS), marched from the Washington Monument to the Capitol to protest the bombing. Johnson and his advisors were not impressed. That day, in a statement that Lady Bird Johnson later said was partly aimed at answering Fulbright's call for a bombing pause, the president reaffirmed his commitment to South Vietnam when he told the protesters in a prepared statement that their outrage "must be visited on those who explode their bombs in cities and villages, ripping the bodies of the helpless. The indignation of this country and the world must extend to all who seek domination over others with a violent and ruthless disregard for life, happiness or security." A few scattered protests would not intimidate Johnson. U.S. forces, he promised, would remain in Vietnam "as long as is necessary, with the might that is required, whatever the risk and whatever the cost."[39]

IN MID-APRIL, Johnson finally gave the Senate a peek into the administration's deliberations over the deployment of ground troops, when he told several groups of senators that his recent decision to use U.S. Marines in an offensive capacity had produced three times the rate of Viet Cong casualties as before. One example of success was found in reports from the coastal province of Binh Dinh, which had been in "critical condition" only two months earlier. On April 13, however, Taylor reported that because of the improved morale caused by the bombing, a more aggressive division commander and "the commitment of five general reserve battalions to the province," the situation "has now been restored to what might be called normalcy."[40]

Despite his glowing reports of recent success, Taylor was far from persuaded that more ground troops were needed. "The mounting number of foreign troops," he cautioned in a cable the next day, "may sap the GVN initiative and turn a defense of the GVN homeland into what appears a foreign war."[41] Reporting Taylor's thoughts to Johnson, McGeorge Bundy predicted that he was sure "we can turn him around if we give him just a little time to come aboard." What concerned Bundy, however, was Johnson's own thinking about additional troops. "I am *not* sure that you yourself currently wish to make a firm decision to put another 10,000–15,000 combat troops in Vietnam today," Bundy said.[42]

Bundy's estimate, of course, was nowhere near the number that Johnson's military advisors—McNamara, Wheeler, William Bundy, Taylor, McNaughton, Sharp, and Westmoreland—discussed when they gathered in Honolulu on April 20. "We considered that since we could not hope to break the will of Hanoi by bombing alone," Taylor wrote in his notes of the conference, "we must do better in the campaign against the Viet Cong in SVN." That meant a significant injection of ground troops into South Vietnam, increasing the current level of American troops in Vietnam from 33,000* to 82,000. Returning to Washington on April 21, McNamara

---

*By then, the officially *approved* level of American troops in South Vietnam was forty thousand.

delivered the sobering news to Johnson and added that the group believed this deployment might only be the beginning of large American troop movements to South Vietnam. In the future, they were prepared to recommend 56,000 additional troops.[43]

Ball, who had not attended the Honolulu conference, was appalled. In emotional language, he urged Johnson not to make such a momentous decision without first searching for a peaceful settlement. Based on the four-point program articulated by the North Vietnamese following Johnson's Johns Hopkins address, Ball believed there was still a chance for meaningful negotiations. "It was a deliberate stalling tactic," Ball later acknowledged, explaining he was willing to employ "all available tactics" to slow down the momentum gathering for what he called "this tragically definitive step." Johnson relented. "All right, George," he said, "I'll give you until tomorrow morning to get me a settlement plan. If you can pull a rabbit out of the hat, I'm all for it!"[44]

That night, Ball sent his proposal to Johnson. "We cannot," he wrote, "continue to bomb the North and use napalm against the South Vietnamese villages without a progressive erosion of our world position." Furthermore, Ball argued, escalation of the war would begin to erode Johnson's domestic standing. "Until now, the American people have gone along out of their great confidence in you and because the United States casualties have been less than a weekend's traffic accidents," Ball wrote. "But even a doubling of the casualties would begin to make a difference." Ball's proposal was simple, but not the hat trick that Johnson wanted. It was a modified version of the failed 1954 Geneva accords: all hostilities would be ended on both sides and the United States would end the bombing; the government in Saigon would declare a general amnesty and permit all Viet Cong guerrillas to return to the north; national elections—supervised by an "international force"—would be held on "an agreed future date" and the National Liberation Front would be recognized as a political party; and, ultimately, the two countries would be reunified "if desired by the people of South Viet-Nam and their government."[45]

Although Johnson was initially intrigued, the proposal suffered a quick death. None of the president's top advisors supported Ball's plan for fear it would precipitate the collapse of the latest Saigon government. "The episode confirmed an opinion I had not wanted to accept," Ball later wrote. "America had become a prisoner of whatever Saigon military clique was momentarily in power. Like a heroine in an eighteenth-century novel who got her way by fainting if anyone spoke crossly, each clique understood how to exploit its own weakness. If we demanded anything significant of it, it would collapse; so we never made any serious demands."[46] In the absence of a viable plan to seek negotiations, Johnson decided to proceed with the troop increases. U.S. forces in Vietnam would soon increase to eighty-two thousand.

IN CONGRESS, MEANWHILE, almost no one rose to the president's defense after sketchy reports of the Honolulu conference recommendations found their way into print. Only Mansfield, who reiterated Johnson's supposed willingness to negotiate a peaceful end to the conflict, had anything kind to say about the administration's policies—and even he chose to stress the need for negotiations, giving no sign that his opposition to escalation had at all weakened. Fulbright, meanwhile, continued to push for a temporary bombing halt—and was supported by Church and Robert Kennedy, now the freshman senator from New York. Javits and Pennsylvania's Joseph Clark also joined Fulbright in urging Johnson not to take the United States any deeper into Vietnam without congressional authorization.[47]

At the White House, Johnson seethed. At an NSC meeting on April 22, the president bitterly complained to his advisors that no one in Congress had risen to support him lately. "He felt that our congressional support was very uncertain and wobbly and we could lose it rapidly," CIA Director McCone wrote in his notes of the meeting. Johnson singled out Morse, Gruening, Clark, and Fulbright. Their statements would have their effect, he cautioned. "He exhorted everyone to carry on an intense personal campaign with sympathetic senators and get them on their feet," McCone wrote. Johnson also believed that McNamara and Rusk should be more visible and he urged them to "take every opportunity" to make speeches and television appearances that pointed out "the reasonableness of U.S. policy and the ridiculousness of the suggestion that we stop bombing." McCone said he understood Johnson's "extended and quite bitter" remarks to mean that the president blamed his advisors for having failed to "carry congressional and public opinion with us."[48]

Rusk took Johnson's exhortation to heart and suggested to the American Society of International Law on April 23 that those who opposed U.S. involvement in Vietnam or who supported a peaceful end to the war were appeasers. "Surely we have learned over the past three decades," Rusk said, "that the acceptance of aggression leads only to a sure catastrophe." Those remarks led Morse to tell the Senate on April 26 that the administration was trying to stifle debate over the war. "I warn the American people," Morse said, "that a propaganda drive has been started by spokesmen for the Johnson administration to interfere with one of their most precious,

fundamental liberties and freedoms, namely the right of freemen to criticize their government." In addition to withholding facts about the war
from the public, Morse charged that "they would like to see us go silent."[49]

Morse was exactly right. Johnson and his advisors had little more than
disdain for members of Congress who meddled in the conduct of foreign
affairs. As Bundy had said in a memorandum to Johnson in March, senators and representatives were "quite free to oppose you if they choose, but
they are not free to make statements that you regard as damaging and pretend that they are speaking as your friends and supporters."[50] Johnson had
no intention of consulting Congress before he made his move toward escalation in South Vietnam. At the most, he would inform them—and, then,
not completely—of his plans. He would not, however, ask for their permission. That, he believed, had already been given in August 1964. He
needed nothing more from Congress—except its vocal support.

Testifying before the Senate Foreign Relations Committee on April
30, Rusk demonstrated the administration's continuing scorn for congressional prerogatives. While he had previously informed Mansfield, Fulbright, and Hickenlooper of the administration's "general" plans for
deploying more American troops to Vietnam, he was less than forthcoming during his testimony to the full committee. While present to talk about
the situation in Vietnam, as well as U.S. military operations in the Dominican Republic, Rusk did not inform the committee that Johnson had already
approved troop increases to a ceiling of 82,000 and that a proposal to send
an additional 56,000 was under consideration. "We have about 34,000
troops," Rusk told committee members. "It is very much under contemplation that it might be necessary to add to those forces additional forces."
Rusk failed to mention that almost 50,000 troops would soon be on their
way to Vietnam. As for Fulbright's contention that another congressional
resolution might be necessary if Johnson decided to significantly increase
the nation's military commitment to Vietnam, Rusk responded that "we do
not have at the present time such a change in the scale of forces I think to
raise that question as an immediate problem."*

Once again, Fulbright insisted that Congress had a right and obligation to participate in any decision to send large numbers of American
troops to Vietnam. He did not believe, he told Rusk, that Congress meant

---

*Asked about his less-than-honest testimony in 1978, Rusk explained, "I was under
instructions from the President not to promise the Congress advance consultation
on the exact numbers of troops. He considered that to be a matter for him to decide
under the Gulf of Tonkin Resolution, and, indeed, independently in his own role
as Commander in Chief. . . . I was never in a position to make any such promise,
because among other things, the president wouldn't let me" (Gibbons, 3:240).

to do anything more when it passed the Gulf of Tonkin Resolution than to affirm the Johnson administration's then-limited and restrained Vietnam policies. "I do not know whether this constitutional practice [of declaring war] is completely outdated or not," he told Rusk, "but it would seem to me not out of order if we are going to send thirty thousand, fifty thousand, one hundred thousand men, that the Congress might have the say about it." Once again, however, Fulbright's friendship for and his political loyalty to Johnson outweighed his mounting concerns about Vietnam. He would not speak publicly about his anxiety over Johnson's apparent refusal to consult Congress. Joseph Clark agreed with Fulbright when he told Rusk that "we do not want to embarrass the administration . . . because we realize this is a very difficult situation."[51]

Fed up with the sniping from Capitol Hill, Johnson called Congress' hand. At a May 2 White House meeting with congressional leaders of both parties, the president revealed his plan to request a $700 million appropriation to meet the mounting military requirements in Vietnam. But it was, as William Bundy later observed, little more than a "gimmick" Johnson used to force Congress into reaffirming its support for his Vietnam policies.[52] Coming only days after Johnson had dispatched twenty-two thousand Marines to quell violence in the Dominican Republic—ostensibly to protect American lives and stop a threatened communist takeover—Johnson's message to Congress took on an unmistakably dramatic air. When he met with congressional leaders at the White House on May 4, Johnson invoked the crisis in the Caribbean to add urgency to his appropriations request for Vietnam. He told the group that the administration now had "unusual and unanticipated needs in both the Vietnam theater and the Dominican Republic."[53] Although his appropriations request was for South Vietnam alone, the unmistakable implication was that fighting communism in Vietnam was just as important as manning the ramparts in the nation's backyard. "This is not a routine appropriation," the president said in his May 4 message to Congress. "For each member of Congress who supports this request is also voting to persist in our effort to halt Communist aggression in South Vietnam. Each is saying that the Congress and the President stand united before the world in joint determination that the independence of South Vietnam shall be preserved and Communist attack will not succeed."[54]

According to the Pentagon, Johnson did not need the supplemental appropriation. The Defense Department had almost $2 billion in unspent funds that could have been transferred to meet the military's needs in Vietnam.[55] But Johnson wanted the appropriation for an entirely different reason. Annoyed by the lack of vocal support from his congressional allies and angered by the second-guessing of Fulbright, Mansfield, Church, Nelson, and McGovern, Johnson would force Congress to register its whole-hearted support for his actions in Southeast Asia.

"What is the difference between voting for a $700 million appropriation and voting for a declaration of war?" Joseph Clark asked Jacob Javits during the Senate's brief debate on Johnson's request that began on May 5. "Would it not be better to be candid and ask for a declaration of war?" Javits shared Clark's reservations and told the Senate that he could not support the president's interpretation of a vote in favor of the appropriation. "I wish to make it crystal clear," Javits said, "that I reserve the right to vote differently than as the president said I would be voting if I were to vote in favor of the appropriation." Making it clear that his vote should not be used as support for escalating the conflict, Javits said:

> I want to be consulted again, I say to the president of the United States, before we send divisions, rather than some of our Air Force and troops to protect our people who fight a war in Asia. I want to be consulted again. I expect to be consulted again. I do not want my vote in favor of the appropriation to stand as my vote for the continuation of that policy. . . . I do not take my vote as a blank-check commitment. . . . If the president is to send divisions to Asia to engage in ground struggles with the Viet Cong, I expect the president to ask Congress for approval, in order to make sure that what they are doing there is being done with the consent of the local people.

Just as concerned about how his vote might be misconstrued was Church, who engaged Mississippi's John Stennis—a senior member of the Armed Services Committee and the resolution's floor manager—in an extensive colloquy about the legislation's intent. Church wanted to know if voting for the resolution meant that "each one of us endorses whatever action may take place in the future?" Although he would become one of the more devoted supporters of Johnson's Vietnam policies, Stennis advised Church that "I do not think we are signing a blank check." Instead, he said, "We are backing up our men and also backing up the present policy of the president." Like many of his Senate colleagues, however, Stennis was confident about Johnson's good-faith relationship with Congress. Satisfied that his intentions were now a prominent part of the record, Church announced his support for the resolution "with the understanding, supported by the colloquy, that no blank-check endorsement of decisions to be made in the future is involved, which would drastically alter the dimensions of the American commitment in this part of the world."

Characteristically, Morse denounced the resolution in the harshest terms. Johnson could have legally found the necessary funds in other areas of the Pentagon's budget, Morse insisted. Therefore, his strategy could only be designed to coerce out of Congress another blank check. "The president wants to commit those senators again," Morse complained, adding that "in my judgment we have a president who is worried about being on top of very thin ice so far as American public opinion is concerned. So the president now wishes senators to come to his rescue again, as they did last August."

Morse's attacks on Johnson's motives brought a harsh, personal rejoinder from Everett Dirksen, who accused the Oregon Democrat of aiding and abetting the Viet Cong. While Dirksen's withering attack on Morse went largely unnoticed, it was significant because it marked the opening salvo in a bitter, personal war of words that Johnson, his advisors, and his congressional supporters would begin to wage with the war's opponents. From this point forward, Johnson and many of his White House aides would perceive those who objected to Johnson's policies as personal enemies, whose motives and patriotism would be questioned. In some extreme cases, the FBI would be employed to investigate their loyalty. Dirksen's words signaled the tactics and rhetoric that were to come:

> I want the word to go out to those who represent us in Vietnam that we back home, on the home front, are in their corner if they need us. It would be a sorry spectacle, indeed, if word should be sent out this afternoon by short-wave: "You have been let down by the U.S. Senate," as the senator from Oregon wants us to do. . . . No word of mine will ever impair their morale; no word of mine will get into an international monitoring service to be broadcast on the radio out of Hanoi, as had been done with the words of the senator from Oregon. . . . It is an amazing thing to listen to excerpts carefully and skillfully excerpted from speeches made on the Senate floor, saying to the Viet Cong, "Hold on a little longer and America will cave in." Is that good for morale in a critical hour like this?

Morse rejected the notion that his vote against the resolution would deny support to American troops in Vietnam. "What the president is doing is using this resolution calling for $700 million to supply funds which he can use—which he does not need because he already has access to the funds—as the vehicle for obtaining a vote of confidence from the Congress of the United States for his policies in Vietnam."

Off the Senate floor, Gaylord Nelson was deeply worried by Johnson's request. Already, he regretted his vote for the Gulf of Tonkin Resolution. The thought of voting again to give Johnson a blank check troubled him deeply. On the morning of May 6, Nelson rose on the Senate floor to join the handful of senators openly opposed to Johnson's Vietnam policies. "I think we should continue our role in Vietnam," he said, "as long as there is some possibility of accomplishing our original goal." Yet Nelson was unwilling to see the war expanded in the ways that many suspected Johnson had in mind. "It would be a tragic mistake to conclude at some stage," he added, "that if they cannot defend their own freedom it then becomes our proper role to throw in the full force of our land army and take on the task of fighting their war for them as well as running their government."

Moments before the final vote, Stennis insisted that "the only question is, Are we going to give the men who we have already sent off to do jungle battle the tools with which to fight?" Appealing to his colleagues' patriotism, Stennis closed by insisting that "if the Senate should refuse to pass the joint resolution or even should pass it by less than an overwhelming vote, that it will be notice to the world that the United States is backing up." The only conclusion that would be drawn from such a vote "would be that the United States will pull out."

> Moreover, it would be a direct message sent by us to our fighting men whom we sent forth to foreign lands, that we are not going to back them up with a sufficient quantity of the tools of war. If the Senate should do that, it would be the first time that this great government ever sent its men to fight on foreign soil, or to fight on any soil, and then failed to provide the necessary money with which to purchase the tools of war. God save our nation from such a day. God save our boys from such a fate.[56]

Minutes later, the Senate voted overwhelmingly, 88–3, to approve the resolution and added its voice to the House's lopsided 408–7 vote of the previous day. In the Senate, only Morse, Gruening, and Nelson opposed the measure.[57]*

When he signed the resolution, Johnson staked out his own interpretation of Congress' intent: "We will do whatever must be done to insure the safety of South Vietnam from aggression. We will use our power with restraint and we will use it with all the wisdom that we can command. But we will use it."[58]

Like the Gulf of Tonkin Resolution before it, the debate on the supplemental appropriations request represented the continuation of what William Conrad Gibbons called a "profound qualitative change in political posture and political rhetoric" regarding Vietnam.[59] Johnson had surreptitiously increased U.S. forces in Vietnam to the point that Congress now felt constrained to support his policies or face the political consequences of refusing to support "our boys" in the field. As Rhode Island's

---

*Fulbright and McGovern were both absent from the debate and did not vote. Russell—who was absent due to illness—was also among the nine senators who did not vote on the resolution.

Claiborne Pell had remarked, going against Johnson on an issue like this would be "like voting against motherhood."[60]

As Gibbons observed, the argument that American troops must be supported, regardless of one's individual views about the war, "was probably the single most determinative factor in Congress' support throughout the war." From 1965 to 1973—when the last combat troops were finally withdrawn—members of Congress consistently resisted all attempts to curtail or eliminate appropriations to continue the war.[61] The notion of tying funds to the troops was so politically intimidating that the senators who would become the most outspoken opponents of the war—Fulbright, Church, and McGovern—would for years continue to support appropriations to finance a war they vociferously opposed. As Mansfield had observed before the vote on the resolution:

> There is not one senator who does not regret, with the president, the necessity for [the resolution]. There is not a senator who would not prefer, with the president, that a decent peace might be achieved quickly in Vietnam. But we will vote for this measure because there is not one member of this body who does not desire to uphold the president and those who are risking their lives in seeking to carry out the policies of this government.[62]

The debate over the joint resolution and the subsequent deployment of American troops to South Vietnam altered more than the manner Congress approached the war in Vietnam. It reordered the balance of power and influence within the administration. As NSC staff member Chester Cooper noted, the troop escalations gave policymaking "a new complexion." Previously, civilian officials in the White House and the State and Defense departments had been primarily responsible for American policy in Vietnam. "Now that the security of American forces was involved," Cooper observed, "military participation in virtually every facet of our Vietnam involvement was taken for granted. . . . Once given a legal hunting license, the Pentagon went after some big game."[63]

CHAPTER 29

This Could Be a Quagmire

1965

IF THERE WAS ONE THING JOHNSON'S CRITICS AND SUPPORTERS could agree on in May 1965, it was that a pause in the three-month-old bombing campaign might have positive results. In late April, Indian President Sarvepalli Radhakrishnam publicly urged Johnson to stop the bombing. Privately, UN Secretary General U Thant urged a similar pause, hoping it might spark a positive response from the North Vietnamese. Robert Kennedy told Johnson in a private meeting in April that a brief respite from the bombing could not hurt and might actually lead to something useful. In the Senate, Mansfield, Fulbright, Church, and others supported this view, as did the *New York Times* in a prominent editorial.

Curiously, supporters of a wider U.S. role in Vietnam also favored a pause, but for completely different reasons. Johnson's military and intelligence advisors, particularly William Raborn, a retired Navy admiral who replaced McCone as CIA director in late April, believed an unproductive halt to the bombing would chasten the president's critics and expose North Vietnam's unwillingness to negotiate.[1] Johnson was skeptical. "One concern I had," he later wrote, "was that a bombing pause might give North Vietnam's leaders the impression that we were so eager for a settlement we would do anything."[2] He also worried that supporters of the war might see the move as a sign of weakness and demand even heavier bombing.[3]

Reluctantly, however, Johnson set aside his concerns. The strategy, after all, did have the attractive potential of silencing Johnson's domestic and international critics all at once. In a cable to Taylor, however, Johnson revealed that the outcome of the upcoming bombing pause would play a decisive role in the direction of future U.S. military policy in Vietnam. "You should understand that my purpose in this plan is to begin a clear path either toward restoration of peace or toward increased military action, depending upon the reaction of the Communists." The pause, Johnson explained, was primarily designed for "use to good effect with world opinion."[4]

As Johnson had expected, North Vietnam refused to acknowledge the six-day pause that began, secretly, on May 13. As North Vietnamese diplomat Luu Doan Huyhn later explained, North Vietnam, like the United States, was not yet prepared to negotiate, believing it could win far more on the battlefield. "Ultimately," Luu said, "we would try to get the U.S. to withdraw its troops from Vietnam through negotiations. But we believed that the prerequisite conditions for withdrawal were [to] . . . defeat the air war, exhaust the troops, and erode your aggressive will."[5] By May 16, after Hanoi had rebuffed administration attempts to officially inform them of the pause, Johnson instructed McNamara to resume the attacks. "If we hold off on this bombing longer," he told them, "people are going to say, 'What in the world is happening?'"

"What do we say to the press?" McNamara asked.

"We don't need to disclose every piece of strategy to the press," Johnson replied. "I would say to Mansfield, Kennedy, Fulbright that we notified the other people [Hanoi, the Soviets, the United Nations]—and for six days we have held off bombing. Nothing happened. We had no illusions that anything would happen. But we were willing to be surprised." Johnson insisted that he was "anxious to pursue every diplomatic adventure to get peace," but added that "we can't throw our gun away." Wary of the right-wing wrath that he might incur if he continued to pursue a strategy urged upon him by Senate liberals, Johnson declared that "we tried out their notion and got no results." The public, he believed, would never have supported a bombing pause—a suspicion supported by a May 16 Gallup poll in which 59 percent of respondents now favored the bombing.[6] "We have stopped in deference to Mansfield and Fulbright," Johnson said, "but we don't want to do it too long, else we lose our [conservative] base of support."[7]

The month of May brought nothing but bad news from Vietnam. First, there was another bloodless coup—the fifth change in government since Diem's demise. Two military officers, Air Marshal Nguyen Cao Ky and General Nguyen Van Thieu, took advantage of the Quat government's impotence and assumed power. Also adding to Johnson's woes was the ineffective two-and-a-half-month air campaign. "Our air strikes to date," Joint Chiefs Chairman Wheeler reported to McNamara on May 17, "have not reduced [North Vietnam's] over-all military capabilities in any major sense." The North Vietnamese economy had also escaped serious damage, Wheeler said. "The North Vietnamese regime, with no apparent opposition from its populace, gives every impression of being determined to continue on its present course."[8]

On June 3, Taylor echoed Wheeler's assessment when he told the State

Department that "we do not believe that any feasible amount of bombing of the North is of itself likely to cause the DRV to cease and desist in its actions in the South."[9] Two days later, Taylor finally gave up his opposition to ground troops and acknowledged that preventing the collapse of the South Vietnamese army would probably require "commit[ting] US ground forces to action."[10] That afternoon, as McNamara, Bundy, Ball, and others gathered in Rusk's State Department office to discuss Taylor's cable, Johnson arrived unexpectedly. Lady Bird was out of town, he told the group. He had dropped by for some company. "What he got," McNamara later observed, "was a cold shower." As Johnson read the telegram, Rusk tried to inject some hope into the situation. "We're looking for no more than a stalemate in the South," the secretary of state said. "Can we achieve it? I don't know. The Communists still think they're winning." Johnson was troubled, worried that the future held only more bad news. "The great danger," he told the group, "is we'll pick up a very big problem any day."[11]

Mansfield, meanwhile, could see the handwriting on the wall. At a June 3 meeting of the Democratic congressional leadership, the majority leader noted Johnson's "pessimistic" attitude about Vietnam. "He said the Joint Chiefs and others within his circle have advocated the bombing of Hanoi," Mansfield wrote in his file memorandum of the meeting, "and he has stalled them off for a week."[12] On June 5, the same day that Johnson received Taylor's recommendations for sending in more ground troops, Mansfield sent another memorandum to Johnson. He applauded Johnson's resistance to the Joint Chiefs' counsel about bombing Hanoi. "The bombing," he said, "would be more than just another military measure. It would also be a political act of the first magnitude." Mansfield warned that the Joint Chiefs' plan would "likely bring about an enlargement and acceleration of the ground war" and would only lead to the "rapid injection of more American forces on the ground, even to hold the situation in that region." Regarding McNamara's suggestion that 300,000 American troops might be needed if the North Vietnamese army invaded the south, Mansfield observed "that is but a beginning. If the expansion goes on to include combat with Chinese forces all over Southeast Asia, we had better start thinking in terms of millions." In his most direct language to date, Mansfield took direct aim at Johnson's military advisors:

> I think it is about time you got an accounting from those who have pressured you in the past to embark on this course and continue to pressure you to stay on it. It is time to ask, not only what immediate advantages it has in a narrow military sense, but where does it lead in the end: What was promised by the initial extension of the war in the air over the North? And what, in fact, has it produced to date?

As I see it, and you know it is a view which I have long held, there
are no significant American interests which dictate an essentially massive,
unilateral American military effort to control the flow of events in Viet
Nam or even on the Southeast Asian mainland as a whole.[13]

Two days later, on June 7, General Westmoreland dropped what
McNamara later called a "bombshell" when he informed the Pentagon
that "the conflict in Southeast Asia is in the process of moving to a higher
level." The Viet Cong had not even employed "their full capabilities,"
Westmoreland said, and yet the South Vietnamese army could not cope.
"I see no course of action open to us," he told the Pentagon, "except to
reinforce our efforts in SVN with additional U.S. or third country forces
as rapidly as is practical during the critical weeks ahead." Westmoreland
needed about 46,000 troops immediately, with another 35,000 to follow.
That would increase the total U.S. troop strength in Vietnam from approx-
imately 75,000 (at the end of August 1965) to more than 150,000. To his
recommendation Westmoreland had added this chilling caveat: "Studies
must continue and plans developed to deploy even greater forces, if and
when required, to attain our objectives or counter enemy initiatives."[14]

It was, McNamara later said, the most disturbing cable he received
during his seven years as Defense secretary. "We were forced to make a
decision," he wrote. "We could no longer postpone a choice about which
path to take. The issue would hang over all of us like a menacing cloud for
the next seven weeks."[15]

The next evening, Johnson shared the news of Westmoreland's request
with Mansfield. The next day, June 9, a troubled Mansfield fired off
another memorandum to Johnson in hopes he could pull the president
back from the brink. Westmoreland, Mansfield said, was responding to
requests from the South Vietnamese military, not the country's civilian
government, and that demonstrated that "we are now at the point where
we are no longer dealing with anyone who represents anybody in a political sense. We are simply acting to prevent a collapse of the Vietnamese military forces which we pay for and supply in any event and who presumably
are going in the same direction that we are going."

Mansfield asked Johnson: "What do we mean when we say we are
going to stay in South Viet Nam and for what specific United States or
Vietnamese ends are we going to stay there?" The question was crucial,
Mansfield told Johnson, "because the answer to it should control the extent
and nature of our military involvement in Vietnam." Did Johnson mean
that the United States would remain until it prevailed "everywhere south
of the 17th parallel down to the smallest hamlet?" If so, "we are talking in
terms of years or decades, and upwards of a million American soldiers on

the ground." If he meant "holding the military situation about where it is now," then Mansfield argued that "the 300,000 McNamara estimate is probably too low." If Johnson meant saying in Vietnam "to hold a bargaining position for negotiations," then Mansfield insisted that committing U.S. forces to defend the entire country would not work. He again advocated the enclave strategy of concentrating forces "into the coastal bases and into Saigon where they would add to our strength, rather than the reverse." At the same time, he argued, the United States should "launch a powerful diplomatic peace-offensive to try to get to a conference table." Unless the U.S. position in Vietnam was already hopeless, Mansfield believed the last alternative "may be feasible—at least for a year or so with something in the order of 100,000 or less United States combat forces on the ground backed by powerful naval and air units." Aware that U.S. forces in the order of 75,000 would soon be in Vietnam, Mansfield knew it was futile to argue against a significant American military presence in Southeast Asia. His fallback position was to urge Johnson to adopt a cautious, moderate approach that limited the now-substantial U.S. role.[16]

Johnson may have agreed with Mansfield more than the majority leader ever knew. "Why must we do it?" a skeptical president asked his national security team on June 10. Wouldn't sending in massive numbers of American troops only lead to the demand for more? he asked. "How do we extricate ourselves?" Yet Johnson appeared equally unsettled by the options proposed by his congressional detractors. They had no real policy, he complained, except to recommend negotiations and greater economic assistance to South Vietnam. "McGovern," he said bitingly, "wants to talk to the Viet Cong." (As the only member of Congress invited to the meeting, Richard Russell said little, other than to express his doubt that Johnson's policy of gradual escalation was the answer. "He wanted a way out," William Bundy recalled of Russell, "but did not see one that would keep our word.")[17] On June 11, Johnson told the National Security Council: "We must delay and deter the North Vietnamese and the Viet Cong as much as we can, and as simply as we can, without going all out." Granting Westmoreland's request, he worried, "means that we get in deeper and it's harder to get out. They think they are winning and we think they are. We must determine which course gives us the maximum protection at the least cost."[18] To aide Bill Moyers, Johnson was more candid. "I feel like a hitchhiker caught in a hailstorm on a Texas highway," he said. "I can't run, I can't hide, and I can't make it stop."[19]

From his State Department office, Ball pondered the enormity of the decision facing Johnson. Sensitive to Johnson's "almost obsessive determination never to lose command," Ball sat down in mid-June to compose a memorandum that spelled out his most compelling argument for going slow in Vietnam. "Ralph Waldo Emerson once wrote: 'Things are in the saddle, and ride mankind.' Your most difficult continuing problem in South Viet-Nam is to prevent 'things' from getting into the saddle—or, in other words, to keep control of policy and prevent the momentum of events from taking command."

Ball's prescription was simple—and Johnson found it appealing. "*Decide* now to authorize an increase in American forces in South Viet-Nam to an aggregate level of 100,000—but no more—additional forces." That, reasoned Ball, would assist the South Vietnamese in dealing with the expected Viet Cong offensive during the country's monsoon season. Less appealing was Ball's advice to stave off the general's aggressive advice indefinitely. "*Instruct* your top advisers," he urged, "that you are *not* committing US forces on an open-ended basis to an all-out land war in South Viet-Nam." Instead, Ball suggested a "*controlled commitment* for a *trial period* of three months" (emphasis Ball's). Ball believed that before Johnson committed "an endless flow of forces to South Viet-Nam, we must have more evidence than we do now that our troops will not bog down in the jungles and rice paddies—while we slowly blow the country to pieces."[20]

Ball sent the memorandum to Johnson on June 18. Several days later, Moyers called to say that the president had read the document over the weekend and agreed with most of Ball's points. "I don't think I should go over one hundred thousand," Johnson told Moyers, "but I think I should go to that number and explain it." Through Moyers, Johnson encouraged Ball to keep sending him his ideas and assured him that "I am not worried about riding off in the wrong direction. I agreed that it might build up bit by bit." Johnson added, however, that if there was no viable alternative to full-scale escalation then "the fellow who had the best program is the way it will probably go." Ball despaired that his advocacy had now "been reduced to a Chinese water torture." As one of the only men around Johnson opposed to a massive expansion of the American role in Vietnam, Ball believed that "all I could do was to keep on an incessant dripping of the by now familiar arguments, increasingly documented by the disappointing events of a futile war, in the hope that I might gradually wear away the resistance of my colleagues and, most of all, the President."[21]

THE DECISION TO RESPOND to Westmoreland's request without fulfilling it completely was entirely consistent with the gradualist approach to Vietnam that Johnson had pursued from his first days in office. Knowing the political perils of full-scale involvement, Johnson resisted the advice of his Pentagon advisors to expand the war with a sudden burst of military force.

The American people would not support it and the conservatives in Congress, he believed, would use the resulting costs of escalation as an excuse to oppose his domestic initiatives. Yet he could not accept the distasteful, defeatist options of withdrawal, negotiation, or maintenance of the status quo; to Johnson and his advisors, all three would result in a communist-dominated South Vietnam and, in each case, they believed, the United States would be blamed for failing to honor the commitments of three previous presidents. This left Johnson with one viable option: a gradual, sometimes clandestine, escalation of military power—never so sudden or so massive to spark widespread protests in Congress or among the public, but just enough to satisfy his military advisors and keep the Viet Cong at bay for another six months. Like the girl in the children's tale of the *Goldilocks and the Three Bears*, Johnson searched for the most politically palatable strategy—not too hot, not too cold, but just right.

Johnson later said that he was determined to prevent the war in Vietnam from "shattering" his Great Society plans. That meant, he explained, "I simply had no choice but to keep my foreign policy in the wings. I knew the Congress as well as I knew Lady Bird, and I knew that the day it exploded into a major debate on the war, that day would be the beginning of the end of the Great Society." Johnson resolved to fight a war on communism as well as a war on poverty and ignorance. "I refused to let my critics push me into choosing one or the other," he said. "I wanted both, I believed in both, and I believed America had the resources to provide for both."[22] Inch by inch, deployment by deployment, Johnson would continue to increase the American commitment in Vietnam so much so that by the summer of 1965, America sank waist deep into the quagmire of Vietnam while a slumbering Congress gave Johnson its reluctant, but tacit support.

Yet Johnson failed to understand why more members of Congress could not see the futility of negotiations and the folly of any strategy that led to a communist victory in Vietnam. In a tempestuous private meeting with Fulbright on June 14, the president urged the Foreign Relations chairman to make a Senate speech in defense of his policies. "All right, Bill, you think we should negotiate?" Johnson said. "Let me show you how many times we have offered to talk to them." Each time, Johnson said, the Communists "have spit in our eyes. How do you negotiate with folks like that?"

Fulbright was resolute. He would make a Senate speech as Johnson requested, but he could not support further escalation of the war. Fine, Johnson said, but at least point out how patient he had been and how he had offered to engage in unconditional negotiations. He did not want to send more American troops to Vietnam, he assured Fulbright. At the same time, however, he had little choice. America's honor was at stake.[23]

The next day, Fulbright rose on the Senate floor to declare that "complete military victory in Vietnam," while "theoretically attainable," would come "only at a cost far exceeding the requirements of our interest and national honor." Yet it was also "equally clear," he observed, that "unconditional withdrawal" from Vietnam would have "disastrous consequences." In light of this dilemma, Fulbright believed that U.S. policy had been and should remain "one of determination to end the war at the earliest possible time by a negotiated settlement *involving major concessions by both sides*" (emphasis added).

Echoing the administration line, Fulbright said he was opposed to an "unconditional withdrawal" because "such action would betray our obligation to people we have solemnly promised to defend" and because withdrawal "would weaken or destroy the credibility of American guarantees to other countries." Yet he was "no less opposed to further escalation of the war, because the bombing thus far of North Vietnam has failed to weaken the military capacity of the Viet Cong in any visible way." True to his word, Fulbright praised Johnson for resisting the pressure to escalate and for his commitment "to the goal of ending the war at the earliest possible time by negotiations without preconditions." But this praise failed to obscure his profound differences with the way Johnson and his advisors viewed communism as a monolithic beast controlled by Moscow and bent on world domination.

> The most striking consequence of a great nation is not the mere possession of power but the wisdom and restraint and largeness of view with which power is exercised. A great nation is one which is capable of looking beyond its own view of the world, or recognizing that, however convinced it may be of the beneficence of its own role and aims, other nations may be equally persuaded of their benevolence and good intent. It is a mark of both greatness and maturity when a nation like the United States, without abandoning its convictions and commitments, is capable at the same time of acknowledging that there may be some merit and even good intent in the views and aims of its adversaries.[24]

The next morning on NBC's "Today" show, Fulbright elaborated on his remarks in an interview with Washington correspondent Sander Vanocur. Asked to explain his suggestion that the Johnson administration might entertain "major concessions," Fulbright became one of the first senior political leaders to suggest direct negotiations with the National Liberation Front. "I think they should recognize the parties involved whether or not they are legitimate in the sense of traditional legitimacy," he said.[25] Fulbright's call for concessions drew sharp rebukes from Republicans leaders. In Miami, Richard Nixon accused Fulbright of statements that would "give our allies and our potential enemies the impression that the United States is divided on the critical importance of prosecuting the war." Any negotiations at this stage, Nixon said, "would be surrender on the installment plan." In Washington, Dirksen chided Fulbright for failing to specify the concessions the United States should be willing to make. "Any who talk of concessions," the Senate Republican leader said, "have an obligation to specify the kinds of concessions which they are prepared to advocate." Moreover, Dirksen said, Fulbright was obligated to "indicate the limits beyond which concessions cannot be made."[26]

Dirksen's and Nixon's statements were indicative of the strong sentiment within the Republican Party for more forceful military action in Vietnam. While leaders like Fulbright, Mansfield, and others worried that Johnson had already gone too far, Republican leaders doubted that the president was willing to go far enough. They goaded him to ratchet up the fighting. "We may be dangerously close to ending Republican support of our present Vietnam policy," Melvin Laird, chairman of the House Republican Conference, said in a June 14 statement. "This possibility exists because the American people do not know how far the administration is prepared to go with large-scale use of ground forces in order to save face in Vietnam." In the absence of a clear answer, Laird said, Republicans could "only conclude that present policy is aimed not at victory over the Communist insurgency nor at driving Communists out of South Vietnam but rather at some sort of negotiated settlement which would include Communist elements in a coalition government." Several days later, in speeches to the Young Republican National Convention, former Senator Barry Goldwater and Bourke Hickenlooper, the senior Republican on the Senate Foreign Relations Committee, echoed Laird's sentiments. Goldwater said that a neutralized Vietnam "would be Communist virtually overnight."[27]

In an impassioned rejoinder from the Senate floor on June 30, Mansfield challenged the Republicans to explain whether their support for the American presence in South Vietnam was "contingent on the president following a course which conforms to a particular course of policy which they advocate." Mansfield said he failed to understand how Republicans, "in view of the extent of the air and naval activity already pursued," could advocate "an indiscriminate slaughter of Vietnamese by air and naval bombardment—a slaughter of combatants and noncombatants alike, of friend and foe alike." Mansfield also worried about what he regarded as a resurgence of the kind of partisan warfare that crippled American foreign policy in the early 1950s:

> That may be ancient history . . . but the scars of partisan politics are still with us years afterward. Let no one doubt that we have paid a massive

price for the politics of foreign policy of an earlier day. We have paid for
its divisiveness with lives and with billions of dollars of foreign aid—much
of which has vanished without a constructive trace into the maw of Asia—
and I hope we are not now beginning to pay for it, once again, in many
lives.[28]

The brewing political feud over Vietnam made Johnson's task only
more difficult. Either way he turned, the growing discontent over Vietnam
threatened to consume his domestic agenda, divide the nation and, perhaps, his own party, and spark another divisive, destructive struggle over
the nation's commitment to fight communism in Asia.

OVER THE NEXT SEVERAL weeks, Ball continued his water-torture
assaults on Westmoreland's troop request. He worked at home late into the
night to produce the arguments he hoped might finally persuade Johnson
to reject a full-scale American war.[29] On July 1, he circulated another
memorandum among Johnson's advisors. "Should we limit our liabilities
in South Viet-Nam and try to find a way out with minimal long-term
costs?" Ball wondered. "The alternative—no matter what we may wish it
to be—is almost certainly a protracted war involving an open-ended commitment of US forces, mounting US casualties, no assurance of a satisfactory solution, and a serious danger of escalation at the end of the road."
His "solution" was "a compromise settlement which achieves less than our
stated objectives and thus cuts our losses while we still have the freedom
of maneuver to do so." Countering the conventional wisdom that any
negotiated settlement reducing the American role in Vietnam would
unsettle American allies around the world, Ball instead argued that "they
would be inclined to regard a compromise solution in South Viet-Nam
more as new evidence of American maturity and judgment than of American loss of face."[30]

On the day that Ball's memorandum landed on Bundy's desk, separate
memoranda from Rusk and McNamara crossed Johnson's. The urgency
with which both men addressed the president was destined to overwhelm
Ball's lonely pleas for caution and deliberation. In presenting a detailed
explanation of how Westmoreland's request would be implemented, McNamara—framing his argument as an effort to "create conditions for a favorable settlement"—argued that Johnson had little choice but to "expand substantially the US military pressure against the Viet Cong." Rusk, meanwhile,
urged Johnson to consider the likely collapse of U.S. prestige and credibility if he withdrew the country's commitment to protecting South Vietnam.

"The integrity of the U.S. commitment is the principal pillar of peace throughout the world," Rusk wrote. "If that commitment becomes unreliable, the communist world would draw conclusions that would lead to our ruin and almost certainly to a catastrophic war. So long as the South Vietnamese are prepared to fight for themselves, we cannot abandon them without disaster to peace and to our interests throughout the world."[31]

Johnson was loath to follow the course Westmoreland and his military advisors were urging on him. But he saw no other viable alternative. First, however, he wanted more information from the field. In mid-July he sent McNamara and Henry Cabot Lodge—whom he summoned in June for another tour as American ambassador—to Vietnam for a first-hand assessment. McNamara's meetings with Westmoreland on July 16–17 reinforced his "worst fears and doubts" about the course of the conflict. Westmoreland wanted 175,000 men in December and another 100,000 the following year. He expected, he told McNamara, that a determined American effort would force the Viet Cong's hand and draw them into fighting a more conventional war—the kind of war the Americans knew how to win. McNamara was skeptical, but he ventured no vigorous challenge to what he later termed "the loose assumptions, unasked questions and thin analyses underlying our military strategy in Vietnam."[32]

Returning to Washington on July 21, the Defense secretary reported his grim assessment to Johnson. "The situation in South Vietnam is worse than a year ago (when it was worse than a year before that)," he said. "After a few months of stalemate, the tempo of the war has quickened. A hard VC push is now on to dismember the nation and to maul the army." As McNamara saw it, Johnson had but three choices: "Cut our losses and withdraw," "continue at about the present level" and lose slowly, or "expand promptly and substantially the US military pressure against the Viet Cong." McNamara clearly favored the third choice. "This alternative would stave off defeat in the short run," he argued, "and offer a good chance of producing a favorable settlement in the longer run." Yet McNamara injected this note of caution: "At the same time, it would imply a commitment to see a fighting war clear through at considerable cost in casualties and materiel and would make any later decision to withdraw even more difficult and even more costly than would be the case today."

McNamara's recommendations were breathtaking: by October, total U.S. military forces in South Vietnam would number 175,000, with perhaps 100,000 added to that in early 1966. "The deployment of additional forces thereafter," he added, "is possible but will depend on developments." He asked Johnson to request congressional authorization to call up 235,000 in reserve and National Guard troops and to increase the regular armed forces by 375,000.[33]

On the morning of July 21, a somber Johnson met with his military and foreign policy advisors in the Cabinet Room to discuss McNamara's alarming report. "What I would like to know is what has happened in recent months that requires this kind of decision on my part. What are the alternatives? I want this discussed in full detail, from everyone around this table." Johnson was clearly skeptical, or at least determined to find some way to avoid committing himself to a decision that he believed he could not avoid. He peppered his aides with questions: "Have we wrung every single soldier out of every country we can? Who else can help? Are we the sole defenders of freedom in the world? Have we done all we can in this direction? What are the compelling reasons for this call-up? What results can we expect? Again, I ask you, what are the alternatives? I don't want to make snap judgments. I want us to consider all our options. We know we can just tell the South Vietnamese we are coming home. Is that the option we should take? What would flow from that? The negotiations, the pause, all the other approaches—have all been explored. It makes us look weak—with cup in hand."

Reaching for a map of Vietnam, McNamara led off by pointing to the predominantly red areas that signified territory controlled by the Viet Cong, areas where he said U.S. troops would be deployed. "It seems dangerous to put U.S. forces in those red areas," Johnson said. "Yes, sir," McNamara said. "You are right. We are placing our people with their backs to the sea, for protection. Our mission would be to seek out the VC in large scale units." Wheeler chimed in. "By constantly harassing them," he said, "they will have to fight somewhere."

"Is anyone of the opinion we should not do what the memo says?" Johnson asked the group. "If so, I'd like to hear from them."

Finally, Ball spoke up. "I can foresee a perilous voyage," he said, adding that he had "great apprehensions that we can win under these conditions. But let me be clear," he added, "if the decision is to go ahead, I'm committed."

Johnson pressed Ball. "But is there another course in the national interest that is better than the McNamara course?" he asked. "We know it's dangerous and perilous. But can it be avoided?"

"There is no course that will allow us to cut our losses," Ball replied. "If we get bogged down, our cost might be substantially greater. The pressures to create a larger war would be irresistible."

Despite all his tough questions and his ostensible doubts, Johnson seemed committed to following McNamara's recommendations. "I feel we have very little alternative to what we are doing," he said. Yet minutes later, he demanded of Wheeler and McNamara: "What makes you think if we put in 100,000 men, Ho Chi Minh won't put in another 100,000?" With all the arrogance and ignorance that had come to characterize the top leadership of the American military, Wheeler answered, "This means greater bodies of men—which will allow us to cream them."

Still not satisfied, Johnson instructed his advisors to return that after-noon to discuss the report again—this time in light of "another course of action" that he instructed Ball to articulate. That afternoon at 2:30, the group reassembled. "We can't win," Ball told Johnson. "The most we can hope for is a messy conclusion." World opinion, he said, would quickly turn against the United States. Domestically, Johnson would also suffer, he predicted. "Every great captain is not afraid to make a tactical withdrawal if conditions are unfavorable to him," Ball said. "The enemy cannot even be seen. He is indigenous to the country." Ball believed the United States had underestimated the seriousness of the situation in Vietnam. Sending hundreds of thousands of American soldiers to fight in South Vietnam was like "giving cobalt treatments to a terminal cancer case. I think a long pro-tracted war will disclose our weakness, not our strength."

Johnson, however, thought of the public relations disaster that would follow an American withdrawal. "Wouldn't all those countries say Uncle Sam is a paper tiger? Wouldn't we lose credibility, breaking the word of three presidents, if we set it up as you proposed? It would seem to be an irreparable blow. But I gather you don't think so."

"The worst blow," Ball answered, "would be that the mightiest power in the world is unable to defeat the guerillas."

Despite the prescience and insight of his arguments, Ball was simply outnumbered. Rusk, McNamara, Bundy, Lodge, and Wheeler all urged Johnson to press ahead. "If the Communist world finds out we will not pur-sue our commitment to the end," Rusk told Johnson near the meeting's end, "I don't know where they will stay their hand." Without explaining, Rusk also added simply that he was "more optimistic" than McNamara. "I don't believe the Viet Cong have made large advances among the Viet-namese people." Falling back on the memory that had so often justified escalation in Vietnam, Lodge compared Johnson's decision to the situation faced by Chamberlain at Munich in 1938. Lodge said he believed that "there is a greater threat of World War III if we don't go in."[34] Johnson agreed with Rusk and Lodge. "If we ran out on Southeast Asia," he later wrote in a fit of apocalyptic fantasy, "I could see trouble ahead in every part of the globe—not just in Asia but in the Middle East and in Europe, in Africa and in Latin America. I was convinced that our retreat from this challenge would open the path to World War III."[35]

As the meeting ended, Johnson had apparently not made his deci-sion—although William Bundy concluded that the president's mind was actually made up well before he sat down. To Bundy, Johnson's probing questions, his nagging doubts, his demands for a thorough examination of all the options, all seemed a show. Johnson's preference for—or at least his resigned acceptance of—McNamara's recommendations was apparent. "It was a bit of a set piece," Bundy later said, adding that he "had the feeling" that the whole meeting "had been scripted."[36] Indeed, that evening, as Bundy ruminated on the issue of announcing the decision to the public, he spoke to Johnson as if the decision had been made.

Tied to Johnson's impending decision about committing one hundred thousand new troops to Vietnam was the daunting question of how to pay for the deployments. Rejecting suggestions that he go to Congress for the $2 billion that McGeorge Bundy and McNamara believed was necessary for 1965 alone, Johnson sought to protect his Great Society initiatives from the inevitable attacks of conservatives who, he knew, would likely slash domestic spending to finance the escalating costs of the war. For now, he would ask for no more than an additional $400 million.[37] Bundy, however, knew Johnson could never fight the war, as Westmoreland and McNamara had recommended, on a shoestring budget. "Bob is afraid we simply cannot get away with the idea that a call-up of the planned magnitude can be paid for by anything so small as another few hundred million," Bundy told Johnson on July 21. The actual cost in 1966, he reported, might go as high as $8 billion.[38]

On July 22, in another meeting of Johnson's national security advisors, McNamara reported that the total bill for 1966 was likely to be closer to $12 billion. "Do you think the Congress and the people will go along with 600,000 people and billions of dollars 10,000 miles away?" Johnson asked. According to the polls, Army Secretary Stanley Resor said, "people are basically behind our commitment." Resor was not entirely correct. Several national surveys taken in June indicated that Americans were badly divided over what course their nation should take in Vietnam. While they generally supported what they believed was a limited bombing campaign, given a choice among several options for the foreseeable future—withdrawal, negotiation, escalation, or continuing the present policy—the public expressed no clear preference. Johnson, who sensed this lack of national consensus, told Resor: "But if you make a commitment to jump off a building, and you find out how high it is, you may withdraw the commitment."[39]

LIKE MOST MEMBERS of Congress, Mansfield sensed that a momentous decision on Vietnam was imminent. Johnson had not only informed the majority leader of Westmoreland's request for troops in early June, he had given public hints of the decision in a July 9 news conference when he told reporters that U.S. troops in Vietnam would soon number seventy-five thousand. "There will be others that will be required," he said. "Whatever is required I am sure will be supplied."[40] Three weeks later, on July 21, the

New York Times, reporting on McNamara's trip, informed its readers that American forces in Vietnam were expected to reach one hundred thousand by year's end "and possibly considerably more depending on the nature of Mr. McNamara's recommendations."[41]

In the Senate that day, Mansfield acknowledged that a fateful decision was at hand. "It appears that the groundwork has been laid for a further intensification of the military effort in Viet Nam," he said, noting "talk" of "a reserve call-up, extended enlistments, added defense appropriations and the like." The time for "wishful thinking" about Vietnam had passed, he said. "We are in, not for a summer of pain and difficulty, but for an ordeal of indefinite duration and increasing sacrifice which will persist until the problem can be resolved at the conference table." He made one last public appeal for a peaceful settlement, suggesting "once again" a reconvening of the 1961 Geneva Conference.[42]

Three days later, Mansfield followed his Senate statement with another memorandum to Johnson in which he again urged him to consider a Geneva Conference or direct negotiations between Saigon and the Viet Cong. Alluding to Westmoreland's troop request, Mansfield told Johnson he had heard that "up to 200,000 and even the figure 300,000 is being brewed about." Mansfield thought those numbers would prove too low. "In my opinion," he wrote, "a figure of one million, if this situation continues to develop as it has, could be considered conservative." As the troop build-up continued, Mansfield warned that the pressure to "pull out all military stops" would increase.[43]

In the days leading up to Johnson's final decision, Mansfield was not the only advisor urging him to back away from committing the United States to Vietnam's war in such a massive way. Supreme Court Justice Arthur Goldberg, soon to be Johnson's UN ambassador, urged the president to take the issue to the United Nations.[44] In blunt language, John Kenneth Galbraith—a Harvard economics professor and former U.S. ambassador to India long skeptical of American involvement in Vietnam— told Johnson that, "much official crap to the contrary, ... Vietnam is of no great intrinsic importance. Had it gone Communist after World War II," he wrote in a July 22 memorandum, "we would be just as strong as now and we would never waste a thought on it."

Sensing correctly that much of Johnson's unyielding commitment to Vietnam was grounded in fear of the political consequences of withdrawal or defeat, Galbraith cautioned that "political questions are partly what we make them." In other words, Vietnam would become a hot-button issue and a potential political problem for his administration only if his advisors and spokesmen continued to stress its overarching importance to the United States. He urged Johnson to instruct his spokesman "to stop saying the future of mankind, the United States and human liberty is being decided in Vietnam. It isn't." If Johnson simply stopped or gradually suspended the bombing and sought negotiations, Galbraith believed "the whole place will go on the back burner. Public attention will come back to areas of sound achievement of the Administration where it belongs." While the Republicans "will bleat," he believed "that will hurt them more than us." Without naming them, Galbraith's contempt for Rusk, McNamara, and Bundy was apparent. None was an astute politician, he seemed to say.[45]

The spirited warnings from knowledgeable and respected advisors like Ball, Mansfield, and Galbraith finally began to spark doubts in Johnson's mind. While he appeared to have already committed himself to filling Westmoreland's call for more troops, he now had momentary second thoughts.[46] Over the July 24–25 weekend, he invited the views of another skeptic—his friend Clark Clifford, the urbane and politically savvy former advisor to Harry Truman and John F. Kennedy. Clifford, who accompanied Johnson to the Camp David presidential retreat on Saturday, saw Johnson's national security advisors as men profoundly influenced by the Cuban Missile Crisis. Their experience of standing up to the Soviet Union had taught them, Clifford believed, the value of what they now called "flexible response" and "controlled escalation." He concluded that "their success in handling a nuclear showdown with Moscow had created a feeling that no nation as small and backward as North Vietnam could stand up to the power of the U.S." While he did not regard them arrogant in the sense that some would later charge, Clifford believed that Johnson's advisors "possessed a misplaced belief that American power could not be successfully challenged, no matter what the circumstances, anywhere in the world."

Clifford made no secret of his opposition to the course that McNamara, Rusk, and Bundy were recommending. "This could be a quagmire," he had told Johnson in May. "It could turn into an open ended commitment on our part that would take more and more ground troops, without a realistic hope of ultimate victory."

In the late afternoon of Sunday, July 25, a subdued Johnson convened a meeting in the camp's rustic Aspen Cabin with Clifford, McNamara, Arthur Goldberg, and several aides. When the men finally settled into their seats around the lodge's dining room table, Johnson turned to Clifford. A successful Washington attorney, Clifford had spent much of the day going over his notes and preparing his strongest argument for his case against escalation, much as he might have prepared for a courtroom appearance. "We must not create an impression that we have decided to replace the South Vietnamese and win a ground war in Vietnam," he told Johnson. Contrary to what Rusk and others had told Johnson, Clifford maintained that foregoing all-out war in Vietnam would not harm U.S. prestige. "This is not the last inning in the struggle against Communism," he said. "We must pick those spots where the stakes are highest for us and we have the greatest ability to prevail."

> I hate this war. I do not believe we can win. If we send in 100,000 more men, the North Vietnamese will match us. If the North Vietnamese run out of men, the Chinese will send in "volunteers." Russia and China don't intend for us to win the war. If we "won" we would face a long occupation with constant trouble. And if we don't win after a big buildup, it will be a huge catastrophe. We could lose more than 50,000 men in Vietnam. It will ruin us. Five years, 50,000 men killed, hundreds of billions of dollars—it is just not for us.

McNamara had been silent during Clifford's forceful presentation. When Clifford finished, however, the Defense secretary responded forcefully. He neither agreed with Clifford's premise nor with his bleak assessment of the chances for success. Without additional American troops, South Vietnam would surely fall, McNamara said. That would harm the United States throughout the world. But before Clifford could respond, Johnson abruptly ended the discussion. "The lines were clearly drawn," Clifford later observed, "and there was little else to say." That evening, a deeply conflicted Johnson drove alone around the Camp David compound for more than an hour and then, for another hour, walked the grounds, apparently lost in thought about the decisions that awaited him when he returned to the White House. Later that evening, Johnson and his guests returned to Washington. Although Johnson invited him to make his presentation once more on Monday to a larger group of advisors, Clifford now had the distinct sense that Johnson had already made up his mind.[47]

Indeed he had. Later that evening the State Department sent out a secret cable to key American embassies alerting them to the impending decision. Although he said he had not reached a final decision, Johnson said that "it now appears certain that it will be necessary to increase United States armed forces in South Vietnam by a number which may equal or exceed the 80,000 already there."[48] In his memoirs, Johnson wrote of the decision: "I had listened to and weighed all the arguments and counterarguments for each of the possible lines of action. I believed that we should do what was necessary to resist aggression but that we should not be provoked into a major war."[49]

At a National Security Council meeting the afternoon of Tuesday, July 27, Johnson announced his conclusion. It came as no surprise to anyone seated around the huge oblong table in the Cabinet Room that he would grant Westmoreland's request—although he would only send the troops the general said were needed. He would not call up additional reserves. He would not acknowledge that his decision signified any major shift in U.S. policy toward Vietnam. "If we do go all out in this fashion," he warned, "Hanoi would be able to ask the Chinese Communists and the Soviets to increase aid and add to their existing commitments."

He would not ask for any new appropriations, he said, insisting that the money be found in current appropriations until January. As for the reserves, Johnson said the Pentagon would rely on existing forces. "We will not deplete them, but there will be a substantial reduction. Quietly," he said, "we will push up the level of our reserve force." Above all, Johnson said, he hoped to keep the escalation from getting out of hand. To do that, he said, meant that the administration would downplay the significance of its actions in Vietnam. "We will neither brag about what we are doing," he instructed, "nor thunder at the Chinese Communists and the Russians." Bundy, however, saw through Johnson's rhetoric about not provoking the Chinese or the Soviets. Based on his discussions with Johnson the previous week, Bundy concluded that "his unspoken object was to protect his legislative program." When Johnson finished he asked if anyone in the room opposed his course of action. No one, not even Ball, spoke up.[50]

Ten minutes later, the congressional leaders—senators Mansfield, Dirksen, Hickenlooper, George Smathers of Florida, and Russell Long of Louisiana, and House members McCormack, Ford, Leslie Arends of Illinois, Hale Boggs of Louisiana, and Carl Albert of Oklahoma—entered the room. Except for Mansfield, none of these men had opposed a more vigorous American presence in Vietnam. More skeptical senior senators—men like Fulbright, Russell, and Aiken—were not invited. While not formal members of the Senate's political leadership, these three were far more knowledgeable on defense and foreign policy matters than most of the assembled leaders. As Johnson knew, however, their presence in the room would have only turned the meeting into a debate over the wisdom of escalation. That they were absent, observed historian Brian VanDeMark, "suggested LBJ's desire for ratification, not debate, of his decision."[51] Indeed, the congressional leaders had not been summoned to the White House so that Johnson could seek their advice. They were present so that Johnson could profess to seek their counsel while pretending that his mind was still open to their suggestions. "Johnson really never, in effect, consulted with you before a decision was made," Ford later said of the meeting. "I think his technique was to have a decision and then you go through the formality of appearing to get advice and counsel. But we were really there just to be told what was going to happen."[52]

Johnson told the group that he had five choices in Vietnam. First, he could "blow them up," presumably meaning the use of nuclear weapons. Second, the United States could withdraw. Third, "we could leave things just as they are with 80,000 to 90,000 men there today" and hope that

Ambassador Lodge "can pull a rabbit out of the hat." The last two options, however, were the only ones that Johnson considered viable. He could declare an emergency, call up the reserves, dispatch thousands of men to Vietnam, and request massive new war appropriations from Congress. That approach, however, might provoke the Soviets or the Chinese, he said. Or, he said, he could give Westmoreland the men and supplies he needed, increase draft calls, extend the enlistment of sailors and Marines, go to Congress for an additional appropriation of $1 to $2 billion, and "defer a full presentation of requirements" until January. Johnson made it clear he favored the last option, as did Lodge, who characterized the thought of withdrawal as "worse than a victory for the Kaiser or Hitler in the two World Wars."

Around the table Johnson heard a chorus of support for his decision. Albert said he agreed with Johnson's assessment about the limited alternatives. Long was particularly supportive and told Johnson that "we should look at the stakes and look at the fact that we have been touched up." The question for Long was whether "we put in more men or take a whipping?" He said the answer was simple: "We'd better go in." Speaker McCormack also agreed with Johnson. He did not see any alternative to escalation. "Dedicated military leaders have asked for more help," he said. The speaker was also impressed by Lodge's comparison of the Communists to Hitler. "The road to appeasement was a road to war," he observed.

More skeptical than the rest was Ford, who wanted to know the fundamental differences between Johnson's fourth and fifth options. Either way, Westmoreland would get his troops, Johnson replied. Under the fourth option, Congress would be asked to appropriate funds immediately, while the fifth option gave Johnson latitude to request additional appropriations in January. "We would ask for the money in any event," Johnson explained, adding that he also would not immediately call up the reserves. Dirksen's primary concern, meanwhile, was how news of the decision would be communicated to an apathetic public unaware of the enormous stakes in Southeast Asia. The president, he said, must tell the country "that we are in a very serious business." Johnson agreed and told Dirksen that he would announce the decision following the meeting.[53]

Throughout the meeting, Mansfield had sat sullen and silent, puffing on his pipe as he listened to the hawkish members of Congress urge Johnson to plunge the nation into a full-scale war in Vietnam. Finally, as the session drew to a close, he spoke up. Pulling a prepared statement from his breast pocket, Mansfield began to read as the rest of the room listened in astonishment. "As the minority leader [Dirksen] has said," he began, "there is apathy among our people. And I would add disquiet and concern, as well, and it applies to the Senate, also."

In the end, the decision was Johnson's to make, Mansfield said, and he would support the president in whatever he decided. "However, I would not be true to my conscience, to the people I represent or to my oath, if I did not, now, *in the confidence of this room*, make known to you my feelings on this matter [emphasis added]. I would not want it said that the opportunity to speak was offered and that it was met with silence on my part." Johnson's decision appeared to have "a certain inevitability" in light of all the previous decisions over the previous months and years. "Yet," he said, "I think we ought to be clear" on several points. "Whatever unbreakable national pledge we may have had was to assist South Vietnam in its own defense, not to take over its defense," Mansfield said. "And whatever the basic commitment, it was abrogated with the assassination of Diem." Lodge, the primary American architect of Diem's downfall, showed no reaction as Mansfield described the tragic legacy of political turmoil left in the wake of Diem's assassination. Since Diem, there had not been a legitimate government in Saigon, Mansfield said. "We do not owe this present government in Saigon anything and we have not owed its predecessors subsequent to Diem anything."

Mansfield told Johnson that he worried that "we are going deeper into a war in which even a total victory would, in the end, be a loss to the nation." A "total victory" would require "a decimation of the Vietnamese people" and would result in "massive destruction" of the country. "The survivors will thank us, not at all," he said. "Nor will the world think more of us for it." Even if the United States won the war, the country would then assume the burden of rebuilding Vietnam, a project that would make Johnson's $1 billion public works proposal "seem trivial." The best hope of "salvaging our national interests," Mansfield believed, was "a quick stalemate and negotiations, but we cannot be to any degree sanguine as to the possibilities of achieving even that limited objective as we go in deeper, even if we pursue it with great vigor."

Mansfield's closing words were filled with stinging criticism of the administration's halfhearted attempts at a peaceful settlement. "We have offered too little, too late in the way of bringing about meaningful negotiations in this situation and we have not, to say the least, encouraged the French who could have and may still be able to play the decisive role in this connection." It was clear, Mansfield said, "that escalation begets escalation as the experiment with this process in the past few months should make crystal clear. If there is any assumption escalation will not continue to beget escalation for a long time to come, and up to and including a devastating and wasting war in Southeast Asia, it is, in my judgment, an unwarranted assumption."[54]

Mansfield was finished. For months, he had given the president his advice, urging him at all times to hold back, search for other options, and pursue the road of a peaceful settlement. Yet at each step along the way, Johnson

had politely, but unmistakably, spurned the advice of the most knowledgeable and astute observer of Southeast Asia in Congress. The process, Mansfield later confessed, was like "butting up against a stone wall."[55]

The next day, Johnson ordered the 1st Air Cavalry Division, with supporting forces, into Vietnam. Within weeks, the number of American
troops in Vietnam would rise by about 50,000—from 75,000 to 125,000.
"Additional forces will be needed later," he added in a public statement on
television, "and they will be sent as requested." While he would not call up
the reserves, Johnson said draft calls would increase from 17,000 to 35,000
a month.[56] Although he portrayed the decision as a continuation of the current U.S. policy and promised to continue searching for a negotiated settlement, his intent was unmistakable and his final words haunting. "*We* will
not surrender," he said. "And *we* will not retreat" (emphasis added).[57] It
was as if the United States itself was under attack.

Quietly and without alarm, Johnson had launched the nation on nine
costly years of warfare in Vietnam. While he agonized over the impact the
decision would have on his beloved Great Society, Johnson had ultimately
heeded the warnings of his national security advisors who confidently
argued that Vietnam represented for the United States the supreme test of
its military might, its resolve against the Soviet Union and Asian communism, and its willingness to honor its solemn commitments. Politically,
Johnson believed that he was boxed in. To withdraw or seek a negotiated
settlement meant withering partisan attacks from Republicans who saw
anything less than a total commitment to South Vietnam's defense as surrender. A revival of the political bickering over foreign policy, he believed,
would only spell disaster for his party, his presidency, and his domestic
agenda. Full-scale commitment had its risks, too. Johnson could not lightly
dismiss the dire warnings of doom that came from respected and knowledgeable men like Mansfield, Fulbright, Ball, Galbraith, and Clifford. Yet
more than anything, Johnson was profoundly influenced by the vivid memories of the political upheaval of the early 1950s, which told him never to
yield an inch of Asian soil to the communists. Coupled with the confident,
near-unanimous advice of his national security advisors, Johnson believed
he had little choice but to commit the United States to war. As the year
began, twenty-three thousand troops had been stationed in South Vietnam. By the end of 1965, the Southeast Asian country would be home to
one hundred eighty-four thousand American soldiers. As Johnson would
soon come to realize, to his profound and everlasting regret, he had taken
his country into war without a clear mandate from either the people or
Congress.

CHAPTER 30

Sliding Farther into
the Morass of War

1965

Mansfield was deeply disturbed by Johnson's decision to deploy more ground troops in South Vietnam. When he returned to his Capitol office on the afternoon of July 27, he had convened his own intimate briefing for several of the Senate's most respected members, all of whom had not been invited to the White House meetings. At 3:30 P.M., five senators settled into their chairs in Mansfield's ornate office on the Capitol's second floor, just a few paces from the Senate chamber.

Looking around the room, Mansfield saw before him men who were widely regarded as among the Senate's wisest hands, especially on matters of defense and foreign policy: Democrat Richard Russell, Johnson's closest friend in the Senate and chairman of the Armed Services Committee; Fulbright, another Johnson intimate and chairman of the Foreign Relations Committee; John Sparkman, a moderate Democrat from Alabama who had been his party's nominee for vice president in 1952; George Aiken of Vermont, the Senate's senior Republican; and John Sherman Cooper, a moderate Republican from Kentucky and former State Department official. Of the group that gathered this day, four—Mansfield, Fulbright, Sparkman, and Aiken—were members of the Foreign Relations Committee.

As the senators discussed the likely course of events in Vietnam, Mansfield realized that Johnson's policies would soon encounter difficulties in the Senate. While he reported to Johnson later that afternoon that the senators were confident Johnson would not "get in deeply," that sentiment was grounded in the belief that he "intend[ed] to do only what was essential in the military line until January, while Rusk and Goldberg were concentrating on attempting to get us out." Johnson could not have been pleased to

459

learn that much of the discussion among these senatorial wise hands involved the ways Johnson might end the war peacefully. Some characterized Soviet support of the North Vietnamese as "not unlike [U.S. help for] a Western European country which might be attacked." Others suggested the United Nations as "an important link in a way out of the situation." One senator urged "underground contact" with the Russians and the Chinese and complained that France had been "virtually ignored as a possible avenue of approach to negotiations." Another suggested that a "cessation of bombing of longer duration than the previous one might be desirable as a means of getting discussions underway."

Perhaps the sharpest areas of disagreement centered on the bombing. Mansfield reported that one senator believed that the "military concept of a greatly extended bombing in Viet Nam is sound," while another maintained that "the President was ill-advised to begin the bombing . . . in the first place and the error was then compounded by the limited character of the bombing."*

In total, Johnson could only have been discouraged by the group's accumulated political wisdom: "The country is backing the President on Viet Nam primarily because he is President," Mansfield concluded in his summary of the senators' views, "not necessarily out of any understanding or sympathy with policies on Viet Nam." Underlying that support, Mansfield explained, "there is deep concern and a great deal of confusion which could explode at any time." In addition, as he reported, some of the senators believed that "the main perplexity in the Vietnamese situation is that even if you win, totally, you still do not come out well. What have you achieved? It is by no means a 'vital' area of U.S. concern."

Mansfield was forthright. Not every senator had agreed with each point in the memorandum. "But there was a very substantial agreement on many of them," he wrote. There was "full agreement," he insisted, that in Vietnam "we are deeply enmeshed in a place where we ought not to be; that the situation is rapidly going out of control; and that every effort should be made to extricate ourselves."[1] While Johnson later responded to most of the nineteen points in Mansfield's memorandum, he ignored the one point with which Mansfield said each member had agreed—that the United States had no business being in Vietnam. Johnson's only defense of the American military presence was to note that "it is a vital US concern to maintain our honor as an ally and our formidability as an opponent."[2]

The message of Mansfield's memorandum was unmistakable, but largely ignored at the White House: Johnson had dramatically altered the dynamics of the war in Vietnam—indeed, had transformed it into, pri-

---

*In his memorandum to Johnson, Mansfield did not identify who said what.

marily, an American conflict—without the informed support of Congress and the American public. He had made his decision about ground troops with minimal consultation of House and Senate members and had hastily informed them in a manner that afforded them little opportunity to register their concerns in substantive ways. While he and his legal advisors regarded the Gulf of Tonkin Resolution as all the congressional authorization that he needed to wage war in Vietnam, Johnson had obtained that measure of legislative assent by deceiving Congress about the extent and nature of the North Vietnamese "aggression." Now, a year later, he had compounded the deception when he excluded Congress from the troop decision, denied that the massive deployments were indicative of a new American policy in Vietnam, and then withheld information about the anticipated costs of the war. On the rare occasions when he had taken members of Congress into his confidence—particularly Russell, Mansfield, and Fulbright—he ignored or disregarded their counsel, especially when it conflicted with the judgment of his advisors. As Russell would tell a constituent in November, he was one of Johnson's "close friends," but he knew "from experience that when my advice is in conflict with McNamara's, it is no longer considered."[3] Like Bundy, Johnson often regarded members of Congress as an annoyance, believed they knew little about foreign policy, and, therefore, had little constructive advice to offer.

In the days following Johnson's low-key announcement, members of Congress generally took the decision in stride. Because he had framed it as nothing more than an extension of existing policy, many members saw no compelling reason to withhold their support. The characterization of the troop deployment as a determined effort to keep South Vietnam from collapse while the administration searched for a peaceful solution appealed to a broad spectrum of Democratic senators like McGee, Frank Lausche, Albert Gore, Thomas Dodd, William Proxmire, Fred Harris, and Mike Monroney—and Republicans like Javits, Aiken, Cooper, and Thomas Kuchel, the Republican whip.[4]

Cooper was particularly pleased that Johnson did not "intend that our troops shall undertake the primary responsibility of South Vietnam to defend itself," although this would be the precise result of Johnson's decision. Although he praised Johnson, Cooper also urged the president to submit the issue to the United Nations and to "seek a new congressional resolution of support."[5] Likewise, in supporting Johnson's decision, Aiken and Lausche—both Foreign Relations Committee members—focused on Johnson's rhetoric about negotiations. Aiken, who had seemed to share Mansfield's trepidation about Vietnam, now said he believed Johnson's July 28 statement "was the most encouraging and farthest step toward peace . . . that we have had up to date." Lausche agreed and told the Senate that "we

have gone beyond the half-way mark" in the search for a peaceful solution.
"We have yielded to the point where some people can justify saying that we
have gone too far."[6] In the House, meanwhile, Johnson's decision attracted
support from a broad array of leaders, including Speaker McCormack and
a significant number of committee leaders, including the chairmen of the
Armed Services, Foreign Affairs, and Appropriations committees.[7]

Mansfield—who only the day before had opposed Johnson in a powerful, dramatic statement in the White House Cabinet Room—now rose
on the Senate floor to defend the president and congratulate him for having amply consulted Congress. Without referring to Johnson's decision to
increase American troops in Vietnam, Mansfield insisted that he knew of
"no president who has ever consulted more with Congress than has Lyndon B. Johnson." In making his televised speech in a "calm and in a deliberately measured manner," Johnson had "tendered both the arrow and the
olive branch."[8] The following day, Mansfield was more enthusiastic in his
defense of Johnson, giving senators no reason for concern over a decision
that he had privately opposed. "He is seeking an honorable and prompt
end to that conflict, not the beginning of a new war," he assured the Senate. "Whatever additional military measures he had to take are cast in that
vein. He has opened the door wide to diplomats, to the United Nations,
all nations, to join in a quest for a prompt peace under honorable conditions on all sides."[9]

Although he supported Johnson, Russell signaled his great displeasure
with the position in which the United States—he diplomatically avoided
specific criticism of Johnson—now found itself. Interviewed on CBS's
"Face the Nation" on August 1, Russell said the country's "greatest mistake there has been in overemphasizing the military and not putting sufficient emphasis on the civilian side." Without a stable government in
Saigon, Russell feared the war would "run on there interminably." Like
Mansfield, Russell did not view the potential loss of South Vietnam as a
"strategic blow" to the United States. "I don't think it has any value strate-
gically," he declared, adding that while he was familiar with the "domino
theory," he did not subscribe to it.[10]

A smaller, less influential group of senators—all Democrats and not
intimate friends of Johnson—was not so supportive. In a speech to the Senate on July 27, the day before Johnson's announcement, McGovern had
lamented the prospect for a "major war involving thousands of American
casualties, the expenditure of billions of dollars, vast bloodshed and
destruction for the Vietnamese people, and an uncertain outcome." He
urged Johnson to stop the bombing and pursue, instead, an enclave strategy that would "keep our casualties at a minimum and hold out indefinitely
for a negotiated settlement." The enclave strategy, McGovern maintained,

would "put the issue of Vietnam in a more reasonable perspective" for the United States. "We must stop talking about it as though the honor of America and our stature in the world depend upon South Vietnam," McGovern insisted. "Our top officials ought to quit preaching that the fate of the human race and the cause of all mankind centers in Saigon."[11] Following McGovern to the Senate floor, Church and Gruening sided with their South Dakota colleague, endorsed the enclave strategy, and agreed that Johnson's advisors had overstated the potential consequences of a communist victory in Vietnam.[12]

Predictably, Morse's criticism was the sharpest. Johnson's impending decision, he told the Senate on July 27, would send the United States and the world "sliding further into the morass of war." While Johnson would justify the troop increase by pointing to increased infiltration of North Vietnamese soldiers, Morse insisted that the stepped up infiltration was the direct result of "American raids on North Vietnamese naval bases" following the Gulf of Tonkin incidents. "I think there is no doubt," Morse warned, "that we are galloping toward a major, massive war in Asia." But Morse also reserved some his harshest words for his own colleagues who would rush to back Johnson's decision. "Congress must stop being a rubberstamp parliament," he said.[13] The next week, Morse pleaded with his colleagues to remain in session through year's end. "Members of Congress of both parties," he said on August 3, "will serve their president a lot better by being here to tell him the truth than by adjourning and leaving his ears to the exclusive talk of the McNamaras and the Lodges and the Bundys and the Rusks and the other architects of Asian policy who have dug us into this pit in the first place."[14]

Silent in the aftermath of Johnson's decision were the Republicans, many of whom had attacked Johnson for his unwillingness to escalate the American effort but now hoped the public would view the war as a Democratic initiative. Unsure of what would happen now that Johnson seemed to be heeding their advice, Republicans generally left it to their leaders to express spiritless support for Johnson. Dirksen, for example, endorsed Johnson's decision, but added that he wished Johnson had talked more about Vietnam's strategic importance to the United States. In supporting Johnson's "firmness against Communist aggression," Ford said that he believed Johnson should bring the issue to Congress and ask for a declaration of war—a view ironically shared by Morse, but for far different reasons.[15] Hickenlooper perhaps best summed up Republican sentiment when he observed that he was supporting the president, but not necessarily his policy.[16]

In the days following Johnson's decision to escalate America's role in Vietnam, the only significant voice of Republican protest came not from

Congress, but from the fiercely independent governor of Oregon, Mark Hatfield. At a meeting of the National Governor's Conference in Minneapolis, one of Hatfield's colleagues offered a resolution of support for Johnson. But when Hatfield asked for an explanation of the resolution, he recalled that his fellow governors glared at him with resentment, alarmed that anyone would dare challenge an expression of support for Johnson's actions. Hatfield, who would later serve in the Senate and join McGovern in an effort to stop funding for the war, was the only governor to oppose the resolution. After the vote, one indignant colleague informed Hatfield that he had "done a disservice to [your] country in not making it a unanimous resolution."[17] As Hatfield would soon learn, it would not be the last time that Johnson's allies would question the patriotism of those who opposed the war.

IN THE WEEKS AFTER Johnson's momentous decision, U.S. troops invaded South Vietnam in massive numbers. Maxwell Taylor, the former ambassador who now served as Johnson's consultant on Vietnam and had once opposed the deployment, now predicted the troops would have a decisive impact. "By the end of 1965," he confidently told Johnson on August 5, "the North Vietnamese offensive will be bloodied and defeated without having achieved major gains." At that point, he said, Hanoi would likely be forced to change its policy. "1966 could be a decisive year."[18]

Westmoreland shared Taylor's optimism and, with the new troops on their way, set about implementing a three-phase strategy. In Westmoreland's mind, the Viet Cong guerrillas were "termites" who were "persistently eating away" at the structural integrity of the South Vietnamese government. At a distance were the main North Vietnamese forces, what he called "the bully boys," whom he likened to vandals "armed with crowbars and waiting for the propitious moment to move in and destroy the weakened building." Westmoreland believed that only by destroying the "bully boys," or at least keeping them away from the building, "was there a possibility of eliminating the termites or enticing them to work for our side."

Westmoreland's approach to exterminating the Viet Cong embodied the time-tested strategies of modern warfare that had guided American military field commanders for more than a generation. His tactics—with certain modifications—were the same conventional methods of World War II and Korea: Allied forces had fought over and conquered certain territory, which they secured while moving forward to conquer even more territory. But Vietnam, sharing a long border with Cambodia, Laos, and China, was much different and far less conducive to the tactics that had served the U.S. military so well in Korea. Moreover, neither World War

II nor Korea had been characterized by the guerrilla strategies employed so effectively by the Viet Cong.

Westmoreland approached Vietnam as if it were Korea. First, American troops would protect the developing "logistical bases" that would be utilized "whenever the enemy's big units posed a threat." In phase 2, Westmoreland expected American troops to "gain the initiative, penetrate, and whenever possible eliminate the enemy's base camps and sanctuaries." There was no hope for victory, he believed "so long as the Communists were free to emerge from those hideouts to terrorize the people, recruit or impress conscripts, glean food, levy taxes, and attack government troops and installations, then to retire with impunity back into their sanctuaries." To win the war, he maintained that communist forces must be identified, engaged, and destroyed. In his ambitious third and final phase of the war, Westmoreland envisioned the Americans engaging in "sustained ground combat," during which they would "mop up the last of the main forces and guerillas, or at least push them across the frontiers where we would try to contain them."

Throughout the three phases, Westmoreland hoped to achieve two crucial goals: pacification of the countryside and an invigorated and well-trained South Vietnamese army. "By the time the war reached the final stage," he later said, "I expected the bulk of the people to be under government control and protection and the [South Vietnamese army] to be so trained and equipped and in such numbers that the South Vietnamese alone could deal with any lingering opposition."[19] Yet Westmoreland's ambitious strategy to pacify the rural populace—that is, reverse inexorable defection of rural villagers to the Viet Cong cause—involved mostly military tactics. While the Americans professed that a sophisticated program of economic and social assistance was under way to prevent further defections among the people, the truth was that they focused almost entirely on military solutions to the problem—an approach that only accelerated desertions. "Grab 'em by the balls," went the common refrain, "and their hearts and minds will follow."[20]

As Westmoreland set about implementing his strategy, a crush of American troops quickly altered the face of South Vietnam. The country underwent, in the words of journalist Stanley Karnow, "a convulsive transformation"—from a sleepy, backwater nation to a vibrant, bustling country that now pulsated to the beat of the sudden, massive influx of American troops and materiel. Vietnam's conflict was now an American conflict, and the U.S. military quickly left its mark on the nation in ways unimaginable only a year earlier. South Vietnam was a nation that, until 1965, boasted little in the way of modern communications or transportation facilities. As hundreds of thousands of American troops began flooding the country, the Americans needed an infrastructure that could accommodate the transportation, housing, feeding, and equipping of its troops. Within months, the U.S. Army had launched an ambitious communications and highway construction project that would eventually leave few regions of the country isolated. Military engineers turned Saigon's primitive port into a world-class facility and repeated the feat in five other spots up and down South Vietnam's coast, including construction of a massive port facility at Camranh Bay.[21] As Frances FitzGerald recalled in her award-winning account of the war, *Fire In the Lake*,

> The troops carried with them the businesslike atmosphere of a country where the telephones worked, where schedules are kept and teamwork is assumed. They carried with them the sense that Americans long in Vietnam tended to lose, of the disproportion between Vietnamese politics and American power. Arriving in their starched summer uniforms from Honolulu, Wake and Guam, the GIs seemed to overawe the small stucco terminal with its public flowers and its damp, tropical smell. The stiff, square carriage of their shoulders set them apart from the limber Vietnamese. Physically, Saigon seemed to change in their direction, the rectilinear shapes of the new American office buildings, billets, and hotels towering above the sloping red-tiled roofs of the French and Vietnamese city. Having established such a visible presence, the United States would surely do whatever was necessary to maintain it. It seemed only natural that the United States should take control of the war.[22]

Armed with new troops and and a new, offensive strategy for defeating the Viet Cong, Westmoreland's men hit the ground fighting. The first serious confrontation between U.S. troops and the Viet Cong came in mid-August, as U.S. Marines launched an offensive against Viet Cong forces on the Battangan peninsula on the north-central coast of South Vietnam. In the engagement—code-named Operation Starlight—four thousand Marines assaulted the Viet Cong stronghold and killed about seven hundred Viet Cong guerrillas. Westmoreland declared the operation a success. Yet more than two-thirds of the Viet Cong regiment had escaped and—in what would become the maddening pattern of engagements between the two sides throughout the rest of the war—returned to capture the area after the "victorious" Marines' departure.[23]

Operation Starlight, however, was only a minor skirmish compared to the fierce confrontation brewing in the central highlands, the first between U.S. troops and North Vietnamese regulars. In late October, Westmoreland became concerned that a North Vietnamese division amassing near Pleiku was preparing to sweep across the country toward the South China Sea, slice the country in half, and then conquer the northern provinces. To blunt the expected attack, he dispatched the 1st Air Cavalry Division on a "search and destroy" mission with orders to "find, fix and defeat the enemy forces." The resulting month-long engagement in the dense forests of the Ia Drang Valley showcased the massive firepower and modern methods of warfare that the Americans would increasingly bring to bear against the Communists. Helicopters conducted reconnaissance, drew an enemy response, and then swooped down on the North Vietnamese troops with massive firepower. B-52 bombers were used for the first time to provide tactical support for American troops on the ground. When the North Vietnamese finally retreated, 3,866 soldiers had died. Of those, 305 were American. It was a favorable "kill ratio" of 12 to 1 that deceived Westmoreland and convinced him that he could fight and win a "war of attrition" in which the enemy would tire of its mounting battlefield losses and eventually sue for peace.[24]

In Hanoi, the story was different. The Ia Drang battle left Ho Chi Minh and his advisors "serenely confident," according to retired Lieutenant General Harold G. Moore, then an army colonel who commanded men of the 1st Battalion, 7th Cavalry, in the first ground engagement of the battle. "Their peasant soldiers had withstood the terrible high-tech fire storm delivered against them by a superpower and had at least fought the Americans to a draw," Moore wrote in his classic account of the battle, *We Were Soldiers Once . . . And Young.* "By their yardstick, a draw against such a powerful opponent was the equivalent of a victory. In time, they were certain, the patience and perseverance that had worn down the French colonialists would also wear down the Americans."[25]

The intensification of the war—the increased bombing, the massive defoliation of forests and fields, the aggressive search and destroy missions—wreaked havoc throughout the country. The newly escalated war drove peasants from their homes and villages by the millions. Mostly, they migrated to the outskirts of larger cities, where they huddled in squalid, makeshift refugee camps and scraped out livings however they could. Some roamed the streets, where they begged for food and money. Thousands of young women turned to prostitution—a rapidly growing industry in a country with thousands of American men—as the only means by which to support themselves or their families. Others fell into the lucrative business of selling narcotics. The conflict in South Vietnam had become, in almost every sense, an American war. The nation was now dominated—militarily, economically, and politically—by the American government of Lyndon Johnson.

THE DEMAND FOR NEW American troops was only beginning. On September 22, McNamara told Johnson that Westmoreland needed 35,000 more troops, a move he predicted, combined with recent troop deployments, would eventually put the total number of American soldiers in Vietnam at 210,000. Johnson and McNamara were hesitant. "We worried that this was the beginning of an open-ended commitment," McNamara recalled. "I sensed things were slipping out of our control."[26] As Ball had warned only months earlier, events were now in the saddle. Yet Johnson finally concluded he had little choice but to go along with Westmoreland. In a compromise decision, he gave McNamara authority to increase troop strength to no more than 195,000. This time, however, there would be no major announcement from the White House. Officials in Saigon would merely announce the troops as they arrived.[27]

More bad news landed on Johnson's desk in late October. The increased troop strength and the intensified bombing were doing little to persuade the North Vietnamese to end their infiltration. Johnson had hoped that escalating the war would force battered and defeated North Vietnamese officials to the negotiating table by early 1966. That now seemed highly unlikely. In fact, the opposite had occurred. As Ball had once predicted, more troops and supplies poured in from the north as the Viet Cong stepped up their recruiting in the south. "Quite simply," McNamara later observed, "they were adapting to the larger U.S. presence."[29] According to an October CIA report, "the cumulative economic losses" in North Vietnam from the bombing were negligible. "There continues to be no basic change in Hanoi's attitude toward the war," the report concluded. "Hanoi continues to assert its determination to press on with the war in South Vietnam despite the continuing attrition of the air war and the increase of US troops in the South."[29]

McNamara's assessment of the war's progress was no more encouraging. While the American troop deployments—one hundred sixty thousand were in place by early November—had "thwarted" the Viet Cong offensive that the Defense secretary had predicted in July, "the pace of the war remains high," he told Johnson. He added that American troops, at the currently approved level, would probably only contain the Viet Cong through March 1966. "US killed-in-action can be expected to increase to 500–800 a month," he predicted. "And the odds are even that the [North Vietnamese and Viet Cong] will hang on doggedly, effectively matching us man-for-man . . . while our efforts may not push the South Vietnamese over the crest of the hill, so that the snow ball begins to roll our way."[30]

While the Ia Drang battle had been—ostensibly, at least—a successful operation for the Americans, it also had confirmed McNamara's worst suspicions about increased infiltration from the north. "The rate of infiltration has increased," McNamara told Johnson, "from three battalion equivalents a month [about 2,400 men] in late 1964 to a high of 9 or 12 [as many as 9,600 men] during one month this past fall." Viet Cong strength had also increased dramatically—from 5 to 12 regiments. "And all this had occurred," McNamara later observed, "amid an intense U.S. interdiction bombing campaign." In late November, Westmoreland responded to this troubling development by requesting 200,000 additional American troops for 1966—a move that, if approved, would increase the total American military presence in Vietnam to 400,000. "The message came as a shattering blow," McNamara later said.[31] When he relayed the news to Johnson, McNamara cautioned that "it should be understood that further deployment (perhaps exceeding 200,000) may be needed in 1967." Even then, McNamara could not promise success, he said, as he upped his predictions of the possible U.S. casualties. "US killed-in-action can be expected to reach 1000 a month, and the odds are even that we will be faced in early 1967 with a 'no-decision' at an even higher level."[32]

McNamara's meeting with Lodge and Westmoreland in late November had only confirmed his worse fears about the direction of the war. "The U.S. presence," he later wrote, "rested on a bowl of jelly: political instability had increased; pacification had stalled; South Vietnamese Army desertions had skyrocketed." Westmoreland's request for more troops, combined with the realization that North Vietnam could continue to move 200 tons of supplies *each day* down the Ho Chi Minh trail, "*despite* heavy interdiction bombing," shook McNamara and, he said, "altered my attitude perceptibly." He returned to Washington with the belief that the only hope for heading off Westmoreland's request was a last-ditch effort at persuading the North Vietnamese to negotiate. On November 30, he proposed "a three- or four-week pause" in the bombing that he believed might "first, lay a foundation in the mind of the American people and in world opinion for such an enlarged phase of the war," while also giving the North Vietnamese "a face-saving chance to stop the aggression."[33]

Several weeks later, McNamara was even more direct. No longer certain that the problems in Vietnam could be solved militarily, he told Johnson that he guessed the odds were only "one out of three or one in two" that U.S. military action would stave off a communist victory. "Ultimately we must find a solution," he said. "We must find a diplomatic solution."

"Then," Johnson asked, "no matter what we do in the military field there is no sure victory?"

"That's right," McNamara replied. "We have been too optimistic. One in three or two in three is my estimate."

Rusk did not agree with McNamara's bleak prediction. "I'm more optimistic," he told Johnson, "but I can't prove it."

McNamara was adamant. "I'm saying we may not find a military solution. We need to explore other means."[34]

Johnson took the suggestion under advisement, but left no doubt where he stood. In the end, he believed, a pause would do more harm than good. As he told his advisors during a December 7 meeting, "I think we'll be spending more time defending ourselves from hawks than from doves." As always, he did not regard the doves as serious critics. "We're spending too much time," he added, "with crybabies."[35]

IN LATE APRIL, Johnson had grappled with another military conflict. Rebellion erupted in the Dominican Republic as prodemocracy rebels overthrew the autocratic, American-backed government of Donald Reid Cabral. Within days, the country was embroiled in a fierce struggle that pitted military leaders against the supporters of former president Juan Bosch, the popularly elected anticommunist president who was overthrown in 1963. Although Kennedy had originally backed Bosch—then-Vice President Johnson, in fact, had attended his inauguration—his penchant for poetry and his idealistic fervor for democratic causes earned him the reputation as an incompetent "demagogue" who could not be trusted to resist the Communists. His departure from the scene was not mourned at the State Department.

Thus, news of Bosch's possible return to power set off alarms in the State Department. On April 28, after pro-Bosch rebels appeared to gain the upper hand, U.S. Ambassador W. Tapley Bennett frantically cabled Washington to report that the struggle was between "Casto-type elements and those who oppose." In other words, communism was again rearing its ugly head in America's backyard. American lives were in danger, Bennett claimed, as he told Johnson that the time had come "to land the Marines."

Intimately involved in the decision-making from the beginning of the crisis, Johnson reacted decisively. Hours after receiving Bennett's request for the Marines, he met with congressional leaders and informed them that American lives were in danger in Santo Domingo. Told by CIA Director William Raborn that "Castro-trained agents" were leading the rebels, Dirksen and Speaker McCormack expressed their grave concern. Johnson explained that he had little choice but to dispatch the Marines immediately to save not only American lives, but the country itself. As he told Rusk several days later, "The last thing we want to happen is a Communist takeover in that country."

That night, Johnson announced that he was sending in the Marines primarily to save American lives. However, two days later, on April 30, the president gave a different reason when he explained his decision in a nationally televised speech. He insisted that "the American nations cannot, must not, and will not permit the establishment of another Communist government in the Western Hemisphere."

Within days, more than twenty-one thousand American troops descended on Santo Domingo. Eager to defend his actions against media charges that the pretext for the American intervention was a series of blatant fabrications, Johnson wildly exaggerated the communist threat, as well as the danger to American citizens. In a meeting with skeptical reporters Johnson angrily defend his actions by explaining that "some 1,500 innocent people were murdered and shot, and their heads cut off." The American embassy had been fired upon, he said. In fact, he said, the ambassador himself had phoned the White House during the attack. "He was talking to us from under a desk while bullets were going through his windows and he had a thousand American men, women and children assembled in the hotel who were pleading with their president for help to preserve their lives." Almost nothing in Johnson's description was true. "He lost his perspective on the thing," said John Barlow Martin, a former American ambassador to Santo Domingo who advised Johnson during the crisis.

Unlike Vietnam, the crisis in the Dominican Republic was a brief affair. On May 5, U.S. officials and representatives of the Organization of American States (OAS) helped broker a deal between the two sides that ended the fighting and set a time frame for elections.* As news of the episode gave way to dispatches from Vietnam, a national poll showed that 69 percent of the American people approved of Johnson's handling of the affair.[36]

In Congress, however, several members of the Senate Foreign Relations Committee grew skeptical as administration officials continued to contradict themselves and each other regarding the rationale for Johnson's sudden decision to inject the Marines into the internal affairs of a Latin American nation. Determined to look beyond the murky, official explanations of the American invasion, Fulbright began summoning administration officials before his committee. In early May, Under Secretary of State Thomas Mann, a strong anti-communist and noted Latin American specialist, stressed the communist threat as the pretext for American military involvement. Mann's testimony annoyed Fulbright, Morse, and other committee members, who noted that he had said almost nothing about the supposed threat to American citizens. Yet, in another hearing almost three weeks later, Rusk assured the committee that Johnson's decision to send in the troops had been motivated almost entirely by the threat to Americans and foreign nationals.

Fulbright smelled a rat. Only the year before, in his celebrated "Old Myths and New Realties" speech, he had decried the reflexive American

---

*In the June 1966 election, Bosch would lose to the American-backed Joaquin Belaguer.

tendency to meddle in Latin America's internal affairs while viewing every popular uprising as a communist-inspired revolution. Although he believed the United States had an obligation to honor defense treaties with its Latin American allies, Fulbright had insisted that "the defense of Latin America is ultimately a Latin American responsibility."[37] Pointedly, Fulbright asked Rusk about the fighting in the Dominican Republic: "Do you consider it now a struggle against Communism?" Rusk danced around the question, as he did additional questions that Fulbright and other committee members posed in their vain attempts to discover the exact motivations for Johnson's decision.[38]

While the hearings produced little more than suspicious explanations and unanswered questions, Fulbright took another route in his effort to get to the bottom of Johnson's Latin American foray. For six weeks, at Fulbright's direction, Foreign Relations Committee staff member Pat Holt sat in Mann's State Department suite and pored over thousands of classified documents, cables, and reports relating to the Dominican Republic incident. By July, Holt returned to Capitol Hill armed with enough evidence to prove that the Johnson administration had used exaggerated—even manufactured—"threats" of communism and the danger to American citizens as a pretext for a breathtaking military intervention designed to influence the internal political affairs of a sovereign Latin American nation. "The real reason" for the intervention, Holt later said, was "that Johnson did not want Juan Bosch to return to power."

> Therefore, it became necessary for the Johnson administration to create reasons which, in their view, would be persuasive, not only with the Congress and the American public, but especially with the OAS [Organization of American States] and the other countries of Latin America, and the one way to do this was to present a picture of public disorder so great that it was threatening the safety of foreigners generally in the Dominican Republic, not just Americans.

Holt's investigation revealed that Dominican Republic military officials had requested U.S. military assistance several times in the days leading up to Johnson's decision. Each time they had been rejected. "They were told, in effect," Holt said, "that the United States would intervene only if the Dominicans formally stated that they could no longer assure the safety of foreigners. The Dominicans interpreted this, correctly, as meaning that if they did make such a statement, then intervention would follow. And that's what happened."[39]

During closed-door committee hearings in July, Fulbright—armed with the evidence from Holt's investigation—left Mann little choice but to admit several of the administration's misdeeds. Americans had, indeed, persuaded the Dominicans to alter their request for assistance so as to stress the threat to American citizens. There had been no American causalities, and virtually no threat to American lives. The invasion, Fulbright concluded, was little more than Johnson's strong-armed effort to keep Bosch out of power. Holt not only uncovered Johnson's lies to Congress and the public; he revealed that Johnson had ordered the CIA to manufacture evidence of communist influence in the Dominican Republic and, when that failed, had ordered FBI Director J. Edgar Hoover to "find me some Communists in the Dominican Republic."[40]

By early August, Fulbright's hearings were completed. While evidence of Johnson's mendacity was abundant, the committee remained deeply split over how to proceed. "We were pretty offended and outraged by this," recalled Seth Tillman, Fulbright's speechwriter and policy advisor.[41] Johnson's overt intervention, Fulbright said later, "made us look silly, the whole idea that we were stopping a Communist takeover."[42] But on this issue, Fulbright commanded something far less than a majority of his own committee. While Morse, Democrats Joseph Clark of Pennsylvania and Eugene McCarthy of Minnesota, and Republican Clifford Case of New Jersey favored publication of a critical committee report, others—including Hickenlooper, Lausche, Long, Symington, McGee, and Dodd—were opposed.

Dodd was especially averse. Slavishly loyal to Johnson and particularly hostile to Fulbright—who had once helped expose the Connecticut senator's financial ties to the Nicaraguan government—Dodd lashed out in a harshly worded press release on August 24. Although he had attended only about a tenth of the hearings into the Dominican affair, Dodd charged that Fulbright had conducted his hearings unfairly and had deliberately withheld exculpatory information about the administration's actions.[43] Dodd's volley, as well as Johnson's other efforts to influence his investigation, seemed to persuade Fulbright that some kind of public report was necessary. Yet knowing that he would never persuade his committee to issue the report, Fulbright concluded that a Senate speech, outlining the conclusions of the investigation, was his best option.

Seth Tillman's hard-hitting speech draft, taken from an extensive memorandum Holt had produced, sparked a vigorous debate among Fulbright's advisors. Fulbright was being asked to say that (1) the invasion was staged not primarily to save lives, but to prevent a revolutionary victory that the administration feared was communist-inspired; (2) the fear of communist influence was based on "fragmentary and inadequate evidence"; (3) U.S. officials let pass an opportunity to facilitate a peaceful settlement because the Johnson administration wanted the antirebel forces to win; (4) the Johnson administration had "turned its back on social revolution in Santo

Domingo and associated itself with a corrupt and reactionary military oligarchy"; (5) U.S. pronouncements on the crisis were "marred by a lack of candor and by misinformation"; and (6) the failure of American policy in the Dominican Republic was Johnson's responsibility, although he was understandably motivated by the "fear of another Cuba."[44]

On the morning of September 15, aide Lee Williams drove to the White House and delivered the final draft of Fulbright's speech. In an accompanying letter, Fulbright assured Johnson that his criticisms were not personal. He simply took exception with "the faulty advice that was given to you."[45] That afternoon, Fulbright rose on the Senate floor to deliver the damning speech which concluded that the "principal reason for the failure of American policy in Santo Domingo was faulty advice given to the president by his representatives in the Dominican Republic at the time of acute crisis. Some of it appears to have been based on inadequate evidence or, in some cases, simply inaccurate information. On the basis of the information and counsel he received, the president could hardly have acted other than he did." While he tried to give Johnson the benefit of the doubt, he left no doubt about the consequences of Johnson's ill-advised policy. Although the administration had helped broker a deal for elections in 1966, "the fact remains," Fulbright said, "that the reaction of the United States at the time of acute crisis was to intervene forcibly and illegally against a revolution which, had we sought to influence it instead of suppressing it, might have produced a strong popular government without foreign military intervention." Johnson's insistence that he had acted to save American lives, he said, "was more a pretext than a reason for the massive U.S. intervention." Fulbright said that the perceived threat of communism was the "primary reason for recommending military intervention."[46]

Fulbright's devastating critique infuriated Johnson. "He was very angry," recalled Harry McPherson, Johnson's special assistant.[47] Johnson's wrath manifested itself in numerous ways. "Your charges are ostensibly directed at Ambassador Bennett," Johnson said in an irate letter, "but in reality they are directed at me. . . . You should not seek to avoid an attack on me by hitting at a man who cannot hit back."[48] For more than a year, Johnson would banish Fulbright from White House social functions; he would not respond to Fulbright's personal communications; and he would snub members of Fulbright's staff. "I got word through associates," Lee Williams recalled, not surprised by the presidential reaction, "that Johnson felt it was a real stab in the back from his chief foreign policy advisor in the Congress."[49]

Publicly, the treatment was just as chilly. In a statement, the White House insisted that it could find no one who believed that "the senator's views are justified." In the Senate, Johnson's allies pounced on Fulbright with a fury. "What's wrong with trying to save a country from Communism?" asked Senator George Smathers of Florida. An impassioned Russell Long declared: "I thank the merciful Lord that our president possesses a sense of urgency and that he possesses initiative." But the most vicious attack came from Dodd, who told the Senate that Fulbright "suffers from an indiscriminate infatuation with revolutions of all kinds, national, democratic or Communist."[50]

In an almost humorous episode in late November, Johnson refused to provide a military jet when Fulbright led a Senate delegation to the Commonwealth Parliamentary Association in New Zealand. Instead, Johnson supplied Fulbright and his party with an antiquated C-118—a painfully slow, but luxurious prop plane that required several refueling stops as it hopscotched across the Pacific. But forcing Fulbright to use a prop plane instead of a jet was not the encumbrance that Johnson had intended. The long trip not only gave Fulbright time to reflect and read about the history of the Vietnamese conflict—he had just finished *Street Without Joy*, Bernard Fall's powerful account of French colonialism in Vietnam—it afforded him the opportunity to discuss Asian history at length with his Democratic colleague, Hiram Fong of Hawaii. By the time he returned from the South Pacific, Fulbright told his staff he was ready to hold public hearings on Vietnam.[51]

But the Dominican Republic incident did more than isolate Fulbright from Johnson and cause him to delve more deeply into Vietnam's political history. To Pat Holt, the episode "demonstrated to Fulbright and others that things were not always as Johnson and the administration were portraying them." That, Holt believed, "became very important in cultivating the seeds of doubt which already existed about the policy in Vietnam."[52] If Johnson could not be trusted to speak candidly about the supposed communist threat in Latin America, why should he be trusted when it came to Southeast Asia? According to Tillman, Fulbright's frustration over Johnson's unwillingness to consider his views on Vietnam partially bred his distrust over the Dominican Republic, which in turn only exacerbated his skepticism about Vietnam. "Finding himself made a pariah," Tillman observed, "he didn't really have any choice in Vietnam, anymore. He had severed his bonds."[53]

MANSFIELD'S FIFTH VISIT to Vietnam in early December confirmed all his worst fears about the ultimate direction of U.S. policy. Several colleagues joined him on the trip: Democrats Edmund Muskie of Maine and Daniel Inouye of Hawaii and Republicans George Aiken and Caleb Boggs of Delaware. His frustrating discussions with Lodge and Westmoreland persuaded the majority leader that the two men were unrealistically optimistic and that despite Westmoreland's refusal to acknowledge it, the United States would soon be increasing its troop strength to half a million men. "It is difficult enough now, as our military participation increases," he wrote to Johnson upon his return, "to maintain the concept that the United States role is to assist the Vietnamese." Soon, he feared, the United States will "have cast ourselves, in the eyes of the Vietnamese, in the role of the French of another era."[54]

THROUGHOUT DECEMBER 1965, McNamara, Bundy, and Ball continued pressing Johnson to order a bombing pause. "We think this is the best single way of keeping it clear," Bundy told Johnson on December 4, "that Johnson is for peace, while Ho is for war."[55] Johnson remained skeptical. Westmoreland, Lodge, and the Joint Chiefs strenuously opposed the pause; Rusk was wary. "It's more a sign of weakness than anything else," the president told his Vietnam advisors on December 21. "All we'll get is distrust from our allies, despair from the troops, and disgruntled generals." Anyway, he said, he doubted that Hanoi would respond favorably. Worse, he added, "if we suffer a severe reverse as a result of this, we'd never explain it." Johnson also worried how he would withstand the inevitable storm of domestic criticism that would occur when he ordered the bombing resumed.[56]

Yet arguments for the pause eventually outweighed Johnson's reluctance, not the least of which was Soviet Ambassador Anatoly Dobrynin's promise that his country would try to persuade Hanoi to negotiate if the United States stopped the bombing for two or three weeks.[57] At 6:00 P.M. on December 24, Johnson reluctantly halted the bombing. U.S. forces were ordered not to fire, except in self-defense, until midnight the next day.[58]

Although his military advisors strongly opposed the stand-down, Johnson would allow the pause to extend into January as he and his diplomats launched a frenetic and very public worldwide search for peace— what NSC staff member Chester Cooper later called "the flying circus"[59]—during which they explained the U.S. position to foreign leaders in capitols around the world. Humphrey went to the Philippines and then to India. Averell Harriman went to several foreign capitols, including Warsaw and Belgrade. Johnson sent UN Ambassador Goldberg to Rome, Paris, and London. He dispatched other State Department officials to Africa and South America. "For twenty days now," Johnson told Congress in his State of the Union Address on January 12, "we and our Vietnamese allies have dropped no bombs in North Vietnam." His emissaries had per-sonally visited leaders in forty countries. "We have talked to more than a hundred governments, all one hundred thirteen that we have relations with, and some that we don't." From Hanoi to New York, Johnson said, he had made it clear "that there are no arbitrary limits to our search for peace." The United States, he insisted, would meet Hanoi's leaders "at any conference table, we will discuss any proposals—four points or fourteen or forty—and we will consider the views of any group." Despite these efforts, Johnson reported no progress. "So far," he said, "we have received no response to prove either success or failure."[60]

Yet the lack of a response may have had more to do with the sincerity of the effort than with the time and energy invested in it. "Don't think these were genuine efforts to get discussions going," Ball later cautioned. "They were foredoomed efforts because we weren't prepared to make any real concessions." In those days, Ball said, negotiations "still consisted pretty much of saying to Hanoi, 'Look, let's work out a deal under which you will capitulate.'"[61] Absent a genuine American desire for peace talks, the bombing would resume.

CHAPTER 31

Let Them Know They
Are in a War

1966

T HE ESCALATION WAS NOT THE ONLY THING ABOUT WHICH JOHN-
son had been less than candid in 1965. For much of the year, he had
deceived Congress and the public about the mounting costs of the conflict.
The $1.7 billion he had requested in September 1965 was only a fraction
of what would eventually be required to transport, support, and equip several hundred thousand troops in the field. But Johnson refused to solicit
the full amount, hoping to delay the painful day of reckoning long enough
to protect his Great Society initiatives from conservatives who, he feared,
would eventually decide that the country could not afford ambitious new
social initiatives *and* a costly war in Asia.

By December, Georgia Senator Richard Russell had reached that conclusion on his own. "It is becoming increasingly apparent to every knowledgeable observer," he told the Atlanta Jaycees, "that this country, for all
its wealth and resources, cannot carry on a war effort of the magnitude we
are reaching in Vietnam and at the same time finance all the domestic programs of the Great Society—however worthy they may be." Russell worried about the "painful prospect" of tax increases unless Johnson got
domestic spending under control. The alternative, he warned, was "an
inflationary new round of deficit financing." When it came to choosing
between Vietnam and Johnson's social program, Russell's choice was an
easy one. "We must provide whatever sums are necessary for the defense
of these United States," he said, despite having maintained that Southeast
Asia was not a vital region. "The nation's security must be placed ahead of
every other consideration."[1]

By early 1966, Johnson could no longer pretend that the war was not a costly affair. On January 19, he asked Congress to appropriate a stunning $12.7 billion in supplemental funding for the fiscal year ending in June 1966. "This $13 billion is only the first drop in the bucket," Republican Senator George Aiken accurately predicted. "Commonsense and experience should tell us that."[2] Several days later, Johnson submitted his Vietnam budget request for the 1967 fiscal year beginning in July and asked Congress for only $10 billion—another deception of enormous proportions.[3] As Johnson and his economic advisors knew, fighting the war for another year would require as much as $18 billion. But Johnson steadfastly refused to make the request. He also rejected the recommendation of his economic advisors to propose a 10 percent income tax surcharge on individual and corporate incomes to prevent a budget deficit. "He engaged in a fudging of the figures—to which stronger language could be applied," William Bundy acknowledged. Bundy, too, saw that Johnson was desperately concerned about the threat that the expanding war in Vietnam posed to the Great Society:

> If he told the Congress what his realistic funding needs were, key conservatives would mobilize powerful support to limit the appropriations for the Great Society—that you couldn't have both together. . . . He did not think the war would be shortchanged. He did think the Great Society would be.[4]

Giving Congress an accurate picture of the war's costs was out of the question, as was a request for the additional revenue needed to avoid a deficit. "I have no question that he was convinced that a tax increase was needed, badly needed, right at the beginning of 1966," recalled Gardner Ackley, head of the president's Council of Economic Advisors. "And that if he didn't get it, the economy really was going to go to hell and all kinds of problems."[5] But submitting a tax increase to Congress would require Johnson to disclose the actual cost projections for the war. Faced with the choice of informing Congress and the American people about the true nature and cost of the war or concealing the truth to save his Great Society, Johnson, once more, chose deception.[6]

JUST AS JOHNSON had predicted, the bombing pause failed to elicit a positive response from Hanoi. As Nguyen Khac Huynh, a North Vietnamese Foreign Ministry official during the war, later explained, Hanoi perceived the bombing pause as little more than a tactic by which Washington could "determine whether the will of the DRV [North Vietnamese] had been broken. That was our understanding of their purpose. In other words, the U.S. more or less 'checked the pulse' of the DRV by an occasional bombing pause." Nguyen also complained that the United States "never, not even once, acknowledged the minimum objectives of our side [cessation of the bombing and no increase in ground troops]. And what did this mean? It means . . . only one thing, and that is unconditional surrender."[7]

In Washington, as Johnson had predicted, the pause had only antagonized the hawks and emboldened the doves. As chairman of the Senate Armed Services Committee, Russell opposed the pause, believing, like Johnson's military advisors, that instead of searching for a peaceful way out, Johnson should press harder for a military solution. "It seems foolish to me," Russell told a constituent in mid-January, "to be losing more fine young men and multi-million dollar airplanes bombing roads and bridges in North Vietnam to prevent the movement of materials of war when we can put the stopper in the bottle very easily by closing and blockading Haiphong."[8] In a speech to the Georgia state assembly on January 17, Russell said that the "time for decision is drawing near." Soon, he believed, Johnson would be forced to decide "whether or not we are willing to take action necessary to win the war in Vietnam and bring a conclusion to our commitment." As Russell saw it, the only alternative would be "to pull out," something he recognized "the overwhelming majority of Americans are not prepared to do."[9]

When he joined Mansfield, Fulbright, and other congressional leaders for a meeting with Johnson on January 25, Russell held nothing back. "This is the most frustrating experience of my life," Russell said. "I didn't want to get in there [Vietnam]," he said, "but we are there." Russell believed that Johnson had allowed the pause to continue for too long and now was the time to resume the bombing—with a fury. "For God sakes, don't start the bombing half way. Let them know they are in a war. We killed civilians in World War II and nobody opposed it. I'd rather kill them than have American boys die. Please, Mr. President, don't get one foot back in it. Go all the way."

Of the seventeen members of Congress who attended the January 25 meeting, only two—Mansfield and Fulbright—raised their voices against renewed bombing. "The best chance of getting to the peace table," Mansfield insisted, "is to minimize our military action." Mansfield believed Johnson should declare a cease-fire, call for a meeting of "all interested parties," and push for nationwide elections within three to six months. He contemplated "withdrawal of our forces" after a secure amnesty and the reunification of the two nations "in conjunction with the Geneva Accords."

Fulbright echoed Mansfield's sentiments and urged Johnson not to resume the bombing. Johnson, of course, already knew Fulbright's position, having seen the front-page story in that morning's *Washington Post* in which Fulbright strongly opposed a resumption of the bombing and endorsed direct negotiations with the Viet Cong. "This is not similar to world wars one and two," Fulbright told Johnson that evening during a White House meeting of House and Senate leaders. "We have never tried to re-impose colonial power on anyone before."* Having undertaken to help France with her colonies, Fulbright said that "we are in a false position now." Urging Johnson to negotiate, Fulbright again invoked his fear that further escalation might provoke the Chinese.[10]

As usual, Johnson was torn. He knew that he could not withstand the political heat that would result if he continued the pause indefinitely. What plaudits a continued pause might win from the likes of Mansfield, Morse, Fulbright, Church, and McGovern would be more than overshadowed by the howls of protest from prominent conservative leaders of both parties. "I think the great majority of the people in the country will believe that you gave them [North Vietnam] a reasonable time, over a month, and there was no movement on their part," McNamara advised Johnson on January 17. But Johnson was not so sure. He still worried about the reaction of the doves. "You sure want to watch that," he warned, "and be prepared on it because I think that's gonna be a campaign issue."[11] Several days later, Johnson raised the issue again with his Defense secretary. Johnson speculated that "we'll be subjected to immense propaganda over the next weeks from [the] peace lovers. They told us [a] bombing cease would help us— now they'll say 'another month or so.'"[12]

That is exactly what Fulbright and Mansfield were saying—and not only Fulbright and Mansfield, but a group of fifteen liberal Democratic senators who signed a January 27 letter to Johnson that urged him not to renew the bombing. Citing statements by Fulbright, Mansfield, and Aiken against the bombing, the group—led by Vance Hartke of Indiana and joined by McGovern, Church, Gruening, Nelson, and McCarthy—gently advised Johnson to extend the pause. Johnson's reply was abrupt and barely concealed his outrage over the growing insurrection in his own party. "I continue to be guided in these matters by the resolution of the Congress on August 10, 1965 [the Gulf of Tonkin Resolution]," Johnson said. Refusing to elaborate, Johnson simply enclosed a copy of a policy statement he had recently sent to a group of House members. Particularly outraged at Hartke's impertinence, Johnson made his displeasure widely known. Through his press secretary, Johnson revealed that he regarded Hartke as "obstreperous." Privately, he called the Indiana senator a "prick." As a sign

---

*Fulbright was wrong. In 1898, the United States had imposed colonial rule on the Philippines, a former Spanish colony.

to others who might step out of line, Johnson made it clear that there would be a price to pay for this particular expression of dissent: he refused to appoint Hartke's nominees to the agricultural stabilization committees in Indiana.[13]

Johnson was not only angry. He was deeply concerned about how the congressional dissent might eventually erode popular support for his Vietnam policies. "I see each day serious difficulties, mounting of pressure," he confessed to his advisors on January 28. "It may result in deep divisions in our government." It had been only a year and a half since Congress, by a 504–2 margin, had "told the president to do what was necessary in Vietnam," Johnson said.* Now the forces opposed to his policies "could muster probably forty votes." Worse, he said, "the majority leader and the chairman of the Foreign Relations Committee are against the general policy of that resolution." It was a fine mess. "I am not happy about Vietnam," Johnson finally concluded, "but we cannot run out—we have to resume bombing."[14]

As Johnson debated the best way to resume the bombing, one thing was clear: the pause had done nothing to move Hanoi closer to the bargaining table. Ho Chi Minh denounced the U.S. offer for unconditional talks as "an effort to fool public opinion" and insisted that "if the United States really wants peace" it would allow the Viet Cong to sit at the conference table, something Johnson and Rusk steadfastly refused to consider. "The Vietnamese people will never submit to the U.S. imperialists' plot," Ho insisted.[15] Based on that negative reaction, Admiral Sharp, the commander in chief in the Pacific, urged the Joint Chiefs to resume the bombing—only this time he wanted the attacks stepped up considerably. "[Rolling Thunder] operations have not been conducted in such a manner as to increase the pressure on Hanoi in recent months," Sharp wrote. "Targets vital to effective military operations have not been struck in significant numbers." The bombing, Sharp concluded, "has not forced Hanoi to the decision which we sought."[16]

Johnson was frustrated and angry with his advisors who had talked him into the pause in the first place. He never should have stopped the bombing, he insisted. "I feel that we have given away a trading point without getting anything in return," he complained. Now he was stuck between the doves, who wanted a longer pause, and the hawks, who believed the pause had gone on for much too long.[17]

However difficult his decision, Johnson knew that he could not ignore the Joint Chiefs. The "unanimous view" of the military commanders, McNamara told Johnson, was that "we must resume bombing." If not, he said, Johnson could expect a "higher level of infiltration." Maxwell Taylor

---

*A reference to the lopsided vote for the Gulf of Tonkin resolution.

warned that the pause was leading some South Vietnamese leaders in Saigon to believe the United States was losing its resolve. "I think they are beginning to suspect things," he said, "and it is beginning to cause them difficulty."[18]

Johnson finally went along with Taylor and the Joint Chiefs. He ordered the bombing resumed. "I think if you stop the bombing they [Hanoi] will go for something else," Johnson said, indicating that he never held much hope that the pause would spur the North Vietnamese to enter into negotiations. "If you let them run you out of your front yard, they'll run you out of your house." But he did not want the kind of aggressive bombing that the Joint Chiefs were urging on him—the kind he feared might spark a confrontation with Russia or China. Yet, he said, "I don't want to back out—and look like I'm reacting to the Fulbrights. We must realize the price we pay for going back in. We'll lose a good part of the Senate."[19]

On January 31, 1966, after a thirty-seven-day pause, American bombs began falling again on targets in North Vietnam. In announcing his decision, Johnson held out an olive branch to the doves. He would ask the UN Security Council to take up the issue of Vietnam in hopes of finding a peaceful solution.[20] The reaction in Congress was mixed. Liberals and some moderate Republicans were dismayed. "I believe the president has erred," Aiken told the Senate, "in taking new steps which may lead to a cataclysmic world conflict."[21] The bombing, said Gruening—echoing the conclusion of some internal administration analyses—had "proved totally ineffective to achieve the objectives which its proponents sought, and indeed, merely stiffened the resistance which our forces encountered."[22]

The harshest rebuke, however, came from Robert Kennedy, an erstwhile supporter of Johnson's policies and one of the unofficial architects of his late brother's commitment to assisting the government of South Vietnam. In 1964, Kennedy had been so supportive of Johnson that he volunteered to resign as attorney general to become ambassador to South Vietnam. Lately, however, the bombing had troubled Kennedy. As early as April 1965, he had urged Johnson to consider a pause. By 1965, Kennedy was in the Senate representing New York and still nominally supportive of Johnson's policies. In May, he had supported the $700 million supplemental appropriations for Vietnam—a vote that Johnson considered a reaffirmation of his policies in Southeast Asia. But Kennedy had made it clear that he did not support escalation of the war—nor did he favor withdrawal of U.S. forces. In a Senate speech explaining his vote, Kennedy called for negotiations to end the conflict. "This, I take it, is the policy of the administration, the policy we are endorsing today."[23]

For years, Kennedy had been among Johnson's bitterest rivals. His public criticism of the administration's Vietnam policy was bound to sting.

On January 31, the day Johnson resumed the bombing, Kennedy urged the administration to quit looking at Vietnam as a military problem. "It is absolutely urgent that we now act to institute new programs of education, land reform, public health, political participation—and that we act to insure honest administration." What disturbed him most, however, was the bombing.

> If we regard bombing as the answer in Vietnam—we are headed straight for disaster. In the past, bombing has not proved a decisive weapon against a rural economy—or against a guerilla army.
>
> And the temptation will now be to argue that if limited bombing does not produce a solution, that further bombing, more extended military action, is the answer. The danger is that the decision to resume may become the first in a series of steps on a road from which there is no turning back—a road which leads to catastrophe for all mankind. That cannot be permitted to happen.[24]

Denied the loyal backing of several leading Democrats in the Senate, Johnson began shoring up Republican support for his policies. He particularly courted Dirksen and Senate Republican Whip Thomas Kuchel of California, both of whom gave their warm endorsement to the renewed bombing campaign.[25] He also spurned Mansfield's efforts to persuade him to reach out to Fulbright. The Foreign Relations chairman might not be a lost cause, Mansfield advised one of Johnson's aides in late January. Invite him over for breakfast, the majority leader advised, and let him explain that he really wants to be helpful. "All in all," the aide told Johnson, "Mansfield thinks that if you were to take a few minutes over breakfast some morning it could be a very rewarding occasion." Johnson rejected that advice and refused to reach out to Fulbright. Such an overture would have likely been futile in any event. Within days, Fulbright's gavel would rap into session the first public hearings by Congress into the Vietnam War—and would transform him, overnight, into the nation's most prominent opponent of Johnson's war.[26]

As JOHNSON HAD FEARED, his party was indeed on the verge of a bruising battle over Vietnam. Some—like Russell, Stennis, Dodd, Long, McGee, Symington, and Lausche—favored an all-out military effort to achieve a quick and decisive victory. And until early 1966 only a handful of senators—Morse, Gruening, Church, McGovern, and Nelson—avidly and publicly opposed Johnson's decision to commit increasing numbers of American troops to Vietnam. But by the time the bombing pause had ended and the number of U.S. troops in Vietnam had swelled to over two hundred thousand, the ranks of open dissenters grew to include Fulbright, Mansfield, McCarthy, Hartke, Gore, Joseph Clark of Pennsylvania, Robert and Edward Kennedy, William Proxmire of Wisconsin, Quentin Burdick of North Dakota, E. L. Bartlett of Alaska, Maurine Neuberger of Oregon, Lee Metcalf of Montana, Harrison Williams of New Jersey, Philip Hart of Michigan, Stephen Young of Ohio, and Claiborne Pell of Rhode Island.

Typical of the dramatic transformation that occurred among Senate Democrats in late 1965 was that of McGovern. While the South Dakota liberal had regarded the U.S. troop escalation as a "highly dangerous development," until late in the year he still had more differences with hawkish Republicans than with Johnson and McNamara. In a July 17, 1965, Senate speech he had derided not the president, but "the recommendation of certain Republican spokesmen who seem to be calling for victory over the Viet Cong guerrilla forces by massive U.S. bombing attacks on China and North Vietnam."[27] More than a month later, on July 27, he praised Johnson in another speech: "The President is searching for a way to peace in Vietnam. He has always been a man of peace and he wants with all his heart to find an honorable settlement to the war in Vietnam. However, the overemphasis on the need for our growing military presence in southeast Asia by those who insist that the honor of our nation rests on the future of Vietnam places a very hazardous political foundation under the administration effort."[28]

Although he defended Johnson, McGovern had also urged the president to "stop the bombing attacks in both North and South Vietnam" and to "consolidate our present position, keep our casualties at a minimum and hold out indefinitely for a negotiated settlement." In his July Senate speech, McGovern had also endorsed the coastal enclave strategy that had become the fallback position of several Senate war critics. All in all, McGovern's position was far from the unyielding posture he would assume in later years. In 1965, he was still willing to give Johnson the benefit of the doubt. For now, at least, he refused to call for unilateral withdrawal of American forces. The enclave strategy, he explained, "would demonstrate that we are not going to be pushed out, thus giving consolation to those who hold the domino theory and fear the paper tiger label."[29] Years later, McGovern argued that his deferential approach to Johnson and McNamara over Vietnam was the result of sound, prudent reasoning:

> I used to react unfavorably to Morse and Gruening talking about McNamara's war and personalizing it. To me, I wanted to make it easier for them to back down by calling for negotiations. Instead of saying, "Let's get

out," my early instinct was to say, "Let's negotiate. Let's talk and see what we can work out." And that was partly designed to make it much easier for the administration to embrace the course we were recommending.[30]*

But what radically changed McGovern's view of Johnson, McNamara, and the Vietnam conflict was his visit to the war-torn country in November 1965. "That trip," he said, "answered any lingering doubts about the rightness of my opposition to the war."[31] During his three-week trip, McGovern met with Lodge and military leaders, toured the Vietnamese countryside, and consulted several of the American journalists assigned to Saigon. One day, as he moved through the streets of Saigon, McGovern's driver made a wrong turn. Suddenly they found themselves blocked by a large flatbed truck which, they realized, was loaded with coffins containing the bodies of U.S. soldiers. "As I sat there momentarily looking at those coffins glistening silently in the sun," he told the Senate upon his return, "I thought what a tragic waste of young life and laughter and love."[32]

His most profound and memorable experiences, however, came during visits to hospitals. His tour of a military hospital visit made him "sick at heart," as he met young Americans "without legs, or arms, or faces, or genitals—all of them victims of land mines, booby traps or sniper fire." When McGovern congratulated a young lieutenant, who had lost both feet, for winning the Purple Heart, the soldier replied, "Senator, that's easy to get in this damn place." The lieutenant became for McGovern "the first of an endless stream of Vietnam veterans who were to tell me in the next few years of their disillusionment and disbelief." Later, in Da Nang, McGovern asked to tour a hospital for wounded civilians. "The scene," he later wrote, "will stay in my memory as long as I live." The ramshackle building was bulging with severely wounded men, women, and children. "Patients were lying on the lawn around the hospital, on the veranda, and two to a cot in the wards inside," he recalled. "One large open ward was jammed with two hundred patients who had been mangled by shrapnel from American bombs and artillery." As he walked among the patients, the room fell eerily silent. "I left that hospital determined," he said, "to redouble my efforts against the war. I was ready not merely to dissent, but to crusade—to join peace marches, sign petitions, lecture across the nation, appear on television, to do whatever might persuade the Congress and the American people to stop the horror."[33]

---

*Despite his criticisms of Morse and Gruening, McGovern was quick to add: "I'm grateful those two men spoke as harshly and directly and as forcefully as they did day after day after day. They performed a great service, but as you know both of them went down to defeat as soon as they faced the electorate" (McGovern, by Mann, 1/27/97).

When McGovern returned to Washington, he was briefly heartened by the bombing pause. As Johnson sent administration officials to foreign capitals to assure world leaders that he was willing to engage in unconditional negotiations, McGovern's spirits lifted. He supported Johnson's efforts publicly. "We have been patient for five years with those who offered a military solution to the problem," McGovern told the Senate on January 20. "Now let us be equally persistent and equally patient in the effort to find a peaceful solution." Yet if the bombing resumed, McGovern warned, "I tremble to think of the staggering blow this would be to our presently favorable position with the many governments whose help we have asked in the search for peace."[34]

That McGovern's resolve to end the war was strengthened by his November visit to Vietnam was not entirely apparent in his public statements of 1966, even during the period after the bombing resumption. During a February 24 interview on NBC's "Today" show, while dropping his usual tribute to Johnson's desire for peace, McGovern limited his criticism of the president to an observation that "the administration at this point has been unwilling to enter into direct negotiations with the Viet Cong or with the National Liberation Front." Asked by correspondent Sander Vanocur if his opposition to the war would lead him to oppose $415 million in supplemental Defense authorization funds for Vietnam, McGovern pledged his support for the measure. While he believed the war was a "mistake," he said that "our soldiers are there and I think we have to provide them the equipment with which to defend themselves and carry out their mission."[35]

But he now believed that America's presence in Vietnam was wrong. As he wrote in an article for *Mademoiselle* magazine in March: "Although it hurts our pride, we need to recognize realistically that there is very little support around the globe—even among our oldest friends—for our present course in Vietnam. But a war-weary world would applaud our initiative for peace."[36]

AT 9:05 ON THE MORNING of Friday, January 28, Dean Rusk pulled up to the witness table in the large, ornate Senate Caucus room on the Old Senate Office Building's second floor. Sitting directly across from him, behind a long table covered with green felt, was Fulbright—a grim, imposing presence as he squinted hard through his black-rimmed glasses into the bright television lights that flooded the room. Flanking the chairman were the eighteen other members of the Senate Foreign Relations Committee.

Rusk was not in the room willingly. Fulbright had demanded his presence, calling on the secretary to appear publicly to defend the administration's request for $415 million in supplemental funding for foreign economic assistance. On this morning, Rusk knew that the subject of his testimony would not be the administration's appropriations request. Instead, Johnson's entire Vietnam policy would be at issue. "The United States has a clear and direct commitment to the security of South Vietnam against external attack," Rusk said in his opening remarks, gamely defending the administration's policy. "The integrity of our commitments is absolutely essential to the preservation of peace right around the globe."

Fulbright wasted no time going on the offensive. "Mr. Secretary," the chairman said after Rusk finished, "I need not tell you many of us are deeply troubled about our involvement in Vietnam and it seems to us that since this is the first bill this session dealing with the subject, now is an appropriate time for some examination of our involvement there for the clarification of the people of this country."

For the rest of the morning, Fulbright and other committee members fired question after question at Rusk in a direct challenge to the administration's Vietnam policies. What had been Rusk's role in the government during our initial involvement in Indochina? Was he concerned at that time about the U.S. role in Indochina? Was not France, in the 1950s, trying to reassert her colonial dominance over the region? Why would our government have assisted in that enterprise? How did the SEATO treaty obligate the United States to assist South Vietnam to this degree? How do you foresee an end to the war? Are we going to be there for five, ten, twenty years? What will be the outcome, even if we are successful in the military realm? Can you describe our objectives in Vietnam? Do you think that the South Vietnamese can really be "free agents" with "our occupation" of their land with two hundred thousand or four hundred thousand men?

"I think there is a great doubt about whether or not we are on the right track, and these doubts need to be cleared up," Fulbright lectured Rusk. While there had been "great discussion about Vietnam," Fulbright maintained, "the discussion has been rather superficial. We had a relatively small commitment even as late as the time of the Bay of Tonkin affair. I personally did not feel at that time that we had undertaken a course of action that could well lead to a world war." What worried him, Fulbright said, were statements he had read in the morning's paper attributed to Senator John Stennis, known to be particularly close to top military leaders in the Pentagon. In remarks the previous day, Stennis had said that the United States might eventually send six hundred ninety thousand troops to Vietnam and employ nuclear weapons against the Chinese. Judging by those statements, and considering the fairly authoritative source, Fulbright said he could only conclude "that the situation has changed a lot, and that we are now engaged in a very serious undertaking."

The growing level of protest around the country, Fulbright said, validated his concerns. "It seems to me that something is wrong or there would not be such great dissent," he said. "I do not regard all of the people who have raised these questions as irresponsible." Like himself, Fulbright said, many people around the country did not see the communist threat to South Vietnam in the same way that Americans had viewed the attack on Pearl Harbor or the North Korean invasion of South Korea. "Vietnam is subtle," Fulbright said, adding that "it needs to be understood if we are to approve of it in the sense of voting these very large sums. If we pursue this policy and resume the bombing, then we are committed, and will have passed the Rubicon. I think that is what justifies some discussion of this."

Rusk fought back. He defended the Johnson administration's decision following the Gulf of Tonkin Resolution, telling Fulbright that "the exact shape of the situation as it developed was not known in August of 1964." So much of what subsequently developed could not have been known at the time, he insisted, "because so much of this turns upon what the other side has been doing during this period. But the policy of the Southeast Asia Treaty [SEATO] and the policy of the resolution has long been known to be the policy of the United States, as expressed both by the executive and the legislative branches."

"Wouldn't you agree though, in light of that, that that should not be interpreted as an authorization or approval of an unlimited expansion of the war?" Fulbright asked.

"Well," Rusk said, "we are not in a position of an unlimited expansion of the war. The steps that have been taken have been taken over a period of time with considerable caution and restraint, while every possibility of peace was being explored. And, on these matters there has been frequent consultation with the various committees and the leadership of the Congress as the situation has developed."

"Well, did you know—"

Rusk interrupted. "We did not lose contact with the Congress in 1964. Both sides have been in business, and we have been discussing this matter in great detail since then."

"Senator Mansfield certainly thinks there is a prospect," Fulbright replied, "a possibility of what he calls an open-ended conflict, which is a euphonious way to say all-out war, and Senator Stennis' statements certainly indicated that he is contemplating the possibility of that or he would not have made such as statement as he made yesterday."

Rusk shot back. "There are some dangers, of course, Mr. Chairman, in any such situation. The problem has been with us in each one of the principal crises we have been faced with since 1945."

"Well, then," Fulbright asked, "the point comes down to: Don't you think we ought to understand what we are in for, and that the Congress should give its further approval of this changed situation?"

Fulbright was not the only committee member subjecting Rusk to tough questioning. Interrogating the secretary about the U.S. reliance on SEATO as the constitutional authority to intervene in Vietnam, Albert Gore asked: "Where are the constitutional processes with respect to the United States that we agreed to follow in SEATO?" Rusk again pointed to the Gulf of Tonkin Resolution. The government, he told Gore, had followed "the processes which have been determined through consultation between the president and the [congressional] leadership and, for example, such processes as the resolution of the Congress of August 1964." Gore rejected that answer and made it clear he did not accept the administration's broad interpretation of the resolution. "I voted for this resolution following the attack upon our ships off Tonkin Bay," he told Rusk. "I interpreted that resolution as approving the specific and appropriate response to this attack, and the chairman of this committee, in presenting such a resolution, stated to the Senate that this was his interpretation. I certainly want to disassociate myself with any interpretation that this was a declaration of war." Fulbright agreed and reminded the committee that, at the time of the 1964 debate, he had shared Gaylord Nelson's concern that Congress should not be "appearing to tell the executive branch or the public that we would endorse a complete change in our mission."[57]

Rusk's testimony left Fulbright strangely dissatisfied and eager for a more complete airing of the administration's Vietnam policies. For weeks, he had considered holding a series of public hearings on Vietnam. It was Church who had first suggested the idea the previous summer.[38] By year's end, several committee staff members had suggested to Fulbright that "carefully prepared public hearings could have a valuable effect for both the Congress and the public." Seth Tillman told Fulbright that the college protests popping up around the country might be due to "the absence of significant debate on United States foreign policy on the official level."[39] Morse had also prodded Fulbright and his committee to assume a more prominent role in the Vietnam debate. Fearing encroachment of the Foreign Relations Committee's jurisdiction by other committees and by the House Foreign Affairs Committee, the Oregon Democrat urged Fulbright to assert himself and end the committee's "lethargy" on Vietnam. In a blunt memorandum on January 11, he told Fulbright that "the Foreign Relations Committee is, as much as anything else, supposed to be a sounding board and an idea factory. Right now, it is too little of either." Morse believed that the committee spent too much time reviewing the foreign aid program at the expense of more pressing problems around the world. "The world is about to blow up in Asia and we can hardly justify limiting the Foreign

Relations Committee to the quiet backwaters of foreign policy problems," he wrote. "Vietnam and relations with China also deserve to be on the list of Committee business."[40]

At first, Fulbright responded cautiously to advice that he lead his committee into the uncharted waters of open opposition to Johnson's Vietnam policy. But after hearing bleak reports on Vietnam from Mansfield and Aiken—who briefed the committee in mid-January on their trip to Vietnam—the idea took on more appeal. But it was Johnson's January 31 decision to resume the bombing that finally convinced Fulbright the time had arrived for an extended public airing of the Vietnam issue. On February 3, five days after Rusk's tempestuous appearance, Fulbright announced that he would begin the first of the hearings the following morning—a subtle but unmistakable message that the Foreign Relations Committee would be taking direct aim at Johnson's Vietnam policies. Any doubt about the relative significance of the hearings was settled when the three television networks announced plans to offer their viewers live coverage of the proceedings.

Fulbright's announcement about the hearings was a bold shot across Lyndon Johnson's bow. Never before had a committee of Congress conducted public hearings into an administration's military policies in the midst of a foreign conflict. Even the Senate's 1951 hearings into Harry Truman's firing of General Douglas MacArthur were held behind closed doors (although edited transcripts were released to the press). Incensed, Johnson immediately resolved to do whatever he could to undermine the committee's proceedings. First, he persuaded Senate Republican leader Everett Dirksen to invoke a rule preventing committees from conducting hearings while the Senate was in session. Dirksen backed down, however, when Fulbright threatened to hold the hearings at night—during television's prime-time viewing hours.[41] Johnson next moved to draw the public's attention away from Fulbright's potentially explosive hearings by hastily convening a high-profile conference in Honolulu with South Vietnam's leaders—Premier Ky and General Thieu—as well as McNamara, Rusk, Westmoreland, Lodge, Wheeler, and Sharp.

Johnson surprised Rusk in a late-afternoon phone call on February 3, just hours after Fulbright's announcement. "I don't want any other human to know this . . . but I fairly think I would like to go out to Honolulu."[42] The next morning, as Fulbright convened his committee to receive the testimony of David Bell, the administrator of U.S. foreign aid programs, Johnson announced plans for the conference that would begin two days hence. The television networks broke away from their coverage of the Foreign Relations Committee hearing to report the news of Johnson's announcement.[43] Hoping to downplay the continuing escalation of the

U.S. role in the war, Johnson said that the conference would focus, not on military matters, but on political, economic, and social issues. That, however, was a ruse. Johnson planned to spend most of his time discussing military strategy with Westmoreland and others. The discussion of nonmilitary matters was, as he told Rusk on February 3, only "a cover."[44] As for the Senate hearings, Johnson said that McNamara, Rusk, and Wheeler would not be available to testify because their public testimony might only aid the communists. Private hearings, he said, were the only appropriate way for the Senate to conduct hearings into such a sensitive national security matter.[45]

"I do not think there is any place in this Republic any more," an angry Morse said during the next morning's hearing, "to have the secretary of defense or any other spokesman of this government hide behind an alleged right to testify in secrecy, and I shall not attend any meeting that sponsors government by secrecy in this country on a matter that is as vital to the welfare of the people of this country." Senators Case and Mundt agreed. But, except for Morse's protest, the first day's testimony by Bell was unremarkable. He was not a senior policymaker and, as he repeatedly informed the committee, he was qualified to speak for the administration only on foreign aid matters.[46]

The testimony of Tuesday, February 8, was far more compelling. Retired Lieutenant General James Gavin, the former U.S. ambassador to France, presented his argument for an enclave strategy in Vietnam—a plan to end the bombing and concentrate American forces into coastal enclaves during the search for a diplomatic solution. Gavin declared that the country's overcommitment in Southeast Asia had caused the United States to ignore "what we are doing in world affairs through our economic endeavors" in favor of "a tactical confrontation that appears to be escalating at the will of the enemy." Describing Vietnam as "a baited trap," Gavin argued that the Communists could not have orchestrated a better way for the United States to become overextended and bogged down. Ultimately, he warned, Vietnam might prove to be "such a costly drain on our resources, that we would lack the ability to respond to other places where it would be a very real challenge to our very vital interests."[47]*

Meanwhile, in Honolulu, Johnson, his advisors, and South Vietnamese

---

*Gavin later reported that within several months of his testimony, the Internal Revenue Service launched an extensive audit of his tax returns, which he believed was instigated by Johnson in retaliation for the views he expressed to Fulbright's committee. While Gavin's specific allegation cannot be substantiated, Johnson made liberal use of the FBI, the CIA, and the IRS to investigate antiwar activity and to harass those who opposed the war (Gibbons, 4:241).

leaders were wrapping up a well-publicized three-day conference that had achieved Johnson's goal of partially overshadowing the committee's hearing. Nothing much was accomplished in Hawaii, beyond a hollow promise by the participants to focus on the social, political, and economic reforms necessary to win what Johnson called "the other war" in Vietnam. Before departing, Johnson, Ky, and Thieu issued a joint statement affirming their resolve to "defeat the Viet Cong and those illegally fighting with them on *our* soil" (emphasis added).[48] Despite having recently expressed his admiration for Adolf Hitler, Ky joined Johnson in the ironic declaration that "we are dedicated to the eradication of social injustice."[49]

Even as he left Honolulu, Johnson could not resist a parting shot at Fulbright and his senatorial tormentors back in Washington. Without specifically naming the committee members, the president said that "special pleaders who counsel retreat in Vietnam" were hampering the war effort.[50] Arriving in Los Angeles, Johnson conferred with Humphrey who, he announced, would travel immediately to Saigon and other Asian capitols to begin building support for the social and economic reforms endorsed in Honolulu. "The road ahead may be long and may be difficult," Johnson said after the conference, but "*we* shall fight the battle against aggression in Vietnam." And, he predicted, "*we* shall prevail" (emphasis added).[51]

Back in Washington, Fulbright and his committee plowed ahead with their hearings. On February 10, the committee heard from one of the country's most distinguished diplomats, George F. Kennan, the former ambassador to Yugoslavia who, as a Foreign Service officer in Moscow, had conceived the nation's "containment" strategy during the Cold War's early years. Kennan told a respectful committee that the United States should liquidate its military involvement in Vietnam "as soon as this can be done without inordinate damage to our own prestige or to the stability" of the region. Kennan expressed "great misgivings about any deliberate expansion of hostilities on our part directed to the achievement of something called victory."

Kennan also questioned Johnson's fundamental premise for the U.S. role in Vietnam—a national responsibility to honor the treaty obligations of the SEATO accords. "What seems to be involved here," he said, "is an obligation on our part not only to defend the frontiers of a certain political entity against outside attack, but to assure the internal security of its government in circumstances where that government is unable to assure that security by its own means." Kennan argued that the United States "should not be asked . . . to shoulder the main burden of determining the political realities in any other country, and particularly not in one remote from our shores, from our culture, and from the experience of our people. This is not only not our business, but I don't think we can do it successfully."[52]

After a week's hiatus, Fulbright convened his committee again on February 17, this time to hear from the first substantial administration witness: Maxwell Taylor, the former Joint Chiefs chairman and ambassador to South Vietnam who now served as Johnson's informal special consultant on Vietnam. Defending Johnson's war as a necessary conflict with "the militant wing of the Communist movement represented by Hanoi, the Viet Cong and Peiping," Taylor argued that American soldiers were in South Vietnam to destroy "the myth of [North Vietnam's] invincibility in order to protect the independence of many weak nations which are vulnerable targets for 'subversive aggression.'"

Taylor's testimony provided the only real sparks of the committee's hearings when he suggested that the dissent of senators like Morse played into the hands of the North Vietnamese. "I happen to hold to the point of view," Morse said, "that it isn't going to be too long before the American people repudiate our war in Southeast Asia."

"That, of course, is good news to Hanoi, senator," Taylor replied.

Incensed, Morse shot back: "I know that that is the smear . . . that you militarists give to those of us who have honest differences of opinion with you, but I don't intend to get down in the gutter with you and engage in that kind of debate, general. I am simply saying that in my judgment the president of the United States is already losing the people of this country by the millions in connection with this war in Southeast Asia. If the people decide that this war should be stopped in Southeast Asia, are you going to take the position that [it] is weakness on the home front in a democracy?"

"I would feel," Taylor said, "that our people were badly misguided and did not understand the consequences of such a disaster."

"Well, we agree on one thing, that they can be badly misguided," Morse said. "You and the president, in my judgment, have been misguiding them for a long time in this war." At that, a number of spectators began applauding, but were quickly silenced by Fulbright.[53]

From the beginning of the two weeks of hearings, Fulbright had wanted the testimony of McNamara, Rusk, Wheeler, and other administration officials. Johnson, however, adamantly refused to send anyone but Rusk, who appeared before the committee on the last day of its public hearings. Rusk argued that the "far-reaching implications of this commitment [to SEATO] were well understood" by the Foreign Relations Committee and the Senate when the treaty was ratified. Rusk explained that under the treaty's provisions "the finding that an armed attack had occurred" did not have to be made collectively by every nation who signed the treaty. The United States, he said, was entirely within its rights to intervene. "If the United States determines that the armed attack has occurred," Rusk explained, "it is obligated to act . . . without regard to the views or actions of any other treaty member."

During his questioning of Rusk, Gore dismissed any notion that the SEATO treaty required the United States to intervene militarily, noting that neither Eisenhower, Kennedy, nor Johnson had supported sending large numbers of troops to protect South Vietnam from communist aggression. If the treaty was so binding, Gore asked, why had Johnson declared only two days after passage of the resolution that "some others are eager to enlarge the conflict. They call upon us to supply American boys to do the job that Asian boys should do. They ask us to take reckless action which might risk the lives of millions and engulf Asia and certainly threaten the peace of the entire world." Gore said that he could not understand "how three presidents could take this limited view of our commitment under SEATO and . . . now you interpret it as being a binding commitment to do what we are doing in Vietnam."[54]

THE HEARINGS CLEARLY invigorated Fulbright. "He was fascinated by those hearings," recalled Seth Tillman. "He never left." Other senators would arrive, ask a few questions, and then leave. Not Fulbright, who remained in the committee room until the gavel fell in the early afternoon. "In many cases," said Tillman, "he'd ask the witnesses to have lunch with him after that and he'd keep interrogating them. He just got absorbed in the subject matter."[55]

Johnson, meanwhile, viewed the committee inquiry, not as an honest policy dispute between his administration and certain senators, but as a very personal attack on him, his administration, and the country. Like Fulbright, he became absorbed by the hearings—but in a nefarious and possibly illegal way. Fulbright's determination to pursue public hearings persuaded an angry president that the chairman, as well as Morse and other liberal members of the committee, were unintentionally—and perhaps intentionally—aiding the communist cause. In mid-March, as the hearings unfolded, Johnson instructed Under Secretary of State Alexis Johnson to begin researching statements that Fulbright and other committee members had previously made about the SEATO treaty. "They're out to destroy Rusk and destroy our position," Johnson said. "And they're taking the position that what they're doing is going to change the foreign policy of this country." The television networks' and the major newspapers' willingness to give the hearings considerable coverage led Johnson to believe that the media had become part of a conspiracy by the Foreign Relations Committee to undermine the war effort. "The infiltration in the networks and in the press on this is rather serious, I think," the president told Alexis Johnson, "and I think it's more serious than any of us realize." By now, the president's paranoia ran amuck. He seemed to equate the military and political objectives of the Viet Cong with the Foreign Relations Committee and the national news media. "I think that they think—the opposition to our system—that they're gonna win this thing right here in Washington."[56]

Complying with a White House directive, the FBI conducted name checks of ordinary citizens who signed telegrams critical of Johnson's Vietnam policies or who wrote Johnson in support of Morse's attacks. At the direction of White House aide Marvin Watson, FBI agents also began monitoring the Foreign Relations Committee hearings so as to brief Johnson on whether Fulbright, Morse, and others were receiving information from communist sources. In mid-March, Johnson met with Assistant FBI Director Cartha DeLoach to give the agency further instructions concerning the monitoring of Foreign Relations Committee members. Johnson wanted FBI agents to record any contacts between representatives of foreign governments, particularly Soviet diplomats, and members of Congress and other prominent citizens. DeLoach recalled that Johnson told him that "he strongly felt that much of this protest concerning his Vietnam policy, particularly the hearings in the Senate, had been generated by" officials of foreign governments. Furthermore, as Johnson told DeLoach, a group of six senators—Fulbright, Morse, Robert Kennedy, Gruening, Clark, and Aiken—had been to the Russian embassy to meet with Ambassador Dobrynin. DeLoach concluded that Johnson suspected that the Soviets were influencing Fulbright's and Morse's positions on Vietnam. Fulbright "doesn't know what the smell of cartridge is," he told DeLoach. "He's a narrow-minded egotist who is attempting to run the country."[57]

Republican leader Dirksen also enlisted in the White House effort to smear Fulbright and Morse, telling DeLoach on March 7 that he believed the two men were heavily involved and obligated to communist interests. Of Fulbright's subsequent decision to hold hearings on U.S. relations with China, Dirksen told DeLoach that "obviously Fulbright had been instructed to do this by certain contacts." Johnson also tried to enlist the State Department to uncover damaging information about Fulbright and instructed the department's Office of Intelligence and Research, headed by Thomas Hughes, to compile a political dossier on Fulbright and other congressional critics of the war. Hughes, a former Senate aide to Humphrey, refused and George Ball rescinded the order. Within days, however, Fulbright learned of the order when Carl Marcy's sources at the State Department apprised him of the aborted effort to uncover damaging information about his boss. "You know who" had ordered the research, Marcy told Fulbright.[58]

Johnson and his aides had feared that the hearings might undermine public confidence in the president's handling of the war, and they were right to a degree that may have even surprised them. For the first time, well-known, respected political, diplomatic, and military leaders had openly questioned the wisdom and direction of America's military role in Vietnam. In the process, observed committee staff member Pat Holt, they had "made dissent respectable." Holt observed that suddenly "the dissenters were no longer a bunch of crazy college kids invading deans' offices and so on; they were people of substance."[59] But it was not merely the strength and stature of Fulbright's witnesses that profoundly influenced the public, rather it was his decision to force the hearings into the open and the television networks' decision to air them. Prior to February 1966, Johnson, Rusk, McNamara, and other proponents of the U.S. role in Vietnam had dominated the public debate over Vietnam. Suddenly, many Americans were exposed to the reasoned, educated views of distinguished military and diplomatic personages like Gavin and Kennan, as well as the persuasive arguments presented by Fulbright, Morse, Church, and Gore. With the cooperation of the news media, Fulbright had engaged the American public in its first true debate over the wisdom of American involvement in Vietnam.

Before the hearings, in January 1966, 63 percent of those surveyed by the Harris polling organization gave Johnson high marks for his handling of Vietnam. After the hearings, in late February, his approval rating on Vietnam dropped precipitously—to 49 percent. But those numbers did not necessarily mean that public opinion was shifting in favor of withdrawing American forces. To the contrary, while most Americans wanted the war ended, they were still badly split on the means to accomplish that end. In fact, only 9 percent of those surveyed by Harris favored withdrawal.

A far greater percentage polled by Harris supported American troops in Vietnam but disagreed on what to do next. Thirty-three percent favored the American presence in Vietnam, but believed that "we should increase our military effort to win a clear military victory." Another 34 percent also agreed with the American military presence, but wanted Johnson "to do more to bring about negotiations, such as a cease-fire." Sixteen percent favored "carrying the war more into North Vietnam" in pursuit of victory. "If there is a movement of opinion in the country," pollster Louis Harris wrote in the *Washington Post* on February 28, "it is toward seeking a military solution to what is generally regarded as a frustrating stalemate."

No matter how they examined the numbers, the poll was bad news for Johnson. The "hawks" believed that Johnson was not doing enough militarily in Vietnam, while the "doves" faulted him for his perceived unwillingness to pursue a peaceful end to the war. "Doubts and reservations have begun to overtake the all-abiding confidence in our effort" in Vietnam, Harris concluded.[60] As Bill Moyers told Johnson on June 9, quoting Harris: "You will continue to go down [in the polls] until there is some movement—either toward a military victory or toward a negotiated settlement."[61] Johnson was not the only politician suffering because of Vietnam.

Democrats across the board were taking a beating. A Gallup poll in July revealed significant erosion in the public's confidence of the Democratic Party to manage the situation in Vietnam.[62]

The hearings not only began to change the public's view of the war, they also transformed Fulbright and his committee into a potent antiwar force. "As long as the committee conducted executive sessions behind closed doors," Church said later, "it was really the captive of the president and the State Department. This, of course, was the device that had been used to reduce the committee over the years to comparative unimportance in the foreign policy of the United States." Until the public 1966 hearings, Church believed that Johnson and his advisors assumed they were free to disregard the Senate and its Foreign Relations Committee. The televised hearings changed that. "It was only at that point that the president really began to take the committee seriously," Church said. Suddenly, when the views of Fulbright, Morse, Church, Gore, Gavin, and Kennan were as well known as those of Johnson, Rusk, McNamara, and Taylor, the president had a problem—one that he could not ignore. As Church noted: "It was the klieg lights that the president feared."[63]

CHAPTER 32

Once Our Flag Is Committed

1966

Hubert Humphrey paid a stiff price for his ill-advised out-spokenness in February 1965. Having advised Johnson to reconsider the bombing of North Vietnam infuriated the temperamental president, who believed Humphrey had violated their preelection arrangement regarding the absolute fealty that Johnson expected from his vice president. For one agonizing year, Humphrey lived in exile, excluded from Johnson's inner circle and particularly banished from foreign policy discussions.

Johnson's "hazing" of Humphrey, as one biographer called it, was humiliating and appallingly severe. Having lived in the subservient darkness of John F. Kennedy's shadow for three years, Johnson expected no less of his vice president. Resentful of any positive press attention that Humphrey received, Johnson would not allow him to invite reporters on out-of-town trips. Humphrey could not even use a government aircraft without Johnson's permission. The president restricted the size of Humphrey's staff and required him to submit all speech drafts to the White House for approval. On the rare occasion that Humphrey did not clear his remarks, he incurred Johnson's wrath. In July 1965, for example, he sparked Johnson's rage when he told a Detroit audience that "the United States must be prepared for a long, ugly, costly war," and inadvertently revealed what Johnson hoped to conceal—the true nature of the armed struggle to which he was committing the nation.[1]

As the end of 1965 approached, Humphrey was still in exile. "I was still outside," he recalled, adding that "it must be said that Johnson probably never intended for me to have any greater role in foreign-policy formation that he himself had had during the Kennedy years." But while Humphrey had no particular foreign policy credentials upon which Johnson relied, he did have something Johnson needed—a better relationship with the

Senate's liberals, men who were the nucleus of the quickly expanding
domestic opposition to the war in Vietnam. For more than a decade, Johnson had used Humphrey as a bridge to these liberals. From his early days
as Senate majority leader, Johnson had assiduously cultivated a friendly
relationship with Humphrey who, in turn, became the leader's ally and
unofficial ambassador to a group of liberal Democrats who distrusted
Johnson and the political expedience with which he often assembled legislative coalitions. By late 1965, Johnson knew that he needed Humphrey's
liberal credentials once again—this time to persuade Senate liberals to
moderate their attacks on his Vietnam policies. While Humphrey's association with Johnson had damaged his own reputation with the liberals, he
realized that Johnson once more "needed bridges over those troubled
waters."[2] Almost overnight, Humphrey's wintry exile began giving way to
signs of spring.

On February 6, with less than a day's notice, Johnson instructed
Humphrey to meet him in Los Angeles, where the president would stop
on his return from the hastily assembled Honolulu conference. Onboard
Air Force One, Johnson briefed Humphrey and sent him, his entourage,
including aides McGeorge Bundy and Jack Valenti, and a large press contingent to Honolulu to pick up Premier Ky and General Thieu for the
flight to Saigon. Ostensibly, Humphrey's assignment was to encourage
South Vietnamese officials to embrace the social reforms discussed in
Honolulu and to secure the cooperation of other Asian nations. What
Johnson really wanted, however, was the enthusiastic, public endorsement
of the U.S. military effort. Humphrey would not disappoint. His desire to
return to Johnson's good graces would far outweigh any doubts he once
nursed about the wisdom of American intervention in South Vietnam. His
unabashed advocacy of Johnson's war in Vietnam would also play an enormous, unforeseen role in the 1968 presidential campaign—a race that
Humphrey would lose to Richard Nixon by the barest of margins.

"LANDING IN SAIGON gave me my first look at a city at war," Humphrey
later wrote, vividly recalling the scenes that greeted him: "Uniforms
everywhere, guns, barricades, checkpoints, barbed-wire fences. Tension
hung in the air. Thunderous planes taking off on missions of destruction,
helicopters thumping rhythmically in the sky. Another world, of civilians,
incredibly quiet considering their numbers, on foot, riding bicycles,
pulling rickshaws. It was a gray and unsmiling world. It was depressing."
During his two days in Saigon, Humphrey talked to Westmoreland,
Lodge, and their staffs, to American soldiers and civilians, to Vietnamese

military leaders, government officials, labor leaders, and civilians, as well as to journalists. Although some U.S. officials privately encouraged him to seek more information beyond the official briefings, Humphrey did not believe "the glimmers of dissent were strong enough" to justify any dispute of the information he received from Westmoreland and Lodge. He would not disappoint Johnson by challenging the administration's orthodoxy on Vietnam. Everything he saw, he argued, confirmed his newly held belief "that this was a war that could be won." Although he said he left still "troubled" by certain aspects of the military effort, Humphrey insisted he was "impressed and heartened by what I saw and heard."[3]

Humphrey returned to Washington an enthusiastic, born-again believer in the American cause in Vietnam. "The big picture must be shown," he told his staff on the return trip, "the big picture that Mansfield, Fulbright, Morse all missed." He now claimed to believe that Vietnam was "a dramatized, concentrated example of what the Communists intend to do elsewhere." He now saw what Johnson, Rusk, McNamara, and Bundy all saw when they looked at Vietnam. "I want to show that there is a master plan," he said, "a designed strategy" by the communists to subjugate South Vietnam. Humphrey saw not a nationalist struggle for control of a single country, but an international communist plot to seize all of Asia. "The danger of China is a plague—an epidemic, and we must stop that epidemic."[4]

After he returned to Washington, Humphrey immediately went to work trying to persuade the public and Congress that Johnson's Vietnam policies were sound. "The tide of battle has turned in Vietnam in our favor," Humphrey declared as he arrived at the White House on February 23.[5] The next day, an approving Johnson orchestrated a White House briefing during which Humphrey told a bipartisan group of congressional leaders that while there was "no easy solution" and no "speedy end" to the war, the U.S. cause was just. There was no doubt, Humphrey argued, that it was Hanoi, not Washington, that had blocked progress toward peace talks. Meanwhile, the only concern in Saigon, he said, was whether the United States possessed the "perseverance to stick it out and stay."[6] Later, Humphrey briefed members of the Senate Foreign Relations and House Foreign Affairs committees, and the Senate and House Armed Services committees. Johnson also invited each member of Congress to attend one of four meetings at the White House at which Humphrey reported on his trip.[7]

Humphrey's fifty-page report to Johnson was not entirely rosy. He cautioned that the road to victory would be long, difficult, and dangerous. He also recommended several policy and personnel changes. None of that, however, was included in the seven-page report, which the White House rewrote and released to the press on March 3. "In Vietnam," Humphrey wrote, "the tide of battle, which less than a year ago was running heavily against the Government of South Vietnam, has begun to turn for the better." While he acknowledged that a "long and costly struggle" lay ahead, he was "confident that we can prevent the success of the aggression in South Vietnam." To Humphrey, the war had become an epic struggle, "not simply the defense of a small nation against powerful neighbors. Vietnam is, in a larger sense, the focus of a broad effort to restrain the attempt by Asian Communists to expand by force—as we assisted our European allies in resisting Communist expansion in Europe after World War II."[8]

Back in Johnson's good graces, Humphrey became, by his own admission, a major "spokesman for the administration" on Vietnam.[9] Casting aside his early, heartfelt opposition to military escalation in Vietnam, Humphrey now shamelessly promoted Johnson's policies to the national press, in speeches around the country, and in the halls of Congress. It was the price that a humiliated and emasculated vice president was willing to pay for Johnson's favor. Finally, he was once more included among Johnson's national security advisors. Despite what it cost him in self-respect and stature among the Senate's liberals, Humphrey loved it.

"Humphrey was a person given to passionate enthusiasm," recalled his chief of staff William Connell, "and wanted very much to believe that Johnson had now turned onto the right path, and this was something that the American people ought to support."[10] But by Humphrey's own admission, his enthusiastic endorsement of Johnson's war policies did nothing to mollify the Senate's liberals. "Inadvertently," he said, "I had helped crystallize the opposition to our Vietnam involvement. If the war was intolerable to critics, then a long-term commitment was inconceivable."[11] No longer a member of the Senate's inner sanctum and now viewed as an unrestrained cheerleader for Lyndon Johnson, the vice president enjoyed minimal credibility with his former colleagues. In fact, his former colleagues on the Senate Foreign Relations Committee subjected him to a withering round of questions when he went before them on March 2 in closed session. According to one account of the meeting, the encounter with Fulbright was so acrimonious that Humphrey began to cry.[12]

Humphrey's outspokenness caused a "terrific row in the liberal community," Connell recalled.[13] His harsh rebuff of Robert Kennedy's suggestion that one path to peace in South Vietnam might be to invite the Viet Cong to share power in the government engendered particular hostility. To Kennedy's proposal, Humphrey had replied: "Putting the Viet Cong in the Vietnamese government would be like putting a fox in the chicken coop." Humphrey's strong views against Viet Cong participation in the South Vietnamese government were certainly not out of the mainstream. But his brusque and dismissive comment outraged liberals in and out of the Senate who believed the rejoinder was disrespectful and insulting. One

Johnson in the Oval Office with his foreign policy advisors on July 27, 1965—the day of his decision to increase the number of U.S. ground troops in South Vietnam from seventy-five thousand to one hundred twenty-five thousand. (LBJ Library)

Johnson meets with congressional leaders at the White House on July 27, 1965, to inform them that he will send fifty thousand additional American ground troops to South Vietnam. Majority Leader Mike Mansfield, the lone dissenter, told Johnson, "We do not owe this present government in Saigon anything." (Yoichi R. Okamoto, LBJ Library)

Johnson and his nemesis, Senator Robert F. Kennedy. Having supported the Vietnam policies of his brother, Robert Kennedy gradually moved into camp of Johnson's Vietnam opponents. His contentious White House meeting with Johnson in 1967 strengthened his opposition, not only to the war, but to Johnson's reelection. (Cecil Stoughon, LBJ Library)

Johnson with Senator Richard Russell, leader of the Senate's southern coalition and one of the president's closest friends. The Georgia Democrat had originally opposed American military involvement in Vietnam, but supported Johnson's policies nonetheless. Vietnam, he told Johnson in 1964, was "the damn worst mess I ever saw." (LBJ Library)

Johnson with Majority Leader Mike Mansfield at a White House meeting in August 1967. While he deplored the bombing in his private discussions with Johnson, Mansfield could not bring himself to break publicly with his president. (Yoichi R. Okamoto, LBJ Library)

Vice President Hubert Humphrey— who was exiled from Johnson's inner circle after opposing early escalation of the war—won his way back into Johnson's good graces in 1966 by becoming an unabashed supporter of the war. (Yoichi R. Okamoto, LBJ Library)

General William Westmoreland before a joint session of Congress in April 1967. The commanding general angered war opponents like McGovern with his warnings about the consequences of congressional dissent. "This, inevitably, will cost lives—American, Vietnamese, and those of our brave allies," the general predicted. (Bettmann/CORBIS)

American forces bomb North Vietnam in June 1966. Flying under radar control with a B-66 Destroyer, Air Force F-105 Thunderchief pilots bomb a military target through low clouds over the southern panhandle of North Vietnam. Despite a massive, four-year U.S. bombing campaign, North Vietnam refused to concede defeat. (CORBIS)

Allies in the effort to stop the Vietnam War, (*left to right*) senators George McGovern and Frank Church. "Perhaps naively," McGovern said of himself and Church, "we still hoped that by avoiding direct attacks on the [Johnson] administration and pressing instead for a negotiated settlement, we might persuade the President to modify his course." (Boise State University Library)

In the wake of the Viet Cong's Tet offensive, the new Defense secretary, Clark Clifford, briefs a somber Johnson in March 1968. "The most serious American casualty at Tet," Clifford later observed, "was the loss of the public's confidence in its leaders." Days later, Johnson would announce a partial bombing halt, as well as his decision not to seek reelection. (LBJ Library)

Senate Foreign Relations Committee Chairman J. William Fulbright gets the "Johnson treatment" from the president in May 1968. Once close friends, the two men were estranged over Vietnam beginning in 1965. "It is really a mystery to me," Fulbright told a friend the year before, "how the President can be persuaded that he is doing the Lord's work in continuing to slaughter those poor people in Vietnam." (LBJ Library)

Delegates to the 1968 Democratic Convention in Chicago protest adoption of the Johnson–Humphrey platform plank on Vietnam. Although Hubert Humphrey emerged as the party's presidential nominee, the violence that marred the convention proceedings gravely damaged his campaign. (Bettmann/CORBIS)

President-elect Richard Nixon confers with Lyndon Johnson just days after his election in November 1968. Nixon had achieved his victory, in part, by sabotaging the Vietnam peace talks. (Yoichi R. Okamoto, LBJ Library)

Nixon visits the troops in Vietnam in July 1969. The new president hoped that precipitate U.S. military action would unnerve the North Vietnamese and force them to make concessions. "I call it the Madman Theory," Nixon told an aide. "I want the North Vietnamese to believe I've reached the point where I might do anything to stop the war." (National Archives)

On April 30, 1970, Nixon told the nation that he had ordered an invasion of Cambodia. "Today is a sad and bloody day," Tennessee Senator Albert Gore told the Senate. (National Archives)

Nixon's national security advisor, and later secretary of state, Henry A. Kissinger. When the *Pentagon Papers* were leaked to the New York Times in 1971, Kissinger encouraged Nixon's overreaction. "It shows you're a weakling, Mr. President," he told Nixon. Nixon's response set in motion a chain of events that ended in the Watergate scandal. (Gerald R. Ford Library)

President Gerald R. Ford presided over the final, turbulent days of American involvement in Vietnam. Hoping to begin healing the deep wounds caused by the war, Ford granted amnesty to disserters and draft dodgers. "All, in a sense, are casualties, still abroad and absent without leave from the real America." (Gerald R. Ford Library)

As Saigon falls to South Vietnamese troops on April 28, 1975, President Ford discusses the situation with Secretary of State Henry Kissinger and Vice President Nelson Rockefeller. "I faced the fact," Ford later acknowledged, "that the end was near." He would order the evacuation of six thousand American personnel still in Vietnam. (Gerald R. Ford Library)

liberal publication labeled him a "hatchet man" for the administration.[14] Another disillusioned liberal was McGovern, Humphrey's friend and next-door neighbor. "It really disappointed me beyond what I can tell," he recalled, adding that Humphrey "was kind of an inspiration to me as a young politician." Vietnam, McGovern said, "was the first major separation we had on anything. It was very painful to me. I think it was to Gaylord [Nelson] and to Frank Church and others."[15]

For Wayne Morse, the conflict in Vietnam had been "McNamara's war." It was the bookish Defense secretary—aided and abetted by Bundy, Rusk, and Taylor and congressional cheerleaders like Dirksen, Long, McCormick, and Ford—who had prodded an unsuspecting Johnson into increasing the U.S. role in Vietnam. Throughout 1965, Morse was charitable enough to hold the somewhat naïve belief that Johnson had merely been the victim of bad advice from his foreign policy advisors. Gradually, however, Morse began to see the war with different eyes. But it was not until he saw that funding for the Great Society was beginning to suffer at the expense of the ever-increasing military appropriations for Vietnam that he reassessed his previous judgment. By the spring of 1966, he was ready to reassign responsibility for the war. "I blame nobody but Johnson for our predicament in Vietnam," he told the *New York Times*, "not his advisors, not anybody but Johnson."

The first clear sign of Morse's change of opinion was his announcement in March that he would support Robert Kennedy for the Democratic nomination in 1968. Kennedy would not announce his candidacy for almost a year, but Morse had already concluded that Kennedy might be the only Democrat who could successfully challenge the president for reelection and, thereby, stop the war. Morse was not particularly close to Kennedy, but such was the depth of his hostility toward Johnson's Vietnam policies that he would take the bold step of opposing the reelection of a popular incumbent president of his own party.[16]

Morse was also eager to force another Senate debate over the Gulf of Tonkin Resolution. In late January, he introduced legislation to repeal the measure that Johnson had used as his blank check in Vietnam. "We owe it to the president to decide whether the American people are entitled to a debate on the issue of a declaration of war," Morse told the Senate on January 29, "rather than a war conducted outside the framework of the Constitution by the president by executive power which he does not possess either legally or constitutionally and which he should not seek to exercise."[17] For once, Morse was not alone in his extreme antipathy to continued American military involvement in Vietnam. Fulbright, working separately from Morse, had instructed his committee staff to draft an amendment to the supplemental military appropriations bill that would effectively supplant the Gulf of Tonkin Resolution by expressing the Senate's sentiment about the Vietnam conflict.[18]

Despite the escalating anxiety about the war among Democratic senators, few were willing to support repealing or reinterpreting the Gulf of Tonkin Resolution—especially during debate over a supplemental military appropriations measure. "Nothing in this legislation can properly be considered as determining foreign policy," said Russell who managed the legislation on the Senate floor when debate began on February 16. Russell's appeal was devastatingly effective—especially with the war's opponents, many of whom still had reservations about opposing appropriations for soldiers already in the field. Comparing approval of Johnson's supplemental funding request to "throwing of a rope to a man in the water," Russell explained: "We may have cause to question how he got there, but he is there, he is a human being, he is our friend, and a member of our family and, therefore, if we have a rope and do not throw it to him to enable him to assist himself out of the water, this would be a callow and heartless attitude for us to take."[19]

Russell's argument carried the day. While many had their doubts about the 1964 resolution's wisdom, few were willing to walk away from Johnson's policies at this point. By the time senators finished a two-week debate on the supplemental request, Fulbright had abandoned his earlier plans to offer an alternative amendment and had even developed brief doubts about the wisdom of voting for Morse's amendment. He feared that Morse's proposal was forcing "a decision on the floor as to whether the Senate should reaffirm policies which I do not wish to reaffirm." Although he would ultimately vote with Morse, Fulbright feared that voting on the Gulf of Tonkin Resolution might only result in an even stronger mandate for Johnson in Vietnam.[20]

Johnson was concerned enough about potential support for Morse's amendment that he worried aloud to Mansfield that the vote on the resolution might "imply" a "dilution of that resolution." If it did, Johnson told the majority leader on the morning of March 1, "I'm in a hell of a shape." Before the vote, Johnson urged Mansfield to explain to the Senate that a rejection of the Morse amendment "leaves the president without a bit of his authority changed or diluted." Mansfield was skeptical that such a point needed to be made. "You have that responsibility and authority even without a resolution," he told Johnson. "I agree with it," Johnson replied. "But all the play, Mike, all the editorials is: What's going to be done [in] this Senate—what this group of twenty or thirty or forty senators—are they going to take away authority? Are they going to hold it back?"[21]

Once more, Mansfield would subjugate concerns about the war to his loyalty to Johnson. Later that day, Mansfield obediently dealt Morse's effort a final deathblow when he submitted a motion to table the amendment. "The pending business is a military nuts-and-bolts measure," he explained. "It is a bill which should stand alone." But unlike Russell, Mansfield stopped short of describing the vote as a referendum on the Gulf of Tonkin Resolution. However, he dutifully complied with Johnson's request to make it clear that the failure of Morse's amendment would keep the Gulf of Tonkin Resolution "in effect with whatever constitutional force it may have."[22] When the Senate voted, only Gruening, Fulbright, McCarthy, and Stephen Young of Ohio sided with Morse to keep the amendment alive. Ninety-two senators cast votes with Russell and, symbolically, with Johnson and the troops. The vote on final passage of the $13 billion supplemental appropriations bill was just as lopsided—92–2—with only Morse and Gruening opposed.* That same day, the House approved the appropriations measure, 393–4.[23]

Even dedicated opponents of the war like McGovern, Nelson, Fulbright, Robert Kennedy and McCarthy had supported the measure, profoundly reflecting the sentiment that, as Russell was fond of saying, "once our flag [is] committed . . . the time for debate is passed."[24] As McGovern explained on NBC's "Today" show, on February 24: "This is a matter of whether you're going to supply equipment to men we've sent overseas, or whether you're going to leave them without the means of defending themselves."[25]

There was another, more subtle argument that helped win overwhelming approval of the appropriations measure: it was the growing belief that actions in Congress could have a profound impact on the will of the communists to continue fighting. As Mansfield told the Senate before the final vote: "We are in too deep now. The situation is one of the utmost delicacy and the risk of misinterpretation is very great."[26]

Few were more offended by this reasoning than Morse. "Oh, I know that when we make statements of this kind, somehow, in some way, we are said to be aiding the enemy," he told the Senate on March 17. "We are supposed to be, somehow, letting down our boys in Southeast Asia. I get lost in that jungle of fallacy. The truth is that those who want to follow the United States' course of action now being followed in Southeast Asia are the ones who are letting down our boys. Those of us who are seeking to try to stop the killing there are the ones who think it is our clear duty to insist on every possible procedure and avenue available to bring about the enforceability of peace and the stopping of the making of war in Southeast Asia."[27]

Johnson was dead wrong if he interpreted the Senate's support for his

---

*Church was among the five senators who did not vote on the measure.

supplemental appropriations request as any indicator of widespread support for his broader Vietnam policies. In truth, as many as thirty senators
and almost one hundred House members were, by now, on record opposing the administration's course in Vietnam. Johnson's victory was merely
an indication that the president and his allies in Congress—Mansfield
among them—still controlled the legislative process. It was also an indication that many members of Congress could, indeed, distinguish between
the relative wisdom of Johnson's foreign and military policies and the perceived need to support American troops overseas.

The dissent came not only from Senate liberals who favored a negotiated settlement and a unified or neutralized Vietnam, but also from conservatives like Russell who agreed with the Joint Chiefs' private complaints
that Johnson was not prosecuting the war aggressively enough. "I have
supported our country's policy in Vietnam because for me there was no
other honorable course that a loyal American could take," Russell told the
Rockdale County Jaycees of Conyers, Georgia, on April 8. "I must, however, state that I do not see how we can permit the present situation to go
on indefinitely. We may no longer be losing the war, as Secretary McNamara has stated, but neither do we appear to be winning it." Russell
believed that Johnson had "no choice but to increase the punishment of
the aggressors in both South and North Vietnam by the measured means
available to us until they are compelled to come to the conference table."
Like his liberal colleagues, Russell also supported what he called "an agonizing reappraisal" of U.S. policy in Vietnam. He said, "if it becomes
clearly evident that a majority of the Vietnamese do not want our help, I
would favor withdrawing immediately both military forces and economic
aid." Although he hoped that "matters will not come to that," he insisted—
sounding more than a little like Morse—that "we must find the means to
bring the war to a conclusion and to stop the maiming and killing of American men."[28]

For Fulbright, meanwhile, the debate over the supplemental appropriations measure marked a crossing of the Rubicon. With his vote for
Morse's amendment, he had finally repudiated the Gulf of Tonkin Resolution—and firmly associated himself with outspoken opponents of the
war like Morse and Gruening. In March, convinced that China held the
key to peace in Vietnam, he again angered administration officials by conducting a series of hearings to examine the history of U.S.-Chinese relations. If there were any lingering doubts about where Fulbright stood, he
dismissed them in April with a series of well-publicized lectures at Johns
Hopkins University in Baltimore. "America," Fulbright declared, "is now
at that historical point at which a great nation is in danger of losing its perspective on what exactly is within the realm of its power and what is beyond

it." Great nations, Fulbright said, were always "susceptible to the idea that its power is a sign of God's favor, conferring upon it a special responsibility for other nations." It was a malady that Fulbright described as the "arrogance of power," something he defined as "a psychological need that nations seem to have in order to prove that they are bigger, better, or stronger than other nations."

It was in Vietnam that Fulbright believed the nation's arrogance was, once again, on display. Although he said he did not doubt Johnson, Humphrey, Rusk, and McNamara when they said American troops were in Vietnam to "defend freedom," he did doubt the country's ability to achieve that end. "What I do question," he said, "is the ability of the United States or any other Western nation to go into a small, alien, underdeveloped Asia nation and create stability where there is chaos, the will to fight where there is defeatism, democracy where there is no tradition of it, and honest government where corruption is almost a way of life."

> The cause of our difficulties in Southeast Asia is not a deficiency of power but an excess of the wrong kind of power, which results in a feeling of impotence when it fails to achieve its desired ends. We are still acting like Boy Scouts dragging reluctant old ladies across streets they do not want to cross. We are trying to remake Vietnamese society, a task which certainly cannot be accomplished by force and which probably cannot be accomplished by any means available to outsiders. The objective may be desirable, but it is not feasible.[29]

In another lecture in which Fulbright examined the roots of American involvement in Vietnam, he concluded that "we have given our opposition to Communism priority over our sympathy for nationalism because we have regarded Communism as a kind of absolute evil, as a totally pernicious doctrine which deprives the people subjected to it of freedom, dignity, happiness and the hope of ever acquiring them." That view, Fulbright believed, was "implicit in much of American foreign policy" and was to him "the principal reason for our involvement in Vietnam."

He dismissed the notion that the United States was opposing nothing more than North Vietnamese aggression. "But what are the North Vietnamese doing," he asked, "except participating in a civil war, not in a foreign country but on the other side of a demarcation line between two sectors of the same country, a civil war in which Americans from ten thousand miles across the ocean are also participating? What are they doing that is different from what the American North did to the American South a hundred years ago, with results that few of my fellow Southerners now regret?" North Vietnam's "crime," Fulbright contended, was that they are Communists—"practitioners of a philosophy we regard as evil." Thus, Fulbright believed, at the foundation of U.S. involvement in Vietnam was "the view of Communism as an evil philosophy and the view of ourselves as God's avenging angels, whose sacred duty it is to combat evil philosophies." To Fulbright, the U.S. view of communism as evil was "a distorting prism through which we see projections of our own minds rather than what is actually there."

The truth, he said, was that Americans, in many cases, were no better than the communists. "Looking through the prism," he said, "we see the Viet Cong who cut the throats of village chiefs as savage murderers but American flyers who incinerate unseen women and children with napalm as valiant fighters for freedom." But the ultimate folly, Fulbright believed, was that "we see China, with no troops in South Vietnam, as the real aggressor while we, with hundreds of thousands of men, are resisting foreign intervention." While he acknowledged that the "greater fault is with the Communists," he insisted that "it is *our* shortcoming, however, that we have the power to overcome and, in doing so, to set a constructive example for our adversaries."[30]

Rejecting the notion that "criticism of the Vietnamese war is illegitimate in the absence of a foolproof plan for ending it," Fulbright articulated his own program "for the eventual restoration of peace" in Vietnam, cautioning that there was no good "alternative policy" to end the war "because our choices are greatly limited by what has already been done." Spelling out an eight-point plan, Fulbright's recommendations included involvement of the NLF in negotiations with the South Vietnamese government; a cease-fire among military representatives of the four separate negotiating parties: the U.S. and South Vietnam, North Vietnam and the NLF; an end to all U.S. bombing of North Vietnam; no additional Americans forces; and the reduction of U.S. military operations. Furthermore, Fulbright said, the United States should pledge to eventually remove its troops from South Vietnam and encourage negotiations among the "four principal belligerents" that would be "directed toward a cease-fire and plans for self-determination in South Vietnam." Like Mansfield, he favored an international conference to "guarantee the arrangements made by the belligerents" and a referendum on the reunification of a neutral Vietnam. If the peace talks failed, Fulbright said, then the United States should pursue an enclave strategy by "consolidat[ing] its forces in highly fortified defensible areas in South Vietnam and keep them there indefinitely."[31]

Fulbright was not alone in his conclusion that U.S. leaders had allowed an intemperate, indiscriminate hatred of communism to guide the country's policies in Southeast Asia for the previous fifteen years. In a May 3 speech to the Senate, McGovern echoed Fulbright's damning analysis of America's recent history in Asia and called for a "fundamental reappraisal" of U.S. policy toward China and Southeast Asia. While the United States had granted independence to the Philippines and encouraged the dissolution of the colonial and imperial possessions of Britain, Japan, and the Netherlands after World War II, McGovern noted that it had applied a different standard in China and Southeast Asia. "In China and Vietnam," McGovern explained, "the revolutionary leaders were Communists, which automatically made them the enemy in American eyes." To U.S. policymakers, Mao Tse-tung and Ho Chi Minh "were part of a world-wide Communist monolith bent upon global conquest." Because the United States had "substituted Communism for the Devil," McGovern said that "we felt sufficiently free from sin to rebuke those who failed to enlist on the side of right."

"Frankly," McGovern concluded, "I have not been able to bring myself to believe that what happens in Vietnam is going to determine the fate of civilization." The United States had "exaggerated the significance of this little country out of all proportion to its relationship to our own security or to its role in international affairs."[32]

Predictably, Johnson did not take the criticism of his controversial policy in stride—particularly Fulbright's remarks, which he interpreted to mean that the Foreign Relations chairman believed the president was "arrogant." Johnson apparently suggested as much to Fulbright at a White House diplomatic reception in early May. "Never at *any* time," Fulbright wrote to Johnson on May 9, "have I spoken, or even thought, of you in connection with arrogance." His theme, he explained, had been the arrogance of power exhibited by nations. "You and I, Mr. President, have the same ultimate interest," Fulbright wrote, "the return to peace and security of our country, and I believe that my opposing *the views of some of your advisors*, who have a different viewpoint from mine, can be of help to you" (emphasis added).[33]

Johnson did not reply to Fulbright immediately. In a May 11 speech, however, he indirectly answered Fulbright's Johns Hopkins lecture when he insisted that "the exercise of power in this century has meant for all of us in the United States not arrogance but agony. We have used our power not willingly and recklessly ever, but always reluctantly and with restraint."[34] The next night he took more direct aim at Fulbright when he addressed a Democratic fund-raising dinner in Washington. Glaring at Fulbright, Johnson told the crowd that he was "glad to be here among so many friends—and some members of the Foreign Relations Committee." That statement was greeted with embarrassed laughter, as was his remark that "you can say one thing about those [Foreign Relations Committee] hearings, but I don't think this is the place to say it." Johnson's call for all Democratic candidates to unite behind his Vietnam policies was no more welcome than his awkward attempts at humor. Indeed, many Democrats in attendance deeply resented the president's tasteless observations. Their party was deeply split over Vietnam and most in the room did not find the war or the debate over it anything to laugh about. "It was, on the whole," observed Johnson biographers Robert Novak and Rowland Evans, "a sour night for Lyndon Johnson and his party, and it reflected how useless Johnson's old and tested political weapons were in dealing with the great crisis of Vietnam."[35]

The next morning, White House aide Harry McPherson told the president in a memorandum that he was "disturbed" by Johnson's remarks which he found "harsh, uncompromising, over-militant. It seemed you were trying to beat Fulbright's ears down before an audience of Democrats who, I am told, had earlier applauded him strongly." While McPherson acknowledged that the speech did not "read as badly as it sounded," he argued that the "tone, emphasis and frequent glances down at Fulbright made it (for me) wrong." Although McPherson said he believed "we are right to stand in Viet Nam" and that he "abhor[ed] the kind of vapid sophomoric bitching Fulbright is producing nowadays," he pointed out that "difficult" questions about Vietnam had been raised—"difficult for anyone, I think, who gives them serious attention. They cannot be shouted out of existence."[36] McPherson later said that his memorandum earned him "the usual pay for doing that kind of thing: about two weeks of silence."[37] His well-intentioned chiding accomplished little. At a Democratic dinner in Chicago on May 17, Johnson served up even harsher criticism of the war's critics when he told those in attendance that although "the road ahead is going to be difficult" some "Nervous Nellies" would continue to oppose the U.S. role in Vietnam. Johnson said they should either offer alternative policies or stifle their criticism.[38]

To McPherson, Johnson was a man caught between hard-liners who wanted the United States to fight more vigorously in Vietnam and the more pacific critics of his policies like Fulbright, McGovern, and Church. "The captious criticism of the left, represented by Fulbright, must have seemed infuriating [to Johnson]," McPherson said. "You know, 'Godamn it! I'm trying not to go in there with hobnail boots and kill a half a million people in Vietnam in order to win this war. I'm trying to be restrained, and you're telling me that I'm a stupid, brutal president to continue the war at all.'"[39]

Finally, on May 27, Johnson responded to Fulbright's May 9 letter. Increasingly worried about the damage the public spat between the two men was inflicting on the Democratic Party, press secretary Bill Moyers had drafted the letter, which he persuaded Johnson to sign. "You are certainly right in saying that statements can be taken out of context and interpreters can draw a different meaning than you meant from your words,"

Johnson wrote. "It has happened to me!" Diplomatically, Johnson took issue with the premise of Fulbright's "Arrogance of Power" lectures. He admitted that while Fulbright's images of "nations in history which were drunk with their own importance are vivid . . . I also believe that there are some very pertinent recent analogies which are applicable, too—and the most significant, as far as I am concerned, is the analogy of what happens when ambitious and aggressive powers are freely permitted in areas where the peace of the world is delicately balanced, to use direct and indirect force against smaller and weaker states in their path."[40]

Meanwhile, the costs of the war were rising almost as rapidly as Johnson's frustration and anger over the dissent in his own party. In an effort to conceal the true extent of the U.S. commitment in Vietnam, Johnson's fiscal 1966 budget had vastly understated the costs of supporting the more than two hundred thousand troops in Vietnam. The extent of the understatement became painfully apparent in March when Congress reluctantly authorized an additional $13 million in military appropriations. In his budget for the 1967 fiscal year (that began in July 1966), Johnson was no more candid. To win congressional support and to keep the public in the dark about the escalating commitment, the president had had requested only $10 billion when he and his advisors knew they would need as much as $20 billion. However, finding the money for another supplemental appropriations would be far more difficult than in March. By the summer of 1966, it was clear that the fiscal 1967 budget deficit would be triple the $1.8 billion that the administration had earlier predicted—and that was not counting the additional money Johnson would need to finance the war. Making matters worse was a slowing economy—the stock market was stagnant while inflation and interest rates were on the rise—that forced Johnson to make critical decisions about how he would continue to finance the war and his domestic programs. As Johnson and his economic advisors knew, a sagging economy meant even slower revenue growth—and an even larger deficit—as well as increased pressure to bleed social programs to pay for the war.

In mid-July, Johnson finally informed congressional leaders of his dilemma, telling them he would need an extra $5 billion to $10 billion to fight the war in fiscal 1967. By early August, Johnson agonized over whether he should consider what he had rejected earlier—some form of income tax increase to pay for the increased military expenditures. "In a perfect world," his domestic policy advisor Joseph Califano later said, "Johnson believed [that] a tax increase might make sense" if it were coupled with an agreement by the Federal Reserve Board to reduce interest rates. "But Johnson feared that a tax increase sufficient to satisfy [board chairman William McChesney] Martin would precipitate a recession." In any event, Califano acknowledged, "he wasn't about to put his Great Society programs on the cutting block by asking for taxes he couldn't persuade Congress to enact."

As he knew, Congress would not like the idea of raising taxes less than three months before the November elections. "You'd have trouble getting more than fifteen votes," House Republican leader Ford told Johnson. Majority Leader Carl Albert agreed, as did House Ways and Means Chairman Wilbur Mills and Senate Finance Committee Chairman Russell Long. The two chairmen would entertain suspension of the investment tax credit, they informed Johnson, but not a tax increase. Eventually, Johnson agreed to a combination of budget cuts—$1.5 billion—and suspension of the investment tax credit. Congress promptly adopted the recommendation. The quick congressional action solved Johnson's problem, but only temporarily. As Califano observed, "There was a gnawing sense that, however many fingers LBJ was able to put in the dike, without a tax increase he could not much longer prevent the waters from flowing over the top."[41]

In one sense, the fiscal woes were the least of Johnson's problems in Vietnam. Public support for his policies in Vietnam had begun to decline in the spring as the costs escalated and domestic unrest in South Vietnam appeared to distract Johnson and U.S. military leaders from their mission of fighting the Viet Cong and the North Vietnamese. Many Americans began to wonder if the South Vietnamese really wanted U.S. assistance. A Gallup poll in June 1966 revealed that a significant minority of Americans now favored withdrawal. While 48 percent of those surveyed said they wanted the U.S. military to continue its mission in Vietnam, 35 percent wanted U.S. forces pulled out. Those numbers were notable, especially considering that in a similar survey the previous June, 66 percent had wanted the United States to continue its military involvement and only 20 percent had favored withdrawal. Other polling confirmed the considerable shift in public opinion about the war. A Louis Harris survey the same month revealed another side of the public's impatience with the conflict— 38 percent of those polled favored taking the war more forcefully to the north. "American public opinion is rising toward increased militancy about the Vietnam war and a 'get it over with' mood," the pollster said of his results. Judging by Harris' analysis, public attitudes bore a striking resemblance to those of Johnson and many members of Congress: "The people show a distaste for what they regard as an indecisive stalemate in which American lives are being spent, but they cannot arrive at any firm conclusion about what should be done to end the war."

Even worse for Johnson was the way the stalemate in Vietnam had damaged his personal standing with the public. Harris reported that public approval of Johnson's handling of the war had dropped from 65 percent in the summer of 1965 to 42 percent in June 1966. Worse was that 58 percent gave Johnson fair or poor marks for his Vietnam policies—an alarming public appraisal of his leadership. As Bill Moyers observed in a memorandum to Johnson, "the people are in a foul mood over Vietnam."[42] Johnson's mood was no better. Moyers told Rusk that Johnson was "deeply disturbed" by the collapsing public support for his policies. "It seems to him," Moyers said, " that internally we cannot permit this thing to go on, it will tear us to pieces and [he] thinks [the] time has come for us to try to push whatever buttons we have to push."[43] As Russell advised Johnson in a June 2 telephone conversation: "Well, you're going to have to do something different out there. If you don't you're going eventually to get in trouble."[44]

The recommendation for "something different" was already on Johnson's desk: a plan to bring more pressure to bear on North Vietnam through the "systematic and sustained bombing" of facilities that refined petroleum, oil, and lubricants (POL). Most of Johnson's military advisors, as well as his new national security advisor, Walt Rostow—an enthusiastic supporter of the war who replaced Bundy in February—urged Johnson to turn the fighting up a notch by denying the North Vietnamese the fuel they needed to transport supplies into the south.* Johnson, however, was resistant, worried that an errant bomb might kill innocent civilians. "I seem to be the only one that's afraid that they'll . . . hit a hospital or hit a school or something." In the end, however, Johnson would relent. As he confessed to Mansfield, "the military and the fellows out there—Westmoreland— just feel like that you're just lettin' 'em shoot our men unnecessarily. That you ought to stop this—you ought to make it as difficult—we can't stop it, but make it as difficult for them to get supplies as possible or you ought'n to be in there."[45]

In addition to bombing the POL sites, the amount of bombs dropped on North Vietnam increased dramatically—from 33,000 tons in 1965 to 128,000 tons in 1966. The number of downed U.S. planes also reflected the increased bombing activity: the United States had lost 171 aircraft in 1965, a number that increased to 318 by 1966. Civilian and military casualties in North Vietnam almost doubled in 1966. The numbers of U.S. troops in Vietnam also swelled—to 265,000 by late June on their way to almost 400,000 by year's end, the result of the president's determination

---

*McNamara's description of Rostow: "Optimistic by nature, he tended to be skeptical of any report that failed to indicate we were making progress" (McNamara, *In Retrospect*, 235).

to give Westmoreland the troops he needed.[46] Yet the increased bombing and the new troops fell far short of expectations. The war in Vietnam was a voracious beast. The more Johnson and his advisors fed it, the hungrier it became. "The more I learn, the more I'm sobered by the realization of how much further we may have to go," Johnson's special assistant Robert Komer acknowledged upon his return from Vietnam in early July. As the CIA reported on July 23, "The recent US air strikes against targets in the Hanoi-Haiphong area do not appear to have weakened the North Vietnamese leadership's resolve to continue to prosecute the war."[47] Two days later, another CIA document—no doubt used to bolster the administration's argument against domestic dissent—concluded that the North Vietnamese were banking on increased U.S. opposition to the war. "In their view," the report said, "these developments may well inhibit substantially greater US ground escalation of the conflict and may, in the long run, force major concessions in Washington's policy which could offer a realization of some Communist objectives in the South. Hanoi *probably* still believes that Washington's determination to pursue the war will crack before curtailed Communist capabilities make it necessary for Hanoi to completely rethink its strategy" (emphasis added).[48]

The apparent failure of the bombing profoundly affected McNamara. For the first time, he began to acknowledge that he had been wrong— badly wrong—about the ability of the bombs to erode the iron will of the North Vietnamese, as well as the effectiveness of U.S. ground troops to break the backs of the Viet Cong. "I myself am more and more convinced that we ought definitely to plan on termination of the bombing in the north," McNamara confessed to Johnson in a September 19 phone conversation, "but not until after the election [in November], and I hate to even talk about it before then for fear of a leak." McNamara also now favored a "ceiling" on U.S. ground troops in South Vietnam. "I don't think we ought to just look ahead to the future and say we're going to go higher and higher and higher and higher—600,000, 700,000, whatever it takes. It will break the economy of that country and will substitute U.S. soldiers for South Vietnamese and will distort the whole pattern of conduct in South Vietnam if we do." McNamara told Johnson he believed in a ceiling of "somewhere between 500,000 and 600,000." No doubt alarmed that his Defense secretary had begun to sound like Fulbright or Mansfield, Johnson did not respond.[49]

In mid-October, after returning from his first trip to Vietnam since the previous November, McNamara told Johnson he saw "no reasonable way to bring the war to an end soon." Pacification efforts had proved "a bad disappointment" and the Rolling Thunder operation had not "significantly affected infiltration or cracked the morale of Hanoi."

In essence, we find ourselves—from the point of view of the important war (for the complicity of the people)—no better, and if anything worse off. This important war must be fought and won by the Vietnamese themselves. We have known this from the beginning. But the discouraging truth is that, as was the case in 1961 and 1963 and 1965, we have not found the formula, the catalyst, for training and inspiring them into effective action.

Despite his growing disillusionment, McNamara was not yet prepared to give up. Although the evidence suggested that the United States could do little to win the conflict, McNamara hoped that a determined military effort would at least persuade the North Vietnamese and the Viet Cong that the United States did, indeed, possess the will to remain in Vietnam indefinitely—a posture, he told Johnson, "that makes trying to 'wait us out' less attractive." Instead of searching for a graceful exit, McNamara advised Johnson to limit increases of U.S. forces in South Vietnam to seventy thousand in 1967. "And we should level off at the total of 470,000 which such an increase would provide." Yet even such an increase of U.S. forces, McNamara cautioned, "would not kill the enemy off in such numbers as to break their morale so long as they think they can wait us out."

But McNamara's visit to Vietnam had finally persuaded him of the futility of the bombing. Upon his return, he argued against any further increases in bombing intensity, telling Johnson that "to bomb the North sufficiently to make a radical impact upon Hanoi's political, economic and social structure, would require an effort which we could make but which would not be stomached either by our own people or by world opinion; and it would involve a serious risk of drawing us into open war with China." Later, "at a proper time," McNamara advised Johnson, he should "consider terminating bombing all of North Vietnam, or at least in the Northeast zones, for an indefinite period in connection with covert moves toward peace." While he was not optimistic that Hanoi would respond positively to "peace overtures," the Defense secretary argued that the North Vietnamese would never agree to talks as long as the bombing continued. "We should see what develops," he suggested, "retaining freedom to resume the bombing if nothing useful was forthcoming."

In one of his more controversial recommendations to Johnson, McNamara advocated diverting as many as twenty thousand American soldiers to begin construction of an "infiltration barrier" that would stretch across the length of the country, from Laos to the South China Sea, near the 17th Parallel. Equipped with acoustic sensors, the wire barrier would be designed to inhibit infiltration of men and supplies from north to south. "The barrier may not be effective at first," McNamara cautioned, "but I believe that it can be made effective in time and that even the threat of its becoming effective can substantially change to our advantage the character of the war."[50]*

It would come as no surprise to McNamara that the Joint Chiefs strongly disputed his bleak assessment of the war's progress. The military situation in Vietnam, they maintained, "has improved substantially over the past year." They strongly objected to his proposal to reduce and eventually end the bombing, explaining that "the likelihood of the war being settled by negotiations is small; and that far from inducing negotiations, another bombing pause will be regarded by North Vietnamese leaders, and our Allies, as renewed evidence of lack of US determination to press the war to a successful conclusion." U.S. troops and the bombing were "the two trump cards in the hands of the President," the Joint Chiefs insisted. "It should not be given up without an end to the NVN aggression in SVN." Instead of imposing a ceiling on U.S. troops, the Joint Chiefs believed they might eventually need as many as seven hundred fifty thousand—as well as a drastic increase in the pace of bombing. Yet even with the massive escalation they thought necessary, they could not promise a quick end to the war, which they acknowledged would last for at least another two years. "Accordingly," they said, "for political, military, and psychological reasons, we should prepare openly for a long-term, sustained military effort."[51]

Once more, a conflicted Johnson faced a crossroads on Vietnam. Publicly, he signaled his determination to press forward, telling American troops in a brief visit to South Vietnam in late October that "we shall never let you down, nor your fighting comrades, nor the 15 million people of Vietnam." He exhorted the troops to continue fighting and to "nail that coonskin to the wall."[52] Privately, however, Johnson reluctantly agreed to McNamara's recommendations. On November 11, he ordered the stabilization of U.S. military operations in Vietnam. Henceforth, the president instructed, primary emphasis would be placed on pacification in South Vietnam and negotiations to end the conflict.[53]

Johnson's decision to stabilize the U.S. military effort in Vietnam coincided with a promising peace plan initiated in June by a Polish diplomat, Janusz Lewandowski—his country's delegate to the International Control Commission that supposedly oversaw the Geneva accords. Lewandowski told U.S. officials that Hanoi might be open to a "political compromise." According to the Polish diplomat, the North Vietnamese would no longer insist on South Vietnam's neutralization and might even accept its present government. Although they wanted some role for the Viet Cong in the peace negotiations, their attitude toward the U.S. military presence had

---

*Although Johnson approved construction of McNamara's barrier, the project soon proved unfeasible and was abandoned.

shifted. They would not insist on an immediate withdrawal of U.S. forces and would accept a "suspension" of U.S. air strikes on the North as an opening to the initiation of peace talks. By November, Ambassador-at-Large Averill Harriman and his deputy, Chester Cooper, concluded that the peace feelers from Hanoi were worth pursuing. U.S. officials gave the operation the code-name "Marigold."

In early December, just as the talks between U.S. and Polish officials turned serious—with the promise of direct discussions with North Vietnamese officials—U.S. military officials staged two ill-timed bombing attacks near Hanoi. Although the air strikes were simply a continuation of a routine bombing operation that had been suspended due to bad weather in November, the Poles and the North Vietnamese viewed the attacks as evidence that the Americans were not serious about negotiations.

If the renewed bombing in early December left any North Vietnamese officials doubting American intentions, the fierce air strikes of December 13 completely dispelled them. Against the advice of McNamara and several other advisors, Johnson continued and intensified the bombing, persuaded by overly optimistic reports out of Saigon that bombs might produce more than the ephemeral negotiations promised by the Poles. "'Marigold' seemed a very perishable flower indeed," Chester Cooper lamented. In despair and disgust, the Poles ended the talks.[54]

CHAPTER 33

Where Does It All End?

1966–1967

THE WAR WAS BEGINNING TO HURT LYNDON JOHNSON AND HIS party. In June 1966, Mansfield informed Johnson that his discussions with seventeen Democratic senators revealed "confusion and deep concern" over the country's inability to find a way out of Vietnam. "The Democratic Party is badly hurt by the war even though individually some Democrats may not be troubled," Mansfield reported. "If war drags on, the Party will suffer badly."[1]

Mansfield's warning proved painfully prophetic. Although the war did not play a primary role in most fall congressional elections, a Gallup poll in September indicated that a wide majority of voters thought the war was now the most important issue facing the nation. The widening rift among Democrats in Congress undoubtedly contributed to the perception of a listless and badly divided party. The urban riots of 1965 and 1966—born of economic disenchantment among black Americans, despite the civil rights laws of 1964 and 1965—only exacerbated that image and confirmed for some that Johnson and the congressional Democrats were unable to govern. Only two years after Barry Goldwater had led his party to its worst presidential defeat in history, the Republicans roared back to life in 1966, gaining more than forty seats in the House and seven in the Senate.[2]

Democrats and Republicans could not ignore the meaning of the 1966 elections, nor could they lightly regard the war's potential as a major issue in 1968. As the war became more unpopular, Democrats knew their party would receive much of the blame—despite overwhelming Republican support for Johnson's Vietnam policies—because the conflict had become indelibly labeled as Johnson's war.

Within the Democratic Party, as well, support for Johnson sagged. The rift over the war would only grow deeper in 1967 and weaken party unity to the breaking point. In response, a frustrated and angry Johnson would increasingly ignore members of his own party and form alliances with friendly Republicans, a strategy that only worsened the alienation of many Democratic liberals.

Mansfield, however, would remain in Johnson's camp, hesitant, unlike Fulbright, to publicly break with his president. Despite his ever-increasing concerns about the futility of the U.S. effort and his doubts about Johnson's readiness to negotiate a peaceful resolution, Mansfield continued to press the administration to engage the North Vietnamese either through direct talks or by taking the issue to the United Nations. Maintaining friendly relations with Johnson at least kept Mansfield in the loop—unlike Fulbright. The president occasionally consulted the majority leader on matters relating to the war. On January 6, 1967, for instance, when Hanoi appeared to soften its conditions for peace talks, Johnson sought Mansfield's counsel. The majority leader responded by urging Johnson to view the "signals" in the best possible light. In a memorandum following their phone conversation, Mansfield speculated that Hanoi's leaders were saying, among other things: "Of course, we are hurting and we want the bombing stopped. But let us be clear about one thing: we are not going to say 'Uncle' to you no matter what you do in the way of bombardment." Mansfield said that since it appeared the United States remained on a course leading to a massive, open-ended military commitment, the North Vietnamese could not conclude that Johnson truly wanted peace talks. "So long as that continues to be the case," Mansfield wrote, "it would not appear to me to be prudent to expect useful negotiations to come from the current Hanoi signals."[3]

Despite Mansfield's frustration over the stalemate, Hanoi's position appeared to be softening, if only slightly. In an interview with *New York Times* assistant managing editor Harrison Salisbury, North Vietnamese Premier Pham Van Dong had seemed to back off his insistence that the United States first agree to its "four-point program" that included an acknowledgment of the "independence, sovereignty, unity and territorial integrity of Vietnam and the withdrawal of United States forces" from the region. Although Pham added the additional demand that the United States permanently end the bombing, he told Salisbury that he considered the four points to be "merely truths," not "conditions" for negotiations.[4] "It is not yet clear whether they are signaling us on their terms for negotiations rather than carrying forward their old campaign to get us unconditionally to stand down bombing of the North," Johnson told Mansfield on January 9. "We don't rule out that there may be something serious here."[5]Indeed, the signal may have been serious, but not in the sense that Johnson hoped. "We felt we were nearing a point of victory," North Vietnamese diplomat

Nguyen Khac Huynh claimed thirty years later, "and we wanted to explore whether the U.S. might be ready to sit down and negotiate with us on the basis of the Four Points."[6]

Johnson's interest in the meaning of the potential peace feelers from North Vietnam did not weaken his determination to prosecute the war more vigorously. Although he had originally agreed with McNamara's plan to "stabilize" the air campaign in the north, in January 1967 Johnson finally acquiesced to his generals' demands for more bombing. Buoyed by reports from Lodge of "sensational military gains" and news from the CIA that chances of a communist military victory in South Vietnam "have vanished," Johnson continued to believe that he could gain more on the battlefield than at the bargaining table.[7]

"The adverse military tide has been reversed," Joint Chiefs Chairman Wheeler confidently told Johnson in mid-January after a trip to Vietnam. "We can win the war if we apply pressure upon the enemy relentlessly in the north and in the south."[8]

Said Rostow: "We have the initiative."[9]

Westmoreland, meanwhile, continued his relentless search-and-destroy missions against the Viet Cong. On January 9, thirty thousand American forces launched the largest such mission of the conflict on a Viet Cong stronghold north of Saigon. Although military leaders hailed "Operation Cedar Falls"—and its even larger successor in February, "Operation Junction City"—as turning points in the war, their successes were largely illusory.

As historian Glen Gendzel noted, Westmoreland's attrition strategy was destined for failure for two important reasons. First, in spite of the massive U.S. military force imposed on Vietnam, "Viet Cong and North Vietnamese forces could control the pace and intensity of battle and hence manage their own attrition." Not only did the enemy commence most of the major engagements, it retreated when losses began to mount and "sought sanctuary across borders that Americans could not cross and received supplies from foreign sources that Americans could not interdict." As one American general observed after the "Cedar Falls" operation: "It was a sheer physical impossibility to keep [the Viet Cong] from slipping away whenever he wished if he were in terrain with which he was familiar—generally the case." Furthermore, the North Vietnamese possessed an astounding ability to absorb significant losses and continue fighting. "You can kill off ten of my men for every one I kill of yours," a brazen Ho Chi Minh once told the French, "but even at those odds, you will lose and I will win." Eventually, as Gendzel noted, "attrition took a greater toll on American public opinion" than on North Vietnam's determination to win.[10]

Hopeful that intensified bombing and more determined search-and-destroy missions would eventually turn the tide in Vietnam, Johnson pressed ahead with the war—keeping one very skeptical eye on potential peace talks. "This is a time of testing for our nation," he told Congress in his January 10 State of the Union Address. Johnson said he wished he could report "that the conflict is almost over. This I cannot do. We face more cost, more loss, and more agony." He could not promise when the end would come. "Our adversary still believes, I think, tonight, that he can go on fighting longer than we can, and longer than we and our allies will be prepared to stand up and resist." Johnson, however, was confident of a military victory. "We have steadily frustrated [the enemy's] main forces," he said. "General Westmoreland reports that the enemy can no longer succeed on the battlefield." The nation would, Johnson insisted, "stand firm in Vietnam."[11]

American public opinion, however, was not as firm as Johnson imagined, especially after Salisbury's *New York Times* dispatches from Hanoi that reported the bombing of civilian targets, including residences, businesses, schools, cemeteries, and churches.[12] Salisbury's reports contradicted official government statements that acknowledged few, if any, civilian casualties and created a firestorm of public protest over what many concluded were administration deceptions about the true nature of the war. That firestorm, McNamara's spokesman later acknowledged, created a "national disaster."[13]

Salisbury's reporting also sparked a minor uprising on college campuses. More than 460 faculty members and administration officials at Yale University, including 5 deans and 15 department chairmen, signed a letter asking Johnson to unconditionally end the bombing. More than 100 members of the Dartmouth College faculty and administration, as well as 239 faculty members from Cornell University, sent similar letters. In late January, a Harvard philosophy professor announced that he had the signatures of 6,000 faculty members from 200 institutions in 37 states who opposed continued bombing of North Vietnam. The protests were not confined to college campuses. In early February, 174 corporate executives, including 89 presidents or board chairmen, petitioned Johnson to scale back the war, stop the bombing and negotiate with the communists, including the Viet Cong. "This war," they wrote, "is against our national interest and world interest."[14]

Meanwhile, Johnson and his advisors began to take the peace feelers more seriously. In early January, Rostow suggested that it was "conceivable, if not probable, that [the North Vietnamese] are trying to get out of the war but don't know how." Rostow speculated that they could not "openly negotiate with us" and might be looking to secure conditions for negotiations which "saves them minimum face with the NLF and the Chinese." Rostow thought the idea of secret communications with the North Vietnamese was worth pursuing. Through its Soviet embassy, the State Department asked North Vietnam's Moscow ambassador to explain the exact nature of Hanoi's new position. "The U.S. Government places the highest priority in finding a mutually agreeable, completely secure arrangement for exchanging communications with the government of the DRV about the possibilities of achieving a peaceful settlement of the Vietnamese dispute," the January 6 message read. "If the DRV is willing to explore such possibilities with us we will attempt to meet any such suggestions they have to offer regarding the time and place of such discussions and we will be prepared to receive such information directly from the North Vietnamese through diplomatic contacts at any capital where we both maintain posts or otherwise."

Back came the response from North Vietnam: What did the United States mean by "completely secure arrangements" and exactly what kind of settlement was contemplated? The State Department immediately responded with a list of possible items for discussion that included "reduction or cessation of hostilities" and the "recognition of the independence and territorial integrity of North and South Vietnam, or all of Vietnam if the people should choose reunification." North Vietnam's January 27 reply was less than encouraging: "The United States must end immediately and unconditionally the bombing and all other acts of war against the Democratic Republic of Vietnam." U.S. officials replied that they were prepared to stop the bombing "to create conditions conducive to the success of talks with the DRV." The bombing could be halted "as a prior and ostensibly unilateral action," the message said, but the United States first wanted a "private understanding" with the North Vietnamese that they were willing to respond with "similar acts of restraint."[15] In early February, into this sensitive exchange between Washington and Hanoi, stumbled the scrappy, charismatic freshman senator from New York, Robert F. Kennedy.

FROM VIRTUALLY THEIR FIRST moment in each other's presence, Kennedy and Johnson had despised each other. "I've never seen two human beings hate the way Lyndon Johnson and Bobby did," Johnson's Senate aide Bobby Baker recalled.[16] By 1967, the mutual hatred was legendary. A sensitive and notoriously insecure man, Johnson had long resented the Kennedys for their wealth, social status, Ivy League educations, and the way the national news media and the East Coast Establishment seemed captivated by the Kennedy mystique. As vice president,

Johnson had made his peace with John F. Kennedy, but he never forgave Robert for his attempt to bump him from the presidential ticket in 1960. As Kennedy's vice president, Johnson "blamed his fallen prestige on Bobby Kennedy," President Kennedy's aide, Kenneth O'Donnell observed. "He felt that Bobby had taken over his rightful position as the number two man in the government, which was true enough."[17] After he became president, Johnson deeply resented the way that Robert and his loyalists treated him as a pretender to the throne—as if Johnson were somehow responsible for Kennedy's death.

Johnson later claimed that he was mystified by his failure to "establish a close relationship" with Robert Kennedy. "Perhaps his political ambitions were part of the problem," Johnson mused in his memoirs. "Maybe it was just chemistry."[18] More likely, it was a severe clash of backgrounds, cultures, and styles that kept the two men constantly at odds. "Johnson was seventeen years older, six inches taller, expansive in manner, coarse in language, emotions near the surface," observed historian Arthur Schlesinger, who knew both men well. "It was southwestern exaggeration against Yankee understatement; frontier tall tales, marvelously but lengthily told, against laconic irony."[19]

Until the spring of 1965, Kennedy had publicly, if not enthusiastically, supported Johnson's Vietnam policies. For years, he had maintained that defending Southeast Asia against encroaching communism was in the U.S. national interest. Without U.S. troops to prop up the shaky regime in Saigon, Kennedy believed that the communists would quickly seize the entire country. But the bombing and the subsequent escalation of troops troubled him. While withdrawal was a bad option, escalation seemed equally inadvisable. As early as April 1965, Kennedy had privately urged Johnson to try a bombing halt and had publicly encouraged him to intensify efforts to convene peace talks with the North Vietnamese.

By early 1966, no longer in Johnson's cabinet, he had quietly but decisively drifted into the camp of the Senate doves. He now supported an end to the bombing and negotiations that included the NLF. Yet, except for some highly publicized remarks about the war in the spring of 1965, Kennedy had been missing in action on the Vietnam debate. One aide later explained that he became "quite reticent" about speaking out for fear that "Lyndon Johnson was so insane that he would literally prolong the war simply because Bobby Kennedy was against it."[20] It was more likely, however, that Kennedy's reticence was the product of his conflicting attitudes about the war. After all, he had strongly supported his brother's Vietnam policies, had backed Johnson's early Vietnam decisions, and had even volunteered to serve as Johnson's ambassador to South Vietnam. Kennedy brought plenty of baggage to the Vietnam debate and that, more than any concern about Johnson's retribution, delayed his emergence as a full-fledged, vocal opponent of the war. Critics were bound to ask how he could so strongly oppose policies that he had supported and helped to formulate.* Whatever the reason, by late 1966, Kennedy's silence on Vietnam was deafening. In October, the liberal journalist I. F. Stone suggested that "while others dodge the draft, Bobby dodges the war." Arriving on college campuses, Kennedy was sometimes greeted with signs that read, "Kennedy: Hawk, Dove or Chicken?"[21]

In late January, Kennedy—traveling throughout Europe on a working vacation and fact-finding tour—arrived in Paris for a series of routine meetings with French officials, including the director of Far Eastern affairs in the French Foreign Office, Étienne Manac'h. As one of France's most knowledgeable experts on Indochina, Manac'h explained to Kennedy that Hanoi had no confidence in U.S. overtures about peace talks. "Recent history has shown that, as soon as President Johnson makes offers of peace, there are parallel actions of war," Manac'h said. Nonetheless, Manac'h told Kennedy, Hanoi remained open to negotiations. But, he said, "the one indispensable condition" was a "cessation of bombing."

Kennedy's French was poor. John Gunther Dean, the U.S. embassy's expert on Vietnam who accompanied him to the meeting, had done his best to translate Manac'h's French into English. But what Kennedy heard Manac'h say, through Dean, was not all that profound. Considerably more sensitive to the nuances of diplomatic language and much more conversant in French, Dean heard something far more significant. Prior to this conversation, U.S. officials believed Hanoi would not negotiate until Washington agreed to its four negotiating points. What Dean heard from Manac'h was far different. Hanoi now seemed to be dropping its preconditions and signaling that a simple cessation of bombing might serve as a prelude to talks. Although Kennedy went on his way without attaching much significance to the conversation, Dean cabled Washington with news of the meeting. Yet, even Dean did not seem to completely comprehend the import of Manac'h's message. Instead of classifying his cable as "Top Secret" or "Eyes Only," Dean gave it the far lower classification of "Confidential." Labeled thusly, senior State Department officials were bound to ignore it when it arrived in Washington.

Unfortunately for Kennedy, the wrong lower-level department employee took notice of the cable and passed a copy not to Rusk but to Edward Weintal, the diplomatic correspondent for *Newsweek*. On Sunday, February 5, the day after Kennedy returned to the United States, the *New York Times* received an advance copy of the *Newsweek* edition containing

---

*Kennedy may also have been hesitant to openly criticize Johnson, who had enthusiastically campaigned on his behalf during his 1964 Senate race.

Weintal's mention of the cable. The *Times*, in turn, prepared a story for its Monday edition, detailing a "significant peace signal . . . unveiled for the benefit of Robert F. Kennedy for reasons best known to the enemy." The story about Kennedy's "peace feeler," which he had not thought significant enough to report to Johnson or the State Department, appeared on the front page of Monday's *Times*.

Johnson exploded when he saw the story. To Johnson and Rusk, the "peace feeler" was nothing of the sort. It was merely Kennedy's attempt to embarrass the White House and force its hand on negotiations at a time when Johnson and his military advisors were flush with new enthusiasm about their prospects for winning the war. Certain that Kennedy had leaked the story to *Newsweek*, Johnson summoned his rival to the White House on Monday afternoon to discuss the matter. "The President started right in by getting mad at me for leaking the story," Kennedy later told his aide, Frank Mankiewicz. Kennedy insisted he had not been the source and had, in fact, not believed that Manac'h was relaying a peace feeler. "I think the leak came from someone in your State Department," Kennedy said. "It's not *my* State Department, God damn it," Johnson replied. "It's *your* State Department."* Johnson insisted that negotiations would be fruitless. "Those guys are out of their minds," Kennedy later told Mankiewicz. "They think they're going to win a military victory in Vietnam by summer. They really believe it." Johnson had, indeed, told Kennedy that the war would likely be over by June or July. "I'll destroy you and every one of your dove friends in six months," Johnson predicted. "You'll be dead politically in six months."

After enduring Johnson's withering tirade for several minutes, Kennedy finally offered his own thoughts about the war. "Say that you'll stop the bombing if they'll come to the negotiating table," Kennedy advised, "and then you should be prepared to negotiate." Kennedy spelled out several possibilities for negotiation, including a cease-fire in stages, expansion of the International Control Commission to discourage further escalation, and extension of the four-day bombing pause that was planned for Tet, the Vietnamese New Year. Doing so, Kennedy said, would put the ball back in Hanoi's court. Failure to negotiate would then be rightly blamed on North Vietnam, not Washington. "There just isn't a chance in hell I will do that," Johnson disdainfully replied, "not the slightest chance." Johnson believed that it was Kennedy and the more vocal war opponents who were responsible for prolonging the war, which had resulted in the

---

*The exact meaning of this statement is unclear, although Johnson appeared to be suggesting that most of the appointed officials at the State Department were people originally installed during the Kennedy administration and, therefore, more loyal to Kennedy than Johnson.

BALSAM LAKE PUBLIC LIBRARY
404 Main St. • P.O. Box 340
Balsam Lake, WI 54810

deaths of American soldiers. Kennedy, he said, had blood on his hands. "Look, I don't have to take that from you," Kennedy said, standing up to leave. Suddenly, Johnson considered the political consequences of an angry Robert Kennedy storming from the Oval Office. Supported by Rostow and Under Secretary of State Nicholas Katzenbach, Johnson urged Kennedy to tell the waiting press corps that there had been no peace feeler. "I didn't know what the hell had been said to me," Kennedy replied. Johnson turned to Rostow and Katzenbach. "We never received any peace feelers at all," Johnson said to them. "Isn't that right?" Both men agreed.

At 6:00 P.M., Kennedy emerged from the Oval Office and informed reporters that "I did not bring home any feelers. . . . I never felt that I was the recipient of any peace feelers." Asked about his talks with foreign leaders, Kennedy said, "I really think that the person who really has to deal with these matters is the president of the United States." Straining his own credibility, Kennedy magnanimously added: "I think not only from his public statements but from my conversations he is dedicated to finding a peaceful solution . . . in Vietnam." Afterwards, a depressed Kennedy described the meeting to his staff. "Well, that wasn't a very pleasant meeting," he said. Later he told a friend that Johnson was "very abusive" and seemed "unstable." Kennedy confessed to thinking "that if he exploded like that with me, how could he ever negotiate with Hanoi."[22]

The result of the stormy meeting with Johnson was a newfound freedom for Bobby Kennedy. Kennedy no longer believed that he owed Johnson his loyalty or acquiescence on Vietnam. In a clumsy attempt to silence him, Johnson had actually driven Kennedy even deeper into the camp of the Senate's war opponents. In only a matter of months, in fact, Kennedy would emerge from his self-imposed silence to become one of the most persuasive and effective critics of the war.

It was a story that repeated itself time and again. Once more, Johnson had taken a bad situation and made it worse. His experience with Kennedy was not unlike his stormy encounters with other erstwhile supporters of his Vietnam policies. Johnson had also banished Fulbright, McGovern, Church, and others (and to some extent Mansfield).

Unable to accept their criticisms or suggestions as sincere policy disagreements, Johnson viewed virtually all dissent as personal disloyalty. To Johnson, the war became not America's war in Vietnam, but *Johnson's* war. Gradually, he had lost the ability to separate himself from the conflict. To oppose or question his policy was to oppose Johnson. To oppose Johnson was an unpatriotic act of betrayal, a decision to oppose "your country" and "the boys" who were fighting and dying in the jungles of South Vietnam. As historian Robert Dallek observed, Johnson's personalization of the war "crimped his capacity to make sensible, detached judgments on what now needed to be done."[23]

Instead of deftly courting his Senate critics—as he had done hundreds of times before on countless other issues—Johnson denounced them, ignored them, or banished them from his presence. When it came to Vietnam, the most effective legislative leader of the twentieth century simply squandered his enormous powers of persuasion. Had he drawn his critics more to his side, listened to them, engaged them in real discussions over the war, and sought to persuade them with honest arguments instead of misleading information, Johnson might have kept men like Fulbright and Kennedy close enough to temper their public criticisms of his policies. He might also have learned something.

As Kennedy had discovered on February 6, Johnson's position on negotiations with Hanoi was hardening. Assured by his advisors that the tide was turning in South Vietnam, Johnson now saw the pursuit of peace talks primarily as a public ploy to mitigate domestic and international opposition to his war policies. In early February, when British Prime Minister Harold Wilson offered to intervene with Soviet Premier Kosygin, Johnson went along with the plan, but only reluctantly. From beginning to end, he undermined the Wilson–Kosygin talks. First, he drastically reordered established U.S. policy concerning the bombing. Previously, the State Department had authorized Wilson to tell Kosygin that (1) Washington would be willing to stop the bombing, if North Vietnam would, in turn, (2) stop the infiltration of troops into South Vietnam. From that point, Johnson would also consider stabilizing the escalation of U.S. forces in South Vietnam.

But just as it appeared the Phase A-Phase B formula might lead to productive intervention on Kosygin's part, Johnson reversed course. At the last minute came word from Washington that the order had been reversed. The United States would stop the bombing only *after* North Vietnam stopped its infiltration. "In short, what we would be saying to the North Vietnamese," recalled NSC staff member Chester Cooper, in London to advise Wilson, "was that a bombing cessation would be directly conditional on their stopping infiltration—a proposition Hanoi had thrown back to us time and time again."*

Wilson was irate, but went ahead with the talks, hopeful there was

---

*Johnson put the same conditions directly to Ho in a February 8 letter. "I am prepared to order a cessation of bombing against your country and the stopping of further augmentation of U.S. forces in South Viet-Nam as soon as I am assured that infiltration into South Viet-Nam by land and by sea has stopped." Ho's response was predictable. "The U.S. Government has unleashed the war of aggression in Vietnam," he wrote on February 15. "If the U.S. Government really wants these talks, it must first of all stop unconditionally its bombing raids and all other acts of war against the Democratic Republic of Vietnam." (Gibbons, 4: 512-20).

something left to salvage. Finally, Wilson and Cooper offered Washington an alternative proposal—a North Vietnamese commitment to keep its forces north of the 17th Parallel in exchange for a U.S. extension of the Tet bombing pause. Worried that the North Vietnamese were taking advantage of the bombing pause to pour men and supplies down the Ho Chi Minh trail, Johnson gave Hanoi less than twelve hours to respond before the bombing resumed. "Several days, perhaps even a week, would be needed to close the loop," Cooper later complained. Johnson, however, was in no mood to give Wilson and Kosygin the time they needed. As Kosygin attempted to negotiate with Hanoi, time ran out. The bombing resumed on February 14. "I believe we got very near" a deal, a bitter Wilson later complained. "Then the whole thing was dashed away." Wilson believed another forty-eight hours might have produced an agreement that would have led to talks. Years later, Cooper was far less certain that more time would have produced results. "Wilson may have been right when he says two more days might have done the trick," Cooper observed. "But then there would still have been a very long way to go even if Hanoi had agreed to our proposal."[24]

On February 13, Johnson issued a disingenuous and misleading statement that characterized the Tet truce, which had been nothing more than a public relations device, as a period in which U.S. leaders had conducted a legitimate and determined search for peace. He had hoped, he said, that the truce "might lead to some abatement of hostilities and to moves toward peace. . . . Despite our efforts and those of third parties, no other response had yet come from Hanoi." Given Hanoi's unwillingness to negotiate, Johnson said he had "no alternative but to resume full-scale hostilities after the cease-fire." Despite having been unwilling to give Kosygin an additional two days to broker a deal with Hanoi, Johnson said: "But the door to peace is and will remain open and we are prepared at any time to go more than halfway to meet any equitable overture from the other side."[25]

The Wilson–Kosygin effort was not the only instance of the administration's ambivalence toward peace talks. In January, Harry Ashmore, director of the Center for the Study of Democratic Institutions and the former editor of the *Arkansas Gazette*, and William Baggs, editor of the *Miami News*, spent nine days in Hanoi. After a two-hour conversation with Ho Chi Minh, the journalists brought back what they considered an important message that Ho wanted relayed to the State Department. "We brought back from Ho Chi Minh the basic proposition that they would not hold a meeting as long as the bombing continued, but they would discuss the terms of a meeting in some fashion on the assumption that if there was agreement, the bombing would stop, that beyond that anything was open for discussion." According to Ashmore and Baggs, Ho accepted the proposition that "the separation of the country could continue for quite a long time as far as the North was concerned." While Ho would insist that the NLF be part of a coalition government, the two men reported that "they were fairly flexible as to how long the American withdrawal would take, et cetera."

After reporting the news of their discussion to officials at the State Department, Ashmore and Baggs heard nothing from the administration for a month. Perplexed, Ashmore finally spoke to Fulbright about the matter. When Fulbright broached the subject at a White House social function, Johnson was dismissive. "You know, Bill," Johnson said, "I can't see everybody that goes over there and talks to Ho Chi Minh." Within days, Johnson—having had second thoughts about the casual way he had disregarded Ashmore and Baggs—invited Fulbright and the two men to meet at the State Department with Katzenbach, Averell Harriman, and William Bundy. Fulbright arrived at the meeting in a foul mood, fully aware that Johnson had ordered the meeting merely to mollify the chairman of the Foreign Relations Committee, not to honestly search for ways to open negotiations with Ho Chi Minh. As Ashmore recalled:

> So Fulbright unloaded. He came in shooting. . . . He told them that he thought this meeting was a bunch of shit. What the hell were we wasting his time and our time and everybody else's time talking? "All you guys," he said, "are committed to a military settlement. You don't want to negotiate; you're not going to negotiate. You're bombing that little piss-ant country up there, and you think you can blow them up. You've been doing this all the time. It's a bunch of crap about wanting to negotiate."

The administration officials assured Fulbright they were serious about negotiations and drafted a conciliatory letter from Ashmore and Baggs to Ho. "There is no doubt in our minds that the American government genuinely seeks peace," the two men would tell the North Vietnamese leader. Only later did they learn that their letter was on its way to Ho about the same time as a hard-line letter from Johnson that demanded an end to North Vietnamese infiltration as a precondition for a U.S. bombing halt. Ashmore angrily concluded that he had been used and that Johnson's communication "was designed to be rejected."[26]

Johnson, meanwhile, pressed ahead with the war. "Hanoi is trying to force us to give up the bombing of North Vietnam," a defiant president told his advisors on February 8, as he vowed give not an inch to the enemy's conditions. "We will keep on until we get something from the North Vietnamese."[27] At a White House briefing for congressmen on February 15, Johnson was even more adamant about staying the course. In 1965, he said, the question had been to "surrender or advance . . . to haul the white flag, tear up *my commitment*" (emphasis added). He was not about to surrender, he insisted. "As long as I have anything to do with it, they're [U.S. troops] going to stay there until we have an honorable and just peace."[28]

THE PUBLIC RESPONSE to Johnson's February 13 statement, announcing resumption of the bombing, was mixed. The following day, two thousand five hundred angry antiwar demonstrators, mostly members of Women Strike for Peace (a group of mothers from Washington, Philadelphia, and New York) marched on the Pentagon and demanded a meeting with McNamara. A week later at Stanford University in California, one hundred students walked out as Humphrey began a speech on campus. As he left for his limousine, an agitated group of about three hundred students rushed the vice president, shouting, "Shame, Shame!" Some of the students banged on his limousine windows and doors as it pulled away, and nervous Secret Service agents ran ahead of the departing vehicle, shoving demonstrators out of the way. The incident left Humphrey visibly shaken. The following day, a group of antiwar students blockaded the president's office at the University of Wisconsin.[29]

That month, the war gained two new influential opponents, Republican Senator Jacob Javits of New York and the Reverend Martin Luther King Jr. For years, Javits had supported America's military role in Vietnam, believing—as he said after a visit to the country in early 1966—that "it is worthy of the cause of freedom." But after Javits learned how Johnson had sabotaged potential peace talks with Saigon in February, he changed his mind. "I concluded that the Vietnam War," Javits later said, "regardless of whether it was desirable for strategic or other reasons, had ceased to be a prudent effort." Javits now believed that Johnson regarded himself as "the savior of the world" who wanted to "earn a place in history by showing that American power could smash this Communist effort."[30]

As the country's preeminent civil rights leader, King and his views were not easily ignored at the White House. In the spring of 1966, King's Southern Christian Leadership Conference had strongly condemned American policy in Vietnam, lamenting that Johnson's "promises of the Great Society top the casualty list of the conflict" because the war had sapped resources from domestic programs. "The intense expectations and hopes of the neglected poor in the United States must be regarded as a priority more urgent than pursuit of a conflict so rapidly degenerating into a sordid military adventure," the SCLC said. Although his organization had been on record opposing the war, King, much like Robert Kennedy, had remained largely silent. By February, he was finally prepared to assume a higher profile. When he did, he called on civil rights and antiwar leaders to join forces against the conflict "until the very foundations of our country are shaken."[31]

Despite these and other portentous displays of public dissent—Kennedy would also publicly denounce the war a month later—national polls on the war in February gave Johnson some comfort and provided what appeared to be a road map for regaining his popularity with the public. Following the perceived successes of the U.S.-led "Operation Cedar Falls" and "Operation Junction City" offensives in January and February, public support for the renewed bombing campaign was strong. Sixty-seven percent of those surveyed by the Gallup polling organization in February said they favored continued bombing, while only 24 percent disapproved. Most of those who wanted more bombing favored it as the best way to bring about a quick end to the fighting. As another pollster, Louis Harris, observed at the time, "the dominant middle-ground opinion is now convinced that intensified military activity, including bombing of North Vietnam, represents the best chance to bring the Communists to the negotiating table."

The public's view of Johnson was another matter. In February, the president's overall approval rating was barely more positive than negative—46 percent approved of his job performance, while 37 percent disapproved. By March, another poll would reveal that national approval of his Vietnam leadership was sinking to an all-time low of 37 percent. Nearly a majority, 49 percent, disapproved of Johnson's handling of the war. As Harris noted, when Johnson "overplayed his hand by raising hopes for a settlement, he has been met with disillusionment among the people." Johnson's "real dilemma," Harris said, "rests squarely with his own behavior in handling the war. If he slips, if he raises false hopes, he will be in irreparable trouble."[32]

Somehow convinced that he had done as much as possible to lure Hanoi to the negotiating table and heartened by the polls, as well as the optimistic reports from his advisors of impending victory, Johnson only intensified the American military effort in Vietnam. On February 22, he approved an extensive program of new and expanded military operations in the north and south, including the bombing of industrial sites that had previously been on the military's restricted list. His goal, he told his advisors in early March, was to put "more pressure—every possible item of pressure on Vietnam."[33] As he told the Tennessee legislature on March 15, he wanted peace, but "the United States cannot and will not reduce its activities unless and until there is some reduction on the other side."[34] Observed James Reston of New York Times: "President Johnson looks more and more like a man who has decided to go for a military victory in Vietnam, and thinks he can make it."[35]

Congress, meanwhile, wrestled with how to pay for Johnson's ever-expanding war. In late January, citing the need to support "the nearly 500,000 American fighting men who are bravely defending the cause of freedom," Johnson asked Congress for an additional $12.2 billion in supplemental military appropriations for the 1967 fiscal year, as well as $21.9 billion to fight the war in fiscal 1968. [36] When Senate debate on the two requests began on February 23, Democrat Joseph Clark of Pennsylvania—joined by Morse—offered a nonbinding "sense-of-the-Congress" amendment that, absent a declaration of war, deplored use of any of the authorized funds for "military operations in or over North Vietnam or to increase the number of United States military personnel in South Vietnam above 500,000." Furthermore, Clark's amendment supported all efforts to "prevent an expansion of the war" and to end it "through a negotiated settlement."

Knowing that his amendment had virtually no chance of passage, Clark next introduced a more limited "fallback" amendment that affirmed congressional support for all U.S. armed forces fighting Vietnam; reiterated support for all efforts toward a peaceful conclusion of the war; and supported the Geneva Conference agreement of 1954 "as a basis for settlement of the Vietnam War."[37]

As floor manager of the appropriations measure, Russell opposed any amendment, even a nonbinding sense-of-Congress resolution, that attempted to tie the president's hands. "I do not think we will hasten the day of peace by stopping the bombing of North Vietnam or by deescalating the war," Russell told the Senate.[38]

Late into the debate, Clark gained an important ally when Mansfield offered a friendly amendment in hopes of making the measure more palatable. Like Clark's amendment, Mansfield's wording expressed support for the troops in Vietnam. But Mansfield's language craftily applauded Johnson for something he had not truly done. Mansfield urged senators to express support for the president's efforts "to prevent an expansion of the war in Vietnam and to bring that conflict to an end through a negotiated settlement which will preserve the honor of the United States . . . and allow the people of South Vietnam to determine the affairs of that nation in their own way." Left intact was Clark's provision calling for implementation of the 1954 Geneva accords provisions.

Mansfield's modification proved a masterstroke. Johnson and his supporters could not oppose it. After all, it applauded the president for his pursuit of peace, despite Mansfield's abundant embellishments. For most members of Congress, the amendment served as a perfect way to express their desire to end the war with "honor." War opponents like Morse, Kennedy, Church, Nelson, McGovern, Gore, and Gruening could rally around the amendment's provision calling for an end to the war, as well as its language about self-determination for the Vietnamese people and the resurrection of the Geneva Conference. On February 28, an unusual collection of the war's opponents and supporters came together to give their overwhelming approval to the nonbinding amendment in a 72–19 vote.* (Several days later, in approving Johnson's supplemental request, the House also adopted the Clark–Mansfield amendment by a wide margin.)

Although it had no force of law, historian William Conrad Gibbons cited the Clark–Mansfield amendment as a significant development. "It was the first statement by Congress," he observed, "about limiting the war and seeking a negotiated settlement." More important, Gibbons believed, the amendment "established the framework for the termination of the war and the withdrawal of American forces." It had also placed Congress on record in support of the 1954 Geneva agreements for the first time, and secured joint administration and congressional assent for complete self-determination for South Vietnam. It also opened the door for a possible coalition government that included the NLF. What the amendment did not do was reflect any significant erosion of support for Johnson's Vietnam policies in Congress. In the House, the supplemental appropriations passed, 385–11, while the Senate approved it, 77–3, with only Morse, Gruening, and Nelson in opposition. Outspoken war opponents like Church, Clark, Fulbright, Robert and Edward Kennedy, McCarthy, and McGovern all supported the bill.[39]

ON MARCH 2, Robert Kennedy finally emerged as a vocal and forceful opponent of U.S. policy in Vietnam. In a lengthy and substantive Senate speech, Kennedy accepted his portion of blame for the policy mistakes of the past. "Three presidents have taken action in Vietnam," Kennedy said to a gallery jammed with reporters and spectators. "As one who was involved in many of those decisions, I can testify that if fault is to be found or responsibility assessed, there is enough to go around for all—including myself." Although Kennedy was not directly critical of Johnson's policies in Vietnam—he rejected unilateral withdrawal—he made it abundantly clear that a wide chasm now separated him and the president over Vietnam. He implied that Johnson had not pursued peace talks vigorously enough. "If our enemy will not accept peace, it cannot come," he said. "Yet, we must also look to ourselves. We must have no doubt that it is not our acts or failures which bar the way; that there is nothing we have left undone

---

*Only nine conservative Southern Democrats, including Russell, and ten conservative Republicans opposed the amendment.

which we might have done." It would do little good, Kennedy said, if peace talks "are simply used to mask continued escalation of the war." Speaking passionately about the devastation the United States had caused in North Vietnam, Kennedy told his colleagues:

> All we say and all we do must be informed by our awareness that this hor- ror is partly our responsibility; not just a nation's responsibility, but yours and mine. It is we who live in abundance and send our young men to die. It is our chemicals that scorch the children and our bombs that level the villages. We are all participants. To know this and to feel the burden of this responsibility is not to ignore important interests, not to forget that freedom and security must, at times, be paid for in blood. Still even though we must know, as a nation, what it is necessary to do, we must also feel, as men, the anguish of what it is we are doing.

Kennedy was not without concrete proposals for extricating the nation from Vietnam. He divided his plan for ending the conflict into three parts. First, he would end the bombing. "Certainly the bombing of the north makes the war more costly and difficult and painful for North Vietnam," he said. "It is a harsh punishment indeed. But we are not in Vietnam to play the role of an avenging angel pouring death and destruction on the roads and factories and homes of a guilty land." By now, Kennedy said— and this was the heart of his speech—it should be clear "that the bombing of the north cannot bring an end to the war in the south; that, indeed, it may well be prolonging that war." Second, Kennedy said the United States should seek to secure agreements that neither side would "substantially increase the size of the war in South Vietnam—by infiltration or rein- forcement" while peace talks were ongoing. Finally, Kennedy suggested that with an "international presence" gradually replacing U.S. troops, "we should move toward a final settlement which allows all the major political elements" to determine the political fate of the nation.[40]

Johnson dismissed Kennedy's proposal out of hand, believing a bomb- ing pause would only give the North Vietnamese time to rebuild damaged facilities and resupply their allies in the south without fear of attack. But even if Johnson had thought his proposals sound, there was little chance that Robert Kennedy would ever get a fair hearing at the White House. What he saw as Kennedy's impertinence infuriated Johnson, as he did his best to deny him the headlines he knew the national press would afford his groundbreaking remarks. Beginning that morning, the president launched a flurry of public appearances in hopes that the news he created would overshadow Kennedy's speech. In one day's time, Johnson held an unscheduled press conference in which he announced that he and Soviet Premier Kosygin had agreed to talks on reducing nuclear weapons; delivered speeches at Howard University and the Office of Education; released the contents of a letter to Democratic Senator Henry Jackson of Washington that defended the bombing; sent public greetings to the people of Puerto Rico on the fiftieth anniversary of their status as U.S. citizens; announced he was inviting the nation's governors to the White House; and confirmed reports that his daughter Luci was pregnant. "The treatment given Kennedy," McGovern observed in the *New Republic* two weeks later, "recalled the president's sudden rush to Honolulu a year ago when Senator Fulbright's hearings were capturing mass television audiences and large news headlines."[41]

In his press conference that morning, Johnson implied strongly that demonstrators and dissident senators like Kennedy should mind their own business when it came to Vietnam. "I think that the American people should know that this is a question between their president, their country, their troops, and Mr. Ho Chi Minh and the troops that he is sending in from the North," Johnson said. "Everyone can take whatever side of the matter that he wants to."[42] That remark prompted the *Washington Post* to observe that Johnson seemed to believe that the war was "no more than a personal vendetta between Lyndon Johnson and Ho Chi Minh." As McGovern later said, Johnson had effectively declared: "Please keep out of this private affair between the White House and Ho Chi Minh!"[43]

McGovern and the *Post* were correct. Johnson *did* regard the war as a personal and political vendetta—especially when critics like Kennedy tried to meddle in his foreign policy. As much as Fulbright's dissent had angered Johnson, Kennedy's enraged him all the more. Fulbright threatened no direct political harm. But Johnson—beyond his intense personal dislike for Kennedy—believed the most recent critic of his war policies posed a serious and very real danger to his political future. That much seemed confirmed on March 15 when *Time*'s Hugh Sidey informed the White House that based on his recent conversation with Kennedy, the New York Democrat had all but "decided to get into the race" for president in 1968. In fact, Kennedy was nowhere near a decision about whether to run for president. But for Johnson, this was all the evidence he needed to conclude that Kennedy and his allies planned to use the Vietnam issue to destroy him politically.[44]

First, Johnson asked Russell to deliver a reply to Kennedy's speech. But Russell refused, telling Johnson he "saw nothing new in the speech or worthy of my involvement." So it was Rusk who eventually delivered the administration's response to Kennedy, insisting that "proposals substantially similar to those put forward by Senator Kennedy were explored prior to, during and since the Tet truce—all without result."[45] Johnson also directed Westmoreland to hold a press conference that highlighted the progress of the war, and especially the bombing's effectiveness.[46] Publicly, Johnson pretended ambivalence.*

Kennedy's speech was just one of several annoying outbursts of protest and dissent that a beleaguered Johnson endured with increasing frequency in the spring of 1967. By the end of 1966, more than 8,400 American soldiers had died in Vietnam. The fighting in 1967 would bring another 11,153 deaths. Those sobering numbers, combined with draft calls now exceeding 30,000 a month, gave many Americans, particularly college students, cause to worry about a never-ending expansion of the U.S. military commitment in Vietnam.[47] On April 15, antiwar rallies in New York and San Francisco attracted large crowds—200,000 in New York and 50,000 in San Francisco. "Stop the bombing, stop the bombing!" Martin Luther King intoned to a crowd that included scattered protesters carrying Viet Cong flags. Some chanted what would become familiar refrains at demonstrations across the country: "Hey, hey, LBJ, how many kids did you kill today?" and "Hell no, we won't go."[48]

The protests in the streets and on the Senate floor angered Johnson and troubled Westmoreland, who suggested in late April that domestic dissenters unwittingly assisted the North Vietnamese. At Johnson's insistence, Westmoreland had reluctantly traveled stateside for a series of speeches touting the success of the U.S. military effort. At a luncheon with the Associated Press in New York on April 24, the general reported that while "the military picture is favorable . . . the end is not in sight." Winning the conflict would require "putting maximum pressure on the enemy anywhere and everywhere we can. We will have to grind him down," he said. "In effect, we are fighting a war of attrition, and the only alternative is a war of annihilation."[49] The centerpiece of Westmoreland's speech was his criticism of the war's critics. From Hanoi's point of view, Westmoreland said, "the military war" was only a portion of the "protracted and carefully coordinated attack, waged in the international arena."

> Regrettably, I see signs of enemy success in the world arena which he cannot match on the battlefield. He does not understand that American democracy is founded on debate, and he sees every protest as evidence of crumbling morale and diminishing resolve. Thus, discouraged by repeated military defeats, but encouraged by what he believes to be popular opposition to our effort in Vietnam, he is determined to continue his

---

*Richard Nixon condemned Kennedy's speech, asserting that "it had the effect of prolonging the war by encouraging the enemy" (Schlesinger, *Robert Kennedy and His Times*, 774).

aggression from the north. This, inevitably will cost lives—American, Vietnamese, and those of our brave allies.[50]

Westmoreland declared that the Vietnamese Communists had "gained support," in the United States and abroad, that "gives [them] hope that [they] can win politically that which [they] cannot accomplish militarily." U.S. troops, he said, were "dismayed, and so am I, by recent unpatriotic acts here at home."[51] Westmoreland's indirect slap at war critics in the Senate and elsewhere incensed McGovern. The next day, backed by Fulbright, Church, Gruening, and Robert Kennedy, McGovern led an indignant Senate attack on the Johnson administration. "I do not blame General Westmoreland because he is obviously doing . . . exactly what he is told to do by his Commander-in-Chief, the President," McGovern said. "In trying to imply that it is American dissent which is causing the Vietnamese to continue the war, the Administration is only confessing the weakness of its own case by trying to silence its critics and confuse the American people." Westmoreland's speech had sapped McGovern of his last measure of forbearance toward Johnson. The deepening U.S. involvement in Vietnam, he said in his strongest language to date,

> represents the most tragic diplomatic and moral failure in our national experience. The mightiest nation in history . . . is, with allegedly good motives, devastating an impoverished little state and ravishing the people whose freedom we would protect. In the process we are sacrificing many of our bravest young men, wasting valuable resources and threatening the peace of the world. . . .
> We seem bent on saving the Vietnamese from Ho Chi Minh even if we have to kill them and demolish their country to do it. As the native people survey bombed-out villages, women and children burned by napalm, rice crops destroyed and cities overrun with our military personnel, they are doubtless saying secretly of the Viet Cong guerrillas and of the American forces, "A plague on both your houses."

Issuing nine "indictments" of American Vietnam policy, McGovern charged that "our Vietnam policymakers have distorted history to justify our intervention in a civil conflict supposedly to defend a free nation against external aggression from another nation." The reality, he said, was that "we are backing a dictatorial group in Saigon against a competing group backed by a dictatorial regime from the north." McGovern alleged that "our Vietnam policymakers are unwittingly advancing the cause of communism while seeking to contain it" and that while they called for negotiations, administration officials "are practicing military escalation and diplomatic rigidity." More serious was McGovern's charge that U.S. officials "have frequently misled the American public, the result being a serious loss of credibility for the U.S. government." And, he added, "we are creating at home a climate of intimidation designed to silence dissent and meaningful discussion of policy."[52]

Like McGovern, Fulbright was alarmed by Westmoreland's assault on the patriotism of the war's vocal opponents. He observed that while a "legitimate difference of opinion" existed over the "best course of action" in Vietnam, "it is quite clear, however, that there is a growing implication that dissent will lead to charges of disloyalty and muddleheadedness and then finally to implications of treason. This, I fear, is one of the last times that anybody will have courage to say anything else about the war."[53] Unbowed by the harsh criticism of his New York speech, Westmoreland addressed a joint session of Congress on April 28 and declared that "it is evident to me that [the North Vietnamese and the Viet Cong believe] our Achilles' heel is our resolve. Your continued strong support is necessary to our mission."[54]

Despite Westmoreland's assertions to Congress that "we will prevail," the conflict he led was actually badly stalemated. The bombs that wreaked such devastation and death on North Vietnam were not turning the tide. "The damage to economic and military targets," a CIA study concluded in May, "has not degraded North Vietnam's ability to support the war sufficiently to affect current levels of combat in the South."[55] Only the previous month, McNamara had created a minor controversy when he confessed as much to the Senate Armed Services Committee during its hearings on Johnson's supplemental appropriations request. The bombing had not "significantly reduced, nor any bombing that I could contemplate in the future would significantly reduce, the actual flow of men and materiel to the South," the Defense secretary told astonished committee members.[56] While the bombs and the American troops, supplies, equipment, and money had, indeed, prevented South Vietnam's collapse, they had done nothing to strengthen the South Vietnamese government and its military to the point that they could begin to withstand an American withdrawal.

Ample evidence of the stalemate was Westmoreland's appeal in late March for more than two hundred thousand additional troops, a request that was strongly supported by the Joint Chiefs and would have eventually raised, by 1969, the total number of U.S. forces in South Vietnam to more than six hundred fifty thousand. On April 27, Westmoreland told Johnson that without at least another one hundred thousand men "we will not be in danger of being defeated, but it will be nip and tuck to oppose the reinforcements the enemy is capable of providing. In the final analysis, we are fighting a war of attrition." Westmoreland was confident—mistakenly so—that the North Vietnamese had finally reached the "crossover point" at which their troops would not be replaced at the rate that American forces killed them.

Johnson was not so sure. "When we add divisions, can't the enemy add divisions?" he asked. "If so, where does it all end?" Westmoreland did not directly answer the question. Instead, he insisted that without at least one hundred thousand additional men "we would be setting up a meat grinder. We would do little better than hold our own." Unless something occurred to break the enemy's will, he told Johnson, "the war could go on for five years." But even with another one hundred thousand troops, Westmoreland predicted the war would last at least three more years.[57]

In addition to more troops, Westmoreland and the Joint Chiefs wanted Johnson's permission to expand the military campaign to include a possible amphibious invasion of North Vietnam, the bombing of the Hanoi–Haiphong area, and the mining of North Vietnamese ports. They also wanted to use South Vietnamese troops to destroy enemy sanctuaries in Cambodia and Laos, areas previously off limits to American troops for fear of sparking a wider war. "The bombing campaign is reaching the point," General Wheeler told Johnson, "where we will have struck all worthwhile fixed targets except the ports." In order to win the war, they argued that Johnson must pour more men into Vietnam. It was a major, mind-boggling expansion of the nation's commitment that would involve mobilizing the reserves and spending an *additional* $10 billion on the war each year.[58]

By now, however, Johnson's advisors were no longer united in pressing for a stronger military effort. Although Rusk, Rostow, and the Joint Chiefs generally favored giving Westmoreland what he said he needed, a dispirited McNamara had finally lost his nerve. To him, the cost of the war in lives and dollars had exceeded whatever legitimate objectives might be achieved in Southeast Asia. As he would tell Johnson in a May 18 memorandum: "There may be a limit beyond which Americans and much of the world will not permit the United States to go."[59]

CHAPTER 34

There Is a Rot in the Fabric

1967

Mᴄɴᴀᴍᴀʀᴀ ɴᴏᴡ ꜱᴀᴡ "ɴᴏ ᴀᴛᴛʀᴀᴄᴛɪᴠᴇ ᴄᴏᴜʀꜱᴇ ᴏꜰ ᴀᴄᴛɪᴏɴ" ɪɴ Vietnam. Hanoi would probably not negotiate until after the 1968 presidential elections. Continuing the current "moderate policy," he advised Johnson in his May 19, 1967, memorandum, might prevent a wider war, but it would not change Hanoi's mind and, therefore, would not satisfy the American people. Nor did it seem likely that more bombs and troops would influence Hanoi's position. An expanded bombing campaign would only mire the nation all the more deeply in Southeast Asia and might ultimately lead to a military confrontation with China or Russia. Since Johnson was "not willing to yield," McNamara added, he must now "choose among imperfect alternatives."

> The Vietnam war is unpopular in this country. It is becoming increasingly unpopular as it escalates—causing more American casualties, more fear of its growing into a wider war, more privation of the domestic sector, and more distress at the amount of suffering being visited on the noncombatants in Vietnam, South and North. Most Americans do not know how we got where we are, and most, without knowing why, but taking advantage of hindsight, are convinced that somehow we should not have gotten this deeply in. All want the war ended and expect their President to end it. Successfully. Or else.
>
> This state of mind in the U.S. generates impatience in the political structure of the United States. It unfortunately also generates patience in Hanoi. (It is commonly supposed that Hanoi will not give anything away pending the trial of the U.S. elections in November 1968.)

What McNamara called the "big war" between the U.S. and the North Vietnamese army was "going well," he told Johnson. "We staved off military defeat in 1965; we gained the military initiative in 1966," he said. Yet, throughout South Vietnam, he reported, "supplies continue to flow in ample quantities" to the Viet Cong and the enemy "retains the ability to initiate both large- and small-scale attacks." Johnson's "other war," the struggle to institute political and economic reforms, was a disaster. "Corruption is widespread," he wrote. "Real government control is confined to enclaves. There is a rot in the fabric."

As for Westmoreland's request for two hundred thousand more troops, McNamara told Johnson that he feared that its approval would "almost certainly set off bitter congressional debate and irresistible domestic pressures for stronger action outside South Vietnam." Proponents of a stronger U.S. effort would soon be insisting that Johnson "take the wraps off the men in the field." That would mean "more intense bombing—not only around-the-clock bombing of targets already authorized, but also bombing of strategic targets such as locks and dikes, mining of the harbors against Soviet and other ships." Pressing for a military victory would also involve "major ground actions in Laos, in Cambodia, and probably in North Vietnam." If the Chinese entered the war, he wrote, the pressure to employ nuclear, chemical, and bacteriological weapons would inevitably increase.

McNamara suggested that perhaps the American people were reaching the outer limits of what they would permit Johnson to do in Vietnam. "The picture of the world's greatest superpower killing or seriously injuring 1000 noncombatants a week, while trying to pound a tiny backward nation into submission on an issue whose merits are hotly disputed, is not a pretty one," he wrote, sounding strangely like Morse or McGovern. McNamara advised against granting Westmoreland's request and urged Johnson to limit the troop increase to thirty thousand and to bomb only the "funnel" area below the 20th Parallel where North Vietnamese men and supplies poured into South Vietnam. He advised Johnson to adopt a more flexible negotiating position on peace talks. Although he acknowledged that more militant voices would advise that "enough pressure" on the North Vietnamese "can pay off," McNamara told Johnson that "the war in Vietnam is acquiring a momentum of its own that must be stopped." Westmoreland's strategy, he warned, "could lead to a major national disaster."[1]

McNamara was not alone in advising Johnson against continued escalation. Backed by UN Ambassador Arthur Goldberg, Mansfield continued to push a reluctant president to seek a negotiated settlement at the United Nations. During a May 1 meeting with Johnson and his advisors, Mansfield bluntly insisted that the United States was "on a road to a direct confrontation with China." The bombing would only "continue to make Hanoi ever more heavily dependent on China."[2] While some of Johnson's advisors generally supported experimenting with Mansfield's UN proposal—if only to prove that the effort had been made—Johnson adamantly opposed the idea. "How would we look in the eyes of the world," seeking a peaceful solution before the United Nations? he asked. "Would it make us look weaker and more foolish than we are? Would we keep fighting while this was happening?"[3]

The next morning, on NBC's "Today" show, Mansfield warned that the "elements" for an "expanded, extended war" would soon fall into place "unless negotiations are brought about through some fashion." Just as he had warned Johnson the day before, Mansfield worried aloud about an expanded war with China. "If that occurs," Mansfield said, "it is my belief, my strong belief, that the differences which now exist between Moscow and Peking—and they are wide and deep and real—will be papered over temporarily, and that the two Socialist states will unite against us."[4]

Politically, Johnson saw nothing but disaster if he stopped the bombing to accelerate the search for a peaceful resolution. Conservative Republicans would attack him mercilessly, while Democrats like Russell, Stennis, Dodd, and Long might abandon him altogether. His only allies in the Senate would be men like Fulbright, Church, McGovern, Morse, and Mansfield—a prospect Johnson refused to countenance. Militarily, Johnson also saw little reason to seek a compromise. One reason was that, other than McNamara's bleak assessment of May 19, the outlook in Vietnam appeared largely positive. At least two CIA assessments that spring suggested that the bombing of North Vietnam was, indeed, reducing Hanoi's will to persist and that communist military strength was waning. Rostow also fed Johnson optimistic reports that affirmed the CIA assessment that "the bombing of the North is having its effect; and the Soviet Union may be reducing its aid to Hanoi." Besides Rostow, Westmoreland, and the CIA, another advisor who talked of future military gains was Robert Komer, the former Kennedy aide now in charge of the U.S. pacification effort in South Vietnam. "I believe that Westy [Westmoreland] *takes much too cautious a view of the momentum we have already achieved in Vietnam*," Komer reported in late April (empasis Komer's). "I believe that by this time next year we can break the back of the VC in South Vietnam."[5]

When Johnson consulted Russell on May 12, the Armed Services chairman strengthened Johnson's resolve against negotiations and advised a tougher military posture. "We've just got to finish it soon," Russell told Johnson over dinner, "because time is working against you both here and there." The only way to win the war, he insisted, was to invade North Vietnam, blockade North Vietnamese ports, and interdict all supply lines into South Vietnam. Even Johnson resisted this hawkish advice, telling Russell that escalation to that degree "would get us into [an expanded] war sooner than anything." Besides, the significant bombing targets had already been hit. "The only thing left," he told Russell, "is a power plant which is located a half mile from Ho's headquarters. Suppose we missed."[6]

Even Johnson knew that Russell's militant approach to Vietnam was increasingly out of step with much of the Senate. One example of the shifting Senate sands on Vietnam came three days later, on May 15, when an erstwhile supporter, Republican John Sherman Cooper of Kentucky—supported by Republicans George Aiken of Vermont, Milton Young of North Dakota, and Thruston Morton of Kentucky—called on Johnson to limit the bombing of North Vietnam. Known for his independence and his foreign policy expertise, Cooper—a former U.S. ambassador to India and Nepal—was well liked among his Senate colleagues. He was also growing disillusioned with the war.

As early as March 1965, Cooper had advocated unconditional negotiations with North Vietnam and suggested that the Johnson administration was applying unreasonable "prerequisites" to negotiations. A year later, Cooper had expressed doubts about a spiraling military escalation in Vietnam. "The war should be limited to its narrowest scope, to South Vietnam," he said, raising questions about the consequences of Johnson's bombing policy. Now, more than a year later, worried about a war involving China, Cooper wanted the bombing all but stopped. Should China enter the war, Cooper feared, all chances for a negotiated settlement would be lost. "The United States would not back down, and I do not believe it likely that Communist China, having made its decision to enter the war, would do so," he said. Overshadowing everything, Cooper feared, was "the dread possibility that the matching of power by power will lead relentlessly to a third world war." Therefore, Cooper outlined a plan similar to McNamara's and called on Johnson to limit the bombing "to infiltration routes near the demilitarized zone where men and supplies enter South Vietnam over the 17th Parallel, or through Laos." If the North Vietnamese responded positively to the curtailment of the bombing, then Cooper argued that "the bombing of North Vietnam in its totality could be suspended."

Congratulating Cooper on his speech, Aiken suggested that Johnson "ought to consider that, instead of escalating the war further, we should undertake to seek means of de-escalation. There is no question that the present policy of escalating higher and higher is bringing us pretty close to a world calamity." Democrat Eugene McCarthy agreed and told Cooper and Aiken that "it appears that we are on the threshold of a period in which demands for some kind of all-out and total war may be made." McCarthy worried that "once that demand is made, the disposition is for the country to make a kind of total response."[7] Frank Church also endorsed Cooper's plan and agreed that a larger war eventually involving China would result in a "tragedy, the costs of which are impossible to calculate and the end impossible to foresee."

Church, however, had also become concerned that perhaps, as Westmoreland and others suggested, his vocal dissent was playing into the Communists' hands. When the State Department suggested that he and other senators might wish to clarify their positions for Hanoi's consumption, Church was worried enough that he agreed and began preparing a statement. The product was "A Plea for Realism," a declaration making it clear that while dissident senators wanted a quick, peaceful end to the war, they were opposed to the unilateral withdrawal of U.S. forces. One of Church's aides later acknowledged that it was an opportunity for Church and other war opponents to take "a cheap hawk position."

The statement did have significant political appeal. Few Americans, even those who opposed Johnson's military policy, wanted the troops withdrawn unilaterally. But Church, Fulbright, McGovern, and others could not assume that their constituents fully understood the nuances of their finely crafted Vietnam positions. Church's statement was a perfect opportunity for these senators—many of whom would face reelection in 1968—to articulate a reasoned, moderate approach to Vietnam.

On May 17, 1967, sixteen senators signed the document, affirming that while "the conflict now appears to have reached an acute phase," Hanoi should have no "misconceptions" about where congressional war opponents stood.* While they supported a peaceful settlement, the senators said they remained "steadfastly opposed to any unilateral withdrawal of American troops from South Vietnam." The declaration, however, did not sit well with some of the war opponents. McCarthy dismissed it as a "retreat." To Gruening it was a "betrayal."[8]

Despite the moderate tone of their statement, despair and alarm was spreading like wildfire among the Senate's doves. "It is really a mystery to me," Fulbright wrote a friend in mid-June, "how the President can be persuaded that he is doing the Lord's work in continuing to slaughter those poor people in Vietnam, and to sacrifice so many of the best people in our country."[9]

McGovern worried that Johnson was inching toward "Armageddon." In May he called on Johnson to stop the bombing and open negotiations

---

*Senators signing the document were Democrats Church, Clark, Fulbright, McGovern, Morse, Nelson, Robert Kennedy, Frank Moss of Utah, E. L. Barlett of Alaska, Lee Metcalf of Montana, Vance Hartke of Indiana, Quentin Burdick of North Dakota, Stephen Young of Ohio, and Claiborne Pell of Rhode Island, and Republicans Cooper and Mark Hatfield of Oregon.

involving the Viet Cong with the North Vietnamese. At a conference on the war at Northern Illinois University, he decried the failure of the bombing to "halt or seriously check the flow of troops to the South" and insisted that in the south U.S. bombs had "killed or maimed countless numbers of innocent people and alienated others whose support we covet." To McGovern, the continued bombing represented "the greatest obstacle" to a peaceful settlement and posed the greatest risk of drawing China or the Soviets into the conflict.[10]

Morse worried that an "inexcusable, nationalistic ego" had overtaken the American people. "What is the matter with us?" he asked the Senate on May 15. "The American people constitute only six percent of the population of the world. Does the United States think it can maintain a permanent, dominating foothold anywhere on the land mass of Asia? If we think that, we should have our heads examined." Furthermore, Morse doubted that a bilateral settlement between the United States and the North Vietnamese would ever produce a lasting peace. Instead, like McGovern, he feared a global catastrophe. "I am willing to let history read the prediction I make this afternoon: a bilateral settlement of the war forced upon North Vietnam and the Viet Cong by the United States will eventually be one of the major causes of world war III."[11]

Perhaps among the most frustrated and conflicted by the stalemate in Vietnam was Mansfield, who still could not bring himself to publicly part ways with Johnson over Vietnam. Although he often disagreed with Johnson and freely shared his frustration over the course of the war in public forums, he would not issue a public demand that the president end the bombing as a first step toward a peaceful settlement of the war. As he told a constituent in June, "The president has the constitutional responsibility in our government for making the fundamental decisions of foreign policy."[12] As for the Senate, Mansfield believed that its role was "primarily that of advice and consent." Therefore, because he so often saw himself as merely Johnson's agent in the Senate, and not as an independent voice in the foreign policy field, Mansfield's dissent was largely repressed.

It was not that Mansfield refused to speak out. He simply would not challenge Johnson's policy in ways that might have made a difference. In one breath, Mansfield would express overwhelming frustration with the war's continuance, pride in the dissent of critics like Fulbright, McGovern and others. Yet, in the next breath, he would wax eloquent in sympathy for Johnson and his sincere desire for a peaceful settlement. "When I think of how much Vietnam is costing us in men and money," Mansfield told the Senate on May 15, "it makes me sad indeed to consider the tragedy which is the lot of this country in that far distant land." Minutes later, however, Mansfield defended the bombing and argued that if the North Vietnamese rejected peace talks after a unilateral American cease-fire "the reaction on our part, both government and people, would be far more bitter and far more dangerous than is the situation at the present time." Defending Johnson in the same speech, Mansfield asserted that "President Johnson's concern with this tragedy is as deep as yours or mine—deeper, perhaps, because he has to live with the responsibility 24 hours a day." He urged senators to give Johnson "our understanding, our prayers, and the support which can be given to him in good conscience." Yet in the same speech, Mansfield extolled the virtues of dissent and revealed something of the frustration and disillusionment building up inside him:

> If we remain silent, future generations will judge us as weaklings, as vacillators, and as cowards. It is to them, and to the generation now fighting in Vietnam, that we owe our chief responsibilities, because those who are over there are not there of their own free will. They are carrying out policy laid down here in Washington.

Noting that the United Nations had "been silent on Vietnam," Mansfield argued for the first time in public that "the time is long past due" for the international organization "to attempt to make some contribution to ending the conflict." While he held no illusions that the UN could broker a peace deal, Mansfield did believe it could serve "as a possible initiator of a face-to-face public confrontation of the conflicting views of the most relevant parties."[13]

Fulbright, Mansfield, McGovern, and others were not the only ones frustrated and fearful of where the war was taking the country. Johnson, increasingly angry with the antiwar protestors and a host of congressional critics, lashed out at the war's most outspoken opponents during a June 23 speech in Los Angeles, again suggesting that their attacks on his policies were undermining American troops in Vietnam. "Those who do not smell the powder or hear the blast of cannon," he said, "who enjoy the luxury and freedom of free speech and the right to exercise it most freely at times really do not understand the burdens that our Marines are carrying there tonight, who are dying for their country, or the burdens that their commanders are carrying, who wish they were home asleep in bed, or even carrying a placard of some kind." For those who urged him to negotiate, Johnson offered a Biblical admonition: "God, forgive them for they know not really what they do." No one, he insisted, "wants to avoid war more than I do. There is no human being in this world who wants peace in Vietnam . . . more than I do." He wanted to negotiate, he assured his audience. "But I just cannot negotiate with myself," he said. "And these protestors haven't been able to deliver Ho Chi Minh any place yet."[14]

It was not, however, the frustration of Johnson's urge to negotiate that kept the war going. Rather, it was Johnson's mistaken belief, bolstered by overly optimistic generals and advisors, that the war could be won. Although his aide Harry McPherson—one of the few advisors unafraid to challenge Johnson directly—warned him against "the hungry optimism that is a part of the military personality," Johnson eagerly gobbled up every shred of positive news out of Vietnam.[15] "The military situation has greatly improved," Ellsworth Bunker, the new American ambassador in Saigon, informed Johnson on June 28.[16] "There is not a military stalemate," a newly optimistic McNamara informed Johnson on July 12 after he and General Wheeler returned from Vietnam. Wheeler agreed. "There is no military stalemate," he echoed. "There has been an unbroken series of military successes. The enemy continues to be off balance." Not only that, but Wheeler assured Johnson that "there are no great military problems in sight."[17] Rostow was just as sanguine. "[The] Viet-Nam situation is not a stalemate," he assured Johnson in July. "We are moving slowly but steadily. [The] enemy is moving downhill, paying a heavy price for aggression."[18]

As biographer Robert Dallek astutely observed, "Johnson's aides were echoing his hopes," not engaging in objective analysis.[19] Wrote the *New York Times*' correspondent in Saigon, R. W. Apple, on August 6: "'Stalemate' is a fighting word in Washington. President Johnson rejects it as a description of the situation. But it is the word used by almost all Americans here, except the top officials, to characterize what is happening." As one anonymous military commander told Apple: "I've chased main-force [communist] units all over the country, and the impact was zilch: It meant nothing to the people." In the words of an unnamed Washington official interviewed by the *Times*: "We are on the way to a policy of occupation in this country. We have found that unless we put enormous numbers of our own troops into a very small area the thing doesn't go."[20] Although Johnson read Apple's story, it did not appear to raise doubts in his mind about the quality or accuracy of official reports out of Vietnam. Instead, he exploded in anger and told aides that Apple was "a Communist" and "a threat to national security."[21]

As evidenced by his reaction to the *Times* story, Johnson was, indeed, deluding himself. He was not so delusional, however, about the perils of negative public opinion about the war. During a meeting with McNamara and Wheeler, after their July mission to Vietnam, Johnson observed that "the U.S. people do think, perhaps, that the war cannot be won." He indicated that a collapse of public confidence in his Vietnam policy frightened him more than any difficulties he had with South Vietnamese leaders. It was just this political concern that prevented Johnson—despite his ostensible determination to press for a military victory—from giving Westmoreland the troops he requested. Doing so would require calling up the reserves and alarming the public to a degree Johnson would not consider. Therefore, while he acknowledged that Westmoreland needed more troops, he urged his advisors to "shave it the best we can."[22]

At a news conference the day after his meeting with McNamara and Wheeler, Johnson—now joined by Westmoreland—refused to disclose the extent of Westmoreland's massive troop request. "We are in accord," Wheeler said disingenuously, suggesting that Johnson had agreed to supply Westmoreland with all the troops he needed. In fact, the opposite was true. The president would soon approve only forty-five thousand of the two hundred thousand additional troops Westmoreland wanted. Johnson, however, encouraged his advisors to show nothing but solidarity before the press. "The troops that General Westmoreland needs and requests, *as we feel it necessary*, will be supplied," Johnson said (Emphasis added). Added Westmoreland: "I agree, Mr. President." Adding to the deception—only this time it was also self-deception—Johnson insisted that "we are generally pleased with the progress we have made militarily. We are very sure that we are on the right track." Westmoreland agreed. "The statement that we are in a stalemate is complete fiction," he declared. "It is completely unrealistic. During the past year tremendous progress has been made."[23]

All of the public and private ebullience emanating from the White House did not sway Fulbright. When he arrived at the White House on July 25 for a meeting of Senate committee chairs, he was in no mood, like Mansfield so often was, to offer Johnson soothing words about the weight of his responsibilities. When it came Fulbright's turn to speak, he was blunt. "Mr. President, what you really need to do is to stop the war," he told Johnson. "That will solve all your problems." Fulbright told Johnson he detected an attitude shift in the Senate over Vietnam. Democrat Frank Lausche of Ohio, a former supporter of Johnson's Vietnam policies, had changed his mind on the bombing, Fulbright said. "The Vietnam War is a hopeless adventure," Fulbright continued. "Vietnam is ruining our domestic and our foreign policy," he insisted, adding that "for the first time in 20 years I may vote against foreign assistance and may try to bottle the whole bill up in the committee."

For the moment, Johnson held his volcanic temper. Congress could "tell the rest of the world to go to hell," he said. "That's their prerogative." Striving not to respond directly to Fulbright, Johnson did not defend his foreign aid bill. Finally, he said, "I understand all of you feel like you are under the gun when you are down here [at the White House], at least according to Bill Fulbright."

"Well," Fulbright said, "my position is that Vietnam is central to the whole problem. We need a new look. The effects of Vietnam are hurting the budget and foreign relations generally."

"Bill," Johnson said, "everybody doesn't have a blind spot like you do. You say don't bomb North Vietnam on just about everything. I don't have the simple solution you have. We haven't delivered Ho yet. Everything which has been proposed to Ho has been rejected." Regarding the bombing, Johnson said he would not "tell our men in the field to put their right hands behind their backs and fight only with their left." Westmoreland had assured him that the bombing was "our offensive weapon," Johnson said, and it would severely hinder his ability to fight the war "if we were to stop it." Knowing that every man in the room was well aware of Fulbright's central role in passage of the Gulf of Tonkin Resolution, Johnson added: "If you want me to get out of Vietnam, then you have the prerogative of taking the resolution under which we are out there now. You can repeal it tomorrow. You can tell the troops to come home. You can tell General Westmoreland that he doesn't know what he is doing." A sullen Fulbright said nothing. Mansfield, ever the peacemaker, quickly changed the subject.[24]

Despite Johnson's strong assurances to the contrary, a majority of Americans appeared to sense the truth about Vietnam. By the end of July, Johnson's public approval ratings—which had temporarily improved in early 1967—had slumped again. Fifty-two percent of those polled disapproved of Johnson's handling of the war, compared to 34 percent who thought the United States was making progress in Vietnam.[25] Although Wheeler and Westmoreland tried to persuade the American people that the press was giving them inaccurate, biased information, much of the public had finally lost faith in the optimistic assessments that military officials had fed them since the early days of the Kennedy administration.[26]

By July, that dispirited attitude toward Vietnam finally claimed Mansfield. Although Johnson continued to consult him on Vietnam, Mansfield's pointed remarks of July 11 revealed a new level of exasperation, particularly for someone of his courtliness and rectitude. Although it is unclear exactly what prompted him to speak out so forcefully, the disgust he expressed over the administration's "progress" reports from Vietnam provides a clue. While he told the Senate he could not challenge the accuracy of the information Johnson received from his advisors, he said that "it must be asked in all frankness what is meant by 'progress' toward our 'objectives' in the context of the present situation in Vietnam?" Such progress reports, he said, would be much more credible "had they not been heard from American leaders in Vietnam at many other times, stretching years into the past." In fact, Mansfield added, "reports of progress are strewn, like burned-out tanks, all along the road which had led this nation ever more deeply into Vietnam and Southeast Asia during the past decade and a half." Quick as always to note that he was not leveling personal criticism at Johnson,

McNamara, or the nation's military leaders, Mansfield made it clear that
he no longer believed their decisions regarding Vietnam were sound:

> We can put another 100,000 men into Vietnam or, I suppose, 200,000 or
> even more; there are a lot of young Americans, even though the supply is
> not unlimited. Yes, we can mine the harbor at Haiphong as we have
> already mined the rivers of North Vietnam; we have most effective mines
> and the best sowing techniques. Yes, we can level the city of Hanoi as we
> have leveled the power plants; we have the ordnance, as the circumlocu-
> tion for bombs now puts it.
>
> It is to be hoped, however, that before we embark on this course of
> expansion toward total war in Vietnam, we will pause for a long and sober
> think. Before we take another significant step deeper into Vietnam, it is
> to be hoped that we will have asked ourselves at what point we intend to
> increase taxes, apply the wage and price controls, tighten the draft exemp-
> tions, call up the Reserves, and make the countless other adjustments in
> our national life which are implicit in further expansions of the American
> involvement. . . .
>
> We have the power . . . to bomb the Vietnamese back into the Stone
> Age. And if that power is unsheathed once in error, we had better be pre-
> pared to move back into the caves, along with the Vietnamese, and the
> rest of the world.

Urging "the greatest restraint in any further increases in the American involvement," Mansfield endorsed John Sherman Cooper's plan to
limit the bombing to that of supporting interdiction of infiltration across
the 17th Parallel and urged Johnson to pursue McNamara's proposal for
constructing a "defensive barrier" south of demilitarized zone from the
Thai/Laotian border to the South China Sea. He continued pressing Johnson to submit the Vietnam conflict to the United Nations. But he stopped
short of advocating withdrawal from Vietnam. "We cannot and should not
withdraw," he said, adding that "we should not and, I hope, will not enlarge
the war in Vietnam against the north."[27]

As Mansfield grew more disillusioned, Fulbright became more determined to address what he regarded as one of the underlying causes of the
U.S. role in Vietnam—the unrestrained freedom with which presidents
often involved the nation's military in foreign conflicts. Vietnam was a
prime example; but so was the Congo, where Johnson—without consulting Congress—had recently dispatched military aircraft and 150 military
personnel, ostensibly to protect U.S. citizens from harm during a rebellion that threatened the government of Joseph Mobutu. Alarmed to learn
that U.S. aircraft were being used to ferry Mobutu's troops around the
country, Russell and a host of liberals and conservatives of both parties
strongly criticized the administration and deplored military intervention

in a country "where we have no commitment or any vital interest whatever." The U.S. role in Vietnam, he noted, had begun with the same kind of limited commitment.

Sensing a potential ally, Fulbright quickly sought Russell's support for a resolution limiting the president's power to make national commitments without legislative approval. On July 31, six days after his White House confrontation with Johnson—during which the president challenged Fulbright to repeal the Gulf of Tonkin Resolution—Fulbright introduced a nonbinding "sense-of-Congress" resolution that declared it unconstitutional for the executive branch to enter into foreign commitments without legislative action. The resolution, he told the Senate, "represents a conservative position, which seeks to recover in some degree the constitutional role of the Senate in the making of foreign policy—a role, which the Senate itself has permitted to be obscured and diminished over the years." Russell immediately offered his support. "I know of nothing that is more in need of clarification," he said, "than the present state of the alleged commitment of the United States all over the world."

Fulbright was in no hurry for a vote on his resolution because he viewed it not so much as a legislative instrument to chasten Johnson, but a public relations effort to educate the Senate and the public. Fulbright was annoyed that many supporters of the war, including Johnson, often justified their positions by citing "commitments" made by Truman, Eisenhower, and Kennedy. As he told the Foreign Relations Committee later in the year, "This business of these people going around and making fine speeches and then coming and saying it is a commitment, I just want to get it out of their minds that it is a commitment."

For five days, beginning on August 16, the Foreign Relations Committee conducted hearings on Fulbright's resolution. The highlight came on August 17 with the testimony of Nicholas Katzenbach, the former attorney general and now under secretary of state, whose impassioned defense of the Gulf of Tonkin Resolution helped to further erode congressional support for the administration's Vietnam policy. Katzenbach said he opposed Fulbright's resolution because it sought to involve Congress in decisions that were the president's primary responsibility. Asked by Fulbright about the congressional power to declare war, Katzenbach argued that the phrase "to declare war" was outmoded, especially in relation to Vietnam, where the nation had limited objectives. In such cases, the president merely had a duty to allow Congress to "express its views." The Gulf of Tonkin Resolution, he explained, was such an expression by Congress. It "fully fulfill[ed] the obligation of the Executive in a situation of this kind to participate with the Congress to give the Congress a full and effective voice, the *functional equivalent*" of "declaring war" (Emphasis added).

"You haven't requested and you don't intend to request a declaration of war, as I understand it," Fulbright asked Katzenbach.

"That is correct, Mr. Chairman," Katzenbach responded testily. He added, "Didn't that [Gulf of Tonkin] resolution authorize the president to use the armed forces of the United States in whatever way was necessary? Didn't it? What could a declaration of war have done that would have given the president more authority and a clear voice of the Congress of the United States than that did?" Indeed, Katzenbach had a point. The resolution that Fulbright supported and Congress had approved had affirmed, in unmistakable language, Johnson's authority "to take *all necessary measures* to repel any armed attack against the forces of the United States and to *prevent further aggression*" (Emphasis added).

But Fulbright gave no ground. The resolution was no substitute for a war declaration, especially, he added, after "having been made under conditions of great emergency. It wasn't a deliberate decision by the Congress to wage war in that full-fledged sense against a foreign government." (Fulbright might also have added that, regardless of its intent or practical implications, the administration had obtained the resolution under false or highly suspicious circumstances.) Gore agreed with Fulbright. "I did not vote for the resolution," he told Katzenbach, "with any understanding that it was tantamount to a declaration of war."[28]

In a press conference the following day, Johnson made it clear that, whatever the congressional intent behind the resolution, he did not need congressional authorization to wage war in Vietnam. Furthermore, he said, "I believe that every congressman and most of the senators knew what that resolution said. That resolution authorized the president—and expressed the Congress' willingness to go along with the president—to do whatever was necessary to deter aggression." Any time Congress wished to withdraw its approval for his actions in Vietnam, Johnson said, "the machinery is there." All Congress had to do was repeal the resolution.[29]

Katzenbach's unfortunate description of the Gulf of Tonkin Resolution as the "functional equivalent" of a war declaration proved difficult for many senators to accept—especially those, like Russell, who were increasingly concerned about the diminution of the Senate's role in foreign policy. As William Conrad Gibbons noted, Katzenbach's words "emphasized the attitude that because a declaration of war was anachronistic and outmoded, Congress' constitutional war power was obsolete and superfluous." What constitutional power Congress had left "could and should be carried out through some mechanism by which Congress could 'participate' in decisions involving the use of the Armed Forces, thus leaving the Executive with the power to determine what the role of Congress should and would be." As Morse had complained, Katzenbach's testimony was nothing more than an attempt "to rationalize a government by executive supremacy." More than one senator took Johnson's remarks about Congress' right to unilaterally repeal the resolution as a taunting dare.

On August 19, when the Associated Press surveyed the Senate, forty-five of the eighty-four senators (twenty-six Democrats and nineteen Republicans) who were willing express a view now reported a lack of confidence in Johnson's Vietnam policies. Although some of the disapproving senators wanted Johnson to prosecute the war more vigorously, the wire service reported that "the substance of the comments of individual senators indicates there is such widespread dissatisfaction with the way the war is going that it would be risky for the president to seek any formal endorsement of his position, as he did in the Gulf of Tonkin Resolution in August, 1964."[30]

Johnson may not have needed congressional authorization to wage the war in Vietnam, but he knew all too well that he could not unilaterally raise the revenue required to continue the conflict. Adding to his woes in mid-1967 was an anticipated federal budget deficit of $28 billion—twice what administration officials had predicted only six months earlier. By August, Johnson reluctantly asked Congress to enact a temporary 10 percent surcharge on corporate and individual taxpayers to offset the war's rising costs. "There are times in a nation's life when its armies must be equipped and fielded, and the nation's business must go on," Johnson said on August 3. "For America that time is now." Johnson also announced that he planned to increase the number of U.S. troops in South Vietnam by forty-five thousand to five hundred twenty-five thousand.[31]

Congressional reaction to Johnson's tax proposal was far from encouraging. As Rusk later told Johnson, "the tax bill made many doves"[32]—but not because members of Congress no longer wished to pay for the war. Instead, much of the waning enthusiasm for Vietnam was tied directly to the difficult and painful domestic spending choices that the nation's expensive venture in Vietnam forced upon them. As Johnson had always predicted, the rising costs in Vietnam posed a far greater danger to his domestic initiatives. Given a choice, he knew that members of Congress would cut domestic spending. Thus, raising taxes was the only way around this dilemma. Instead of choosing between guns and butter, a tax increase would give Johnson both. Unfortunately for Johnson, the chairmen of the tax writing committees in both houses—Wilbur Mills of Arkansas in the House and Russell Long of Louisiana in the Senate—both had grave reservations about a tax increase. Both doubted that their House and Senate colleagues would ever approve the plan. Supported by Republican leaders in the House, Mills insisted on deep cuts in welfare spending. To Johnson's dismay, Mills would bottle up the tax request in his committee for the rest of 1967.[33]

WITH EACH SUCCESSIVE troop increase, McGovern grew more despondent. The additional forty-five thousand troops, he told the Senate on August 11, was a "turning point" that would take the country "more deeply into war."[34]

Republicans Cooper and Clifford Case of New Jersey agreed. The North Vietnamese were not fighting hard enough to defend their country. Case was particularly alarmed that Johnson, ignoring public opinion, planned to press ahead with further escalation. "Is the Johnson administration blind to the signs of growing public unrest about Vietnam?" Case asked the Senate. "Is it deaf to the continuing advice of members of Congress?"[35]

Among the Senate's Republicans, Johnson's decision to commit more troops to Vietnam particularly outraged New York's Jacob Javits, who reassessed his support for military appropriations to continue fighting the war. Like many members of Congress, Javits had not allowed his opposition to U.S. Vietnam policy—first expressed in February—to influence his vote on appropriations. But by August, after Johnson's decision to deploy more troops and amidst the continuing reports of military stalemate and the skyrocketing costs of the war, Javits had changed his mind.

Given that Johnson believed he needed no congressional authorization to continue the war, the New York Republican now concluded that limiting appropriations was the only way for Congress to impose its will. "We cannot go on endorsing the administration's policy in the Vietnam War by voting successive supplemental appropriations without limitation," he told the Senate on August 11. He believed that "the country is deeply troubled and highly dubious about this war. The momentum of the past decade in Vietnam is threatening to push us into a new and disastrous commitment." When he finished, Democrat Joseph Clark of Pennsylvania cheerfully welcomed his New York colleague "to the ranks of the 'nervous Nellies' and the 'doves.' "[36]

The next month brought an even more disturbing defection from the ranks of Johnson's supporters when Representative Thomas P. "Tip" O'Neill of Massachusetts, a prominent House Democrat, changed course and informed his constituents in a newsletter that the war in Vietnam was unwinnable. It was time to get out, he said. When Johnson learned about O'Neill's new position, he flew into a rage and regarded O'Neill's statement as a personal affront. "I can understand these assholes over on the [House] floor opposing the war," Johnson told O'Neill. "But Jesus, you, my friend, to come out against *me* [emphasis added], I can't believe it." Johnson only calmed down when O'Neill persuaded him that his decision was based on an honest assessment of the American military posture in Vietnam, and not on political expediency.[37]

Unbowed by the hemorrhaging support for his policies in the Senate, a troubled and emotionally exhausted Johnson pressed his advisors to try harder. He wanted more bombing. Although McNamara advised him in early August that intensified air strikes around Hanoi would "compound the problems with the doves," Johnson worried that "it doesn't look as though we have escalated enough to win." More concerned about congressional critics who believed he was not pushing hard enough in Vietnam, Johnson told McNamara, "We've got to do something to win. We aren't doing much now."[38]

Yet nothing he did pleased either side. Military leaders and conservatives in Congress knew that forty-five thousand additional troops would not change the course of the conflict, while Johnson's dovish congressional critics regarded the deployment as further evidence of a tragic, open-ended commitment. Johnson wanted more out of his advisors. "Search for imaginative ideas to put pressure to bring this war to a conclusion," he ordered on September 12.[39] But as long as U.S. military leaders persisted in fighting a conventional war, a victory—as defined by Johnson and his generals—was virtually impossible.[40]

All the talk about limiting the bombing alarmed Democrat John Stennis of Mississippi and other members of the Armed Services Committee—a panel far more hawkish on Vietnam than the Foreign Relations Committee. Through his Pentagon contacts, Stennis—a loyal supporter of the nation's armed forces—learned of McNamara's recommendation to confine the bombing's objectives. He quickly scheduled closed-doors hearings of his Preparedness Investigating subcommittee and summoned McNamara and a host of top military commanders, including all five of the Joint Chiefs. For the first time, the deep philosophical divide that separated Johnson's military and civilian advisors would be exposed to astonished lawmakers. During six days of hearings, a parade of distinguished military leaders informed trusting subcommittee members that the bombing was an important, indispensable, and highly effective element of the strategy for fighting the war in the south. Absent the bombing, they told the subcommittee, North Vietnam would have doubled the size of its troops in the south. Stopping or limiting the bombing now would be "disaster." The answer was not to limit the bombing, but to step it up, they said. The bombing had not achieved all of its goals simply because civilian leaders like McNamara had imposed too many restrictions. A pliant Stennis made it quite clear where he stood on the question. "In my opinion," he told his colleagues, "this is no time to reduce or diminish the pressure or to throw away any military advantage."

On August 25, the subcommittee gave McNamara his chance to respond. In anguish over the consequences of exposing a congressional committee to the hard truth he had delivered to Johnson, McNamara finally resolved to speak his mind. While he did not characterize the bombing as unsuccessful, he did insist that it had "always been considered a supplement to and not a substitute for an effective counterinsurgency land and air campaign in South Vietnam." The "discriminating use of air power," he said, was working to reduce the infiltration of men and supplies. "A less discriminating bombing campaign against North Vietnam would, in my opinion, do no more," he said. "We have no reason to believe it would break the will of the North Vietnamese people or sway the purpose of their leaders." McNamara noted that he and Johnson had approved 302 of the 359 bombing targets (84 percent) recommended by the Joint Chiefs. Many of the unapproved sites, he added, were minor civilian targets, militarily insignificant or too close to the Chinese border.

Those senators not skeptical were downright hostile. "Mr. Secretary," Republican Strom Thurmond of South Carolina said, "I am terribly disappointed with your statement. I think it is a statement of placating the Communists. It is a statement of no-win." Members of Stennis's subcommittee were not the only ones shocked by McNamara's testimony. Johnson was furious and summoned his Defense secretary to the White House that afternoon. In a tense confrontation, the president upbraided McNamara for exposing the split between Johnson's civilian and military advisors. That evening, the Joint Chiefs—reportedly "stunned" by McNamara's testimony—met at the Pentagon and vowed to resign en masse the next morning. McNamara, they believed, had betrayed them and had put forth a bad-faith defense of a fatally flawed strategy. Backing off the bombing would cost American lives, they believed, concluding that their only option was resignation. By the next morning, however, Chairman Wheeler thought better of the plan and dissuaded his colleagues.

The damage, however, was done. Johnson's Vietnam policy was in disarray and now that fact was apparent to the Senate Armed Services Committee, which eagerly accepted the generals' hawkish testimony as gospel. The bombing campaign directed by Johnson and his civilian advisors "has not done the job," a unanimous subcommittee report concluded. "What is needed now is the hard decision to do whatever is necessary! [sic] take the risks that have to be taken, and apply the force that is required to see the job through." Ground troops could no longer be expected to perform their duties without a more vigorous air war in North Vietnam. "This," the subcommittee said, "requires closing the port of Haiphong, isolating it from the rest of the country, striking all meaningful targets with a military significance, and increasing the interdiction of the lines of communication from Red China." Once more, conflicting military and political interests swirled around Johnson, squeezing him mercilessly. In the words of the *Pentagon Papers'* authors, the president was again "caught unhappily in the middle, satisfying neither his critics of the right nor the left."[41] Lyndon Johnson was a miserable man.

ALTHOUGH THE BOMBS continued dropping, Johnson's men had not completely given up on a peaceful settlement. In mid-June Henry Kissinger, then a Harvard government professor, had reported a possible channel to North Vietnam through two Frenchmen who claimed friendships with Ho Chi Minh and Premier Pham Van Dong. According to Kissinger, who had been in Paris for a conference, the two men were willing to serve as intermediaries between Hanoi and Washington in hopes of exploring possible terms for peace talks. Encouraged that Hanoi's position on talks might be softening, McNamara urged Johnson to take the possible opening and told him on August 8 that it was "the most interesting message on the matter of negotiations, which we have ever had." Johnson and Rusk were skeptical. The president refused to consider any reduction or pause in the bombing "until we have their assurance they will not take advantage of the bombing halt."[42] Reluctantly, however, Johnson had allowed McNamara to pursue the lead. Later that month, Kissinger delivered the following message from Johnson to the French conduits:

> The United States is willing to stop the aerial and naval bombardment of North Vietnam if this will lead promptly to productive discussions between representatives of the U.S. and DRV looking toward a resolution of the issues between them. We would assume that, while discussions proceed either with public knowledge or secretly, the DRV would not take advantage of the bombing cessation or limitation. Any such move on their part would obviously be inconsistent with the movement toward resolution of the issues between the U.S. and the DRV which the negotiations are intended to achieve.[43]

In the meantime, Johnson agreed to temporarily suspend all bombing in a 10-mile radius around Hanoi. But that decision, combined with his message to Ho and Pham, did nothing to bring Hanoi closer to the negotiating table. Unmoved by the moratorium on air strikes near its capital, North Vietnam demanded an end to all bombing. Although he remained skeptical that anything would come of the effort, Johnson agreed with Kissinger's advice to regard the messages out of Hanoi "as [the] first step in a complicated bargaining process."[44] At a September 12 luncheon meeting with his advisors, Johnson suggested that Washington simplify its message to Hanoi. Why not quit explaining so much and simply declare that "we will stop bombing if a conference is arranged and if it will lead to fruitful discussions?"[45] The following day, another message went out to Hanoi: the U.S. proposal "contained neither conditions nor threats and should not be rejected on these grounds." The United States merely assumed that North Vietnam would be willing to participate in "productive discussions leading to peace when there was a cessation of aerial and naval bombardment."[46]

Hanoi responded to Johnson's message with stony silence. Meanwhile, the Joint Chiefs—edgy and angry over the pause—pushed Johnson to begin bombing Hanoi. But McNamara and Katzenbach pleaded for more time. Seeing a glimmer of hope in the communications between Hanoi and Washington, Katzenbach urged Johnson to continue the bombing pause around Hanoi. "It's worth doing," he said. Johnson, however, sympathized with the Joint Chiefs, who were urging him to destroy several targets near Hanoi before imposing a more permanent pause. "A pause won't change the political situation," Johnson said. "It will give them an answer, though, that we are prepared to go the last mile. But," he then added, "I do want to get all those targets before a pause."

Doubting the targets were as important as the Joint Chiefs maintained, McNamara responded that "we are not going to be able to have a pause without the military saying there are still targets to be hit." Furthermore, as he reminded Johnson, the administration was also fighting a war of domestic public relations. "The serious problem is that you must show the American people that you are willing to walk that last mile," he said. But Johnson doubted the whole exercise with Hanoi would lead to anything productive. "I think they are playing us for suckers," he complained. "They have no more intention of talking than we have of surrendering. In my judgment, everything you hit is important. It makes them hurt more."[47]

Reluctantly, however, Johnson accepted the advice. Three days later—heeding McNamara's counsel to issue a strong statement about his willingness to end the bombing in exchange for productive, good-faith negotiations—Johnson went public with his new terms for negotiations. The United States would halt the bombing, he said to a conference of state lawmakers in San Antonio on September 29, "when this will lead promptly to productive discussions." But so far, he added, "Hanoi has not accepted any of these proposals."[48]

Nor would they. Hanoi deeply distrusted Johnson—and, perhaps, for good reason. In August, prior to imposing the moratorium on bombing in the 10-mile perimeter around Hanoi, the United States had subjected the North Vietnamese capital to heavy air strikes, leading communist leaders to conclude that Johnson hoped to bomb them into submitting to talks. Furthermore, as Hanoi recognized, the restrictions on bombing around the capital did not constitute a real reduction in the number of American bombs falling on North Vietnam. The U.S. military had simply diverted its bombers to Haiphong, Cam Pha, and other North Vietnamese cities. By the time Johnson articulated his "San Antonio Formula," Hanoi's reluctance to proceed with the talks had only intensified, although concerns about "conditions" in the formula had replaced the August complaints about the coercion they said the American bombs represented. On October 3 Hanoi appeared to reject Johnson's bid when the North Vietnamese Communist Party newspaper, *Nham Dan*, characterized the San Antonio Formula as a "faked desire for peace" and "sheer deception."[49]

Despite this public rebuff, Johnson sometimes appeared genuinely eager for talks that might end the conflict. Discussing the issue with his advisors on October 3, he asked about the impact on the war if he did not seek reelection. He speculated that a national election with the war as the dominant issue might give the next president a clear mandate to keep fighting or to negotiate a settlement.

"You must not go down," Rusk implored. "You are the commander-in-chief, and we are in a war. This would have a very serious effect on the country."

"What I am asking," Johnson said, "is what would this do to the war?"

"I think they [Hanoi] would think they have got it made," Rusk answered.

McNamara agreed. "I do think they would not negotiate under any circumstances and they would wait for the 1968 elections," he said.[50]

Johnson was torn between thinking that the bombing was effective militarily and his knowledge that it was a major obstacle to peace talks. "I know this bombing must be hurting them," he told McNamara, Rusk, and Rostow on October 4. "Despite any reports to the contrary, I can feel it in my bones." In a very hawkish mood on this day, Johnson insisted that "we need to pour the steel on. Let's hit them every day and go every place except Hanoi."[51] The following day, however, Johnson returned to the pursuit of talks and told McNamara and Rusk that "I'm for stopping the bombing" as long as Hanoi did not take advantage of the pause to reinforce its troops in the south.[52]

Hanoi would not be coming to the negotiating table any time soon. On October 20, after interviewing Pham Van Dong, communist journalist Wilfred Burchette reported that "there is no possibility of any talks or even contacts between Hanoi and the U.S. government unless the bombardment and other acts of war against North Vietnam are definitively halted." The conditions each side imposed on the other were impossible. Politically and militarily, Johnson could not afford to be seen capitulating to Hanoi's demand for an unconditional bombing halt. Yet what Johnson considered a wise strategy designed to protect American troops during the talks, Hanoi viewed as unacceptable conditions. By mid-October, it was becoming clear that there would be no meeting of the minds. North Vietnam's rejection of the talks, Rusk told reporters on October 12, meant that "Hanoi has not abandoned its effort to seize South Vietnam by force."[53]

As the fighting and the bombing continued, the protests grew larger and more impassioned. A series of antiwar rallies around the country culminated on October 21 with a huge protest at the Lincoln Memorial in which more than one hundred thousand protesters demanded an end to the bombing, withdrawal of American forces from Vietnam, and immediate peace talks with the North Vietnamese. The huge demonstration, the largest antiwar rally in Washington to date, alarmed and angered Johnson, who believed the Communists controlled the protesters.[54] "We've almost lost the war in the last two months in the court of public opinion," Johnson groused to his advisors on October 23. "These demonstrators and others are trying to show that we need somebody else to take over this country." Yet despite his frustrating and fruitless effort to convene a peace conference, Johnson knew the whole exercise had not been for naught. His very public bid for talks would persuade some Americans that he sincerely hoped for a peaceful end to the fighting. "People who want us to stop the bombing should know all we have gone through in this exchange," Johnson said.[55]

Even so, Johnson was more frustrated and felt increasingly hemmed in by a restless public—popular support for his Vietnam policies plunged to 28 percent in early October[56]—by his belligerent military advisors and a divided Congress that assailed him from both sides of the issue. He saw no option but to pour on the bombs. "If we cannot get negotiations," he told McNamara and Rusk, "why don't we hit all the military targets short of provoking Russia and China?" But Johnson knew he could not escalate the bombing without persuading Congress and the public of his dogged pursuit of peace. "We've got to do something about public opinion," he said. "We must show the American people we have tried and failed after going the very last mile."[57]

On October 23, when Johnson consulted a group of Republican and Democratic congressional leaders, everyone but Mansfield urged him to abandon the idea of a bombing pause as an inducement to peace talks. "If we stop the bombing," Hickenlooper told Johnson, "we will surrender in effect." Dirksen agreed. "I am still in your corner," he said. Russell Long, one of Johnson's most bellicose Senate supporters, not only opposed a halt, he urged Johnson to "step it up. Anytime you want to lose a war you can. If we lose Vietnam, we lose influence in this entire area of the world. We must make a stand here."

Only Mansfield spoke against the bombing. "We could bomb North

Vietnam into the Stone Age if we wanted to," he told Johnson, adding that the objective of bombing—interdiction of men and supplies from the north—had failed. Mansfield, instead, urged Johnson to continue pursuing peace talks through an innovative idea, first proposed by John Sherman Cooper, to drive a wedge between the Viet Cong and the North Vietnamese. "We should think of contact between the NLF and Saigon," he advised, "to try to cut them out from North Vietnam." Johnson, however, made it clear that he no longer entertained the idea of a bombing pause. "I am not prepared to act simply on hope," he said. The North Vietnamese, he concluded, "are not seriously interested in meaningful peace negotiations at this time."[58]

Prodded by his bellicose military advisors and their hawkish supporters in Congress, and stymied by Hanoi's seeming hostility to negotiations, Johnson saw no alternative to more bombs. Although he asserted that he was willing to stop the attacks "if they [the North Vietnamese] will talk promptly and not take advantage of us," Johnson and his advisors resigned themselves to more war. But the problem of public perception remained. As Harry McPherson told Johnson in an October 27 memorandum, the bombing "has just about become *the war* in the eyes of the press and the minds of the public" (emphasis McPherson's). And it was hurting Johnson politically. "It appears to some people that you are escalating the air war, and running a kind of numbers game on remaining targets, solely in order to quiet or escape criticism from right-wing Senators and Congressmen and your own military leaders." Another damaging perception, McPherson told Johnson, was the notion that "there is a vindictiveness in prosecution of the air war. America and her President are angry that this little two-bit country will not come to terms, despite the bombardment."[59]

There was a tragic degree of truth to McPherson's blunt assessment. Fearful as always of being the president who allowed another Asian domino to fall, Johnson was allowing his generals and strident members of Congress like John Stennis to guide his Vietnam policy. But even as he marched to the drumbeats of the hawks, he knew he could not lightly dismiss those advisors, like McNamara and McPherson, who urged him to alter course. "Continuation of our present course of action," McNamara warned Johnson on November 1, "would be dangerous, costly in lives, and unsatisfactory to the American people." McNamara urged Johnson to consider a sustained bombing pause and announce that he would send no more American troops to Vietnam.[60]

Hoping to settle the ongoing dispute between McNamara and his military advisors, Johnson called together a group of military and national security experts that included Dean Acheson, George Ball, Omar Bradley, McGeorge Bundy, Clark Clifford, Abe Fortas, Henry Cabot Lodge, and

Maxwell Taylor. On the morning of November 2, the president met with the group in the White House Cabinet Room. Johnson posed a series of questions. What could he be doing differently in Vietnam? Should he stop the bombing of the north? How should he pursue negotiations, if at all? Should the United States withdraw? What could his administration do to unite the country and better communicate its policies to the people?

Because of the one-sided way that military and White House officials had briefed the group the night before, Johnson was almost guaranteed to get the advice he wanted. The "Wise Men," as they were later called, had not been told of McNamara's recommendations about the bombing. Johnson withheld a Navy report concluding that a military victory in Vietnam was unlikely, as well as a CIA analysis judging the risks of U.S. withdrawal from Vietnam as minimal. "The Wise Men had no clue that all this was going on," McNamara later said. "Unsurprisingly, in the absence of new information, their preconceived notions about the military and political situation in South Vietnam determined their answers."[61] Nonetheless, the group's collective, if uninformed advice seriously undercut McNamara's credibility. Instead of stopping the bombing, Acheson recommended that Johnson simply "play it down." By now, Johnson doubted that he had much control over the public's impression of the bombing campaign. "I'm like the steering wheel of a car without any control," he complained. "The Senate won't let us play down the bombing issue." Acheson sympathized. "The cross you have to bear is a lousy Senate Foreign Relations Committee," he said. "You have a dilettante fool at the head of the committee." Virtually every member of the group echoed Acheson's basic conclusion: "We certainly should not get out of Vietnam." Even Ball, once Johnson's house dove and now an investment banker in New York, urged his former boss to hang tough, although he did urge him to adopt Cooper's recommendation to focus the bombing on interdiction of men and supplies near the Demilitarized Zone.[62]

Having stacked the deck so that he would receive the advice he wanted, Johnson was free to ignore McNamara's recommendation. The bombing continued—although there was little left in the way of strategic targets. By the end of October, American bombers had hit virtually every military and economic site that the Joint Chiefs and the Stennis subcommittee had recommended—except for the port of Haiphong and a few other targets that they feared might provoke China or the Soviet Union. "Except for simply keeping it up," the authors of the *Pentagon Papers* observed, "almost everything bombing could do to pressure the NVN had been done." By early December, the bombing in North and South Vietnam exceeded the 1.5 million tons that U.S. forces dropped in the entire European Theater during World War II. Of the 1.6 million tons of American bombs dropped in the Vietnam War thus far, 864,000 tons had been dumped on North Vietnam—an amount that exceeded the tonnage dropped during the Korean War or in the Pacific Theater during World War II.[63] Yet the North Vietnamese and the Viet Cong continued fighting. A confidential Defense Department report confirmed McNamara's judgment about the bombing campaign's ineffectiveness: "As of October 1967, the U.S. bombing of North Vietnam has had no measurable effect on Hanoi's ability to mount and support military operations in the South."[64*]

Mansfield hoped that diplomacy would accomplish what the bombing clearly could not. Throughout the year, he had pushed his proposal to request UN intervention on Vietnam. In October—heartened by the knowledge that McNamara no longer supported a military solution to the conflict—Mansfield launched another attempt to get the UN involved. On October 9, he sent letters to Rusk, UN Ambassador Arthur Goldberg, and each of his Senate colleagues soliciting support for a nonbinding resolution expressing the "sense of the Senate" that Johnson should "consider taking the appropriate initiative" to bring the subject of Vietnam before the UN Security Council. "In my judgment," he told his colleagues, "much might be gained and nothing is to be lost" in attempting to get the UN involved. Mansfield quickly discovered that his resolution had more appeal than he might have imagined. In a matter of weeks, thirty-seven senators had enlisted as co-sponsors (and he would eventually gain thirteen more).[65]

Ostensibly, Johnson supported Mansfield's proposal. It was Johnson who had originally suggested the UN initiative when he told Mansfield in August that he should recruit Senator John Sherman Cooper, who had been ambassador to India, to help him secure the support of India's UN diplomats. Johnson, in fact, had no real enthusiasm for the UN proposal. He saw it merely as a way to keep Mansfield occupied and to distract him

---

*Why was the air war so ineffective? As military historian Colonel Herbert Y. Schandler, writing in Robert McNamara's *Argument Without End* observed, North Vietnam was far from the ideal place to wage a successful air campaign. It was an agriculturally based country, with a poor transportation system and virtually no industry. In other words, few strategic targets were available to military planners from the beginning. Schandler noted that when the Pentagon first selected bombing targets, the Joint Chiefs of Staff "found only eight industrial installations worth listing on a par with airfields, military supply dumps, barracks complexes, port facilities, bridges, and oil tanks. Even by the end of 1965, after the JCS had lowered the standards and more than doubled the number of targets, the list included only twenty-four industrial installations, eighteen of which were power plants that were used mainly for such ordinary uses as lighting streets and pumping water" (McNamara, *Argument Without End*, 343–44).

from further criticism of his Vietnam policy. Mansfield undoubtedly discovered the truth in late October, when Goldberg told him that the growing Senate momentum for Mansfield's resolution had Johnson "as nervous as a kitten." Mansfield was puzzled. He could not imagine why Johnson was nervous. "In effect," he told Goldberg, "this is his idea."

Mansfield blamed Rusk for Johnson's antipathy toward the UN proposal. In truth, however, the blame belonged to Johnson and his fear that once the conflict reached the United Nations, the United States might lose its grip on the war. When Mansfield phoned Johnson on November 1 to discuss the resolution, Fulbright's Senate Foreign Relations Committee had already conducted two days of hearings on the measure, something that undoubtedly annoyed the president. Indeed, Mansfield found Johnson to be "a little excited. He talked loudly and seemed to be disturbed about what the Senate was attempting to do and the consequences which might well be attributed to him should the . . . resolution fail." Yet Mansfield resisted the urge to "recall to him that it was he Johnson who started this discussion about going to the UN."[66]

Johnson, however, could do nothing but allow the measure to run its course. On November 21, the Foreign Relations Committee unanimously reported Mansfield's resolution to the Senate. It was time, Mansfield announced, for the administration to "energetically and earnestly" urge the UN to take up the Vietnam issue, "not in whispers in the corridors but in open view and with firm voice." For those UN members who had openly criticized the U.S. role in Vietnam, Mansfield had tough words. It was time, he said, "that the nations which talk a great deal ought to put their money where their words are, face up to their responsibility and undertake in their own way to do what they can" to bring about a peaceful settlement. "Win, lose or draw, if we only received our own vote, we better go in and find out where the members of the Security Council stand, and let the world know." But Mansfield knew that Johnson would have the final say regarding the United Nations. "He can pursue the sense of the resolution or not as he sees fit," Mansfield said, giving Johnson, as always, wide berth. "It remains his responsibility . . . to decide if, when and how to act."[67]

On November 30, the Senate endorsed Mansfield's resolution in an 82–0 vote. Afterwards, Mansfield observed that the Senate had spoken "with a loud and clear voice on the issue—one whose purpose and intention cannot be misunderstood." Johnson, however, was less than impressed with the Senate vote. Despite his early, insincere support for Mansfield's initiative, he had no plans to ask for the UN's involvement. UN officials, fully aware that Johnson refused to stop the bombing without the requisite assurances from North Vietnam, demonstrated little interest in getting involved.[68]

If Mansfield was bitter about Johnson's refusal to seek UN intervention, he did not reveal it publicly. But the overwhelming Senate support for his resolution did serve to place more distance between Johnson and his usually loyal majority leader. But nothing symbolized the growing gulf between the two men more than Mansfield's public support for direct negotiations between South Vietnam and the NLF. "Perhaps negotiation between Saigon and the Viet Cong might prove fruitful," Mansfield said in the Senate on November 20, noting that the bombing of the north had proved a failure. "The main area of conflict is not North Vietnam, but South Vietnam."[69]

Despite his policy differences with Johnson, Mansfield still saw himself as a loyal soldier, especially when it came to keeping the peace between Fulbright's committee and the administration. In late November, when Fulbright, Gore, and Morse were demanding that Rusk testify about the war in a public session of the Foreign Relations Committee, White House officials—fearing a televised thrashing of the secretary like the one in early 1966—turned to Mansfield to keep Gore and Fulbright in line. "This is really a procedural matter," Harry McPherson told Mansfield, distinguishing between Mansfield's opposition to the war and his fundamental sense of fairness toward Rusk and Johnson. "The president knows how you feel about Vietnam. But he hopes you can support him on the procedural question." Presented this way, the pliant Mansfield could hardly refuse to uphold Johnson's hand. Reluctantly, he agreed to help shield his president from congressional wrath. "All right," he told McPherson, "I'll try to support him. I think he's wrong, but I'll try to support him. But you ought to be aware that this could develop into a Constitutional crisis."[70] For the next three and a half months, Mansfield would mediate the dispute between Rusk and the Foreign Relations Committee. Rusk would not testify before the committee in open session until March 11, 1968.[71]

"MY NOVEMBER 1 MEMORANDUM did do one thing," McNamara later observed. "It raised the tension between two men who loved and respected each other—Lyndon Johnson and me—to the breaking point."[72] By October, Johnson had grown deeply concerned about the physical health and emotional stability of his defense secretary—and not simply because McNamara had recommended an end to the bombing. Johnson and others had begun to notice the toll that the Defense job exacted on McNamara. "Bob McNamara was hanging on by his fingernails," recalled While House aide John Roche, one of Johnson's Vietnam advisors. From his observations of McNamara, Roche concluded that he suffered from a "very serious psychological condition."[73] George Christian, Johnson's press secretary, remembered McNamara as "emotionally wrought up."[74] Others recalled that Johnson mentioned to more than one person his concern that McNamara might become another James Forrestal (Truman's Defense secretary who had committed suicide).[75]

Although McNamara denied that he was near physical or emotional collapse, those around him recognized a man near the breaking point. Even McNamara acknowledged that "I was indeed feeling stress." Worse, he recognized that "I was at loggerheads with the president of the United States; I was not getting answers to my questions; and I was tense as hell."[76] In November, when McNamara informed Johnson that he was interested in leaving the Defense Department to become president of the World Bank, Johnson quickly engineered the job switch and on November 29 announced McNamara's departure.

Having rejected much of McNamara's advice, Johnson was now determined to disprove his Defense secretary's bleak assessment of the war. In that endeavor Humphrey became a willing accomplice. In November 1967, Humphrey approached his second vice presidential trip to Asia with characteristic enthusiasm and vigor. What he saw in Saigon, however, rattled his faith in the U.S. mission. "Americanization of the war was total," he later wrote. "We had taken over the economy, we had taken over the fighting, we had taken over South Vietnam." Humphrey said that he began to understand "that the American people would not stand for this kind of involvement much longer."

Humphrey's mission, however, was to represent Johnson at the inauguration of newly elected President Nguyen Van Thieu. But he failed to convince the new South Vietnamese leader that the American commitment to South Vietnam was not, despite all appearances, open-ended. American public opinion was shifting, he informed the new president, and that meant Congress would eventually withdraw its support for the war. If Thieu wanted continued American support, Humphrey said, then he must institute significant political and economic reforms and force South Vietnam's military to assume more responsibility for the fighting.

Smoking a cigarette, Thieu listened impassively. "No," he told Humphrey, "you will be here for a long time. We are aware of what you say, but we realize that your support will have to continue, and perhaps increase for the next five or six years."

"Perhaps I haven't made myself clear," Humphrey said, repeating his message more firmly and in greater detail. "What we are doing to Vietnamese society is not healthy for either you or us."

Again, Thieu ignored Humphrey's message. "Oh, yes . . . yes," he said, dismissively.[77]

Despite his serious concerns about the direction of the war, in public at least, Humphrey played the role Johnson dictated. He was unflinching in his enthusiasm for the U.S. military effort in Vietnam. At the U.S. embassy, he delivered an embarrassingly optimistic speech to a group of American officials. "I believe that Vietnam will be marked as the place where the family of man has gained the time it needed to finally break through to a new era of hope and human development and justice. This is the chance we have. This is our great adventure—and a wonderful one it is!"[78]

When Humphrey returned to Washington on November 8, Johnson's aides whisked him back to the White House to brief a gathering of Johnson's cabinet and the bipartisan congressional leaders. Although he had reportedly told a friend that "America is throwing lives and money down a corrupt rat hole," Humphrey now flawlessly—and shamelessly—played the role of hawk. He was "impressed" and "encouraged" by what he saw. Asked by Fulbright exactly who the enemy was in Vietnam, the North Vietnamese or the Chinese, an emotional Humphrey replied that the South Vietnamese "know who the enemy is. Those boys out there who are being shot and maimed don't have any difficulty recognizing who the enemy is. For them it is the North Vietnamese and the Viet Cong." Humphrey's briefing was persuasive. Even Mansfield said he was "mildly" encouraged.[79]

Privately, Humphrey told Johnson that while he supported the American effort to stop communist aggression in Southeast Asia, the time had arrived to begin directing U.S. efforts toward helping the South Vietnamese government assume a greater role in the country's defense. "The critical task of months ahead," he wrote in a memorandum to Johnson, "will be to help the Thieu–Ky government build a base of popular support throughout the country and follow through on the establishment of a constructive relationship with the new parliament. Unless this is achieved, there is danger of a fallback into chaos and decomposition." Humphrey urged Johnson to abandon Westmoreland's "search and destroy" missions for a more defensive, less destructive "clear and hold" strategy. He advocated phasing down the U.S. combat presence and advised reforms in the country's economic aid program, including cutting the U.S. aid mission in half.[80]

Humphrey was not alone in recognizing the need to accelerate an end to American involvement in Vietnam—or at least the perception of American dominance. Despite his public assurances of continued military success, Lyndon Johnson could no longer avoid the bitter truth about the American effort. Throughout November, he was increasingly impatient. He pushed his military and civilian advisors to do everything possible to bring the war to a speedy conclusion. At a November 4 meeting, he demanded to know how the military proposed to do a better job of winning the war in the south. "We've been on dead center for the last year," he complained. Johnson also wondered if the bombing of small tire factories, steel mills, and airfields—relatively insignificant sites—was "worth all the hell we are catching here."[81]

On November 21, he told Westmoreland, Wheeler, and McNamara that "the clock is ticking." Torn between his need to placate his generals and satisfy a restless public and Congress, Johnson told the generals to quickly "get the targets you have to hit. The bombing arouses so much opposition in this country." But McNamara, still on the job until March 1968, continued arguing against the strikes. The targets were not worth the losses in aircraft, he said, noting that five U.S. aircraft were recently lost in an attack on one North Vietnamese site. Johnson reluctantly agreed and observed that "it does not appear the targets are worth the loss in planes." The important thing, he said, was to make certain "the Vietnamese, by what they do—even if it is limited—must gradually emerge towards the center of the stage."[82]

Despite his private doubts, Johnson continued trying to give Americans hope, as if the progress of the war would improve merely by the force of his will. On November 17, he told reporters at a White House press conference that although the fighting was difficult, "we are making progress. We are pleased with the results we are getting."[83]

By late November, the administration's public relations effort appeared to yield limited, but encouraging results. Public opinion of Johnson's Vietnam policies, which had fallen to a record low of 23 percent in late October, climbed slightly to 34 percent by late November. Despite that slight improvement, a vast majority of Americans—66 percent in a Harris survey—disapproved his handling the war. By year's end, however, Johnson found even more hope in a Harris poll that revealed that Americans, by a large margin, 63 to 37 percent, favored escalation over curtailment of the military effort. In the same survey, public opinion was divided on whether Johnson should send American group troops into North Vietnam. "This is a high water mark for feelings that the military effort should be intensified," Harris reported. But as the pollster also noted, public opinion was fluid. Only the previous July a majority had favored deescalation. In analyzing the shift in public attitudes, Harris pointed to three potential factors: a negative reaction to the tactics of antiwar protesters, the difficulty of the war's opponents in outlining a "convincing alternative" course in Vietnam, and the "reassurances" by Westmoreland and Bunker "that the war is now going better and will go better in the future with the implication that future U.S. troop demands in Vietnam may level off."[84]

With public opinion on Vietnam climbing out of the cellar, Johnson and his advisors closed the year cautiously optimistic. While the tide had not turned in Vietnam, they now hoped the American public might be willing to give them enough time to finish the job. "All in all," White House aide Fred Panzer told Johnson on December 28, "it looks like the public has greater understanding of what the Administration is trying to do in Vietnam—and accepts it." Vietnam, Panzer concluded, "is well in hand. The time has now come, I believe, to shift gears to the domestic side."[85]

Perhaps nothing captured the administration's renewed spirit of optimism and bravado more than Westmoreland's remarks. So confident of an eventual victory in Vietnam, Westmoreland, like French general Henri Navarre at Dien Bien Phu, dared the Communists to attack. "I hope they try something," Westmoreland told an interviewer from *Time*, "because we are looking for a fight."[86]

CHAPTER 35

A Very Near Thing

1968

"WE ARE MAKING STEADY PROGRESS WITHOUT ANY QUESTION," General Westmoreland had declared unequivocally at a White House briefing for members of Congress on November 16, 1967.[1] Later, briefing reporters, he was even more optimistic. "I have never been more encouraged in my four years in Vietnam." Speaking to the National Press Club on November 19, the general claimed the war had reached the point "when the end begins to come into view." Although he would not put a specific date on that end, during meetings with other groups he guessed that the United States could begin recalling troops within two years. The general was not alone in his optimism. Ambassador Bunker was equally hopeful in testimony before the Senate Foreign Relations Committee. On November 16 he told senators that "the military situation has greatly improved" and predicted that the United States would "win" the war.[2]

Johnson eagerly accepted the good news delivered by the country's top two officials in Vietnam. Where others saw stalemate and defeat, Johnson saw progress and a light at the end of the tunnel. "The enemy has been defeated in battle after battle," the president insisted in his annual State of the Union Address to Congress on the evening of January 17, 1968. "The number of South Vietnamese living in areas under government protection tonight has grown by more than a million since January of last year."

In the previous year, Johnson reported, three elections had been conducted and national leaders elected and installed. Unfortunately, despite the American and South Vietnamese successes that Johnson touted in his speech, the North Vietnamese and the Viet Cong seemed to be unaware that they were on the verge of losing the war. Johnson wisely made no mention of the U.S. bombing campaign that had wreaked havoc and massive destruction throughout the north and south but had done very little to weaken the enemy's fighting spirit. As for the American spirit, Johnson declared that his administration was as resolute and determined as ever. The enemy "continues to hope that America's will to persevere can be broken," Johnson said. "Well, he is wrong. America will persevere. Our patience and our perseverance will match our power. Aggression will never prevail."[3]

While the progress that Johnson described was mostly illusory, he continued to press Westmoreland and his generals for better results. A presidential election year had dawned and the president was still feuding with House Ways and Means Chairman Wilbur Mills over how to eliminate a budget deficit of $11.3 billion, the result of Johnson's stubborn refusal to choose between domestic and military spending. But Johnson's desire for positive developments in Vietnam was motivated by far more than the simple yearning to end the war on terms favorable to the United States. At stake was the future of his presidency and that of his political party. Unless the general direction of the war changed, and soon, not only would Congress grow more intransigent and less likely to approve Johnson's tax surcharge proposal, but the Democratic Party—already badly split over the war—might face a buzz saw of public outrage in November.

Within days of Johnson's State of the Union speech it appeared that he and Westmoreland would finally get their much-desired decisive confrontation with the enemy. On January 20, the North Vietnamese commenced a fierce assault on a U.S. marine base in the hills of northwestern South Vietnam near the Laotian border at Khe Sanh. Westmoreland was "confident that whatever the enemy attempted, American and South Vietnamese forces could eventually foil it."[4] But the fighting at Khe Sanh was bloody and fierce and, as it dragged on, it began to appear that perhaps the Marines, like the French at Dien Bien Phu, had picked the wrong place to confront their enemy. Unlike the French in 1954, however, the Americans at Khe Sanh enjoyed use of a fortified air strip and, equally significant, benefited from air support provided by Air Force and Navy aircraft that relentlessly attacked the thirty-five thousand North Vietnamese soldiers surrounding the American garrison. In a meeting with congressional leaders on January 23, Johnson acknowledged the similarity between Dien Bien Phu and Khe Sanh, but informed them, as Westmoreland had assured him, of "a rapid deterioration of the strength of the Viet Cong. They are having to replace their manpower with North Vietnamese. The current campaign is a short-term surge effort designed to gain political advantages."[5]

Johnson was partly correct. The siege at Khe Sanh suggested an attempt by the Viet Cong and their North Vietnamese allies to achieve a short-term military advantage. It did not, however, reveal any diminution of the Viet Cong's fighting strength. Khe Sanh may have been the battle that Westmoreland wanted, but it was actually a clever diversion, part of a "general offensive, general uprising" that the Viet Cong and the North Vietnamese had planned for the early months of 1968. The attack was primarily designed to lure American commanders into shifting combat troops from the large population centers to remote battlefields, leaving the cities vulnerable to military attack and the general uprisings that the North Vietnamese hoped would destabilize the Saigon government and force the Americans to concede defeat. Westmoreland took the bait and shifted six thousand American troops from Saigon and other cities to the defense of Khe Sanh.

In the early morning hours of January 30—during the traditional cease-fire period of Tet, the Vietnamese New Year—a squad of Viet Cong commandos laid siege to the U.S. embassy in Saigon and killed a young U.S. army guard who vainly attempted to stop the raid.[6] Before their assault was over six hours later, the commandos would kill five U.S. soldiers in fierce fighting that was amply covered by American network television crews. Elsewhere in the city, the Viet Cong attacked Westmoreland's headquarters, as well as the South Vietnamese general staff offices. That evening in the United States, millions of Americans who watched the network news broadcasts were shocked to learn that, despite years of fierce bombing and the presence of half a million American troops in South Vietnam, the Viet Cong appeared as strong and viable as ever.

By the time officials in Washington learned of the attack, more than eighty-four thousand Viet Cong and North Vietnamese troops were staging well-coordinated attacks on forty-four provincial capitals, sixty-four district capitals, and five of the six major cities in South Vietnam. Taken by surprise, the American and South Vietnamese forces acquitted themselves well. In Saigon, American troops inflicted heavy causalities, took hundreds of prisoners, and quickly regained control of the city. The same was true in a number of other cities and towns where the Viet Cong made early tactical mistakes. Within two weeks, American and South Vietnamese troops gained the upper hand. Only in Hue, the ancient and picturesque imperial capital, did the Viet Cong establish a viable stronghold.* Suddenly, American military officials reluctantly acknowledged—but only to themselves—a bitter truth about the war in Vietnam: but for Viet Cong mis-

---

*But the price to loosen the Viet Cong grip on the city was severe: three weeks of brutal fighting, some of the fiercest of the entire war, in which five hundred Americans, five thousand Viet Cong, and countless civilians were killed and one hundred thousand refugees were forced to evacuate. In one of the more inhumane acts of the war, Viet Cong troops were said to have murdered as many as five thousand seven hundred civilians (Young, 217–18).

takes, and Westmoreland's decision to move American troops quickly back to the urban areas, the Viet Cong offensive might have resulted in much higher American and South Vietnamese casualties. "It was a very near thing," General Wheeler cabled from Hawaii in late February.[7]

While Viet Cong attacks were quashed in every city and town except Hue, the Tet offensive had a devastating impact on American public opinion. For months, Johnson, Westmoreland, and other administration officials had assured Congress and the public that Viet Cong strength was on the wane. It was only a matter of months, they said, before the U.S. military could begin gradually turning over the fighting to the South Vietnamese. "Well, Tet changed all that," observed Clark Clifford, Johnson's Defense secretary nominee, who added that "after Tet, I assure you, there was no suggestion that we could see any light at the end of the tunnel, nor was there any thought of sending any American boys home."[8]

Many Americans, including many in Congress, now realized that Johnson had deceived them about the strength of the Viet Cong. Despite three years of difficult fighting and bombing and the presence of more than five hundred thousand American troops on the ground, the Viet Cong were still viable enough to stage simultaneous attacks on more than one hundred cities and towns throughout the country. "They were trying to portray an enemy which was going downhill," recalled CIA analyst Samuel Adams, "which really wasn't true."[9]

Despite Ambassador Bunker's technically accurate assurances that "the enemy has suffered a major military defeat,"[10] members of Congress, the news media, and a significant percentage of the American people were left with a vivid and disheartening image of an American fighting force so vulnerable that it could barely repel an assault on the U.S. embassy in Saigon. "In my judgment," Jacob Javits told the Senate on February 5, "this lesson of the guerilla raids and the impending battle at Khe Sanh is this: The situation in Vietnam is in a stalemate, despite our apparent victories, which seem to evaporate so soon."[11] The next morning, on April 6, at a briefing for congressional leaders, the new Senate Democratic whip, Robert Byrd of West Virginia—previously a strong supporter of Johnson's Vietnam policy—surprised Johnson and his aides with a withering assessment of the administration's handling of Tet and its underestimation of Viet Cong strength. Byrd complained that "we had poor intelligence . . . were not prepared for these attacks, we underestimated the morale and vitality of the Viet Cong [and] we overestimated the support of the South Vietnamese government in its people."

"I don't agree with any of that," Johnson angrily shot back, explaining that U.S. intelligence had predicted "a general uprising around Tet."

Byrd was persistent. "I have never caused you any trouble on this matter on the Hill," he said. "But I do have very serious concerns about Vietnam."

Johnson denied that he had mischaracterized the strength of the Viet Cong. "I have never underestimated the Viet Cong," he insisted. "They are not pushovers. I do not think we have bad intelligence or have underestimated the Viet Cong morale."

"Something is wrong over there," Byrd replied.

"The intelligence wasn't bad," Johnson said, ignoring the import of Byrd's astute observation.

"That does not mean the Viet Cong did not succeed in their efforts," Byrd correctly noted. "Their objective was to show that they could attack all over the country and they did."

"That was not their objective at all," Johnson said. Weary of the argument, Johnson finally said, "I am of the opinion that criticism is not worth much. I look at all of these speeches that are in the [*Congressional*] *Record*. I look at all the people who are going around the country saying our policy is wrong. Where do they get us? Nowhere."

It was easy to talk about mismanagement in Vietnam, Johnson complained. "I think there has been very little." Turning on Mansfield, he said, "I wish Mike would make a speech on Ho Chi Minh. Nothing is as dirty as to violate a truce during the [Tet] holidays. But nobody says anything bad about Ho. They call me a murderer. But Ho has a great image." Mansfield said nothing. But Johnson made it abundantly clear that he had little use for criticism from men like Byrd and Mansfield. "I believe that our military and diplomatic men in the field know more than many of our congressmen and senators back here." Criticism was cheap, he complained. "Anybody can kick a barn down," he said, quoting one of his political mentors, the late House Speaker Sam Rayburn. "It takes a good carpenter to build one."

"Personally," Johnson added, "I think they [the Viet Cong] suffered a severe defeat." In the meantime, however, he appealed for forbearance from his congressional critics.

"I do not want to argue with the President," Byrd finally said. "But I am going to stick by my convictions."[12]

Despite his insistence that the Tet offensive had ended in a resounding victory for U.S. forces, Johnson knew that in the arena of public opinion it had been a major disaster. The *Wall Street Journal*, hardly a bastion of liberal opinion on the war, cautioned that Americans "should be getting ready to accept, if they haven't already, the prospect that the whole Vietnam effort may be doomed."[13] Any lingering doubts about Tet's impact were confirmed for Johnson on February 27, when the nation's most respected broadcast journalist, CBS News anchorman Walter Cronkite, returned from Vietnam and declared that the U.S. effort was stalemated. "To say we are closer to victory today," Cronkite told his viewers, "is to believe, in the face of the evidence, the optimists who have been wrong in the past. To suggest we are on the edge of defeat is to yield to unreasonable pessimism. To say that we are mired in stalemate seems the only realistic, yet unsatisfactory, conclusion." Stunned by Cronkite's blunt assessment, Johnson reportedly remarked to aides that the newsman's gloomy report would likely undermine support for the war among middle-class Americans—previously the bedrock of public support for the war.[14] As Rostow told Johnson, "If the war goes well, the American people are with us. If the war goes badly, they are against us."[15]

Night after night, for more than a month, the grisly images from Vietnam continued flashing across television screens in millions of American homes. A particularly horrifying incident that would come to symbolize for many the horror of the war occurred in the midst of the Tet attacks on February 3, when General Nguyen Ngoc Loan, director of the South Vietnamese National Police and an intimate of Vice President Ky, summarily executed a Viet Cong guerrilla on a Saigon street. As an NBC television camera and a newspaper photographer recorded the event, Loan took his revolver and shot the guerrilla in the head. The guerrilla was no mere bystander; he had killed several South Vietnamese civilians.[16] But to many Americans, the incident brought home the brutality and oppression of the Saigon regime and suggested that the South Vietnamese were no longer worthy of continued American military assistance.

In the wake of Tet, Johnson's overall job approval ratings plunged to new lows, as did public opinion about his handling of the war. In the six weeks after the first communist attacks on Saigon, the percentage of Americans polled who approved of Johnson's overall performance as president dropped from 48 percent to 36 percent. At the same time, public approval of his Vietnam policies fell from 40 percent to 26 percent. "The country's trust in his authority had evaporated," journalist Stanley Karnow observed. "His credibility—the key to a president's capacity to govern—was gone."[17]

Indeed, as Clark Clifford later wrote, "the most serious American casualty at Tet was the loss of the public's confidence in its leaders. Tet hurt the administration where it needed support most, with Congress and the American public—not because of the reporting, but because of the event itself, and what it said about the credibility of America's leaders." Like Johnson, Clifford was badly shaken by the public reaction to Tet:

> The pressure grew so intense that at times I felt the government itself might come apart at its seams. Leadership was fraying at its very center— something very rare in a nation with so stable a governmental structure.

In later years, almost every one of the men who lived through the crisis claimed that he had reacted calmly to events. In fact, everyone, both military and civilian, was profoundly affected by the Tet Offensive. This was true equally for those whose positions on Vietnam changed, and those who later viewed Tet as a great victory. There was, for a brief time, something approaching paralysis, and a sense of events spiraling out of control of the nation's leaders.[18]

Even as the fighting raged during Tet, Johnson saw no option but to give Westmoreland more troops. "If we lose this big build-up [the Tet offensive], we can't endure many losses," he told his advisors on February 12, adding that "*I* have a mighty big stake in this. I am more unsure every day" (emphasis added).[19] Consulted by McNamara the same day, Richard Russell strongly urged against sending any more troops "until after there was a complete reappraisal of Vietnam." The Tet offensive had shaken Russell's confidence in U.S. policy in Vietnam, particularly the "half-way measures" that Johnson had taken in his approach to the war.[20]

For now, Johnson was inclined to ignore Russell's cautionary advice and send Westmoreland only 10,500 troops—a move that would increase the number of U.S. forces in South Vietnam to 510,500. He urged Rusk, McNamara and Rostow to begin studying whether he should send even more, in addition to extending enlistments and calling up the reserves. "There is a very strange contradiction in what we are saying and doing," Defense Secretary nominee Clark Clifford observed during the February 9 meeting. "On one hand, we are saying that we have known of this build up." And, as Clifford noted, Johnson had told the American people that the Tet offensive was a defeat for the Viet Cong, had cost them as many as twenty-five thousand combat troops, and had produced no uprising among the South Vietnamese people. "Now our reaction to all of that is to say that the situation is more dangerous today than it was before all of this. We are saying that we need more troops, that we need more ammunition and that we need to call up the reserves." Clifford urged Johnson to consider the obvious contradictions. "I think we should give some very serious thought to how we explain saying on one hand the enemy did not take a victory and yet we are in need of many more troops and possibly an emergency call up." Replied Johnson: "The only explanation I can see is that the enemy has changed its tactics."[21]

One bright spot on the horizon was Clifford's appointment to replace the departing McNamara. Emotionally exhausted and inextricably tied to the war in the public's mind, McNamara had outlived his usefulness to Johnson. Clifford, on the other hand—with the independence befitting the elder-statesman status he had earned as a valued advisor to three presidents—may have been the perfect man for the job. "There was a feeling [in Congress]," recalled Foreign Relations Committee staff director Carl Marcy, "that he was not necessarily dovish, but more rational, less committed to carrying out the war in Vietnam, and was looking for a way out."[22] Clifford was, House Armed Services Committee Chairman F. Edward Hebert recalled, the "greatest pitchman I ever met in my life. A real con artist. And you loved it. And you knew it was happening to you." Such were descriptions that also applied to Johnson. And like Johnson, Hebert observed, "Clifford knew men. He knew human nature."[23]

Clifford also knew that the war must end. But having observed the physical and emotional toll the war had exacted on McNamara, he vowed to reporters that he would not use his new position as a stepping stone to political office. "I am sixty-one years old," he said, "and I'm sure this will finish me off."[24]

THE GULF OF TONKIN incidents and the resulting congressional resolution had nagged at Fulbright for years. Had the events of August 1964 occurred as Johnson claimed? If so, were they the result of provocative actions by a U.S. government that also directed the South Vietnamese OPLAN 34-A raids—a relationship that McNamara and others had so vigorously denied? Had Fulbright, the floor manager of the Gulf of Tonkin Resolution, been duped by Johnson into supporting a resolution that gave the administration what Under Secretary of State Nicholas Katzenbach later described as the functional equivalent of a war declaration?

Fulbright had privately nursed these questions since his investigation into the 1965 Dominican Republic crisis. At the time of the Foreign Relations Committee's original hearings on the Gulf of Tonkin incidents, he had dismissed Wayne Morse's informed, probing questions about the whereabouts of the logbooks for the *Maddox* and the *C. Turner Joy*.* But as his doubts about Johnson's truthfulness grew and the administration's hostility toward him increased, Fulbright kept going back in his mind to the missing logbooks. In March 1966, when he had received a letter from a retired Navy admiral telling him that the administration's account of the events in the Gulf of Tonkin "sound[ed] unrealistic," Fulbright was curious enough to contact George Ball. Had the incidents really occurred? Fulbright asked. "I'll tell you what the president told me," Ball replied. "He said, 'Those goddamn admirals; they see a bunch of flying fish and they

---

*Although McNamara had informed the committee that the books were not available, they were, in fact, in Washington at that very moment.

think they're ships. They don't know how to run the goddamn navy.'" At the time, Fulbright wanted to pursue the matter. But he was also cautious, especially since he had little more than anonymous sources and his suspicions to go on—certainly not enough to justify a full-scale investigation.[25]

But his confrontation in August 1967 with Katzenbach finally provoked Fulbright to action. During the tense committee hearing, Fulbright had asked Katzenbach to explain why the administration had gone to war without a formal declaration by Congress. Katzenbach's petulant response offended Fulbright: "Didn't that resolution authorize the President to use the armed forces of the United States in whatever way was necessary? Didn't it?" Fulbright protested that the resolution was offered as a response to a specific, emergency situation. Administration officials had never sold it to him as a national policy statement to guide the president in formulating his overall Vietnam policy. Knowing that he had Fulbright on the defensive, Katzenbach pressed his case. "You explained that resolution," he said with relish, "and you made it clear as it could be what Congress was committing itself to."[26]

Within days, an indignant Fulbright instructed Bill Bader, a committee staff member with experience in naval intelligence, to begin a quiet investigation of the Gulf of Tonkin incidents. At first, Pentagon officials were cooperative and provided Bader with the logs of the *Maddox* and the *C. Turner Joy*, undoubtedly believing that a committee staff person would find the arcane terminology indecipherable. But Bader was far more knowledgeable and industrious than the Pentagon imagined. When he asked Fulbright to formally request certain communications mentioned in the logs, Defense Department officials refused. "They were getting suspicious that we were on to something," Carl Marcy later speculated, "and the higher-ups took over."[27]

By January 1968, Bader—aided by at least two confidential Pentagon informants—had uncovered information that confirmed Fulbright's worst suspicions about the incidents of August 1964. According to Bader's twenty-page report, Pentagon documents confirmed that the American DeSoto patrols and the OPLAN 34-A raids had, indeed, been related. It was highly doubtful that the second incident had ever occurred. On January 31, the day the Tet offensive began, Fulbright announced that the Foreign Relations Committee would reexamine the Gulf of Tonkin events. Reluctantly, McNamara agreed to testify.[28]

In describing the relationship between the American naval patrols and the North Vietnamese raids on the North Vietnamese coast, McNamara insisted on February 20 that "our naval vessels played absolutely no part in, and were not associated with, this activity." He insisted that the August 2 and 4 incidents had occurred. To suggest that the U.S. government "induced the incident on August 4 with the intent of providing an excuse to take the retaliatory action which we in fact took" was, McNamara told the committee, "monstrous."

McNamara maintained that the attacks on the American vessels "were in no sense provoked or justified by any participation or association of our ships with South Vietnamese naval operations." To bolster his case, he cited "intelligence reports received from a highly classified and unimpeachable source" that described plans for a North Vietnamese attack on the American destroyers and which later reported on the events of August 4. Asked to share his information with the committee, however, McNamara retreated. Committee staff members, despite their Top Secret security clearances, were not approved to view the documents and McNamara said he would only share the information if the committee's staff left the room.

Fulbright, however, confronted McNamara with evidence that the U.S. destroyers knew of the North Vietnamese 34-A attacks, that they may have crossed into North Vietnamese territorial waters, and that, furthermore, the U.S. commander in the Gulf of Tonkin was unsure about the second incident. McNamara defiantly held his ground. "The *Maddox* was operating in international waters, was carrying out a routine patrol of the type we carry out all over the world at all time," he told the committee. "It was not informed of, was not aware of, had no evidence of, and so far as I know today has no knowledge of any possible South Vietnamese actions [off the North Vietnamese coast]."

Even when Fulbright read a cable sent from the *Maddox*, referring to the 34-A operations, McNamara refused to budge. "We can find no basis for the commander making this statement," he asserted, as though the cable had never been sent. When pressed, however, McNamara reluctantly acknowledged the cable's existence. Later, Fulbright cited another cable in which a naval commander warned that his "review of action [regarding the second incident] makes many recorded contacts and torpedoes fired appear doubtful." Again, McNamara refused to give any ground and insisted that a Pentagon investigation confirmed the second attack. "I was convinced it had taken place," he said.

To Fulbright, Morse, and Gore, the evidence was clear enough. Johnson had acted precipitously at best and provocatively at worst. "I think it was very unfair to ask us to vote upon a resolution when the state of the evidence was as uncertain as I think it now is, even if your intercepts are correct," Fulbright told McNamara at the end of the day-long hearing. "We have taken what is called the functional equivalent of a declaration of war upon evidence of this kind, and action as precipitate as this was." Had he known of the naval telegram casting doubt on the second attack, Fulbright insisted that he would not have been as eager to push Johnson's resolution through the Senate. "We accepted your statement completely without doubt," he told McNamara.

> I went on the floor to urge passage of the resolution. You quoted me, as saying these things on the floor. Of course, all my statements were based upon your testimony. I had no independent evidence, and now I think I did a great disservice to the Senate. I feel very guilty for not having enough sense at that time to have raised these questions and asked for evidence. I regret it. . . . I regret it more than anything I have ever done in my life, that I was the vehicle which took that resolution to the floor and defended it in complete reliance upon information which, to say the very least, is somewhat dubious at this time.

Morse was just as harsh in his assessment of the events leading up to the resolution's passage. While he was confident that it "was not a put-up job," Morse believed that "it was not the inexcusable and flagrant attack upon U.S. ships that it seemed to be, and that would have justified the resolution and retaliation had there been so. It was a confused bungle which was used by the President to justify a general course of action and policy that he had been advised by the military to follow."[29]

For McNamara, his last appearance before the committee as Defense secretary had been a grueling ordeal. He left the hearing room angry, with no intention of accepting Fulbright's critical assessment of the administration's questionable actions following the Gulf of Tonkin incidents. Although he and Fulbright had agreed in advance to say nothing to the public about the hearing, McNamara promptly released to eager reporters a twenty-one-page document claiming that he and Johnson had acted responsibly. Furthermore, he condemned Fulbright and other critical members of the committee for the way they had attempted to impugn his integrity. Repeating the words he used in his testimony, McNamara said it was "monstrous" to suggest that the Johnson administration had provoked the incidents as a way to justify escalation of the war.

On February 22, Fulbright responded to McNamara's attack by insisting that administration officials had not only misled Congress and the American public about the Gulf of Tonkin incidents, they had engaged in unethical behavior to hide the truth from his committee. Then, Fulbright dropped a minor bombshell. He revealed that when a Navy commander had contacted the committee in November with information about McNamara's duplicity, Pentagon officials retaliated by confining the officer to a mental ward for a month. During his testimony, McNamara had acknowledged the incident, but explained that the officer had indeed suffered mental problems, which were successfully treated during his confinement.[30]

In the weeks following McNamara's statement and the committee's release of the hearing transcripts, it became clear to many Americans that the Johnson administration had lied about the events in the Gulf of Tonkin. As the liberal journalist I. F. Stone concluded after examining transcripts of the hearing: "The more one studies the evidence so far available the more one does begin to see the outlines of a conspiracy, not to fabricate the incident of August 4, but to plan and to put into motion a sharp escalation of the Vietnamese war in the very year Johnson was campaigning for election as a man of peace."[31]

The publication of Fulbright's hearings, and the subsequent news media examination, further damaged Johnson's faltering credibility. Not only was the war increasingly unpopular; not only did most Americans disagree with Johnson's policies in Vietnam; they were now faced with the likelihood that a pivotal event in the American role in Vietnam—congressional authorization for Johnson's massive escalation—had been secured by lies and deceptions to which the Johnson administration continued to cling. Although Fulbright now believed he had enough evidence for a damning indictment, not just of the Gulf of Tonkin incidents, but the entirety of Lyndon Johnson's war policies, he held his fire. The Tet offensive was still underway. At first, he believed it would be unseemly and would expose him and the antiwar cause to harsh criticism were he to assail the president during a fierce battle between American troops and the Viet Cong.

Yet news reports in early March that Johnson was considering a massive new deployment of American troops began to change everything. Fulbright and the other Senate doves knew that they could not wait for the outcome of the Tet offensive before sounding the alarms. Worried that Johnson was about to take the country over a cliff in Vietnam, Fulbright, Mansfield, and several other senators began preparing their demands that Johnson reconsider his hopelessly flawed policy.

AT JOHNSON'S DIRECTION, the Joint Chiefs Chairman, General Earl Wheeler, had gone to Vietnam in late February. His mission: determine, in consultation with Westmoreland, how many additional American troops were needed in South Vietnam. The news that Wheeler brought back to Washington was alarming. Although Westmoreland's troops had blunted the Viet Cong attacks during Tet, Wheeler reported that the enemy now had the initiative. They were "operating with relative freedom in the countryside," he told Johnson. American and South Vietnamese forces were now in a defensive posture, protecting the cities and towns the Viet Cong had attacked with such ferocity. The pacification program was in shambles. To maintain the country's northern provinces, Westmoreland had dispatched half of his American maneuver battalions, a decision that robbed "the rest of the country of adequate reserves" and eliminated the American military's "offensive capability." In short, Wheeler said, the situation was bleak. "Under these circumstances, we must be prepared to accept some losses."

To regain the initiative, Wheeler argued, would require 206,000 more men, an act that would raise the ceiling of American troops in Vietnam to more than 731,000. Of that number, Westmoreland said that he needed half by May 1. To supply a force of that size presented Johnson with a decision he had thus far resisted: calling up 280,000 civilian reservists. "A fork in the road had been reached," the *Pentagon Papers* observed. "Now the alternatives stood out in stark reality. To accept and meet General Westmoreland's request for troops would mean a total U.S. military commitment to [South Vietnam]—an Americanization of the war, a call-up of reserve forces, vastly increased expenditures." But to deny Westmoreland the forces he needed would be tantamount to conceding defeat on an installment plan.[32]

Within days, reports about Westmoreland's request for troops made their way into print. Anxiety spread like wildfire throughout Congress. News that Johnson might soon send another two hundred thousand troops to Vietnam "has brought Congress as close to mutiny as I have ever seen it," reported *Newsweek* congressional correspondent Samuel Shaffer. "Hawks are being converted overnight to doves and House members in particular are falling over each other to get resolutions in the hopper demanding that no more troops be sent."[33] On March 7, a frustrated Fulbright—who was still holding his fire after the McNamara hearings—rose on the Senate floor to question Johnson's authority to commit additional troops without congressional approval, particularly in light of recent revelations about the Gulf of Tonkin incidents. "Insofar as the consent of this body is said to derive from the Gulf of Tonkin resolution, it can only be said that that resolution, like any other contract based on misrepresentation, in my opinion, is null and void," Fulbright said.

Fulbright's provocative remarks—aimed not so much at Johnson, but at senators who had refused to defend the Senate's constitutional warmaking prerogatives—sparked one of the liveliest Senate Vietnam debates in months. His demand that the Senate assume greater responsibility for decision-making in Vietnam generated a chorus of support, but also howls of protest from hawks like Stennis, Lausche, and Republican John Tower of Texas who attempted to shut down the debate.

Republican Clifford Case of New Jersey: "I think we cannot any longer evade the responsibility of a share in the decision as to whether we are to continue in the present way, for it is now a question as to whether or not the war is winnable without the destruction of South Vietnam and much of American might itself." Frank Church: "The Constitution vests in Congress a fundamental responsibility in the matter of war and peace. We have abdicated that responsibility in recent years. . . . This is the time to reassert our prerogative, to insist on full congressional participation in that decision. . . . If we fail now to assert our constitutional responsibilities, we shall have only ourselves to blame for any disaster that the future may hold." Republican Mark Hatfield of Oregon: "Congress should say to the president very clearly that if he deems it absolutely necessary, in the interests of our country, to expand the war, we should, therefore, share in the decision making, that it should not be the decision of one man, that it should not be a matter of ratifying that which he has already decided upon."

It was Robert Kennedy, now actively contemplating a campaign against Johnson for the Democratic presidential nomination, whose words were among the most passionate. To continue the bombing would be "immoral and intolerable," Kennedy said.

> I think it would be a mistake for the executive branch and for the President to take a step toward escalation of the conflict in the next several weeks without having the support and understanding of the Senate, and of the American people. . . . It seems to me if we have learned anything over the period of the last seven years, it is the fact that just continuing to send more troops, or increasing the bombing, is not the answer in Vietnam. We have tried that. . . . Moreover, there is a question of our moral responsibility. Are we like the God of the Old Testament that we can decide in Washington, D.C., what cities, what towns, what hamlets in Vietnam are going to be destroyed? Is it because we think it may possibly protect the people of Thailand, the people of Malaysia, the people of Hawaii, or keep certain people out of Texas or California or Massachusetts or New York? Or do we have that authority to kill tens and tens of thousands of people because we say we have a commitment to the South Vietnamese people?

For the first time, Kennedy went out of his way to ridicule Johnson's Vietnam policies, complaining that thousands of South Vietnamese citizens had responded to the American liberation of Hue by looting the city. "Do we have to accept that?" he said. "Do we have to accept the situation in which we are told that a young man in South Vietnam is running his father's factory because he paid off his draft board and does not have to go?" Johnson's answer, Kennedy told the Senate, was "that there is stealing in Beaumont, Texas. If there is stealing in Beaumont, Texas," Kennedy said bitingly, "it is not bringing about the death of American boys."

Rebutting Fulbright's indictment of Johnson was the fiercely conservative Tower, one of a large group of conservatives who faulted Johnson for not prosecuting the war aggressively enough. Tower suggested that he would eagerly support the kind of escalation that press reports indicated Johnson was considering. The administration, he said, was finally "doing what a number of us have been saying for two and a half years—that you cannot win a war by a graduated response." Tower rejected the notion that American forces had "suffered a series of very great defeats in South Vietnam," explaining that the Viet Cong's "major achievement" was "to frighten so many people in this country into wanting to get out, into negotiating, into believing that we cannot win, into believing that we are losing and we have to just withdraw unilaterally." To that argument, Democrat Vance Hartke of Indiana replied: "If the Senator wants to defend the policies of the administration, why does he not want the administration to tell us what the policies are?"[34]

As the debate ended, Mansfield finally rose to speak. For four years now, the majority leader had waged a patient, determined, and wholly unsuccessful effort to influence Johnson's Vietnam policies. At every turn, he had diplomatically, but firmly urged Johnson to reject escalation.[35] Yet even as he prepared to speak harshly of Johnson's Vietnam policies, he was careful as always to signal his personal loyalty to his president: "It is my intention to uphold the hand of the president as much as I can in this particular matter, and at the same time stick to my own conviction." While insisting that Johnson had "tried hard and vigorously and consistently to find a way to the negotiating table," Mansfield acknowledged that he had not gone far enough. To Mansfield, the fundamental philosophy behind the American involvement in Vietnam—the fears of four presidents and countless American leaders about the spreading influence of communism in Southeast Asia—was fatally flawed:

> We are in the wrong place, and we are fighting the wrong kind of war; and those of us who try to say that if we do not fight there, we will be forced back to Hawaii or California, ought to think and think again. Those who talk about the domino theory ought to get away from that cliché and look at the map and understand it; because there have been too many clichés. In that respect, I confess that I have been as guilty as the next man, in trying to explain this struggle in which we are engaged.
>
> There are those who say, "Win, go all the way, or get out." That sounds fine on the stump, and that may go well in our states, but it does not hold up in a consideration of the reality of the situation which confronts this nation today, and those who say it know it.

As for the reports about Westmoreland's request for two hundred thousand additional troops, Mansfield urged even greater emphasis on a peaceful settlement of the conflict. "I do not believe that we should confess diplomatic failure and fall back on military answers only," he said. "Is that all we can think of? If we confess diplomatic failure—and I do not—then we face only a continuance of a grim escalation upon escalation on both sides. Are we prepared to face up to that gruesome prospect?"[36]

At the White House, meanwhile, gloom had settled over Johnson's staff in the aftermath of Wheeler's depressing report. Harry McPherson's handwritten notes indicate that William Bundy told a gathering of Johnson's advisors on February 27 that the administration should begin preparing "for the worst. South Vietnam is very weak. Our position may be truly untenable. Contingency planning should proceed toward the possibility that we will withdraw with the best possible face and defend the rest of Asia." McNamara could not fathom why Wheeler and the Joint Chiefs thought two hundred thousand additional men would accomplish what five hundred thousand could not. "It is neither enough to do the job," he told the group, "nor an indication that our role must change." The bombing had utterly failed, McNamara said. Barely able to speak and overcome with emotion, he told the group: "The goddamned Air Force, they're dropping more on North Vietnam than we dropped on Germany in the last year of World War II, and it's not doing anything!" Now McNamara was crying. "We just simply have to end this thing," he said. "I just hope you can get hold of it. It is out of control." Stunned, Clifford, Rostow, Bundy, and McPherson went on with the conversation as if nothing had happened. "Everyone in the room understood what had happened," Clifford later wrote. "This proud, intelligent, and dedicated man was reaching the end of his strength on his last full day in office. He was leaving the Pentagon just in time."[37]

On February 28, torn between two unattractive alternatives, Johnson handed the issue to Clifford, who would take office the next day. Johnson gave him three days to develop a preliminary recommendation based on Wheeler's report.[38] Clifford and a task force of Johnson's military and civilian advisors immediately went to work and, under the new secretary's leadership, began approaching the issue of Vietnam with a healthy skepticism that Johnson and his aides had eschewed for years. He demanded that the Joint Chiefs justify their requests for additional troops. Will 206,000 more men do the job? Clifford asked. The Joint Chiefs could make no promises. If that was not enough, how many might be eventually needed? No one could say. If Westmoreland got his troops, could not the enemy respond in kind? Indeed, they could. Would more bombing stop the war? No. Although it was inflicting heavy damage on North Vietnam, it could not, by itself, do the job. How long until South Vietnam would be ready to carry the burden of fighting the war? The South Vietnamese might never be ready. These and other exchanges with military leaders "disturbed me greatly," Clifford said. "The military was utterly unable to provide an acceptable rationale for the troop increase." "Appalled," Clifford recalled that "nothing had prepared me for the weakness of the military's case."

Clifford knew what he had to do. He also acknowledged the need to move cautiously if he ever hoped to persuade Johnson to reject the Joint Chiefs' plan. "After only four days at the Pentagon," he said later, "I was not ready to take on the collective weight of Rusk, the Joint Chiefs, Westmoreland, and Rostow."[39] For now, he would recommend that Johnson give Westmoreland only 22,000 additional troops, a call-up of 262,000 reserves and an extension of the terms of service of U.S. soldiers in Vietnam. While he was understandably hesitant to confront Johnson's advisors directly, Clifford presented a fourth recommendation that contained the seeds of an eventual deescalation of the war: A final decision on the Joint Chiefs' request, he insisted, should be contingent on a week-by-week assessment of the situation, improved performance by Saigon and its army, and a thorough review of U.S. political and strategic options in Vietnam.

In his presentation to Johnson, Clifford was direct, as usual. "We are not sure the present strategy is the right strategy—that of being spread out all over the country with a seek-and-destroy policy." Furthermore, Clifford said that he and his task force were no longer confident that a military solution in Vietnam was possible. "Perhaps we should not be trying to protect all of the countryside," he said, "and instead concentrate on the cities and important areas in the country."[40]

Aware of the rising anxiety in the Senate, confident that the Tet offensive had been blunted, and in no mood to enlarge the war further, Johnson did not challenge Clifford's recommendations. Although he did not explicitly say so, by tacitly approving of Clifford's presentation Johnson signaled that he, like McNamara, had finally acknowledged there would be no American military solution in Vietnam. What about peace negotiations? Johnson asked. Things were "quite bleak," Rusk replied. But when pressed by Deputy Defense Secretary Paul Nitze to consider a bombing halt, Rusk paused for a moment. He had long been disabused of the notion that bombing could win the war. "Well," Rusk said, "we could try stopping the bombing during the rainy season in the north. It would not cost us much militarily, since our air sorties are way down at that time anyway." Suspecting that Viet Cong losses during the Tet invasion had strengthened the U.S. negotiating position, Johnson seized the idea. "Dean, I want you to *really* get on your horse on that one—right away."

BY MARCH 1968, it had been almost two years since the secretary of state had testified in open session before the Senate Foreign Relations Committee, although not for lack of an invitation. In his memoirs Rusk claimed that while he had always been eager to testify about the war before Fulbright's committee, Johnson had adamantly refused for fear of giving Fulbright another public forum to attack the administration. But every time Fulbright and other committee members saw Rusk appear on "Meet the Press" and other television news programs, it angered them more. Rusk was willing to talk to reporters about the nation's Vietnam policy, but not to the elected representatives of the American people.[41]

On February 7, after the committee voted 8 to 4 to request Johnson's acquiescence for Rusk's testimony, Fulbright wrote the president. "Certain members felt strongly that what is now at stake is no less urgent a question than the Senate's constitutional duty to advise, as well as consent, in the sphere of foreign policy," Fulbright said.[42] In a reply that Johnson prepared, but did not mail, he wrote that while he understood and agreed with the Senate's desire to obtain relevant information on the war, "I cannot, however, take the further step of agreeing that those presentations and discussions should take place before television cameras and sometimes in a divisive, argumentative atmosphere."[43] Meanwhile, Johnson angrily complained to Rusk, McNamara, and Clifford that "Fulbright has an obsession on Vietnam."[44]

Fulbright, however, had the upper hand. He let it be known that without the chairman's support—which would not be forthcoming so long as Rusk refused to testify in open session—there would be no foreign aid bill for fiscal 1969. In the end, Johnson and Rusk had no choice. Rusk would have to testify. On the morning of March 11, the secretary strolled into the committee room and into the bright glare of the television klieg lights. The questioning from Fulbright and others was tougher and more skeptical than he could have imagined—and the Senate's support for Johnson's Vietnam policies was weaker than anyone could have predicted. Republican Karl Mundt of South Dakota acknowledged that public opinion about the war had shifted dramatically. "Some more convincing," he said, "has to come from the Administration as to what this is all about." Stuart Symington, the Missouri Democrat and former Air Force secretary who had strongly supported Johnson's policies, now revealed his "increasing doubts" about American involvement in Vietnam.

When Rusk advanced his well-worn argument that the United States should remain in Vietnam in order to honor its treaty obligations, Clifford Case asked, "[If] our success in South Vietnam can only be accomplished by the destruction of South Vietnam" must the United States "inexorably . . . pursue this course?" For almost eleven hours over two full days of testimony, Rusk gave the senators little new information that could enhance their understanding of the war. Asked about reports that Johnson and his advisors were considering increasing the U.S. troop ceiling in Vietnam by two hundred thousand, Rusk dodged. On the first day of testimony, he would only say that the entire U.S. Vietnam policy was under review "from A to Z." That answer did little to satisfy skeptical senators. Johnson, who watched much of the hearing on television, finally gave Rusk permission to elaborate during his second day before the committee. If more troops were needed, Rusk assured the senators, "we will, as we have in the past, consult with *appropriate members* of the Congress" (emphasis added). But he stopped well short of promising to consult Fulbright or his committee.[45]

While the televised hearings focused new attention on the growing, bipartisan Senate opposition to the war, it appeared to have little impact on public opinion. Of the 31 percent of Americans who said they watched the hearings, only 6 percent told pollsters in one survey that they had changed their minds about Vietnam—and most of those appeared to move toward Johnson's position. "Basically all the Fulbright investigation achieved was moving a mountain of exposure to get at some mole hills of public opinion," an aide gleefully told Johnson. "Thus, Fulbright and the Doves threw a 100-pound punch and struck a three-ounce blow, which had a seven-ounce kick back."[46] In the weeks after the hearing, Fulbright endured criticism from the conservatives for the direct and aggressive questions that he and other committee members had fired at Rusk. "I really do not think the Committee was rough on him at all," Fulbright protested to a friend in Arkansas, "in view of the fact that he refused to budge one inch on the question of consulting the Committee before a decision is made to send additional troops to Vietnam." Fulbright argued that Congress was entitled to information about such a momentous decision. "If the Senate is not entitled to know what our war plans are," he wrote, "it really does not have much of a function to play."[47]

CHAPTER 36

Everyone Has Turned into a Dove

1968

"W E SEEM TO HAVE A SINKHOLE," A GLUM CLARK CLIFFORD TOLD
Johnson during a March 4 meeting of the president's senior policy advisors. Giving Westmoreland the 206,000 additional troops he wanted was
not the answer, Clifford insisted. "We put in more, they match it." Not
only that, but Clifford believed the Viet Cong were now better armed than
the South Vietnamese army. They were better trained, and had better rifles
and more sophisticated weapons, he told the president. "I see more fighting with more and more casualties on the U.S. side," Clifford said, "and
no end in sight to the action."[1]

At best, Johnson's war was stalemated. At worst, it was a foreign policy
disaster that would destroy him politically by inviting a potent challenge to
his renomination. Johnson, however, was not entirely persuaded of the
severity of the situation. "I had much greater confidence in Westmoreland
and his staff in Vietnam than many people in Washington," he wrote later,
reflecting on Clifford's briefing.[2] Although the president had spent little
time worrying about how the war might invigorate the nascent, insurgent
challenge of Democratic Senator Eugene McCarthy of Minnesota, an
objective survey of the nation's political landscape in early 1968 should have
given him reason for profound concern. Half a million American men were
mired in the morass of South Vietnam in pursuit of a military objective that
seemed more illusory than ever. In large numbers, Americans not only
opposed Johnson's handling of the war, they now disapproved of his overall performance as president. Leaders of his party were badly split over Vietnam. Ironically, much of Johnson's support in Vietnam now came from
Republicans—but even this had dwindled as an election year dawned and
the failure of Johnson's military policies became apparent in the wake of Tet.
Despite towering domestic legislative achievements—civil rights, voting

rights, Medicare and a host of Great Society initiatives—Johnson and his presidency were now irrevocably defined, or stained, by a war he had expanded partly for fear that doing otherwise would doom his presidency and his party.

Adding to Johnson's woes was Senator Eugene McCarthy—a most unusual politician. Although many saw a talented, witty man with a superior intellect (others, not so charitably, regarded him as aloof, cynical, and annoying), he was no natural politician like Johnson or Humphrey. A former university professor and amateur poet, McCarthy had little passion for the hard work of legislating. In fact, in almost twenty years in Congress (he was first elected to the Senate in 1958), the 51-year-old McCarthy had accomplished little of consequence. "McCarthy spent a lot of time in the Senate restaurant, delivering bon mots about the political situation to infatuated reporters," recalled Johnson's aide Harry McPherson, who nonetheless admitted he might have supported the Minnesota Democrat in 1968 "had I not been committed to the man he was attacking."[3] But what McCarthy *did* have in his favor was his role as the first—and for several months, the only—prominent Democrat to oppose Johnson's reelection.

For much of 1967, a young Democratic Party antiwar activist, Allard Lowenstein, had worked tirelessly in hopes of recruiting a leader of sufficient stature to challenge Johnson's renomination. Robert Kennedy had been a natural first choice. Young, popular, energetic, and now opposed to the war, Kennedy seemed to promise a revival of the hopeful era of Camelot so abruptly ended in November 1963. It was not just Lowenstein who yearned for an alternative to Johnson's leadership. Discontent with the war—and the way it burdened the economy and stalled many of Johnson's domestic initiatives—had spawned a small but passionate movement within the party to dump the incumbent president. "Kennedy was an alternate pole of attraction because his candidacy simply made sense," Jeff Shesol observed in his examination of the Kennedy–Johnson feud, *Mutual Contempt*. "Unlike Fulbright or McCarthy or McGovern, Bobby had Kennedy money, Kennedy glamour, the Kennedy name, and the Kennedy organization."[4] That earned him support from a wide variety of Democrats who opposed the war or who believed that Vietnam had irreparably damaged Johnson.

Yet Kennedy was not ready to take on Johnson. In fact, throughout the latter part of 1967, the New York senator had devoted himself to making peace with his longtime rival, explaining to a friend that running for president would only give Johnson cause to blame him for the country's domestic and foreign policy troubles. "I would have a problem if I ran first against Johnson," Kennedy told his advisors when they met with Lowenstein. "People would say that I was splitting the party out of ambition and envy.

No one would ever believe that I was doing it because of how I feel about Vietnam and poor people. I think Al is doing the right thing, but I think that someone else will have to be the first to run. It can't be me because of my relationship with Johnson." Kennedy also worried that his candidacy might imperil Senate war opponents like McGovern, Clark, Nelson, Gruening, Church, and Morse—all who faced reelection in 1968. If he ran, Kennedy knew that he would force each man to take sides in the presidential race. Those who sided with Kennedy would likely become targets for Johnson's retribution. By his own estimate, Kennedy believed he might be responsible for the loss of six Democratic Senate seats.

Kennedy was not the only one aware that his candidacy might split the party down the middle. For that reason, few if any of his Senate colleagues urged him to run. After a cursory check of his Democratic colleagues, McGovern—although he had originally backed a Kennedy candidacy—admitted that "I cannot in all conscience recommend to Bobby that he run."[5]

For now, at least, Kennedy would remain on the sidelines. Lowenstein went looking elsewhere. His next stop was McGovern's office. But McGovern was no more eager than Kennedy for a bruising presidential battle. The South Dakota Democrat had won by fewer than six hundred votes in 1962 and was anticipating a tough reelection battle. While he agreed to give the proposition some thought, McGovern eventually demurred and sent Lowenstein to see his friend McCarthy.

As bored by the Senate as he was disgusted with the nation's course in Vietnam, McCarthy jumped at the idea and almost immediately began making plans to challenge Johnson. Near the end of October, when McGovern encountered McCarthy on the Senate floor, he apologized for having sent Lowenstein. But to McGovern's amazement, McCarthy said, "Not at all. I think I may do it."[6] On November 30, 1967, McCarthy did it—announcing that he would enter the Wisconsin, Oregon, and Nebraska Democratic primaries, and would also consider running in Massachusetts and New Hampshire.

More than any other issue, the Vietnam War would shape and characterize McCarthy's insurgent campaign. But he also capitalized on the political apathy among younger voters that was the war's by-product. He hoped, he told his mostly young antiwar supporters, that his campaign might "counter the growing sense of alienation from politics, which I think is currently reflected in a tendency to withdraw from political action and talk of non-partisan efforts." He was against the war, but was also quick to add that "I am not—as I'm sure I'll be charged—for peace at any price, but for an honorable, rational, and political solution to this war."[7]

At first, few took McCarthy's campaign seriously—least of all the complacent Johnson and his self-assured political advisors. "McCarthy is doing so badly," one overconfident aide told Johnson, "that I am tempted to float a rumor that he is actually working for you to dispirit the 'peace movement.'"[8] But as the news from Vietnam went from bad to worse, Johnson found his reelection unexpectedly imperiled by the low-key campaign of a maverick Minnesota senator who had opted to run in the New Hampshire primary—the nation's first and, in many respects, most significant primary contest. Backed by dozens of energetic young workers who stormed the state for their candidate—some called them "the children's crusade"—the McCarthy campaign became David to Johnson's Goliath. Although Johnson would not campaign in person, and his name would not even appear on the ballot, his supporters organized a last-minute write-in campaign hoping to hasten McCarthy's political demise.

But Johnson's supporters committed several tactical blunders that played into their opponent's hands. Trying to portray McCarthy's positions on Vietnam as something less than American, Governor John King a Johnson supporter, warned that a McCarthy victory would spark "dancing in the streets of Hanoi." He also labeled him "a champion of appeasement and surrender." Several days before the March 11 primary, Democratic supporters of Johnson bought a newspaper ad that claimed "the communists in Vietnam are watching the New Hampshire primary. . . . They are hoping for a divided America. Don't vote for fuzzy thinking and surrendering. Support our fighting men . . . by writing in the name of President Johnson." Freshman Democratic Senator Thomas McIntyre of New Hampshire labeled McCarthy a friend of "draft-dodgers and deserters." These and other attacks would backfire. The war on McCarthy smacked of the smear tactics once employed by a Republican senator of the same name, a coincidence that did not escape some New Hampshire voters.[9]

Throughout the primary campaign, McCarthy was unfazed by the attacks and left many with the impression—largely accurate—that his was a campaign of principle, fueled by idealism and run mostly by political amateurs. To many voters, McCarthy seemed like the antipode of Lyndon Johnson—an honest, forthright politician wholly lacking the raw political ambition upon which most men in Washington thrived. He was also self-deprecating in a way that would have never occurred to Johnson. Asked if his campaign was not a case of political suicide, McCarthy jokingly replied, "I don't think it will be a case of suicide. It might be an execution." But when he addressed the war in Vietnam, McCarthy was forceful and passionate and took direct aim at Johnson's failures and deceit. "The Democratic Party in 1964 promised 'no wider war,'" he told a blue-collar audience in Manchester. "Yet the war is getting wider every month. Only a few months ago we were told that 65 percent of the population was secure. Now we know that even the American embassy is not secure."[10]

As the primary approached, Johnson's supporters sensed a McCarthy upset and did their best to raise expectations for their opponent. Although McCarthy had been but a blip in the polls in early 1968 (Johnson enjoyed a 71 to 18 percent lead in a January Gallup survey), the organizer of Johnson's write-in effort now declared that the Minnesota senator would be disgraced if he drew less than 40 percent of the vote.[11] When the votes came in, McCarthy scored an upset of historic proportions. Although he finished second, his 42.2 percent of the vote to Johnson's 49.4 percent was widely perceived as an astounding victory. A little-known senator with an amateur campaign staff on shoestring budget had scored a decisive psychological victory over an incumbent president. As with the Tet offensive, Johnson had lost while winning.

On the Republican side, former Vice President Richard Nixon, unchallenged, polled 79 percent of the vote. Nixon pledged that if elected he would "end the war," but refused to elaborate, except to say that the Soviet Union was "very possibly the key" to a negotiated settlement. "His position up to this point," Nixon speechwriter Richard Whalen observed, "was a grab bag of phrases, from which audiences could draw whatever general conclusions they pleased."[12] Although Nixon favored "keeping the pressure on militarily," the Republican front-runner faulted Johnson for placing "too much emphasis" on a military solution. "Unless you go forward politically and economically in South Vietnam," Nixon told the *New York Times* on March 10, "you could be there another 10 years."[13]

In the days leading up to McCarthy's earth-shattering upset, Robert Kennedy's reluctance to enter the presidential race had begun to evaporate—the inevitable consequence of an environment influenced by Johnson's failures in Vietnam, growing domestic unrest, deepening economic woes, and a surprisingly strong political rival. Prior to McCarthy's entry in the New Hampshire primary, Kennedy had assumed Johnson's hold on the nomination was sound. But McCarthy's surprising strength in New Hampshire changed the equation. The day after the New Hampshire primary, Kennedy told reporters in Washington that since the Democratic Party was already split, "I am actively reassessing the possibility of whether I will run against President Johnson."[14]

In fact, Kennedy had already decided to run. By now he was merely searching for a graceful way to enter the campaign.[15] On March 16, only five days after the New Hampshire primary, the New York senator declared his candidacy in the crowded caucus room of the Old Senate Office Building, the same room in which his older brother had announced his candidacy eight years earlier. Kennedy told the audience that "I do not run for the Presidency merely to oppose any man, but to propose new policies." The nation's "disastrous, divisive policies" toward Vietnam and the growing urban violence could only be changed, Kennedy said, "by changing the men who are now making them." While he said he harbored no personal animus toward Johnson, Kennedy claimed that their "profound differences over where we are heading and what we want to accomplish" had prompted his candidacy. "At stake is not simply the leadership of our party or even our country—it is our right to moral leadership on this planet."[16]

At a press conference afterwards, Kennedy tried again to explain that his campaign was not motivated by any personal animus toward Johnson, but rather by a new political climate created in New Hampshire. McCarthy's success had "established that the division that exists in this country [and] the division that exists in the Democratic Party are there." Kennedy insisted that "I haven't brought that about. . . . What has brought that about is . . . the *policies* that are being followed by President Johnson" (emphasis Kennedy's).[17]

Kennedy's estimation of the party division was correct. Even before his candidacy, disputes over the war were ripping the Democratic Party apart. In the Senate, two of the most prominent Democrats—the majority leader, Mansfield, and the chairman of the Foreign Relations Committee, Fulbright—strongly opposed the bombing. Fulbright and much of his committee, in particular, were in open revolt against the secretary of state. Outside the nucleus of the Democratic leadership, the dissent was even more profound: two leading Democratic liberals, McCarthy and Kennedy, were challenging Johnson's renomination, while at least a dozen other Democrats had strongly questioned the wisdom of the administration's policies.

Outside Washington, among Democratic Party leaders, the divisions were just as profound. "The war is increasingly unpopular," North Dakota Governor William Guy told Johnson in early March, describing discussions with Democrats in his state. "Without any coaching and without leading questions by our Party leaders, I find wholesale abandonment of confidence in our mission in Vietnam."[18] Newspaper columnist Drew Pearson reported to Johnson that during his travels around the country he had "found increasing resentment, even bitterness, over the war, with much of it being personally directed against you. In my opinion we cannot continue tearing the country asunder over an issue so distant and so unrelated to the mainstream of our lives."[19]

The polls bore out Pearson's bleak assessment of public opinion. By March, Johnson's job approval rating on Vietnam had dropped to 26 percent. Sixty-nine percent said they now wanted a "phase-out plan" to withdraw American troops and replace them with South Vietnamese units.[20] Johnson, who could not help but notice the collapsing public support, told his advisors on March 22 that "there has been a dramatic shift in public opinion on the war, that a lot of people are really ready to surrender without knowing they are following a party line."[21]

Yet in his public remarks, Johnson continued beating the drums of war. To an audience in Beaumont, Texas, on March 2, he had insisted that "we are not going to be quislings, and we are not going to be appeasers, and we are not going to cut and run." (Johnson also revived a 1964 campaign theme when he said, "We are going to do all we can to avoid a wider war. We are not going to fight the war that Asians ought to fight for themselves.") The following week, to a veterans group in Washington, he said that while he and Rusk continued to pursue a peaceful resolution of the conflict "we shall never retreat."[22] On March 18, speaking to the National Farmers Union in Minnesota, Johnson called for a "total national effort to win the war." Should Hanoi continue to refuse peace talks, Johnson vowed that "we will win peace on the battlefield by supporting our men who are doing that job there now."[23]

Johnson's militant bluster did little to calm the public's fears about where the nation was headed in Vietnam. In a blunt, ten-page memorandum that same day, Harry McPherson warned Johnson that his unwillingness to publicly project anything other than steely resolve to continue the fighting "will lead either to Kennedy's nomination or Nixon's election, or both." Johnson had become the defender of the status quo, McPherson explained. "Therefore, you are the most conservative [of all the current and potential presidential candidates]—the man who is not calling for change, but resisting it. That is a tough position today." McPherson also noted that "you ask people to support the continuation of an administration *that was in office while*" U.S. casualties in Vietnam skyrocketed, the cost of the war increased to $30 billion a year, and "anti-Americanism in Europe grew to unparalleled dimensions, largely because of Vietnam" (emphasis McPherson's). In addition, McPherson noted, under Johnson's watch racial divisions had increased, youth were increasingly alienated from their elders, the government, and the American system, and the crime rate had continued to rise.

> Your culpability or lack of it, for any of these things is beside the point [McPherson wrote]. This is all "bad news." To the voter, it is like going deeper and deeper into debt. What a man wants when this happens to him is *not* someone who will say, "You should be proud of your situation. It's the price of responsibility, and there's nothing so good as responsibility. I recommend that you go deeper into debt." He wants someone to show him how to get *out* of debt, even if that will take time. He needs "good news": a word of encouragement that says, "Sure, you can get out of debt. You just have to change the way you're doing things right now."

McPherson's advice was simple: Johnson must change his policies in several areas, but particularly in Vietnam. But a change in the status quo, McPherson warned, would mean either pursuit of a military victory and a massive escalation to as many as one million troops or "deescalating the fighting by changing our tactics, and ultimately even bringing a few Americans home. I pray we choose the latter."[24] Johnson knew McPherson was right. Press Secretary George Christian told McPherson that Johnson had agreed with much of the memorandum.[25]

It was time for Johnson to decide how he would proceed in Vietnam. Would he stick to his tentative decision of early March—give Westmoreland twenty-two thousand extra troops, call up the reserves, and give Rusk time to see if another bombing pause might lure Hanoi to the negotiating table—or would he give in to the hawks in Congress and the Pentagon who continued to press for a decisive military victory? Few now advised him to choose the latter route. "It seems to me that requests for any increase above the 525,000 assigned level ought to be resisted," Mansfield advised in a March 13 memorandum. "That does not mean we have to get out of Viet Nam. It does mean we have to concentrate and consolidate the already great commitment we have there."[26]

When Johnson met with Dean Acheson on March 14, he tried to persuade the former secretary of state that the ground war against the Viet Cong was finally picking up. "Mr. President," Acheson said bluntly, "you are being led down the garden path." Acheson now doubted the military was capable of providing objective information about the war. He also thought it much more important to determine whether the South Vietnamese would ever be capable of fighting alone. If not, he urged Johnson to launch the country "on a path looking towards progressive disengagement."[27]

Several days later, Johnson's old friend James Rowe was equally straightforward when he told the president that "somehow or other, somewhere or other the picture of the President as the man who would go anywhere, do anything in his desperate search for Peace has been lost. McCarthy and Kennedy are the candidates of peace and the President is the war candidate." As Rowe noted, with some exaggeration, "everyone has turned into a dove."[28] UN Ambassador Arthur Goldberg also advised Johnson against escalation and went further than even Rusk in proposing a total bombing halt. Johnson was furious at what he perceived as Goldberg's betrayal. "Let's get one thing clear!" he bellowed at his advisors. "I'm telling you now that I am not going to stop the bombing. Now I don't want to hear any more about it."[29] But Johnson's former national security advisor, McGeorge Bundy, had not gotten that word. "This damned war is much tougher than—and very different from—World War II and Korea," Bundy wrote on March 22, "and I just don't think the country can be held together much longer by determination and patriotism alone." While he was opposed to "empty peace gestures," Bundy said that "I have to admit that Goldberg is right when he says the only one thing that the whole world—and Kennedy and McCarthy too—will call serious is a bombing halt."[30]

The fact that Johnson's inner circle was now full of doves would not make it easier to stop or reduce the bombing. As he told Rusk, Clifford, and Rostow on March 19, he would make "the hawks furious" if he stopped the bombs. Rusk, however, was direct. The "element of hope has been taken away by the Tet offensive. People don't think there is likely to be an end."[31] Something had to give, and soon. To Rusk and Clifford, reducing the bombing had grown even more enticing in light of renewed hints coming from Hanoi that North Vietnam might be open to negotiations. But as Johnson continued to discuss his options, he knew that he could not delay his decision on the troops much longer. The public, as well as members of Congress, had grown anxious their Tet's wake, an uneasiness only exacerbated by continued media speculation about Westmoreland's request for additional troops.

Hoping to calm the public about Vietnam, Johnson had decided on a nationally televised speech, scheduled for March 31. In the meantime, he had put his advisors, led by Harry McPherson, to work preparing that speech and—and the same time—formulating the new policy he would unveil in the address. But, as he told Clifford and McPherson, he wanted a tough speech. On March 20, when Clifford tried to persuade him to instead make a peace overture the centerpiece of the speech, Johnson refused. "Let's get 'peace' out of the speech except [to say] that we're ready to talk," Johnson ordered. "We are mixing up two different things when we include peace initiatives in this speech. Let's just make it troops and war."[32] When Clifford saw the draft that Johnson ordered McPherson to write, he was thoroughly depressed. "I thought it would be a calamity for the President to make that speech," he later said.[33]

By now, Clifford had moved considerably further away from the administration's Vietnam policy—much further than Johnson would ever have imagined. Disturbed by the growing domestic unrest and the erosion of public support for Johnson's policies and persuaded that the bombing had long since failed, the Defense secretary knew that Johnson could no longer sustain his Vietnam policies and his presidency at the same time. "I was convinced," he later said, "that the military course we were pursuing . . . was not only endless, but hopeless" and that "our primary goal should be to level off our involvement, and to work toward gradual disengagement."[34]

Hoping to move Johnson away from "troops and war" and toward a significant bombing reduction, Clifford urged Johnson to convene again the group of distinguished political, legal, and foreign policy experts—the "Wise Men" who had advised him to stay the course in their meeting the previous November. Johnson respected these men. Each represented some aspect of the unassailable Cold War orthodoxy that had guided the foreign and military policies of the past four presidential administrations. Johnson trusted men like Acheson; McGeorge Bundy; Averell Harriman; Supreme Court Justice Abe Fortas; Generals Maxwell Taylor and Omar Bradley, both former chairmen of the Joint Chiefs; Douglas Dillon, Kennedy's Treasury secretary; George Ball, the former under secretary of state; Henry Cabot Lodge, the former senator who had twice served as ambassador to South Vietnam; and, Arthur Dean, former law partner of John Foster Dulles and negotiator of the Korean armistice.

On Monday, March 25, the "Wise Men" gathered at the State Department for another briefing on the war. Except for General Matthew Ridgway, the former commander of U.S. forces in Korea, and Cyrus Vance, former deputy secretary of defense, the group was identical to the one that had met with Johnson in November. Briefed by officials from the State and Defense departments and the CIA, the group now reached a radically different conclusion. "In November," Douglas Dillon later said, "we were told that it would take us a year to win." In the wake of Tet, however, the military landscape looked far different. "Now it looked like five or ten, if that. I knew the country wouldn't stand for it." Vance arrived already knowing how he would advise Johnson. "I could sense that the country was being torn up," he said. "We had to find a way out." The next morning, the group met again to formulate their recommendations. "There must have been a mistake in the invitation list," Ball thought as he watched the group of erstwhile hawks discuss ways to disengage the United States from Vietnam. But the decision was not unanimous. Taylor, for one, scolded the group for its change of heart. He later complained that "the same mouths that said a few months before to the President, 'You're on the right course, but do more,' were now saying that the policy was a failure."[35]

Early that afternoon, Johnson heard the verdict. "There is a very significant shift in our position," McGeorge Bundy began. "When we last met, we saw reasons for hope." Today, however, Bundy reported that most of the group—Taylor, Fortas, and Bradley excepted—believed that "we must begin to take steps to disengage." One by one the "Wise Men" gave Johnson the dreaded news. Acheson: "The issue is can we do what we are trying to do in Vietnam. I do not think we can." Arthur Dean: "All of us got the impression that there is no military conclusion in sight." Dillon: "The briefing last night led me to conclude we cannot achieve a military victory." Ball: "Our objectives are not attainable. . . . As long as we continue to bomb, we alienate ourselves from the civilized world."[36] Deeply disturbed by the gloomy tone of the report, Johnson demanded to hear the State Department's briefing for himself. "I don't know why they've drawn that conclusion," he said afterwards.[37] The briefing, Clifford later said, "was a very bitter pill" for Johnson.[38]

Clifford, however, was elated. His gambit appeared to have worked. He had forced Johnson to face the truth that military victory, short of a million or more American soldiers, was impossible. But as preparations for the president's March 31 speech proceeded, Clifford's euphoria quickly dissolved. Johnson was far from prepared to renounce his bellicosity. He remained adamantly opposed to including language about negotiation or deescalation in the speech. "The President cannot give that speech!" Clifford said, in an uncharacteristic display of emotion, when he saw an early draft. "It would be a disaster! This speech is about war. What the President needs is a speech about peace! The first sentence reads, 'I want to talk to you about the war in Vietnam.' It should read, 'I want to talk to you about *peace* in Vietnam [emphasis Clifford's].'"

To Clifford's surprise, Rusk agreed. In fact, the secretary of state had been working quietly for weeks—since he had first proposed a partial bombing halt on March 4—to persuade Johnson that it was time to aggressively seek a negotiated settlement. "My own mind is running close to that of Harry McPherson about a possible peace move," Rusk told Johnson before his meeting with the "Wise Men. "Still skeptical about the likelihood that negotiations with the North Vietnamese would succeed, he had concluded that it was at least worth a try. "Even a blind hog sometimes finds the chestnut," Rusk told Johnson.[39]

McPherson was astonished that none of Johnson's civilian advisors now argued against a determined peace initiative. "Here were five men [Rusk, Clifford, Rostow, William Bundy, and McPherson], all associated with the war," McPherson recalled. "All of whom had either urged its prosecution, helped to form its strategies, argued its rationale, or written its leader's speeches; and not one of whom spoke out against 'winding it down'—which would mean, inevitably, accepting a result that was less than satisfactory by the standards they had set for it."[40] But it was Johnson's opinion that counted and until he acknowledged the futility of further escalation, the peace process could not begin.

The day after his meeting with the "Wise Men," Johnson sent word to Mansfield through their mutual friend, James Rowe, that he wanted to talk about Vietnam. At first, Mansfield demurred, undoubtedly certain from experience that nothing he could say would ever influence Johnson to change course in Vietnam. "He's got too much on his mind," Mansfield said, politely declining the invitation. But Rowe was persistent and finally persuaded Mansfield to call the White House for an appointment. Later that evening, Mansfield met with Johnson in the Cabinet Room.

"Westmoreland wants 200,000 more troops," Johnson told Mansfield. "We can't give it to him. But I've talked it over with Clark Clifford and I want 40,000."

"Isn't 40,000 too much?" Mansfield replied.

"Well, I sent the Marines over from [Camp] Pendleton, and the Airborne from Fort Bragg with no support."

"You may have to support them," said Mansfield, the ex-Marine, "but it doesn't take anywhere near 40,000."

Johnson phoned Clifford and, after a fifteen-minute discussion, turned back to Mansfield and said, "You won't go for 40,000?"

"No," Mansfield said. "You're not offering any hope for the American people. You're just getting us involved deeper."

Johnson then showed Mansfield a draft of the speech he planned to give on March 31. After reading the entire draft, Mansfield said, "It won't sell. . . . You've got to offer the American people some hope. You've got to get out some way. You're in too deep. It's costing too much in lives. And it's going to cost you more if you don't change your opinion."

Johnson did not argue with Mansfield. But as he left, Johnson—with uncharacteristic equanimity—said, "Mike, I wish we'd agree more often, but I want you to know I appreciate your candor."[41]

It is not clear whether Mansfield's conversation with Johnson was decisive, or only added to cumulative opposition to more escalation. It is clear, however, that Johnson—with the exception of Westmoreland and a few military advisors—was now almost entirely surrounded by men who recognized the futility of pressing for a military victory in Vietnam.*

Outside his administration, in Congress, the opposition was even more virulent and potentially more problematic. "If the street demonstrations could not convince the President to alter his course," McPherson observed later, "word that Congress no longer supported it could. Along that armature between the Capitol and the White House, the current flowed—not, this time, from President to Congress to country, but in reverse."[42] Everywhere he looked, the message was clear: Congress and the public would no longer support the mindless pursuit of a military victory. It was time to pursue a peaceful solution.

Finally, on Thursday, March 28, Johnson relented. He told his aides to prepare the kind of speech that Clifford had wanted all along. Throughout the weekend, Johnson and his aides painstakingly rewrote the speech line by line. On Sunday evening, Johnson would announce suspension of the air attacks over North Vietnam, "except in the area north of the demilitarized zone" where enemy troops directly threatened American and

---

*When Johnson consulted Richard Russell about Rusk's proposal to severely limit the bombing, Russell was adamantly opposed, "unless there was some indication of reciprocity on the part of the North Vietnamese." But later he candidly acknowledged that "I have no solution of my own to bring the war to a successful conclusion without considerable escalation" (Fite, 459).

South Vietnamese troops and through which the North Vietnamese continued to move their troops and supplies southward. The partial bombing halt, he hoped, might prompt the North Vietnamese to agree to talks.

As they wrapped up work on the speech on Saturday night, Johnson asked McPherson why he had removed the speech's peroration. "I didn't like it, Mr. President," McPherson answered. "I'm going upstairs to write another. I'll make it short. The speech is already pretty long." Johnson smiled. "That's O.K.," he said. "Make it as long as you want. I may even add one of my own." When Johnson left, McPherson turned to Clifford. "Jesus, is he going to say sayonara?" Clifford had missed Johnson's signal. "What?" he asked. McPherson tried to explain what he thought he had heard. "Is he going to say goodbye tomorrow night?" McPherson recalled that Clifford simply dismissed his suspicions and "looked at me with pity, as if I were too tired to be rational."[43]

For almost a year, a weary Johnson had suggested to Lady Bird and various staff members that he might not run again. His popularity was at its lowest ebb. The war, a sluggish economy, and the urban riots had left severe physical and emotional scars on Johnson and his presidency. The Tet offensive, as well as Eugene McCarthy's surprising strength in New Hampshire—presaging an ugly, protracted struggle to recapture the nomination—had only added more weight to the immense burdens Johnson carried in early 1968. For weeks, Johnson had been able to sleep only a few hours each night. Sometimes, he would rise at 3:00 A.M.—clad in pajamas and bathrobe—to monitor the bombing from the Situation Room or the Oval Office.[44]

It was about this time that his old friend Richard Russell began to dread his private visits with Johnson. In meetings during the early months of 1968, Russell recalled that Johnson often cried uncontrollably.[45] As Johnson told Doris Kearns, "I felt that I was being chased on all sides by a giant stampede coming at me from all directions. On one side, the American people were stampeding me to do something about Vietnam. . . . The whole situation was unbearable for me. After thirty-seven years of public service, I deserved something more than being left alone in the middle of the plain, chased by stampedes on every side."[46]

At 9:00 P.M. on Sunday, March 31, a solemn Johnson, bathed in the glow of the bright klieg lights, sat at his Oval Office desk and peered into the television cameras. "Tonight I want to speak to you of peace in Vietnam and Southeast Asia," he began, adding that his pursuit of a peaceful solution in Vietnam had been sincere. But at every turn, he said, the North Vietnamese had spurned his overtures, most recently with "a savage assault on the people, the government and the allies of South Vietnam." Should the war continue, Johnson warned of the inevitable causalities on both sides. "There is no need to delay the talks that could bring an end to this long and this bloody war," he declared. With that, he renewed the offer he had made the previous August—"to stop the bombardment of North Vietnam. We ask that talks begin promptly, that they be serious talks on the substance of peace." To hasten North Vietnam's acquiescence, Johnson said, "I am taking the first step to deescalate the conflict. We are reducing—substantially—the present level of hostilities. And we are doing so unilaterally, and at once." The bombing over all of North Vietnam north of the Demilitarized Zone would stop. Instead of sending the 206,000 men that Westmoreland requested, Johnson said he would send only 13,500 new troops spread out over the next five months.

At the end of his speech, Johnson dropped another bombshell. He had concluded, he said, "that I should not permit the Presidency to becoming involved in the partisan divisions that are developing in this political year." With peace hanging the balance, Johnson said he believed he should avoid "partisan causes" as long as the war continued. "Accordingly, I shall not seek, and I will not accept, the nomination of my party for another term as your President."[47] Afterwards, at a press conference, Johnson told reporters that he hoped that his decision would permit him to "concentrate more of our energies and efforts on trying to bring about peace in the world and we will have a better chance to do it." Later, in answer to a question about the irrevocability of his decision, Johnson said, "I don't feel very good about asking half a million men to stand out there and defend us, and offer their lives and die for us, and for me not to do everything I can to put myself in a position to do a job as successfully as they do theirs."[48]

But Johnson's was not a completely altruistic decision aimed at achieving peace in Vietnam. It was also based on cold political calculations that his reelection prospects were dim, primarily because of the war but also because of the domestic unrest and growing congressional exasperation with his leadership. Exhausted and doubtful of victory, Johnson had chosen to play the role of statesman instead of politician.

Politically, it was a masterstroke that brought him accolades from Democrats on both sides of the Vietnam issue. The announcement had represented Johnson's "finest hour," McGovern said. "I believe it will go down in history as the most imaginative and significant action of his Administration."[49] Russell believed Johnson had demonstrated "the good faith of his efforts for peace" and had proved "the sincerity of his overwhelming desire to end the war in Vietnam and bring peace to the whole world."[50] Morse magnanimously called it one of Johnson's "great speeches."[51] Robert Byrd described Johnson's decision as "an act of selfless devotion to duty."[52] In light of Johnson's announcement, Church said that "no one, at home or abroad, can any longer doubt his sincerity of purpose."[53] Said Mansfield: "I hope there will be no question raised in this country about the credibility of Lyndon B. Johnson in this or any other respect."[54]

Among Republicans, Richard Nixon—worried that a quick end to the war might scuttle his own campaign for the White House—greeted Johnson's announcement far more skeptically. While he said he hoped the peace initiative succeeded, Nixon said that "in my judgment, a bombing halt by itself would not be a step toward peace." Pointing to the "lesson" of Korea, he noted that most of the U.S. casualties in that conflict had occurred "*after* peace talks began." He left the door open to attack any Johnson-brokered peace plan: "This is a time for both hope and realism—a time to explore every avenue toward settlement, but at the same time, to keep up our guard against the temptation of a camouflaged surrender."[55]

Although he had guided the process that produced Johnson's decision to curtail the bombing, Clifford still wondered: Exactly what had the president intended? Had he given up his political career in the pursuit of peace, "or had he put forward a series of half measures designed to shore up domestic support, at a lower cost, without changing our objective in Vietnam?" Clifford suspected that Johnson "was torn between a search for an honorable exit and his desire not to be the first President to lose a foreign war." As Clifford noted, because Johnson's objectives were not entirely clear in his own mind, "he sent conflicting signals and possibly lost the opportunity to end the war during his term in office." For his part, Clifford hoped the speech would mark the beginning of a renewed and deadly serious bid for peace talks. But Rusk, Bunker, Rostow, and Johnson's military advisors—fearing that an aggressive push for talks might only weaken the already shaky government in Saigon—saw the speech primarily as a way to shore up domestic support for the war.[56]

Johnson himself acknowledged that his speech was motivated more by domestic concerns. "My biggest worry was not Vietnam itself," he later wrote. "It was the divisiveness and pessimism at home. I knew the American people were deeply worried. I had seen the effects of Tet on some of the Wise Men. I looked upon my approaching speech as an opportunity to help right the balance and provide better perspective."[57]

Rhetoric is often a poor indicator of intentions. Actions are more reliable. Thus, Johnson's actions of April 1 may have answered Clifford's questions more definitively than his words ever could. That morning, U.S. planes flew bombing missions deep into North Vietnam, 205 miles north of the Demilitarized Zone and only 80 miles south of Hanoi. In fact, on that day American bombers flew one hundred missions against North Vietnam—nearly twice the daily average prior to Johnson's speech. It was clear that, despite the speech, the fundamental American policy in Vietnam had not changed substantially. Only the tactics in pursuit of that policy had changed. The next day, from the Senate floor, Fulbright understandably expressed confusion over Johnson's motives and appealed to the White House to clarify exactly what the president had meant when he announced the bombing halt over most of North Vietnam.*

The intensified bombing, he said, "is a great tragedy because I cannot imagine how this President or hardly anyone else can ever say anything or do anything that would impress the Vietnamese or the enemy with our intentions hereafter to move in a significant way to bring the war to a close."[58] Fulbright's criticism, and a resulting chorus of attacks from other critics, enraged Johnson, but also forced him to retreat further by restricting the bombing to an area between the Demilitarized Zone and the 20th Parallel.[59]

Johnson's decision to curtail the bombing, despite the April 1 forays deep into North Vietnam, appeared to be working. On April 3, Hanoi said it was interested in "contact with U.S. representatives to decide . . . the unconditional cessation of bombing and all other war acts against the DRV so that talks can begin." Johnson greeted the North Vietnamese statement with cautious optimism, saying only "we will establish contact with the representatives of North Vietnam."[60] On May 3, after a month of negotiation over the location of the potential talks, Johnson announced that American and North Vietnamese officials would soon begin meeting in Paris to open "conversations" to discuss a formal peace process. "This is only the very first step," Johnson warned reporters at a press conference. "There are many, many hazards and difficulties ahead."[61]

One of those difficulties was the exact nature of the U.S. negotiating position at Paris. Although Johnson's more hawkish advisors—Rusk, Rostow, Bunker, Taylor, and the Joint Chiefs—wanted the American delegation to assume a tough, unrelenting stance, Johnson finally sided with doves like Harriman, Clifford, Goldberg, and Katzenbach, who advanced a more flexible approach. He also appointed Deputy Defense Secretary Cyrus Vance, sympathetic to a flexible U.S. position, to lead the American delegation. "I'm glad we're going to talk," Johnson told the delegation on May 6 before they left for Paris, "but I'm not overly hopeful. I think it's going to be tough going, very tough." Johnson warned the delegation not to concern itself with domestic politics. "Some of you may think that we

---

*Technically, Johnson had not promised to bomb only those areas in the Demilitarized Zone, although he may have purposely tried to leave that impression. Johnson had merely said he would stop bombing everywhere *except* "north of the demilitarized zone where the continuing enemy buildup directly threatens allied forward positions."

want a resolution of this because it is an election year. Now be clear, I want it resolved, but not because of this or any election."[62]

On May 13, formal discussions between the United States and North Vietnam opened in Paris. From the beginning, however, the talks deadlocked. The North Vietnamese maintained that their participation was aimed at obtaining the "unconditional cessation of the U.S. bombing raids and all other acts of war so that talks may start."[63] Johnson later complained that "the opening statement by the chief North Vietnamese delegate could have been an editorial in Hanoi's Communist party newspaper. We were the 'aggressors.' All right was on their side, all wrong on ours. Their solution was for us to stop the bombing and pull out all our forces." Johnson also believed, correctly, that another North Vietnamese objective was the manipulation of U.S. and world public opinion. North Vietnamese delegates quoted antiwar statements made by Fulbright and Robert Kennedy. Johnson complained that "they began to turn the Paris talks into a propaganda sideshow."[64]

JOHNSON'S WITHDRAWAL FROM the presidential race only intensified the struggle for the Democratic nomination. Within days, Humphrey entered the race. By then, however, it was too late to organize a campaign organization to effectively compete against Kennedy and McCarthy in the primaries. Instead, the vice president chose to avoid most direct electoral confrontations with his Democratic rivals and focus on the delegate-rich nonprimary states.

In any event, as the man who had suffered defeat at the hands of John F. Kennedy in the 1960 presidential primaries, Humphrey dreaded the thought of another direct Kennedy encounter. When Johnson had first disclosed that he would not seek reelection and urged Humphrey to run, the vice president's stunned reaction had been, "There's no way I can beat the Kennedy machine."[65] But as he would soon prove, backed by the money and organization of the Democratic Party establishment, Humphrey *could* successfully challenge Kennedy and his machine. Within weeks, Humphrey assembled an impressive, well-funded coalition that included labor, business, civil rights and Jewish leaders, party regulars, and even some pro-war southern segregationists. But no matter how hard he would try, Humphrey could not remove the stains of his intimate association with Johnson. Since 1966, the vice president had been among the most vocal and unequivocal supporters of Johnson's Vietnam policies—the steep price he had paid to return to and remain in Johnson's good graces. Humphrey had, indeed, rehabilitated himself in the White House. But that rehabilitation had also come at a steep price. Now, in the public's mind, Humphrey was intimately associated with a very unpopular war—a war that he had publicly and enthusiastically championed at home and abroad.

The Kennedy juggernaut, meanwhile, rolled effortlessly through the primaries. On May 7, Kennedy won in Indiana with 42 percent of the vote to McCarthy's 27 percent. Determined to remain in the race, McCarthy blithely dismissed the results by telling reporters that it did not matter who finished first. "That's not what my father told me," Kennedy replied. One week later, Kennedy rolled up another victory, this time in Nebraska, where he won 51.5 percent of the vote. McCarthy finished at 31 percent. Kennedy saw his vote, combined with McCarthy's, as a resounding repudiation of the Johnson–Humphrey administration. "The people want to move in a different direction," he said. "We can't have the politics of happiness and joy [a slap at Humphrey's unfortunate "politics of joy" campaign theme] when we have so many problems in our own country." Kennedy's only disappointing showing would come in Oregon on May 28, when McCarthy beat him, 45 to 39 percent. The next morning, Kennedy headed to California where he hoped a strong victory there would propel him, victorious, toward the Democratic nomination in August.[66]

Nixon, meanwhile, had assumed—hoped even—that Johnson would be his general election rival. Weakened by an unpopular war, a struggling economy, and the growing, often violent domestic unrest that had spilled into the nation's streets, the incumbent president seemed like the perfect opponent. Now, however, Nixon faced the possibility that he would confront not a weakened, unpopular president, but a strong, charismatic antiwar Democrat like Kennedy. Like Humphrey, Nixon did not relish the prospect of running against another Kennedy for the presidency.

For Nixon, Vietnam was a problem. For years, he had cast himself as an unrepentant hawk. He had steadfastly opposed most efforts aimed at a diplomatic solution in Vietnam, telling a reporter in 1965 that he would only "support a settlement of the kind the Eisenhower Administration reached in Korea, in which South Vietnam retained independence and security." However, by late 1967—planning another run for the White House and pragmatic enough to know that a military victory in Vietnam was unlikely—Nixon began to relax his hard-line opposition to peace talks. The nation was tired of war and Nixon knew that while a strong, pro-military stance might have won him votes in 1966, that position would not play well with a growing segment of the public. While he had hinted at a plan to end the war (he had pledged to "end the war and win the peace"), Nixon knew that he needed a new strategy for the changing times.

In early March, he unveiled his new approach when he told an NBC radio audience that Johnson had "frittered away" the nation's military power "in a misguided policy of gradualism." Had Johnson employed "our power quickly, we could have ended it with far less than we are now using," Nixon asserted, without offering specifics. Yet at the same time Nixon insisted that military power alone would not be decisive. Better and more determined diplomacy was needed. Instead of questioning the need for a diplomatic solution—as he had done for more than two years—Nixon would now claim that *stronger* diplomatic efforts were needed because the war was harming U.S.-Soviet relations. The solution to Vietnam, Nixon said, could lie in Moscow, where Soviet officials—hoping for better relations with the United States—might be persuaded to urge their North Vietnamese allies to accept a negotiated settlement.[67]

Nixon's new strategy was imaginative, politically canny, and highly cynical. His stance on the war had something for everyone. All at once, he portrayed himself as a hawk who faulted Johnson for not using enough military force soon enough; a dove who advocated a negotiated settlement, believing that the opportunity for a military victory had passed; and a clever moderate who advocated an imaginative effort to involve the Soviets in a peace plan, while opposing a hasty withdrawal of American troops and warning against an overly flexible bargaining position at Paris. Nixon's political strategy also reflected his desire for maximum diplomatic and military latitude should he win the election. "I've come to the conclusion that there's no way to win the war," Nixon confessed to his aides on March 29 after learning from his sources that the "Wise Men" had advised Johnson to give up on a military solution. "But we can't say that, of course. In fact, we have to seem to say the opposite, just to keep some degree of bargaining leverage."[68]

But for Nixon, Johnson's March 31 announcement changed everything. With Johnson out of the picture, and Kennedy's star rising, Nixon feared that public frustration over the war might not shape the election to the degree he had anticipated. "He had expected to face a bloodied, beatable opponent," recalled speechwriter Richard Whalen, who observed that "Johnson's withdrawal left [Nixon] a bit scared."[69]

But Johnson's ostensible decision to remove himself from politics also let Nixon off the hook and devalued Vietnam as an issue for Kennedy and McCarthy. Now Nixon could claim that he was merely following Johnson's lead by declaring a temporary "moratorium" on statements about Vietnam.* "In order to avoid anything that might, even inadvertently, cause difficulty for our negotiators, I shall not make the comprehensive statement

---

*This is virtually the same Vietnam strategy that Barry Goldwater had adopted in 1964, when he offered Johnson a secret truce on campaign rhetoric about the war.

on Vietnam which I had planned for this week," Nixon said of a major policy speech he had scheduled for March 31. For the remainder of the campaign, Nixon would strike the pose of responsible statesman—so patriotic
and committed to the delicate peace process that he would not make public statements about the war while the Paris talks continued.[70] As long as
Johnson had the opportunity to negotiate a peace settlement, as Nixon
would insist in late May, it was wrong to "make some statement that would
lead the enemy to believe that he could wait and get a different deal. . . .
In other words, let's not destroy the chances for a peaceful settlement by a
mouthful of words."[71]

Meanwhile, running behind Humphrey in the delegate hunt,
Kennedy's campaign gained momentum and now enjoyed a certain air of
high expectation and even inevitability. "If the New York Senator is going
to be stopped," *U.S. News & World Report* said, "Hubert Humphrey will
have to do the stopping."[72] Indeed, Kennedy's primary victories in South
Dakota and California on June 4 put him in a strong position to make a
powerful case for his candidacy in the two-and-a-half months leading up
to the Democratic National Convention in Chicago. Kennedy, after all,
had won most of his delegates, not in the backrooms like Humphrey, but
in electoral contests across the nation.

Despite Humphrey's lead in the delegate count, Kennedy was closing
in fast. "What I think is clear," a victorious Kennedy told a rally in Los
Angeles after the California primary returns were in, "is that we can work
together in the last analysis, and that what has been going on with the
United States over a period of the last three years—the division, the violence, the disenchantment with our society; the divisions, whether it's
between blacks and whites, between poor and the more affluent, or
between age groups or on the war in Vietnam—is that we can start to work
together. We are a great country, an unselfish country, and a compassion-
ate country." Moments later, Kennedy lay dying, the victim of three bullets from an assassin's gun.[73]

CHAPTER 37

The Vice President
Has Very Few Guns

1968

If the experiences of 1965 and 1966 had deepened George McGovern's opposition to the war, the presidential election year of 1968 marked the beginning of a new phase of his effort to end the conflict. Throughout the year, McGovern had tried to remain neutral in the presidential race, refusing to endorse McCarthy, Humphrey, or Kennedy. But despite his official neutrality, McGovern made no secret of his affection for Kennedy. If Kennedy were elected, McGovern said when introducing the New York senator to a South Dakota audience in April 1968, "he will, in my judgment, become one of the three or four greatest presidents in our national history."[1] The sudden void left by Kennedy's death sent the slain senator's supporters looking forlornly for a candidate around whom they could rally. McGovern, the antiwar champion who had regarded Kennedy as one of his closest Senate friends, suddenly became that rallying point.

Like many others, McGovern had doubted his or anyone's ability to build a serious candidacy around opposition to the Vietnam War. But McCarthy's strong showing in the early days of the campaign caused almost everyone, including McGovern, to reconsider. "If I had sensed that such a groundswell of support were possible," McGovern later wrote, "I would have entered the race—even at the sacrifice of my Senate seat."[2] By the time New Hampshire exposed Johnson's political weakness, it was too late. Kennedy quickly jumped into the race and McGovern again demurred.

But after Kennedy's death, a presidential campaign became more appealing, if only, in McGovern's words, "to maximize the impact of the antiwar movement at the coming convention."[3] On August 10, less than three weeks before the Chicago convention, McGovern announced he would seek the nomination. But his primary aim, he told supporters, was to gain a voice for the antiwar movement in writing the party's platform:

> The loss of American youth and the slaughter of the Vietnamese should stop now. The next president of the United States, if he has the will to do so, can soon end this war on terms fully acceptable to the American people.
>
> As Democrats, we bear a special burden to the voters, because four years ago we sought their confidence on a platform of peace. "We seek no wider war" was the pledge of 1964. Now, 25,000 young American lives and $100 billion later, it is our responsibility to take to the American people a platform and a leadership determined to reverse the grievous error—not rationalize it.[4]

McGovern was waging a losing cause—and he knew it. In the aftermath of Kennedy's death, Humphrey had moved swiftly to sew up the nomination. But the nomination he sought was, in many respects, devalued currency. Kennedy's assassination had, in Humphrey's words, worked to "sour the whole public, and particularly the Democratic party, on the election and on the democratic process." What Humphrey did not say was that much of the public's resentment and anxiety over the war, and the domestic unrest that it had sparked, was now laid at the vice president's doorstep, particularly by many of Kennedy's young former supporters. In a strange way, many of them resented Humphrey, like Johnson before him, for benefiting from the death of a Kennedy. "I was doing everything I could to get the nomination," Humphrey said later, "but God knows I didn't want it that way."[5]

Although Kennedy's death had ensured Humphrey's nomination, it did little to enhance his prospects for November. Now that there was no serious contest for the nomination, Humphrey's fund-raising lagged and Johnson's interest in his candidacy, fed primarily by his intense animosity for Kennedy, evaporated. With McCarthy's campaign at a standstill, Humphrey's candidacy lost what little luster it had left. Nothing, however, was more damaging to Humphrey's image than his fatal association with Lyndon Johnson and his war. Although campaign advisors continually urged him to distance himself from Johnson, especially on the war, Humphrey vacillated. "Anyone who would repudiate a government and a policy of which he has been a part in order to gain votes," Humphrey told Oklahoma Democrats in June, "is not the kind of person you can trust to keep the promises he makes in a campaign and deliver on them in a general election."[6]

The crisis of Humphrey's ill-fated association with Johnson only deepened in early July when Johnson ordered resumption of B-52 bombing raids along the infiltration routes north of the Demilitarized Zone. Despite Johnson's earlier decision to curtail the bombing north of the 20th Parallel, the intensity of the attacks along those infiltration routes had nearly doubled in 1968—to more than one million tons of bombs for the year. The notion of a deescalating American presence in Vietnam ran counter to the news coming out of Southeast Asia in early 1968. In March and April, for example, General Creighton Abrams*—the new American commanding general in South Vietnam—ordered the most extensive search-and-destroy mission of the war and sent more than one hundred thousand troops into battle against enemy forces in the Mekong Delta region.

Everywhere Humphrey went, protesters heckled him, chanting "Dump the Hump!" One sign that confronted him in Los Angeles said: HITLER, HUBERT AND HIROHITO. Meanwhile, there was little to cheer about in the polling data. One national survey in mid-July showed him only narrowly ahead of Nixon, while McCarthy enjoyed an eight-point lead over the presumptive Republican nominee. "Humphrey's problem, one he can't escape," observed a *Time* writer, "is that he carries on his back the past. He is the candidate of the past no matter how much he talks about his programs and the future." Humphrey knew his predicament. "I'm in the position of walking a tightrope," he told staff members.[7]

Finally, in July, Humphrey relented. He allowed campaign staff members to draft a Vietnam platform plank putting just enough space between Johnson and him to convince voters that a Humphrey presidency would mean a quicker end to the war. The draft that aides produced in July represented a significant departure from administration policy. It advocated a cease-fire and "de-Americanizing" the war. The draft also included this statement: "I am encouraged by recent reports of a lull in the fighting, a decline in the infiltration rate from North Vietnam, and at least a temporary curtailing of the shelling of Saigon. If these trends should continue, they might at some point approximate the reciprocal action that our government has called for on previous occasions. If this should develop I would favor an immediate halt in the bombing of North Vietnam."

When Humphrey showed the statement to the president, Johnson balked and told him that he would publicly oppose it. Johnson tried to soften the blow, however, when he hinted at an imminent breakthrough in the peace talks. "We have some things under way now that can lead to very important developments," he cryptically told the vice president of the United States with no elaboration. Later, when Humphrey returned to Johnson with a softened version of the plank, Johnson again urged him to reconsider. Within the week, he promised without offering details, there

---

*Johnson had promoted General Westmoreland to Army chief of staff.

would be an important development in Paris. This time, Humphrey dropped the idea, greatly encouraged that a negotiated settlement was probable—a development he knew would provide a spectacular boost to his campaign. Within days, however, Johnson informed Humphrey that there would be no breakthrough. North Vietnam was mounting a major offensive and in a speech to the Veterans of Foreign Wars on August 19, the president renounced the bombing halt that he had imposed on March 31. "We are not going to stop the bombing just to give them a chance to step up their bloodbath," Johnson declared.[8]

That Johnson appeared to be again escalating the war in Vietnam just weeks before Humphrey's nomination was bad enough; what was worse was that despite having pledged to stay out of politics for the remainder of the year, Johnson and his aides refused to allow Humphrey to control his own convention. Down to the smallest detail, the Chicago convention held during the last week in August would be a Lyndon Johnson affair—including the drafting and approval of the Vietnam platform plank. Humphrey tried his best to influence the platform, but it was only as a supplicant. In the weeks leading up the convention, Humphrey's campaign reluctantly negotiated a delicate compromise draft in consultation with Rusk, Rostow, Eugene McCarthy, and several former Kennedy staff members. Finally, the group agreed to language promising an end to the bombing of North Vietnam that included this proviso: "The action and its timing shall take into account the security of our troops and the likelihood of a response from Hanoi."[9] Having obtained the assent of Johnson's top two foreign policy advisors, Humphrey assumed that Johnson's support was automatic. It was not.

"Well, this plank just undercuts our whole policy and, by God, the Democratic party ought not to be doing that to me and you ought not to be doing it," Johnson complained to Humphrey. "You've been a part of this policy." Humphrey protested, but when Johnson's handpicked Platform Committee chairman, Louisiana Congressman Hale Boggs, threatened to oppose the plank, Humphrey capitulated. "The Vice President has very few guns in a battle with the presidential artillery," Humphrey later explained. "He can be shot down before he takes off."[10]

In the wake of Humphrey's unconditional surrender, McGovern and his supporters immediately set about to put their imprint on the convention's Vietnam plank. Testifying before the platform committee on August 20, McGovern characterized the war in his strongest language ever: "Our involvement in this struggle," he said, "has been the most tragic diplomatic and moral catastrophe in our national history." No longer would he advocate a moderate coastal enclave strategy. Now, he wanted three hundred thousand U.S. troops out of Vietnam in sixty days, a position far more dramatic than that of any other congressional war opponent, McCarthy included.[11]

Humphrey, meanwhile, was strangely unable or unwilling to do anything but watch the farce unfold. The convention that would soon award
him its nomination would also endorse Johnson's position on Vietnam. But
if Humphrey would not fight to save his campaign by standing up to Johnson, McGovern and McCarthy would. In Chicago, the two men joined
forces to substitute a "peace" plank for language that the White House,
with Humphrey's acquiescence, had written. McGovern and McCarthy
insisted on language calling for an immediate end to the bombing, a mutual
withdrawal of all U.S. and North Vietnamese forces from South Vietnam,
a reduction of offensive operations in the Vietnamese countryside, and
U.S. encouragement of a negotiated settlement between the Viet Cong
and the South Vietnamese government.[12]

Not surprisingly, the pro-Johnson committee rejected the McGovern–McCarthy plank by an almost 2 to 1 margin. "Now the lines are clearly
drawn, between those who want more of the same and those who think it
necessary to change our course in Vietnam," McCarthy said after the committee vote. "The convention as a whole will decide."[13] After more than two
hours of acrimonious debate on the afternoon of August 28, the full convention rejected the McGovern–McCarthy substitute, 1,567 to 1,048.[14] The
divisive platform debate over the McGovern–McCarthy substitute,
observed *Congressional Quarterly*, "had no parallel in American convention
politics and the vote was a record of the party opinion that could not help
but influence the party's eventual nominee, Hubert Humphrey. That 40 percent of the delegates had voted against his position was a signal that he would
have grave difficulty holding his party's vote in November."[15]

As the delegates debated Vietnam inside the convention hall, bedlam
reigned on the streets of Chicago. As many as fifteen thousand antiwar
demonstrators violently clashed with members of Mayor Richard Daley's
police force, supported by national guardsmen and state police. "Police
violence is always sickening," wrote the authors of the 1968 campaign
chronicle, *An American Melodrama*. "But what distinguished the police
action in Chicago from anything previously seen . . . was the fact that the
police went, quite literally, berserk."[16] When the young demonstrators—
some of them waving Viet Cong flags—tried to march on the convention
hall, Daley's police force staged a ferocious attack, assaulting them with
clubs and rifle butts. Teargas was everywhere. The angry demonstrators
responded by hurling rocks and bottles. More than one hundred protesters were injured; another 175 were arrested.

The police brutality prompted a horrified Connecticut Senator Abraham
Ribicoff to tell the convention, during his speech to nominate McGovern,
that "with George McGovern we wouldn't have Gestapo tactics on the streets
of Chicago." Delegates erupted in wild applause, as an angry Daley, seated
just below the podium, mouthed profanities at Ribicoff.[17] Unfortunately for

Humphrey, the street violence received more attention than the platform debate and, as journalist Stanley Karnow observed, the televised scenes "alienated many Americans sympathetic to the antiwar movement."[18]

From his hotel suite, Humphrey was barely cognizant of the drama unfolding on the streets below. Eventually, however, teargas wafted into his suite and forced him to take refuge in his shower. That evening, red-eyed from the teargas, Humphrey blamed the protesters for the violence.[19]* McGovern, meanwhile, watched the mayhem from his hotel room and said the experience left him "sick at heart." Although some of the demonstrators' extreme acts—the waving of Viet Cong flags—deeply troubled him, his public remarks indicated that his sympathies were clearly with the protestors. "I saw American youth beaten with police clubs while they lay prostrate on the pavement on Michigan Avenue for the crime of protesting policies in which those young Americans have had no voice."[20]

In accepting the nomination of his party, Humphrey appealed for peace in Vietnam. "Let those who believe our cause in Vietnam has been right—and those who believe it has been wrong—agree here and now," he told the delegates, many of whom had voted for Kennedy or McCarthy in the primaries, "[that] neither vindication nor repudiation will bring peace or be worthy of our country." Humphrey deplored the violence that had enveloped the convention the previous day. "May America tonight resolve that never, never again shall we see what we have seen."

Although McGovern joined Humphrey on the podium in a symbolic statement of unity, McCarthy refused and the Democrats left Chicago bitterly divided over the war. Observed James Reston of the *New York Times* in a column the next morning: "The convention presented to the vast nation-wide audience a picture of division, of old-fashioned city bossism, of clashes between the young and old, of events out of control and of a party unable even to govern itself or maintain order." There was, Reston concluded, "little Humphrey can do to heal his party."[21]

The disarray among Democrats was a boon for Nixon, to whom delegates had awarded their nomination at a peaceful, largely unified Republican National Convention earlier that month in Miami. When compared to Humphrey, who was tied inextricably to Johnson and his policies, the

---

*Later, in his memoirs, Humphrey acknowledged that "decent young people expressing their democratic right to dissent were beaten and injured needlessly and sometimes brutally." But he also defended the police, arguing that they were "provoked in an environment created in large part by a few people" (Humphrey, 387).

recently bellicose Nixon was a dove. At the convention, Nixon explained that his failure to offer specific recommendations to end the war was a patriotic impulse, an expression of his sincere desire to give Johnson a completely free hand in the Paris peace talks. He would reject, he said, any action "in the political arena that might undercut [the] hand" of Johnson's negotiators in Paris. But there was still much that could be discussed, he maintained. "The war must be ended," he said, sounding almost like McGovern and McCarthy. "It must be ended honorably, consistent with America's limited aims and with the long-term requirements of peace in Asia." Nixon said he favored "a negotiated settlement" to the war. But that would require patience, he said.

> Until it *is* ended—and in order to hasten a negotiated end—it must be waged more effectively. But rather than further escalation on the military front, what it requires now is a dramatic escalation of our efforts on the economic, political, diplomatic and psychological fronts. It requires a new strategy, which recognizes that this is a new and different kind of war. And it requires a fuller enlistment of our Vietnamese allies in their own defense.

Attacking Johnson's credibility, Nixon charged a failure "in candor at home and in leadership abroad. By not taking the American people into *its* confidence, the Administration has lost *their* confidence." While Nixon did not explicitly say that he had a plan to end the war, his rhetoric strongly suggested he did. "There is no Republican way or Democratic way to end the war," Nixon said, "but there *is* a difference between an administration that inherits the errors of the past, and an administration that can make a fresh beginning free from the legacy of those errors" (emphasis Nixon's). At the very least, Nixon promised that his administration would bring into office a new era of candor and forthrightness regarding Vietnam. If the war was not over by January of 1969, Nixon said, then it

> can best be ended by a new administration that has given no hostages to the mistakes of the past; an administration neither defending old errors nor bound by the old record. A new Republican administration will be pledged to conduct a thorough reappraisal of every aspect of the prosecution of the war and the search for peace. It will accept nothing on faith, reputation or statistics. In waging the war and making the peace, it will come with a fresh eye and act with a free hand. And it will do what the present administration has so signally failed to do: it will arm the American people with the truth.[22]

Still, Nixon offered few specifics, other than to suggest that the United States "keep the pressure on" North Vietnam militarily, while engaging in more aggressive diplomatic, economic, and political initiatives in South Vietnam. He also suggested that the Soviet Union might also intervene diplomatically, an approach he cited as a possible "key to peace."[23] Nixon's clever ambiguity on Vietnam enabled him to court both the supporters and the opponents of the war. At a press conference during the convention, Nixon appealed to both hawks and doves when he advocated the pursuit of a negotiated settlement—but from a position of strength. "I certainly do not seek the Presidency for the purpose of presiding over the destruction of the credibility of American power throughout the world," he said, adding that "I believe there must be a negotiated settlement." But such a settlement was not possible, Nixon argued, "unless you have the strong military and economic and political presence and policy which will encourage the enemy to negotiate rather than continue to fight." What Nixon seemed to say, couched in reassuring rhetoric about peace, was that the U.S. military should be employed more forcefully to strong-arm the North Vietnamese into making real concessions at the bargaining table—a position barely different from that of the Joint Chiefs of Staff.[24]

Nixon's clever, if disingenuous, strategy of appealing to both sides was working. Humphrey trailed badly in the polls, dogged by a war he had once opposed but later championed. At virtually every campaign stop, boisterous antiwar protesters interrupted his speeches. "The gestalt that the American people had about Humphrey," said the vice president's chief of staff, William Connell, "was Humphrey and those damn, loud kids and banners and so on—an inability to control, inability to be in control." Nixon, meanwhile, serenely promised law and order and an honorable end to the war—a vivid contrast to the uproar, violence, and confusion that dogged his Democratic opponent. While Nixon talked about peace, Humphrey defended Johnson's Vietnam policies. "Every single time that Humphrey would have a press conference—be it Dubuque, Iowa, or New York City," Connell recalled, "the first question was always Vietnam, and the second question was Vietnam, and the third question was Vietnam. He couldn't get on the attack."[25]

Despite Nixon's unwillingness to elaborate on a peace plan, ending the war in Vietnam had become his issue. "If Humphrey would have broken with Johnson on the war," said Republican Congressman Melvin Laird, soon to be Nixon's Defense secretary, "Nixon wouldn't have had a chance." Nixon and Laird always feared that Humphrey would "walk away from Johnson." But throughout September, Humphrey resolutely refused to separate himself from the president and the war that was dragging down his campaign. "Old Johnson had him," Laird said, an observation that few of Humphrey's supporters would ever dispute.[26]

SINCE JUNE, GEORGE BALL—Johnson's house dove during his early years as president—had served as U.S. ambassador to the United Nations. Ball had not wanted the job, but Johnson would not relent. "I need you, George," Johnson had said. "No one else ever disagreed with me as much as you, but I need you." Finally, Ball agreed. But by the late summer, he was in despair as he watched the "nightmare" of protest and violence that had unfolded at the Democratic convention now spread to college campuses around the country—"a fever of hysteria and revulsion induced by the Vietnam War." In even greater frustration, Ball watched as Humphrey tried "futilely to make himself heard against the mindless yammering of enraged hell-raisers." That frustration was only magnified by Ball's intense disdain for Nixon, whom he regarded as "intellectually corrupt." In September, Ball resigned his UN post, telling Johnson that he would devote the next two months to Humphrey's campaign. While he hoped to defeat Nixon, Ball at least wanted to deny him an overwhelming victory.

Ball went out with a bang when he told a press conference at the State Department that he was joining Humphrey's campaign because Nixon "lamentably lacks" the qualities needed for presidential leadership. He was optimistic that there would be "a political solution to the Vietnamese War fairly early in the term of the next President—if he is President Humphrey." Then Ball added, "if he is Mr. Nixon, I have no idea what he would do. . . . I don't think he has any kind of settled principles." Several days later, on CBS's "Face the Nation," Ball attacked Nixon's running mate, Maryland Governor Spiro Agnew, as a "preposterous" choice and described him as "a fourth-rate political hack." Ball's strategy was shrewd. Just as he had hoped, his resignation and his subsequent attacks on Nixon distracted the press and the public just long enough to slow Nixon's momentum.[27]

Nixon, meanwhile, refined his crafty strategy of dual poses on Vietnam. He remained a hawkish dove who refused to give his specific plan for ending the war because it might undermine Johnson's position in Paris. "I am not going to make the practical military judgments as to what it should be," he told a Seattle radio audience in late September, "and I certainly don't want to pull the rug out from under our negotiators in Paris by indicating now that we are going to start cutting back our forces and leave the enemy encouraged to believe that if they just want, they don't really have to negotiate now." At the same time, Nixon said he opposed any weakening of the U.S. military position in Vietnam because "in order to negotiate a settlement the enemy must be convinced that he isn't going to be able

to win something militarily at the time we are talking."²⁸ Asked in a newspaper questionnaire if he was a hawk or a dove, Nixon said simply: "I don't
accept either label. . . . But let me say this: The war must be ended. It must
be ended honorably, consistent with America's limited aims and with the
long-term requirements of peace in Asia."²⁹

Nixon's artful dodges on Vietnam were maddening to Humphrey's
campaign advisors like Ball and Larry O'Brien, who knew the time had
come for Humphrey to make a decision: he would either screw up the
courage to separate himself from Johnson on Vietnam or he would lose the
race. "Let's face it, Mr. Vice President," O'Brien told Humphrey in mid-
September, "as of now, we've lost. It's on everybody's lips. You're not your
own man. Unless you change direction on this Vietnam thing, and become
your own man, you're finished." This time, Humphrey did not fight, but
he insisted that his advisors give him something "positive." He told
O'Brien that he, unlike Nixon, could offer the American people "peace."
He would tell the public that "we have to start pulling our ground forces
out as soon as the Vietnamese are ready—de-Americanizing it." But
O'Brien did not think this was enough. "How can you say that, without a
break [with Johnson]? Johnson hasn't said, 'Phase out.' Listen, we have to
make a clean break this week or never. Do it now—maybe even a white
paper." Humphrey listened, but he was still unsure.

Several days later in South Dakota, with McGovern at his side,
Humphrey began to inch away from Johnson. "I'm going to seek peace in
every way possible, but only the President can do it now. Come January,
it's a new ball game. Then I will make peace." The crowd cheered wildly.
The next day, in Louisville, Humphrey again roused his audience when he
pledged to work for peace in Vietnam. Peace. It was just a word, but
Humphrey finally began to realize the vast potential for his campaign if he
decisively separated himself from Johnson.

Finally, Humphrey agreed to take the plunge. He began making plans
for a major address in Salt Lake City in late September during which he
would spell out his vision for peace in Vietnam. Ball and other Humphrey
aides went to work on the speech and drafted, in Ball's words, "some foggy
language" that would somehow separate Humphrey from Johnson by
"inventing a sufficiently fuzzy shibboleth." The crux of Humphrey's
planned separation from Johnson was this: instead of waiting for North
Vietnamese concessions before stopping the bombing—Johnson's position—Humphrey would "stop the bombing of North Vietnam as an
acceptable risk for peace." If the North Vietnamese failed to respond, then
Humphrey reserved "the right to resume the bombing." That condition
to the bombing halt was added to satisfy Harriman and Vance in Paris, who

worried that Humphrey's promise of an unconditional bombing halt might undermine the U.S. negotiating position.[30]

On the evening of September 30, Humphrey made the speech. "As President," he said, "I would be willing to stop the bombing of North Vietnam as an acceptable risk for peace, because I believe that it could lead to success in the negotiations and a shorter war."[31] So hungry were the American people for an end to the war—and so distrustful were many of them of Nixon's ability to end it—that this one statement transformed Humphrey's campaign. "Instead of students getting up and raising hell with him, people were cheering him," Connell recalled. "He got cheering crowds the next day. And the press accepted it, didn't ask any more questions. Vietnam became a non-issue."[32] Money poured into the campaign—almost $300,000 in the days after the speech. Antiwar liberals returned to the fold and Humphrey, now invigorated, began to energize Democratic regulars, dissuading many of them from voting for third-party candidate George Wallace, the segregationist former governor of Alabama. Even Johnson seemed to take Humphrey's speech in stride.[33] Suddenly, Humphrey's candidacy was on the rise. He was closing in on Nixon.

NIXON WAS WORRIED. Not only had Humphrey's promise to end the bombing revived the flagging Democratic campaign, placing the two major candidates neck-and-neck in public opinion polls, now there was word of a potential breakthrough in the Paris peace talks. In mid-October, Vance and Harriman finally believed they had struck a deal—Harriman called it an "understanding"—with North Vietnam: under the assumption that serious peace talks would follow, the United States would stop all bombing in North Vietnam, confident that the North Vietnamese would not take advantage of the bombing halt to reinforce or resupply their forces in the south and would stop all attacks on South Vietnamese cities. Vance and Harriman also had resolved an ongoing dispute that would finally allow the NLF and the South Vietnamese government to participate in the talks as equals.[34]

At first, Johnson was skeptical of the "understanding," concerned that an announcement less than a month before the presidential election would be labeled a "cheap political trick."[35] Indeed, Nixon had sent word to Johnson that he knew about the breakthrough and suspected that Johnson was trying to "throw the election to Humphrey by pulling something in Paris."[36] Rusk, however, believed the best way to put Nixon at ease was to officially inform him—along with Humphrey and Wallace—of the developments. At an October 14 meeting, Rusk naively assured Johnson that the Republican nominee could be trusted. "Nixon has been honorable on Vietnam," Rusk said. "He has actually been more responsible on this than our own candidate." Clifford agreed. "I expect Nixon would play it fair with you," he said.[37] What Johnson, Rusk, and Clifford did not know, but would soon discover, was that Nixon not only knew about deal, he saw it as a direct threat to his campaign—and he was actively working to sabotage the peace talks by turning the South Vietnamese government against any preelection peace agreement.

Early in 1968, Nixon had opened up a confidential channel of communication with Bui Diem, South Vietnam's ambassador to Washington. His conduit was Madame Anna Chennault, the well-connected China-born widow of General Claire Chennault, famed leader of World War II's Flying Tigers. Well aware of Chennault's extensive contacts throughout Asia, including Saigon, Nixon eagerly embraced her as a campaign advisor. "I know you consider [Chennault] a friend," Nixon had told Bui in a private meeting earlier in the year. "So please rely on her from now on as the only contact between myself and your government."[38]

When she learned of the deal between U.S. negotiators and the North Vietnamese, Chennault immediately contacted Nixon's campaign, whereupon she was instructed to advise South Vietnamese leaders that they should hold out for a better deal under a Nixon administration. Humphrey's Salt Lake City speech, during which he pledged to end the bombing of North Vietnam, persuaded the South Vietnamese government that Nixon and Chennault were right. The message to Thieu was unmistakable: unlike Humphrey, Nixon would negotiate with North Vietnam only from a position of strength. Nixon would keep the pressure on Hanoi. There would be no bombing halts under a Nixon administration. "The longer the present situation continues, the more we are favored," Ambassador Bui cabled President Thieu on October 27, reflecting the advice he had received from the Nixon campaign via Chennault. "I am still in contact with the Nixon entourage. If Nixon is elected, he would first send an unofficial representative to Saigon, and consider going himself to Saigon before taking office."[39] Recalled William Bundy: "Thieu was in one hell of a spot, and a lot of voices in Saigon must have been raised, 'Don't do this [agree to negotiate with the North Vietnamese]! Certainly don't do it to affect the election.'"[40]

Nixon was playing a cynical and deadly game. On October 25, he issued a public statement in which he noted a "flurry of meetings in the White House and elsewhere on Vietnam." He also reported that he had been advised that "top officials in the administration have been driving very hard for an agreement on a bombing halt, accompanied by a cease-

fire, in the immediate future. I have since learned these reports are true."
Nixon then added that he had also been told that "this spurt of activity is
a cynical, last-minute attempt by President Johnson to salvage the candidacy of Mr. Humphrey. This I do not believe."[41] Of course, this was exactly
what Nixon believed—and wanted the voters to believe. "It was an old
standard Nixon ploy," observed journalist Jules Witcover, "giving wide
publicity to a serious charge and then knocking it down himself. It was also
standard Nixon to give testimony to his own purity in not taking political
advantage of the rumor, which he proceeded to do."[42]

Johnson, who had remained mostly above the fray, could not ignore
the attack. Two days later, in a speech in New York, he effusively praised
Humphrey and labeled Nixon as "a man from the past—a veteran of the
time when America's problems were deferred and her needs were ignored."
Nixon was "a man who distorts the history of his time in office," Johnson
said, reminding his audience that Cuba had been "lost to Communism"
under the Eisenhower administration and that Nixon, in 1954, had urged
U.S. intervention on behalf of the beleaguered French at Dien Bien Phu.[43]

Nixon's hypocrisy apparently knew no bounds, as evidenced by his
remarks in a speech on the CBS Radio Network on October 27, when he
reaffirmed his commitment to the success of the Paris talks at the very time
his personal emissary was actively working to undermine them. "As long as
there is a chance for an honorable peace through the Paris talks, candidates
should offer nothing in the political arena that would risk undercutting our
negotiators," Nixon said. "I hope President Johnson can honorably end this
war. I hope it can be done quickly. When the Paris talks began last April, I
pledged that I would do nothing that might interfere." Reminding listen-
ers that he had told the Republican convention's platform committee that
"the pursuit of peace is too important for politics-as-usual," Nixon said that
"tonight, I reaffirm that pledge and commitment."[44]

Relying on information from CIA sources, and an FBI wiretap that
Johnson ordered placed on the South Vietnamese embassy in Washington,
administration officials and Humphrey knew of Nixon's clandestine efforts
to sabotage the talks.[45] "This is treason!" Johnson exploded when presented
with the evidence of Nixon's subversive activities. Days later, fearful that
Johnson would publicly disclose his activities, Nixon frantically phoned the
president to argue his innocence and then contacted Democratic Senator
George Smathers of Florida to protest his purity, pleading with him to reassure Johnson of the same.[46] Johnson, of course, knew better. He had seen
the cables and the transcripts of phone conversations. But the question was:
What to do with the potentially explosive information that surfaced only
days before the election. "There wasn't anything we could do about it,"
Harry McPherson later insisted. "You couldn't, without jeopardizing the

whole ball of wax [the peace talks]."[47] As Johnson told his advisors on October 29, "If we go public—and they [the South Vietnamese] object— we have a real problem on our hands."[48] But Johnson thought Thieu was being duped. "Nixon will doublecross them after November 5," he said.[49]

Humphrey was furious when he received the information about Nixon's stunning duplicity, but was persuaded to do nothing because, as William Connell explained, "It would be considered by the American people as a last-minute, last-ditch" charge leveled by Humphrey out of desperation.[50] Said Ted Van Dyk, one of Humphrey top campaign advisors: "We would have had to explain how we came by the information. [Are] you going to explain that an illegal wiretap was what led you to it? Who's going to confirm that's what you did?" As Van Dyk noted, the latest Harris poll showed Humphrey barely ahead of Nixon. "Why on earth throw a wild, last-minute allegation?" he said. "I thought it would look like a desperate measure which we could not have explained or validated."[51]

Regardless of the intentions or protestations of either side, presidential politics had become inextricably a part of the peace negotiations. "There were so many currents and crosscurrents running it was hard sometimes to know what was happening and why," Johnson observed in his memoirs.[52]

Encouraged by Nixon, via Chennault, Thieu finally balked at the agreement, clearly expecting more favorable treatment from a Republican administration. In the end, Nixon's intervention may have been superfluous. Thieu was already wary of negotiations and firmly opposed to any talks that included representatives of the NLF. Furthermore, he and other government leaders had long been hostile to Humphrey, a consequence of the vice president's frank admonitions about South Vietnamese self-sufficiency during his 1967 conversation with Thieu in Saigon.[53]

The North Vietnamese, meanwhile, sensed a Nixon victory and, expecting a better deal from the Johnson–Humphrey administration, were more eager than ever to compromise on October 23. On that day, the Hanoi delegation proposed a hard-and-fast deal: a complete bombing halt that would begin on October 30, to be followed by four-way negotiations beginning on November 3.

Johnson was torn. To reject the deal would be to walk away from a possible peace agreement under his watch and almost certainly turn the presidency over to Nixon. But to negotiate without Saigon also had its risks—particularly if Nixon charged that the agreement was merely a political deal to help Humphrey. Worse, Saigon's absence from the talks would make it highly unlikely that a lasting peace agreement could be negotiated. "All of us know that, with all its uncertainties, we have the best deal we now can get," advised Rostow. "Vastly better that we thought we could get since 1961."[54]

Johnson decided to take the deal. On the afternoon of October 31, less than five days before the election, Johnson taped a speech to be aired that evening on network television. He would announce an end to all air, naval, and artillery bombardment of North Vietnam as of the next morning. "We have reached the stage where productive talks can begin," he said, offering the assurance that the announcement had nothing to do with the presidential election.[55] Early that evening, Johnson placed a conference call to Humphrey, Nixon, and Wallace and briefed them on the details of his decision. Although he knew of Nixon's machinations, he kept his cool. He did, however, take one indirect slap at the Republican nominee. "Some old China hands are going around and implying to some of the Embassies and some others that they might get a better deal out of somebody that was not involved in this," Johnson said. "Now that's made it difficult and it's held up things a bit, and I know that none of you candidates are aware of it or responsible for it."[56]

Johnson's announcement of the bombing halt was less than triumphant. Although Humphrey's poll numbers had begun to climb, his momentum stalled on November 3 when Thieu poured cold water on the deal, rejecting the North Vietnamese peace overture and reiterating his intention to boycott the talks. On November 5, in one of the closest presidential elections in American history—thanks to a conservative, third-party challenge by Wallace who won 13.5 percent of the vote—Nixon beat Humphrey by fewer than five hundred thousand votes out of more than 62 million. While other issues played a role in the Republican victory, the Vietnam War was paramount. Nixon had campaigned skillfully and encouraged voters to believe he had a plan to end the conflict, although he never discussed its specifics. When an agreement appeared imminent, Nixon—through Chennault—slowed it down by persuading Thieu to object with the assurance that Nixon would be tougher on Hanoi than Humphrey. Even after Johnson announced the bombing halt, Thieu played right into Nixon's hand by rejecting the deal.

For Humphrey, Vietnam had been a millstone. In retrospect, Humphrey acknowledged that his candidacy had been doomed by his failure to oppose Johnson's war. "It would have been better that I stood my ground and remembered that I was fighting for the highest office in the land," Humphrey lamented after the election. "I ought not to have let a man who was going to be a former President dictate my future."[57] Nixon, of course, had demonstrated none of Humphrey's compunctions about exploiting the Vietnam issue for his own political purposes. Although he had campaigned on the need to end the war, Nixon now had every reason to continue the fighting: he believed that he owed his razor-thin victory to Thieu's intransigence and the way the South Vietnamese leader had diminished the import of Johnson's October 31 announcement. As Nixon's aide William Safire noted: "Nixon probably would not be President were it not for Thieu. Nixon remembered."[58] Nixon and Thieu had one final indignity in store for Humphrey and Johnson. Four days before Nixon's January 20, 1969, inauguration, Thieu changed his mind. He agreed to send representatives of his government to the peace talks in Paris.

Because neither major candidate had dealt honestly with the American people about Vietnam, the public's voice on the war was muted and diffuse in November 1968. Humphrey had suggested that he would end the bombing, but never separated himself enough from Johnson to give most voters the sense that his administration would result in any radical change. After all, the vice president had, since 1966, been one of the nation's most vocal cheerleaders for Johnson's war. When given the chance to clearly articulate a different approach to Vietnam, Humphrey had proved cowardly and indecisive. Nixon, on the other hand, was deceitful and, perhaps, even treasonous. He had worked to scuttle plans for peace talks to further his own campaign and suggested, deceptively, that he had a plan to end the war. He campaigned as a peace candidate, despite having supported the bombing and the subsequent escalation, but also talked of achieving an "honorable peace."* But because both men had equivocated on Vietnam, the election returns held no clear public mandate for how Americans wanted the war ended. Therefore, Nixon had what he most wanted: maximum flexibility to end it on his own terms.

The 1968 elections were a mixed bag for the Senate doves as well. Although voters reelected several of the most prominent dissenters like Fulbright, McGovern, Church and Ribicoff, the two earliest public critics of the war, Morse and Gruening, went down in defeat, as did another war opponent, Pennsylvania's Joseph Clark. In all, Democrats forfeited five seats in the Senate and four in the House. As Johnson returned to Texas, five hundred thirty-five thousand American soldiers were still in Vietnam. During his more than five years in the White House, more than thirty thousand American soldiers had died in a conflict that a stubborn and proud president—haunted by political ghosts from the early 1950s—had vowed never to lose.

---

*Later, voters would learn that this meant at least five more years of bloody fighting in Vietnam.

PART FIVE

NIXON'S WAR

I'm not going to end up like LBJ, holed up in the White House afraid to show my face on the street. I'm going to stop that war. Fast.

— President Richard Nixon, 1969

Every senator in this chamber is partly responsible for sending 50,000 young Americans to an early grave. This chamber reeks of blood.

— Senator George McGovern, 1970

CHAPTER 38

Win the Peace

1969

Ironically, Mansfield, Fulbright, McGovern, and the other war opponents in the Senate regarded Richard Nixon, if only briefly, as a breath of fresh air. "The greatest honor history can bestow is the title of peacemaker," the new president said in his inaugural address. "This honor now beckons America. . . . If we succeed, generations to come will say of us now living that we mastered our moment, that we helped make the world safe for mankind. This is our summons to greatness."[1] Nixon meant to end the war. "I'm not going to end up like LBJ," he told a friend, "holed up in the White House afraid to show my face on the street. I'm going to stop that war. Fast."[2] To Republican Congressman Donald Riegle of Michigan, Nixon predicted that he could end the conflict in six months.[3]

If Nixon wanted to make peace, Mansfield was ready to help. Two days into Nixon's presidency, the majority leader commented that Nixon was off to "a good beginning" in taking over the peace talks in Paris.[4] Several days later, Mansfield told a constituent, "I am in accord with President Nixon's views" on ending the war.[5]

In his public remarks, Fulbright expressed a similar degree of confidence in the new president when he cautioned against any premature decision about withdrawing American troops. "I think we ought to give these people [in Paris] an opportunity to negotiate without making any serious change in the status quo."[6] *Washington Evening Star* columnist Mary McGrory called it "Fulbright's bombing pause," and speculated that the reason for his cease-fire "seems to be that Fulbright is persuaded that Richard Nixon wants to end the war and is prepared to let him use any means he wishes to go about it."[7] According to his chief of staff, Lee Williams, Fulbright was attempting to do "the opposite of what he had done with Johnson: Don't challenge him head-on, don't call him a liar.

Let's try to work with these people and maybe we can establish a relationship through which I can have some influence."[8]

When Nixon's nominee for secretary of state, William Rogers, came before the Foreign Relations Committee, Fulbright warmly welcomed and praised Rogers—a marked difference from the harsh treatment his committee had afforded Rusk. "My feeling is that he is a broad-gauged man, not doctrinaire and capable of adjusting to change," Fulbright said of Rogers.[9] What Fulbright did not know, however, was that the new secretary would play a pitifully minor role in the formulation of U.S. foreign policy. Nixon reserved the right to formulate his own foreign policy—with help from national security advisor Henry Kissinger. A pragmatic and seasoned Harvard professor with close ties to the foreign affairs establishment that had guided U.S. international relations through several administrations, Kissinger had opened many doors with his bipartisan approach to foreign policy. In the span of about two years, he had represented Johnson in several diplomatic missions and had advised New York Governor Nelson Rockefeller, Humphrey, and, finally, Nixon.

Widely respected for his agile mind and a sophisticated view of the world, Kissinger thought of himself as a realist who understood that the war in Vietnam had diverted America's attention away from more important issues, particularly the prospects for improving relations with the Soviet Union. While Kissinger was not as convinced as Nixon that the key to a peaceful settlement in Vietnam resided in the Kremlin, he did share Nixon's view that war had diverted far too much of America's time, energy, and resources. Both men agreed that the war had to be ended, but "honorably," so as to preserve U.S. prestige around the world. Likewise, neither Nixon nor Kissinger was opposed to using American military force to compel the North Vietnamese to come to terms. Yet Nixon and Kissinger differed on at least one important point. Plagued by political demons that were partly his own creation—that is, the severe recriminations that threatened any president who presided over a communist triumph in any part of Asia—Nixon would not consider a rapid withdrawal from Vietnam. A communist victory in South Vietnam might threaten his own political future.

"Of all choices," Kissinger later observed, Nixon was "probably the least suited for the act of grace that might have achieved reconciliation with the responsible members" of the antiwar movement. "Seeing himself in any case the target of a liberal conspiracy to destroy him, he could never bring himself to regard the upheaval caused by the Vietnam war as anything other than a continuation of the long-lived assault on his political existence."[10] Less the politician and more the realist, Kissinger believed it far more important for the United States to extricate itself from South Vietnam with the hope that a peace agreement would give the Saigon regime a "reasonable" chance to survive.[11]

However, Nixon was saddled with many of the same conventional Cold War assumptions about a Soviet-inspired communist monolith that had shaped the Vietnam policies of every White House occupant since Harry Truman. "Our primary interest in Vietnam," Nixon would write confidently in 1985, "was to prevent the fall of Indochina to the Communists. We wanted to prevent the loss of Vietnam because we believed it would lead to the fall of the rest of Southeast Asia." Even more than Johnson, Nixon was determined to preserve the nation's credibility as the world's foremost bulwark against communist aggression. Nixon believed that America was fighting in Vietnam, first, to prevent a communist totalitarian government in South Vietnam and, second, because a communist victory would, among other things, "damage American strategic interests and pose a threat to our allies and friends in other non-Communist nations."[12]

The nuances of their foreign policy views aside, Nixon and Kissinger had persuaded Mansfield and Fulbright—two of the most influential congressional critics of American involvement in Vietnam—that the new administration was determined to end the war as soon as possible. "I think [Fulbright] really wanted to believe that they were going to do the sensible and logical thing and get the hell out of there," recalled Norvill Jones, a member of the Foreign Relations Committee staff. "He was willing to lean over backwards to give them the benefit of the doubt and to give them some time. I'm sure that was part of Kissinger's message to him, 'Give us some time, give us some time. Don't press us too hard.'"[13]

In a meeting with Nixon and Kissinger in late March, Fulbright bluntly warned that unless the new president ended the war by the middle of his term, his administration "will be on an irreversible path toward repudiation." Whatever you do, he advised Nixon, do not escalate the war. Nixon and Kissinger assured Fulbright they had no such plans. "Just give us a year," they told him.[14]

Despite those assurances, Fulbright was nagged by doubts about Nixon's commitment to moving quickly on a peaceful settlement. In fact, after returning to his office from his White House meeting, Fulbright received confidential information from a reporter suggesting that Nixon—despite his soothing words about winding down the war—had already intensified the bombing above and below the 17th Parallel and had issued orders to step up the pace of ground operations. Furthermore, the reporter relayed information that Nixon was considering a plan to bomb several sites in Cambodia near the South Vietnamese border, through which passed the Ho Chi Minh Trail and where numerous North Vietnamese sanctuaries were located.[15] Indeed, on March 18, only three days before his meeting with Fulbright, Nixon had secretly ordered the bombing in response to a broad North Vietnamese military offensive launched in late February throughout South Vietnam.[16]

Militarily, the bombing in Cambodia was aimed at destroying the sanctuaries. Nixon, however, had other reasons for sending the bombers over Cambodia. He believed that he, unlike Johnson, could find the key to ending the war quickly—at least within the first year of his presidency. He hoped that precipitate U.S. military action would unnerve the North Vietnamese and cause them to begin dealing seriously with American negotiators in Paris. "I call it the Madman Theory, Bob," Nixon had told his chief of staff Bob Haldeman during the campaign. "I want the North Vietnamese to believe I've reached the point where I might do *anything* to stop the war. We'll just slip the word to them that, 'for God's sake, you know Nixon is obsessed about Communism. We can't restrain him when he's angry—and he has his hand on the nuclear button'—and Ho Chi Minh himself will be in Paris in two days begging for peace."[17]

Nixon likely had an additional reason not to seek a quick, peaceful end to the war. By refusing to accede to the plan Johnson's negotiators had proposed in the campaign's final weeks, Thieu may have helped, at least in Nixon's mind, to guarantee a Republican victory. If Thieu wanted a continuation of some level of American military activity in South Vietnam in order to preserve his regime—and he did—then Nixon might have felt obligated to repay the considerable debt by giving it to him. That apparent obligation, as William Bundy later observed, was an enormous burden to Nixon's Vietnam policies at a time when the United States should have been applying considerable pressure on Thieu to reform his government and his military—and using the threat of an American military withdrawal as an incentive. "That a new American President started with a heavy and recognized debt to the leader he had above all to influence," Bundy wrote, "was surely a great handicap, brought on by Nixon for domestic political reasons."[18]

Fulbright was obviously troubled by the information about the Cambodian bombing. The day after his White House meeting, at a Capitol Hill symposium on the military budget, he lamented that because Nixon was determined to achieve an "honorable peace"—which generally meant a tough military stance in Vietnam and an inflexible negotiation position in Paris—this was "probably the calm before the storm." Unless a diplomatic breakthrough occurred soon, Fulbright worried aloud that "we face a bad time." Fulbright was not sure exactly what Nixon and Kissinger would do to end the war, but he feared that the new administration's course would not be markedly different from Johnson's.[19]

Fulbright was not the only Senate dove growing concerned about the trim of Nixon's sails. Mansfield had also heard rumors about the Cambodia bombing, as well as news that Cambodia's chief of state, Prince Norodom Sihanouk, would not object if the United States attacked communist sanctuaries in his country. The majority leader refused to give credibility to the information. But he was worried enough to tell senators on March 26 that he was "disturbed" by the reports. Mansfield refused to believe Nixon would try something so foolhardy and that his friend Sihanouk would agree to it. "I question this allegation," Mansfield told the Senate, "because an attack on Cambodia would very possibly bring that nation into the conflict, very likely bring about an increase in American forces, and would reduce all prospects, in my opinion, for a reduction in the war, a possible de-escalation, and would hinder the chances of American withdrawals at a future date."[20]*

McGovern also had sources who informed him that the new president was escalating the conflict. In March, after Nixon rejected an immediate withdrawal of U.S. forces from Vietnam and declared that the United States was considering an "appropriate response" to the communist offensive in South Vietnam, McGovern reacted indignantly in a Senate speech so strident that it startled even some of his antiwar allies:

> It is nearly a year since President Johnson announced the first steps to negotiate an end to the war. It was a year ago almost to the day that the voters of New Hampshire gave us the first clear manifestation that the American conscience and will were shocked and disgusted by the war. . . . Today, the killing continues. American battle casualties have exceeded 200,000. The toll of American lives lost will shortly pass 33,000. . . .
>
> I believe that the American people had every hope and expectation that the Paris talks would bring a military disengagement; that we would minimize clashes with the enemy and seek to hold down the loss of life on both sides while the Paris discussions were pending.
>
> And yet, in defiance of all the dictates of common sense and respect for human life, we have pursued the opposite course. We invoked the old, disingenuous slogan, claiming the need to "negotiate from strength," and launched a so-called accelerated pacification campaign designed to keep constant, intensive military pressure on the enemy. . . . If the administration is truly flirting with plans to pursue the military effort toward some undefinable victory, then it is setting a disaster course for our country and for the cause of peace. The new Commander in Chief must grasp what his predecessor learned to his sorrow—that in any continuance of the war in Vietnam lies the seed of national tragedy and the certainty of personal political disaster. . . .
>
> The war in Vietnam must be ended. . . . There is no more time for "considering military options," no more time for "improving the bargaining

---

*Here can be seen the approaching shadow of the Watergate scandal. News reports about the bombing—which appeared in the *New York Times*, the *Washington Post*, the *Wall Street Journal*, and *Newsweek*—infuriated Nixon, who approved an FBI plan to place wire taps on the phones of thirteen administration officials and four reporters (Kissinger, *White House Years*, 252–53).

position." In the name of decency and common sense, there must be no further continuation of the present war policy, however disguised in rhetoric or more hollow predictions of victory yet to come. . . . I believe the only acceptable objective now is an immediate end to the killing.[21]

Unwilling to trust the administration's characterizations of the peace talks, McGovern went to Paris in May to meet personally with the top negotiators representing North Vietnam and the National Liberation Front. He came away, he said upon his return, "with enhanced respect for the intelligence, shrewdness and the absolute devotion to their cause of both the North Vietnamese and their NLF allies." McGovern had always believed that the North Vietnamese and the Viet Cong were more profoundly motivated by nationalistic passions than by a blind devotion to communism. "These Vietnamese who follow Ho Chi Minh and the National Liberation Front," he told the Senate afterwards, "see those Vietnamese who have resisted the 'liberation' struggle—Bao Dai, the late President Diem, Ky and Thieu—not as patriots but as Benedict Arnolds."

The result of his twelve hours of talks with the two negotiating teams was a clearer understanding of the enemy's peace proposal. "First of all, they insist on the unconditional withdrawal of all American forces from Vietnam," he informed the Senate. "Neither Hanoi nor the NLF is willing to talk about 'mutual withdrawal' since they insist we are the only foreigners in Vietnam. I have no doubt, however, that if we began withdrawing our troops while moving toward a defensive, cease-fire strategy, the other side would quickly respond by easing off their military pressure." When McGovern informed the communist delegations that "some Americans fear a bloodbath during or after an American withdrawal," he said they replied "that just the opposite would happen—the killing would stop."[22]

McGovern's description of the communists' rigid negotiating stance was correct. On May 8, Viet Cong representatives finally released their own terms for a peaceful settlement—a ten-point plan that insisted on the unilateral, unconditional withdrawal of U.S. forces from South Vietnam, as well as Saigon's acquiescence in free country-wide elections, a new constitution, and a coalition government that included the NLF.[23] Nixon rejected the proposal, but countered with one of his own. In a nationally televised address on May 14, Nixon effectively ended any pretense that the United States hoped to achieve a military victory in Vietnam when he proposed a cease-fire, followed by a signed agreement in which both sides would agree to a phased pullout of most forces from South Vietnam within a year. "I want to end this war," Nixon said. "The American people want to end this war. The people of South Vietnam want to end this war." Although he rejected a unilateral U.S. withdrawal, Nixon did hold out the promise of significant U.S. force reductions. "The time is approaching,"

Nixon said, "when South Vietnamese forces will be able to take over some of the fighting fronts now being manned by Americans."

Nixon's speech had something for the hawks and the doves, but its purpose was to shore up the support of the hawks. His message to them was that while the United States would no longer try to win the war with military force, it would at least employ its remaining forces to prevent an American defeat. In other words, the war would go on, but only to preserve the Saigon regime and American prestige.

The communists, considering the earlier Viet Cong proposal, were not likely to accept the Nixon plan. As Nixon said, he would not allow Saigon to fall to communism without a struggle. His message was clear. Like Johnson and Kennedy before him, he would not be the president who allowed another Asian nation to go communist. In his own tribute to the Munich analogy, Nixon told the national television audience on May 14: "If Hanoi were to succeed in taking over South Vietnam by force—even after the power of the United States had been engaged—it would greatly strengthen those leaders who scorn negotiation, who advocate aggression and who minimize the risks of confrontation with the United States. It would bring peace now, but it would enormously increase the danger of a bigger war later."[24]

Nixon's speech offered little hope of a shortened war. In the Senate, Albert Gore wondered if Nixon's real goal was to simply prop up the Thieu–Ky regime at the expense of true self-rule in South Vietnam. Nixon's plan would accomplish little, Gore told the Senate on May 8, "if the Pentagon-Saigon axis has in mind the withdrawal of increments of U.S. troops over a period of years, leaving behind U.S. troops to back up the South Vietnamese Army and to prop up a corrupt military dictatorship in Saigon."[25] At the White House, Kissinger soon realized that the timing of Nixon's first major speech on Vietnam as president had been a diplomatic error. U.S. allies, who learned of the gambit through regular news channels, should have been notified in advance. As for the speech itself, Kissinger thought the "whole thing was too complex with too many nuances that are totally unintelligible to the ordinary guy."[26]

While a peace proposal—even one likely to be rejected in Paris—was news, it was nothing compared to the domestic impact of the drastic changes in the Selective Service System that Nixon proposed on May 19. In one fell swoop, Nixon deprived the student antiwar protest movement of much of its fuel by asking Congress to begin drafting eligible 19-year-old men first and to reduce the period from seven years to one during which young men were exposed to the draft. When Congress finally approved the changes, the practical impact was that most young men over age 19 no longer feared the draft. Those most vulnerable to being called would participate in a lottery system that gave them a clear idea of the extent of their liability. Nixon's move was a masterstroke. Relieved of the threat of being forced into combat in Vietnam, the intensity of student protests declined significantly.[27]

By June, aware that Congress and the American people expected some movement toward an end to the war, Nixon announced that he would withdraw the first U.S. troops from Vietnam. At a meeting with Thieu at Midway Island, Nixon said that twenty-five thousand American troops— the equivalent of a combat division—would be sent home by the end of August. Nixon also challenged North Vietnam to do the same. The withdrawal of about 5 percent of the total U.S. force in Vietnam was no earthshattering event. But it was, in the words of *New York Times* reporter Robert Semple, "a strategy with a built-in device designed to hold public support for the long negotiating process ahead."[28] Nixon tried to relieve the pressure for quick progress in Vietnam in a meeting with House leaders on June 12. "Whatever happens," he pledged, "a year from now, next July, the situation is going to be better. One way or another, we are going to have Vietnam cooled."[29]

A gradual withdrawal would assuage the public for a while, but Nixon knew he needed something more. Bombing supplies lines and the communist sanctuaries in Cambodia might slow down the pace of the enemy's infiltration, but these actions alone would never turn the tide. As the summer ended, Nixon knew that Congress would be back in session and college students back on campus. He feared—his changes in draft procedures notwithstanding—that "a massive new antiwar tide would sweep the country during the fall and winter." With Vietnam's fall dry season approaching, the president also anticipated a renewed communist offensive during the Tet holiday in February. "By early spring," he speculated, "the pressures of the November 1970 elections would make congressional demands for more troop withdrawals impossible to stop and difficult to ignore." In July, Nixon decided to jump-start the negotiations in Paris with a "go for broke" strategy. "I would attempt to end the war one way or another," he wrote, "either by negotiated agreement or by an increased use of force."[30]

On July 15, Nixon contacted Jean Sainteny, a French businessman and diplomat who enjoyed friendly relations with U.S. and North Vietnamese officials. He invited Sainteny to the White House and asked him to deliver a personal message to Ho Chi Minh. Nixon instructed Sainteny to inform the North Vietnamese that unless "some serious breakthrough" was achieved by November 1—the first anniversary of Johnson's bombing halt—Nixon would likely resort "to measures of great consequence and force." As Sainteny departed, Nixon believed that he had "put the choice between war and peace in [Ho's] hands."[31]

What Nixon had in mind, but did not say to Ho, was a massive bombing operation—proposed by Kissinger and code-named "Duck Hook"—

aimed at Hanoi, Haiphong, and other key industrial areas of North Vietnam. Nixon also envisioned the mining of harbors and rivers, the bombing of North Vietnam's dike system to cause massive flooding and destruction, a possible invasion of North Vietnam, and a proposal to strike the Ho Chi Minh Trail with tactical nuclear weapons. Within days word came back from Paris. The North Vietnamese were willing to talk; they proposed secret meetings between Kissinger and Xuan Thuy, the head of Hanoi's negotiating team.

Nixon sent Kissinger to Paris to begin secret negotiations in early August. The United States, Kissinger told the North Vietnamese delegates during a meeting in Sainteny's apartment, was prepared to withdraw all its forces from South Vietnam, as long as the communists agreed to do the same. Furthermore, Kissinger said the United States was willing to accept "the outcome of any free political process" in South Vietnam. If negotiations toward this end proved fruitful, Kissinger said, Nixon was also prepared to "adjust military operations to facilitate an agreement." But Kissinger also had tough words for Xuan and his colleagues. "If by November 1 no progress had been made, the United States would have to consider steps of grave consequence." Kissinger warned Xuan that his government should stop its attempt to label the conflict "Mr. Nixon's war." This was not in their best interests, he said, "because if it is Mr. Nixon's war, then he cannot afford not to win it."[32]

Xaun was impassive. Despite the fact that Kissinger had, in his words, "presented the most comprehensive American peace plan yet," the North Vietnamese delegate insisted that any military agreement must also be accompanied by a political settlement that removed Thieu and Ky from office. "In other words," Kissinger later explained, "not even a unilateral United States withdrawal would end the war or secure the release of our prisoners." To Kissinger, the situation was now clear: Hanoi wanted victory more than it wanted peace.

In early August, communist guerrillas ended their months-long lull in the fighting when they attacked the American base at Cam Ranh Bay, on the central coast of South Vietnam. Several days later, the Viet Cong staged attacks in more than one hundred cities, towns, and bases in South Vietnam. "The most generous interpretation could not avoid the conclusion," Kissinger observed, "that Hanoi did not believe in gestures, negotiation, goodwill or reciprocity."[33] Rebuffed by the intransigent North Vietnamese and their Viet Cong allies, Nixon prepared for a wider war.

ALTHOUGH HE HAD MADE NO actual progress in the quest for a peaceful solution in Vietnam, the public, for now, generally approved of Nixon's performance. But a national opinion poll conducted for the Republican National Committee in August revealed that "while just over half the public believes the Administration is doing as well as can be expected in handling the Vietnam war, six persons in ten are of the opinion that the Administration should be more actively seeking some way to stop the fighting." Yet two-thirds of those surveyed also appeared to be generally in line with Nixon's public strategy, telling the pollster that they supported a "compromise settlement within the next six months on terms that are reasonably favorable to the United States and taking necessary military actions during this time."[34]

Indeed, despite the fact that he was secretly escalating and expanding the war into Cambodia, Nixon *appeared* to be making solid progress toward ending American involvement in Vietnam. "I believe the record is clear as to which side has gone the extra mile in behalf of peace," Nixon said in a speech at the Presidential Palace in Saigon during a quick visit to Vietnam on July 30. "We have stopped the bombing of North Vietnam. We have withdrawn 25,000 American troops. They have been replaced by South Vietnamese. We have made, and [the South Vietnamese] have made a peace offer which is as generous as any ever made in the history of warfare."[35]

Despite the "generosity" of Nixon's peace offer and his simultaneous threat of "grave consequences," the North Vietnamese remained stubbornly intransigent. On September 4, Ho Chi Minh died, but not before he had personally responded to Nixon's ultimatum of early August. If the United States wanted a "just peace," Ho said in a letter that arrived on August 25, then it "must cease the war of aggression and withdraw their troops from South Vietnam, respect the right of the population of the South and of the Vietnamese nation to dispose of themselves, without foreign influence." Nixon took the letter as "a cold rebuff." He now had to consider how he would respond, given the threat Kissinger had issued on his behalf. But Ho's response also gave Nixon pause. "I knew that I had to prepare myself for the tremendous criticism and pressure that would come with stepping up the war," he later wrote.[36]

Nixon got a strong taste of that criticism in mid-September after ordering a brief, one-day cease-fire on the day of Ho's funeral. Mansfield, Gore, Javits, Fulbright, McGovern, and others had hoped the funeral might serve as the occasion for an even longer pause that would, in turn, lead to more constructive peace talks and further withdrawals of U.S. troops. "I am curious and confused," Mansfield said on ABC's "Issues and Answers" on September 14. "I thought there was an opportunity to do something to speed withdrawals of American troops." Asked if his patience with Nixon's approach to Vietnam was beginning to "wear a little thin," Mansfield responded passionately. "Well," he said, "my patience began to wear thin with the start of this tragic, useless, barbaric war, some years ago. I have never been in favor of it. I think that it is in an area where we have no vital interests."[37]

On September 9, Gore expressed his growing impatience with Nixon's handling of the war. "How long must American boys fight and die in Vietnam?" the Tennessee senator asked the Senate. "We have suffered more than 60,000 casualties since the inauguration of President Nixon on January 20." Fulbright agreed, adding that Nixon's continued support of the Thieu government was an obstacle to peace. "It does not matter how much we talk about settlement," he said, "the war cannot be settled as long as we insist on maintaining the puppet government in South Vietnam."[38] The next day, the Republican Javits chimed in and called on Nixon to end American involvement in Vietnam by speeding up the troop withdrawals with a goal of removing two hundred thousand by the end of 1970. He shared Fulbright's conclusions about Nixon's blind loyalty to Thieu. "Only when it is unmistakably clear to the Saigon government—and to the U.S. officials in Saigon—that the United States will no longer support the status quo, can there be any expectation of the kind of political evolution which may assure the survival of an independent government in South Vietnam."[39]

Aware that making good on his military threats would only inflame public opinion and turn more Americans against the war, Nixon and Kissinger also worried that continued troop withdrawals and a moribund peace process would do little to give the United States the honorable peace that Nixon had promised. "I am not optimistic about the ability of the South Vietnamese armed forces to assume a larger part of the burden than current MACV plans allow," Kissinger informed Nixon on September 10. Kissinger also worried, correctly, that the troop withdrawals might get out of hand and become "like salted peanuts to the American public: The more U.S. troops come home, the more will be demanded."[40] At an NSC meeting on September 12, Kissinger insisted that "we need a plan to end the war, not only to withdraw troops." What Kissinger had in mind was the massive "Duck Hook" military operation that his NSC staff had developed in the early summer.[41]

Tempted as he was by Kissinger's plan to throw a massive, war-ending blow at North Vietnam, Nixon also knew the furor such action would provoke in Congress and among the antiwar activists who were planning nationwide "Moratorium" rallies for October 15. Hoping instead to rob the antiwar movement of some of its pre-Moratorium momentum, Nixon announced on September 16 that sixty thousand additional American troops would be withdrawn from South Vietnam by December 15. Three days later, he announced that the withdrawals meant that draft calls for November and December had been cancelled.[42]

Those actions—welcome as they were—did little to stem a rising tide of frustration in Congress, born of a growing fear that Nixon's plan to end the war would take years, not months. On September 25, Republican Senator Charles Goodell of New York—a moderate Republican appointed to serve out Robert Kennedy's term—introduced one of the strongest antiwar measures ever offered in the Senate: an amendment to the foreign assistance bill that required a complete suspension of funds for the war on December 1, 1970. Fulbright liked Goodell's proposal and promised to hold hearings on the measure.[43]

Hoping to discourage talk of an "arbitrary cutoff time" for U.S. troops, Nixon argued at a September 26 press conference that a deadline "inevitably leads to perpetuating and continuing the war until that time" and would reduce the chances of "ending the war before the end of 1970 or before the middle of 1971." Nixon said that Goodell's proposal, if approved, would "undercut and destroy the negotiating position we now have in Paris." While he acknowledged that "we have not made significant progress" in the peace talks, Nixon insisted that "any incentive for the enemy to negotiate is destroyed if he is told in advance that if he just waits for 18 months we'll be out anyway."[44]

Goodell's amendment, however, captured the sentiment of a growing number of war critics in the Senate who had rejected Nixon's Vietnam policy of increased bombing, gradual troop withdrawals, and painfully slow and unproductive peace negotiations. Tired of war, frustrated by the pace of Nixon's efforts to end the fighting, and increasingly persuaded that the new president's Vietnam policies were remarkably similar to Johnson's, Goodell and others believed the only way to persuade Nixon to change his policies was to give him a specific date for the war's end. Nixon cynically and deftly negotiated his way around this potential minefield when he suggested an even earlier end to the war. At his September 27 press conference, he told reporters that while Goodell's proposal was "well-intentioned," it would perpetuate the belief "that the United States is going to be stuck in Vietnam till the end of 1970, that there's no hope of ending the war before then."[45]*

---

*Goodell's was not the only congressional resolution aimed at ending U.S. involvement in Vietnam. That fall, Frank Church and Mark Hatfield introduced a moderate resolution that mostly urged Nixon to adopt "a more rapid withdrawal of American troops, and a commitment by the United States to fully disengage from South Vietnam." Another resolution, offered by Democratic senators Thomas Eagleton of Missouri and Harold Hughes of Iowa, called for terminating all U.S. assistance to the regime in Saigon in the absence of political reforms (*CR*, 10/8/69, 29114; *CQA*, 1969, 1002).

Two days later, in a meeting with Republican leaders in Congress, Nixon again encouraged the notion that his unspecific actions and policies would result in an early end to the fighting. In this meeting, however, Nixon was far more bellicose than in public. He did not intend to be the "first American President to lose a war," he told them—echoing Lyndon Johnson—and added that he would not withdraw U.S. troops precipitously because it would constitute a "retreat from the world." This "first defeat in American history," he said, would "destroy the confidence of the American people in themselves." By the November 1970 elections, Nixon promised, the war would be over.[46]

Despite these assurances, most opponents of the war were not mollified, particularly the organizers of the national Moratorium events planned for October 15. Asked about how he would respond to the expected outpouring of public opposition to the war, Nixon dismissed the protests as irrelevant. "Under no circumstances," he said, "will I be affected whatever by it."[47] That remark infuriated the war's opponents in and out of Congress, even as Nixon began dropping prominent hints that he was still considering implementation of Kissinger's "Duck Hook" proposal. When newspaper columnist Rowland Evans and Robert Novak reported in early October that Nixon was considering a plan to blockade Haiphong and invade North Vietnam, Republican Senator Howard Baker of Tennessee called the White House to register his alarm. Nixon had no reaction. According to biographer Stephen Ambrose, "The President himself was the one who had leaked the story."[48]

On October 1, Fulbright delivered his most passionate broadside against the war—and Nixon—when he ridiculed a suggestion by Senate Republican leader Hugh Scott of Pennsylvania for a sixty-day moratorium on criticism of Nixon's Vietnam policies. "It has been nine months since the President took office," Fulbright told the Senate, "the normal period of gestation for humans to bring forth their issue. No one expected a miracle, but many of us did expect the President to make progress in delivering on his campaign promises to give new birth to his plan to end the war." Rather than a moratorium on criticism of Nixon, "which kills no one," Fulbright said, "we who criticize continuation of the war seek, instead, a moratorium on killing. When will this administration bite the bullet instead of firing it and present to the American people the plan to end this war which practically all knowledgeable observers now believe we should never have been involved in?"[49]

FREED FROM ANY self-imposed constraints of party loyalty, McGovern and other Democrats were now to free assail the war and the Republican president in ways they might not have if Johnson still occupied the White House—or if Humphrey had won the 1968 election. Beginning in 1969, McGovern had begun voting against military appropriations bills, a protest he had earlier rejected as detrimental to the troops in the field. He also began to associate himself more closely with the antiwar movement outside the Senate.

To McGovern, Nixon's Vietnam policies only guaranteed the deaths of additional U.S. soldiers. "It is time to say 'Enough,'" he said on October 9 as he joined a group of his colleagues to introduce a resolution directing that "all U.S. forces now be withdrawn from Vietnam." The pace of the withdrawal, McGovern explained, would "be limited only by steps to ensure: first, the safety of our troops; second, the mutual release of prisoners of war; and third, the assurance of safety through arrangements for amnesty or asylum in friendly countries for those Vietnamese who might be endangered by our disengagement."[50] The resolution received less than twenty votes. Another resolution the next month—seeking to cut off all funds for Vietnam after December 1970—attracted even fewer supporters.[51]

On October 15, McGovern delivered three major Vietnam speeches in Washington, Boston and Bangor, Maine, as part of the nationwide Moratorium. "The president has described Vietnam as our finest hour," McGovern said. "It is not. It is our worst hour." He applauded the actions of students and citizens who were peacefully protesting the war. "This is the highest patriotism," he said of their dissent.[52] From the East Coast to the West Coast, and the Midwest in between, people from all walks of life took time out of their day to express their opposition to the war—almost all of it peaceful—in a variety of ways, quiet, boisterous, and solemn. In Boston an estimated 100,000 people gathered at Boston Common to hear antiwar speeches and music. Meanwhile, in New York City, organizers staged rallies and memorial services that attracted a quarter million people. Similar events were held in Philadelphia and Baltimore. In Washington, 1,500 congressional aides held a silent vigil on the Capitol steps during their lunch hour. That evening, Coretta Scott King led as many as 40,000 peaceful protestors in a candlelight march from the Lincoln Memorial to the White House. In Hudson, Ohio, 40,000 people gathered to pray for peace in the town square, while in Chicago 100,000 people took part in a variety of teach-ins, vigils, and rallies. Ten thousand people, including Hubert Humphrey, gathered to protest the war in Minneapolis. In Los Angeles, 20,000 people assembled on the UCLA campus, while several thousand more attended a rally on the campus of the University of Southern California. Even at Nixon's alma mater, Whittier College, a group of students lit a "flame of life" that they said would burn until the war ended.[53]

As historian Charles DeBenedetti observed in his chronicle of the anti-war movement, *An American Ordeal*, the nationwide expressions of protest and dissent

> reflected the changing nature of the war for America. With U.S. troops headed home, and given the general consensus that Saigon could not survive without them, continuing warfare was hard to defend in terms of upholding national security and international credibility. At an unparalleled moment of military retreat, with the risk of political defeat, Vietnam became a metaphor for a struggle over the national identity. It expressed a nation longing to find meaning in its losses—something more than empty humiliation. Participation in the Moratorium implied that it was all right and even patriotic to be against the war, that it was not a betrayal of earlier sacrifices to want to stop the carnage, that divisive misjudgment could be redeemed by getting beyond the conflict.

Overall, the Moratorium attracted surprisingly broad support across the country—in every region but the South, where traditional support for the military, and thus the war, remained strong.[54]* Organizers next summoned opponents of the war to Washington on November 15 for a Mobilization rally of massive proportions—a gathering that administration officials feared might give the antiwar movement unstoppable momentum. This was an especially frightful prospect for Nixon, given the lukewarm national support for his Vietnam policies. Although some Republican leaders voiced strong support of the president's policies, veterans' organizations and other strong supporters of the early American military role in Vietnam had fallen strangely silent since Nixon had taken office. The same broad spectrum of groups that had once supported Lyndon Johnson's war now declined to support to Nixon at a time of rising public discontent over a seemingly endless war.

Why was it that Nixon enjoyed no broad public support for a continued American presence in Vietnam? In May, when he had ruled out a military victory and had begun withdrawing troops, the issue had shifted from *whether* American involvement in Vietnam would end to *when*. Even some hawks who had avidly supported military action no longer saw the purpose

---

*Several factors may explain the lack of substantial protest in the South, beyond the deep, historical affection of many southerners for the military. One of every three soldiers in Vietnam came from a southern state at a time when the South represented 25 percent of the country's population. In addition, an inordinate share (40 percent in the House and 37 percent in the Senate) of southern members of Congress served on military committees, proving a potent source of public opinion leadership in their states. The South also had a large share of the nation's military bases, as well as a large number of military retirees.

of remaining in Vietnam once the objective shifted from achieving a military victory to finding an honorable peace. "The war had always been a hard sell," Stephen Ambrose observed. "Once Nixon began to withdraw, it was nearly an impossible one."[55]

This, of course, did not make the massive public response to the Moratorium any easier to swallow. Nixon failed to see patriotism and a principled expression of frustration in the Moratorium protests, believing that, by demonstrating a lack of national resolve to stay in the war, they had actually "destroyed whatever small possibility may still have existed of ending the war in 1969."

In reality, even though its organizers did not realize it, the Moratorium had finally eliminated any possibility that Nixon would initiate the "Duck Hook" operation he had obliquely threatened in his message to Hanoi. Nixon bitterly complained that the protests "had undercut the credibility" of that ultimatum. Later, he said that he viewed public dissent as a subjugation of the democratic process, arguing that "if a President—any President—allowed his course to be set by those who demonstrate, he would betray the trust of all the rest. Whatever the issue, to allow government policy to be made in the streets would destroy the democratic process." Yet by abandoning "Duck Hook" in partial reaction to the Moratorium, Nixon had, indeed, allowed his government's policy to be set in the streets. In fact, he later acknowledged that following the October 15 protests he "began to think more in terms of stepping up Vietnamization* while continuing the fighting at its present level rather than trying to increase it."[56]

Nixon, however, left it to his vice president to make the definitive public statement about the protests. Speaking in New Orleans several days later, Agnew attacked the protesters as "an effete corps of impudent snobs who characterize themselves as intellectuals." If the Moratorium had any purpose at all, Agnew said disdainfully, "it served as an emotional purgative for those who feel the need to cleanse themselves of their lack of ability to offer a constructive solution to the problem."[57]

Nixon, meanwhile, stewed in private and continued to threaten Hanoi through Russian intermediaries as he began writing a major Vietnam speech that he planned to deliver on November 3. As he later confessed to aide William Safire, he hoped the speech would help him "to go over the heads of the columnists" and appeal directly to public opinion. "We've got to hold American public opinion with us for three or four months," he told Safire, "and then we can work this Vietnam thing out."[58] As he labored on

---

*"Vietnamization" was the term Nixon coined in 1969 to characterize his plan for withdrawing U.S. troops from Vietnam while gradually turning over the fighting to the South Vietnamese.

the speech, Nixon suffered from no shortage of advice about what to say. Rogers wanted him to emphasize the administration's effort to jump-start the Paris talks. Defense Secretary Melvin Laird urged Nixon to stress the prospects of Vietnamization. Many of the White House staffers, members of Nixon's cabinet, and the congressional leaders he consulted urged him to establish "beyond any doubt" his sincere desire for a peaceful end to the war. Kissinger, meanwhile, pushed a hard line. "He felt that if we backed off," Nixon recalled, "the Communists would become totally convinced that they could control our foreign policy through public opinion."

The week before the speech, Mansfield weighed in with his views and sent Nixon a memorandum that the president took with him to Camp David just days before the speech. "The continuance of the war in Vietnam, in my judgment, endangers the future of this nation," Mansfield wrote. More than wasted lives or money worried Mansfield. "Most serious are the deep divisions within our society to which this conflict of dubious origin and purpose is contributing." Should Nixon act to bring about a "rapid termination of the war," Mansfield pledged his strong public support.

While Nixon saw Mansfield's memorandum as an appeal for "a unilateral cease-fire and withdrawal," he also recognized that the Democratic majority leader was offering a Republican president a politically palatable way to the end the war with minimum political damage. In effect, as Nixon realized, Mansfield was suggesting that Nixon declare an end to "Johnson's and Kennedy's war." Nixon said that he interpreted Mansfield's references to a "conflict of dubious origin" and to the military positions "unfortunately" assumed during previous years "as signals that he would allow me to claim that I was making the best possible end of a bad war my Democratic predecessors had begun." But Nixon rejected Mansfield's appeal, later explaining that "it would be wrong to end the Vietnam war on any terms I believed to be less than honorable."[59]

That meant, of course, that while Nixon's policies were profoundly influenced—or moderated—by the growing antiwar sentiment in Congress and around the country, the potential political impact of a precipitate withdrawal influenced him more. Like Kennedy and Johnson before him, Nixon was unwilling to assume the blame for the communist domination of South Vietnam.

On the evening of Monday, November 3, Nixon delivered the second major Vietnam speech of his nine-month presidency. From his desk in the Oval Office, he began by recalling that after he became president some advisors had urged him to "end the war at once by ordering the immediate withdrawal of all American forces." Such a course would have been popular, Nixon acknowledged, and would have allowed him to blame the war on Johnson. "Some put it to me quite bluntly: This was the only way to avoid allowing Johnson's war to become Nixon's war." But Nixon insisted that he had a "greater obligation" than his reelection. The question before Americans was now, "How can we win America's peace?"

After a brief historical review of American involvement in Vietnam—during which he falsely claimed that he had opposed Johnson's initial troop commitments in 1965—Nixon turned to explaining why he could not authorize "the precipitate withdrawal" of American forces from Vietnam. To do so, he insisted, "would be a disaster not only for South Vietnam, but for the United States and for the cause of peace," resulting in defeat for the United States. "This first defeat in our nation's history," Nixon said, relying on the same philosophy that kept Johnson in Vietnam for so long, "would result in a collapse of confidence in American leadership not only in Asia but throughout the world." Ultimately, he predicted, "this would cost more lives. It would not bring peace; it would bring more war."

The obstacle to peace, Nixon insisted, was not America's unwillingness to abandon Vietnam, but "the other side's absolute refusal to show the least willingness to join us in seeking a just peace." The North Vietnamese would not come to terms with the United States "while it is convinced that all it has to do is to wait for our next concession, and our next concession after that one, until it gets everything it wants." Johnson had "Americanized the war in Vietnam," Nixon said. "In this administration we are Vietnamizing the search for peace." Nixon's "plan," in cooperation with Saigon, was "the complete withdrawal of all U.S. combat ground forces and their replacement by South Vietnamese forces on an orderly scheduled timetable." Nixon boiled his, and the nation's, choices down to two distinct courses of actions:

> I can order an immediate, precipitate withdrawal of all Americans from Vietnam without regard to the effects of that action.
>
> Or we can persist in our search for a just peace, through a negotiated settlement if possible or through continued implementation of our plan for Vietnamization if necessary—a plan in which we will *withdraw all our forces from Vietnam* on a schedule in accordance with our program, *as the South Vietnamese become strong enough to defend their own freedom.* (emphasis added)
>
> I have chosen this second course. It is not the easy way. It is the right way.

Although he set no firm timetable for withdrawal and did not articulate how he would measure the ability of Saigon to assume greater responsibility for the fighting, Nixon referred to his policy as "a plan for peace." As he closed, Nixon made an overt appeal to the patriotism of his viewers—and, indirectly, a slap at the antiwar protesters who would converge by the thousands on Washington in less than two weeks—using a phrase that would serve as a rallying cry for many domestic supporters of the war. "And so tonight—to you, the great silent majority of my fellow Americans—I ask for your support." In his campaign Nixon recalled that he had pledged to end the war "in a way that we could win the peace." He said that he had articulated a "plan" that would enable him to honor that pledge. "The more support I can have from the American people," he said, "the sooner that pledge can be redeemed; for the more divided we are at home, the less likely the enemy is to negotiate in Paris. Let us also be united against defeat. Because let us understand: North Vietnam cannot defeat or humiliate the United States. Only Americans can do that."[60]

As Nixon hoped, the speech generated a massive outpouring of public support for his "plan" to end the war. Within days, more than fifty thousand telegrams and thirty thousand letters, the vast majority supportive, poured into the White House. Three hundred House members and fifty-eight senators signed a letter endorsing Nixon's policies. "For the first time," Nixon wrote years later, "the Silent Majority had made itself heard." Although a majority of the public undoubtedly favored Nixon's policy—a Gallup poll immediately after the speech showed 77 percent approval—many expressions of support were less than spontaneous.[61] Years later, Nixon's aide Alexander Butterfield acknowledged that the highly touted public response to the speech was "manufactured." Weeks before the speech, Butterfield was instructed "to make damn sure that the response to the Silent Majority speech was fantastic." By prearrangement, labor unions, veterans organization, Republican governors, and state party chairmen worked with the White House to ensure a massive public response. "Everything," Butterfield said, "was spring-loaded."[62]

While a majority of the House and Senate—mostly Republicans and conservative southern Democrats—publicly supported Nixon, the speech dejected many prominent Democratic senators, including Mansfield, Fulbright, McGovern, Gore, and Edward Kennedy. To them, Nixon's speech was merely an effort to build public support for a protracted period of continued American military involvement in Vietnam while questioning the patriotism of those who opposed the war. The morning after the speech, a despondent Mansfield appeared on NBC's "Today" show and expressed disappointment that Nixon had failed to "offer the people more hope." Disputing Nixon's argument that a speedy withdrawal would diminish America's prestige, Mansfield maintained that "we've lost prestige and standing among the nations of the world because of Vietnam. Vietnam is a cancer. It's a tragedy. It's eating out the heart of America. It's doing us no good. And the sooner we can come to a responsible solution, which the President is trying to achieve, the better off we'll all be."[63]

That afternoon in the Senate, Mansfield opened the Senate's session by again voicing his profound disappointment with Nixon's speech. Although he believed that Nixon "spoke sincerely" and wanted to get the nation out of Vietnam, he observed that "what is still not clear is the how or when. There were no specifics." Edward Kennedy agreed. "The President's speech, simply stated, was more of the same—no new hopes, no new considerations, no new inspiration, for an American people who have waited so long and given so much for peace."[64] Meanwhile, a disappointed Fulbright told reporters that Nixon "now has fully and truthfully taken on himself the Johnson war, and I think that is a fundamental error."[65] To a friend, Fulbright ruefully wrote of his distress at finally realizing "that we eliminated LBJ only to end up with this, which is almost more than the human spirit can endure."[66] McGovern, in a prepared statement, attacked the speech as "an echo from the past," and called it "the exercise of the same tired Cold War policy in which our actions are devoid of initiative and totally dependent upon the actions of our adversaries."[67]

The day after the speech, Gore came to the Senate floor to ridicule Nixon's plea for national unity. "To urge the public to unite behind the President in support of a policy which has not been defined—after years of erosion of public confidence in the Nation's leadership because of the war," Gore said, "is, as the song popular with the young people says, like 'blowing in the wind.'" Challenging Gore's dim view of the speech was Republican Senator Robert Dole of Kansas, soon to become one of Nixon's most vociferous Senate defenders, who trumpeted the White House line. "I got the opposite impression," Dole said, "that we are on the road to peace, that we do have a program and do have a plan, that there has been a reduction in the fighting, that there has been a reduction in infiltration, that some 60,000 Americans will be home by December."[68] Among other vocal Nixon supporters in the Senate that day was Democrat Herman Talmadge of Georgia, who elaborated on the president's veiled condemnation of the antiwar movement. "To persist in demonstrating against our own Government," he said, "provides aid and comfort to the enemy."[69]

Despite growing Senate dissent, there would always be a crippling and pronounced lack of cohesion and organization among the Senate's doves. Unlike the impregnable southern forces that Richard Russell had led in opposition to civil rights in the 1950s, the Senate's antiwar forces were disorganized and without a clear leader. The antiwar liberals neither enjoyed nor seemed to desire a similar degree of unity and coordination. In the first instance, they simply lacked a leader with the stature and organizational skills of Russell. While Fulbright and Mansfield might have filled that role, neither man was a strong legislative leader or strategist in the tradition of Russell, Humphrey, or Johnson. Mansfield, in particular, was averse to twisting arms or providing the kind of coercive leadership that would have been necessary to stop the war by denying appropriations to continue the fighting. After Johnson's autocratic rule in the 1950s, the new majority leader had apparently determined that his colleagues desired a far less imposing style of leadership. "Mansfield didn't *want* to be the [majority] leader," complained Democratic Senator Frank Moss of Utah. "He never tried to exert leadership."[70]

Like Fulbright, Mansfield often saw the Senate as a forum for airing dissenting views, not a place to enforce them—especially in the realm of foreign affairs, where he believed the president's authority to formulate policy was paramount. "Mike Mansfield is a monk," Johnson's aide Harry McPherson once observed. "He has no desire to impose his imprint on legislation."[71] So averse to doing anything that might suggest he wanted his colleagues to follow his lead, Mansfield often withheld his vote on controversial issues until the rest of the Senate had voted. "Mansfield saw his role as harmonizing the various viewpoints held by the Senate Democrats," explained his aide Francis Valeo.[72]

Fulbright, who saw himself primarily as an intellectual and not a legislator, was just as ill suited for the kind of coalition building the Senate's antiwar minority needed to maximize its effectiveness. Despite his preeminent role as chairman of the Foreign Relations Committee, Fulbright believed his panel's duty was merely to *educate* the Senate and the American public about the inadvisable policies that Johnson and Nixon had pursued in Vietnam. "He didn't believe it was his role to personally, one on one, try to alter people's views," explained Fulbright's top aide, Lee Williams. "He thought the Senate should be a forum through which these things were discussed and debated."[73] Recalled speechwriter Seth Tillman: "He always thought it was embarrassing to try to persuade somebody to do something, to lobby somebody to do anything."[74]

Had Mansfield and Fulbright regarded the Senate more as a legislative body and less a debating society, the antiwar forces might have enjoyed more success. But the fault was not entirely attributable to Mansfield's and Fulbright's reticence to lead. By their very nature, the Senate's liberals were averse to the kind of strong-willed, coercive leadership that might have been required. "In some sense," observed Bryce Nelson, then an aide to Frank Church, "they were all lone wolves."[75] No group had been more troublesome to Majority Leader Lyndon Johnson in the 1950s than the Senate's liberals—men who had despised their leader's propensity for compromise and who chaffed under his oppressive rule. It is doubtful that many of these same senators—as well as the younger, independent war opponents like McGovern, Kennedy, and Church—would have been any more willing to follow a strong leader, even one less forceful and imposing than Johnson.

Another reason the antiwar forces lacked cohesion was the absence of a rallying point or a single plan for extricating the U.S. military from

Southeast Asia. While almost all of the war's opponents talked of the need
to negotiate with Hanoi and the NLF, they did not agree on what to do in
the meantime. Some favored an immediate withdrawal; others simply
wanted an acceleration of Nixon's Vietnamization policy; still others
favored an enclave strategy. Some wanted to stop all appropriations for
U.S. forces in Vietnam as a way of forcing Nixon's hand; others—fearing
the political backlash—hesitated to take such a drastic step. Even with a
plan around which to rally, the fact remained that, short of congressional
action to end military appropriations, there would have been little the antiwar forces could have done to change Nixon's policy or force a rapid withdrawal of U.S. forces. With Mansfield and Fulbright unwilling to provide
the leadership necessary to stop appropriations for the war, the awesome
task of defying the commander in chief during wartime was often left to
more junior senators like McGovern, Church, and Mark Hatfield. For lack
of effective, seasoned leadership, and a single plan of action, the Senate's
antiwar movement foundered.

NIXON HAD HOPED that his Silent Majority speech would rob the November 15 Mobilization rally of its momentum. While it may have had the effect
of marginalizing the protesters with some segment of the public, speech did
nothing to dampen their determination to join voices in a massive statement
of dissatisfaction with the administration's policies. What the *New York
Times* called a "vast throng of Americans"—the largest mass march in
Washington's history—descended on the city and stretched ten blocks from
the foot of the Capitol down to the Washington Monument. City officials
estimated the crowd at more than three hundred thousand.[76]

"We meet today at this historic place because we love America," said
McGovern, who addressed the crowd against the advice of several of his
staff members and joined McCarthy and Goodell as the only senators
attending the rally.

> We love America enough to call her to a higher standard. We love Amer-
> ica enough to call her away from the folly of war to the blessings of peace.
> . . . We are here as American patriots, young and old, to build a country,
> to build a world, that seeks the ways of peace—that teaches war no more.
> We meet today to reaffirm those ageless values that gave us birth—"life,
> liberty and the pursuit of happiness." We meet to declare peace—to put
> an end to war, not in some vanishing future, but to end it *now*.[77]

The antiwar movement gained even more momentum on November
17, when the *New York Times* broke the story of the My Lai massacre. On
March 16, 1968—during the Tet offensive—a small American infantry unit

on a search and destroy mission had summarily murdered more than 300 unarmed civilians, most of them women and children, in the South Vietnamese hamlet of My Lai. Army investigators had covered up the story for eighteen months, but had appointed Lieutenant General William Peers to investigate "the nature and scope" of the incident. The week after the *Times* first reported details of the massacre, Army officials announced that Peers' report had concluded that a 26-year-old first lieutenant, William Calley, leader of the platoon that had killed the civilians, was primarily to blame. Military prosecutors charged Calley with the premeditated killing of at least 109 men, women, and children, including a 2-year-old child. Reports later indicated that the American soldiers had raped many of the women before shooting them.[78]

In many respects, My Lai had been inevitable—the tragic and deadly result of sending heavily armed, emotionally frayed young men into a guerrilla war in which they could not distinguish between civilians and the Viet Cong and that was populated by people they grew to regard as subhuman. Combined with the military's insatiable demand for positive enemy kill ratios and body counts, tragedies like My Lai—and there were others—were virtually guaranteed. Back home, Americans had mixed reactions about the incident. By a narrow 41–40 percent margin, those interviewed by the Harris polling organization in January 1970 condemned the shooting of civilians even if they were "believed to be helping the enemy in war." However, a lopsided majority—66–15 percent—opposed any efforts to courtmartial those involved if they had killed the civilians under orders from a superior.[79]

McGovern's reaction to the news about My Lai was among the strongest in Congress. He demanded that "the Nixon administration . . . stop our participation in the horrible destruction of this tiny country and its people."[80] But several days later, appearing on CBS's "Face the Nation," McGovern actually defended Calley, who some viewed as a scapegoat for the institutional and cultural ills that had led to the massacre. "Many people will see the lieutenant and his men as a convenient target on which to unload what should be a sense of national guilt," McGovern told host George Herman. "We put these men into a situation where it was almost inevitable that sooner or later events of this kind would take place." McGovern failed to see the difference between killing on a massive scale and the crimes committed at My Lai. "Now, really," said the former World War II bomber pilot, "what is the difference between a bombing plane or an artillery piece destroying a village, including its inhabitants—men, women and children—and what Lieutenant Calley did?"[81]

Nixon, meanwhile, could not help but sense the nation's escalating unease over the events in Vietnam and the seemingly endless American commitment. He knew it was time again to stave off the antiwar movement with additional troop withdrawals. Throughout November, Nixon badgered Kissinger in a stream of memoranda about doing something "drastic" to reduce the number of American civilian and military personnel in Vietnam. "We have been in [office] almost a year now," he complained on November 24, "and there is no cut of significance. The place has swollen to the bursting point with Americans falling all over each other."[82]

On December 15, Nixon announced that fifty thousand additional troops would be home by April 15, 1970. "It marks further progress in turning over the defense of South Vietnam to the South Vietnamese," Nixon explained. "It is another clear sign of our readiness to bring an end to the war and achieve a just peace." In his first year in office, Nixon had announced troop withdrawals totaling over one hundred thousand. But even with those reductions, four hundred thirty-four thousand American troops would remain in Vietnam—a number still far too high for opponents of the war like Mansfield and other Senate critics who wanted the pace vastly accelerated.[83]

Nixon worried about that criticism, but he was undeterred. On New Year's Day 1970, he sat alone in the study of his San Clemente, California, home and reviewed the past year. As he recalled in his memoirs, he allowed himself a feeling of "cautious optimism." Despite the strong criticism of Fulbright, Mansfield, McGovern, and others, he still enjoyed the support of a fairly broad majority of Congress. On December 2, the House had overwhelmingly passed a resolution commending him for his efforts toward "peace with justice" in Vietnam. Finally, Nixon believed, the worst had passed. At last he had what many Americans believed was a "plan" to end the war. He concluded that now was the time to hold steady and resist the urge to tailor his policy to suit his congressional detractors and the louder critics in the increasingly radical antiwar movement. Nixon admitted to himself that he had underestimated the "willingness of the North Vietnamese to hang on and resist a negotiated settlement on any other than their own terms." But he was also confident that the North Vietnamese had "underestimated my own willingness to hold on despite the domestic and international pressures that would be ranged against me."[84]

Believing that he had weathered the worst of the storm, Nixon "was determined to lead a slow, disguised American retreat from Vietnam," one former campaign speechwriter, Richard Whalen, observed from afar. "The disguise came from clouds of misleading rhetoric and prospects of 'Vietnamization.'" Regardless, Whalen said, as long as Nixon could "execute the retreat without dishonor and collapse abroad and permanent disunity at home, he would earn the nation's gratitude."[85] But Nixon's optimism was premature. The worst, as he would soon discover, was yet to come.

CHAPTER 39

This Chamber Reeks of Blood

1970

Arthur Schlesinger was deeply troubled as he wrote to Fulbright in late January from his office at the City University of New York. He found himself in concert with an increasing band of observers confused by Nixon's dual approaches to Vietnam. At first, as the noted historian and former Kennedy aide recalled, Nixon had stressed negotiations as a way to end American involvement in Vietnam. "However," Schlesinger observed, "if he had been in dead earnest about negotiation, he would surely have slowed down the fighting, begun to cut loose from the Saigon regime, taken measures to protect the potential leaders of a coalition government and responded promptly and imaginatively to the Ho Chi Minh letter and to other signals from Hanoi." As Schlesinger correctly observed, Vietnamization required "an incompatible set of actions: the prosecution of the fighting; the strengthening of the Saigon government; acquiescence in Thieu's repression of opposition; rejection of signals from Hanoi." It was as if the two policies had different goals, he concluded. "The negotiation idea is designed to bring the war to an end; the Vietnamization plan is designed to keep the war going, though with much reduced American participation, and even apparently in some sense to 'win' the war." Schlesinger mournfully concluded that Nixon "has practically abandoned negotiation."

Fulbright agreed. "I have the feeling," he lamented in his reply on January 30, "that many of the President's advisors in the military and in the State Department are not very anxious to give up the war without a victory—therefore, he finds it difficult to move vigorously toward a negotiated settlement that might not look like a victory."[1]

Although Nixon had declared in his State of the Union Address that "the prospects for peace are far greater today than they were a year ago,"

651

sure signs were not so easy to find.[2] Indeed, as Schlesinger and Fulbright worried, a stepped-up war seemed the likelier prospect in the interim—with or without U.S. involvement—as Nixon poured hundreds of millions of dollars into modernizing, equipping, and training the South Vietnamese armed forces for the day when U.S. withdrawal was complete. But to the public, at least, the U.S. mission in Vietnam appeared to have changed. "The top priority of U.S. fighting men in South Viet Nam," *Time* reported in early January, "is no longer killing the enemy. It is teaching and equipping South Viet Nam's army to do so."[3]

What the public saw and heard of Vietnamization it liked—and believed. Although 40 percent of those questioned in a *Time*–Louis Harris poll in December opposed Nixon's policies, a majority of 54 percent approved his handling of the war—representing a 9 percent gain in support in the months after his November "Silent Majority" speech. Asked if they supported immediate withdrawal, a faster pace of withdrawals, or the Vietnamization "plan put forward by the President," those surveyed favored Nixon's plan by a more than 2-to-1 margin.[4]

By all official accounts, Vietnamization was a success. Indeed, in the year since Nixon had taken office, the South Vietnamese military was being amply equipped to fight on its own. Indigenous force levels grew from eight hundred fifty thousand to more than a million. Saigon's military was now armed to the teeth—with ships, planes, helicopters, vehicles, more than a million M-16 rifles, twelve thousand M-60 machine guns, forty thousand M-79 grenade launchers—all courtesy of the U.S. taxpayer.[5] Despite this Herculean public effort—and in direct contradiction of Nixon's campaign to convince the citizenry that the Americanization of the war was virtually over—the war in Vietnam remained a very American enterprise. The truth was that the South Vietnamese army, still rife with corruption and hopelessly disorganized, was woefully incapable of fighting the war on its own. "We have not seen proof that ARVN [the South Vietnamese army] has really improved," Kissinger warned Nixon on January 16.[6] Furthermore, as Nixon and Kissinger knew, Thieu—clinging desperately to power—had absolutely no interest in political or economic reforms, nor did he desire an end to the war.

Several weeks after Kissinger's warning about ARVN inadequacies, the Senate Foreign Relations Committee echoed the national security advisor's private counsel when it disclosed the conclusions of two committee consultants—James Lowenstein and Richard Moose—who had investigated the Vietnamization program in December. While senior American officials had informed the two men that the North Vietnamese were "no longer capable of mounting a sufficiently powerful attack to defeat" the American-backed South Vietnamese army, junior officials and journalists told a far different and more realistic story. Those officials cautioned Lowenstein and Moose that "the South Vietnamese Army could not now defend the country against a massive North Vietnamese attack, even with United States artillery and air support. A number doubt that the army will ever be able to do so." Despite Nixon's soothing words about the improving prospects for peace that his Vietnamization policies had reaped, the consultants concluded that the war "appears to be not only far from won but far from over."[7]

McGovern was among those thoroughly disgusted with the Vietnamization program and the way it seemed geared toward propping up Thieu's government, which he regarded as hopelessly corrupt. "Indeed," he told the Foreign Relations Committee in early February, "self-determination and independence are probably far stronger among the Vietnamese guerillas and their supporters than within the Saigon government camp."[8] Peace would not come to Vietnam, McGovern said in the Senate on March 3, "until we loosen our embrace of the Thieu–Ky regime. That regime will never be accepted by the people of Vietnam and as long as we insist on keeping it in power, we will have to stay there to hold it in power."[9]

To McGovern, it was appalling enough that Nixon insisted on backing the corrupt government in Saigon. He now appeared to be expanding the fighting in Southeast Asia by sending American troops into Laos. Rumors of American involvement in Laos abounded, but the White House denied them all. "There are no American combat troops in Laos," Nixon said flatly on March 6. "We have no plans for introducing ground combat forces."[10] In fact, American ground forces had been in Laos for some time, engaging in hundreds of cross-border operations to stop the flow of men and supplies southward through the poorly defended neutral country via the Ho Chi Minh Trail. In addition, Nixon's Pentagon dispatched hundreds of military advisors to advise the Laotian army and had directed a secret airlift. For months, American planes based in Thailand had flown in and out of Laos, supporting the government's armed struggle against the communist Pathet Lao in the Plain of Jars near the border of Laos and northwestern North Vietnam. In mid-February, Nixon upped the ante by sending in more American troops after a North Vietnamese invasion. At an NSC meeting on February 16, Nixon extended even more help to the government of Laotian Premier Souvanna Phouma when he ordered B-52 strikes against the Pathet Lao.

Nixon could not much longer conceal the truth about the U.S. role in Laos. On March 8, the *Los Angeles Times* reported that an American captain had been killed in combat in Laos. By day's end, embarrassed Pentagon officials acknowledged that he had not been the first. In fact, twenty-seven Americans had lost their lives in Laos in the past year. The next night, Nixon went on national television to acknowledge that the United States was no longer fighting only in Vietnam. The nation had entered the war in Laos. While he disclosed the presence of four hundred American "advisors" stationed in the neighboring country, as well as the American bombing and airlift missions that had supported the Laotian government, he denied that they were combat ground troops. Technically, he was correct. American combat troops had engaged only in cross-border operations. Those troops were not stationed in Laos. To prove his determination to limit the fighting, Nixon promised to observe a 1969 congressional directive—sponsored by Church, Cooper, and Mansfield in December—against sending American troops to Laos.[11]

McGovern was among the most outraged at Nixon's duplicity. "Are we about to sacrifice more young Americans in another war in Southeast Asia?" he said in a speech to the National Newspaper Association. "Have we learned nothing from the long years of bloodshed and blunders in Vietnam?"[12] Doubting Nixon's pledge to keep ground troops out of Laos, Fulbright offered a broad resolution prohibiting the use of U.S. forces "in combat in or over Laos" without congressional approval. "If the Senate is to remain silent while the President uses air forces in an Asian country without authorization from Congress," Fulbright said, "we should remain silent about his use of ground combat forces."[13]

FULBRIGHT HAD LONG AGO discounted the domino theory, as well as the idea that Southeast Asia was somehow a vital U.S. interest. On April 2, he rose in the Senate to deliver a bold speech that attacked the myths he believed surrounded and supported the continued U.S. military presence in Southeast Asia. The core of his speech was a heretical argument against the notion of an international communist conspiracy, as well as a plea for American leaders to tolerate communism in Asia. "The master myth of Vietnam— that is, the country as distinguished from the war—is the greatly inflated importance which has been attached to it," Fulbright said. "From the standpoint of American security and interests, the central fact about Indochina, including Vietnam is that it does not matter very much who rules in those small and backward lands." Fulbright wondered how "we come to inflate so colossally the importance of Indochina to our own security?" The answer, he concluded, was in "that hoariest, hardiest, most indestructible myth of them all: the myth of the international Communist conspiracy."

Fulbright believed the American commitment in Vietnam was sustained because "the Vietnamese Communists are perceived as no more than spearbearers for the world—or the Asian—Communist conspiracy."

He maintained, however, that North Vietnam, "though materially dependent and politically influenced" by China and the Soviet Union, was "an authentically independent country" and "the dominant power of Indochina." Even so, in spite of its communist government and its military power, Fulbright argued that it was a small, undeveloped country "without the resources to become a significant imperialist power, much less a threat to the United States." Even less important to Fulbright was the corrupt government of South Vietnam. "The preservation of a non-Communist—as against a Communist—dictatorship in South Vietnam is not going to protect us, or anybody else, from Soviet or Chinese missiles," he said. "It simply does not matter very much for the United States, in cold, unadorned strategic terms, who rules the states of Indochina."

> We ought in a way to welcome North Vietnam's preeminence in Indochina, because while North Vietnam has shown itself strong enough to dominate Indochina if left alone by outside powers, it has also shown itself willing and able to resist Chinese domination. At the same time North Vietnam is far too small a power to have any serious hope of conquering all of Southeast Asia, much less posing any kind of a threat to the United States.

Fulbright made it clear that he did not advocate a communist-controlled Indochina. "I merely propose to accept it," he explained, "if it arises from the local power situation, as something unwelcome but tolerable, and most emphatically not worth the extravagant costs of a war like the one we are now fighting."[14] Fulbright's speech was a courageous statement that challenged twenty-five years of reflexive American hostility to communism of all stripes. It was not, however, a philosophy that his Senate colleagues, beyond his usual allies like McGovern and Church, would soon embrace.

If Fulbright was appalled by the costs of the U.S. war in Vietnam, he was to be doubly alarmed at the price Nixon was willing to pay in Cambodia. For years, Cambodian leader Prince Norodom Sihanouk had labored to maintain his country's neutrality in the war that threatened to engulf his own corner of Southeast Asia. He knew that the North Vietnamese had established sanctuaries just over the Cambodian-South Vietnamese border and had routinely trekked the Ho Chi Minh Trail that passed through the eastern part of his country. Sihanouk tolerated the North Vietnamese, just as he turned a blind eye to the American bombing aimed at the southerly flow of communist men and supplies from North Vietnam. He did not, however, wish to give the United States carte blanche to wage war in his country.

Nixon, however, had another agenda. He desperately wanted to deprive the North Vietnamese of their Cambodian sanctuaries and reduce the threat to American and South Vietnamese forces. In mid-March, he finally got his opening, when General Lon Nol overthrew Sihanouk in a bloodless coup. Aware that the general had plans to expand his army by ten thousand men in order to move against the communists, Nixon was ready to help. "Let's get a plan to aid the new government on this goal," he told his aides. But Rogers, Laird, and CIA Director Richard Helms opposed the idea, arguing that a precipitous rush to Lon Nol's side would only convince Hanoi, Moscow, and Peking that the United States was behind the coup. The North Vietnamese, they believed, would then have a perfect excuse to stage a preemptive attack. Nixon reluctantly put the plan on hold. By mid-April, however, the fighting in Cambodia intensified. South Vietnamese forces clashed with the Viet Cong inside Cambodian territory and forced communist troops deeper into the Cambodian interior. Fearing that the capital of Phnom Penh might soon be under communist attack, Nixon was itching to order U.S. intervention.

Indeed, April found Nixon in a poor frame of mind to make decisions about war in Cambodia. The month was filled with indignities and insults, courtesy of the Democratic-controlled Senate and the antiwar movement. On April 8, the Senate rejected G. Harold Carswell, the man Nixon had nominated to fill the Supreme Court seat vacated by Justice Abe Fortas. To make matters worse, it was the second Senate rebuff Nixon had suffered in three-and-a-half months. In November, senators had enraged Nixon by rejecting his first nominee, Clement Haynesworth.

Carswell and Haynesworth were both conservative Southerners, roundly assailed by civil rights groups as racist and derided by liberals as unqualified. But Nixon stubbornly clung to his nominees and forced the Senate to vote them down. To *Time*, Carswell's rejection was "the most serious reversal of [Nixon's] young presidency."[15] Nixon took it as such. After the vote, he seethed and lashed out at the Senate for its "hypocrisy" and regional prejudice.[16] Two days later, the Senate again took aim at Nixon's authority in Vietnam when the Foreign Relations Committee voted unanimously to repeal the Gulf of Tonkin Resolution.

The final indignity was private, although just as exasperating. Fearful of violence from radical antiwar groups, Nixon reluctantly cancelled plans to attend college graduation ceremonies for his daughter Julie and son-in-law David Eisenhower. Like Johnson before him, he was becoming a prisoner in the White House. The antiwar movement had become his jailer.[17]

Thus Nixon was in a particularly foul mood when he finally faced the challenge of Cambodia in mid-April. "Those senators think they can push me around," he warned Kissinger, "but I'll show them who's tough. The liberals are waiting to see Nixon let Cambodia go down the drain just the way Eisenhower let Cuba go down the drain."[18] Nixon's disgust with the protest movement and his opponents in Congress had begun to cloud his judgment. Cambodia, it seemed, assumed a degree of importance in Nixon's mind all out of proportion to its importance to the United States. Regardless of the risks of wider war posed by American intervention, Nixon told Kissinger that he was prepared to order "a bold move in Cambodia."[19]

As Nixon pondered his options in Cambodia, Laird forced him to face up to the need for additional troop withdrawals in Vietnam. Although Kissinger worried that the continued diminution of troop strength, despite its enormous domestic popularity, was "evaporating Hanoi's need to bargain about our disengagement," Laird worried about the increasing congressional pressure to curtail defense spending. Withdrawing troops, he believed, was a perfect way to increase Nixon's domestic popularity while appeasing congressional critics who demanded budget cuts. Kissinger, on the other hand, cautioned against announcing a large, precipitous troop withdrawal that would undermine or stall the negotiations still underway in Paris. On April 20, Nixon compromised and told the nation in a televised statement that he was bringing home one hundred fifty thousand troops in a phased withdrawal—sixty thousand by year's end and the remaining ninety thousand troops by the end of 1971. Kissinger called the announcement a "tour de force" that "met the political need for a withdrawal schedule and the military necessity to retain the largest possible number of troops during the next three critical months while Hanoi's forces were assaulting Cambodia and pressing forward in Laos."[20] Unspoken, however, was Nixon's tacit acknowledgment that he would not end American involvement in the war by the 1970 election, as he had promised congressional leaders the year before.

Nixon's statement was full of false hope for an early end to the fighting. "The decision I have announced tonight means that we finally have in sight the just peace we are seeking." Yet at the very moment Nixon spoke of peace, he was nursing a plan to inject the United States more deeply into war by sending American troops into Cambodia, a fact he hinted at when he said, "If I conclude that increased enemy action [in Laos or Cambodia] jeopardizes our remaining forces in Vietnam, I shall not hesitate to take strong and effective measures to deal with that situation."[21]

While Nixon did not brief leading members of Congress on what he had in mind in Cambodia, he hinted at his intentions to Armed Services Committee Chairman John Stennis on April 24. That afternoon Kissinger met with Stennis in the Mississippian's office and explained, Kissinger recalled, "that a US-supported incursion into Cambodia was a military necessity if Vietnamization were to proceed." During the conversation, by prearrangement, Nixon phoned. A compliant Stennis told Nixon that he supported the proposed operation, although it is not clear that he knew that a "US-supported incursion" meant that U.S. forces would invade Cambodia. Except for the conversation with Stennis, there is no evidence that Nixon consulted any other member of Congress prior to the planned Cambodian incursion. Other than his veiled public allusions to the invasion, Nixon was determined to deny his critics the opportunity to attack his policies beforehand.[22]

On the evening of April 30, Nixon showed the Senate just how tough he was when he told a stunned national television audience that he was sending U.S. combat troops into Cambodia. "Tonight, American and South Vietnamese units will attack the headquarters for the entire Communist military operation in South Vietnam," Nixon said. It was no "invasion" of Cambodia, Nixon assured his viewers. "The areas in which these attacks will be launched are completely occupied and controlled by North Vietnamese forces. Our purpose is not to occupy the areas. Once enemy forces are driven out of these sanctuaries and once their military supplies are destroyed, we will withdraw." After explaining the rationale for his action, Nixon added a gratuitous and demagogic slap at his antiwar critics:

> My fellow Americans, we live in an age of anarchy, both abroad and at home. We see mindless attacks on all the great institutions, which have been created by free civilizations in the last 500 years. Even here in the United States, great universities are being systematically destroyed. Small nations all over the world find themselves under attack from within and without.
>
> If when the chips are down, the world's most powerful nation, the United States of America, acts like a pitiful, helpless giant, the forces of totalitarianism and anarchy will threaten free nations and free institutions throughout the world.
>
> It is not our power but our will and character that is being tested tonight.*

Nixon disingenuously claimed he had "rejected all political considerations" in making his decision. "Whether my party gains in November is nothing compared to the lives of 400,000 brave Americans fighting for our country and for the cause of peace and freedom in Vietnam." He would

---

*Historian Marilyn B. Young noted the irony that another politician had once delivered a strikingly similar speech in turbulent times: "The streets of our country are in turmoil. The universities are filled with students rebelling and rioting. Communists are seeking to destroy our country. Russia is threatening us with her might. And the republic is in danger. Yes! Danger from within and without. We need law and order! Without law and order our nation cannot survive." The speaker: Adolf Hitler in 1932 (Young, 244).

rather be a "one-term President," he said, "and do what I believe is right than to be a two-term President at the cost of seeing America become a second-rate power and to see this nation accept the first defeat in its proud 190-year history."[23]

Condemnation was swift and furious. "The invasion of Cambodia ordered by President Nixon," wrote Tom Wicker in the *New York Times*, "makes it clear that he does not have and never has had a 'plan to end the war.'"[24] The speech sparked outrage in Congress and riots on college campuses throughout the country. Only days before, in testimony before the Senate Foreign Relations Committee, Secretary of State Rogers had reassured members that the United States had no plans for a Cambodian operation. "I didn't think the president would do it," complained the Republican dean of the Senate, George Aiken of Vermont. "I was wrong. It's all-out war now, short of atomic bombs."[25] "Today is a sad and bloody day," Albert Gore declared the next afternoon in the Senate.[26]

"I think the effect is going to be—and already is—a terrible destruction to a rather fine little country that was not bothering anybody," Fulbright told reporters. Mansfield condemned the Cambodian incursion in harsh terms, saying the time had arrived for the nation's leaders to show "a fitting sense of humility."[27] The United States, he added later, was "sinking deeper into the morass."[28] Days later, in a private memorandum to his file, the majority leader wrote that "it is about time that we wrote off this mistaken war, this tragedy for our country, this penetration into an area in which we have no business and which is not tied to the security of this country." Mansfield wrote that for the first time he was prepared to give "most serious consideration to a termination date after which no more funds will be appropriated for military operations in Indochina."[29]

On May 1, McGovern and Republican Mark Hatfield of Oregon offered just the kind of measure that Mansfield had in mind—an amendment to the military procurement bill stopping all funds for the war after December 1970 and requiring withdrawal of all U.S. troops by June 30, 1971, "unless Congress shall have declared war."[30] "The way to save American lives is not by saving face or by spreading the war to yet another Asian country," McGovern said, explaining that the amendment would force Congress to share the burden of the war with Nixon. "This amendment will place that burden on each Senator—a political risk that we should gladly bear rather than further risking the lives of our men in Southeast Asia."[31]

But Senate consideration of the McGovern–Hatfield amendment would wait until senators disposed of a milder, less encompassing measure proposed by Church and Cooper. In a Senate speech the same day, Church lamented that the amendment he and Cooper had sponsored the previous

December—prohibiting the introduction of U.S. ground forces into Laos and Thailand—had not included Cambodia. It now seemed "appropriate," he said, "to go a step beyond exhortation" and begin using "the explicit war and appropriations powers vested in Congress" to stop Nixon's Cambodian foray. "Torn between its stubborn adherence to the war and its political need to get out of it," Church said, "the Nixon administration has devised a policy with no chance of winning the war, little chance of ending it, and every chance of perpetuating it into the indefinite future." Eventually, Church argued, "we are going to have to plunge into Indochina all the way and face the enormous consequences at home and abroad, or we are going to have to get out."[32]

On May 11, the Senate Foreign Relations Committee, in a 9-to-5 vote, adopted a Cooper–Church amendment to the House-passed Foreign Military Sales Act that halted funds for U.S. ground troops and military advisors in Cambodia. Although he acknowledged that the amendment would not likely force Nixon out of Cambodia—the president had said most troops would be out of the country by June 30—Church thought the measure might at least cause him to honor his pledge about keeping the operation temporary. He said he hoped to "draw the purse strings tight against a deepening American involvement in Cambodia." In an effort to attract support from some of the milder of Nixon's defenders, Church and Cooper modified their amendment to prohibit spending on Cambodia after July 1, 1970—the day after Nixon had promised to end the operation.[33]

Defiant, Nixon was unbowed by the withering criticism from Capitol Hill. He told his aides in a May 3 staff meeting that congressional supporters should be encouraged to "say that not supporting the President is sticking a knife in the back of the U.S. troops, and attacking us on this is giving aid and comfort to the enemy—use that phrase, because that's what it really is." As he spoke, Nixon could sense that some staff members were uncomfortable with his tough stance. "Don't worry about divisiveness," he told them. "Having drawn the sword, don't take it out—stick it in hard, because for people to go squealing around while a combat operation is underway, undermining the very purpose of the action where good men are losing their lives—that's beyond the pale. Hit 'em in the gut. No defensiveness."[34]

One presidential aide, Tom Charles Huston, took Nixon's advice to heart, advising Haldeman and Kissinger that "unless we meet this assault directly and rebuff it, we will have presided over a constitutional revolution." To Nixon's men, the Cooper–Church amendment was not a challenge to Nixon's Southeast Asia policy, but to the presidency itself. To meet the Senate challenge, Haldeman looked for "3–4 good gut fighters"—like Republicans Barry Goldwater of Arizona and Bob Dole of Kansas—who could "really ram" Cooper and Church in Senate debate and portray them, following Nixon's instructions, as those who would "stab" America's fighting men "in the back."[35]

News of the Cambodian invasion sparked new protests as a temporarily waning antiwar movement roared back to life. In Ohio, three days after the invasion, National Guardsmen killed four Kent State students as they protested the invasion.[36] A defiant and insensitive Nixon only compounded the outrage by refusing to condemn the trigger-happy guardsmen who fired the shots. "When dissent turns to violence," he said, failing to acknowledge his personal role in inciting the protests, "it invites tragedy." College campuses across the country erupted. In all, students at more than 440 schools took to the streets. Demonstrations shut down hundreds of universities. In Washington, more than one hundred thousand protestors marched on a barricaded White House to protest the invasion and the Kent State killings. It seemed clear, *Time* observed on May 18, "that even if the Cambodian expedition should accomplish more than now appears likely, it has already destroyed far more American resources of morale and cohesion than any North Vietnamese supplies could be worth."[37] *Newsweek* described the events in Cambodia in even harsher terms. Nixon had become "perilously insensitive to the expectations of millions of his countrymen that the war would be steadfastly wound down rather than suddenly cranked up. And the abrupt manner of his decision suggested that Mr. Nixon had allowed himself to become isolated not only from the American people, not only from their representatives in Congress but also from many of his own chief advisors."[38]

ON MAY 13, as the Senate began debating the Foreign Military Sales Act—legislation that included the Cooper–Church amendment—Armed Services Chairman John Stennis insisted that keeping the amendment would be a "grave mistake . . . while the battle is still going on." But in a strong retort, Church told his colleagues that "the dispatch of American troops into Cambodia, though presently limited in scope, could easily become the first step toward committing the United States to the defense of still another government in Southeast Asia." Endorsing the amendment, he said, "presents Congress with a historic opportunity to draw the limits on American intervention in Indochina."[39]

At the White House, officials were beginning to panic in the face of growing Senate support for the measure. Worried that the efforts of Goldwater, Dole, Stennis, Strom Thurmond, and others might fall short in the poisonous post-Cambodian invasion environment, the White House looked for ways to mobilize public opinion against Cooper–Church.

Administration officials joined forces with the American Legion and the Veterans of Foreign Wars to organize a massive grassroots mailing directed at members of Congress. In a letter to thousands of his members, the American Legion president warned that the Cooper–Church amendment represented "the first time the Senate has debated a 'declaration of surrender.'" He urged veterans to pressure their members of Congress to oppose the bill. "This is urgent," he wrote. "The enemy *within our country* have a long head start in opposing our President" (emphasis added).[40]

Evidence of the amendment's strength was reflected in the sudden willingness of the opponents, prodded by the White House, to amend the measure rather than attempt to defeat it outright. Mansfield's role in this effort was instrumental. "By adopting the Cooper–Church amendment," the majority leader told his colleagues on May 20, "the Senate will be acting in concert—and let me emphasize those words, 'in concert'—with [the president's] intent" to withdraw the troops from Cambodia by the end of June. "The amendment is not a rash and reckless step. It is the surest way of protecting the safety of the U.S. forces in Cambodia" by mandating their withdrawal "in accordance with the President's own timetable."[41] Mansfield's message was shrewd and unmistakable. Given that the amendment was likely to prevail, despite the intense White House lobbying, Nixon's choices were to suffer another humiliating defeat at the hands of the Senate's doves, or pragmatically embrace its language and acknowledge that it mandated a policy he had already endorsed.

While Republican leader Hugh Scott of Pennsylvania was interested in the idea—he agreed that the Senate should declare its reluctance to assist the Cambodian government—Assistant Minority Leader Robert Griffin of Michigan was far more skeptical. "I know it is not the intention of the sponsors to aid the enemy," he said, "but the amendment, if it were adopted in its present form, would have the effect of aiding the enemy by tying the hands of the Commander-in-Chief."

"The President himself tied his own hands," Mansfield replied, pointing out that it was Nixon, not the Senate, who had declared that U.S. forces would not go more than 21 miles into Cambodian territory and that the troops would be out by June 30. The next day, Mansfield handed Nixon his way out of the Senate jungle when he introduced a revised preamble to the amendment declaring that it was "in concert with the declared objectives of the President . . . to avoid the involvement of the United States in Cambodia after July 1, 1970." On May 26, the Senate adopted Mansfield's change, 82–11. Cooper, like Mansfield, shrewdly insisted that his amendment merely reaffirmed Nixon's position. "Our amendment could be more correctly and properly called an amendment to support the President," he said, "to assist him in his effort to end the war in Vietnam." On June 11,

Mansfield made the amendment even more palatable to the hawks when the Senate overwhelmingly approved his language declaring that nothing in the Cooper-Church measure would be "deemed to impugn" Nixon's prerogatives as commander in Chief.[42]

No one, however, mistook the votes as honest affirmations of Nixon's policies in Southeast Asia. In the first real test of the strength of both sides, on June 3 the Senate narrowly rejected Democrat Robert Byrd's amendment allowing Nixon to send troops back into Cambodia "to protect the lives of U.S. forces in South Vietnam or to facilitate the withdrawal of U.S. forces." Byrd's amendment was clearly aimed at weakening the amendment, and its defeat—however narrow—served as a strong signal that the White House was losing the fight to stop its passage.[43]

Boxed in by Mansfield's clever maneuvers, the White House abruptly changed tactics. This time, officials persuaded Nixon's Senate allies to slow down the debate long enough for Nixon to withdraw the troops according to his previously announced plan. Sensing victory, Mansfield pressed for a quick vote. He warned his colleagues that if the debate dragged on much longer a backlog of legislation would keep the Senate in session for the remainder of 1970 and would permit only two weeks of campaigning before the November elections. Nixon's forces would not budge and refused to allow a vote. The Senate Republican leadership, Nixon aide Bryce Harlow had told Haldeman, "is willing to try to continue to debate up to at least the middle of June. At that point, we may have to own up the fact that Republicans, with Administration approval, are definitely engaging in a filibuster."[44]

Mansfield laid the amendment aside for several days, but when debate resumed on June 22, Byrd returned with another modification—and this one sealed the amendment's victory. Approved by the Senate, 79–5, Byrd's second amendment—in the spirit of Mansfield's and Cooper's efforts to cast the measure as an affirmation of Nixon's goals for withdrawing troops from Cambodia—declared that nothing would prevent the president from exercising his constitutional power "to protect the lives of U.S. armed forces wherever deployed."

After approving a series of minor modifications, the Senate finally accepted the Cooper–Church amendment, 58–37, on June 30—the date Nixon had set for withdrawing American troops from Cambodia. The debate had lasted more than six weeks.

In the end, both sides could claim a semblance of victory. Nixon had staved off outright defeat, first by persuading his Senate allies to prolong the debate long enough to permit him to remove the troops from Cambodia on his own terms and, second, by tacitly approving the modifying language that cast the amendment as an endorsement of his deadline for withdrawing the troops. But the import of the vote was unmistakable: the Senate had finally voted to limit Nixon's war-making powers.

But the doves' victory, while more celebrated, was mostly illusory. Although Cooper, Church, and Mansfield could comfort themselves with the knowledge that Nixon would not be sending more troops into Cambodia, they had been unable or unwilling to stop him when they might have made a difference. Moreover, Church and Cooper were forced to rely on weakening compromises in order to win a majority. Despite the sound and fury, most senators were still reluctant to take on Nixon directly—and they were far from ready to assume responsibility for ending the war on anything other than Nixon's terms. In the House, members were even more reluctant to challenge Nixon. The amendment languished for the rest of the year, as a House–Senate conference committee grappled with Cooper–Church and other contentious issues in the Foreign Military Sales Bill. On December 31, the conferees finally dropped the Cooper–Church language from the bill. But the decision was largely meaningless. The Cambodian crisis was over, and Congress had already approved a revised version of the amendment—attached to a supplemental foreign aid bill—on December 22.[45]

The Senate-passed measure contained one other important amendment left in limbo until the House and Senate conferees agreed on the bill's final version—a repeal of the 1964 Gulf of Tonkin Resolution. In April, the Foreign Relations Committee had approved separate legislation repealing the joint resolution. On June 22, however, Dole moved mischievously to scuttle the committee's action by offering his own repealing amendment to the Foreign Military Sales Bill. Dole's amendment, because it would require the president's signature to take effect, ran counter to the language of the original resolution, which provided for its dissolution merely by concurrent resolution.

Fulbright vehemently opposed Dole's maneuver, arguing that it was "improper in this form." He also noted a glaring contradiction created by the amendment: as the Senate moved to repeal the Gulf of Tonkin Resolution it would, in the same bill, give the president—by virtue of Byrd's amendment—the power "to initiate military action whenever and wherever he might wish."[46]

Dole's surprise move struck Democrat Sam Ervin of North Carolina as incredibly ironic. While Nixon was actively engaged in an effort to defeat the Cooper–Church amendment—a bill to limit his authority in Cambodia—Ervin observed that "his spokesmen propose to the Senate an amendment which would not only take away his power to act in Cambodia and Laos, but also take away his power to act in South Vietnam." Fulbright tried to stop the Dole amendment, but ultimately failed. The Senate—with Fulbright voting no—overwhelming adopted the repeal language on June 24.[47]

Not satisfied to leave the repeal of the resolution in the uncertain hands of a conference committee that might not finish its work until year's end and which had the power to eliminate the provision altogether, Fulbright pressed for a concurrent resolution. Three weeks after the Senate voted for the first repeal measure, Fulbright brought the committee's resolution to the floor. This time the Senate approved the measure in an 81–10 vote. The year would end, however, with both measures dying in the House.[48]

Dole's end run on the Gulf of Tonkin Resolution was not the only assault on the Senate doves staged by Nixon's supporters that summer. On June 25, Republican Gordon Allott of Colorado, the third-ranking Republican in the Senate, introduced the McGovern–Hatfield End the War amendment—a measure halting all funds for Vietnam, except for withdrawal purposes, after December 31, 1970—with the clear intent of sabotaging it. "At the risk of being deemed crude or cynical," Allott told the Senate while it debated the Foreign Military Sales Bill, "this is a proper and sensible time to come to grips with the various measures [on Southeast Asia]." Then, Allott urged the Senate to reject the amendment on the grounds that it was unconstitutional and would aid the enemy. The only problem was that McGovern and Hatfield planned to push their amendment as a modification to an entirely different measure, the defense procurement authorization bill, scheduled for debate later in the year.

The brief but contentious debate that ensued reminded senators that Cooper–Church was not the only antiwar game in town. In fact, to McGovern and Hatfield—whose much more potent amendment was aimed at ending American military involvement altogether, not just meekly limiting Nixon's latitude in Cambodia—the Cooper–Church amendment had been little more than a momentum-killing distraction.

McGovern angrily deplored Allott's attempt to undermine his amendment, arguing that those who wanted to call it up "want to see it defeated. By bringing it up out of order, they would confuse the debate, confuse the public and prevent the kind of discussion this most seriously deserves." Allott's motives were all the clearer, McGovern noted, "when we consider that its architects have for the past six weeks prevented, through extended discussion and a series of amendments, the vote on the Cooper–Church amendment." McGovern acknowledged that it was not "discourteous and irregular" for Allott to vote against an amendment he introduced. "What is discourteous and irregular is for him to seize a piece of legislation authored by other Senators that has not yet even been brought to the Senate floor and then offer it as his own for the express purpose of defeating it." Allott had gone too far. Even opponents of the amendment like Gold-water, Stennis, Gale McGee, and Spessard Holland of Florida objected to the strategy and joined the McGovern–Hatfield forces to table the amendment, 69–29, on June 29.[49]

Once the Cooper–Church debate ended, the Hatfield–McGovern proposal—introduced in the wake of the violent antiwar protests of early May—quickly became, in Hatfield's words, the true "rallying point" for the radical antiwar forces in and out of the Senate. "We realized the nest was getting fouled pretty quickly—unless there could be something positive and something that could be used as a focal point of the anti-war feeling," Hatfield said, referring to the violent protests erupting throughout the country.[50]

Compared with Nixon's ambiguous plan for a steady, but seemingly endless series of withdrawals, the McGovern–Hatfield amendment held enormous appeal in the antiwar movement. As one McGovern aide put it at the time, McGovern and Hatfield were offering "a clear distinction between an irreversible, timed-limited withdrawal" and "the President's reversible, no-time-limited withdrawal."[51]

Before introducing the amendment, the two men had consulted Ful-bright, who counseled against putting the matter to a vote. Fulbright advised that "there'll be so few votes that the administration will take it as a further affirmation of the rightness of their policy." More than six years earlier, McGovern had yielded to Fulbright's counsel on Gaylord Nelson's amendment to the Gulf of Tonkin Resolution—to his everlasting regret. This time, he and Hatfield would heed their own counsel. "We were not dissuaded," Hatfield said.[52]

But McGovern and Hatfield also knew that an outpouring of public opinion was their only chance for victory. Restricting Nixon's latitude in Cambodia was one thing; cutting off all funds for the fighting by the end of 1970 was another. Facing almost impossible odds, in mid-May the two men enlisted Republican Charles Goodell of New York and Democrat Harold Hughes of Iowa to join them in touting their prospective amendment on a half-hour program on one of the three national television networks. Rejected by CBS and ABC, they finally approached NBC. They could buy the air time, the network told them, but only if they delivered $60,000 within three days. Raising that amount was a daunting challenge, but McGovern quickly made the bold decision to secure a second mortgage on his Washington, D.C., home to finance the lion's share of the cost. The rest, he borrowed from a friend. "That certainly brought into proper focus in my own mind how strongly he felt about this thing," recalled McGovern's aide George Cunningham.[53] On the evening of Sunday, May 12, NBC aired the edited, thirty-minute result of a four-hour antiwar panel discussion by McGovern, Hatfield, Hughes, Goodell, and Church. At the end of the broadcast, the senators made an appeal for money to defray the costs of the broadcast and to continue the campaign to build public support for the amendment.[54]

The success of the appeal exceeded their wildest dreams. For several weekends, McGovern's staff worked overtime counting and depositing the thousands of contributions that poured into his and the other Senate offices. In all, viewers mailed in more than a half million dollars. The money enabled McGovern and Hatfield to create and staff an organization—the Committee to End the War—dedicated to the passage of their legislation. Meanwhile, the two senators enlisted other Senate doves and their staffs—Church, Nelson, Thomas Eagleton of Missouri, and Alan Cranston of California—to help lobby other senators for the amendment. "Those few months were like standing in a pile of marbles," recalled McGovern's principal Vietnam staff advisor, John Holum, as he described the ebb and flow of support for the amendment during the tense summer months of 1970. For a time, McGovern and Hatfield thought they stood a chance of persuading at least forty senators to vote with them—and they made the necessary compromises to gain several supporters, including moving back the date for the cutoff of funds to support the fighting. During the summer, the two men moved the date back several times, finally agreeing on December 31, 1971—a full year later than the original proposal—to win the support of Republican Jacob Javits of New York.

McGovern and Hatfield had hoped their willingness to compromise around the edges of the amendment would attract support from other influential senators like Cooper, George Aiken of Vermont, and Clinton Anderson of New Mexico. But by late August, it became apparent that the amendment's support would come primarily from the small, hardcore band of antiwar senators—and not the very desirable group of moderate Republicans and Democrats who were tired of the war, but not yet ready to force a dramatic showdown with the commander in chief.[55]

"Well, you're right," McGovern heard from a colleague, "but I just can't interfere with the president's prerogatives." Others told him, "You're right on the war, but I just can't vote to cut off the funds for our troops." To McGovern's aide John Holum, the explanations were really nothing more than "lame excuses" from senators unwilling to assert the Senate's constitutional responsibilities for the conduct of the war.[56]

The rebuffs outraged and frustrated McGovern. "Congress just abdicated on Vietnam, beginning to end," he later complained, not mentioning his own abdication in 1964. As he lobbied his colleagues, he encountered the same mind-set that had persuaded most of the Senate, McGovern included, to support the Gulf of Tonkin Resolution in 1964. "Some of that same attitude was always there," McGovern recalled many years later: "It's up to the commander-in-chief to make these decisions, these military judgments. We don't have the information to do this."[57]

Many senators, especially those facing reelection that year, were reluctant to take the bold political step of opposing Nixon so blatantly, especially in the face of potential attacks from two political influence groups sponsored by the White House. Americans for Winning the Peace and The Tell It to Hanoi Committee were both geared toward persuading senators that a vote for McGovern–Hatfield would be portrayed as un-American. At the suggestion of Charles Colson, the White House aide charged with coordinating the opposition to the amendment, the group described McGovern, Hatfield, and the two co-sponsors of the amendment as "apostles of retreat and defeat," "unilateral disarmers," "neo Neville Chamberlains," and "salesmen of surrender, selling the 'sell-out' like some sell used cars or potato chips." Playing directly to the sentiment that McGovern repeatedly encountered, Tell It to Hanoi Committee literature warned that "it is the President, and the President alone who is authorized to conduct the foreign policy of the United States."[58]

Vice President Agnew, displaying his legendary gift for invective and vituperation, labeled the amendment "a blueprint for the first defeat in the history of the United States and for chaos and communism for the future of South Vietnam." Then Agnew turned personal and told the Veterans of Foreign Wars in Miami that "one wonders if they really give a damn." Hatfield responded that Agnew's "inflammatory" speech was an attempt at intimidation and a direct attack on the constitutional process. Said McGovern in response to Agnew: "It is not a defeat to recognize that we have been on a mistaken course in Vietnam that has needlessly sacrificed American life."[59]

As Hatfield deftly described it during the Senate debate on September 1, the amendment did nothing more than affirm Nixon "in his currently announced withdrawal plan, that the Congress believes that the withdrawal should be completed by the end of 1971—an opinion shared by the majority of Americans—and that if the President finds it necessary or advisable to maintain troops beyond that time, then he should simply obtain the authorization of the Congress." Hatfield reminded senators that the Constitution gave them "an obligation and a duty to exercise a role in the determination of the policies guiding our Nation." The amendment, he insisted, was in that spirit, not in opposition to Nixon, "but simply as a means to share in the responsibility that is ours. Today, we shall choose to assume that responsibility, or to continue to abdicate it."[60]

By the time McGovern rose to speak, he had known for days that he and Hatfield would certainly fall short of a majority and would likely fail to attract the forty votes they believed were necessary to claim a symbolic victory. Even so, he was frustrated and angry at what he saw as the Senate's cowardly refusal to accept and exercise its constitutional responsibilities regarding Vietnam. "He thought he saw it so clearly that he couldn't understand for the life of him why everybody else couldn't," recalled George Cunningham. For days, Cunningham and others on McGovern's staff noted the anger and exasperation with recalcitrant Senate colleagues building inside of their boss.[61] Minutes before the voting began, McGovern appealed for support with the strongest and most emotional language he had ever used regarding the war. His brief, passionate speech would stun his Senate colleagues:

> Every senator in this chamber is partly responsible for sending 50,000 young Americans to an early grave. This chamber reeks of blood. Every senator here is partly responsible for that human wreckage at Walter Reed and Bethesda Naval [hospitals] and all across our land—young men without legs, or arms, or genitals, or faces, or hopes.
>
> There are not very many of these blasted and broken boys who think this war is a glorious adventure.* Do not talk to them about bugging out, or national honor, or courage.
>
> It does not take any courage at all for a congressman, or a senator, or a president to wrap himself in the flag and say we are staying in Vietnam, because it is not our blood that is being shed. But we are responsible for those young men and their lives and their hopes.
>
> And if we do not end this damnable war, those young men will some day curse us for our pitiful willingness to let the Executive carry the burden that the Constitution places on us.
>
> So before we vote, let us ponder the admonition of Edmund Burke, the great parliamentarian of an earlier day: "A conscientious man would be cautious how he dealt in blood."[62]

As McGovern took his seat, most senators sat in stunned silence. "You could have heard a pin drop," recalled John Holum.[63] Until now, they had never heard a colleague so angrily blame them, personally, for the carnage and bloodshed in Vietnam. Other than Morse, who was no longer in the Senate, they had never witnessed such passion and anger directed at the members of Congress who refused to assert their constitutional prerogatives to bring about an end to the war. As the Senate prepared to begin voting, one senator (he could not recall whom) approached McGovern and indignantly told him that he had been personally offended by the speech. McGovern did not flinch. "That's what I meant to do," he told his stunned

---

*Possibly an indirect slap at McGovern's old friend Hubert Humphrey, who had once described the war as "our great adventure."

colleague.[64] In the end, McGovern's dramatic speech had little or no effect. Despite a poll showing that 55 percent of Americans favored the Hatfield–McGovern amendment—up 10 percent from a poll in late July—it failed in a 55–39 vote.[65]

In reality, the amendment, even had it passed the Senate, would have faced rough waters in the more conservative and militaristic House. Even if the House had approved the measure, Nixon could have vetoed it. For McGovern and Hatfield, however, it was just as important to put senators on record and determine exactly where they stood on ending the war. "I would liked to have seen a stronger showing," McGovern said after the vote. "But I suppose it's the first time in the history of the country that thirty-nine Senators have stood up in the middle of a war and voted to cut off funds."[66] Observed *Time:* "The willingness of more than a third of the Senators to take the unprecedented step of handing the President a deadline for terminating a shooting war was a clear warning that senatorial patience was precariously thin."[67]

Holum recalled that McGovern, despite the anger he expressed in his speech, also took the long view. "We never expected to win the first time around," he said. "We thought of it as a longer campaign."[68] At the White House, Kissinger worried that this was only the beginning. "The pattern was clear," he later wrote. "Senate opponents of the war would introduce one amendment after another, forcing the Administration into unending rearguard actions to preserve a minimum of flexibility for negotiations." From Kissinger's point of view, senators like McGovern and Hatfield were only undermining the peace talks. "Hanoi could only be encouraged to stall, waiting to harvest the results of our domestic dissent."[69]

In many ways, Nixon and his aides were just as angry and frustrated with the Senate as was McGovern—only for different reasons. Where McGovern saw vacillation and an appalling lack of resolve, the White House saw appeasement and recklessness. Fighting the Communists in Southeast Asia was tough enough without the difficulty caused by the small band of determined opponents in the Senate. But they had to be challenged. Nixon believed that he could not sit and watch their numbers grow. So he now opened another front in the war, not in Cambodia or Laos, but a new offensive against his political opponents in Washington.

CHAPTER 40

We'll Bomb the Bastards Off the Earth

1970–1971

Nixon REFUSED TO BELIEVE THAT THE COLLEGE DEMONSTRATIONS were completely spontaneous. His critics, he complained to aides, "want the United States to surrender to the Communists." Aide Bob Haldeman later recalled that Nixon suspected that the demonstrators "were being aided and abetted, if not actually inspired, by Communist countries." Nixon wanted the evidence—as well as the identities of those officials who were leaking sensitive information about the war to reporters. Ever since the *New York Times* had broken news of Nixon's secret bombing of Cambodia in May 1969, the president—inflamed by Kissinger—had pushed the FBI to plug the leaks and investigate the antiwar groups. To do so, Nixon ordered illegal wiretaps and surveillance of White House and State Department officials, as well as reporters.

But it was the Kent State killings that, in Haldeman's words, "marked a turning point for Nixon; a beginning of his downhill slide toward Watergate." Angrier and more defiant than ever, Nixon was persuaded that the FBI was not equal to the task of ferreting out the sources of administration leaks. He now pushed for even more aggressive surveillance. On June 5, Nixon called together the heads of the CIA, FBI, the Defense Intelligence Agency, and the National Security Agency. His message was clear: he was dissatisfied with the way they had coordinated the gathering of foreign and domestic intelligence, especially information about the antiwar demonstrations. Nixon demanded a special task force and a plan to better investigate the sources of the domestic unrest.[1]

Nixon was not simply concerned about communist infiltration in the antiwar movement. He worried about the impact of the dissidents on the country. He believed they "were developing their own brand of indigenous revolutionary activism which is as dangerous as anything they could import from Cuba, China or the Soviet Union." The investigative and intelligence agencies took Nixon's directive seriously. The FBI lowered its age requirement for college informants from 21 to 18. In San Diego and Minneapolis, FBI field agents worked with local businessmen and right-wing activists to harass antiwar dissidents. By one estimate, as much as 40 percent of the FBI fieldwork in the fall of 1970 was devoted to domestic dissent.

While Nixon fought his secret war against the antiwar protestors, the White House and its conservative allies staged a sophisticated public relations offensive to drive a patriotic wedge between supporters and opponents of the war. On one side were loyal Americans—the "silent majority"—who supported the president and his "plan" to end the war with "honor." On the other side were the disloyal turncoats who wanted "peace at any price" and were willing to sell out their country to achieve it. "We simply have got to keep the label of radical sympathizers on the Democrats," argued Charles Colson.[2] The "patriots" were easy to distinguish from the "radicals." Thanks to another White House-sponsored initiative, Americans who supported the war were encouraged to adopt the American flag as a symbol for their nationalistic fervor. Nixon and his supporters took to wearing flag pins on their lapels, while the conservative publishers of the *Reader's Digest* distributed 68 million flag decals. Meanwhile, the symbol of the antiwar movement, the peace sign, was derided by veterans and conservative groups as a communist-inspired, anti-Christian symbol.[3]

Much like Johnson before him, Nixon divided his world into his enemies and his allies—"us" versus "them." To Nixon, "them" was the enemy, especially the young, disheveled antiwar protesters. They were perfect foils. "'They' could be useful to 'us,'" speechwriter William Safire later explained, "as the villain, the object against which all of our supporters, as well as those who might become our supporters, could be rallied." Safire described Nixon's strategy as "superpartisan—that is, aggressively majoritarian, building a new coalition by playing off the unpopularity of the minority."[4] Occasionally, however, the lines between "us" and "them" became blurred, as it did in August when supporters of his Vietnam policy, like Democrat Harry Byrd of Virginia and Republican Gordon Allott of Colorado, surprised Nixon by urging him to get out of Vietnam quickly. Several weeks later, Republican Senate Leader Hugh Scott joined Mansfield and a dozen other senators in signing a letter that asked Nixon to consider a comprehensive cease-fire in Vietnam. Such defections rattled Nixon. As he told Kissinger in August: "We've got the Left where we want it now. All they've got to argue for is a bug-out, and that's their problem. But when the Right starts wanting to get out, for whatever reason, that's *our* problem."[5]

Nixon knew that many of his conservative supporters in Congress would stay with him to the end; others, however, might not prove so loyal. In the Senate—as the thirty-nine votes for the McGovern–Hatfield amendment had proved—a shift of only six senators would mean serious trouble and might dramatically undermine his policy of Vietnamization. Given Nixon's stubborn loyalty to Thieu's regime and his opposition to the "coalition" Saigon government the North Vietnamese negotiators demanded, the Paris peace talks remained moribund. Sensing that he needed something dramatic to prevent the hemorrhaging of his congressional and public support—especially with the midterm congressional elections less than a month away—Nixon went on national television and radio on October 7 to announce yet another peace offer. This time, Nixon proposed an internationally supervised standstill cease-fire throughout Indochina and a peace conference to negotiate an end to the fighting throughout Southeast Asia, including Cambodia and Laos. Conceding that a cease-fire might be difficult to implement and even harder to sustain, Nixon said that "an unconventional war may require an unconventional truce; our side is ready to stand still and cease firing."[6]

Even such vehement critics like McGovern, Fulbright, and Hatfield signed their names to a resolution endorsing the president's proposal—which the Senate approved unanimously. "The President has joined us," Frank Church said. "He is now on the same perch with the doves. So what is there to argue about? We've won this argument."[7] But it was clear to many, especially Nixon's aides, that the announcement was primarily for domestic political consumption, not a genuine effort to restart the peace process. Knowing the response from Hanoi would be negative, Nixon had merely wanted the voters to give him and his party credit for making a peace proposal that had no chance of succeeding. At a press conference the next morning, Nixon scoffed at that notion. "If we had intended it for that," he told skeptical reporters, "I am politically enough astute to have done it just about four days before the election. Then we would not have known what the results would have been and people would have voted their hopes rather than the realities." Five days later, Nixon sweetened the pot further when he announced that his Vietnamization program had been so successful that he would accelerate the troop withdrawals. Forty thousand troops would be home by Christmas, he said. What he did not say, however, was that the troop withdrawals had already been announced; he was merely speeding up their departure from Vietnam by a month.[8]

Nixon took to the campaign trail with partisan gusto, traveling to twenty-three states on behalf of Republican candidates, touting a return to "law-and-order" and his plan for "a just peace" in Vietnam. Agnew, meanwhile, campaigned for candidates in thirty-two states. While each man touted Republican gubernatorial and House candidates, the clear target was the Senate—the body that had dogged Nixon for most of 1970. "One issue dominates this election," Agnew said. "Will the radical-liberalism that controls the Senate of the United States prevail in the nation?"[9]

But the Vietnam War had waned as a campaign issue—the result of the common perception that Nixon's Vietnamization plan was working, although American troop strength would still stand at two hundred eighty thousand by year's end. In place of Vietnam as a compelling theme was the lingering domestic discord caused by the war. Indeed, Nixon took particular delight in exploiting popular fears of radical domestic dissent.

As he crisscrossed the country, the president actively sought out confrontation with demonstrators, hoping that his provocation would result in a popular backlash against the Democrats. Nixon even worried that his staff and the Secret Service were doing "too good a job of keeping the demonstrators out of the halls," thereby reducing the chance of politically advantageous confrontations. "The President's whole pitch is built around having a few demonstrators in the hall heckling him so that he can refer to them and their 'obscenities,'" aide Dwight Chapin wrote to a White House aide, who was ordered to allow "fifty to a hundred" demonstrators into all of Nixon's rallies. "This should give the President the opportunity to strike out at them should he desire to do so."[10]

One confrontation in San Jose, California, on October 27 turned violent during the final week of campaigning, when Nixon taunted a group of protestors by climbing on the hood of his limousine and striking a familiar and defiant pose—arms spread above his head and his fingers wagging the trademark Nixon "V" salute. "That's what they hate to see," Nixon proudly told his aides. Thusly incited, the protesters began throwing eggs and rocks at Nixon's motorcade, smashing windows in the press and staff buses. Days later in a speech in Phoenix—which the Republican National Committee replayed for a national television audience—an angry Nixon milked the incident for all it was worth. He denounced the protesters and what they represented. "It is about time we cut out the nonsense about repression being the cause of violence," he said. "Violence in America today is not caused by the war, not caused by repression. There is no romantic ideal involved. Let's recognize them for what they are—not romantic revolutionaries, but the same thugs and hoodlums that have always plagued a good people." Nixon blamed "appeasement" for breeding the dissent.

> When you permit an imbalance to exist that favors the accused over the victim, you are inviting more violence and breeding more bullies. For too long, the strength of freedom in our society has been eroding by a creeping permissiveness—in our legislatures, in our courts, in our universities. For too long, we have appeased aggression here at home—and as with all appeasement, the results have been more aggression, more violence. The time has come to draw the line.

The White House's them-versus-us theme had blossomed into full maturity. No longer was patriotism simply determined by one's support for the war. Now the overriding issue was the nation's response to the violent protests the war had sparked. On one side were the good Americans, those who favored law and order and an end to violent dissent; in other words, those who backed the president. On the other side, were those who rioted and engaged in violent protest or who appeased those who did; in other words, those who opposed the president and, therefore, were less than loyal to their country. In his divisive, black-and-white speeches, Nixon left no room for the millions of Americans in the middle—opposed to the war, but dedicated to peaceful dissent aimed at changing national policy. "It is time for us to recognize," Nixon said in a speech in Anaheim, California, "that candidates for the Senate and the House who in the past have either condoned this, defended it, excused it or failed to speak against it—that these are men who do not have the qualifications now to take the strong stand that needs to be taken." Agnew, as always, phrased the same sentiment more bluntly: "It is time to sweep that kind of garbage out of our society."[11]

On Election Day, Nixon's bold gambit to influence the election failed. Republicans gained only two Senate seats, leaving them far short of the majority Nixon wanted. Opponents of the war—like Mansfield, Philip Hart of Michigan, Vance Hartke of Indiana, Edward Kennedy of Massachusetts, and Edmund Muskie of Maine—won reelection handily. Even worse, the Republicans lost eleven governorships and nine House seats. Nixon "and his party," one political reporter observed, "emerged weaker than before."[12] But the news was not entirely bad for Nixon. Conservative Nixon allies defeated three Senate doves—Democrats Albert Gore of Tennessee and Joseph Tydings of Maryland and Republican Charles Goodell of New York.

Despite the stridency of the attacks by Nixon and Agnew, Mansfield urged his Democratic colleagues to stay the course, and resist the urge to engage in retribution against Nixon. In a speech to the first postelection meeting of the Senate Democratic Conference on November 16, the majority leader decried the continuance of the war, Vietnamization notwithstanding. "Americans still die," he said. "Billions still disappear into the morass of Southeast Asia. Rather than apologize for the Cambodian resolution, the Senate has a responsibility to remain ever alert to possibilities for strengthening its intent." Underlying his displeasure about Vietnam was Mansfield's advice to "let the election recede into history. What matters is not what party may have lost but what the nation may have won."

Fulbright, however, was furious about Nixon's divisive campaign tactics. "I am not as disposed to heal old wounds as the Majority Leader," he said when Mansfield finished. Describing the "malicious" and "fraudulent" Republican tactics that led to Tydings' defeat, Fulbright protested that "being agreeable with the Administration doesn't set too well with me. The Vice President came to Arkansas to attack me." Fulbright worried that "if we allow the Senate to become a nonentity by turning the other cheek, we also destroy the democratic process. I don't think the Senate should lie down and take it."[13]

But for now, at least, there was not much that senators were willing to do. In spite of Nixon's failure to cut deeply into the Senate's Democratic majority in the November elections, his Vietnamization policy still commanded a clear—albeit shrinking—majority of the Senate. The troops continued to come home and the 6,083 combat deaths in 1970 were almost half of what had been reported in 1969.[14] "In Vietnam," *Time* reported in a New Year's assessment of Nixon's presidency, "things seem to be going according to Mr. Nixon's plan. The result, no doubt, is not all that either the fluttery doves or the militant hawks might have wished, but Vietnam no longer seems like the morass Mr. Nixon inherited two years ago." *Time* also noticed a significant reduction in the volume and stridency of public dissent over the war. "Today, the sirens in the night no longer wail as urgently as they once did. An uneasy but palpable calm has settled over the cities and the campuses. Voices have been lowered and, if the President has not succeeded in bringing us together, at least things are no longer falling apart."[15]

Despite the *Time*'s portrait of a placid domestic scene, things in Vietnam were indeed falling apart. Nixon's determination to fight a rearguard action to prop up Thieu's corrupt, authoritarian regime during the slow, steady withdrawal he called Vietnamization had taken a heavy toll on the demoralized American troops. No longer were they fighting to win the war, but to preserve a regime that everyone but the Nixon administration acknowledged was shot through with corruption. The news on the American side was no better. In the spring of 1971 estimates were that of the roughly 300,000 American troops still in Vietnam, as many as forty thousand were heroin addicts. Marijuana use was even more prevalent.[16] On January 4, the *New York Times* reported news of a Defense Department study that identified "increasing drug abuse" among military personnel and described "a breakdown in leadership and discipline particularly at or below the company command levels."[17]

Ignoring all the warning signs, Nixon pressed ahead, determined to prove that his Vietnamization policy was working. He approved a major offensive against the Ho Chi Minh Trail in Laos—code-named "Dewey Canyon II"—that involved about twenty thousand South Vietnamese ground troops protected by American air power and artillery. Technically, the operation did not violate the congressional Cooper–Church mandate against ground troops in Laos because American troops would be employed only from the air.

That fact, however, did not make the operation any more palatable to frustrated Democrats and some Republicans in Congress who viewed the action as a violation of the spirit of Cooper–Church. Complained Mansfield: "The people of this country want out of Southeast Asia—lock, stock and barrel. I doubt many of them think the way to do that is to go into Laos."[18] Humphrey, back in the Senate after a six-year hiatus, said the invasion represented "a stepping up instead of a toning down of the war. The shortest distance between peace and war is not through Cambodia and Laos. It is from Saigon to Washington." McGovern compared the offensive to the Cambodian operation a year earlier. "It is more likely a reminder," he said, "that the Administration clings to the mistaken belief that we can yet achieve a military decision in Vietnam, where our military involvement stands as the most serious blunder in our national history."[19]

As usual, Dole assumed his role as the most ferocious Republican defender of Nixon's Vietnam policy, assailing his colleagues who were "unable to wait for the facts or results" before complaining about the operation. Armed Services Committee Chairman John Stennis also threw his wholehearted support behind the Laotian operation and even suggested that the time had come for Congress to lift its prohibition against U.S. involvement in Cambodia. "Very frankly," an angry McGovern told reporters when he learned of Stennis' proposal, "any senator who talks about sending American forces into Cambodia ought to lead the charge himself. I'm fed up with old men dreaming up wars for young men to die in, particularly stupid wars of this kind that add nothing to our security."[20]

Appearing before the Senate Foreign Relations Committee, Secretary of State Rogers assured senators that Nixon was honoring the spirit of the Cooper–Church amendment and that the invasion would not lead to another full-scale American operation in Laos. "My God, Bill," an astonished Stuart Symington told Fulbright at the end of Rogers' testimony, "that sounded just like a recording I first heard played here in 1965." Despite their pique over the operation, there was little that the Senate could do. Congress had passed no clear prohibition against American air and logistical support of an action of this sort. "For the time being, at least," *Newsweek* observed, "President Nixon appeared to have a free hand to test his theory that the war can be ended by expanding it."[21]

Although the White House pretended that the operation was a huge success and proof positive of the viability of Vietnamization, media reports suggested that the South Vietnamese troops were very nearly routed by superior, better-trained North Vietnamese forces that outnumbered them almost 2 to 1. The invasion ended ignominiously in April with panicked South Vietnamese troops fighting each other for places on U.S. evacuation helicopters. Even the Americans suffered substantial losses. Enemy ground fire damaged 608 U.S. helicopters and downed 104.[22]

In the end, the operation revealed that almost nothing stood between the South Vietnamese and utter defeat except marginal U.S. air superiority. Far from proving the success of Vietnamization, the invasion of Laos, in the words of the *New York Times,*

> underscored weaknesses in South Vietnam's army and its almost total dependence on American warplanes and helicopters, handed Hanoi a propaganda victory, dramatized the limitations of American air power, fell so short of expected results as to be devoid of long-term benefits and created new strains at unofficial levels between Americans and South Vietnamese arising out of the oft-expressed concern among the Vietnamese that the Americans were skimping on air support.[23]

The foray into Laos also revealed new fissures in Nixon's congressional support. White House aide Bryce Harlow informed the president on April 1 that "in the last two days perhaps twenty hawkish Congressmen—Democrats and Republicans—have contacted me to report a swift change in their constituents' attitude toward Vietnam . . . brought on by the negative press over the Laos operation." Another aide told Nixon that House Republican Leader Gerald Ford, Republican Senator Howard Baker of Tennessee, and Republican Congressman Peter Frelinghuysen of New Jersey were badly shaken by the bleak news out of Laos. "Laos is one more straw—and a substantial one—on the camel's back," Frelinghuysen said. "Most Americans—myself included—have come to feel that this war has gone on too long."[24]

In mid-April, a group of nine moderate Republican congressmen and senators, worried about the political fallout for their party if the war dragged on, gathered at Jacob Javits' Washington penthouse apartment for dinner and a conversation with Defense Secretary Laird. After dinner, over cigars and cognac, the lawmakers gave the secretary their blunt assessments. "You don't see any hawks around here," Senate Leader Hugh Scott bluntly told Laird. "The hawks are all ex-hawks. There's a feeling that the Senate ought to tell the President that we should get the hell out of the war." Scott warned that, in the future, he could no longer promise success in defeating antiwar amendments by the Senate's doves. "We just can't hold the line any longer on numbers," Scott said. "The President must think in terms of finality. He must make public some formula that clearly indicates the end of American participation in the war." Alaska Congressman Ted Stevens agreed. "I come from the most hawkish state in the union," Stevens said. "I ran in '70 as a hawk. I can't do it again in '72."[25]

Nixon was defiant. He would exit Vietnam at his own pace, not one set by others, even his allies in Congress. On April 7, the president added to the aura of Vietnamization by announcing that he would withdraw one hundred thousand additional troops from Vietnam by December 1, leaving one hundred eighty-four thousand troops in the country less than a year before the 1972 elections. "Tonight I can report that Vietnamization has succeeded," Nixon declared, noting that as a presidential candidate he had promised to end American involvement in the war. "I am keeping that pledge," he said, "and I expect to be held accountable by the American people if I fail."[26] Despite Nixon's promise of additional troop withdrawals and his declaration about the success of Vietnamization, his basic policy had changed little.

Time called it a "foxhole speech, digging in tenaciously in defense of his existing position."[27] Nixon had primarily acted to draw the public's attention away from the aborted Laotian operation and the conviction in late March of Lieutenant William Calley on the My Lai murder charges. He had accelerated the pace of troop withdrawals from 12,500 a month to 14,300—an increase of less 2,000 a month. Those who had expected a more dramatic announcement—an end to American ground combat operations or a specific deadline for the complete withdrawal of American troops—were disappointed. "I expected an elephant and we got a mouse," complained Mark Hatfield. But, as one anonymous administration official confessed to a reporter, domestic political considerations had prevented Nixon from setting a specific time for withdrawal of the remaining American troops. "If we set a withdrawal date now," the official said, "the domestic reaction would be worse than it was to the fall of China and the McCarthy period."[28] But that official was missing the point, as well as exaggerating the potential domestic political fallout. The most immediate threat to Nixon's policy was a nervous Congress, moving cautiously toward cutting off funds for the war.[29]

Nixon was enraged by the deafening silence from his supporters in Congress—as well as members of his own cabinet. "Screw the Cabinet and the rest," he belligerently told Kissinger, one of the few advisors who had called to praise the speech. Nixon was so exorcised by the lack of enthusiasm for his speech that he temporarily toyed with the idea of reversing field on Vietnam. "I'll turn right so goddamn hard it'll make your head spin," he told Kissinger. "We'll bomb the bastards off the Earth."[30]

In spite of his bravado, Nixon knew his back was against the wall. Vietnamization was ending American involvement in Vietnam, but not soon enough for most Americans, and far too slowly for a growing number of Senate and House members. By month's end, the Foreign Relations Committee went back to work, as Fulbright convened hearings on the Vietnam Disengagement Act, a modified version of the Hatfield–McGovern amendment that set a cutoff date of December 31, 1971, for funding of American ground, air, and naval forces. Under the legislation, Congress would only authorize funds for arranging the return of prisoners of war, ensuring the safety of South Vietnamese citizens, and continued economic and military assistance to Saigon. On the first day of testimony, McGovern attacked Vietnamization as a cruel, inhumane policy that "accelerates indiscriminate air power and artillery as it seeks to reduce ground forces. It subsidizes the continued killing of the people of Indochina by technology and mercenaries. This is not an acceptable moral, diplomatic, or military posture for a great country such as ours."[31]

In his testimony, Hatfield took a different tack, arguing that while Nixon possessed the constitutional authority to protect and withdraw U.S. troops, his Vietnamization policy was on far shakier ground. "Now we may agree or disagree with the policy of Vietnamization," Hatfield said, "but regardless of our preferences, I do not believe the President has the legal, constitutional authority for pursuing the objectives and goals of that policy." It fell, however, to Richard A. Falk, a professor of international law at Princeton University, to illuminate the underlying political rationale for Nixon's slow, but steady withdrawal policy. "President Nixon, like his predecessors in office, has no illusions of achieving victory in South Vietnam," Falk told the committee on May 26. "The objective remains, as before, to avoid or at least to defer defeat. The effects of troop withdrawal and so-called Vietnamization are to defer the evidence of defeat past the 1972 election date."[32]

Fulbright's committee also heard testimony from a highly decorated 27-year-old Navy lieutenant, John Kerry, who represented the Vietnam Veterans Against the War (VVAW). Kerry, who would be elected to the U.S. Senate from Massachusetts in 1984, urged Congress to impose a date for leaving Vietnam. "In our opinion and from our experience," the gaunt, fatigues-clad Kerry told the committee, "there is nothing in South Vietnam that threatens the United States. To attempt to justify the loss of one American life in Vietnam, Cambodia and Laos by linking such loss to the preservation of freedom is to us the height of criminal hypocrisy."[33] Later, about 700 VVAW members gathered near the Capitol steps, acknowledged their own war crimes, and protested the war by ceremoniously discarding their medals.[34] Kerry's testimony and the demonstration by the VVAW members coincided with a massive antiwar demonstration on the Capitol grounds attended by more than 200,000 people on May 1. That same day, as many as 150,000 protesters marched against the war in San Francisco.

While most of the demonstrators in Washington were peaceful, they did engage in various acts of civil disobedience—mostly "lie-ins" designed to block entrances to government buildings and snarl traffic at bridges and busy intersections. Having long ago lost his tolerance for protests of this sort, Nixon gave Mitchell and Washington, D.C., authorities wide latitude to control the crowds. The result was an embarrassing overreaction by police that ended with more than 13,400 arrests—most of them illegal. The 7,200 arrests on the first day set a record for the largest mass arrest in U.S. history.[35]

The May Day protestors were not alone in assaulting Nixon's Vietnam policy. Inside the Capitol building, senators were planning a legislative offensive against the war that, while more conventional in approach, was no less threatening to the White House in its execution. The vehicle for the latest Senate attack on Nixon was a routine administration-backed bill to extend the draft by two years, through June 1973. The bill came to the Senate floor on May 6 and was a natural measure for antiwar senators to test their growing strength. From the very beginning, Nixon and his allies found themselves on the defensive as senators offered one hostile amendment after another, among them a measure by Gaylord Nelson prohibiting the assignment of draftees to combat roles in Southeast Asia unless they specifically volunteered or reenlisted. Although Stennis, as the bill's floor manager, argued that the draft extension bill should not be debated as a Vietnam issue, Nelson insisted that "the central issue of the draft is the issue of Vietnam. The draft feeds the war. The war becomes the argument for continuing the draft." As if to make Nelson's point, Stennis responded, "No one relishes the idea or likes to draft these men. No one wants to reenact this law. All of us want the war to end. However, . . . we are in the war and we cannot abruptly cut and run."

Perhaps the most hostile attack on the bill came from Hatfield, who offered an unsuccessful amendment to abolish the draft by June 30, 1971. "There are 95,000 soldiers doing nothing but KP duty and mowing lawns," Hatfield told the Senate. "There are many more who are bartenders in officers clubs and who are driving as chauffeurs for admirals and generals. Those duties could be turned over from the military to civilians and those men who are trained for military duty could perform military functions." Hatfield's amendment failed by a large margin, as did most other amendments that senators perceived as direct assaults on the Selective Service program.

Nonetheless, senators did act on several amendments aimed at shortening the war. One measure sponsored by Edward Kennedy, designed to limit Nixon's authority as commander in chief, passed with a substantial majority. Although existing law imposed a one hundred fifty thousand-man ceiling on the number of men the president could draft each year, a loophole allowed the president to exceed the limit by a simple executive order. No one, not even Stennis, spoke against Kennedy's amendment to remove that escape clause. In fact, Stennis successfully modified Kennedy's amendment to *lower* the ceiling to one hundred thirty thousand in 1972 and to one hundred forty thousand in 1973. "The unfettered power of the President to draft young men," Kennedy said, "has become a central factor in a loss of congressional influence in the design and execution of American foreign policy." The Senate adopted Kennedy's amendment, 78–4.[36]

Mansfield offered another of the successful amendments—a nonbinding resolution urging Nixon to withdraw all U.S. forces from Vietnam when North Vietnam released American prisoners of war. Nixon regarded that proposal as "the least irresponsible of the irresponsible resolutions" coming out of the Senate. The Senate agreed when it approved Mansfield's amendment, 61–37, on June 22. The next day, however, Nixon complained to Mansfield that his amendment might wreck the Paris negotiations. In that event, the president later told his aides, he planned to blame the collapse on the Senate and Mansfield. "If so," Haldeman wrote in his diary that evening,

> the P[resident] will have to go on to the people and explain that the reason for the collapse was the action of the Senate and that Mansfield will have to take that blame. He made the point to us that if we do not get to the point where we have to withdraw because the negotiations failed, he will do it with a total bombing of the North to eliminate their capability of attacking, so in order to get out, we escalate to accelerate our withdrawal.[37]

No modification to the bill, however, generated more controversy than the Hatfield–McGovern amendment that the Senate began debating on June 10. Ten months after the first disappointing defeat of their to End the War Amendment, McGovern and Hatfield roared back. This time, public opinion polls were even more favorable to their cause. Nixon's approval rating on Vietnam had slumped to 31 percent. A solid majority of those polled, 72 percent, now favored a deadline for ending American involvement in Vietnam. With those numbers, success at least seemed plausible, if not entirely likely.

Again, the White House took no chances. Nixon's aides mobilized allies in and out of the Senate to defeat the measure. As the most aggressive champion of Nixon's policies, Dole derided the amendment as the "lose-the-peace" proposal. "I have seen some of the publicity of the groups and organizations supporting the legislation," he added. "Their rosters read like a Who's Who of has-beens, would-be's, professional second-guessers and apologists for the policies which led us into this tragic conflict in the first place." Dole was undoubtedly referring to former Deputy Defense Secretary Cyrus Vance and Clark Clifford, both supporters of the amendment. "If these people wish to salve their consciences for errors committed while they were entrusted with the responsibility of leading this nation," Dole said, "they should do so in private. If these people are seeking to relive the glories of past high office, they should repair their scrapbooks and press clippings." Of course, Dole neglected to note that the leaders of his own party, including Nixon, were among those who had consistently and enthusiastically supported the initial policies that led to the massive American military role in Vietnam in the mid-1960s.[38]

McGovern believed correctly that the amendment would be a test of whether the Senate finally was ready to assert the constitutional war-making role it had gradually abdicated beginning in the 1950s. "I suggest that those who oppose this amendment would do well," he told the Senate on June 16, "to avoid the grave error of confusing their support for the President's Vietnam policy with an imaginary constitutional mandate for the Congress to abandon duties imposed upon it by that document." McGovern assured his colleagues that the amendment would not

> declare illegal the past actions of any President. It is not an amendment to find scapegoats or to crucify anyone for decisions made in the past. It applies only to the future. It applies not to the 50,000 young Americans who are dead, whom we cannot recall, but it applies to the thousands of young men who will die if we do not end this war. It applies to our prisoners of war who have been sitting in their cells in Hanoi for these past five or six years.[39]

Hoping to pick up additional votes, McGovern and Hatfield modified their amendment in one significant respect: if American prisoners of war were not released within sixty days of the amendment's enactment, the withdrawal deadline would be extended by an additional sixty days and Congress would be permitted, by joint resolution, to authorize "further action" to secure the prisoners' release. As the vote approached, however, the two senators realized they would again fall short of a majority. At the last minute, hoping to salvage the amendment, they entertained a modification, offered by moderate Democrat Lawton Chiles of Florida, to move back the funding moratorium by six months, to June 1972. "I believe I can get at least three Southern votes," Chiles told Hatfield, "but I can't if George McGovern's name is on the proposal." Chiles also proposed to void the amendment "if [the] North Vietnamese and other adversary forces" did not release all American prisoners by April 1972.[40]

McGovern gladly stepped aside. But even with Chiles' leadership, the effort fell far short. On June 16, the Senate rejected the Chiles modification in a 52–44 vote and then rejected the remaining Hatfield–McGovern language, 55–42. The doves had gained only three votes since the previous September.[41] The next day, the House ducked the issue, as well. In a 256–158 vote, representatives rejected an amendment to forbid use of new military appropriations to support U.S. forces in Indochina after December 31.[42] Even in defeat, McGovern was hopeful. After all, he reasoned, "this must be the only time in American history that [more than] 40 senators have stood up in the middle of a war and told the commander-in-chief to end it."[43]

In the end, however, the Senate was still unwilling to take responsibility for terminating a war that, according to the polls, a vast majority of Americans wanted ended by the very means specified in the Hatfield–McGovern amendment. "The Senate doesn't want to assume responsibility for the war and its aftermath," one unidentified Republican "insider" told a *Newsweek* correspondent after the vote. "The senators want a time-table, but they don't want to set it themselves."[44]

ON SUNDAY, JUNE 13, 1971, the *New York Times* stunned the White House and many Americans with the first in a series of stories about "a massive study of how the United States went to war in Indochina," commissioned by Robert McNamara in mid-1967. It was the first time that the public had heard of the *Pentagon Papers*—an ambitious, seven thousand-page Defense Department history of American involvement in Indochina from World War II to mid-1968. Leaked to *Times* reporter Neil Sheehan by a former Defense Department official, Daniel Ellsberg, the thousands of confidential and classified documents shed considerable light on the origins of the U.S. role in Vietnam. The excerpts published by the *Times* detailed, among other things, the Kennedy administration's decisions broadening American involvement in Vietnam, as well as evidence that the Johnson administration had discussed, beginning in the spring of 1964, an increase in the U.S. military presence in Vietnam—despite Johnson's insistence that he would seek "no wider war."[45]

A talented defense analyst who worked for McNamara in 1967 and 1968, and had been among those who assembled the *Pentagon Papers*, Ellsberg had once advised Kissinger on Vietnam policy. By 1969, however, the former hawk joined the Rand Corporation—a think tank with close Pentagon ties—and had repented of his involvement in the war. He had become a committed dove who concluded from his reading of the papers that there was "very little hope" changing Nixon's mind about the war "from inside the executive branch . . . by giving him good advice or by giving him realistic estimates of what was happening in Vietnam." Since 1945, Ellsberg concluded, presidents had been receiving, and ignoring, gloomy predictions from their advisors about the risks of American involvement in Vietnam. He believed that the war would end only when the pressure to do so came from "outside the executive branch." Telling the truth about the history of American involvement in Vietnam, Ellsberg hoped, just might be enough to spark a tidal wave of public protest against Nixon's policies.[46] With the help of a Rand colleague, Ellsberg began photocopying the study from copies in his safe. In the fall of 1969, he was ready to share those copies with members of Congress. On November 6, he went first to Fulbright, giving him an envelope containing a number of documents he hoped would pique the senator's interest and prompt him to use them as the basis for extensive hearings on the war.

Fulbright was uncertain about how to handle secret papers that he knew had been stolen. Hoping to obtain them from a source other than Ellsberg, he wrote to Defense Secretary Laird on November 11, requesting copies of the entire study. Citing national security, Laird denied the request. By February 1970, however, Ellsberg solved that problem when he shipped, by air freight, two boxes of documents—representing about half of the complete study—to Fulbright's staff at the Senate Foreign Relations Committee. After he reviewed the documents, committee staff director Norvill Jones was not impressed. "I found many of them dull and boring and most of interest only for historical purposes," he later recalled. "I was unable to see how the papers would reveal anything of significance to the Committee that would have a bearing on the current situation in Congress relating to the war."[47] Fulbright shared Jones' ambivalence. "I didn't know what to do with [the papers]," Fulbright later said, explaining that he did not wish to endanger Ellsberg by leaking or releasing the documents. Furthermore, he said, "it wasn't clear then of what use they actually were in stopping the war."[48] Doubtful that they would prove helpful in ending the conflict, Jones filed the documents in the committee's safe.[49]

When Ellsberg testified before the Foreign Relations Committee on May 13, 1970—shortly after Nixon's Cambodian invasion—he did not refer to the documents, but spoke about Vietnamese politics and how Congress and the public had been misled about the war. In private, however, Ellsberg kept pushing Fulbright and his staff to convene hearings on the papers. But Fulbright thought it best to continue pushing a recalcitrant Laird to release the documents to Congress. On August 7, Fulbright took the bold step of inserting copies of his correspondence with Laird into the *Congressional Record*. "Instead of an open-minded cooperative approach which would help both branches profit from the mistakes of the past," Fulbright told the Senate, "the executive branch—in what has become a reflexive action—has again slammed the door on the Congress." Knowing that Ellsberg would eventually share the documents with others, Fulbright added that "I hope that the first enterprising reporter who obtains a copy of this history will share it with the committee."[50]

Persuaded that he was on much safer legal ground leaking the information to members of Congress who were protected by legislative immunity, Ellsberg also shopped the papers to McGovern in January 1971. Initially, McGovern told Ellsberg that he was willing to accept the papers, but then changed his mind after developing concerns about the national security and legal implications of accepting stolen classified material. "I figured that if anybody was to go to jail," McGovern acknowledged in a 1972 interview, "it would be better for him to go than me, since I was a United States senator, doing what I think is important work."[51] McGovern referred Ellsberg to his staff aide on Vietnam, John Holum, and suggested that it might be better to give the documents to someone other than a presidential candidate whose decision to release them would inevitably become entangled in partisan politics. When Holum met with Ellsberg, he was intrigued by his visitor's description of the papers, but shared McGovern's concerns about receiving stolen classified material. Furthermore, Holum later said, the papers were "really a description of the previous administration's misleading the country. . . . Our job was to end the war, not to prove that Johnson was a jerk."[52]

Ellsberg was having no luck with members of Congress. He had also approached Republican Senator Charles Mathias of Maryland and Republican Representative Pete McCloskey of California. In March 1971, Ellsberg finally gave up and contacted Neil Sheehan, the *New York Times* reporter he had known in Vietnam when Sheehan was a foreign correspondent for United Press International. Three months later, after a fierce internal debate, the *Times* began publishing excerpts of the papers, followed by the *Washington Post*, which published more excerpts. Nixon, meanwhile, had not known of the Pentagon study until he read Sheehan's initial story. While some of his advisors believed their publication was politically advantageous because it exposed Johnson's and Kennedy's duplicity, a furious Kissinger persuaded Nixon otherwise. "It shows you're a weakling, Mr. President," Kissinger said, cleverly appealing to Nixon's manly insecurities. "The fact that some idiot can publish all of the diplomatic secrets of this country on his own, is damaging to your image, as far as the Soviets are concerned, and it could destroy our ability to conduct foreign policy. If the other foreign powers feel that we can't control internal leaks, they will never agree to secret negotiations."[53]

Persuaded, Nixon ordered the Justice Department to pursue the person who leaked the material—soon identified by the FBI as Ellsberg—and to seek court injunctions against the *Times* and other newspapers to prevent them from publishing additional excerpts. Justice Department lawyers quickly obtained the desired injunctions, the first time in American history the federal government had gone to court to prevent a newspaper from printing a story that, ostensibly, threatened national security.

The newspapers appealed, and on June 30 in a landmark decision, the Supreme Court ruled against Nixon and declared that he had "not met the heavy burden of showing justification" for imposing prior restraint on the newspapers.[54]

The release of the papers infuriated Nixon, prompting him to mobilize his aides to plug leaks throughout his administration. Mistakenly believing that the Brookings Institution had obtained secret information for a study similar to the *Pentagon Papers*, Nixon ordered a break-in of the organization's offices in search of documents embarrassing to Lyndon Johnson. Nixon had long suspected that Johnson halted the bombing in September 1968 as a way to boost Hubert Humphrey's candidacy. Finding and releasing documents that confirmed his suspicion, he hoped, would embarrass those former Johnson administration officials now critical of his Vietnam policies. "Goddammit, get in and get those files," Nixon ordered. "Blow the safe and get them."[55] Despite direct orders from their president, Nixon's aides never followed through with the burglary. Where the spirit of Nixon's orders *was* followed had to do with Ellsberg, whom White House officials targeted for particular scorn. Acting with Ehrlichman's specific approval—and under general orders from Nixon to "find out what Ellsberg was up to"—the "Plumbers" antileak unit burglarized the offices of Ellsberg's Los Angeles psychiatrist in hopes of finding information to disgrace him. Thus, with Nixon's zeal for illegal wiretaps and burglary aimed at the critics of his Vietnam policies, was born the scandal known as Watergate.[56]

THE FAILURE OF THE End the War amendment heightened McGovern's alienation from his colleagues. He was now far less tolerant of his pro-war colleagues. As biographer Robert Sam Anson noted, "he also seemed to grow in his admiration for the enemy, and he became far less circumspect about saying so." In an interview for the September 1971 issue of *Playboy*, McGovern said that he sympathized with the North Vietnamese and the Viet Cong. "I think their posture is more legitimate than General Thieu. . . . I think he is completely out of stride with the nationalistic aspirations of the Vietnamese people, whereas the Viet Cong and Hanoi have been on the side of expelling first the Japanese and then the French and now us." Asked by interviewer Milton Viorst if he saw any similarities between the Vietnamese communists and the leaders of the American Revolution, McGovern replied: "I think they're very close." Did that mean that Ho Chi Minh had been the "North Vietnam George Washington?" Viorst asked. "That's right," McGovern said.[57]

In mid-September, McGovern visited Vietnam again, this time as a candidate for the 1972 Democratic presidential nomination and one of the most outspoken and passionate congressional critics of the war. On his way, he stopped off in Paris, where peace negotiators from all sides briefed him on their slow progress and the Vietcong and North Vietnamese assured him that they would guarantee the safety of withdrawing American soldiers. It was in Saigon, however, that McGovern experienced the full extent of the anti-American sentiment spreading throughout South Vietnam. While he was visiting a Catholic school, the South Vietnamese secret police tossed firebombs and rocks at the building. McGovern and his party barely escaped with their lives. The next day, when he met with South Vietnamese President Thieu, McGovern said, "I hold you personally responsible for what happened last night, Mr. President. It's no wonder this country is in such a mess, if, after ten years of war and 50,000 American lives, the capital is not safe for a U.S. senator to visit." McGovern warned Thieu "that you are in considerable difficulty with the American people, and I would think with large elements of your own people."[58]

Thieu was not in as much trouble as McGovern might have expected. In South Vietnam's constitutionally mandated elections in October, Thieu bullied all of his opponents out of the race and then rigged the returns. Although they expressed disappointment that the election farce further tarnished Saigon's already dismal record of antidemocratic excesses, Nixon and American embassy officials in South Vietnam did virtually nothing. Still loyally supporting the leader who he believed had been so instrumental in his election as president, Nixon told quizzical reporters that there was little the United States could do to change the political climate in Saigon. Of the ninety-one countries that received U.S. military or economic assistance, only thirty were democracies, Nixon said. Why should South Vietnam be treated differently than the rest? The reporters pressed him harder. Could not the United States influence the South Vietnamese in some manner? Twisting the question, Nixon said that if the reporter was suggesting that "the United States should use its leverage now to overthrow Thieu, I would remind all concerned that the way we got into Vietnam was through overthrowing Diem."[59*]

THE FUROR OVER THE *Pentagon Papers* only strengthened Mansfield's resolve to force Nixon to end the war through Senate action. He had voted for the unsuccessful McGovern–Hatfield amendment and watched as the

---

*Left unspoken was the Nixon administration's acquiescence in the 1970 overthrow of Cambodia's leader, Prince Sihanouk, in a bloodless coup.

Nixon administration persuaded the House to water down his own non-binding amendment to the draft extension bill. In late September, he returned to the Senate floor and offered a nonbinding amendment to the military procurement bill that urged Nixon to establish a specific date for withdrawal of American forces, although it was tied to the release of the American prisoners of war. Previously, Mansfield had set a nine-month timetable for the withdrawal. This time, he asked the Senate to call on Nixon to complete the process in six months. He told his colleagues that the measure "proposes, in a sentence, a decisive end to this tragic chapter in the Nation's history."[60]

Again, the Senate approved the bill, but Mansfield watched helplessly as the House undermined his efforts by removing the deadline from language that urged the troop withdrawal. Although Mansfield vowed to continue pushing for a specific date for the U.S. withdrawal, he was unaware that Nixon had rejected a secret North Vietnamese offer to end the war on terms virtually identical to those in the majority leader's Senate amendment. Nonetheless, Nixon signed the procurement bill containing Mansfield's weakened amendment, noting that it was "without binding force or effect" and did not "represent the policies of the Administration." That remark prompted Frank Church to say, "What is he going to do next? Dispatch Henry Kissinger to Capitol Hill and disband the Congress?"[61]

When the foreign aid authorization bill for fiscal years 1972 and 1973 came to the Senate floor in late October, it became yet another magnet for antiwar provisions by senators like Mansfield, Church, and Cooper, all of whom attached amendments to it during Foreign Relations Committee deliberations. A Cooper–Church amendment, for example, declared that funds for U.S. forces in South Vietnam could be used only for completing their withdrawal. U.S. forces could not engage in combat, except to protect withdrawing American troops from "imminent danger."

Mansfield argued for the bill with a newfound passion. When Republican leader Hugh Scott warned that Nixon might veto the measure if the Cooper–Church language remained, Mansfield responded that the Senate should stand up to Nixon's threats, despite the potential loss of the "many goodies" (special interest provisions inserted by members) in the bill. "Nobody seems to mention the Americans in Vietnam," he said. "Nobody seems to understand that what the Cooper–Church amendment does is to protect them fully, completely, constitutionally, as they withdraw, as the President is withdrawing and as we anticipate without question that he will continue to withdraw."

This time, Cooper and Church came close. But in a series of three narrow roll-call votes on October 28, the Senate removed the amendment from the bill.[62] Left standing, however, was Mansfield's nonbinding amendment calling for a withdrawal of U.S. troops in six months, contingent on the release of U.S. prisoners.

This time, it was the bill itself and not any Vietnam amendments that threatened its survival. For years, foreign aid had been a controversial issue. Many conservatives opposed the program as a wasteful giveaway program that did little to win friends for the United State abroad. Some liberals believed much of the money could be better spent on domestic programs or at least more effectively funneled through existing international aid programs. When these natural opponents of foreign aid were joined by a group of frustrated doves—eager to assert congressional authority over foreign policy and fearful that continued foreign aid to Cambodia would only prolong the war—the bill was doomed. On October 29, the Senate rejected the bill, 41–27, the first time either house of Congress had objected to a foreign aid bill since the program was established in the years following World War II.

Explaining his vote, Church said that he could no longer "endorse with my vote a foreign aid program, which has been twisted into a parody and a farce." Mansfield agreed. "I think the only solution," he said, "is to bring an end to a program which has outlived its usefulness, and keep the good parts and get away from the discrepancies which have come into existence and the kind of aid which has been so prevalent and so profligate."[63]

But the bill was not dead, despite the Senate action. After the Senate adopted two scaled-back measures authorizing foreign economic and military assistance, the House tried to revive the larger foreign aid bill it had originally passed. After a month of negotiation, a group of House and Senate conferees finally resolved their major differences over the legislation. All that remained was the sticky issue of Mansfield's withdrawal amendment. That was settled on December 16, when House members blocked efforts to force their conferees to accept Mansfield's language. Frustrated and angry, Mansfield warned the House to expect more amendments from him. He would continue working for enactment of his amendment "until this involvement [in Vietnam] is cut loose from the life of this nation."[64]

As the year ended, the vanquished antiwar amendments of Mansfield, Church, Cooper, McGovern, and Hatfield littered the Senate's political landscape. Despite a war that had claimed more than fifty-five thousand lives and was now strongly opposed by a large majority of Americans (who could not, however, agree on the best way out), Congress steadfastly refused to assume responsibility for ending it. That duty would continue to rest with Nixon. Besides a fundamental aversion to being labeled as a dove, many moderate senators were not yet willing to force Nixon's hand as long as he continued the slow-but-steady process of Vietnamization. On

November 12, Nixon let even more steam out of the Senate doves' imperative when he announced that he would withdraw an additional forty-five thousand American soldiers by February 1, 1972, leaving one hundred thirty-nine thousand American troops behind. Despite the illusion of a rapidly vanishing war—Vietnam had all but disappeared as a major topic on the nightly television network news programs—the fighting and dying continued.

CHAPTER 41

Peace Is at Hand

1972

As THE PRESIDENTIAL ELECTION YEAR OF 1972 DAWNED, NIXON proclaimed the American military role in Vietnam all but over. "The issue of Vietnam will not be an issue in the [presidential] campaign," the president confidently told CBS newsman Dan Rather in an interview on January 2, "because we will have brought the American involvement to an end." Nixon's statement was intriguing. Did that mean, Rather asked, that no U.S. troops would be in South Vietnam on Election Day? Nixon dodged the question, explaining that the answer depended on the actions of North Vietnam, which held at least four hundred American prisoners of war. "Can the President," Nixon said, "withdraw all of our forces as long as the enemy holds one American as a prisoner of war? The answer is no." If Hanoi refused to release the prisoners, then Nixon said "we will have to continue the possibility of air strikes on the North Vietnamese." Rather asked, "Then how can you campaign saying you have ended the American involvement?" "Well," Nixon replied, revealing the political motivations behind his assertion, "the important thing is whether the American people are convinced that the President of the United States had done everything that he can do to bring this desperately difficult war to an end."[1]

In other words, Nixon's talk about ending American involvement in Vietnam by the election was only soothing rhetoric designed for domestic political consumption. In fact, he had no idea how long it would take to bring home the troops. He only hoped that the American people would credit him with drastically reducing American involvement and forget his vague 1968 campaign promise about a plan to end the war. Nonetheless, Nixon had the upper hand. Despite the reality of a raging war—more than one hundred thousand troops remained in Vietnam—the perception among much of the public was that America's role was virtually over.

Congress was more problematic. As the November election approached and the war grew even more unpopular, Nixon knew that congressional support for a specific date to withdraw all U.S. troops might again become an irresistible temptation. Exasperated and eager to court antiwar voters, Congress might finally take the drastic step of cutting off funds for the war. A worst case scenario, although highly unlikely, would be an abrupt end to the war forced upon Nixon by congressional Democrats, an act that would prevent him from claiming he had achieved an "honorable peace." To avoid any such humiliating turn of events—and to neutralize the administration's congressional critics—Nixon and Kissinger staged a dramatic announcement on January 25. Any notion that Nixon had not been trying to end the war through peaceful means was dispelled when the president went on national television to reveal that Kissinger had been engaged in a series of secret talks with the North Vietnamese. Nixon reported that he had proposed a deal under which the United States would withdraw all its forces six months after a cease-fire agreement and the return of American POWs. Furthermore, he said, Thieu had offered to resign one month before a new presidential election.[2]

Nixon's speech was a political masterstroke that suddenly placed his congressional critics on the defensive. Having attacked Nixon for months for his seeming refusal to seek a peaceful settlement, most of his congressional critics could now do little more than praise him for his efforts. John Sherman Cooper called the proposal "fair and just."[3] Mansfield said it was "a long step forward in laying the cards on the table and letting the American people and the Congress know of the many attempts over the past thirty months to arrive at a basis for negotiations."[4] Although Mansfield was too modest to make note of the fact, Nixon's proposal—a withdrawal of troops following release of the POWs—was virtually the same plan the majority leader had advanced for months in the Senate, in the face of Nixon's opposition. As Democrat Philip Hart of Michigan observed, "It's not the Mansfield Amendment, but it certainly adopts the underlying elements of it."* Church was more skeptical and criticized Nixon's plan for a

---

*There were important differences between the Mansfield and Nixon proposals. Mansfield had simply proposed that the United States withdraw from Indochina within six months and stop all military operations in exchange for release of the POWs. "No political quid pro quo or cease fire," as Foreign Relations Committee staff member Norvill Jones explained to Fulbright. "Just get out." Nixon's plan, however, was more involved. It called for a cease-fire as part of any withdrawal-and-POW release agreement—requiring the far-more-complicated process of achieving a political and military settlement before the ultimate withdrawal of American forces. (Jones to Fulbright, 1/26/72, 78:8, Box 51:3, Fulbright Papers)

new South Vietnamese presidential election. "This has been suggested before and rejected" by the North Vietnamese, Church said. Nonetheless, he grudgingly applauded Nixon's proposal as "a starting point for serious negotiations." McGovern, on the other hand, was entirely skeptical. He bitterly accused the president of contributing to the "credibility gap" with his secret negotiations. "At the same time Mr. Nixon was bitterly opposed to the McGovern–Hatfield proposal to end the war," he said, "he was at the very same time offering it to the other side."[5]

Fulbright was also wary of Nixon's plan. To Western eyes, at least, Fulbright said the plan seemed "fair and generous." But, he added, "what looks generous to us may not look generous to North Vietnam. We may have to do more to get a favorable response from North Vietnam." The "sticking point," Fulbright added, was whether the United States was "willing to get out and leave the Thieu Government to its own devices."[6] As aide Norvill Jones explained to Fulbright the day after the president's speech, Nixon's peace plan was not as reasonable as it seemed. "Nixon's proposal, in effect, asks the North Vietnamese to go back home and rely on the good faith of the United States and South Vietnam to ensure that it gets a fair shake in determining who controls South Vietnam in the future," Jones wrote. "North Vietnam has had sad experiences in the past, 1946 and 1954 in particular, in relying on political promises by Western powers. They are not likely to do it again."[7]

But critics of Nixon's plan found few friendly forums for their complaints. Because the North Vietnamese had not formally rejected Nixon's proposal, White House aides hit Nixon's detractors with accusations that they "are consciously giving aid and comfort to the enemy. They want the United States to surrender."[8] White House officials leveled charges of sabotage against McGovern and his rival for the Democratic presidential nomination, Democratic Senator Edmund Muskie of Maine, who had criticized Nixon's peace proposal. "Such ugly and un-American accusations impugning the loyalty and patriotism of elected officials have no place in a country that was founded on the right of free speech," McGovern angrily shot back when White House Chief of Staff H. R. Haldeman attacked him in early February.[9]

Despite the criticism of a few critics, Nixon's peace plan disarmed many of his congressional opponents and forced them to pay him grudging tribute. Just as disarming was Nixon's bold and historic trip to Communist China on February 17, 1972, when he became the first sitting president to set foot on Chinese soil. As an election-year gambit, Nixon's visit was brilliant. Just as he was claiming victory in his effort to extricate the United States from Vietnam, his dramatic journey to China and the normalization of relations between the two former enemies further solidified his image as an international statesman and man of peace—an image he would burnish further with a visit to the Soviet Union in May. In a geopolitical sense, Nixon's visits to China and the Soviet Union would also undoubtedly aggravate tensions between Hanoi's two major benefactors and put pressure on both to reduce their support for the war. Although Hanoi had complained bitterly to Chinese officials about Nixon's trip, they could do nothing to prevent it. In fact, even before Nixon arrived, Chairman Mao Tse-tung urged Hanoi to find a compromise solution to the war. The North Vietnamese watched bitterly as their Chinese allies warmly toasted Nixon while American bombs continued raining on them.[10]

Nixon's visit to China, and his historic sojourn to Moscow three months later, made it almost impossible for his congressional critics to argue that the president—a man so visibly dedicated to world peace—was needlessly prolonging the war in Vietnam. From his secret negotiations and an ostensibly generous peace proposal to his earth-shattering summit meetings in Beijing and Moscow, Nixon appeared the consummate statesman devoted to reordering the world's balance of power in an American context. The fierce anti-communist who had eagerly attacked Democratic leaders who tolerated the 1949 communist victory in China and had warned for years of an international communist conspiracy aimed at world domination, had now embraced Hanoi's two principal allies at a perilous but opportune moment in the drive for a resolution of the Vietnam War.

In the short term, however, Nixon's visit to China did not appear to advance the cause of peace in Vietnam. Far from it, on March 30, the North Vietnamese launched a massive, surprise military offensive as one hundred twenty thousand communist troops charged into South Vietnam in three waves: the first, a thrust into South Vietnam's northern provinces; the second, a sweep across the central highlands to the coast; and the third, an offensive in the region just north of Saigon. Within days, major towns and cities in all three regions were threatened in some of the most furious fighting of the war. That prompted new calls for a quick end to American involvement. In an interview on CBS's "Face the Nation" on April 2, McGovern said the time had come for the United States to set a date, "perhaps 90 days hence," for termination of all American military operations in Vietnam. "I'm willing to say the time has come for General Thieu to worry about his own political future," McGovern said. "If he has the support on the part of his own people, he'll demonstrate that now. If he doen't have support, I don't want Americans dying to save a government that doesn't have the respect and confidence of its own people."[11]

Although McGovern and the other doves had long ago given up on Thieu and his corrupt regime, Nixon—ever loyal to the leader whose intransigence he believed was partly responsible for his 1968 election victory—had not. With the 1972 election only six months away, Nixon was even more determined to keep Thieu in power. Toward that end, he responded to the communist invasion with a furious American military response. "The bastards have never been bombed like they're going to be bombed this time,"[12] Nixon fumed before he unleashed American B-52s for strikes north of the Demilitarized Zone and sent bombers to attack fuel depots near Haiphong and Hanoi. Although the number of American ground troops stationed in Vietnam had dropped to 68,000 by early April, Nixon increased the numbers of air and naval personnel stationed in Southeast Asia from 47,000 to 77,000.[13]

The communist forces, battered but undeterred, seemed determined to prove that Vietnamization was a failure and hoped that the evidence of this fact would finally force Nixon to settle the war on communist terms. Although administration officials hailed the American and South Vietnamese response to the attacks as "astonishingly successful," the truth was that the South Vietnamese army would never be equal to the task of defending its country against the communists. "The real problem," Nixon wrote in his diary, "is that the enemy is willing to sacrifice in order to win, while the South Vietnamese simply aren't willing to pay that much of a price in order to avoid losing."[14] Publicly, however, Nixon declared that Vietnamization had been so successful that he could "continue our goal of withdrawing American forces without detriment to our overall goal of insuring South Vietnam's survival as an independent country." In late April, Nixon announced that Vietnamization had worked so well that he would bring home an additional twenty thousand American troops by the end of June, cutting the troop ceiling to forty-nine thousand, for a total reduction of a half million men since he had entered the White House.[15]

In Congress, however, the doves were not about to fade away, despite the popularity of Nixon's response to the North Vietnamese invasion. Working its way to the Senate floor in late March was legislation passed unanimously by the Foreign Relations Committee to impose strict limits on the presidential use of armed forces without specific congressional authorization. Written by Republican Jacob Javits and Armed Services Committee Chairman John Stennis—no dove, but deeply concerned about the circumstances by which the nation had become embroiled in Vietnam—the War Powers Act of 1972 envisioned a series of checks on presidential war-making authority: in the absence of a congressional war declaration, American forces could be sent into battle only to (1) repel an armed attack on the United States or to prevent the "direct and imminent threat of such an attack"; (2) repel an attack on U.S. armed forces or to prevent the threat of such an attack; and (3) protect and evacuate U.S. citizens and nationals in another country whose lives were threatened. Once the president had committed U.S. troops, he would be required to report promptly to Congress the reasons for his actions and could not continue the military operation beyond thirty days without specific congressional authorization. In the meantime, however, Congress could pass legislation terminating the military operation before the end of the thirty-day period.

The bill's purpose, the committee concluded in its report to the full Senate, was to "fulfill—not to alter, amend or adjust—the intent of the framers of the . . . Constitution in order to assure that the collective judgment of both the Congress and the President will be brought to bear in decisions" regarding the deployment of U.S. forces. The bill, the committee argued, had made "ample provision for the exigencies of modern warfare and international politics."[16] The war powers legislation would put the president and the military in a stronger position, Stennis explained to the Senate, because the commander in chief "will not be tempted to risk a war which the nation will not support. I lean toward military preparedness, everybody knows that, but that doesn't mean I have to abandon common sense and throw away this safeguard."

Stennis' role as a primary sponsor of the bill was crucial. Known for his vocal support for a vigorous effort to win the war and his opposition to measures that limited Nixon's latitude in Vietnam, Stennis had for years nursed reservations about the suspicious circumstances by which Lyndon Johnson had first escalated the war in Vietnam. By the time Nixon took office, Stennis had finally concluded that the American intervention in Vietnam, although prompted by lofty motives, had been initiated by a series of unconstitutional presidential actions. Stennis' high-profile role of support for the bill made it much easier to win the support of other erstwhile hawks. Majority Whip Robert Byrd of West Virginia was typical. In declaring his support, Byrd explained that although the power to declare war had always been vested in the legislative branch, "the actual power to initiate war . . . has, practically speaking, shifted since World War II from Congress to the Executive." Echoing liberals like McGovern and Church, Byrd declared: "This power of Congress must be reasserted in no uncertain terms."

Democrat Herman Talmadge of Georgia—another vocal supporter of the conflict—agreed and argued that the "single most important decision we as a nation can make is the decision to go to war." In recent years, Talmadge noted, "the President, acting virtually alone, has determined whether we followed a course of war or peace. The decision is too great for one man to make, no matter how thick his hide or how broad his shoulders."

Although Nixon's supporters vigorously attacked the bill as an unconstitutional restriction on the president's authority, the Senate overwhelmingly approved the bill on April 13, 68–16. The bill's passage was assured when senators overwhelmingly beat back attempts by Fulbright and

Democratic Senator Mike Gravel of Alaska to apply its provisions retroactively to Vietnam. For once, most of the Senate's doves—fearing that a retroactive application would doom the bill—joined the hawks in opposing the amendments. But in a passionate appeal for his modifications, Gravel pointed out the absurdity of a situation in which Congress reasserted its prerogative to restrict the president's latitude in future wars, while continuing to abdicate responsibility for the one in progress.

> We have been waging war in Southeast Asia but . . . have never bothered to declare war. Yet senators stand on this floor to insist and appeal that we should do more bombing. . . . If we are going to double, as we have done in the last few days, the number of B-52s with which we have been bombing these poor people . . . then we at least ought to have the gumption, the honesty and the straightforwardness to look them in the face and say, "We declare war against you." . . . If we voted not to declare war, it would make our actions in Indochina look somewhat ridiculous.

Even though the bill would not apply to Vietnam, Senate passage of the war powers bill marked the beginning of a new attitude in Congress toward American involvement in Vietnam. Although it would come too late to have any momentous impact—most troops had been withdrawn by the time the Senate considered the bill—the debate identified a growing political fault line in Congress over the war. Conservative southern Democrats, formerly resolute in their support of presidential prerogatives in the conduct of war, had finally been persuaded to back away from Nixon—not because they opposed the war, but because they had finally acknowledged just how badly the constitutional powers and prerogatives of their institution had been eroded. To their discredit, it was only after Nixon had virtually ended the war that these conservatives mustered the "courage" to finally take a stand and reassert those constitutional powers. Each senator who had voted for the Gulf of Tonkin resolution—and its predecessors of the late 1950s and early 1960s—had been responsible for the massive shift of constitutional powers that he now decried.

Despite the historic implications of the vote, the legislation was doomed. When it arrived in the House, representatives watered down the bill at the White House's behest and removed all requirements for congressional approval for military action beyond the Senate's thirty-day limitation. The year ended with no agreement between the two houses on a final version of the bill.[17]

In South Vietnam, meanwhile, fierce fighting to stave off a North Vietnamese rout continued. Despite the severe damage inflicted around Hanoi and Haiphong by American bombers, the Communists stubbornly pressed on and sparked mass panic in the coastal area around Hué, where as many as one hundred fifty thousand frantic refugees streamed southeastward toward Da Nang. North Vietnam refused to negotiate with Kissinger, despite a new American willingness to negotiate a "standstill" cease-fire that allowed North Vietnamese forces to remain in the south. When a secret trip to Moscow to enlist the aid of Soviet leader Leonid Brezhnev failed to produce the desired results, Nixon responded with even more intense bombing. Suspecting that the communists were delaying in hopes that they could come to terms with the Democratic "supporters of Hanoi" after the November elections, Nixon resolved to bomb his enemy into submission. On May 8, he announced to a stunned nation that he had ordered the long-contemplated mining of all North Vietnamese ports, including Haiphong, and a massive intensification of the bombing—steps he knew might scuttle his summit with Brezhnev, scheduled for late May.

Nixon first briefed congressional leaders just prior to giving the news to the nation. Mansfield was stunned and visibly angry. When Nixon left the room to deliver his televised address, the majority leader interrupted Admiral Thomas Moorer's briefing.

"How long ago were these orders issued?" Mansfield asked in a voice trembling with anger.

"Today, this afternoon."

"What it means is that the war is enlarged," Mansfield insisted. "It appears to me that we are embarking on a dangerous course. We are courting danger here that that could extend the war, increase the number of war prisoners and make peace more difficult to achieve."

Moorer was unmoved and did not respond. Finally, Laird spoke up. "As far as extension is concerned, Mike, it was extended by the enemy. It's not a fair charge to charge us with that responsibility."

"Compared with bombing Haiphong," Rogers chimed in, "this is much more limited, wouldn't you say, Admiral Moorer?"

"Yes," Moorer responded. "Mines are a passive weapon."

After discussion of the logistics of the mining and bombing operation, Fulbright spoke up. He agreed with Mansfield. "It seems like an enlargement of the war," he said. "There is no longer a Gulf of Tonkin Resolution, and I don't know your legal justification under the Constitution. You are going to the U.N. with legal justification of the mining—but what will you tell the American people?"[18] Despite the protests, it was too late to affect the outcome, even if Nixon had cared what Mansfield and Fulbright thought. The decision had been made. Like Johnson, Kennedy, and Truman before him, Nixon had informed, not consulted the congressional leaders.

As the congressmen watched, Nixon appeared on television to explain his decision. Somberly, Nixon said that the mining of ports, the American

attacks on Chinese rail lines within North Vietnam, and the effort to intercept the movement of supplies over water would not end until the North
Vietnamese agreed to return all American POWs and accept an internationally supervised cease-fire. "Then," he said, "we will stop all acts of force
throughout Indochina and proceed with the complete withdrawal of all
forces within four months." For the first time, however, Nixon conceded
that his Vietnamization program had not yet succeeded. While the South
Vietnamese forces had fought bravely, he acknowledged that "the Communist offensive has now reached the point where it gravely threatens the
lives of sixty thousand troops who are still in Vietnam." Although he
expressed his continued support for the Saigon government, Nixon was
addressing the South Vietnamese people when he said that "it is your spirit
that will determine the outcome of the battle."[19]

Although the Soviets protested the attacks, they would not scuttle the
summit—one more indication that Hanoi's benefactors were tiring of the
war and the toll it had taken on East-West relations. Domestic reaction to
the renewed bombing campaign was mixed.[20] As the president's most reliable and strident defender in the Senate, Dole praised Nixon on May 9 for
adding a "new dimension to the effort for peace" and indirectly attacked
the president's critics as disloyal. Dole said he hoped that "those of us who
speak could from time to time support our Government in its efforts to
end the war in Southeast Asia." Republican Strom Thurmond of South
Carolina echoed Dole's call for unity. "The time has come for the leadership of these United States to unite behind our Commander in Chief,"
Thurmond told the Senate. "We can owe nothing less to a man who has
put the welfare of freedom-loving people above his own political fortunes."[21] But Nixon's actions were not as damaging to his own poll numbers as Thurmond might have imagined. In the speech's wake, Nixon's
public approval ratings shot up—a reflection of the broad support that the
bombing still enjoyed and how it was now viewed as a relatively safe and
painless means to stave off disaster in South Vietnam while forcing Hanoi
to capitulate.[22]

Nixon's critics, however, were incensed. The *Washington Post* called the
attacks "reckless" and observed that "it is hard to imagine a more damning indictment of the vaunted Vietnamization program. . . . The North
Vietnamese are no less resilient, no less resourceful and no less resolved
than they were two or five or twenty years ago."[23] Castigating Nixon for
his "willingness to risk confrontation with other superpowers by blockading North Vietnam and mining its harbors," the *St. Louis Post-Dispatch*
termed the gambit "strange and risky." "The people want to get out of this
disastrous, tragic war that is ruining a little nation and racking a big one,"
the paper added.[24] Nixon's renewed reliance on "the old and discredited

assumptions of a possible military solution in Vietnam," the *Christian Science Monitor* observed, suggested that his Vietnamization policy was "tottering on the brink of failure."[25]

The day after Nixon's announcement, the Senate Democratic caucus overwhelmingly endorsed a Fulbright-sponsored resolution "disapproving the escalation of the war in Vietnam" and resolved to support the latest end-the-war measure sponsored by Church and New Jersey's Clifford Case.[26] In a particularly emotional Senate speech later that day, Mansfield worried that that the president's actions would expand the war, jeopardize arms control negotiations with the Soviets, delay or scuttle the Moscow summit, and lessen the chances that North Vietnam would release American POWs. Acknowledging the climate of fear in which White House officials labeled dissenting congressmen as un-American, Mansfield added:

> Every member of this body is entitled to the use of free speech and the exercise of his conscience. As far as I am concerned personally, the sooner this horrible, tragic war is brought to a close and every American is brought home, the better off I will feel, because to me 358,918 casualties in a twelve-year period is 358,918 too many in a war in which we have no business and which is not vital to the security of this Nation, a war which, in my opinion, is the greatest tragedy which has ever befallen this Republic.[27]

Nixon's actions, McGovern said later in the Senate, had demonstrated "that the President must not have a free hand in Indochina any longer." Worried that the president had now escalated the war into "a confrontation between great powers," McGovern added: "A President who promised a 'generation of peace' has made the world more dangerous for all mankind. And he has done it without so much as a glance toward Capitol Hill." Announcing his support for an amendment to force Nixon to withdraw the troops, McGovern called for congressional "action to tie the President's hands, to stop the insanity in Indochina, and to choose the course of decency and responsibility, which the American people overwhelmingly want."[28]

Fulbright was no less critical in his remarks on May 11. He praised Soviet "restraint" for not cancelling the summit, while attacking Nixon for his recklessness. "We now seem to be threatening world peace in order to preserve it," Fulbright told the Senate. "That kind of mistaken logic led us into Vietnam originally, has continued to keep us there and has now led us, a Nation founded on the rule of law and a 'decent respect to the opinions of mankind,' to take actions which violate the law and offend mankind."[29]

Within a week, during Foreign Relations Committee hearings on the military assistance authorization bill, Mansfield proposed another amendment designed to end American involvement in Vietnam. This time, he proposed a two-stage approach to disengagement. No funds for supporting U.S. troops would be authorized beyond August 31, 1972, and no U.S. forces—naval, air, or ground—could participate in hostile actions in Vietnam once a cease-fire agreement had been reached and all POWs had been released and accounted for. As Mansfield later explained his amendment to senators, "There are no preconditions. There are no ifs, ands, or buts. Every last serviceman on the ground in Vietnam will be out by August 31, whether he plays a combat role or a supporting role." In adding the amendment to the military aid bill, the committee cleverly sought to cast Mansfield's measure as a legislative endorsement of Nixon's policy, explaining in its report to the Senate that the provision "continues the President's troop withdrawal policy and places legislative force behind that policy."[30]

If Mansfield hoped to force removal of all American ground forces from Vietnam he would have to compete with Defense Secretary Laird, who had begun quietly accelerating the troop withdrawals during the communist offensive for fear Nixon might, in desperation, reverse the exodus. By June, only forty-seven thousand ground troops remained. But the removal of those troops would not mean an end to the fighting. In fact, the numbers of American military personnel assigned to the air war dramatically increased at air bases around the region—in places like Thailand, Guam, and the six aircraft carriers offshore.[31] Indeed, air and naval resources in the region were almost doubled. Another hundred B-52 bombers were mobilized. Almost overnight, the Pentagon increased the number of tactical air squadrons devoted to the bombing campaign from thirty-five to seventy-four. The ferocious bombing that ensued served its purpose. In only a matter of days, the bombs had halted all rail traffic heading south out of Hanoi. The city's main power plant lay in ruins. With all the nation's major ports mined, virtually all ship traffic in and out of North Vietnam ceased.[32]

The bombing missions—a campaign of enormous proportions comprising more than fifty-five thousand sorties, during which American planes dropped more than 100,000 tons of bombs on North Vietnam by early June—were finally yielding the deadly and destructive results Nixon and Kissinger had desired. In the face of furious American bombing attacks, the communist offensive sputtered and the war returned to its pre-offensive, status quo stalemate. By early summer, North Vietnamese intransigence began melting as the bombing and the naval blockade dried up communist supply lines. Further impetus for negotiations came from communist leaders in Peking and Moscow who were eager for improved U.S. relations. Leaders in both countries signaled their desire for a quick end to the war. Realizing they could not overpower the South Vietnamese army—weak as it was—so long as it was backed by such massive American air power, the North Vietnamese were now more favorably inclined to

American proposals for a cease-fire. Secretly, in May, Kissinger and the North Vietnamese negotiators resumed their peace talks. Nixon, meanwhile, kept up the steady drumbeat of ground troop withdrawals.[33] On June 28, he announced that an additional ten thousand would be home by September and added that, henceforth, no draftees would be sent to Vietnam unless they volunteered. (The administration had rejected the latter provision when Gaylord Nelson first proposed it.)[34]

Just as the American ground combat role in Vietnam had dwindled to virtually nothing, the Senate finally moved to stop the fighting, approving the End the War amendment that McGovern and Hatfield had originally proposed in May 1970. On July 24, in a 50–45 vote, the Senate voted to end funding for air, naval, and ground combat in Vietnam, Cambodia, and Laos as soon as the communist-held POWs were released. That day, the Senate also turned back an attempt by Stennis to delete Mansfield's End the War amendment, which had been modified to mandate American troop withdrawals by October 1.* Senators voted 49–46 to retain the provision. This time, Mansfield defended his amendment by suggesting that without a congressional mandate Nixon might be tempted to leave a "residual force" in South Vietnam for years to come. "The question," he said, "is whether we want to be tied to the apron strings of South Vietnam and have them determine what we should do or whether we want to sever those strings."[35]

Nixon's "defeat," however, was short-lived. Almost as soon as they suffered their stunning rebuke, Nixon's Senate allies moved quickly to kill the entire military aid bill rather than tolerate its End the War amendment. To Frank Church's surprise, Mansfield and Fulbright supported the move, regarding it as a more practical way to deny Nixon the funds for fighting the war. While he had no abiding love for the military aid program, Church saw the move as a trap. In the end, he argued, House and Senate leaders would revive the military aid bill, minus the End the War provision. Mansfield and Fulbright, however, saw their opposition to the bill as a pragmatic acknowledgment that the amendment stood no chance of passage in the House. It would be far easier to kill the entire bill, they argued, than to persuade House members to sustain the controversial provision. Later that day, with Mansfield, Church, and other doves in the majority, the Senate rejected the military aid bill, 48–42. A dejected Church complained that his erstwhile allies had allowed Nixon to "snatch victory from the jaws of defeat." The antiwar forces, he observed, had "marched all the way up the hill and conquered the summit," but had then "marched back down again" by rejecting the entire measure. Even in victory—after years of pushing for

---

*In a compromise move, Mansfield agreed to move back the date for the final withdrawal of U.S. troops from August to October.

an End the War measure—the doves had engineered their own defeat, a direct result of their own lack of cohesion.

A week after the Senate spared, then killed Mansfield's groundbreaking provision, the House made history when the Foreign Affairs Committee, voting mostly along party lines, passed its own End the War amendment in an 18–17 vote. The House provision—its approval marking the first time any House committee had taken a stand in opposition to Nixon on the war—was virtually identical to Mansfield's language. It required the withdrawal of U.S. ground, air, and naval forces from Vietnam by October 1, subject to a cease-fire agreement; the release of all U.S. POWs; and an accounting of all soldiers missing in action. But the House doves' measure was destined for the same fate as Mansfield's scuttled amendment. On August 10, Nixon's allies prevailed in the House, just as Mansfield and Fulbright had expected. Before passing their own version of the military aid bill, House members voted to strike the amendment.[36]

The Senate and House actions, although aborted, worried Nixon's advisors. "Sooner or later," Kissinger later wrote, "one of the amendments to cut off funds would pass." Far from trying to bomb Hanoi into submission, Nixon and Kissinger now admitted what Hanoi had itself acknowledged: neither side would ever score a decisive military victory as long as both sides remained committed to the fight. "We were therefore determined," Kissinger wrote, "to see a fair compromise."[37]

FOR ALL GEORGE McGOVERN's passion about Vietnam, his best opportunity to bring about a quick end to the war had come in 1968—and he had walked away from it. Had he challenged Lyndon Johnson in the New Hampshire primary, McGovern, with his impressive pedigree of dissent, would have captured the almost unanimous support of the antiwar movement. McGovern, not Eugene McCarthy, might have vanquished Johnson. Robert Kennedy, a close associate, probably would not have run, thereby pitting McGovern and the antiwar forces against Humphrey and Johnson. Had he become the Democratic nominee—by no means a certain outcome—much of the violence and unrest at the Democratic National Convention in Chicago might have been averted and McGovern would have led a more unified party into the November election. McGovern would have undoubtedly forced Nixon to articulate a clearer vision of how and when he would remove American forces from Vietnam. Moderate and liberal Republicans might have found him more appealing than Nixon. "A lot of us on the Republican side," Mark Hatfield later said, "would have certainly been much more willing to support McGovern."[38]

Four years later, Vietnam remained McGovern's abiding passion. His years of forceful opposition to the war had earned him the enthusiastic support of the antiwar movement and had played no small role in his successful bid to capture the Democratic presidential nomination. Appointed chairman of the Democratic Party's reform commission, McGovern successfully advocated changes in the party's rules that encouraged young voters, women, and minorities to participate at the 1972 convention. The new inclusive party procedures were instrumental in paving the way to McGovern's presidential nomination in 1972. Unfortunately, the Democratic nomination of 1972 was devalued currency. Despite what McGovern and most liberals thought about Nixon's conduct of the war, much of the American electorate saw Nixon as a strong leader determined to secure an "honorable" peace in Vietnam. Despite the president's ill-advised forays into Laos and Cambodia and the renewed bombing of North Vietnam, Vietnamization had resulted in the withdrawal of most U.S. troops. Nixon appeared strong, steady, and determined to end the war on American, not communist terms.

McGovern, meanwhile, appeared bellicose and inextricably tied to the most radical elements of the antiwar movement. "McGovern was simply their vehicle," campaign advisor Ted Van Dyk said of the radical antiwar protesters, recalling his candidate's unfortunate image as the "acid, amnesty and abortion" candidate. "George McGovern, who was a very straight arrow personally, was made to look like the standard bearer for the counter culture."[39] It was also unhelpful that his allies in the presidential quest included not only the more radical antiwar leaders, but also the communist government of North Vietnam, which had characterized his program to end the war as "positive."[40] McGovern, the distinguished World War II veteran who should have been extolled as one of the most prescient and outspoken opponents of the war, was instead vilified as a weak leader unwilling to stand up to the communist leaders of North Vietnam.

Four years earlier, before Nixon's Vietnamization had stolen much of the antiwar thunder, McGovern's pledge to end the war might have captured the hearts of working-class America. His was a simple, swift prescription for ending the war: (1) "All American bombing in Indochina would be immediately stopped—with no preconditions." (2) "All American ground forces would be withdrawn from Indochina within 90 days—with no preconditions." (3) "All military assistance to the Thieu regime would be immediately terminated—with no preconditions." (4) "Vigorous diplomatic efforts would be undertaken to achieve the release of U.S. prisoners of war." (5) Upon the release of U.S. prisoners of war, U.S. bases in Thailand would be closed and U.S. naval forces off the shores of Southeast Asia would be removed.[41]

Nixon, meanwhile, exuded confidence as his Vietnamization policy slowly drained Vietnam of American troops and the new, massive bombing campaign sparked the North Vietnamese interest in negotiations to end the fighting. Having previously desired a peace settlement before the presidential elections, Nixon now reversed course—skeptical of what could be achieved through negotiations and fearful that a last-minute deal would be viewed not as a triumph for peace but a political maneuver designed to attract votes. In fact, Nixon believed that delaying a settlement beyond the election might actually help him with voters. As long as the president was viewed as a wartime leader, directing a vigorous air campaign against the communists in North Vietnam, his pollsters believed that he would hold the support of patriotic blue-collar voters who had traditionally voted the Democratic ticket in national elections, but supported Nixon's strong stand in Vietnam. Nixon's advisors reasoned that as soon as the war was over—and was no longer a major public concern—many erstwhile Democrats would have little reason to continue backing a Republican president against a liberal opponent more attuned to the economic issues that had traditionally attracted them to the Democratic fold.

Nixon also believed the United States could negotiate from a strong position after the election. Then, he wrote in his diary, the enemy "either has to settle or face the consequences of what we could do to them." In short, Nixon was prepared to forego a negotiated settlement—no matter how much the communists wanted it—in the belief that he could exact more generous concessions with a continuation of the bombing and mining campaign. Years later, Nixon explained that "after a tremendous mandate, after the antiwar crowd had been totally defeated, I thought that then we could get these people to, shall we say, cry uncle."[42]

Kissinger, however, knew the communists were eager to negotiate for peace prior to the election and more apt to make concessions, believing—correctly—that Nixon might turn even more bellicose after his almost certain reelection. As he looked at the Senate, with sentiment growing for legislation to force Nixon to end the war, Kissinger believed the United States might never again possess the kind of leverage in negotiations that it enjoyed in the summer of 1972. "For I thought—contrary to both Hanoi's probable analysis and our own conventional wisdom—that we would actually be *worse* off after the election[emphasis Kissinger's]," Kissinger explained. "All the polls that I had seen suggested that the composition of the new Congress would be substantially the same as of the old or even slightly less favorable." Kissinger believed this meant "the pressures for ending the war by legislation were certain to resume after November. And the opposition would have a convenient target when we submitted a supplemental budget in January to pay for the costs of reinforcements during the [spring 1972] offensive."[43]

While Hanoi initially held back, hesitant to make concessions until the shape of the presidential race became more defined, it was clear by September that Nixon enjoyed a commanding lead over McGovern. When the North Vietnamese negotiators finally concluded that their best terms in negotiations with Nixon would come before, not after the elections, they began moderating their position and hinted that Thieu's removal from office would no longer be a prerequisite for successful peace talks. On October 8, a month before the elections, North Vietnam's chief negotiator, Le Duc Tho, made a dramatic peace offer during a secret meeting with Kissinger in Paris. The proposal was simple: a standstill cease-fire with the complete withdrawal of American troops within sixty days and an exchange of all prisoners of war (North Vietnamese troops would remain, but could not be reinforced). Under the proposal, Thieu would remain in office, but would be forced to recognize the NLF as an "administrative entity." The remaining political problems were not addressed by the peace plan. Rather, Le Duc Tho proposed to leave those issues to the two "entities," which would negotiate the formation of a National Council of Concord and Reconciliation and oversee national elections and the eventual reunification of North and South. Meanwhile, both sides could continue to support their respective allies in the South—the South Vietnamese army and the Viet Cong.[44]

Kissinger was elated—despite the fact that the proposal would expedite the American withdrawal and leave Saigon at the mercy of the North Vietnamese army. When staff members questioned the wisdom of the proposal and expressed doubts about Thieu's willingness to accede to the plan, Kissinger exploded. "You don't understand," he snapped. "I want to meet their terms. I want to reach an agreement. I want to end this war before the election. It can be done, and it will be done."[45] For days, Kissinger continued the negotiations without informing Nixon or Thieu of the details. On October 11, he and Le Duc Tho struck a deal along the basic lines of the October 8 proposal. In almost every way, it was a deal that ensured—or recognized the inevitability of—South Vietnam's defeat. Thieu could stay in office, but would share power with the Viet Cong's Provisional Revolutionary Government, which would govern the patchwork quilt of areas in South Vietnam controlled by communist forces. When the standstill cease-fire began, American troops would leave the country (but North Vietnamese troops would remain) and both sides would release their POWs.

Delighted with the deal, Kissinger believed that it would also generate a huge electoral turnout for Republican candidates in the November elections, regardless of the impact on South Vietnam's security. But there was one major problem: Kissinger had failed to inform North Vietnamese negotiators that the deal was invalid without Thieu's acquiescence—a tall order given Kissinger's readiness to force the South Vietnamese leader into a power-sharing arrangement with an enemy that had waged war against his government for almost two decades. Even after he and Le Duc Tho had signed the agreement, Kissinger kept Saigon in the dark. In a White House meeting the next day, an ecstatic Kissinger explained the terms of the deal to Nixon, who wholeheartedly approved. So sure were they of success that the two men, joined by Kissinger's aide Alexander Haig, celebrated their diplomatic feat with steaks and a bottle of Château Lafite-Rothschild.

Next, Kissinger and Nixon agreed to a wildly optimistic schedule for completing the peace accords: Kissinger would return to Paris on October 17 to complete details of the agreement, including the negotiation of several minor changes that Nixon had insisted upon. On October 18, he would go to Saigon to present the plan to Thieu. Four days later, he would travel to Hanoi to initial the agreement and return to Washington on October 24. Nixon would announce the agreement on October 26 and would sign it on October 31—one week before the presidential elections. All went according to plan until Kissinger arrived in Saigon. Thieu immediately balked, furious that Kissinger had negotiated—"over our head with the Communists"—an agreement that allowed the North Vietnamese to remain in his country and forced him to share power with the Viet Cong. "Now for years I say never, never a coalition, never accept a coalition," Thieu said. "I say that the life of South Vietnam rely on those two main points [no Communist troops and no coalition government]." Despite Kissinger's reassurances that the United States would strictly enforce the agreement, Thieu was reluctant to see U.S. troops leave his country and refused to budge. "It is hard to exaggerate the toughness of Thieu's position," a frustrated Kissinger complained to Nixon in an October 22 cable. "His demands verge on insanity."[46] Not nearly as eager as Kissinger for a preelection peace agreement, Nixon refused to sign the agreement without Saigon's approval. "It cannot be a shotgun marriage," he told Kissinger.[47]

Frustrated by Thieu's refusal to bow to the inevitable, Nixon nonetheless viewed his intransigence as merely a temporary detour on a steady road to peace. While Kissinger worried about the election, Nixon contemplated his place in history. "I still felt that if we abandoned [Thieu] South Vietnam would fall to the Communists within a matter of months, and our entire effort there would have been for naught," Nixon later wrote, attesting to his determination not to suffer the blame for America's first loss in war. Nixon was confident that Thieu would eventually come around and sign the agreement "at some point before Congress returned in January and took matters out of our hands by voting to cut off all appropriations for the war and for aid to South Vietnam."[48]

Kissinger had other ideas. In an attempt to force Nixon to force

Thieu's hand, he leaked details of the agreement to the *New York Times*. That infuriated Nixon, who believed Kissinger was trying to steal credit for the expected landslide over McGovern. The next day, however, the plot thickened when impatient officials in Hanoi began releasing details of the agreement and accused the Nixon administration of belaboring the talks in order to conceal a "scheme of maintaining the Saigon puppet regime for the purpose of continued war of aggression."[49] In the Senate, many of the doves were skeptical. Why had the Nixon administration not negotiated the same agreement four years before—especially considering the liberal concessions that Kissinger had made to Hanoi?

At a televised press conference the next day, Kissinger sought to reassure Hanoi of his good intentions, while signaling Saigon that the United States would stand by the agreement. "We must remember that, having come this far, we cannot fail and we will not fail over what still remains to be accomplished," Kissinger told reporters. "We believe," he added, "that peace is at hand."* When Nixon learned of Kissinger's unfortunate, inaccurate, and overly optimistic phrase, he immediately realized "that our bargaining position with the North Vietnamese would be seriously eroded and our problem of bringing Thieu and the South Vietnamese along would be made even more difficult." Just as disturbing to Nixon was the risk of premature hopes for an agreement that might lend credence to charges by McGovern that Nixon was manipulating the peace talks for domestic political gain. "He had no plan for ending the war," McGovern charged in the campaign's final week. "He's not going to let that corrupt Thieu regime in Saigon collapse.... He's going to stay there. He's going to keep our troops there. He's going to keep the bombers flying. He's going to confine our prisoners to their cells in Hanoi for whatever time it takes for him to keep his friend General Thieu in office."[50]

Hoping to reassure the public about his intentions, Nixon delivered a very persuasive televised campaign speech on November 2 during which he insisted that the peace talks would not be influenced by the elections. "We are going to sign the agreement when the agreement is right," he said, "not one day before." That same day, however, Nixon began again gradually to intensify the bombing raids over North Vietnam in a plan to slowly ratchet up the pressure on Hanoi to return to the bargaining table. Nixon's ploy worked. Within two days, the North Vietnamese agreed to reopen talks in Paris on November 14, a week after the elections.[51]

---

*The remark was painfully reminiscent of British Prime Minister Neville Chamberlain's claim to have achieved "peace in our time" following his Munich conference with Hilter in 1938.

ON NOVEMBER 7, American voters reelected Nixon in a landslide. The president carried every state but Massachusetts en route to winning 60.7 percent of the vote to McGovern's 37.5 percent. McGovern's passion for ending the war was never a factor with most voters. Because Nixon had ended the draft and withdrawn most of the ground troops, most Americans believed the war was virtually over. Peace, they believed, *was* at hand. In any event, voters refused to judge McGovern on his defense and foreign policies alone. Nixon won for a variety of reasons besides his success in winding down the war, including a strong economy; the shooting of Alabama Governor George Wallace, which removed the possibility of a conservative, third-party threat to Nixon; McGovern's oft-ridiculed program for redistributing income through guaranteed income grants to every citizen; and, most of all, McGovern's disastrous handling of the vice presidential nomination of Missouri Senator Thomas Eagleton, forced off the ticket following revelations about psychiatric treatments. In the end, voters simply concluded that despite all his faults, Nixon was far more qualified to serve as president than McGovern. "As many of you know," McGovern would later joke to audiences, "for many years, I wanted to run for the Presidency in the worst possible way—and last year I sure did."[52]

The measured, moderate man who opposed the Vietnam War out of principled devotion to country was far removed from the radical, strident McGovern that most voters perceived during the campaign. "The trouble was," he later observed, "all people saw on television were a few of my outspoken supporters out front, and they came away thinking that was me."[53] In defeat, McGovern tried to frame his campaign in terms of its contribution to peace. "If we pushed the day of peace just one day closer," he told supporters on election night, "then every minute and every hour and every bone-crushing effort in this campaign was worth the entire sacrifice."[54]

Nixon reached the end of the election-year marathon on November 7 with barely a scratch. The real wounds from Watergate would not be inflicted until 1973. Until then, Nixon basked in the glow of having earned the second largest share of popular vote in a presidential election—and the largest ever accorded a Republican candidate. "I was confident," Nixon later wrote, "that a new era was about to begin, and I was eager to begin it."[55]

CHAPTER 42

A Spirit of Doubt and Contrition

1972–1975

PEACE WAS NOT AT HAND. AFTER THE U.S. ELECTIONS, THIEU STILL did not budge, stubbornly refusing to approve any peace agreement that did not call for a withdrawal of North Vietnamese troops and that forced him to share power with the Viet Cong. When General Alexander Haig, Kissinger's deputy, traveled to Saigon in hopes of persuading the South Vietnamese leader, Thieu noted that both men were generals. "Would you as a general," he bluntly asked Haig, "accept this agreement? If Russia invaded the U.S., would you accept an agreement where they got to stay and then say that it was a peace?" Haig had no reply.[1]

Thieu insisted on sixty-nine modifications to the agreement. Kissinger returned to the negotiating table on November 20 and dutifully presented the desired changes to Le Duc Tho. By that time, however, both men were operating in vastly different environments and approaching the talks from radically different perspectives. Relying on American assurances that the agreement would be signed no later than October 31, the North Vietnamese had launched a costly, last-minute offensive to secure as much land as possible in South Vietnam. They were not of a mood to continue negotiations with an adversary they increasingly distrusted as unreliable at best or duplicitous at worst. As later Kissinger acknowledged, to his colleagues in the Hanoi Politburo, "Le Duc Tho must have appeared guilty of the unforgivable sin of having been tricked by a wily capitalist." He would not make the same mistake again.

Kissinger, too, had his own domestic problems. "What was left of Congressional support for continuing the war evaporated," he observed, expressing his belief that an expectation of congressional opposition to further hostilities had been an "inherent" factor in Hanoi's October peace proposal. "Once it was apparent that it [the new agreement] *improved* [emphasis Kissinger's] the terms we had put forward on January 25 and May 8, 1972," Kissinger later explained, "we would lose all public and Congressional support if we did not sign." He believed that at least one resolution cutting off funds would surely pass, especially if Hanoi released the American POWs. Nixon feared that Congress would stop all funds for the war within two weeks of convening in January 1973; a White House official responsible for congressional liaison reported that the Senate of 1973 would have at least three fewer votes in support of Nixon's Vietnam policies. "For whatever reasons," Kissinger observed, "we were facing the nightmare I had dreaded since the summer: of negotiating against the deadline of the return of Congress, with no additional leverage on Hanoi to hold the process together."[2]

As Kissinger feared, the North Vietnamese were in no mood for further concessions. On December 13, after several weeks of unfruitful negotiations, Le Duc Tho broke off the talks and left for Hanoi. Returning to Washington, Kissinger gave Nixon two options: "taking a massive, shocking step to impose our will on events and end the war quickly, or letting matters drift into another round of inconclusive negotiations, prolonged warfare, bitter national divisions, and mounting casualties." For Nixon, the choice was not terribly difficult. But, prompted by the rift between Washington and Saigon and believing that Congress had left Nixon little choice but to come to terms with the enemy, Hanoi misjudged the president's reaction to their intransigence. "They cornered him," Kissinger believed, adding that "Nixon was never more dangerous than when he seemed to have run out of options." Nixon was eager for a quick end to the war, but not so eager to risk the political consequences of having ended it on terms imposed by Hanoi.[3]

On December 14, Nixon instructed the military to plant new mines in Haiphong harbor and gave the orders for a massive B-52 bombing campaign against military targets in and around Hanoi, including transportation, power and radio sites, and shipyards and docks at Haiphong. Kissinger called it "jugular diplomacy."[4] "I don't want any more of this crap about the fact that we couldn't hit this target or that one," Nixon told Joint Chiefs chairman Admiral Thomas Moorer. "This is your chance to use military power effectively to win this war, and if you don't, I'll consider you responsible."[5] On December 18, the bombs began falling. For the next eleven days, through Christmas, American aircraft flew three thousand missions and dropped as much as 40,000 tons of bombs on North Vietnam. The destruction around Hanoi was extensive. But Nixon's infamous "Christmas bombing" campaign came at a steep price. North Vietnamese antiaircraft brought down twenty-six American aircraft; fifteen of them were B-52s.[6]

Another price Nixon paid was in public opinion. Almost overnight, his approval rating in the polls slumped to 39 percent.[7] Among those members of Congress most outraged by the renewed bombing was Mansfield, who denounced it as a "Stone Age tactic," noting that bombing had failed for eight years to end the war. "It is long since past time to stop worrying about saving face," Mansfield said, "and concentrate on saving lives and our own sense of decency and humanity." If Nixon wanted to negotiate an end to the war, Mansfield said the Senate "would be more than willing to give of its advice, counsel, and its full support to the President."[8]

Despite its intensity and callous brutality, Nixon's bombing gambit worked again. In late December, the North Vietnamese finally signaled their willingness to return to the negotiating table on January 8. While the intense bombing had been largely responsible for North Vietnam's sudden eagerness to settle, Congress had exerted the same kind of influence on Nixon. On January 2, the House Democratic caucus—angry over the renewed bombing campaign—voted, 154–75, in favor of ending appropriations for the war as soon as the POWs were released and arrangements were made for the withdrawal of American troops. Two days later, the Senate's Democratic caucus approved a similar resolution, 36–12.[9]

In Paris, Kissinger and Le Duc Tho resumed their negotiations. As for Thieu, Nixon had made clear the terms of the new pragmatic Washington–Saigon relationship: "You must decide now whether you desire to continue our alliance or whether you want me to seek a settlement with the enemy which serves U.S. interests alone."[10] Given that ultimatum, Thieu would have no choice but to capitulate.* Nixon's gratitude for Thieu's help in sabotaging the 1968 peace talks had finally expired. On January 9, during the second day of talks, Kissinger and Le Duc Tho struck a deal in which they agreed on the outline of a basic plan to end the war in Vietnam and Laos (Cambodia was omitted from the agreement). The following week, the White House signaled an imminent end to the hostilities by announcing a suspension of all offensive actions throughout North Vietnam.[11] Two weeks later, Nixon went on national television to deliver the

---

*"Brutality is nothing," Nixon told Kissinger as they discussed Thieu's anticipated intransigence. "You have never seen it if this son-of-a-bitch doesn't go along, believe me." In a threatening letter to Thieu, Nixon explained his decision to sign the peace agreement, with or without the South Vietnamese leader. Should he be forced to sign it without Thieu, Nixon said that "I shall have to explain publicly that your Government obstructs peace. The result will be inevitable and immediate termination of U.S. economic and military assistance which cannot be forestalled by a change of personnel in your government" (Kissinger, *White House Years*, 1469).

good news: Kissinger and Le Duc Tho had initialed an agreement "to end the war and bring peace with honor in Vietnam and Southeast Asia."[12]

While the agreement was hailed as a breakthrough, in reality it differed little from the plan the two men had negotiated the previous October. In Paris, on January 27, Secretary of State William Rogers joined representatives of North Vietnam, South Vietnam, and the Viet Cong in signing the accords, bringing about an official end to what the *New York Times* called "the longest, most divisive foreign war in America's history."[13] In all, more than 55,000 American soldiers had died in Vietnam since the early 1960s—more than 20,000 of them in the four years since Nixon had taken office with a promise to end the fighting. As much as the United States had suffered, the toll sustained by the Vietnamese people was staggering by comparison. More than 200,000 South Vietnamese soldiers had died in battle (another 570,000 were wounded), while the death toll among the North Vietnamese Army and the Viet Cong stood at about half a million. In addition, another two million civilians in the north and south were killed. By virtue of hundreds of thousands of bombs and untold tons of defoliant and napalm, much of Vietnam's countryside was left a barren wasteland. Millions of homeless civilians roamed the countryside or crowded into the cities in search of food and shelter. And the country's economy was a shambles, only worsened by the withdrawal of American troops and the millions of dollars they had to spend.

In Washington and throughout the nation, the war had also taken its toll. Since the mid-1960s, Vietnam had been the most divisive issue, other than race, in American life. The draft, disproportionately aimed at young men in the ranks of the lower and middle classes and those not otherwise eligible for college deferments, had helped sharpen the distinctions and heighten the tensions between the economically disadvantaged and those in the middle and upper economic classes. On college campuses and in major cities, opposition to the war often sparked violence and the kind of angry, boisterous protest that unsettled many Americans and added to the disturbing sense that the nation and its society was spinning out of control. Excessive deficit spending on the war had dragged down the U.S. economy and created inflation that would not subside until the early 1980s.

Politically, the division over the war had laid waste to the Democratic Party in 1968, ensuring Hubert Humphrey's defeat and helping elect Nixon, with his ephemeral plan to end the war. For the Republicans, the price exacted by the war was not immediately apparent. In early 1973, Nixon was basking the glow of the "peace with honor" he claimed to have finally achieved. But his "victory" was short-lived. Despite the peace agreement, the fighting in Vietnam would continue—only without direct

American military participation. In Cambodia, meanwhile, deadly American bombs would fall for another six months. In the White House, Nixon's excessive paranoia over leaks and his irrational hatred for the antiwar movement and congressional doves had led him and his aides to commit crimes that had only begun coming to light and which would soon be known to the world as the Watergate scandal.

In early 1973, however, optimism reigned. The war appeared a conflict of the past. On March 29, the last American combat troops left South Vietnam, leaving behind an eight hundred-person American truce observation force and just over two hundred Marine guards and military attaches. By April, Hanoi had released the last of the American POWs. But the war was far from over, as was the American role. American dollars would continue to pour into South Vietnam to prop up Thieu and his regime. Knowing he would face uphill battles in Congress to provide as much economic assistance as Thieu would demand, Nixon could only promise to seek a "sufficient" level of funding for South Vietnam's "economic stability and rehabilitation."[14]

Although he sought to assure Thieu that he would be willing to use American military might to force North Vietnamese compliance with the accords, Nixon knew he could not make good on his promise. Although the U.S. Navy continued to ply the waters off Vietnam and Air Force bombers remained stationed in Thailand and Guam, the threat to intervene was more implied than real. Once the bombing had stopped over North Vietnam and the troops left the South, Congress would never stand by as Nixon sent them back, no matter how few in number. The North Vietnamese, meanwhile, were in no mood to force Nixon's hand—or to antagonize Congress—and focused instead on consolidating and reinforcing their military position in South Vietnam and worked to undermine Thieu through political means. The big offensive aimed at seizing control of South Vietnam would come soon enough. After more than a quarter century of struggle to unify Vietnam under communist rule, Hanoi was willing to wait for another year or two.

Despite Nixon's inability to continue direct military assistance to Thieu, the American government did continue supporting South Vietnam with military supplies—although it was forced by the provisions of the peace agreement to do so furtively. Before the agreements were signed, Nixon had hurriedly shipped massive amounts of military supplies and equipment to South Vietnam and bequeathed even more American military assets to Thieu—including U.S. military bases. As many as nine thousand military advisors stayed behind after they went through the charade of leaving military service, only to be reassigned as civilians to assist the South Vietnamese government.

Although the bombing over North Vietnam had ended, Nixon continued his air campaign over Cambodia in support of the government of Lon Nol—the American-friendly leader who had seized power in 1970— that struggled to defend itself against a fierce uprising by North Vietnam's client, the Khmer Rouge. Throughout the spring, Nixon issued veiled warnings that North Vietnamese violations of the peace accords in Cambodia and elsewhere might force him to order renewed bombing in the North. By summer, however, that threat lost its punch as Congress moved dramatically to strip Nixon of his power to conduct war anywhere in Southeast Asia. In June, both houses of Congress passed legislation sponsored by Democratic Senator Thomas Eagleton of Missouri that contained a provision mandating an immediate cessation of all funds for American combat activities in Cambodia and Laos.

Nixon promptly vetoed the bill. "After more than ten arduous years of suffering and sacrifice," he said in his veto statement, "it would be nothing short of tragic if this great accomplishment [the peace accord], bought with the blood of so many Asians and Americans, were to be undone by congressional action." But it was clear to most members of Congress that Nixon's senseless bombing was one of the major impediments to a lasting cease-fire in Cambodia. The same day, the House sustained Nixon's veto. But he knew he had lost the battle. Mansfield vowed that the provision would be introduced "again and again and again, until the will of the people prevails."[15]

Among Nixon's aides, Kissinger resigned himself to the inevitable. Only two days before, former White House counselor John Dean had begun describing to a special Senate committee the details of the Watergate cover-up masterminded by Nixon. Dean's testimony was devastating. "With every passing day Watergate was circumscribing our freedom of action," Kissinger later wrote. In any event, Kissinger knew that the failure of the Cambodia funding halt, by virtue of a presidential veto, "was technical and parliamentary; the steamroller could not be arrested for long." One by one, Nixon's aides advised against a protracted fight. "No one had the stomach," Kissinger said, "to refight the Vietnam debate in the midst of Watergate."[16]

Finally recognizing "that I could not win these battles forever," Nixon compromised and agreed to end the bombing over Cambodia on August 15. Congress quickly accepted the deal and passed legislation on June 29 that prohibited further U.S. military action in Cambodia after the August deadline without specific congressional approval.[17] An uncharacteristically angry Mansfield was among the handful of senators opposing the compromise. The majority leader reminded the Senate that "the warmaking power is that of Congress exclusively, and the war in Cambodia does not have a shred of validity attached to it. It is illegal, it is unconstitutional, it is immoral. Why should we be afraid of a confrontation with the executive branch of this Government? The bombing must stop . . . not on August 15, but now."[18] Mark Hatfield agreed and observed bitterly that "one does not compromise about the slaughter of innocents."[19]

Nixon signed the bill, but responded by warning North Vietnam that it should "not draw the erroneous conclusion from this congressional action that they are free to launch a military offensive in other areas in Indochina." In such an event, Nixon said, "the American people would respond to such aggression with appropriate action."[20] But it was nothing more than bluster. Despite the fact that he dramatically intensified the bombing in the final weeks, Nixon could do little more without the permission of Congress. "I had only words with which to threaten," he later complained. "The Communists knew it too."[21]

The bloody war in Cambodia—a conflict that Nixon had exacerbated with years of bombing beginning in 1970—eventually led to tragic consequences of epic proportions. By year's end, as many as 2 million of the nation's 7 million inhabitants were refugees. Ultimately, in 1978, the madness sparked by the spread of the Vietnam conflict into Cambodia would claim millions of lives in a holocaust perpetrated by the murderous Khmer Rouge.[22]

By the fall, the spreading Watergate scandal had so weakened Nixon that he was powerless to withstand a congressional assault on his war-making prerogatives. On November 6, Congress overrode his veto of the War Powers Act and enacted legislation strictly limiting the ability of presidents to send U.S. troops into combat for more than sixty days without congressional assent. Seeking to restore the balance of power that had tilted toward the White House after World War II, Congress decreed that presidents could no longer send U.S. troops into battle without congressional approval, except in the most extraordinary situations. Even so, presidents would heretofore be required to explain their actions to the leaders of both houses within forty-eight hours and would be forced to terminate the military action within sixty days unless Congress declared war or specifically authorized the commitment of forces.[23]*

It had been a long, bumpy ride since August 1964, when Congress had completed the abdication of its constitutional authority by passing the Gulf of Tonkin Resolution—a measure that vested in the president, not Congress, the power to decide whether, when, where, and how U.S. troops should be sent to Southeast Asia to fight a protracted war. It had taken nine years, more than fifty-eight thousand American deaths, and a president weakened by scandal before members of Congress awakened to the costly

---

*The act would be routinely ignored and flouted by future presidents.

price paid for their repeated refusal to exercise the powers the Constitution had vested in them. But now that they had the feel of rebuffing Nixon, members of Congress went a step beyond the War Powers Act and flexed their muscles by asserting control of the nation's military purse strings. The day before overriding Nixon's veto, Congress passed a $21.3 billion defense appropriations bill that contained a provision prohibiting U.S. military assistance to any country in Indochina without specific congressional authorization.[24]

By the spring of 1974, Nixon was on his last political legs. Watergate had robbed him of the power and moral authority to force Congress to go along with his plan to increase military assistance to South Vietnam by $266 million. In May, the Senate narrowly rejected his request to raise the spending ceiling on military aid to South Vietnam to $1.6 billion. "We came out there [in Vietnam] with our flags flying," complained John Stennis, the administration's chief Senate proponent for increased military funding, who said the extra money was "an obligation to an ally" and "part of the process of winding down and getting out as fast as we reasonably can." But Edward Kennedy of Massachusetts, and a majority of those voting, rejected that reasoning. "How long are we going to hear that argument?" Kennedy asked the Senate. "We have heard it long enough."[25]

Congress had only begun the process of cutting U.S. aid to South Vietnam. When a House–Senate conference committee began working on the bill in August, it had barely agreed to limit military aid to South Vietnam to $1 billion in 1975 when one member suggested an additional cut of $300 million. When military officials at the Pentagon offered no objection—believing that Thieu had more than enough military equipment and munitions if only his government would rein in rampant waste and corruption—the committee overwhelmingly approved the additional reduction. Both houses approved the scaled-down aid package by wide margins. In the Senate, opponents of military aid to South Vietnam came within three votes of cutting an additional $150 million out of the bill.[26] "It has been a twenty-year war," complained Democrat William Proxmire of Wisconsin, who proposed the additional reduction. "We are now out of it by a year and a half or so. It seems like an endless, hopeless expenditure."[27]

But it was the demands of domestic programs in the midst of a sagging economy that weighed on the minds of many members of Congress, weary from having spent more than $145 billion dollars in Vietnam during the previous two decades. "Today we are having problems," Democrat John O. Pastore of Rhode Island told the Senate on August 20. "We are in a bad way. Let me say very frankly, I believe what we do for Americans will never bankrupt this Nation, but the way we are spending our money abroad will bring us to bankruptcy, and the sooner we begin to realize that, the better off we are going to be."[28]

On August 9, Richard Nixon resigned in disgrace, leaving town as Congress moved toward impeachment over the many crimes of Watergate. Only the day before, in the fiercest fighting since the 1973 peace accords, communist troops—in violation of the cease-fire agreement—took control of a strategic outpost 330 miles north of Saigon, near Da Nang. The region north of the southern capital, the coastal plain between Saigon and Da Nang, was now under siege. While the new president, Gerald Ford, assured Thieu that he supported the government of South Vietnam, he had little more than words to back up his promises. In late August, despite supporting the increase in military assistance that Nixon had requested, Ford reluctantly accepted the scaled-back $700 million appropriations that Congress had passed.

A decent man, eager to heal the deep, festering wounds left by five and a half years of Nixon's duplicity and his loathsome attitude toward critics of the war, Ford acted quickly. He pardoned Nixon in early September and then, a week later, began the process of reconciliation by announcing a program of "earned" amnesty for the fifty thousand draft evaders and deserters from the Vietnam War. As long as the deserters and draft dodgers were willing to engage in a brief stint of public service, Ford was willing to grant them immunity from prosecution. "All, in a sense, are casualties, still abroad and absent without leave from the real America," Ford told a veterans' convention. "I want them to come home if they want to *work* their way back [emphasis Ford's]."[29]

The mood of forgiveness and healing that a wise and benevolent Ford hoped to bring to the national debate over Vietnam was what most Americans wanted in general, but not in particular. Ford's pardon of Nixon angered liberal Democrats, while his amnesty program found little support among Republicans and conservative Democrats. By late September, the new president's public approval ratings dropped significantly. Ford was not the only political leader suffering the vicissitudes of public opinion in Vietnam's aftermath. In Arkansas that spring, Fulbright had reluctantly decided to seek a sixth Senate term. But as he quickly learned, times had changed. In many ways the veteran senator was now a remote figure alienated from an Arkansas electorate that increasingly viewed him as more concerned about arcane matters of foreign policy than the domestic issues most important to Arkansans. In some respects, they were right.[30] Fulbright's chief of staff, Lee Williams, estimated that in the six years preceding the 1974 Senate election, Fulbright had made only thirty public appearances in Arkansas. "He was involved in trying to end that damn war," Williams explained, adding that Fulbright also refused to adapt to the changing political times. "He didn't believe in modern political campaigning techniques."[31]

By the time that Dale Bumpers, the young, enormously popular two-term Democratic governor of Arkansas, announced his plan to challenge Fulbright, the campaign was virtually over. Fulbright found himself suffering not only from his woeful neglect of the political home fires, but from a general backlash against incumbent politicians generated by the Watergate scandal and the forced resignation of Vice President Spiro Agnew after his indictment on bribery charges. "The truth was that Fulbright was vulnerable not only because of his neglect of the state and his stands on Vietnam, Watergate," and other foreign policies issues, biographer Randall Bennett Woods observed, "but also because his heart was not in the race." In the May Democratic primary election, Bumpers drubbed Fulbright and went on to win the November general election.[32]

It was a bitter and ironic end to a distinguished and legendary political career. Fulbright's principled, determined opposition to the war during the height of Johnson's popularity in 1965 had earned him the respect and admiration of his constituents and an easy reelection in 1968. But when the war that Fulbright had helped initiate—and then ultimately terminate—was over, his constituents found little for which to thank him. To many, the conflict in Vietnam was history, Nixon a bad memory, and Fulbright a politician hopelessly out of touch with his state's interests. It was an ignominious and undeserving end to a remarkable political career.

IN SOUTH VIETNAM, meanwhile, Thieu's political position was barely stronger than Nixon's or Fulbright's. The drastic reduction in American military and economic assistance had taken its toll on Thieu's stature, as well as his regime's ability to withstand the encroaching communist forces. Public morale sagged to all-time lows, as public demonstrations against Thieu's autocratic and corrupt regime broke out in Saigon and quickly spread to other cities. Thieu reacted badly and in ways virtually guaranteed to bring about a swift end to his rule. In a repressive move reminiscent of Ngo Dinh Diem, Thieu shut down newspapers, fired hundreds of military officers, and outlawed public demonstrations. Nothing, however, could contain the unrest for long. Rising inflation combined with falling wages decimated South Vietnam's army. In 1974, alone, two hundred thousand men deserted.

By January 1975, the North Vietnamese had captured the province of Phuoc Long, 50 miles north of Saigon on the Cambodian border, including its provincial capital, Phuoc Binh. As March passed, the communists enjoyed control over thirteen provinces, most of them taken after South Vietnamese forces offered little or no defense. Thieu frantically adopted a last-minute enclave strategy, pulling back his country's forces to defend the Mekong Delta area around Saigon.

Ford, his options limited, was eager to help. On April 10, in a speech to Congress, he made an impassioned appeal for increased military assistance, asking members to appropriate $1 billion in military and economic assistance. Kissinger, now secretary of state, had urged Ford to "tell the American people that Congress was solely to blame for the debacle in Southeast Asia," a statement as breathtakingly absurd as it was reckless and demagogic. Ford wisely rejected the advice and opted instead to simply inform members of the dire circumstances facing South Vietnam—and hope for the best.

> The situation in South Vietnam and Cambodia has reached a critical phase requiring immediate and positive decisions by this government. The options before us are few, and the time is very short.
>
> Members of the Congress, my fellow Americans, this moment of tragedy for Indochina is a time of trial for us. It is a time for national resolve.
>
> It has been said that the United States is overextended, that we have too many commitments too far from home, that we must examine what our truly vital interests are and shape our strategy to conform to them. I find no fault with this as a theory, but . . . we cannot, in the meantime, abandon our friends while our adversaries support and encourage theirs. We cannot dismantle our defenses, our diplomacy or our intelligence capability while others increase and strengthen theirs. Let us put an end to self-inflicted wounds. Let us remember that national unity is a most priceless asset. Let us deny our adversaries the satisfaction of using Vietnam to pit Americans against Americans. At this moment the United States must present the world a united front.

At that point, two freshman Democratic House members—Toby Moffet of Connecticut and George Miller of California—demonstrated the degree of their opposition to Ford's request by rising and walking out of the chamber as he continued his speech. Ford knew that the odds for congressional approval were long, a fact confirmed on April 14 in a White House meeting with members of the Senate Foreign Relations Committee, now chaired by Democrat John Sparkman of Alabama. After a briefing by Kissinger and other administration officials, Ford invited the senators' comments. "The message," Ford recalled, "was clear: get out, fast." Javits told Ford that "I will give you large sums for evacuation [of refugees], but not one nickel for military aid." Church, however, had problems even assisting in an evacuation, fearing that it "could involve us in a very large war." Democrat Joseph Biden of Delaware agreed. "I will vote for any amount for getting Americans out," he said. "I don't want it mixed with getting the Vietnamese out."[33]

Reluctant to order a precipitous withdrawal of the remaining American personnel, for fear of creating a panic among the South Vietnamese, Ford resolved to wait and see. On April 17, Cambodia's capital of Phnom Penh fell to the invading Khmer Rouge, prompting Ford to order the evacuation of eighty-two Americans. In South Vietnam, meanwhile, Saigon was under attack. On April 20, under pressure from American officials, Thieu resigned and six days later fled the country for Thailand. The day before, the final battle for control of the capital had begun, with communist troops laying siege to the city. "I faced the fact," Ford finally acknowledged, "that the end was near." He finally ordered the evacuation of the six thousand American personnel still in Vietnam. In Saigon, pandemonium reigned, as thousands of South Vietnamese citizens flocked to the airport, hoping for a ride on departing U.S. military aircraft. Frantic refugees streamed onto the runway and prevented planes from landing. "The only option left," Ford explained, "was to remove the remaining Americans, and as many South Vietnamese as possible, by helicopter from the roof of the U.S. embassy in Saigon." With the helicopters standing by on the decks of navy ships off the coast, Ford finally ordered the commencement of the final, desperate evacuation in the early morning hours of April 29. For sixteen grueling hours, U.S. Navy helicopters ferried six thousand five hundred American and South Vietnamese citizens to safety.[34]

THE U.S. PHASE of the war was finally over. America's twenty-five-year effort to vanquish communism in Southeast Asia lay in ruins. For the first time in its 199-year history, the United States had lost a war. Less than a year before the country would begin its Bicentennial Celebration, American citizens were forced to consider, for the first time during the twentieth century, the limitations of their country's awesome power. "The high hope and wishful idealism with which the American nation had been born had not been destroyed," *Newsweek* astutely observed, "but they had been chastened by the failure of America to work its will in Indochina. Now, the world and the ability of the United States to influence it have changed. It was still far too soon to tell what the third century of America's independence would bring, but there was no question that it was dawning in a spirit of doubt and contrition."[35]

Conclusion

Five successive American presidents and scores of senators and congressmen had insisted that the preservation of a small, isolated Southeast Asian nation was vital to U.S. national security. During a period of twenty-five years, these leaders first funded the war fought by the French and then supported and sponsored a policy under which the fighting in Vietnam was eventually assumed by the U.S. military—to the point that it became, almost entirely, an American war.

America's involvement in Vietnam began, in 1950, as a political reaction to events elsewhere in Asia. While the communist victory in China in 1949 and the subsequent invasion of South Korea in 1950 had not directly threatened the United States, the political fallout from these events had tarnished President Harry Truman's presidency and elevated the importance of Southeast Asia to his administration. Siding with France in opposition to the "communist" Vietminh insurgency in Indochina was a proposition Truman could not afford to reject. Fighting communism in Indochina had been a tempting path out of the political jungle of recrimination and humiliation created by the foreign and domestic turmoil of the early days of the Cold War.

Thus Truman willingly, but out of apparent political necessity, made the first down payment on the tragedy that would become America's Vietnam War. Because he and his party had been painted soft on communism, especially communism in Asia, Democrats would vow never again to take lightly the communist threat in Asia. Because of Truman's painful experience, John F. Kennedy, Lyndon Johnson, and even Republican Richard Nixon, each entered the White House acutely aware of the potential political consequences of insufficient vigilance against encroaching communism in the region.

But the down payment that Truman made in Indochina was not his alone. As a president labeled by his partisan and unyielding political opponents as a communist sympathizer, Truman could hardly be singularly condemned for seizing the opportunity for atonement in Asia. His decision to assist the French in what they persuaded American officials was a noble effort to resist Chinese communist aggression in Indochina may have been naive and misguided, but it was hardly a tragic and irreversible mistake. Besides providing Truman and the Democrats with some measure of political inoculation against further charges of appeasement, Truman's decision to assist the French was prompted by a very legitimate desire to strengthen France's ability to resist Soviet communism in its European backyard.

Perhaps Truman's greatest shortcoming in Indochina was his inability to devote adequate attention to the region in the crucial months after World War II. Had the new president and his State Department responded to Ho Chi Minh's entreaties in the war's aftermath, the charismatic Vietnamese leader might never have turned so completely to China for help with his war of national independence against the oppressive French colonialists. But in the period when State Department officials were debating whether to side with the legitimate nationalistic passions of many in Indochina, a preoccupied Truman was absent from the debate. Eventually, he blindly heeded the counsel of American officials far more sympathetic to the desires of French leaders. Ho was snubbed and a potential ally was lost to the Chinese.

Dwight Eisenhower and John Foster Dulles were no less committed to vigilance against communism in Asia (although Eisenhower approved an armistice agreement that accepted the communist government of North Korea). But where Truman and Acheson had stressed their successful containment policy against Soviet and Chinese communism, especially in Europe, Eisenhower and Dulles promised a far more ambitious and aggressive strategy for liberating the "captive peoples" under communist domination. In Indochina, at least, the Republican president and his secretary of state never seemed to understand that the real captors in Indochina were the French colonialists who were determined to reestablish their former empire using American money, arms, and assistance. The foreign troops on Vietnamese soil were French.

That mattered little to Eisenhower and Dulles, who spoke boldly of liberating those enslaved by communism, but merely refined Truman's successful containment policy under the label of "New Look." What really occurred in Indochina during Eisenhower's tenure as president was a congressional-executive consensus on the need to assist the French in what was widely characterized as their valiant struggle against the Soviet-backed Chinese communist threat in Indochina. Persuaded by Eisenhower that preserving democracy in the region—if it ever really existed—was crucial to U.S. national security, members of Congress were more than willing to subsidize the lion's share of France's expenses. That was primarily because as long as France continued the fight, the United States could remain on the sidelines. That was good politics so soon after the end of the recent, unpopular war in Korea. Few, if any officials, ever bothered to explain the contradiction inherit in official pronouncements that while U.S. national security was at stake in Indochina, French troops, and not American soldiers, were expected to defend American interests.

When the French finally fled Indochina after the debacle at Dien Bien Phu, the United States assumed responsibility for financing and training the South Vietnamese. The real purpose of the American aid, however, was to build a bastion strong enough to withstand the communist tide that Eisenhower and Dulles believed threatened all of Southeast Asia. That endeavor, of course, required hundreds of millions of American dollars. But it also required the active support and willing participation of the leaders and citizens of South Vietnam—something that Eisenhower, Dulles, and almost everyone associated with the American-led enterprise recognized but were never able to obtain. American leaders, it seemed, always cared more about South Vietnam's "salvation" than the people they were saving.

Despite that major stumbling block, Eisenhower and Congress persisted. What kept the United States in Vietnam throughout the 1950s was the experience of just enough success—or, rather, the absence of abject failure—to suggest that real reforms and military advances might someday be possible. But the optimism was always excessive, the faith in the power of old-fashioned Yankee know-how usually naive, and the knowledge of Vietnam's culture and history woefully inadequate. But even had American officials come to their senses, the story might not have changed much. Eisenhower and Dulles believed that to abandon Vietnam meant a communist victory in Saigon and a Democratic takeover in Washington. Politically, Eisenhower could not afford to abandon Vietnam any more than Truman could have afforded to ignore it.

Except for dissuading Eisenhower from a military operation he had already rejected at Dien Bien Phu, leading members of Congress were either quiescent or ignorant about U.S. policy toward Indochina during much of the 1950s. When they found the voice to find fault, it was usually to complain, as did Kennedy, about the French or, as did Mansfield, that American support for Ngo Dinh Diem was insufficient. Because the conflict seemed under control and Diem appeared to be the leader that South Vietnam needed, few leaders in Congress bothered to notice the increasing Vietminh strength, as well as Diem's troubling lack of enthusiasm for political and economic reforms that might have deprived the communist fires of the oxygen they needed to survive. In the process, few noticed that the so-called democratic government in South Vietnam was nothing of the sort.

By 1960, Eisenhower and Dulles had done little to improve the situation in South Vietnam. But the massive influx of American dollars and

BALSAM LAKE PUBLIC LIBRARY
404 Main St. • P.O. Box 340
Balsam Lake, WI 54810

military equipment did buy Diem's regime time, meaning that John F. Kennedy inherited that nation's chronic problems when he became president in 1961. Kennedy had the misfortune to become president at a time when Eisenhower's status quo policy in Indochina had run its course.

But Kennedy was no innocent bystander. Just as wedded to the domino theory in Southeast Asia as his predecessors, the new president regarded Vietnam as vital to U.S. security and believed the conflict was a proxy war in which the Soviets were testing the American will to resist communism. Following the debacle at the Bay of Pigs and his disastrous summit with Khrushchev in Vienna, Kennedy—like Truman before him—found Indochina to be just the place to prove his commitment to the anticommunist struggle.

When the time came to decide whether to give up on Vietnam or pour in more American men and resources, it was Kennedy who willingly played the hand that Eisenhower and Dulles had dealt him. Those cards were being played less than twelve years after China had gone communist and Harry Truman was labeled a communist dupe for having "allowed" Mao Tse-tung's ascendancy. No matter how troubling and distasteful another Asian conflict might have been, Kennedy believed that he and his party could not withstand the political gales resulting from any decision that turned Diem into a Vietnamese Chiang kai-Shek. Kennedy's decision to send substantial numbers of military "advisors" was a monumental move that opened the door to the future escalation of the war during the Johnson years. Yet it was a decision made with too little thought about Vietnam's importance to U.S. national security and without a realistic assessment of the chances for success absent a democratic leader amenable to political and economic reforms. Furthermore, it was accomplished with little more than minor grumbling from compliant members of Congress who were still blissfully ignorant and uninformed about the stakes in Southeast Asia.

But it was Kennedy's fateful decision to put his administration on the side of the South Vietnamese military officers planning Diem's demise that virtually ensured that the Southeast Asian country would be enveloped in domestic strife, political corruption, and military lethargy for the remainder of the war. As bad as he was, Diem proved a more skillful leader than the parade of rouges, incompetents, and dictators who succeeded him. While historians will debate for years whether Kennedy, had he lived, would have escalated the war to the degree that Johnson did in 1965, it is clear that Kennedy, at the very least, left Johnson a Vietnam plagued by problems too daunting for any American army or nation-building enterprise. Even had he wanted to withdraw U.S. forces from Vietnam, Kennedy would have been unwilling—prior to the 1964 elections, at least—to invite the inevitable political firestorm from conservatives of both political parties.

Johnson, as a new president unsure of his political standing and facing an election in less than a year, would prove even more reticent to tamper with the Eisenhower–Kennedy policy in Vietnam. Advised by the very men Kennedy had hired and whose advice he had heeded, Johnson vowed to carry out Kennedy's policies, foreign and domestic. He had no interest in any fundamental reappraisal of the policy that had resulted in the murder of the popularly elected president of a nation the United States supported in its struggle against the Viet Cong. Even as he campaigned for election in his own right, pledging "no wider war," Congress eagerly gave him permission to widen the war as much as he liked. While the Gulf of Tonkin Resolution might not have given Johnson any powers he did not already possess, its near-unanimous passage ensured that he would never again feel the need to engage members of Congress in any meaningful or substantive consultation as he took the nation headlong into the "wider war" he had once decried.

Despite his mandate for reducing or maintaining the status quo in Vietnam, Johnson feared the political consequences of anything short of an outright victory over the Viet Cong—and also how a full-scale American war might erode support and funding for his domestic initiatives. Although he considered other options, the graduated, sustained bombing of North Vietnam seemed the only viable option in early 1965 after the Viet Cong had demonstrated alarming strength throughout South Vietnam beginning in the summer of 1964. But when the bombs failed to bring North Vietnam to the negotiating table, Johnson agonized before taking the fateful step of ordering massive numbers of ground troops. Like his predecessors, Johnson believed he was fighting against a Soviet-Chinese puppet regime in Hanoi. The degree to which the North Vietnamese and their Viet Cong allies were primarily concerned with the independence and unification of their nation was ignored. Instead, Johnson stressed his belief in the Munich analogy and said repeatedly that the U.S. presence in South Vietnam was aimed at preventing World War III.

It often seemed, however, that Johnson's motives were more personal. Besides his obvious intense personal dislike of Ho, whom he never met, Johnson believed that any diminution of the U.S. effort in Vietnam would violate the SEATO treaty and the commitments of three presidents, bringing upon him embarrassment and discredit. To "tuck tail and run," Johnson believed, would mean that he, and by extension his country, would stand accused of cowardice and mendacity.

But Johnson never fully informed the American people about the war being fought in their name. To share the real nature of the escalation and its expected costs with members of Congress and their constituents would have jeopardized his beloved Great Society. In any event, Johnson knew that some in Congress would loudly oppose the escalation that he and his national security advisors had in mind. Therefore, a policy grounded in the deceptions of the Gulf of Tonkin incidents was now expanded by deceiving members of Congress, for political reasons, about its cost as well as its very nature and extent. But once the real extent and cost of the war became known, many of the most skeptical members of Congress were generally supportive of Johnson. The United States, after all, seemed to be fighting communism in Asia in support of the democratic government of South Vietnam in adherence with the nation's solemn obligations and in support of America's continued stature among the community of nations.

Wrapped thusly in the American flag by Johnson and his congressional supporters, the administration's policies enjoyed widespread support. The vast majority of members of Congress—despite having been deceived about the Gulf of Tonkin incidents—enthusiastically gave Johnson carte blanche to fight the war on his terms. More tragic, however, were those like Mansfield, Fulbright, Nelson, and McGovern who subjugated their serious doubts about Johnson's policies during an election year and gave him their support and then, in the ensuing months, gave him their silence.

Even among the most highly skeptical members of Congress— McGovern, Church, and Mansfield—support for continued appropriations for Vietnam was strong. Indeed, support for "our boys in the field" would remain an article of faith in Congress for the remainder of the decade and would prove the most influential argument against withholding funds to force a troop withdrawal.

Withdrawal was never the only alternative to escalation. But calls for a negotiated settlement, which Johnson embraced rhetorically, were always spurned in practice. Johnson believed, and most certainly correctly, that any negotiated settlement would result in a communist-dominated South Vietnam. (Of course, after twenty-five years of war and millions of lost lives, including almost sixty thousand Americans, the result was no different.) But Johnson and his aides were transfixed on the evils of monolithic communism and the domino theory. They never entertained the idea, advanced by Fulbright and others, that the United States might have been able to peacefully coexist with a South Vietnamese communist regime that would have served as a buffer with Communist China, or at least one that would have been equally hostile to the United States and China. Encouraged by Rusk, McNamara, Bundy, and Rostow, Johnson equated a negotiated settlement with appeasement, recalling the perceived "lessons" of Munich that aggression unchecked is aggression unleashed. As long the Americans believed, as did the North Vietnamese, that more could be gained on the battlefield than at the negotiating table, a peaceful settlement was impossible.

Only when one or both sides realized the futility of continued war were negotiations conceivable. Johnson and Westmoreland, enamored of their war of attrition, always believed the next troop deployment would finally sap the Communists of their will to fight. While Westmoreland was correct in assuming that the conflict was one of attrition, he never seemed to understand that it was the Americans whose patience for fighting was limited. Meanwhile, those without patience—the Fulbrights, McGoverns, Mansfields, and the antiwar protesters—were also, in Johnson's estimation, lacking patriotism.

Johnson's problem, however, was not the incessant cries of his critics for negotiations, but rather his mistaken belief that the conflict in Vietnam could be won entirely on the battlefield. Vietnam was also a political conflict in which the hearts and minds of the people were at stake. No matter how much Johnson and the U.S. military wished it to be, more bombs and more troops could never force the political and economic changes necessary to persuade millions of South Vietnamese that their government in Saigon was worth fighting for. Persuaded that he and his country would be labeled cowards or appeasers if he refused to fight, Johnson sometimes doubted that the application of military force was sufficient but he never seriously—until 1968—considered deescalation or engaging the North Vietnamese in peace talks.

Although he agonized over the 1965 decisions to begin the bombing campaign and to drastically increase the number of ground troops in South Vietnam, Johnson—having achieved a popular mandate for a more limited American role in Vietnam—allowed himself to become captive to his fear of the partisan political ghosts of the early 1950s. His errors were compounded by the ways he and his advisors deceived the public and Congress about the administration's policy and then ignored or spurned the cautionary advice of Ball, Mansfield, Fulbright, Church, McGovern, and others. Instead of listening and learning from men like Mansfield and Ball, Johnson merely humored them. To his detriment, Johnson also mishandled his detractors in Congress—particularly Robert Kennedy and Fulbright—and forced them to fight him and his war with even more passion and intensity.

But the failed policy in Vietnam was not Johnson's alone. While many members of Congress can be faulted for abdicating their constitutional responsibilities regarding Vietnam, Mansfield, Fulbright, and Richard Russell deserve special mention. Even when it became obvious that Johnson could not achieve his objectives in Vietnam, Mansfield and Russell were loyal soldiers. While possessing enough power and influence to force Johnson to alter course, their perverse, singular sense of loyalty to Johnson prevented them from speaking out in ways that might have saved thousands of lives. At a time when the Senate might have benefited from the passion and initiative of a strong leader, Mansfield and Fulbright were absent, handicapped by their tragic unwillingness to assume the legitimate leadership roles their positions demanded. Yet it is not clear that such leadership would have made a difference. Even the more vociferous opponents of the war proved ineffective because of their fundamental reluctance to coalesce behind any leader, as well as their inability to agree on a single coherent plan to end the war.

Few members of Congress, Morse and Gruening excepted, could ever claim to have clean hands regarding Vietnam. From almost the beginning of the war to its end, the story of Congress was one of a tragic abdication of power and responsibility. While some would later claim the war in Vietnam was mostly a political conflict, hampered by the meddling of politicians who tied the hands of the military commanders in the field, the truth was that Congress meddled in Vietnam almost not at all, and certainly not before 1966 and not substantially until 1969. It was not until 1975, after the war was virtually over, that members of Congress finally mustered the "courage" to withhold funding for the conflict.

Only when Richard Nixon took office did Mansfield begin to lose his reluctance to challenge the commander in chief over Vietnam. By then it was too late. The issue in 1969 was not whether to end the war, but how and how soon. Like Johnson, the American people gave Nixon a mandate to end the fighting. Like Johnson, Nixon—slavishly loyal to Thieu, his perceived political benefactor—squandered it in favor of a deceitful, excruciatingly slow, and deadly withdrawal strategy in pursuit of an illusive "honorable peace." To Nixon and Kissinger, that meant withdrawing U.S. troops slowly enough to leave all parties dissatisfied but not outraged. Nixon did not quite achieve that objective, but Vietnamization, along with his dissolution of the draft, did disarm his critics and allow him to continually claim, even as he escalated and widened the fighting, that the incremental troop withdrawals were proof that the war was all but over.

Nixon refused to stop the fighting for many of the same reasons as Johnson. Like the four presidents before him, the Republican president believed he could not withstand the partisan attacks after a precipitate withdrawal. But by 1969, Nixon knew what Johnson, in 1965, did not: a military victory in Vietnam was impossible short of a massive, overwhelming application of U.S. firepower. That, Nixon knew, would have been political suicide and still would not guarantee a U.S. victory. Nixon, therefore, attempted to split the difference by escalating the bombing in hopes of driving the North Vietnamese to the bargaining table, while he simultaneously deescalated the ground war with his gradual troop withdrawals.

Like a gunslinger in a Western movie, Nixon shot his way out, escaping the barroom brawl while he walked backwards toward the door with guns blazing. It was a retreat disguised as an offensive. The ruse worked. By 1972, most Americans assumed the war was over and that Vietnamization had been marginally successful. Nixon won another term in a landslide over McGovern, the war's most visible and vociferous opponent. But Nixon had not won the war, or the honorable peace that he had promised. He had merely delayed the day of the communist victory, with deadly and disastrous consequences.

THE VIETNAM WAR was America's longest armed conflict, a tragic crusade that cost millions of lives and ruined millions more. The war dispelled the widespread and erroneous belief that, in its foreign and military policies, the United States had always exhibited the purest of motives and actions. This, of course, had never been the case, particularly in the twentieth century. From Truman to Nixon, the decisions about Vietnam were almost always made by presidents and other political leaders seeking to preserve or enhance their domestic or international political standings.

While these presidents talked of preserving democratic institutions in Southeast Asia, the massive influx of American manpower and military might in the 1960s actually undermined the ideal of a free and independent South Vietnam and transformed the nation into a client of the United States. By the time the war ended, the region that America had sought to protect from communism was, instead, ruled by it.

At home, the United States became, in some ways, a stronger nation because of its tragic experience in Vietnam. Organized public dissent became a widely accepted and effective way of influencing public policy. The American people and the news media exhibited a more healthy distrust of government officials and their public pronouncements. These and other positive changes, however, came at a horrible cost. In the name of fighting for freedom in Vietnam, the political and military leadership of the United States inflicted untold damage on a proud nation and its people.

Whatever good may have come from the war, and no matter how honorable and brave the soldiers on both sides, the Vietnam War should be remembered as the kind of tragedy that can result when presidents—captivated by grand delusions—enforce their foreign and military policies without the informed support of Congress and the American people.

Notes

AFPC	American Foreign Policy Center, Louisiana Tech University
CQA	*Congressional Quarterly Almanac*
CR	*Congressional Record*
CRS	Congressional Research Service (William C. Gibbons Vietnam project)
CUOHC	Columbia University Oral History Collection
ExSess SFRC	Executive Sessions of the Senate Foreign Relations Committee
FMOC	Former Members of Congress Oral History Project, Library of Congress
FRUS	*Foreign Relations of the United States*
HGDOHP	Helen G. Douglas Oral History Project, University of California, Berkeley
JFKL	John F. Kennedy Library
JFDOHP	John Foster Dulles Oral History Project, Seeley G. Mudd Manuscript Library, Princeton University
LBJL	Lyndon B. Johnson Library
NARA	National Archives and Records Administration, Washington, D.C.
NARA-LN	National Archives and Records Administration, Laguna Nigel, CA
NARA-CP	National Archives and Records Administration, College Park, MD
NYT	*New York Times*
NYTM	*New York Times Magazine*
NPMP	Nixon Presidential Materials Project, National Archives and Records Administration, College Park, MD
PP, GE	*Pentagon Papers*, Gravel Edition
RBRL	Richard B. Russell Library, University of Georgia
SGM	Seeley G. Mudd Manuscript Library, Princeton University
USGPO	U.S. Government Printing Office
USSHO	U.S. Senate Historical Office
WP	Washington Post.

PROLOGUE

1. David F. Schmitz and Natalie Fousekis, "Frank Church, the Senate, and the Emergence of Dissent on the Vietnam War," *Pacific Historical Review*, November 1994.

2. Bundy to LBJ, 2/7/65, Barrett, *Lyndon B. Johnson's Vietnam Papers*, 108.

3. *CR*, 1/12/65, 540.

4. *CQA*, 1965, 451.

5. *NYTM*, 2/14/65.

6. *CR*, 2/17/65, 2869–72.

7. Ibid., 2878–79.

8. McGovern, 104.

9. Schmitz and Fousekis.

10. McGovern, by Mann, 9/10/97.

11. Ibid.; Ashby and Gramer, 193–94; Schmitz and Fousekis.

12. *CR*, 2/18/65, 3146–47.

13. Ibid., 3/26/64, 6438.

14. Ibid., 3/26/64, 6438–41.

15. Dallek, *Lone Star Rising*, 197.

16. Church OH, LBJL, 5/1/69.

17. Ibid.; Ashby and Gramer, 194–96.

18. Nelson, by Mann.

19. Ashby and Gramer, 196; Bethine Church, by Mann.

20. Raskin and Fall, 31–37.

21. Langer and Gleason, 13.

22. Ibid., 144, 146; McKenna, 237–241, 345–368; Maddox, 215–247.

23. Patterson, *Mr. Republican*, 243, 247.

24. Ibid., 288–90.

25. *Time*, 1/22/65.

26. *CR*, 3/26/64, 6441.

27. *CQA*, 1965, 451.

28. *Time*, 1/22/65.

CHAPTER ONE

1. Hamby, 551; WP, 11/8/50; NYT, 11/8/50; Donovan, 297–98.

2. *Chicago Daily News*, 11/8/50.

3. *Newsweek*, 11/20/50.

4. Nixon speech, 9/18/50, PPS 208(1950).24, Nixon Library.

5. *Newsweek*, 11/20/50.

6. Burns, 232.

7. Patterson, *Grand Expectations*, 128; *PP, GE*, 1:34–35; Cooper, 13.

8. *CR*, 1/20/50, 673; *U.S. News & World Report*, 1/20/50.

9. Bernstein and Matusow, 344.

10. *Time*, 8/15/49.

11. *CR*, 1/5/50, 85.

12. George Reedy, by Mann, 6/11/97; Wilcox OH, USSHO.

13. *CR*, 1/5/50, 85–89.

14. Ibid., 1/11/50, 298.

15. Reeves, *The Life and Times of Joe McCarthy*, 218; CR, 1/25/50, 904.

16. For an excellent discussion of how China became enmeshed in American politics, see Parmet, *Richard Nixon and His America*, 200–213.

17. *U.S. News & World Report*, 2/24/50.

18. *New Republic*, 1/16/50.

19. *Boston Post*, 1/13/50, For more about Harry Truman's China policy, see Purifoy; Hamby, 509–33; Truman, 80–114.

20. *CR*, 1/25/50, 902, 904.

21. Patterson, *Grand Expectations*, 202.

22. Holt OH, USSHO, 9/29/80.

23. Hamby, 529.

CHAPTER TWO

1. Reeves, *The Life and Times of Joe McCarthy*, 224, 227–28.

2. Griffith, 11; Ambrose, *Nixon: The Eduction*, 129.

3. Dugger, 314, 320.

4. Harper, 76–78; Dugger, 349.

5. Rovere, 11.

6. Truman to Acheson, 3/31/50, HST's Office Files, 1945–53, part 2, Correspondence Files, AFPC.

7. *CR*, 5/19/50, A3786–89.

8. Keith, 67.

9. *CR*, 4/25/50, 5698–99.

10. Ibid., 2/14/50, A1041–43.

11. *Time*, 4/3/50.

12. Ibid.; Patterson, *Mr. Republican*, 446.

13. Griffith, 75.

14. Patterson, *Mr. Republican*, 446.

15. Reeves, *The Life and Times of Joe McCarthy*, 297–98, For more about Joseph McCarthy, see Griffith; Rovere; and Keith.

16. Theoharis, *Seeds of Repression*, 205.

17. Hamby, 488–505.

18. "NSC 68: United States Objectives and Programs for National Security," 4/7/50:

19. http://www.seattleu.edu/artsci/departments/history/us1945/docs/nsc68–1.htm.

20. Patterson, *Grand Expectations*, 176.

21. Ibid., 176–78; McCollough, 772–73.

CHAPTER THREE

1. Hamby, 538.

2. Ferrell, *Harry S. Truman*, 124.

3. *CR*, 1/20/50, 672–76; *Time*, 1/23/50.

4. *Newsweek,* 7/10/50.

5. Patterson, *Mr. Republican,* 452.

6. *Newsweek,* 7/10/50.

7. Patterson, *Mr. Republican,* 453.

8. *Time,* 8/28/50.

9. *NYT,* 8/13/50.

10. *Time,* 8/28/50.

11. Ibid., 8/21/50.

12. *CR,* 8/14/50, 12418–19.

13. Ibid., 8/16/50, 12590–91.

14. *Time,* 8/28/50.

15. *Newsweek,* 8/28/50.

16. *NYT,* 9/16/50.

17. *Time,* 9/25/50.

18. *CR,* 9/15/50, 14915.

19. Ibid., 14913–17.

20. Ibid., 14917–26; Miller, *Plain Speaking,* 238; *NYT,* 9/16/50; Pogue, 427–28; *CR,* 14917–18; *Time,* 9/25/50.

21. Griffith, 117.

22. *CQA,* 1950, 390–98; Donovan, 295–96.

23. *CR Appendix,* 1950, A6899.

24. *Chicago Daily News,* 11/2/50.

25. *Time,* 10/9/50, 23.

26. Ambrose, *Nixon: The Education,* 211.

27. Aitken, 188–89.

28. Meyers OH, 3/23/78, HGDOHP.

29. Aitken, 188–89.

30. Morris, 542.

31. Ambrose, *Nixon: The Education,* 213.

32. *WP,* 9/20/50.

33. *Newsweek,* 11/6/50, 20.

CHAPTER FOUR

1. White, *The Taft Story,* 173, 103.

2. Patterson, *Mr. Republican,* 472.

3. *Time,* 1/1/51.

4. White, *The Taft Story,* 160.

5. *Time,* 1/15/51.

6. Qtd. by Arthur M. Schlesinger Jr., "The New Isolationism," *The Atlantic Monthly,* 5/52.

7. Tucker, *A New Isolationism,* 29.

8. Acheson, *Present at the Creation,* 517.

9. Truman, 437.

10. Acheson, 518.

11. McCullough, 836.

12. Spanier, 161.

13. *Newsweeek*, 4/16/51.

14. Acheson, 520.

15. Truman, 506.

16. Ferrell, *Harry S. Truman*, 334.

17. Manchester, 781.

18. *CR*, 4/11/51, 3618–19.

19. Ibid., 3623.

20. Ibid., 3640.

21. Ibid., 3655.

22. Ibid., 3649.

23. White, *The Taft Story*, 167.

24. *Time*, 4/30/51.

25. Patterson, *Mr. Republican*, 491.

26. *Time*, 5/14/51.

27. Manchester, 799.

CHAPTER FIVE

1. Deane to HST, 10/19/49, HST's Office Files, 1945–53, part 3, Subject Files, AFPC.

2. Hatfield, 153–54.

3. Gibbons, 1:19–21.

4. Ibid.

5. Anderson, *Shadow on the White House*, 24.

6. Gettleman, 57–59.

7. Lacouture, 271.

8. *PP*, GE, 1:4–5.

9. Schulzinger, 33.

10. *PP*, GE, 1:14; Gardner, *Approaching Vietnam*, 65–66; Hess, 174–75.

11. Hess, 175.

12. Patti, 51; Lacouture, 266–73.

13. Lacouture, 266–73; Patti, 51.

14. *PP*, GE, 1:54.

15. Tucker, 45–47.

16. *FRUS*, 1947, 6:54–55

17. Gibbons, 1:26.

18. *FRUS*, 1947, 6:120–22.

19. Ibid., 6:122.

20. Gibbons, 1:26.

21. *FRUS*, 1948, 6:45.

22. Ibid., 1950, 6:713, 746; Schulzinger, 37–38.

23. *FRUS*, 1949, 7:67.

24. *New Republic*, 2/13/50.

25. Memorandum of Conversation, Acheson and Bonnet, 3/13/50, U.S. State Department Papers, Microfiche Collection, Louisiana State University Library.

26. Karnow, 190.

27. *FRUS*, 1950, 6:713.

28. *NYT*, 1/20/50.

29. *U.S. News*, 2/24/50.

30. *PP*, GE, 1:37–38.

31. *NYT*, 1/20 and 1/31/50.

32. *FRUS*, 1950, 6:711.

33. Ibid., 6:708.

34. Ibid., 6:714.

35. Ibid., 6:744–47.

36. PP, GE, 1:66.

37. Ibid., 1:55.

38. Truman, 269.

39. *PP*, GE, 1:370–72.

40. *CQA*, 1950, 204–5.

41. Ibid., 215.

42. Gibbons, 1:70.

43. *Time*, 5/27/50, 27.

44. Fall, *The Two Vietnams*, 219.

CHAPTER SIX

1. JFK speech text, 11/14/51, Pre-presidential Papers, Box 102, JFKL.

2. JFK speech text, 11/19/51, Pre-presidential Papers, Box 102, JFKL.

3. Lasky, 99–100.

4. Reeves, *The Life and Times of Joe McCarthy*, 442–43; Griffith, 211.

5. Rusk, 75–83; Karnow, 179.

6. Khong, 175.

7. *Hearings Before the Committee on Foreign Relations and the Committee on Armed Services*, United States Senate, 82nd Congress, 1st Sess., On S. 1762, Mutual Security Act of 1951, USGPO, 1951, 532–33.

8. *CR*, 8/30/51, 10840.

9. Ibid., 8/29/51, 10756.

10. Gibbons, 1:80–81.

11. *FRUS*, 1951, 6:492.

12. Ibid., 6:506–08.

13. *NYT*, 9/21/51.

14. *PP*, GE, 1:67–68.

15. Shaplen, 84.

16. Rusk, 422.

17. *PP*, GE, 1:79.

18. *Hearings Before the Committee on Foreign Relations and the Committee on Armed Services*, United States Senate, 82nd Congress, 1st Sess., On S. 1762, Mutual Security Act of 1951, USGPO, 1951, 537–38.

19. Sorenson, 41.

20. Schlesinger, *Robert Kennedy and His Times*, 92.

21. Schlesinger, *A Thousand Days*, 320–21; *PP*, GE, 1:72.

22. Upon returning to the United States in late 1951, Robert Blum—who directed the U.S. economic aid program in Vietnam and was Gullion's ally in pressing for a larger U.S. role—offered his frank and bleak assessment of the French effort. The situation, he concluded, "is not satisfactory and shows no substantial prospect of improving, . . . no decisive military victory can be achieved, . . . the Bao Dai government gives little promise of developing competence and winning the loyalty of the population, . . . French policy is uncertain and often ill-advised, and . . . the attainment of American objectives is remote (*PP*, GE, 1:73).

23. Schlesinger, *A Thousand Days*, 320–21.

24. Schlesinger, *Robert Kennedy and His Times*, 92.

25. Ibid., 93.

26. JFK radio speech text, 11/14/51, Pre-Presidential Papers, Box 102, JFKL.

27. JFK speech text, 11/19/51, Pre-Presidential Papers, Box 102, JFKL.

28. *CR*, 4/9/51, 3524.

29. Ibid., 12/22/50, 17000.

30. *Hearings Before the Committee on Foreign Relations and the Committee on Armed Services*, United States Senate, 82nd Congress, 1st Sess., On S. 1762, Mutual Security Act of 1951, USGPO, 1951, 540.

31. *ExSess SFRC, Historical Series*, vol. IV, 82nd Congress, 2nd Sess., 1952, 150–51.

32. Ibid., 178.

CHAPTER SEVEN

1. Ferrell, *The Eisenhower Diaries*, 190.

2. Fall, *The Two Vietnams*, 108–11.

3. *FRUS*, 1952–54, 13:57.

4. Ibid., 13:81.

5. Eden, 83–84; *FRUS*, 1952–54, 13:158–61; Shaplen, 84–85; Acheson, 676.

6. Eden, 83–84.

7. Ibid., 84; Herring, *America's Longest War*, 18, 20; Arnold, 79–80.

8. *PP*, GE, 1:375.

9. *FRUS*, 1952–54, 13:22–24.

10. Patti, 410–11.

11. Herring, *America's Longest War*, 18; *FRUS*, 1952–54, 13:57.

12. *ExSess SFRC*, 1952, 30.

13. *NYT*, 6/27/52.

14. *Life*, 5/19/52.

15. Ibid.

16. *CQA*, 1952, 490.

17. Ibid. 490–91.

18. Manchester, 780.

19. *Time*, 11/3/52.

20. Morris, 748.

21. Parmet, *Richard Nixon and His America*, 228; Republican National Committee research memo, 12/2/52, PPS 205.2987, Nixon Library.

22. *Time*, 9/15/52

23. Parmet, *Eisenhower and the American Crusades*, 145.
24. Ibid., 141.
25. *Time*, 11/3/52.
26. Parmet, *Eisenhower and the American Crusades*, 145.
27. McCullough, 914.
28. Rusk OH, Tape T, RBRL.
29. Arnold, 61.

CHAPTER EIGHT

1. Urofsky, 304.
2. Douglas, 9–10.
3. Ibid., 201–2.
4. Baldwin, 13–15.
5. *CR*, 1/16/45, 277–83.
6. Olson, 13–16; Mansfield radio speech transcript, 11/3/52, Series XIX, Box 593, Mansfield Papers.
7. Douglas, 180–81.
8. *FRUS*, 1952–54, 13:553–54.
9. Mansfield interview with BBC, 12/13/76, Oral History Project, Mansfield Papers.
10. Mansfield, "Reprieve in Viet Nam," *Harper's Magazine*, 1/56.
11. JFK to Dulles, 5/7/53 and State Department letter of reply, Pre-Presidential Files, General, Box 488, JFKL.
12. Memoranda of 4/17/53 and 4/22/53, Pre-Presidential Files, General, Box 481, JFKL.
13. Gibbons, 1:52.
14. *FRUS*, 1952–54, 13:551–52.
15. Ibid., 13:368.
16. *ExSess SFRC*, 1953, 9.
17. *FRUS*, 1952–54, 13:429–32; Eisenhower, 167–68.
18. *FRUS*, 1952–54, 13:517–18
19. Ibid., 13:426–28.
20. Ambrose, *Eisenhower*, 179–80.
21. Eisenhower, 169.
22. *FRUS*, 1952–54, 13:542.
23. Ibid., 13:547–48.
24. Ibid., 13:550.
25. Radford, 362.
26. *FRUS*, 1952–54, 13:649–50.
27. Ibid., 13:780–83.
28. *CR*, 7/1/53, 7779–89.
29. Ibid., 6/30/53, 7622–25.
30. Ibid., 7/1/53, 7784, 7789.
31. *FRUS*, 1952–54, 13:714–17.
32. Morton, CRS interview; FRUS, 1952–54, 13:806–07.

33. *FRUS*, 1952–54, 13:811–12.

34. Ibid., 13:747.

35. Fall, *The Two Viet-Nams*, 225.

36. *CQA*, 1952, 491.

37. *PP*, I, 412–29; Hoopes, *The Devil and John Foster Dulles*, 194–201.

CHAPTER NINE

1. *U.S. News*, 9/25/53.

2. *Time*, 9/28/53.

3. *CQA*, 1953, 218–19.

4. Foreign Service Dispatch, 9/16/53, Knowland press conference of 9/15/53, Nixon Pre-Presidential Papers, 1952 Far East Trip, Series 364, Box 3, NARA-LN.

5. *Time*, 6/29/53.

6. Valeo OH, USSHO, 85–96.

7. *Indochina: Report of Senator Mike Mansfield on a Study Mission to the Associated States of Indochina*, 10/27/53, Printed for the U.S. Senate Foreign Relations Committee, Washington: USGPO, 1953.

8. Nixon, *RN*, 119.

9. Nixon memo, 10/18/53, Nixon Pre-Presidential Papers, 1953 Far Eastern Trip , Series 378, Box 1, NARA-LN.

10. Nixon, *RN*, 122; Foreign Service Dispatch, No. 181, from Heath, "Conversations of Vice President Nixon with Bao Dai," 11/2/53, Nixon Pre-Presidential Papers, 1953 Far Eastern Trip, Series 366, Box 2, NARA-LN.

11. Gibbons, 1:142; Foreign Service Dispatch, No. 181, 11/2/53, from Heath, "Conversations of Vice President Nixon with Bao Dai," and Nixon Toast of Bao Dai, Nixon Pre-Presidential Papers, 1953 Far Eastern Trip, Series 366, Box 2, NARA-LN; Nixon, *RN*, 122.

12. Nixon, *RN*, 123.

13. Nixon dinner speech at Hanoi, 10/3/53, Nixon Pre-Presidential Papers, 1953 Far Eastern Trip, Series 366, Box 2, NARA-LN.

14. Nixon, *RN*, 124–25; Nixon speech at Hanoi, 11/4/53, Nixon Pre-Presidential Papers, 1953 Far Eastern Trip, Series 366, Box 2, NARA-LN.

15. Nixon, *RN*, 125–26.

16. *FRUS*, 1952–54, 13:929–31.

17. *State Department Bulletin*, 1/4/54.

18. McCormick, 48.

CHAPTER TEN

1. Arnold, 143.

2. *ExSess SFRC*, 1954, 113, 123, 127

3. Ibid., 136–37, 169–70.

4. Ibid., 6:142.

5. Fall, *Hell in a Very Small Place*, viii.

6. *Time*, 3/29/54.

7. Gardner, *Approaching Vietnam*, 153–54.

8. *FRUS*, 1952–54, 13:937.

9. Gardner, *Approaching Vietnam*, 166.

10. *FRUS*, 1952–54, 13:947–52.

11. Ibid., 13:961–64.

12. Ibid., 13:1002–4.

13. *Time*, 2/15/54.

14. *FRUS*, 1952, 13:1023–24; Diaries of DDE, 1953–61, AFPC.

15. *NYT*, 2/11/54.

16. *CR*, 2/8/54, 1504.

17. Ibid., 2/9/54, 1550–52.

18. *FRUS*, 1952–54, 13:1034–35.

19. Mansfield to Thomas Delaney, 2/25/54, Series XIX, Box 515, Mansfield Papers.

20. *NYT*, 2/11/54.

21. *Time*, 5/3/54.

22. Billings-Yun, 36.

23. *FRUS*, 1952–54, 13:1141.

24. Billings-Yun, 48–50.

25. *FRUS*, 1952–54, 1163–68; *PP*, GE, 1:459–60.

26. Hoopes, *The Devil and John Foster Dulles*, 209; *FRUS*, 1952–54, 13:1150.

27. *FRUS*, 1952–54, 13:1163.

28. Nixon, *RN*, 151.

29. Dulles speech text, Overseas Press Club of America, 3/29/54, Dulles Papers; *NYT*, 3/25/54.

30. Billings-Yun, 65.

31. *CR*, 4/14/54, 5112.

32. *NYT*, 4/5/54.

33. White, *Citadel*, 129.

34. *CR*, 3/31/54, 4207–12.

35. *CQA*, 1954, 254–55.

36. Gibbons, 1:181.

37. *FRUS*, 1952–54, 13:1200–2.

38. Ibid., 13:1211–12.

39. Gibbons, 1:184.

40. *FRUS*, 1952–54, 13:1210–11.

CHAPTER ELEVEN

1. Chalmers M. Roberts, "The Day We Didn't Go to War," *The Reporter*, 9/15/54.

2. *FRUS* , 1952–54, 13:1210–11.

3. Roberts, "The Day We Didn't Go to War," *The Reporter*, 9/15/54; *FRUS*, 1952–54, 13:1224–25.

4. Roberts, "The Day We Didn't Go to War," *The Reporter*, 9/15/54; Knowland OH, CUOHP; *FRUS*, 1952–54, 13:1224–25.

5. Fite, 358–59.

6. *FRUS*, 1952–54, 13:1224–25.

7. Ibid., 13:1224–25.

8. Billings-Yun, 92.

9. Roberts, "The Day We Didn't Go to War," *The Reporter*, 9/15/54.

10. *FRUS*, 1952–54, 13:1230.

11. Adams, 122.

12. *FRUS*, 1952–54, 13:1236–37.

13. Ibid., 13:1241–42.

14. Ibid., 13:1238–40.

15. Ibid., 13:1238, 2fn.

16. Ibid., 13:1250–65.

17. Nixon, *RN*, 151.

18. *FRUS*, 1952–54, 13:1250–65.

19. *CR*, 4/6/54, 4671–77.

20. Gibbons, 1:206–07.

21. *FRUS*, 1952–54, 13:1280–81.

22. *NYT*, 4/8/54.

23. *CR*, 4/14/54, 5111–20.

24. *FRUS*, 1952–54, 13:1328–34.

25. Billings-Yun, 123–30; Hoopes, *The Devil and John Foster Dulles*, 213–16.

26. *NYT*, 4/20/54.

27. *U.S. News*, 4/30/54; Transcript of *RN* remarks, PPS 208 (1954), uncatalogued, Nixon Library.

28. *New York Herald Tribune*, 4/17/54.

29. *NYT*, 4/18/54; Parmet, *Richard Nixon and His America*, 319.

30. *CR*, 4/19/54, 5281.

31. *NYT*, 4/15 and 4/18/54.

32. *CR*, 4/19/54, 5289–94.

33. *NYT*, 4/20/54.

34. *CR*, 4/19/54, 5290.

35. *WP*, 4/20/54.

36. *New York Herald Tribune and NYT*, 4/18/54.

37. Parmet, *Richard Nixon and His America*, 318.

38. *WP*, 4/20/54.

39. "Telephone Conversation with Vice President Nixon," 4/19/54, Dulles Papers.

40. *FRUS*, 1952–54, 13:1347.

41. Billings-Yun, 132.

42. *FRUS*, 1952–54, 13:1258, 1263.

43. *NYT*, 4/20/54.

44. Ambrose, *Eisenhower: The President*, 184.

45. Billings-Yun, 120.

46. Nixon, *RN*, 154.
47. Billings-Yun, 130–35.
48. *CQA*, 1952, 491.
49. Anderson, *Trapped by Success*, 42.
50. Dulles to Bidault, 4/24/54, Dulles Papers.
51. *NYT*, 4/25/54.
52. Cooper, 78.
53. *FRUS*, 1952–54, 13:1410–12.
54. Nixon, *RN*, 153.
55. *FRUS*, 1952–54, 13:1410–12.

CHAPTER TWELVE

1. *Indochina: Report of Senator Mike Mansfield*, 10/27/53, iii, U.S. Government Printing Office; Mansfield interview, "Man of the Week," 4/25/54, CBS, Series XIX, Box 593, Mansfield Papers.
2. *FRUS*, 1952–54, 13:1431–45.
3. Ibid., 13:1437–38.
4. Ibid., 13:1466–70.
5. Cooper, 79.
6. Hoopes, *The Devil and John Foster Dulles*, 227.
7. Gibbons, 1:224.
8. SFRC *Historical Series*, vol. VI, 257–81.
9. *FRUS*, 1952–54, 13:1538–40.
10. *NYTM*, 5/16/54.
11. Hoopes, *The Devil and John Foster Dulles*, 228.
12. SFRC hearings on Mutual Security Act of 1954, 83rd Congress, 2nd Sess., 6/4–22/54, 210.
13. Hoopes, *The Devil and John Foster Dulles*, 229.
14. Ibid., 230.
15. SFRC hearings on Mutual Security Act of 1954, 83rd Congress, 2nd Sess., 6/4–22/54, 228–29.
16. Karnow, 236–37; Gibbons, 1:259–60.
17. Gibbons, 1:234.
18. Hoopes, *The Devil and John Foster Dulles*, 222.
19. Gibbons, 1:252–53.
20. *CR*, 7/8/54, 9997–10004.
21. Gibbons, 1:253–54.
22. Kutler, *Encyclopedia of the Vietnam War*, 206–8.
23. *NYT*, 7/21/54.
24. Dulles statement of 7/23/54, Dulles Papers.
25. *Time*, 8/2/54.
26. *NYT*, 7/22/54.
27. *CR*, 7/21 and 22/54, 11302, 11316, 11486–87.
28. Dulles statement of 7/23/54, Dulles Papers.
29. *CR*, 7/8/54, 10007.

30. *FRUS*, 1952–54, 13:1869.

31. Gibbons, 1:267–69; *PP*, GE,1:204.

32. *FRUS*, 1952–54, 13:1869.

33. *NYT*, 7/26/54.

CHAPTER THIRTEEN

1. JFK speech to The Executives Club, 5/28/54, Pre-Presidential Papers, Senate Files, Legislation, Box 647, JFKL.

2. *FRUS*, 1952–54, 13:1977–78.

3. Fall, *The Two Vietnams*, 236–37.

4. Arnold, 232–33; Herring, *America's Longest War*, 50–52.

5. *FRUS*, 1952–54, 13:1783–84.

6. Ibid., 13:1990–91.

7. "The Leading Question," CBS Radio, 5/16/54, Series XIII, Container 7, Mansfield Papers.

8. Mansfield's notes of meetings, 8/28 and 8/30/54, Series XXII, Container 95, Mansfield Papers.

9. *Viet Nam, Cambodia and Laos, Report by Senator Mike Mansfield*, 10/6/55, SFRC.

10. Mansfield meeting notes, 9/2/54, Series XXII, Container 95, Mansfield Papers.

11. *FRUS*, 1952–54, 13:2001–2.

12. Valeo OH, 7/3/85,103, USSHO.

13. Hanes OH, JFDOHP.

14. *FRUS*, 1952–54, 13:2007–12.

15. Ibid., 13:2012–13.

16. Meeting notes, 9/10/54, Series XXII, Container 95, Mansfield Papers.

17. Olson, 38.

18. Mansfield message of 9/24/54, Series XXII, Container 95, Mansfield Papers; also found in *FRUS*, 1952–54, 13:2055–56.

19. Olson, 39.

20. *FRUS*, 1952–54, 13:2069.

21. Olson, 39.

22. *PP*, GE, 1:222–23.

23. *Report on Indochina: Report of Senator Mike Mansfield on a Study Mission to Vietnam, Cambodia, Laos*, 10/15/54, Committee Print, SFRC.

24. Olson, 42.

25. *FRUS*, 1952–54, 13:2141–42.

26. Ibid., 13:2142ff., 2378–79.

27. Ibid., 13:2166–67; *NYT*, 10/25/54; Cooper, 134–35.

28. Hearing on Southeast Asia Collective Defense Treaty, SFRC, 1/19/54, part 2, 43.

29. *ExSess SFRC*, 1/13/55, 7:57.

30. *CQA*, 1955, 281.

31. *FRUS*, 1952–54, 13:2153–57.

32. Herring, *America's Longest War,* 49.

33. *FRUS,* 1952–54, 13:2205–7; *NYT,* 11/4/54.

34. Collins, Dulles JFDOHP; Transcript, *Vietnam: A Television History,* "America's Mandarin (1954–1963)," Public Broadcasting System: http://www.pbs.org/wgbh/amex/vietnam/103ts.html.

35. *FRUS,* 1952, 13:2341–44.

36. Ibid., 13:2350–52.

37. Ibid., 13:2379.

38. Ibid., 13:2393–94.

39. Ibid., 13:2362–65.

40. Ibid., 1:55; Herring, *America's Longest War,* 52.

41. *FRUS,* 1952, 1:66.

42. Ibid., 1:102.

43. Ibid., 1:162; Herring, *America's Longest War,* 52; Cooper, 138–40.

44. *FRUS,* 1955–57, 1:169.

45. Ibid., 1:175–76.

46. Ibid., 1:177.

47. Ibid., 1:219.

48. Ibid., 1:221–22.

49. Ibid., 1:229–31.

50. Ibid., 1:234.

51. Ibid., 1:239–41.

CHAPTER FOURTEEN

1. *FRUS,* 1955–57, 1:277.

2. *Report on Indochina: Report of Senator Mike Mansfield on a Study Mission to Vietnam, Cambodia, Laos,* 10/15/54, Committee Print, SFRC.

3. *FRUS,* 1955–57, 1:281, 284–85.

4. *NYT,* 4/28/55.

5. *FRUS,* 1955–57, 1:294.

6. Ibid., 1:297.

7. Morgan, 28.

8. *CR,* 5/2/90, 5289–91.

9. *FRUS,* 1955–57, 1:338.

10. Mansfield to Heath, 5/2/55, Series XIII, Box 8, Mansfield Papers.

11. *NYT,* 4/30/55.

12. *FRUS,* 1955–57, 1:344–45.

13. Diem to Mansfield, 5/4/55, Series XXII, Box 95, Mansfield Papers.

14. Anderson, *Trapped by Success,* 118.

15. *FRUS,* 1955–57, 1:220.

16. Cooper, 145–46; FRUS, 1955–57, 1:407.

17. Herring, *America's Longest War,* 56–58.

18. Ibid., 59.

19. Gibbons, 1:314.

20. *FRUS,* 1955–57, 1:421–22.

21. Mansfield to Anderson, 3/1/55, Series XIII, Box 14, Mansfield Papers.

22. JFK speech, 11/22/55, Pre-Presidential, Speech Files, Box 894, JFKL.

23. Cooper, 149; *FRUS*, 1955–57, 1:489; NYT, 8/11/55.

24. Valeo OH, USSHO.

25. Mansfield travel memoranda, 8/18/55, Series XXII, Box 95, Mansfield Papers.

26. *Viet Nam, Cambodia and Laos, Report by Senator Mike Mansfield*, 10/6/55, SFRC; *FRUS*, 1955–57, 1:518–21.

27. *FRUS*, 1955–57, 1:589–94.

28. Fall, *The Two Viet-Nams*, 257.

29. Anderson, *Trapped by Success*, 132.

30. Fall, *The Two Viet-Nams*, 258.

31. Anderson, *Trapped by Success*, 130.

32. Morgan, 15–45.

33. JFK speech of 6/1/56, Vital Speeches, 8/1/56.

34. *FRUS*, 1955–57, 1:624.

35. Ibid., 1:639.

36. *NYT*, 7/7/56.

37. Parmet, *Eisenhower and the American Crusades*, 494.

CHAPTER FIFTEEN

1. Gibbons, 1:276–81.

2. *CQA*, 1957, 57–59, 573–74.

3. Gibbons, 1:345.

4. *CR*, 3/1/57, 2877–81.

5. Gibbons, 1:347.

6. Ibid., 1:346–47.

7. Ibid., 1:347–48; *CQA*, 1957, 578.

8. *CQA*, 1957, 573–79.

9. Gibbons, 1:348–49, 2:302.

CHAPTER SIXTEEN

1. *Time*, 5/20/57.

2. *NYT*, 5/9/57.

3. *FRUS*, 1955–57, 1:787–88.

4. Shaplen, 143–45; Fall, *The Two Vietnams*, 309–11.

5. *FRUS*, 1955–57, 1:794–99.

6. Ibid., 1:820–22.

7. Ibid., 1:822–23.

8. *New Republic*, 11/25/57.

9. *FRUS*, 1955–57, 1:869–84.

10. Ibid., 1:853.

11. Schulzinger, 93.

12. *FRUS*, 1955–57, 1:871.

13. Ibid., 1:854–55.

14. Ibid., 1:863–64.

15. *CR*, 2/16/56, 2637–38.

16. *CQA*, 1959, 191.

17. *Foreign Aid Program: Compilation of Studies and Surveys*, The Special Committee to Study the Foreign Aid Program, United States Senate, July 1957, 85th Congress, 1st Session, 1429–36.

18. Gibbons, 1:322.

19. Anderson, *Trapped by Success*, 180; Olson, 80; *CQA*, 1959, 189–90; Anderson, *Shadow on the White House*, 56–58.

20. *FRUS*, 1958–60, 1:185–86.

21. Woods, *Fulbright*, 238–39; *CQA*, 1957, 601–10.

22. *CQA*, 1959, 182–83.

23. *Washington Daily News*, 7/20–25/59.

24. *CQA*, 1959, 730.

25. Berman, *William Fulbright and the Vietnam War*, 10.

26. Gibbons, 1:324.

27. "Current Situation in the Far East," Hearings before the Subcommittee on the Far East and the Pacific of the Committee on Foreign Relations, House of Representatives, 86th Congress, 1st Sess., 7/27/59, 8/3,11,14/59, 328–38; Gibbons, 1:325.

28. *Situation in Vietnam*, Hearings Before the Subcommittee on State Department Organization and Public Affairs of the Committee on Foreign Relations, United States Senate, 86th Congress, 1st Sess., 7/30–31/59.

29. Gibbons, 1:326.

30. Ibid., 1:327.

31. Schulzinger, 94.

32. *FRUS*, 1958–60, 1:579.

33. Ibid., 1:487.

34. Ibid., 1:598–602.

35. Ibid., 1:707–11.

36. Kutler, *Encyclopedia of the Vietnam War*, 347–48; Schulzinger, 95–96; Herring, *America's Longest War*, 67.

CHAPTER SEVENTEEN

1. JFK inaugural address, Columbia University Bartley Archive, Internet, Available: http://www.columbia.edu/acis/bartleby/inaugural/index.html.

2. Strober and Strober, *'Let Us Begin Anew,'* 68.

3. McNamara, *Argument Without End*, 40.

4. *Boston Post*, 1/13/50.

5. Walton, 6.

6. *FRUS*, 1961–63, 1:1–12; Gibbons, 2:13–14.

7. *FRUS*, 196–63, 1:16ff.

8. Rostow OH, 45, JFKL.

9. *FRUS*, 1961–63, 1:15ff.

10. Gibbons, 2:7.

11. Komer to JFK, 2/1/61, NSF Files, Kennedy Papers, Vietnam, AFPC.

12. JFK memo on 1/19/61 meeting, Presidential Office Files, Special Correspondence, Box 29a, JFKL.

13. Sorenson, *Kennedy*, 640.

14. JFK memo on 1/19/61 meeting, Clifford 1/24/61 memo to JFK, Presidential Office Files, Special Correspondence, Box 29a, JFKL.

15. Reeves, *Profile of Power*, 75.

16. Sorenson, 644.

17. Gilpatric OH, 13–14, JFKL.

18. RFK OH, 52, 609, JFKL; Reeves, 112.

19. Gibbons, 2:29; Johnson, *The Right Hand of Power*, 324.

20. Schlesinger, *A Thousand Days*, 338–39; Sorenson, 644.

22. Sorenson, 644.

22. Gibbons, 2:112–17.

23. Rostow to JFK, 4/21/61, Newman Papers, JFKL.

24. Gibbons, 2:41.

25. *FRUS*, 1961–63, 1:74.

26. Ibid., 93–96.

27. Ibid., 125.

28. Ibid., 84.

29. Ibid., 132–33.

CHAPTER EIGHTEEN

1. Reeves, *Profile of Power*, 118–19.

2. Rowan, 182; Newman, 67–68.

3. Miller, *Lyndon*, 273.

4. Krock OH, LBJL.

5. Gibbons, 2:41.

6. Rusk OH, NN, Russell Library.

7. Valeo OH, USSHO.

8. Gibbons, 2:42.

9. *FRUS*, 1961–63, 1:136–38; Saigon embassy telegram 1748, 5/15/61, Newman Papers, JFKL.

10. *FRUS*, 1961–63, 1:145.

11. Valeo OH, USSHO.

12. Department of State, incoming telegram 1739, 5/13/61, NSF, Box 238–242, JFKL; Saigon embassy telegram 1748, 5/15/61, Newman Papers, JFKL.

13. Saigon embassy telegram 1748, 5/15/61, Newman Papers, JFKL.

14. Bangkok embassy telegram 2101, 5/20/61, NSF, Box 238–342, JFKL.

15. Gibbons, 2:44–46; *NYT*, 5/13/61; Valeo OH, Senate Historical Office; *FRUS*, 1961–63, 1:156; LBJ to JFK, 5/23/61, Vice Presidential Security File, Box 1, LBJL.

16. *FRUS*, 1961–63, 1:149–57.

17. *ExSess SFRC*, 5/25/61, 633.

18. *FRUS*, 1961–63, 1:157.
19. Halberstam, *The Best and the Brightest*, 76.
20. Meyer, 128.
21. Johnson and Gwertzman, 7.
22. Marcy OH, 128, USSHO.
23. Rusk OH, 12/2/69, JFKL.
24. *CR*, 6/29/61, 11702–5.
25. *FRUS*, 1961–63, 1:274–75.
26. Ibid., 1:296.
27. Ibid., 1:234–35.
28. Gibbons, 2:63.
29. Schulzinger, 107.
30. *FRUS*, 1961–63, 1:248.
31. Ibid., 1:345.
32. Ibid., 1:344–45.
33. Ibid., 1:477–532.
34. Ibid., 1:532–33.
35. Reeves, *Profile of Power*, 255.
36. Mansfield to JFK, 11/2/61, NSF, Box 194, JFKL.
37. Herring, *America's Longest War*, 81–82.
38. *FRUS*, 1961–63, 1:458–60.
39. Ball, 366; *FRUS*, 1961–63, 1:532–33.
40. Ball, 365–67; Ball OH, CRS.
41. Roberts, 131.
42. McNamara, *In Retrospect*, 30–31.
43. *FRUS*, 1961–63, 1:559–61.
44. Ibid., 1:573–75.
45. Ibid., 1:532.
46. Ibid., 1:512–14.
47. Reeves, *Profile of Power*, 257.
48. Gibbons, 2:101.
49. *FRUS*, 1961–63, 1:577.
50. Schlesinger, *A Thousand Days*, 547.
51. *FRUS*, 1961–63, 1:607–10.
52. *FRUS*, 1961–63, 1:656–57.
53. *FRUS*, 1961–63, 1:643.
54. Bradlee, 58.
55. *PP*, GE, 2:121–24.
56. Gibbons, 2:100–101.
57. *PP*, GE, 2:126–27.

CHAPTER NINETEEN

1. *ExSess SFRC*, 1962, 31–65.
2. Holt OH, 10/17/80, USSHO.
3. McPherson, 47.

4. *ExSess SFRC*, 1962, 47–48.

5. Karnow, 275.

6. *NYT*, 2/14/62; *PP*, GE, 2:807.

7. *NYT*, 2/14/62.

8. *Newsweek*, 2/12/62 and 2/26/62.

9. Ibid., 2/26/62; *NYT*, 2/14/62.

10. *CR*, 2/15/62, 2325–26.

11. *FRUS*, 1961–63, 2:124.

12. Ibid., 2:129–31, 156, 159–60.

13. Karnow, 275; *NYT*, 2/25/62.

14. *ExSess SFRC*, 1962, 189–213.

15. Karnow, 274.

16. Newhouse to JWF, 2/23/62, Series 48, 35:1, JWF Papers.

17. *FRUS*, 1961–63, 2:249.

18. Ibid., 2:379–87.

19. *PP*, GE, 2:152–53.

20. *FRUS*, 1961–63, 2:237.

21. Ibid., 2:284.

22. Ibid., 2:164.

23. *New Republic*, 3/12/62.

24. *CR*, 6/11/62, 10047–50.

25. Olson, 101.

26. Mecklin, 130–31.

27. Valeo to Mansfield, 6/15/62, XXII, 105, Mansfield Papers.

28. Bowles to JFK, 6/13/62, Sorenson Papers, Classified Subject Files, 1961–64, Box 43–47, JFKL.

29. *PP*, GE, 2:813–14.

30. Olson, 101.

31. Valeo, 25.

32. Gibbons, 2:127.

33. Ibid., 2:128.

34. *CR*, 6/8/62, 10034.

35. *FRUS*, 1961–63, 2:650.

36. Ibid., 2:655–57.

37. Mecklin, 100.

38. *NYT*, 10/21/62.

39. *PP*, GE, 2:162; *FRUS*, 1961–63, 2:683.

40. Forrestal to JFK, 9/18/62, NSF, Box 196, JFKL.

41. *FRUS*, 1961–63, 2:743–48.

42. Mecklin, 105.

43. Prochnau, 196.

CHAPTER TWENTY

1. Briefing summary, 11/30/62, XXII, 96, Mansfield Papers.

2. Trueheart OH, LBJL.

3. Mansfield memo, 12/2/62, XXII, 95, Mansfield Papers.

4. Valeo OH, USSHO.

5. Mansfield OH, 12/13/76, BBC interview, Mansfield Papers.

6. Mansfield memo, 12/2/62, XXII, 95, Mansfield Papers.

7. Memorandum of conversation, 12/1/62, XXII, 96, Mansfield Papers.

8. Gibbons, 2:131.

9. Prochnau, 209.

10. Proposed statement, 12/2/62, XXII, 53, Mansfield Papers.

11. Gibbons, 2:131; Halberstam, *The Best and the Brightest*, 208; New *Republic*, 12/15/62.

12. Trueheart OH, LBJL.

13. *FRUS*, 1961–63, 3:169–73.

14. Karnow, 284–85; Halberstam, *The Best and the Brightest*, 208–9; Reeves, *President Kennedy*, 442.

15. *Southeast Asia—Vietnam*, 12/18/62, XXII, 95, Mansfield Papers.

16. Mansfield, by Mann; Reeves, *President Kennedy*, 443.

17. Mansfield to Joe McCarthy, 10/6/69, XIX, 587, Mansfield Papers.

18. Mansfield OH, JFKL.

19. Nolting OH, JFKL.

20. *FRUS*, 1961–63, 3:19–22.

CHAPTER TWENTY-ONE

1. Karnow, 275–79; Sheehan, 203–65.

2. *WP*, 1/3/63.

3. *NYT*, 1/3, 5, 7, and 11/63.

4. *FRUS*, 1961–63, 3:1–3.

5. Qtd. in Strober, *'Let Us Begin Anew,'* 409.

6. *FRUS*, 1961–63, 3:126–28.

7. *PP*, GE, 2:717–19.

8. *FRUS*, 1961–63, 3:97, 89–91.

9. *NYT*, 5/8/63.

10. *FRUS*, 1961–63, 3:243.

11. *PP*, GE, 2:817.

12. *Newsweek*, 3/11/63; see also *NYT*, 2/28/63.

13. *Newsweek*, 3/11/63.

14. Mansfield to McCarthy, 10/6/69, XIX, 587, Mansfield Papers.

15. O'Donnell and Powers, 15–16.

16. Bartlett OH, LBJL.

17. Rusk OH, 3/30/70, JFKL; see also Rusk OH, NN, Russell Library.

18. Rusk, 441–42.

19. Bundy OH, CRS.

20. Qtd. in Strober, *'Let Us Begin Anew,'* 413.

21. *WP*, 5/12/63.

22. *NYT*, 6/10/63.

23. Browne, 11.

24. Mecklin, 157.

25. Colby OH, LBJL.

26. Karnow, 297.

27. *FRUS*, 1961–63, 3:381–83.

28. Ibid., 3: 411–12.

29. *NYT*, 6/14/63.

30. Herring, *America's Longest War*, 94.

31. *FRUS*, 1961–63, 3:402.

32. Mansfield to JFK, 8/19/63, XXII, 102, Mansfield Papers; see also *FRUS*, 1961–63, 3:585–88.

33. Cooper OH, JFKL.

34. *FRUS*, 1961–63, 3:644.

35. Ball OH, CRS; Ball, 371.

36. Hilsman OH, JFKL.

37. *FRUS*, 1961–63, 3:620–21.

38. Department of State cable 243, 8/24/63, NSF, 198, JFKL; see also *FRUS*, 1961–63, 3:628–29.

39. Ball OH, CRS.

40. Ball, 371; Ball OH, CRS; Gilpatric OH, LBJL.

41. *FRUS*, 1961–63, 3: 628–29.

42. Robert Kennedy OH, JFKL; Cline OH, LBJL.

43. Robert Kennedy OH, JFKL.

44. Nolting OH, JFKL; Gilpatric OH, LBJL.

45. *FRUS*, 1961–63, 3:659–65.

46. Ibid., 3:668–70.

47. Ibid., 4:20–21; see also, *PP*, GE, 2:738.

48. Ibid., 4:35–36.

49. Helms OH, LBJL.

50. Comments by President Kennedy, Hilsman Papers, Countries, 4, JFKL; see also *FRUS*, 1961–63, 4:93.

51. State Department telegram 341, 9/6/63, NSF, 199, JFKL.

52. *FRUS*, 1961–63, 4:113.

53. Ibid., 4:140–43.

54. Bryce Nelson, by Mann; *FRUS*, 1961–63, 4:167–68.

55. *FRUS*, 1961–63, 4:168ff.

56. Ibid., 4:166–67.

57. Ibid., 4:185–93.

58. Gibbons, 2:169.

59. *CR*, 9/12/63, 16824–25.

60. NBC interview transcript, 9/9/63, NSF, 199, JFK.

61. *FRUS*, 1961–63, 4:176.

62. Ibid., 4:173.

63. Ibid., 4:161–62.

CHAPTER TWENTY-ONE

1. *CR*, 9/9/63, 16488.

2. Anson, 60.

3. McGovern, by Mann, 1/27/97.

4. *CR*, 9/24/63, 17881–85.

5. Ibid., 9/26/63, 18205..

6. Rusk OH, JFKL.

7. Gibbons, 2:180.

8. Rusk OH, JFKL.

9. McGovern, by Mann, 9/10/97.

10. McGovern OH, LBJL.

11. White House to Saigon, 9/17/63, *FRUS*, 1961–63, 4:252–54.

12. "Report of McNamara–Taylor Mission," 10/1/63, Hilsman Papers, Countries, 4, JFKL; see also *FRUS*, 1961–63, 4:336–46.

13. Bird, 258.

14. Harriman OH, 6/6/65, JFKL.

15. Sullivan OH, LBJL.

16. White House news conference transcript, 10/2/63, NSF, 200, JFKL; see also *FRUS*, 1961–63, 4:353.

17. Herring, *America's Longest War*, 103.

18. *FRUS*, 1961–63, 4:435–36.

19. Ibid., 4:437.

20. Ibid., 4:454.

21. Ibid., 4:472.

22. Ibid., 4:517.

23. Ibid., 4:513.

24. Taylor, 301.

25. RN to DDE, PPS 324.220 and DDE to RN, PPS 324.223, Nixon Library.

26. Mansfield, by Mann.

27. Mansfield, BBC interview, 12/13/76, Mansfield Papers.

28. *CR*, 11/5/63, 21061.

29. Ball, 374.

30. Valeo OH, #13, USSHO.

31. Strober and Strober, *'Let Us Begin Anew,'* 424.

CHAPTER TWENTY-THREE

1. Kearns, 177–78.

2. Ball, 313.

3. Miller, *Lyndon*, 381.

4. McNamara, *In Retrospect*, 101.

5. Ball, 376.

6. *CQA*, 1963, 1019.

7. *NYT*, 12/6/63.

8. *FRUS*, 1961–63, 4:732–35.

9. Miller, *Lyndon*, 381.

10. Barrett, *Lyndon B. Johnson's Vietnam Papers*, 7–8.

11. William Bundy OH, LBJL.

12. *FRUS*, 1961–63, 4:637–40.

13. Beschloss, 73–74.

14. Ball OH, LBJL.

15. McGovern OH, LBJL.

16. Beschloss, 87–88, 95.

17. *NYT*, 5/1/66.

18. Mansfield to LBJ, 12/7/63, XXII, 102, Mansfield Papers.

19. Wicker, *JFK and LBJ*, 205.

20. *FRUS*, 1961–63, 4:745–46.

21. Beschloss, 123–24.

22. Mansfield to LBJ, 1/6/64, XXII, 103, Mansfield Papers.

23. *FRUS*, 1964–68, 1:8–11.

24. Ibid., 1:12–13.

25. Ibid., 1:28–29.

26. *PP, GE*, 3:496–99.

27. *FRUS*, 1964–68, 1:43–45.

28. Halberstam, *The Best and the Brightest*, 352.

29. Mansfield to LBJ, 2/1/64, XXII, 103, Mansfield Papers.

30. *FRUS*, 1964–68, 1:56; Gardner, *Pay Any Price*, 115.

31. Beschloss, 213–14.

32. *FRUS*, 1964–68, 1:67.

33. *CR*, 2/19/64, 3114–15.

34. *WP*, 1/22/64.

35. Garnder, *Pay Any Price*, 115.

36. *CR*, 2/20/64, 3226.

37. Javits, 393.

38. *CR*, 2/20/64, 3277–79.

39. Beschloss, 250.

40. *ExSess SFRC*, 1964, 117.

41. Beschloss, 263–64.

42. *FRUS*, 1964–68, 1:129.

43. *CR*, 3/2/64, 4087.

44. *ExSess SFRC*, 1964, 141.

45. *CR*, 3/4/64, 4357–58.

46. Ibid., 4359.

47. Sundborg, by Mann.

48. *CR*, 3/10/64, 4835.

49. Ibid., 4832.

50. Gibbons, 2:225.

51. Ibid.

52. *FRUS*, 1964–68, 1:153–67.

53. Ibid., 1:171.

54. Ibid., 1:174.

55. Johnson, *The Vantage Point*, 65.

56. Fulbright OH, FMOC.

57. *CR*, 3/25/64, 6227–32.

58. Woods, *Fulbright*, 336.

59. *NYT*, 3/26/64.
60. Woods, *Fulbright*, 337.
61. *Washington Evening Star*, 3/27/64.
62. *St. Louis Globe-Democrat*, 3/27/64.
63. Woods, *Fulbright*, 334, 337.
64. Beschloss, 297–98.

CHAPTER TWENTY-FOUR

1. Gibbons, 2:249.
2. Drukman, 406.
3. McGovern, by Mann, 9/10/97.
4. *NYT*, 3/21/64.
5. Ibid.
6. *CR*, 3/26/64, 6468–69.
7. Drukman, 408.
8. *CR*, 3/30/64, 6579.
9. Ibid., 3/31/64, 6629–30.
10. Ibid., 4/2/64, 6793–94.
11. *FRUS*, 1964–68, 1: 222–24.
12. *CR*, 4/9/64, 7427.
13. *FRUS*, 1964–68, 1:244.
14. Ibid., 1:288.
15. Ibid., 1:284–85.
15. Ibid., 1:296–97.
17. Beschloss, 338.
18. *FRUS*, 1964–68, 1:306.
19. Ibid., 1:308–9.
20. Ibid., 1:322–23.
21. Ibid., 1:328–32.
22. Ibid., 1: 337; *NYT*, 5/19/64.
23. Gibbons, 2:264–65.
24. Beschloss, 361.
25. Ibid., 363–64.
26. *FRUS*, 1964–68, 1:374–77.
27. Beschloss, 364–73.
28. Ibid.
29. Mansfield to LBJ, 5/26/64, XXII, 102, Mansfield Papers.
30. Beschloss, 370–72.
31. Ibid., 373–74.
32. *FRUS*, 1964–68, 1:400–401.
33. Ibid., 1:442–46.
34. *Johnson Presidential Press Conferences*, 1:144–45.
35. Gibbons, 2:265.
36. Beschloss, 380–82.
37. Rusk OH, U, Russell Library.

38. Beschloss, 390.

39. *FRUS*, 1964–68, 1:349–50.

40. Ibid., 1:356–58.

41. Beschloss, 390.

42. Notes on telephone conversation between Ball and LBJ, Ball Papers, Box 7, LBJ Library, Barrett, *Lyndon B. Johnson's Vietnam Papers*, 44.

43. *FRUS*, 1964–68, 1:487–93.

44. Valenti, 105.

45. Beschloss, 393.

46. Ibid., 394–95.

47. Mansfield to LBJ, 6/9/64, XXII, 102, Mansfield Papers.

48. Beschloss, 403.

49. Ibid., 401.

50. Ibid., 398.

51. *FRUS*, 1964–68, 1:523.

52. Beschloss, 415.

53. *Johnson Presidential Press Conferences*, 1:146–47.

54. *ExSess SFRC*, 1964, 177–211.

55. *CR*, 6/23/64, 14788–93.

56. Ibid., 14790–96.

57. Humphrey, 482–83.

58. Gibbons, 2:277.

59. *CR*, 6/23/64, 14801–2.

60. Gibbons, 2:278.

61. Ibid., 2:279; *NYT*, 6/30/64.

62. *Johnson Presidential Press Conferences*, 1:148.

CHAPTER TWENTY-FIVE

1. *FRUS*, 1964–68, 1:563–65.

2. *NYT*, 7/20/64.

3. *FRUS*, 1964–68, 1:563–65.

4. Clifford OH, 7/2/69, LBJL.

5. Dietz, 64.

6. *NYT*, 8/3/64.

7. Goldberg, 2–3.

8. Edwards, 272; *NYT*, 7/17/64.

9. Goldberg, 217–16; Goldwater, 244–45.

10. *FRUS*, 1964–68, 1:566–68.

11. Ibid., 1:569–70.

12. Ibid., 1:547; Gibbons, 2:282.

13. Moïse, 4–7, 50–68; Gibbons, 2:282–83; Windchy, 54–70.

14. Moïse, 68.

15. *FRUS*, 1964–68, 1:487–92.

16. *PP*, GE, 3:560–61.

17. Rusk OH, LBJL.

18. Gibbons, 2:285; Ball OH, CRS.
19. Moïse, 101.
20. *FRUS*, 1964–68, 1:590.
21. Ibid.
22. Johnson, *The Vantage Point*, 113.
23. Gibbons, 2:286.
24. Miller, *Lyndon*, 382.
25. Windchy, 4–5.
26. Ball, 379.
27. Ibid.
28. Johnson, *Vantage Point*, 113.
29. *PPP*, 1963–64, 2:926–27.
30. Ball, 379.
31. Gibbons, 2:287.
32. *FRUS*, 1964–68, 1:603.
33. Beschloss, 495–97.
34. Gibbons, 2:289.
35. Beschloss, 498.
36. *FRUS*, 1964–68, 1:608.
37. Dallek, *Flawed Giant*, 150.
38. *FRUS*, 1964–68, 1:609.
39. Ibid.,
40. McNamara–Sharo phone conversation, 8/4/64, Reference File, Vietnam, Box 2, LBJL, in Barrett, *Lyndon B. Johnson's Vietnam Papers*, 63–64.
41. Gibbons, 2:292.
42. Moïse, 107.
43. Ibid., 183; *FRUS*, 1964–68, 1:609.
44. Moïse, 183–84.
45. *FRUS*, 1964–68, 1:611.
46. Ibid., 1:611–12.
47. LBJ phone conversation with McNamara, 9/18/64, Johnson Presidential Recordings, WH6409.08, Prog. 1, LBJL.
48. *FRUS*, 1964–68, 1:631–32.
49. Ibid., 1:612–13.
50. Ibid., 1:615–21.
51. Beschloss, 504.
52. *PPP*, 1963–64, 2:927–28.
53. Karnow, 388.
54. *PPP*, 1963–64, 2:928–30.
55. *FRUS*, 1964–68, 1:615.
56. Woods, *Fulbright*, 353.
57. Tillman, by Mann, 9/11/97.
58. Williams, by Mann, 3/26/97.
59. Gibbons, 2:313.
60. Tillman, by Mann, 2/13/97.
61. McGovern, by Mann, 1/27/97.

62. Holt OH, 10/19/80, USSHO.

63. Ibid.

64. Gibbons, 2:305; Goulden, 51.

65. Holt OH, 10/19/80, USSHO.

66. Valeo OH, 379, 383, USSHO.

67. Gibbons, 2:307–8.

68. Ibid., 2:305.

69. "Southeast Asia Resolution," *ExSess SFRC*, 1964, 291–92.

70. Windchy, 150–51; Goulden, 48–49.

71. "Southeast Asia Resolution," *ExSess SFRC*, 1964, 291–94; Austin, 62–80.

72. Gibbons, 2:310–11.

73. SFRC Report, 8/6/64, "Promoting the Maintenance of International Peace and Security in Southeast Asia," *ExSess SFRC*, 1964, 374–82.

74. *CR*, 8/6/64, 18399–410; Austin, 81–105.

75. *CR*, 8/6/64, 18410–411.

76. Marcy OH, 153, USSHO.

77. "Southeast Asia Resolution," *ExSess SFRC*, 1964, 295.

78. *CR*, 8/7/64, 18443, 18447.

79. Goulden, 48.

80. Nelson, by Mann.

81. McGovern, by Mann, 9/10/64.

82. *CR*, 8/7/64, 18458–59.

83. Nelson, by Mann.

84. McGovern, by Mann, 1/27/97.

85. *CR*, 8/7/64, 18456–57.

86. Gibbons, 2:308, 329.

87. *PPP*, 1963–64, 2:936.

88. *WP*, 8/10/64.

89. Young, 121.

90. Humphrey, 352.

91. *CR*, 8/6/64, 18421.

92. Ibid., 8/8/64, 18667–68.

93. Ibid.

94. Gibbons, 2:342ff.

95. *FRUS*, 1964–68, 1:662.

CHAPTER TWENTY-SIX

1. *FRUS*, 1964–68, 1:646.

2. Ibid., 1:669.

3. Ibid., 1:723–24.

4. Ibid., 1:749–55; *ExSess SFRC*, 1964, 295.

5. "The Situation in South Vietnam," *ExSess SFRC*, 9/10/64, 317–33.

6. *PPP*, 1963–64, 2:1126–27.

7. Ibid., 2:1164–65.

8. Humphrey speech text, 10/26/64, Thompson Papers, 12, JFKL.

9. *PPP*, 1963–64, 2:1165.
10. Powers, 17.
11. Dallek, *Flawed Giant*, 240.
12. *PPP*, 1963–64, 2:1242–43.
13. Ibid., 2:1260.
14. Ibid., 2:1267.
15. Moyers to LBJ, 10/3/64, Reference File, Vietnam, Box 1, LBJL, qtd. in Barrett, *Lyndon B. Johnson's Vietnam Papers*, 89.
16. Bundy, Memorandum for the Record, 8/10/64, NS File, NS History, Tonkin, 38, LBJL, qtd. in Barrett, *Lyndon B. Johnson's Vietnam Papers*, 78–79.
17. *FRUS*, 1964–68, 1:723.
18. Ibid., 1:689–91.
19. Ibid., 1:847.
20. *PPP*, 1963–64, 2:719.
21. Fulbright OH, FMOC.
22. *FRUS*, 1964–68, 1:873; Gibbons, 2:364.
23. Gibbons, 2:364.
24. William Bundy OH, 5/29/69, LBJL.
25. Halberstam, *The Best and the Brightest*, 606.
26. *FRUS*, 1964–68, 1:914–16.
27. Ibid., 1: 916–25.
28. Ibid., 1:914–16.
29. Ibid., 1:932–35.
30. VanDeMark, 32.
31. *Johnson Presidential Press Conferences*, 1:243–44.
32. *FRUS*, 1964–68, 1:958–59.
33. *PP*, GE, 3:678.
34. *FRUS*, 1964–68, 1:965–69.
35. "The Situation in South Vietnam," *ExSess SFRC*, 12/3/64, 351–70.
36. Mansfield to LBJ, 12/9/64, XXII, 103, Mansfield Papers.
37. Moss OH, FMOC.
38. McPherson, 45.
39. "Issues and Answers" transcript, 2/1/70, XIX, 597, Mansfield Papers.
40. LBJ to Mansfield, 12/17/64, XXII, 102, Mansfield Papers.
41. Ball, 380–83; *Atlantic Monthly* July 1972, 35–49.
42. Ball OH, 7/8/71, LBJL.
43. Ball, 383.
44. William Bundy OH, 5/29/69, LBJL.
45. Forrestal OH, LBJL.
46. Kearns, 262.
47. VanDeMark, 45.
48. *FRUS*, 1965–68, 2:12–13.
49. Ibid., 2:30–32.
50. VanDeMark, 47–48.
51. Valenti, 239–40.
52. *FRUS*, 1965–68, 2:33, 21.

53. "The Situation in Vietnam," *ExSess SFRC*, 1/8/65, 93–142.

54. "The United Nations and Southeast Asia," *ExSess SFRC*, 1/15/65, 231.

55. *FRUS*, 1965–68, 2:63–69.

56. Kearns, 251–52.

CHAPTER TWENTY-SEVEN

1. *FRUS*, 1965–68, 2:91–93.

2. Ibid., 2:93–94.

3. Ibid., 2:60–61, 95–97.

4. Gibbons, 3:51.

5. Cooper OH, 7/9/69, LBJL.

6. Gibbons, 3:57–59.

7. Johnson, *The Vantage Point*, 128.

8. Cooper OH, 7/9/69, LBJL; Gibbons, 3:61.

9. Karnow, 429.

10. *FRUS*, 1965–68, 2:155–60.

11. Bundy OH, CRS.

12. Gibbons, 3:63.

13. Ibid., 3:63–64; *FRUS*, 1965–68, 2:158–60; Halberstam, *The Best and the Brightest*, 522.

14. *FRUS*, 1965–68, 2:165.

15. Ibid., 2:169–72.

16. Johnson, *The Vantage Point*, 125.

17. *FRUS*, 1965–68, 2:169–72.

18. Ibid., 2:166–72.

19. *Newsweek*, 1/18/65.

20. Ibid., 3/1/65.

21. *NYT*, 1/7/65.

22. *Newsweek*, 3/1/65.

23. *FRUS*, 1965–68, 2:174–85.

24. Ibid., 2:187–88.

25. Ibid., 2:188–89.

26. Gibbons, 3:67.

27. Berman, *William Fulbright*, 34.

28. "The Situation in Vietnam," 2/9/65, *ExSess SFRC*, XVII, 273–302.

29. *NYT*, 1/7/65.

30. Ibid., 2/9/65.

31. Johnson and Gwertzman, 221.

32. *FRUS*, 1965–68, 2:203–6.

33. Ibid., 2: 208–11.

34. Johnson, *The Vantage Point*, 129.

35. Ball, 390.

36. Humphrey, 319.

37. *CR*, 8/6/64, 18420.

38. Van Dyk, by Mann, 9/8/97.

39. "The Situation in Vietnam," *ExSess SFRC*, 1/7/64, 35–91.

40. *FRUS*, 1965–68, 2:216–23.

41. Ibid., 2:223–24.

42. Ibid., 2:225–26.

43. Ibid., 2:226–27.

44. Ibid., 2:237–38.

45. Ibid., 2:252–61,

46. Ball, 390–91.

47. *FRUS*, 1965–68, 2:263.

48. Ibid., 2:282–83.

49. Ibid., 2:290–91.

50. Humphrey, 319; Van Dyk, by Mann, 9/8/97.

51. Gibbons, 3:92.

52. Humphrey, 320–24; *FRUS*, 1964–68, 2:309–13.

53. Solberg, 273; VanDeMark, 75.

54. *FRUS*, 1964–68, 2:282–83.

55. Ibid.

56. Ibid., 2:290–91.

57. Gibbons, 3:107.

58. *FRUS*, 1964–68, 2:298–308.

59. Ibid., 2:390.

60. *CR*, 1/15/65, 784–86.

61. *Ramparts* interview, January–February 1965, qtd. in *CR*, 1/12/65, 538–41.

62. *NYT*, 2/14/65.

63. *CR*, 2/17/65, 2869–75.

64. Ibid., 2877–78.

65. Ibid., 2886–87.

66. Gibbons, 3:130.

67. *Newsweek*, 3/1/65.

68. Church OH, LBJL.

69. McGovern, by Mann, 1/27/97.

70. Gibbons, 3:134.

71. Ibid., 3:140.

72. Ibid., 3:140–41.

73. Nelson, by Mann.

CHAPTER TWENTY-EIGHT

1. Halberstam, *The Best and the Brightest*, 564.

2. *FRUS*, 1964–68, 2:402.

3. NYT, 3/8/65; LBJ phone conversation with Russell, 3/6/65, Johnson Presidential Recordings, WH6503.03, Prog. 1, LBJL.

4. *FRUS*, 1964–68, 2:347; LBJ phone conversation with McNamara, 3/6/65, Johnson Presidential Recordings, WH6503.03, Prog. 3, LBJL.

5. Ibid., 2:407.

6. Ibid., 2:454.

7. Ibid., 2:465–67.

8. Gibbons, 3:180.

9. LBJ OH, LBJL.

10. *FRUS*, 1964–68, 2:473.

11. Phone conversation notes, 3/6/65, XXII, 103, Mansfield Papers.

12. Gibbons, 3:205; Olson, 147.

13. Mansfield to LBJ, 3/24/65, XXII, 102, Mansfield Papers.

14. McGovern, 104.

15. Transcript of "Vietnam: The Hawks and the Doves," CBS News Special Report, 3/8/65.

16. McGovern, 104; McGovern memo to LBJ, 3/26/65, WHCF, Aides Files, Busby, Box 6, LBJL; McGovern OH, 4/30/69, LBJL.

17. Coffin, 241–44.

18. Johnson and Gwertzman, 205–6; Powell, 239; Coffin, 243–44.

19. "The Situation in Vietnam," *ExSess SFRC*, 4/2/65, 359–407.

20. *FRUS*, 1964–68, 2:231–16.

21. Ibid., 2:524–25ff.

22. Ibid., 2:512–54.

23. Gibbons, 3:215.

24. *CQA*, 1965, 1370–71.

25. Karnow, 434.

26. Johnson and Gwertzman, 206.

27. Anson, 159; McGovern OH, LBJL; Diary index card for 4/7/65, Diaries and Appointment Logs, Special Files, LBJL.

28. McGovern OH, LBJL.

29. *New Republic*, 3/18/67.

30. Karnow, 434.

31. Miller, *Lyndon*, 466.

32. Gibbons, 3:220.

33. Ibid.

34. Woods, *Fulbright*, 368.

35. Johnson and Gwertzman, 206.

36. *FRUS*, 1964–68, 2:544.

37. Herring, *America's Longest War*, 136.

38. Marcy to JWF, 3/30/65, Chron 1965, 5, Marcy Papers, National Archives.

39. DeBenedetti, 107–8; Gibbons, 3:221–22.

40. *FRUS*, 1964–68, 2:549.

41. Ibid., 2:554–55.

42. Ibid., 2:556.

43. Ibid., 2:572–77.

44. Ball, 393.

45. *FRUS*, 1964–68, 2:582–92.

46. Ball, 395.

47. *CR*, 4/21/65, 8124–25; Gibbons, 3:238.

48. *FRUS*, 1964–68, 2:597–600.

49. *CR*, 4/26/65, 8440–43.

50. Woods, *Fulbright*, 371.

51. "Situation in the Domincan Republic and Vietnam," *ExSess SFRC*, 4/30/65, 461, 468–80.

52. Gibbons, 3:242.

53. VanDeMark, 133.

54. *CQA*, 1965, 1372.

55. Ibid., 180–81.

56. Nelson, by Mann; Senate debate in *CR*, 5/5 and 5/6/65, 9453–55, 9492–9507, 9729–72.

57. *CR*, 5/6/65, 9772; *CQA*, 1965, 180–81.

58. Gibbons, 3:249.

59. Ibid., 3:250.

60. VanDeMark, 134.

61. Gibbons, 3:250.

62. *CR*, 5/6/65, 9770.

63. Cooper, 275.

CHAPTER TWENTY-NINE

1. VanDeMark, 134–35; Johnson, *Vantage Point*, 136.

2. Johnson, *Vantage Point*, 136.

3. McNamara, *In Retrospect*, 185.

4. *FRUS*, 1964–68, 2:629–30.

5. Qtd. in McNamara, *Argument Without End*, 226–27.

6. McMaster, 284.

7. *FRUS*, 1964–68, 2:665–67.

8. Ibid., 2:670–71.

9. Ibid., 2:710.

10. Ibid., 2:719–24.

11. McNamara, *In Retrospect*, 186–87.

12. Memorandum by Mansfield, 6/3/65, XXII, 102, Mansfield Papers.

13. Mansfield to LBJ, 6/5/65, XXII, 102, Mansfield Papers.

14. *FRUS*, 1964–68, 2:733–41 and 3:174.

15. McNamara, *In Retrospect*, 187–88.

16. Mansfield to LBJ, 6/9/65, XXII, 102, Mansfield Papers.

17. *FRUS*, 1964–68, 2:745–48.

18. Ibid., 2:757–59.

19. Transcript, *Vietnam: A Television History*, "LBJ Goes to War (1964–1965)," Public Broadcasting System: http://www.pbs.org/wgbh/amex/vietnam/104ts.html.

20. *FRUS*, 1964–68, 3:16–21.

21. Ball, 396.

22. Kearns, 282–83.

23. Coffin, 252–53.

24. *CR*, 6/15/65, 13656.

25. "Today" show transcript, 6/15/65, 48, 44:1, JWF Papers.

26. *Arkansas Gazette*, 6/20/65.

27. Gibbons, 3:305–6.

28. *CR*, 6/30/65, 15319.

29. Ball OH, CRS.

30. *FRUS*, 1964–68, 3:106–15.

31. Ibid., 3:97–106.

32. McNamara, *In Retrospect*, 201.

33. *FRUS*, 1964–68, 3:171–79.

34. Ibid., 3:189–205.

35. Johnson, *Vantage Point*, 147.

36. Bundy OH, 5/29/69, LBJL.

37. Gardner, *Pay Any Price*, 243.

38. *FRUS*, 1964–68, 3:206–07.

39. Ibid., 3:209–17; Gibbons, 3:351–53.

40. Gibbons, 3:367.

41. *NYT*, 7/21/65.

42. *CR*, 7/21/65, 17797–99.

43. Mansfield to LBJ, 7/23/65, XXII, 102, Mansfield Papers.

44. *FRUS*, 1964–68, 3:231–32.

45. Ibid., 3:221–23.

46. William Bundy OH, CRS.

47. Clifford, 410–11, 418–21; *FRUS*, 1964–68, 3:238.

48. VanDeMark, 206.

49. Johnson, *The Vantage Point*, 149.

50. *FRUS*, 1964–68, 3:260–63.

51. VanDeMark, 208.

52. Ford, by Mann.

53. *FRUS*, 1964–68, 3:264–69.

54. Notes on Vietnam, 7/28/65, XXII, 102, Mansfield Papers; VanDeMark, 210; Valenti, 282; Olson, 160–61.

55. Mansfield, by Mann, 9/8/97.

56. *FRUS*, 1964–68, 3:273; Gibbons, 3:436–38.

57. Valenti, 283–84.

CHAPTER THIRTY

1. Mansfield to LBJ, 7/27/65, XXII, 102, Mansfield Papers.

2. LBJ to Mansfield and McNamara to LBJ, 7/28/65, XXII, 102, Mansfield Papers.

3. Russell to Carl T. Sutherland, 11/5/65, Dictation Series, 11, Russell Library.

4. Gibbons, 3:445.

5. *CR*, 7/28/65, 18506.

6. Ibid., 7/29/65, 18815.

7. Gibbons, 3:447.

8. *CR*, 7/28/65, 18507.

9. Ibid., 7/29/65, 18811.

10. Gibbons, 4:23.

11. *CR*, 7/27/65, 18308–9.

12. Ibid., 18309.

13. Ibid., 18316–18.

14. Ibid., 8/3/65, 19132.

15. Gibbons, 3:447.

16. Ibid., 4:22.

17. Ibid., 3:451; Hatfield, by Mann.

18. *FRUS*, 1964–68, 3:307–8.

19. Westmoreland, 175–76.

20. Karnow, 450.

21. Ibid., 451.

22. FitzGerald, 272.

23. Bonds, *The Vietnam War*, 102; Young, *The Vietnam Wars*, 161.

24. See Moore and Galloway for the definitive account of the Ia Drang battle; Bonds, 102; Karnow, 493–94; Young, 161–63.

25. Moore and Galloway, 399.

26. McNamara, 213.

27. *FRUS*, 1964–68, 3:411–12, 417, 419–21.

28. McNamara, *In Retrospect*, 213.

29. *FRUS*, 1964–68, 3:500–504.

30. Ibid., 3:514–28.

31. McNamara, *In Retrospect*, 221.

32. *FRUS*, 1964–68, 3:591–94.

33. Ibid., 3:594.

34. Ibid., 3:658–69; Johnson, *Vantage Point*, 234.

35. *FRUS*, 1964–68, 3:619–22.

36. Miller, *Lyndon*, 424–27; Dallek, *Flawed Giant*, 262–68; Johnson and Gwertzman, 208–13; Woods, *Fulbright*, 376–81.

37. Fulbright, *Old Myths and New Realities*, 34.

38. Johnson and Gwetzman, 212–13.

39. Holt OH, 10/19/80, USSHO.

40. Woods, *Fulbright*, 382.

41. Tillman, by Mann, 9/11/97.

42. Miller, *Lyndon*, 427.

43. Woods, *Fulbright*, 383.

44. *CR*, 9/15/65, 23859; Holt OH, 11/10/80, USSHO.

45. Williams, by Mann, 3/27/97; Johnson and Gwertzman, 218.

46. *CR*, 9/15/65, 23855–64.

47. McPherson, by Mann, 9/12/97.

48. Woods, *Fulbright*, 387.

49. Williams, by Mann, 3/27/97.

50. *Newsweek*, 9/27/65.

51. Jones, by Mann, 7/21/97; Tilmann, by Mann, 9/11/97; Marcy to Valenti, 10/14/65 and Marcy to McNamara, 11/15/65, Box 2, Carl Marcy Misc., 1953 and 1961–62, Legislative Records, Carl Marcy Papers, NARA.

52. Holt OH, 11/10/80, USSHO.

53. Tillman, by Mann, 9/11/97.

54. Olson, 167–68; Mansfield Report, "vietnam: The Situation and Outlook," 12/17/65, Senate Doc. 93-11,1

55. *FRUS*, 1964–68, 3:599–600.

56. Ibid., 3:677–79.

57. Ibid., 3:607–9.

58. Ibid., 3:691–92.

59. Cooper OH, 7/9/69, LBJL.

60. Johnson, 239.

61. Ball OH, 7/8/71, LBJL.

CHAPTER THIRTY-ONE

1. Russell press release, 12/30/65, III B. Media, 23, RBRL.

2. *CR*, 1/31/66, 1577.

3. Gibbons, 4:219–20.

4. Bundy OH, CRS.

5. Ackley OH, 4/13/73, LBJL.

6. Miller, *Lyndon*, 453.

7. McNamara, *Argument Without End*, 228, 258–59.

8. RBR to Jim Rovig, 1/18/66, XVI, International Series, Subject: Vietnam, 39, RBRL.

9. RBR speech to Georgia Assembly, III. Speech/Media, B. Media, 22, RBRL.

10. *FRUS*, 1964–68, 4:141–45.

11. Ibid., 4:74–80.

12. Ibid., 4:98.

13. Joint letter to LBJ, 1/27/66, and LBJ response, 1/28/66, NSF, Country File, Vietnam, Box 102, LBJL; Gibbons, 4:157–58.

14. *FRUS*, 1964–68, 4:174–81.

15. *NYT*, 1/29/66.

16. *FRUS*, 1964–68, 4:47–52.

17. Gardner, *Pay Any Price*, 284.

18. *FRUS*, 1964–68, 4:105–10.

19. Ibid., 4:164–70.

20. Ibid., 4:192; Gibbons, 4:164.

21. *CR*, 1/31/66, 1577.

22. Ibid., 2/4/66, 2132.

23. Schlesinger, *Robert Kennedy and His Times*, 729–30.

24. *CR*, 1/31/66, 1603.

25. Dietz, 150–51.

26. Gibbons, 4:170.

27. *CR*, 6/17/65, 14038–39.

28. Ibid., 7/27/65, 18308–10.

29. Ibid.

30. McGovern, by Mann, 1/27/97.

31. McGovern, 106.

32. *CR*, 1/20/66, 778.

33. McGovern, 106–7; McGovern, by Mann, 1/27/97; *CR*, 1/20/66, 778.

34. *CR*, 1/20/66, 775–76.

35. "Today" show transcript, 2/24/66, Speeches, Box 24, McGovern Papers, SGM.

36. *Mademoiselle*, 3/66.

37. *The Truth About Vietnam: Report on the U.S. Senate Hearings*, 22–71; Berman, *William Fulbright*, 54.

38. Berman, *William Fulbright*, 54.

39. Gibbons, 4:222–23.

40. Morse memorandum, 1/11/66, Marcy Files, Box 7, NARA.

41. Woods, *Fulbright*, 403.

42. *FRUS*, 1964–68, 4:203.

43. Gibbons, 4:230.

44. *FRUS*, 1964–68, 4:203.

45. Dallek, *Flawed Giant*, 352.

46. *The Truth About Vietnam: Report on the U.S. Senate Hearings*, 72–124.

47. Ibid., 125–88.

48. Johnson, *Vantage Point*, 244.

49. Powell, 273; Johnson, *Vantage Point*, 244.

50. Woods, *Fulbright*, 404.

51. Johnson, *Vantage Point*, 245.

52. *The Truth About Vietnam: Report on the U.S. Senate Hearings*, 189–253.

53. Ibid., 254–331.

54. Ibid., 332–403.

55. Tillman, by Mann, 9/11/97.

56. *FRUS*, 1964–68, 4:220–22.

57. Theoharis, *Spying on Americans: Political Surveillance from Hoover to the Huston Plan*, 176–77; Theoharis, *From the Secret Files of J. Edgar Hoover*, 236–37.

58. Theoharis, *From the Secret Files of J. Edgar Hoover*, 238.
Gibbons, 4:228–30; Marcy to JWF, 2/22/66, Marcy Files, Box 7, NARA.

59. Holt OH, 10/19/80, USSHO.

60. *WP*, 1/3/66 and 2/28/66.

61. Moyers to LBJ, 6/9/66, Office Files of Bill Moyers, Box 12, LBJL.

62. Roche to Redmon, 7/26/66, Office Files of Bill Moyers, Box 12, LBJL.

63. Church OH, LBJL.

CHAPTER THIRTY-TWO

1. Solberg, 278.

2. Humphrey, 329; Connell OH, LBJL.

3. Humphrey, 331.

4. Solberg, 288–89.

5. Ibid., 290.

6. *FRUS*, 1964–68, IV, 255–57.

7. Gibbons, 4:236.

8. HHH to LBJ, 3/3/66, Thompson Papers, Box 12, JFKL.

9. Humphrey, 337.

10. Connell OH, LBJL.

11. Humphrey, 338.

12. Gibbons, 4:237.

13. Connell OH, LBJL.

14. Solberg, 290; *NYT*, 2/20/66.

15. McGovern, by Mann, 9/10/97.

16. Drukman, 424–25.

17. *CR*, 1/29/66, 1510.

18. Gibbons, 4:251.

19. *CR*, 2/16/66, 3135–38.

20. Gibbons, 4:257–58.

21. *FRUS*, 1964–68, 4:267–68.

22. *CR*, 3/1/66, 4376–77.

23. Gibbons, 4:258.

24. Russell to H. B. Rackley, 2/22/66, XVI, Vietnam, Box 38, RBRL.

25. "Today" show transcript, 2/24/66.

26. *CR*, 3/1/66, 4377.

27. Ibid., 3/17/66, 6151.

28. Speech text, Rockdale County Jaycees, 4/8/66, III, B.Media, 22, RBRL.

29. Fulbright, *The Arrogance of Power*, 3, 5, 15, 18.

30. Ibid., 106–8.

31. Ibid., 178–81, 188–97.

32. *CR*, 5/3/66, 9609–15.

33. Fulbright to LBJ, 5/9/66, 1:1, 3:5, Fulbright Papers.

34. Gibbons, 4:309.

35. Evans and Novak, 572–73.

36. McPherson to LBJ, 5/13/66, Barrett, *Lyndon B. Johnson's Vietnam Papers*, 341–42.

37. McPherson, by Mann, 9/12/97.

38. Gibbons, 4:310; *CQA*, 1996, 379.

39. Ibid., 4:311.

40. LBJ to Fulbright, 5/27/66, Barrett, *Lyndon B. Johnson's Vietnam Papers*, 343–44.

41. Gibbons, 4:424–26; Califano, 147–48.

42. Gibbons, 4:334–39.

43. *FRUS*, 1964–68, 4:397.

44. Ibid., 4:410–11.

45. Ibid., 4:417–18.

46. Schulzinger, 213; *FRUS*, 1964–68, 4:468; Herring, *America's Longest War*, 151–52.

47. *FRUS*, 1964–68, 4:517.

48. Ibid., 4:530.

49. Ibid., 4:649.

50. Ibid., 4:727–35.

51. Ibid., 4:738–42; Dallek, *Flawed Giant*, 387.

52. Dallek, *Flawed Giant*, 385; *CQA*, 1966, 382; *PPP*, 1966, 2:1269–70.

53. Gibbons, 4:464.

54. Cooper, 333–39; Karnow, 505–7; Herring, *LBJ and Vietnam*, 104–6.

CHAPTER THIRTY-THREE

1. FRUS, 1964–68, 4:465–67.

2. Schulzinger, 234–35.

3. Mansfield to LBJ, 1/6/67, XXII, 103, Mansfield Papers.

4. NYT, 12/25, 27, 28, 29, 30/66 & 1/1, 8, and 13/67.

5. LBJ to Mansfield, 1/9/67, XXII, 103, Mansfield Papers.

6. McNamara, *Argument Without End*, 281.

7. Cooper, 501; "The War in Vietnam," Abbot Smith to Richard Helms, 1/9/67, in Barrett, *Lyndon B. Johnson's Vietnam Papers*, 381–83.

8. Gibbons, 4:558.

9. Rostow to LBJ, 1/26/67, NSF, Country File, Vietnam, Box 10, LBJL.

10. Kutler, *Encyclopedia of the Vietnam War*, 75–76; Gibbons, 4:540–43.

11. *PPP*, 1967, 1:2–14.

12. *NYT*, 1/13/67.

13. Gibbons, 4:499–500.

14. Ibid., 4:553–54.

15. Ibid., 4:501–11.

16. Strober and Strober, *'Let Us Begin Anew,'* 197.

17. O'Donnell, 4.

18. Johnson, *Vantage Point*, 539.

19. Schlesinger, *Robert Kennedy and His Times*, 623.

20. Shesol, 299.

21. Ibid., 303.

22. Schlesinger, *Robert Kennedy and His Times*, 765–69; Shesol, 363–67.

23. Dallek, Flawed Giant, 453.

24. Cooper, 350–68; Cooper OH, 8/7/69, LBJL.

25. *PPP*, 1967, 1:178.

26. Miller, *Lyndon*, 472–76.

27. NSC meeting summary notes, 2/8/67, in Barrett, *Lyndon B. Johnson's Vietnam Papers*, 392.

28. Congressional briefing transcript, 2/15/67, Congressional Briefings on Vietnam, Box 1, LBJL.

29. DeBenedetti, 54–55; Gibbons, 4:554–55.

30. Javits, 397–98.

31. Garrow, 469–70; Schulzinger, 236.

32. Gibbons, 4:555–56; Dallek, *Flawed Giant*, 450.

33. Gibbons, 4:562–70.

34. *PPP*, 1967, 1:353–54.

35. *NYT*, 3/16/67.

36. *PPP*, 1967, 1:61; *CQA*, 1967, 917.

37. *CR*, 2/23/67, 4295–96.

38. Ibid., 2/28/67, 4723.

39. Gibbons, 4:585–602.

40. *CR*, 3/2/67, 5279–96.

41. "Why Don't You Speak Out, Senator?" *New Republic*, 3/18/67.

42. *PPP*, 1967, 1:261.

43. "Why Don't You Speak Out, Senator?" *New Republic*, 3/18/67.

44. Dallek, *Flawed Giant*, 454.

45. Ibid.

46. Gibbons, 4:594.

47. Herring, *America's Longest War*, 173; http://www.thwall-usa.com/stats/index.html.

48. Garrow, 556–57; Schulzinger, 237.

49. Westmoreland, 273–74.

50. Gibbons, 4:617–18.

51. CQA, 1967, 926.

52. CR, 4/25/67, 10610–14.

53. Ibid., 4/25/67, 10624.

54. Gibbons, 4:619.

55. CIA Intelligence Memorandum, "The Effectiveness of the Rolling Thunder Program," 5/23/67, NSF, Country File, Vietnam, Box 43, LBJL.

56. Gibbons, 4:587.

57. Westmoreland cable to Joint Chiefs, 3/28/67; Joint Chiefs' report to McNamara, 4/20/67; and, Notes on LBJ's discussion with Westmoreland, 4/27/67, PP, NYT, 560–65; Notes on Westmoreland-Wheeler discussion with LBJ, 4/27/67, in Barrett, *Lyndon B. Johnson's Vietnam Papers*, 412–414.

58. Notes on Westmoreland–Wheeler discussion with LBJ, 4/27/67, in Barrett, *Lyndon B. Johnson's Vietnam Papers*, 412–14; McNamara, In Retrospect, 264–65.

59. PP, NYT, 580.

CHAPTER THIRTY-FOUR

1. PP, NYT, 577–85; McNamara, *In Retrospect*, 266–71.

2. Mansfield memorandum to file, 5/1/67 and Mansfield to LBJ, 4/29/67, XXII, 105, Mansfield Papers.

3. Mansfield memo to file, 5/1/67, XXII, 105, Mansfield Papers.

4. "Today" show transcript, 5/2/67, XIX, 596, Mansfield Papers.

5. Dallek, *Flawed Giant*, 464–65.

6. Gibbons, 4:685–86; Russell's "Notes on White House visit," 5/12/67, XVIII, Exhibit B, RBRL.

7. *CR*, 5/15/67, 12578–83; Gibbons, 4:683–85.

8. *CR*, 5/15/67, 12582; Ashby and Gramer, 225–27.

9. Fulbright to W. S. Atkins, 6/13/67, FR—Vietnam, 48:18, 51:1, Fulbright Papers.

10. McGovern press release, "The Lessons of Vietnam," 5/13/67, Speeches, Box 30, McGovern Papers, SGM.

11. *CR*, 5/15/67, 12608–9.

12. Mansfield to Lauren McKinsey, 6/20/67, XIII, 75, Mansfield Papers.

13. *CR*, 5/15/67, 12593–94.

14. *PP*, GE, 1967, 1:649.

15. McPherson to LBJ, 6/13/67, in Barrett, *Lyndon B. Johnson's Vietnam Papers*, 433–36.

16. Bunker to LBJ, 6/28/67, in Barrett, *Lyndon B. Johnson's Vietnam Papers*, 438.

17. Notes of 7/12/67 meeting, Thomas Johnson Meeting Notes, Box 1, LBJL.

18. Rostow to LBJ, 7/1/67, NSF, Country File, Vietnam, Box 55, LBJL.

19. Dallek, *Flawed Giant*, 471.

20. NYT, 8/7/67.

21. Dallek, *Flawed Giant*, 475.

22. Notes of 7/12/67 meeting, Thomas Johnson Meeting Notes, Box 1, LBJL.

23. PPP, 1967, 2:690–95.

24. Meeting with Senate committee chairs, 7/25/67, Thomas Johnson's Meeting Notes, Box 1, LBJL.

25. Dallek, *Flawed Giant*, 474.

26. Bundy, 6/2/69, LBJL.

27. CR, 7/11/67, 18368–70.

28. Gibbons, 4:808–24; Woods, *Fulbright*, 456–58.

29. *PP*, GE, 1967, 2:794–95.

30. Gibbons, 4:813, 815, 817.

31. *PP*, GE, 1967, 2:733–37.

32. Meeting notes, 10/3/67, Thomas Johnson's Meeting Notes, Box 1, LBJL.

33. Gibbons, 4:754–63; Califano, 242–46.

34. *CR*, 8/11/67, 22355–56.

35. Gibbons, 4:758.

36. *CR*, 8/11/67, 22348–52.

37. Clancy and Elder, 102–07.

38. Notes of meeting, 8/8/67, Thomas Johnson Meeting Notes, Box 1, LBJL.

39. Meeting notes, 9/12/67, Meeting Notes File, Box 2, LBJL.

40. Herring, *America's Longest War*, 179.

41. *PP*, IV, 199–204; Gibbons, 4:743–54; McNamara, *In Retrospect*, 283–90.

42. Meeting notes, 8/8/67, Thomas Johnson Meeting Notes, Box 1, LBJL.

43. McNamara, *In Retrospect*, 298.

44. Dallek, *Flawed Giant*, 480.

45. Meeting notes, 9/12/67, Meeting Notes File, Box 2, LBJL.

46. Dallek, *Flawed Giant*, 481.

47. Meeting notes, 9/26/67, Thomas Johnson Meeting Notes, Box 1, LBJL.

48. *PPP*, 1967, 2:876–79.

49. *PP*, GE, 4:205–6.

50. Meeting notes, 10/3/67, Thomas Johnson Meeting Notes, Box 1, LBJL.

51. Ibid., 10/4/67.

52. Ibid., 10/5/67.

53. *PP*, GE, 4:206–7.

54. Schulzinger, 240–41.

55. Meeting notes, 10/23/67, Thomas Johnson Meeting Notes, Box 1, LBJL.

56. Dallek, *Flawed Giant*, 486.

57. Meeting notes, 10/23/67, Thomas Johnson Meeting Notes, Box 1, LBJL.

58. Meeting with congressional leaders, 10/23/67, Thomas Johnson Meeting Notes, Box 1, LBJL.

59. McPherson to LBJ, 10/27/67, McPherson Office Files, Box 53, LBJL.

60. McNamara to LBJ, 11/1/67, in Barrett, *Lyndon B. Johnson's Vietnam Papers*, 515–22.

61. McNamara, *In Retrospect*, 305–9.

62. Meeting notes, 11/2/67, Meeting Notes File, Box 2, LBJL.

63. *PP*, GE, 4:216.

64. Ibid., 4:222–21.

65. *CQA*, 1967, 942; Mansfield to Russell Long, 10/9/67, U.S. Senate Series, 96, Long Papers, LSU.

66. Olson, 185–89.

67. *CQA*, 1967, 943-44.

68. Olson, 188.

69. *CR*, 11/20/67, 33130–31.

70. Gibbons, 4:908–15.

71. Olson, 191.

72. McNamara, *In Retrospect*, 311.

73. Roche OH, LBJL.

74. Christian OH, 7/1/71, LBJL.

75. Dallek, *Flawed Giant*, 495.

76. McNamara, *In Retrospect*, 313.

77. Humphrey, 348–49; Van Dyk, by Mann, 9/8/97.

78. Solberg, 311–12.

79. Gibbons, 4:894–96; Notes of NSC meeting, 11/9/67, in Barrett, *Lyndon B. Johnson's Vietnam Papers*, 531–33.

80. Humphrey, 349–50.

81. Meeting notes, 11/4/67, Meeting Notes File, Box 2, LBJL.

82. Meeting notes, 11/21/67, Thomas Johnson Meeting Notes, Box 1, LBJL.

83. *PP*, GE, 1967, 2:495.

84. Gibbons, 4:900–902.

85. Ibid., 4:902.

86. Karnow, 527.

CHAPTER THIRTY-FIVE

1. Congressional briefing transcript, 11/16/67, Congressional Briefings on Vietnam, Box 1, LBJL.

2. Gibbons, 4:896–900; *NYT*, 11/20/67.

3. *PP*, GE, 1968–69, 1:25.

4. Westmoreland, 384.

5. Gardner, *Pay Any Price*, 417.

6. Schulzinger, 259.

7. Gardner, *Pay Any Price*, 435.

9. Adams OH, 9/20,84, LBJL.

10. Bunker to LBJ, 2/8/68, in Barrett, *Lyndon B. Johnson's Vietnam Papers*, 590.

11. *CR*, 2/5/68, 2087.

12. Meeting notes, 2/6/8/68, Thomas Johnson Meeting Notes, Box 2, LBJL.

13. Karnow, 560.

14. Dallek, *Flawed Giant*, 506; Christian OH, (Culbert interview), LBJL.

15. Meeting notes, 2/6/68, Thomas Johnson Meeting Notes, Box 2, LBJL.

16. Schulzinger, 261.

17. Karnow, 559.

18. Clifford, 174–76.

19. Meeting notes, 2/12/68, Thomas Johnson Meeting Notes, Box 2, LBJL.

20. Russell's handwritten notes, 2/12/68, XVIII, Exhibit B, RBRL.

21. Meeting notes, 2/9/68, in Barrett, *Lyndon B. Johnson's Vietnam Papers*, 592–98.

22. Marcy OH, USSHO, 206.

23. Hebert OH, LBJL.

24. Clifford, 464.

25. Woods, *Fulbright*, 474–75.

26. Gibbons, 4:813; Berman, *William Fulbright and the Vietnam War*, 88.

27. Goulden, 203.

28. Woods, *Fulbright*, 476.

29. *The Gulf of Tonkin, The 1964 Incidents*, Hearing before the Committee on Foreign Relations, 2/20/68.

30. Woods, *Fulbright*, 478–79; Goulden, 204–5.

31. *CR*, 3/22/68, 7384.

32. *PP, NYT*, 596–98.

33. *Newsweek*, 3/25/68.

34. *CR*, 3/7/68, 5644–61.

35. "Issues and Answers" transcript, 1/14/68, Series XIX, Personal, Box 596, Mansfield Papers.

36. *CR*, 3/7/68, 5644–61.

37. Clifford, 484–85.

38. LBJ to Clifford, 2/28/68, in Barrett, *Lyndon B. Johnson's Vietnam Papers*, 635.

39. Clifford, 493.

40. Meeting notes, 3/4/68, Thomas Johnson Meeting Notes, Box 2, LBJL.

41. Rusk, 478; Woods, *Fulbright*, 470.

42. Fulbright to LBJ, 2/7/68, Series 1:1, 4:1, Fulbright Papers; Woods, *Fulbright*, 470.

43. LBJ to Fulbright, 2/7/68, in Barrett, *Lyndon B. Johnson's Vietnam Papers*, 588–89; After he dictated the letter, Johnson told a secretary: "Don't file. Tear up. Flush away. We didn't send it. I don't want a record of it."

44. Meeting notes, 2/9/68, Thomas Johnson Meeting Notes, 2/9/68, Box 2, LBJL.

45. *Newsweek*, 3/25/68.

46. Panzer to LBJ, 3/25/68, Confidential File FG400, FG431 Senate Committees, Box 34, LBJL.

47. Fulbright to Joe Martin, 3/22/68, FR Vietnam, Fulbright Papers.

CHAPTER THIRTY-SIX

1. Meeting notes, 3/4/68, Thomas Johnson Notes, Box 2, LBJL.

2. Johnson, 398.

3. McPherson, 199, 427.

4. Shesol, 400.

5. Ibid., 397, 400, 403–4; Schlesinger, *Robert Kennedy and His Times*, 837.

6. McGovern OH, LBJL; Chester, Hodgson, and Page, 66–67.

7. Witcover, 37–38; Miller, *Lyndon*, 504.

8. Shesol, 411.

9. Chester, Hodgson, and Page, 98; Witcover, 93.

10. Miller, 505.

11. Schlesinger, *Robert Kennedy and His Times*, 839; Chester, Hodgson, and Page, 99.

12. Whalen, 128.

13. *NYT*, 3/11/68.

14. Shesol, 418.

15. Memorandum of conversation, 3/14/68, in Barrett, *Lyndon B. Johnson's Vietnam Papers*, 671–74; Schlesinger, *Robert Kennedy and His Times*, 851–54.

16. Shesol, 422.

17. Ibid, 423.

18. Guy to LBJ, 3/7/68, in Barrett, *Lyndon B. Johnson's Vietnam Papers*, 656.

19. Pearson to LBJ, 3/11/68, in Barrett, *Lyndon B. Johnson's Vietnam Papers*, 663–64.

20. Dallek, *Flawed Giant*, 506–7.

21. Meeting notes, 3/22/68, Meeting Notes File, Box 2, LBJL.

22. *PP*, GE, 1968, 1:318, 382.

23. Ibid,. 1:410.

24. McPherson to LBJ, 3/18/68, Office Files of Harry McPherson, Box 53, LBJL.

25. McPherson, 430.

26. Mansfield to LBJ, 3/13/68, in Barrett, *Lyndon B. Johnson's Vietnam Papers*, 668.

27. Isaacson and Thomas, 694; Rostow to LBJ, 3/14/68, in Barrett, *Lyndon B. Johnson's Vietnam Papers*, 674–75.

28. Rowe to LBJ, 3/19/68, in Barrett, *Lyndon B. Johnson's Vietnam Papers*, 674–75, 686–88.

29. Isaacson and Thomas, 695.

30. Bundy to LBJ, 3/22/68, in Barrett, *Lyndon B. Johnson's Vietnam Papers*, 700.

31. Meeting notes, 3/19/68, Meeting Notes File, Box 2, LBJL.

32. Clifford, 510.

33. Clifford OH, 7/14/69, LBJL.

34. Herring, *America's Longest War*, 202.

35. Isaacson and Thomas, 698–700.

36. Meeting notes, 3/26/68, Meeting Notes File, Box 2, LBJL.

37. Isaacson and Thomas, 703.

38. Transcript, *Vietnam: A Television History*, "The Tet Offensive (1968)," Public Broadcasting System: http://www.pbs.org/wgbh/amex/vietnam/107ts.html.

39. Ibid., 703–5.

40. McPherson, 435.

41. Mansfield OH, 12/13/76, BBC, Mansfield Papers; Mansfield, by Mann; Ferris, by Mann.

42. McPherson, 436.

43. Ibid., 438.

44. Dallek, *Flawed Giant*, 526–27.

45. Powell Moore OH, RBRL.

46. Kearns, 343.

47. *PPP*, 1968–69, 2:469–76.

48. Ibid., 2:476–78.

49. McGovern statement, 4/1/68, Speeches, Box 35, McGovern Papers.

50. Russell statement, 4/1/68, III. Speech/Media, B.Media, Box 22, RBRL.

51. *CR*, 4/2/68, 8575.

52. Ibid., 4/1/68, 8417.

53. Ibid., 4/3/68, 8865.

54. Ibid., 4/1/68, 8414.

55. Nixon statement, 4/1/68, Speech File, PPS 208 (1968).15, Nixon Library.

56. Clifford, 528.

57. Johnson, *Vantage Point*, 422.

58. *CR*, 4/2/68, 8570.

59. Dallek, *Flawed Giant*, 537.

60. *PPP*, 1968–69, 2:492.

61. Ibid., 2:556.

62. Johnson, *Vantage Point*, 505.

63. Herring, *America's Longest War*, 207.

64. Johnson, *Vantage Point*, 507–8.

65. Solberg, 322.

66. Schlesinger, *Robert Kennedy and His Times*, 883, 889, 906–7.

67. Nixon speech transcript, 3/7/68, PPS 208(1968).11.3, Nixon Library; Wicker, *One of Us*, 313.

68. Whalen, 137.

69. Ibid., 143.

70. Wicker, *One of Us*, 322.

71. Nixon interview, 5/26/68, Speech File: Oregon telethon, PPS 208 (1968).36, Nixon Library.

72. Shesol, 450.

73. Schlesinger, *Robert Kennedy and His Times*, 914.

CHAPTER THIRTY-SEVEN

1. McGovern introduction of RFK, Speeches, Box 35, McGovern Papers.

2. McGovern, 111.

3. Ibid., 118.

4. McGovern announcement, 8/10/68, Speeches, Box 37, McGovern Papers.

5. Solberg, 340.

6. Witcover, 275.

7. Solberg, 346.

8. Ibid., 350; *PPP*, 1969–68, 2:901.

9. Solberg, 353.

10. Humphrey, 389–90.

11. McGovern statement, 8/20/68, Box 37, McGovern Papers.

12. McGovern/McCarthy proposal, 8/23/68, Speeches, Box 37, McGovern Papers.

13. Chester, Hodgson, and Page, 537.

14. *CQA*, 1968, 1021.

15. Ibid., 1021–24.

16. Chester, Hodgson and Page, 581–82.

17. Ibid., 584–85; Wicker, *One of Us*, 354–55.

18. Karnow, 595.

19. Witcover, 336.

20. McGovern statement, 8/29/68, Box 37, McGovern Papers.

21. *NYT*, 8/29/68.

22. Nixon statement, 8/1/68, PPS 208(1968).54, Nixon Library.

23. *NYT*, 3/6/69.

24. Press conference transcript, Speech File, Press Conference, PPS 208 (1968). 56, Nixon Library.

25. Connell OH, LBJL.

26. Laird OH, FMOC.

27. Ball, 436–37, 444–45.

28. Nixon interview, 9/24/68, PPS 208(1968).121.1, Nixon Library.

29. *Detroit Free Press*, 9/29/68.

30. Ball, 445–46; Solberg, 380–84; Van Dyk, by Mann, 9/8/97.

31. Chester, Hodgson, and Page, 649.

32. Connell OH, LBJL.

33. Solberg, 386–87; Ball, 447.

34. Herring, *America's Longest War*, 213–14.

35. Meeting notes, 10/14/68, Thomas Johnson Meeting Notes, Box 4, LBJL.

36. Kimball, 59.

37. Meeting notes, 10/14/68, Thomas Johnson Meeting Notes, Box 4, LBJL.

38. Chennault, 175.

39. Solberg, 394–95.

40. William Bundy OH, #5, LBJL.

41. Nixon statement, 10/25/68, Speech File, PPS(1968).226, Nixon Library.

42. Witcover, 404.

43. *PPP*, 1968–69, 2:1087–93.
44. Nixon speech text, 10/27/68, Speech File, PPS 208(1968).232, Nixon Library.
45. Nguyen and Schecter, 24; Solberg, 395.
46. Witcover, 410–12.
47. McPherson,4/9/69, LBJL.
48. Meeting notes, 10/29/68, Thomas Johnson Meeting Notes, Box 4, LBJL.
49. Ibid.
50. Connell OH, LBJL.
51. Van Dyk, by Mann, 9/8/97.
52. Johnson, *Vantage Point*, 516.
53. Bundy, 46–47.
54. Johnson, *Vantage Point*, 518.
55. *PPP*, 1968–69, 2:1099–1103.
56. Clifford, 593.
57. Solberg, 407.
58. Safire, 88.

CHAPTER THIRTY-EIGHT

1. Nixon, *RN*, 366.
2. Haldeman, *The Ends of Power*, 81.
3. Riegle, 20; Anderson, *Shadow on the White House*, 130, 146.
4. *Washington Evening Star*, 1/27/69.
5. Olson, 203.
6. *Washington Evening Star*, 1/27/69.
7. Ibid., 1/29/69.
8. Williams, by Mann, 9/8/97.
9. *Arkansas Democrat*, 1/16/69.
10. Kissinger, *White House Years*, 227.
11. Karnow, 603–4; Schulzinger, 275–76.
12. Nixon, *No More Vietnams*, 29, 46.
13. Jones, by Mann, 8/25/97.
14. Woods, *Fulbright*, 505.
15. Ibid., 504–5; Ambrose, *Nixon*, 256–58.
16. Tucker, 156.
17. Haldeman, *The Ends of Power*, 83.
18. Nguyen and Schecter, 39–40, 483n1; Bundy, 48, 65.
19. Berman, *William Fulbright and the Vietnam War*, 107–8.
20. *CR*, 3/26/69, 7634.
21. Ibid., 3/17/69, 6576–78.
22. Ibid., 7/2/69, 18198–18208.
23. *NYT*, 5/9/69.
24. Ibid., 5/15/69.
25. *CR*, 5/8/69, 11826.
26. Haldeman, *The Haldeman Diaries*, 56.

27. Ambrose, *Nixon*, 265.

28. *NYT*, 6/9 and 6/11/69.

29. Meeting notes, 6/12/69, President's Meeting Files, 1969–74, Nixon Papers, University Publications of America.

30. Nixon, *RN*, 393.

31. Ibid., 393–94.

32. Kissinger, *White House Years*, 277–80; Nixon, *RN*, 396.

33. Kissinger, *White House Years*, 281–82.

34. RNC poll, August 1969, WHSF: Haldeman, Box 406, NPM, NARA.

35. *NYT*, 7/31/69.

36. Nixon, *RN*, 397.

37. "Issues and Answers" transcript, 9/14/69, XIX, 539, Mansfield Papers.

38. *CR*, 9/9/69, 24860–61.

39. Ibid., 9/10/69, 25044.

40. Kissinger to Nixon, 9/10/69, NSC, Lake Chron, 1047, NPM, NARA.

41. Ambrose, *Nixon*, 299.

42. Ibid., 300.

43. Woods, *Fulbright*, 533.

44. *NYT*, 9/27/69.

45. Ibid., 9/27/69.

46. Meeting notes, 9/29/69, The President's Meeting File, 1969–74, Nixon Papers, University Publications of America.

47. *NYT*, 9/27/69.

48. Ambrose, *Nixon*, 301.

49. *CR*, 10/1/69, 27861.

50. Ibid., 10/9/69, 29397–98.

51. Anson, 174–75.

52. *CR*, 10/27/69, 31514; Anson, 172.

53. DeBenedetti, 255–57; *NYT*, 10/16/69.

54. DeBenedetti, 255–57.

55. Ambrose, 302.

56. Nixon, *RN*, 403, 405.

57. *NYT*, 10/20/69.

58. Safire, 177.

59. Nixon, *RN*, 408–9.

60. McMahon, 447–52.

61. Nixon, *RN*, 410; Schulzinger, 282.

62. *WP*, 1/23/99.

63. "Today" show transcript, 11/4/69, XIX, 597, Mansfield Papers.

64. *CR*, 11/4/69, 32781–82.

65. Woods, *Fulbright*, 538.

66. Fulbright to Coffin, 11/8/69, 48:18, Box 56:3, Fulbright Papers.

67. McGovern release, 11/5/69, Speeches, Box 43, McGovern Papers.

68. *CR*, 11/4/69, 32790–92.

69. Ibid., 32782.

70. Moss OH, FMOC.

71. McPherson OH, 12/5/68, LBJL.

72. Valeo, 35.

73. Williams, by Mann, 9/8/97.

74. Tillman, by Mann, 9/11/97.

75. Bryce Nelson, by Mann.

76. *NYT*, 11/16/69.

77. Anson, 172.

78. DeBenedetti, 265–66; *NYT*, 11/17 and 25/69; Young, 243.

79. *Chicago Tribune*, 1/8/70 and 2/5/70.

80. *CR*, 11/21/69, 35351–52

81. *Face the Nation* transcript, 11/30/69, *Face the Nation: The Collected Transcripts from the CBS Radio and Television Broadcasts*.

82. Nixon to Kissinger, 11/24/69, WHSF, Subject Files, CO 165, Box 84, NPM, NARA-CP.

83. *NYT*, 12/16/69.

84. Nixon, *RN*, 414; *CQA*, 1969, 1003.

85. Whalen, 236.

CHAPTER THIRTY-NINE

1. Schlesinger to Fulbright, 1/26/70; Fulbright to Schlesinger, 1/30/70, 48:18, 61:4, Fulbright Papers.

2. Ambrose, *Nixon*, 327.

3. *Time*, 1/5/70.

4. Ibid., 1/12/70.

5. Herring, *America's Longest War*, 226.

6. Ambrose, *Nixon*, 324; Kissinger to Nixon, 1/16/70, NSC Files, Lake Chron, Box 1046, NPM, NARA-CP.

7. *NYT*, 2/2/70; *Time*, 2/9/70.

8. McGovern press release, 2/4/70, Speeches, Box 45, McGovern Papers.

9. *CR*, 3/3/70, 5610.

10. *Time*, 3/16/70.

11. Ambrose, *Nixon*, 335–36; Woods, *Fulbright*, 552–53.

12. McGovern speech, 3/5/70, Speeches, Box 45, McGovern Papers.

13. Woods, *Fulbright*, 554.

14. *CR*, 4/2/70, 10150–51.

15. *Time*, 4/20/70.

16. Ibid.

17. Nixon, *RN*, 422–23; Ambrose, *Nixon*, 337–38.

18. Shawcross, 134.

19. Nixon to Kissinger, 4/22/70, President's Personal File, Memoranda from the President, Box 2, NPM, NARA-CP.

20. Kissinger, *White House Years*, 475–81.

21. *NYT*, 4/21/70.

22. Kissinger, *White House Years*, 496; Bundy, 153.

23. McMahon, 452–55.

24. *NYT*, 5/3/70.

25. *Newsweek*, 5/11/70.

26. *CR*, 5/1/70, 13885.

27. Woods, *Fulbright*, 564.

28. *Time*, 5/11/70.

29. Mansfield memorandum, 5/11/70, XXII, 103, Mansfield Papers; See also, Valeo, 227–29.

30. McGovern statements, 4/29 and 5/1/70, Box 46, McGovern Papers.

31. McGovern statement, 5/1/70, Speeches, Box 47, McGovern Papers.

32. *CR*, 5/1/70, 13829–34.

33. Ashby and Gramer, 313; *CQA*, 1970, 932–33; *NYT*, 5/9/70.

34. Safire, 190.

35. Ashby and Gramer, 314.

36. *NYT*, 5/5/70.

37. *Time*, 5/18/70.

38. *Newsweek*, 5/18/70.

39. *CQA*, 1970, 933–35.

40. Ashby and Gramer, 313–14; *NYT*, 5/9/70.

41. *CQA*, 1970, 936.

42. Ibid., 937–38.

43. Ibid., 937, 940.

44. Ashby and Gramer, 315.

45. *CQA*, 1970, 947.

46. *CR*, 7/10/70, 23711.

47. *CQA*, 1970, 941.

48. Ibid., 948–49.

49. Ibid., 942.

50. Hatfield, by Mann.

51. DeBenedetti, 287.

52. Michaelson and Hatfield, by Mann.

53. Cunningham, by Mann.

54. Ashby and Gramer, 317; Anson, 176.

55. Anson, 176–77.

56. Holum, by Mann, 9/10/97.

57. McGovern, by Mann, 1/27/97.

58. Ashby and Gramer, 331–32.

59. *CQA*, 1970, 397.

60. *CR*, 9/1/70, 30664.

61. Cunningham, by Mann.

62. *CR*, 9/1/70, 30682.

63. Holum, by Mann, 9/10/97.

64. Ibid.; McGovern could not recall the senator's name.

65. *CR*, 9/1/70, 30683; Mueller, 96.

66. Anson, 178.

67. *Time*, 9/14/70.

68. Anson, 178.

69. Kissinger, *White House Years*, 513.

CHAPTER FORTY

1. Kutler, *The Wars of Watergate*, 158; Haldeman, *The Ends of Power*, 100–108.

2. Ashby and Gramer, 334.

3. DeBenedetti, 288–89.

4. Safire, 308–9.

5. Kissinger, *White House Years*, 969.

6. *NYT*, 10/8/70.

7. Ambrose, *Nixon*, 390; *Time*, 10/19/70.

8. Ambrose, *Nixon*, 390.

9. *Time*, 10/26/70.

10. Chapin to Walker, 10/21/70, WHSF:Subject Files, Confidential Files, CO 165, Box 46, NPM, NARA-CP.

11. *Time*, 11/9/70.

12. Ibid., 11/16/70.

13. Minutes of Senate Democratic Conference, 11/16/70, XXII, 90, Mansfield Papers.

14. The Vietnam Veterans Memorial Wall Page: http://thewall-usa.com/stats/index.html#year.

15. *Time*, 1/25/71.

16. Ibid., 6/7/71; Ambrose, *Nixon*, 418.

17. *NYT*, 1/4/71.

18. *Newsweek*, 2/15/71.

19. *CQA*, 1971, 354.

20. *Newsweek*, 2/8/71.

21. Ibid.

22. *NYT*, 4/5 and 4/22/71; Ambrose, *Nixon*, 420.

23. *NYT*, 3/24/71.

24. Ambrose, *Nixon*, 421.

25. *Newsweek*, 4/19/71.

26. *NYT*, 4/8/71.

27. *Time*, 4/19/71.

28. Ibid.

29. *Newsweek*, 4/19/71.

30. *WP*, 12/27/98.

31. McGovern testimony, 4/20/71, Speeches, Box 55, McGovern Papers.

32. *CQA*, 1971, 351–53.

33. *Time*, 5/3/71.

34. Ibid.; Herring, *America's Longest War*, 235.

35. *NYT*, 4/25/71; *Newsweek*, 5/3 and 5/17/71; *Time*, 5/3 and 5/17/71.

36. *CQA*, 1971, 272–82; *Time*, 5/24/71.

37. Olson, 225; Haldeman, *Haldeman Diaries*, 305.

38. *CQA*, 1971, 282–83.

39. *CR*, 6/16/71, 20176–79.

40. *CQA*, 1971, 284; *Newsweek*, 6/28/71.

41. *CQA*, 1971, 282.

42. *Newsweek*, 6/28/71.

43. McGovern, by Mann, 1/27/97.

44. *Newsweek*, 6/28/71.

45. *NYT*, 6/13/71.

46. Ellsberg interview, 7/29/98, "Conversations with History," Institute of International Studies, UC Berkley: http://globetrotter.berkeley.edu/people/Ellsberg/ellsberg98–7.html.

47. Jones to Fulbright, undated, "Background of Contacts with Daniel Ellsberg," Norvill Jones Papers (private collection).

48. *WP*, 4/30/72.

49. Jones to Fulbright, undated, "Background of Contacts with Daniel Ellsberg," Norvill Jones Papers (private collection).

50. *CR*, 8/7/70, 27827–28.

51. *WP*, 4/30/72.

52. Holum, by Mann, 9/10/97.

53. Rudenstine, 46; Haldeman, *The Ends of Power*, 110.

54. Schulzinger, 291.

55. *WP*, 11/23/96 and 1/24/97; Kutler, *Abuse of Power*, 3–9.

56. Wicker, *One of Us*, 645; Karnow, 649; Ambrose, *Nixon*, 465–66.

57. Anson, 180.

58. Ibid., 184; McGovern notes on Thieu conversation and notes of *Time* interview, 9/15/71, Box 58, McGovern Papers; Time, 9/27/71; *NYT*, 9/14 and 9/15/71.

59. *NYT*, 9/17/71, 10/3 and 10/4/71; Ambrose, Nixon, 463–64.

60. *CR*, 9/27/71, 33458.

61. Olson, 227; CR, 9/27/71, 33458.

62. CQA, 1971, 402–3.

63. Ibid., 406.

64. Ibid., 387; *CR*, 12/15/71, 47118–20.

CHAPTER FORTY-ONE

1. Ambrose, *Nixon*, 493–94.

2. *NYT*, 1/26/72; Young, 268; Schulzinger, 293.

3. *NYT*, 1/26/72.

4. *CR*, 1/26/72.

5. *NYT*, 1/26/72.

6. *Ibid.*

7. Jones to Fulbright, 1/26/72, 78:8, Box 51:3, Fulbright Papers.

8. Young, 268.

9. McGovern press release, 2/10/72, Campaign Issues–1972, Box 26, McGovern Papers; Young, 268.

10. Young, 266–68; Wicker, *One of Us*, 596–97; Schulzinger, 293–94.

11. "Face the Nation" transcript, 4/2/72.

12. See Hersch, *Price of Power*, 506.

13. Schulzinger, 295; Herring, *America's Longest War*, 240–41; Young, 269.

14. Karnow, 657.

15. *NYT*, 4/27/72.

16. *CQA*, 1972, 842–44.

17. Ibid., 842–51.

18. Safire, 422–27.

19. *NYT*, 5/9/72.

20. Herring, *America's Longest War*, 242.

21. *CR*, 5/9/72, 16353, 16361–62.

22. Herring, *America's Longest War*, 242.

23. *WP*, 5/10/72.

24. *St. Louis Post-Dispatch*, 5/9/72.

25. *Christian Science Monitor*, 5/10/72.

26. Woods, *Fulbright*, 615–16.

27. *CR*, 5/9/72, 16355.

28. Ibid., 16359–60.

29. Ibid., 5/11/72, 16977.

30. *CQA*, 1972, 453–55; *CR*, 6/12/72, 20516.

31. Young, 272.

32. Sorley, 326–27.

33. Herring, *America's Longest War*, 243; Young, 272; Isaacson, *Kissinger*, 439.

34. *NYT*, 6/29/72.

35. *CR*, 7/24/72, 25053–54; *CQA*, 1972, 456–63.

36. *CQA*, 1972, 468–71.

37. Kissinger, *White House Years*, 1307.

38. Hatfield, by Mann.

39. Ted Van Dyk, by Mann, 1/30/97.

40. *NYT*, 7/30/72.

41. McGovern statement, July 12, 1972, Box 67, McGovern Papers, SGM.

42. Isaacson, *Kissinger*, 440–41.

43. Kissinger, *White House Years*, 1308.

44. Young, 273; Karnow, 662; Isaacson, *Kissinger*, 447–48; Schulzinger, 298–99.

45. Karnow, 663.

46. *NYT*, 4/29/2000.

47. Kissinger, *White House Years*, 1352–61; Nixon, *RN*, 693–94; Isaacson, *Kissinger*, 454; *NYT*, 10/25/72.

48. Nixon, *RN*, 701–2.

49. Ibid., 704–5.

50. White, *The Making of the President—1972*, 363.

51. Nixon, *RN*, 704–7; *NYT*, 10/27/72; Ambrose, *Nixon*, 648–49.

52. *NYTM*, 5/5/73.

53. Ibid.

54. McGovern concession speech, November 7, 1972, Box 73, McGovern Papers, SGM.

55. Nixon, *RN*, 717.

CHAPTER FORTY-TWO

1. Isaacson, *Kissinger*, 462.
2. Kissinger, *White House Years*, 1415–16.
3. Ibid., 1447–48.
4. Herring, 247; Schulzinger, 300–302; Young, 278–79.
5. Nixon, *RN*, 733–34.
6. Karnow, 667–68.
7. Herring, 249.
8. Olson, 233.
9. Nixon, *RN*, 742; Young, 279.
10. Kissinger, *White House Years*, 1459.
11. Karnow, 668–69; *NYT*, 1/16/73.
12. *NYT*, 1/24/73.
13. Ibid., 1/28/73.
14. Ibid., 3/30 and 4/4/73.
15. Olson, 237.
16. Kissinger, *Years of Upheaval*, 124, 358–57.
17. *CQA*, 1973, 95–107; Nixon, *RN*, 887–88.
18. Olson, 237–38.
19. Ashby and Gramer, 406.
20. *CQA*, 1973, 862.
21. Nixon, *RN*, 888.
22. Tucker, 191–99.
23. *CQA*, 1973, 905–8.
24. Ibid., 886–87.
25. *NYT*, 5/7/74.
26. Kolko, 502–6.
27. *CR*, 8/20/74, 29179.
28. Ibid.
29. Ford, 141–42.
30. Jones, by Mann, 7/21/97.
31. Williams, by Mann, 9/8/97.
32. Woods, *Fulbright*, 669–70.
33. Ford, 250–55; *NYT*, 4/11/75.
34. Ford, 255–56.
35. *Newsweek*, 4/28/75.

Bibliography

ARCHIVES AND SPECIAL COLLECTIONS

American Foreign Policy Center, Louisiana Tech University, Ruston, LA
Presidential Papers of Harry S. Truman (microfilm)
Presidential Papers of Dwight D. Eisenhower (microfilm)
Presidential Papers of John F. Kennedy (microfilm)
Papers of John Foster Dulles (microfilm)
John F. Kennedy Library, Boston, MA
Papers of John F. Kennedy
Library of Congress
Manuscript Division
Oral History Project, Association of Former Members of Congress
Lyndon B. Johnson Library, Austin, TX
Papers of Lyndon B. Johnson
National Archives and Records Administration, College Park, MD
Nixon Presidential Materials
National Archives and Records Administration, Laguna Nigel, CA
Richard Nixon Pre-Presidential Papers
National Archives and Records Administration, Washington, D.C.
Legislative Archives
Records of the Committee on Foreign Relations
Records of Carl Marcy
Records of J. William Fulbright
Richard Nixon Library, Yorba Linda, CA
Richard Nixon Pre-Presidential Papers
Richard B. Russell Library, University of Georgia, Athens
Dean Rusk Oral History Collection
Richard B. Russell Jr. Senatorial Papers
Richard B. Russell Oral History Project
University of Arkansas, University Libraries Special Collections, Fayetteville
J. William Fulbright Papers
University of California, Berkeley, The Bancroft Library
Helen G. Douglas Oral History Project

University of Montana, Mansfield Library, K. Ross Toole Archives, Missoula, MT
Mike Mansfield Collection
University of New Orleans Library, New Orleans, LA
Papers of the Nixon White House (microfiche), University Publications of America
Columbia University Oral History Collection
Seeley G. Mudd Manuscript Library, Princeton University, Princeton, NJ
John Foster Dulles Papers
George McGovern Papers
U.S. Senate Historical Office, U.S. Senate, Washington, D.C.
Senate Staff Oral History Program

GOVERNMENT PUBLICATIONS

Congressional Record. U.S. Congress. 1949–74.
Executive Sessions of the Senate Foreign Relations Committee. (Historical Series) 1949–1966. U.S. Senate. Washington: USGPO, 1976–93.
Foreign Relations of the United States, 1947—The Far East. Vol. VI. USDS. Washington: USGPO, 1972.
———, *1948—The Far East and Australasia (sic).* Vol. VI. USDS. Washington: USGPO, 1974.
———, *1949—The Far East and Australasia.* Vol. VII. USDS. Washington: USGPO, 1975.
———, *1950—East Asia and The Pacific.* Vol. VI. USDS. Washington: USGPO, 1976.
———, *1950—Indochina.* Vol. VI. USDS. Washington: USGPO, 1974.
———, *1951—Indochina.* Vol. VI. USDS. Washington: USGPO, 1977.
———, *1951—Asia and the Pacific.* Vol. VI. Washington: USGPO, 1977.
———, *1952–1954—Indochina.* Vol. XIII. Washington: USGPO, 1982.
———, *1955–1957—Vietnam.* Vol. I. USDS. Washington: USGPO, 1985.
———, *1958–1960—Vietnam.* Vol. I. USDS. Washington: USGPO, 1986.
———, *1961–1963—Vietnam.* Vols. I–IV. Washington: USGPO, 1988–91.
———, *1964–1968—Vietnam.* Vols. I–IV. Washington: USGPO, 1992–98.
Public Papers of the Presidents of the United States: Lyndon B. Johnson. Washington: USGPO, 1964–69.
The Gulf of Tonkin, The 1964 Incidents. U.S. Senate. Committee on Foreign Relations. 90th Cong., 2d sess., 2/20/68.

MEMOIRS, DOCUMENTARIES, PERSONAL ACCOUNTS, ORAL HISTORY COLLECTIONS, AND OTHER PRIMARY SOURCES

Acheson, Dean. *Present at the Creation: My Years in the State Department.* New York: W. W. Norton, 1969.
Adams, Sherman. *Firsthand Report: The Story of the Eisenhower Administration.* New York: Harper, 1961.

Ball, George W. *The Past Has Another Pattern: Memoirs.* New York: W. W. Norton, 1982.

Barrett, David M., ed. *Lyndon B. Johnson's Vietnam Papers: A Documentary Collection.* College Station: Texas A&M, 1997.

Bernstein, Barton J., and Matusow, Allen, J. *The Truman Administration: A Documentary History.* New York: Harper and Row, 1966.

Beschloss, Michael R., ed. *Taking Charge: The Johnson White House Tapes, 1963–1964.* New York: Simon and Schuster, 1997.

Bradely, Benjamin C. *Conversations With Kennedy.* New York: W. W. Norton, 1975.

Browne, Malcolm. *Muddy Boots and Red Socks: A Reporter's Life.* New York: Times, 1993.

Califano, Joseph A., Jr. *The Triumph and Tragedy of Lyndon Johnson: The White House Years.* New York: Simon and Schuster, 1991.

Chennault, Anna. *The Education of Anna.* New York: Times, 1980.

Clifford, Clark. *Counsel to the President: A Memoir.* New York: Random House, 1971.

Douglas, William O. *North from Malaya: Adventure on Five Fronts.* Garden City, NY: Doubleday, 1953.

Eden, Sir Anthony. *Full Circle.* London: Cassell, 1960.

Eisenhower, Dwight D. *Mandate for Change, 1953–1956: The White House Years.* Garden City, NY: Doubleday, 1963.

Ferrell, Robert H. *The Eisenhower Diaries.* New York: W. W. Norton, 1981.

Ford, Gerald R. *A Time to Heal: The Autobiography of Gerald R. Ford.* New York: Harper and Row, 1979.

Galloway, John. *The Gulf of Tonkin Resolution.* Rutherford: Fairleigh Dickenson University, 1970.

Gittinger, Ted, ed. *The Johnson Years: A Vietnam Roundtable.* Austin: LBJ Library, 1993.

Goldwater, Barry. *Goldwater.* New York: St. Martin's, 1988.

Gruening, Ernest. *Many Battles: The Autobiography of Ernest Gruening.* New York: Liveright, 1973.

Haldeman, H. R. *The Haldeman Diaries: Inside the Nixon White House.* New York: Putnam, 1994.

———. *The Ends of Power.* New York: Times, 1978.

Hatfield. Mark O. *Not Quite So Simple.* New York: Harper and Row, 1968.

Hilsman, Roger. *To Move a Nation: The Politics of Foreign Policy in the Administration of John F. Kennedy.* Garden City, NY: Doubleday, 1967.

Hoopes, Townsend. *The Limits of Intervention.* New York: David McKay, 1969.

Hull, Cordell. *The Memoirs of Cordell Hull.* Vol. II. London: Hodder and Stoughton, 1948.

Humphrey, Hubert H. *The Education of a Public Man: My Life and Politics.* Garden City, NY: Doubleday, 1976.

Javits, Jacob. *Javits: The Autobiography of a Public Man.* Boston: Houghton, Mifflin, 1981.

Johnson, Lyndon Baines. *The Vantage Point: Perspectives of the Presidency, 1963–1969.* New York: Holt, Rinehart and Winston, 1971.

Johnson, U. Alexis. *The Right Hand of Power*. Englewood Cliffs: Prentice Hall, 1984.

The Johnson Presidential Press Conferences. Vol. I. New York: Earl M. Coleman, 1978.

Just, Ward. *To What End: Report from Vietnam*. New York: Public Affairs, 1968, 2000.

Kissinger, Henry. *White House Years*. Boston: Little, Brown, 1979.

———. *Years of Upheaval*. Boston: Little, Brown, 1982.

Kutler, Stanely I., ed. *Abuse of Power: The New Nixon Tapes*. New York: Free Press, 1997.

McGovern, George. *Grassroots: The Autobiography of George McGovern*. New York: Random House, 1977.

McMahon, Robert J. *Major Problems in the History of the Vietnam War: Documents and Essays*. Lexington: D. C. Heath, 1990.

McNamara, Robert S., Blight, James G., and Brigham, Robert K. *Argument Without End: In Search of Answers to the Vietnam Tragedy*. New York: Public Affairs, 1999.

McNamara, Robert S. *In Retrospect: The Tragedy and Lessons of Vietnam*. New York: Times, 1995.

McPherson, Harry. *A Political Education*. Boston: Little, Brown, 1972.

Mecklin, John. *Mission in Torment: An Intimate Account of the U.S. Role in Vietnam*. Garden City, NY: Doubleday, 1965.

Miller, Merle. *Lyndon: An Oral Biography*. New York: G. P. Putnam, 1980.

———. *Plain Speaking: An Oral Biography of Harry S. Truman*. New York: Putnam, 1974.

Nixon, Richard. *No More Vietnams*. New York: Arbor House, 1985.

———. *RN: The Memoirs of Richard Nixon*. New York: Grossett and Dunlap, 1978.

O'Donnell, Kenneth P., and Powers, David F. *'Johnny, We Hardly Knew Ye': Memories of John Fitzgerald Kennedy*. Boston: Little, Brown, 1972.

The Pentagon Papers: The Defense Department History of United States Decisionmaking on Vietnam, The Senator Gravel Edition. Vols. I–V. Boston: Beacon, 1971.

The Pentagon Papers. New York: Bantam, 1971.

Radford, Arthur W. *From Pearl Harbor to Vietnam: The Memoirs of Admiral Arthur W. Radford*. Stanford, CA: Hoover Institution, 1980.

Raskin, Marcus G., and Fall, Bernard B., eds. *The Viet-Nam Reader: Articles and Documents on American Foreign Policy and the Viet-Nam Crisis*. New York: Vintage, 1965.

Riegle, Donald S. *O Congress*. Garden City, NY: Doubleday, 1972.

Robinson, Frank M., and Kemp, Earl., eds. *The Truth About Vietnam: Report on the U.S. Senate Hearings*. San Diego: Greenleaf, 1966.

Rowan, Carl T. *Breaking Barriers: A Memoir*. Boston: Little, Brown, 1991.

Rusk, Dean. *As I Saw It*. New York: W. W. Norton, 1990.

Safire, William. *Before the Fall: An Inside View of the Pre-Watergate White House*. New York: Doubleday, 1975.

Salisbury, Harrison E. *Behind the Lines–Hanoi*. New York: Harper and Row, 1967.

Schlesinger, Arthur M., Jr. *A Thousand Days: John F. Kennedy in the White House*. Boston: Houghton Mifflin, 1965.

Sharp, U. S. Grant. *Strategy for Defeat: Vietnam in Retrospect.* San Rafael, CA: Presidio, 1978.

Sorenson, Theodore C. *Kennedy.* New York: Harper and Row, 1965.

Strober, Gerald S. and Deborah H. *'Let Us Begin Anew': An Oral History of the Kennedy Presidency.* New York: HarperCollins, 1993.

———. *Nixon: An Oral History of His Presidency.* New York: HarperCollins, 1994.

Taylor, Maxwell D. *Swords and Plowshares.* New York: Norton, 1972.

Theoharis, Athan. *From the Secret Files of J. Edgar Hoover.* Chicago: Ivan R. Dee, 1991.

Truman, Harry S. *Years of Trial and Hope: Memoirs by Harry S. Truman.* Vol. II. New York: Time, 1956.

Urofsky, Melvin I. *The Douglas Letters: Selections from the Private Papers of Justice William O. Douglas.* Bethesda, MD: Adler and Adler, 1987.

Valeo, Francis R. *Mike Mansfield, Majority Leader: A Different Kind of Senate, 1961–1976.* Armonk, NY: M. E. Sharp, 1999.

Valenti, Jack. *A Very Human President.* New York: W. W. Norton, 1976.

Vietnam: A Television History, Public Broadcasting System, 1983, 13 parts, transcripts: http://www.pbs.org/wgbh/amex/vietnam.

Westmoreland, William C. *A Soldier Reports.* New York: Doubleday, 1976.

Whalen, Richard J. *Catch the Falling Flag: A Republican's Challenge to His Party.* Boston: Houghton, Mifflin, 1972.

Williams, William A., McCormick, Thomas, Gardner, Lloyd C., and LaFeber, Walter. *America in Vietnam: A Documentary History.* New York: W. W. Norton, 1985.

BOOKS

Aitken, Jonathan. *Nixon: A Life.* Washington: Regenry, 1993.

Ambrose, Stehphen E. *Nixon: The Education of a Politician, 1913–1962.* New York: Simon and Schuster, 1987.

———. *Nixon: The Triumph of a Politician, 1962–1972.* New York: Simon and Schuster, 1989.

Anderson, David L., ed. *Shadow on the White House: Presidents and the Vietnam War, 1945–1975.* Lawrence: University Press of Kansas, 1993.

———. *Trapped by Success: The Eisenhower Administration and Vietnam, 1953–1961.* New York: Columbia University, 1991.

Anson, Robert Sam. *McGovern: A Biography.* New York: Holt, Rinehart and Winston, 1972.

Arnold, James R. *The First Domino: Eisenhower, the Military, and America's Intervention in Vietnam.* New York: William Morrow, 1991.

Ashby, LeRoy, and Gramer, Rod. *Fighting the Odds: The Life of Senator Frank Church.* Pullman: Washington State University, 1994.

Austin, Anthony. *The President's War: The Story of the Tonkin Gulf Resolution and How the Nation Was Trapped in Vietnam.* Philadelphia: J. B. Lippincott, 1971.

Baldwin, Louis. *Hon. Politician: Mike Mansfield of Montana.* Missoula, MT: Mountain Press, 1979.

Baritz, Loren. *Backfire: Vietnam—The Myths That Made Us Fight the Illusions That Helped Us Lose, The Legacy That Haunts Us Today*. New York: Ballantine, 1985.

Barnet, Richard J. *The Rocket's Red Glare: When America Goes to War*. New York: Simon and Schuster, 1990.

Barrett, David M. *Uncertain Warriors: Lyndon Johnson and His Vietnam Advisors*. Lawrence: University Press of Kansas, 1993.

Berman, Larry. *Planning a Tragedy: The Americanization of the War in Vietnam*. New York: W. W. Norton, 1982.

Berman, William C. *William Fulbright and the Vietnam War*. Kent: Kent State, 1988.

Billings-Yun, Melanie. *Decision Against War: Eisenhower and Dien Bien Phu, 1954*. New York: Columbia University, 1988.

Bird, Kai. *The Color of Truth. McGeorge Bundy and William Bundy: Brothers in Arms*. New York: Simon and Schuster, 1998.

Brandon, Henry. *Anatomy of Error: The Inside Story of the Asian War on the Potomac, 1954–1969*. Boston: Gambit, 1969.

Bundy, William. *A Tangled Web: The Making of Foreign Policy in the Nixon Administration*. New York: Hill and Wang, 1998.

Burns, James MacGregor. *The Crosswinds of Freedom*. New York: Knopf, 1989.

Chester, Lewis, Hodgson, Godfrey, and Page, Bruce. *An American Melodrama: The Presidential Campaign of 1968*. New York: Viking, 1969.

Clancy, Paul, and Elder, Shirley. *Tip: A Biography of Thomas P. O'Neill*. New York: Macmillan, 1980.

Coffin, Tristam. *Fulbright: Portrait of a Public Philosopher*. New York: Dutton, 1966.

Congressional Quarterly Almanac. Washington: CQ, 1950–74.

Cooper, Chester L. *The Lost Crusade: America in Vietnam*. New York: Dodd, Mead, 1970.

———. *Lone Star Rising: Lyndon Johnson and His Time, 1908–1960*. New York: Oxford, 1991.

Dallek, Robert. *Flawed Giant: Lyndon Johnson and His Times, 1961–1973*. New York: Oxford, 1998.

DeBenedetti, Charles. *An American Ordeal: The Antiwar Movement of the Vietnam Era*. Syracuse: Syracuse University, 1990.

Dietz, Terry. *Republicans and Vietnam, 1961–1968*. New York: Greenwood, 1986.

DiLeo, David L. *George Ball, Vietnam, and the Rethinking of Containment*. Chapel Hill: University of North Carolina Press, 1991.

Doenecke, Justus D. *Not to the Swift: The Old Isolationists in the Cold War Era*. Lewisburg, PA: Bucknell University, 1979.

Donovan, Robert J. *Tumultuous Years: The Presidency of Harry S. Truman, 1949–1953*. New York: W. W. Norton, 1982.

Drukman, Mason. *Wayne Morse: A Biography*. Portland: Oregon Historical Society, 1997.

Dugger, Ronnie. *The Politician: The Life and Times of Lyndon Johnson*. New York: W. W. Norton, 1982.

Edwards, Lee. *Goldwater: The Man Who Made a Revolution*. Washington: Regenry, 1995.

Evans, Rowland, and Novak, Robert. *Lyndon B. Johnson: The Exercise of Power.* New York: New American Library, 1966.

Fairbank, John King. *The United States and China.* New York: Viking, 1962.

Fall, Bernard B. *Hell in a Very Small Place: The Siege of Dien Bien Phu.* Philadelphia: J. B. Lippincott, 1967.

———. *The Two Viet-Nams: A Political and Military Analysis.* New York: Frederick A. Praeger, 1964.

Ferrell, Robert. *Harry S. Truman: A Life.* Columbia: Missouri Press, 1994.

Fite, Gilbert C. *Richard B. Russell, Jr., Senator from Georgia.* Chapel Hill: University of North Carolina, 1991.

———. *Harry S. Truman and the Modern American Presidency.* Boston: Little, Brown, 1983.

FitzGerald, Frances. *Fire in the Lake: The Vietnamese and the Americans in Vietnam.* Boston: Little, Brown, 1972.

Fulbright, J. W. *Old Myths and New Realities and Other Commentaries.* New York: Random House, 1964.

———. *Senator Fulbright: A Legislator's Thoughts on World Issues.* New York: Mac-Fadden, 1964.

———. *The Arrogance of Power.* New York: Vintage, 1966.

Gardner, Lloyd C. *Approaching Vietnam: From World War II through Dienbienphu.* New York: W. W. Norton, 1988.

———. *Pay Any Price: Lyndon Johnson and the Wars for Vietnam.* Chicago: Ivan R. Dee, 1995.

Garrow, David J. *Bearing the Cross: Martin Luther King, Jr., and the Southern Christian Leadership Conference.* New York: William Morrow, 1986.

Gelb, Leslie H., and Betts, Richard K. *The Irony of Vietnam: The System Worked.* Washington: Brookings, 1979.

Gettleman, Marvin E., ed. *Vietnam: History, Documents, and Opinions on a Major World Crisis.* New York: Fawcett, 1965.

Gibbons, William Conrad. *The U.S. Government and the Vietnam War: Executive and Legislative Roles and Relationships.* Vols. I–IV. Princeton: Princeton University, 1986–95.

Goldberg, Robert Alan. *Barry Goldwater.* New Haven: Yale, 1995.

Goodman, Walter. *The Committee: The Extraordinary Career of the House Committee on Un-American Activities.* New York: Farrar, Straus and Giroux, 1968.

Goulden, Joseph C. *Truth Is the First Casualty: The Gulf of Tonkin—Illusion and Reality.* Chicago: Rand McNally, 1969.

Griffith, Robert. *The Politics of Fear: Joseph R. McCarthy and the Senate.* Amherst: University of Massachusetts, 1987.

Halberstam, David. *The Best and the Brightest.* New York: Fawcett, 1992.

———. *The Making of a Quagmire.* New York: Random House, 1965.

Hamby, Alonzo L. *Man of the People: A Life of Harry Truman.* New York: Oxford, 1995.

Hamilton, John Maxwell. *Edgar Snow: A Biography.* Bloomington: Indiana University Press, 1988.

Hendrickson, Paul. *The Living and the Dead: Robert McNamara and Five Lives of a Lost War.* New York: Knopf, 1996.

Herring, George C. *America's Longest War: The United States and Vietnam, 1950–1975*. New York: John Wiley, 1979.

———. *LBJ and Vietnam: A Different Kind of War*. Austin: University of Texas, 1994.

Hersh, Seymour. *The Price of Power: Kissinger in the Nixon White House*. New York: Summit, 1983.

Hess, Gary R. *The United States' Emergence as a Southeast Asian Power, 1940–1950*. New York: Columbia University, 1987.

Hoopes, Townsend. *The Devil and John Foster Dulles*. Boston: Little, Brown. 1973.

Hunt, Michael H. *Lyndon Johnson's War: America's Cold War Crusade in Vietnam, 1945–1968*. New York: Hill and Wang, 1996.

Isaacson, Walter. *Kissinger: A Biography*. New York: Simon and Schuster, 1992.

Isaacson, Walter, and Thomas, Evan. *The Wise Men: Six Friends and the World They Made*. New York: Simon and Schuster, 1986.

Johnson, Haynes, and Gwertzman, Bernard M. *Fulbright: The Dissenter*. Garden City, NY: Doubleday, 1968.

Kaiser, David. *American Tragedy: Kennedy, Johnson and the Origins of the Vietnam War*. Cambridge, MA: Harvard University Press, 2000.

Kalb, Marvin and Bernard. *Kissinger*. Boston: Little, Brown, 1974.

Karnow, Stanley. *Vietnam: A History*. New York: Penguin, 1991.

Kearns, Doris. *Lyndon Johnson and the American Dream*. New York: Harper and Row, 1976.

Keith, Caroline H. *'For Hell and a Brown Mule': The Biography of Senator Millard E. Tydings*. New York: Madison, 1991.

Kendrick, Alexander. *The Wound Within: America in the Vietnam Years, 1945–1974*. Boston: Little, Brown, 1974.

Khong, Yuen Foong. *Analogies at War: Korea, Munich, Dien Bien Phu, and the Vietnam Decisions of 1965*. Princeton: Princeton University, 1992.

Kimball, Jeffery. *Nixon's Vietnam War*. Lawrence: University of Kansas, 1998.

Kissinger, Henry. *Diplomacy*. New York: Simon and Schuster, 1994.

Kolko, Gabriel. *Anatomy of a War: Vietnam, the United States, and the Modern Historical Experience*. New York: Pantheon, 1985.

Kutler, Stanley I. *Encyclopedia of the Vietnam War*. New York: Charles Scribner's, 1996.

———. *The Wars of Watergate: The Last Crisis of Richard Nixon*. New York: Knopf, 1990.

Langer, William L., and Gleason, S. Everett. *The Challenge to Isolationism, 1937–1940*. New York: Harper, 1952.

Lasky, Victor. *J.F.K.: The Man and the Myth*. New York: Macmillan, 1963.

Logevall, Fredrik. *Choosing War: The Lost Chance for Peace and the Escalation of War in Vietnam*. Berkeley: University of California, 1999.

McCarthy, Joseph R. *America's Retreat from Victory: The Story of George Catlett Marshall*. New York: Devin-Adair, 1951.

McCormick, Thomas J. *America's Half Century: United States Foreign Policy in the Cold War and After*. Baltimore: Johns Hopkins University Press, 1995.

McCullough, David. *Truman*. New York: Simon and Schuster, 1992.

McKenna, Marian C. *Borah*. Ann Arbor: University of Michigan, 1961.

McMaster, H. R. *Dereliction of Duty: Lyndon Johnson, Robert McNamara, the Joint Chiefs of Staff, and the Lies That Led to Vietnam*. New York: HarperCollins, 1997.

Maclear, Michael. *The Ten Thousand Day War, Vietnam: 1945–1975*. New York: Avon, 1981.

Manchester, William. *American Caesar: Douglas MacArthur 1880–1964*. Boston: Little, Brown, 1978.

Meyer, Karl E., ed. *Senator Fulbright: A Legislator's Thoughts on World Issues*. New York: Macfadden, 1964.

Miles, Michael W. *The Odyssey of the American Right*. New York: Oxford, 1980.

Maddox, Robert James. *William E. Borah and American Foreign Policy*. Baton Rouge: LSU Press, 1969.

Moïse, Edwin E. *Tonkin Gulf and the Escalation of the Vietnam War*. Chapel Hill: University of North Carolina, 1996.

Moore, Harold G., and Galloway, Joseph L. *We Were Soldiers Once . . . And Young, Ia Drang: The Battle that Changed the War in Vietnam*. New York: Random House, 1992.

Morgan, Joseph G. *The Vietnam Lobby: The American Friends of Vietnam, 1955–1975*. Chapel Hill: University of North Carolina, 1997.

Morris, Roger. *Richard Milhous Nixon: The Rise of An American Politician*. New York: Henry Holt, 1990.

Mueller, John E. *War, Presidents and Public Opinion*. New York: John Wiley, 1973.

Newman, John M. *JFK and Vietnam: Deception, Intrigue, and the Struggle for Power*. New York: Warner, 1992.

Nguyen Tien Hung, and Schecter, Jerrold L. *The Palace File*. New York: Harper & Row, 1986.

Olson, Gregory Allen. *Mansfield and Vietnam: A Study in Rhetorical Adaptation*. East Lansing: Michigan State University, 1995.

Parmet, Herbert S. *Eisenhower and the American Crusades*. New York: Macmillan, 1972.

———. *JFK: The Presidency of John F. Kennedy*. New York: Dial, 1983.

———. *Richard Nixon and His America*. New York: Smithmark, 1990.

Patterson, James T. *Grand Expectations: The United States, 1945–1974*. New York: Oxford, 1996.

———. *Mr. Republican: A Biography of Robert A. Taft*. Boston: Houghton, Mifflin, 1972.

Patti, Archimedes L. A. *Why Viet Nam? Prelude to America's Albatross*. Berkeley: University of California, 1980.

Podhoretz, Norman. *Why We Were in Vietnam*. New York: Touchstone, 1983.

Pogue, Forrest C. *George C. Marshall: Statesman*. New York: Viking, 1987.

Powell, Lee Riley. *J. William Fulbright and His Times*. Memphis: Guild Bindery Press, 1996.

Powers, Thomas. *The War at Home: Vietnam and the American People, 1964–1968*. New York: Grossman, 1973.

Prados, John. *The Hidden History of the Vietnam War*. Chicago: Ivan R. Dee, 1995.

Prochnau, William. *Once Upon a Distant War: David Halberstam, Neil Sheehan, Peter Arnett—Young War Correspondents and Their Early Vietnam Battles.* New York: Times Books, 1995.

Purifoy, Lewis McCarroll. *Harry Truman's China Policy: McCarthyism and the Diplomacy of Hysteria, 1947–1951.* New York: New Viewpoints, 1976.

Reeves, Richard. *President Kennedy: Profile of Power.* New York: Touchstone, 1994.

Reeves, Thomas C. *The Life and Times of Joe McCarthy.* New York: Stein and Day, 1982.

Roberts, Charles. *LBJ's Inner Circle.* New York: Delacorte, 1965.

Rovere, Richard H. *Senator Joe McCarthy.* New York: Harcourt, Brace, Jovanovich, 1959.

Rudenstine, David. *The Day the Presses Stopped: A History of the Pentagon Papers Case.* Berkeley: University of California Press, 1996.

Rust, William J. *Kennedy in Vietnam.* New York: Scribner, 1985.

———. *The Bitter Heritage: Vietnam and American Democracy, 1941–1966.* Boston: Houghton Mifflin, 1967.

Schlesinger, Arthur M., Jr. *Robert Kennedy and His Times.* New York: Ballentine, 1978.

Schoenbaum, Thomas J. *Waging Peace and War: Dean Rusk in the Truman, Kennedy, and Johnson Years.* New York: Simon and Schuster, 1988.

Schulzinger, Robert D. *A Time for War: The United States and Vietnam, 1941–1975.* New York: Oxford, 1997.

Shaplen, Robert. *The Lost Revolution.* New York: Harper and Row, 1965.

Shapley, Deborah. *Promise and Power: The Life and Times of Robert McNamara.* Boston: Little, Brown, 1993.

Shawcross, William. *Sideshow: Kissinger, Nixon and the Destruction of Cambodia.* New York: Simon and Schuster, 1979.

Shesol, Jeff. *Mutual Contempt: Lyndon Johnson, Robert Kennedy and the Feud That Defined a Decade.* New York: W. W. Norton, 1997.

Sidey, Hugh. *John F. Kennedy, President.* New York: Atheneum, 1964.

Siff, Ezra Y. *Why the Senate Slept.* Westport, CT: Praeger, 1999.

Solberg, Carl. *Hubert Humphrey: A Biography.* New York: W. W. Norton, 1984.

Sorley, Lewis. *A Better War: The Unexamined Victories and Final Tragedy of America's Last Years in Vietnam.* New York: Harcourt, Brace, 1999.

Stokesbury, James L. *A Short History of the Korean War.* New York: William Morrow, 1988.

Theoharis, Athan. *Seeds of Repression: Harry S. Truman and the Origins of McCarthyism.* Chicago: Quadrangle, 1971.

———. *Spying on Americans: Political Surveillance from Hoover to the Huston Plan.* Philadelphia: Temple University, 1978.

Tucker, Robert W. *A New Isolationism: Threat or Promise?* New York: Universe Books, 1972.

Tucker, Spencer C. *Vietnam.* Lexington: University Press of Kentucky, 1999.

VanDeMark, Brian. *Into the Quagmire: Lyndon Johnson and the Escalation of the Vietnam War.* New York: Oxford, 1995.

Walton, Richard J. *Cold War and Counterrevolution: The Foreign Policy of John F. Kennedy.* New York: Viking, 1972.

White, Theodore H. *The Making of the President, 1960.* New York: Atheneum, 1961.

———. *The Making of the President, 1964.* New York: Atheneum, 1965.

———. *The Making of the President, 1972.* New York: Atheneum, 1973.

White, William S. *Citadel: The Story of the U.S. Senate.* New York: Harper, 1957.

———. *The Taft Story.* New York: Harper, 1954.

Wicker, Tom. *JFK and LBJ: The Influence of Personality Upon Politics.* New York: William Morrow, 1969.

———. *One of Us: Richard Nixon and the American Dream.* New York: Random House, 1991.

Windchy, Eugene G. *Tonkin Gulf.* New York: Doubleday, 1971.

Witcover, Jules. *The Year the Dream Died: Revisiting 1968 in America.* New York: Warner, 1997.

Woods, Randall Bennett. *Fulbright: A Biography.* Cambridge: Cambridge University, 1995.

———. *J. William Fulbright, Vietnam, and the Search for a Cold War Foreign Policy.* Cambridge: Cambridge University, 1998.

Young, Marilyn B. *The Vietnam Wars, 1945–1990.* New York: HarperCollins, 1991.

INTERVIEWS AND ORAL HISTORIES

Abel, Elie. 1/70. LBJL.

Abel, Elie. 12/10/70. CUOHP.

Ackley, Gardner. 4/13/73. LBJL.

Adams, Samuel A. 9/20/84. LBJL.

Adams, Sherman. 8/15/64. JFDOHP.

Aiken, George. 4/27/67. CUOHP.

Allen, George. 3/7/67. CUOHP.

Alsop, Joseph. 3/4/66. JFDOHP.

Alsop, Stewart. 7/15/69. LBJL.

Anderson, Dillon. 12/30/69. CUOHP.

Ball, George. 7/8 & 7/9/71. LBJL.

Ball,George. 9/30/80. CRS.

Barr, Joseph. 8/25/69. LBJL.

Bartlett, Charles L. 5/6/69. LBJL.

Beech, Keyes. 3/22 & 5/30/83. LBJL.

Bell, Elliot. 7/7/64. JFDOHP.

Bennett, Charles. 12/17/70. CUOHP.

Berding, Andrew. 6/13/67. CUOHP.

Bohlen, Charles. 11/20/68. LBJL.

Bowles, Chester. 2/2/65. JFKL.

Bowles, Chester. 5/23/63. CUOHP.

Bricker, John. 3/14/74. FMOC.

Brown, Harold. 1/17/69. LBJL.

Brzezinski, Zbigniew. 11/12/71. LBJL.

Bundy, McGeorge. Tape CCC. RBRL.

Bundy, William. 8/3/78. CRS.

Bundy, William. 5/29/69. LBJL.

Bush, Prescott. 7/22/66. CUOHP.

Cabot, John M. 11/15/65. JFDOHP.

Childs, Marquis. 1/12/66. JFDOHP.

Church, Bethine. 3/4/98. By Mann.

Church, Frank. 5/1/69. LBJL.

Christian, George. 11/11/68. LBJL.

Cleveland, Harlan. 8/13/69. LBJL.

Clifford, Clark. 7/2, 7/14, 8/7 & 12/15/69. LBJL.

Clifford, Clark. 3/85. Tape XX. RBRL.

Cline, Ray. 3/21 & 5/31/83. LBJL.

Colby, William. 6/2/81. LBJL.

Collins, Lawton. 1/12/66. JFDOHP.

Connell, William. 3/18/85. LBJL.

Cooper, Chester. 7/9, 7/17 & 8/7/69. LBJL.

Cooper, Chester. 5/6/66. JFKL.

Crockett, William J. 5/28/74 & 8/19/85. LBJL.

Crawford, Kenneth. 6/13/67. CUOHP.

Couve de Murville, Maurice. 6/19/64. JFDOHP.

Cunningham, George. 10/3/97. By Mann.

Davidson, Phillip. 3/30/82. LBJL.

D'Ewart, Wesley. 7/25/67. CUOHP.

Dillon, Douglas. LBJL.

Dole, Robert. 4/23/98. By Mann.

Donovan, Patricia. 2/9/98. By Mann.

Douglas, William O. 11/9/67. JFKL.

Drummond, Roscoe. 6/21/67, CUOHP.

Durbrow, Elbridge. 6/3/81. LBJL.

Dutton, Frederick. 5/3/65. JFKL.

Eisenhower, Dwight D. 7/28/64. JFDOHP.

Eisenhower, Milton. 6/21/67. JFDOHP.

Ferris, Charles. 10/20/97. By Mann.

Folliard, Edward. 9/7/67. CUOHP.

Ford, Gerald. 10/20/97. By Mann.

Forrestal, Michael. 11/3/69. LBJL.

Fowler, Henry. 4/22/69. LBJL.

Fulbright, J. William. 3/5/79. FMOC.

Fulbright, J. William. JFKL.

Goldberg, Arthur. 3/23/83. LBJL.

Graham, Daniel O. 5/24/82.

Halaby, Najeeb. 11/6/72. CUOHP.

Hanes, John W. 1/29 & 8/12/66. JFDOHP.

Harkins, Paul. 11/10/81. LBJL.

Harsch, Joseph C. 3/29/66. JFDOHP.

Harriman, W. Averell. 4/13/64. JFKL.

Harriman, W. Averell. 6/16/69. LBJL.

Harris, Fred. 6/29/70. JFKL.

Hatfield, Mark O. 2/14/97. By Mann.

Hays, Wayne. 3/11/69. LBJL.

Hebert, F. Edward. 7/15/69. LBJL.

Helms, Richard. 9/16/81. LBJL.

Hilsman, Roger. 8/14/70. JFKL.

Hilsman, Roger. 5/15/69. LBJL.

Holbrooke, Richard. 3/85. Tape VV. RBRL.

Holt, Pat. 10/19/80. USSHO.

Holum, John. 6/5 & 9/10/97, By Mann.

Gilpatric, Roswell. 5/5/70. JFKL.

Gilpatric, Roswell. 11/2/82. LBJL.

Goodpaster, Andrew. 6/21/71. LBJL.

Gruening, Ernest. 4/23/74. LBJL.

Johnson, Lyndon B. 4/12/69. LBJL.

Johnson, U. Alexis. JFKL.

Johnson, U. Alexis. 6/14/69. LBJL.

Jones, Norvill. 7/21 & 8/25/97. By Mann.

Jorden, William J. 3/22/69. LBJL.

Judd, Walter H. 12/11/65. JFDOHP.

Judd, Walter H. 8/29/68. CUOHP.

Karnow, Stanley. 4/30/84. LBJL.

Katzenbach, Nicholas. 3/85. Tape AAA. RBRL.

Katzenbach, Nicholas. 11/23/68. LBJL.

Kennedy, Robert F. 2/29, 3/1, 4/13, 4/30, 5/14 & 2.27/64. JFKL.

Knowland, William. 6/22/67. CUOHP.

Krock, Arthur. 11/21/68. LBJL.

Laird, Melvin. 5/14/79. FMOC.

Levinson, Lawrence. 9/12/97. By Mann.

Lindsley, Byron. 12/8/76. HGDOHP.

McBride, Charles. 4/22/98. By Mann.

McCulloch, Frank. 5/13/80. LBJL.

McGee, Gale. 2/10 & 3/10/69. LBJL.

McGee, Gale. 6/8/79. FMOC.

McGovern, George. 1/27 & 9/10/97. By Mann.

McGovern, George. 4/30/69. LBJL.

McGovern, George. 7/16/70. JFKL.

McPherson, Harry. 7/10 & 9/12/97. By Mann.

McPherson, Harry. 12/5/68, 1/16, 3/24 and 4/9/69. LBJL.

McNamara, Robert S. 4/4/64. JFKL.
Macomber, William B. 12/17/68.
    LBJL.
Mansfield, Mike. 9/8/97. By Mann.
Mansfield, Mike. 6/23/64. JFKL.
Mansfield, Mike. 12/13/76. BBC.
    Mansfield Library.
Mansfield, Mike. 5/10/66. JFDOHP.
Marks, Leonard. 1/26/76. LBJL.
Michaelson, Wesley. 3/27/97. By
    Mann.
Moore, Powell. 4/24/98. By Mann.
Moore, Powell. 1/23/76. LBJL.
Myers, Alvin. 3/23/78. HGDOHP.
Morton, Thruston. 1/29/79. CRS.
Moss, Frank. 9/20/78. FMOC.
Nelson, Bryce. 12/30/97. By Mann.
Nelson, Gaylord. 9/9/97. By Mann.
Newhouse, John. 4/23/98. By Mann.
Nixon, Richard. 3/5/65. JFDOHP.
Nolting, Frederick. 5/14/66. JFKL.
Nolting, Frederick. 12/11/82. LBJL.
Oberdorfer, Don. 6/3/81. LBJL.
Pike, Douglas. 6/4/81. LBJL.
Purvis, Hoyt. 4/21/97. By Mann.
Radford, Arthur W. 5/8/65. JFDOHP.
Reedy, George. 6/11/97. By Mann.
Reedy, George. 10/27/82. LBJL.
Roberts, Chalmers. 4/23/69. LBJL.
Roberts, Chalmers. 8/29/67. CUOHP.
Roberts, Charles. 1/14/70. LBJL.
Robertson, Walter S. 6/23 & 6/24/65.
Robertson, Walter S. 4/18/67.
    CUOHP.
Roche, John. 7/16/70. LBJL.
Rostow, Walt. 4/11/64. JFKL.
Rostow, Walt. 3/21/69.
Rovere, Richard. 2/22/68. CUOHP.
Rovere, Richard. 5/6/69. LBJL.
Rubottom, R. Richard. 6/12/66.
    JFDOHP.

Rusk, Dean. 7/28 & 9/26/69, 1/2/70.
    LBJL.
Rusk, Dean. Tapes C, D, E, G, J, T,
    U, KK, MM, NN, OO, PP,
    RBRL.
Rusk, Dean. 12/2/69. JFKL.
Saltonstall, Leverett. 1/11/67.
    CUOHP.
Scherer, Raymond. 1/20/68. CUOHP.
Shepley, James. 8/23/67. CUOHP.
Sherrod, Robert. 2/26/72. CUOHP.
Sidey, Hugh. 6/22/71. LBJL.
Simpson, Charles. 5/2/84. LBJL.
Smith, Bromley. 7/29/69. LBJL.
Smith, Howard K. 1/19/67. CUOHP.
Sullivan, William H. 7/21/71. LBJL.
Sundborg, George. 9/5/97. By Mann.
Taylor, Maxwell. 1/9 & 2/10/69, 6/1 &
    9/14/81. LBJL.
Taylor, Maxwell. 4/26/64. JFKL.
Thomson, James C. 7/22/71. LBJL.
Tillman, Seth. 2/13 & 9/11/97. By
    Mann.
Truehart, William. 3/2/82. LBJL.
Twining, Nathan. 3/16/65. JFDOHP.
Vance, Cyrus. 3/9/70. LBJL.
Van Dyk, Ted. 1/30 & 9/8/97. By
    Mann.
Valeo, Francis. 7/3, 7/10, 8/14, 8/21,
    8/28, 9/4, 9/12, 9/18, 9/25, 10/2,
    10/23, 11/6, 11/13 & 12/4/85.
    USSHO.
Westmoreland, William C. 2/8/69.
    LBJL.
Wheeler, Earle. 8/21/69 & 5/7/70.
    LBJL.
White, William s. 3/10/69. LBJL.
Williams, Lee. 3/27 & 9/8/97. By
    Mann.
Williams, Samuel T. 3/2/81. LBJL.

Index

Acknowledgments

MANY PEOPLE HELPED ME DURING THE RESEARCH AND WRITING OF this book. I am indebted to the staffs of the following libraries and archival collections: the Middleton Library and the Hill Memorial Library at Louisiana State University; the Lyndon B. Johnson Library; the Mansfield Library at the University of Montana; the Seeley G. Mudd Library at Princeton University; the Special Collections Division at the University of Arkansas; the Richard Russell Library at the University of Georgia; the John F. Kennedy Library; the National Archives facilities in Washington, D.C., Laguna Nigel, California, and College Park, Maryland; the Richard Nixon Library; the American Foreign Policy Center at Louisiana Tech University; the Frank Church Papers at Boise State University Library; the Gerald R. Ford Library; and the Library of Congress.

Several people helped me improve this work immensely with their honest and insightful critiques of the manuscript: Tony Gaughan, Dave Norris, Jack Bresch, Mark Carson, Mike Skinner, and Ward Bond. For their proofreading assistance, I am grateful to Paul Mann, Roger Guissinger, and Frank Snellings. For his careful and caring approach to the manuscript, I am particularly indebted to my editor at Basic Books, Tim Bartlett. I am also grateful to all the other fine people at Basic Books who helped produce this book, including Don Fehr, Christine Marra, Rob Kirkpatrick, and Vanessa Mobley. I also appreciate the fine job of copy editing performed on the manuscript by Maria E. denBoer at Nighthawk Design.

While I am grateful to everyone who gave freely of their time to share recollections of the political history of the Vietnam War, several people were especially generous and helpful: George McGovern, Norvill Jones (who shared copies of his private files with me), Gaylord Nelson (who also shared his private files), Harry McPherson (who helped me obtain interviews with several reluctant subjects), Seth Tillman, Lee Williams, Gerald Ford, Mike Mansfield, Bob Dole, Mark Hatfield, John Holum, Ted Van Dyk, and the late George Reedy. Thanks also to: William Conrad Gibbons for sharing with me the oral histories in his files collected for the four volumes of his monumental work, *The U.S. Government and the Vietnam War;*

and to David M. Barrett, author of *Uncertain Warriors: Lyndon Johnson and His Vietnam Advisors*, for sharing documents from his collection.

For their support and encouragement, I thank my friends, including: Clyde Taylor (who is also my literary agent), John and Diane Copes, Roger and Gayle Guissinger, Jim and Susan Nickel, Chris and Glo Andrews, Jerry and Margaret Johnson, Russell and Carolyn Long, Jim and Tammie Oakes, Chris Peacock, Frank Snellings, Rich Masters, Ron LeLeux, Stan Tiner, Martin Walke, Max Holland, David Barrett, Kyle France, Kevin McGill, Ross Atkins, Lanny Keller, Jim Brady, Leo Honeycutt, Joy Erwin, Kathryn Flournoy, Jeff Day, John Maxwell Hamilton, Cecil Eubanks, Wayne Parent, Richard Baxter, Vincent Marsala, Douglas Brinkley, Hal Kilshaw, Steve and Mary Kay Carleton, Robert and Judith Levy, Harvill Eaton, Wendy Wilson, Fred Loy, Paula Roughton, Derrick Whitfield, Bill and Patsy Arceneaux, David and Robbie Madden, and Benny and Myra Crawford. A special word of thanks to all my friends and brothers at Louisiana State Penitentiary at Angola, Main Prison, and Camps C and D, for their prayers and support.

I am deeply indebted to my friend and boss, U.S. Senator John Breaux, and my current and former colleagues on his staff, including Jim Nickel, Aliscia Rogers, Mike Jefferson, Suzy Sonnier, Fred Hatfield, Tommy Hudson, Norma Jane Sabiston, Bette Phelan, Susie Owens, Judy Siegel, Diana Bostic, Raymond Cordova, Donnie Barthelemy, Heather Liles, Jean Bates, Jan Becker, Gail Wolfe, Mark Herbert, Lynette Savoie, Malcolm Myer, Kristan Roetker, Shantrice Norma-Dial, and Suzanne Perilloux.

During the final phase of this book, my wife, Cindy, gave birth to twins. While this was a wonderful and blessed occasion, it more than complicated the process of completing this work. I am forever indebted to the dozens of friends, neighbors, and family members who lightened our burdens in countless ways that brought a semblance of sanity to our home and enabled me, occasionally, to steal away from my duties as a new father to tend to this book. I am especially thankful to the members of First United Methodist Church of Baton Rouge for their prayers and support during this very stressful period. More than anything, I was sustained by my faith in God, who constantly amazes me with his grace and always shows me how to fulfill my duties as a father, husband, employee, and writer. There were many times when I was certain that I was not up to the task of completing this book. As much as I would like to boast that this is the product of my own initiative and talent, it was God—revealed to me in the faces of countless friends, family members, and a few strangers—who saw me through.

I am thankful for the support and love of my family. My parents, Robert and Charlene Mann; my brother, Paul Mann and his wife Marlo;

my sister, Sarah Luker and her husband Gary; my father- and mother-in-law, Alfred and Gerry Horaist. More than anyone, I am grateful to my wife, Cindy, whose support and love sustains me in every aspect of my personal and professional life. It is largely because of Cindy that I believe so strongly in divine grace. Her love, her life, and her example are true expressions of God's unmerited favor in my life. While I do not deserve someone so beautiful, loving, and forgiving, I thank God for the profound way he has blessed me through Cindy. My love for her has only deepened in the months since she bore our son, Robert Townley III, and our daughter, Avery Frances. It is to these two beautiful and blessed children that this book is lovingly dedicated.

About the Author

Robert Mann, a veteran U.S. Senate aide, has worked as press secretary to U.S. Senator Russell B. Long of Louisiana and his successor, Senator John Breaux. A former award-winning newspaper reporter, he is the author of two previous books about the U.S. Congress: *The Walls of Jericho: Lyndon Johnson, Hubert Humphrey, Richard Russell, and the Struggle for Civil Rights*, a highly praised political history of the civil rights movement; and *Legacy to Power: Senator Russell Long of Louisiana*.

A journalism graduate of the University of Louisiana at Monroe, he has taught on the history of civil rights at Louisiana State University and has lecture widely on congressional history and current affairs. Mann lives in Baton Rouge, Louisiana, with his wife, Cindy, and their two children.